# CONTENTS

Comment by Stuart Barnes ...

World Cup round-up ...

World Cup results/teams ...

World Cup – The things they say ...

World Cup Facts/figures ...

World Cup summaries ...

Diary ...

English tables ...

English League results ... 48

Premier League highlights ... 52

How Manchester City won the title ... 63

End of season play-offs ... 65

History of the play-offs ... 70

English honours ... 77

Annual awards ... 91

Club reviews, appearances, scorers ... 95

English League managers ... 152

Managerial changes ... 154

FA Cup ... 156

FA Cup Final teams ... 161

League Cup ... 173

League Cup results ... 175

Other competitions ... 177

Changing homes ... 184

Scottish tables ... 185

Scottish League results ... 187

Celtic's record-breaking title win ... 191

Scottish honours ... 193

Scottish Premiership roll call ... 200

Scottish League Cup ... 204

Scottish League Cup Finals ... 205

Scottish FA Cup ... 207

Scottish FA Cup Finals ... 208

National League table ... 210

National League results ... 211

National League north/south ... 212

Other leagues ... 213

UEFA Cup/Europa League Finals ... 241

Fairs Cup Finals ... 242

Cup-winners' Cup Finals ... 242

Super Cup results ... 243

Inter-Continental Cup ... 244

European club tables ... 246

British & Irish internationals ... 249

Other British & Irish results ... 257

International appearances ... 283

International scorers ... 306

Home Internationals ... 311

Nations Cup ... 317

Under-21s ... 318

Toulon tournament ... 322

England under-17 World Cup win ... 323

Transfer trail ... 325

Milestones ... 330

Obituaries ... 338

Records section (separate index) ... 349

Premier League club details & squads ... 451

English Football League squads ... 472

Scottish Premiership squads ... 517

Fixtures 2018–19 ... 520

English Leagues ... 520

Scottish Leagues ... 535

National League ... 541

# THE NATIONWIDE FOOTBALL ANNUAL 2018–2019

Published by SportsBooks Limited, 9 St Aubyns Place, York, YO24 1EQ
First published in 1887


www.sportsbooks.ltd.uk

**ALBERT SEWELL 1927–2018**

The 132nd edition of this publication is tinged with sadness following the death of renowned statistician Albert Sewell shortly before we went to press. He was editor from 1983-97, when it was the *News of the World Annual*, and continued to supply the records section, including the present one. Albert, who lost his wife Betty last year, was football statistician with BBC TV from 1968 until retiring in 2005. He edited Chelsea's match-day programme for nearly 30 years, wrote several books and was mentor to many young journalists who went on from the Hayters sports agency in Fleet Street to become leading football writers. Albert was awarded an MBE for services to the game in 2005.



A CIP catalogue record for this book is available from the British Library.

Editorial compilation by Stuart Barnes

ISBN-13 9781907524561

Front cover: England manager Gareth Southgate consoles his captain Harry Kane, who went on to win the Golden Boot as top scorer, after the World Cup semi-final defeat by Croatia. (Mladen Antonov, Getty Images)
Back cover: Manchester City celebrate their Premier League title. (PA Images)

Printed and bound in the UK by CPI Group (UK) Ltd, Croydon CR0 4YY

# COMMENT

**By Stuart Barnes**

Football didn't quite make it all the way home, but is certainly heading in the right direction on the evidence of England's performance at the World Cup. Unrated by many of their own supporters and largely ignored abroad, they exceeded all expectations, restoring pride in the national team and bringing the nation together to such an extent that almost half the population were said to have watched the semi-final against Croatia. While the players merited all the praise coming their way, much of the transformation in fortunes was down to manager Gareth Southgate. Ruthless in discarding some established internationals, shrewd in fostering team spirit and adept in his tactical decisions, he commanded respect in all quarters. Who would have thought that his faith in Jordan Pickford, Harry Maguire and Kieran Trippier, with just 13 international starts between them before the tournament, would be totally justified. Southgate also won admirers after the defeat, consoling every member of his squad, embracing his backroom staff and congratulating the Croatian management team. If he can now develop an influential midfield playmaker as the one missing link – could Ruben Loftus-Cheek be the answer? – there is no reason why, as the manager believes, they cannot go on to greater things. The immediate target is the new Nations League, which UEFA have introduced as a replacement for most international friendlies. In their group, England renew rivalry with Croatia, together with Spain. That is followed by the start of qualifying for Euro 2020, the draw for which is on December 2.

•

There was one aspect of an outstanding tournament which left much to be desired – the standard of some referees. Despite the presence for the first time of video assistants, too many officials were allowed to pay lip service to proper control. England's game against Colombia was a prime example. The Premier League has some accomplished men in the middle, so it was a mystery why there was no domestic referee on duty at the finals for the first time since 1938.

•

John Motson covered ten World Cups during 50 years with the BBC, along with ten European Championships, 29 FA Cup Finals and more than 200 England games. Now, he has relinquished his commentary position and one of the game's most familiar voices will be missing from the new season. His career took off at one of the FA Cup's biggest upsets – Hereford's victory over Newcastle in 1972. It came to an end with Crystal Palace against West Bromwich Albion on Match of the Day, after which Palace manager Roy Hodgson presented him with a framed copy of the match programme from his first and last games at Selhurst Park, along with a crystal microphone. That night, there was a special presentation at the British Television Academy Awards. BBC Two then dedicated an evening of programmes to mark his retirement, including The Man Behind the Sheepskin. The tributes truly reflected an outstanding contribution to sports broadcasting.

•

While England were doing the nation proud in Russia, former captain Steven Gerrard was preparing for his first taste of management with Rangers. His task: to restore the club as a domestic force, while filling a void in Scottish football. Ever since Rangers paid the price for financial mismanagement and were demoted to the bottom division, Celtic have steamrollered their way to seven successive titles, most of them by a big margin. The game is crying out for a more competitive Premiership. For Gerrard to bring that about in his first season is asking a lot. 'Glasgow is not a city where you can sit pretty and develop,' he admitted after being appointed. Yet Gerrard has already revitalised the club and supporters. Attracting 41,000 to Ibrox for a pre-season friendly against Bury was evidence of that. He has made several signings, reshaped the squad and it would not be surprising if Celtic were finally given a run for their money.

# ENGLAND ON THE WAY UP AFTER A WORLD CUP TO REMEMBER

Among the many messages of support for England's squad ahead of the World Cup was one from Sir Bobby Charlton. He told Harry Kane during a visit to the National Football Centre at St George's Park: 'I do hope you can give me something I will always remember.' Sir Bobby, whose two goals against Portugal at Wembley took England to the 1966 final, was not disappointed. Gareth Southgate's side couldn't repeat that feat, losing their semi-final to Croatia. But after being largely written off at home and ignored abroad, they upset the odds to reach the last four and had chances to have gone all the way. If only Kane had taken one to add gloss to his Golden Boot award; if only Jesse Lingard had not missed another opportunity to add to Kieran Trippier's fifth-minute free-kick; if only a John Stones header had gone in instead of being cleared off the line in extra-time. Such are the fine lines between success and failure at the highest level that caught up with Southgate's young players. They knew a golden opportunity had been lost when Croatia seized the initiative in the second-half and were rewarded when a moment's indecision by Stones enabled Mario Mandzukic to steal in for the winner.

England had less cause to argue about defeat in the play-off for third place by Belgium, one of the four or five teams Southgate rated ahead of his own in terms of experience and know-how. Even so, had Eric Dier not been denied an equaliser by a goal-line clearance they could have got something out of the match. Overall, a bright future seems to beckon for a side who overcame a shortage of creativity in midfield areas with a strong sense of togetherness, the ability to exploit dead-ball situations and making full use of a draw which opened up in front of them after the demise of some fancied sides - defending champions Germany, Spain, Brazil and Argentina. In the months to come, we can expect Ruben Loftus-Cheek and Trent Alexander-Arnold to press strongly for regular starting positions and it would not be surprising to see the youthful talent of Fulham's Ryan Sessegnon and Manchester City's Phil Foden given a chance. Southgate will also have to address the reliance on Kane for goals. The Tottenham player made less of an impact the longer the tournament went on, prompting speculation that he might be carrying an injury, and with Raheem Sterling drawing a blank it may be time for Marcus Rashford to have an extended run. Despite this, England certainly made a significant contribution to what was widely regarded as one of the best-ever World Cups – and not just on the field. In the past, they were perceived as remote and unwelcoming. This time, with Southgate an excellent ambassador as well as a shrewd coach, the squad embraced the media, instead of keeping them at arm's length, and the local community. Most importantly, they reconnected with an ever-willing public at home.

We didn't have to wait long for the tournament to take off – Cristiano Ronaldo scoring a hat-trick in a 3-3 thriller with Spain. Germany fell to two South Korea goals in time added on and Japan looked on course for another upset until Marouane Fellaini sparked Belgium into life after trailing 2-0. Lionel Messi, like Ronaldo, could have played his last World Cup after a 4-3 defeat by France in which 19-year-old Kylian Mbappe announced himself on the world stage with two goals in a dazzling performance. France went on to defeat Belgium in a fascinating match between the two remaining heavyweights and started strong favourites for the final. Croatia matched them for an hour, despite an own goal by Mandzukic and a controversial penalty confirmed when referee Nestor Pitana consulted the VAR system in use for the first time. But two goals in six minutes by Paul Pogba, finally revealing his true colours after an up-and-down season with Manchester United, and Mabappe turned the match and France were able to survive a gift goal conceded by Tottenham's Hugo Lloris to Mandzukic to win 4-2 – the highest-scoring final since England's defeat of West Germany half a century ago. It was a fitting end to a tournament initially beset by fears about racism, hooliganism, security and infrastructure. But they proved unfounded and Russia were able to celebrate not just a sporting success but also a public relations triumph which changed the perception of many of the host country – **STUART BARNES**

# WORLD CUP FINALS – RUSSIA 2018

## GROUP A

**RUSSIA 5 SAUDI ARABIA 0**
**Moscow Luzhniki (78,011); Thursday, June 14**

**Russia** (4-4-2): Akinfeev, Fernandes, Kutepov, Ignashevich, Zhirkov, Samedov (Kuziaev 63), Gazinsky, Zobnin, Golovin, Dzagoev (Cheryshev 23), Smolov (Dzyuba 69). **Scorers**: Gazinsky (12), Cheryshev (43, 90+1), Dzyuba (71), Golovin (90+4). **Booked**: Golovin
**Saudi Arabia** (4-4-1-1): Al-Mayouf, Al-Burayk, Osama Hawsawi, Omar Hawsawi, Al-Shahrani, Al-Faraj, Otayf (Al-Muwallad 63), Al-Jassim, Al-Dawsari, Al-Shehri (Bahebri 74), Al-Sahlawi (Assiri 85). **Booked**: Al-Jassim
**Referee**: N Pitana (Argentina). **Half-time**: 2-0

**EGYPT 0 URUGUAY 1**
**Ekaterinburg (27,015); Friday, June 15**

**Egypt** (4-2-3-1): El-Shenawy, Fathi, Gaber, Hegazi, Abdel-Shafi, Hamed (Morsy 49), Elneny, Warda (Sobhi 83), Said, Trezeguet, Mohsen (Kahraba 63). **Booked**: Morsy, Hegazi
**Uruguay** (4-4-2): Muslera, Varela, Gimenez, Godin, Caceres, Nandez (Sanchez 60), Vecino (Torreira 87), Betancur, De Arrascaeta (Rodriguez 60), Suarez, Cavani. **Scorer**: Gimenez (89)
**Referee**: B Kuipers (Holland). **Half-time**: 0-0

**RUSSIA 3 EGYPT 1**
**St Petersburg (64,468); Tuesday, June 19**

**Russia** (4-4-2): Akinfeev, Fernandes, Kutepov, Ignashevich, Zhirov (Kudriashov 86), Samedov, Gazinsky, Zobnin, Cheryshev (Kuziaev 74), Dzyuba (Smolov 79), Golovin. **Scorers**: Fathi (47 og), Cheryshev (59), Dzyuba (62). **Booked**: Smolov
**Egypt** (4-2-3-1): El-Shenawy, Fathi, Gaber, Hegazi, Abdel-Shafi, Hamed, Elneny (Warda 64), Salah, Said, Trezeguet (Sobhi 68), Mohsen (Kahraba 82). **Scorer**: Salah (73 pen). **Booked**: Trezeguet
**Referee**: E Caceres (Paraguay). **Half-time**: 0-0

**URUGUAY 1 SAUDI ARABIA 0**
**Rostov (42,678); Wednesday, June 20**

**Uruguay** (4-4-2): Muslera, Varela, Gimenez, Godin, Caceres, Sanchez (Nandez 82, Vecino (Torreira 59), Betancur, Rodriguez (Laxalt 59), Suarez, Cavani. **Scorer**: Suarez (23)
**Saudi Arabia** (4-2-3-1): Al-Owais, Al-Burayk, Osama Hawsawi, Al-Bulayhi, Al-Shahrani, Al-Jassim (Al-Moqahwi 44), Otayf, Bahebri (Kanno 75), Al-Faraj, Al-Dawsari, Al-Muwallad (Al-Sahlawi 75)
**Referee**: C Turpin (France). **Half-time**: 1-0

**SAUDI ARABIA 2 EGYPT 1**
**Volgograd (36,823); Monday, June 25**

**Saudi Arabia** (4-3-3): Al-Mosaileem, Al-Burayk, Osama Hawsawi, M Hawsawi, Al-Shahrani, Al-Faraj, Otayf, Al-Moqahwi, Bahebri (Assiri 65), Al-Muwallad (Al-Shehri 79), Al-Dawsari. **Scorers**: Al-Faraj (45+6), Al-Dawsari (90+5)
**Egypt** (4-2-3-1): El Hadary, Fathi, Gaber, Hegazi, Abdel-Shafi, Hamed, Elneny, Salah, Said (Warda 46), Trezeguet (Kahraba 81), Mohsen (Sobhi 64). **Scorer**: Salah (22). **Booked**: Fathi, Gaber
**Referee**: W Rodan (Colombia). **Half-time**: 1-1

**URUGUAY 3 RUSSIA 0**
**Samara (41,970); Monday, June 25**

**Uruguay** (4-3-1-2): Muslera, Caceres, Coates, Godin, Laxalt, Nandez (Rodriguez 73), Vecino

Torreira, Betancur (De Arrascaeta 63), Suarez, Cavani (Gomez 90+3). **Scorers**: Suarez (10), Cheryshev (23 og), Cavani (90). **Booked**: Betancur
**Russia** (4-2-3-1): Akinfeev, Smolnikov, Kutepov, Ignashevich, Kudriashov, Samedov, Gazinsky, Zobnin, Miranchuk (Smolov 60), Cheryshev (Fernandes 38), Dzyuba. **Booked**: Gazinsky, Smolnikov. **Sent off**: Smolnikov (36)
**Referee**: M Diedhiou (Senegal). **Half-time**: 2-0

| | P | W | D | L | F | A | Pts |
|---|---|---|---|---|---|---|---|
| Uruguay Q | 3 | 3 | 0 | 0 | 5 | 0 | 9 |
| Russia Q | 3 | 2 | 0 | 1 | 8 | 4 | 6 |
| Saudi Arabia | 3 | 1 | 0 | 2 | 2 | 7 | 3 |
| Egypt | 3 | 0 | 0 | 3 | 2 | 6 | 0 |

## GROUP B

**MOROCCO 0 IRAN 1**
**St Petersburg (62,548); Friday, June 15**

**Morocco** (4-2-3-1): El Kajoui, N Amrabat (S Amrabat 75), Benatia, Saiss, Hakimi, El Ahmadi, Boussoufa, Belhanda, Ziyech, Harit (Da Costa 81), El Kaabi (Bouhaddouz 76). **Booked**: El Ahmadi
**Iran** (4-1-4-1): Beiranvand, Rezaein, Cheshmi, Pouraliganji, Hajisafi, Jahanbakhsh (Ghoddos 83), Shojaei (Taremi 66), Ebrahimi (Montazeri 79), Amiri, Ansarifard, Azmoun. **Scorer**: Bouhaddouz (90+5 og). **Booked**: Shojaei, Jahanbakhsh, Ansarifard
**Referee**: C Cakir (Turkey). **Half-time**: 0-0

**PORTUGAL 3 SPAIN 3**
**Sochi (43,866); Friday, June 15**

**Portugal** (4-4-2): Rui Patricio, Soares, Pepe, Fonte, Guerreiro, Bernardo Silva (Ricardo Queresma 69), Joao Moutinho, William Carvalho, Bruno Fernandes (Joao Mario 68), Ronaldo, Guedes (Andre Silva 80). **Scorer**: Ronaldo (4 pen, 44, 88). **Booked**: Bruno Fernandes
**Spain** (4-2-3-1): De Gea, Nacho, Pique, Sergio Ramos, Jordi Alba, Busquets, Koke, D Silva (Lucas Vazquez 86), Isco, Iniesta (Thiago Alcantara 70), Diego Costa (Aspas 77). **Scorers**: Diego Costa (24, 55), Nacho (58). **Booked**: Busquets
**Referee**: G Rocchi (Italy). **Half-time**: 2-1

**PORTUGAL 1 MOROCCO 0**
**Moscow Luzhniki (78,011); Wednesday, June 20**

**Portugal** (4-4-2): Rui Patricio, Soares, Pepe, Fonte, Guerreiro, Bernardo Silva (Gelson Martins 58), Joao Moutinho (Adrien Silva 88), William Carvalho, Joao Mario (Bruno Fernandes 69), Ronaldo, Guedes. **Scorer**: Ronaldo (4). **Booked**: Bernardo Silva
**Morocco** (4-2-3-1): El Kajoui, Dirar, Benatia, Da Costa, Hakimi, El Ahmadi (Fajr 86), Boussoufa, N Amrabat, Belhanda (Carcela 75), Ziyech, Boutaib (El Kaabi 69). **Booked**: Benatia
**Referee**: M Geiger (USA). **Half-time**: 1-0

**IRAN 0 SPAIN 1**
**Kazan (42,718): Wednesday, June 20**

**Iran** (4-1-4-1): Beiranvand, Rezaein, Pouraliganji, Hosseini, Hajisafi (Mohammadi 69), Ezatolahi, Taremi, Ebrahimi, Amiri (Ghoddos 86), Ansarifard (Jahanbakhsh 75), Azmoun. **Booked**: Amiri, Ebrahimi
**Spain** (4-2-3-1): De Gea, Dani Carvajal, Pique, Sergio Ramos, Jordi Alba, Busquets, Iniesta (Koke 70), D Silva, Isco, Lucas Vazquez (Marco Asensio 80), Diego Costa (Rodrigo 88). **Scorer**: Diego Costa (54)
**Referee**: A Cunha (Uruguay). **Half-time**: 0-0

**IRAN 1 PORTUGAL 1**
**Saransk (41,685); Monday, June 25**

**Iran** (4-5-1): Beiranvand, Rezaein, Pouraliganji, Hosseini, Hajisafi (Mohammadi 56), Taremi, Jahanbakhsh (Ghoddos 70), Ezatolahi (Ansarifard 76), Ebrahimi, Amiri, Azmoun. **Scorer**: Ansarifard (90+3 pen). **Booked**: Hajisafi, Azmoun

**Portugal** (4-4-2): Rui Patricio, Soares, Pepe, Fonte, Guerreiro, Ricardo Quaresma (Bernardo Silva 70), William Carvalho, Adrien Silva, Joao Mario (Joao Moutinho 84), Andre Silva (Guedes 90+5), Ronaldo. **Scorer**: Ricardo Quaresma (45). **Booked**: Guerreiro, Ricardo Quaresma, Ronaldo, Soares

**Referee**: E Caceres (Paraguay). **Half-time**: 0-1

**SPAIN 2 MOROCCO 2**
**Kaliningrad (33,973); Monday, June 25**

**Spain** (4-2-3-1): De Gea, Dani Carvajal, Pique, Sergio Ramos, Jordi Alba, Busquets, Thiago Alcantara (Marco Asensio 74), Iniesta, D Silva (Rodrigo 84), Isco, Diego Costa (Aspas 74)). **Scorer**: Isco (19), Aspas (90+1)

**Morocco** (4-2-3-1): El Kajoui, Hakimi, Da Costa, Saiss, Ziyech (Bouhaddouz 85), El Ahmadi Boussoufa, N Amrabat, Belhanda (Fajr 63), Ziyech, Boutaib (En-Nesyri 70). **Scorers**: Boutaib (14), En-Nesyri (81). **Booked**: El Ahmadi, N Amrabat, Boussoufa, Da Costa, El Kajoui, Hakimi

**Referee**: R Irmatov (Ukbekistan). **Half-time**: 1-1

| | P | W | D | L | F | A | Pts |
|---|---|---|---|---|---|---|---|
| Spain Q | 3 | 1 | 2 | 0 | 6 | 5 | 5 |
| Portugal Q | 3 | 1 | 2 | 0 | 5 | 4 | 5 |
| Iran | 3 | 1 | 1 | 1 | 2 | 2 | 4 |
| Morocco | 3 | 0 | 1 | 2 | 2 | 4 | 1 |

## GROUP C

**FRANCE 2 AUSTRALIA 1**
**Kazan (41,279): Saturday, June 16**

**France** (4-3-3): Lloris, Pavard, Varane, Umtiti, Hernandez, Pogba, Kante, Tolisso (Matuidi 79), Dembele (Fekir 69), Griezmann (Giroud 69), Mbappe. **Scorers**: Griezmann (58 pen), Behich (80 og). **Booked**: Tolisso

**Australia** (4-2-3-1): Ryan, Risdon, Sainsbury, Milligan, Behich, Mooy, Jedinak, Leckie, Rogic (Irvine 71), Kruse (Arzani 85), Nabbout (Juric 65). **Scorer**: Jedinak (62 pen). **Booked**: Risdon, Behich, Leckie

**Referee**: A Cunha (Uruguay). **Half-time**: 0-0

**PERU 0 DENMARK 1**
**Saransk (40,502); Saturday, June 16**

**Peru** (4-2-3-1): Gallese, Advincula, Rodriguez, Ramos, Trauco, Tapia (Aquino 87), Yotun, Carrillo, Cueva, Flores (Guerrero 62), Farfan (Ruidiaz 85). **Booked**: Tapia

**Denmark** (4-2-3-1): Schmeichel, Dalsgaard, Kjaer, Christensen (M Jorgensen 81), Larsen, Kvist (Schone 36), Delaney, Poulsen, Eriksen, Sisto (Braithwaite 67), N Jorgensen. **Scorer**: Poulsen (59). **Booked**: Delaney, Poulsen

**Referee**: B Gassama (Gambia). **Half-time**: 0-0

**DENMARK 1 AUSTRALIA 1**
**Samara (40,727); Thursday, June 21**

**Denmark** (4-2-3-1): Schmeichel, Dalsgaard, Kjaer, Christensen, Larsen, Delaney, Schone, Eriksen, Poulsen (Braithwaite 59), N Jorgensen (Cornelius 68), Sisto. **Scorer**: Eriksen (7). **Booked**: Poulsen, Sisto

**Australia** (4-2-3-1): Ryan, Risdon, Sainsbury, Milligan, Behich, Jedinak, Mooy, Leckie, Rogic (Irvine 82), Kruse (Arzani 68), Nabbout (Juric 75). **Scorer**: Jedinak (38 pen)

**Referee**: A Mateu Lahoz (Spain). **Half-time**: 1-0

**FRANCE 1 PERU 0**

**Ekaterinburg (32,789); Thursday, June 21**

**France** (4-2-3-1): Lloris, Pavard, Varane, Umtiti, Hernandez, Pogba (Nzonzi 85), Kante, Mbappe (Dembele 75), Griezmann (Fekir 79), Matuidi, Giroud. **Scorer**: Mbappe (34). **Booked**: Matuidi, Pogba

**Peru** (4-2-3-1): Gallese, Advincula, Rodriguez (Santamaria 46), Ramos, Trauco, Aquino, Yotun (Farfan 46), Carrillo, Cueva (Ruidiaz 82), Flores, Guerrero. **Booked**: Guerrero, Aquino

**Referee**: M Hassan (United Arab Emirates). **Half-time**: 1-0

**AUSTRALIA 0 PERU 2**

**Sochi (44,073); Tuesday, June 26**

**Australia** (4-4-1-1): Ryan, Risdon, Sainsbury, Milligan, Behich, Leckie, Jedinak, Mooy, Kruse (Arzani 58), Rogic (Irvine 71), Juric (Cahill 53). **Booked**: Jedinak, Arzani, Rogic, Milligan

**Peru** (4-2-3-1): Gallese, Advincula, Ramos, Santamaria, Trauco, Tapia (Hurtado 64), Yotun (Aquino 46), Carrillo (Cartagena 79), Cueva, Flores, Guerrero. **Scorers**: Carrillo (18), Guerrero (50). **Booked**: Yotun, Hurtado

**Referee**: S Karasev (Russia). **Half-time**: 0-1

**DENMARK 0 FRANCE 0**

**Moscow Luzhniki (78,011); Tuesday, June 26**

**Denmark** (4-2-3-1): Schmeichel, Dalsgaard, Kjaer, Christensen, Larsen, M Jorgensen, Delaney (Lerager 90), Braithwaite, Eriksen, Sisto (Fischer 59), Cornelius (Dolberg 75). **Booked**: Jorgensen

**France** (4-2-3-1): Mandanda, Sidibe, Varane, Kimpembe, Hernandez (Mendy 49), N'Zonzi, Kante, Dembele (Mbappe 77), Griezmann (Fekir 68), Lemar, Giroud

**Referee**: S Ricci (Brazil)

| | P | W | D | L | F | A | Pts |
|---|---|---|---|---|---|---|---|
| France Q | 3 | 2 | 1 | 0 | 3 | 1 | 7 |
| Denmark Q | 3 | 1 | 2 | 0 | 2 | 1 | 5 |
| Peru | 3 | 1 | 0 | 2 | 2 | 2 | 3 |
| Australia | 3 | 0 | 1 | 2 | 2 | 5 | 1 |

## GROUP D

**ARGENTINA 1 ICELAND 1**

**Moscow Spartak (44,190); Saturday, June 16**

**Argentina** (4-2-3-1): Cabellero, Salvio, Otamendi, Rojo, Tagliafico, Biglia (Banega 54), Mascherano, Meza (Higuain 84), Messi, Di Maria (Pavon 75), Aguero. **Scorer**: Aguero (19)

**Iceland** (4-4-1-1): Halldorsson, Saevarsson, Arnason, R Sigurdsson, Magnusson, B Gudmundsson (Gislason 63), Gunnarsson (Skulason 76), Hallfredsson, Bjarnason, G Sigurdsson, Finnbogason (Sigurdarson 89). **Scorer**: Finnbogarson (23)

**Referee**: S Marcinak (Poland). **Half-time**: 1-1

**CROATIA 2 NIGERIA 0**

**Kaliningrad (31,136); Saturday, June 16**

**Croatia** (4-2-3-1): Subasic, Vrsaljko, Lovren, Vida, Strinic, Modric, Rakitic, Rebic (Kovacic 79), Kramaric (Brozovic 61), Perisic, Mandzukic (Pjaca 85). **Scorers**: Etebo (32 og), Modric (71 pen). **Booked**: Rakitic, Brozovic

**Nigeria** (4-2-3-1): Uzoho, Shehu, Troost-Ekong, Balogun, Idowu, Ndidi, Etebo, Moses, Mikel, Iwobi (Musa 62), Ighalo (Iheanacho73). **Booked**: Troost-Ekong

**Referee**: S Ricci (Brazil). **Half-time**: 1-0

### ARGENTINA 0 CROATIA 3

**Nizhny Novgorod (43,319); Thursday, June 21**

**Argentina** (3-4-3): Cabellero, Tagliafico, Otamendi, Mercado, Acuna, Mascherano, Perez (Dybala 68), Salvio (Pavon 56), Meza, Aguero (Higuain 54), Messi. **Booked**: Mercado, Otamendi, Acuna

**Croatia** (4-2-3-1): Subasic, Vrsaljko, Lovren, Vida, Strinic, Modric, Rakitic, Rebic (Kramaric 57), Brozovic, Perisic (Kovacic 82), Mandzukic (Corluka 90+2). **Scorers**: Rebic (53), Modric (80), Rakitic (90+1). **Booked**: Rebic, Mandzukic, Vrsaljko

**Referee**: R Irmatov (Uzbekistan). **Half-time**: 0-0

### NIGERIA 2 ICELAND 0

**Volgograd (40,904); Friday, June 22**

**Nigeria** (3-5-2): Uzoho, Balogun, Troost-Ekong, Omeruo, Moses, Ndidi, Mikel, Etebo (Iwobi 90), Idowu (Ebuehi 46), Musa, Iheanacho (Ighalo 84). **Scorers**: Musa (49, 75). **Booked**: Idowu

**Iceland** (4-4-2): Halldorsson, Saevarsson, Arnason, R Sigurdsson (Ingason 65), Magnusson, Gislason, G Sigurdsson, Gunnarsson (Skulason 86), Bjarnason, Finnbogason, Bodvarsson (Sigurdarson 71)

**Referee**: M Conger (New Zealand). **Half-time**: 0-0

### ICELAND 1 CROATIA 2

**Rostov (43,472): Tuesday, June 26**

**Iceland** (4-2-3-1): Halldorsson, Saevarsson, Ingason, R Sigurdsson (Sigurdarson 71), Magnusson, Hallfredsson, Gunnarsson, Gudmundsson, G Sigurdsson, Bjarnason (Traustason 90), Finnbogason. **Scorer**: Sigurdsson (76 pen). **Booked**: Hallfredsson, Saevarsson, Finnbogason

**Croatia** (4-3-2-1): Kalinic, Jedvaj, Corluka, Caleta-Car, Pivaric, Modric, Badelj, Kovacic (Rakitic 81), Pjaca (Lovren 69), Perisic, Kramaric. **Scorers**: Badelj (53), Perisic (90), **Booked**: Jedvaj, Pjaca

**Referee**: A Mateu Lahoz (Spain). **Half-time**: 0-0

### NIGERIA 1 ARGENTINA 2

**St Petersburg (64,468): Tuesday, June 26**

**Nigeria** (3-5-2): Uzoho, Balogun, Troost-Ekong, Omeruo (Iwobi 90), Moses, Ndidi, Mikel, Etebo, Idowu, Musa (Nwanko 90+2), Iheanacho (Ighalo 46). **Scorer**: Moses (50 pen). **Booked**: Balogun, Mikel

**Argentina** (4-3-3): Armani, Mercado, Otamendi, Rojo, Tagliafico (Aguero 80, Mascherano, Perez (Pavlon 61), Banega, Messi, Higuain, Di Maria (Meza 72). **Scorers**: Messi (14), Rojo (86). **Booked**: Mascherano, Banega, Messi

**Referee**: C Cakir (Turkey). **Half-time**: 0-1

| | P | W | D | L | F | A | Pts |
|---|---|---|---|---|---|---|---|
| Croatia Q | 3 | 3 | 0 | 0 | 7 | 1 | 9 |
| Argentina Q | 3 | 1 | 1 | 1 | 3 | 5 | 4 |
| Nigeria | 3 | 1 | 0 | 2 | 3 | 4 | 3 |
| Iceland | 3 | 0 | 1 | 2 | 2 | 5 | 1 |

## GROUP E

### COSTA RICA 0 SERBIA 1

**Samara (41,432): Sunday, June 17**

**Costa Rica** (5-4-1): Navas, Gamboa, Acosta, Gonzalez, Duarte, Calvo, Venegas (Bolanos 60), Guzman (Colindres 73), Borges, Ruiz, Urena (Campbell 67). **Booked**: Calvo, Guzman

**Serbia** (4-2-3-1): Stojkovic, Ivanovic, Milenkovic, Tosic, Kolarov, Milivojevic, Matic, Tadic (Rukavina 83), Milinkovic-Savic, Ljajic (Kostic 70), Mitrovic (Prijovic 90). **Scorer**: Kolarov (56). **Booked**: Ivanovic, Prijovic

**Referee**: M Diedhiou (Senegal). **Half-time**: 0-0

**BRAZIL 1 SWITZERLAND 1**
**Rostov (43,109): Sunday, June 17**

**Brazil** (4-2-3-1): Alisson, Danilo, Thiago Silva, Miranda, Marcelo, Casemiro (Fernandinho 60), Paulinho (Renato Augusto 68), Willian, Coutinho, Neymar, Gabriel Jesus (Firmino 79). **Scorer**: Coutinho (20). **Booked**: Casemiro
**Switzerland** (4-2-3-1): Sommer, Lichtsteiner (Lang 87), Schar, Akanji, Rodriguez, Behrami (Zakaria 71), Xhaka, Shaqiri, Dzemaili, Zuber, Seferovic (Embolo 80). **Scorer**: Zuber (50). **Booked**: Lichtsteiner, Schaer, Behrami
**Referee**: A Ramos (Mexico). **Half-time**: 1-0

**BRAZIL 2 COSTA RICA 0**
**St Petersburg (64,468); Friday, June 22**

**Brazil** (4-3-3): Alisson, Fagner, Thiago Silva, Miranda, Marcelo, Casemiro, Paulinho (Firmino 68), Coutinho, Willian (Costa 46), Neymar, Gabriel Jesus (Fernandinho 90+3). **Scorer**: Coutinho (90+1), Neymar (90+6). **Booked**: Neymar, Coutinho
**Costa Rica** (5-4-1): Navas, Gamboa (Calvo 75), Acosta, Gonzalez, Duarte, Oviedo, Venegas, Guzman (Tejeda 83), Borges, Ruiz, Urena (Bolanos 54)). **Booked**: Acosta
**Referee**: B Kuipers (Holland). **Half-time**: 0-0

**SERBIA 1 SWITZERLAND 2**
**Kaliningrad (33,167); Friday, June 22**

**Serbia** (4-2-3-1): Stojkovic, Ivanovic, Milenkovic, Tosic, Kolarov, Milivojevic (Radonjic 81), Matic, Tadic, Milinkovic-Savic, Kostic (Ljajic 65), Mitrovic. **Scorer**: Mitrovic (5). **Booked**: Milinkovic-Savic, Milivojevic, Matic, Mitrovic
**Switzerland** (4-2-3-1): Sommer, Lichtsteiner, Schar, Akanji, Rodriguez, Behrami, Xhaka, Shaqiri, Dzemaili (Embolo 73), Zuber (Dmic 90+4), Seferovic (Gavranovic 46). **Scorers**: Xhaka (52), Shaqiri (90). **Booked**: Shaqiri
**Referee**: F Brych (Germany). **Half-time**: 1-0

**SERBIA 0 BRAZIL 2**
**Moscow Spartak (44,190); Wednesday, June 27**

**Serbia** (4-2-3-1): Stojkovic, Rukavina, Milenkovic, Veljkovic, Kolarov, Milinkovic-Savic, Matic, Tadic, Ljajic (Zivkovic 75), Kostic (Radonjic 82), Mitrovic (Jovic 89). **Booked**: Ljajic, Matic, Mitrovic
**Brazil** (4-3-3): Alisson, Fagner, Thiago Silva, Miranda, Marcelo (Filipe Luis 10), Casemiro, Paulinho (Fernandinho 65), Coutinho (Renato Augusto 80), Willian, Neymar, Gabriel Jesus, **Scorers**: Paulinho (36), Thiago Silva (68)
**Referee**: A Faghani (Iran). **Half-time**: 0-1

**SWITZERLAND 2 COSTA RICA 2**
**Nizhny Novgorod (43,319); Wednesday, June 27**

**Switzerland** (4-2-3-1): Sommer, Lichtsteiner, Schar, Akanji, Rodriguez, Behrami (Zakaria 60), Xhaka, Shaqiri (Lang 81), Dzemaili, Embolo, Gavranovic (Drmic 69). **Scorers**: Dzemaili (31), Drmic (88). **Booked**: Lichtsteiner, Zakaria, Schar
**Costa Rica** (3-4-2-1): Navas, Acosta, Gonzalez, Waston, Gamboa (Smith 90+3), Borges, Guzman (Azofeifa 90+1), Oviedo, Ruiz, Colindres (Wallace 81), Campbell. **Scorers**: Waston (56), Sommer (90+3 og). **Booked**: Gamboa, Campbell, Waston
**Referee**: C Turpin (France). **Half-time**: 1-0

| | P | W | D | L | F | A | Pts |
|---|---|---|---|---|---|---|---|
| Brazil Q | 3 | 2 | 1 | 0 | 5 | 1 | 7 |
| Switzerland Q | 3 | 1 | 2 | 0 | 5 | 4 | 5 |
| Serbia | 3 | 1 | 0 | 2 | 2 | 4 | 3 |
| Costa Rica | 3 | 0 | 1 | 2 | 2 | 5 | 1 |

## GROUP F

**GERMANY 0 MEXICO 1**
**Moscow Luzhniki (78,011); Sunday, June 17**

**Germany** (4-2-3-1): Neuer, Kimmich, Boateng, Hummels, Plattenhardt (Gomez 79), Khedira (Reus 60), Kroos, Muller, Ozil, Draxler, Werner (Brandt 86). **Booked**: Muller, Hummels
**Mexico** (4-2-3-1): Ochoa, Salcedo, Ayala, Moreno, Gallardo, Guardado (Marquez 74), Herrera, Layun, Lozano (Jimenez 66), Vela (Alvarez 58), Hernandez. **Scorer**: Lozano (35). **Booked**: Moreno, Herrera
**Referee**: A Faghani (Iran). **Half-time**: 0-1

**SWEDEN 1 SOUTH KOREA 0**
**Nizhny Novgorod (42,300); Monday, June 18**

**Sweden** (4-4-2): Olsen, Lustig, Granqvist, Jansson, Augustinsson, Claesson, Ekdal (Hiljemark 71), Larsson (Svensson 81), Forsberg, Toivonen (Thelin 76), Berg. **Scorer**: Granqvist (65 pen). **Booked**: Claesson
**South Korea** (4-3-3): Cho Hyun-Woo, Lee Yong, Kim Young-Gwon, Jang Hyun-Soo, Park Joo-Ho (Kim Min-Moo 29), Koo Ja-Cheol (Lee Seung-woo 73), Ki Sung-Yueng, Lee Jae-Sung, Hwang Hee-Chan, Kim Shin-Wook (Jung Woo-Young 66), Son Heung-Min. **Booked**: Kim Shin-Wook, Hwang Hee-Chan
**Referee**: J Aguillar (El Salvador. **Half-time**: 0-0

**SOUTH KOREA 1 MEXICO 2**
**Rostov (43,472): Saturday, June 23**

**South Korea** (4-2-3-1): Cho Hyun-Woo, Lee Yong, Jang Hyun-Soo, Kim Young-Gwon, Kim Min-Moo (Hong Chul 84), Ju Se-Jong (Lee Seung-Woo 64), Ki Sung-Yueng, Lee Jae-Sung, Hwang Hee-Chan, Moon Seon-Min (Jung Woo-Young 77), Son Heung-Min. **Scorer**: Son Heung-Min (90+3). **Booked**: Kim Young-Gwon, Lee Yong, Lee Seung-Woo, Jung Woo-Young
**Mexico** (4-2-3-1): Ochoa, Alvarez, Salcedo, Moreno, Gallardo, Guardado (Marquez 68), Herrera, Layun, Lozano (Jesus Corona 71), Vela (G dos Santos 77), Hernandez. **Scorers**: Vela (26 pen), Hernandez (66)
**Referee**: M Mazic (Serbia). **Half-time**: 0-1

**GERMANY 2 SWEDEN 1**
**Sochi (44,287); Saturday, June 23**

**Germany** (4-2-3-1): Neuer, Kimmich, Boateng, Rudiger, Hector (Brandt 87), Rudy, (Gundogan 31), Kroos, Muller, Reus, Draxler (Gomez 46), Werner. **Scorers**: Reus (48), Kroos (90+5). **Booked**: Boateng. **Sent off**: Boateng (82)
**Sweden** (4-4-2): Olsen, Lustig, Lindelof, Granqvist, Augustinsson, Claesson (Durmaz 74), Ekdal Larsson, Forsberg, Berg (Thelin 90), Toivonen (Guidetti 78). **Scorer**: Toivonen (32)
**Referee**: S Marciniak (Poland). **Half-time**: 0-1

**MEXICO 0 SWEDEN 3**
**Ekaterinburg (33,061); Wednesday, June 27**

**Mexico** (4-2-3-1): Ochoa, Alvarez, Salcedo, Moreno, Gallardo (Fabian 65), Guardado (Jesus Corona 75), Herrera, Layun (Peralta 89), Lozano, Vela, Hernandez. Vela (26 pen), Hernandez (66). **Booked**: Gallardo, Moreno, Layun
**Sweden** (4-4-2): Olsen, Lustig, Lindelof, Granqvist, Augustinsson, Claesson, Ekdal (Hiljemark 80), Larsson (Svensson 57), Forsberg, Berg (Thelin 68), Toivonen. **Scorers**: Augustinsson (50), Granqvist (62 pen), Alvarez (74 og). **Booked**: Larsson, Lustig
**Referee**: N Pitane (Argentina). **Half-time**: 0-0

**SOUTH KOREA 2 GERMANY 0**
**Kazan (41,835); Wednesday, June 27**

**South Korea** (4-2-3-1): Cho Hyun-Woo, Lee Yong, Yun Young-Sun, Kim Young-Gwon, Hong

Chul, Lee Jae-Sung, Jang Hyun-Soo, Jung Woo-Young, Moon Seon-Min (Ju Se-Jong 69), Son Heung-Min, Koo Ja-Cheol (Hwang Hee-Chan 56) (Ko Yo-Han 79). **Scorers**: Kim Young-Gwon (90+2). Son Heung-Min (90+6). **Booked**: Jung Woo-Young, Lee Jae-Sung, Moon Seon-Min, Son Heung-Min

**Germany** (4-2-3-1): Neuer, Kimmich, Hummels, Sule, Hector (Brandt 78), Khedira (Gomez 58), Kroos, Goretzka (Muller 63), Ozil, Reus, Werner

**Referee**: M Geiger (USA). **Half-time**: 0-0

| | P | W | D | L | F | A | Pts |
|---|---|---|---|---|---|---|---|
| Sweden Q | 3 | 2 | 0 | 1 | 5 | 2 | 6 |
| Mexico Q | 3 | 2 | 0 | 1 | 3 | 4 | 6 |
| South Korea | 3 | 1 | 0 | 2 | 3 | 3 | 3 |
| Germany | 3 | 1 | 0 | 2 | 2 | 4 | 3 |

## GROUP G

**BELGIUM 3 PANAMA 0**
**Sochi (43,257; Monday, June 18**

**Belgium** (3-4-3): Courtois, Alderweireld, Boyata, Vertonghen, Meunier, Witsel (Chadli 90), De Bruyne, Carrasco (Dembele 74), Mertens (T Hazard 83), Lukaku, E Hazard. **Scorers**: Mertens (47), Lukaku (69, 75). **Booked**: Meunier, Vertonghen, De Bruyne

**Panama** (4-1-4-1): Penedo, Murillo, Escobar, R Torres, Davis, Gomez, Barcenas (G Torres 64), Godoy, Cooper, Rodriguez (Diaz 64), Perez (Tejeda 73). **Booked**: Davis, Barcenas, Cooper, Murillo, Godoy

**Referee**: J Sikazwe (Zambia). **Half-time**: 1-0

**TUNISIA 1 ENGLAND 2**
**Volgograd (41,064); Monday, June 18**

**Tunisia** (4-1-4-1): Hassen (Ben Mustapha 15), Bronn, S Ben Youssef, Meriah, Maaloul, Skhiri, F Ben Youssef, Sassi, Badri, Sliti (Ben Amor 74), Khazri (Khalifa 85). **Scorer**: Sassi (35 pen)

**England** (3-1-4-2): Pickford, Walker, Stones, Maguire, Henderson, Trippier, Lingard (Dier 90), Alli (Loftus-Cheek 80), Young, Sterling (Rashford 68), Kane. **Scorer**: Kane (11, 90+1). **Booked**: Walker

**Referee**: W Roldan (Colombia). **Half-time**: 1-1

**BELGIUM 5 TUNISIA 2**
**Moscow Spartak (44,190); Saturday, June 23**

**Belgium** (3-4-3): Courtois, Alderweireld, Boyata, Vertonghen, Meunier, Witsel, De Bruyne, Carrasco, Mertens (Tielemans 86), Lukaku (Fellaini 59), E Hazard (Batshuayi 67). **Scorers**: E Hazard (6 pen, 51), Lukaku (16, 45+3), Batshuayi (90)

**Tunisia** (4-3-3): Ben Mustapha, Bronn (Nagguez 24), S Ben Youssef (Benalouane 41), Meriah, Maaloul, Skhiri, Sassi (Sliti 60), Khaoui, F Ben Youssef, Khazri, Badri. **Scorers**: Bronn (18), Khazri (90+3). **Booked**: Sassi

**Referee**: J Marrufo (USA). **Half-time**: 3-1

**ENGLAND 6 PANAMA 1**
**Nizhny Novgorod (43,319); Sunday, June 24**

**England** (3-1-4-2): Pickford, Walker, Stones, Maguire, Henderson, Trippier (Rose 70, Lingard (Delph 63), Loftus-Cheek, Young, Sterling, Kane (Vardy 63). **Scorers**: Stones (8, 40), Kane (22 pen, 45+1 pen, 62), (Lingard 36). **Booked**: Loftus-Cheek

**Panama** (4-1-4-1): Penedo, Murillo, Escobar, R Torres, Davis, Gomez (Baloy 69), Barcenas (Arroyo 69) Godoy (Avila 63), Cooper, Rodriguez, Perez. **Scorer**: Baloy (78). **Booked**: Cooper, Escobar, Murillo

**Referee**: G Grisha (Egypt). **Half-time**: 5-0

**ENGLAND 0 BELGIUM 1**
**Kaliningrad (33,973): Thursday, June 28**

**England** (3-1-4-2): Pickford, Jones, Stones (Maguire 46), Cahill, Dier, Alexander-Arnold (Welbeck 79), Loftus-Cheek, Delph, Rose, Rashford, Vardy

**Belgium** (3-4-3): Courtois, Dendoncker, Boyata, Vermaelen (Kompany 74), Chadli, Dembele, Fellaini, T Hazard. Januzaj (Mertens 86), Batshuayi, Tielemans. **Scorer**: Januzaj (51). **Booked**: Tielemans, Dendoncker

**Referee**: D Skomina (Slovenia). **Half-time**: 0-0

**PANAMA 1 TUNISIA 2**
**Saransk (37,168); Thursday, June 28**

**Panama** (4-1-4-1): Penedo, Machado, Escobar, R Torres (Tejeda 56), Ovalle, Gomez, Rodriguez, Godoy, Avila (Arroyo 81), Barcenas, G Torres (Cummings 46). **Scorer**: Meriah (33 og). **Booked**: Avila, Gomez, Tejeda

**Tunisia** (4-1-4-1): Mathlouthi, Nagguez, Bedoui, Meriah, Haddadi, Skhiri, F Ben Youssef, Chalali, Sassi (Badri 46), Sliti (Khalil 77), Khazri (Srarfi 89). **Scorers**: Ben Youssef (51), Khazri (66). **Booked**: Sassi, Badri, Chalali

**Referee**: N Shukralla (Bahrain). **Half-time**: 1-0

| | P | W | D | L | F | A | Pts |
|---|---|---|---|---|---|---|---|
| Belgium Q | 3 | 3 | 0 | 0 | 9 | 2 | 9 |
| England Q | 3 | 2 | 0 | 1 | 8 | 3 | 6 |
| Tunisia | 3 | 1 | 0 | 2 | 5 | 8 | 3 |
| Pamana | 3 | 0 | 0 | 3 | 2 | 11 | 0 |

## GROUP H

**COLOMBIA 1 JAPAN 2**
**Saransk (40,842); Tuesday, June 19**

**Colombia** (4-2-3-1): Ospina, Arias, D Sanchez, Murillo, Mojica, Lerma, C Sanchez, Cuadrado (Barrios 31), Quintero (Rodriguez 59), Izquierdo (Bacca 70), Falcao. **Scorer**: Quintero (39). **Booked**: Barrios, Rodriguez. **Sent off**: C Sanchez (4)

**Japan** (4-2-3-1): Kawashima, H Sakai, Yoshida, Shoji, Nagatomo, Shibasaki (Yamaguchi 80), Hasebe, Haraguchi, Kagawa (Honda 70), Inui, Osako (Okazaki 85). **Scorers**: Kagawa (6 pen), Osako (73). **Booked**: Kawashima

**Referee**: D Skomina (Slovenia). Half-time: 1-1

**POLAND 1 SENEGAL 2**
**Moscow Spartak (44,190); Tuesday, June 19**

**Poland** (4-3-2-1)): Szczesny, Piszczek (Bereszyski 81), Pazdan, Cionek, Rybus, Blaszczykowski (Bednarek 46), Krychowiak, Zielinski, Grosicki, Milik (Kownacki 73), Lewandowski. **Scorer**: Krychowiak (85). **Booked**: Krychowiak

**Senegal** (4-4-2): K N'Diaye, Wague, Sane, Koulibaly, Sabaly, Sarr, Gueye, A N'Diaye (Kouyate 87, Mane, Diouf (N'Doye 60), Niang (Konate 74). **Scorers**: Cionek (37 og), Niang (60). **Booked**: Sane, Gueye

**Referee**: N Shukralla (Bahrain). **Half-time**: 0-1

**JAPAN 2 SENEGAL 2**
**Ekaterinburg (32,572); Sunday, June 24**

**Japan** (4-2-3-1): Kawashima, H Sakai, Yoshida, Shoji, Nagatomo, Shibasaki, Hasebe, Haraguchi (Okazaki 75), Kagawa (Honda 72), Inui (Usami 87), Osako. **Scorers**: Inui (34), Honda (78). **Booked**: Inui, Hasebe

**Senegal** (4-1-4-1): K N'Diaye, Wague, Sane, Koulibaly, Sabaly, A N'Diaye (Kouyate 65), Sarr, B N'Diaye (N'Doye 81), Gueye, Mane, Niang (Diouf 86). **Scorers**: Mane (11), Wague (71). **Booked**: Niang, Sabaly, N'Doye

**Referee**: G Rocchi (Italy). **Half-time**: 1-1

**POLAND 0 COLOMBIA 3**
**Kazan (42,873); Sunday, June 24**

**Poland** (3-4-3): Szczesny, Piszczek, Bednarek, Pazdan (Glik 80), Bereszynski (Teodorzyk 72) Krychowiak, Goralski, Rybus, Sielinski, Lewandowski, Kownacki (Grosicki 57). **Booked**: Bednarek, Goralski

**Colombia** (4-2-3-1): Ospina, Arias, Mina, D Sanchez, Mojica, Aguilar (Uribe 32), Barrios, Cuadrado, Rodriguez, Quintero, (Lerma 73), Falcao (Bacca 78). **Scorers**: Mina (40), Falcao (70), Cuadrado (75)

**Referee**: C Ramos (Mexico). **Half-time**: 0-1

**JAPAN 0 POLAND 1**
**Volgograd (42,189); Thursday, June 28**

**Japan** (4-2-3-1): Kawashima, H Sakai, Yoshida, Makino, Nagatomo, Yamaguchi, Shibasaki, G Sakai, Okazaki (Osako 47), Usami (Inui 65), Mutom (Hasebe 82). **Booked**: Makino

**Poland** (3-4-3): Fabianski, Bereszynski, Glik, Bednarek, Kurzawa (Peszko 80), Krychowiak, Goralski, Jedrzejczyk, Zielinski (Teodorczyk 79), Lewandowski, Grosicki. **Scorer**: Bednarek (59)

**Referee**: J Sikazwe (Zambia). **Half-time**: 0-0

**SENEGAL 0 COLOMBIA 1**
**Samara (41,970): Thursday, June 28**

**Senegal** (4-4-2): K N'Diaye, Gassama, Sane, Koulibaly, Sabaly (Wague 74), Sarr, Kouyate, Gueye, Balde (Konate 80), Niang (Sakho 86), Mane. **Booked**: Niang

**Colombia** (4-3-2-1): Ospina, Arias, Mina, D Sanchez, Mojica, Quintero, C Sanchez, Uribe (Lerma 83), Cuadrado, Rodriguez (Muriel 31), Falcao (Borja 89). **Scorer**: Mina (74). **Booked**: Mojica

| | P | W | D | L | F | A | Pts |
|---|---|---|---|---|---|---|---|
| Colombia Q | 3 | 2 | 0 | 1 | 5 | 2 | 6 |
| Japan Q | 3 | 1 | 1 | 1 | 4 | 4 | 4 |
| Senegal | 3 | 1 | 1 | 1 | 4 | 4 | 4 |
| Poland | 3 | 1 | 0 | 2 | 2 | 5 | 3 |

## ROUND OF 16

**FRANCE 4 ARGENTINA 3**
**Kazan (42,873); Saturday, June 30**

**France** (4-2-3-1): Lloris, Pavard, Varane, Umtiti, Hernandez, Pogba, Kante, Mbappe (Thauvin 89), Griezmann (Fekir 83), Matuidi (Tolisso 73), Giroud. **Scorers**: Griezmann (13 pen), Pavard (57), Mbappe (64, 68). **Booked**: Matuidi, Pavard, Giroud

**Argentina** (4-3-3): Armani, Mercado, Otamendi, Rojo (Fazio 46), Tagliafico, Mascherano, Perez (Aguero 66), Banega, Pavon, (Meza 73), Messi, Di Maria. **Scorers**: Di Maria (41), Mercado (48), Aguero (90+3). **Booked**: Rojo, Tagliafico, Mascherano, Banega, Otamendi

**Referee**: A Faghani (Iran). **Half-time**: 1-1

**URUGUAY 2 PORTUGAL 1**
**Sochi (44,287); Saturday, June 30**

**Uruguay** (4-3-1-2): Muslera, Caceres, Gimenez, Godin, Laxalt, Nandez (Sanchez 81), Vecino Torreira, Betancur (Rodriguez 63), Suarez, Cavani (Stuani 74). **Scorer**: Cavani (7, 62)

**Portugal** (4-4-2): Rui Patricio, Ricardo Pereira, Pepe, Fonte, Guerreiro, Bernardo Silva, William Carvalho, Adrien Silva (Ricardo Quaresma 65), Joao Mario (Fernandes 84), Guedes (Andre Silva 74), Ronaldo. **Scorer**: Pepe (55). **Booked**: Ronaldo

**Referee**: A Ramos (Mexico). **Half-time**: 1-0

**SPAIN 1 RUSSIA 1 (aet, Russia won 4-3 on pens)**
**Moscow Luzhniki (78,011); Sunday, July 1**

**Spain** (4-2-3-1): De Gea, Nacho (Dani Carvajal 70), Pique, Sergio Ramos, Jordi Alba, Koke, Busquets, Silva (Iniesta 67), Isco, Marco Asensio (Rodrigo 104), Diego Costa (Aspas 80). **Scorer**: Ignashevich (12 og). **Booked**: Pique
**Russia** (5-3-1-1): Akinfeev, Fernandes, Kutepov, Ignashevich, Kudriashov, Zhirkov (Granat 46), Samedov (Cheryshev 61), Zobnin, Kuziaev (Erokhin 97), Golovin, Dzyuba (Smolov 65). **Scorer**: Dzyuba (41 pen). **Booked**: Kutepov, Zobnin
**Referee**: B Kuipers (Holland). **Half-time**: 1-1

**CROATIA 1 DENMARK 1 (aet, Croatia won 3-2 on pens)**
**Nizhny Novgorod (40,851); Sunday, July 1**

**Croatia** (4-3-3): Kalinic, Vrsalijko, Lovren, Vida, Strinic (Pivaric 81), Modric, Brozovic (Kovacic 71), Rakitic, Rebic, Mandzukic (Badelj 108), Perisic (Kramaric 97). **Scorer**: Mandzukic (4)
**Denmark** (4-2-3-1): Schmeichel, Dalsgaard, Kjaer, M Jorgensen, Knudsen, Christensen (Schonne 46), Delaney (Krohn-Dehli 98), Yurary, Eriksen, Braithwaite (Sisto 105), Cornelius (N Jorgensen 66). **Scorer**: M Jorgensen (1). **Booked**: M Jorgensen
**Referee**: N Pitana (Argentina). **Half-time**: 1-1

**BRAZIL 2 MEXICO 0**
**Samara (41,970); Monday, July 2**

**Brazil** (4-3-3): Alisson, Fagner, Thiago Silva, Miranda, Filipe Luis, Casemiro, Paulinho (Fernandinho 81), Coutinho (Firmino 86)), Willian (Marquinos 90+1), Neymar, Gabriel Jesus. **Scorers**: Neymar (51), Firmino (88). **Booked**: Filipe Luis, Casemiro
**Mexico** (4-3-3): Ochoa, Alvarez (J dos Santos 55), Ayala, Salcedo, Gallardo, Herrera, Guardado, Marquez (Layun 46), Vela, Hernandez (Jimenez 59), Lozano. **Booked**: Alvarez, Herrera, Salcedo, Guardado
**Referee**: G Rocchi (Italy). **Half-time**: 0-0

**BELGIUM 3 JAPAN 2**
**Rostov (41,466); Monday, July 2**

**Belgium** (3-4-2-1): Courtois, Alderweireld, Kompany, Vertonghen, Meunier, Witsel, De Bruyne, Carrasco (Chadli 64), Mertens (Fellaini 64), E Hazard, Lukaku. **Scorers**: Vertonghen (69), Fellaini (74), Chadli (90+4)
**Japan** (4-2-3-1): Kawashima, H Sakai, Yoshida, Shoji, Nagatomo, Shibasaki (Yamaguchi 81), Hasebe, Haraguchi (Honda 81), Kagawa, Inui, Osako. **Scorers**: Haraguchi (48), Inui (52). **Booked**: Shibasaki
**Referee**: M Diedhiou (Senegal). **Half-time**: 0-0

**SWEDEN 1 SWITZERLAND 0**
**St Petersburg (64,042); Tuesday, July 3**

**Sweden** (4-4-2): Olsen, Lustig (Krafth 82), Lindelof, Granqvist, Augustinsson, Claesson, Ekdal Svensson, Forsberg (Olsson 82), Berg (Thelin 90+1), Toivonen. **Scorer**: Forsberg (64). **Booked**: Lustig
**Switzerland** (4-2-3-1): Sommer, Lang, Akanji, Djourou, Rodriguez, Behrami, Xhaka, Shaqiri, Dzemaili (Seferovic 73), Zuber (Embolo 73), Drmic. **Booked**: Behrami, Xhaka. **Sent off**: Lang (90+4)
**Referee**: D Skomina (Slovenia). **Half-time**: 0-0

**COLOMBIA 1 ENGLAND 1 (aet, England won 4-3 on pens)**
**Moscow Spartak (44,190); Tuesday, July 3**

**Colombia** (4-3-2-1): Ospina, Arias (Zapata 116), Mina, D Sanchez, Mojica, Barrios, C Sanchez (Uribe 79), Lerma (Bacca 61), Cuadrado, Quintero (Muriel 88), Falcao. **Scorer**: Mina (90+3). **Booked**: Barrios, Arias, C Sanchez, Falcao, Bacca, Quadrado

**England** (3-1-4-2): Pickford, Walker (Rashford 113), Stones, Maguire, Henderson, Trippier, Lingard, Alli (Dier 81), Young (Rose 102), Sterling (Vardy 88), Kane. **Scorer**: Kane (57 pen). **Booked**: Henderson, Lingard

**Penalty shoot-out** (Colombia first): Falcao 1-0, Kane 1-1, Quadrado 2-1, Rashford 2-2, Muriel 3-2, Henderson saved, Uribe missed, Trippier 3-3, Bacca saved, Dier 3-4

**Referee**: M Geiger (USA). **Half-time**: 0-0

## QUARTER-FINALS

**URUGUAY 0 FRANCE 2**

**Nizhny Novgorod (43,319); Friday, July 6**

**Uruguay** (4-3-1-2): Muslera, Caceres, Gimenez, Godin, Laxalt, Nandez (Urretaviscaya 73), Vecino, Torreira, Betancur (Rodriguez 59), Suarez, Stuani (Gomez 59). **Booked**: Betancur, Rodriguez

**France** (4-2-3-1): Lloris, Pavard, Varane, Umtiti, Hernandez, Pogba, Kante, Mbappe (Dembele 88), Griezmann (Fekir 90), Tolisso (Nzonzi 80), Giroud. **Scorers**: Varane (40), Griezmann (61). **Booked**: Hernandez, Mbappe

**Referee**: N Pitana (Argentina). **Half-time**: 0-1

**BRAZIL 1 BELGIUM 2**

**Kazan (42,873); Friday, July 6**

**Brazil** (4-3-3): Alisson, Fagner, Thiago Silva, Miranda, Marcelo, Coutinho, Fernandinho, Paulinho (Renato Augusto 73), Neymar, Gabriel Jesus (Douglas Costa 58), Willian (Firmino 46). **Scorer**: Renato Augusto (76). **Booked**: Fernandinho, Fagner

**Belgium** (3-4-3): Courtois, Alderweireld, Kompany, Vertonghen, Meunier, Fellaini, Witsel, Chadli, (Vermaelen 83), Lukaku, (Tielemans 87), De Bruyne, E Hazard. **Scorers**: Fernandinho (13 og), De Bruyne (31). **Booked**: Alderweireld, Meunier

**Referee**: M Mazic (Serbia). **Half-time**: 0-2

**SWEDEN 0 ENGLAND 2**

**Samara (39,991); Saturday, July 7**

**Sweden** (4-4-2): Olsen, Krafth (Jansson 85), Lindelof, Granqvist, Augustinsson, Claesson, Larsson, Ekdal, Forsberg (Olsson 65), Berg, Toivonen (Guidetti 65). **Booked**: Guidetti, Larsson

**England** (3-1-4-2): Pickford, Walker, Stones, Maguire, Henderson (Dier 84), Trippier, Lingard, Alli (Delph 77), Young, Sterling (Rashford 90+1), Kane. **Scorers**: Maguire (30), Alli (58). **Booked**: Maguire

**Referee**: B Kuipers (Holland). **Half-time**: 0-1

**RUSSIA 2 CROATIA 2 (aet, Croatia won 4-3 on pens)**

**Sochi (44,287); Saturday, July 7**

**Russia** (4-2-3-1): Akinfeev, Fernandes, Kutepov, Ignashevich, Kudriashov, Kuziaev, Samedov (Erokhin 54), Zobnin, Golovin (Drazoev 102), Cheryshev (Smolov 67), Dzyuba (Gazinsky 79). **Scorers**: Cheryshev (31), Fernandes (115). **Booked**: Gazinsky

**Croatia** (4-2-3-1): Subasic, Vrsalijko (Corluka 97), Lovren, Vida, Strinic (Pivaric 72), Modric, Rakitic, Rebic, Kramaric (Kovacic 88), Perisic (Brozovic 62), Mandzukic. **Scorers**: Kramaric (39), Vida (100). **Booked**: Lovren, Strinic, Vida, Pivaric

**Referee**: S Ricci (Brazil). **Half-time**: 1-1

## SEMI-FINALS

**FRANCE 1 BELGIUM 0**

**St Petersburg (64,286); Tuesday, July 10**

**France** (4-2-3-1): Lloris, Pavard, Varane, Umtiti, Hernandez, Pogba, Kante, Mbappe, Griezmann, Matuidi (Tolisso 86), Giroud (Nzonzi 84). **Scorer**: Umtiti (51). **Booked**: Kante, Mbappe

**Belgium** (4-2-3-1): Courtois, Chadli (Batshuayi 90+1), Alderweireld, Kompany, Vertonghen, Witsel, Dembele (Mertens 60), De Bruyne, Fellaini (Carrasco 80), Lukaku, E Hazard.
**Booked**: E Hazard, Alderweireld, Vertonghen
**Referee**: A Cunha (Uruguay). **Half-time**: 0-0

**CROATIA 2 ENGLAND 1 (aet)**
**Moscow Luzhniki (78,011); Wednesday, July 11**

**Croatia** (4-1-4-1): Subasic, Vrsaljko, Lovren, Vida, Strinic (Pivaric 95), Brozovic, Rebic (Kramaric 101), Modric (Badelj 119), Rakitic, Perisic, Mandzukic (Corluka 115). **Scorers**: Perisic (68), Mandzukic (109). **Booked**: Mandzukic, Rebic
**England** (3-1-4-2): Pickford, Walker (Vardy 112), Stones, Maguire, Henderson (Dier 97), Trippier, Lingard, Alli, Young (Rose 90), Sterling (Rashford 74), Kane. **Scorer**: Tripper (5).
**Booked**: Walker
**Referee**: C Cakir (Turkey). **Half-time**: 1-0

## THIRD PLACE PLAY-OFF

**BELGIUM 2 ENGLAND 0**
**St Petersburg (64,406); Saturday, July 14**

**Belgium** (3-4-3): Courtois, Alderweireld, Kompany, Vertonghen, Meunier, Tielemens (Dembele 78), Witsel, Chadli (Vermaelen 39), De Bruyne, Lukaku (Mertens 60), E Hazard.
**Scorers**: Meunier (4), E Hazard (82). **Booked**: Witsel
**England** (3-1-4-2): Pickford, Jones, Stones, Maguire, Dier, Trippier, Loftus-Cheek (Alli 85), Delph, Rose (Lingard 46), Sterling (Rashford 46), Kane B**ooked**: Stones, Maguire
**Referee**: A Faghani (Iran). **Half-time**: 1-0

## FINAL

**FRANCE 4 CROATIA 2**
**Moscow Luzhniki (78,011); Sunday, July 15**

**France** (4-2-3-1): Lloris, Pavard, Varane, Umtiti, Hernandez, Pogba, Kante (Nzonzi 55), Mbappe, Griezmann, Matuidi (Tolisso 73), Giroud (Fekir 81). **Subs not used**: Mandanda, Areola, Kimpembe, Lemar, Dembele, Rami, Sidibe, Thauvin. Mendy. **Scorers**: Mandzukic (18 og), Griezmann (38 pen), Pogba (59), Mbappe (65). **Booked**: Kante, Hernandez.
**Coach**: Didier Deschamps
**Croatia** (4-1-4-1): Subasic, Vrsaljko, Lovren, Vida, Strinic (Pjaca 81)), Brozovic, Rebic (Kramaric 71), Modric, Rakitic, Perisic, Mandzukic. **Subs not used**: Livakovic, Kalinic, Corluka, Kovacic, Jedvaj, Bradaric, Caleta-Car, Badelj, Pivaric. **Scorers**: Perisic (28), Mandzukic (69). **Booked**: Vrsaljko. **Coach**: Zlatko Dalic
**Referee**: N Pitana (Argentina). **Half-time**: 2-1

# THE THINGS THEY SAY ...

'It hurt so much to lose the Euro final two years ago. But it made us learn. We worked so hard and this was the supreme coronation' – **Didier Deschamps**, coach of champions France.

'I told the players to hold their heads high. There is nothing to feel dissatisfied about. You can be proud of your performances' – **Zlatko Dalic**, Croatia coach, whose side went to extra-time in three previous rounds.

'We were so close to what was unimaginable at the start. Now we have a new benchmark, a new level of expectation, a new scenario. Many of these players have come of age on an international stage' – **Gareth Southgate**, England manager.

'It hurts a lot and it will hurt for a while. But this has been a fantastic journey. I'm proud of what we achieved and it's a great foundation for the future' – **Harry Kane,** England captain.

# RUSSIA 2018 FACTS AND FIGURES

● Didier Deschamps, captain of France's successful 1998 side, joined an elite list of World Cup winners as player and coach. He followed West Germany's Franz Beckenbauer (1974, 1990) and Brazil's Mario Zagallo, who lifted the trophy in 1958 and 1962 and was in charge in 1970.

● Beaten finalist Luka Modric was named the tournament's outstanding player, ahead of Eden Hazard and Antoine Griezmann. Kylian Mbappe won the best young player award and Thibaut Courtois was voted top goalkeeper.

● Harry Kane's six goals – three penalties, two from corners and one from open play – gave him the Golden Boot award. That was two more than Russia's Denis Cheryshev, Belgium's Romelu Lukaku and Portugal's Cristiano Ronaldo.

● Harry Kane was the first player since Tommy Lawton in 1939 to score in six successive appearances for England – three in pre-World Cup matches and three in the finals.

● England's total of 12 goals was their best-ever at a World Cup, one more than the winning team of 1966.

● John Stones became the first defender to score twice for England in the finals, in their record 6-1 win over Panama.

● Germany were the fourth defending champions to be eliminated at the group stage in the last five tournaments, following France (2002), Italy (2010) and Spain (2014).

● Russia's 5-0 victory over Saudi Arabia was a record scoreline for the opening match, overtaking Brazil's 4-0 win over Mexico in 1950.

● Mexico's Jesus Gallardo was booked after 15 seconds for charging into the back of Sweden striker Ola Toivonen – the fastest in the tournament's history.

● The oldest player to feature at a World Cup, 45-year-old Egypt goalkeeper Essam El Hadary, saved a penalty against Saudi Arabia.

● With a hat-trick against Spain, Cristiano Ronaldo joined Miroslav Klose, Uwe Seeler and Pele in scoring in four World Cups.

● For the first time since 1982, no African team made it beyond the group stage.

● There were just four red cards in the tournament – Carlos Sanchez (Colombia), Jerome Boateng (Germany) and Igor Smolnikov (Russia) in group matches and Michael Lang (Switzerland) in the first knockout round. The total was six fewer than in Brazil four years ago and the lowest since the 1978 finals in Argentina.

● The Football Association were fined £53,000 after the quarter-final win over Sweden for their players wearing unauthorised commercial branding on their playing socks.

● **England squad**: Butland (Stoke), Pickford (Everton), Pope (Burnley); Alexander-Arnold (Liverpool), Cahill (Chelsea), Delph (Man City), Jones (Man Utd), Maguire (Leicester), Rose (Tottenham), Stones (Man City), Trippier (Tottenham), Walker (Man City), Young (Man Utd); Alli (Tottenham), Dier (Tottenham), Henderson (Liverpool), Lingard (Man Utd), Loftus-Cheek (Chelsea); Kane (Tottenham), Rashford (Man Utd), Sterling (Man City), Vardy (Leicester), Welbeck (Arsenal)

# WORLD CUP SUMMARIES 1930–2014

## 1930 – URUGUAY

**WINNERS: Uruguay RUNNERS-UP: Argentina THIRD: USA FOURTH: Yugoslavia**
Other countries taking part: Belgium, Bolivia, Brazil, Chile, France, Mexico, Paraguay, Peru, Romania. **Total entries:** 13
**Venue:** All matches played in Montevideo
**Top scorer:** Stabile (Argentina) 8 goals
**Final** (30/7/30): **Uruguay 4** (Dorado 12, Cea 55, Iriarte 64, Castro 89) **Argentina 2** (Peucelle 29, Stabile 35). **Att:** 90,000
**Uruguay:** Ballesteros; Nasazzi (capt), Mascheroni, Andrade, Fernandez, Gestido, Dorado, Scarone, Castro, Cea, Iriarte
**Argentina:** Botasso; Della Torre, Paternoster, J Evaristo, Monti, Suarez, Peucelle, Varallo, Stabile, Ferreira (capt), M Evaristo
**Referee:** Langenus (Belgium). **Half-time:** 1-2

## 1934 – ITALY

**WINNERS: Italy RUNNERS-UP: Czechoslovakia THIRD: Germany FOURTH: Austria**
Other countries in finals: Argentina, Belgium, Brazil, Egypt, France, Holland, Hungary, Romania, Spain, Sweden, Switzerland, USA. **Total entries:** 29 (16 qualifiers)
**Venues:** Bologna, Florence, Genoa, Milan, Naples, Rome, Trieste, Turin
**Top scorers:** Conen (Germany), Nejedly (Czechoslovakia), Schiavio (Italy), each 4 goals. **Final** (Rome, 10/6/34): **Italy 2** (Orsi 82, Schiavio 97) **Czechoslovakia 1** (Puc 70) after extra-time. **Att:** 50,000
**Italy:** Combi (capt); Monzeglio, Allemandi, Ferraris, Monti, Bertolini, Guaita, Meazza, Schiavio, Ferrari, Orsi
**Czechoslovakia:** Planicka (capt); Zenisek, Ctyroky, Kostalek, Cambal, Krcil, Junek, Svoboda, Sobotka, Nejedly, Puc
**Referee:** Eklind (Sweden). **Half-time:** 0-0 (90 mins: 1-1)

## 1938 – FRANCE

**WINNERS: Italy RUNNERS-UP: Hungary THIRD: Brazil FOURTH: Sweden**
Other countries in finals: Belgium, Cuba, Czechoslovakia, Dutch East Indies, France, Germany, Holland, Norway, Poland, Romania, Switzerland. **Total entries:** 25 (15 qualifiers)
**Venues:** Antibes, Bordeaux, Le Havre, Lille, Marseille, Paris, Reims, Strasbourg, Toulouse
**Top scorer:** Leonidas (Brazil) 8 goals
**Final** (Paris, 19/6/38): **Italy 4** (Colaussi 6, 36, Piola 15, 81) **Hungary 2** (Titkos 7, Sarosi 65). **Att:** 45,000
**Italy:** Olivieri; Foni, Rava, Serantoni, Andreolo, Locatelli, Biavati, Meazza (capt), Piola, Ferrari, Colaussi
**Hungary:** Szabo; Polgar, Biro, Szalay, Szucs, Lazar, Sas, Vincze, Sarosi (capt), Szengeller, Titkos
**Referee:** Capdeville (France). **Half-time:** 3-1

## 1950 – BRAZIL

**WINNERS: Uruguay RUNNERS-UP: Brazil THIRD: Sweden FOURTH: Spain**
Other countries in finals: Bolivia, Chile, England, Italy, Mexico, Paraguay, Switzerland, USA, Yugoslavia. **Total entries:** 29 (13 qualifiers)
**Venues:** Belo Horizonte, Curitiba, Porto Alegre, Recife, Rio de Janeiro, Sao Paulo
**Top scorer:** Ademir (Brazil) 9 goals
**Deciding Match** (Rio de Janeiro, 16/7/50): **Uruguay 2** (Schiaffino 64, Ghiggia 79) **Brazil 1** (Friaca 47). **Att:** 199,850
(For the only time, the World Cup was decided on a final pool system, in which the winners of the four qualifying groups met in a six-match series So, unlike previous and subsequent

tournaments, there was no official final as such, but Uruguay v Brazil was the deciding match in the final pool)
**Uruguay:** Maspoli; Gonzales, Tejera, Gambetta, Varela (capt), Andrade, Ghiggia, Perez, Miguez, Schiaffino, Moran
**Brazil:** Barbosa; Augusto (capt), Juvenal, Bauer, Danilo, Bigode, Friaca, Zizinho, Ademir, Jair, Chico
**Referee:** Reader (England). **Half-time:** 0-0

## 1954 – SWITZERLAND

**WINNERS: West Germany RUNNERS-UP: Hungary THIRD: Austria FOURTH: Uruguay**
Other countries in finals: Belgium, Brazil, Czechoslovakia, England, France, Italy, Korea, Mexico, Scotland, Switzerland, Turkey, Yugoslavia. **Total entries:** 35 (16 qualifiers)
**Venues:** Basle, Berne, Geneva, Lausanne, Lugano, Zurich
**Top scorer:** Kocsis (Hungary) 11 goals
**Final** (Berne, 4/7/54): **West Germany 3** (Morlock 12, Rahn 17, 84) **Hungary 2** (Puskas 4, Czibor 9). **Att:** 60,000
**West Germany:** Turek; Posipal, Kohlmeyer, Eckel, Liebrich, Mai, Rahn, Morlock, O Walter, F Walter (capt), Schaefer
**Hungary:** Grosics; Buzansky, Lantos, Bozsik, Lorant, Zakarias, Czibor, Kocsis, Hidegkuti, Puskas (capt), J Toth
**Referee:** Ling (England). **Half-time:** 2-2

## 1958 – SWEDEN

**WINNERS: Brazil RUNNERS-UP: Sweden THIRD: France FOURTH: West Germany**
Other countries in finals: Argentina, Austria, Czechoslovakia, England, Hungary, Mexico, Northern Ireland, Paraguay, Scotland, Soviet Union, Wales, Yugoslavia. **Total entries:** 47 (16 qualifiers)
**Venues:** Boras, Eskilstuna, Gothenburg, Halmstad, Helsingborgs, Malmo, Norrkoping, Orebro, Sandviken, Stockholm, Vasteras
**Top scorer:** Fontaine (France) 13 goals
**Final** (Stockholm, 29/6/58): **Brazil 5** (Vava 10, 32, Pele 55, 88, Zagalo 76) **Sweden 2** (Liedholm 4, Simonsson 83). **Att:** 49,737
**Brazil:** Gilmar; D Santos, N Santos, Zito, Bellini (capt), Orlando, Garrincha, Didi, Vava, Pele, Zagallo
**Sweden:** Svensson; Bergmark, Axbom, Boerjesson, Gustavsson, Parling, Hamrin, Gren, Simonsson, Liedholm (capt), Skoglund
**Referee:** Guigue (France). **Half-time:** 2-1

## 1962 – CHILE

**WINNERS: Brazil RUNNERS-UP: Czechoslovakia THIRD: Chile FOURTH: Yugoslavia**
Other countries in finals: Argentina, Bulgaria, Colombia, England, Hungary, Italy, Mexico, Soviet Union, Spain, Switzerland, Uruguay, West Germany. **Total entries:** 53 (16 qualifiers)
**Venues:** Arica, Rancagua, Santiago, Vina del Mar
**Top scorer:** Jerkovic (Yugoslavia) 5 goals
**Final** (Santiago, 17/6/62): **Brazil 3** (Amarildo 17, Zito 69, Vava 77) **Czechoslovakia 1** (Masopust 16). **Att:** 68,679
**Brazil:** Gilmar; D Santos, Mauro (capt), Zozimo, N Santos, Zito, Didi, Garrincha, Vava, Amarildo, Zagallo
**Czechoslovakia:** Schroiff; Tichy, Novak, Pluskal, Popluhar, Masopust (capt), Pospichal, Scherer, Kvasnak, Kadraba, Jelinek
**Referee:** Latychev (Soviet Union). **Half-time:** 1-1

## 1966 – ENGLAND

**WINNERS: England RUNNERS-UP: West Germany THIRD: Portugal FOURTH: USSR**
Other countries in finals: Argentina, Brazil, Bulgaria, Chile, France, Hungary, Italy, Mexico, North Korea, Spain, Switzerland, Uruguay. **Total entries:** 53 (16 qualifiers)

**Venues:** Birmingham (Villa Park), Liverpool (Goodison Park), London (Wembley and White City), Manchester (Old Trafford), Middlesbrough (Ayresome Park), Sheffield (Hillsborough), Sunderland (Roker Park)
**Top scorer:** Eusebio (Portugal) 9 goals
**Final** (Wembley, 30/7/66): **England 4** (Hurst 19, 100, 120, Peters 78) **West Germany 2** (Haller 13, Weber 89) after extra-time. **Att:** 93,802
**England:** Banks; Cohen, Wilson, Stiles, J Charlton, Moore (capt), Ball, Hurst, Hunt, R Charlton, Peters
**West Germany:** Tilkowski; Hottges, Schnellinger, Beckenbauer, Schulz, Weber, Haller, Held, Seeler (capt), Overath, Emmerich
**Referee:** Dienst (Switzerland). **Half-time:** 1-1 (90 mins: 2-2)

## 1970 – MEXICO

**WINNERS: Brazil RUNNERS-UP: Italy THIRD: West Germany FOURTH: Uruguay**
Other countries in finals: Belgium, Bulgaria, Czechoslovakia, El Salvador, England, Israel, Mexico, Morocco, Peru, Romania, Soviet Union, Sweden. **Total entries:** 68 (16 qualifiers)
**Venues:** Guadalajara, Leon, Mexico City, Puebla, Toluca
**Top scorer:** Muller (West Germany) 10 goals
**Final** (Mexico City, 21/6/70): **Brazil** 4 (Pele 18, Gerson 66, Jairzinho 71, Carlos Alberto 87) **Italy** 1 (Boninsegna 38). **Att:** 107,412
**Brazil:** Felix; Carlos Alberto (capt), Brito, Piazza, Everaldo, Clodoaldo, Gerson, Jairzinho, Tostao, Pele, Rivelino
**Italy:** Albertosi; Burgnich, Facchetti (capt), Cera, Rosato, Bertini (Juliano 72), Domenghini, De Sisti, Mazzola, Boninsegna (Rivera 84), Riva
**Referee:** Glockner (East Germany). **Half-time:** 1-1

## 1974 – WEST GERMANY

**WINNERS: West Germany RUNNERS-UP: Holland THIRD: Poland FOURTH: Brazil**
Other countries in finals: Argentina, Australia, Bulgaria, Chile, East Germany, Haiti, Italy, Scotland, Sweden, Uruguay, Yugoslavia, Zaire. **Total entries:** 98 (16 qualifiers)
**Venues:** Berlin, Dortmund, Dusseldorf, Frankfurt, Gelsenkirchen, Hamburg, Hanover, Munich, Stuttgart
**Top scorer:** Lato (Poland) 7 goals
**Final** (Munich, 7/7/74): **West Germany** 2 (Breitner 25 pen, Muller 43) **Holland** 1 (Neeskens 2 pen). **Att:** 77,833
**West Germany:** Maier; Vogts, Schwarzenbeck, Beckenbauer (capt), Breitner, Bonhof, Hoeness, Overath, Grabowski, Muller, Holzenbein
**Holland:** Jongbloed; Suurbier, Rijsbergen (De Jong 69), Haan, Krol, Jansen, Van Hanegem, Neeskens, Rep, Cruyff (capt), Rensenbrink (R Van der Kerkhof 46)
**Referee:** Taylor (England). **Half-time:** 2-1

## 1978 – ARGENTINA

**WINNERS: Argentina RUNNERS-UP: Holland THIRD: Brazil FOURTH: Italy**
Other countries in finals: Austria, France, Hungary, Iran, Mexico, Peru, Poland, Scotland, Spain, Sweden, Tunisia, West Germany. **Total entries:** 102 (16 qualifiers)
**Venues:** Buenos Aires, Cordoba, Mar del Plata, Mendoza, Rosario
**Top scorer:** Kempes (Argentina) 6 goals
**Final** (Buenos Aires, 25/6/78): **Argentina** 3 (Kempes 38, 104, Bertoni 115) **Holland** 1 (Nanninga 82) after extra-time. **Att:** 77,000
**Argentina**: Fillol; Passarella (capt), Olguin, Galvan, Tarantini, Ardiles (Larrosa 66), Gallego, Ortiz (Houseman 74), Bertoni, Luque, Kempes
**Holland**: Jongbloed; Krol (capt), Poortvliet, Brandts, Jansen (Suurbier 73), Haan, Neeskens, W Van der Kerkhof, Rep (Nanninga 58), R Van der Kerkhof, Rensenbrink
**Referee:** Gonella (Italy). **Half-time:** 1-0 (90 mins: 1-1)

## 1982 – SPAIN

**WINNERS: Italy RUNNERS-UP: West Germany THIRD: Poland FOURTH: France**
Other countries in finals: Algeria, Argentina, Austria, Belgium, Brazil, Cameroon, Chile, Czechoslovakia, El Salvador, England, Honduras, Hungary, Kuwait, New Zealand, Northern Ireland, Peru, Scotland, Soviet Union, Spain, Yugoslavia. **Total entries:** 109 (24 qualifiers)
**Venues:** Alicante, Barcelona, Bilbao, Coruna, Elche, Gijon, Madrid, Malaga, Oviedo, Seville, Valencia, Valladolid, Vigo, Zaragoza
**Top scorer:** Rossi (Italy) 6 goals
**Final** (Madrid, 11/7/82): **Italy** 3 (Rossi 57, Tardelli 69, Altobelli 81) **West Germany** 1 (Breitner 84). **Att:** 90,089
**Italy:** Zoff (capt); Bergomi, Scirea, Collovati, Cabrini, Oriali, Gentile, Tardelli, Conti, Rossi, Graziani (Altobelli 18 – Causio 88)
**West Germany:** Schumacher; Kaltz, Stielike, K-H Forster, B Forster, Dremmler (Hrubesch 63), Breitner, Briegel, Rummenigge (capt) (Muller 70), Fischer, Littbarski
**Referee:** Coelho (Brazil). **Half-time:** 0-0

## 1986 – MEXICO

**WINNERS: Argentina RUNNERS-UP: West Germany THIRD: France FOURTH: Belgium**
Other countries in finals: Algeria, Brazil, Bulgaria, Canada, Denmark, England, Hungary, Iraq, Italy, Mexico, Morocco, Northern Ireland, Paraguay, Poland, Portugal, Scotland, South Korea, Soviet Union, Spain, Uruguay. **Total entries:** 118 (24 qualifiers)
**Venues:** Guadalajara, Irapuato, Leon, Mexico City, Monterrey, Nezahualcoyotl, Puebla, Queretaro, Toluca
**Top scorer:** Lineker (England) 6 goals
**Final** (Mexico City, 29/6/86): **Argentina** 3 (Brown 23, Valdano 56, Burruchaga 85) **West Germany** 2 (Rummenigge 74, Voller 82). **Att:** 115,026
**Argentina:** Pumpido; Cuciuffo, Brown, Ruggeri, Olarticoechea, Batista, Giusti, Maradona (capt), Burruchaga (Trobbiani 89), Enrique, Valdano
**West Germany:** Schumacher; Berthold, K-H Forster, Jakobs, Brehme, Briegel, Eder, Matthaus, Magath (Hoeness 62), Allofs (Voller 45), Rummenigge (capt)
**Referee:** Filho (Brazil). **Half-time:** 1-0

## 1990 – ITALY

**WINNERS: West Germany RUNNERS-UP: Argentina THIRD: Italy FOURTH: England**
Other countries in finals: Austria, Belgium, Brazil, Cameroon, Colombia, Costa Rica, Czechoslovakia, Egypt, Holland, Republic of Ireland, Romania, Scotland, Spain, South Korea, Soviet Union, Sweden, United Arab Emirates, USA, Uruguay, Yugoslavia. **Total entries:** 103 (24 qualifiers)
**Venues:** Bari, Bologna, Cagliari, Florence, Genoa, Milan, Naples, Palermo, Rome, Turin, Udine, Verona
**Top scorer:** Schillaci (Italy) 6 goals
**Final** (Rome, 8/7/90): **Argentina** 0 **West Germany** 1 (Brehme 85 pen). **Att:** 73,603
**Argentina:** Goycochea; Ruggeri (Monzon 45), Simon, Serrizuela, Lorenzo, Basualdo, Troglio, Burruchaga (Calderon 53), Sensini, Maradona (capt), Dezotti **Sent-off:** Monzon (65), Dezotti (86) – first players ever to be sent off in World Cup Final
**West Germany:** Illgner; Berthold (Reuter 75), Buchwald, Augenthaler, Kohler, Brehme, Matthaus (capt), Littbarski, Hassler, Klinsmann, Voller
**Referee:** Codesal (Mexico). **Half-time:** 0-0

## 1994 – USA

**WINNERS: Brazil RUNNERS-UP: Italy THIRD: Sweden FOURTH: Bulgaria**
Other countries in finals: Argentina, Belgium, Bolivia, Cameroon, Colombia, Germany, Greece, Holland, Mexico, Morocco, Nigeria, Norway, Republic of Ireland, Romania, Russia, Saudi

Arabia, South Korea, Spain, Switzerland, USA. **Total entries:** 144 (24 qualifiers)
**Venues:** Boston, Chicago, Dallas, Detroit, Los Angeles, New York City, Orlando, San Francisco, Washington
**Top scorers:** Salenko (Russia), Stoichkov (Bulgaria), each 6 goals
**Final** (Los Angeles, 17/7/94): **Brazil** 0 **Italy** 0 after extra-time; Brazil won 3-2 on pens
**Att:** 94,194
**Brazil:** Taffarel; Jorginho (Cafu 21), Aldair, Marcio Santos, Branco, Mazinho, Mauro Silva, Dunga (capt), Zinho (Viola 105), Romario, Bebeto
**Italy:** Pagliuca; Mussi (Apolloni 35), Baresi (capt), Maldini, Benarrivo, Berti, Albertini, D Baggio (Evani 95), Donadoni, R Baggio, Massaro
**Referee:** Puhl (Hungary)
**Shoot-out:** Baresi missed, Marco Santos saved, Albertini 1-0, Romario 1-1, Evani 2-1, Branco 2-2, Massaro saved, Dunga 2-3, R Baggio missed

## 1998 – FRANCE

**WINNERS: France RUNNERS-UP: Brazil THIRD: Croatia FOURTH: Holland**
Other countries in finals: Argentina, Austria, Belgium, Bulgaria, Cameroon, Chile, Colombia, Denmark, England, Germany, Iran, Italy, Jamaica, Japan, Mexico, Morocco, Nigeria, Norway, Paraguay, Romania, Saudi Arabia, Scotland, South Africa, South Korea, Spain, Tunisia, USA, Yugoslavia. **Total entries:** 172 (32 qualifiers)
**Venues:** Bordeaux, Lens, Lyon, Marseille, Montpellier, Nantes, Paris (St Denis, Parc des Princes), Saint-Etienne, Toulouse
**Top scorer:** Davor Suker (Croatia) 6 goals
**Final** (Paris St Denis, 12/7/98): **Brazil** 0 **France** 3 (Zidane 27, 45, Petit 90). **Att:** 75,000
**Brazil:** Taffarel; Cafu, Junior Baiano, Aldair, Roberto Carlos; Dunga (capt), Leonardo (Denilson 46), Cesar Sampaio (Edmundo 74), Rivaldo; Bebeto, Ronaldo
**France:** Barthez; Thuram, Leboeuf, Desailly, Lizarazu; Karembeu (Boghossian 56), Deschamps (capt), Petit, Zidane, Djorkaeff (Viera 75); Guivarc'h (Dugarry 66) **Sent-off**: Desailly (68)
**Referee:** Belqola (Morocco). **Half-time:** 0-2

## 2002 – JAPAN/SOUTH KOREA

**WINNERS: Brazil RUNNERS-UP: Germany THIRD: Turkey FOURTH: South Korea**
Other countries in finals: Argentina, Belgium, Cameroon, China, Costa Rica, Croatia, Denmark, Ecuador, England, France, Italy, Japan, Mexico, Nigeria, Paraguay, Poland, Portugal, Republic of Ireland, Russia, Saudi Arabia, Senegal, Slovenia, South Africa, Spain, Sweden, Tunisia, USA, Uruguay. **Total entries:** 195 (32 qualifiers)
**Venues: Japan** – Ibaraki, Kobe, Miyagi, Niigata, Oita, Osaka, Saitama, Sapporo, Shizuoka, Yokohama. **South Korea** – Daegu, Daejeon, Gwangju, Incheon, Jeonju, Busan, Seogwipo, Seoul, Suwon Ulsan
**Top scorer:** Ronaldo (Brazil) 8 goals
**Final** (Yokohama, 30/6/02): **Germany** 0, **Brazil** 2 (Ronaldo 67, 79). **Att:** 69,029
**Germany:** Kahn (capt), Linke, Ramelow, Metzelder, Frings, Jeremies (Asamoah 77), Hamann, Schneider, Bode (Zeige 84), Klose (Bierhoff 74), Neuville
**Brazil:** Marcos, Lucio, Edmilson, Roque Junior, Cafu (capt) Kleberson, Gilberto Silva, Roberto Carlos, Ronaldinho (Juninho 85), Rivaldo, Ronaldo (Denilson 90)
**Referee:** Collina (Italy). **Half-time:** 0-0

## 2006 – GERMANY

**WINNERS: Italy RUNNERS-UP: France THIRD: Germany FOURTH: Portugal**
Other countries in finals: Angola, Argentina, Australia, Brazil, Costa Rica, Croatia, Czech Republic, Ecuador, England, Ghana, Holland, Iran, Ivory Coast, Japan, Mexico, Paraguay, Poland, Saudi Arabia, Serbia & Montenegro, South Korea, Spain, Sweden, Switzerland, Trinidad & Tobago, Togo, Tunisia, Ukraine, USA. **Total entries:** 198 (32 qualifiers)
**Venues:** Berlin, Cologne, Dortmund, Frankfurt, Gelsenkirchen, Hamburg, Hanover,

Kaiserslautern, Leipzig, Munich, Nuremberg, Stuttgart
**Top scorer:** Klose (Germany) 5 goals
**Final** (Berlin, 9/7/06): **Italy** 1 (Materazzi 19) **France** 1 (Zidane 7 pen) after extra-time: Italy won 5-3 on pens. **Att:** 69,000
**Italy:** Buffon; Zambrotta, Cannavaro (capt), Materazzi, Grosso, Perrotta (De Rossi 61), Pirlo, Gattuso, Camoranesi (Del Piero 86), Totti (Iaquinta 61), Toni
**France:** Barthez; Sagnol, Thuram, Gallas, Abidal, Makelele, Vieira (Diarra 56), Ribery (Trezeguet 100), Malouda, Zidane (capt), Henry (Wiltord 107) **Sent-off**: Zidane (110)
**Referee:** Elizondo (Argentina). **Half-time:** 1-1 90 mins: 1-1
**Shoot-out:** Pirlo 1-0, Wiltord 1-1, Materazzi 2-1, Trezeguet missed, De Rossi 3-1, Abidal 3-2, Del Piero 4-2, Sagnol 4-3, Grosso 5-3

## 2010 – SOUTH AFRICA

**WINNERS: Spain RUNNERS-UP: Holland THIRD: Germany FOURTH: Uruguay**
Other countries in finals: Algeria, Argentina, Australia, Brazil, Cameroon, Chile, Denmark, England, France, Ghana, Greece, Honduras, Italy, Ivory Coast, Japan, Mexico, New Zealand, Nigeria, North Korea, Paraguay, Portugal, Serbia, Slovakia, Slovenia, South Africa, South Korea, Switzerland, USA. **Total entries**: 204 (32 qualifiers)
**Venues:** Bloemfontein, Cape Town, Durban, Johannesburg (Ellis Park), Johannesburg (Soccer City), Nelspruit, Polokwane, Port Elizabeth, Pretoria, Rustenburg
**Top scorers:** Forlan (Uruguay), Muller (Germany), Sneijder (Holland), Villa (Spain) 5 goals
**Final** (Johannesburg, Soccer City, 11/7/10): **Holland** 0 **Spain** 1 (Iniesta 116) after extra-time; **Att:** 84,490
**Holland:** Stekelenburg; Van der Wiel, Heitinga, Mathijsen, Van Bronckhorst (capt) (Braafheid 105), Van Bommel, De Jong (Van der Vaart 99), Robben, Sneijder, Kuyt (Elia 71), Van Persie. **Sent off:** Heitinga (109)
**Spain:** Casillas (capt); Sergio Ramos, Puyol, Piquet, Capdevila, Busquets, Xabi Alonso (Fabregas 87), Iniesta, Xavi, Pedro (Jesus Navas 60), Villa (Torres 106)
**Referee:** Webb (England). **Half-time:** 0-0

## 2014 – BRAZIL

**WINNERS: Germany RUNNERS-UP: Argentina THIRD: Holland FOURTH: Brazil**
Other countries in finals: Algeria, Argentina, Australia, Belgium, Bosnia-Herzegovina, Brazil, Cameroon, Chile, Colombia, Costa Rica, Croatia, Ecuador, England, France, Germany, Ghana, Greece, Holland, Honduras, Iran, Italy, Ivory Coast, Japan, Mexico, Nigeria, Portugal, Russia, South Korea, Spain, Switzerland, Uruguay, USA. **Total entries:** 204 (32 qualifiers)
**Venues:** Belo Horizonte, Brasilia, Cuiaba, Curitiba, Fortaleza, Manaus, Natal, Porto Alegre, Recife, Rio de Janeiro, Salvador, Sao Paulo
**Top scorer:** Rodriguez (Colombia) 6 goals
**Final** (Rio de Janeiro, 13/7/14): **Germany** 1 (Gotze 113) **Argentina** 0 after extra-time; **Att:** 74,738
**Germany:** Neuer; Lahm (capt), Boateng, Hummels, Howedes, Kramer (Schurrle 32), Schweinsteiger, Muller, Kroos, Ozil (Mertesacker 120), Klose (Gotze 88)
**Argentina:** Romero; Zabaleta, Demichelis, Garay, Rojo, Biglia, Mascherano, Perez (Gago 86), Messi (capt), Lavezzi (Aguero 46), Higuain (Palacio 78)
**Referee:** Rizzoli (Italy). **Half-time:** 0-0

# DAY BY DAY DIARY 2017–18

## JULY 2017

**17** England goalkeeper Joe Hart, frozen out at Manchester City, joins West Ham on a season's loan.

**18** Antonio Conte, manager of Premier League champions Chelsea, signs an improved two-year contract.

**19** Kieran Trippier signs a new five-year deal with Tottenham, following the sale of Kyle Walker to Manchester City.

**20** Chelsea break their transfer record with the £57.2m acquisition of Spain striker Alvaro Morata from Real Madrid.

**21** Liverpool turn down a £72m bid from Barcelona for Philippe Coutinho.

**22** West Ham pay £24m for Stoke's Marko Arnautovic – a record fee for both clubs.

**23** Manchester City take their summer spending to more than £200m with the signing of Benjamin Mendy from Monaco for £52m and fellow defender Danilo from Real Madrid for £26.5m.

**24** Tottenham chairman Daniel Levy claims that the spending spree by Premier League clubs is 'unsustainable.' Manchester United's Eric Bailly, sent off in their Europa League semi-final against Celta Vigo, has his one-match ban extended to three games by UEFA.

**25** Chelsea send Brazilian winger Kenedy home from their tour of China and Singapore for two social media posts which the club admit is offensive to the Chinese people.

**26** Joey Barton's 18-month ban for breaching FA betting rules is reduced to 13 months on appeal.

**27** England top their group with maximum points from three games at the European Women's Championship in Holland.

**28** Celtic are fined £20,600 by UEFA for an 'illicit' banner and blocked stairways at their Champions League qualifier against Linfield.

**30** Jodie Taylor's fifth goal of the tournament gives England women a 1-0 quarter-final win over France. The victory is clouded by the loss of goalkeeper Karen Bardsley, who sustains a broken leg in a collision with captain Steph Houghton.

**31** UEFA ban Phil Jones for two European matches for verbally abusing an anti-doping officer after Manchester United's Europa League Final win over Ajax. Jones is also fined £4,450, along with team-mate Daley Blind, for a delay in reporting to doping control. United are fined £8,900.

## AUGUST 2017

**1** Four days before the start of the season, Hearts manager Ian Cathro is sacked after his team fail to qualify from the group stage of the Scottish League Cup.

**2** The world transfer record is shattered when Paris Saint-Germain, owned by a Qatar investment fund linked to the state's royal family, sign Barcelona's Neymar for £198m. The fee dwarfs the £89.3m paid by Manchester United to Juventus for Paul Pogba in August 2016. Neymar is reported to be earning nearly £600,000 a week after tax with his new club.

**3** England's women lose 3-0 to Holland in the semi-finals of Euro 2017. Aberdeen are beaten 3-2 on aggregate by Apollon Limassol in the third qualifying round of the Europa League, following defeats for Rangers and St Johnstone in previous qualifying matches.

**4** Danny Murphy, Lee Dixon and Terry Butcher are among 13 former internationals and managers named by the FA to be used during the course of the season to decide whether players have dived and should be banned retrospectively under new rules.

**5** Burnley's pre-season friendly with Hannover at Turf Moor is abandoned at half-time after crowd trouble involving supporters of the German club. Both the Football League's newcomers kick-off with 2-2 draws, Forest Green against Barnet and Lincoln at Wycombe. Yeovil players and staff promise to refund fans who watched their side's 8-2 defeat at Luton.

6 Arsenal beat Chelsea 4-1 on penalties after a 1-1 scoreline in the Community Shield at Wembley.

7 Two clubs break their transfer records for midfield players. Southampton pay Juventus £18.1m for Mario Lemina. Brighton sign Colombia winger Jose Izquierdo from Club Bruges for £13.5m.

8 Europa League champions Manchester United lose 2-1 to Champions League winners Real Madrid in the European Super Cup in Skopje.

9 Watford pay a club-record £18.5m for Burnley's Andre Gray. Liverpool turn down another bid from Barcelona for Philippe Countinho, this time for £90m.

10 Danny Rose is fined by Tottenham for questioning in a newspaper interview the club's wage policy and lack of summer transfer activity.

11 West Bromwich Albion manager Tony Pulis signs a new contract through to 2019.

12 Chelsea open their defence of the Premier League title with a 3-2 home defeat by Burnley after having Gary Cahill and Cesc Fabregas sent off.

14 Chinese businessman Gao Jisheng becomes Southampton's majority owner, buying an 80 per cent share of the club from Katharina Liebherr for £210m.

15 Everton sign Swansea's Gylfi Sigurdsson for £45m – a record fee for both clubs.

16 England women's manager Mark Sampson, accused of bullying and discrimination by striker Eniola Aluko, is cleared by an independent inquiry. Sampson admits the need to improve his communication skills.

17 Winston Reid signs a new six-year contract with West Ham.

18 Tottenham, the only Premier League club without a summer signing, buy Ajax central defender Davinson Sanchez for a club-record £42m.

21 Burnley sign Chris Wood from Leeds for a club-record £15m.

22 Celtic reach the Champions League group stage by beating Kazakhstan side Astana 8-4 on aggregate in the play-offs.

23 Wayne Rooney announces his retirement from international football after 119 England appearances and a record 53 goals. Liverpool defeat Hoffenheim 6-3 on aggregate in their Champions League play-off tie, giving England five teams in the group stage for the first time. Manchester City acquire 44 per cent of Spanish club Girona for around £3.5m.

24 Record-signing Gylfi Sigurdsson scores with a lob from 57 yards as Everton reach the group stage of the Europa League with a 3-1 aggregate win over Hajduk Split. Zlatan Ibrahimovic, released by Manchester United after a serious knee injury, re-signs for the club on a one-year contract.

25 Watford are fined £3.95m, with £350,000 costs, by the English Football League after admitting that former chairman Raffaele Riva faked a bank letter to smooth the way for a takeover of the club.

26 Grimsby, beaten 3-2 at home by Wycombe, have a fifth player sent off in five league and cup games. Matty James signs a new four-year contract with Leicester.

27 Barcelona use the world record fee for Neymar to buy France striker Ousmane Dembele from Borussia Dortmund for an initial £96.8m, rising to £135.5m.

28 Liverpool break their transfer record by agreeing a fee of £55m for Leipzig's Guinea midfielder Naby Keita to join the club in July, 2018. So do West Bromwich Albion, who sign Leipzig winger Oliver Burke for £15m. Director of Football Craig Levein is named the new Hearts manager.

29 Josh King signs a new four-year contract with Bournemouth.

30 Aleksandar Mitrovic is banned for three matches by the FA after being caught on camera elbowing Manuel Lanzini in Newcastle's match against West Ham.

31 Spending by Premier League clubs in the summer transfer window reaches £1.4bn, a record for the sixth successive year. The total for deadline day is £210m, topped by £35m fees which take Alex Oxlade-Chamberlain from Arsenal to Liverpool and Danny Drinkwater from Leicester to Chelsea, followed by Mamadou Sakho's £26m move from Liverpool to Crystal Palace. Northampton's Justin Edinburgh becomes the season's first managerial casualty, sacked after his side lose their first four League One matches.

## SEPTEMBER 2017

1 Harry Kane, goalless for Tottenham in August, scores twice and Ryan Bertrand nets his first for his country in England's 4-0 World Cup qualifying victory in Malta. Stuart Armstrong opens his account for Scotland, who win 3-0 in Malta. Josh Magennis is on the mark twice as Northern Ireland beat San Marino by the same scoreline away from home.

2 Four minutes after coming off the bench for his international debut, 17-year-old Liverpool striker Ben Woodburn scores from 25 yards to give Wales a 1-0 win over Austria to keep alive their chances of qualifying for the finals. Shaun Duffy's first international goal gives the Republic of Ireland a 1-1 draw in Georgia.

3 Arsene Wenger reveals Arsenal made an unsuccessful £92m bid on transfer deadline-day for Monaco's Thomas Lemar.

4 Northern Ireland defeat the Czech Republic 2-0 to guarantee a World Cup play-off place. Scotland keep alive their chances of finishing runners-up to England in their group by beating Malta 2-0. England come from behind to move to the brink of an automatic place in the finals with a 2-1 victory over Slovakia. Jimmy Floyd Hasselbaink, former Queens Park Rangers and Burton manager, takes over at Northampton.

5 Ben Woodburn makes another significant impact off the bench, supplying the cross for Hal Robson-Kanu to put Wales on the way to a 2-0 success in Moldova. The Republic of Ireland suffer a potentially damaging 1-0 home defeat by Serbia, who protect a goal from former Manchester City defender Aleksandar Kolarov for the last 28 minutes with ten men.

6 Commentator John Motson announces he will retire at the end of the season after 50 years with the BBC.

7 Former Sutton goalkeeper Wayne Shaw, who ate a pie before their FA Cup defeat by Arsenal after a bookmaker offered odds of 8-1 on him doing so on camera, is banned for two months and fined £375 by the FA for breaching betting rules.

8 Premier League clubs vote to close the transfer window before the season kicks off, instead of at the end of August. Bolton manager Phil Parkinson is fined £2,000 by the FA for leaving his technical area during the match against Sheffield Wednesday.

9 Carlos Carvalhal, manager of Sheffield Wednesday, receives a two-match touchline ban and £4,000 fine from the FA for an altercation with Bolton's Phil Parkinson, who is fined £2,000.

10 The English Football League sign a new five-year TV deal with Sky worth £120m a year.

11 Frank de Boer is sacked by Crystal Palace after four games – the shortest-lived manager in Premier League history.

12 Former England manager Roy Hodgson takes over at Selhurst Park, where he started his playing career. Celtic suffer the club's worst home defeat since 1895 – 5-0 against Paris Saint-Germain in their opening Champions League group game.

13 Mame Biram Diouf signs a new three-year-contract with Stoke.

14 Arsenal's opening Europa League game against Cologne is delayed for an hour amid safety fears after ticketless supporters of the German club try to gain entry to the Emirates.

15 Tom Heaton, Burnley's England goalkeeper, is ruled out for seven months after surgery on a dislocated shoulder.

16 Harry Redknapp, manager of Birmingham for five months, is sacked after six successive league and cup defeats. Two other managers pay the price for poor starts to the season – Chesterfield's Gary Caldwell and Port Vale's Michael Brown, with their respective teams in the bottom two places in League Two.

18 Wayne Rooney is fined by Everton after being banned from the road for two years and given 100 hours of community service for drink-driving.

20 The day after England launch their qualifying campaign for the Women's World Cup by beating Russia 6-0, manager Mark Sampson is sacked by the FA for unspecified 'inappropriate conduct' during his time coaching Bristol Academy.

21 The FA and chief executive Martin Glenn come under pressure over a previous 'safeguarding' inquiry which cleared Mark Sampson of wrongdoing.

**22** Chelsea agree to sell Diego Costa, frozen out by manager Antonio Conte after their title-winning season, back to Atletico Madrid for £57m – three years after signing him for £32m. UEFA fine Everton £8,800 and Hajduk Split £35,300 for crowd trouble at the Europa League match at Goodison Park.

**23** Plymouth, beaten 3-0 by Doncaster, have a player sent off for the fourth successive home match.

**24** The FA give their backing to chief executive Martin Glenn at a board meeting.

**25** Two League One managers are dismissed – John Sheridan with Oldham at the foot of the table and Ady Pennock with Gillingham third from bottom. Jim McIntyre is fired by Ross County with his side third from bottom of the Scottish Premiership.

**26** Harry Kane scores his sixth hat-trick of 2017 for Tottenham in a 3-0 Champions League win over Apoel Nicosia.

**27** Brighton's Tomer Hemed, caught on camera stamping on Newcastle's DeAndre Yedlin, is banned for three matches by the FA.

**28** West Ham and Tottenham are both fined £20,000 by the FA for a players' melee. Manchester City's Sergio Aguero sustains a broken rib in a taxi crash and misses three games. Former Wolves and Reading striker Kevin Doyle, 34, capped 63 times by the Republic of Ireland, announces his retirement. Owen Coyle, former Blackburn, Bolton and Burnley manager, takes charge at Ross County.

**29** Dele Alli is given a one-match international ban and £3,800 fine by FIFA for an 'offensive and unsporting' gesture towards team-mate Kyle Walker during England's win over Slovakia. Benjamin Mendy, Manchester City's £52m signing, has an operation on a ruptured cruciate ligament in his right knee and is ruled out for seven months. Former Bristol City manager Steve Cotterill takes charge at Birmingham, the club's fourth in ten months. Former Chesterfield striker Jack Lester becomes their new manager.

**30** Former England women's captain Mo Marley is appointed interim manager following the dismissal of Mark Sampson.

## OCTOBER 2017

**1** Lee McCulloch, manager of the Scottish Premiership's bottom club Kilmarnock, is sacked.

**2** Rickie Lambert, who scored with his first touch in international football for England against Scotland, won 11 caps and played for nine clubs, announces his retirement.

**3** Reading's Chris Gunter is named Wales Player of the Year, ending Gareth Bale's four years as recipient of the award.

**4** Former long-serving Port Vale defender Neil Aspin leaves Gateshead to become the League Two club's new manager.

**5** A goal by Harry Kane four minutes into extra-time gives England a 1-0 win over Slovenia, confirming their place in the World Cup Finals. Scotland beat Slovakia with an 89th minute Martin Skrtel own goal to move into second place in Group F. Northern Ireland lose 3-1 at home to Germany, who maintain a 100 per cent qualifying record.

**6** Tom Lawrence scores his first international goal as Wales win 1-0 in Georgia. The Republic of Ireland defeat Moldova 2-0 with two goals from Daryl Murphy to set up a winner-takes-all final match against the Welsh in Group D.

**7** Republic of Ireland manager Martin O'Neill and assistant manager Roy Keane extend their contracts through to the Euro 2018 campaign.

**8** Scotland lose out on a play-off place to Slovakia on goal difference after a 2-2 draw in Slovenia in their final group match. England complete an unbeaten qualifying campaign with a 1-0 win in Lithuania, with Harry Kane again on the mark, this time from the penalty spot. Northern Ireland finish with a 1-0 defeat away to Norway.

**9** James McClean scores the only goal of the game to send the Republic of Ireland into the play-offs and leave Wales in despair.

**10** Holland, runners-up in 2010 and third in 2014, fail to qualify on goal difference.

**11** Aston Villa owner Tony Xia is fined £4,000 by the FA for questioning the integrity of referee Jeremy Simpson. Barnsley manager Paul Heckingbottom receives a two-match touchline ban and £3,000 fine for confronting match officials during the game against Millwall.

12 Gordon Strachan, Scotland manager since January 2013, leaves the position by 'mutual consent' after the team's failure to qualify.

13 Liverpool honour club legend Kenny Dalglish by renaming Anfield's Centenary Stand after him. Malky Mackay, the Scottish FA's performance director, takes interim charge of the national team.

14 England top their group at the Under-17 World Cup in India with maximum points from three matches. Steve Clarke, former Reading and West Bromwich Albion manager, takes charge at Kilmarnock.

15 League One Shrewsbury achieve their target of raising £65,000 from supporters for the first safe standing area in English football.

16 Mike Ashley, owner of Newcastle for ten years, goes public with his intention to sell the club in an attempt for a quick sale.

17 Four months after signing a three-year contract to become permanent manager, Craig Shakespeare is sacked by Leicester with his side third from bottom. Liverpool equal a Champions League record with a 7-0 away win over the Slovenian side Maribor. England's under-17 team reach the quarter-finals by beating Japan 5-3 on penalties after a goalless draw.

18 The FA apologise at a parliamentary inquiry to two players, Eniola Aluko and Drew Spence, for racist comments by sacked England women's manager Mark Sampson. Oldham coach Richie Wellens is appointed manager after winning four games and drawing the other as caretaker.

19 The Premier League decide against having three matches on Christmas Eve, including Arsenal v Liverpool, following pressure from supporters.

20 Carlisle's Shaun Miller becomes the first player to be given a two-match retrospective ban for diving under new FA rules. He is punished by an independent commission for 'successful deception of a match official' after winning a penalty against Wycombe. Everton ban for life a supporter who, with a child in his arms, lashed out at a Lyon playing during the teams' Europa League match at Goodison Park.

21 Liverpool's Rhian Brewster scores a hat-trick as England under-17s beat the United States 4-1 to reach the semi-finals.

23 Everton manager Ronald Koeman is sacked following a 5-2 home defeat by Arsenal which leaves his side third from bottom.

24 Queens Park Rangers face a multi-million pound fine for breaking spending limits after their claim that the English Football League's Financial Fair Play rules are unlawful is dismissed by an arbitration panel. The club announce their intention to appeal.

25 Former Southampton manager Claude Puel takes over at Leicester. England under-17s defeat Brazil 3-1 to reach the final with another hat-trick from Rhian Brewster.

26 Pedro Caixinha is sacked by Rangers after seven months in charge – the shortest serving manager in the club's history – with his side out of the League Cup and Europa League and fourth in the Scottish Premiership.

27 Chairman Greg Clarke admits that the FA have 'lost the trust of the public' over their handling of the Mark Sampson affair and promises a 'fundamental' review to make the governing body more inclusive and representative.

28 England under-17s retrieve a two-goal deficit to beat Spain 5-2 in the Under-17 World Cup Final. Rhian Brewster, scorer of their first goal, wins the Golden Boot award with eight to his credit, while Manchester City's Phil Foden is named the tournament's best player.

30 Lee Clark is sacked after eight months as Bury manager, with his side second from bottom. Cologne are fined £53,000 by UEFA for crowd trouble at their Europa League match against Arsenal at the Emirates. Celtic's Kieran Tierney signs a new six-year contract.

31 Simon Grayson, manager of Sunderland for four months, is dismissed immediately after a 3-3 draw with Bolton leaves his team third from bottom. Watford captain Troy Deeney is banned for three games by the FA for gouging the cheeks of Stoke's Joe Allen. The governing body fine Preston £10,000 and Wolves £5,000 for a players' melee. Celtic fail to qualify for the knockout stage of the Champions League after a second group defeat by Bayern Munich.

## NOVEMBER 2017

1 Sergio Aguero becomes Manchester City's all-time record scorer in all competitions with his 178th goal in a 4-2 away win over Napoli which confirms their place in the Champions League's knockout phase. On an outstanding night for English teams, Tottenham also go through with a 3-1 win over Real Madrid, while Liverpool take a firm grip on their group by beating Maribor 3-0. Notts County are ordered by a tribunal to pay John Sheridan £125,000 after their former manager wins an appeal against the grounds for his dismissal.

2 Arsenal reach the knockout stage of the Europa League. Everton fail to qualify from their group, effectively ending caretaker David Unsworth's hopes of the permanent manager's job. Demarai Gray signs a new four-year contract with Leicester. Bristol City's Bailey Wright is banned for two matches by the FA for diving against Fulham. Former Rangers manager Pedro Caixinha and Motherwell's Stephen Robinson receive one-match bans from the Scottish FA for a touchline confrontation during the League Cup semi-final.

3 The English Football League warn that fans taking fireworks into grounds face a minimum ban of three seasons. James Collins announces his retirement from international football after winning 50 Wales caps.

4 Celtic set a British record of 63 games without defeat in domestic competitions when beating St Johnstone 4-0 to overtake the mark set by the club 100 years ago.

6 Slaven Bilic is sacked as West Ham manager after a 4-1 home defeat by Liverpool leaves his side third from bottom.

7 West Ham move quickly for a replacement – former Sunderland, Manchester United and Everton manager David Moyes.

8 Tammy Abraham, Swansea striker on loan from Chelsea, commits his international future to England after being offered a place in Nigeria's World Cup squad.

9 Steven Davis wins his 100th cap in the first leg of Northern Ireland's World Cup play-off against Switzerland, a match they lose 1-0 at Windsor Park to a disputed penalty awarded for handball against Corry Evans which manager Michael O'Neill calls 'staggering.' Scotland, with performance director Malky Mackay in temporary charge following the departure of Gordon Strachan, lose by the same scoreline to Holland in a friendly international. Watford and Stoke are both fined £25,000 by the FA for a clash between players.

10 England, with five players making their debuts in a squad hit by injuries, draw 0-0 with Germany. Wales are beaten 2-0 by France in another friendly. In a statement issued by the Irish FA, Corry Evans apologises for his wife's foul-mouthed comments on social media about the Romanian referee, Ovidiu Hategan, who awarded the controversial penalty.

11 The Republic of Ireland draw 0-0 in the away leg of their World Cup play-off against Denmark.

12 Jonny Evans has a stoppage-time header cleared off the line, ending Northern Ireland's World Cup hopes in the return match against Switzerland, who qualify 1-0 on aggregate. Aaron Hughes makes his 109th appearance for the Irish, passing England's Bobby Moore as the Home Nations' most capped defender. Former England captain Alan Shearer presents a BBC documentary on potential links between former players and dementia.

13 Italy, four-time World Cup winners and an ever-present at the finals since 1958, lose 1-0 on aggregate to Sweden in the play-offs. Mark McGhee, former assistant to Scotland manager Gordon Strachan, takes over at Barnet from Rossi Eames after the team go 11 league games without a win.

14 After scoring first in the return leg, the Republic of Ireland are crushed 5-1 by Denmark, for whom Tottenham's Christian Eriksen scores a hat-trick. In friendlies, England share a goalless draw with Brazil, while Wales concede a stoppage-time equaliser in their first international against Panama.

15 Aston Villa's Mile Jedinak scores all three goals – two penalties and a deflected free-kick – as Australia qualify for the finals in Russia with a 3-1 win over Honduras in the second leg of their play-off.

16 The English Football League sign a five-year extension to their title sponsorship with Sky Bet

for a reported £8.5m a year. Gillingham appoint caretaker Steve Lovell as manager until the end of the season.

**17** Chris Coleman, manager of Wales for nearly six years, resigns after their failure to reach the World Cup Finals.

**18** Sunderland become the first club in English football history to go 20 successive home games without a win in all competitions. Luton's Olly Lee scores with a shot from 65 yards in the 7-0 victory over Cambridge

**19** Chris Coleman is appointed Sunderland's ninth manager in six years with the club bottom of the Championship.

**20** West Bromwich Albion sack manager Tony Pulis after a 4-0 home defeat by Chelsea extends their run to just two wins in 21 Premier League games. Manchester United extend Ander Herrera's contract until 2019.

**21** Phil Foden, named best player of the tournament after England's triumph at the Under-17 World Cup, makes his Manchester City debut in a Champions League group match against Feyenoord.

**22** The FA ban Everton's Oumar Niasse for two matches for diving to win a penalty against Crystal Palace. Everton are fined £26,000 by UEFA over the incident in which a supporter carrying a toddler lashed out at a Lyon playing during the teams' Europa League match at Goodison Park. Chelsea reach the last 16 of the Champions League with a group match to spare. Chris Lucketti, Scunthorpe's assistant manager, takes charge at Bury, where he spent six seasons as a player.

**23** The FA commission research into possible links between players heading the ball and dementia, to be funded jointly with the players' union, the PFA.

**24** Manchester United's Michael Carrick reveals he has had minor surgery to correct an irregular heartbeat.

**26** Goals by James Forrest and Moussa Dembele with a penalty enable Celtic to retain the Scottish League Cup with a 2-0 win over Motherwell, who have Cedric Kipre sent off for conceding the spot-kick.

**27** Peter Crouch, 36, signs a new one-year contract with Stoke.

**28** Rebuffed in their approach for Watford's Marco Silva, Everton turn to Sam Allardyce, his ninth club managerial appointment.

**29** Alan Pardew returns to management 11 months after being sacked by Crystal Palace, taking charge of West Bromwich Albion.

**30** London Mayor Sadiq Khan agrees to take control of the former Olympic Stadium after an independent review shows the cost of transforming it into West Ham's new ground rose from the original estimate of £190m to £323m.

## DECEMBER 2017

**1** Manager Gareth Southgate is satisfied with England's World Cup draw in a group with Belgium, Tunisia and Panama.

**3** Leonid Slutsky is sacked after six months as Hull manager, with his side fifth from bottom of the Championship.

**4** Chelsea manager Antonio Conte accepts an £8,000 fine from the FA for berating fourth official Lee Mason during the game with Swansea.

**5** Manchester United make sure of a place in the last 16 of the Champions League by beating CSKA Moscow 2-1 in their final group match.

**6** Liverpool defeat Spartak Moscow 7-0 to join both Manchester sides, Chelsea and Tottenham in the knockout phase – the first time any country has had five sides through.

**7** Nigel Adkins, former Sheffield United, Reading, Southampton and Scunthorpe manager, takes charge at Hull. The FA fine Wolves manager Nuno Espirito Santo £2,000 and Bolton's Phil Parkinson £3,000 for a touchline clash.

**8** Aberdeen's Derek McInnes turns down the chance to become the new Rangers manager.

**9** Cristiano Ronaldo is voted the world's best player for the fifth time, equalling the record of Lionel Messi, who is runner-up, with Neymar third.

10 Manchester City's 2-1 win over Manchester United, which put them 11 points clear at the top of the Premier League, is followed by a tunnel brawl between rival players and staff.
11 The FA ask both clubs for their observations before deciding on whether to take disciplinary action.
12 AFC Wimbledon are given the go-ahead by their local council for a new £25m stadium in Plough Lane – 250 yards from where the former club played.
13 Manchester City set an all-time record for English top-flight football with a 15th successive Premier League victory – 4-0 at Swansea.
15 Cardiff manager Neil Warnock, sent off after confronting fourth official Andy Woolmer during the game against Reading, is fined £2,000 by the FA for misconduct.
16 Real Madrid become the first team to retain the Club World Cup, beating Gremio of Brazil 1-0 with a goal by Cristiano Ronaldo.
17 Celtic's British record run of 69 games without defeat in domestic competitions comes to an end when they lose 4-0 to Hearts in the Scottish Premiership.
18 West Ham's Manuel Lanzini is banned by the FA for two matches for diving to win a penalty against Stoke.
19 A consortium including Chinese billionaire Chien Lee and baseball pioneer Billy Beane, who inspired the Hollywood film *Moneyball*, take control of Barnsley from owner Patrick Cryne.
20 Paul Clement is dismissed as Swansea manager with his side bottom of the Premier League. Holders Manchester United are knocked out of the League Cup by Bristol City.
21 The FA decide to take no disciplinary action over the tunnel brawl at Old Trafford. Burnley's James Tarkowski is banned for three matches by the governing body after being caught on camera elbowing Brighton's Glenn Murray.
23 Two Championship managers are sacked for struggling to keep pace with the leading teams – Garry Monk after six months at Middlesbrough and Carlos Carvalhal, in charge of Sheffield Wednesday for two years.
24 Charlie Austin is banned for three matches by the FA on video evidence for kicking goalkeeper Jonas Lossl in Southampton's match against Huddersfield.
26 Harry Kane breaks Alan Shearer's Premier League record of 36 goals in a calendar year with a hat-trick for Tottenham against Southampton, taking his tally for 2017 to 39. Tony Pulis succeeds Garry Monk at the Riverside, a month after his dismissal by West Bromwich Albion.
27 Liverpool break the world record transfer fee for a defender with the signing of Southampton's Virgil van Dijk, who officially becomes their player on January 1.
28 Carlos Carvalhal makes a rapid return to management, taking charge at Swansea.
29 Former Manchester United youth team manager Eric Harrison, who helped develop the careers of David Beckham, Ryan Giggs, Paul Scholes, Nicky Butt and Gary Neville, is awarded an MBE in the New Year Honours.
30 Mark Warburton, manager of Nottingham Forest for nine months, is sacked with his side ten points adrift of a play-off place.
31 Manchester City's record run comes to an end after 18 successive Premier League wins. They are held to a goalless draw by Crystal Palace, but go into the New Year with a 14-point lead at the top. Two players are banned for three games on video evidence – Ashley Young for elbowing Dusan Tadic in Manchester United's match against Southampton; Swansea's Kyle Naughton for stamping on Watford's Stefano Okaka.

## JANUARY 2018

1 Jose Mourinho reacts angrily to criticism of his Manchester United side by former United sta
Paul Scholes.
2 James Tarkowski signs a new contract with Burnley through to 2022.
3 Manchester City's David Silva reveals that he missed matches against Newcastle and Crysta
Palace because of the premature birth of son Mateo.
4 Mohamed Salah is voted African Player of the Year, with his Liverpool team-mate Sadio Man
the runner-up.
5 Arsenal manager Arsene Wenger is given a three-match touchline ban and £40,000 fin

by the FA for abusive language and questioning the integrity of Mike Dean after the game against West Bromwich Albion. Sheffield Wednesday appoint former Hertha Berlin and Stuttgart coach Jos Luhukay as their new manager. Everton sign Turkey striker Cenk Tosun from Besiktas for £27m.

**6** Mark Hughes, under pressure with his side in the Premier League relegation zone, is sacked after an FA Cup third round defeat by League Two Coventry.

**7** Liverpool's Philippe Coutinho joins Barcelona for £142m, four years after moving to Anfield from Inter Milan for £8.5m. Holders Arsenal, with nine changes in the side, are knocked out of the FA Cup 4-2 by Nottingham Forest.

**8** The Video Assistant Referee system is used for the first time in English football – at Brighton's FA Cup third round tie against Crystal Palace. Leeds forward Samuel Saiz is banned for six matches by the FA for spitting at Newport's Robbie Willmott in another third round tie.

**9** Former Middlesbrough manager Aitor Karanka takes over at Nottingham Forest.

**10** The FA introduce a rule requiring at least one candidate from an ethnic minority background to be interviewed when the next England manager is appointed.

**11** The FA decide to take no disciplinary action against West Bromwich Albion's Jake Livermore over a confrontation with a West Ham fan taunting him about the death of his son.

**12** A ticket pricing dispute between Manchester United and Sevilla over their Champions League tie results in both clubs deciding to subsidise their own travelling fans.

**13** Southampton manager Mauricio Pellegrino and Swansea's Carlos Carvalhal call for video assistant referees in the Premier League after points dropped to hand-ball decisions against their teams.

**14** Chris Lucketti, without a goal in eight league games as Bury manager, is sacked after 54 days in the job, with his side 12 points adrift at the bottom of League One.

**15** Ryan Giggs, winner of 64 caps for his country, is named the new Wales manager. Paul Lambert, former Wolves, Blackburn, Aston Vila and Norwich manager, takes charge at Stoke. Cyrille Regis, a pioneer for black players in British football, dies aged 59. Barnet make another managerial change in a bid to stay in the Football League – former Newport, Peterborough and Preston manager Graham Westley taking over from Mark McGhee, who becomes the club's technical head.

**16** Kelechi Iheanacho becomes the first player to be awarded a goal by a video assistant referee, who overrules an offside flag against the Leicester striker in their FA Cup tie against Fleetwood. Newcastle owner Mike Ashley calls off takeover talks with financier Amanda Staveley and her investment fund.

**17** Theo Walcott ends 12 years at Arsenal with a £20m move to Everton. Phil Brown, manager of Southend for nearly five years, is sacked after a run of seven defeats in eight matches.

**18** Manchester City's Fernandinho signs a two-year contract extension with the club through to 2020.

**19** Kevin De Bruyne agrees a new five-and-a-half-year contract with Manchester City. The Premier League bow to pressure from supporters for a minute's applause at all weekend matches as a tribute to Cyrille Regis. Brighton pay a club-record £14m for PSV Eindhoven striker Jurgen Locadia.

**20** MK Dons manager Robbie Neilson is sacked with his side fourth from bottom after a single win in 11 games.

**21** Marco Silva becomes the season's eighth Premier League manager to lose his job, with Watford's owners blaming an approach by Everton for his services in November for a subsequent poor run of results. Within hours, he is replaced by Javi Gracia, former Rubin Kazan and Malaga coach.

**22** Alexis Sanchez becomes the highest-earning Premier League player, at a reported salary of more than £500,000 a week, when joining Manchester United from Arsenal. Henrikh Mkhitaryan moves the other way in a swop deal, with both players valued at £35m because Sanchez has only four months of his Arsenal contract remaining. Jimmy Armfield, former England captain, winner of 43 caps and a member of the 1966 World Cup-winning squad, dies aged 82. Northern Ireland manager Michael O'Neill turns down the vacant Scotland job.

Pep Clotet, manager of Oxford for six months, is dismissed after a home defeat by bottom-of-the-table Bury.

**23** Phil Neville, winner of 59 England caps, is appointed new manager of the national women's team. Manchester City reach the League Cup Final with a 5-3 aggregate win over Bristol City. Burnley manager Sean Dyche signs a new contract through to 2022. Two League One clubs name new managers. Chris Powell, formerly in charge of Huddersfield and Charlton, takes over at Southend, for whom he made 290 appearances as a player. Former Academy coach Dan Micciche is appointed by MK Dons, his first managerial appointment. Otis Khan is ruled out of Yeovil's FA Cup tie against Manchester United by the FA, who decide that his appeal against a red card for shoving referee Kevin Johnson has 'no prospect of success' and increase his ban from three to five matches.

**24** On his first day in the new job, Phil Neville is rebuked by the FA for historic messages posted on social media about women. Arsenal beat Chelsea 2-1 on aggregate in the second League Cup semi-final.

**25** Southampton pay a club-record £19.1m for Monaco's Argentine striker Guido Carrillo. Moroccan football agent Abdallah Lemsagam takes over League One Oldham, ending Simon Corney's 14 years as owner.

**26** Manchester United retain their position as world football's richest club according to accountancy firm Deloitte, earning £581m in season 2016-17, £1,5m more than Real Madrid. Manchester City, Arsenal, Chelsea and Liverpool are also in the top ten.

**27** West Ham are knocked out of the FA Cup by Wigan in a fourth round tie and have Arthur Masuaku sent off for spitting at Nick Powell. He is banned for six matches by the FA.

**29** Former England captain David Beckham launches his long-planned Major League Soccer team in Miami. The BBC pay £211m to extend their Premier League highlights contract until 2022.

**30** Manchester City break their transfer record with the £57m signing of Athletic Bilbao's French centre-back Aymeric Laporte. Doncaster manager Darren Ferguson is fined £1,000 by the FA for saying he would 'shoot' League One's 'appalling' referees.

**31** Arsenal pay a club-record £56m for Borussia Dortmund's Gabon striker Pierre-Emerick Aubameyang, sell Olivier Giroud to Chelsea for £18m and make Mesut Ozil their highest earner, at a reported weekly salary of £350,000, on a new three-and-a-half-year contract. Swansea also break their transfer record, re-signing Andre Ayew from West Ham for £18m. Premier League clubs spend a record £150m on deadline day, bringing the total in the January window to a record £430m

## FEBRUARY 2018

**1** Riyad Mahrez fails to turn up for training after Leicester reject Manchester City's bid of around £50m for the player on deadline day. Stewart Regan resigns after eight years as chief executive of the Scottish FA, citing the 'need for change.'

**2** West Ham dismiss director of recruitment Tony Henry after his comments about not wanting to sign any more African players for the club.

**3** Riyad Mahrez misses Leicester's Premier League match against Swansea to 'clear his head,' according to manager Claude Puel.

**4** Thomas Christiansen, manager of Leeds for eight months, is sacked after his side concede eight goals in two successive home matches and fall seven points adrift of a play-off place.

**5** Bradford dismiss manager Stuart McCall after six successive defeats in League One and FA Cup matches.

**6** Four days after signing a new rolling contract with Barnsley, Paul Heckingbottom leaves the club to become Leeds' new manager. Former Everton manager Ronald Koeman succeeds Dick Advocaat as coach to the Dutch national team.

**7** Alexis Sanchez, Manchester United's new signing, is given a suspended 16-month priso sentence in Spain for a tax fraud amounting to nearly £900,000.

**8** Norwich midfielder Wes Hoolahan retires from international football after winning 4 Republic of Ireland caps. Businessman Paul Barry, Cambridge's largest shareholder becomes the club's owner.

**9** Minutes after a goalless draw with Lincoln, Cambridge announce the departure of manager Shaun Derry, the club claiming by mutual agreement. Northern Ireland manager Michael O'Neill signs a four-year extension to his contract.

**10** Riyad Mahrez is named in Leicester's squad against Manchester City after ending his self-imposed exile from training.

**11** Russell Slade, manager of Grimsby for ten months, is sacked after a run of 12 matches without a win. Simon Grayson, dismissed by Sunderland earlier in the season, takes over at Bradford.

**12** The Premier League sell live TV rights for 2019-22 for £4.46bn, down from £5.13bn for the current deal which covers slightly more matches. Sky, with most games, pay £3.57bn and BT £885m.

**13** Hull midfielder Ryan Mason, who fractured his skull in a Premier League match against Chelsea in January 2017, announces his retirement on medical advice. West Bromwich Albion chairman John Williams and chief executive officer Martin Goodman are sacked by club owner Guochuan Lai

**14** Sadio Mane scores a hat-trick in Liverpool's 5-0 away win over Porto in the first leg of their Champions League round of 16 match.

**15** Alex McLeish is appointed Scotland manager for the second time, having held the job for ten months in 2007 before resigning to become Birmingham's manager. Paul Dummett signs a new four-and-a-half-year contract with Newcastle.

**16** Four West Bromwich Albion players, Gareth Barry, Jonny Evans, Jake Livermore and Boaz Myhill, apologise for breaking a midnight curfew and allegedly stealing a taxi during a training break in Barcelona. Portuguese coach Jose Morais, who worked alongside Jose Mourinho at Inter Milan, Real Madrid and Chelsea, is appointed Barnsley's new manager.

**17** A troubled week for West Bromwich Albion ends with a 2-1 FA Cup fifth round home defeat by Southampton. Fleetwood manager Uwe Rosler is sacked after five successive defeats leave his side one place above the relegation zone.

**18** Arsenal extend their shirt sponsorship with Emirates for a further five years in a deal reported to be in excess of £200m.

**19** Wigan end Manchester City's bid for an unprecedented four trophies in an FA Cup fifth round tie. A goal by Will Grigg gives the League One club a repeat of their 1-0 victory over City in the 2013 final. Former coach Barry Bennell, who had links with Crewe, Manchester City and Stoke, is jailed for 30 years for 50 counts of sexual abuse against boys. The sentencing judge at Liverpool Crown Court brands him the 'Devil incarnate.'

**20** The FA decide not to take disciplinary action against Manchester City manager Pep Guardiola and Wigan's Paul Cook over their half-time altercation following the red card for City's Fabian Delph. The governing body also rule out sanctioning City's Sergio Aguero, who was abused by a Wigan fan after the game. Everton's Idrissa Gueye signs a new contract through to 2022.

**21** Liverpool's Roberto Firmino is told he will not face any disciplinary action from the FA following an allegation he racially abused Everton's Mason Holgate. Leicester agree to pay the Football League £3.1m to settle a Financial Fair Play dispute arising from the club's 2013-14 Championship-winning season. Thai businessman Sumrith Thanakarnjanasuth takes over ownership of Oxford United from Darryl Eales.

**22** Arsenal beat Ostersunds 4-2 on aggregate in the Europa League's first knockout round. Celtic lose 3-1 to Zenit St Petersburg.

**23** Football League clubs fall in line with the Premier League by voting to close the transfer window before the season kicks off, instead of at the end of August.

**24** John Sheridan, former Oldham and Notts County manager, takes charge at Fleetwood until the end of the season.

**25** Manchester City win their first trophy under Pep Guardiola, beating Arsenal 3-0 in the League Cup Final. Peterborough manager Grant McCann is sacked after a single win in ten matches in all competitions.

**26** Celtic captain Scott Brown retires from international football for the second time, after winning 55 Scotland caps.

**27** Mansfield manager Steve Evans resigns amid speculation that he will take over at Peterborough.

**28** Steve Evans is confirmed as Peterborough's new manager, his sixth Football League appointment.

## MARCH 2018

**1** Phil Neville makes a successful start as England women's team manager with a 4-1 win over France in a four-team tournament in Columbus, Ohio. David Flitcroft resigns as Swindon manager to take charge at Mansfield.

**2** Manchester City are fined £50,000 by the FA after their players surrounded referee Anthony Taylor with protests over the dismissal of Fabian Delph in the FA Cup defeat by Wigan. Grimsby appoint former Burnley under-23 coach Michael Jolley as their new manager. Owen Coyle resigns after five months as Ross County manager with his side bottom of the Scottish Premiership. Peterborough owner Darragh MacAnthony sells half his stake in the club to Canada-based investors Jason Neale and Stewart Thompson.

**3** Steve Cotterill, manager of Birmingham for five months, is sacked after five successive defeats leave his side third from bottom. The International FA Board approve video assistant referees for the World Cup in Russia. Snow and ice cause the postponement of 24 Football League games and all league fixtures in Scotland.

**4** Garry Monk, dismissed by Middlesbrough two days before Christmas, succeeds Steve Cotterill at St Andrew's, the club's fifth manager in 15 months. England's women draw 2-2 with Germany in their second match in New York.

**5** Scott McTominay, Manchester United's emerging midfielder, pledges his international future to Scotland, the country of his father, rather than England. Martin Glenn, FA chief executive, apologises for comparing the Star of David with symbols such as the Nazi swastika when discussing Manchester City manager Pep Guardiola wearing a yellow ribbon in support of imprisoned politicians in Catalonia.

**6** Liverpool reach the last eight of the Champions League with a 5-0 aggregate victory over Porto.

**7** Manchester City go through by beating Basle 5-2 over the two legs. Tottenham lose 4-3 to Juventus.

**8** West Ham are fined £30,000 for a breach of the FA's anti-doping regulations concerning the whereabouts of players. England's women miss out on winning the tournament when going down 1-0 to the USA in Orlando.

**9** Pep Guardiola is fined £20,000 by the FA for wearing the yellow ribbon – a 'politica message' – during his side's FA Cup defeat by Wigan.

**10** West Ham launch an immediate investigation after ugly scenes at the London Stadium or the day the club mark the 25th anniversary of Bobby Moore's death. During a 3-0 defea by Burnley, there are four separate pitch invasions, captain Mark Noble grapples with a supporter and fans abuse owners David Sullivan and David Gold in the directors' box.

**11** Celtic twice come from behind to beat Rangers 3-2 at Ibrox and prevent their rivals fron closing the gap at the top of the Scottish Premiership. The win puts them nine points clea with nine games remaining. After working for the BBC for nearly 50 years, John Motso delivers his final live commentary, at the Arsenal-Watford match for Radio 5.

**12** Jamie Carragher is suspended from his job as a Sky pundit for the rest of the seaso after being caught on camera spitting through his car window at a man goading him ove Liverpool's defeat by Manchester United. Southampton's Mauricio Pellegrino becomes th season's ninth Premier League managerial casualty, sacked after a single win in 17 games Walsall manager Jon Whitney is also dismissed, following four defeats in five matches. Tw months after his sacking by Southend, Phil Brown takes charge at Swindon until the end c the season.

**13** After a goalless first leg, Manchester United lose 2-1 to Sevilla at Old Trafford and go out c the Champions League at the round of 16 stage.

**14** Chelsea are also knocked out, losing 4-1 on aggregate to Barcelona as Lionel Messi reache

100 Champions League goals with two in the return leg. Mark Hughes, sacked by Stoke, is appointed Southampton manager until the end of the season.

**15** Arsenal reach the last eight of the Europa League with a 5-1 aggregate victory over AC Milan. Hibernian manager Neil Lennon is given a three-match touchline ban by the Scottish FA for his reaction to being sent to the stands against Kilmarnock and subsequent criticism of referee Kevin Clancy.

**16** Wrexham's Dean Keates is appointed manager of his home-town club Walsall, where he had two spells as a player.

**18** Stevenage manager Darren Sarll is sacked after a run of two league victories in 11 matches.

**19** Martin Allen is appointed manager of Barnet for the fifth time, following the dismissal of Graham Westley after two months in charge, with his side seven points adrift at the bottom of the table.

**20** Dino Maamria leaves Nuneaton to take charge at Stevenage, where he was a player and former assistant manager.

**21** West Ham ban five supporters for life for pitch invasions during the match against Burnley. Reading sack manager Jaap Stam after a single victory in 18 matches leaves his team three points away from the relegation zone.

**22** Gareth Bale becomes Wales's all-time leading scorer with a hat-trick in a 6-0 victory over China in the China Cup tournament – Ryan Giggs's first match as manager. Bale moves ahead of Ian Rush with 29 goals. Chris Gunter, on his 86th appearance, becomes their most-capped outfield player. Harry Wilson scores his first international goal on his 21st birthday. Karl Robinson parts company with Charlton by mutual agreement and is immediately named Oxford's new manager. Fulham manager Slavisa Jokanovic is fined £3,000 by the FA for calling on referee Simon Hooper for 'protection' for his players ahead of the match against Preston.

**23** Jesse Lingard scores his first international goal to give England a 1-0 victory in Holland. It is marred by clashes between England fans and police. Scotland lose by the same scoreline to Costa Rica in another friendly – the first match of Alex McLeish's second spell as manager The managerial merry-go-round continues, Paul Clement taking over at Reading three months after being sacked by Swansea.

**24** Paul Smyth comes off the bench for his international debut and scores four minutes later to give Northern Ireland a 2-1 victory over South Korea. Scunthorpe's Graham Alexander becomes the latest managerial casualty, despite his side clinging to a top-six place after a single win in 13 games.

**26** Wales are beaten 1-0 by Uruguay in the final of the China Cup. Arsenal's Mohamed Elneny signs a new contract, the length of which is not disclosed.

**27** Matt Phillips scores his first international goal to give Scotland a 1-0 victory in Hungary. England draw 1-1 with Italy.

**28** Ten days after being sacked as Stevenage manager, Darren Sarll returns to oversee the club's youth system.

**29** Ipswich announce that Mick McCarthy, appointed in November 2012 and the Championship's longest-serving manager, will leave the club when his contract expires at the end of the season. Dundee manager Neil McCann is given a two-match touchline ban by the Scottish FA following a confrontation with St Johnstone goalkeeper Zander Clark, who is also banned for two games.

**30** FIFA announce there will be no British referee at the World Cup – for the first time since 1938.

**31** Queen's Park, owners of the stadium since 1903, agree in principle to sell Hampden Park to the Scottish FA.

## APRIL 2018

**2** Alan Pardew, manager for four months, leaves West Bromwich Albion by mutual consent with his side almost certain to be relegated after a single win in 18 Premier League matches. Jimmy Floyd Hasselbaink, in charge of Northampton for seven months, is sacked with his team third from bottom.

3 Figures show Premier League clubs paying £211m to agents over the last two transfer windows, an increase of £37m. Liverpool (£26.8m), Chelsea (£25.1m) and Manchester City (£23.5m) are the biggest spenders, with Aston Villa (£5.5m), Blackburn (£764,000) and Coventry (£113,000) paying the most in the other divisions.

4 Former Chelsea, Manchester United and Rangers midfielder Ray Wilkins, capped 84 times by England, dies aged 64 after a heart attack. Liverpool beat Manchester City 3-0 in the first leg of their Champions League quarter-final.

5 Liverpool are charged by UEFA following an attack by supporters on the Manchester City team bus arriving at Anfield.

6 A 25,600 crowd at Southampton watch Phil Neville's first home match as England women's team manager – a goalless World Cup qualifier against Wales.

8 Lincoln defeat Shrewsbury 1-0 in the Football League's Checkatrade Trophy Final at Wembley.

9 West Bromwich Albion's application for a safe-standing section at The Hawthorns is turned down by the Government.

10 Liverpool win the return leg 2-1 at the Etihad to reach the semi-finals 5-1 on aggregate. Pep Guardiola is sent to the stands for protesting at the decision to disallow a second Manchester City goal. Barcelona, 4-1 winners of their first leg against Roma, go out on the away goals rule after losing the second match 3-0. Ipswich manager Mick McCarthy walks away from the club, earlier than planned, after more protests from fans. Newcastle are fined £7,500 by the FA for their under-18 team wearing shirts bearing the logo of a betting company.

11 Premier League referee Michael Oliver awards Real Madrid a last-minute penalty and sends off Juventus goalkeeper Gianlugi Buffon for protesting in a dramatic finish at the Bernabeu. Cristiano Ronaldo converts it to send the holders through 4-3 on aggregate. Tottenham's appeal for Harry Kane, not Christian Eriksen, to be awarded their second goal in a 2-1 win at Stoke – to boost his chances of winning the Golden Boot award – is upheld by the Premier League.

12 Arsenal reach the semi-finals of the Europa League by beating CSKA Moscow 6-3 on aggregate.

13 Premier League clubs postpone a decision on the use of video assistant referees in favour of extensive testing next season. West Bromwich Albion striker Jay Rodriguez is cleared of racially abusing Brighton's Gaetan Bong by an FA commission which finds the allegation 'not proven.'

14 Championship leaders Wolves become the first team to win promotion. League One Bury are the first to be relegated. Motherwell reach the Scottish Cup Final by beating Aberdeen 3-0.

15 Manchester City are crowned Premier League champions for the third time in seven years. Manchester United's defeat by West Bromwich Albion means City cannot be overtaken in their five remaining games. Celtic defeat Rangers 4-0 in the second Scottish Cup semi-final.

16 Ryan Sessegnon, Fulham's 17-year-old winger, is named the Championship's Player of the Year. Hull and Queens Park Rangers are both fined £5,000 by the FA for a players' confrontation.

17 Manchester United are reported to be willing to let £89m record-signing Paul Pogba leave the club in the summer.

18 Joey Barton is named Fleetwood's new manager, the appointment to take effect on June 2 at the end of his 13-month FA ban for betting on matches. John Sheridan, appointed until the end of the season, will leave the club he saved from relegation.

19 Chelsea's Marcos Alonso is banned for three matches by the FA for violent conduct and misses the FA Cup semi-final against Southampton after his tackle on Shane Long in the Premier League win over Southampton is caught on camera. Former Lincoln defender Bradley Wood, 26, is banned for six years for match-fixing offences, having been found guilty of deliberately getting himself booked in the club's FA Cup wins over Ipswich and Burnley in the 2016-17 season.

20 Arsene Wenger, manager of Arsenal since October 1996, announces he will leave the club at the end of the season.

21 Manchester United come from behind to beat Tottenham 2-1 in the first FA Cup semi-final. Wolves win the Championship title. Sunderland are relegated for the second successive season. Macclesfield return to the Football League after six years as National League champions.

22 Chelsea beat Southampton 2-0 to reach the FA Cup Final. Liverpool's Mohamed Salah is named the Professional Footballers' Association Player of the Year. Dan Micciche is sacked after three months as MK Dons manager with his side on the brink of being relegated.

23 Millwall's Tim Cahill is banned for three matches after being caught on camera elbowing Fulham's Ryan Fredericks. Manager Jack Lester has his contract terminated with Chesterfield on the brink of being relegated to the National League. Ian Maxwell, Partick Thistle's managing director, is named the new Scottish FA chief executive. Chelsea lose 3-0 to Barcelona in the UEFA Youth League Final.

24 Mohamed Salah scores twice and lays on goals for Sadio Mane and Roberto Firmino in Liverpool's 5-2 over Roma in the first leg of their Champions League semi-final. Michael Oliver is appointed to referee the FA Cup Final. Chesterfield are relegated after 97 years in the Football League.

25 Alex Oxlade-Chamberlain is ruled out for the rest of the season and misses the World Cup with a knee injury sustained against Roma. Wolves are cleared by the Football League over allegations of an improper relationship with agent Jorge Mendes.

26 Fulham owner Shahid Khan, a billionaire businessman, makes a £600m bid to buy Wembley Stadium from the FA. Wigan are fined £12,500 by the FA for a pitch invasion following their FA Cup win over Manchester City. Carlisle manager Keith Curle announces he will leave the club at the end of the season.

28 Liverpool's Roberto Firmino agrees a new five-year contract. Accrington, a club with one of the lowest budgets and smallest crowds, become champions of League Two.

29 Sunderland owner Ellis Short sacks manager Chris Coleman, clears debts of around £140m and sells the club to a consortium headed by Stewart Donald, chairman of National League side Eastleigh. Celtic are crowned Scottish champions for the seventh successive season after beating arch-rivals Rangers 5-0. Their captain, Scott Brown, is named PFA Scotland Player of the Year. Jack Ross, of Championship title winners St Mirren, takes the Manager of the Year award, ahead of Celtic's Brendan Rodgers. Arsene Wenger is presented with an engraved silver vase by Sir Alex Ferguson and Jose Mourinho before his final match against Manchester United as Arsenal manager.

30 Chelsea win the FA Youth Cup for the fifth successive year, beating Arsenal 7-1 on aggregate to match the achievement of Manchester United's Busby Babes in the 1950s.

## MAY 2018

1 Mohamed Salah completes the double by winning the Football Writers' Association Footballer of the Year award. Graeme Murty, appointed Rangers manager until the end of the season, is sacked after the defeat by Celtic. Arsenal's Rob Holding signs a new four-year contract. Morecambe are taken over by a London-based investment company, four days before a match which decides whether the club retain Football League status.

2 Liverpool reach the Champions League Final against Real Madrid with a 7-6 aggregate win over Roma in the tournament's highest-scoring semi-final for 58 years. Caretaker Joe Dunne is given the Cambridge manager's job on a permanent basis.

3 Arsenal are beaten 2-1 over two legs in the Europa League semi-finals by a goal from Atletico Madrid's former Chelsea striker Diego Costa. Islam Slimani, on loan at Newcastle from Leicester, is banned for three matches by the FA after being caught on camera kicking West Bromwich Albion's Craig Dawson.

4 Steven Gerrard, former Liverpool and England captain, is appointed manager of Rangers.

5 Sir Alex Ferguson, 76-year-old former Manchester United manager, has emergency surgery for a brain haemorrhage. Stoke are relegated from the Premier League. Barnet are relegated to the National League. Wigan win the League One title. Chelsea beat Arsenal 3-1 in the

Women's FA Cup Final at Wembley, watched by a record crowd for the competition of 45,423.

**6** Arsene Wenger, in his last home game as Arsenal manager, sends a public message of support to Sir Alex Ferguson. So does Pep Guardiola as Manchester City are presented with the Premier League trophy. Neil Warnock's record eighth promotion as a manager takes Cardiff into the Premier League. Jose Morais, Barnsley's manager for three months, is sacked after his team are relegated.

**7** Marc Albrighton is banned from Leicester's final two matches and fined £25,000 by the FA for misconduct following his sending-off against Crystal Palace. Simon Grayson turns down the chance to continue as Bradford manager after his short-term deal expires.

**8** West Bromwich Albion are relegated from the Premier League. Liverpool's Joe Gomez is ruled out of the Champions League Final, and misses the chance of a place in England's World Cup squad, after ankle surgery.

**9** Sir Alex Ferguson comes out of intensive care and Manchester United manager Jose Mourinho suggests he will make a full recovery.

**10** Queens Park Rangers manager Ian Holloway is sacked, with former England manager Steve McClaren lined up to replace him.

**11** Celtic captain Scott Brown completes the double by winning the Scottish Football Writers' Association Footballer of the Year award. Caretaker Ryan Lowe is appointed Bury manager on a permanent basis. Martin Allen turns down an offer to stay at Barnet after relegation.

**12** Caretaker Dean Austin is appointed permanent manager of Northampton. Tranmere have defender Liam Ridehalgh sent off for a two-footed challenge after 48 seconds of the National League Play-of Final, but defeat Boreham Wood 2-1 and return to the Football League after a three-year absence. Ross County are relegated from the Scottish Premiership.

**13** Manchester City goalkeeper Ederson signs a two-year contract extension, keeping him at the club until 2025.

**14** Davinson Sanchez, Tottenham's record-signing, signs a new contract through to 2024. Manager Chris Hughton is rewarded for keeping Brighton in the Premier League with a new deal until 2021.

**15** Manchester City's Pep Guardiola is named Manager of the Year by the League Managers' Association. Martin Allen is appointed manager of Chesterfield, the other club relegated from League Two. Chelsea win the Women's Super League title to complete a domestic double.

**16** England manager Gareth Southgate names two uncapped players, 19-year-old Liverpool full-back Trent Alexander-Arnold and goalkeeper Nick Pope, in his 23-man World Cup squad. Joe Hart and Jack Wilshere are among those omitted. Sam Allardyce is sacked after six months as Everton manager. David Moyes leaves West Ham at the end of a six-month contract. Ray Wilson, England's World Cup-winning left-back in 1966, dies aged 83. Chelsea are fined £20,000 by the FA after protesting players and coaches surrounded referee Lee Mason at half-time of the match against Huddersfield.

**17** Darren Moore is named West Bromwich Albion manager after 11 points from six games as caretaker. Manchester City's Pep Guardiola signs a two-year contract extension through to the end of the 2020-21 season.

**18** Two more managers join the Premier League casualty list, both after their teams are relegated. Paul Lambert leaves Stoke by mutual consent. Carlos Carvalhal's contract is not renewed at Swansea. Steve McClaren's appointment is confirmed by Queens Park Rangers.

**19** Chelsea defeat Manchester United 1-0 in the FA Cup Final. Owner Roman Abramovich misses his team's win because of problems over renewing his UK visa. Celtic beat Motherwell 2-0 to become the first Scottish side to win back-to-back domestic trebles.

**20** Livingston are promoted to the Scottish Premiership with a 3-1 aggregate Play-off Final win over Partick, who are relegated. Brackley beat Bromley 5-4 on penalties after a 1-1 scoreline in the FA Trophy Final.

**21** Arsenal appoint former Paris Saint-Germain and Sevilla coach Unai Emery to succeed Arsene Wenger as manager.

**22** Tottenham's Harry Kane is named England's World Cup captain. Gary Rowett leaves Derby to become Stoke's new manager.

**23** Bristol City's Famara Diedhiou is banned for six matches by the FA for spitting at an opponent during their match against Birmingham. Arsenal are fined £20,000 for players surrounding referee Graham Scott after a penalty award to Leicester.

**24** Tottenham manager Mauricio Pochettino ends speculation about his future by signing a new five-year contract. Three flights scheduled to take Liverpool fans to the Champions League Final in Kiev are cancelled.

**25** St Mirren's Jack Ross, Scotland's Manager of the Year, takes charge at relegated Sunderland. Caretaker-manager Nick Daws is given the Scunthorpe job on a full-time basis.

**26** Two mistakes by goalkeeper Loris Karius and a wonder goal by Gareth Bale condemn Liverpool to a 3-1 defeat by Real Madrid in the Champions League Final. Fulham defeat Aston Villa 1-0 in the Championship Play-off Final.

**27** Mohamed Salah has scans on a damaged shoulder sustained in Kiev which threatens his place in Egypt's World Cup team. Rotherham beat Shrewsbury 2-1 after extra-time in the League One Play-off Final.

**28** Liverpool sign Monaco's Brazil midfielder Fabinho for £43.7m. Coventry defeat Exeter 3-1 in the League Two Play-off Final. The Republic of Ireland lose 2-0 to France, one of the World Cup favourites.

**29** Wales hold Mexico to a goalless draw in front of a crowd of more than 82,000 in Pasadena, California. Manager David Wagner signs a new three-year contract after keeping Huddersfield in the Premier League.

**30** Frank Lampard, former Chelsea and England midfielder, is appointed Derby's new manager. Paul Hurst leaves Shrewsbury to become Ipswich manager. Northern Ireland share a goalless draw with Panama, one of England's World Cup opponents. Seven Scotland players win their first caps in a 2-0 defeat by another team heading for Russia, Peru.

**31** Chelsea owner Roman Abramovich orders work to stop on a new 60,000-seater stadium at Stamford Bridge after the Home Office delay renewing his visa at a time of political tension between Russia and Britain. Zinedine Zidane steps down as Real Madrid coach. Livington manager David Hopkin turns down a contract extension after leading the club into the Scottish Premiership.

## JUNE 2018

**1** Former Watford and Hull manager Marco Silva takes charge at Everton. Paul Heckingbottom, manager of Leeds for four months, is sacked. Paul Tisdale, appointed in 2006 and the league's longest-serving manager after Arsene Wenger's departure from Arsenal, leaves Exeter. Tisdale is replaced by former team captain Matt Taylor. John Askey, who led Macclesfield back to the Football League, is appointed Shrewsbury's new manager. Raheem Sterling apologises to England manager Gareth Southgate after reporting late to the squad's St George's Park training base.

**2** John O'Shea makes his 118th and final appearance for the Republic of Ireland in a 2-1 win over the United States. Graham Burke and Alan Judge score for the first time. Harry Kane is on the mark for the eighth time in seven matches as England defeat Nigeria 2-1.

**3** Scotland lose 1-0 to Mexico and Northern Ireland are beaten 3-0 by another World Cup-bound team, Costa Rica.

**4** Manchester United agree a £52m fee for Shakhtar Donetsk's Brazil midfielder Fred. Darren Ferguson resigns as manager of Doncaster.

**5** Goalkeeper Gianluigi Buffon is banned by UEFA for three matches for his red card and outburst at referee Michael Oliver after Juventus's Champions League defeat by Real Madrid. John Sheridan, who led Fleetwood away from the threat of relegation, is named Carlisle's new manager.

**6** Two more clubs appoint new managers. Daniel Stendel, former Hannover coach, takes over at Barnsley. Paul Tisdale joins MK Dons.

**7** Marcus Rashford stakes a claim for a World Cup place with a 30-yard strike in England's 2-0 win over Costa Rica at Elland Road. Richard Scudamore, one of the game's most influential figures, announces he will step down as executive chairman of the Premier League by the end of 2018 after 20 years as head of the organisation. American tech giants Amazon agree a three-year deal to stream 20 Premier League games a season.

**8** The Premier League decide on a fortnight's winter break during the 2019-20 season, with half the clubs using it for the first week and the remainder for the second week. To accommodate it, FA Cup fifth round ties will take place in midweek and be decided on the night. Harry Kane signs a new six-year contract with Tottenham. Oldham sack manager Richie Wellens after being relegated. Huddersfield pay a club-record £12m to sign Monaco's Holland defender Terence Kongolo on a permanent basis.

**9** Liverpool legend Kenny Dalglish is knighted in the Queen's Birthday Honours. Former England striker Jermain Defoe receives an OBE for his charity work.

**10** The Football League give clubs the option to scrap matchday programmes. Former Hibernian manager Alan Stubbs takes charge of newly-promoted St Mirren.

**11** Chelsea secure a shirt-sleeve sponsorship deal with Hyundai, reported to be worth a record £40m.

**12** Former Oldham striker Frankie Bunn returns to the club as the new manager.

**13** Spain, one of the World Cup favourites, sack coach Julen Lopetegui the day after his appointment to succeed Zinedine Zidane at Real Madrid. The USA, Canada and Mexico, in a 'united' bid, win the right to stage the 2026 World Cup.

**14** The finals in Russia get under way with the hosts defeating Saudi Arabia 5-0 – a record scoreline for the opening match. Nottingham Forest break their transfer record with the £13.2m signing from Benfica of Portugal under-21 midfielder Joao Carvalho.

**15** Cristiano Ronaldo scores a hat-trick in Portugal's 3-3 draw with Spain. Granit Xhaka agrees a new five-year contact with Arsenal.

**16** Former Argentina and Chile coach Marcelo Bielsa is appointed the new Leeds manager.

**18** A stoppage-time goal by captain Harry Kane, his second of the game, gives England a 2-1 win over Tunisia in their opening game. Manchester United's Romelu Lukaku scores twice as Belgium beat Panama 3-0. Bradford appoint 32-year-old Michael Collins, their under-18 coach, as the clubs's new manager. He is the youngest manager in the top four divisions.

**19** West Ham pay a club-record £22m for Issa Diop, a France under-21 defender, from Toulouse. Macclesfield appoint Solihull's Mark Yates as their new manager.

**20** England manager Gareth Southgate suffers a dislocated shoulder when falling while out on a run near the team's World Cup hotel in Repino.

**21** Norwich receive a club-record £22m from Leicester for midfielder James Maddison.

**22** Romelu Lukaku and Chelsea's Eden Hazard both score twice in Belgium's 5-2 victory over Tunisia.

**24** England record their biggest-ever win in a World Cup finals to qualify for the knockout stage with a match to spare. They defeat Panama 6-1 – scoring five times in the first-half – with a hat-trick from Harry Kane, including two penalties, two headers from John Stones, his first international goals, and a brilliant finish by Jesse Lingard.

**25** Grant McCann, sacked by Peterborough, is appointed Doncaster's new manager.

**26** An 86th minute winner against Nigeria by Manchester United's Marcos Rojo keeps Argentina in the World Cup.

**27** Defending champions Germany concede two goals in stoppage-time to South Korea and are knocked out of the tournament.

**28** England lose 1-0 to Belgium and finish runners-up in their group, Gareth Southgate and Roberto Martinez both saving most of their first-choice players for the knockout stage. Wayne Rooney leaves Everton to join Washington club DC United of the MLS on a three-and-a-half year contract.

**29** Marouane Fellaini signs a new two-year contract with Manchester United.

**30** The World Cup's two biggest names bow out of the tournament in the round of 16. Lionel Messi's Argentina lose 4-3 to France. Cristiano Ronaldo's Portugal are beaten 2-1 by Uruguay. Former Rangers striker Kenny Miller is appointed player-manager of Scottish Premiership newcomers Livingston.

## JULY 2018

**1** Spain, another of the fancied teams, are beaten by Russia on penalties in the first knockout round.

**2** Liverpool's Mohamed Salah signs a new contract through to the summer of 2023. So does Ruben Neves, an influential figures in Wolves winning promotion to the Premier League. Jamie Carragher, suspended by Sky for spitting through his car window at a car carrying a 14-year-old girl, is reported to have kept his job as a pundit.

**3** England win a World Cup penalty shootout for the first time, defeating Colombia to reach the quarter-finals.

**4** Ahead of their last eight match against Sweden, Gareth Southgate says England will never have a better chance of winning the World Cup.

**5** Tony Henry, sacked as West Ham's director of recruitment for comments about African players, is banned from football for a year by the FA.

**6** A crowd of 41,000 watch Steven Gerrard's first Ibrox match as Rangers manager – a friendly against Bury. In a dispute over wages and bonuses, Bolton's players refuse to appear in a friendly against St Mirren and the match is cancelled.

**7** England reach the World Cup semi-finals for the first time since 1990, defeating Sweden with Harry Maguire's first international goal and another header from Dele Alli.

**8** Thousands of England fans scramble to book to see the semi-final against Croatia, who beat beat Russia on penalties to go through.

**9** Arsenal agree a £26m fee with Sampdoria for Uruguay's World Cup midfielder Lucas Torreira.

**10** Manchester City sign Riyad Mahrez from Leicester for £60m – a record fee or both clubs. Cristiano Ronaldo leaves Real Madrid for Juventus for £99.2m. France reach the World Cup Final with a 1-0 victory over Belgium.

**11** Kieran Trippier gives England a fifth minute lead with a free-kick, but they miss chances to increase it and go out of the tournament 2-1 to Croatia in extra-time.

**12** Summer-long speculation about the future of Antonio Conte comes to an end with the sacking of the Chelsea manager after two years in the job. Promoted Fulham pay a club-record £25m to Nice for Ivory Coast midfielder Jean Michael Seri.

**13** Former Napoli coach Maurizio Sarri replaces Antonio Conte.

**14** England lose 2-0 to Belgium in the match to decide third place. Chelsea sign Italy midfielder Jorginho from Napoli for £50m.

**15** West Ham sign Brazil midfielder Felipe Anderson from Lazio for a club-record £36m. France defeat Croatia 4-2 4-1 in a final in keeping with one of the best-ever World Cups.

# THINGS THEY SAID...

One hundred points, fifty at home, fifty away. I don't have the words to describe it. Incredible, incredible' – **Pep Guardiola**, manager of champions Manchester City.

They have brought a brand of football to the Premier League we have never seen before' – **Alan Shearer**, *Match of the Day* analyst and former England captain.

'This is not a dynasty. It is one title. There is a lot more to do to unlock our full potential' – **Vincent Kompany**, Manchester City captain.

'The scenes are still running through my head again and again. I know that I messed up and let you all down. It's even worse as we all felt we could have beaten Real Madrid' – **Loris Karius**, Liverpool goalkeeper, takes the blame for their Champions League defeat

'I'm grateful for having had the privilege to serve the club for so many memorable years. I managed with full commitment and integrity' – **Arsene Wenger** on leaving Arsenal after nearly 22 years in charge.

# ENGLISH TABLES 2017–2018

## PREMIER LEAGUE

| | | | Home | | | | | Away | | | | | | |
|---|---|---|---|---|---|---|---|---|---|---|---|---|---|---|
| | | P | W | D | L | F | A | W | D | L | F | A | GD | Pts |
| 1 | Manchester City | 38 | 16 | 2 | 1 | 61 | 14 | 16 | 2 | 1 | 45 | 13 | 79 | 100 |
| 2 | Manchester Utd | 38 | 15 | 2 | 2 | 38 | 9 | 10 | 4 | 5 | 30 | 19 | 40 | 81 |
| 3 | Tottenham | 38 | 13 | 4 | 2 | 40 | 16 | 10 | 4 | 5 | 34 | 20 | 38 | 77 |
| 4 | Liverpool | 38 | 12 | 7 | 0 | 45 | 10 | 9 | 5 | 5 | 39 | 28 | 46 | 75 |
| 5 | Chelsea | 38 | 11 | 4 | 4 | 30 | 16 | 10 | 3 | 6 | 32 | 22 | 24 | 70 |
| 6 | Arsenal | 38 | 15 | 2 | 2 | 54 | 20 | 4 | 4 | 11 | 20 | 31 | 23 | 63 |
| 7 | Burnley | 38 | 7 | 5 | 7 | 16 | 17 | 7 | 7 | 5 | 20 | 22 | -3 | 54 |
| 8 | Everton | 38 | 10 | 4 | 5 | 28 | 22 | 3 | 6 | 10 | 16 | 36 | -14 | 49 |
| 9 | Leicester | 38 | 7 | 6 | 6 | 25 | 22 | 5 | 5 | 9 | 31 | 38 | -4 | 47 |
| 10 | Newcastle | 38 | 8 | 4 | 7 | 21 | 17 | 4 | 4 | 11 | 18 | 30 | -8 | 44 |
| 11 | Crystal Palace | 38 | 7 | 5 | 7 | 29 | 27 | 4 | 6 | 9 | 16 | 28 | -10 | 44 |
| 12 | Bournemouth | 38 | 7 | 5 | 7 | 26 | 30 | 4 | 6 | 9 | 19 | 31 | -16 | 44 |
| 13 | West Ham | 38 | 7 | 6 | 6 | 24 | 26 | 3 | 6 | 10 | 24 | 42 | -20 | 42 |
| 14 | Watford | 38 | 7 | 6 | 6 | 27 | 31 | 4 | 2 | 13 | 17 | 33 | -20 | 41 |
| 15 | Brighton | 38 | 7 | 8 | 4 | 24 | 25 | 2 | 5 | 12 | 10 | 29 | -20 | 40 |
| 16 | Huddersfield | 38 | 6 | 5 | 8 | 16 | 25 | 3 | 5 | 11 | 12 | 33 | -30 | 37 |
| 17 | Southampton | 38 | 4 | 7 | 8 | 20 | 26 | 3 | 8 | 8 | 17 | 30 | -19 | 36 |
| 18 | Swansea | 38 | 6 | 3 | 10 | 17 | 24 | 2 | 6 | 11 | 11 | 32 | -28 | 33 |
| 19 | Stoke | 38 | 5 | 5 | 9 | 20 | 30 | 2 | 7 | 10 | 15 | 38 | -33 | 33 |
| 20 | WBA | 38 | 3 | 9 | 7 | 21 | 29 | 3 | 4 | 12 | 10 | 27 | -25 | 31 |

Manchester City, Manchester Utd, Tottenham, Liverpool all into Champions League group stage; Chelsea, Arsenal into Europa League group stage, Burnley into second qualifying round

**Prize money** (league position = amount received): 1 £149.4m, 2 £149.8m, 3 £144.5m, 4 £145.9m, 5 £141.7m, 6 £142m, 7 £119.7m, 8 £128m, 9 £118.2m, 10 £123m, 11 £114.3m, 12 £111.2m, 13 £116.1m,14 £106.2m, 15 £107.7m, 16 £102.4m, 17 £107.2m, 18 £98.5m, 19 £98.9m. 20 £94.6m

**Biggest win**: Watford 0 Manchester City 6
**Highest aggregate score**: Manchester City 7 Stoke 2; Tottenham 5 Leicester 4
**Highest attendance**: 83,222 (Tottenham v Arsenal, Wembley)
**Lowest attendance**: 10,242 (Bournemouth v WBA)
**Player of Year**: Mohamed Salah (Liverpool)
**Manager of Year**: Pep Guadiola (Manchester City)
**Golden Boot**: 32 Mohamed Salah (Liverpool)
**Golden Glove**: 18 clean sheets David de Gea (Manchester Utd)
**PFA Team of Year**: De Gea (Manchester Utd), Walker (Manchester City), Otamendi (Manchester City), Vertonghen (Tottenham), Alonso (Chelsea), David Silva (Manchester City), Eriksen (Tottenham), De Bruyne (Manchester City), Salah (Liverpool), Kane (Tottenham), Aguero (Manchester City)
**Leading league scorers**: 32 Salah (Liverpool), 30 Kane (Tottenham); 21 Aguero (Manchester City); 20 Vardy (Leicester); 18 Sterling (Manchester City); 16 Lukaku (Manchester Utd); 15 Firmino (Liverpool); 14 Lacazette (Arsenal); 13 Gabriel Jesus (Manchester City); 12 Hazard (Chelsea), Mahrez (Leicester), Murray (Brighton), Son Heung-Min (Tottenham); 11 Arnautovic (West Ham), Morata (Chelsea); 10 Aubameyang (Arsenal), Eriksen (Tottenham), Mane (Liverpool), Milivojevic (Crystal Palace), Rooney (Everton), Sane (Manchester City), Wood (Burnley)

## SKY BET CHAMPIONSHIP

| | | Home | | | | | | Away | | | | | | |
|---|---|---|---|---|---|---|---|---|---|---|---|---|---|---|
| | | P | W | D | L | F | A | W | D | L | F | A | GD | Pts |
| 1 | Wolves | 46 | 16 | 5 | 2 | 47 | 18 | 14 | 4 | 5 | 35 | 21 | 43 | 99 |
| 2 | Cardiff | 46 | 16 | 4 | 3 | 40 | 16 | 11 | 5 | 7 | 29 | 23 | 30 | 90 |
| 3 | Fulham* | 46 | 13 | 8 | 2 | 40 | 17 | 12 | 5 | 6 | 39 | 29 | 33 | 88 |
| 4 | Aston Villa | 46 | 14 | 7 | 2 | 42 | 19 | 10 | 4 | 9 | 30 | 23 | 30 | 83 |
| 5 | Middlesbrough | 46 | 14 | 3 | 6 | 33 | 17 | 8 | 7 | 8 | 34 | 28 | 22 | 76 |
| 6 | Derby | 46 | 12 | 5 | 6 | 41 | 22 | 8 | 10 | 5 | 29 | 26 | 22 | 75 |
| 7 | Preston | 46 | 9 | 8 | 6 | 27 | 22 | 10 | 8 | 5 | 30 | 24 | 11 | 73 |
| 8 | Millwall | 46 | 12 | 7 | 4 | 33 | 21 | 7 | 8 | 8 | 23 | 24 | 11 | 72 |
| 9 | Brentford | 46 | 9 | 11 | 3 | 37 | 24 | 9 | 4 | 10 | 25 | 28 | 10 | 69 |
| 10 | Sheffield Utd | 46 | 12 | 5 | 6 | 33 | 20 | 8 | 4 | 11 | 29 | 35 | 7 | 69 |
| 11 | Bristol City | 46 | 11 | 6 | 6 | 41 | 28 | 6 | 10 | 7 | 26 | 30 | 9 | 67 |
| 12 | Ipswich | 46 | 9 | 6 | 8 | 29 | 27 | 8 | 3 | 12 | 28 | 33 | -3 | 60 |
| 13 | Leeds | 46 | 10 | 6 | 7 | 32 | 27 | 7 | 3 | 13 | 27 | 37 | -5 | 60 |
| 14 | Norwich | 46 | 8 | 8 | 7 | 25 | 25 | 7 | 7 | 9 | 24 | 35 | -11 | 60 |
| 15 | Sheffield Wed | 46 | 8 | 7 | 8 | 37 | 31 | 6 | 8 | 9 | 22 | 29 | -1 | 57 |
| 16 | QPR | 46 | 12 | 5 | 6 | 38 | 31 | 3 | 6 | 14 | 20 | 39 | -12 | 56 |
| 17 | Nottm Forest | 46 | 10 | 3 | 10 | 25 | 27 | 5 | 5 | 13 | 26 | 38 | -14 | 53 |
| 18 | Hull | 46 | 7 | 8 | 8 | 41 | 32 | 4 | 8 | 11 | 29 | 38 | 0 | 49 |
| 19 | Birmingham | 46 | 10 | 3 | 10 | 21 | 24 | 3 | 4 | 16 | 17 | 44 | -30 | 46 |
| 20 | Reading | 46 | 5 | 8 | 10 | 25 | 35 | 5 | 6 | 12 | 23 | 35 | -22 | 44 |
| 21 | Bolton | 46 | 9 | 4 | 10 | 25 | 33 | 1 | 9 | 13 | 14 | 41 | -35 | 43 |
| 22 | Barnsley | 46 | 5 | 9 | 9 | 25 | 32 | 4 | 5 | 14 | 23 | 40 | -24 | 41 |
| 23 | Burton | 46 | 4 | 5 | 14 | 19 | 43 | 6 | 6 | 11 | 19 | 38 | -43 | 41 |
| 24 | Sunderland | 46 | 3 | 7 | 13 | 23 | 39 | 4 | 9 | 10 | 29 | 41 | -28 | 37 |

*Also promoted

**Biggest win**: Fulham 6 Burton 0
**Highest aggregate score**: Bristol City 5 Hull 5
**Highest attendance**: 41,745 (Aston Villa v Derby)
**Lowest attendance**: 2,750 (Burton v Reading)
**Player of Year**: Ryan Sessegnon (Fulham)
**Manager of Year**: Neil Warnock (Cardiff)
**PFA Team of Year**: Ruddy (Wolves), Fredericks (Fulham), Bamba (Cardiff), Boly (Wolves), Sessegnon (Fulham), Maddison (Norwich), Ruben Neves (Wolves), Cairney (Fulham), Reid (Bristol City), Clarke (Sheffield Utd), Vydra (Derby)
**Leading league scorers**: 21 Vydra (Derby); 19 Clarke (Sheffield Utd), Reid (Bristol City); 17 Jota (Wolves); 16 Waghorn (Ipswich); 15 Assombalonga (Middlesbrough), Sessegnon (Fulham); 14 Adomah (Aston Villa), Bowen (Hull), Maddison (Norwich); 13 Diedhiou (Bristol City), Sharp (Sheffield Utd); 12 Leo Bonatini (Wolves), Maupay (Brentford), Mitrovic (Fulham); 11 Bamford (Middlesbrough), Hourihane (Aston Villa), Nuhiu (Sheffield Wed), Roofe (Leeds), Smith (QPR)
Also: 20 Grabban (12 Sunderland, 8 Aston Villa)

## SKY BET LEAGUE ONE

| | | | Home | | | | | Away | | | | | | |
|---|---|---|---|---|---|---|---|---|---|---|---|---|---|---|
| | | P | W | D | L | F | A | W | D | L | F | A | GD | Pts |
| 1 | Wigan | 46 | 13 | 8 | 2 | 37 | 11 | 16 | 3 | 4 | 52 | 18 | 60 | 98 |
| 2 | Blackburn | 46 | 15 | 6 | 2 | 46 | 20 | 13 | 6 | 4 | 36 | 20 | 42 | 96 |
| 3 | Shrewsbury | 46 | 14 | 4 | 5 | 32 | 17 | 11 | 8 | 4 | 28 | 22 | 21 | 87 |
| 4 | Rotherham* | 46 | 15 | 3 | 5 | 45 | 23 | 9 | 4 | 10 | 28 | 30 | 20 | 79 |
| 5 | Scunthorpe | 46 | 9 | 8 | 6 | 28 | 23 | 10 | 9 | 4 | 37 | 27 | 15 | 74 |
| 6 | Charlton | 46 | 11 | 6 | 6 | 31 | 24 | 9 | 5 | 9 | 27 | 27 | 7 | 71 |
| 7 | Plymouth | 46 | 13 | 3 | 7 | 37 | 30 | 6 | 8 | 9 | 21 | 29 | -1 | 68 |
| 8 | Portsmouth | 46 | 12 | 3 | 8 | 33 | 21 | 8 | 3 | 12 | 24 | 35 | 1 | 66 |
| 9 | Peterborough | 46 | 12 | 4 | 7 | 37 | 26 | 5 | 9 | 9 | 31 | 34 | 8 | 64 |
| 10 | Southend | 46 | 12 | 7 | 4 | 38 | 21 | 5 | 5 | 13 | 20 | 41 | -4 | 63 |
| 11 | Bradford | 46 | 9 | 4 | 10 | 28 | 32 | 9 | 5 | 9 | 29 | 35 | -10 | 63 |
| 12 | Blackpool | 46 | 9 | 8 | 6 | 37 | 29 | 6 | 7 | 10 | 23 | 26 | 5 | 60 |
| 13 | Bristol Rov | 46 | 11 | 6 | 6 | 38 | 30 | 5 | 5 | 13 | 22 | 36 | -6 | 59 |
| 14 | Fleetwood | 46 | 7 | 6 | 10 | 32 | 35 | 9 | 3 | 11 | 27 | 33 | -9 | 57 |
| 15 | Doncaster | 46 | 7 | 9 | 7 | 30 | 25 | 6 | 8 | 9 | 22 | 27 | 0 | 56 |
| 16 | Oxford | 46 | 9 | 6 | 8 | 34 | 32 | 6 | 5 | 12 | 27 | 34 | -5 | 56 |
| 17 | Gillingham | 46 | 5 | 11 | 7 | 26 | 26 | 8 | 6 | 9 | 24 | 29 | -5 | 56 |
| 18 | AFC Wimbledon | 46 | 8 | 6 | 9 | 25 | 30 | 5 | 8 | 10 | 22 | 28 | -11 | 53 |
| 19 | Walsall | 46 | 9 | 6 | 8 | 30 | 31 | 4 | 7 | 12 | 23 | 35 | -13 | 52 |
| 20 | Rochdale | 46 | 6 | 12 | 5 | 24 | 24 | 5 | 6 | 12 | 25 | 33 | -8 | 51 |
| 21 | Oldham | 46 | 8 | 6 | 9 | 31 | 33 | 3 | 11 | 9 | 27 | 42 | -17 | 50 |
| 22 | Northampton | 46 | 7 | 5 | 11 | 20 | 35 | 5 | 6 | 12 | 23 | 42 | -34 | 47 |
| 23 | MK Dons | 46 | 6 | 8 | 9 | 24 | 30 | 5 | 4 | 14 | 19 | 39 | -26 | 45 |
| 24 | Bury | 46 | 7 | 4 | 12 | 20 | 30 | 1 | 8 | 14 | 21 | 41 | -30 | 36 |

*Also promoted

**Biggest win**: Oxford 0 Wigan 7
**Highest aggregate score**: MK Dons 4 Oldham 4
**Highest attendance**: 27,600 (Blackburn v Oxford)
**Lowest attendance**: 2,088 (Fleetwood v Gillingham)
**Player of Year**: Bradley Dack (Blackburn)
**Manager of Year**: Paul Hurst (Shrewsbury)
**PFA Team of Year**: Henderson (Shrewsbury), Byrne (Wigan), Mulgrew (Blackburn), Burn (Wigan), Bell (Blackburn), Dack (Blackburn), Oztumer (Walsall), Powell (Wigan), Graham (Blackburn), Marriott (Peterborough), Grigg (Wigan)
**Leading league scorers**: 27 Marriott (Peterborough); 23 Pitman (Portsmouth); 19 Grigg (Wigan); 18 Dack (Blackburn); 17 Eaves (Gillingham); 15 Oztumer (Walsall), Powell (Wigan), Wyke (Bradford); 14 Carey (Plymouth), Doyle (Oldham), Graham (Blackburn), Marquis (Doncaster), Mulgrew (Blackburn), Taylor (AFC Wimbledon); 13 Henderson (Rochdale), Moore (Rotherham); 12 Harrison (Bristol Rov), Jacobs (Wigan); 11 Davies (Oldham), Morris (Scunthorpe), Payne (Shrewsbury), Vassell (Blackpool)
Also: 12 Toney (4 Wigan, 8 Scunthorpe)

## SKY BET LEAGUE TWO

| | | | Home | | | | | Away | | | | | | |
|---|---|---|---|---|---|---|---|---|---|---|---|---|---|---|
| | | P | W | D | L | F | A | W | D | L | F | A | GD | Pts |
| 1 | Accrington | 46 | 17 | 3 | 3 | 42 | 19 | 12 | 3 | 8 | 34 | 27 | 30 | 93 |
| 2 | Luton | 46 | 17 | 2 | 4 | 62 | 24 | 8 | 11 | 4 | 32 | 22 | 48 | 88 |
| 3 | Wycombe | 46 | 12 | 5 | 6 | 43 | 35 | 12 | 7 | 4 | 36 | 25 | 19 | 84 |
| 4 | Exeter | 46 | 15 | 4 | 4 | 34 | 19 | 9 | 4 | 10 | 30 | 35 | 10 | 80 |
| 5 | Notts Co | 46 | 14 | 7 | 2 | 43 | 19 | 7 | 7 | 9 | 28 | 29 | 23 | 77 |
| 6 | Coventry* | 46 | 13 | 4 | 6 | 36 | 24 | 9 | 5 | 9 | 28 | 23 | 17 | 75 |
| 7 | Lincoln | 46 | 12 | 8 | 3 | 38 | 23 | 8 | 7 | 8 | 26 | 25 | 16 | 75 |
| 8 | Mansfield | 46 | 10 | 10 | 3 | 42 | 26 | 8 | 8 | 7 | 25 | 26 | 15 | 72 |
| 9 | Swindon | 46 | 9 | 5 | 9 | 29 | 36 | 11 | 3 | 9 | 38 | 29 | 2 | 68 |
| 10 | Carlisle | 46 | 7 | 10 | 6 | 31 | 23 | 10 | 6 | 7 | 31 | 31 | 8 | 67 |
| 11 | Newport | 46 | 9 | 10 | 4 | 32 | 24 | 7 | 6 | 10 | 24 | 34 | -2 | 64 |
| 12 | Cambridge | 46 | 13 | 5 | 5 | 38 | 23 | 4 | 8 | 11 | 18 | 37 | -4 | 64 |
| 13 | Colchester | 46 | 9 | 7 | 7 | 30 | 23 | 7 | 7 | 9 | 23 | 29 | 1 | 62 |
| 14 | Crawley | 46 | 8 | 4 | 11 | 30 | 30 | 8 | 7 | 8 | 28 | 36 | -8 | 59 |
| 15 | Crewe | 46 | 10 | 4 | 9 | 32 | 32 | 7 | 1 | 15 | 30 | 43 | -13 | 56 |
| 16 | Stevenage | 46 | 9 | 9 | 5 | 42 | 27 | 5 | 4 | 14 | 18 | 38 | -5 | 55 |
| 17 | Cheltenham | 46 | 8 | 6 | 9 | 31 | 31 | 5 | 6 | 12 | 36 | 42 | -6 | 51 |
| 18 | Grimsby | 46 | 6 | 9 | 8 | 20 | 26 | 7 | 3 | 13 | 22 | 40 | -24 | 51 |
| 19 | Yeovil | 46 | 8 | 5 | 10 | 29 | 26 | 4 | 7 | 12 | 30 | 49 | -16 | 48 |
| 20 | Port Vale | 46 | 7 | 6 | 10 | 26 | 29 | 4 | 8 | 11 | 23 | 38 | -18 | 47 |
| 21 | Forest Green | 46 | 10 | 2 | 11 | 35 | 36 | 3 | 6 | 14 | 19 | 41 | -23 | 47 |
| 22 | Morecambe | 46 | 6 | 9 | 8 | 22 | 27 | 3 | 10 | 10 | 19 | 29 | -15 | 46 |
| 23 | Barnet | 46 | 8 | 6 | 9 | 24 | 25 | 4 | 4 | 15 | 22 | 40 | -19 | 46 |
| 24 | Chesterfield | 46 | 8 | 3 | 12 | 27 | 33 | 2 | 5 | 16 | 20 | 50 | -36 | 38 |

*Also promoted

**Biggest win**: Luton 7 Cambridge 0
**Highest aggregate score**: Luton 8 Yeovil 2
**Highest attendance**: 28,343 (Coventry v Accrington)
**Lowest attendance**: 893 (Morecambe v Colchester)
**Player of Year**: Billy Kee (Accrington)
**Manager of Year**: John Coleman (Accrington)
**PFA Team of Year**: Stech (Luton), Grimmer (Coventry), Sheehan (Luton), Hughes (Accrington), Potts (Luton), Grant (Notts Co), Berry (Luton), McConville (Accrington), Akinfenwa (Wycombe), Kee (Accrington), Hylton (Luton)
**Leading league scorers**: 25 Kee (Accrington); 23 Eisa (Cheltenham), McNulty (Coventry); 21 Hylton (Luton); 20 Doidge (Forest Green); 19 Collins (Luton), Dennis (Chesterfield); 17 Akinfenwa (Wycombe), Pope (Port Vale); 16 Jackson (Accrington); 15 Grant (Notts Co), Hemmings (Mansfield); 14 Newton (Stevenage), Rose (Mansfield); 13 Amond (Newport), Green (Lincoln), Ikpeazu (Cambridge), Norris (Swindon), Zoko (Yeovil)
Also: 13 Reid (7 Exeter, 6 Forest Green)

# PREMIER LEAGUE RESULTS 2017–2018

| | Arsenal | Bournemouth | Brighton | Burnley | Chelsea | Crystal Palace | Everton | Huddersfield | Leicester | Liverpool | Man City | Man Utd | Newcastle | Southampton | Stoke | Swansea | Tottenham | Watford | WBA | West Ham |
|---|---|---|---|---|---|---|---|---|---|---|---|---|---|---|---|---|---|---|---|---|
| Arsenal | – | 3–0 | 2–0 | 5–0 | 2–2 | 4–1 | 5–1 | 5–0 | 4–3 | 3–3 | 0–3 | 1–3 | 1–0 | 3–2 | 3–0 | 2–1 | 2–0 | 3–0 | 2–0 | 4–1 |
| Bournemouth | 2–1 | – | 2–1 | 1–2 | 0–1 | 2–2 | 2–1 | 4–0 | 0–0 | 0–4 | 1–2 | 0–2 | 2–2 | 1–1 | 2–1 | 1–0 | 1–4 | 0–2 | 2–1 | 3–3 |
| Brighton | 2–1 | 2–2 | – | 0–0 | 0–4 | 0–0 | 1–1 | 1–1 | 0–2 | 1–5 | 0–2 | 1–0 | 1–0 | 1–1 | 2–2 | 4–1 | 1–1 | 1–0 | 3–1 | 3–1 |
| Burnley | 0–1 | 1–2 | 0–0 | – | 1–2 | 1–0 | 2–1 | 0–0 | 2–1 | 1–2 | 1–1 | 0–1 | 1–0 | 1–1 | 1–0 | 2–0 | 0–3 | 1–0 | 0–1 | 1–1 |
| Chelsea | 0–0 | 0–3 | 2–0 | 2–3 | – | 2–1 | 2–0 | 1–1 | 0–0 | 1–0 | 0–1 | 1–0 | 3–1 | 1–0 | 5–0 | 1–0 | 1–3 | 4–2 | 3–0 | 1–1 |
| Crystal Palace | 2–3 | 2–2 | 3–2 | 1–0 | 2–1 | – | 2–2 | 0–3 | 5–0 | 1–2 | 0–0 | 2–3 | 1–1 | 0–1 | 2–1 | 0–2 | 0–1 | 2–1 | 2–0 | 2–2 |
| Everton | 2–5 | 2–1 | 2–0 | 0–1 | 0–0 | 3–1 | – | 2–0 | 2–1 | 0–0 | 1–3 | 0–2 | 1–0 | 1–1 | 1–0 | 3–1 | 0–3 | 3–2 | 1–1 | 4–0 |
| Huddersfield | 0–1 | 4–1 | 2–0 | 0–0 | 1–3 | 0–2 | 0–2 | – | 1–1 | 0–3 | 1–2 | 2–1 | 1–0 | 0–0 | 1–1 | 0–0 | 0–4 | 1–0 | 1–0 | 1–4 |
| Leicester | 3–1 | 1–1 | 2–0 | 1–0 | 1–2 | 0–3 | 2–0 | 3–0 | – | 2–3 | 0–2 | 2–2 | 1–2 | 0–0 | 1–1 | 1–1 | 2–1 | 2–0 | 1–1 | 0–2 |
| Liverpool | 4–0 | 3–0 | 4–0 | 1–1 | 1–1 | 1–0 | 1–1 | 3–0 | 2–1 | – | 4–3 | 0–0 | 2–0 | 3–0 | 0–0 | 5–0 | 2–2 | 5–0 | 0–0 | 4–1 |
| Man City | 3–1 | 4–0 | 3–1 | 3–0 | 1–0 | 5–0 | 1–1 | 0–0 | 5–1 | 5–0 | – | 2–3 | 3–1 | 2–1 | 7–2 | 5–0 | 4–1 | 3–1 | 3–0 | 2–1 |
| Man Utd | 2–1 | 1–0 | 1–0 | 2–2 | 2–1 | 4–0 | 4–0 | 2–0 | 2–0 | 2–1 | 1–2 | – | 4–1 | 0–0 | 3–0 | 2–0 | 1–0 | 1–0 | 0–1 | 4–0 |
| Newcastle | 2–1 | 0–1 | 0–0 | 1–1 | 3–0 | 1–0 | 0–1 | 1–0 | 2–3 | 1–1 | 0–1 | 1–0 | – | 3–0 | 2–1 | 1–1 | 0–2 | 0–3 | 0–1 | 3–0 |
| Southampton | 1–1 | 2–1 | 1–1 | 0–1 | 2–3 | 1–2 | 4–1 | 1–1 | 1–4 | 0–2 | 0–1 | 0–1 | 2–2 | – | 0–0 | 0–0 | 1–1 | 0–2 | 1–0 | 3–2 |
| Stoke | 1–0 | 1–2 | 1–1 | 1–1 | 0–4 | 1–2 | 1–2 | 2–0 | 2–2 | 0–3 | 0–2 | 2–2 | 0–1 | 2–1 | – | 2–1 | 1–2 | 0–0 | 3–1 | 0–3 |
| Swansea | 3–1 | 0–0 | 0–1 | 1–0 | 0–1 | 1–1 | 1–1 | 2–0 | 1–2 | 1–0 | 0–4 | 0–4 | 0–1 | 0–1 | 1–2 | – | 0–2 | 1–2 | 1–0 | 4–1 |
| Tottenham | 1–0 | 1–0 | 2–0 | 1–1 | 1–2 | 1–0 | 4–0 | 2–0 | 5–4 | 4–1 | 1–3 | 2–0 | 1–0 | 5–2 | 5–1 | 0–0 | – | 2–0 | 1–1 | 1–1 |
| Watford | 2–1 | 2–2 | 0–0 | 1–2 | 4–1 | 0–0 | 1–0 | 1–4 | 2–1 | 3–3 | 0–6 | 2–4 | 2–1 | 2–2 | 0–1 | 1–2 | 1–1 | – | 1–0 | 2–0 |
| WBA | 1–1 | 1–0 | 2–0 | 1–2 | 0–4 | 0–0 | 0–0 | 1–2 | 1–4 | 2–2 | 2–3 | 1–2 | 2–2 | 2–3 | 1–1 | 1–1 | 1–0 | 2–2 | – | 0–0 |
| West Ham | 0–0 | 1–1 | 0–3 | 0–3 | 1–0 | 1–1 | 3–1 | 2–0 | 1–1 | 1–4 | 1–4 | 0–0 | 2–3 | 3–0 | 1–1 | 1–0 | 2–3 | 2–0 | 2–1 | – |

# SKY BET CHAMPIONSHIP RESULTS 2017–2018

| | Aston Villa | Barnsley | Birmingham | Bolton | Brentford | Bristol City | Burton | Cardiff | Derby | Fulham | Hull | Ipswich | Leeds | Middlesbrough | Millwall | Norwich | Nottm Forest | Preston | QPR | Reading | Sheffield Utd | Sheffield Wed | Sunderland | Wolves |
|---|---|---|---|---|---|---|---|---|---|---|---|---|---|---|---|---|---|---|---|---|---|---|---|---|
| Aston Villa | – | 3–1 | 2–0 | 1–0 | 0–0 | 5–0 | 3–2 | 1–0 | 1–1 | 2–1 | 1–1 | 2–0 | 1–0 | 0–0 | 0–0 | 4–2 | 2–1 | 1–1 | 1–3 | 3–0 | 2–2 | 1–2 | 2–1 | 4–1 |
| Barnsley | 0–3 | – | 2–0 | 2–2 | 2–0 | 2–2 | 1–2 | 0–1 | 0–3 | 1–3 | 0–1 | 1–2 | 0–2 | 2–2 | 0–2 | 1–1 | 2–1 | 0–0 | 1–1 | 1–1 | 3–2 | 1–1 | 3–0 | 0–0 |
| Birmingham | 0–0 | 0–2 | – | 0–0 | 0–2 | 2–1 | 1–1 | 1–0 | 0–3 | 3–1 | 3–0 | 1–0 | 1–0 | 0–1 | 0–1 | 0–2 | 1–0 | 1–3 | 1–2 | 0–2 | 2–1 | 1–0 | 3–1 | 0–1 |
| Bolton | 1–0 | 3–1 | 0–1 | – | 0–3 | 1–0 | 0–1 | 2–0 | 1–2 | 1–1 | 1–0 | 1–1 | 2–3 | 0–3 | 0–2 | 2–1 | 3–2 | 1–3 | 1–1 | 2–2 | 0–1 | 2–1 | 1–0 | 0–4 |
| Brentford | 2–1 | 0–0 | 5–0 | 2–0 | – | 2–2 | 1–1 | 1–3 | 1–1 | 3–1 | 1–1 | 1–0 | 3–1 | 1–1 | 1–0 | 0–1 | 3–4 | 1–1 | 2–1 | 1–1 | 1–1 | 2–0 | 3–3 | 0–0 |
| Bristol City | 1–1 | 3–1 | 3–1 | 2–0 | 0–1 | – | 0–0 | 2–1 | 4–1 | 1–1 | 5–5 | 1–0 | 0–3 | 2–1 | 0–0 | 0–1 | 2–1 | 1–2 | 2–0 | 2–0 | 2–3 | 4–0 | 3–3 | 1–2 |
| Burton | 0–4 | 2–4 | 2–1 | 2–0 | 0–2 | 0–0 | – | 0–1 | 3–1 | 2–1 | 0–5 | 1–2 | 1–2 | 1–1 | 0–1 | 0–0 | 0–0 | 1–2 | 1–3 | 1–3 | 1–3 | 1–1 | 0–2 | 0–4 |
| Cardiff | 3–0 | 2–1 | 3–2 | 2–0 | 2–0 | 1–0 | 3–1 | – | 0–0 | 2–4 | 1–0 | 3–1 | 3–1 | 1–0 | 0–0 | 3–1 | 2–1 | 0–1 | 2–1 | 0–0 | 2–0 | 1–1 | 4–0 | 0–1 |
| Derby | 2–0 | 4–1 | 1–1 | 3–0 | 3–0 | 0–0 | 1–0 | 3–1 | – | 1–2 | 5–0 | 0–1 | 2–2 | 1–2 | 3–0 | 1–1 | 2–0 | 1–0 | 2–0 | 2–4 | 1–1 | 2–0 | 1–4 | 0–2 |
| Fulham | 2–0 | 2–1 | 1–0 | 1–1 | 1–1 | 0–2 | 6–0 | 1–1 | 1–1 | – | 2–1 | 4–1 | 2–0 | 1–1 | 1–0 | 1–1 | 2–0 | 2–2 | 2–2 | 1–0 | 3–0 | 0–1 | 2–1 | 2–0 |
| Hull | 0–0 | 1–1 | 6–1 | 4–0 | 3–2 | 2–3 | 4–1 | 0–2 | 0–0 | 2–2 | – | 2–2 | 0–0 | 1–3 | 1–2 | 4–3 | 2–3 | 1–2 | 4–0 | 0–0 | 1–0 | 0–1 | 1–1 | 2–3 |
| Ipswich | 0–4 | 1–0 | 1–0 | 2–0 | 2–0 | 1–3 | 0–0 | 0–1 | 1–2 | 0–2 | 0–3 | – | 1–0 | 2–2 | 2–2 | 0–1 | 4–2 | 3–0 | 0–0 | 2–0 | 0–0 | 2–2 | 5–2 | 0–1 |
| Leeds | 1–1 | 2–1 | 2–0 | 2–1 | 1–0 | 2–2 | 5–0 | 1–4 | 1–2 | 0–0 | 1–0 | 3–2 | – | 2–1 | 3–4 | 1–0 | 0–0 | 0–0 | 2–0 | 0–1 | 1–2 | 1–2 | 1–1 | 0–3 |
| Middlesbrough | 0–1 | 3–1 | 2–0 | 2–0 | 2–2 | 2–1 | 2–0 | 0–1 | 0–3 | 0–1 | 3–1 | 2–0 | 3–0 | – | 2–0 | 0–1 | 2–0 | 0–0 | 3–2 | 2–1 | 1–0 | 0–0 | 1–0 | 1–2 |
| Millwall | 1–0 | 1–3 | 2–0 | 1–1 | 1–0 | 2–0 | 0–1 | 1–1 | 0–0 | 0–3 | 0–0 | 3–4 | 1–0 | 2–1 | – | 4–0 | 2–0 | 1–1 | 1–0 | 2–1 | 3–1 | 2–1 | 1–1 | 2–2 |
| Norwich | 3–1 | 1–1 | 1–0 | 0–0 | 1–2 | 0–0 | 0–0 | 0–2 | 1–2 | 0–2 | 1–1 | 1–1 | 2–1 | 1–0 | 2–1 | – | 0–0 | 1–1 | 2–0 | 3–2 | 1–2 | 3–1 | 1–3 | 0–2 |
| Nottm Forest | 0–1 | 3–0 | 2–1 | 3–2 | 0–1 | 0–0 | 2–0 | 0–2 | 0–0 | 1–3 | 0–2 | 2–1 | 0–2 | 2–1 | 1–0 | 1–0 | – | 0–3 | 4–0 | 1–1 | 2–1 | 0–3 | 0–1 | 1–2 |
| Preston | 0–2 | 1–1 | 1–1 | 0–0 | 2–3 | 2–1 | 2–1 | 3–0 | 0–1 | 1–2 | 2–1 | 0–1 | 3–1 | 2–3 | 0–0 | 0–0 | 1–1 | – | 1–0 | 1–0 | 1–0 | 1–0 | 2–2 | 1–1 |
| QPR | 1–2 | 1–0 | 3–1 | 2–0 | 2–2 | 1–1 | 0–0 | 2–1 | 1–1 | 1–2 | 2–1 | 2–1 | 1–3 | 0–3 | 2–2 | 4–1 | 2–5 | 1–2 | – | 2–0 | 1–0 | 4–2 | 1–0 | 2–1 |
| Reading | 2–1 | 3–0 | 0–2 | 1–1 | 0–1 | 0–1 | 1–2 | 2–2 | 3–3 | 1–1 | 1–1 | 0–4 | 2–2 | 0–2 | 0–2 | 1–2 | 3–1 | 1–0 | 1–0 | – | 1–3 | 0–0 | 2–2 | 0–2 |
| Sheffield Utd | 0–1 | 1–0 | 1–1 | 0–1 | 1–0 | 1–2 | 2–0 | 1–1 | 3–1 | 4–5 | 4–1 | 1–0 | 2–1 | 2–1 | 1–1 | 0–1 | 0–0 | 0–1 | 2–1 | 2–1 | – | 0–0 | 3–0 | 2–0 |
| Sheffield Wed | 2–4 | 1–1 | 1–3 | 1–1 | 2–1 | 0–0 | 0–3 | 0–0 | 2–0 | 0–1 | 2–2 | 1–2 | 3–0 | 1–2 | 2–1 | 5–1 | 3–1 | 4–1 | 1–1 | 3–0 | 2–4 | – | 1–1 | 0–1 |
| Sunderland | 0–3 | 0–1 | 1–1 | 3–3 | 0–2 | 1–2 | 1–2 | 1–2 | 1–1 | 1–0 | 1–0 | 0–2 | 0–2 | 3–3 | 2–2 | 1–1 | 0–1 | 0–2 | 1–1 | 1–3 | 1–2 | 1–3 | – | 3–0 |
| Wolves | 2–0 | 2–1 | 2–0 | 5–1 | 3–0 | 3–3 | 3–1 | 1–2 | 2–0 | 2–0 | 2–2 | 1–0 | 4–1 | 1–0 | 1–0 | 2–2 | 0–2 | 3–2 | 2–1 | 3–0 | 3–0 | 0–0 | 0–0 | — |

# SKY BET LEAGUE ONE RESULTS 2017–2018

| | AFC Wimbledon | Blackburn | Blackpool | Bradford | Bristol Rov | Bury | Charlton | Doncaster | Fleetwood | Gillingham | MKs Dons | Northampton | Oldham | Oxford | Peterborough | Plymouth | Portsmouth | Rochdale | Rotherham | Scunthorpe | Shrewsbury | Southend | Walsall | Wigan |
|---|---|---|---|---|---|---|---|---|---|---|---|---|---|---|---|---|---|---|---|---|---|---|---|---|
| AFC Wimbledon | – | 0–3 | 2–0 | 2–1 | 1–0 | 2–2 | 1–0 | 2–0 | 0–1 | 1–1 | 0–2 | 1–3 | 2–2 | 2–1 | 2–2 | 0–1 | 0–2 | 0–0 | 3–1 | 1–1 | 0–1 | 2–0 | 1–2 | 0–4 |
| Blackburn | 0–1 | – | 3–0 | 2–0 | 2–1 | 2–0 | 2–0 | 1–3 | 2–2 | 1–0 | 4–1 | 1–1 | 2–2 | 2–1 | 3–1 | 1–1 | 3–0 | 2–0 | 2–0 | 2–2 | 3–1 | 1–0 | 3–1 | 2–2 |
| Blackpool | 1–0 | 2–4 | – | 5–0 | 0–0 | 2–1 | 1–0 | 1–2 | 2–1 | 1–1 | 1–0 | 3–0 | 2–1 | 3–1 | 1–1 | 2–2 | 2–3 | 0–0 | 1–2 | 2–3 | 1–1 | 1–1 | 2–2 | 1–3 |
| Bradford | 0–4 | 0–1 | 2–1 | – | 3–1 | 2–2 | 0–1 | 2–0 | 0–3 | 1–0 | 2–0 | 1–2 | 1–1 | 3–2 | 1–3 | 0–1 | 3–1 | 4–3 | 1–0 | 1–2 | 0–0 | 0–2 | 1–1 | 0–1 |
| Bristol Rov | 1–3 | 1–1 | 3–1 | 3–1 | – | 2–1 | 1–1 | 0–1 | 3–1 | 1–1 | 2–0 | 1–1 | 2–3 | 0–1 | 1–4 | 2–1 | 2–1 | 3–2 | 2–1 | 1–1 | 1–2 | 3–0 | 2–1 | 1–1 |
| Bury | 2–1 | 0–3 | 1–1 | 3–1 | 2–3 | – | 0–1 | 0–1 | 0–2 | 2–1 | 0–2 | 2–3 | 2–2 | 3–0 | 0–1 | 0–0 | 1–0 | 0–2 | 0–3 | 0–1 | 1–0 | 0–0 | 1–0 | 0–2 |
| Charlton | 1–0 | 1–0 | 1–1 | 1–1 | 1–0 | 1–1 | – | 1–0 | 0–0 | 1–2 | 2–2 | 4–1 | 1–0 | 2–3 | 2–2 | 2–0 | 0–1 | 2–1 | 3–1 | 0–1 | 0–2 | 2–1 | 3–1 | 0–3 |
| Doncaster | 0–0 | 0–1 | 3–3 | 2–0 | 1–3 | 3–3 | 1–1 | – | 3–0 | 0–0 | 2–1 | 3–0 | 1–1 | 0–1 | 0–0 | 1–1 | 2–1 | 2–0 | 1–1 | 0–1 | 1–2 | 4–1 | 0–3 | 0–1 |
| Fleetwood | 2–0 | 1–2 | 0–0 | 1–2 | 2–0 | 3–2 | 1–3 | 0–0 | – | 0–2 | 1–1 | 2–0 | 2–2 | 2–0 | 2–3 | 1–1 | 1–2 | 2–2 | 2–0 | 2–3 | 1–2 | 2–4 | 2–0 | 0–4 |
| Gillingham | 2–2 | 0–0 | 0–3 | 0–1 | 4–1 | 1–1 | 1–0 | 0–0 | 2–1 | – | 1–2 | 1–2 | 0–0 | 1–1 | 1–1 | 5–2 | 0–1 | 2–1 | 0–1 | 0–0 | 1–2 | 3–3 | 0–0 | 1–1 |
| MK Dons | 0–0 | 1–2 | 0–0 | 1–4 | 0–1 | 2–1 | 1–2 | 1–2 | 1–0 | 1–0 | – | 0–0 | 4–4 | 1–1 | 1–0 | 0–1 | 1–2 | 3–2 | 3–2 | 0–2 | 1–1 | 1–1 | 1–1 | 0–1 |
| Northampton | 0–1 | 1–1 | 1–0 | 0–1 | 0–6 | 0–0 | 0–4 | 1–0 | 0–1 | 1–2 | 2–1 | – | 2–2 | 0–0 | 1–4 | 2–0 | 3–1 | 0–1 | 0–3 | 0–3 | 1–1 | 3–1 | 2–1 | 0–1 |
| Oldham | 0–0 | 1–0 | 2–1 | 2–1 | 1–1 | 2–1 | 3–4 | 0–0 | 1–2 | 1–1 | 1–0 | 5–1 | – | 0–2 | 3–2 | 1–2 | 0–2 | 3–1 | 1–1 | 2–3 | 1–2 | 0–3 | 1–1 | 0–2 |
| Oxford | 3–0 | 2–4 | 1–0 | 2–2 | 1–2 | 1–2 | 1–1 | 1–0 | 0–1 | 3–0 | 3–1 | 1–2 | 0–0 | – | 2–1 | 0–1 | 3–0 | 2–1 | 3–3 | 1–1 | 1–1 | 2–0 | 1–2 | 0–7 |
| Peterborough | 1–1 | 2–3 | 0–1 | 1–3 | 1–1 | 3–0 | 4–1 | 1–1 | 2–0 | 0–1 | 2–0 | 2–0 | 3–0 | 1–4 | – | 2–1 | 2–1 | 0–1 | 2–1 | 2–2 | 1–0 | 0–1 | 2–1 | 3–2 |
| Plymouth | 4–2 | 2–0 | 1–3 | 1–0 | 3–2 | 3–0 | 2–0 | 0–3 | 1–2 | 2–1 | 0–1 | 2–0 | 4–1 | 0–4 | 2–1 | – | 0–0 | 1–1 | 2–1 | 0–4 | 1–1 | 4–0 | 1–0 | 1–3 |
| Portsmouth | 2–1 | 1–2 | 0–2 | 0–1 | 3–0 | 1–0 | 0–1 | 2–2 | 4–1 | 1–3 | 2–0 | 3–1 | 1–2 | 3–0 | 2–0 | 1–0 | – | 2–0 | 0–1 | 1–1 | 0–1 | 1–0 | 1–1 | 2–1 |
| Rochdale | 1–1 | 0–3 | 1–2 | 1–1 | 1–0 | 0–0 | 1–0 | 2–1 | 0–2 | 3–0 | 0–0 | 2–2 | 0–0 | 0–0 | 2–0 | 1–1 | 3–3 | – | 0–1 | 1–1 | 3–1 | 0–0 | 1–1 | 1–4 |
| Rotherham | 2–0 | 1–1 | 1–0 | 2–0 | 2–0 | 3–2 | 0–2 | 2–1 | 3–2 | 1–3 | 2–1 | 1–0 | 5–1 | 3–1 | 1–1 | 1–1 | 1–0 | 0–1 | – | 2–0 | 1–2 | 5–0 | 5–1 | 1–3 |
| Scunthorpe | 1–1 | 0–1 | 0–0 | 1–1 | 1–0 | 1–0 | 2–0 | 1–1 | 1–1 | 1–3 | 2–2 | 2–2 | 0–2 | 1–0 | 2–1 | 2–0 | 2–0 | 1–1 | 1–2 | – | 1–2 | 3–1 | 1–0 | 1–2 |
| Shrewsbury | 1–0 | 1–1 | 1–0 | 0–1 | 4–0 | 1–1 | 0–2 | 2–2 | 1–0 | 1–1 | 0–1 | 1–0 | 1–0 | 3–2 | 3–1 | 1–2 | 2–0 | 3–2 | 0–1 | 2–0 | – | 1–0 | 2–0 | 1–0 |
| Southend | 1–0 | 2–1 | 2–1 | 1–2 | 0–0 | 1–0 | 3–1 | 0–0 | 1–2 | 4–0 | 4–0 | 2–2 | 2–0 | 1–1 | 1–1 | 1–1 | 3–1 | 0–0 | 2–0 | 3–2 | 1–2 | – | 0–3 | 3–1 |
| Walsall | 2–3 | 1–2 | 1–1 | 3–3 | 0–0 | 1–0 | 2–2 | 4–2 | 4–2 | 0–1 | 1–0 | 1–0 | 2–1 | 2–1 | 1–1 | 2–1 | 0–1 | 0–3 | 1–2 | 1–0 | 1–1 | 0–1 | – | 0–3 |
| Wigan | 1–1 | 0–0 | 0–2 | 1–2 | 3–0 | 4–1 | 0–0 | 3–0 | 2–0 | 2–0 | 5–1 | 1–0 | 3–0 | 1–0 | 0–0 | 1–0 | 1–1 | 1–0 | 0–0 | 3–3 | 0–0 | 3–0 | 2–0 | – |

# SKY BET LEAGUE TWO RESULTS 2017–2018

| | Accrington | Barnet | Cambridge | Carlisle | Cheltenham | Chesterfield | Colchester | Coventry | Crawley | Crewe | Exeter | Forest Green | Grimsby | Lincoln | Luton | Mansfield | Morecambe | Newport | Notts Co | Port Vale | Stevenage | Swindon | Wycombe | Yeovil |
|---|---|---|---|---|---|---|---|---|---|---|---|---|---|---|---|---|---|---|---|---|---|---|---|---|
| Accrington | – | 4–1 | 1–0 | 3–0 | 1–1 | 4–0 | 3–1 | 1–0 | 2–3 | 1–0 | 1–1 | 3–1 | 1–2 | 1–0 | 0–2 | 2–1 | 1–0 | 1–1 | 1–0 | 3–2 | 3–2 | 2–1 | 1–0 | 2–0 |
| Barnet | 1–1 | – | 3–1 | 1–3 | 0–2 | 3–0 | 0–1 | 0–0 | 1–2 | 2–1 | 1–2 | 1–0 | 0–2 | 1–1 | 1–0 | 1–1 | 2–1 | 2–0 | 1–0 | 1–1 | 0–1 | 1–2 | 0–2 | 1–1 |
| Cambridge | 0–0 | 1–0 | – | 1–2 | 4–3 | 2–1 | 1–0 | 2–1 | 3–1 | 3–1 | 2–3 | 3–0 | 3–1 | 0–0 | 1–1 | 0–0 | 0–0 | 1–2 | 1–0 | 5–0 | 1–0 | 1–3 | 1–3 | 2–1 |
| Carlisle | 3–1 | 1–1 | 1–1 | – | 3–0 | 2–0 | 1–1 | 0–1 | 2–2 | 1–0 | 0–1 | 1–0 | 2–0 | 0–1 | 1–1 | 1–1 | 1–1 | 1–1 | 1–1 | 1–2 | 0–2 | 1–2 | 3–3 | 4–0 |
| Cheltenham | 0–2 | 1–1 | 0–0 | 0–1 | – | 1–1 | 3–1 | 1–6 | 1–0 | 1–0 | 3–4 | 0–1 | 2–3 | 1–0 | 2–2 | 3–0 | 3–0 | 1–1 | 1–1 | 5–1 | 0–1 | 2–1 | 0–2 | 0–2 |
| Chesterfield | 1–2 | 2–1 | 2–3 | 2–2 | 0–2 | – | 0–0 | 0–0 | 1–2 | 0–2 | 1–0 | 3–2 | 1–3 | 1–3 | 2–0 | 0–1 | 0–2 | 1–0 | 3–1 | 2–0 | 0–1 | 2–1 | 1–2 | 2–3 |
| Colchester | 0–1 | 0–1 | 0–0 | 0–1 | 1–4 | 1–1 | – | 2–1 | 3–1 | 3–1 | 3–1 | 5–1 | 1–1 | 1–0 | 2–1 | 2–0 | 0–0 | 2–0 | 1–3 | 1–1 | 1–1 | 0–0 | 1–2 | 0–1 |
| Coventry | 0–2 | 1–0 | 3–1 | 2–0 | 2–1 | 1–0 | 0–0 | – | 1–1 | 1–0 | 2–0 | 0–1 | 4–0 | 2–4 | 2–2 | 0–1 | 0–0 | 0–1 | 3–0 | 1–0 | 3–1 | 3–1 | 3–2 | 2–6 |
| Crawley | 2–1 | 2–0 | 0–1 | 0–1 | 3–5 | 0–2 | 0–2 | 1–2 | – | 1–2 | 3–1 | 1–1 | 3–0 | 3–1 | 0–0 | 2–0 | 1–1 | 1–2 | 0–1 | 1–3 | 1–0 | 1–1 | 2–3 | 2–0 |
| Crewe | 0–2 | 1–0 | 0–1 | 0–5 | 2–1 | 5–1 | 1–0 | 1–2 | 3–0 | – | 1–2 | 3–1 | 2–0 | 1–4 | 1–2 | 2–2 | 1–0 | 1–1 | 2–0 | 2–2 | 1–0 | 0–3 | 2–3 | 0–0 |
| Exeter | 2–0 | 2–1 | 1–0 | 1–1 | 2–1 | 2–1 | 1–0 | 1–0 | 2–2 | 3–0 | – | 2–0 | 2–0 | 1–0 | 1–4 | 0–1 | 4–1 | 1–0 | 0–3 | 0–1 | 2–1 | 3–1 | 1–1 | 0–0 |
| Forest Green | 0–1 | 2–2 | 5–2 | 0–1 | 1–1 | 4–1 | 1–2 | 2–1 | 2–0 | 3–2 | 1–3 | – | 0–3 | 0–1 | 0–2 | 2–0 | 2–0 | 0–4 | 1–2 | 1–0 | 3–1 | 0–2 | 1–2 | 4–3 |
| Grimsby | 0–3 | 2–2 | 0–0 | 0–1 | 1–1 | 1–0 | 2–2 | 0–2 | 0–0 | 1–0 | 0–1 | 1–0 | – | 0–0 | 0–1 | 1–1 | 0–2 | 1–2 | 2–1 | 1–1 | 0–0 | 3–2 | 2–3 | 2–1 |
| Lincoln | 2–0 | 2–1 | 0–0 | 4–1 | 1–0 | 2–1 | 2–1 | 1–2 | 0–0 | 1–4 | 3–2 | 2–1 | 3–1 | – | 0–0 | 0–1 | 1–1 | 3–1 | 2–2 | 3–1 | 3–0 | 2–2 | 0–0 | 1–1 |
| Luton | 1–2 | 2–0 | 7–0 | 3–0 | 2–2 | 1–0 | 3–0 | 0–3 | 4–1 | 3–1 | 1–0 | 3–1 | 2–0 | 4–2 | – | 2–1 | 1–0 | 3–1 | 1–1 | 2–0 | 7–1 | 0–3 | 2–3 | 8–2 |
| Mansfield | 0–1 | 3–1 | 2–1 | 3–1 | 3–2 | 2–2 | 1–1 | 1–1 | 1–1 | 3–4 | 1–1 | 2–0 | 4–1 | 1–1 | 2–2 | – | 2–1 | 5–0 | 3–1 | 1–1 | 1–0 | 1–3 | 0–0 | 0–0 |
| Morecambe | 1–2 | 0–1 | 0–0 | 1–1 | 2–1 | 2–2 | 0–0 | 2–0 | 0–1 | 0–1 | 2–1 | 1–1 | 0–0 | 0–0 | 0–0 | 1–2 | – | 2–1 | 1–4 | 0–3 | 1–1 | 0–1 | 2–1 | 4–3 |
| Newport | 2–1 | 1–2 | 2–1 | 3–3 | 1–0 | 4–1 | 1–2 | 1–1 | 2–1 | 1–2 | 2–1 | 3–3 | 1–0 | 0–0 | 1–1 | 1–1 | 1–1 | – | 0–0 | 1–1 | 0–1 | 2–1 | 0–0 | 2–0 |
| Notts Co | 2–2 | 2–1 | 3–3 | 2–1 | 3–1 | 2–0 | 2–1 | 2–1 | 1–2 | 4–1 | 1–2 | 1–1 | 0–0 | 4–1 | 0–0 | 1–1 | 2–0 | 3–0 | – | 1–0 | 2–0 | 1–0 | 0–0 | 4–1 |
| Port Vale | 1–2 | 1–0 | 2–0 | 1–2 | 3–1 | 2–1 | 2–2 | 1–0 | 1–2 | 0–1 | 0–1 | 1–1 | 1–2 | 1–0 | 4–0 | 0–4 | 0–0 | 0–0 | 0–1 | – | 2–2 | 0–3 | 2–3 | 1–1 |
| Stevenage | 3–2 | 4–1 | 0–2 | 0–0 | 4–1 | 5–1 | 0–1 | 1–1 | 1–1 | 2–2 | 3–1 | 1–2 | 3–1 | 1–2 | 1–1 | 1–1 | 2–1 | 3–3 | 1–1 | 2–0 | – | 0–1 | 0–0 | 4–1 |
| Swindon | 3–0 | 1–4 | 2–0 | 0–0 | 0–3 | 2–2 | 2–3 | 1–2 | 0–3 | 4–3 | 1–1 | 1–0 | 0–1 | 0–1 | 0–5 | 1–0 | 1–1 | 0–1 | 1–0 | 3–2 | 3–2 | – | 1–0 | 2–2 |
| Wycombe | 0–4 | 3–1 | 1–1 | 4–3 | 3–3 | 1–0 | 3–1 | 0–1 | 4–0 | 3–2 | 0–0 | 3–1 | 2–1 | 2–2 | 1–2 | 1–2 | 2–4 | 2–0 | 2–4 | 0–0 | 1–0 | 3–2 | – | 2–1 |
| Yeovil | 3–2 | 2–0 | 2–0 | 0–1 | 0–0 | 1–2 | 0–1 | 2–0 | 1–2 | 2–0 | 3–1 | 0–0 | 3–0 | 0–2 | 0–3 | 2–3 | 2–2 | 0–2 | 1–1 | 1–1 | 3–0 | 1–2 | 0–1 | – |

# HIGHLIGHTS OF THE PREMIER LEAGUE SEASON 2017–18

## AUGUST 2017

**11** The season gets off to a rousing start. Alexandre Lacazette, Arsenal's record-signing, scores the fastest-ever Premier League opening goal after 94 seconds, Jamie Vardy nets twice for Leicester, then substitute Olivier Giroud gives the home side a 4-3 win with an 85th minute header.

**14** Champions Chelsea, without the injured Eden Hazard, Pedro and Tiemoue Bakayoko, the suspended Victor Moses and the exiled Diego Costa, have a nightmare start. New captain Gary Cahill receives a straight red for a lunging tackle on Steven Defour and Cesc Fabregas is sent off for a second yellow card. Record-signing Alvaro Morata opens his account, but they lose 3-2 to Burnley, for whom Sam Vokes scores twice. Two more record buys are on the mark. A brace by Steve Mounie points Huddersfield to a 3-0 success at Crystal Palace on the club's return to the top division after a 45-year absence. Mohamed Salah puts Liverpool 3-2 ahead at Watford, a lead they maintain until stoppage-time when Miguel Britos equalises. Wayne Rooney marks his return to Everton by heading the only goal against Stoke, while 6ft 5in central defender Ahmed Hegazi marks his West Bromwich Albion debut with a header for a 1-0 victory over Bournemouth. A record crowd of 30,415 at the Amex Stadium for Brighton's return to the big time see the promoted side hold out for 70 minutes before Sergio Aguero puts Manchester City on the way to a 2-0 win.

**15** New-signing Romelu Lukaku scores twice as Manchester United make an impressive start, beating West Ham 4-0. Newcastle captain Jonjo Shelvey is shown a straight red card for treading on Dele Alli in the 2-0 home defeat by Tottenham.

**19** Eric Bailly puts Manchester United ahead at Swansea with his first goal for the club and they score three more in the space of three minutes 41 seconds for a 4-0 success. Former United striker Javier Hernandez is off the mark for West Ham with a brace as his new side overcome the dismissal of Marko Arnautovic for elbowing Jack Stephens by retrieving a 2-0 deficit. But they go down 3-2 to substitute Charlie Austin's 91st minute penalty for Southampton. On-loan Jese Rodriguez marks his debut for Stoke with the only goal of the game against Arsenal, while two more players score for the first time for new clubs. The Brazilian Richarlison puts Watford on the way to a 2-0 win at Bournemouth; Harry Maguire heads the second for Leicester, who beat Brighton by the same scoreline. Delight turns to despair for West Bromwich Albion substitute Hal Robson-Kanu, whose match-winner at Burnley is followed by a straight red card for catching Matthew Lowton with an outstretched arm.

**20** Chelsea are up and running with two goals by Marcos Alonso for a 2-1 victory at Wembley to spoil Tottenham's Premier League debut at the national stadium. Huddersfield win again, 1-0, with Aaron Mooy's strike sending Newcastle away empty-handed.

**21** Wayne Rooney scores his 200th Premier League goal in Everton's 1-1 draw with Manchester City. Two players are sent off for second yellow cards – Everton's Morgan Schneiderlin and the home side's Kyle Walker.

**26** Raheem Sterling scores in the 97th minute to give Manchester City a 2-1 victory at Bournemouth and is then shown a second yellow card for celebrating with City fans. Kasper Schmeichel saves a penalty from Romelu Lukaku, but is beaten by goals from substitutes Marcus Rashford and Marouane Fellaini which deliver a 2-0 success for Manchester United against Leicester. Joselu puts Newcastle on the way to a 3-0 win over West Ham with his first goal for the club, while on-loan Tammy Abraham nets his first in the league for Swansea, who overcome Crystal Palace 2-0 at Selhurst Park. Watford's Miguel Britos is sent off for the third time in 20 matches – a straight red for a studs-up lunge on Anthony Knockaert – in the goalless draw with Brighton.

**27** Liverpool outclass Arsenal 4-0 with dazzling attacking play and would have been even more convincing winners but for Petr Cech's work in goal. At Wembley, Chris Wood comes off the bench for his Burnley debut and fires a stoppage-time equaliser to frustrate Tottenham. Manchester United, with maximum points from three games, are the early leaders.

## SEPTEMBER 2017

**9** Gabriel Jesus and Leroy Sane both score twice as Manchester City crush ten-man Liverpool 5-0 after Sadio Mane is shown a straight red card for a boot in the face of goalkeeper Ederson at 1-0. Four other players are on the mark twice. Harry Kane, goalless in August, opens his account for the season as Tottenham win 3-0 away to Everton, taking his tally for the club to 101. Pascal Gross nets his first two for Brighton, who chalk up their first victory, 3-1 against West Bromwich Albion. So does Maxim Choupo-Moting for Stoke in a 2-2 draw with Manchester United, while Danny Welbeck's brace for Arsenal helps see off Bournemouth 3-0.

**10** Four defeats without a goal in his four Premier League matches in charge – the latest a 1-0 reversal at Burnley – cost Crystal Palace manager Frank de Boer his job. Newcastle's Matt Ritchie directs a high boot at Alfie Mawson in their 1-0 victory at Swansea, but unlike Sadio Mane the previous day he escapes with a yellow card.

**15** Jermain Defoe's first goal for Bournemouth delivers a 2-1 win over Brighton.

**16** Manchester City overwhelm Watford 6-0 at Vicarage Road – Sergio Aguero netting a hat-trick – to make it 15 goals in three Premier League and Champions League games in eight days. Crystal Palace, under new manager Roy Hodgson, lose 1-0 at home to Southampton and become the first top-flight team in English football to lose their first five matches without scoring. Laurent Depoitre scores his first Huddersfield goal in a 1-1 draw with Leicester. Captain Jamaal Lascelles is again Newcastle's match-winner, following up his goal against Swansea with the decisive strike for a 2-1 result against Stoke.

**17** Wayne Rooney's return to Old Trafford is an unhappy one as Antonio Valencia puts Manchester United ahead with a spectacular 30-yard volley and his team score three more goals in the final ten minutes for a 4-0 success against Everton. Chelsea's David Luiz receives a straight red card for an over-the-top challenge on Sead Kolasinac in the goalless draw with Arsenal.

**23** On the day Chelsea outcast Diego Costa prepares to rejoin Atletico Madrid, record-signing Alvaro Morata scores a hat-trick in the 4-0 win at Stoke. Manchester City become the first Premier League team to record five or more goals in three successive matches, defeating Crystal Palace 5-0 with Raheem Sterling on the mark twice. Substitute Oumar Niasse, back in favour at Everton after a loan spell with Hull, scores two for a 2-1 victory over Bournemouth. Harry Kane's brace looks to have put Tottenham out of sight at West Ham, but Serge Aurier receives two yellow cards on his first league start and his new side are hanging on for 3-2 at the end. Watford win a record third successive away game 2-1 at Swansea, helped by a first goal from their record-signing Andre Gray. Liverpool, knocked out of the League Cup by Leicester in midweek, return to the King Power Stadium for a 3-2 success, courtesy of Simon Mignolet's penalty save from Jamie Vardy. Manchester United register the day's fifth away win, 1-0 against Southampton, with Jose Mourinho watching the final moments from the stand after being sent off for leaving his technical area and stepping over the touchline.

**25** Gareth Barry surpasses Ryan Giggs's record of 632 Premier League appearances in West Bromwich Albion's 2-0 defeat by Arsenal. Alexandre Lacazette scores both goals, one a penalty.

**30** In the biggest match of the season so far, a goal by Kevin De Bruyne at Stamford Bridge gives Manchester City a 1-0 win over Chelsea. Romelu Lukaku equals Andy Cole's Manchester United record of seven goals in his first seven league games. His side defeat Crystal Palace 4-0, with Marouane Fellaini netting twice. City head United on goal difference at the end of the month, five points ahead of Tottenham and six clear of Chelsea. A brace for Harry Kane brings his September tally for Tottenham and England to 13, while Moussa Sissoko scores his first for the club in a 4-0 success at Huddersfield. The pressure on West Ham manager Slaven Bilic eases with a 90th minute goal by Diafra Sakho, the only one of the game against Swansea. Another substitute, Peter Crouch, delivers in the 85th minute to give Stoke a 2-1 victory over Southampton which looks to have eluded them following Fraser Forster's penalty save from Saido Berahino. Another late goal, from Richarlison in stoppage-time, completes Watford's comeback from 2-0 down for a 2-2 draw away to West Bromwich Albion.

## OCTOBER 2017

**1** The pressure builds on Everton's Ronald Koeman following a 1-0 home defeat by Burnley, inflicted by Jeff Hendrick's goal at the end of a move involving 24 passes.

**14** Manchester City, at the top, and Crystal Palace, at the bottom, share pride of place. City hammer Stoke 7-2 to become the first side to score 29 goals in their first eight league games since Everton in the 1894-95 season. Kevin De Bruyne, on his 100th appearance, has a hand in four goals, while Bernardo Silva scores his first for the club. After seven successive goalless defeats, Palace are lifted by the return of Wilfried Zaha, who marks his first appearance since a knee injury sustained on the opening day of the season with a goal in their 2-1 victory over Chelsea. Antonio Conte's side look to be out of the title reckoning after just eight games, along with Arsenal and Liverpool, who are also left nine points behind City. Arsenal lose 2-1 at Watford to Tom Cleverley's stoppage-time goal. Liverpool share a forgettable goalless draw with Manchester United, predictably relegated to a footnote appearance on BBC's *Match of the Day*. Tammy Abraham scores both goals as Swansea see off Huddersfield 2-0, but it's a bad day for another striker, West Ham's Andy Carroll, who is sent off for two elbowing offences in the space of two first-half minutes during the 1-1 draw at Burnley.

**15** Southampton twice come from behind with goals by Manolo Gabbiadini, his second a penalty, to draw 2-2 with Newcastle.

**16** A 1-1 draw against West Bromwich Albion leaves Leicester without a win in six league games and manager Craig Shakespeare is sacked the following day.

**20** Two goals by Glenn Murray, one a penalty, and a first for the club from record-signing Jose Izquierdo deliver Brighton's 3-0 victory at West Ham.

**21** Manager David Wagner hails Huddersfield's 2-1 success against Manchester United as 'a special moment for the town.' Aaron Mooy and Laurent Depoitre score first-half goals in front of a record crowd for the John Smith's Stadium of 24,426. The result leaves previously unbeaten United five points adrift of Manchester City, 3-0 winners over Burnley. Southampton's Sofiane Boufal comes off the bench to deliver the day's individual highlight, evading five players in a 70-yard run to score the only goal of the game with West Bromwich Albion. Two more substitutes make their mark. Newcastle's Mikel Merino opens his account for the club with the only goal against Crystal Palace, while two by Michy Batshuayi help Chelsea turn a 2-1 deficit into a 4-2 victory over Watford.

**22** Wayne Rooney puts Everton ahead from 20 yards against Arsenal, evoking memories of his spectacular winner against them as a 16-year-old in 2002. This time it's not enough as Idrissa Gueye is sent off midway through the second-half for a second yellow card and Arsene Wenger's side take advantage with a 5-2 victory. The result brings to an end Ronald Koeman's time as manager at Goodison Park. Two more goals from Harry Kane fire Tottenham to a 4-1 success win over Liverpool in front of a record Premier League crowd of 80,827 at Wembley.

**28** Lifted by a midweek League Cup win over Tottenham, West Ham look like delivering another much-needed victory for Slaven Bilic. Instead, the manager is left fuming as Michail Antonio elects to cross instead of keeping the ball in the corner and Crystal Palace break for Wilfried Zaha to make it 2-2 in the seventh minute of stoppage-time. Darren Fletcher scores his first goal for the club to give Stoke a 1-0 success at Watford, while substitute Anthony Martial gives Manchester United victory by the same scoreline against a Tottenham side missing Harry Kane with a tight hamstring. Manchester City's 3-2 win away to West Bromwich Albion, keeps them five points ahead of United and eight clear of Tottenham. Arsenal's Arsene Wenger marks his 800th league game in charge with a 2-1 win over Swansea. Huddersfield's Jonas Lossl saves a penalty from Mohamed Salah before Daniel Sturridge nets his 100th goal in club football to put Liverpool on the way to a 3-0 win.

**29** Claude Puel, Leicester's new manager, starts with a 2-0 win over Everton.

**30** Sean Dyche marks five years as Burnley manager with a 1-0 victory over Newcastle.

## NOVEMBER 2017

**4** West Ham's 4-1 home defeat by Liverpool, for whom Mohamed Salah scores twice, proves to be the last match for manager Slaven Bilic, who is sacked two days later and replaced by David Moyes. Steve Cook's 92nd minute header gives Bournemouth the points at Newcastle, substitute Sam Vokes heads Burnley to victory at Southampton, while Brighton are also 1-0 away winners, over Swansea, courtesy of Glenn Murray's fourth goal in three games. Huddersfield, at home to West Bromwich Albion, have Christopher Schindler sent off for a second yellow card, but hold on for the final half-hour to Rajiv van La Parra's winning goal. Vicente Iborra's strike for Leicester in a 2-2 draw at Stoke is his first for the club.

**5** Manchester City stretch their lead at the top by beating Arsenal 3-1, Gabriel Jesus scoring the decisive third goal after provider David Silva is shown, by replays, to be offside. Arsenal face a £25,000 fine for six bookings. City lead by eight points from Manchester United, who lose 1-0 at Chelsea to a header from Alvaro Morata. A dramatic 12 minutes of stoppage-time bring to an end Everton's eight-match run in all competitions without a win. After retrieving a two-goal deficit against Watford, they go 3-2 ahead with a record 24th successful penalty for the club by Leighton Baines – and stay ahead when Tom Cleverley puts his spot-kick at the other end wide. Injury-hit Tottenham give third-choice goalkeeper Paulo Gazzaniga his debut against Crystal Palace – and the Argentine goalkeeper makes vital saves in 1-0 victory.

**18** A 2-0 defeat by arch-rivals Arsenal at the Emirates effectively kills off Tottenham's title chances. It leaves them 11 points behind Manchester City, 2-0 victors at Leicester and showing no sign of losing their momentum. Manchester United now seem the only side capable of challenging following the 4-1 defeat of Newcastle in which Paul Pogba scores on his return from two months out with a hamstring injury and Zlatan Ibrahimovic is back after a knee injury threatened to end his career. Callum Wilson, sidelined by two separate knee injuries and without a Premier League goal for nearly a year, delivers a hat-trick for Bournemouth, who make light of the dismissal of Simon Francis for a second yellow card in first-half stoppage-time to double their lead after the interval for a 4-0 success against Huddersfield. Eden Hazard is on the mark twice as Chelsea match that scoreline away to West Bromwich Albion, whose manager Tony Pulis is sacked two days later. Mohamed Salah makes it eight goals in six Premier League and Champions League games with two in Liverpool's 3-0 win over Southampton.

**19** David Moyes has nothing to celebrate in his 500th game as a top-flight manager – and his first in charge of West Ham. They lose 2-0 at Watford, for whom Will Hughes records his first goal for the club.

**20** On-loan Kurt Zouma scores his first goal for Stoke in a 2-2 draw at Brighton.

**25** Two players score for the first time for Crystal Palace – on-loan Ruben Loftus-Cheek, then Mamadou Sakho in stoppage-time for a 2-1 victory over Stoke. Manchester United need a Lewis Dunk own goal to overcome Brighton 1-0, while West Bromwich Albion, under interim manager Gary Megson, hold Tottenham to 1-1 at Wembley. Pick of the day is Watford's 3-0 success away to Newcastle.

**26** Raheem Sterling, enjoying the most productive season of his career, scores for the 12th time in all competitions for Manchester City. An 84th goal delivers a 2-1 away victory over Huddersfield, who have Rajiv van La Parra shown a straight red card at full-time for raising his hands to Leroy Sane. Everton, beaten 5-1 at home by Atalanta in the Europa League, complete a wretched week by going down 4-1 at Southampton, for whom Charlie Austin is on the mark with two identical near-post headers. For the third successive match between the teams, Arsenal defeat Burnley with a controversial stoppage-time goal, this time a penalty from Alexis Sanchez for a 1-0 scoreline.

**28** Two goals by Ashley Young, his first since May 2016 and both from outside the penalty box, pave the way for Manchester United's 4-2 win at Watford. Nineteen-year-old Sam Field, with his first goal for the club, puts West Bromwich Albion 2-0 ahead against Newcastle, who hit back to draw 2-2.

**29** Wayne Rooney's spectacular hat-trick arrests Everton's slide in David Unsworth's final match as caretaker. With new manager Sam Allardyce watching from the directors' box, Rooney heads in the rebound after his penalty is saved by West Ham's Joe Hart, converts a cross from Tom Davies, then returns Hart's clearance back over the goalkeeper and into the net from 60 yards in a 4-0 victory. Manchester City re-establish an eight-point lead at the top by beating Southampton 2-1, courtesy of Raheem Sterling's strike in the sixth minute of stoppage-time. At the end of the month, City have 40 points, ahead of Manchester United, with Chelsea third on 29 followed by Arsenal on 28. Chelsea manager Antonio Conte is sent to the stands for berating fourth official Lee Mason during a 1-0 win over Swansea. Arsenal score three times in four second-half minutes to beat Huddersfield 5-0, substitute Olivier Giroud netting twice. The prolific Mohamed Salah also gets two off the bench as Liverpool win 3-0 at Stoke after goalkeeper Simon Mignolet escapes with a yellow card when taking out Mame Biram Diouf with the score 1-0.

## DECEMBER 2017

**2** Two goals from Jesse Lingard and a Premier League record 14 saves by David de Gea deliver Manchester United's 3-1 success against Arsenal at the Emirates. For United, the result is clouded by a straight red card for Paul Pogba for stamping on Hector Bellerin. For Arsenal, it brings to an end a run of 12 successive Premier League home wins. Two other players score twice – Roberto Firmino, as Liverpool sweep aside Brighton 5-1 away from home, and Eden Hazard, as Chelsea come from behind to defeat Newcastle 3-1. Hazard's second is a penalty. Everton see off Huddersfield 2-0 in Sam Allardyce's first game in charge, while Alan Pardew's first as West Bromwich Albion manager is a goalless draw with his former club Crystal Palace. Tottenham's Davinson Sanchez receives a straight red for an arm across the face of Richarlison in a 1-1 draw at Watford.

**3** For the third successive match, Manchester City win 2-1 with a late goal, this time from David Silva in the 83rd minute against West Ham.

**9** Christian Benteke comes under fire from manager Roy Hodgson and Crystal Palace fans after selfishly demanding the ball for a stoppage-time penalty and having it saved by Asmir Begovic, denying his side the chance of a 3-2 win over Bournemouth. Hodgson is angry that Luka Milivojevic should have taken it, having scored from the spot earlier in the game. Jermain Defoe's brace for Bournemouth moves him to 200 career league goals and two other players are on the mark twice. Harry Kane takes his tally to 50 in 2017 for club and country as Tottenham beat Stoke 5-1 to become the first team in top-flight football to score four or more against the same opponents in four successive games. Steve Mounie, without a goal since the opening day of the season, sets up a 2-0 victory for Huddersfield against Brighton. Marko Arnautovic's winner against Chelsea, his first goal for the club, delivers West Ham's first three points under David Moyes. But they have six players booked and face a £25,000 FA fine. Watford lose by the same 1-0 scoreline at Burnley after Marvin Zeegelaar receives a straight red card for lunging at Steven Defour.

**10** Manchester City move 11 points clear by beating Manchester United 2-1 with goals from David Silva and Nicolas Otamendi, ending United's 40-match unbeaten run at Old Trafford. Liverpool manager Jurgen Klopp rests Philippe Coutinho and Roberto Firmino from his starting line-up against Everton, who draw 1-1 at Anfield with Wayne Rooney's penalty.

**12** Burnley climb to fourth in the table – albeit briefly – with an 89th minute goal from substitute Ashley Barnes, the only one of the game against Stoke. Late drama, too, at Selhurst Park, where Watford have Tom Cleverley sent off for a second yellow card in the 87th minute, Crystal Palace equalise through Bakary Sako two minutes later, then James

McArthur scores a stoppage-time winner for Roy Hodgson's side.

**13** David Silva scores twice as Manchester City set an all-time record for English top-flight football with a 15th successive victory – 4-0 at Swansea. There is also a brace for Shinji Okazaki in Leicester's 4-1 success at Southampton – a hugely satisfying result for manager Claude Puel against the club who sacked him six months previously. Serge Aurier's first goal for Tottenham comes in a 2-0 win over Brighton, while Wayne Rooney makes it five in four matches as Everton win 1-0 at Newcastle, who have Jonjo Shelvey sent off for a second yellow card.

**16** Crystal Palace and West Ham move out of the relegation zone with emphatic performances. A week after defying orders and taking a stoppage-time penalty, Christian Benteke scores Palace's first away goal of the season to launch a 3-0 win over in-form Leicester, who have Wilfred Ndidi sent off for two yellow cards. At Stoke, where kick-off is delayed for an hour because of a power cut, Mark Noble's penalty puts West Ham on the way to a 3-0 success, piling further pressure on Mark Hughes in the process. Despite losing Jonathan Hogg to a second yellow, Huddersfield prosper on their travels for the first time since the opening day. Aaron Mooy scores two goals, one a penalty, in a 4-1 victory over Watford, who have Troy Deeney shown a straight red for lunging at Collin Quaner. At the top, Manchester City make light of a penalty miss by Gabriel Jesus to sweep aside Tottenham 4-1, Raheem Sterling netting twice. Manchester United are 2-1 winners over West Bromwich Albion, who have Gareth Barry on the scoresheet for the first time.

**17** Liverpool overwhelm Bournemouth 4-0 to become the first Premier League side to win four successive away games by at least three goals. Mohamed Salah takes his tally to 20 in all competitions, the first Anfield player to do so before Christmas since Ian Rush in 1986.

**18** Two Wayne Rooney penalties point Everton to a 3-1 win over Swansea. The first, kept out by Lukasz Fabianski and a post, is knocked in on the rebound by Dominic Calvert-Lewin. The second is converted cleanly. Swansea manager Paul Clement is sacked two days later.

**22** The holiday programme gets off to a cracking start, with Arsenal scoring three times in five minutes in the second-half to lead Liverpool, who then equalise for a 3-3 scoreline.

**23** Sergio Aguero is on the mark with two headers and Danilo registers his first goal for the club as Manchester City continue to set new standards in this one-sided title race. City's 13-point lead after a 4-0 win over Bournemouth at the top is the biggest in English top-flight history at Christmas. They also become the first in the Premier League to score more than 100 goals in a calendar year. Manchester United fall further behind when Harry Maguire's stoppage-time strike gives ten-man Leicester a 2-2 draw after they lose substitute Daniel Amartey to a second yellow card and concede twice to Juan Mata. Tottenham's ambitions may be limited to a top-four place, but there is no stopping Harry Kane, who puts them ahead with a penalty at Burnley and goes on to complete a hat-trick in a 3-0 success to equal Alan Shearer's record of 36 Premier League goals in a calendar year. Henri Saivet scores his first for Newcastle and Rob Elliot saves a penalty from Andre Ayew as Newcastle end a run of one point from nine games by winning 3-2 away to West Ham.

**26** Harry Kane claims the record outright with his eighth hat-trick of 2017 in all competitions. It comes in a 5-2 win over Southampton and takes his tally for club and country to 56 goals, establishing him as the leading marksman in Europe's top leagues for the year, ahead of Lionel Messi, Robert Lewandowski and Cristiano Ronaldo. Manchester United drop more points and need a stoppage-time goal from substitute Jesse Lingard, his second of the game, for a 2-2 draw with Burnley, who incur a £25,000 fine for six bookings. Callum Wilson's equaliser in added time for Bournemouth against West Ham (3-3) is clouded in controversy, with assistant Simon Long's flag for offside overruled by referee Bobby Madley. Marko Arnautovic nets twice for West Ham and there is a brace for Roberto Firmino as Liverpool overwhelm Swansea 5-0. On-loan Molla Wague scores on his first start for Watford, who defeat Leicester 2-1. Tom Ince's first for Huddersfield comes in a 1-1 draw with Stoke.

**27** Manchester City equal the top-flight record of 11 successive away wins by beating Newcastle 1-0.

**28** Amid speculation about his future, Alexis Sanchez scores twice in Arsenal's 3-2 away win over Crystal Palace.

**30** Carlos Carvalhal makes a successful start as Swansea new manager at Vicarage Road. On-loan Andre Carrillo's scores his first goal for Watford, but Jordan Ayew equalises after 86 minutes and substitute Luciano Narsingh opens his account for the club in stoppage-time. Danny Drinkwater nets his first for Chelsea in a 5-0 victory over Stoke, whose manager Mark Hughes leaves out key players ahead of the home match with fellow-strugglers Newcastle. Liverpool come from behind to defeat Leicester 2-1 with two from Mohamed Salah, who takes his tally to 23 in all competitions for the season, becoming the club's first player to reach that tally before the New Year since Roger Hunt in 1961. Bournemouth gain three points for the first time in nine matches, thanks to an 88th minute goal by Ryan Fraser, his second of the afternoon, for a 2-1 scoreline against Everton.

**31** Manchester City's record run comes to an end after 18 successive wins. They are held to a goalless draw by Crystal Palace and need Ederson's stoppage-time penalty save from Luka Milivojevic to preserve an unbeaten record. City lose Gabriel Jesus and Kevin De Bruyne to injuries, but are still 14 points clear of Chelsea, with Manchester United dropping more points after a third successive draw, against Southampton.

## JANUARY 2018

**1** Ayoze Perez scores the only goal of the game to give Newcastle some breathing space and leave Stoke in trouble. Their manager Mark Hughes is sacked five days later. Ragnar Klavan heads his first Premier League goal in stoppage-time to give Liverpool a 2-1 victory at Burnley. In-form Jesse Lingard scores his seventh in nine matches as Manchester United return to winning ways – 2-0 at Everton.

**2** Raheem Sterling strikes after 38 seconds to put Manchester City on the way to a 3-1 success against Watford. West Ham's Andy Carroll, without a goal all season, gets two for a 2-1 win over West Bromwich Albion, his second coming in stoppage-time. Shane Long ends his drought, stretching back the best part of a year, but it's not enough to prevent sinking Southampton's ninth winless game as Crystal Palace prevail 2-1 at St Mary's. With Harry Kane nursing a cold, Fernando Llorente marks his first league start for Tottenham with a goal against former club Swansea, who are beaten 2-0.

**3** Full-back Hector Bellerin scores in stoppage-time to give Arsenal a 2-2 draw against Chelsea.

**13** As West Bromwich Albion end a run of 20 matches without a win, two other teams in the bottom four complain, justifiably, about costly hand-ball decisions. Defenders Jonny Evans and Craig Dawson both head in corners to give a delighted Alan Pardew his first three points as Albion manager – 2-0 against Brighton. In sharp contrast, Southampton's Mauricio Pellegrino calls for video assistant referees in the Premier League after Abdoulaye Doucoure punches a 90th minute equaliser into the net to complete Watford's comeback from a 2-0 deficit, established by two goal from James Ward-Prowse. Pellegrino is backed by Swansea's Carlos Carvalhal, who sees Mike Van der Hoorn's goal-bound effort blocked by Mohamed Diame's arm during the 1-1 draw at Newcastle. Harry Kane chalks up another record in Tottenham's 4-0 dismissal of Everton, with two goals to overtake Teddy Sheringham's Premier League total of 97 for the club. Manuel Lanzini also gets two for West Ham, who win 4-1 at Huddersfield. Leicester's Ben Chilwell is sent off for two yellow cards against Chelsea, who are involved in a third successive goalless draw in all competitons for the first time in the club's history.

**14** Manchester City lose their unbeaten record in a match living up to its top-of-the-table billing. Mohamed Salah returns a clearance from Ederson over the goalkeeper from 35 yards as Liverpool score three times in nine minutes to lead 4-1. Then, they then face an anxious finish as the leaders pull two goals back. Former Liverpool midfielder Jordon Ibe's first goal for Bournemouth delivers a 2-1 success against Arsenal.

**15** Hours after being appointed their new manager, Paul Lambert watches from the stands as Stoke lose 3-0 away to Manchester United.

**20** Sergio Aguero marks his 200th Premier League appearance for Manchester City with a hat-trick in their 3-1 win over Newcastle, taking his tally to 138 for the club. Newcastle's reply is a first for Jacob Murphy. Eden Hazard passes 100 career league goals for Chelsea and his previous club Lille with a brace in the 4-0 success at Brighton. Arsenal, in their first match without Alexis Sanchez, also score four, all in the opening 22 minutes, to overcome Crystal Palace 4-1. Paul Lambert's first match in charge is a success as Stoke beat Huddersfield 2-0 in front of a record stadium crowd of 29,785. Marco Silva's last as Watford manager before his sacking is a defeat by the same scoreline at Leicester. Everton's Sam Allardyce takes change of his 1,000th game as a manager, but the afternoon is overshadowed when his midfielder James McCarthy sustains a double leg fracture during a 1-1 draw with West Bromwich Albion.

**22** Liverpool's 18-match unbeaten run in all competitions comes to an end at Swansea, where Alfie Mawson scores the only goal of the match.

**30** Swansea move out of the bottom three by defeating Arsenal 3-1 with two goals from Sam Clucas.

**31** A record Premier League crowd of 81,978 sees Christian Eriksen score after 11 seconds, third fastest goal in the competition's history, to put Tottenham on the way to a 2-0 victory over Manchester United at Wembley. Manchester City ease past West Bromwich Albion 3-0 to go 15 points clear of United and 18 ahead of Chelsea. The deposed champions are outplayed 3-0 at Stamford Bridge by Bournemouth, whose manager Eddie Howe rates his team's performance as their best in the top division. Theo Walcott opens his account for Everton with two goals for a 2-1 victory over Leicester in which new team-mate Seamus Coleman returns after ten months out with a broken leg. Nick Pope's penalty save from Joselu helps Burnley to a 1-1 draw at Newcastle.

## FEBRUARY 2018

**3** On an emotional afternoon at The Hawthorns, West Bromwich Albion wear commemorative shirts and join former players and managers in a tribute to the late Cyrille Regis. His former side take an early lead. But Southampton respond to end a run of 12 games without a win, Mario Lemina striking a spectacular first goal for the club from 28 yards in a 3-2 scoreline to underline Albion's precarious position, four points adrift at the bottom of the table. Alexis Sanchez also scores his first, for Manchester United, converting the rebound after his penalty is saved by Jonas Lossl in a 2-0 victory over Huddersfield, who drop into the bottom three for the first time. Aaron Ramsey takes the day's scoring honours with a hat-trick as Arsenal dismantle Everton 5-1. Record-signing Pierre-Emerick Aubameyang marks his debut with a goal, allowed to stand despite his offside position. Manchester City's Raheem Sterling looks certain to add to his tally, but misses from three yards and Burnley take advantage to draw 1-1 with the runaway leaders. City manager Pep Guardiola defends his decision to name only six substitutes, insisting he has no more available first-teamers to fill the bench. Bournemouth extend their unbeaten run to seven matches by beating Stoke 2-1 to move further away from trouble.

**4** Harry Kane scores his 100th Premier League goal in a dramatic period of stoppage-time at the end of one of the games of the season. Mohamed Salah's second of the afternoon, a brilliant solo effort after 92 minutes, puts Liverpool 2-1 ahead at Anfield. Three minutes later, Kane makes amends for an earlier penalty saved by Loris Karius with a decisive spot-kick awarded for a hotly-disputed foul by Virgil van Dijk.

**5** Another crushing defeat for Chelsea, who lose 4-1 to Watford and have Tiemoue Bakayoko sent off for a second yellow card. New-signing Gerard Deulofeu opens his accounts for the home side, who score three times in the final ten minutes to give new manager Javi Gracia his first victory.

**10** Sergio Aguero is on the mark four times in the second-half as Manchester City overwhelm Leicester 5-1. It's his third hat-trick of the season and makes him the first Premier League player to score four or more goals on three separate occasions. Tottenham's Harry Kane delivers the only one of the north London derby in front of another Premier League record crowd of 83,222, leaving Arsenal facing the prospect of missing out again on a Champions League place unless they begin to strike some consistent form. Swansea defeat Burnley by the same scoreline to continue an impressive revival under Carlos Carvalhal which has netted 14 points from seven games. Ki Sung-yueng's winner is his first goal since May 2016. Stoke also record a new attendance high, 29,876, against Brighton, who earn a 1-1 draw thanks to Mathew Ryan's 90th minute penalty save from Charlie Adam, followed by Anthony Knockaert's clearance off the line from Kurt Zouma's header.

**11** Matt Ritchie secures a big win for Newcastle, scoring the only goal against Manchester United. Alex Pritchard's first for Huddersfield puts his new side on the way to their first league victory of 2018 – 4-1 against Bournemouth.

**12** Two goals by Eden Hazard spark Chelsea's return to form and increase the pressure on West Bromwich Albion, who lose 3-0.

**24** Brighton and Huddersfield give themselves breathing space in matches between teams battling to stay up. Two goals by Glenn Murray, one a penalty, point Chris Hughton's side to a 4-1 victory over Swansea. Huddersfield are 2-1 away winners over bottom-of-the-table West Bromwich Albion, who are left seven points from safety. A brace by Dwight Gayle look to have eased the pressure on Newcastle until the final ten minutes when they concede two to Bournemouth and have to be satisfied with a point. Burnley are left cursing their luck when referee Bobby Madley inadvertently impedes Ashley Westwood, enabling Southampton to break away and level at 1-1 through Manolo Gabbiadini.

**25** Romelu Lukaku scores one goal and sets up another for Jesse Lingard as Manchester United come from behind to defeat Chelsea 2-1. They end the month on 59 points, 13 behind Manchester City – League Cup winners at Wembley – with Liverpool on 57. Tottenham have 55 after Harry Kane's 88th minute winner at Crystal Palace.

## MARCH 2018

**1** Manchester City repeat their 3-0 victory over Arsenal in the League Cup Final with three goals in the opening 33 minutes at the Emirates to go 16 points clear. Ederson's second-half penalty save from Pierre-Emerick Aubameyang rubs it in.

**3** Goals by Ashley Barnes and substitute Chris Wood give Burnley their first three points in 12 games. They come from behind for a 2-1 victory over Everton, who surrender the lead established by Cenk Tosun's first goal for the club and have captain Ashley Williams shown a straight red card for swinging an arm into the face of Barnes. On-loan Andy King nets his first for Swansea, who see off West Ham 4-1, while the prolific Harry Kane turns provider with one of the assists of the season. Kane's pin-point cross is headed in by Son Heung-Min for the second of his two goals in Tottenham's 2-0 victory over Huddersfield. Mohamed Salah's seventh in seven games in all competitions, as Liverpool beat Newcastle 2-0, takes him level on 24 with Kane in the race for the Golden Boot award.

**4** After four own goals this season, Lewis Dunk scores one at the right end to put Brighton on the way to a 2-1 success against Arsenal, whose manager Arsene Wenger admits his side can no longer finish in a Champions League place. Bernardo Silva's strike 35 seconds into the second-half gives Manchester City a 1-0 win over Chelsea.

**5** Manchester United retrieve a two-goal deficit to defeat Crystal Palace 3-2 at Selhurst Park with a stoppage-time goal from Nemanja Matic, his first for the club.

**10** A day when the good, the bad and the ugly face of Premier League football is on show. Marcus Rashford, making his first start since Boxing Day, takes the honours with both goals as Manchester United defeat Liverpool 2-1. Jamie Vardy scores one of the best of the season in Leicester's 4-1 away win over West Bromwich Albion, collecting and controlling a 50-yard lofted pass from Riyad Mahrez and volleying in with his weaker left foot. Chelsea loanee Kenedy, opens his account for Newcastle with two goals in a 3-0 success against Southampton, whose manager Mauricio Pellegrino is sacked two days later. Substitute Chris Wood gets two in Burnley's victory over West Ham by the same scoreline. That match is scarred by four separate pitch invasions at the London Stadium, West Ham captain Mark Noble grappling with a fan and club owners David Sullivan and David Gold being abused.

Trouble, too, for Brighton's Anthony Knockaert and Swansea's Jordan Ayew. Knockaert is sent off for a two-footed lunge at Leighton Baines in a 2-0 defeat by Everton, who can afford Wayne Rooney having a penalty saved by Mathew Ryan. Ayew is also shown a straight red card, for his studs-up challenge on Jonathan Hogg in a goalless draw at Huddersfield.

**11** Petr Cech achieves his 200th Premier League clean sheet with a penalty save from Troy Deeney in Arsenal's 3-0 victory over Watford. Harry Kane goes off with an ankle injury at Bournemouth, but Tottenham make light of his absence by winning 4-1, with Son Heung-Min's two goals taking his tally to seven in four matches in all competitions.

**12** Manchester City close to within two wins of the title with a 2-0 success at Stoke, achieved by two goals from David Silva.

**17** The prolific Mohamed Salah scores four goals as Liverpool overwhelm Watford 5-0. Cenk Tosun, staring to flourish after a difficult start at Everton, nets twice for a 2-1 win at Stoke, who have Charlie Adam shown a straight red card for lunging at Wayne Rooney. Bournemouth record the same scoreline against West Bromwich Albion, thanks to an 89th minute goal by Junior Stanislas, while Crystal Palace are 2-0 winners at Huddersfield in a meeting of teams struggling to beat the drop.

**31** Manchester City, 3-1 winners over Everton at Goodison Park, move to 84 points, ahead of Manchester United (68) and Liverpool (66). West Ham also score three times in the first-half to put a smile back on the faces of their fans with a 3-0 success against Southampton, Marko Arnautovic netting twice and on-loan Joao Mario on the mark for the first time. Romelu Lukaku scores his 100th Premier League goal in Manchester United's 2-0 victory over Swansea, who along with Southampton and three other sides striving to avoid relegation are all defeated. Glenn Murray has a penalty saved by Kasper Schmeichel as Brighton lose 2-0 to Leicester, who have Wilfred Ndidi sent off for a second yellow card. Crystal Palace also go down at home, 2-1 to an 84th minute goal from Liverpool's Mohamed Salah. Another late goal, the only one of the match, from Newcastle's Ayoze Perez after 80 minutes, leaves Huddersfield empty-handed. Championship-bound West Bromwich Albion's 2-1 defeat by Burnley proves to be Alan Pardew's last match as manager.

## APRIL 2018

**1** Pierre-Emerick Aubameyang passes up the chance of a hat-trick against Stoke by handing the ball over to Arsenal team-mate Alexandre Lacazette, who rounds off a 3-0 win with his spot-kick. The official attendance at the Emirates is given as 59,371, but with rows and rows of empty seats it is estimated to be nearer to 40,000. Stoke stay second from bottom with 27 points, below Southampton (28), Crystal Palace (30), Huddersfield and Swansea (31), West Ham (33) and Brighton (34). Two goals by Dele Alli in the space of four second-half minutes point Tottenham to their first victory at Stamford Bridge since 1990. They come from behind to win 3-1 and move eight points ahead of Chelsea for the fourth Champions League place.

**7** Manchester City are poised to clinch the title when leading Manchester United 2-0 at the Etihad with goals from Vincent Kompany and Ilkay Gundogan. But Raheem Sterling misses two gilt-edged chances to finish United off and his team pay the price as Paul Pogba scores twice in the space of 97 seconds and Chris Smalling volleys the winner. Bookings for six players cost City a £25,000 fine. Christian Eriksen, enjoying the most productive season of his career, also claims a brace in Tottenham's 2-1 win at Stoke. But his club's appeal for Harry Kane to be awarded the second, to boost his chances of winning the Golden Boot award, is upheld by the Premier League. Substitutes Lys Mousset and Josh King are both on the mark for Bournemouth, whose 2-2 draw with Crystal Palace takes their tally of points gained from losing positions to 18 – highest in the league. Sam Vokes also makes his mark when coming off the bench, scoring after 22 seconds in a 2-1 victory at Watford which keeps Burnley on course for a Europa League place. Liverpool manager Jurgen Klopp shuffles his side ahead of the Champions League quarter-final second leg against Manchester City and the normally frenetic Merseyside derby with Everton is a sterile goalless draw. Brighton have Davy Propper shown a straight red card for lunging at

Jonathan Hogg in the 1-1 draw with Huddersfield

**8** Two goals by Danny Welbeck point Arsenal to a 3-2 win over Southampton in a game which ends with two straight red cards in stoppage-time. Jack Stephens is dismissed for retaliating after Jack Wilshere rips his shirt, Arsenal's Mohamed Elneny for raising his hands and pushing Cedric Soares. Elneny's card is rescinded on appeal.

**14** After three Champions League and Premier League defeats in a week, Manchester City are back on track with a 3-1 success against Tottenham in front of an 80,000 crowd at Wembley. It's Tottenham's first league reversal for four months, since City beat them 4-1 at the Etihad. Southampton's survival bid looks set for a boost when Polish defender Jan Bednarek puts them 2-0 ahead against Chelsea on his league debut. But they concede three goals in the space of nine minutes, two of them to substitute Olivier Giroud, go down 3-2 and fall five points adrift. A stoppage-time strike by substitute Tom Ince, the only one of the match, gives Huddersfield the verdict against Watford, while Crystal Palace also collect a vital three points, 3-2 against Brighton with Wilfried Zaha on the mark twice. Burnley win a fifth successive top-flight victory for the first time since 1968, defeating Leicester 2-1 as Kevin Long nets his first league goal for the club. Liverpool boost their bid for the runners-up spot with a 3-0 victory over Bournemouth in which Mohamed Salah takes his tally for the season to 40 goals – 30 of them in the league – with Liverpool's second.

**15** Manchester City are crowned champions in the most unlikely fashion. – a defeat for Manchester United against West Bromwich Albion leaving them 16 points in the clear with five fixtures remaining. Jay Rodriguez scores the only goal at Old Trafford to give Albion, under caretaker Darren Moore, only their fourth win all season.

**16** Andy Carroll, making his first appearance for more than three months after injury, comes off the bench to score a 90th minute equaliser, edge West Ham a point nearer safety and deprive Stoke of a much-needed win.

**21** West Bromwich Albion again give their supporters something to cheer about by retrieving a two-goal deficit to draw 2-2 with Liverpool, who have injured-dogged Danny Ings scoring for the first time since October 2015.

**22** Alexandre Lacazette scores twice in the final five minutes to round off Arsenal's 4-1 defeat of West Ham in their first match since Arsene Wenger's announcement that he is leaving the club at the end of the season. Manchester City celebrate their title win by overwhelming Swansea 5-0. Badou Ndiaye scores his first goal for Stoke in a 1-1 draw against Burnley.

**28** Crystal Palace all but ensure safety with their biggest–ever Premier League victory – 5-0 against Leicester, who lose Marc Albrighton to a straight red card for pulling down Wilfried Zaha. Dusan Tadic scores both goals as Southampton win at home for the first time since November, 2-1 against Bournemouth, to improve their chances of staying up. Stoke, with the worst away record in the four divisions, gain an unlikely point in a goalless draw against Liverpool, while West Bromwich Albion continue to salvage some respect under Darren Moore by winning 1-0 at Newcastle. But home defeats for Huddersfield (2-0 against Everton) and Swansea (1-0 by Chelsea) add to their worries.

**29** Arsene Wenger is feted by Sir Alex Ferguson and Jose Mourinho in his final match at Old Trafford as Arsenal manager. Wenger fields a weakened side ahead of the Europa League semi-final second leg against Atletico Madrid and Manchester United win 2-1 with Marouane Fellaini's stoppage-time header. West Ham's 4-1 home defeat by Manchester City leaves them still in trouble. With a fortnight to go, Albion have 28 points, below Stoke (30), Southampton (32), Swansea (33), Huddersfield (35), West Ham (35) and Brighton (37).

## MAY 2018

**4** Brighton are safe after a 1-0 win over Manchester United, goal-line technology confirming the winner from Pascal Gross.

**5** Stoke are relegated after ten years in the Premier League, beaten 2-1 at home by Crystal Palace in their 13th successive match without a win. Swansea continue to struggle for goals, a 1-0 defeat at Bournemouth leaving them with just two in seven games. But West Ham break free of the pack as captain Mark Noble completes a 2-0 success at Leicester with a spectacular 25-yard volley. Nathan Redmond puts Southampton ahead at Goodison Park and they look like holding on, despite an 85th minute second yellow card for Maya Yoshida. But Everton win a disputed free-kick, are allowed to take it ten yards further up the field and equalise deep into stoppage-time courtesy of a deflected Tom Davies shot. West Bromwich Albion, meanwhile, maintain their remarkable late rally, a stoppage-time winner by Jake Livermore seeing off Tottenham and raising just a glimmer of hope for a great escape.

**5** Arsenal treat Arsene Wenger to a 5-0 win over Burnley his final match at the Emirates, with Pierre-Emerick Aubameyang scoring twice. After Manchester City receive the Premier League trophy, Huddersfield succeed in dampening the party mood by gaining a priceless goalless draw. Chelsea close to within two points of Tottenham in the fourth Champions League spot by beating Liverpool 1-0.

**8** Southampton all-but ensure survival by winning 1-0 at Swansea with a goal by substitute Manolo Gabbiadini. The result sends West Bromwich Albion down.

**9** Huddersfield stay up after a 1-1 draw at Chelsea which effectively seals Swansea's fate. Tottenham defeat Newcastle 1-0 to make sure of a Champions League place. Manchester City beat Brighton 3-1 and overtake Chelsea's Premier League records for most points (95), most wins (30) and most goals (103). Arsenal have Konstantinos Mavropanos shown a straight red card for bringing down Kelechi Iheanacho in their seventh successive away defeat – 3-1 against Leicester.

**13** Manchester City become the first team in English top-flight history to reach 100 points when a 94th minute goal by Gabriel Jesus delivers a 1-0 success at Southampton on the final day of the season. Southampton's survival is confirmed as Swansea lose 2-1 at home to Stoke and go down. Liverpool make sure of fourth place at Chelsea's expense with a 4-0 victory over Brighton, Golden Boot winner Mohamed Salah taking his record-breaking tally to 32 and both Dominic Solanke and Andrew Robertson scoring their first goals for the club. Chelsea lose 3-0 at Newcastle for whom Ayoze Perez scores twice. West Ham's 3-1 win over Everton, featuring a brace from Manuel Lanzini, proves to be the final match in charge for respective managers David Moyes and Sam Allardyce. Arsene Wenger bows out with a 1-0 scoreline at Huddersfield, where a standing ovation in the 22nd minute marks his 22 years as manager. Tottenham's last match is a goal feast against Leicester. They prevail 5-4, Harry Kane and Erik Lamela sharing four of them and Jamie Vardy netting two for Leicester. Michael Carrick makes his 464th and final appearance for Manchester United, before joining the Old Trafford coaching staff, in a 1-0 win over Watford. John Motson also bids farewell, after a distinguished career at the BBC. His final commentary for *Match of the Day* is Crystal Palace's 2-0 defeat of West Bromwich Albion.

# HOW RECORD-BREAKING MANCHESTER CITY WON THE TITLE

## AUGUST 2017

**12** Brighton 0 Manchester City 2 (Aguero 70, Dunk 75 og). Att: 30,415

**21** Manchester City 1 (Sterling 82) Everton 1 (Rooney 35). Att: 49,108

**26** Bournemouth 1 (Daniels 13) Manchester City 2 (Gabriel Jesus 21, Sterling 90+7). Att: 10,419

## SEPTEMBER 2017

**9** Mancheste City 5 (Aguero 24, Gabriel Jesus 45, 53, Sane 77, 90+1) Liverpool 0. Att: 54,172

16 Watford 0 Manchester City 6 (Aguero 27, 31, 81, Gabriel Jesus 37, Otamendi 63, Sterling 89 pen). Att: 20,305

23 Manchester City 5 (Sane 44, Sterling 51, 59, Aguero 79, Delph 89) Crystal Palace 0. Att: 53,526

30 Chelsea 0 Manchester City 1 (De Bruyne 67). Att: 41,530

## OCTOBER 2017

14 Manchester City 7 (Gabriel Jesus 17, 55, Sterling 19, D Silva 27, Fernandinho 60, Sane 62, Bernardo Silva 79) Stoke 2 (Diouf 44, Walker 47 og). Att: 54,128

21 Manchester City 3 (Aguero 30 pen, Otamendi 73, Sane 75) Burnley 0. Att: 54,118

28 WBA 2 (Rodriguez 13, Phillips 90+2) Manchester City 3 (Sane 10, Fernandinho 15, Sterling 64). Att: 24,003

## NOVEMBER 2017

5 Manchester City 3 (De Bruyne 19, Aguero 50 pen, Gabriel Jesus 74) Arsenal 1 (Lacazette 65). Att: 54,286

18 Leicester 0 Manchester City 2 (Gabriel Jesus 45, De Bruyne 45). Att: 31,908

26 Huddersfield 1 (Otamendi 45 og) Manchester City 2 (Aguero 47 pen, Sterling 84). Att: 24,121

29 Manchester City 2 (De Bruyne 47, Sterling 90+6) Southampton 1 (Romeu 75). Att: 53,407

## DECEMBER 2017

3 Manchester City 2 (Otamendi 57, D Silva 83) West Ham 1 (Ogbonna 44). Att: 54,203

10 Manchester Utd 1 (Rashford 45) Manchester City 2 (D Silva 43, Otamendi 54). Att: 74,847

13 Swansea 0 Manchester City 4 (D Silva 27, 52, De Bruyne 34, Aguero 85). Att: 20,870

16 Manchester City 4 (Gundogan 14, De Bruyne 71. Sterling 80, 90) Tottenham 1 (Eriksen 90+3). Att: 54,214

23 Manchester City 4 (Aguero 27, 79, Sterling 53, Danilo 85) Bournemouth 0. Att: 54,270

27 Newcastle 0 Manchester City 1 (Sterling 31). Att: 52,311

31 Crystal Palace 0 Manchester City 0. Att: 25,804

## JANUARY 2018

2 Manchester City 3 (Sterling 1, Kabasele 13 og, Aguero 63) Watford 1 (Gray 82). Att: 53,556

14 Liverpool 4 (Oxlade-Chamberlain 9, Firmino 60, Mane 62, Salah 68) Manchester City 3 (Sane 41, Bernardo Silva 84, Gundogan 90+1). Att: 53,285

20 Manchester City 3 (Aguero 34, 63 pen, 83) Newcastle 1 (Murphy 67). Att: 54,452

31 Manchester City 3 (Fernandinho 19, De Bruyne 68, Aguero 89) WBA 0. Att: 53,241

## FEBRUARY 2018

3 Burnley 1 (Gudmundsson 82) Manchester City 1 (Danilo 22). Att: 21,658

10 Manchester City 5 (Sterling 3, Aguero 48, 53, 77, 90) Leicester 1 (Vardy 24). Att: 54,416

## MARCH 2018

1 Arsenal 0 Manchester City 3 (Bernardo Silva 15, D Silva 28, Sane 33). Att: 58,420

4 Manchester City 1 (Bernardo Silva 46) Chelsea 0. Att: 54,328

12 Stoke 0 Manchester City 2 (D Silva 10, 50). Att: 29,138

31 Everton 1 (Bolasie 63) Manchester City 3 (Sane 4, Gabriel Jesus 12, Sterling 37). Att: 39,221

## APRIL 2018

**7** Manchester City 2 (Kompany 25, Gundogan 31) Manchester Utd 3 (Pogba 53, 55, Smalling 69). Att: 54,259
**14** Tottenham 1 (Eriksen 42) Manchester City 3 (Gabriel Jesus 22, Gundogan 25 pen, Sterling 75). Att: 80,811 (City became champions the following day after Manchester Utd lost to WBA
**21** Manchester City 5 (D Silva 12, Sterling 16, De Bruyne 54, Bernardo Silva 64, Gabriel Jesus 88) Swansea 0. Att: 54,387
**29** West Ham 1 (Cresswell 42) Manchester City 4 (Sane 13, Zabaleta 27 og, Gabriel Jesus 53, Fernandinho 64). Att: 56,904

## MAY 2018

**6** Manchester City 0 Huddersfield 0. Att: 54,350
**9** Manchester City 3 (Danilo 16, Bernardo Silva 34, Fernandinho 72) Brighton 1 (Ulloa 20). Att: 54,013
**13** Southampton 0 Manchester City 1 (Gabriel Jesus 90+4)

*Manchester City became the first team in English top-flight history to accumulate 100 points. Their other Premier League records: goals 106 (previous best 103, Chelsea 2009-10); goal difference +79 (+71 Chelsea 2009-10); wins 32 (30 Chelsea 2016-17); away wins 16 (15 Chelsea 2004-05); consecutive wins 18 (14 Arsenal 2002), away points 50 (48 Chelsea 2004-05), points gap to second place 19 (18 Manchester Utd 1999-2000)

# ENGLISH FOOTBALL LEAGUE PLAY-OFFS 2018

Slavisa Jokanovic followed in the footsteps of David Wagner to lead **Fulham** into the Premier League. The German coach transformed Huddersfield from relegation candidates to Wembley winners in 2017. When Jokanovic, a former international midfielder with the old Yugoslavia, took over at Craven Cottage, they were 18th in the Championship. He kept them up, reached the semi-finals of the play-offs in his first full season and in the second organised Fulham's return to the top-flight after a four-year absence. They defeated Aston Villa 1-0, overcoming the dismissal of central defender Denis Odoi for a second yellow card after 70 minutes to protect a lead established by a goal from captain Tom Cairney set up by 18-year-old Ryan Sessegnon, the Championship Player of the Year. It meant there was no instant return for Villa, nor a record fifth promotion to the Premier League for Steve Bruce. The manager lost both his parents in the previous three months and earned tremendous admiration for keeping his side in the running. There was another captain's performance in the League One Final. Richard Wood scored both goals in **Rotherham**'s 2-1 victory over Shrewsbury, each time converting a set-play delivery from Joe Newell. **Coventry** ended years of decline, during which the club dropped from the Premier League to the fourth tier, by beating Exeter 3-1 in the League Two Final with second-half goals from goals from Jordan Willis, Jordan Shipley and Jack Grimmer. **Tranmere** had Liam Ridehalgh sent off for a two-footed challenge with just 48 seconds gone of the National League Final against Boreham Wood . But they were back in the Football League after a three-year absence with a 2-1 win secured by goals from Andy Cook and James Norwood.

## QUARTER-FINALS (one match)

**NATIONAL LEAGUE**
**Aldershot** 1 (Kabamba 106) **Ebbsfleet** 1 (Winfield 119). Att: 3,319 (aet, Ebbsfleet won 5-4 on pens). **Boreham Wood** 2 (Turley 6, Andrade 17) **AFC Fylde** 1 (Grand 30). Att: 1,244

## SEMI-FINALS (one match)

**NATIONAL LEAGUE**
**Sutton** 2 (Bolarinwa 82, Lafayette 90+2) **Boreham Wood** 3 (Balanta 42, Lafayette 53 og,

Folivi 88). Att: 2,730. **Tranmere** 4 (Norwood 33, 103, Ginnelly 56, Cole 106) **Ebbsfleet** 2 (Coulson 16, Weston 51). Att: 8,898 (aet)

## SEMI-FINALS, FIRST LEG

**CHAMPIONSHIP**

**Derby** 1 (Jerome 34) **Fulham** 0. Att: 27,163. **Middlesbrough** 0 **Aston Villa** 1 (Jedinak 15). Att: 29,233.

**LEAGUE ONE**

**Charlton** 0 **Shrewsbury**1 (Nolan 80). Att: 14,367. **Scunthorpe** 2 (Ihieklwe 18 og, McGeehan 88) **Rotherham** 2 (Taylor 17, Newell 64). Att: 6,591

**LEAGUE TWO**

**Coventry** 1 (McNulty 87 pen) **Notts Co** 1 (Forte 49). Att: 17,404. **Lincoln** 0 **Exeter** 0. Att: 9,509

## SEMI-FINALS, SECOND LEG

**CHAMPIONSHIP**

**Aston Villa** 0 **Middlesbrough** 0. Att: 40,505 (Aston Villa won 1-0 on agg). **Fulham** 2 (Sessegnon 47, Odoi 66) **Derby** 0. Att: 23,529 (Fulham won 2-1 on agg)

**LEAGUE ONE**

**Rotherham** 2 (Wood 45, Vaulks 63) **Scunthorpe** 0. Att: 11,061 (Rotherham won 4-2 on agg). **Shrewsbury** 1 (C Morris 58) **Charlton** 0. Att: 9,016 (Shrewsbury won 2-0 on agg)

**LEAGUE TWO**

**Exeter** 3 (Stockley 27, Boateng 47, Harley 69) **Lincoln** 1 (Green 78). Att: 5,645 (Exeter won 3-1 on agg). **Notts Co** 1 (Grant 45) **Coventry** 4 (Biamou 6, 71, McNulty 37, Bayliss 86). Att: 17,615 (Coventry won 5-2 on agg)

## FINALS

**CHAMPIONSHIP – SATURDAY, MAY 26, 2018**

**Aston Villa** 0 **Fulham** 1 (Cairney 23). Att: 85,243 (Wembley)

**Aston Villa** (4-1-4-1): Johnstone, Elmohamady (Kodija 77), Chester, Terry (capt), Hutton, Snodgrass, Jedinak (Onomah 77). Hourihane (Hogan 81). Adomah, Grealish, Grabban. **Subs not used**: Bunn, Bree, Whelan, Bjarnason. **Booked**: Chester, Grealish, Jedinak, Hutton. **Manager**: Steve Bruce

**Fulham** (4-3-3): Bettinelli, Fredericks (Christie 82), Odoi, Ream, Targett, McDonald, Cairney (capt), Johansen (Norwood 72), Kamara (Kalas 77), Mitrovic, Sessegnon. **Subs not used** Button, Ayite, Fonte, Piazon. **Booked**: Odoi, Kamara. **Sent off**: Odoi (70). **Manager**: Slavisa Jokanovic

**Referee**: A Taylor (Cheshire). **Half-time**: 0-1

**LEAGUE ONE – SUNDAY, MAY 27, 2018 – aet**

**Rotherham United** 2 (Wood 32, 103) **Shrewsbury Town** 1 (Rodman 58). Att: 26,218 (Wembley)

**Rotherham United** (4-2-3-1): Rodak, Emmanuel, Ajayi, Wood (capt), Mattock, Towell, Vaulks, Taylor (R Williams 75), Ball (Lavery 71), Newell (Forde 110), Smith. **Subs not used**: Price, Palmer, Purrington, Cummings. **Manager**: Paul Warne

**Shrewsbury Town** (4-4-2): Henderson, Bolton (Riley 73), Nsiala, Sadler (capt), Beckles, Whalley, B Morris (Payne 56), Godfrey, Rodman, Nolan, C Morris (John-Lewis 66). **Subs not used**: MacGillivray, Lowe, Brown, Jones. **Booked**: Whalley, Bolton, Sadler. **Manager**: Paul Hurst

**Referee**: R Jones (Merseyside). **Half-time**: 1-0

**LEAGUE TWO – MONDAY, MAY 28, 2018**
**Coventry City** 3 (Willis 49, Shipley 54, Grimmer 68) **Exeter City** 1 (Edwards 89). Att: 50,196 (Wembley)
**Coventry City** (4-4-2): Burge, Grimmer, Willis, Hyam, Stokes, Bayliss, Kelly, Doyle (capt), Shipley (Reid 73), McNulty (Ponticelli 82), Biamou (Clarke-Harris 51). **Subs not used**: O'Brien, McDonald, Maguire-Drew, Thompson. **Manager**: Mark Robins
**Exeter City** (4-1-4-1): Pym, Sweeney, Storey, Moore-Taylor (capt), Woodman (James 63), Taylor, Boateng (Edwards 73), Tillson, Moxey (Jay 63), Harley, Stockley. **Subs not used**: Jones, Archibald-Henville, Simpson, Wilson. **Manager**: Paul Tisdale
**Referee**: D Webb (Co Durham). **Half-time**: 0-0

**NATIONAL LEAGUE - SATURDAY, MAY 12, 2018**
**Boreham Wood** 1 (Andrade 45) **Tranmere Rovers** 2 (Cook 6, Norwood 80). Att: 16,306 (Wembley)
**Boreham Wood** (3-4-1-2): Smith; Champion, Stephens, Doe, Shakes, Murtagh, Ricketts (capt), Balanta, Woodards (Thomas 83), Folivi (Quigley 70), Andrade. **Subs not used**: Burbidge, Harfield, Davey. **Booked**: Balanta, Folivi. **Manager**: Luke Garrard
**Tranmere Rovers** (4-4-2): Davies, Sutton (Harris 45), Monthe, McNulty (capt), Ridehalgh, Ginnelly (Jennings 34), Norburn, Hughes, Cole (Clarke 9), Cook, Norwood. **Subs not used**: Taylor, Mangan. **Booked**: Jennings. **Sent off**: Ridehalgh (1). **Manager**: Micky Mellon
**Referee**: N Hair (Cambs). **Half-time**: 1-1

# PLAY-OFF FINALS – HOME & AWAY

**1987: Divs 1/2: Charlton** beat Leeds 2-1 in replay (Birmingham) after 1-1 agg (1-0h, 0-1a). Charlton remained in Div 1 Losing semi-finalists: Ipswich and Oldham. **Divs 2/3: Swindon** beat Gillingham 2-0 in replay (Crystal Palace) after 2-2 agg (0-1a, 2-1h). Swindon promoted to Div 2. Losing semi-finalists: Sunderland and Wigan; Sunderland relegated to Div 3. **Divs 3/4: Aldershot** beat Wolves 3-0 on agg (2-0h, 1-0a) and promoted to Div 3. Losing semi-finalists: Bolton and Colchester; Bolton relegated to Div 4

**1988: Divs 1/2: Middlesbrough** beat Chelsea 2-1 on agg (2-0h, 0-1a) and promoted to Div 1; Chelsea relegated to Div 2. Losing semi-finalists: Blackburn and Bradford City. **Divs 2/3: Walsall** beat Bristol City 4-0 in replay (h) after 3-3 agg (3-1a, 0-2h) and promoted to Div 2. Losing semi-finalists: Sheffield Utd and Notts County; Sheffield Utd relegated to Div 3. **Divs 3/4: Swansea** beat Torquay 5-4 on agg (2-1h, 3-3a) and promoted to Div 3. Losing semi-finalists: Rotherham and Scunthorpe.; Rotherham relegated to Div 4

**1989: Div 2: Crystal Palace** beat Blackburn 4-3 on agg (1-3a, 3-0h). Losing semi-finalists: Watford and Swindon. **Div 3: Port Vale** beat Bristol Rovers 2-1 on agg (1-1a, 1-0h). Losing semi-finalists: Fulham and Preston **Div.4: Leyton Orient** beat Wrexham 2-1 on agg (0-0a, 2-1h). Losing semi-finalists: Scarborough and Scunthorpe

**PLAY-OFF FINALS AT WEMBLEY**

**1990: Div 2: Swindon** 1 Sunderland 0 (att: 72,873). Swindon promoted, then demoted for financial irregularities; Sunderland promoted. Losing semi-finalists: Blackburn and Newcastle Utd **Div 3: Notts County** 2 Tranmere 0 (att: 29,252). Losing semi-finalists: Bolton and Bury. **Div 4: Cambridge Utd** 1 Chesterfield 0 (att: 26,404). Losing semi-finalists: Maidstone and Stockport County

**1991: Div 2: Notts County 3** Brighton 1 (att: 59,940). Losing semi-finalists: Middlesbrough and Millwall. **Div 3: Tranmere** 1 Bolton 0 (att: 30,217). Losing semi-finalists: Brentford and Bury. **Div 4: Torquay 2** Blackpool 2 – Torquay won 5-4 on pens (att: 21,615). Losing semi-finalists: Burnley and Scunthorpe

**1992: Div 2: Blackburn** 1 Leicester 0 (att: 68,147). Losing semi-finalists: Derby and Cambridge Utd. **Div 3: Peterborough** 2 Stockport 1 (att: 35,087). Losing semi-finalists: Huddersfield and Stoke. **Div 4: Blackpool** 1 Scunthorpe 1 aet, Blackpool won 4-3 on pens (att: 22,741). Losing semi-finalists: Barnet and Crewe

**1993: Div 1: Swindon** 4 Leicester 3 (att: 73,802). Losing semi-finalists: Portsmouth and Tranmere. **Div 2: WBA** 3 Port Vale 0 (att: 53,471). Losing semi-finalists: Stockport and Swansea. **Div 3: York** 1 Crewe 1 aet, York won 5-3 on pens (att: 22,416). Losing semi-finalists: Bury and Walsall

**1994: Div 1: Leicester** 2 Derby 1 (att: 73,671). Losing semi-finalists: Millwall and Tranmere. **Div 2: Burnley** 2 Stockport 1 (att: 44,806). Losing semi-finalists: Plymouth Argyle and York. **Div 3: Wycombe** 4 Preston 2 (att: 40,109). Losing semi-finalists: Carlisle and Torquay

**1995: Div 1: Bolton** 4 Reading 3 (att: 64,107). Losing semi-finalists: Tranmere and Wolves. **Div 2: Huddersfield** 2 Bristol Rov 1 (att: 59,175). Losing semi-finalists: Brentford and Crewe. **Div 3: Chesterfield** 2 Bury 0 (att: 22,814). Losing semi-finalists: Mansfield and Preston

**1996: Div 1: Leicester** 2 Crystal Palace 1 aet (att: 73,573). Losing semi-finalists: Charlton and Stoke. **Div 2: Bradford City** 2 Notts Co 0 (att: 39,972). Losing semi-finalists: Blackpool and Crewe. **Div 3: Plymouth Argyle** 1 Darlington 0 (att: 43,431). Losing semi-finalists: Colchester and Hereford

**1997: Div 1: Crystal Palace** 1 Sheffield Utd 0 (att: 64,383). Losing semi-finalists: Ipswich and Wolves. **Div 2: Crewe** 1 Brentford 0 (att: 34,149). Losing semi-finalists: Bristol City and Luton. **Div 3: Northampton** 1 Swansea 0 (att: 46,804). Losing semi-finalists: Cardiff and Chester

**1998: Div 1: Charlton** 4 Sunderland 4 aet, Charlton won 7-6 on pens (att: 77, 739). Losing semi-finalists: Ipswich and Sheffield Utd. **Div 2: Grimsby** 1 Northampton 0 (att: 62,988). Losing semi-finalists: Bristol Rov and Fulham. **Div 3: Colchester** 1 Torquay 0 (att: 19,486). Losing semi-finalists: Barnet and Scarborough

**1999: Div 1: Watford** 2 Bolton 0 (att: 70,343). Losing semi-finalists: Ipswich and Birmingham. **Div 2: Manchester City** 2 Gillingham 2 aet, Manchester City won 3-1 on pens (att: 76,935). Losing semi-finalists: Preston and Wigan. **Div 3: Scunthorpe** 1 Leyton Orient 0 (att: 36,985). Losing semi-finalists: Rotherham and Swansea

**2000: Div 1: Ipswich** 4 Barnsley 2 (att: 73,427). Losing semi-finalists: Birmingham and Bolton. **Div 2: Gillingham** 3 Wigan 2 aet (att: 53,764). Losing semi-finalists: Millwall and Stoke. **Div 3: Peterborough** 1 Darlington 0 (att: 33,383). Losing semi-finalists: Barnet and Hartlepool

**PLAY-OFF FINALS AT MILLENNIUM STADIUM**

**2001: Div 1: Bolton** 3 Preston 0 (att:. 54,328). Losing semi-finalists: Birmingham and WBA. **Div 2: Walsall** 3 Reading 2 aet (att: 50,496). Losing semi-finalists: Stoke and Wigan. **Div 3: Blackpool** 4 Leyton Orient 2 (att: 23,600). Losing semi-finalists: Hartlepool and Hull.

**2002: Div 1: Birmingham** 1 Norwich 1 aet, Birmingham won 4-2 on pens, (att: 71,597). Losing semi-finalists: Millwall and Wolves. **Div 2: Stoke** 2 Brentford 0 (att: 42,523). Losing semi-finalists: Cardiff and Huddersfield. **Div 3: Cheltenham** 3 Rushden & Diamonds 1 (att: 24,368). Losing semi-finalists: Hartlepool and Rochdale

**2003: Div 1: Wolves** 3 Sheffield Utd 0 (att: 69,473). Losing semi-finalists: Nott'm Forest and Reading. **Div 2: Cardiff** 1 QPR. 0 aet (att: 66,096). Losing semi-finalists: Bristol City and Oldham. **Div 3: Bournemouth** 5 Lincoln 2 (att: 32,148). Losing semi-finalists: Bury and Scunthorpe

**2004: Div 1: Crystal Palace** 1 West Ham 0 (att: 72,523). Losing semi-finalists: Ipswich and Sunderland. **Div 2: Brighton** 1 Bristol City 0 (att: 65,167). Losing semi-finalists: Hartlepool and Swindon. **Div 3: Huddersfield** 0 Mansfield 0 aet, Huddersfield won 4-1 on pens (att: 37,298). Losing semi-finalists: Lincoln and Northampton

**2005: Championship: West Ham** 1 Preston 0 (att: 70,275). Losing semifinalists: Derby Co and Ipswich. **League 1: Sheffield Wed** 4 Hartlepool 2 aet (att: 59,808). Losing semi-finalists:

Brentford and Tranmere **League 2: Southend** 2 Lincoln 0 aet (att: 19532). Losing semi-finalists: Macclesfield and Northampton

**2006: Championship: Watford** 3 Leeds 0 (att: 64,736). Losing semi-finalists: Crystal Palace and Preston. **League 1: Barnsley** 2 Swansea 2 aet (att: 55,419), Barnsley won 4-3 on pens. Losing semi-finalists: Huddersfield and Brentford. **League 2: Cheltenham** 1 Grimsby 0 (att: 29,196). Losing semi-finalists: Wycombe and Lincoln

## PLAY-OFF FINALS AT WEMBLEY

**2007: Championship: Derby** 1 WBA 0 (att: 74,993). Losing semi-finalists: Southampton and Wolves. **League 1: Blackpool** 2 Yeovil 0 (att: 59,313). Losing semi-finalists: Nottm Forest and Oldham. **League 2: Bristol Rov** 3 Shrewsbury 1 (att: 61,589). Losing semi-finalists: Lincoln and MK Dons

**2008: Championship: Hull** 1 Bristol City 0 (att: 86,703). Losing semi-finalists: Crystal Palace and Watford. **League 1: Doncaster** 1 Leeds 0 (att: 75,132). Losing semi-finalists: Carlisle and Southend. **League 2: Stockport** 3 Rochdale 2 (att: 35,715). Losing semi-finalists: Darlington and Wycombe

**2009: Championship: Burnley** 1 Sheffield Utd 0 (att: 80,518). Losing semi-finalists: Preston and Reading. **League 1: Scunthorpe** 3 Millwall 2 (att: 59,661). Losing semi-finalists: Leeds and MK Dons. **League 2: Gillingham** 1 Shrewsbury 0 (att: 53,706). Losing semi-finalists: Bury and Rochdale

**2010: Championship: Blackpool** 3 Cardiff 2 (att: 82,244). Losing semi-finalists: Leicester and Nottm Forest. **League 1: Millwall** 1 Swindon 0 (att:73,108). Losing semi-finalists: Charlton and Huddersfield. **League 2: Dagenham & Redbridge** 3 Rotherham 2 (att: 32,054). Losing semi-finalists: Aldershot and Morecambe

**2011: Championship: Swansea** 4 Reading 2 (att: 86,581). Losing semi-finalists: Cardiff and Nottm Forest. **League 1: Peterborough** 3 Huddersfield 0 (Old Trafford, att:48,410). Losing semi-finalists: Bournemouth and MK Dons. **League 2: Stevenage** 1 Torquay 0 (Old Trafford, att: 11,484. Losing semi-finalists: Accrington and Shrewsbury

**2012: Championship: West Ham** 2 Blackpool 1 (att: 78,523). Losing semi-finalists: Birmingham and Cardiff. **League 1: Huddersfield** 0 Sheffield Utd 0 aet, Huddersfield won 8-7 on pens (att: 52,100). Losing semi-finalists: MK Dons and Stevenage. **League 2: Crewe** 2 Cheltenham 0 (att: 24,029). Losing semi-finalists: Southend and Torquay

**2013: Championship: Crystal Palace** 1 Watford 0 (att: 82,025). Losing semi-finalists: Brighton and Leicester. **League 1: Yeovil** 2 Brentford 1 (att: 41,955). Losing semi-finalists: Sheffield Utd and Swindon. **League 2: Bradford** 3 Northampton 0 (att: 47,127). Losing semi-finalists: Burton and Cheltenham

**2014: Championship: QPR** 1 Derby 0 (att: 87,348). Losing semi-finalists: Brighton and Wigan. **League 1: Rotherham** 2 Leyton Orient 2 aet, Rotherham won 4-3 on pens (att: 43,401). Losing semi-finalists: Peterborough and Preston. **League 2: Fleetwood** 1 Burton 0 (att: 14,007). Losing semi-finalists: Southend and York)

**2015: Championship: Norwich** 2 Middlesbrough 0 (att: 85,656). Losing semi-finalists: Brentford and Ipswich. **League 1: Preston** 4 Swindon 0 (att: 48,236). Losing semi-finalists: Chesterfield and Sheffield Utd. **League 2: Southend** 1 Wycombe 1 aet, Southend won 7-6 on pens (att: 38,252). Losing semi-finalists: Stevenage and Plymouth

**2016: Championship: Hull** 1 Sheffield Wed 0 (att 70,189). Losing semi-finalists: Brighton and Derby. **League 1: Barnsley** 3 Millwall 1 (att 51,277). Losing semi-finalists: Bradford and Walsall. **League 2: AFC Wimbledon** 2 Plymouth 0 (att 57,956). Losing semi-finalists: Accrington and Portsmouth)

**2017: Championship: Huddersfield** 0 Reading 0 aet, Huddersfield won 4-3 on pens (att 76,682). Losing semi-finalists: Fulham and Sheffield Wed. **League 1: Millwall** 1 Bradford 0 (att 53,320. Losing semi-finals: Fleetwood and Scunthorpe. **League 2: Blackpool** 2 Exeter 1 (att 23,380). Losing semi-finalists: Carlisle and Luton

# HISTORY OF THE PLAY-OFFS

Play-off matches were introduced by the Football League to decide final promotion and relegation issues at the end of season 1986-87. A similar series styled 'Test Matches' had operated between Divisions One and Two for six seasons from 1893-98, and was abolished when both divisions were increased from 16 to 18 clubs.

Eighty-eight years later, the play-offs were back in vogue. In the first three seasons (1987-88-89), the Finals were played home-and-away, and since they were made one-off matches in 1990, they have featured regularly in Wembley's spring calendar, until the old stadium closed its doors and the action switched to the Millennium Stadium in Cardiff in 2001.

Through the years, these have been the ups and downs of the play-offs:

**1987:** Initially, the 12 clubs involved comprised the one that finished directly above those relegated in Divisions One, Two and Three and the three who followed the sides automatically promoted in each section. Two of the home-and-away Finals went to neutral-ground replays, in which **Charlton** clung to First Division status by denying Leeds promotion while **Swindon** beat Gillingham to complete their climb from Fourth Division to Second in successive seasons, via the play-offs, Sunderland fell into the Third and Bolton into Division Four, both for the first time. **Aldershot** went up after finishing only sixth in Division Four; in their Final, they beat Wolves, who had finished nine points higher and missed automatic promotion by one point.

**1988:** Chelsea were relegated from the First Division after losing on aggregate to **Middlesbrough**, who had finished third in Division Two. So Middlesbrough, managed by Bruce Rioch, completed the rise from Third Division to First in successive seasons, only two years after their very existence had been threatened by the bailiffs. Also promoted via the play-offs: **Walsall** from Division Three and **Swansea** from the Fourth. Relegated, besides Chelsea: Sheffield Utd (to Division Three) and Rotherham (to Division Four).

**1989:** After two seasons of promotion-relegation play-offs, the system was changed to involve the four clubs who had just missed automatic promotion. That format has remained. Steve Coppell's **Crystal Palace**, third in Division Two, returned to the top flight after eight years, beating Blackburn 4-3 on aggregate after extra time. Similarly, **Port Vale** confirmed third place in Division Three with promotion via the play-offs. For **Leyton Orient**, promotion seemed out of the question in Division Four when they stood 15th on March 1. But eight wins and a draw in the last nine home games swept them to sixth in the final table, and two more home victories in the play-offs completed their season in triumph.

**1990:** The play-off Finals now moved to Wembley over three days of the Spring Holiday weekend. On successive afternoons, **Cambridge Utd** won promotion from Division Four and **Notts Co** from the Third. Then, on Bank Holiday Monday, the biggest crowd for years at a Football League fixture (72,873) saw Ossie Ardiles' **Swindon** beat Sunderland 1-0 to reach the First Division for the first time. A few weeks later, however, Wembley losers **Sunderland** were promoted instead, by default; Swindon were found guilty of "financial irregularities" and stayed in Division Two.

**1991:** Again, the season's biggest League crowd (59,940) gathered at Wembley for the First Division Final in which **Notts Co** (having missed promotion by one point) still fulfilled their ambition, beating Brighton 3-1. In successive years, County had climbed from Third Division to First via the play-offs – the first club to achieve double promotion by this route. Bolton were denied automatic promotion in Division Three on goal difference, and lost at Wembley to an extra-time goal by **Tranmere**. The Fourth Division Final made history, with Blackpool beaten 5-4 on penalties by **Torquay** – first instance of promotion being decided by a shoot-out. In the table, Blackpool had finished seven points ahead of Torquay.

**1992:** Wembley that Spring Bank Holiday was the turning point in the history of **Blackburn.** Bolstered by Kenny Dalglish's return to management and owner Jack Walker's millions, they beat Leicester 1-0 by Mike Newell's 45th-minute penalty to achieve their objective – a place in the new Premier League. Newell, who also missed a second-half penalty, had recovered from a broken leg just in time for the play-offs. In the Fourth Division Final **Blackpool** (denied by penalties the previous year) this time won a shoot-out 4-3 against Scunthorpe., who were unlucky in the play-offs for the fourth time in five years. **Peterborough** climbed out of the Third Division for the first time, beating Stockport County 2-1 at Wembley.

**1993:** The crowd of 73,802 at Wembley to see **Swindon** beat Leicester 4-3 in the First Division Final was 11,000 bigger than that for the FA Cup Final replay between Arsenal and Sheffield Wed Leicester rallied from three down to 3-3 before Paul Bodin's late penalty wiped away **Swindon**'s bitter memories of three years earlier, when they were denied promotion after winning at Wembley. In the Third Division Final, **York** beat Crewe 5-3 in a shoot-out after a 1-1 draw, and in the Second Division decider, **WBA** beat Port Vale 3-0. That was tough on Vale, who had finished third in the table with 89 points – the highest total never to earn promotion in any division. They had beaten Albion twice in the League, too.

**1994:** Wembley's record turn-out of 158,586 spectators at the three Finals started with a crowd of 40,109 to see Martin O'Neill's **Wycombe** beat Preston 4-2. They thus climbed from Conference to Second Division with successive promotions. **Burnley**'s 2-1 victory in the Second Division Final was marred by the sending-off of two Stockport players, and in the First Division decider **Leicester** came from behind to beat Derby Co and end the worst Wembley record of any club. They had lost on all six previous appearances there – four times in the FA Cup Final and in the play-offs of 1992 and 1993.

**1995:** Two months after losing the Coca-Cola Cup Final to Liverpool, Bruce Rioch's **Bolton** were back at Wembley for the First Division play-off Final. From two goals down to Reading in front of a crowd of 64,107, they returned to the top company after 15 years, winning 4-3 with two extra-time goals. **Huddersfield** ended the first season at their new £15m. home with promotion to the First Division via a 2-1 victory against Bristol Rov – manager Neil Warnock's third play-off success (after two with Notts Co). Of the three clubs who missed automatic promotion by one place, only **Chesterfield** achieved it in the play-offs, comfortably beating Bury 2-0.

**1996:** Under new manager Martin O'Neill (a Wembley play-off winner with Wycombe in 1994), **Leicester** returned to the Premiership a year after leaving it. They had finished fifth in the table, but in the Final came from behind to beat third-placed Crystal Palace by Steve Claridge's shot in the last seconds of extra time. In the Second Division **Bradford City** came sixth, nine points behind Blackpool (3rd), but beat them (from two down in the semi-final first leg) and then clinched promotion by 2-0 v Notts County at Wembley. It was City's greatest day since they won the Cup in 1911. **Plymouth Argyle** beat Darlington in the Third Division Final to earn promotion a year after being relegated. It was manager Neil Warnock's fourth play-off triumph in seven seasons after two with Notts County (1990 and 1991) and a third with Huddersfield in 1995.

**1997:** High drama at Wembley as **Crystal Palace** left it late against Sheffield Utd in the First Division play-off final. The match was scoreless until the last 10 seconds when David Hopkin lobbed Blades' keeper Simon Tracey from 25 yards to send the Eagles back to the Premiership after two seasons of Nationwide action. In the Second Division play-off final, **Crewe** beat Brentford 1-0 courtesy of a Shaun Smith goal. **Northampton** celebrated their first Wembley appearance with a 1-0 victory over Swansea thanks to John Frain's injury-time free-kick in the Third Division play-off final.

**1998:** In one of the finest games ever seen at Wembley, **Charlton** eventually triumphed 7-6 on penalties over Sunderland. For Charlton, Wearside-born Clive Mendonca scored a hat-trick and Richard Rufus his first career goal in a match that lurched between joy and despair for both sides as it ended 4-4. Sunderland defender Michael Gray's superb performance ill deserved to end with his weakly struck spot kick being saved by Sasa Ilic. In the Third Division, the penalty spot also had a role to play, as **Colchester**'s David Gregory scored the only goal to defeat Torquay, while in the Second Division a Kevin Donovan goal gave **Grimsby** victory over Northampton.

**1999:** Elton John, watching via a personal satellite link in Seattle, saw his **Watford** side overcome Bolton 2-0 to reach the Premiership. Against technically superior opponents, Watford prevailed with application and teamwork. They also gave Bolton a lesson in finishing through match-winners by Nick Wright and Allan Smart. **Manchester City** staged a remarkable comeback to win the Second Division Final after trailing to goals by Carl Asaba and Robert Taylor for Gillingham. Kevin Horlock and Paul Dickov scored in stoppage time and City went on to win on penalties. A goal by Spaniard Alex Calvo-Garcia earned **Scunthorpe** a 1-0 success against Leyton Orient in the Third Division Final.

**2000:** After three successive play-off failures, **Ipswich** finally secured a place in the Premiership. They overcame the injury loss of leading scorer David Johnson to beat Barnsley 4-2 with goals by 36-year-old Tony Mowbray, Marcus Stewart and substitutes Richard Naylor and Martijn Reuser. With six minutes left of extra-time in the Second Division Final, **Gillingham** trailed Wigan 2-1. But headers by 38-year-old player-coach Steve Butler and fellow substitute Andy Thomson gave them a 3-2 victory. Andy Clarke, approaching his 33rd birthday, scored the only goal of the Third Division decider for **Peterborough** against Darlington.

**2001: Bolton**, unsuccessful play-off contenders in the two previous seasons, made no mistake at the third attempt. They flourished in the new surroundings of the Millennium Stadium to beat Preston 3-0 with goals by Gareth Farrelly, Michael Ricketts – his 24th of the season – and Ricardo Gardner to reach the Premiership. **Walsall**, relegated 12 months earlier, scored twice in a three-minute spell of extra time to win 3-2 against Reading in the Second Division Final, while **Blackpool** capped a marked improvement in the second half of the season by overcoming Leyton Orient 4-2 in the Third Division Final.

**2002:** Holding their nerve to win a penalty shoot-out 4-2, **Birmingham** wiped away the memory of three successive defeats in the semi-finals of the play-offs to return to the top division after an absence of 16 years. Substitute Darren Carter completed a fairy-tale first season as a professional by scoring the fourth spot-kick against Norwich. **Stoke** became the first successful team to come from the south dressing room in 12 finals since football was adopted by the home of Welsh rugby, beating Brentford 2-0 in the Second Division Final with Deon Burton's strike and a Ben Burgess own goal. Julian Alsop's 26th goal of the season helped **Cheltenham** defeat League newcomers Rushden & Diamonds 3-1 in the Third Division decider.

**2003: Wolves** benefactor Sir Jack Hayward finally saw his £60m investment pay dividends when the club he first supported as a boy returned to the top flight after an absence of 19 years by beating Sheffield Utd 3-0. It was also a moment to savour for manager Dave Jones, who was forced to leave his previous club Southampton because of child abuse allegations, which were later found to be groundless. **Cardiff**, away from the game's second tier for 18 years, returned with an extra-time winner from substitute Andy Campbell against QPR after a goalless 90 minutes in the Division Two Final. **Bournemouth**, relegated 12 months earlier, became the first team to score five in the end-of-season deciders, beating Lincoln 5-2 in the Division Three Final.

**2004:** Three tight, tense Finals produced only two goals, the lowest number since the Play-offs were introduced. One of them, scored by Neil Shipperley, gave **Crystal Palace** victory over West Ham, the much-travelled striker tapping in a rebound after Stephen Bywater parried Andy Johnson's shot. It completed a remarkable transformation for Crystal Palace, who were 19th in the table when Iain Dowie left Oldham to become their manager. **Brighton** made an immediate return to Division One in a poor game against Bristol City which looked set for extra-time until Leon Knight netted his 27th goal of the campaign from the penalty spot after 84 minutes. **Huddersfield** also went back up at the first attempt, winning the Division Three Final in a penalty shoot-out after a goalless 120 minutes against Mansfield.

**2005:** Goals were few and far between for Bobby Zamora during **West Ham**'s Championship season – but what a difference in the Play-offs. The former Brighton and Tottenham striker scored three times in the 4-2 aggregate win over Ipswich in the semi-finals and was on the mark again with the only goal against Preston at the Millennium Stadium. **Sheffield Wed** were eight minute away from defeat against Hartlepool in the League One decider when Steven MacLean made it 2-2 from the penalty spot and they went on to win 4-2 in extra-time. **Southend**, edged out of an automatic promotion place, won the League Two Final 2-0 against Lincoln, Freddy Eastwood scoring their first in extra-time and making the second for Duncan Jupp. **Carlisle** beat Stevenage 1-0 with a goal by Peter Murphy in the Conference Final to regain their League place 12 months after being relegated.

**2006:** From the moment Marlon King scored his 22nd goal of the season to set up a 3-0 win over Crystal Palace in the semi-final first leg, **Watford** had the conviction of a team going places. Sure enough, they went on to beat Leeds just as comfortably in the final. Jay DeMerit, who was playing non-league football 18 months earlier, headed his side in front. James Chambers fired in a shot that hit a post and went in off goalkeeper Neil Sullivan. Then Darius Henderson put away a penalty after King was brought down by Shaun Derry, the man whose tackle had ended Boothroyd's playing career at the age of 26. **Barnsley** beat Swansea on penalties in the League One Final, Nick Colgan making the vital save from Alan Tate, while Steve Guinan's goal earned **Cheltenham** a 1-0 win over Grimsby in the League Two Final. **Hereford** returned to the Football League after a nine-year absence with Ryan Green's extra-time winner against Halifax in the Conference Final.

**2007:** Record crowds, plenty of goals and a return to Wembley for the finals made for some eventful and entertaining matches. Stephen Pearson, signed from Celtic for £650,000 in the January transfer window, took **Derby** back to the Premier League after an absence of five seasons with a 61st minute winner, his first goal for the club, against accounted for West Bromwich Albion.. It was third time lucky for manager Billy Davies, who had led Preston into the play-offs, without success, in the two previous seasons. **Blackpool** claimed a place in the game's second tier for the first time for 30 years by beating Yeovil 2-0 – their tenth successive victory in a remarkable end-of-season run. Richard Walker took his tally for the season to 23 with two goals for **Bristol Rov**, who beat Shrewsbury 3-1 in the League Two Final. Sammy McIlroy, who led Macclesfield into the league in 1997, saw his Morecambe side fall behind in the Conference Final against Exeter, but they recovered to win 2-1.

**2008:** Wembley has produced some unlikely heroes down the years, but rarely one to match 39-year-old Dean Windass. The **Hull** striker took his home-town club into the top-flight for the first time with the only goal of the Championship Final against Bristol City – and it was a goal fit to grace any game. In front of a record crowd for the final of 86,703, Fraizer Campbell, his 20-year-old partner up front, picked out Windass on the edge of the penalty box and a sweetly-struck volley flew into the net. **Doncaster**, who like Hull faced an uncertain future a few years earlier, beat Leeds 1-0 in the League One Final with a header by James Hayer from Brian Stock's corner. Jim Gannon had lost four Wembley finals with **Stockport** as a player, but his first as manager brought a 3-2 win against Rochdale in the League Two Final with goals by Anthony Pilkington and Liam Dickinson and a Nathan Stanton own goal. Exeter's 1-0 win over Cambridge United in the Conference Final took them back into the Football League after an absence of five years.

**2009:** Delight for Burnley, back in the big time after 33 years thanks to a fine goal from 20 yards by Wade Elliott, and for their town which became the smallest to host Premier League football. Despair for Sheffield Utd, whose bid to regain a top-flight place ended with two players, Jamie Ward and Lee Hendrie, sent off by referee Mike Dean. Martyn Woolford capped a man-of-the match performance with an 85th minute winner for Scunthorpe, who beat Millwall 3-2 to make an immediate return to the Championship, Matt Sparrow having scored their first two goals. Gillingham also went back up at the first attempt, beating Shrewsbury with Simeon Jackson's header seconds from the end of normal time in the League Two Final. Torquay returned to the Football League after a two-year absence by beating Cambridge United 2-0 in the Conference Final.

**2010: Blackpool**, under the eccentric yet shrewd Ian Holloway, claimed the big prize two years almost to the day after the manager was sacked from his previous job at Leicester. On a scorching afternoon, with temperatures reaching 106 degrees, they twice came back from a goal down to draw level against Cardiff through Charlie Adam and Gary Taylor-Fletcher, then scored what proved to be the winner through Brett Ormerod at the end of a pulsating first half. **Millwall**, beaten in five previous play-offs, reached the Championship with the only goal of the game against Swindon from captain Paul Robinson. **Dagenham & Redbridge** defeated Rotherham 3-2 in the League Two Final, Jon Nurse scoring the winner 20 minutes from the end. **Oxford** returned to the Football League after an absence of four years with a 3-1 over York in the Conference Final.

**2011:** Scott Sinclair scored a hat-trick as **Swansea** reached the top flight, just eight years after almost going out of the Football League. Two of his goals came from the penalty spot as Reading were beaten 4-2 in the Championship Final, with Stephen Dobbie netting their other goal. The day after his father's side lost to Barcelona in the Champions League Final, Darren Ferguson led **Peterborough** back to the Championship at the first attempt with goals by Tommy Rowe, Craig Mackail-Smith and Grant McCann in the final 12 minutes against Huddersfield. John Mousinho scored the only one of the League Two Final for **Stevenage**, who won a second successive promotion by beating Torquay. **AFC Wimbledon**, formed by supporters in 2002 after the former FA Cup-winning club relocated to Milton Keynes, completed their rise from the Combined Counties to the Football League by winning a penalty shoot-out against Luton after a goalless draw in the Conference Final.

**2012**: **West Ham** were third in the Championship and second best to Blackpool in the final. But they passed the post first at Wembley, thanks to an 87th minute goal from Ricardo Vaz Te which gave Sam Allardyce's side a 2-1 victory. Allardyce brought the Portuguese striker to Upton Park from Barnsley for £500,000 – a fee dwarfed by the millions his goal was worth to the club. Goalkeepers took centre stage in the League One Final, with **Huddersfield** and Sheffield United still locked in a marathon shoot-out after a goalless 120 minutes. Alex Smithies put the 21st penalty past his opposite number Steve Simonsen, who then drove over the crossbar to give Huddersfield victory by 8-7. Nick Powell, 18, lit up the League Two Final with a spectacular volley as **Crewe** beat Cheltenham 2-0. **York** regained a Football League place after an absence of eight years by beating Luton 2-1 in the Conference decider.

**2013:** Veteran Kevin Phillips, a loser in three previous finals, came off the bench to fire **Crystal Palace** into the Premier League with an extra-time penalty. Wilfried Zaha was brought down by Marco Cassetti and 39-year-old Phillips showed nerves of steel to convert the spot-kick. A goalline clearance by Joel Ward then denied Fernando Forestieri as Watford sought an equaliser. **Yeovil** upset the odds by reaching the Championship for the first time. They defeated Brentford 2-1, Paddy Madden scoring his 23rd goal of the season and on-loan Dan Burn adding the second. **Bradford**, back at Wembley three months after their Capital One Cup adventure, swept aside Northampton 3-0 in the League Two Final with goals from James Hanson, Rory McArdle and Nahki Wells. **Newport** returned to the Football League after a 25-year absence by defeating Wrexham 2-0 in the Conference Final.

**2014**: An immediate return to the Premier League for **Queens Park Rangers** seemed unlikely when Gary O'Neil was sent off for bringing down Derby's Johnny Russell. There was still more than half-an-hour to go of a match Derby had dominated. But Rangers held on and with 90 minutes nearly up Bobby Zamora punished a mistake by captain Richard Keogh to score the only goal. **Rotherham** retrieved a 2-0 deficit against Leyton Orient with two goals by Alex Revell in the League One Final and won the eventual penalty shoot-out 4-3 for a second successive promotion. **Fleetwood** achieved their sixth promotion in ten seasons with a 1-0 victory over Burton, courtesy of a free-kick from Antoni Sarcevic in the League Two Final. Liam Hughes and Ryan Donaldson were on the mark as **Cambridge United** returned to the Football League after a nine-year absence by beating Gateshead 2-1 in the Conference Final, two months after winning the FA Trophy at Wembley

**2015: Norwich** were rewarded for a flying start with a return to the Premier League at the first attempt. Cameron Jerome put them ahead against Middlesbrough after 12 minutes of the Championship Final and Nathan Redmond made it 2-0 three minutes later, a scoreline they maintained without too many problems. Jermaine Beckford's hat-trick put **Preston** on the way to a record 4-0 victory over Swindon in the League One Final. **Southend**, who like Preston were denied automatic promotion on the final day of the regular season, beat Wycombe 7-6 on penalties after the League Two Final ended 1-1. **Bristol Rovers** were also penalty winners, by 5-3 against Grimsby in the Conference decider, so making an immediate return to the Football League.

**2016:** A goal worthy of winning any game took Hull back to the Premier League at the first attempt. Mohamed Diame, their French-born Senegal international midfielder, curled a 25-yard shot into the top corner after 72 minues for a 1-0 win over Sheffield Wednesday. Another spectacular goal, by Adam Hammill, helped Barnsley beat Millwall 3-1 on their return to Wembley for the League One Final after winning the Johnstone's Paint Trophy. AFC Wimbledon achieved their sixth promotion since being formed by supporters in 2002, defeating favourites Plymouth 2-0 in the League Two Final. Grimsby ended a six-year absence from the Football League with a 3-1 victory over Forest Green in the National League decider

**2017**: David Wagner transformed **Huddersfield** from relegation candidates into a Premier League club – with the help of German penalty-taking expertise. After a goalless Championship Play-off Final, they beat Reading 4-3 in a shoot-out clinched by Christopher Schindler'spot-kick. Steve Morison followed up his two goals in **Millwall**'s League One semi-final against Scunthorpe with the only one against Bradford, in the 85th minute at Wembley. Brad Potts and Mark Cullen were on the mark to give **Blackpool** a 2-1 victory over Exeter in the League Two Final. **Forest Green** beat Tranmere 3-1 in the National League Final, on-loan Kaiyne Woolery scoring twice.

## Play-off attendances

| | | | | | |
|---|---|---|---|---|---|
| 1987 | 20 | 310,000 | 2003 | 15 | 374,461 |
| 1988 | 19 | 305,817 | 2004 | 15 | 388,675 |
| 1989 | 18 | 234,393 | 2005 | 15 | 353,330 |
| 1990 | 15 | 291,428 | 2006 | 15 | 340,804 |
| 1991 | 15 | 266,442 | 2007 | 15 | 405,278 (record) |
| 1992 | 15 | 277,684 | 2008 | 15 | 382,032 |
| 1993 | 15 | 319,907 | 2009 | 15 | 380,329 |
| 1994 | 15 | 314,817 | 2010 | 15 | 370,055 |
| 1995 | 15 | 295,317 | 2011 | 15 | 310,998 |
| 1996 | 15 | 308,515 | 2012 | 15 | 332,930 |
| 1997 | 15 | 309,085 | 2013 | 15 | 346,062 |
| 1998 | 15 | 320,795 | 2014 | 15 | 307,011 |
| 1999 | 15 | 372,969 | 2015 | 15 | 367,374 |
| 2000 | 15 | 333,999 | 2016 | 15 | 393,145 |
| 2001 | 15 | 317,745 | 2017 | 15 | 323,727 |
| 2002 | 15 | 327,894 | 2018 | 15 | 373,295 |

# THE THINGS THEY SAY ...

'It's a long time since I came home from a night out in the daylight' – **David Wagner**, Huddersfield manager, after celebrating his team's Premier League survival.

'With three teams you need a bandleader and I'm happy to hold the baton' – **Roy Hodgson**, Crystal Palace manager, thanking his players, coaches and medical staff for preserving Premier League status.

'I didn't think we would get into the play-offs, never mind the Premier League' – **Neil Warnock**, Cardiff manager, after his team's promotion.

'Someone said to me it's like winning the world snooker championship with a toothpick. I wouldn't go that far, but......' – **John Coleman**, Accrington manager, after his side won League Two against all the odds.

'Glasgow isn't a city where you can sit pretty and develop. It's either triumph or disaster.' – **Steven Gerrard** on his appointment as manager of Rangers.

This is not a box office, showbiz appointment just to boost the profile of the club' – **Andy Pilley**, Fleetwood chairman, on giving Joey Barton the manager's job

'I wouldn't leave for any other club. Barcelona is a place of magic for me' – **Philippe Coutinho** on his £142m move from Liverpool.

# ENGLISH HONOURS LIST

## PREMIER LEAGUE

| | First | Pts | Second | Pts | Third | Pts |
|---|---|---|---|---|---|---|
| 1992–3*a* | Manchester Utd | 84 | Aston Villa | 74 | Norwich | 72 |
| 1993–4*a* | Manchester Utd | 92 | Blackburn | 84 | Newcastle | 77 |
| 1994–5*a* | Blackburn | 89 | Manchester Utd | 88 | Nottm Forest | 77 |
| 1995–6*b* | Manchester Utd | 82 | Newcastle | 78 | Liverpool | 71 |
| 1996–7*b* | Manchester Utd | 75 | Newcastle | 68 | Arsenal | 68 |
| 1997–8*b* | Arsenal | 78 | Manchester Utd | 77 | Liverpool | 65 |
| 1998–9*b* | Manchester Utd | 79 | Arsenal | 78 | Chelsea | 75 |
| 1999–00*b* | Manchester Utd | 91 | Arsenal | 73 | Leeds | 69 |
| 2000–01*b* | Manchester Utd | 80 | Arsenal | 70 | Liverpool | 69 |
| 2001–02*b* | Arsenal | 87 | Liverpool | 80 | Manchester Utd | 77 |
| 2002–03*b* | Manchester Utd | 83 | Arsenal | 78 | Newcastle | 69 |
| 2003–04*b* | Arsenal | 90 | Chelsea | 79 | Manchester Utd | 75 |
| 2004–05*b* | Chelsea | 95 | Arsenal | 83 | Manchester Utd | 77 |
| 2005–06*b* | Chelsea | 91 | Manchester Utd | 83 | Liverpool | 82 |
| 2006–07*b* | Manchester Utd | 89 | Chelsea | 83 | Liverpool | 68 |
| 2007–08*b* | Manchester Utd | 87 | Chelsea | 85 | Arsenal | 83 |
| 2008–09*b* | Manchester Utd | 90 | Liverpool | 86 | Chelsea | 83 |
| 2009–10*b* | Chelsea | 86 | Manchester Utd | 85 | Arsenal | 75 |
| 2010–11*b* | Manchester Utd | 80 | Chelsea | 71 | Manchester City | 71 |
| 2011–12*b* | *Manchester City | 89 | Manchester Ud | 89 | Arsenal | 70 |
| 2012–13*b* | Manchester Utd | 89 | Manchester City | 78 | Chelsea | 75 |
| 2013–14*b* | Manchester City | 86 | Liverpool | 84 | Chelsea | 82 |
| 2014–15*b* | Chelsea | 87 | Manchester City | 79 | Arsenal | 75 |
| 2015–16*b* | Leicester | 81 | Arsenal | 71 | Tottenham | 70 |
| 2016–17*b* | Chelsea | 93 | Tottenham | 86 | Manchester City | 78 |
| 2017–18*b* | Manchester City | 100 | Manchester Utd | 81 | Tottenham | 77 |

* won on goal difference. Maximum points: *a*, 126; *b*, 114

## FOOTBALL LEAGUE

### FIRST DIVISION

| | First | Pts | Second | Pts | Third | Pts |
|---|---|---|---|---|---|---|
| 1992–3 | Newcastle | 96 | West Ham | 88 | ††Portsmouth | 88 |
| 1993–4 | Crystal Palace | 90 | Nottm Forest | 83 | ††Millwall | 74 |
| 1994–5 | Middlesbrough | 82 | ††Reading | 79 | Bolton | 77 |
| 1995–6 | Sunderland | 83 | Derby | 79 | ††Crystal Palace | 75 |
| 1996–7 | Bolton | 98 | Barnsley | 80 | ††Wolves | 76 |
| 1997–8 | Nottm Forest | 94 | Middlesbrough | 91 | ††Sunderland | 90 |
| 1998–9 | Sunderland | 105 | Bradford City | 87 | ††Ipswich | 86 |
| 1999–00 | Charlton | 91 | Manchester City | 89 | Ipswich | 87 |
| 2000–01 | Fulham | 101 | Blackburn | 91 | Bolton | 87 |
| 2001–02 | Manchester City | 99 | WBA | 89 | ††Wolves | 86 |
| 2002–03 | Portsmouth | 98 | Leicester | 92 | ††Sheffield Utd | 80 |
| 2003–04 | Norwich | 94 | WBA | 86 | ††Sunderland | 79 |

### CHAMPIONSHIP

| | First | Pts | Second | Pts | Third | Pts |
|---|---|---|---|---|---|---|
| 2004–05 | Sunderland | 94 | Wigan | 87 | ††Ipswich | 85 |
| 2005–06 | Reading | 106 | Sheffield Utd | 90 | Watford | 81 |
| 2006–07 | Sunderland | 88 | Birmingham | 86 | Derby | 84 |
| 2007–08 | WBA | 81 | Stoke | 79 | Hull | 75 |
| 2008–09 | Wolves | 90 | Birmingham | 83 | ††Sheffield Utd | 80 |
| 2009–10 | Newcastle | 102 | WBA | 91 | ††Nottm Forest | 79 |
| 2010–11 | QPR | 88 | Norwich | 84 | Swansea | 80 |

| | | | | | | |
|---|---|---|---|---|---|---|
| 2011–12 | Reading | 89 | Southampton | 88 | West Ham | 86 |
| 2012–13 | Cardiff | 87 | Hull | 79 | ††Watford | 77 |
| 2013–14 | Leicester | 102 | Burnley | 93 | ††Derby | 85 |
| 2014–15 | Bournemouth | 90 | Watford | 89 | Norwich | 86 |
| 2015–16 | Burnley | 93 | Middlesbrough | 89 | ††Brighton | 89 |
| 2016–17 | Newcastle | 94 | Brighton | 93 | ††Reading | 85 |
| 2017–18 | Wolves | 99 | Cardiff | 90 | Fulham | 88 |

Maximum points: 138 ††Not promoted after play–offs

## SECOND DIVISION

| | | | | | | |
|---|---|---|---|---|---|---|
| 1992–3 | Stoke | 93 | Bolton | 90 | ††Port Vale | 89 |
| 1993–4 | Reading | 89 | Port Vale | 88 | ††Plymouth Argyle | 85 |
| 1994–5 | Birmingham | 89 | ††Brentford | 85 | ††Crewe | 83 |
| 1995–6 | Swindon | 92 | Oxford Utd | 83 | ††Blackpool | 82 |
| 1996–7 | Bury | 84 | Stockport | 82 | ††Luton | 78 |
| 1997–8 | Watford | 88 | Bristol City | 85 | Grimsby | 72 |
| 1998–9 | Fulham | 101 | Walsall | 87 | Manchester City | 82 |
| 1999–00 | Preston | 95 | Burnley | 88 | Gillingham | 85 |
| 2000–01 | Millwall | 93 | Rotherham | 91 | ††Reading | 86 |
| 2001–02 | Brighton | 90 | Reading | 84 | ††Brentford | 83 |
| 2002–03 | Wigan | 100 | Crewe | 86 | ††Bristol City | 83 |
| 2003–04 | Plymouth Argyle | 90 | QPR | 83 | ††Bristol City | 82 |

## LEAGUE ONE

| | | | | | | |
|---|---|---|---|---|---|---|
| 2004–05 | Luton | 98 | Hull | 86 | ††Tranmere | 79 |
| 2005–06 | Southend | 82 | Colchester | 79 | ††Brentford | 76 |
| 2006–07 | Scunthorpe | 91 | Bristol City | 85 | Blackpool | 83 |
| 2007–08 | Swansea | 92 | Nottm Forest | 82 | Doncaster | 80 |
| 2008–09 | Leicester | 96 | Peterborough | 89 | ††MK Dons | 87 |
| 2009–10 | Norwich | 95 | Leeds | 86 | Millwall | 85 |
| 2010–11 | Brighton | 95 | Southampton | 92 | ††Huddersfield | 87 |
| 2011–12 | Charlton | 101 | Sheffield Wed | 93 | ††Sheffield Utd | 90 |
| 2012–13 | Doncaster | 84 | Bournemouth | 83 | ††Brentford | 79 |
| 2013–14 | Wolves | 103 | Brentford | 94 | ††Leyton Orient | 86 |
| 2014–15 | Bristol City | 99 | MK Dons | 91 | Preston | 89 |
| 2015–16 | Wigan | 87 | Burton | 85 | ††Walsall | 84 |
| 2016–17 | Sheffield Utd | 100 | Bolton | 86 | ††Scunthorpe | 82 |
| 2017–18 | Wigan | 98 | Blackburn | 96 | ††Shrewsbury | 87 |

Maximum points: 138 †† Not promoted after play–offs

## THIRD DIVISION

| | | | | | | |
|---|---|---|---|---|---|---|
| 1992–3*a* | Cardiff | 83 | Wrexham | 80 | Barnet | 79 |
| 1993–4*a* | Shrewsbury | 79 | Chester | 74 | Crewe | 73 |
| 1994–5*a* | Carlisle | 91 | Walsall | 83 | Chesterfield | 81 |
| 1995–6*b* | Preston | 86 | Gillingham | 83 | Bury | 79 |
| 1996–7*b* | Wigan | 87 | Fulham | 87 | Carlisle | 84 |
| 1997–8*b* | Notts Co | 99 | Macclesfield | 82 | Lincoln | 75 |
| 1998–9*b* | Brentford | 85 | Cambridge Utd | 81 | Cardiff | 80 |
| 1999–00*b* | Swansea | 85 | Rotherham | 84 | Northampton | 82 |
| 2000–01*b* | Brighton | 92 | Cardiff | 82 | *Chesterfield | 80 |
| 2001–02*b* | Plymouth Argyle | 102 | Luton | 97 | Mansfield | 79 |
| 2002–03*b* | Rushden & D | 87 | Hartlepool Utd | 85 | Wrexham | 84 |
| 2003–04*b* | Doncaster | 92 | Hull | 88 | Torquay | 81 |

* Deducted 9 points for financial irregularities

## LEAGUE TWO

| | | | | | | |
|---|---|---|---|---|---|---|
| 2004–05*b* | Yeovil | 83 | Scunthorpe | 80 | Swansea | 80 |

| | | | | | | |
|---|---|---|---|---|---|---|
| 2005–06*b* | Carlisle | 86 | Northampton | 83 | Leyton Orient | 81 |
| 2006–07*b* | Walsall | 89 | Hartlepool | 88 | Swindon | 85 |
| 2007–08*b* | MK Dons | 97 | Peterborough | 92 | Hereford | 88 |
| 2008–09*b* | Brentford | 85 | Exeter | 79 | Wycombe | 78 |
| 2009–10*b* | Notts Co | 93 | Bournemouth | 83 | Rochdale | 82 |
| 2010–11*b* | Chesterfield | 86 | Bury | 81 | Wycombe | 80 |
| 2011–12*b* | Swindon | 93 | Shrewsbury | 88 | Crawley | 84 |
| 2012–13*b* | Gillingham | 83 | Rotherham | 79 | Port Vale | 78 |
| 2013–14*b* | Chesterfield | 84 | Scunthorpe | 81 | Rochdale | 81 |
| 2014–15*b* | Burton | 94 | Shrewsbury | 89 | Bury | 85 |
| 2015–16*b* | Northampton | 99 | Oxford | 86 | Bristol Rov | 85 |
| 2016–17*b* | Portsmouth | 87 | Plymouth | 87 | Doncaster | 85 |
| 2017–18*b* | Accrington | 93 | Luton | 88 | Wycombe | 84 |

Maximum points: *a*, 126; *b*, 138;

## FOOTBALL LEAGUE 1888–1992

| | | | | | | |
|---|---|---|---|---|---|---|
| 1888–89*a* | Preston | 40 | Aston Villa | 29 | Wolves | 28 |
| 1889–90*a* | Preston | 33 | Everton | 31 | Blackburn | 27 |
| 1890–1*a* | Everton | 29 | Preston | 27 | Notts Co | 26 |
| 1891–2*b* | Sunderland | 42 | Preston | 37 | Bolton | 36 |

## OLD FIRST DIVISION

| | | | | | | |
|---|---|---|---|---|---|---|
| 1892–3*c* | Sunderland | 48 | Preston | 37 | Everton | 36 |
| 1893–4*c* | Aston Villa | 44 | Sunderland | 38 | Derby | 36 |
| 1894–5*c* | Sunderland | 47 | Everton | 42 | Aston Villa | 39 |
| 1895–6*c* | Aston Villa | 45 | Derby | 41 | Everton | 39 |
| 1896–7*c* | Aston Villa | 47 | Sheffield Utd | 36 | Derby | 36 |
| 1897–8*c* | Sheffield Utd | 42 | Sunderland | 39 | Wolves | 35 |
| 1898–9*d* | Aston Villa | 45 | Liverpool | 43 | Burnley | 39 |
| 1899–1900*d* | Aston Villa | 50 | Sheffield Utd | 48 | Sunderland | 41 |
| 1900–1*d* | Liverpool | 45 | Sunderland | 43 | Notts Co | 40 |
| 1901–2*d* | Sunderland | 44 | Everton | 41 | Newcastle | 37 |
| 1902–3*d* | The Wednesday | 42 | Aston Villa | 41 | Sunderland | 41 |
| 1903–4*d* | The Wednesday | 47 | Manchester City | 44 | Everton | 43 |
| 1904–5*d* | Newcastle | 48 | Everton | 47 | Manchester City | 46 |
| 1905–6*e* | Liverpool | 51 | Preston | 47 | The Wednesday | 44 |
| 1906–7*e* | Newcastle | 51 | Bristol City | 48 | Everton | 45 |
| 1907–8*e* | Manchester Utd | 52 | Aston Villa | 43 | Manchester City | 43 |
| 1908–9*e* | Newcastle | 53 | Everton | 46 | Sunderland | 44 |
| 1909–10*e* | Aston Villa | 53 | Liverpool | 48 | Blackburn | 45 |
| 1910–11*e* | Manchester Utd | 52 | Aston Villa | 51 | Sunderland | 45 |
| 1911–12*e* | Blackburn | 49 | Everton | 46 | Newcastle | 44 |
| 1912–13*e* | Sunderland | 54 | Aston Villa | 50 | Sheffield Wed | 49 |
| 1913–14*e* | Blackburn | 51 | Aston Villa | 44 | Middlesbrough | 43 |
| 1914–15*e* | Everton | 46 | Oldham | 45 | Blackburn | 43 |
| 1919–20*f* | WBA | 60 | Burnley | 51 | Chelsea | 49 |
| 1920–1*f* | Burnley | 59 | Manchester City | 54 | Bolton | 52 |
| 1921–2*f* | Liverpool | 57 | Tottenham | 51 | Burnley | 49 |
| 1922–3*f* | Liverpool | 60 | Sunderland | 54 | Huddersfield | 53 |
| 1923–4*f* | *Huddersfield | 57 | Cardiff | 57 | Sunderland | 53 |
| 1924–5*f* | Huddersfield | 58 | WBA | 56 | Bolton | 55 |
| 1925–6*f* | Huddersfield | 57 | Arsenal | 52 | Sunderland | 48 |
| 1926–7*f* | Newcastle | 56 | Huddersfield | 51 | Sunderland | 49 |
| 1927–8*f* | Everton | 53 | Huddersfield | 51 | Leicester | 48 |
| 1928–9*f* | Sheffield Wed | 52 | Leicester | 51 | Aston Villa | 50 |

| | | | | | | |
|---|---|---|---|---|---|---|
| 1929–30*f* | Sheffield Wed | 60 | Derby | 50 | Manchester City | 47 |
| 1930–1*f* | Arsenal | 66 | Aston Villa | 59 | Sheffield Wed | 52 |
| 1931–2*f* | Everton | 56 | Arsenal | 54 | Sheffield Wed | 50 |
| 1932–3*f* | Arsenal | 58 | Aston Villa | 54 | Sheffield Wed | 51 |
| 1933–4*f* | Arsenal | 59 | Huddersfield | 56 | Tottenham | 49 |
| 1934–5*f* | Arsenal | 58 | Sunderland | 54 | Sheffield Wed | 49 |
| 1935–6*f* | Sunderland | 56 | Derby | 48 | Huddersfield | 48 |
| 1936–7*f* | Manchester City | 57 | Charlton | 54 | Arsenal | 52 |
| 1937–8*f* | Arsenal | 52 | Wolves | 51 | Preston | 49 |
| 1938–9*f* | Everton | 59 | Wolves | 55 | Charlton | 50 |
| 1946–7*f* | Liverpool | 57 | Manchester Utd | 56 | Wolves | 56 |
| 1947–8*f* | Arsenal | 59 | Manchester Utd | 52 | Burnley | 52 |
| 1948–9*f* | Portsmouth | 58 | Manchester Utd | 53 | Derby | 53 |
| 1949–50*f* | *Portsmouth | 53 | Wolves | 53 | Sunderland | 52 |
| 1950–1*f* | Tottenham | 60 | Manchester Utd | 56 | Blackpool | 50 |
| 1951–2*f* | Manchester Utd | 57 | Tottenham | 53 | Arsenal | 53 |
| 1952–3*f* | *Arsenal | 54 | Preston | 54 | Wolves | 51 |
| 1953–4*f* | Wolves | 57 | WBA | 53 | Huddersfield | 51 |
| 1954–5*f* | Chelsea | 52 | Wolves | 48 | Portsmouth | 48 |
| 1955–6*f* | Manchester Utd | 60 | Blackpool | 49 | Wolves | 49 |
| 1956–7*f* | Manchester Utd | 64 | Tottenham | 56 | Preston | 56 |
| 1957–8*f* | Wolves | 64 | Preston | 59 | Tottenham | 51 |
| 1958–9*f* | Wolves | 61 | Manchester Utd | 55 | Arsenal | 50 |
| 1959–60*f* | Burnley | 55 | Wolves | 54 | Tottenham | 53 |
| 1960–1*f* | Tottenham | 66 | Sheffield Wed | 58 | Wolves | 57 |
| 1961–2*f* | Ipswich | 56 | Burnley | 53 | Tottenham | 52 |
| 1962–3*f* | Everton | 61 | Tottenham | 55 | Burnley | 54 |
| 1963–4*f* | Liverpool | 57 | Manchester Utd | 53 | Everton | 52 |
| 1964–5*f* | *Manchester Utd | 61 | Leeds | 61 | Chelsea | 56 |
| 1965–6*f* | Liverpool | 61 | Leeds | 55 | Burnley | 55 |
| 1966–7*f* | Manchester Utd | 60 | Nottm Forest | 56 | Tottenham | 56 |
| 1967–8*f* | Manchester City | 58 | Manchester Utd | 56 | Liverpool | 55 |
| 1968–9*f* | Leeds | 67 | Liverpool | 61 | Everton | 57 |
| 1969–70*f* | Everton | 66 | Leeds | 57 | Chelsea | 55 |
| 1970–1*f* | Arsenal | 65 | Leeds | 64 | Tottenham | 52 |
| 1971–2*f* | Derby | 58 | Leeds | 57 | Liverpool | 57 |
| 1972–3*f* | Liverpool | 60 | Arsenal | 57 | Leeds | 53 |
| 1973–4*f* | Leeds | 62 | Liverpool | 57 | Derby | 48 |
| 1974–5*f* | Derby | 53 | Liverpool | 51 | Ipswich | 51 |
| 1975–6*f* | Liverpool | 60 | QPR | 59 | Manchester Utd | 56 |
| 1976–7*f* | Liverpool | 57 | Manchester City | 56 | Ipswich | 52 |
| 1977–8*f* | Nottm Forest | 64 | Liverpool | 57 | Everton | 55 |
| 1978–9*f* | Liverpool | 68 | Nottm Forest | 60 | WBA | 59 |
| 1979–80*f* | Liverpool | 60 | Manchester Utd | 58 | Ipswich | 53 |
| 1980–1*f* | Aston Villa | 60 | Ipswich | 56 | Arsenal | 53 |
| 1981–2*g* | Liverpool | 87 | Ipswich | 83 | Manchester Utd | 78 |
| 1982–3*g* | Liverpool | 82 | Watford | 71 | Manchester Utd | 70 |
| 1983–4*g* | Liverpool | 80 | Southampton | 77 | Nottm Forest | 74 |
| 1984–5*g* | Everton | 90 | Liverpool | 77 | Tottenham | 77 |
| 1985–6*g* | Liverpool | 88 | Everton | 86 | West Ham | 84 |
| 1986–7*g* | Everton | 86 | Liverpool | 77 | Tottenham | 71 |
| 1987–8*h* | Liverpool | 90 | Manchester Utd | 81 | Nottm Forest | 73 |
| 1988–9*j* | ††Arsenal | 76 | Liverpool | 76 | Nottm Forest | 64 |
| 1989–90*j* | Liverpool | 79 | Aston Villa | 70 | Tottenham | 63 |
| 1990–1*j* | Arsenal | 83 | Liverpool | 76 | Crystal Palace | 69 |

| | | | | | | |
|---|---|---|---|---|---|---|
| 1991–2*g* | Leeds | 82 | Manchester Utd | 78 | Sheffield Wed | 75 |

Maximum points: *a*, 44; *b*, 52; *c*, 60; *d*, 68; *e*, 76; *f*, 84; *g*, 126; *h*, 120; *j*, 114
*Won on goal average †Won on goal diff ††Won on goals scored No comp 1915–19 –1939–46

## OLD SECOND DIVISION 1892–1992

| | | | | | | |
|---|---|---|---|---|---|---|
| 1892–3*a* | Small Heath | 36 | Sheffield Utd | 35 | Darwen | 30 |
| 1893–4*b* | Liverpool | 50 | Small Heath | 42 | Notts Co | 39 |
| 1894–5*c* | Bury | 48 | Notts Co | 39 | Newton Heath | 38 |
| 1895–6*c* | *Liverpool | 46 | Manchester City | 46 | Grimsby | 42 |
| 1896–7*c* | Notts Co | 42 | Newton Heath | 39 | Grimsby | 38 |
| 1897–8*c* | Burnley | 48 | Newcastle | 45 | Manchester City | 39 |
| 1898–9*d* | Manchester City | 52 | Glossop | 46 | Leicester Fosse | 45 |
| 1899–1900*d* | The Wednesday | 54 | Bolton | 52 | Small Heath | 46 |
| 1900–1*d* | Grimsby | 49 | Small Heath | 48 | Burnley | 44 |
| 1901–2*d* | WBA | 55 | Middlesbrough | 51 | Preston | 42 |
| 1902–3*d* | Manchester City | 54 | Small Heath | 51 | Woolwich Arsenal | 48 |
| 1903–4*d* | Preston | 50 | Woolwich Arsenal | 49 | Manchester Utd | 48 |
| 1904–5*d* | Liverpool | 58 | Bolton | 56 | Manchester Utd | 53 |
| 1905–6*e* | Bristol City | 66 | Manchester Utd | 62 | Chelsea | 53 |
| 1906–7*e* | Nottm Forest | 60 | Chelsea | 57 | Leicester Fosse | 48 |
| 1907–8*e* | Bradford City | 54 | Leicester Fosse | 52 | Oldham | 50 |
| 1908–9*e* | Bolton | 52 | Tottenham | 51 | WBA | 51 |
| 1909–10*e* | Manchester City | 54 | Oldham | 53 | Hull | 53 |
| 1910–11*e* | WBA | 53 | Bolton | 51 | Chelsea | 49 |
| 1911–12*e* | *Derby | 54 | Chelsea | 54 | Burnley | 52 |
| 1912–13*e* | Preston | 53 | Burnley | 50 | Birmingham | 46 |
| 1913–14*e* | Notts Co | 53 | Bradford PA | 49 | Woolwich Arsenal | 49 |
| 1914–15*e* | Derby | 53 | Preston | 50 | Barnsley | 47 |
| 1919–20*f* | Tottenham | 70 | Huddersfield | 64 | Birmingham | 56 |
| 1920–1*f* | *Birmingham | 58 | Cardiff | 58 | Bristol City | 51 |
| 1921–2*f* | Nottm Forest | 56 | Stoke | 52 | Barnsley | 52 |
| 1922–3*f* | Notts Co | 53 | West Ham | 51 | Leicester | 51 |
| 1923–4*f* | Leeds | 54 | Bury | 51 | Derby | 51 |
| 1924–5*f* | Leicester | 59 | Manchester Utd | 57 | Derby | 55 |
| 1925–6*f* | Sheffield Wed | 60 | Derby | 57 | Chelsea | 52 |
| 1926–7*f* | Middlesbrough | 62 | Portsmouth | 54 | Manchester City | 54 |
| 1927–8*f* | Manchester City | 59 | Leeds | 57 | Chelsea | 54 |
| 1928–9*f* | Middlesbrough | 55 | Grimsby | 53 | Bradford City | 48 |
| 1929–30*f* | Blackpool | 58 | Chelsea | 55 | Oldham | 53 |
| 1930–1*f* | Everton | 61 | WBA | 54 | Tottenham | 51 |
| 1931–2*f* | Wolves | 56 | Leeds | 54 | Stoke | 52 |
| 1932–3*f* | Stoke | 56 | Tottenham | 55 | Fulham | 50 |
| 1933–4*f* | Grimsby | 59 | Preston | 52 | Bolton | 51 |
| 1934–5*f* | Brentford | 61 | Bolton | 56 | West Ham | 56 |
| 1935–6*f* | Manchester Utd | 56 | Charlton | 55 | Sheffield Utd | 52 |
| 1936–7*f* | Leicester | 56 | Blackpool | 55 | Bury | 52 |
| 1937–8*f* | Aston Villa | 57 | Manchester Utd | 53 | Sheffield Utd | 53 |
| 1938–9*f* | Blackburn | 55 | Sheffield Utd | 54 | Sheffield Wed | 53 |
| 1946–7*f* | Manchester City | 62 | Burnley | 58 | Birmingham | 55 |
| 1947–8*f* | Birmingham | 59 | Newcastle | 56 | Southampton | 52 |
| 1948–9*f* | Fulham | 57 | WBA | 56 | Southampton | 55 |
| 1949–50*f* | Tottenham | 61 | Sheffield Wed | 52 | Sheffield Utd | 52 |
| 1950–1*f* | Preston | 57 | Manchester City | 52 | Cardiff | 50 |
| 1951–2*f* | Sheffield Wed | 53 | Cardiff | 51 | Birmingham | 51 |
| 1952–3*f* | Sheffield Utd | 60 | Huddersfield | 58 | Luton | 52 |

| | | | | | | |
|---|---|---|---|---|---|---|
| 1953–4*f* | *Leicester | 56 | Everton | 56 | Blackburn | 55 |
| 1954–5*f* | *Birmingham | 54 | Luton | 54 | Rotherham | 54 |
| 1955–6*f* | Sheffield Wed | 55 | Leeds | 52 | Liverpool | 48 |
| 1956–7*f* | Leicester | 61 | Nottm Forest | 54 | Liverpool | 53 |
| 1957–8*f* | West Ham | 57 | Blackburn | 56 | Charlton | 55 |
| 1958–9*f* | Sheffield Wed | 62 | Fulham | 60 | Sheffield Utd | 53 |
| 1959–60*f* | Aston Villa | 59 | Cardiff | 58 | Liverpool | 50 |
| 1960–1*f* | Ipswich | 59 | Sheffield Utd | 58 | Liverpool | 52 |
| 1961–2*f* | Liverpool | 62 | Leyton Orient | 54 | Sunderland | 53 |
| 1962–3*f* | Stoke | 53 | Chelsea | 52 | Sunderland | 52 |
| 1963–4*f* | Leeds | 63 | Sunderland | 61 | Preston | 56 |
| 1964–5*f* | Newcastle | 57 | Northampton | 56 | Bolton | 50 |
| 1965–6*f* | Manchester City | 59 | Southampton | 54 | Coventry | 53 |
| 1966–7*f* | Coventry | 59 | Wolves | 58 | Carlisle | 52 |
| 1967–8*f* | Ipswich | 59 | QPR | 58 | Blackpool | 58 |
| 1968–9*f* | Derby | 63 | Crystal Palace | 56 | Charlton | 50 |
| 1969–70*f* | Huddersfield | 60 | Blackpool | 53 | Leicester | 51 |
| 1970–1*f* | Leicester | 59 | Sheffield Utd | 56 | Cardiff | 53 |
| 1971–2*f* | Norwich | 57 | Birmingham | 56 | Millwall | 55 |
| 1972–3*f* | Burnley | 62 | QPR | 61 | Aston Villa | 50 |
| 1973–4*f* | Middlesbrough | 65 | Luton | 50 | Carlisle | 49 |
| 1974–5*f* | Manchester Utd | 61 | Aston Villa | 58 | Norwich | 53 |
| 1975–6*f* | Sunderland | 56 | Bristol City | 53 | WBA | 53 |
| 1976–7*f* | Wolves | 57 | Chelsea | 55 | Nottm Forest | 52 |
| 1977–8*f* | Bolton | 58 | Southampton | 57 | Tottenham | 56 |
| 1978–9*f* | Crystal Palace | 57 | Brighton | 56 | Stoke | 56 |
| 1979–80*f* | Leicester | 55 | Sunderland | 54 | Birmingham | 53 |
| 1980–1*f* | West Ham | 66 | Notts Co | 53 | Swansea | 50 |
| 1981–2*g* | Luton | 88 | Watford | 80 | Norwich | 71 |
| 1982–3*g* | QPR | 85 | Wolves | 75 | Leicester | 70 |
| 1983–4*g* | †Chelsea | 88 | Sheffield Wed | 88 | Newcastle | 80 |
| 1984–5*g* | Oxford Utd | 84 | Birmingham | 82 | Manchester City | 74 |
| 1985–6*g* | Norwich | 84 | Charlton | 77 | Wimbledon | 76 |
| 1986–7*g* | Derby | 84 | Portsmouth | 78 | ††Oldham | 75 |
| 1987–8*h* | Millwall | 82 | Aston Villa | 78 | Middlesbrough | 78 |
| 1988–9*j* | Chelsea | 99 | Manchester City | 82 | Crystal Palace | 81 |
| 1989–90j | †Leeds | 85 | Sheffield Utd | 85 | †† Newcastle | 80 |
| 1990–1*j* | Oldham | 88 | West Ham | 87 | Sheffield Wed | 82 |
| 1991–2*j* | Ipswich | 84 | Middlesbrough | 80 | †† Derby | 78 |

Maximum points: *a*, 44; *b*, 56; *c*, 60; *d*, 68; *e*, 76; *f*, 84; *g*, 126; *h*, 132; *j*, 138 * Won on goal average † Won on goal difference †† Not promoted after play–offs

## THIRD DIVISION 1958–92

| | | | | | | |
|---|---|---|---|---|---|---|
| 1958–9 | Plymouth Argyle | 62 | Hull | 61 | Brentford | 57 |
| 1959–60 | Southampton | 61 | Norwich | 59 | Shrewsbury | 52 |
| 1960–1 | Bury | 68 | Walsall | 62 | QPR | 60 |
| 1961–2 | Portsmouth | 65 | Grimsby | 62 | Bournemouth | 59 |
| 1962–3 | Northampton | 62 | Swindon | 58 | Port Vale | 54 |
| 1963–4 | *Coventry | 60 | Crystal Palace | 60 | Watford | 58 |
| 1964–5 | Carlisle | 60 | Bristol City | 59 | Mansfield | 59 |
| 1965–6 | Hull | 69 | Millwall | 65 | QPR | 57 |
| 1966–7 | QPR | 67 | Middlesbrough | 55 | Watford | 54 |
| 1967–8 | Oxford Utd | 57 | Bury | 56 | Shrewsbury | 55 |
| 1968–9 | *Watford | 64 | Swindon | 64 | Luton | 61 |
| 1969–70 | Orient | 62 | Luton | 60 | Bristol Rov | 56 |
| 1970–1 | Preston | 61 | Fulham | 60 | Halifax | 56 |

| | | | | | | |
|---|---|---|---|---|---|---|
| 1971–2 | Aston Villa | 70 | Brighton | 65 | Bournemouth | 62 |
| 1972–3 | Bolton | 61 | Notts Co | 57 | Blackburn | 55 |
| 1973–4 | Oldham | 62 | Bristol Rov | 61 | York | 61 |
| 1974–5 | Blackburn | 60 | Plymouth Argyle | 59 | Charlton | 55 |
| 1975–6 | Hereford | 63 | Cardiff | 57 | Millwall | 56 |
| 1976–7 | Mansfield | 64 | Brighton | 61 | Crystal Palace | 59 |
| 1977–8 | Wrexham | 61 | Cambridge Utd | 58 | Preston | 56 |
| 1978–9 | Shrewsbury | 61 | Watford | 60 | Swansea | 60 |
| 1979–80 | Grimsby | 62 | Blackburn | 59 | Sheffield Wed | 58 |
| 1980–1 | Rotherham | 61 | Barnsley | 59 | Charlton | 59 |
| †1981–2 | **Burnley | 80 | Carlisle | 80 | Fulham | 78 |
| †1982–3 | Portsmouth | 91 | Cardiff | 86 | Huddersfield | 82 |
| †1983–4 | Oxford Utd | 95 | Wimbledon | 87 | Sheffield Utd | 83 |
| †1984–5 | Bradford City | 94 | Millwall | 90 | Hull | 87 |
| †1985–6 | Reading | 94 | Plymouth Argyle | 87 | Derby | 84 |
| †1986–7 | Bournemouth | 97 | Middlesbrough | 94 | Swindon | 87 |
| †1987–8 | Sunderland | 93 | Brighton | 84 | Walsall | 82 |
| †1988–9 | Wolves | 92 | Sheffield Utd | 84 | Port Vale | 84 |
| †1989–90 | Bristol Rov | 93 | Bristol City | 91 | Notts Co | 87 |
| †1990–1 | Cambridge Utd | 86 | Southend | 85 | Grimsby | 83 |
| †1991–2 | Brentford | 82 | Birmingham | 81 | ††Huddersfield | 78 |

* Won on goal average ** Won on goal difference † Maximum points 138 (previously 92) †† Not promoted after play–offs

## FOURTH DIVISION 1958–92

| | | | | | | | | |
|---|---|---|---|---|---|---|---|---|
| 1958–9 | Port Vale | 64 | Coventry | 60 | York | 60 | Shrewsbury | 58 |
| 1959–60 | Walsall | 65 | Notts Co | 60 | Torquay | 60 | Watford | 57 |
| 1960–1 | Peterborough | 66 | Crystal Palace | 64 | Northampton | 60 | Bradford PA | 60 |
| 1961–2 | Millwall | 56 | Colchester | 55 | Wrexham | 53 | Carlisle | 52 |
| 1962–3 | Brentford | 62 | Oldham | 59 | Crewe | 59 | Mansfield | 57 |
| 1963–4 | *Gillingham | 60 | Carlisle | 60 | Workington | 59 | Exeter | 58 |
| 1964–5 | Brighton | 63 | Millwall | 62 | York | 62 | Oxford Utd | 61 |
| 1965–6 | *Doncaster | 59 | Darlington | 59 | Torquay | 58 | Colchester | 56 |
| 1966–7 | Stockport | 64 | Southport | 59 | Barrow | 59 | Tranmere | 58 |
| 1967–8 | Luton | 66 | Barnsley | 61 | Hartlepool Utd | 60 | Crewe | 58 |
| 1968–9 | Doncaster | 59 | Halifax | 57 | Rochdale | 56 | Bradford City | 56 |
| 1969–70 | Chesterfield | 64 | Wrexham | 61 | Swansea | 60 | Port Vale | 59 |
| 1970–1 | Notts Co | 69 | Bournemouth | 60 | Oldham | 59 | York | 56 |
| 1971–2 | Grimsby | 63 | Southend | 60 | Brentford | 59 | Scunthorpe | 57 |
| 1972–3 | Southport | 62 | Hereford | 58 | Cambridge Utd | 57 | Aldershot | 56 |
| 1973–4 | Peterborough | 65 | Gillingham | 62 | Colchester | 60 | Bury | 59 |
| 1974–5 | Mansfield | 68 | Shrewsbury | 62 | Rotherham | 58 | Chester | 57 |
| 1975–6 | Lincoln | 74 | Northampton | 68 | Reading | 60 | Tranmere | 58 |
| 1976–7 | Cambridge Utd | 65 | Exeter | 62 | Colchester | 59 | Bradford City | 59 |
| 1977–8 | Watford | 71 | Southend | 60 | Swansea | 56 | Brentford | 59 |
| 1978–9 | Reading | 65 | Grimsby | 61 | Wimbledon | 61 | Barnsley | 61 |
| 1979–80 | Huddersfield | 66 | Walsall | 64 | Newport | 61 | Portsmouth | 60 |
| 1980–1 | Southend | 67 | Lincoln | 65 | Doncaster | 56 | Wimbledon | 55 |
| †1981–2 | Sheffield Utd | 96 | Bradford City | 91 | Wigan | 91 | Bournemouth | 88 |
| †1982–3 | Wimbledon | 98 | Hull | 90 | Port Vale | 88 | Scunthorpe | 83 |
| †1983–4 | York | 101 | Doncaster | 85 | Reading | 82 | Bristol City | 82 |
| †1984–5 | Chesterfield | 91 | Blackpool | 86 | Darlington | 85 | Bury | 84 |
| †1985–6 | Swindon | 102 | Chester | 84 | Mansfield | 81 | Port Vale | 79 |
| †1986–7 | Northampton | 99 | Preston | 90 | Southend | 80 | ††Wolves | 79 |
| †1987–8 | Wolves | 90 | Cardiff | 85 | Bolton | 78 | ††Scunthorpe | 77 |
| †1988–9 | Rotherham | 82 | Tranmere | 80 | Crewe | 78 | ††Scunthorpe | 77 |
| †1989–90 | Exeter | 89 | Grimsby | 79 | Southend | 75 | ††Stockport | 74 |
| †1990–1 | Darlington | 83 | Stockport | 82 | Hartlepool Utd | 82 | Peterborough | 80 |
| 1991–2*a* | Burnley | 83 | Rotherham | 77 | Mansfield | 77 | Blackpool | 76 |

* Won on goal average Maximum points: †, 138; *a*, 126; previously 92 †† Not promoted after play–offs

## THIRD DIVISION – SOUTH 1920–58

| | | | | | | |
|---|---|---|---|---|---|---|
| 1920–1*a* | Crystal Palace | 59 | Southampton | 54 | QPR | 53 |
| 1921–2*a* | *Southampton | 61 | Plymouth Argyle | 61 | Portsmouth | 53 |
| 1922–3*a* | Bristol City | 59 | Plymouth Argyle | 53 | Swansea | 53 |
| 1923–4*a* | Portsmouth | 59 | Plymouth Argyle | 55 | Millwall | 54 |
| 1924–5*a* | Swansea | 57 | Plymouth Argyle | 56 | Bristol City | 53 |
| 1925–6*a* | Reading | 57 | Plymouth Argyle | 56 | Millwall | 53 |
| 1926–7*a* | Bristol City | 62 | Plymouth Argyle | 60 | Millwall | 56 |
| 1927–8*a* | Millwall | 65 | Northampton | 55 | Plymouth Argyle | 53 |
| 1928–9*a* | *Charlton | 54 | Crystal Palace | 54 | Northampton | 52 |
| 1929–30*a* | Plymouth Argyle | 68 | Brentford | 61 | QPR | 51 |
| 1930–31*a* | Notts Co | 59 | Crystal Palace | 51 | Brentford | 50 |
| 1931–2*a* | Fulham | 57 | Reading | 55 | Southend | 53 |
| 1932–3*a* | Brentford | 62 | Exeter | 58 | Norwich | 57 |
| 1933–4*a* | Norwich | 61 | Coventry | 54 | Reading | 54 |
| 1934–5*a* | Charlton | 61 | Reading | 53 | Coventry | 51 |
| 1935–6*a* | Coventry | 57 | Luton | 56 | Reading | 54 |
| 1936–7*a* | Luton | 58 | Notts Co | 56 | Brighton | 53 |
| 1937–8*a* | Millwall | 56 | Bristol City | 55 | QPR | 53 |
| 1938–9*a* | Newport | 55 | Crystal Palace | 52 | Brighton | 49 |
| 1946–7*a* | Cardiff | 66 | QPR | 57 | Bristol City | 51 |
| 1947–8*a* | QPR | 61 | Bournemouth | 57 | Walsall | 51 |
| 1948–9*a* | Swansea | 62 | Reading | 55 | Bournemouth | 52 |
| 1949–50*a* | Notts Co | 58 | Northampton | 51 | Southend | 51 |
| 1950–1*d* | Nottm Forest | 70 | Norwich | 64 | Reading | 57 |
| 1951–2*d* | Plymouth Argyle | 66 | Reading | 61 | Norwich | 61 |
| 1952–3*d* | Bristol Rov | 64 | Millwall | 62 | Northampton | 62 |
| 1953–4*d* | Ipswich | 64 | Brighton | 61 | Bristol City | 56 |
| 1954–5*d* | Bristol City | 70 | Leyton Orient | 61 | Southampton | 59 |
| 1955–6*d* | Leyton Orient | 66 | Brighton | 65 | Ipswich | 64 |
| 1956–7*d* | *Ipswich | 59 | Torquay | 59 | Colchester | 58 |
| 1957–8*d* | Brighton | 60 | Brentford | 58 | Plymouth Argyle | 58 |

## THIRD DIVISION – NORTH 1921–58

| | | | | | | |
|---|---|---|---|---|---|---|
| 1921–2*b* | Stockport | 56 | Darlington | 50 | Grimsby | 50 |
| 1922–3*b* | Nelson | 51 | Bradford PA | 47 | Walsall | 46 |
| 1923–4*a* | Wolves | 63 | Rochdale | 62 | Chesterfield | 54 |
| 1924–5*a* | Darlington | 58 | Nelson | 53 | New Brighton | 53 |
| 1925–6*a* | Grimsby | 61 | Bradford PA | 60 | Rochdale | 59 |
| 1926–7*a* | Stoke | 63 | Rochdale | 58 | Bradford PA | 57 |
| 1927–8*a* | Bradford PA | 63 | Lincoln | 55 | Stockport | 54 |
| 1928–9*a* | Bradford City | 63 | Stockport | 62 | Wrexham | 52 |
| 1929–30*a* | Port Vale | 67 | Stockport | 63 | Darlington | 50 |
| 1930–1*a* | Chesterfield | 58 | Lincoln | 57 | Wrexham | 54 |
| 1931–2*c* | *Lincoln | 57 | Gateshead | 57 | Chester | 50 |
| 1932–3*a* | Hull | 59 | Wrexham | 57 | Stockport | 54 |
| 1933–4*a* | Barnsley | 62 | Chesterfield | 61 | Stockport | 59 |
| 1934–5*a* | Doncaster | 57 | Halifax | 55 | Chester | 54 |
| 1935–6*a* | Chesterfield | 60 | Chester | 55 | Tranmere | 54 |
| 1936–7*a* | Stockport | 60 | Lincoln | 57 | Chester | 53 |
| 1937–8*a* | Tranmere | 56 | Doncaster | 54 | Hull | 53 |
| 1938–9*a* | Barnsley | 67 | Doncaster | 56 | Bradford City | 52 |
| 1946–7*a* | Doncaster | 72 | Rotherham | 64 | Chester | 56 |
| 1947–8*a* | Lincoln | 60 | Rotherham | 59 | Wrexham | 50 |
| 1948–9*a* | Hull | 65 | Rotherham | 62 | Doncaster | 50 |
| 1949–50*a* | Doncaster | 55 | Gateshead | 53 | Rochdale | 51 |
| 1950–1*d* | Rotherham | 71 | Mansfield | 64 | Carlisle | 62 |
| 1951–2*d* | Lincoln | 69 | Grimsby | 66 | Stockport | 59 |

| | | | | | | |
|---|---|---|---|---|---|---|
| 1952–3*d* | Oldham | 59 | Port Vale | 58 | Wrexham | 56 |
| 1953–4*d* | Port Vale | 69 | Barnsley | 58 | Scunthorpe | 57 |
| 1954–5*d* | Barnsley | 65 | Accrington | 61 | Scunthorpe | 58 |
| 1955–6*d* | Grimsby | 68 | Derby | 63 | Accrington | 59 |
| 1956–7*d* | Derby | 63 | Hartlepool Utd | 59 | Accrington | 58 |
| 1957–8*d* | Scunthorpe | 66 | Accrington | 59 | Bradford City | 57 |

Maximum points: *a*, 84; *b*, 76; *c*, 80; *d*, 92 * Won on goal average

## TITLE WINNERS

### PREMIER LEAGUE

Manchester Utd.............. 13
Chelsea ............................ 5
Arsenal ............................ 3
Manchester City................. 3
Blackburn .......................... 1
Leicester............................ 1

### FOOTBALL LEAGUE CHAMPIONSHIP

Newcastle.......................... 2
Reading............................. 2
Sunderland ........................ 2
Wolves............................... 2
Bournemouth ...................... 1
Burnley.............................. 1
Cardiff............................... 1
Leicester............................ 1
QPR .................................. 1
WBA.................................. 1

### DIV 1 (NEW)

Sunderland ........................ 2
Bolton ............................... 1
Charlton............................. 1
Crystal Palace .................... 1
Fulham............................... 1
Manchester City.................. 1
Middlesbrough .................... 1
Newcastle........................... 1
Norwich............................. 1
Nottm Forest....................... 1
Portsmouth ........................ 1

### DIV 1 (ORIGINAL)

Liverpool.......................... 18
Arsenal ............................ 10
Everton.............................. 9
Aston Villa ......................... 7
Manchester Utd................... 7
Sunderland ........................ 6
Newcastle.......................... 4
Sheffield Wed..................... 4
Huddersfield ...................... 3
Leeds ............................... 3
Wolves.............................. 3
Blackburn .......................... 2
Burnley.............................. 2
Derby ............................... 2
Manchester City.................. 2
Portsmouth ........................ 2
Preston.............................. 2
Tottenham.......................... 2
Chelsea ............................. 1
Ipswich.............................. 1
Nottm Forest....................... 1
Sheffield Utd...................... 1
WBA.................................. 1

### LEAGUE ONE

Wigan................................ 2
Brighton ............................ 1
Bristol City......................... 1
Charlton............................. 1
Doncaster .......................... 1
Leicester............................ 1
Luton ................................ 1
Norwich............................. 1
Scunthorpe ........................ 1
Sheffield Utd...................... 1
Southend........................... 1
Swansea ............................ 1
Wolves............................... 1

### DIV 2 (NEW)

Birmingham ........................ 1
Brighton ............................ 1
Bury.................................. 1
Chesterfield........................ 1
Fulham............................... 1
Millwall ............................. 1
Plymouth ........................... 1
Preston.............................. 1
Reading............................. 1
Stoke ................................ 1
Swindon ............................ 1
Watford.............................. 1
Wigan................................ 1
Notts Co ............................ 1

### DIV 2 (ORIGINAL)

Leicester............................ 6
Manchester City.................. 6
Sheffield Wed..................... 5
Birmingham ........................ 4
Derby ............................... 4
Liverpool............................ 4
Ipswich.............................. 3
Leeds ................................ 3
Middlesbrough .................... 3
Notts County ...................... 3
Preston.............................. 3
Aston Villa ......................... 2
Bolton ............................... 2
Burnley.............................. 2
Chelsea ............................. 2
Grimsby............................. 2
Manchester Utd................... 2
Norwich............................. 2
Nottm Forest....................... 2
Stoke ................................ 2
Tottenham.......................... 2
WBA.................................. 2
West Ham .......................... 2
Wolves............................... 2
Blackburn .......................... 1
Blackpool........................... 1
Bradford City...................... 1
Brentford ........................... 1
Bristol City......................... 1
Bury.................................. 1
Coventry ............................ 1
Crystal Palace .................... 1
Everton.............................. 1
Fulham............................... 1
Huddersfield ...................... 1
Luton ................................ 1
Millwall ............................. 1
Newcastle........................... 1
Oldham ............................. 1
Oxford Utd.......................... 1
QPR .................................. 1
Sheffield Utd...................... 1
Sunderland ......................... 1

### LEAGUE TWO

Chesterfield ....................... 2
Accrington ......................... 1
Brentford ........................... 1
Burton............................... 1
Carlisle.............................. 1
Gillingham ......................... 1
MK Dons ............................ 1
Northampton....................... 1
Notts County ...................... 1
Portsmouth ........................ 1
Swindon ............................ 1
Walsall .............................. 1
Yeovil ............................... 1

## APPLICATIONS FOR RE–ELECTION (System discontinued 1987)

| | | | | | |
|---|---|---|---|---|---|
| 14 | Hartlepool | 4 | Norwich | 2 | Oldham |
| 12 | Halifax | 3 | Aldershot | 2 | QPR |
| 11 | Barrow | 3 | Bradford City | 2 | Rotherham |
| 11 | Southport | 3 | Crystal Palace | 2 | Scunthorpe |
| 10 | Crewe | 3 | Doncaster | 2 | Southend |
| 10 | Newport | 3 | Hereford | 2 | Watford |
| 10 | Rochdale | 3 | Merthyr | 1 | Blackpool |
| 8 | Darlington | 3 | Swindon | 1 | Brighton |
| 8 | Exeter | 3 | Torquay | 1 | Bristol Rov |
| 7 | Chester | 3 | Tranmere | 1 | Cambridge Utd |
| 7 | Walsall | 2 | Aberdare | 1 | Cardiff |
| 7 | Workington | 2 | Ashington | 1 | Carlisle |
| 7 | York | 2 | Bournemouth | 1 | Charlton |
| 6 | Stockport | 2 | Brentford | 1 | Mansfield |
| 5 | Accrington | 2 | Colchester | 1 | Port Vale |
| 5 | Gillingham | 2 | Durham | 1 | Preston |
| 5 | Lincoln | 2 | Gateshead | 1 | Shrewsbury |
| 5 | New Brighton | 2 | Grimsby | 1 | Swansea |
| 4 | Bradford PA | 2 | Millwall | 1 | Thames |
| 4 | Northampton | 2 | Nelson | 1 | Wrexham |

## RELEGATED CLUBS (TO 1992)

1892–3 In Test matches, Darwen and Sheffield Utd won promotion in place of Accrington and Notts Co
1893–4 Tests, Liverpool and Small Heath won promotion Darwen and Newton Heath relegated
1894–5 After Tests, Bury promoted, Liverpool relegated
1895–6 After Tests, Liverpool promoted, Small Heath relegated
1896–7 After Tests, Notts Co promoted, Burnley relegated
1897–8 Test system abolished after success of Burnley and Stoke, League extended Blackburn and Newcastle elected to First Division
Automatic promotion and relegation introduced

## FIRST DIVISION TO SECOND DIVISION

**1898–9** Bolton, Sheffield Wed
**1899–00** Burnley, Glossop
**1900–1** Preston, WBA
**1901–2** Small Heath, Manchester City
**1902–3** Grimsby, Bolton
**1903–4** Liverpool, WBA
**1904–5** League extended Bury and Notts Co, two bottom clubs in First Division, re–elected
**1905–6** Nottm Forest, Wolves
**1906–7** Derby, Stoke
**1907–8** Bolton, Birmingham
**1908–9** Manchester City, Leicester Fosse
**1909–10** Bolton, Chelsea
**1910–11** Bristol City, Nottm Forest
**1911–12** Preston, Bury
**1912–13** Notts Co, Woolwich Arsenal
**1913–14** Preston, Derby
**1914–15** Tottenham, *Chelsea
**1919–20** Notts Co, Sheffield Wed
**1920–1** Derby, Bradford PA
**1921–2** Bradford City, Manchester Utd
**1922–3** Stoke, Oldham
**1923–4** Chelsea, Middlesbrough
**1924–5** Preston, Nottm Forest
**1925–6** Manchester City, Notts Co
**1926–7** Leeds, WBA
**1927–8** Tottenham, Middlesbrough
**1928–9** Bury, Cardiff
**1929–30** Burnley, Everton
**1930–1** Leeds, Manchester Utd
**1931–2** Grimsby, West Ham
**1932–3** Bolton, Blackpool
**1933–4** Newcastle, Sheffield Utd
**1934–5** Leicester, Tottenham
**1935–6** Aston Villa, Blackburn
**1936–7** Manchester Utd, Sheffield Wed
**1937–8** Manchester City, WBA
**1938–9** Birmingham, Leicester
**1946–7** Brentford, Leeds
**1947–8** Blackburn, Grimsby
**1948–9** Preston, Sheffield Utd
**1949–50** Manchester City, Birmingham
**1950–1** Sheffield Wed, Everton
**1951–2** Huddersfield, Fulham
**1952–3** Stoke, Derby
**1953–4** Middlesbrough, Liverpool

**1954–5** Leicester, Sheffield Wed
**1955–6** Huddersfield, Sheffield Utd
**1956–7** Charlton, Cardiff
**1957–8** Sheffield Wed, Sunderland
**1958–9** Portsmouth, Aston Villa
**1959–60** Luton, Leeds
**1960–61** Preston, Newcastle
**1961–2** Chelsea, Cardiff
**1962–3** Manchester City, Leyton Orient
**1963–4** Bolton, Ipswich
**1964–5** Wolves, Birmingham
**1965–6** Northampton, Blackburn
**1966–7** Aston Villa, Blackpool
**1967–8** Fulham, Sheffield Utd
**1968–9** Leicester, QPR
**1969–70** Sheffield Wed, Sunderland
**1970–1** Burnley, Blackpool
**1971–2** Nottm Forest, Huddersfield
**1972–3** WBA, Crystal Palace
**1973–4** Norwich, Manchester Utd, Southampton
**1974–5** Chelsea, Luton, Carlisle
**1975–6** Sheffield Utd, Burnley, Wolves
**1976–7** Tottenham, Stoke, Sunderland
**1977–8** Leicester, West Ham, Newcastle
**1978–9** QPR, Birmingham, Chelsea
**1979–80** Bristol City, Derby, Bolton
**1980–1** Norwich, Leicester, Crystal Palace
**1981–2** Leeds, Wolves, Middlesbrough
**1982–3** Manchester City, Swansea, Brighton
**1983–4** Birmingham, Notts Co, Wolves
**1984–5** Norwich, Sunderland, Stoke
**1985–6** Ipswich, Birmingham, WBA
**1986–7** Leicester, Manchester City, Aston Villa
**1987–8** Chelsea**, Portsmouth, Watford, Oxford Utd
**1988–9** Middlesbrough, West Ham, Newcastle
**1989–90** Sheffield Wed, Charlton, Millwall
**1990–1** Sunderland, Derby
**1991–2** Luton, Notts Co, West Ham

*** Subsequently re–elected to First Division when League extended after the war**
**** Relegated after play–offs**

## SECOND DIVISION TO THIRD DIVISION

**1920–1** Stockport
**1921–2** Bradford City, Bristol City
**1922–3** Rotherham, Wolves
**1923–4** Nelson, Bristol City
**1924–5** Crystal Palace, Coventry
**1925–6** Stoke, Stockport
**1926–7** Darlington, Bradford City
**1927–8** Fulham, South Shields
**1928–9** Port Vale, Clapton Orient
**1929–30** Hull, Notts County
**1930–1** Reading, Cardiff
**1931–2** Barnsley, Bristol City
**1932–3** Chesterfield, Charlton
**1933–4** Millwall, Lincoln
**1934–5** Oldham, Notts Co
**1935–6** Port Vale, Hull
**1936–7** Doncaster, Bradford City
**1937–8** Barnsley, Stockport
**1938–9** Norwich, Tranmere
**1946–7** Swansea, Newport
**1947–8** Doncaster, Millwall
**1948–9** Nottm Forest, Lincoln
**1949–50** Plymouth Argyle, Bradford PA
**1950–1** Grimsby, Chesterfield
**1951–2** Coventry, QPR
**1952–3** Southampton, Barnsley
**1953–4** Brentford, Oldham
**1954–5** Ipswich, Derby
**1955–6** Plymouth Argyle, Hull
**1956–7** Port Vale, Bury
**1957–8** Doncaster, Notts Co
**1958–9** Barnsley, Grimsby
**1959–60** Bristol City, Hull
**1960–1** Lincoln, Portsmouth
**1961–2** Brighton, Bristol Rov
**1962–3** Walsall, Luton
**1963–4** Grimsby, Scunthorpe
**1964–5** Swindon, Swansea
**1965–6** Middlesbrough, Leyton Orient
**1966–7** Northampton, Bury
**1967–8** Plymouth Argyle, Rotherham
**1968–9** Fulham, Bury
**1969–70** Preston, Aston Villa
**1970–1** Blackburn, Bolton
**1971–2** Charlton, Watford
**1972–3** Huddersfield, Brighton
**1973–4** Crystal Palace, Preston, Swindon
**1974–5** Millwall, Cardiff, Sheffield Wed
**1975–6** Portsmouth, Oxford Utd, York
**1976–7** Carlisle, Plymouth Argyle, Hereford
**1977–8** Hull, Mansfield, Blackpool
**1978–9** Sheffield Utd, Millwall, Blackburn
**1979–80** Fulham, Burnley, Charlton
**1980–1** Preston, Bristol City, Bristol Rov
**1981–2** Cardiff, Wrexham, Orient
**1982–3** Rotherham, Burnley, Bolton
**1983–4** Derby, Swansea, Cambridge Utd
**1984–5** Notts Co, Cardiff, Wolves
**1985–6** Carlisle, Middlesbrough, Fulham
**1986–7** Sunderland**, Grimsby, Brighton
**1987–8** Sheffield Utd**, Reading, Huddersfield
**1988–9** Shrewsbury, Birmingham, Walsall
**1989–90** Bournemouth, Bradford City, Stoke
**1990–1** WBA, Hull
**1991–2** Plymouth Argyle, Brighton, Port Vale

**** Relegated after play–offs**

## THIRD DIVISION TO FOURTH DIVISION

**1958–9** Rochdale, Notts Co, Doncaster, Stockport
**1959–60** Accrington, Wrexham, Mansfield, York
**1960–1** Chesterfield, Colchester, Bradford City, Tranmere

**1961–2** Newport, Brentford, Lincoln, Torquay
**1962–3** Bradford PA, Brighton, Carlisle, Halifax
**1963–4** Millwall, Crewe, Wrexham, Notts Co
**1964–5** Luton, Port Vale, Colchester, Barnsley
**1965–6** Southend, Exeter, Brentford, York
**1966–7** Doncaster, Workington, Darlington, Swansea
**1967–8** Scunthorpe, Colchester, Grimsby, Peterborough (demoted)
**1968–9** Oldham, Crewe, Hartlepool Utd, Northampton
**1969–70** Bournemouth, Southport, Barrow, Stockport
**1970–1** Gillingham, Doncaster, Bury, Reading
**1971–2** Mansfield, Barnsley, Torquay, Bradford City
**1972–3** Scunthorpe, Swansea, Brentford, Rotherham
**1973–4** Cambridge Utd, Shrewsbury, Rochdale, Southport
**1974–5** Bournemouth, Watford, Tranmere, Huddersfield
**1975–6** Aldershot, Colchester, Southend, Halifax
**1976–7** Reading, Northampton, Grimsby, York
**1977–8** Port Vale, Bradford City, Hereford, Portsmouth
**1978–9** Peterborough, Walsall, Tranmere, Lincoln
**1979–80** Bury, Southend, Mansfield, Wimbledon
**1980–1** Sheffield Utd, Colchester, Blackpool, Hull
**1981–2** Wimbledon, Swindon, Bristol City, Chester
**1982–3** Reading, Wrexham, Doncaster, Chesterfield
**1983–4** Scunthorpe, Southend, Port Vale, Exeter
**1984–5** Burnley, Orient, Preston, Cambridge Utd
**1985–6** Lincoln, Cardiff, Wolves, Swansea
**1986–7** Bolton**, Carlisle, Darlington, Newport
**1987–8** Doncaster, York, Grimsby, Rotherham**
**1988–9** Southend, Chesterfield, Gillingham, Aldershot
**1989–90** Cardiff, Northampton, Blackpool, Walsall
**1990–1** Crewe, Rotherham, Mansfield
**1991–2** Bury, Shrewsbury, Torquay, Darlington
**** Relegated after plays–offs**

## DEMOTED FROM FOURTH DIVISION TO CONFERENCE

**1987** Lincoln
**1988** Newport
**1989** Darlington
**1990** Colchester
**1991** No demotion
**1992** No demotion

## DEMOTED FROM THIRD DIVISION TO CONFERENCE

**1993** Halifax
**1994–6** No demotion
**1997** Hereford
**1998** Doncaster
**1999** Scarborough
**2000** Chester
**2001** Barnet
**2002** Halifax
**2003** Exeter, Shrewsbury
**2004** Carlisle, York

## DEMOTED FROM LEAGUE TWO TO CONFERENCE/NATIONAL LEAGUE

**2005** Kidderminster, Cambridge Utd
**2006** Oxford Utd, Rushden & Diamonds
**2007** Boston, Torquay
**2008** Mansfield, Wrexham
**2009** Chester Luton
**2010** Grimsby, Darlington
**2011** Lincoln, Stockport
**2012** Hereford, Macclesfield
**2013** Barnet, Aldershot
**2014** Bristol Rov, Torquay
**2015** Cheltenham, Tranmere
**2016** Dagenham, York
**2017** Hartlepool, Leyton Orient
**2018** Barnet, Chesterfield

## RELEGATED CLUBS (SINCE 1993)

### 1993

**Premier League to Div 1**: Crystal Palace, Middlesbrough, Nottm Forest
**Div 1 to Div 2**: Brentford, Cambridge Utd, Bristol Rov
**Div 2 to Div 3**: Preston, Mansfield, Wigan, Chester

### 1994

**Premier League to Div 1**: Sheffield Utd, Oldham, Swindon

**Div 1 to Div 2**: Birmingham, Oxford Utd, Peterborough
**Div 2 to Div 3**: Fulham, Exeter, Hartlepool Utd, Barnet

### 1995
**Premier League to Div 1**: Crystal Palace, Norwich, Leicester, Ipswich
**Div 1 to Div 2**: Swindon, Burnley, Bristol City, Notts Co
**Div 2 to Div 3**: Cambridge Utd, Plymouth Argyle, Cardiff, Chester, Leyton Orient

### 1996
**Premier League to Div 1**: Manchester City, QPR, Bolton
**Div 1 to Div 2**: Millwall, Watford, Luton
**Div 2 to Div 3**: Carlisle, Swansea, Brighton, Hull

### 1997
**Premier League to Div 1**: Sunderland, Middlesbrough, Nottm Forest
**Div 1 to Div 2**: Grimsby, Oldham, Southend
**Div 2 to Div 3**: Peterborough, Shrewsbury, Rotherham, Notts Co

### 1998
**Premier League to Div 1**: Bolton, Barnsley, Crystal Palace
**Div 1 to Div 2**: Manchester City, Stoke, Reading
**Div 2 to Div 3**: Brentford, Plymouth Argyle, Carlisle, Southend

### 1999
**Premier League to Div 1**: Charlton, Blackburn, Nottm Forest
**Div 1 to Div 2**: Bury, Oxford Utd, Bristol City
**Div 2 to Div 3**: York, Northampton, Lincoln, Macclesfield

### 2000
**Premier League to Div 1**: Wimbledon, Sheffield Wed, Watford
**Div 1 to Div 2:** Walsall, Port Vale, Swindon
**Div 2 to Div 3**: Cardiff, Blackpool, Scunthorpe, Chesterfield

### 2001
**Premier League to Div 1**: Manchester City, Coventry, Bradford City
**Div 1 to Div 2:** Huddersfield, QPR, Tranmere
**Div 2 to Div 3**: Bristol Rov, Luton, Swansea, Oxford Utd

### 2002
**Premier League to Div 1**: Ipswich, Derby, Leicester
**Div 1 to Div 2:** Crewe, Barnsley, Stockport
**Div 2 to Div 3**: Bournemouth, Bury, Wrexham, Cambridge Utd

### 2003
**Premier League to Div 1**: West Ham, WBA, Sunderland
**Div 1 to Div 2:** Sheffield Wed, Brighton, Grimsby
**Div 2 to Div 3**: Cheltenham, Huddersfield, Mansfield, Northampton

### 2004
**Premier League to Div 1**: Leicester, Leeds, Wolves
**Div 1 to Div 2:** Walsall, Bradford City, Wimbledon
**Div 2 to Div 3**: Grimsby, Rushden & Diamonds, Notts Co, Wycombe

### 2005
**Premier League to Championship**: Crystal Palace, Norwich, Southampton
**Championship to League 1**: Gillingham, Nottm Forest, Rotherham
**League 1 to League 2**: Torquay, Wrexham, Peterborough, Stockport

**2006**
**Premier League to Championship**: Birmingham, WBA, Sunderland
**Championship to League 1**: Crewe, Millwall, Brighton
**League 1 to League 2**: Hartlepool Utd, MK Dons, Swindon, Walsall

**2007**
**Premier League to Championship**: Sheffield Utd, Charlton, Watford
**Championship to League 1**: Southend, Luton, Leeds
**League 1 to League 2**: Chesterfield, Bradford City, Rotherham, Brentford

**2008**
**Premier League to Championship:** Reading, Birmingham, Derby
**Championship to League 1**: Leicester, Scunthorpe, Colchester
**League 1 to League 2**: Bournemouth, Gillingham, Port Vale, Luton

**2009**
**Premier League to Championship**: Newcastle, Middlesbrough, WBA
**Championship to League 1**: Norwich, Southampton, Charlton
**League 1 to League 2**: Northampton, Crewe, Cheltenham, Hereford

**2010**
**Premier League to Championship:** Burnley, Hull, Portsmouth
**Championship to League 1:** Sheffield Wed, Plymouth, Peterborough
**League 1 to League 2:** Gillingham, Wycombe, Southend, Stockport

**2011**
**Premier League to Championship**: Birmingham, Blackpool, West Ham
**Championship to League 1**: Preston, Sheffield Utd, Scunthorpe
**League 1 to League 2**: Dagenham & Redbridge, Bristol Rov, Plymouth, Swindon

**2012**
**Premier League to Championship**: Bolton, Blackburn, Wolves
**Championship to League** 1: Portsmouth, Coventry, Doncaster
**League 1 to League 2**: Wycombe, Chesterfield, Exeter, Rochdale

**2013**
**Premier League to Championship**: Wigan, Reading, QPR
**Championship to League 1**: Peterborough, Wolves, Bristol City
**League 1 to League 2**: Scunthorpe, Bury, Hartlepool, Portsmouth

**2014**
**Premier League to Championship**: Norwich, Fulham, Cardiff
**Championship to League 1**: Doncaster, Barnsley, Yeovil
**League 1 to League 2**: Tranmere, Carlisle, Shrewsbury, Stevenage

**2015**
**Premier League to Championship**: Hull, Burnley QPR
**Championship to League** 1: Millwall, Wigan, Blackpool
**League 1 to League 2**: Notts Co, Crawley, Leyton Orient, Yeovil

**2016**
**Premier League to Championship**: Newcastle, Norwich, Aston Villa
**Championship to League** 1: Charlton, MK Dons, Bolton
**League 1 to League 2**: Doncaster, Blackpool, Colchester, Crewe

**2017**
**Premier League to Championship**: Hull, Middlesbrough, Sunderland
**Championship to League 1**: Blackburn, Wigan, Rotherham
**League 1 to League 2**: Port Vale, Swindon, Coventry, Chesterfield

**2018**
**Premier League to Championship**: Swansea, Stoke, WBA
**Championship to League 1**: Barnsley, Burton, Sunderland
**League 1 to League 2**: Oldham, Northampton, MK Dons, Bury

# ANNUAL AWARDS

## FOOTBALL WRITERS' ASSOCIATION

**Footballer of the Year: 1948** Stanley Matthews (Blackpool); **1949** Johnny Carey (Manchester Utd); **1950** Joe Mercer (Arsenal); **1951** Harry Johnston (Blackpool); **1952** Billy Wright (Wolves); **1953** Nat Lofthouse (Bolton); **1954** Tom Finney (Preston); **1955** Don Revie (Manchester City); **1956** Bert Trautmann (Manchester City); **1957** Tom Finney (Preston); **1958** Danny Blanchflower (Tottenham); **1959** Syd Owen (Luton); **1960** Bill Slater (Wolves); **1961** Danny Blanchflower (Tottenham); **1962** Jimmy Adamson (Burnley); **1963** Stanley Matthews (Stoke); **1964** Bobby Moore (West Ham); **1965** Bobby Collins (Leeds); **1966** Bobby Charlton (Manchester Utd); **1967** Jack Charlton (Leeds); **1968** George Best (Manchester Utd); **1969** Tony Book (Manchester City) & Dave Mackay (Derby) – shared; **1970** Billy Bremner (Leeds); **1971** Frank McLintock (Arsenal); **1972** Gordon Banks (Stoke); **1973** Pat Jennings (Tottenham); **1974** Ian Callaghan (Liverpool); **1975** Alan Mullery (Fulham); **1976** Kevin Keegan (Liverpool); **1977** Emlyn Hughes (Liverpool); **1978** Kenny Burns (Nott'm Forest); **1979** Kenny Dalglish (Liverpool); **1980** Terry McDermott (Liverpool); **1981** Frans Thijssen (Ipswich); **1982** Steve Perryman (Tottenham); **1983** Kenny Dalglish (Liverpool); **1984** Ian Rush (Liverpool); **1985** Neville Southall (Everton); **1986** Gary Lineker (Everton); **1987** Clive Allen (Tottenham); **1988** John Barnes (Liverpool); **1989** Steve Nicol (Liverpool); Special award to the Liverpool players for the compassion shown to bereaved families after the Hillsborough Disaster; **1990** John Barnes (Liverpool); **1991** Gordon Strachan (Leeds); **1992** Gary Lineker (Tottenham); **1993** Chris Waddle (Sheffield Wed); **1994** Alan Shearer (Blackburn); **1995** Jurgen Klinsmann (Tottenham); **1996** Eric Cantona (Manchester Utd); **1997** Gianfranco Zola (Chelsea); **1998** Dennis Bergkamp (Arsenal); **1999** David Ginola (Tottenham); **2000** Roy Keane (Manchester Utd); **2001** Teddy Sheringham (Manchester Utd); **2002** Robert Pires (Arsenal); **2003** Thierry Henry (Arsenal); **2004** Thierry Henry (Arsenal); **2005** Frank Lampard (Chelsea); **2006** Thierry Henry (Arsenal); **2007** Cristiano Ronaldo (Manchester Utd); **2008** Cristiano Ronaldo (Manchester Utd), **2009** Steven Gerrard (Liverpool), **2010** Wayne Rooney (Manchester Utd), **2011** Scott Parker (West Ham), **2012** Robin van Persie (Arsenal), **2013** Gareth Bale (Tottenham), **2014** Luis Suarez (Liverpool), **2015** Eden Hazard (Chelsea), **2016** Jamie Vardy (Leicester), **2017** N'Golo Kante (Chelsea), **2018** Mohamed Salah (Liverpool)

## PROFESSIONAL FOOTBALLERS' ASSOCIATION

**Player of the Year: 1974** Norman Hunter (Leeds); **1975** Colin Todd (Derby); **1976** Pat Jennings (Tottenham); **1977** Andy Gray (Aston Villa); **1978** Peter Shilton (Nott'm Forest); **1979** Liam Brady (Arsenal); **1980** Terry McDermott (Liverpool); **1981** John Wark (Ipswich); **1982** Kevin Keegan (Southampton); **1983** Kenny Dalglish (Liverpool); **1984** Ian Rush (Liverpool); **1985** Peter Reid (Everton); **1986** Gary Lineker (Everton); **1987** Clive Allen (Tottenham); **1988** John Barnes (Liverpool); **1989** Mark Hughes (Manchester Utd); **1990** David Platt (Aston Villa); **1991** Mark Hughes (Manchester Utd); **1992** Gary Pallister (Manchester Utd); **1993** Paul McGrath (Aston Villa); **1994** Eric Cantona (Manchester Utd); **1995** Alan Shearer (Blackburn); **1996** Les Ferdinand (Newcastle); **1997** Alan Shearer (Newcastle); **1998** Dennis Bergkamp (Arsenal); **1999** David Ginola (Tottenham); **2000** Roy Keane (Manchester Utd); **2001** Teddy Sheringham (Manchester Utd); **2002** Ruud van Nistelrooy (Manchester Utd); **2003** Thierry Henry (Arsenal); **2004** Thierry Henry (Arsenal); **2005** John Terry (Chelsea); **2006** Steven Gerrard (Liverpool); **2007** Cristiano Ronaldo (Manchester Utd); **2008** Cristiano Ronaldo (Manchester Utd), **2009** Ryan Giggs (Manchester Utd), **2010** Wayne Rooney (Manchester Utd), **2011** Gareth Bale (Tottenham), **2012** Robin van Persie (Arsenal), **2013** Gareth Bale (Tottenham), **2014** Luis Suarez (Liverpool), **2015** Eden Hazard (Chelsea), **2016** Riyad Mahrez (Leicester), **2017** N'Golo Kante (Chelsea), **2018** Mohamed Salah (Liverpool)

**Young Player of the Year: 1974** Kevin Beattie (Ipswich); **1975** Mervyn Day (West Ham); **1976** Peter Barnes (Manchester City); **1977** Andy Gray (Aston Villa); **1978** Tony Woodcock (Nott'm Forest); **1979** Cyrille Regis (WBA); **1980** Glenn Hoddle (Tottenham); **1981** Gary Shaw (Aston Villa); **1982** Steve Moran (Southampton); **1983** Ian Rush (Liverpool); **1984** Paul Walsh (Luton); **1985** Mark Hughes (Manchester Utd); **1986** Tony Cottee (West Ham); **1987**

Tony Adams (Arsenal); **1988** Paul Gascoigne (Newcastle); **1989** Paul Merson (Arsenal); **1990** Matthew Le Tissier (Southampton); **1991** Lee Sharpe (Manchester Utd); **1992** Ryan Giggs (Manchester Utd); **1993** Ryan Giggs (Manchester Utd); **1994** Andy Cole (Newcastle); **1995** Robbie Fowler (Liverpool); **1996** Robbie Fowler (Liverpool); **1997** David Beckham (Manchester Utd); **1998** Michael Owen (Liverpool); **1999** Nicolas Anelka (Arsenal); **2000** Harry Kewell (Leeds); **2001** Steven Gerrard (Liverpool); **2002** Craig Bellamy (Newcastle); **2003** Jermaine Jenas (Newcastle); **2004** Scott Parker (Chelsea); **2005** Wayne Rooney (Manchester Utd); **2006** Wayne Rooney (Manchester Utd); **2007** Cristiano Ronaldo (Manchester Utd); **2008** Cesc Fabregas (Arsenal), **2009** Ashley Young (Aston Villa), **2010** James Milner (Aston Villa), **2011** Jack Wilshere (Arsenal), **2012** Kyle Walker (Tottenham), **2013** Gareth Bale (Tottenham), **2014** Eden Hazard (Chelsea), **2015** Harry Kane (Tottenham), **2016** Dele Alli (Tottenham), **2017** Dele Alli (Tottenham), **2018** Leroy Sane (Manchester City)

**Merit Awards: 1974** Bobby Charlton & Cliff Lloyd; **1975** Denis Law; **1976** George Eastham; **1977** Jack Taylor; **1978** Bill Shankly; **1979** Tom Finney; **1980** Sir Matt Busby; **1981** John Trollope; **1982** Joe Mercer; **1983** Bob Paisley; **1984** Bill Nicholson; **1985** Ron Greenwood; **1986** England 1966 World Cup–winning team; **1987** Sir Stanley Matthews; **1988** Billy Bonds; **1989** Nat Lofthouse; **1990** Peter Shilton; **1991** Tommy Hutchison; **1992** Brian Clough; **1993** Manchester Utd, 1968 European Champions; Eusebio; **1994** Billy Bingham; **1995** Gordon Strachan; **1996** Pele; **1997** Peter Beardsley; **1998** Steve Ogrizovic; **1999** Tony Ford; **2000** Gary Mabbutt; **2001** Jimmy Hill; **2002** Niall Quinn; **2003** Sir Bobby Robson; **2004** Dario Gradi; **2005** Shaka Hislop; **2006** George Best; **2007** Sir Alex Ferguson; **2008** Jimmy Armfield; **2009** John McDermott, **2010** Lucas Radebe, **2011** Howard Webb, **2012** Graham Alexander, **2013** Eric Harrison/Manchester Utd Class of '92, **2014** Donald Bell (posthumously; only footballer to win Victoria Cross, World War 1), **2015** Steven Gerrard & Frank Lampard, **2016** Ryan Giggs, **2017** David Beckham, **2018** Cyrille Regis (posthumously)

## MANAGER OF THE YEAR 1 (chosen by media and sponsors)

**1966** Jock Stein (Celtic); **1967** Jock Stein (Celtic); **1968** Matt Busby (Manchester Utd); **1969** Don Revie (Leeds); **1970** Don Revie (Leeds); **1971** Bertie Mee (Arsenal); **1972** Don Revie (Leeds); **1973** Bill Shankly (Liverpool); **1974** Jack Charlton (Middlesbrough); **1975** Ron Saunders (Aston Villa); **1976** Bob Paisley (Liverpool); **1977** Bob Paisley (Liverpool); **1978** Brian Clough (Nott'm Forest); **1979** Bob Paisley (Liverpool); **1980** Bob Paisley (Liverpool); **1981** Ron Saunders (Aston Villa); **1982** Bob Paisley (Liverpool); **1983** Bob Paisley (Liverpool); **1984** Joe Fagan (Liverpool); **1985** Howard Kendall (Everton); **1986** Kenny Dalglish (Liverpool); **1987** Howard Kendall (Everton); **1988** Kenny Dalglish (Liverpool); **1989** George Graham (Arsenal); **1990** Kenny Dalglish (Liverpool); **1991** George Graham (Arsenal); **1992** Howard Wilkinson (Leeds); **1993** Alex Ferguson (Manchester Utd); **1994** Alex Ferguson (Manchester Utd); **1995** Kenny Dalglish (Blackburn); **1996** Alex Ferguson (Manchester Utd); **1997** Alex Ferguson (Manchester Utd); **1998** Arsene Wenger (Arsenal); **1999** Alex Ferguson (Manchester Utd); **2000** Sir Alex Ferguson (Manchester Utd); **2001** George Burley (Ipswich); **2002** Arsene Wenger (Arsenal); **2003** Sir Alex Ferguson (Manchester Utd); **2004** Arsene Wenger (Arsenal); **2005** Jose Mourinho (Chelsea); **2006** Jose Mourinho (Chelsea); **2007** Sir Alex Ferguson (Manchester Utd); **2008** Sir Alex Ferguson (Manchester Utd); **2009** Sir Alex Ferguson (Manchester Utd), **2010** Harry Redknapp (Tottenham), **2011** Sir Alex Ferguson (Manchester Utd), **2012**: Alan Pardew (Newcastle), **2013** Sir Alex Ferguson (Manchester Utd), **2014** Tony Pulis (Crystal Palace), **2015** Jose Mourinho (Chelsea), **2016** Claudio Ranieri (Leicester), **2017** Antonio Conte (Chelsea), **2018** Pep Guardiola (Manchester City)

## MANAGER OF THE YEAR 2 (Chosen by the League Managers' Association)

**1993** Dave Bassett (Sheffield Utd); **1994** Joe Kinnear (Wimbledon); **1995** Frank Clark (Nott'm Forest); **1996** Peter Reid (Sunderland); **1997** Danny Wilson (Barnsley); **1998** David Jones (Southampton); **1999** Alex Ferguson (Manchester Utd); **2000** Alan Curbishley (Charlton Athletic); **2001** George Burley (Ipswich); **2002** Arsene Wenger (Arsenal); **2003** David Moyes (Everton); **2004** Arsene Wenger (Arsenal); **2005** David Moyes (Everton); **2006** Steve Coppell (Reading); **2007** Steve Coppell (Reading); **2008** Sir Alex Ferguson (Manchester Utd); **2009** David Moyes (Everton), **2010** Roy Hodgson (Fulham), **2011** Sir Alex Ferguson (Manchester

Utd), **2012**: Alan Pardew (Newcastle), **2013** Sir Alex Ferguson (Manchester Utd), **2014** Brendan Rodgers (Liverpool), **2015** Eddie Howe (Bournemouth), **2016** Claudio Ranieri (Leicester), **2017** Antonio Conte (Chelsea), **2018** Pep Guardiola (Manchester City)

## SCOTTISH FOOTBALL WRITERS' ASSOCIATION

**Footballer of the Year: 1965** Billy McNeill (Celtic); **1966** John Greig (Rangers); **1967** Ronnie Simpson (Celtic); **1968** Gordon Wallace (Raith); **1969** Bobby Murdoch (Celtic); **1970** Pat Stanton (Hibernian); **1971** Martin Buchan (Aberdeen); **1972** David Smith (Rangers); **1973** George Connelly (Celtic); **1974** World Cup Squad; **1975** Sandy Jardine (Rangers); **1976** John Greig (Rangers); **1977** Danny McGrain (Celtic); **1978** Derek Johnstone (Rangers); **1979** Andy Ritchie (Morton); **1980** Gordon Strachan (Aberdeen); **1981** Alan Rough (Partick Thistle); **1982** Paul Sturrock (Dundee Utd); **1983** Charlie Nicholas (Celtic); **1984** Willie Miller (Aberdeen); **1985** Hamish McAlpine (Dundee Utd); **1986** Sandy Jardine (Hearts); **1987** Brian McClair (Celtic); **1988** Paul McStay (Celtic); **1989** Richard Gough (Rangers); **1990** Alex McLeish (Aberdeen); **1991** Maurice Malpas (Dundee Utd); **1992** Ally McCoist (Rangers); **1993** Andy Goram (Rangers); **1994** Mark Hateley (Rangers); **1995** Brian Laudrup (Rangers); **1996** Paul Gascoigne (Rangers); **1997** Brian Laudrup (Rangers); **1998** Craig Burley (Celtic); **1999** Henrik Larsson (Celtic); **2000** Barry Ferguson (Rangers); **2001** Henrik Larsson (Celtic); **2002** Paul Lambert (Celtic); **2003** Barry Ferguson (Rangers); **2004** Jackie McNamara (Celtic); **2005** John Hartson (Celtic); **2006** Craig Gordon (Hearts); **2007** Shunsuke Nakamura (Celtic); **2008** Carlos Cuellar (Rangers); **2009** Gary Caldwell (Celtic), **2010** David Weir (Rangers), **2011** Emilio Izaguirre (Celtic), **2012** Charlie Mulgrew (Celtic), **2013** Leigh Griffiths (Hibernian), **2014** Kris Commons (Celtic), **2015** Craig Gordon (Celtic), **2016** Leigh Griffiths (Celtic), **2017** Scott Sinclair (Celtic), **2018** Scott Brown (Celtic)

## PROFESSIONAL FOOTBALLERS' ASSOCIATION SCOTLAND

**Player of the Year: 1978** Derek Johnstone (Rangers); **1979** Paul Hegarty (Dundee Utd); **1980** Davie Provan (Celtic); **1981** Mark McGhee (Aberdeen); **1982** Sandy Clarke (Airdrieonians); **1983** Charlie Nicholas (Celtic); **1984** Willie Miller (Aberdeen); **1985** Jim Duffy (Morton); **1986** Richard Gough (Dundee Utd); **1987** Brian McClair (Celtic); **1988** Paul McStay (Celtic); **1989** Theo Snelders (Aberdeen); **1990** Jim Bett (Aberdeen); **1991** Paul Elliott (Celtic); **1992** Ally McCoist (Rangers); **1993** Andy Goram (Rangers); **1994** Mark Hateley (Rangers); **1995** Brian Laudrup (Rangers); **1996** Paul Gascoigne (Rangers); **1997** Paolo Di Canio (Celtic) **1998** Jackie McNamara (Celtic); **1999** Henrik Larsson (Celtic); **2000** Mark Viduka (Celtic); **2001** Henrik Larsson (Celtic); **2002** Lorenzo Amoruso (Rangers); **2003** Barry Ferguson (Rangers); **2004** Chris Sutton (Celtic); **2005** John Hartson (Celtic) and Fernando Ricksen (Rangers); **2006** Shaun Maloney (Celtic); **2007** Shunsuke Nakamura (Celtic); **2008** Aiden McGeady (Celtic); **2009** Scott Brown (Celtic), **2010** Steven Davis (Rangers), **2011** Emilio Izaguirre (Celtic), **2012** Charlie Mulgrew (Celtic), **2013** Michael Higdon (Motherwell), **2014** Kris Commons (Celtic), **2015** Stefan Johansen (Celtic), **2016** Leigh Griffiths (Celtic), **2017** Scott Sinclair (Celtic), **2018** Scott Brown (Celtic)

**Young Player of the Year: 1978** Graeme Payne (Dundee Utd); **1979** Ray Stewart (Dundee Utd); **1980** John McDonald (Rangers); **1981** Charlie Nicholas (Celtic); **1982** Frank McAvennie (St Mirren); **1983** Paul McStay (Celtic); **1984** John Robertson (Hearts); **1985** Craig Levein (Hearts); **1986** Craig Levein (Hearts); **1987** Robert Fleck (Rangers); **1988** John Collins (Hibernian); **1989** Billy McKinlay (Dundee Utd); **1990** Scott Crabbe (Hearts); **1991** Eoin Jess (Aberdeen); **1992** Phil O'Donnell (Motherwell); **1993** Eoin Jess (Aberdeen); **1994** Phil O'Donnell (Motherwell); **1995** Charlie Miller (Rangers); **1996** Jackie McNamara (Celtic); **1997** Robbie Winters (Dundee Utd); **1998** Gary Naysmith (Hearts); **1999** Barry Ferguson (Rangers); **2000** Kenny Miller (Hibernian); **2001** Stilian Petrov (Celtic); **2002** Kevin McNaughton (Aberdeen); **2003** James McFadden (Motherwell); **2004** Stephen Pearson (Celtic); **2005** Derek Riordan (Hibernian); **2006** Shaun Maloney (Celtic); **2007** Steven Naismith (Kilmarnock); **2008** Aiden McGeady (Celtic); **2009** James McCarthy (Hamilton), **2010** Danny Wilson (Rangers), **2011:** David Goodwillie (Dundee Utd), **2012** James Forrest (Celtic), **2013** Leigh Griffiths (Hibernian), **2014** Andy Robertson (Dundee Utd), **2015** Jason Denayer (Celtic), **2016** Kieran Tierney (Celtic), **2017** Kieran Tierney (Celticl), **2018** Kieran Tierney (Celtic)

## SCOTTISH MANAGER OF THE YEAR

**1987** Jim McLean (Dundee Utd); **1988** Billy McNeill (Celtic); **1989** Graeme Souness (Rangers); **1990** Andy Roxburgh (Scotland); **1991** Alex Totten (St Johnstone); **1992** Walter Smith (Rangers); **1993** Walter Smith (Rangers); **1994** Walter Smith (Rangers); **1995** Jimmy Nicholl (Raith); **1996** Walter Smith (Rangers); **1997** Walter Smith (Rangers); **1998** Wim Jansen (Celtic); **1999** Dick Advocaat (Rangers); **2000** Dick Advocaat (Rangers); **2001** Martin O'Neill (Celtic); **2002** John Lambie (Partick Thistle); **2003** Alex McLeish (Rangers); **2004** Martin O'Neill (Celtic); **2005** Alex McLeish (Rangers); **2006** Gordon Strachan (Celtic); **2007** Gordon Strachan (Celtic); **2008** Billy Reid (Hamilton); **2009** Csaba Laszlo (Hearts), **2010** Walter Smith (Rangers), **2011:** Mixu Paatelainen (Kilmarnock), **2012** Neil Lennon (Celtic), **2013** Neil Lennon (Celtic), **2014** Derek McInnes (Aberdeen), **2015** John Hughes (Inverness), **2016** Mark Warburton (Rangers), **2017** Brendan Rodgers (Celtic), **2018** Jack Ross (St Mirren)

## EUROPEAN FOOTBALLER OF THE YEAR

**1956** Stanley Matthews (Blackpool); **1957** Alfredo di Stefano (Real Madrid); **1958** Raymond Kopa (Real Madrid); **1959** Alfredo di Stefano (Real Madrid); **1960** Luis Suarez (Barcelona); **1961** Omar Sivori (Juventus); **1962** Josef Masopust (Dukla Prague); **1963** Lev Yashin (Moscow Dynamo); **1964** Denis Law (Manchester Utd); **1965** Eusebio (Benfica); **1966** Bobby Charlton (Manchester Utd); **1967** Florian Albert (Ferencvaros); **1968** George Best (Manchester Utd); **1969** Gianni Rivera (AC Milan); **1970** Gerd Muller (Bayern Munich); **1971** Johan Cruyff (Ajax); **1972** Franz Beckenbauer (Bayern Munich); **1973** Johan Cruyff (Barcelona); **1974** Johan Cruyff (Barcelona); **1975** Oleg Blokhin (Dynamo Kiev); **1976** Franz Beckenbauer (Bayern Munich); **1977** Allan Simonsen (Borussia Moenchengladbach); **1978** Kevin Keegan (SV Hamburg); **1979** Kevin Keegan (SV Hamburg); **1980** Karl-Heinz Rummenigge (Bayern Munich); **1981** Karl-Heinz Rummenigge (Bayern Munich); **1982** Paolo Rossi (Juventus); **1983** Michel Platini (Juventus); **1984** Michel Platini (Juventus); **1985** Michel Platini (Juventus); **1986** Igor Belanov (Dynamo Kiev); **1987** Ruud Gullit (AC Milan); **1988** Marco van Basten (AC Milan); **1989** Marco van Basten (AC Milan); **1990** Lothar Matthaus (Inter Milan); **1991** Jean-Pierre Papin (Marseille); **1992** Marco van Basten (AC Milan); **1993** Roberto Baggio (Juventus); **1994** Hristo Stoichkov (Barcelona); **1995** George Weah (AC Milan); **1996** Matthias Sammer (Borussia Dortmund); **1997** Ronaldo (Inter Milan); **1998** Zinedine Zidane (Juventus); **1999** Rivaldo (Barcelona); **2000** Luis Figo (Real Madrid); **2001** Michael Owen (Liverpool); **2002** Ronaldo (Real Madrid); **2003** Pavel Nedved (Juventus); **2004** Andriy Shevchenko (AC Milan); **2005** Ronaldinho (Barcelona); **2006** Fabio Cannavaro (Real Madrid); **2007** Kaka (AC Milan); **2008** Cristiano Ronaldo (Manchester United), **2009** Lionel Messi (Barcelona)

## WORLD FOOTBALLER OF YEAR

**1991** Lothar Matthaus (Inter Milan and Germany); **1992** Marco van Basten (AC Milan and Holland); **1993** Roberto Baggio (Juventus and Italy); **1994** Romario (Barcelona and Brazil); **1995** George Weah (AC Milan and Liberia); **1996** Ronaldo (Barcelona and Brazil); **1997** Ronaldo (Inter Milan and Brazil); **1998** Zinedine Zidane (Juventus and France); **1999** Rivaldo (Barcelona and Brazil); **2000** Zinedine Zidane (Juventus and France); **2001** Luis Figo (Real Madrid and Portugal); **2002** Ronaldo (Real Madrid and Brazil); **2003** Zinedine Zidane (Real Madrid and France); **2004** Ronaldinho (Barcelona and Brazil); **2005** Ronaldinho (Barcelona and Brazil); **2006** Fabio Cannavaro (Real Madrid and Italy); **2007** Kaka (AC Milan and Brazil); **2008** Cristiano Ronaldo (Manchester United and Portugal), **2009** Lionel Messi (Barcelona and Argentina)

## FIFA BALLON D'OR (replaces European and World Footballer of the Year)

**2010:** Lionel Messi (Barcelona). **2011** Lionel Messi (Barcelona), **2012** Lionel Messi (Barcelona), **2013** Cristiano Ronaldo (Real Madrid), **2014**: Cristiano Ronaldo (Real Madrid), **2015** Lionel Messi (Barcelona), **2016** Cristiano Ronaldo (Real Madrid), **2017** Cristiano Ronaldo (Real Madrid)

## FIFA WORLD COACH OF THE YEAR

**2010:** Jose Mourinho (Inter Milan). **2011** Pep Guardiola (Barcelona), **2012** Vicente del Bosque (Spain), **2013** Jupp Heynckes (Bayern Munich), **2014** Joachim Low (Germany), **2015** Luis Enrique (Barcelona), **2016** Claudio Ranieri (Leicester), **2017** Zinedine Zidane (Real Madrid)

# REVIEWS, APPEARANCES, SCORERS 2017–18

(figures in brackets denote appearances as substitute)

# PREMIER LEAGUE

## ARSENAL

Arsene Wenger received widespread acclaim – not least from arch-rivals Sir Alex Ferguson and Jose Mourinho at Manchester United – after announcing his departure from the club after nearly 22 years and 1,235 games as manager. But there would be no trophy to mark the end of an era when his side were knocked out of the Europa League in the semi-finals by Atletico Madrid. Arsenal had every chance to build a solid lead in the first leg against a side who had a man sent off with just ten minutes gone. Instead, a goal by Alexandre Lacazette was cancelled out by Antoine Griezmann eight minutes from the end of normal time and Atletico went through after winning the return match in Spain 1-0. It meant another season out of the Champions League, with any hopes of a title challenge having disappeared with three Premier League defeats in the opening eight matches, then Wenger admitting a top-four place was beyond them after losing to Brighton and falling 13 points adrift. Even before the sale of Alexis Sanchez in the January transfer window, Arsenal's inconsistency had been exposed by the teams above them, resulting in attendances at the Emirates dipping significantly well before the end of the campaign. A 3-0 League Cup Final defeat by Manchester City, followed four days later by the same scoreline against the same team, exposed their shortcomings. So did seven successive away defeats towards the end, along with a 4-2 FA Cup third round defeat by Nottingham Forest. Wenger was replaced by former Paris Saint-Germain coach Unai Emery.

| | | |
|---|---|---|
| Aubameyang P-E ...... 12 (1) | Kolasinac S ............. 25 (2) | Ospina D ..................... 4 (1) |
| Bellerin H ............... 34 (1) | Koscielny L ..................... 25 | Oxlade-Chamberlain A ...... 3 |
| Cech P .......................... 34 | Lacazette A ............. 26 (6) | Ozil M ...................... 24 (2) |
| Chambers C ............ 10 (2) | Maitland-Niles A ......... 8 (7) | Ramsey A ................. 21 (3) |
| Coquelin F ................. 1 (6) | Mavropanos K ................... 3 | Sanchez A ............... 17 (2) |
| Nketiah E .................. - (3) | Mertesacker P ............ 4 (2) | Walcott T ..................... - (6) |
| Elneny M ................ 11 (2) | Mkhitaryan H ............. 9 (2) | Welbeck D ............. 12 (16) |
| Giroud O ................. 1 (15) | Monreal N ............... 26 (2) | Willock J ..................... 1 (1) |
| Holding R ................. 9 (3) | Mustafi S ................ 25 (2) | Wilshere J ................ 12 (8) |
| Iwobi A .................... 22 (4) | Nelson R .................... 2 (1) | Xhaka G .................. 37 (1) |

**League goals** (74): Lacazette 14, Aubameyang 10, Ramsey 7, Sanchez 7, Welbeck 5, Monreal 5, Giroud 4, Ozil 4, Iwobi 3, Mustafi 3, Bellerin 2, Kolasinac 2, Koscielny 2, Mkhitaryan 2, Mertesacker 1, Wilshere 1, Xhaka 1, Opponents 1

**FA Cup goals** (2): Mertesacker 1, Welbeck 1. **League Cup goals** (6): Nketiah 2, Walcott 1, Welbeck 1, Xhaka 1, Opponents 1. **Community Shield goals** (1): Kolasinac 1

**Europa League goals** (30): Ramsey 4, Giroud 3, Lacazette 3, Walcott 3, Welbeck 3, Kolasinac 2, Bellerin 1, Debuchy M 1, Elneny 1, Holding 1, Mkhitaryan 1, Monreal 1, Ozil 1, Sanchez 1, Wilshere 1, Xhaka 1, Opponents 2

**Average home league attendance**: 59,323. **Player of Year**: Aaron Ramsey

## BOURNEMOUTH

Eddie Howe continued to remind his players they had no divine right to be in the Premier League and had to work every day to maintain it. The response was positive, enabling Bournemouth to take another step towards becoming an established top-flight club. They took some beatings on the way, conceding four goals to Liverpool, Manchester City, Huddersfield and Tottenham. But the character of the side was reflected in their ability to recover losing position in many other matches. When Lys Mousset and Josh King came off the bench to earn a 2-2 draw against Crystal Palace, it took Bournemouth's tally of points gained from losing positions to 18 – highest in the league. There was a sticky start to the season with successive defeats by West Bromwich Albion, Watford, Manchester City and Arsenal. At the half-way stage, they were still in the bottom three. Then, a run of seven unbeaten games, launched by Callum Wilson's stoppage-time equaliser for 3-3 against West Ham, netted 15 points and a move clear of the relegation pack. The sequence included a 3-0 win at Chelsea which Howe rated their best performance since being promoted.

Afobe B .................. 5 (12)
Ake N ..................... 37 (1)
Arter H .................... 11 (2)
Begovic A .....................38
Cook L .................... 25 (4)
Cook S .................... 31 (3)
Daniels C ................. 34 (1)
Defoe J ................. 11 (13)
Francis S ................. 31 (1)
Fraser R .................. 23 (3)
Gosling D ................ 21 (7)
Hyndman E .....................1
Ibe J ..................... 22 (10)
King J ..................... 27 (6)
Mings T ...................... 3 (1)
Mouset L ................. 4 (19)
Pugh M .................... 11 (9)
Simpson J ........................1
Smith A .................. 22 (5)
Stanislas J ............... 17 (2)
Surman A ................ 20 (5)
Wilson C .................. 23 (5)

**League goals** (45): King 8, Wilson 8, Fraser 5, Stanislas 5, Defoe 4, Ake 2, Cook S 2, Gosling 2, Ibe 2, Mousset 2, Surman 2, Arter 1, Daniels 1, Smith 1
**FA Cup goals** (2): Cook S 1, Mousset 1. **League Cup goals** (7): Afobe 1, Fraser 1, Gosling 1, King 1, Pugh 1, Simpson 1, Wilson 1
**Average home league** attendance: 10,640. **Player of Year**: Nathan Ake

## BRIGHTON AND HOVE ALBION

Glenn Murray fired Brighton clear of the bottom three at a time when a serious shortage of goals was threatening an immediate return to the Championship. The 34-year-old striker scored five in five games to insulate them against any late slide – and the toughest run-in of all the relegation candidates, with four of the final five matches against top-four teams. At the time, Chris Hughton's side were a single point away from a relegation place following a 4-0 home defeat by Chelsea. They had won just once in 13 league matches, failing to score in nine of them, and conceding too many goals from set pieces. Murray delivered a confidence-boosting FA Cup third round win at Middlesbrough, then continued to make his mark as Brighton defeated West Ham, Swansea and Arsenal at the Amex Stadium and held Southampton and Stoke away from home. The reward was a place in the top half of the table, Brighton were unable to maintain it, but a point against Tottenham was followed by victory over Manchester United – earned by a Pascal Gross header confirmed by goalline technology – which ensured staying up.

Baldock S .................. - (2)
Bong G .........................25
Brown I ...................... 4 (9)
Bruno ...................... 23 (2)
Duffy S .........................37
Dunk L .........................38
Goldson C ................. 2 (1)
Gross P ................... 35 (3)
Hemed T .................... 9 (7)
Hunemeier U .............. - (1)
Izquierdo J .............. 23 (9)
Kayal B .................... 8 (11)
Knockaert A ............. 27 (6)
Locadia J .................. 3 (3)
March S ................. 18 (18)
Murphy J ................... 1 (3)
Murray G ................ 25 (10)
Propper D .....................35
Rosenior L ................. 1 (2)
Ryan M .........................38
Schelotto E ............... 15 (5)
Stephens D ...................36
Suttner M ................ 13 (1)
Ulloa L ...................... 2 (8)

**League goals** (34): Murray 12, Gross 7, Izquierdo 5, Knockaert 3, Hemed 2, Dunk 1, Locadia 1, March 1, Ulloa 1, Opponents 1
**FA Cup goals** (6): Murray 2, Goldson 1, Locadia 1, Stephens 1, Ulloa 1. **League Cup goals** (1): Tilley J 1
**Average home league attendance**: 30,402. **Player of Year**: Pascal Gross

## BURNLEY

When Burnley opened the season with a 3-2 win against defending champions Chelsea at Stamford Bridge, there were many who dismissed it as a one-off performance. When they held Tottenham at Wembley and earned another 1-1 draw against Liverpool at Anfield, the spotlight began to follow Sean Dyche's team. And with wins at Everton, Southampton and Bournemouth came the realisation that something special was in the making away from the normal Premier League hot-spots. A side with just one victory away from home in the previous season were fourth in the table. That momentum couldn't be maintained. But Burnley held on to seventh place in pursuit of the club's first appearance in Europe since the Fairs Cup in 1967. After entering the final phase of the season neck-and-neck with Leicester, they reeled off five successive victories, one of them against their rivals, to open up a nine-point advantage, earned with a spate of goals from Ashley Barnes and Chris Wood. The reward was a place in the Europa League and the club's highest finish since the sixth spot delivered in the old First Division in 1974. Motivated and highly organised, Burnley were difficult to beat, with goalkeeper Nick Pope a key player after replacing the injured Tom Heaton and proving so capable that he won a place in England's World Cup squad.

Arfield S .................. 15 (3)
Bardsley P ......................13
Barnes A............... 21 (15)
Brady R .........................15
Cork J.............................38
Defour S ........................24
Gudmundsson J B..... 32 (3)
Heaton T...........................4
Hendrick J............... 29 (5)
Lennon A ................ 13 (1)
Long K...........................16
Lowton M ................ 25 (1)
McNeil D..................... - (1)
Mee B ...........................29
Nkoudou G-K............. 2 (6)
Pope N..................... 34 (1)
Tarkowski J.....................31
Taylor C....................10 (1)
Vokes S....................7 (23)
Walters J ....................- (3)
Ward S...........................28
Wells N ......................- (9)
Westwood A..............12 (7)
Wood C ....................20 (4)

**League goals** (36): Wood 10, Barnes 9, Vokes 4, Arfield 2, Cork 2, Gudmundsson 2, Hendrick 2, Brady 1, Defour 1, Long 1, Ward 1, Opponents 1
**FA Cup goals** (1): Barnes 1. **League Cup goals** (4): Brady 2, Cork 1, Wood 1
**Average home league attendance**: 20,688. **Player of Year**: Nick Pope

## CHELSEA

A below-par season dominated by speculation about the position of Antonio Conte was rescued by victory in the FA Cup. Eden Hazard's winner from the penalty spot went some to compensating for a poor defence of the Premier League title and defeat by Barcelona in the last-16 of the Champions League. But it did little to disguise prolonged tension between the manager and the club's hierarchy over transfer business – and his falling-out with Diego Costa which led eventually to the leading scorer's return to Atletico Madrid. Conte blamed insufficient team-strengthening during the summer for their title chances falling by the wayside barely two months into the campaign. By then, they had lost three of the opening eight matches and were nine points adrift of Manchester City after a 2-1 defeat by previously goalless Crystal Palace. Chelsea retained a top-four place for another four months until successive defeats by Manchester United and Manchester City, followed closely by a home loss to Tottenham, left them eight points adrift of the top-four with little chance of retrieving the deficit. They went to Wembley on the back of a poor finish – 1-1 at home to Huddersfield and a 3-0 defeat at Newcastle. But Conte successfully set up his side to frustrate Manchester United only to be dismissed a few weeks later. He was replaced by former Napoli coach Maurizio Sarri.

Alonso M .......................33
Ampadu E.................... - (1)
Azpilicueta C..................37
Bakayoko T .............. 24 (5)
Barkley R..........................2
Batshuayi M............... 3 (9)
Boga J ..............................1
Caballero W......................3
Cahill G .................. 24 (3)
Christensen A........... 23 (4)
Courtois T .......................35
Drinkwater D............. 5 (7)
Emerson .................... 3 (2)
Fabregas C.............. 25 (7)
Giroud O.................... 6 (7)

Hazard E.................. 28 (6)
Hudson-Odoi C ........... - (2)
Kante N.........................34
Luiz D ...................... 9 (1)
Morata A.................. 24 (7)
Moses V................... 25 (3)
Musonda C................. - (3)
Pedro ................... 17 (14)
Rudiger A ............... 25 (2)
Willian.................. 20 (16)
Zappacosta D ......... 12 (10)

**League goals** (62): Hazard 12, Morata 11, Alonso 7, Willian 6, Pedro 4, Giroud 3, Moses 3, Azpilicueta 2, Bakayoko 2, Batshuayi 2, Fabregas 2, Rudiger 2, Drinkwater 1, Kante 1, Luiz 1, Zappacosta 1, Opponents 2
**FA Cup goals** (13): Batshuayi 3, Giroud 2, Morata 2, Pedro 2, Willian 2, Alonso 1, Hazard 1.
**League Cup goals** (10): Batshuayi 3, Willian 2, Hazard 1, Kenedy 1, Morata 1, Musonda 1, Rudiger 1. **Community Shield goals** (1): Moses 1
**Champions League goals** (17): Hazard 3, Willian 3, Batshuayi 2, Azpilicueta 1, Bakayoko 1, Fabregas 1, Luiz 1, Morata 1, Pedro 1, Zappacosta 1, Opponents 2
**Average home league attendance**: 41,282. **Player of Year**: N'Golo Kante

## CRYSTAL PALACE

Roy Hodgson came through one of the biggest tests of his 40-year career in management to lift the relegation cloud over Selhurst Park. He replaced Frank de Boer, who was sacked after four goalless defeats, making him the shortest-lived manager in Premier League history. Another left Palace as the first top-flight team in English football to lose five without scoring. That was followed by 5-0 and 4-0 defeats by Manchester City and Manchester United respectively. The former England manager, who started his playing days at the club, called it 'a baptism of fire' before Wilfried Zaha returned from a knee injury to lift the gloom with a goal in a 2-1 win over defending champions Chelsea. Zaha went on to prove an influential figure in his side's revival. Palace remained bottom into November before four victories in seven games – Watford, Leicester, Southampton and Burnley – were accompanied by a move towards mid-table. In a tightly packed lower part of the division, a run of seven without a win had them back in the bottom three. Then came two vital victories over relegation rivals – 2-0 against Huddersfield, 3-2 against Brighton in which Zaha scored twice. That put Palace six points above the drop and they rounded off the season in style with three more victories, including their biggest in the Premier League – 5-0 against Leicester.

Benteke C................ 24 (7)
Cabaye Y.................. 28 (3)
Dann S.................... 16 (1)
Delaney D.................. 1 (1)
Fosu-Mensah T......... 17 (4)
Hennessey W..................27
Kaikai S...................... - (1)
Kelly M.................... 12 (3)
Ladapo F .................... - (1)
Lee Chung-Yong.......... 1 (6)
Loftus-Cheek R......... 21 (3)
Lumeka L.................... - (1)
McArthur J ............... 27 (6)
Milivojevic L............ 35 (1)
Souare P..................... - (1)
Puncheon J ............... 6 (4)
Riedewald J............... 4 (8)
Sakho M.................. 18 (1)
Sako B .................... 4 (12)
Schlupp J................ 21 (3)
Sorloth A.........................4
Speroni J.......................11
Tomkins J.................27 (1)
Townsend A.............35 (1)
Wan-Bissaka A.................7
Ward J ..........................19
Zaha W ...................28 (1)
Van Aanholt P...........25 (3)

**League goals** (45): Milivojevic 10, Zaha 9, McArthur 5, Van Aanholt 5, Benteke 3, Sako 3, Tomkins 3, Loftus-Cheek 2, Townsend 2, Dann 1, Sakho 1, Opponents 1
**FA Cup goals** (1): Sako 1. **League Cup goals** (4): McArthur 2, Sako 2
**Average home league attendance**: 25,063. **Player of Year**: Wilfried Zaha

## EVERTON

An outlay of more than £180m on players was not matched by Everton's results throughout a season which brought the dismissal of one manager, the unsuccessful pursuit of a second and the controversial appointment of a third. Ronald Koeman's £135m summer spending included club-record fees for Jordan Pickford and Gylfi Sigurdsson. He also took Wayne Rooney back to

Goodison Park, but was sacked in October following a 5-2 home defeat by Arsenal which left his side third from bottom with two wins out of nine. The club were rebuffed in their approach for Watford's Marco Silva, while failure to qualify from their Europa League group ended under-23 coach David Unsworth's chances of the job permanently after a spell as caretaker. They turned to Sam Allardyce, who started his ninth club managerial appointment with 2-0 win over Huddersfield and 12 points from the first six games in charge. A further £47m was spent on Theo Walcott and Turkish striker Cenk Tosun in the winter transfer window. But conceding five more goals to Arsenal in the return fixture and four to Tottenham fuelled unrest among supporters. Allardyce eventually completed the job he was hired to do – avoid a relegation struggle – while securing an eighth-place finish. He was then sacked and the club finally got their man, with Silva now available after his dismissal by Watford.

Baines L........................22
Baningime B.............. 1 (7)
Besic M........................- (2)
Bolasie Y................. 11 (5)
Calvert-Lewin D...... 18 (14)
Cenk Tosun.............. 12 (2)
Coleman S.....................12
Davies T................ 20 (13)
Funes Mori R............. 1 (3)
Gueye I.................... 32 (1)
Holgate M............... 13 (2)
Jagielka P................ 23 (2)
Keane M.................. 29 (1)
Kenny J.................... 17 (2)
Klaassen D................. 3 (4)
Lennon A................... 9 (6)
Lookman A................. 1 (6)
Mangala E.........................2
Martina C................. 20 (1)
McCarthy J................. 3 (1)
Mirallas K...................2 (3)
Niasse O................10 (12)
Pickford J.......................38
Rooney W.................27 (4)
Sandro........................3 (5)
Schneiderlin M.........24 (6)
Sigurdsson G............25 (2)
Vlasic N......................7 (5)
Walcott T..................13 (1)
Williams A................20 (4)

**League goals** (44): Rooney 10, Niasse 8, Cenk Tosun 5, Calvert-Lewin 4, Sigurdsson 4, Walcott 3, Baines 2, Davies 2, Gueye 2, Bolasie 1, Williams 1, Opponents 2
**FA Cup goals** (1); Sigurdsson 1. **League Cup goals** (4): Calvert-Lewin 3, Niasse 1
**Europa League goals** (12): Lookman 2, Vlasic 2, Baines 1, Calvert-Lewin 1, Gueye 1, Keane 1, Rooney 1, Sandro 1, Sigurdsson 1, Williams 1
**Average home league attendance**: 38,797. **Player of Year**: Jordan Pickford

## HUDDERSFIELD TOWN

Jubilant players hoisted manager David Wagner aloft on the Stamford Bridge pitch in celebration of staying up against all the odds. A second defiant display in the space of five days delivered a 1-1 draw against Chelsea, took them to 37 points and ensured they could not be overtaken in the final round of matches. Previously, they had interrupted Manchester City's title party by earning a goalless draw at the Etihad. That Huddersfield collected all-important points at two of the Premier League's biggest clubs was a fitting testimony to collective commitment and organisation. The club had prepared well for the season with three record-breaking signings and all transfer activity wrapped up weeks before the start. It was not enough to alter the widespread belief that victory in the 2017 Play-off Final would be the limit of their ambitions. That perception was immediately challenged by wins over Crystal Palace and Newcastle in the opening two fixtures. Then came a 2-0 win over Manchester United, earned by goals from Aaron Mooy and Laurent Depoitre and described by Wagner as 'a special moment for the town.' After that, times were often tough, notably when a run of eight games without a victory in mid-winter left them second from bottom. It was ended by a 4-1 win over Bournemouth and from then on Huddersfield did just enough to stay out of the bottom three.

Billing P.................... 8 (8)
Cranie M.................... 2 (1)
Depoitre L.............. 18 (15)
Hadergjonaj F........... 19 (4)
Hefele M.....................- (2)
Hogg J..................... 29 (1)
Ince T...................... 27 (6)
Jorgensen M...................38
Kachunga E............. 17 (2)
Kongolo T............... 11 (2)
Lolley J...................... 2 (4)
Lossl J...........................38
Lowe C.................... 19 (4)
Malone S.............. 12 (10)
Mooy A.................... 34 (2)
Mounie S................. 21 (7)
Palmer K.................. 1 (3)
Pritchard A.............. 12 (2)

| | | |
|---|---|---|
| Quaner C .............. 13 (13) | Smith T .................. 21 (3) | Van La Parra R ........ 26 (7) |
| Sabiri A .................... 2 (3) | Whitehead D .............. - (4) | |
| Schindler C ....................37 | Williams D .............. 11 (9) | |

**League goals** (28): Mounie 7, Depoitre 6, Mooyn 4, Van La Parra 3, Ince 2, Kachunga 1, Lolley 1, Pritchard 1, Opponents 3

**FA Cup goals** (7): Mounie 2, Van La Parra 2, Ince 1, Williams 1, Opponents 1. **League Cup goals** (2): Billing 1, Lolley 1

**Average home league attendance**: 24,040. **Player of Year**: Christopher Schindler

## LEICESTER CITY

Leicester's bid for a place in Europe to brighten a largely anonymous season was undermined from the moment Riyad Mahrez showed his annoyance at a winter move to Manchester City falling through. Until the midfielder's self-imposed exile from the club, Claude Puel's side were running neck-and-neck with Burnley for a Europa League spot. By the time he returned to training, Mahrez had missed matches against Everton and Swansea and been restricted to a substitute's appearance against Manchester City. He was back in the side against Stoke and Bournemouth. But the failure to win any of those five matches enabled Burnley to open up a gap, which they extended with a 2-1 victory over their rivals, then went on to tie down seventh place. Soon after, Leicester's last chance of something tangible from the campaign went with an extra-time defeat by Chelsea in the FA Cup quarter-finals Former Southampton manager Puel replaced Craig Shakespeare, who was sacked four months into a three-year contract as permanent manager, with his side third from bottom after eight matches.

| | | |
|---|---|---|
| Adrien Silva ............. 9 (3) | Fuchs C ................. 21 (4) | Mahrez R ................34 (2) |
| Albrighton M........... 30 (4) | Gray D .................. 17 (18) | Morgan W......................32 |
| Amartey D................. 6 (2) | Hamer B ................... 3 (1) | Ndidi O.........................33 |
| Barnes H .................... - (3) | Iborra V.................... 17 (2) | Okazaki S..............17 (10) |
| Benalouane Y....................1 | Iheanacho K............ 7 (14) | Schmeichel K................33 |
| Chilwell B ................ 20 (4) | Jakupovic E.......................2 | Simpson D ..............27 (1) |
| Choudhury H............. 4 (4) | James M ................ 11 (2) | Slimani I.................2 (10) |
| Diabate F.................. 5 (9) | King A ...................... 5 (6) | Ulloa L.......................- (4) |
| Dragovic A ................ 7 (4) | Maguire H.....................38 | Vardy J.........................37 |

**League goals** (56): Vardy 20, Mahrez 12, Okazaki 6, Gray 3, Iborra 3, Iheanacho 3, Albrighton 2, Maguire 2, King 1, Slimani 1, Opponents 3

**FA Cup goals** (9): Iheanacho 4, Diabate 2, Vardy 2, Ndidi 1. **League Cup goals** (10): Slimani 4, Gray 1, Iheanacho 1, Mahrez 1, Musa A 1, Okazaki 1, Vardy 1

**Average home league attendance**: 31,583. **Player of Year**: Harry Maguire

## LIVERPOOL

Liverpool were in good company when they lost interest in the title reckoning before the clocks went back. Jurgen Klopp then lost Philippe Coutinho to Barcelona in the winter transfer winter and Emre Can (back) and Alex Oxlade-Chamberlain (knee) to injuries towards the end of the season. And his side lost the Champions League Final to Real Madrid after another injury, this time to record marksman Mohamed Salah (shoulder). Yet there was still plenty to admire about the club's season after a dodgy start when 16 goals were conceded in nine games – the most since 1964. Klopp plugged the holes by acquiring Southampton's Virgil van Dijk for £75m, a world record for a defender, and their goals against ratio halved. The goals for column continued to bulge, with the front three of Salah, Roberto Firmino and Sadio Mane all on the mark to inflict Manchester City's first defeat of the campaign 4-3 at Anfield. Late on, their top-four place came under threat with points dropped against struggling West Bromwich Albion and Stoke, followed by a 1-0 defeat at Stamford Bridge. But Chelsea blew the chance and Liverpool made sure of holding on to fourth place by beating Brighton 4-0. Salah, named Player of the Year by the PFA and football writers, brought his tally to 32 to win the Golden Boot and set a Premier League record for 38 games.

Alexander-Arnold T ... 18 (1)
Clyne N ..................... 2 (1)
Coutinho P............... 13 (1)
Emre Can................. 24 (2)
Firmino R ................ 32 (5)
Gomez J .................. 21 (2)
Grujic M ..................... - (3)
Henderson J............. 25 (2)
Ings D ....................... 3 (5)
Karius L.........................19
Klavan R .................. 16 (3)
Lallana A.................. 1 (11)
Lovren D .................. 24 (5)
Mane S .................... 28 (1)
Matip J .................... 22 (3)
Mignolet S.......................19
Milner J ................. 16 (16)
Moreno A ................. 14 (2)
Origi D ........................- (1)
Oxlade-Chamberlain A 14 (18)
Robertson A.................. 22
Salah M ...................34 (2)
Solanke D.................5 (16)
Sturridge D.................5 (4)
Wijnaldum G.............27 (6)
Woodburn B.................- (1)
Van Dijk V ..................... 14

**League goals** (84): Salah 32, Firmino 15, Mane 10, Coutinho 7, Emre Can 3, Oxlade-Chamberlain 3, Lovren 2, Sturridge 2, Alexander-Arnold 1, Henderson 1, Ings 1, Klavan 1, Matip 1, Robertson 1, Solanke 1, Wijnaldum 1, Opponents 2
**FA Cup goals** (4): Firmino 1, Milner 1, Salah 1, Van Dijk 1. **League Cup goals**: None
**Champions League goals** (47): Firmino 11, Salah 11, Mane 10, Coutinho 5, Emre Can 3, Alexander-Arnold 2, Oxlade-Chamberlain 2, Sturridge 1, Wijnaldum 1, Opponents 1
**Average home league attendance**: 53,049. **Player of Year**: Mohamed Salah

## MANCHESTER CITY

The superlatives had been exhausted well before the end of the season. What more was there to acclaim, apart from even more records waiting to be broken? Manchester City blew apart the Premier League like no other club except, perhaps, Manchester United in 1999-2000. They had everything in place, concluding more than £200m worth of major transfer business weeks before the campaign kicked-off. One by one, pretenders to the title fell away, until only United presented a realistic challenge. And when they were beaten 2-1 at Old Trafford in early December, Pep Guadiola's side were out on their own. They became the first in the Premier League to score five or more in three successive matches, defeating Liverpool 5-0, Watford 6-0 and Crystal Palace 5-0. By overwhelming Stoke 7-2 City were the first to accumulate 29 goals in their first eight games since Everton in 1894-95, followed by an all-time record for English top-flight football of 18 successive victories. On the way, Sergio Aguero became the club's all-time record marksman in all competitions with his 178th goal in a 4-2 away win over Napoli which confirmed their place in the Champions League's knockout phase. City dismissed Arsenal in the League Cup Final before falling to Liverpool over two legs in Europe, then surrendering a two-goal lead and losing to Manchester United. But they were crowned champions with five matches to play after United lost to West Bromwich Albion and became the first ever to reach 100 points when a 94th minute goal by Gabriel Jesus delivered victory at Southampton on the final day. Other Premier League records were for goals scored, goal difference, overall wins, away victories, away points and the points gap to second place.

Aguero S.................. 22 (3)
Bernardo Silva........ 15 (20)
Bravo C...................... 2 (1)
Danilo .................. 13 (10)
De Bruyne K............. 36 (1)
Delph F .................. 21 (1)
Diaz B ....................... - (5)
Ederson .........................36
Fernandinho............ 33 (1)
Foden P ...................... - (5)
Gabriel Jesus.......... 19 (10)
Gundogan I............. 15 (15)
Kompany V.....................17
Laporte A .........................9
Mangala E................. 4 (5)
Mendy B ................... 4 (3)
Nmecha L ................... - (2)
Otamendi N............. 33 (1)
Sane L.....................27 (5)
Silva D.....................28 (1)
Sterling R................29 (4)
Stones J..................16 (2)
Toure Y ...................... 1 (9)
Walker K ...................... 32
Zinchenko A ..............6 (2)

**League goals** (106): Aguero 21, Sterling 18, Gabriel Jesus 13, Sane 10, Silva D 9, De Bruyne 8, Bernardo Silva 6, Fernandinho 5, Gundogan 4, Otamendi 4, Danilo 3, Delph 1, Kompany 1, Opponents 3
**FA Cup goals** (6): Aguero 2, Bernardo Silva 1, De Bruyne 1, Sane 1, Sterling 1. **League Cup goals**

(11): Aguero 3, Sane 3, De Bruyne 2, Bernardo Silva 1, Kompany 1, Silva D 1
**Champions League goals** (20): Aguero 4, Gabriel Jesus 4, Sterling 4, Stones 3, Gundogan 2, Bernardo Silva 1, De Bruyne 1, Otamendi 1,
**Average home league attendance**: 53,812. **Player of Year**: Kevin De Bruyne

## MANCHESTER UNITED

Dominated by their next-door neighbours, knocked out of the Champions League in front of their own supporters and unable to go some way to balancing the books in the FA Cup. Manchester United's season was hardly a failure and would have more than met the expectations of many teams. But it still fell short of the demands of a club of such stature, both in terms of missing out on the silverware and, probably more importantly, lacking the vibrancy of their top-four rivals. United matched Manchester City stride for stride for the first month or so, accumulating 19 points and 21 goals from the opening seven matches. But while their rivals motored on, they stalled against Huddersfield and Chelsea, then had a 40-match unbeaten home run ended by City, after which even Jose Mourinho had to concede the title. United drew some degree of satisfaction by overturning a two-goal deficit in the return fixture to win 3-2 with two goals from Paul Pogba in the space of 97 seconds and Chris Smalling's volley for the decider. It meant City had to wait another week before clinching the title and eventually removing United's 18-point margin of success in 1999-200 from the record books. A 2-1 defeat by Sevilla in the last 16 at Old Trafford put paid to thoughts of Champions League success, leaving the FA Cup as the only hope of a trophy. Mourinho felt Chelsea's victory at Wembley was undeserved. The wider viewpoint concentrated more on his side's failings.

Bailly E.................... 11 (2)
Blind D...................... 4 (3)
Carrick M................... 1 (1)
Darmian M................. 5 (3)
De Gea D........................37
Fellaini M ................ 5 (11)
Herrera A.............. 13 (13)
Ibrahimovic Z............ 1 (4)
Jones P..........................23
Lindelof V................ 13 (4)
Lingard J............... 20 (13)
Lukaku R ................ 33 (1)
Martial A............... 18 (12)
Mata J ..................... 23 (5)
Matic N................... 35 (1)
McTominay S............. 7 (6)
Mkhitaryan H............ 11 (4)
Pogba P .................. 25 (2)
Rashford M............17 (18)
Rojo M .......................8 (1)
Romero S ........................ 1
Sanchez A..................... 12
Shaw L.......................8 (3)
Smalling C ..............28 (1)
Tuanzebe A.................- (1)
Valencia A..................... 31
Young A ..................28 (2)

**League goals** (68): Lukaku 16, Martial 9, Lingard 8, Rashford 7, Pogba 6, Fellaini 4, Smalling 4, Mata 3, Valencia 3, Sanchez 2, Young 2, Bailly 1, Matic 1, Mkhitaryan 1, Opponents 1
**FA Cup goals** (12): Lukaku 5, Herrera 2, Lingard 2, Matic 1, Rashford 1, Sanchez 1
**League Cup goals** (7): Lingard 3, Rashford 2, Ibrahimovic 1, Martial 1
**Champions League goals** (13): Lukaku 5, Rashford 3, Blind 1, Fellaini 1, Martial 1, Mkhitaryan 1, Opponents 1. **European Super Cup** (1): Lukaku 1
**Average home league attendance**: 74,976. **Player of Year**: David de Gea

## NEWCASTLE UNITED

A late season run of success lifted the relegation cloud over St James' Park. Four successive victories pointed Newcastle to safety at a time when they looked set for a nail-biting run-in to the end of the season. Rafael Benitez blamed the threat of an immediate return to the Championship on a lack of summer investment by owner Mike Ashley, arguing that £40m was nowhere near enough to meet the demands of the Premier League. Well into the second half of the campaign, the manager continued to argue his case, with his side one of seven struggling to avoid dropping into the bottom three. Then, two winter loan signings, goalkeeper Martin Dubravka from Sparta Prague and Chelsea winger Kenedy, began to make an important impact. A 1-0 win over Manchester United set the ball rolling. Kenedy's two goals against Southampton was followed by more success against Huddersfield, Leicester and Arsenal, in which Ayoze Perez scored three times, resulting in a climb to mid-table. Two more by Perez came on the final day of the campaign when a 3-0 win over Chelsea confirmed tenth place.

Aarons R.................... 1 (3)
Atsu C..................... 19 (9)
Clark C.................. 19 (10)
Darlow K........................10
Diame M................. 23 (8)
Dubravka M....................12
Dummett P............. 19 (1)
Elliot R..........................16
Gayle D................ 23 (12)
Haidara M.................. - (1)
Hayden I............... 15 (11)
Jesus Gamez................ (1)
Joselu.................... 19 (11)
Kenedy.........................13
Lascelles J.............. 32 (1)
Lejeune F.......................24
Manquillo J............. 20 (1)
Mbemba C................. 7 (2)
Merino M...............14 (10)
Mitrovic A.....................- (6)
Murphy J...............13 (12)
Perez A.................. 28 (8)
Ritchie M................32 (3)
Saivet H..........................1
Shelvey J..................25 (5)
Slimani I....................1 (3)
Yedlin D..................31 (3)

**League goals** (39): Perez 8, Gayle 6, Joselu 4, Lascelles 3, Ritchie 3, Atsu 2, Clark 2, Diame 2, Kenedy 2, Hayden 1, Merino 1, Mitrovic 1, Murphy 1, Saivet 1, Shelvey 1, Opponents 1
**FA Cup goals** (3): Perez 2, Shelvey 1. **League Cup goals** (2): Aarons 1, Mitrovic 1
**Average home league attendance**: 51,992. **Player of Year**: Jamaal Lascelles

## SOUTHAMPTON

Mark Hughes returned to the club he once helped save from relegation as a player and led them to safety as manager. Southampton were in the bottom three with a month of the season remaining after four successive defeats and 12 goals conceded. Two goals by Dusan Tadic against Bournemouth delivered a first home win for five months. Then, they came through two demanding away matches. First, Nathan Redmond's goal at Goodison Park looked like delivering three more points until Everton won a disputed free-kick, were allowed to take it ten yards further up the field and equalised deep into stoppage-time with a deflected Tom Davies shot. Preparations for a crucial fixture against fellow-strugglers Swansea were disrupted by the mysterious cancellation of hotel rooms booked for an overnight stay. But amid a suggestion of 'dirty tricks,' Hughes used the incident to fire up his team and a 1-0 victory, secured by substitute Manolo Gabbiadini, effectively brought survival and sent Swansea down. Sacked by Stoke, Hughes, was brought in when Southampton's season turned sour under Mauricio Pellegrino after a 4-1 win over Everton at St Mary's had consolidated a mid-table position. They conceded five goals to Tottenham, four to Leicester and after a lifeless display at Newcastle, had won only once in 17 matches. Pellegrino was dismissed ahead of an FA Cup tie against Wigan, which they won in Hughes's first match in charge, before losing by the same 2-0 scoreline to Chelsea in the semi-finals.

Austin C............... 10 (14)
Bednarez J.......................5
Bertrand R.....................35
Boufal S............... 11 (15)
Carrillo G.................. 5 (2)
Davis S................... 17 (6)
Forster F........................20
Gabbiadini M......... 11 (17)
Hoedt W........................28
Hojbjerg P............... 19 (4)
Lemina M............... 20 (5)
Long S.................. 15 (15)
McCarthy A.....................18
McQueen S................ 1 (6)
Obafemi M................ - (1)
Pied J..............................2
Redmond N............. 22 (9)
Romeu O........................34
Sims J.......................1 (5)
Soares C........................32
Stephens J.....................22
Tadic D...................34 (2)
Targett M.........................2
Ward-Prowse J........20 (10)
Yoshida M...............23 (1)
Van Dijk V...............11 (1)

**League goals** (37): Austin 7, Tadic 6, Gabbiadini 5, Davis 3, Ward-Prowse 3, Boufal 2, Long 2, Stephens 2, Yoshida 2, Bednarek 1, Lemina 1, Redmond 1, Romeu 1, Opponents 1
**FA Cup goals** (6): Hoedt 1, Hojbjerg 1, Soares 1, Stephens 1, Tadic 1, Ward-Prowse 1. **League Cup goals**: None
**Average home league attendance**: 30,794. **Player of Year**: Alex McCarthy

## STOKE CITY

Ten successive seasons of Premier League football came to an end for Stoke, who collapsed in the second half of the season and paid the penalty. They had never been lower than 14th and recorded top-ten finishes in three of the previous four seasons under Mark Hughes. This time, his side drifted just above the relegation zone for much of the first part of the campaign, winning sufficient enough games to compensate for heavy defeats by Manchester City (7-2), Tottenham (5-1) and Chelsea (4-0). The return match at Stamford Bridge delivered another beating (5-0) and Hughes was sacked in the wake of an FA Cup third round defeat by League Two Coventry. Paul Lambert, former Wolves, Blackburn, Aston Vila and Norwich manager, took charge after Martin O'Neill reportedly turned down the job. Lambert watched a 3-0 defeat by Manchester United, then supervised a 2-0 victory over Huddersfield with goals from Joe Allen and Mame Biram Diouf. It proved to be his only one until the final fixture which brought a 2-1 win over relegated Swansea. By then, Stoke had taken just seven points from 13 games, paying the price for dropping 12 points from leading positions. They went down after a 2-1 home defeat by Crystal Palace and finished second from bottom. Lambert left the club by mutual consent and was replaced by Stoke's Gary Rowett.

Adam C..................... 5 (6)
Afellay I..................... 1 (5)
Allen J...........................36
Bauer M ........................15
Berahino S............... 3 (12)
Biram Diouf M.......... 30 (5)
Butland J........................35
Cameron G............... 17 (3)
Campbell T................. - (4)
Choupo-Moting E...... 26 (4)
Crouch P............... 14 (17)
Edwards T..........................6
Fletcher D................ 25 (2)
Grant L .............................3
Ireland S.................... 1 (3)
Jese............................ 8 (5)
Johnson G................. 7 (2)
Krkic B ..............................1
Martins Indi B .......... 14 (3)
Ndiaye B.........................13
Ngoy J .........................- (1)
Pieters E.................30 (1)
Shaqiri X.......................36
Shawcross R..................27
Sobhi R..................12 (12)
Sorenson L.......................1
Stafylidis K.................4 (1)
Tymon J .....................2 (1)
Wimmer K................14 (3)
Zouma K..................32 (2)

**League goals** (35): Shaqiri 8, Diouf 6, Choupo-Moting 5, Crouch 5, Allen 2, Ndiaye 2, Sobhi 2, Fletcher 1, Jese 1, Shawcross 1, Zouma 1, Opponents 1
**FA Cup goals** (1): Adam 1. **League Cup goals** (4): Allen 2, Crouch 1, Sobhi 1
**Average home league attendance**: 29,280. **Player of Year**: No award

## SWANSEA CITY

A chronic shortage of goals brought an end to seven seasons in the Premier League. Swansea were unable to compensate for the loss of leading scorers Fernando Llorente and Gylfi Sigurdsson and failed to score in almost half of their 38 matches. The writing was on the wall with blanks in four of their opening five matches. There was little improvement under Paul Clement, who was replaced midway through the campaign by Carlos Carvalhal, returning to management a week after himself being sacked by Sheffield Wednesday. The Portuguese made a successful start against Watford, closely followed by victories over Liverpool and Arsenal. His first five games yielded ten points, lifting Swansea off the bottom of the table. That boost was followed by the club spending a record £18m on transfer deadline-day to bring back Andre Ayew from West Ham. But just when a 4-1 victory over West Ham looked to have sealed a move away from trouble, the tide turned during eight games without a win – six of them goalless. There was still a golden chance of survival in the last of those at home to Southampton. But a 1-0 defeat condemned them, while effectively guaranteeing their rivals stayed up. The club decided not to renew Carvalhal's contract, instead turning to Graham Potter from the Sweden club Ostersunds.

Abraham T............ 15 (16)
Ayew A.................... 10 (2)
Ayew J..................... 33 (3)
Bartley K ................... 2 (3)
Bony W....................... 8 (7)
Britton L.................... 4 (1)
Carroll T ................. 28 (9)
Clucas S.................. 23 (6)
Dyer N.................... 16 (8)
Fabianski L.....................38
Fer L........................ 15 (5)
Fernandez F ...................30
Fulton J ....................... - (2)
Ki Sung-Yueng.......... 21 (4)
King A ....................... 9 (2)
Mawson A........................38
McBurnie O................ 2 (9)
Mesa R ...................... 9 (2)
Narsingh L ...............5 (13)
Naughton K...................34
Olsson M.......................36
Rangel A....................2 (2)
Roberts C...................3 (1)
Routledge W............4 (11)
Sanches R..................9 (3)
Van der Hoorn M...........24

**League goals** (28): Ayew J 7, Abraham 5, Clucas 3, Bony 2, Ki Sung-Yueng 2, King 2, Mawson 2, Fer 1, Fernandez 1, Narsingh 1, Van der Hoorn 1, Opponents 1
**FA Cup goals** (13): Dyer 3, Abraham 2, Ayew J 2, Bony 1, Carroll 1, James D 1, Narsingh 1, Naughton 1, Routledge 1. **League Cup goals** (6): Ayew J 2, Fer 2, Abraham 1, Mawson
**Average home league attendance**: 20,623. **Player of Year**: Lukasz Fabianski

## TOTTENHAM HOTSPUR

Along with the rest of the supporting cast, Tottenham's title challenge was effectively over with barely a dozen games completed, a 2-0 defeat by arch-rivals Arsenal leaving them 11 points behind Manchester City. Mauricio Pochettino admitted the club's transfer business – five signings in the final two weeks of the summer window – had not been the ideal preparation. And there were more questions to face after his side faltered in the knockout competitions. After holding their own in the away leg of the Champions League last 16 tie against Juventus, they were beaten 2-1 at Wembley. Then, after leading against Manchester United, Tottenham were beaten by the same scoreline in the semi-finals of the FA Cup at what again was their home ground ahead of the return to a new stadium at White Hart Lane. The consolation was another top-four place, ahead of Chelsea and Arsenal, and finishing London's leading club for the first time for 23 years. Harry Kane continued his prolific form. An eighth hat-trick of 2017 in all competitions took him to 39 Premier League goals for the calendar year, overhauling Alan Shearer's 1995 record for Blackburn. It also brought his tally for club and country to 56, establishing him as Europe's leading marksman for the year ahead of Lionel Messi, Robert Lewandowski and Cristiano Ronaldo. Kane, however, had to settle for second place behind Liverpool's Mohamed Salah in the race for the season's Golden Boot

Alderweireld T.......... 13 (1)
Alli D....................... 34 (2)
Aurier S.................. 16 (1)
Davies B.................. 26 (3)
Dembele M ............. 21 (7)
Dier E....................... 32 (2)
Eriksen C.......................37
Gazzaniga P.....................1
Janssen V................... - (1)
Kane H .................... 35 (2)
Lamela E................. 7 (18)
Llorente F................ 1 (15)
Lloris H..........................36
Lucas Moura.............. 2 (4)
Nkoudou G-K.............. - (1)
Rose D....................... 9 (1)
Sanchez D............... 29 (2)
Sissoko M.............. 15 (18)
Son Heung-Min.......27 (10)
Trippier K................21 (3)
Vertonghen J..................36
Vorm M ........................... 1
Walker-Peters K ..........2 (1)
Wanyama V...............8 (10)
Winks H .....................9 (7)

**League goals** (74): Kane 30, Son Heung-Min 12, Eriksen 10, Alli 9, Aurier 2, Davies 2, Lamela 2, Llorente 1, Sissoko 1, Wanyama 1, Opponents 4
**FA Cup goals** (18): Kane 4, Llorente 3, Eriksen 2, Lamela 2, Son Heung-Min 2, Alli 1, Lucas Moura 1, Vertonghen 1, Walker-Peters 1, Opponents 1. **League Cup goals** (3): Alli 2, Sissoko 1
**Champions League goals** (18): Kane 7, Son Heung-Min 4, Alli 2, Eriksen 2, Llorente 1, Nkoudou 1, Opponents 1
**Average home league attendance**: 67,953. **Player of Year**: Jan Vertonghen

## WATFORD

Another season of managerial change; another poor finish costing the chance of a first top-ten finish in the Premier League. Watford's season had a familiar ring about it, even though there was a change of emphasis about the club's business in the summer transfer market. Previously it had been defined by signings and loan recruits from abroad. This time, Marco Silva acquired England under-21 midfielders Nathaniel Chalobah and Will Hughes and paid a club-record £18.5m for Andre Gray. Unluckily, Chalobah sustained a fractured kneecap after five games, while Hughes later missed three months with a hamstring injury. Gray struggled for goals, but his side were still up to eighth after a 3-0 win at Newcastle. Then came a change of fortune, blamed on an approach by Everton for their manager. Watford dropped points from winning positions, a dozen matches delivered a single victory and Silva was sacked, the owners claiming he had lost focus after the approach was rebuffed. Within hours, he was replaced by Javi Gracia, former Rubin Kazan and Malaga coach, the club's eighth manager in four years. A 4-1 win over Chelsea ended the lean run and was closely followed by maximum points against Everton and West Bromwich Albion. But in an echo of the previous campaign, there was only one more victory, sending them down to 14th.

Amrabat N........................3
Britos M.................. 10 (2)
Capoue E................. 18 (5)
Carrillo A.............. 16 (12)
Cathcart C.................. 5 (2)
Chalobah N................ 5 (1)
Cleverley T.............. 22 (1)
Deeney T................. 20 (9)
Deulofeu G................. 5 (2)
Doucoure A....................37
Gomes H........................24
Gray A.................... 16 (15)
Holebas J................. 26 (2)
Hughes W................ 11 (4)
Janmaat D................ 21 (2)
Kabasele C............... 27 (1)
Kaboul Y..........................2
Karnezis O................ 14 (1)
Kiko......................... 19 (4)
Lukebakio D................ - (1)
Mariappa A..............24 (4)
Okaka S...................3 (12)
Pereyra R..............18 (14)
Prodl S....................17 (4)
Richarlison...............32 (6)
Sinclair J......................- (4)
Wague M....................5 (1)
Watson B....................6 (2)
Zeegelaar M..................12

**League goals** (44): Doucoure 7, Deeney 5, Gray 5, Pereyra 5, Richarlison 5, Janmaat 3, Hughes 2, Kabasele 2, Britos 1, Capoue 1, Carrillo 1, Cleverley 1, Deulofeu 1, Kiko 1, Okaka 1, Wague 1, Opponents 2
**FA Cup goals** (3): Capoue 1, Carrillo 1, Deeney 1. **League Cup goals** (2): Capoue 1, Mariappa 1
**Average home league attendance**: 20,231. **Player of Year**: Abdoulaye Doucoure

## WEST BROMWICH ALBION

A troubled season, on and off the field, ended with Albion rock bottom. It started with back-to-back wins over Bournemouth and Burnley, but soon developed into a fight for survival which neither Tony Pulis nor Alan Pardew could counter. Pulis was sacked after ten matches without a win, culminating in a 4-0 home defeat by Chelsea. Under his successor, returning to management 11 months after being dismissed by Crystal Palace, the run extended to 20 games before defenders Jonny Evans and Craig Dawson both headed in corners for a 2-0 success against Brighton. It proved Pardew's only one. Not even the encouragement of an early goal against Southampton in the tribute match to the late Cyrille Regis on an emotional afternoon at The Hawthorns could add to it. Significantly, a 3-2 defeat took the total of points lost from leading position to 18, leaving Albion adrift at the foot of the table. There was more turmoil at the club. Four players broke a midnight curfew and allegedly stole a taxi during a training break in Barcelona. And chairman John Williams and chief executive officer Martin Goodman were sacked by owner Guochuan Lai. Pardew was also dismissed, with Albion ten points from safety and six games remaining. Coach Darren Moore managed to introduce some spirit to the side, accumulating 11 points as caretaker and earning the job on a permanent basis. It was ironic he won a Premier League Manager of the Month award just hours before relegation was confirmed by Southampton's win at Swansea.

Hegazi A........................38
Barry G.................... 22 (3)
Brunt C.................... 22 (4)
Burke O.................. 2 (13)
Chadli N.................... 2 (3)
Dawson C.......................28
Evans J.................... 26 (2)
Field S...................... 7 (3)
Foster B.........................37
Gibbs K.................... 32 (1)
Harper R...................... - (1)
Krychowiak G............ 20 (7)
Livermore J.............. 30 (4)
McAuley G.................. 5 (4)
McClean J............. 14 (16)
Morrison J................. 2 (2)
Myhill B..........................1
Nyom A....................25 (4)
Phillips M................23 (7)
Robson-Kanu H.........8 (13)
Rodriguez J.............31 (6)
Rondon S.................32 (4)
Sturridge D.................2 (4)
Yacob C......................9 (7)

**League goals** (31): Rodriguez 7, Rondon 7, Hegazi 2, Dawson 2, Evans 2, Livermore 2, Phillips 2, Robson-Kanu 2, Barry 1, Chadli 1, Field 1, McClean 1, Morrison 1
**FA Cup goals** (6): Rodriguez 3, Rondon 2, Opponents 1. **League Cup goals** (4): Phillips 1, Rodriguez 1, Rondon 1, Yacob 1
**Average home league attendance**: 24,520. **Player of Year**: Ben Foster

## WEST HAM UNITED

West Ham negotiated an uneasy path through the lower reaches of the table before ensuring safety with two matches remaining. The first steps, under Slaven Bilic, were particularly hazardous – three defeats to start with and two wins in 11. Bilic was sacked after a 4-1 home defeat by Liverpool to be replaced immediately by David Moyes, the former Sunderland, Manchester United and Everton manager, who lifted his new side out of the bottom three with victories over Chelsea and Stoke. They moved towards mid-table by beating Huddersfield 4-1, but four defeats by the same scoreline – at the hands of Liverpool, Swansea, Arsenal and Manchester City – in an eight-match sequence delivering a single success put them back under pressure. West Ham were hanging on three points above the drop zone until Mark Noble capped a captain's performance with a spectacular 25-yard volley for a 2-0 victory at Leicester which completed the survival job Moyes was asked to undertake. He departed at the end of a short-term contract and was replaced by former Manchester City manager Manuel Pellegrini.

Adrian ..........................19
Antonio M ............... 16 (5)
Arnautovic M............ 28 (3)
Ayew A ...................... 9 (9)
Byram S .................... 2 (3)
Carroll A .................... 7 (9)
Collins J ................. 12 (1)
Cresswell A ............. 35 (1)
Cullen J ...................... - (2)
Evra P....................... 3 (2)
Fernandes E .............. 9 (5)
Fonte J...........................8
Hart J ..........................19
Hernandez J .......... 16 (12)
Hugill J ....................... - (3)
Joao Mario............... 12 (1)
Kouyate C................ 32 (1)
Lanzini M................ 23 (4)
Masuaku A ..............21 (6)
Noble M ..................28 (1)
Obiang P .................18 (3)
Ogbonna A ....................32
Oxford R.......................- (1)
Reid W............................ 17
Rice D ...................15 (11)
Sakho D .....................- (14)
Zabaleta P.....................37

**League goals** (48): Arnautovic 11, Hernandez 8, Lanzini 5, Noble 4, Antonio 3, Ayew 3, Carroll 3, Joao Mario 2, Kouyate 2, Obiang 2, Sakho 2, Collins 1, Cresswell 1, Ogbonna 1
**FA Cup goals** (1): Burke R 1. **League Cup goals** (8): Ayew 3, Ogbonna 2, Sakho 2, Masuaku 1
**Average home league attendance**: 56,885. **Player of Year**: Marko Arnautovic

# SKY BET CHAMPIONSHIP

## ASTON VILLA

The omens were in their favour, but there would be no return to the Premier League for Villa. They lost 1-0 to Fulham in the Play-off Final, 36 years to the day of the club's greatest triumph – beating Bayern Munich to lift the European Cup. Manager Steve Bruce had taken teams up from the Championship four times and there was the chance of a fifth when Fulham had Denis Odoi sent off 20 minutes from the end of normal time for a second yellow card. Instead, Bruce was left to reflect on injuries to key players Jonathan Kodija and Jack Grealish during the season – and how his side were unable to build on the momentum of a 4-1 victory over champions-to-be Wolves. It followed wins over Sheffield Wednesday (4-2) and Sunderland (3-0) and left them four points behind Cardiff with ten games remaining. The opportunity was lost over the next three matches in which Villa took a single point against opponents in the bottom half of the table – Queens Park Rangers, Bolton and Hull – and it was Fulham who went closest to going up automatically. After winning only one of their first seven games, Villa were up and running with a steady flow of goals from Albert Adomah. Then, after dropping out of the top-six over Christmas, they came through strongly by winning seven successive fixtures.

Adomah A............... 34 (5)
Agbonlahor G ............ 2 (4)
Bacuna L.........................1
Bjarnason B .......... 11 (12)
Bree J........................ 3 (3)
Bunn M ..........................1
Chester J ......................46
Davis K................. 17 (11)
De Laet R ................. 1 (4)
Elmohamady A......... 36 (7)
Elphick T.................. 3 (1)
Grabban L............... 10 (5)
Grealish J ............... 19 (8)
Green A ..................... 4 (1)
Hepburn-Murphy R ...... - (3)
Hogan S ............... 19 (18)
Hourihane C............ 40 (1)
Hutton A................. 26 (3)

Jedinak M ................ 17 (8)
Johnstone S ....................45
Kodija J ...................... 9 (6)
Lansbury H ............... 6 (4)
O'Hare C ..................... - (4)
Onomah J ............. 20 (13)
Samba C .................... 5 (7)
Snodgrass R ............ 38 (2)
Taylor N .................. 27 (2)
Terry J ...........................32
Tuanzebe A ................ 4 (1)
Whelan G ................ 30 (3)

**Play-offs – appearances**: Adomah 3, Chester 3, Hourihane 3, Hutton 3, Jedinak 3, Grabban 3, Grealish 3, Johnstone 3, Snodgrass 3, Terry 3, Elmohamady 2, Bree 1, Kodjia – (3), Whelan – (2), Bjarnason – (1), Hogan – (1), Onomah – (1)
**League goals** (72): Adomah 14, Hourihane 11, Grabban 8, Snodgrass 7, Hogan 6, Chester 4, Onomah 4, Bjarnason 3, Grealish 3, Davis 2, Lansbury 2, Agbonlahor 1, Green 1, Jedinak 1, Kodija 1, Samba 1, Terry 1, Whelan 1, Opponents 1. **Play-offs – goals** (1): Jedinak 1
**FA Cup goals** (1): Davis 1. **League Cup goals** (6) Hogan 3, Adomah 1, Bjarnason 1, Opponents 1
**Average home league attendance**: 32,097. **Player of Year**: James Chester

## BARNSLEY

Not even a helping hand from Jose Mourinho could save Barnsley from relegation at the end of a season of bitter managerial recriminations. On a dramatic final day, despite losing at Derby they looked to be safe when Bolton trailed Nottingham Forest with minutes to go. Instead, Bolton found salvation with two goals in a minute to condemn their fellow-strugglers to the drop. The 4-1 defeat at Pride Park was followed immediately by the dismissal of Portuguese manager Jose Morais, who worked alongside Mourinho at Inter Milan, Real Madrid and Chelsea, and was in constant contact throughout his three months in south Yorkshire. Morais was brought in after Paul Heckingbottom walked away from the club, four days after signing a new rolling contract, to take over at Leeds. The board said it was 'shocked and disappointment' at his decision to leave. Heckingbottom, who supported his home-town side when growing up and later played at Oakwell, argued that the criticism was 'out of order' and the board was 'trying to save face.' Whatever the rights and wrongs, Barnsley dropped more points at home from winning positions than any other team and under Morais won only three out of 15, including a 2-0 success against Brentford in the final home game to move briefly out of the bottom three. It was a sad legacy for long-standing owner Patrick Cryne, who sold the club midway through the season and died soon after of cancer. Former Hannover coach Daniel Stendel was appointed the new manager.

Barnes H ................ 18 (5)
Bird J ......................... - (3)
Bradshaw T ........... 26 (13)
Cavare D .................... 7 (2)
Davies A ........................35
Fryers E .........................22
Gardner G ............... 28 (1)
Hammill A .............. 30 (8)
Hedges R ................ 6 (17)
Isgrove L ................. 10 (6)
Jackson A ......................22
Knasmullner C ........... 1 (2)
Lindsay L .......................42
MacDonald A ........... 10 (1)
Mahoney C ................ 3 (5)
Mallan S .................... 5 (3)
McBurnie O ............. 16 (1)
McCarthy J .............. 17 (4)
McGeehan C .............. 6 (3)
Mills M ...........................4
Moncur G .............. 22 (12)
Moore K .................. 16 (4)
Mottley-Henry D .......... - (1)
Mowatt A .........................1
Payne S ...................... - (2)
Pearson M ............... 14 (3)
Pinillos D ................... 7 (1)
Pinnock E .................. 9 (3)
Potts B .................... 35 (2)
Thiam M ............... 12 (17)
Townsend N .....................8
Ugbo I ....................... 7 (9)
Walton J ..........................3
Williams J ............... 33 (1)
Yiadom A ................. 31 (1)

**League goals** (48): Bradshaw 9, McBurnie 9, Barnes 5, Moore 4, Potts 3, Gardner 2, Hedges 2, Moncur 2, Pinnock 2, Cavare 1, Fryers 1, Isgrove 1, Jackson 1, Lindsay 1, McGeehan 1, Thiam 1, Ugbo 1, Williams 1, Opponents 1
**FA Cup goals** (1): Potts 1. **League Cup goals** (7): Bradshaw 3, Hammill 1, Hedges 1, Jackson 1, Opponents 1
**Average home league attendance**: 13,704. **Player of Year**: Oliver McBurnie

## BIRMINGHAM CITY

Garry Monk restored a measure of stability at St Andrew's, although not enough to prevent another nail-biting finish to the season. For the third time in five years, Birmingham's fate was decided in the final round of matches, this time with five clubs battling against the drop. They were among the survivors, with a 3-1 win over Fulham ensuring safety irrespective of what happened elsewhere, while at the same time ending their opponents' chance of automatic promotion. The club's fifth manager in 15 months came in when five successive defeats, and a single goal scored, cost Steve Cotterill his job after five months in charge. Monk, himself dismissed by Middlesbrough two days before Christmas, had to contend with two more defeats before successive wins over Hull, Ipswich and Bolton transformed the pictured. His side were not yet out of the woods, but gained some breathing space when coming from behind to overcome Sheffield United with goals from Marc Roberts and Jacques Maghoma. Cotterill had replaced Harry Redknapp – in the job for five months – after six successive league and cup defeats. A 6-1 thrashing at Hull spelled out the problems and Birmingham were bottom going into the New Year.

Adams C................ 16 (14)
Boga J..................... 24 (7)
Bramall C ................. 3 (2)
Colin M..........................35
Cotterill D.................. 2 (5)
Dacres-Cogley J.......... 1 (2)
Davis D.................... 33 (5)
Dean H...........................34
Donaldson C.....................4
Gallagher S............ 23 (10)
Gardner C................ 20 (6)
Gleeson S.................. 3 (2)
Grounds J.......................26
Harding W.........................9
Jenkinson C.......................7
Jota........................ 24 (8)
Jutkiewicz L.......... 19 (16)
Keita C......................... - (1)
Kieftenbeld M........... 33 (2)
Kuszczak T.....................10
Lowe J....................... 6 (3)
Lubula B..................... - (1)
Maghoma J...............32 (9)
Morrison M.....................33
Ndoye C..................28 (9)
Nsue E....................15 (3)
Roberts M...............26 (4)
Robinson P..................- (2)
Shotton R....................- (1)
Stockdale D...................36
Vassell I.....................3 (6)
Walsh L......................1 (2)

**League goals** (38): Gallagher 6, Adams 5, Jota 5, Jutkiewicz 5, Maghoma 5, Boga 2, Colin 2, Davis 2, Gardner 2, Dean 1, Morrison 1, Roberts 1, Vassell 1
**FA Cup goals** (3): Adams 1, Gallagher 1, Jutkiewicz 1. **League Cup goals** (6): Adams 3, Davis 1, Kkieftenbeld 1. Tesche R 1,
**Average home league attendance**: 21,042. **Player of Year**: Jacques Maghoma

## BOLTON WANDERERS

In terms of great escapes, this ranked alongside the best of them. With the clock ticking at the Macron Stadium, Bolton faced the consequences of a wretched run of form at the most important stage of the season. Seven matches had yielded a single point – and that felt like a defeat after relegation rivals Barnsley scored a 93rd minute equaliser. In the final match, they trailed Nottingham Forest 2-1 in the 85th minute and looked set for an immediate return to League One. Instead, goals by defender David Wheater and 38-year-old striker Aaron Wilbraham delivered an astonishing recovery which lifted them above Burton and Barnsley. It had been a tough campaign throughout for Phil Parkinson's side. The first 15 games brought just one victory – 2-1 against Sheffield Wednesday. They climbed out of the bottom three with three wins out of four over the Christmas/New Year programme, beating Cardiff, Sheffield United and Hull, with Gary Madine scoring three goals in those games. Leading scorer Madine was sold to Cardiff on transfer deadline-day to ease financial pressure on the club and Bolton struggled for goals for the remainder of the campaign.

Alnwick B.......................39
Ameobi S................. 33 (2)
Armstrong A............. 14 (6)
Beevers M.......................44
Buckley W............. 14 (10)
Burke R................... 22 (3)
Charsley H.......................1
Clough Z.................... 2 (7)
Cullen J..................... 9 (3)
Darby S............................3
Derik........................ 13 (4)
Dervite D.................. 13 (1)
Flanagan J.................. 8 (1)
Henry K..........................33
Howard M.................. 7 (1)
Karacan J................. 14 (2)
King J...............................1
Kirchoff J.................. 2 (2)
Le Fondre A........... 15 (20)
Little M.................... 27 (1)
Madine G.......................28
Morais F................17 (16)
Noone C..................6 (18)
Pratley D..................31 (1)
Robinson A..............26 (4)
Taylor A.........................20
Vela J.......................26 (4)
Walker T.....................3 (2)
Wheater D................32 (1)
Wilbraham A.............3 (20)

**League goals** (39): Madine 10, Le Fondre 7, Ameobi 4, Buckley 2, Pratley 2, Wilbraham 2, Armstrong 1, Beevers 1, Burke 1, Clough 1, Henry 1, Little 1, Morais 1, Noone 1, Vela 1, Wheater 1, Opponents 2
**FA Cup goals** (1): Derik 1. **League Cup goals** (5): Armstrong 2, Derik 1, Dervitie 1, Karacan 1
**Average home league attendance**: 15,887. **Player of Year**: Ben Alnwick

## BRENTFORD

Brentford continued to punch above their weight, overcoming a sticky start to claim a fourth successive top-ten finish. The second smallest club in the Championship looked to be in for a tough season when failing to win any of the opening eight games. Instead, they developed a commendable challenge for a play-off place which lasted until the penultimate match. It included a satisfying four points gathered from both west London rivals, Fulham and Queens Park Rangers. The opening eight matches produced four draws and four defeats before quality strikes from Yoann Barbet, Nico Yennaris and Ollie Watkins delivered a 3-0 success at Bolton. They were up into the top half of the table midway through the campaign and pushed on from there, helped by a 5-0 victory over Birmingham. March proved a lean month, but three successive 1-0 wins in April restored momentum and with two games remaining Brentford were still in with a chance, three points behind sixth-place Derby. It disappeared in a 2-0 defeat away to relegation-threatened Barnsley, leaving them ninth to follow tenth, ninth and fifth placings in previous seasons

Archibald T................. - (2)
Barbet Y.................. 32 (2)
Bentley D.......................45
Bjelland A............... 32 (2)
Canos S................ 17 (13)
Clarke J.................. 23 (5)
Colin M............................3
Dalsgaard H...................29
Daniels L.........................1
Dean H............................3
Egan J..................... 32 (1)
Henry R...........................8
Jota.................................4
Jozefzoon F............. 31 (8)
Judge A................... 3 (10)
MacLeod L................. 5 (5)
Marcondes E............ 2 (10)
Maupay N............... 25 (17)
McEachran J........... 14 (12)
Mepham C............... 17 (4)
Mokotjo K..............25 (10)
Ogbene C.....................- (2)
Sawyers R...............36 (6)
Shaibu J......................- (2)
Vibe L......................14 (5)
Watkins O.................39 (6)
Woods R...................35 (4)
Yennaris N.............31 (10)

**League goals** (62): Maupay 12,Watkins 10, Jozefzoon 7, Vibe 7, Sawyers 4, Yennaris 4, Barbet 3, Canos 3, Egan 2, Bjelland 1, Clarke 1, Dalsgaard 1, MacLeod 1, Mepham 1, Mokotjo 1, Woods 1, Opponents 3
**FA Cup goals**: None. **League Cup goals** (8): Clarke 2, Egan 1, Maupay 1, Sawyers 1, Shaibu 1, Watkins 1, Opponents 1
**Average home league attendance**: 10,234. **Player of Year**: Ryan Woods

## BRISTOL CITY

Lee Johnson's side supplemented a solid season in the Championship with outstanding performances in the League Cup. City knocked out Watford, Stoke and Crystal Palace and reached the semi-finals by overcoming holders Manchester United 2-1 in front of a 26,000 crowd at Ashton Gate with a goal by Joe Bryan and the winner from Korey Smith in stoppage-time. Then, they made Manchester City work hard to reach Wembley, taking the lead through Bobby Reid's penalty in the first leg at the Etihad and losing 2-1 only to Sergio Aguero's strike in added time. There was more praise from Pep Guardiola after the return tie in which Marlon Pack and Aden Flint scored in a 3-2 defeat. The league campaign gathered momentum after a modest start, a run of eight victories in 11 matches rewarded with second place behind Wolves by Boxing Day. Expectation was dampened by a 5-0 beating by Aston Villa, but City remained in a play-off place for the next two months and were still in touch until losing to Middlesbrough, then sharing a remarkable 5-5 draw with Hull.

Baker N..........................34
Brownhill J.............. 41 (4)
Bryan J.................... 42 (1)
Diedhiou F.............. 28 (4)
Diony L..................... 1 (6)
Djuric M ................. 4 (12)
Eliasson N .............. 3 (11)
Engvall G.................... - (2)
Fielding F......................43
Flint A.................... 38 (1)
Hegeler J.................... 3 (1)
Hinds F....................... - (1)
Kelly L....................... 7 (4)
Kent R....................... 6 (4)
Leko J........................ 5 (6)
Magnusson H........... 15 (9)
O'Dowda C ............ 13 (11)
O'Neil G..................... - (4)
Pack M .................. 36 (6)
Paterson J .............. 34 (7)
Pisano E.................. 13 (3)
Reid B ..........................46
Semenyo A..................- (1)
Smith K ..................44 (1)
Steele L .....................3 (2)
Taylor M..................4 (14)
Vyner Z ..........................1
Walsh L......................3 (3)
Woodrow C ..............3 (11)
Wright B.......................36

**League goals** (67): Reid 19, Diedhiou 13, Flint 8, Brownhill 5, Bryan 5, Paterson 5, Djuric 3, Pack 3, Woodrow 2, Kelly 1, O'Dowda 1, Smith 1, Taylor 1
**FA Cup goals**: None. **League Cup goals** (19): Bryan 2, Hinds 2, Reid 2, Smith 2, Taylor 2, Baker 1, Diedhiou 1, Djuric 1, Eliasson 1, Flint 1, Hegeler 1, O'Dowda 1, Pack 1, Paterson 1
**Average home league attendance**: 20,953. **Player of Year**: Bobby Reid

## BURTON ALBION

They defied all the odds to preserve Championship status by a single point the previous season. This time, there was no escape – but what a fight they put up. Nigel Clough's side looked dead and buried when a 5-0 beating by Hull left them seven points adrift with four fixtures remaining. Instead, a glimmer of hope came with a 3-1 victory over big-club rivals Derby. A week later, Darren Bent in the 86th minute and Liam Boyce in stoppage-time delivered a 2-1 success at Sunderland, who were relegated for the second successive season. Then, Hope Akpan scored his first goal for the club as fellow-strugglers Bolton were beaten 2-0. Remarkably, Burton went into the final round of matches with a chance of staying up. But the dream died with a 93rd minute goal conceded at Preston, while Bolton's two late ones against Nottingham Forest made them safe. In the end, Burton paid dearly for poor home form. They were in and out of the bottom three for the first-half of the campaign before this inability to win in front of their own supporters caught up with them – seven months and 17 games in all, including a club-record eight successive defeats.

Akins L.................... 39 (3)
Akpan H ................. 19 (7)
Allen J.................. 19 (10)
Barker S ..................... - (1)
Bent D.................... 10 (5)
Boyce L.................. 12 (4)
Brayford J ............... 27 (1)
Buxton J ................. 29 (4)
Bywater S ......................44
Davenport J............. 15 (2)
Dyer L: ................... 30 (8)
Egert T........................ - (3)
Flanagan T .............. 20 (7)
Irvine J............................3
Lund M ................... 10 (2)
Mason J .................... 3 (3)
McCrory D ................. 9 (2)
McFadzean K........... 39 (3)
Mousinho J.......................1
Murphy L ................ 34 (4)
Naylor T.................. 32 (1)
Palmer M .................. 8 (3)
Ripley C..........................2
Samuelsen M.............7 (2)
Sbarra J ..................4 (13)
Scannell S...............13 (5)
Sordell M ..............30 (10)
Turner B..................26 (4)
Varney L..................1 (17)
Warnock S...............13 (1)
Miller W .....................7 (3)

**League goals** (38): Dyer 7, Akins 5, Boyce 3, Naylor 3, Sordell 3, Akpan 2, Bent 2, Flanagan 2, Turner 2, Allen 1, Davenport 1, Irvine 1, Lund 1, Mason 1, Murphy 1, Palmer 1, Warnock 1, Opponents 1
**FA Cup goals**: None. **League Cup goals** (6): Akins 1, Dyer 1, Fox B 1, Lund 1, Naylor 1, Varney 1
**Average home league attendance**: 4,645. **Player of Year**: Lucas Akins

## CARDIFF CITY

Which was the greater achievement – a record eight promotions, or leading Cardiff into the Premier League against all the odds? Neil Warnock took pride in making the record his own after sharing it on seven with Graham Taylor, Dave Bassett and Jim Smith. But the transformation of a club languishing second from bottom when he took over October 2016 was something else. The 69-year-old Yorkshireman, in his 38th year of management, did it with a succession of largely low-key signings who proved the backbone of a reshaped squad. These players were not expected to take such a demanding division by storm – until the perception changed with five successive wins to start the season. Nathaniel Mendez-Laing a free transfer signing from Rochdale, typified Warnock's successful recruitment with four goals in those games. His side were in the top two for most of the first half of the season before faltering over Christmas and New Year, losing four successive matches. Then came eight victories in a row, along with a new contract through to 2020 for the manager. That closed the gap on runaway leaders Wolves and his side would have been right on their heels had Gary Madine and Junior Hoilett not missed stoppage-time winners at Molineux, where a 1-0 defeat put Wolves back in charge of the title. Four days later, Cardiff lost to an 89th minute goal at Aston Villa and were overtaken for second place by Fulham. But they made full use of a game in hand, kept their nerve and a goalless draw against Reading in the final round of matches proved enough to confirm the runners-up spot, with Fulham losing at Birmingham.

| | | |
|---|---|---|
| Bamba S.................. 43 (3) | Gunnarsson A ........... 17 (3) | Peltier L..................27 (3) |
| Bennett J........................38 | Halford G ................. 2 (10) | Pilkington A................1 (7) |
| Bogle O ..................... 4 (6) | Harris K ..................... 1 (2) | Ralls J ..........................37 |
| Bryson C.................. 19 (3) | Healey R .................... 1 (2) | Richards A .................5 (1) |
| Connolly M.......................4 | Hoilett J................... 44 (2) | Tomlin L......................5 (8) |
| Damour L................ 18 (9) | Kennedy M.................. - (1) | Traore A .....................3 (1) |
| Ecuele Manga B ....... 35 (3) | Madine G ................... 5 (8) | Ward D.....................6 (12) |
| Etheridge N....................45 | Mendez-Laing N........ 33 (5) | Ward J ........................2 (2) |
| Feeney L.................. 4 (11) | Morrison S............... 38 (1) | Wildschut Y................3 (7) |
| Gounongbe F............... - (3) | Murphy B ........................1 | Zohore K ..................30 (6) |
| Grujic M .................. 12 (1) | Paterson C............... 23 (9) | |

**League goals** (69): Paterson 10, Hoilett 9, Zohore 9, Morrison 7, Ralls 7, Mendez-Laing 6, Bamba 4, Ward D 4, Bogle 3, Pilkington 3, Bryson 2, Bennett 1, Grujic 1, Gunnarsson 1, Tomlin 1, Traore 1

**FA Cup goals** (4): Hoilett 2, Ecuele-Manga 1, Pilkington 1. **League Cup goals** (3): Halford 1, Mendez-Lang 1, Pilkington 1

**Average home league attendance**: 20,164. **Player of Year**: Sean Morrison

## DERBY COUNTY

Derby supporters have now become used to the ups and downs of the Championship. For the third time in five years their team reached the play-offs – and for the third time hopes of a return to the Premier League were dashed. Cameron Jerome's fifth goal in four games gave them the edge, securing a 1-0 victory over Fulham in the first leg of their semi-final. But it was overtaken at Craven Cottage as Ryan Sessegnon showed why is one of English football's hottest young prospects by scoring his side's first goal and setting up their winner. It was indicative of much of Derby's season, a modest first two months in the middle reaches of the division followed by just two defeats in 15 matches to the end of the year, plenty of goals and second place behind runaway leaders Wolves. Then came a dip in form which put a top-six place in jeopardy. Finally, there was Jerome's scoring burst which accounted for Cardiff, earned a point at Villa Park, then helped make sure the season would continue in a 4-1 victory over Barnsley which also sent their opponents down. At the end of it, manager Gary Rowett left for Stoke and was replaced by the former Chelsea and England midfielder Frank Lampard.

| | | |
|---|---|---|
| Anya I........................ 3 (4) | Butterfield J............... 2 (1) | Hanson J ..................... - (6) |
| Baird C.................... 21 (1) | Carson S........................46 | Huddlestone T...............44 |
| Bennett M.................. 1 (2) | Davies C ........................46 | Jerome C ................ 8 (10) |
| Bryson C...................... - (4) | Forsyth C ........................31 | Johnson B................ 25 (8) |

| | | |
|---|---|---|
| Keogh R ........................42 | Olsson M ................ 14 (1) | Thorne G................. 9 (11) |
| Lawrence T ............. 36 (3) | Palmer K ................ 2 (13) | Vydra M .................. 34 (6) |
| Ledley J.................. 23 (3) | Pearce A.................... 5 (2) | Weimann A .............. 32 (8) |
| Martin C .................. 5 (18) | Russell J............... 13 (10) | Winnall S................. 6 (11) |
| Nugent D................ 29 (8) | Thomas L.................... - (2) | Wisdom A ............... 29 (1) |

**Play-offs – appearances**: Carson 2, Davies 2, Forsyth 2, Huddlestone 2, Jerome 2, Johnson 2, Keogh 2, Lawrence 2, Weimann 2, Wisdom 2, Anya 1 (1), Vydra 1 (1), Nugent – (2), Hanson – (1), Palmer – (1)
**League goals** (70): Vydra 21, Nugent 9, Lawrence 6, Winnall 6, Jerome 5, Weimann 5, Johnson 4, Russell 4, Huddlestone 2, Palmer 2, Bryson 1, Davies 1, Keogh 1, Ledley 1, Martin 1, Pearce 1. **Play-offs – goals** (1): Jerome 1
**FA Cup goals**: None. **League Cup goals** (3): Bennett 1, Russell 1, Vydra 1
**Average home league attendance**: 27,175. **Player of Year**: Matej Vydra

## FULHAM

Fulham returned to the Premier League after a four-year absence and it was fitting that two of the season's outstanding players made it possible at Wembley. Ryan Sessegnon delivered the pass midway through the first-half and captain Tom Cairney scored the goal which defeated Aston Villa in the Play-off Final. Their side held the lead in the final 20 minutes with ten men after Denis Odoi was sent off for two yellow cards. Sessegnon, 18-year-old Championship Player of the Year, was also the club's top scorer, while Aleksandar Mitrovic proved the season's best signing with 12 goals in 17 appearances after a winter loan move from Newcastle. With Cairney pulling the strings in midfield, Fulham rewrote their record books after a patchy first half of the campaign. Marooned in mid-table eight points adrift of the top-six, they went on an unbeaten run of 23 matches, 18 of them wins and five draws. Despite conceding a 94th minute equaliser at home to Brentford, they went into the final day a point behind second-place Cardiff with every chance of continuing the run. Instead, a 3-1 defeat at Birmingham ruled out automatic promotion as Cardiff shared a goalless draw with Reading in their last fixture. Fulham lost the first leg of the semi-final 1-0 at Derby and won the return 2-0 with goals by Sessegnon and Odoi.

| | | |
|---|---|---|
| Aluko S...........................4 | Graham J ................... - (3) | Ojo S ...................... 18 (4) |
| Ayite F..................... 23 (5) | Johansen S.............. 43 (2) | Piazon L.................. 14 (8) |
| Bettinelli M....................26 | Kalas T .................. 29 (4) | Rafa ..........................- (3) |
| Button D.......................20 | Kamara A................ 8 (22) | Ream T ........................ 44 |
| Cairney T ................ 30 (4) | Kebano N.............. 10 (16) | Rui Fonte .............. 16 (11) |
| Christie C.................. 1 (4) | McDonald K ..................42 | Sessegnon R............45 (1) |
| Cisse I ...................... 2 (4) | Mitrovic A................ 15 (2) | Targett M................. 17 (1) |
| De La Torre L .............. - (5) | Mollo Y ...................... 2 (4) | Edun T....................... 1 (1) |
| Djalo M....................... - (2) | Norwood O ............ 22 (14) | |
| Fredericks R..................44 | Odoi D .................... 30 (8) | |

**Play-offs – appearances**: Bettinelli 3, Cairney 3, Fredericks 3, Johansen 3, Odoi 3, McDonald 3, Mitrovic 3, Ream 3, Sessegnon 3, Targett 3, Kamara 2, Ayite 1, Norwood – (3), Kalas – (2), Christie – (1), Kebano – (1), Piazon – (1)
**League goals** (79): Sessegnon 15, Mitrovic 12, Johansen 8, Kamara 7, Cairney 5, Piazon 5, Norwood 5, Ayite 4, Ojo 4, Kebano 3, McDonald 3, Rui Fonte 3, Odoi 1, Ream 1, Targett 1, Opponents 2. **Play-offs – goals** (3): Cairney 1, Odoi 1, Sessegnon 1
**FA Cup goals**: None. **League Cup goals** (2): Odoi 1, Piazon 1
**Average home league attendance**: 19,896. **Player of Year**: Tim Ream

## HULL CITY

Relegation stripped Hull of some of their best players – the likes of Andrew Robertson, Sam Clucas and Tom Huddlestone – suggesting there was little prospect of a challenge for an immediate return to the Premier League. So it proved during a season in which they spent most of the time in the lower reaches of the table. At one stage only a superior goal difference kept them out of the bottom three after just two goals in eight matches. With a prolonged relegation struggle looming, Liverpool loanee Harry Wilson sparked a change of fortune with six goals in nine games as Hull put five past Burton, scored four against Norwich and Queens Park Rangers and three against Ipswich. There was also a remarkable game against Bristol City which ended 5-5, with Hull by then well clear of trouble. The revival came under the club's fifth manager in 18 months, Nigel Adkins, formerly in charge at Sheffield United, Reading, Southampton and Scunthorpe. He came in when Leonid Slutsky was sacked in mid-season, six months into the job, after a run of seven matches without a win.

| | | | | | |
|---|---|---|---|---|---|
| Batty D | 1 | Hector M | 33 (3) | Mazuch O | 10 (4) |
| Bowen J | 37 (5) | Henriksen M | 25 (6) | McGregor A | 44 |
| Campbell F | 23 (13) | Hernandez A | 8 (2) | Meyler D | 17 (8) |
| Clark M | 25 (2) | Irvine J | 27 (7) | Ola Aina | 42 (2) |
| Clucas S | 3 | Keane W | 3 (6) | Stewart K | 10 (7) |
| Dawson M | 40 | Kingsley S | 10 | Tomori F | 23 (2) |
| Dicko N | 19 (10) | Larsson S | 37 (3) | Toral J-M | 16 (10) |
| Diomande A | 3 (13) | Luer G | - (1) | Weir J | - (3) |
| Goebel E | 3 (5) | MacDonald A | 12 | Wilson H | 11 (2) |
| Grosicki K | 22 (15) | Marshall D | 2 | | |

**League goals** (70): Bowen 14, Grosicki 9, Hernandez 8, Wilson 7, Campbell 6, Meyler 5, Dicko 4, Dawson 3, Henriksen 2, Irvine 2, Larsson 2, Diomande 1, Goebel 1, Hector 1, Keane 1, Toral 1, Opponents 3
**FA Cup goals** (3): Bowen 1, Dicko 1, Ola Aina. **League Cup goals**: None
**Average home league attendance**: 15,622. **Player of Year**: Allan McGregor

## IPSWICH TOWN

A season which started so promisingly, settled into mid-table mediocrity and ended with Mick McCarthy walking away from the club, fed up with protesting supporters. The Championship's longest-serving manager, appointed in November 2012, agreed in talks with owner Marcus Evans to go when his contract expired at the end of the campaign. Instead, he walked after more jeers from fans during a 1-0 win over Barnsley, declaring: 'I'm out of here'. It was a bitter finale to the sweet opening McCarthy enjoyed when summer signings Joe Garner and Martyn Waghorn were both among the goals as straight wins over Birmingham, Barnsley, Millwall and Brentford left his side joint top with Cardiff. But while Cardiff continued to flourish under Neil Warnock, Ipswich fell off the pace. They returned to within three points of a play-off place approaching Christmas before a lean holiday programme set them back and they spent the rest of the campaign well adrift. But there was some satisfaction at the end with a place above arch-rivals Norwich in the table. McCarthy was succeeded by Shrewsbury's Paul Hurst.

| | | | | | |
|---|---|---|---|---|---|
| Adeyemi T | 4 (1) | Folami B | 1 (3) | Morris B | 1 (2) |
| Bialkowski B | 45 | Garner J | 29 (3) | Nydam T | 12 (6) |
| Bishop E | 1 (3) | Gerken D | 1 | Rowe D | - (2) |
| Bru K | 3 (6) | Gleeson S | 5 (5) | Sears F | 15 (21) |
| Carayol M | 5 (3) | Huws E | 3 (2) | Skuse C | 39 |
| Carter-Vickers C | 17 | Hyam L | 6 (11) | Smith T | 3 |
| Celina B | 23 (12) | Iorfa D | 20 (3) | Spence J | 37 (3) |
| Chambers L | 37 | Kenlock M | 15 (1) | Waghorn M | 39 (5) |
| Connolly C | 29 (5) | Knudsen J | 42 | Ward G | 25 (12) |
| Cotter B | 1 (1) | McDonnell A | - (1) | Webster A | 25 (3) |
| Downes F | 3 (7) | McGoldrick D | 18 (4) | Woolfenden L | 1 (1) |
| Dozzell A | 1 | McLoughlin S | - (1) | | |

**League goals** (57): Waghorn 16, Garner 10, Celina 7, McGoldrick 6, Connolly 4, Spence 4, Sears 2, Ward 2, Carayol 1, Chambers 1, Iorfa 1, Knudsen 1, Skuse 1, Opponents 1
**FA Cup goals**: None. **League Cup goals** (3): McGoldrick 2, Celina 1
**Average home league attendance**: 16,272. **Player of Year**: Bartosz Bialkowski

## LEEDS UNITED:

Thomas Christiansen made the best start by a new manager in the club's history, raising hopes of a long-overdue meaningful challenge for a return to the Premier League. With nine new signings in the squad, Leeds accumulated 20 points from the opening nine fixtures to go top. Just as quickly the optimism faded, with six defeats in the next seven games and a fall to tenth in the table. By the half-way point of the season, they appeared to be back on track, moving into a play-off place after beating Hull. But again promotion prospects faded as six more matches delivered just two points. Four goals were conceded in successive home games against Millwall and Cardiff and Christiansen, in charge for eight months, was sacked seven points adrift. Paul Heckingbottom, the club's tenth manager in five years, left Barnsley four days after signing a new rolling contract, to face a disciplinary problem accompanying his new side's inconsistency. There had been six red cards and there was to be a seventh when Gaetano Berardi was sent off for the third time, against Sunderland. Of those seven games, Leeds lost five, drew one and won one, statistics that told their own story. Leeds duly finished in the bottom half of the table and Heckingbottom was dismissed after four months in the job. In came former Argentina and Chile coach Marcelo Bielsa.

Alioski E .................. 40 (2)
Anita V .................... 14 (4)
Ayling L .........................27
Berardi G ................. 29 (2)
Borthwick-Jackson C .........1
Cibicki P .................... 5 (2)
Cooper L ........................30
Dallas S ................ 14 (15)
De Bock L ........................7
Diaz H ........................ - (1)
Edmondson R .............. - (1)
Ekuban C .................... - (1)
Ekuban C ................ 12 (8)
Forshaw A ................. 9 (3)
Grot J-R .................. 1 (19)
Hernandez P ............ 34 (7)
Jansson P ................ 41 (1)
Klich M ...................... 1 (3)
Lasogga P-M ........... 21 (10)
Lonergan A .......................7
O'Connor P .......................4
O'Kane E ................. 27 (5)
Peacock-Farrell B ........... 11
Pearce T ..........................5
Pennington M ........... 15 (9)
Phillips K ................. 36 (5)
Roofe K .................... 27 (9)
Sacko H ................... 1 (13)
Saiz S ...................... 28 (6)
Shaughnessy C ........... 5 (4)
Vieira R ................... 23 (5)
Wiedwald F .................... 28
Wood C ...........................3

**League goals** (59): Roofe 11, Lasogga 10, Alioski 7, Hernandez 7, Phillips 7, Saiz 5, Jansson 3, Dallas 2, Cooper 1, Ekuban 1, Grot 1, Pearce 1, Wood 1, Opponents 2
**FA Cup goals** (1): Berardi 1. **League Cup goals** (12): Saiz 4, Roofe 3, Hernandez 2, Ekuban 1, Sacko 1, Vieira 1
**Average home league attendance**: 31,521. **Player of Year**: Pablo Hernandez

## MIDDLESBROUGH

Tony Pulis took a rational view of Middlesbrough's failure to make an immediate return to the Premier League. The pre-season favourites squeezed into the play-offs with a productive late run of form, but were beaten 1-0 at home by Aston Villa and Stewart Downing's 89th minute free-kick which hit the bar left the return leg goalless. The manager admitted they did not create sufficient chances, despite being on top over the two legs, and had no argument with the clubs who finished third and fourth, Fulham and Villa, contesting the final. He had taken over midway through the season when Garry Monk was sacked two days before Christmas after six months in the job, his side having struggled to keep pace with the leading teams. Pulis, himself dismissed by West Bromwich Albion a month earlier, had a mixed introduction before Patrick Bamford sparked a run of 13 points and 13 goals from five games to put them back in the running. Bamford contributed eight of them, including a hat-trick against Leeds, and Middlesbrough went on to a clinch a place in the knockout phase by ending Millwall's bid to overtake them by defeating their rivals in the penultimate fixture.

Assombalonga B..... 32 (12)
Ayala D.......................33
Baker L..................... 6 (6)
Bamford P ............ 23 (16)
Besic M.......................15
Braithwaite M.......... 17 (2)
Christie C................ 24 (1)
Clayton A.............. 22 (10)
Cranie M.................... 1 (8)
Downing S .............. 38 (2)
Fabio ....................... 18 (4)
Fletcher A ............... 3 (13)
Forshaw A ................. 5 (6)
Friend G.................. 29 (4)
Fry D ....................... 11 (2)
Gestede R ............... 10 (9)
Gibson B.......................45
Guedioura A ....................1
Harrison J.................... - (4)
Howson J ................ 37 (6)
Johnson M...............6 (11)
Leadbitter G ............29 (3)
Randolph D..................46
Roberts C.........................1
Shotton R................23 (1)
Tarvernier M ..............4 (1)
Traore A ..................26 (8)
De Roon M ......................1

**Play-offs – appearances**: Assombalonga 2, Besic 2, Clayton 2, Downing 2, Friend 2, Gibson 2, Howson 2, Randolph 2, Shotton 2, Traore 2, Ayala 1, Fry 1, Bamford – (2), Fabio – (2), Gestede – (1)
**League goals** (67): Assombalonga 15, Bamford 11, Ayala 7, Braithwaite 5, Traore 5, Downing 3, Gestede 3, Howson 3, Leadbitter 3, Friend 2, Baker 1, Besic 1, Christie 1, Fabio 1, Fletcher 1, Gibson 1, Johnson 1, Shotton 1, Tavernier 1, Opponents 1. **Play-offs – goals**: None
**FA Cup goals** (2): Braithwaite 1, Gestede 1. **League Cup goals** (6): Bamford 2, Baker 1, Fabio 1, Fletcher 1, Tavernier 1
**Average home league attendance**: 25,544. **Player of Year**: Adama Traore

## MILLWALL

Millwall proved to be the dark horses in the race for promotion, moving through the field largely unnoticed before faltering at the final hurdle. That Neil Harris and his players missed out on the play-offs took nothing away from a splendid season's work. Promoted in 2017, they won just one of the first seven matches – albeit 4-0 against Norwich – and at the midway point of the campaign the target seemed to be to avoid being drawn into a relegation struggle. Instead, Millwall launched run of 17 unbeaten games, 11 wins and six draws, with the help of a dramatic 4-3 win at Leeds earned by an 87th minute equaliser from Tom Elliott and a Jed Wallace effort in the second minute of stoppage-time. They broke into a play-off place with goals from Elliott and Ben Marshall at Bolton and were still there with three matches remaining. These were all against teams above them in the table and the challenge this time proved too much. Millwall's run came to an end with a 3-0 home defeat by Fulham, themselves in the midst of a long undefeated sequence. Then, a 2-0 reversal at Middlesbrough effectively put them out of the running, after which Middlesbrough manager Tony Pulis said Harris 'should be proud of his players.'

Archer J.........................45
Cahill T..................... - (10)
Cooper J ................. 35 (3)
Craig T ..................... 1 (3)
Elliott T .................. 8 (16)
Ferguson S.............. 9 (15)
Gregory L................. 40 (3)
Hutchinson S.................46
Marshall B.....................16
Martin D...........................1
McLaughlin C .......... 23 (1)
Meredith J.....................46
Morison S................ 38 (6)
O'Brien A ................ 23 (7)
Onyedinma F ........... 8 (29)
Romeo M ................ 22 (5)
Saville G ......................44
Shackell J ..................- (7)
Thompson B...............- (3)
Tunnicliffe R............19 (5)
Twardek K ..................- (2)
Wallace J.................42 (1)
Webster B ....................10
Williams S...............30 (5)

**League goals** (56): Gregory 10, Saville 10, Wallace 6, Morison 5, Cooper 4, Elliott 4, O'Brien 4, Marshall 3, Hutchinson 2, Williams 2, McLaughlin 1, Onyedinma 1, Romeo 1, Tunnicliffe 1, Opponents 2
**FA Cup goals** (6): O'Brien 2, Thompson 2, Onyedinma 1, Wallace 1. **League Cup goals** (3): Elliott 2, Ferguson 1
**Average home league attendance**: 13,368. **Player of Year**: Shaun Hutchinson

## NORWICH CITY

Marooned in mid-table for much of the season, Norwich never developed a serious threat to the Championship's leading group of teams. The club had taken a leaf out of promoted Huddersfield's book with the appointment as manager of a little-known German coach, Daniel Farke, who signed nine players during the summer, including four from lower divisions in Germany. His team set a club-record in the game's second tier with five successive clean sheets in September, closely followed by victory over arch-rivals Ipswich at Portman Road with a goal by James Maddison. That took Norwich to sixth, but three months without a home win left them in the bottom half of the table, after which there was little to suggest they were capable of retrieving the situation. Best moments were a 3-1 win over Aston Villa and recovering from 2-0 down to earn a point at Wolves with Nelson Oliveira's stoppage-time goal. They also defeated Leeds on an emotional afternoon when Wes Hoolahan, making his 352nd and final appearance after ten years with the club, scored an equaliser and laid on the winner for Josh Murphy. But a 5-1 defeat by Sheffield Wednesday in the final match left them below Ipswich in the table.

Edwards M.................. - (1)
Franke M..........................5
Gunn A...........................46
Hanley G.................. 28 (4)
Hernandez O............. 5 (7)
Hoolahan W.......... 14 (15)
Husband J............... 14 (4)
Ivo Pinto................. 31 (4)
Jerome C................. 11 (4)
Klose T.................... 36 (1)
Leitner M................ 10 (2)
Lewis J..................... 19 (3)
Maddison J.............. 42 (2)
Martin R..................... 4 (1)
Murphy J................. 34 (7)
Naismith S.......................2
Nelson Oliveira ....... 26 (11)
Pritchard A................ 5 (3)
Raggett S.................... - (2)
Reed H.................... 36 (3)
Srbeny D....................7 (7)
Stiepermann M.........15 (8)
Tettey A....................21 (2)
Trybull T...................17 (3)
Vrancic M.................29 (6)
Watkins M..............12 (12)
Wildschut Y................7 (9)
Zimmermann C.........30 (9)

**League goals** (49): Maddison 14, Nelson Oliveira 8, Murphy 7, Klose 4, Ivo Pinto 2, Trybull 2, Hanley 1, Hoolahan 1, Jerome 1, Pritchard 1, Reed 1, Srbeny 1, Stiepermann 1, Vrancic 1, Wildschut 1, Zimmermann 1, Opponents 2
**FA Cup goals** (1): Lewis 1. **League Cup goals** (11): Murphy 4, Vrancic 2, Hoolahan 1, Jerome 1, Maddison 1, Trybull 1, Watkins 1,
**Average home league attendance**: 25,785. **Player of Year**: James Maddison

## NOTTINGHAM FOREST

Three wins in the opening four matches fired the hopes of Forest fans after a nail-biting finish to the previous season when relegation was averted on goal difference. That optimism quickly faded. Their team lacked the consistency needed for a promotion push, costing Mark Warburton, manager for six months, his job after a home defeat by Sunderland left them ten points adrift of a play-off place. His successor, former Middlesbrough manager Aitor Karanka, had a notable first win over runaway leaders Wolves at Molineux in his second match in charge. He made six winter transfer deadline-day signings during a run of eight league matches in nine without a goal – starting under Warburton – and five successive home defeats. Bizarrely, during this bleak spell, Forest defeated FA Cup holders Arsenal 4-2 at the City Ground with two goals from Eric Lichaj and penalties from Ben Brereton and Kieran Dowell. The goal drought ended with victories over Queens Park Rangers (5-2) and Birmingham (2-1) before six more games without scoring. They eventually finished 17th after losing the final match 3-2 against Bolton, who scored two late goals to avoid the drop.

Bouchalakis A........ 11 (10)
Brereton B............ 25 (10)
Bridcutt L............... 24 (3)
Carayol M ............... 2 (13)
Cash M.................... 14 (9)
Clough Z................... 4 (9)
Cohen C...................... - (2)
Colback J.......................16
Cummings J.............. 7 (7)
Darikwa T ............... 29 (1)
Dejagah A.................. - (1)
Dowell K................. 31 (7)
Figueiredo T..................12
Fox D ............................23
Guedioura A.............. 6 (5)
Hobbs J...........................2
Juan Fuentes....................1
Kapinos S........................4
Lichaj E.................. 22 (1)
Lolley J.................... 13 (3)
Mancienne M .......... 27 (2)
McKay B.................. 22 (4)
Mills M.................... 11 (2)
Murphy D................ 22 (5)

| | | |
|---|---|---|
| Osborn B ................ 42 (4) | Traore A.................. 15 (3) | Ward J....................... - (8) |
| Pantilimon C..................13 | Vaughan D.....................14 | Watson B.......................14 |
| Smith J..........................29 | Vellios A .................... 4 (8) | Worrall J ................. 28 (3) |
| Tomlin L................. 12 (3) | Walker T.................... 7 (5) | |

**League goals** (51): Dowell 9, Murphy 7, Brereton 5, McKay 5, Osborn 4, Tomlin 4, Lolley 3, Walker 3, Bouchalakis 2, Cash 2, Bridcutt 1, Carayol 1, Colback 1, Cummings 1, Lichaj 1, Vellios 1, Worrall 1
**FA Cup goals** (5): Lichaj 2, Brereton 1, Dowell 1, Vellios 1. **League Cup goals** (6): Cummings 3, Carayol 1, Darikwa 1, Walker 1
**Average home league attendance**: 24,680. **Player of Year**: Ben Osborn

## PRESTON NORTH END

Preston achieved their highest finish since 2009 in Alex Neil's first season as manager, maintaining a play-off bid until the final round of matches. His side, who had been on the fringes since a nine-match unbeaten run going into the New year, closed with a 2-1 win over Burton, courtesy of a stoppage-time goal from Louis Moult. But it was not enough to dislodge Derby, who held on to a two-point advantage in sixth place by beating Barnsley 4-1. Neil praised his players for going so close, while admitting they did not score enough goals to make it over the line. Crucially, there was a run of three successive defeats which left them six points adrift with a month of the campaign remaining. It included a 1-0 setback against Derby at Deepdale in which Alan Browne missed a penalty. Preston made up ground by coming from behind to defeat Leeds and Queens Park Rangers, then beating Sheffield United with a goal by Player of the Year Browne. However, Derby's win over promoted Cardiff proved decisive during the run-in.

| | | |
|---|---|---|
| Barkhuizen T........... 43 (3) | Harrop J................ 11 (27) | Pearson B......................35 |
| Bodin B.................. 14 (3) | Horgan D................. 2 (18) | Robinson C............30 (11) |
| Boyle A...........................3 | Hugill J................... 26 (1) | Rudd D........................ 16 |
| Browne A................ 38 (6) | Huntington P.................44 | Simpson C .................- (1) |
| Clarke T.................. 14 (4) | Johnson D............... 25 (8) | Spurr T ..........................5 |
| Cunningham G ..............20 | Maguire S................ 19 (5) | Vermijl M ...................- (2) |
| Davies B................. 33 (1) | Mavididi S................. 3 (7) | Welsh J......................5 (4) |
| Earl J ..................... 16 (3) | Maxwell C......................30 | Woods C..................11 (5) |
| Fisher D........................34 | Moult L...................... 3 (7) | |
| Gallagher P........... 22 (10) | O'Connor K................ 4 (4) | |

**League goals** (57): Maguire 10, Barkhuizen 8, Hugill 8, Robinson 8, Browne 6, Johnson 3, Clarke 2, Gallagher 2, Harrop 2, Moult 2, Bodin 1, Cunningham 1, Davies 1, Horgan 1, Huntington 1, Opponents 1
**FA Cup goals** (5): Browne 2, Harrop 2, Horgan 1. **League Cup goals** (2): Hugill 2
**Average home league attendance**: 13,774. **Player of Year**: Alan Browne

## QUEENS PARK RANGERS

Ian Holloway's second spell as manager came to an end five days after the final match of the season. The club admitted he had developed young talent and reduced the wage bill, while remaining competitive in the Championship. But they now wanted to 'take the next step' and brought in former England manager Steve McClaren, who had a brief spell on the Loftus Road coaching staff under Harry Redknapp in 2013. The season was clouded by a £40m fine imposed for breaking spending limits under the Football League's Financial Fair Play rules. The club are continuing an appeal, arguing the rules are unlawful under competition law. Rangers made a decent start to the campaign, including a 2-1 win over the eventual champions Wolves. There were other notable victories, particularly in the closing stages – 3-1 against Aston Villa and four goals scored against Norwich and Sheffield Wednesday – but not the consistency required to carry them, beyond a 16th place finish.

Baptiste A......................26
Bidwell J................. 45 (1)
Caulker S..........................2
Chair I.............................4
Cousins J................ 13 (2)
Eze E ........................ 8 (8)
Freeman L .............. 43 (2)
Furlong D................ 18 (4)
Hall G........................ 1 (3)
Ingram M.........................2
Kakay O...........................2
LuaLua K .................. 2 (6)
Lumley J ..........................2
Luongo M................ 38 (1)
Lynch J ................... 22 (3)
Mackie J ................. 16 (4)
Manning R .............. 10 (9)
Ngbakoto Y..................2 (3
Onuoha N................ 28 (1)
Osayi-Samuel B ........ 6 (12)
Oteh A ...................... 3 (3)
Perch J ..................... 6 (1)
Robinson J ...............29 (2
Scowen J.......................42
Smith M.................17 (24)
Smithies A ..............42 (1)
Smyth P.....................7 (6)
Sylla I....................13 (13)
Washington C...........24 (9)
Wheeler D ..................5 (4)
Wszolek P.................28 (8)

**League goals** (58): Smith 11, Sylla 7, Luongo 6, Washington 6, Freeman 5, Mackie 4, Bidwell 2, Eze 2, Manning 2, Robinson 2, Smyth 2, Wszolek 2, Chair 1, Lynch 1, Osayi-Samuel 1, Oteh 1,Scowen 1, Wheeler 1, Opponents 1
**FA Cup goals**: None. **League Cup goals** (2): Furlong 1, Ngbakoto 1
**Average home league attendance**: 13,928. **Player of Year**: Massimo Luongo

## READING

Championship status was preserved on an anxious final day of the season. Reading went into a demanding match at Cardiff as one of five teams under threat of joining Sunderland in League One if results went against them. They emerged with a goalless draw – overshadowed by Cardiff sealing a place in the Premier League – and it was Barnsley and Burton who went down after losing. It proved a poor follow-up season to the one under Jaap Stam which took the club so close to a return to the top division in a goalless Play-off Final which Huddersfield won in a penalty shoot-out. Reading had a reasonable first half of the campaign before a single victory in 18 matches left them three points away from the relegation zone with eight games remaining. Stam was dismissed and replaced by sacked Swansea manager Paul Clement, who started with an edgy 1-0 win over Queens Park Rangers, his side playing for the final ten minutes with ten men after Yann Kermorgant's red card and needing Vito Mannone's penalty save from Jake Bidwell. They defeated Preston by the same scoreline, but conceded seven in successive defeats by Sheffield Wednesday and Ipswich which increased the pressure.

Aluko S.................... 36 (3)
Bacuna L................. 29 (4)
Barrow M................. 37 (4)
Beerens R.................. 9 (8)
Blackett T................ 19 (6)
Bodvarsson J D....... 20 (13)
Clement P............. 10 (13)
Edwards D .............. 27 (5)
Elphick T................... 2 (2)
Evans G..................... 9 (9)
Gunter C ........................46
Holmes T .........................1
Ilori T....................... 26 (3)
Jaakkola A.......................5
Kelly L.................... 28 (6)
Kermorgant Y.......... 13 (12)
Mannone V.....................41
Martin C..................... 4 (6)
McCleary G................. 9 (9)
McShane P.............. 23 (2)
Mendes J ..................1 (2)
Moore L ........................46
Obita J.........................- (2)
Popa A.......................3 (3)
Richards O .................9 (4)
Smith S ......................4 (4)
Swift J .....................17 (7)
Van den Berg J..........31 (2)

**League goals** (48): Barrow 10, Bodvarsson 7, Kelly 5, Aluko 3, Edwards 3, Moore 3, Beerens 2, Kermorgant 2, Richards 2, Swift 2, Bacuna 1, Evans 1, Gunter 1, Martin 1, Smith 1, Van den Berg 1, Opponents 3
**FA Cup goals** (4): Bodvarsson 3, Opponents 1. **League Cup goals** (5): Kelly 2, Bacuna 1, Evans1, Smith 1
**Average home league attendance**: 16,656. **Player of Year**: Liam Moore

## SHEFFIELD UNITED

Chris Wilder's promoted side adapted well to life back in the Championship. They were in contention for the play-offs for much of the season before tailing off in the final few weeks and having to settle for a top-half finish. Boosted by Leon Clarke's goals, United were one of four teams to hold the leadership of the division in the first three months. Clarke scored four goals in successive wins over Sheffield Wednesday and eventual champions Wolves. Then, he struck ten times in a run of six games, including all four against Hull and three against Fulham. But his side were set back by the loss of influential midfielder Paul Coutts with a broken leg, winning just twice in a 13-match spell and sliding to eighth. They were up and running again when beating Leeds, Queens Park Rangers and Reading in quick succession to regain a top-six place, with Billy Sharp among the goals. This time it was just a fleeting appearance. Clarke regained some of his scoring touch, while a brace by Lee Evans, his first for the club, brought victory against Middlesbrough. However, back-to-back defeats by Birmingham and Preston proved costly.

| | | | | | |
|---|---|---|---|---|---|
| Baldock G | 30 (4) | Eastwood J | - (1) | Lundstram J | 21 (15) |
| Basham C | 44 (1) | Evans C | 2 (7) | Moore S | 15 (3) |
| Blackman J | 31 | Evans L | 18 (1) | O'Connell J | 46 |
| Brooks D | 9 (21) | Fleck J | 41 | Sharp B | 28 (6) |
| Carruthers S | 4 (10) | Freeman K | 10 | Slater R | - (1) |
| Carter-Vickers C | 17 | Hanson J | - (1) | Stearman R | 28 |
| Clarke L | 38 (1) | Holmes R | 1 (4) | Stevens E | 45 |
| Coutts P | 16 | Lafferty D | 1 (7) | Thomas N | - (1) |
| Donaldson C | 9 (17) | Lavery C | 1 (2) | Wilson J | 4 (4) |
| Duffy M | 28 (8) | Leonard R | 6 (7) | Wright J M | 13 (4) |

**League goals** (62): Clarke 19, Sharp 13, Donaldson 5, Brooks 3, Duffy 3, Lundstram 3, Basham 2, Evans L 2, Fleck 2, Stearman 2, Baldock 1, Carruthers 1, Carter-Vickers 1, Coutts 1, Freeman 1, Stevens 1, Wilson 1, Opponents 1

**FA Cup goals** (2): Sharp 1, Thomas 1. **League Cup goals** (4): Lafferty 1, Lavery 1, Thomas 1, Opponents 1

**Average home league attendance**: 26,854. **Player of Year**: John Fleck

## SHEFFIELD WEDNESDAY

A bleak winter ruled out any chance of reaching the play-offs for the third successive season. Wednesday were on the fringe of the top-six after goals by Adam Reach and Jordan Rhodes secured a 2-1 victory at Villa Park. Three months later, there was just one more win – 3-0 away to Nottingham Forest – to show from a run of 15 matches. By then, they were in the bottom half of the table and manager Carlos Carvalhal had been sacked two days before Christmas. He was replaced by former Hertha Berlin and Stuttgart coach Jos Luhukay, whose first game in charge was a goalless draw in the Sheffield derby, earned with ten men after the dismissal of Glenn Loovens. The Dutchman's first league success in his sixth game, 2-0 against Derby, was followed by four straight defeats and 12 goals conceded. Then came three wins against Leeds, Preston and Sunderland in which 6ft 5in Kosovo striker Atdhe Nuhiu scored five goals. Wedenesday went on to finish strongly, Nuhiu scoring a hat-trick in the 5-1 defeat of Norwich, without much improvement in their position.

| | | | | | |
|---|---|---|---|---|---|
| Abdi A | 1 (3) | Hutchinson S | 7 (1) | Pudil D | 24 (3) |
| Baker A | 1 | Jones D | 20 (7) | Reach A | 45 (1) |
| Bannan B | 28 (1) | Kirby C | - (1) | Rhodes J | 17 (14) |
| Boyd G | 13 (7) | Lee K | 10 (5) | Stobbs J | 2 (1) |
| Butterfield J | 12 (8) | Lees T | 28 (1) | Thorniley J | 7 (4) |
| Clare S | 4 (1) | Loovens G | 20 | Van Aken J | 14 |
| Dawson C | 3 | Lucas Joao | 17 (14) | Venancio F | 20 |
| Fletcher S | 13 (6) | Matias M | 2 (7) | Wallace R | 24 (3) |
| Forestieri F | 6 (4) | Nielsen F | - (3) | Westwood K | 18 |
| Fox M | 26 (2) | Nuhiu A | 15 (13) | Wildsmith J | 25 (1) |
| Hooper G | 22 (2) | Palmer L | 16 (9) | Winnall S | 1 (1) |
| Hunt J | 28 (1) | Pelupessy J | 17 | | |

**League goals** (59): Nuhiu 11, Hooper 10, Lucas Joao 9, Forestieri 5, Rhodes 5, Reach 4, Lee 3, Boyd 2, Fletcher 2, Wallace 2, Clare 1, Jones 1, Lees 1, Pelupessy 1, Venancio 1, Winnall 1
**FA Cup goals** (5): Nuhiu 3, Boyd 1, Matias 1. **League Cup goals** (6): Rhodes 2, Bannan 1, Fletcher 1, Hooper 1, Hutchinson 1
**Average home league attendance**: 25,995. **Player of Year**: Adam Reach

## SUNDERLAND

Sunderland suffered a second successive relegation in a calamitous season which ended with owner Ellis Short selling the club and Chris Coleman losing his job. Their ninth manager in almost six years admitted to a 'brutal experience' after swopping international success with Wales for rock-bottom reality at the Stadium of Light. He came in after Simon Grayson, in charge or just four months, was dismissed with his side third from bottom and on the way to becoming the first in English football history to go 20 successive home games without a win in all competitions. There was one more to add to that total before Coleman gave Josh Maja his league debut and the 18-year-old scored the goal which delivered a 1-0 win over Fulham. That result lifted Sunderland briefly out of the relegation zone and offered some hope that the tide had turned. There was also the boost of retrieving a 3-0 deficit for a point against Bristol City and winning 4-1 at Derby. In between those results, however, they continued to struggle, with a last-minute equaliser conceded at home to Norwich leaving them six points adrift, together with an inferior goal difference, and just four games remaining. The drop was confirmed after another embarrassing performance at home as fellow-strugglers Burton scored twice in the final six minutes to win 2-1. A 3-0 victory over champions Wolves on the final day did little to lift the gloom. Short sacked Coleman, cleared debts of around £140m and sold out to a consortium headed by Stewart Donald, chairman of National League side Eastleigh. St Mirren's Jack Ross, Scotland's Manager of the Year, replaced Coleman.

Asoro J .................. 11 (15)
Browning T .............. 26 (1)
Camp L..................... 11 (1)
Cattermole L ............ 34 (1)
Clarke-Salter J............ 8 (3)
Embleton E................. - (2)
Ejaria O ..................... 9 (2)
Fletcher A................ 15 (1)
Galloway B................. 5 (2)
Gibson D.................. 12 (3)
Gooch L................. 12 (12)
Grabban L................ 18 (1)
Honeyman G ............ 37 (5)
Hume D ...................... - (1)
Jones B.................... 19 (3)
Khazri W ..................... - (3)
Kone L...........................24
Love D ...........................11
LuaLua K .................... - (6)
Maja J...................... 6 (11)
Matthews A ............. 25 (9)
McGeady A.............. 28 (7)
McManaman C........ 13 (11)
McNair P................. 12 (4)
Molyneux L.......................1
Mumba B .................. - (1)
Ndong D.................. 16 (2)
O'Shea J .................. 34 (3)
Oviedo B ................. 31 (3)
Robson E ................... 6 (3)
Rodwell J ................... 1 (1)
Ruiter R....................... 20
Steele J........................ 15
Vaughan J ............... 15 (8)
Watmore D ................. 4 (2)
Williams J .................. 7 (5)
Wilson M.................. 20 (1)

**League goals** (52): Grabban 12, McGeady 7, Honeyman 6, McNair 5, Asoro 3, Fletcher 2, Oviedo 2, Vaughan 2, Cattermole 1, Ejaria 1, Gooch 1, Jones 1, Maja 1, Matthews 1, McManaman 1, O'Shea 1, Rodwell 1, Williams 1, Opponents 3
**FA Cup goals**: None. **League Cup goals** (3): Gooch 1, Honeyman 1, Love 1
**Average home league attendance**: 27,635. **Player of Year**: John O'Shea

## WOLVERHAMPTON WANDERERS

Wolves completed their rehabilitation with a return to the Premier League in some style. Relegated in 2012, then condemned to the third tier the following season, they flourished with a new manager and new-look team to finish champions by a nine-point margin. Nuno Espirito Santo, the club's fourth man in charge in ten months, built a squad around his fellow Portuguese, including £15m record-signing midfielder Ruben Neves from Porto. He also retained a solid British core and the blend paid off handsomely, with victory in the opening three matches elevating the expectancy at Molinuex. They contested the leadership with Cardiff in the first half of the season before accelerating on the back of run of ten victories and two draws in 12 matches. The only wobble, which included a 4-1 defeat by Aston Villa, resulted in a 12-point lead being cut in half. It could have more serious had Cardiff not missed two stoppage-time penalties, enabling Wolves to preserve a 1-0 lead in the meeting of the top two. The leaders made certain of promotion when third-place Fulham dropped points against Brentford, and clinching the title a week later with a 4-0 victory at Bolton with two matches to spare.

Afobe B ..................... 7 (9)
Batth D.................... 15 (1)
Bennett R ................ 27 (2)
Boly W...........................36
Bonatini L.............. 29 (14)
Burgoyne H................. - (1)
Buur O ........................ - (1)
Coady C.........................45
Deslandes S................ - (1)
Dicko N ....................... - (5)
Diogo Jota................ 43 (1)
Doherty M .......................45
Douglas B................. 38 (1)
Edwards D................... - (1)
Enobakhare B .......... 5 (16)
Gibbs-White M.......... 1 (12)
Graham J .................... - (1)
Hause K....................... - (1)
Helder Costa........... 21 (15)
Ivan Cavaleiro ......... 31 (11)
Marshall B................ 1 (5)
Mir R .......................... - (2)
Miranda R ................ 16 (1)
N'Diaye A.............. 13 (20)
Norris W.......................... 1
Price J ........................- (5)
Ruben Neves ................ 42
Ruben Vinagre ........... 8 (1)
Ronan C......................- (3)
Ruddy J ........................ 45
Saiss R .................... 37 (5)

**League goals** (82): Diogo Jota 17, Leo Bonatini 12, Ivan Cavaleiro 9, Afobe 6, Ruben Neves 6, Helder Costa 5, Douglas 5, Doherty 4, Saiss 4, Boly 3, N'Diaye 3, Batth 1, Bennett 1, Buur 1, Coady 1, Dicko 1, Enobakhare 1, Ruben Vinagre 1, Opponents 1
**FA Cup goals** (1): Diogo Jota 1. **League Cup goals** (4): Batth 1, Dicko 1, Enobakhare 1, Wilson D 1
**Average home league attendance**: 28,298. **Player of Year**: Ruben Neves

# SKY BET LEAGUE ONE

## AFC WIMBLEDON

What a difference a few days can make to a side threatened by relegation. With six matches remaining, Wimbledon were in all sorts of trouble, a point above the bottom four and teams poised the overtake them. A home fixture against promotion-chasing Charlton looked a difficult one. But a goal by leading scorer Lyle Taylor delivered a priceless 1-0 win and there was even better to follow. Trailing 2-0 at Walsall, they replied through Taylor and Joe Pigott, then completed a fine recovery with a stoppage-time penalty from Dean Parrett. That took them four points clear of trouble and safety was ensured with a goalless draw at Doncaster in the penultimate game. Wimbledon's troubles stemmed from a poor start to the season – two wins in the opening 12 games. They slipped to third from bottom at the turn of the year before wins over Southend and Blackpool, followed by a 4-0 success at Bradford – their biggest away win in the Football League. The upsurge followed news that the club had been given approval to build a new £25m stadium at Plough Lane – site of the old team. But the new one were unable to maintain that momentum and slipped back into trouble.

Abdou N .................. 26 (8)
Appiah K ................... 8 (6)
Barcham A............... 38 (7)
Charles D................. 26 (5)
Egan A ....................... - (2)
Forrester H............ 20 (16)
Francomb G ............ 31 (6)
Fuller B ........................42
Hartigan A ................ 6 (5)
Kaja E...................... 7 (12)
Kennedy C............... 11 (3)
Long G..........................45
McDonald C............. 23 (9)
McDonnell J ....................1
Meades J................. 19 (7)
Nightingale W.......... 15 (3)
Oshilaja A................ 41 (1)
Parrett D ................. 16 (7)
Pigott J .................... 10 (8)
Robinson P.............. 11 (4)
Sam L........................- (2)
Sibbick T ....................- (1)
Soares T.................. 27 (4)
Taylor L.................... 42 (4)
Trotter L.................. 41 (1)

**League goals** (47): Taylor 14, McDonald 5, Pigott 5, Barcham 4, Appiah 3, Forrester 3, Trotter 3, Abdou 2, Meades 2, Oshilaja 2, Parrett 2, Nightingale 1, Soares 1
**FA Cup goals** (4): Taylor 3, McDonald 1. **League Cup goals** (1): Robinson 1. **League Trophy goals** (9): Kaja 2, Sibbick 2, Hartigan 1, McDonald 1, Parrett 1, Taylor 1, Opponents 1
**Average home league attendance**: 4,325. **Player of Year**: Deji Oshilaja

## BLACKBURN ROVERS

Tony Mowbray took Blackburn straight back to the Championship in his first full season as manager, his side gathering momentum after an indifferent start, breaking into the promotion race with a burst of scoring and eventually disputing the title with Wigan. They were 12 points adrift of their rivals at one stage before six successive victories and 18 goals scored transformed the picture at the top of the table. Rovers went top for the first time with 2-0 win over Bury, by which time they had lost just once in 22 games. Adam Armstrong, on loan from Newcastle, scored nine goals in nine games to maintain the momentum which accounted for Shrewsbury, the third side looking to fill one of the automatic promotion places. Rovers made sure of going up with Charlie Mulgrew's winner at Doncaster. But points dropped against Gillingham and Bristol Rovers had cost them the leadership and defeat at Charlton gave Wigan the chance to open a two-point advantage going into the final round of matches. A crowd of more than 27,000 was a reminder of the good times at Ewood Park, although victory over Oxford was not enough to prevent their rivals remaining on top.

Antonsson M ............ 22 (9)
Armstrong A............. 17 (4)
Bell A......................... 6 (6)
Bennett E ................ 40 (1)
Caddis P.................. 13 (1)
Chapman H.............. 1 (11)
Conway C................. 19 (5)
Dack B ..................... 37 (5)
Downing P ............... 26 (2)
Evans C................... 25 (7)
Feeney L...................... - (1)
Gladwin B ................... - (5)
Graham D............... 29 (13)
Harper R .................... 1 (3)
Hart S.......................... - (3)
Lenihan D ................ 13 (1)
Leutwiler J .......................1
Mulgrew C.......................41
Nuttall J.................... 3 (10)
Nyambe R ................ 27 (2)
Payne J.................... 7 (11)
Raya D...........................45
Samuel D............... 19 (17)
Smallwood R .................46
Tomlinson W................- (4)
Travis L.........................- (5)
Ward E.......................9 (1)
Whittingham P..........14 (6)
Williams D......................45

**League goals** (82): Dack 18, Graham 14, Mulgrew 14, Armstrong 9, Antonsson 7, Samuel 5, Bennett 2, Conway 2, Nuttall 2, Smallwood 2, Chapman 1, Downing 1, Lenihan 1, Payne 1, Williams 1, Opponents 2
**FA Cup goals** (7): Graham 3, Samuel 2, Antonsson 1, Nuttall 1. **League Cup goals** (3): Evans 1, Samuel 1, Smallwood 1. **League Trophy goals** (2): Nuttall 2
**Average home league attendance**: 12,823. **Player of Year**: Bradley Dack

## BLACKPOOL

A rousing finish to the season completed Blackpool's resurgence after a barren winter had threatened an immediate return to League Two. They were lodged comfortably in mid-table after Kyle Vassell returned from injury to score the only goal at Peterborough against his former club. But his side won only one of the next 14 games to slide to within two points of a relegation place. They were boosted by a 2-0 victory against Wigan, with Armand Gnanduillet and Kevin Mellor on the mark to knock their hosts off the top spot. Two more promotion-chasing sides, Portsmouth and Charlton, were beaten. Then, with safety still not secured, Blackpool scored 13 goals in four successive victories to move completely out of trouble. Nathan Delfouneso netted a hat-trick in a 5-0 success over Bradford, followed by maximum points against Northampton (3-0), Fleetwood (2-1) and Gillingham (3-0) which brought a place in the top half of the table.

Aygei D..................... 1 (8)
Aimson W ................ 13 (4)
Allsop R........................22
Clayton M .................. - (2)
Cooke C.................. 19 (1)
Cullen M................... 3 (6)

| | | |
|---|---|---|
| D'Almeida S........... 12 (11) | Mellor K .................. 26 (3) | Solomon-Otabor V..... 35 (9) |
| Daniel C .................. 43 (1) | Menga D..................... - (8) | Spearing J................ 30 (3) |
| Delfouneso N ......... 29 (11) | Osayi-Samuel B.......... 2 (2) | Taylor A ..................... 4 (3) |
| Gnanduillet A........... 9 (17) | Philliskirk D............. 7 (12) | Tilt C............................42 |
| Longstaff S .............. 37 (5) | Quigley S.................... - (9) | Turton O ........................41 |
| Lumley J.........................17 | Roache R.................... - (1) | Vassell K.........................29 |
| Mafoumbi C.....................4 | Robertson C...................39 | Williams B .......................3 |
| McAlister J.................. - (1) | Ryan J...........................36 | Wilmer-Anderton N ..... 3 (1) |

**League goals** (60): Vassell 11, Delfouneso 9, Longstaff 8, Mellor 6, Solomon-Otabor 5, Daniel 4, Gnanduillet 4, Robertson 3, Ryan 3, Cooke 2, Philliskirk 2, Tilt 1, Turton 1, Opponents 1 **FA Cup goals** (1): Philliskirk 1. **League Cup goals** (1): Gnanduillet 1. **League Trophy goals** (8): Philliskirk 3, Clayton 1, D'Almeida 1, Longstaff 1, Mellor 1, Sinclair-Smith 1
**Average home league attendance**: 4,178. **Player of Year**: Clark Robertson

## BRADFORD CITY

Bradford's season fell apart alarming after a third successive appearance in the play-offs looked on the cards. They spent five months in the top-six, thanks largely to productive away form compensating for poor results at Valley Parade. With that place under threat after five successive defeats home and away – along with an FA Cup loss to Yeovil – manager Stuart McCall was sacked and replaced by Simon Grayson, himself dismissed by Sunderland earlier in the season. Five more matches came and went without a win, by which time his side were down to mid-table. They broke the sequence by defeating Gillingham, but a 5-0 trouncing at Blackpool underlined the slide. Even so, there was still a crowd of more than 19,000 to see Portsmouth defeated, before a tenth home defeat, inflicted by Southend, left them struggling to maintain a place in the upper half of the table. Grayson, who was on a short-term contract, declined the chance to stay on and was replaced by 32 year-old Michael Collins, their under-18 coach.

| | | |
|---|---|---|
| Barr L......................... - (1) | Hawkes C.................... - (2) | Pybus D .......................- (1) |
| Brunker K.................. 5 (4) | Hendrie L.................. 9 (4) | Raeder L ......................... 1 |
| Chicksen A............... 16 (2) | Jones A...................... 4 (3) | Reeves J...................24 (1) |
| Devine D...................... - (3) | Kilgallon M.....................42 | Robinson T...............13 (8) |
| Dieng T.................... 19 (7) | Knight-Percival N...... 40 (1) | Sattelmaier R ...........10 (1) |
| Doyle C..........................35 | Law N...................... 33 (5) | Staunton R..................- (1) |
| Field T....................... 7 (1) | Lund M...................... 7 (3) | Taylor P....................18 (9) |
| Gibson J .................... 1 (4) | McCartan S ........... 13 (11) | Thompson A ...............4 (5) |
| Gillieard A............... 36 (6) | McGowan R......................3 | Vincelot R ................37 (1) |
| Grodowski J................. - (1) | McMahon T....................38 | Warnock S..................... 13 |
| Guy C...................... 15 (2) | Omari P .................. 8 (11) | Wyke C.....................38 (2) |
| Hanson J .................. 1 (2) | Poleon D............... 16 (16) | |

**League goals** (57): Wyke 15, Poleon 6, Taylor 6, Kilgallon 4, Knight-Percival 4, McCartan 4, Vincelot 4, Robinson 3, Dieng 2, Lund 2, Omari 2, Gibson 1, Gillieard 1, McMahon 1, Opponents 2 **FA Cup goals** (5): Jones 1, Gillieard 1, Knight-Percival 1, Vincelot 1, Wyke 1. **League Cup goals** (2): Jones 1, Poleon 1. **League Trophy goals** (6): Jones 3, Hanson 1, Omari 1, Thompson 1
**Average home league attendance**: 19,787. **Player of Year**: Matt Kilgallon

## BRISTOL ROVERS

Rovers transformed a potentially precarious position with some free-scoring performances, but lost momentum when closing to within sight of a play-off spot. They were four points away from the relegation zone before wins over Bradford, Doncaster and Rochdale delivered nine goals to ease the pressure. Further victories at Oxford and MK Dons left them four points away from the leading group of six, offering the chance of further progress. Instead, relegation-bound Northampton, down to ten men for the final quarter-of-an-hour, came away from the Memorial

Ground with a point, while promotion-chasing Plymouth twice came from behind to win with an 85th minute penalty. Rovers were also pegged back late on by Wigan and Gillingham, by which time their chance had long gone. The final 11 matches yielded a single victory, 2-1 against Bury, and the result was a finishing place in the bottom half of the table.

Andre A ...................... - (1)
Baghdadi M ................ - (2)
Bennett K................ 15 (2)
Bodin B................... 20 (1)
Bola M .................... 15 (3)
Broadbent T............. 19 (3)
Broom R..................... - (3)
Brown L................... 31 (2)
Burn J .............................1
Clarke J ..................... 9 (2)
Clarke O .................. 37 (3)
Craig T...........................17
Dunnwald K................. - (1)
Gaffney R.............. 21 (21)
Harrison E................ 41 (3)
Kelly M ....................... - (1)
Leadbitter D............ 15 (2)
Lines C.................... 36 (6)
Lockyer T.......................37
Menayesse R ............. 2 (1)
Mensah B.................. 3 (5)
Moore B................. 10 (10)
Nichols T ..............18 (21)
Partington J.............30 (2)
Russe L......................1 (2)
Sercombe L.............40 (2)
Sinclair S.................24 (5)
Slocombe S................... 23
Smith A ........................ 23
Sweeney R ...............17 (6)
Telford D..................1 (18)

**League goals** (60): Harrison 12, Bodin 9, Sercombe 8, Gaffney 7, Lines 5, Bennett 3, Partington 3, Sweeney 3, Telford 3, Sinclair 2, Brown 1, Clarke O 1, Craig 1, Lockyer 1, Nichols 1
**FA Cup goals** (2): Sercombe 1, Sinclair 1. **League Cup goals** (5): Bodin 2, Harrison 2, Sercombe 1. **League Trophy goals** (8) Broom 2, Sercombe 2, Telford 2, Nichols 1, Sweeney
**Average home league attendance**: 8,933. **Player of Year**: Ellis Harrison

## BURY

Bury finished a point clear of the relegation zone in 2017, but there was no escape this time as three managers tried and failed to arrest their slide. Lee Clark was sacked at the end of October, after eight months in charge, with his side second from bottom. Chris Lucketti, Scunthorpe's assistant manager, took over at a club where he spent six seasons as a player. But he was without a goal in eight league games and paid the price after 54 days in the job with Bury 12 points adrift at the bottom. Caretaker Ryan Lowe, appointed until the end of the campaign, won his first match 2-1 at Oxford. That was followed by victories by the same score against AFC Wimbledon and Gillingham, offering a glimpse of survival. Instead, six successive defeats left them isolated and a seventh, 3-2 at home to fellow-strugglers Northampton, confirmed the drop, 16 points adrift with four matches remaining. Lowe, who had three spells with the club as a player, was appointed on a permanent basis.

Adams J ...................... - (2)
Ajose N...................... 8 (1)
Aldred T ................. 18 (1)
Beckford J .....................15
Bruce A..........................2
Bunn H................... 28 (9)
Cameron N.....................21
Clarke P.................. 16 (2)
Cooney R .................. 9 (3)
Danns N .................. 22 (3)
Dawson S.................. 9 (4)
Dobre M-A ................ 3 (7)
Edwards P............... 35 (2)
Fasan L .................. 14 (1)
Hanson J.................... 8 (9)
Humphrey C .............. 8 (2)
Ince R..................... 18 (4)
Ismail Z ................. 18 (3)
Jones C..................... 6 (1)
Laurent J................. 20 (2)
Leigh G................... 40 (1)
Lowe R...................... 2 (4)
Maguire C.............. 13 (11)
Mayor D ................. 16 (4)
Miller G.................. 16 (3)
Murphy J.......................17
Nyaupembe D............... (1)
O'Connell E...................12
O'Shea J .................19 (8)
Reilly C...................15 (3)
Ripley C....................... 15
Sang C........................- (2)
Shotton S........................4
Skarz J......................3 (1)
Smith M..................16 (3)
Styles C .....................9 (2)
Thompson A ............13 (2)
Tsun Dai.....................2 (6)
Tutte A....................4 (12)
Whitmore A ...............7 (1)
Williams J .................5 (4)

**League goals** (41): Beckford 8, Miller 8, Danns 5, O'Shea 4, Bunn 3, Cameron 2, Maguire 2, Ajose 1, Aldred 1, Bruce 1, Clarke 1, Laurent 1, Leigh 1, Mayor 1, Smith 1, Opponents 1
**FA Cup goals** (1): Smith 1. **League Cup goals**: None. **League Trophy goals** (8): Ajose 3, Bunn 2, Leigh 1, Riley 1, Tsu Dai 1
**Average home league attendance**: 3,931

## CHARLTON ATHLETIC

Lee Bowyer achieved a measure of success in his first managerial appointment. The former Newcastle and West Ham midfielder led Charlton into the play-offs and his team had plenty of momentum going into the semi-finals against Shrewsbury. But they were beaten 1-0 at home in the first leg and by the same scoreline in the return, Bowyer insisting they were superior over the two games without taking the chances that came their way. He was given the job until the end of the season after Karl Robinson parted company with the club by mutual agreement and was immediately named Oxford's new manager. A dream start brought successive victories over Plymouth, Northampton and Rotherham, nine goals scored and a place in the top-six. Two 1-0 defeats were a damper, but Charlton bounced back for maximum points against Shrewsbury, Portsmouth and Blackburn which provided sufficient insurance for a defeat in the final round of fixtures by Rochdale, who survived as a result.

Ahearne-Grant K....... 4 (18)
Ajose N...................... 7 (5)
Amos B..........................46
Aribo J..................... 19 (7)
Bauer P.................. 33 (1)
Best L....................... 2 (3)
Clarke B................. 16 (1)
Crofts A...................... - (1)
Dasilva J.................. 34 (4)
Dijksteel A................. 8 (2)
Dodoo J...................... - (5)
Forster-Caskey J........ 40 (1)
Fosu-Henry T........... 26 (4)
Hackett-Fairchild R...... - (5)
Holmes R................ 22 (1)
Jackson J.................. 4 (7)
Kaikai S.................... 8 (6)
Kashi A.................... 33 (1)
Konsa E.................. 32 (7)
Lapslie G..................... - (1)
Lennon H................... 6 (4)
Magennis J.............. 37 (5)
Maloney T...................- (1)
Marshall M..............20 (7)
Mavididi S..................6 (6)
Novak L.....................1 (1)
Page L...........................8
Pearce J...................24 (1)
Reeves B..................21 (8)
Sarr N......................14 (5)
Solly C..........................27
Watt T.........................- (1)
Zyro M.......................8 (5)

**Play-offs – appearances**: Ajose 2, Amos 2, Bauer 2, Dasilva 2, Forster-Caskey 2, Konsa 2, Magennis 2, Pearce 2, Aribo 1 (1), Fosu-Henry 1 (1), Mavididi 1 (1), Dijksteel 1, Kashi 1, Reeves 1, Kaikai – (1), Sarr – (1), Zyro – (1)
**League goals** (58): Magennis 10, Fosu-Henry 9, Holmes 6, Aribo 5, Forster-Caskey 5, Bauer 3, Reeves 3, Zyro 3, Kashi 2, Mavididi 2, Pearce 2, Ahearne-Grant 1, Ajose 1, Clarke 1, Dodoo 1, Marshall 1, Page 1, Opponents 2. **Play-offs – goals**: None
**FA Cup goals** (4): Reeves 2, Ahearne-Grant 1, Marshall 1. **League Cup** (3): Charles-Cook R 1, Clarke 1, Novak 1. **League Trophy goals** (9): Ahearne-Grant 2, Hackett-Fairchild 2, Reeves 2, Aribo 1, Dodoo 1, Lapslie 1
**Average home league attendance**: 11,846. **Player of Year**: Jay Dasilva

## DONCASTER ROVERS

Darren Ferguson's side consolidated on their return to League One, but missed the chance of a top-half position when firing blanks at the end of the season. Wins over Bradford, Blackpool and MK Dons, in which John Marquis scored four goals, enabled Rovers to make up ground on teams immediately above them. And with five of the final six matches at the Keepmoat, they were well placed to go higher. Instead, they were held 3-3 by relegated Bury after surrendering a two-goal lead, then failed to score against Oxford, Blackburn – who clinched promotion with a 1-0 victory – and AFC Wimbledon. There was no joy, either, at Oldham or in the final fixture against Wigan, which Ferguson missed after his father, Sir Alex Ferguson, was taken ill. His side finished 15th. Ferguson, unhappy with the future direction of the club, resigned in the summer and was replaced by former Peterborough manager Grant McCann

Alcock C................... 6 (3)
May A................... 13 (14)
Amos D...................... 2 (1)
Anderson T......................7
Andrew D.........................4
Baudry M................ 19 (3)
Beestin A................ 17 (9)
Ben Khemis I............ 2 (1)
Blair M.................. 32 (8)
Boyce A...........................6
Butler A.................. 34 (2)
Coppinger J............. 34 (4)
Fletcher J.................. - (1)
Garrett T................ 10 (3)
Houghton J............. 33 (4)

Kiwomya A ................. 5 (7)
Kongolo R .............. 17 (18)
Lawlor I ..........................34
Mandeville L ............ 7 (10)
Marosi M ................. 12 (1)
Marquis J.........................45
Mason N .................. 37 (3)
McCullough L........... 10 (3)
Rowe T ...........................40
Toffolo H.................. 11 (2)
Whiteman B ............ 34 (8)
Williams A .................. 3 (6)
Wright J.................. 32 (1)

**League goals** (52): Marquis 14, Whiteman 6, May 4, Butler 4, Rowe 4, Coppinger 3, Mason 3, Anderson 2, Beestin 2, Blair 2, Baudry 1, Boyle 1, Kiwomya 1, Mandeville 1, Opponents 4
**FA Cup goals** (9): Rowe 4, Coppinger 2, Houghton 1, Mandeville 1, Marquis 1. **League Cup goals** (5): May 2, Kongolo 1, Rowe 1, Whiteman 1. **League Trophy goals** (4): Mandeville 2, Ben Khemis 1, Williams 1
**Average home league attendance**: 8,213. **Player of Year**: James Coppinger

## FLEETWOOD TOWN

An eventful season ended with League One status preserved and the high-profile appointment of Joey Barton as manager. Although Fleetwood failed to maintain the momentum of winning the three opening matches without conceding a goal, they were still comfortably placed just above halfway going into the New Year. Players came and went in the winter transfer window, among them leading scorer Devante Cole to Wigan. The turnaround was followed by five successive defeats, a slide to one place above the relegation zone and the sacking of manager Uwe Rosler after a 3-0 reversal at Doncaster. John Sheridan was appointed until the end of the season in the hope that the former Oldham and Notts County manager could maintain his record of having an immediate effect at clubs in trouble. So it proved, with seven unbeaten matches yielding 15 points and lifting his side within sight of mid-table. With three matches remaining, the club announced that Sheridan would leave as planned, to be replaced when Barton completed a 13-month FA ban for betting on matches while a player.

Bell A............................27
Biggins H.................. 2 (5)
Bolger C .........................41
Burns W ............... 12 (16)
Cairns A.........................38
Cargill B .................... 9 (2)
Oliver C ...................... - (1)
Cole D .................... 24 (4)
Coyle L.................... 41 (1)
Dempsey K ....................45
Diagouraga T ..................17
Eastham A......................45
Ekpolo G .................... 1 (2)
Glendon G............... 23 (7)
Grant R................. 19 (10)
Hiwula J................ 21 (22)
Hunter A .............. 24 (20)
Maguire J .........................2
Jones G...................... 8 (2)
Madden P................ 17 (3)
McAleny C............ 15 (14)
Nadesan A.................. - (1)
Neal C ............................8
O'Connor K......................4
O'Neill A .................13 (8)
Pond N ....................27 (3)
Schwabi M .................8 (2)
Sowerby J................15 (7)

**League goals** (59): Cole 10, Hunter 9, Hiwula 8, Madden 6, McAleny 5, Bell 4, Bolger 3, Eastham 3, Grant 3, Burns 2, Sowerby 2, Dempsey 1, Diagouraga 1, O'Neill 1, Opponents 1
**FA Cup goals** (5): Bolger 2, Cole 2, Sowerby 1. **League Cup goals** (1): Hiwula 1. **League Trophy goals** (14): Burns 3, Hiwula 3, Sowerby 2, Bolger 1, Cargill 1, Ekpolo 1, Grant 1, Reid 1, Opponents 1
**Average home league attendance**: 3,140. **Player of Year**: Ashley Eastham

## GILLINGHAM

Gillingham turned successfully to former player Steve Lovell to rescue a season that was becoming increasingly fraught. Lovell, a prolific scorer in his five years at Priestfield, was appointed caretaker after the club's worst start in 40 years under Ady Pennock, then Peter Taylor's brief, third spell as manager. He took over a side second from bottom with a single win in 12 matches and made an immediate impact with a 1-0 success at Peterborough. A month later, he was given the job until the end of the season, with Gillingham on the way to a run of 14 matches and just one defeat. And four successive victories over Charlton, Rochdale, Scunthorpe and Fleetwood brought the Manager of the Month award for January. By then they were in the top half of the table and Lovell was further rewarded with a two-year contract. When Lee Martin scored twice in a 3-1 win at Portsmouth, there was an outside chance of making the play-offs. Instead, the next nine matches delivered just three goals and a slide into the bottom half before a rousing 5-2 finish against Plymouth in which Tom Eaves scored a hat-trick.

Bingham B......................9
Byrne M.................. 41 (1)
Clare S .................. 20 (1)
Cundle G .................. 1 (5)
Eaves T.................. 34 (7)
Ehmer M.................. 41 (1)
Garmston B............. 16 (3)
Hadler T..........................1
Hessenthaler J.......... 33 (4)
Holy T..........................45
Lacey A.................. 10 (1)
List E...................... 7 (16)
Martin L.................. 33 (2)
Moussa F .................. - (2)
Murphy R.........................1
Nash L.................... 2 (10)
Nasseri N.................. 2 (2)
Nugent B................. 17 (6)
O'Mara F.................... 1 (1)
O'Neill L................. 36 (2)
Ogilvie C.................28 (9)
Oldaker D....................- (3)
Parker J ..................35 (7)
Reilly C.........................15
Starkey J.....................- (1)
Tucker J......................- (1)
Wagstaff S.............19 (12)
Wilkinson C...........17 (17)
Wright J......................2 (1)
Zakuani G.....................40

**League goals** (50): Eaves 17, Parker 10, Martin 6, Byrne 3, Wilkinson 3, Ehmer 2, List 2, Clare 1, Garmston 1, Lacey 1, Nasseri 1, O'Neill 1, Ogilvie 1, Opponents 1
**FA Cup goals** (4): Eaves 1, O'Neill 1, Parker 1, Wagstaff 1. **League Cup goals**: None. **League Trophy goals** (11): Oldaker 2, Byrne 1, Cundle 1, Ehmer 1, Mbo N 1, O'Neill 1, Parker 1, Wagstaff 1, Wilkinson 1, Opponents 1
**Average home league attendance**: 5,370. **Player of Year**: Mark Byrne

## MILTON KEYNES DONS

Former manager Karl Robinson continued to cast a shadow over the club during a second relegation in three seasons. Robinson was in charge for six-and-a-half years before being dismissed in October 2016 and chairman Pete Winkelman insisted his legacy was still being felt. Winkelman also admitted mistakes were made in the appointment of Robinson's successors, Robbie Neilson and Dan Micciche, who shared the drop from League One. Neilson was sacked early in the New Year after 14 months, his side having slipped into the relegation zone after a single win in 11 games – 1-0 against Peterborough in which Joe Walsh and Osman Sow were sent off and the manager sent to the stands. Former Academy coach Micciche lasted three months before he was fired in the wake of a 4-0 defeat at Southend after three victories in 16 games. Three days later, under assistant manager Keith Millen, Dons were effectively relegated when losing 2-0 at Bradford. Paul Tisdale left Exeter to try to revive the club's fortunes.

Agard K................. 24 (17)
Aneke C.................. 26 (5)
Ariyibi G ................. 17 (5)
Brittain C................ 26 (3)
Cisse O................... 28 (4)
Ebanks-Landell E...... 25 (4)
Gilbey A.................. 22 (1)
Golbourne S............ 24 (1)
Kasumu D................... - (1)
Lewington D............ 21 (1)
McGrandles C.......... 13 (6)
Muirhead R........... 13 (17)
Nesbitt A................ 5 (14)
Nicholls L.......................41
Nombe S.................... - (6)
Pawlett P ................ 20 (4)
Rasulo G.................... - (1)
Seager R.................... 8 (6)
Sietsma W.......................5
Sow O...................... 17 (2)
Tavernier M ................5 (2)
Thomas-Asante B.......- (15)
Tshibola A.....................12
Tymon J ......................8 (1)
Ugbo I.....................11 (4)
Upson E...................32 (5)
Walsh J.........................10
Ward E.........................15
Williams G................41 (2)
Wootton S ...............37 (1)

**League goals** (43): Aneke 9, Agard 6, Ariyibi 3, Gilbey 3, Muirhead 3, Pawlett 3, Upon 3, Brittain 2, Ebanks-Landell 2, Nesbitt 2, Sow 2, Ugbo 2, Seager 1, Williams 1, Opponents 1
**FA Cup goals** (9): Agard 2, Nesbitt 2, Aneke 1, Cisse 1, Ebanks-Landell 1, Pawlett 1, Upson 1
**League Cup goals** (2): Ariyibi 1, Seager 1. **League Trophy goals** (6): Ariyibi 3, Seager 1, Thomas-Asante 1, Tshibola 1
**Average home league attendance**: 9,202. **Player of Year**: No award

## NORTHAMPTON TOWN

Two changes of manager and a late rally were unable to prevent Northampton from relegation after two seasons in League One. Justin Edinburgh was the Football League's first casualty of the campaign after his side lost their first four matches. He was replaced by Jimmy Floyd Hasselbaink, formerly in charge of Queens Park Rangers and Burton, who made a successful start with seven points from his first three games to supervise a move out of the bottom four. Fortunes continued to fluctuate, with Hasselbaink busy in the January window in a bid to bring about some stability. John-Joe O'Toole scored in four successive matches which netted ten points for another move out of the bottom four. Then it was back to square one after no wins in nine resulted in the club's second sacking and left them third from bottom. Under caretaker Dean Austin, Northampton won 3-2 at fellow-strugglers Bury and defeated promotion-chasing Plymouth 2-0. But they conceded a stoppage-time winner to Walsall and despites one fixture remaining, a vastly inferior goal difference effectively left them with no chance of surviving. Austin was given the job permanently.

| | | |
|---|---|---|
| Ariyibi G .......... 3 (9) | Hoskins S .......... 18 (9) | Phillips A .......... 2 |
| Barnett L .......... 13 (2) | Ingram M .......... 20 | Pierre A .......... 19 |
| Bowditch D .......... 3 (8) | Kasim Y .......... 4 (2) | Poole R .......... 18 (4) |
| Bridge J .......... 1 (3) | Long C .......... 30 (8) | Powell D .......... 21 (8) |
| Buchanan D .......... 32 | Luckassen K .......... 1 (3) | Revell A .......... 10 (5) |
| Bunney J .......... 11 (1) | Mathis B .......... 2 (3) | Richards M .......... 7 (12) |
| Coddington L .......... 1 | McGivern R .......... - (1) | Roberts M .......... - (1) |
| Cornell D .......... 6 | McGugan L .......... 7 (2) | Smith G .......... 5 (1) |
| Crooks M .......... 29 (1) | McWilliams S .......... 15 (4) | Taylor A .......... 45 |
| Facey S .......... 13 (2) | Moloney B .......... 31 (3) | Taylor M .......... 1 |
| Foley S .......... 15 (9) | O'Donnell R .......... 19 | Turnbull J .......... 14 |
| Grimes M .......... 43 (1) | O'Toole J-J .......... 25 (4) | Waters B .......... 9 (8) |
| Hanley R .......... 3 (1) | Pereira H .......... 4 (8) | Van Veen K .......... 6 (4) |

**League goals** (43): Long 9, O'Toole 6, Taylor A 6, Crooks 4, Grimes 4, Foley 2, Hoskins 2, Powell 2, Revell 2, Barnett 1, Buchanan 1, Facey 1, Luckassen 1, Richards 1, Opponents 1
**FA Cup goals**: None. **League Cup goals**: None. **League Trophy goals** (5): Foley 1, McGugan 1, Revell 1, Taylor A 1, Opponents 1
**Average home league attendance**: 5,830. **Player of Year**: Ash Taylor

## OLDHAM ATHLETIC

Twenty one years in the game's third tier came to an end in a see-saw season which delivered relegation in a tense final round of matches. Going into a make-or-break fixture at Northampton a point clear of Rochdale, Oldham took the lead through George Edmundson's first goal for the club. Then, after they trailed at the interval, Thomas Haymer's header put his side back in the driving seat. But Rochdale's winner against Charlton proved decisive, leaving Richie Wellens and his players to reflect on too many drawn matches at the business end of the campaign – seven out of eight. Oldham had lost the first five games, leading to the end of John Sheridan's third spell as manager following a 5-1 defeat by Rotherham. Wellens, in a caretaker role, supervised successive wins over Peterborough, Portsmouth and Blackburn to earn a permanent appointment. And a 5-1 victory over Northampton suggested a move clear of the relegation area. Instead, there was a barren run stretching over nine games and Oldham slipped back into trouble. Wellens was sacked in the summer and replaced by their former striker Frankie Bunn.

| | | |
|---|---|---|
| Banks O .......... 5 (2) | Davies C .......... 34 (6) | Fawns M .......... 1 (3) |
| Benteke J .......... - (1) | Doyle E .......... 28 (2) | Flynn R .......... 2 (5) |
| Benyu K .......... 3 (1) | Duffus C .......... - (6) | Gardner D .......... 42 (1) |
| Bryan K .......... 32 | Dummigan C .......... 28 (2) | Gerrard A .......... 30 (1) |
| Byrne J .......... 37 (3) | Edmundson G .......... 14 (1) | Green P .......... 3 (3) |
| Clarke P .......... 18 (1) | Fane O .......... 38 (3) | Haymer T .......... 5 (2) |

Holloway A............... 7 (29)
Hunt R .................... 32 (1)
Kyeremeh G .....................1
Mantack K .................. - (1)
Maouche M................. - (1)
McEleney P................ 4 (5)
McLaughlin R........... 10 (6)
Menig Q.................. 4 (10)
Moimbe W ....................11
Nazon D ................. 13 (3)
Nepomuceno G......... 20 (6)
Obadeyi T ............. 10 (12)
Omrani A ................... 1 (7)
Osei D ...................... 1 (2)
Placide J.......................36
Pringle B ......................13
Ruddy J ..........................5
Wilson Ben .....................5
Wilson Brian ........... 13 (6)

**League goals** (58): Doyle 14, Davies 11, Nazon 6, Byrne 5, Bryan 2, Clarke 2, Dummigan 2, Gerrard 2, Holloway 2, Edmundson 1, Gardner 1, Haymer 1. McEleney 1, McLaughlin 1, Menig 1, Nepomuceno 1, Obadeyi 1, Osei 1, Pringle 1, Opponents 2
**FA Cup goals** (2): Clarke 1, Holloway 1. **League Cup goals** (2): Davies 1, Green 1. **League Trophy goals** (11): Byrne 3, Davies 2, Doyle 2, Obadeyi 2, Gerrard 1, Holloway 1
**Average home league attendance**: 4,442. **Player of Year**: Dan Gardner

## OXFORD UNITED

A shattering home defeat undermined what had been promised to be a decent season. Oxford were four points off a top-six place approaching the midway point when they suffered a club-record 7-0 loss to leaders Wigan. Another reversal at the Kassam Stadium, this time against bottom-of-the-table Bury a month later, was followed by the dismissal of manager Pep Clotet after six months in the job. The slide continued under caretaker Derek Fazackerley, who took charge for two months until Karl Robinson was appointed hours after parting company with Charlton. His first match was a 3-0 defeat at Portsmouth, followed by four more without a win. Oxford had slipped to 18th before the new manager was off the mark with goals from James Henry and the Brazilian Ricardinho for a 2-0 victory over Southend. Henry's goal secured three more points against Doncaster to virtually ensure safety, while penalties from John Mousinho and Todd Kane against Rochdale confirmed it. This late flourish was not enough to lift them higher than 16th – down from eighth in 2017.

Brannagan C ..................12
Buckley-Ricketts I ...... 8 (3)
Carroll C .................. 10 (2)
Dickie R .........................15
Eastwood S ....................46
Hall R...................... 10 (3)
Henry J.................... 34 (8)
James O ..................... - (1)
Johnson M .......................2
Kane T ...........................17
Ledson R.................. 37 (7)
Martin A.................. 10 (2)
Mehmeti A .............. 3 (10)
Mousinho J.....................40
Mowatt A............... 20 (10)
Napa M................... 3 (11)
Nelson C .................. 18 (2)
Obika J ................. 20 (15)
Payne J .................... 25 (3)
Ribeiro C........................10
Ricardinho................29 (7)
Roberts J.....................- (1)
Rothwell J .............26 (10)
Ruffles J...................33 (5)
Smith-Brown A ................ 9
Thomas W ................32 (5)
Tiendalli D................12 (1)
Williamson M...........13 (1)
Xemi ..........................4 (6)
Van Kessel G ............8 (15)

**League goals** (61): Henry 10, Thomas 10, Obika 5, Rothwell 5, Ruffles 5, Kane 3, Ledson 3, Payne 3, Ricardinho 3, Van Kessel 3, Hall 2, Mowatt 2, Carroll 1, Dickie 1, Mehmeti 1, Mousinho 1, Nelson 1, Ribeiro 1, Xemi 1
**FA Cup goals**: None. **League Cup goals** (3): Johnson 1, Obika 1, Xemi 1. **League Trophy goals** (14): Payne 4, Hall 3, Van Kessel 2, Henry 1, Mowatt 1, Obika 1, Rothwell 1, Thomas 1
**Average home league attendance**: 7,376. **Player of Year**: Ryan Ledson

## PETERBOROUGH UNITED

A promotion push petered out just when it looked like a change of manager had revived their bid for a play-off place. Steve Evans left Mansfield to take over when Grant McCann was sacked after a single win in nine matches in all competitions. Evans watched from the stands as his new side defeated Walsall, then supervised a 4-1 victory over Charlton in which Jack Marriott scored his 20th and 21st goals of the season. Marriott continued his prolific form in wins over Bury and Northampton, by which time Peterborough had climbed back into the top-six. But a season-long failure to retain winning positions came back to haunt them, with four successive defeats resulting in a slide to ninth and not enough games remaining to make up lost ground. A 3-1 reversal against below-strength Shrewsbury meant that 30 points had been dropped after going ahead, convincing Evans of the need to shake-up his squad during the summer. Marriott, who scored a hat-trick against Bristol Rovers, early in the campaign finished League One's top scorer on 27.

| | | |
|---|---|---|
| Anderson J.............. 7 (10) | Forrester C .............. 22 (7) | Morias J................12 (13) |
| Baldwin J................ 32 (1) | Freestone L ............... 2 (2) | O'Malley C......................9 |
| Bogle O .................... 4 (5) | Grant A .................... 37 (1) | Penny A .....................6 (1) |
| Bond J..........................37 | Hughes A ................ 35 (8) | Shephard L..............23 (1) |
| Chettle C .................... - (2) | Kanu I ..................... 1 (17) | Tafazolli R ...............32 (1) |
| Cooper G.................... 8 (5) | Lloyd D ................ 17 (14) | Taylor S....................43 (1) |
| Da Silva Lopes L..... 28 (11) | Maddison M ...................41 | Ward J ......................9 (8) |
| Doughty M ............... 28 (6) | Marriott J .......................44 | |
| Edwards G .............. 25 (1) | Miller R...................... 4 (6) | |

**League goals** (68): Marriott 27, Lloyd 8, Maddison 8, Morias 6, Edwards 4, Taylor 3, Baldwin 2, Cooper 2, Hughes 2, Bogle 1, Doughty 1, Tafazolli 1, Opponents 3
**FA Cup goals** (16): Marriott 5, Lloyd 3, Maddison 2, Tafazolli 2, Baldwin 1, Doughty 1, Edwards 1, Hughes 1. **League Cup goals** (1): Edwards 1. **League Trophy goals** (9): Lloyd 2, Maddison 2, Edwards 1, Marriott 1, Morias 1, Taylor 1, Opponents 1
**Average home league attendance**: 5,669. **Player of Year**: Jack Marriott

## PLYMOUTH ARGYLE

One of the season's finest comebacks failed narrowly to secure a play-off place. Plymouth registered a single win in the opening 14 games and had four players sent off in successive home matches – Antoni Sarcevic, Graham Carey, Ryan Edwards and Sonny Bradley. They were still bottom after 20 fixtures, undermined by a weakness in defending corners. But manager Derek Adams received a vote of confidence from the board and his side were transformed with five wins out of the next seven to go clear of the relegation zone. A 2-1 win over Oldham then left them almost half-way up table and after beating Bradford 1-0 in late February they were up to sixth. By then, Plymouth had taken 36 points from 15 games. Graham Carey won and converted a stoppage-time penalty for a 2-1 victory over Rotherham before they faltered, losing to struggling Northampton and dropping points to Portsmouth and Rochdale. The crunch came in the penultimate match at Scunthorpe, where a 2-0 defeat by rivals for a play-off place ended their chances.

| | | |
|---|---|---|
| Ainsworth L............. 3 (16) | Fox D...................... 42 (3) | Roos K..........................4 |
| Battle A..................... - (1) | Grant J.................. 24 (9) | Sangster C..................- (2) |
| Blissett N ................. 6 (7) | Jervis J.................... 17 (7) | Sarcevic A................25 (5) |
| Bradley S................ 39 (1) | Lameiras R.............. 25 (9) | Sawyer G......................46 |
| Carey G.........................42 | Letheren K .......................7 | Sinclair A..............10 (14) |
| Church S ................... - (2) | Makasi M ................ 6 (1) | Sokolik J ....................- (2) |
| Ciftci N..................... 6 (1) | Matthews R ....................26 | Songo'o Y................24 (9) |
| Cooper M................... - (1) | McCormick L ....................9 | Taylor R........................21 |
| Diagouraga T.................15 | Miller G.................. 11 (4) | Threlkeld O...................24 |
| Edwards R .....................25 | Ness J..................... 26 (1) | Vyner Z ........................ 17 |
| Fletcher A................ 3 (12) | Paton P..................... 1 (2) | Wylde G ....................2 (7) |

**League goals** (58): Carey 14, Grant 6, Lameiras 6, Taylor 5, Bradley 4, Jervis 4, Diagouraga 3, Edwards 3, Ness 3, Sarcevic 3, Blissett 1, Fletcher 1, Fox 1, Makasi 1, Sawyer 1, Vyner 1, Wylde 1
**FA Cup goals** (2): Carey 2. **League Cup goals**: None. **League Trophy goals** (5): Fletcher 2, Blissett 1, Edwards 1, Taylor 1
**Average home league attendance**: 10,413. **Player of Year**: Graham Carey

## PORTSMOUTH

Portsmouth's push for a second successive promotion ran out of steam at a critical time. The 2017 League Two champions reached the play-off fringes with seven wins out of nine going into the New Year, struggled through a loss of home form, then forced their way back into contention with four straight wins, the most significant against former manager Paul Cook's Wigan. Brett Pitman was on the mark five times in that run and he added another two in a 3-3 draw at Rochdale. His side were then level on 62 points with Charlton for the fourth play-off place. But a 3-1 defeat at Bradford was followed by a 1-0 reversal at home to Charlton, the eighth in front of their own supporters. That left their chances hanging by a thread and defeat by the same scoreline at relegated Bury ended all hope. Pitman took his tally for the season to 23 in the final match against Peterborough, second to Peterborough's Jack Marriott in the division's rankings.

Baker C .................... 1 (1)
Bass A ...........................1
Bennett K ............... 11 (7)
Burgess C ............... 34 (1)
Chaplin C.............. 11 (15)
Clarke M .......................42
Close B ................... 37 (3)
Deslandes S ....................2
Donohue D .............. 29 (4)
Evans G .................. 26 (6)
Haunstrup B ........... 13 (3)
Hawkins O ............... 22 (9)
Henderson S....................1
Holmes-Dennis T..............1
Kabamba N ................. - (1)
Kennedy M .............. 20 (9)
Lalkovic M.......................1
Lowe J .................... 39 (5)
Main C...................... 2 (3)
May A ..................... 10 (3)
McCrory D .......................3
McGee L .......................44
Naismith K...............19 (7)
O'Keefe S................17 (4)
Pitman B.................35 (3)
Ronan C.....................8 (8)
Rose D....................13 (2)
Talbot D .........................4
Thompson N............34 (2)
Walkes A .......................12
Whatmough J.................14

**League goals** (57): Pitman 23, Hawkins 7, Lowe 7, Chaplin 5, Kennedy 3, Clarke 2, Close 2, Evans 2, Naismith 2, Walkes 1, Opponents 3
**FA Cup goals**: None. **League Cup goals** (1): Opponents 1. **League Trophy goals** (10): Lowe 2, O'Keefe 2, Clarke 1, Evans 1, Hawkins 1, Main 1, Naismith 1, Pitman 1
**Average home league attendance**: 17,917. **Player of Year**: Matt Clarke

## ROCHDALE

Joe Thompson reckoned 'it was written in the stars' after scoring the goal which preserved the club's League One status. The 29-year-old midfielder, who returned to the side after recovering from a second bout of cancer, came off the bench to deliver a 1-0 victory over Charlton on the final day of the regular season. It enabled Keith Hill's team to move above Oldham and finish one point ahead of their local rivals, who drew at Northampton in their last fixture and were relegated. Rochdale had retrieved an 11-point deficit with the help of games in hand built up after a memorable FA Cup run. But it proved a close thing, with points dropped against Oldham in a goalless draw after Joe Rafferty's penalty was saved and against Bradford who scored a stoppage -time equaliser. In the Cup, Ian Henderson's goal knocked out Millwall in a fourth round replay. Then, Rochdale held Tottenham 2-2 on the newly-laid Spotland pitch, thanks to a stoppage-time equaliser by substitute Steve Davies, before losing the replay 6-1 at Wembley.

Adshead D ................. - (1)
Allen J ...................... 3 (1)
Andrew C ................ 26 (5)
Brown R ................... 2 (1)
Bunney J ................ 18 (2)
Camps C ................. 41 (1)
Canavan N .......................3
Cannon A................ 18 (3)
Daniels D................ 14 (1)
Davies S ................. 8 (24)
Delaney R ............... 16 (2)
Dobre M-A.................. - (5)
Done M ................... 40 (6)
Gillam M ................... 1 (7)
Hart S....................... 1 (2)
Henderson I.....................39
Humphrys S ............ 11 (5)
Inman B................ 25 (12)
Keane K...........................3
Kitching M .............. 10 (3)
Knott B ..................... 1 (3)
Lillis J............................40
McGahey H..............41 (1)
McNulty J.......................40
Moore B ..........................6
Ntlhe K...................11 (9)
Rafferty J ................30 (3)
Rathbone O .............30 (3)
Slew J.........................- (5)
Thompson J ................3 (7)
Williams J (midfield)....6 (5)
Williams J (defender)...... 12
Wiseman S ................7 (6)

**League goals** (49): Henderson 13, Davies 7, Done 6, Inman 4, Andrew 3, Camps 2, Cannon 2, Delaney 2, Humphrys 2, Kitching 2, Dobre 1, Gillam 1, McNulty 1, Rafferty 1, Rathbone 1, Thompson 1

**FA Cup goals** (15): Henderson 6, Andrew 2, Done 2, Inman 2, Camps 1, Davies 1, Humphrys 1. **League Cup goals** (1): Camps 1. **League Trophy goals** (6): Inman 2, Bunney 1, Gillam 1, Henderson 1, Slew 1

**Average home league attendance**: 3,503. **Player of Year**: Ian Henderson

## ROTHERHAM UNITED

The club kept faith with manager Paul Warne after relegation and were rewarded with an immediate return to the Championship. Two goals by captain Richard Wood delivered a 2-1 Play-off Final win over Shrewsbury, who had finished eight points ahead of them in the table. The central-defender converted set-play deliveries from Joe Newell to follow his goal against Scunthorpe in the semi-finals and take his tally for the season to seven. After losing three of their opening four matches, Rotherham climbed into the top-six with seven wins out of nine, including 5-1 scorelines against Walsall and Oldham. There was a mid-season dip in form which pushed them down to mid-table, then a decisive run of 14 unbeaten matches featuring 11 victories, the last of those against Doncaster earned by Newell's penalty in the 13th minute of stoppage-time. The successful sequence wasn't enough to pose a threat to the top three, Wigan, Blackburn and Shrewsbury. But Rotherham held on comfortably to a play-off spot and made sure of going through by beating Bristol Rovers 2-0 in the penultimate home game.

| | | | | | |
|---|---|---|---|---|---|
| Ajayi S | 29 (6) | Mattock J | 34 (1) | Rodak M | 35 |
| Ball D | 26 (7) | Moore K | 19 (3) | Smith M | 18 (2) |
| Clarke-Harris J | 1 (13) | Newell J | 22 (17) | Taylor J | 13 (12) |
| Cummings S | 11 (1) | O'Donnell R | 10 | Towell R | 34 (5) |
| Emmanuel J | 30 (1) | Palmer M | 10 (4) | Vaulks W | 38 (6) |
| Forde A | 27 (14) | Potter D | 16 | Williams R | 33 (9) |
| Frecklington L | 17 (2) | Price L | 1 | Wood R | 34 (2) |
| Ihiekwe M | 26 (5) | Proctor J | 4 | Yates J | 7 (10) |
| Lavery C | 1 (13) | Purrington B | 10 | | |

**Play-offs – appearances**: Emmanuel 3, Mattock 3, Rodak 3, Smith 3, Towell 3, Vaulks 3, Wood 3, Newell 2 (1), Taylor 2 (1), Williams 2 (1), Palmer 2, Ihiekwe 2, Ajayi 1 (2), Ball 1, Forde – (3), Lavery – (1)

**League goals** (73): Moore 13, Ball 8, Newell 7, Smith 6, Towell 5, Vaulks 5, Ajayi 4, Frecklington 4, Taylor 4, Williams 4, Wood 4, Forde 2, Lavery 2, Ihiekwe 1, Mattock 1, Yates 1, Opponents 2.

**Play-offs – goals** (6): Wood 3, Newell 1, Taylor 1, Vaulks 1

**FA Cup goals** (1): Vaulks 1. **League Cup goals** (3): Ajayi 1, Forde 1, Proctor 1. **League Trophy goals** (5): Ball 1, Clarke-Harris 1, Towell 1, Vaulks 1, Yates 1

**Average home league attendance**: 8,514. **Player of Year**: Will Vaulks

## SCUNTHORE UNITED

Another seesaw season, another place in the play-offs and another defeat in the knockout phase. This time, Scunthorpe were second best to Rotherham, rescuing a 2-2 draw with an 88th minute goal from on-loan Cameron McGeehan at Glanford Park and losing the second leg 2-0. Caretaker Nick Daws, however, had done enough to be given the manager's job permanently after overseeing a strong finish which sealed fifth place. They had been clinging on after a single win in 13 matches when Graham Alexander was sacked and replaced by his assistant, initially until the end of the campaign. Daws supervised four consecutive wins, the last of which was a 2-0 success against Plymouth which put Scunthorpe through and left their opponents on the outside. Under Alexander, they were up to third, helped by six straight wins and the ability to accumulate points from losing positions. Against that, was a tendency to concede costly stoppage-time goals, along with an 87th minute equaliser which denied them a 3-2 win at champions-to-be Wigan.

| | | |
|---|---|---|
| Adelakun H ............ 29 (10) | Hopper T ............... 27 (11) | Sutton L .................. 12 (3) |
| Bishop N ................ 33 (2) | Lewis C ...................... 1 (3) | Toney I ..................... 13 (3) |
| Burgess C ............... 22 (3) | Madden P ................ 15 (5) | Townsend C ............. 24 (6) |
| Butroid L .................. 6 (1) | Mantom S ................. 1 (7) | Vermijl M .................... 3 (3 |
| Goode C .................. 10 (3) | McArdle R ......................36 | Wallace M ..................... 45 |
| Church S ..................... - (4) | McGeehan C ............ 3 (10) | Watson R ......................... 4 |
| Clarke J .................. 20 (3) | Morris J .................... 43 (1) | Williams L .................... - (2) |
| Crofts A ..................... 1 (3) | Novak L ................. 16 (16) | Wootton K ..................... - (1) |
| Gilks M .........................42 | Ojo F ....................... 40 (1) | Yates R ..................... 14 (2) |
| Holmes D .............. 34 (11) | Redmond D ................. - (1) | Van Veen K .............. 12 (9) |

**Play-offs – appearances**: Adelakun 2, Holmes 2, McArdle 2, Morris 2, Ojo 2, Toney 2, Townsend 2, Wallace 2, Yates 2, Watson 1 (1), Clarke 1, Gilks 1, Vermijl 1, Hopper – (2), McGeechan – (2), Novak – (1)

**League goals** (65): Morris 11, Toney 8, Holmes 7, Hopper 7, Novak 6, Van Veen 5, Adelakun 4, Townsend 4, Burgess 2, Madden 2, Ojo 2, Yates 2, Bishop 1, Goode 1, McArdle 1, Wallace 1, Opponents 1. **Play-offs – goals** (2): McGeehan 1, Opponents 1

**FA Cup goals** (1): Adelakun 1. **League Cup goals** (3): Madden 2, Holmes 1. **League Trophy goals** (7): Hopper 2, Van Veen 2, Holmes 1, Lewis 1, Morris 1

**Average home league attendance**: 4,364. **Player of Year**: Duane Holmes

## SHREWSBURY TOWN

It was a measure of what Shrewsbury achieved throughout the season against all the odds that Paul Hurst was named League One's Manager of the Year – even though his side were beaten in the Play-off Final by Rotherham. The second favourites to be relegated finished third on 87 points, a total good enough to have gained automatic promotion in the two previous years. They also reached the Checkatrade Trophy Final, losing 1-0 to Lincoln. Shrewsbury were alone in the Football League in remaining undefeated for the first 15 games. The run came to an end with a 1-0 defeat at Peterborough, but they remained in the top two for more than six months until a 3-1 loss at Rochdale allowed Wigan and Blackburn to take over and eventually pull away. Momentum lost towards the end of the campaign returned in the semi-finals, bringing a 2-0 semi-final victory over Charlton, helped by Jon Nolan's spectacular 20-yard half-volley in the first leg at The Valley. Dean Henderson saved a penalty and Alex Rodman netted a second-half equaliser at Wembley. But Rotherham scored another goal from a set-play in extra-time and returned to the Championship at the first attempt. Hurst left to become the new Ipswich manager and was replaced by John Askey, who led Macclesfield back into the Football League.

| | | |
|---|---|---|
| Adams E ..................... - (5) | Henderson D ...................38 | Nsiala A ........................ 44 |
| Beckles O ................ 29 (4) | Hendrie L .................. 9 (1) | Ogogo A ........................ 35 |
| Bolton J .................. 32 (1) | John-Lewis L ............ - (34) | Payne S ................ 17 (21) |
| Brown J ........................15 | Jones S ...................... 3 (2) | Riley J ......................... 8 (2) |
| Dodds L ..................... 5 (4) | Lowe M ...................... 8 (4) | Rodman A ............... 36 (5) |
| Eisa A ........................ 3 (2) | MacGillivray C ..................8 | Sadler M ....................... 42 |
| Ennis N ...................... - (1) | Morris B .................. 13 (5) | Thomas N ................... 7 (4) |
| Gnahoua A ................. 4 (7) | Morris C ................ 32 (10) | Whalley S ................ 40 (4) |
| Godfrey B ................ 35 (5) | Nolan J .........................43 | |

**Play-offs – appearances**: Beckles 3, Bolton 3, Godfrey 3, Henderson 3, Morris B 3, Morris C 3, Nolan 3, Nsiala 3, Rodman 3, Sadler 3, Whalley 3, John-Lewis – (3), Payne – (3), Riley – (3),

**League goals** (60): Payne 11, Nolan 9, Whalley 8, Morris C 6, Rodman 5, Beckles 3, Nsiala 3, John-Lewis 2, Ogogo 2, Thomas 2, Bolton 1, Brown 1, Eisa 1, Gnahoua 1, Godfrey 1, Jones 1, Riley 1, Sadler 1, Opponents 1. **Play-offs – goals** (2): Nolan 1 Morris C 1

**FA Cup goals** (7): Rodman 2, Whalley 2, Gnahoua 1, Morris C 1, Payne 1. **League Cup goals** (1): Whalley 1. **League Trophy goals** (11): Dodds 2, Morris C 2, Payne 2, Gnahoua 1, John-Lewis 1, Riley 1, Rodman 1, Whalley 1
**Average home league attendance**: 6,249. **Player of Year**: Jon Nolan

## SOUTHEND UNITED

Chris Powell brought stability to Southend's season at a time when seven defeats in eight matches had heightened fears of a relegation struggle ahead. The run ended Phil Brown's near five-year spell as manager and brought in a man who made 290 appearances for the club as a player. Powell, formerly in charge of Huddersfield and Charlton, started with a 3-2 victory over Scunthorpe, earned by Michael Turner's stoppage-time goal. It was followed by wins against two more teams chasing promotion, Peterborough and leaders Wigan, enabling Powell to become the club's first permanent manager to take maximum points from his first three games. His team also dented the ambitions of Portsmouth and Rotherham, then after a sequence of goalless performance, Southend ended in the top half of the table on the back of nine goals against MK Dons, Oldham and Bradford, Theo Robinson scoring a hat-trick in the first of those wins.

Amadou Ba ................. - (5)
Bishop N ..................... - (1)
Bridge J ...................... - (1)
Bwomono E................ 9 (2)
Coker B ................... 21 (1)
Cox S ...................... 40 (2)
Demetriou J ............ 41 (1)
Ferdinand A ............ 29 (2)
Fortune M-A........... 26 (12)
Gard L........................ - (2)
Harrison S................. 5 (8)
Hendrie S................... 8 (4)
Kiernan R.................... - (1)
Kightly M ................ 26 (3)
Kyprianou H ............ 12 (1)
Ladapo F.................... 3 (7)
Leonard R ......................25
Mantom S .................. 6 (1)
McGlashan J............. 9 (17)
McLaughlin S ......... 35 (10)
Oxley M.........................46
Ranger N.................11 (7)
Robinson T...............7 (18)
Timlin M .................32 (2)
Turner M .......................25
Wabo N.........................- (3)
White J ....................26 (5)
Wordsworth A...........21 (3)
Wright J ...................19 (4)
Yearwood D..............24 (2)

**League goals** (58): Cox 10, Demetriou 8, Kightly 6, McLaughlin 6, Robinson 5, Fortune 4, Leonard 4, Turner 4, Wordsworth 3, Ranger 2, White 2, McGlashan 1, Wright 1, Opponents 2
**FA Cup goals**: None. **League Cup goals**: None. **League Trophy goals** (4): Robinson 2, McLaughlin 1, Wright 1
**Average home league attendance**: 7,376. **Player of Year**: Mark Oxley

## WALSALL

A stoppage-time goal by George Dobson lifted a relegation cloud hanging over the club. The midfielder rounded off a 91st minute counter-attack with a fine strike to deliver a 1-0 victory over fellow-strugglers Northampton, his first goal since rejoining the club from Sparta Rotterdam in the January transfer window. It left them on the brink of surviving and effectively sealed their opponents' fate. A 1-1 draw at Bradford in the penultimate match made sure. Walsall seemed to be settling into a secure mid-table spot after a convincing 3-0 win at Southend. Instead, alarm bells were ringing when the next eight games yielded just four points. The slide was accompanied by the dismissal of Jon Whitney after a 15-year association with the club during which he had been physio, head of medicine and assistant manager before stepping up in June 2016. Wrexham's Dean Keates, talking take charge of his home-town club where he had two spells as a player, came in to home defeats against promotion-chasing Wigan and Portsmouth. More worrying was a 2-0 lead surrendered to AFC Wimbledon and punished by a 3-2 loss.

Agyei D................... 7 (11)
Bakayoko A............. 33 (8)
Candlin M.................. - (3)
Chambers A ..................43
Cockerill-Mollett C...........1
Cuvelier F ............. 10 (13)
Devlin N ................. 30 (3)
Dobson G................ 19 (2)
Donnellan S .............. 7 (3)
Edwards J ................ 29 (1)
Fitzwater J .....................16
Flanagan R ............... 3 (6)

Gillespie M ....................23
Guthrie J.........................46
Ismail Z.................. 12 (4)
Jackson S ................. 1 (7)
Kinsella L ................ 17 (2)
Kouhyar Q............... 5 (10)
Leahy L .........................46
Morris K ................ 35 (7)
Ngoy J ...................... 9 (4)
Oztumer E............... 41 (4)
Roberts K ............... 17 (3)
Roberts L................ 23 (1)
Roberts T................ 11 (6)
Shaibu J ................ 3 (11)
Shorrock W ............... - (1)
Wilson J.........................19

**League goals** (53): Oztumer 15, Edwards 7, Bakayoko 5, Roberts T 5, Agyei 4, Fitzwater 3, Morris 3, Ngoy 3, Leahy 2, Dobson 1, Guthrie 1, Ismail 1, Kouhyar 1, Wilson 1, Opponents 1
**FA Cup goals** (1) Bakayoko 1. **League Cup goals** (2): Bakayoko 1, Oztumer 1. **League Trophy goals** (7): Ismail 2, Agyei 1, Bakayoko 1, Flanagan 1, Leahy 1, Oztumer 1
**Average home league attendance**: 4,760. **Player of Year**: Joe Edwards

## WIGAN ATHLETIC

League One champions, FA Cup quarter-finalists, winners against Manchester City. Seasons don't come much better than this one. Most importantly, Wigan made an immediate return to the Championship, outscoring every team in the division, notably away from home where they piled up 52 goals, including a club-record 7-0 victory against Oxford. Will Grigg scored a hat-trick and got another as MK Dons were beaten 5-1. Wigan also put four past Bury, AFC Wimbledon, Rochdale and Fleetwood on the way to overhauling early leaders Shrewsbury, then holding off Blackburn's challenge for the title. In the Cup, they knocked out Bournemouth, after a replay, and West Ham before Grigg's breakaway goal delivered a repeat of the 1-0 win over City in the 2013 Wembley final. The Northern Ireland striker, whose team lost 2-0 to Southampton in the last eight, finished with 26 in all competitions. Another influential player was former Manchester United midfielder Nick Powell, reportedly the subject of a £10m bid turned down by the club, while manager Paul Cook's reward was a new four-year contract.

Bruce A ..................... 4 (2)
Burn D ..........................45
Byrne N.........................44
Colclough R ........... 11 (15)
Cole D ........................ - (6)
Daniels D.........................1
Dunkley C.......................43
Elder C.................... 24 (3)
Evans L .........................20
Fulton J ..................... 4 (1)
Gilbey A....................... - (2)
Grigg W................. 29 (14)
Hunt N......................... - (7)
Jacobs M........................44
James R..........................22
Jones J............................15
Massey G ................. 35 (7)
Morsy S..........................41
Perkins D .................2 (11)
Powell N ..................38 (1)
Power M.................29 (11)
Roberts G.................6 (21)
Thomas T....................- (3)
Toney I...................10 (14)
Vaughan J ................7 (12)
Walker J.....................1 (7)
Walton C .......................31

**League goals** (89): Grigg 19, Powell 15, Jacobs 12, Dunkley 7, Massey 6, Burn 5, Power 5, Colclough 4, Toney 4, Vaughan 3, Morsy 2, Bruce 1, Evans 1, Fultlon 1, Perkins 1, Roberts 1, Opponents 2
**FA Cup goals** (14): Grigg 7, Toney 2, Burn 1, Elder 1, Evans 1, Morsy 1, Opponents 1. **League Cup goals** (3): Colclough 1, Flores J 1, Laurent J 1. **League Trophy goals** (5): Colclough 1, Evans 1, Gilbey, Hunt 1, Maffeo V 1
**Average home league attendance**: 9,152. **Player of Year**: Nathan Byrne

# SKY BET LEAGUE TWO

## ACCRINGTON STANLEY

Who would have thought that the new season's fixture list would include Accrington v Sunderland? The little club with the big heart were the toast of the lower divisions, overcoming a tiny budget and even smaller crowds, upsetting all the odds and reaching the third tier of English football for the first time they reformed in 1968. John Coleman's side did it with a remarkable run of success in the second half of the season. After a Boxing Day defeat at Carlisle, they were ninth in the table, 14 points behind leaders Luton and heading, it would seem, for a repeat of the previous season's comfortable, mid-table finish. Instead, a 3-0 victory over Grimsby launched a run of 17 wins, two draws and a single defeat by Crawley. A 2-0 victory at Coventry took them into the top three; a stoppage-time winner by leading marksman Billy Kee at Kenilworth Road knocked Luton off top spot; two more by Kee, the division's Player of the Year, for a 2-0 win over Yeovil in front of their own fans, clinched automatic promotion. It didn't end there. Accrington clinched the title by beating Lincoln 1-0 in the penultimate match with a goal by Jordan Clark in front of record crowd 4,753. Then, Coleman was named Manager of the Year after they finished five points clear of Luton.

Beckles O ........................2
Brown S................... 28 (8)
Chapman A............. 44 (1)
Clark J..........................43
Conneely S.....................33
Dallison T........................2
Donacien J.....................45
Dunne J................... 18 (2)
Edwards J................. 1 (1)
Hmami J.....................- (1)
Hornby-Forbes T......... 2 (4)
Hughes M.......................46
Jackson K.......................44
Johnson C............... 29 (2)
Kee B...........................46
Leacock-McLeod M .... - (10)
Maxted J..........................1
McConville S ..................43
Nolan L.................... 27 (2)
Ogle R ........................ - (3)
Rawson F......................12
Richards-Everton B ... 18 (4)
Rodgers H ................. 4 (1)
Sousa E ......................- (6)
Stryjek M ........................ 1
Sykes R.......................- (2)
Thorniley J .................... 14
Watson N ....................- (2)
Wilks M.................... 3 (16)
Williams D...................- (1)
Zanzala O....................- (6)

**League goals** (76): Kee 25, Jackson 16, McConville 12, Clark 8, Hughes 4, Wilks 3, Conneely 2, Beckles 1, Brown 1, Johnson 1, Richards-Everton 1, Zanzala 1, Opponents 1
**FA Cup goals** (1): McConville 1. **League Cup goals** (4): Clark 1, Dallison 1, Kee 1, Richards-Everton 1. **League Trophy goals** (10): Sousa 3, Wilks 2, Brown 1, Edwards 1, Leacock-McLeod 1, Nolan 1 Opponents 1
**Average home league attendance**: 1,979. **Player of Year**: Billy Kee

## BARNET

So near, yet so far. Martin Allen led his side to within touching distance of safety, only for goal difference to send them back to the National League in the final round of fixtures. A last throw of the dice by chairman Tony Kleanthous was to appoint Allen manager for the fifth time, with Barnet seven points adrift and eight games to play. Four wins and a draw transformed what looked like a lost cause into a position two points behind third-from-bottom Morecambe with one to play. John Akinde, Richard Brindley and Alex Nicholls delivered a 3-0 victory over already-relegated Chesterfield in front of a record 5,539 crowd. But Morecambe secured a goalless draw away to promotion-chasing Coventry and stayed up with a superior goals ratio. Allen was the club's fourth manager of the season. They started solidly with ten points from the opening six matches under Rossi Eames. He was replaced by Mark McGhee, former assistant to Scotland manager Gordon Strachan, after failing to win any of the next 11. Another change brought in Graham Westley, formerly in charge of Newport, Peterborough and Preston, but that too failed to take Barnet out of the bottom two, a position they occupied through the second half of the campaign. Allen turned down an offer to stay on and took over at Chesterfield.

| | | |
|---|---|---|
| Aghadiuno B ....................1 | Hinckson-Mars M ......... - (1) | Santos R ......................42 |
| Akinde J .................. 30 (2) | Izquierdo R................ 8 (5) | Shomotun F...............2 (4) |
| Akinola S.............. 10 (19) | Johnson E .......................2 | Stephens J ...................11 |
| Akpa Akpro J-L....... 14 (12) | Kyei N ...................... 2 (1) | Sule F........................- (1) |
| Amaluzor J.................- (4) | Legg G ...........................3 | Sweeney D ..............20 (1) |
| Blackman A ............ 15 (4) | Mason-Clark E ............ - (8) | Taylor H ..................14 (2) |
| Briggs M......................- (1) | Nelson M ................ 24 (3) | Taylor J .................27 (11) |
| Brindley R................ 17 (1) | Nicholls A ............... 19 (6) | Tutonda D ...............35 (6) |
| Campbell-Ryce J....... 23 (1) | Nicholson J ............... 3 (5) | Vilhete M.................27 (5) |
| Clough C.................. 29 (7) | Pascal D..........................1 | Watson R.................25 (3) |
| Coulthirst S............. 34 (6) | Payne J ...................... 1 (2) | Weston C.......................22 |
| Tarpey D .........................2 | Plavotic T.................... - (1) | |
| Fonguck W............. 10 (10) | Ross C .................... 32 (1) | |

**League goals** (46): Coulthirst 10, Akinde 7, Nicholls 7, Akinola 4, Campbell-Ryce 4, Akpa Akpro 3, Santos 3, Vilhete 3, Taylor J 2, Brindley 1, Watson 1, Weston 1
**FA Cup goals** (1): Akinola 1. **League Cup goals** (3): Akpa-Akpro 1, Coulthirst 1, Vilhete 1. **League Trophy goals** (6): Blackman 1, Coulthirst 1, Izquierdo 1, Nicholls 1, Taylor J 1, Opponents 1
**Average home league attendance**: 2,113

## CAMBRIDGE UNITED

A takeover and a change of manager proved the major talking points during a season of modest achievement on the pitch. Businessman Paul Barry, the largest shareholder, becomes the club's owner in early February. The following day, minutes after a goalless draw with Lincoln, he announced the departure of manager Shaun Derry by 'mutual agreement.' Derry's assistant, Joe Dunne, took over as caretaker and was given the job on a permanent basis before the final fixture after winning six and drawing four of his 14 games. Dunne, formerly in charge of Colchester, targeted an improvement in his side's away record after Cambridge lost 11 times on their travels. Those included a 7-0 drubbing by leaders Luton and a 3-3 draw against second-place Notts County after surrendering a 3-0 lead, established with goals from Jevani Brown (2) and Uche Ikpeazu with 68 minutes gone. After sustaining a promotion challenge until the final round of fixtures the previous season, Cambridge spent most of this season in mid-table, neither threatening a play-off place nor in danger of a dropping into trouble.

| | | |
|---|---|---|
| Amoo D .................. 6 (18) | Elito M.................... 24 (8) | Mingoia P................17 (5) |
| Azeez A .................... 5 (8) | Forde D.........................43 | Mitov D ...........................3 |
| Berry L ...........................3 | Halliday B .....................43 | O'Neil L ..................19 (7) |
| Brown J .................. 35 (6) | Howkins K.................. - (2) | Osadebe E..................- (4) |
| Carroll J.................. 24 (9) | Ibehre J .................. 19 (8) | Phillips A ........................4 |
| Corr B....................... 2 (8) | Ikpeazu U................ 36 (4) | Taft G .....................26 (2) |
| Darling H ........................3 | Knowles T .................. - (1) | Taylor G.........................43 |
| Davies L ................... 3 (1) | Legge L................... 24 (3) | Waters B .................15 (3) |
| Deegan G.......................42 | Lewis P ..................... 5 (7) | |
| Dunk H................... 28 (9) | Maris G................... 34 (6) | |

**League goals** (56): Ikpeazu 13, Maris 10, Ibehre 7, Brown 6, Corr 4, Elito 4, Amoo 2, Dunk 2, Legge 2, Waters 2, Halliday 1, Lewis 1, Taft 1, Taylor 1
**FA Cup goals** (1): Ibehre 1. **League Cup goals** (1): Ikpeazu 1. **League Trophy goals** (1): Mingoia 1
**Average home league attendance**: 4,523

## CARLISLE UNITED

Keith Curle's side fell short of another play-off appearance in his fourth and final season as manager. Despite a single defeat in the final 14 matches, they paid the price for indifferent home form and were well adrift of a top-seven place. There were just seven wins in 23 games in front of their own supporters, with points dropped against seven teams in the bottom half of the table. Carlisle were more productive away from Brunton Park, a 2-1 win over Port Vale the tenth on their travels. This imbalance meant they spent much of the season in the middle reaches of the table. Successive wins over Chesterfield, Barnet, Yeovil and Grimsby took them to within three points of Swindon in seventh place, raising hopes of a late challenge. Instead, they were held at home by Crawley and Cambridge and lost touch again. Curle announced he would leave the club at the end of the campaign to seek a new challenge. He was replaced by John Sheridan.

Adams N................. 15 (2)
Bennett R.............. 24 (14)
Bonham J......................42
Brown J.........................27
Campbell-Ryce J......... 4 (5)
Cosgrove S................. 3 (5)
Devitt J.................. 30 (10)
Ellis M..................... 21 (2)
Etuhu K................... 13 (7)
George S..........................4
Grainger D............... 32 (2)
Hill C.............................38
Hope H................. 29 (12)
Jones M.................. 39 (4)
Joyce L................... 35 (3)
Kennedy J.................. 1 (5)
Lambe R.................. 28 (6)
Liddle G................... 37 (4)
Miller T.................... 13 (4)
Miller S................. 11 (12)
Nadesan A.................. 9 (6)
O'Sullivan J.............. 2 (16)
Parkes T.................. 34 (3)
Rigg S......................- - (3)
Stockton C............... 10 (2)
Twardek K.................. 5 (7)

**League goals** (62): Devitt 10, Hope 9, Grainger 8, Bennett 6, Lambe 6, Nadesan 4, Etuhu 3, Miller S 3, Ellis 2, Joyce 2, Miller T 2, Cosgrove 1, Hill 1, O'Sullivan 1, Parkes 1, Stockton 1, Opponent 2
**FA Cup goals** (7): Hope 3, Bennett 2, Grainger 1, Miller S 1. **League Cup goals** (3): Grainger 1, Miller S 1, Miller T 1. **League Trophy goals** (3): Hope 1, Kennedy 1, Miller S 1
**Average home league attendance**: 4,609. **Player of Year**: Clint Hill

## CHELTENHAM TOWN

There were rarely any half measures about Cheltenham's season, with a sackful of goals scored and conceded. They netted three or more in ten matches, usually involving Sudanese striker Mohamed Eisa. Signed from Greenwich Borough, Eisa delivered a hat-trick in a 5-1 win over Port Vale on the way to club-record 23 for the campaign, overtaking Julian Alsop's mark from the 2001-02 season, plus two in the League Cup. It put him on the shortlist for League Two's Player of the Year alongside Accrington's Billy Kee, who took the award, and Wycombe's Adebayo Akinfenwa. Cheltenham shipped three or more goals in 11 games, including ten in successive fixtures at the tail-end of the season against Cambridge and promotion-chasing Coventry. Gary Johnson's side had a difficult start – two wins in nine – before spending the rest of the campaign in the lower reaches of the table, without ever looking like falling into trouble. After the 6-1 home defeat by Coventry, Johnson admitted he needed to strengthen the squad to become competitive.

Adebayo E................. 2 (5)
Andrews J.................. 4 (3)
AtanganaN.............. 23 (9)
Bower M....................- (3)
Boyle W.................. 33 (1)
Chatzitheodoridis I..........18
Cranston J............... 17 (5)
Dawson K................ 32 (2)
Eisa M.........................45
Flatt J............................4
Flinders S......................41
Forster J..........................4
Gordon J....................- (4)
Graham B............... 15 (12)
Grimes J.................. 41 (2)
Hinds F.................. 1 (11)
Holman D..................- (2)
Lloyd G..................... 3 (4)
Lovett R..........................1
Moore T................... 35 (1)
Morrell J.........................38
O'Shaughnessy D........ 5 (5)
Odelusi S................... 3 (6)
Onariase E.................. 4 (1)
Pell H...................... 32 (5)
Rodon J..................... 7 (5)
Sellars J................ 21 (10)
Storer K.................. 17 (4)
Winchester C..................44
Wright D................ 16 (17)

**League goals** (67): Eisa 23, Boyle 5, Dawson 5, Graham 5, Pell 5, Winchester 5, Grimes 3, Morrell 3, Wright 3, Adebayo 2, Lloyd 2, Sellars 2, Andrews 1, Atangana 1, Holman 1, Odelusi 1
**FA Cup goals** (2): Dawson 1, Opponents 1. **League Cup goals** (4): Eisa 2, Wright 2. **League Trophy goals** (4): Graham 1, Hinds 1, Pell 1, Storer 1
**Average home league attendance**: 3,172. **Player of Year**: Mohamed Eisa

## CHESTERFIELD

Ninety seven years of Football League membership came to an end after a second successive relegation. Chesterfield finished bottom of League One in 2017 and met the same fate this time after spending almost the whole season in the drop zone. The club turned to their former striker Jack Lester after manager Gary Caldwell was sacked after a single win in the opening eight matches. His side were still second from bottom by the midway point of the campaign before successive wins over leaders Luton and Yeovil offered hope of better things. Instead, successive home defeats by Stevenage, Crawley and Cambridge set them back and there were few signs from then on of escaping. Even a 3-1 success against promotion-minded Notts County had little impact. An 88th minute penalty conceded to fellow-strugglers Grimsby left Chesterfield six points from safety, needing to rely on games in hand on teams above them. Kristian Dennis scored his 20th goal in all competitions at Forest Green, but his side conceded three late goals to lose 4-1 and with an inferior goal difference were effectively doomed . Lester was sacked after that defeat and replaced later by Martin Allen, who just failed to save Barnet from going down.

Anyon J ........................14
Barry B ..........................29
Binnom-Williams J.... 13 (6)
Brewster D ................. - (2)
Briggs M .................... 8 (3)
Brown J ..................... 8 (5)
Coke G ...................... 1 (1)
Dawson C.........................2
De Girolamo D............ 6 (9)
Dennis K................. 38 (5)
Dimaio C.................... 2 (8)
Dodds L..................... 7 (5)
Donohue D.......................2
Eastwood J.......................4
Evatt I...........................21
Flores J .................... 11 (2)
German R.................... - (2)
Hines Z ...................... 9 (2)
Hird S............................24
Jules Z.............................6
Kay J ......................... 8 (3)
Kellett A.................. 29 (7)
Lee T ...............................7
Maguire L................. 13 (5)
McCourt J............... 21 (13)
Mitchell R .................. - (4)
Mottley-Henry D.......... 1 (1)
Nelson S .......................15
O'Grady C..............20 (15)
Ramsdale A..................19
Rawson L ....................- (1)
Reed L.....................41 (1)
Rowley J...................23 (5)
Sinnott J ....................4 (4)
Smith G .....................6 (2)
Talbot D ........................14
Ugwu G......................3 (9)
Wakefield C ....................1
Weir R......................39 (2)
Whitmore A .............14 (1)
Wiseman S ..............23 (1)

**League goals** (47): Dennis 19, McCourt 5, Kellett 4, Reed 4, Rowley 3, O'Grady 2, Weir 2, Flores 1, Hines 1, Nelson 1, Sinnott 1, Whitmore 1, Opponents 3
**FA Cup goals**: None. **League Cup goals** (1): Dennis 1. **League Trophy goals** (6): De Girolamo 1, Dennis 1, McCourt 1, O'Grady 1, Rowley 1, Sinnott 1
**Average home league attendance**: 5,354

## COLCHESTER UNITED

A Boxing Day treat and an Easter parade raised hopes of a promotion bid. Each time, Colchester lost momentum and finished in mid-table. They were up to fifth after a 2-0 win over Crawley on December 26, Sammie Szmodics clinching the points with his seventh goal in eight matches. Six games without a win set them back and it was not until the next holiday programme that hopes were revived. This time, there were 2-1 victories over leaders Luton and Forest Green, with Drey Wright scoring after 16 seconds after getting on the end of a Szmodics cross against the league newcomers. It put his side within four points of the leading group. But a tough run-in proved too much. Colchester lost to the eventual champions Accrington and also went down at home to Notts County after leading at half-time with another goal from Wright. They conceded a 94th minute winner to ten-man Lincoln, then lost to Exeter in the final match after a fourth penalty miss of the campaign

Barnes D..........................2
Comley B................ 31 (7)
Dickenson B.............. 4 (3)
Eastman T .............. 41 (1)
Gondoh R ................. 1 (1)
Guthrie K.................. 7 (5)
Hanlan B ................ 10 (8)
Inniss R........................18
Issan T ...................... - (2)
Jackson R ............... 41 (1)
James C.................... 3 (4)
Johnstone D.............. 1 (1)

Kabamba N................ 3 (5)
Kent F..........................37
Kinsella L................. 4 (5)
Kpekawa C................. 4 (2)
Lapslie T................. 27 (2)
Loft D..................... 10 (2)
Mandeville L .............. 1 (6)
Mandron M ............. 42 (2)
Murray S............... 18 (19)
O'Sullivan T ................ - (1)
Odelusi S.................... - (9)
Ogedi-Uzokwe J......... 3 (6)
Prosser L ................ 14 (2)
Reid K.................... 13 (4)
Senior C ................. 10 (8)
Shodipo O................. 2 (4)
Slater C ...................... 1 (5)
Stevenson B............. 10 (3)
Szmodics S............. 29 (8)
Vincent-Young K....... 37 (1)
Walker S.........................44
Wright D ................. 38 (6)

**League goals** (53): Szmodics 12, Mandron 10, Senior 4, Eastman 3, Murray 3, Reid 3, Wright 3, Hanlan 2, Jackson 2, Kent 2, Stevenson 2, Comley 1, Guthrie 1, Odelusi 1, Ogedi-Uzokwe 1, Prosser 1, Vincent-Young 1, Opponents 1
**FA Cup goals**: None. **League Cup goals** (1): Kent 1. **League Trophy goals** (2: McKeown E 1, Szmodics 1
**Average home league attendance**: 3,321. **Player of Year**: Tom Eastman

## COVENTRY CITY

Coventry started the season with a flourish and finished it in style to put a smile back on the face of the club. They defeated Exeter 3-1 in the Play-off Final, roared on by nearly 38,000 supporters, to end years of decline which started with relegation from the Premier League. There were two further demotions, a temporary relocation to play home matches at Northampton and ongoing protests against the owners. Dropping into to the game's fourth tier in 2017 was softened somewhat by victory over Oxford in the Checkatrade Trophy Final under Mark Robins at the start of his second spell as manager. Robins then rebuilt the team, who opened with a Jodi Jones hat-trick against Notts County and went on spend most of the campaign in or around the top-seven. Marc McNulty, with hat-tricks against Grimsby and Cheltenham, was the club's highest scorer since Bobby Gould in 1967, with 23 to his credit. Coventry squeezed into the play-offs on the final day, five points behind Exeter in the table. But they were 5-2 aggregate winners over Notts County in the semi-finals and a rousing second-half performance, rewarded with goals from Jordan Willis, Jordan Shipley and Jack Grimmer, meant a successful return to Wembley.

Andreu A .................. 2 (3)
Barrett J .................... 1 (5)
Bayliss T........................24
Beavon S .................. 9 (5)
Biamou M............. 20 (19)
Burge L .........................40
Clarke-Harris J.......... 12 (5)
Davies T ................. 15 (6)
Kelly-Evans D............. 8 (6)
Doyle M ........................44
Grimmer J ......................42
Haynes R ................ 18 (3)
Hyam D................... 11 (3)
Jones J...........................19
Kelly L.................... 30 (3)
Kelly-Evans D ............ 1 (1)
Maguire-Drew J.................3
Maycock C................... - (1)
McDonald R ............ 36 (1)
McNulty M .............. 40 (2)
Nazon D.................11 (10)
O'Brien L ...................6 (1)
Ponticelli J ...............4 (15)
Reid K ......................2(11)
Shipley J..................25 (5)
Stevenson B ...............2 (3)
Stokes C...................28 (1)
Vincenti P ...............18 (6)
Willis J...........................35

**Play-offs – appearances**: Bayliss 3, Biamou 3, Burge 3, Doyle 3, Grimmer 3, Hyam 3, Kelly 3, McNulty 3, Shipley 3, Stokes 3, Willis 2, Davies 1, Clarke-Harris – (3), Ponticelli – (3), Reid – (1)
**League goals** (64): McNulty 23, Nazon 6, Bayliss 5, Biamou 5, Jones 5, Shipley 4, Clarke-Harris 3, Doyle 3, Ponticelli 3, Vincenti 3, Grimmer 1, Kelly 1, Opponents 2. **Play-offs – goals** (8): Biamou 2, McNulty 2, Bayliss 1, Grimmer 1, Shipley 1, Willis 1
**FA Cup goals** (9): Ponticelli 2, Biamou 1, Clarke-Harris 1, Grimmer 1, McNulty 1, Nazon 1, Shipley 1, Willis 1. **League Cup goals** (1): Nazon 1. **League Trophy goals** (6): McNulty 2, Andreu 1, Biamou 1. Ponticelli 1, Stevenson 1
**Average home league attendance**: 9,255. **Player of Year**: Marc McNulty

## CRAWLEY TOWN

Impressive scoring bursts by Enzio Boldewijn and Karlan Ahearne-Grant highlighted Crawley's campaign. Dutch striker Boldewijn netted eight times in nine games to fire his side away from the threat of dropping into relegation trouble and raise hopes of developing a genuine challenge for a play-off place. Charlton loanee Ahearne-Grant then matched that sequence as Crawley made it nine wins out of 12 with a 3-1 victory over Lincoln. They were then within two points of a top-seven spot. But that was as good as it got. They struggled against teams from the lower reaches of the table, including a 5-3 home defeat by Cheltenham. By the time Boldewijn was on the mark again, against Exeter, their chances were fading. And although Ahearne-Grant added to his tally in the final match against Mansfield, Crawley had won just once more in 12 matches. They finished 14th, albeit an improvement of five on the previous season.

Ahearne-Grant K............15
Boldewijn E.............. 44 (1)
Bulman D................ 34 (3)
Camara P............... 14 (15)
Clifford B.................... 4 (3)
Connolly M.....................40
Cox D........................ 3 (1)
Djalo A...................... 1 (1)
Doherty J................. 11 (4)
Evina C.................... 32 (2)
Harrold M.................... - (2)
Lelan J..................... 29 (2)
Lewis D...................... 3 (7)
McNerney J............. 10 (6)
Meite I..................... 6 (13)
Mersin Y..........................2
Morris G..........................44
Payne J................. 23 (12)
Randall M...............24 (8)
Roberts J...............25 (10)
Sanoh M....................4 (8)
Smith J....................36 (1)
Tajbakhsh A................8 (9)
Verheydt T...............16 (4)
Yorwerth J...............37 (2)
Young L.........................41

**League goals** (58): Boldewijn 10, Smith 10, Ahearne-Grant 9, Roberts 6, Payne 5, Young 3, Camara 2, Meite 2, Verheydt 2, McNerney 1, Randall 1, Yorwerth 1, Opponents 5
**FA Cup goals** (1): Roberts 1. **League Cup goals** (1): Camara 1. **League Trophy goals** (2: Meite 1, Sanoh 1
**Average home league attendance**: 2,268. **Player of Year**: Glenn Morris

## CREWE ALEXANDRA

Just when it looked as if Crewe were in danger of becoming embroiled in a relegation struggle, Jordan Bowery ended his goal drought to spark a revival. A single win in eight games, including a home defeat by Exeter, who scored twice in stoppage-time, left them fourth from bottom. Four days after that setback, Bowery ended 18 games without scoring with two goals at Lincoln. Harry Pickering and on-loan Paul Green scored their first goals for the club in a 4-1 victory, their best of the season and the perfect tonic. Crewe went on to win seven of their final 12 fixtures, including a 4-3 away success against another promotion-chasing team, Mansfield, with Bowery again on the mark in a spell of eight goals in nine games. Shuan Miller's brace for a 2-1 victory over Cheltenham in the last match enabled his side to overtake the previous season's 55 points with a starting 11 made up entirely of players who came through the club's youth system. They finished 15th and it would have been higher but for a weakness in surrendering points from leading positions.

Ainley C.................. 37 (8)
Bakayogo Z............. 28 (4)
Barlaser D.................. - (4)
Bowery J................ 32 (13)
Cooper G................. 22 (5)
Dagnall C................ 24 (8)
Dale O....................... - (4)
Finney O..................... - (1)
Garratt B................. 35 (1)
Grant C.................. 13 (4)
Green P.................... 19 (1)
Jones J....................... 5 (1)
Kirk C.................... 15 (10)
Lowery T................. 28 (3)
McKirdy H............... 5 (11)
Miller S.................... 13 (2)
Ng P........................ 36 (2)
Nolan E.................... 41 (1)
Pickering H ...............27 (8
Porter C.................. 23 (8)
Ray G..........................12
Raynes M................27 (2)
Reilly L.......................2 (3)
Richards D...................11
Sterry J..........................9
Stubbs S....................3 (2)
Walker B.................22 (5)
Wintle R..................17 (1)

**League goals** (62): Bowery 12, Porter 9, Dagnall 7, Miller 6, Kirk 5, Ainley 4, Ng 4, McKirdy 3, Pickering 3, Raynes 2, Wintle 2, Cooper 1, Green 1, Jones 1, Walker 1, Opponents 1
**FA Cup goals** (5): Porter 2, Ainley 1, Nolan 1, Walker 1 **League Cup goals** (1): Porter 1. **League Trophy goals** (3): Reilly 2, Bowery 1
**Average home league attendance**: 3,876. **Player of Year**: Eddie Nolan

## EXETER CITY

Exeter bade farewell to manager Paul Tisdale, director of football Steve Perryman and to the chance of League One football after losing the Play-off Final for the second successive season. They were beaten by Blackpool in 2017 and this time conceded three second-half goals before a consolation from substitute Kyle Edwards against Coventry. Tisdale, appointed in 2006 and the league's longest-serving manager following Arsene Wenger's departure from Arsenal, turned down the offer of a new contract to take over at MK Dons. Former Tottenham captain Perryman retired after a 15-year association with the club. Despite selling leading scorers Dave Wheeler and Ollie Watkins during the summer, Exeter went close to gaining automatic promotion, winning seven of the opening eight matches and remaining in contention until a 3-1 defeat at Stevenage in the penultimate match of the regular campaign. They were five points ahead of Coventry in the table, but after leading marksman Jayden Stockley put them on the way to a 3-1 win over Lincoln in the semi-finals, his side were below their best at Wembley. Tisdale was succeeded by former club captain Matt Taylor.

| | | |
|---|---|---|
| Archibald-Henville T . 12 (3) | Jay M ........................ 5 (12) | Stockley J.................34 (7) |
| Boateng H.............. 28 (10) | Loft R ................................1 | Storey J.....................11 (2) |
| Brown T..........................25 | McAlinden L........... 17 (12) | Sweeney P......................40 |
| Brunt R ...................... - (1) | Moore-Taylor J ................24 | Taylor J ....................43 (1) |
| Byrne A ...................... - (1) | Moxey D.................. 30 (4) | Tillson J ...................35 (2) |
| Croll L ....................... 7 (3) | Pym C.............................46 | Wheeler D ........................2 |
| Edwards K .............. 7 (16) | Reid R .................... 18 (3) | Wilson K ..................14 (5) |
| Harley R ................. 14 (5) | Seaborne D................ 4 (1) | Woodman C..............28 (5) |
| Holmes L................. 20 (7) | Simpson R ................. 5 (6) | |
| James L.................. 36 (4) | Sparkes J .................... - (3) | |

**Play-offs – appearances**: Boateng 3, Harley 3, Moore-Taylor 3, Moxey 3, Pym 3, Stockley 3, Storey 3, Sweeney 3, Taylor 3, Tillson 3, James 1 (2), Simpson 1 (1), Woodman 1, Archibald-Henville – (2), Edwards – (1), Jay – (1)
**League goals** (64): Stockley 19, Sweeney 8, Taylor 8, Reid 7, Moxey 3, Holmes 2, James 2, McAlinden 2, Moore-Taylor 2, Simpson 2, Storey 2, Boateng 1, Brown 1, Harley 1, Jay 1, Tillson 1, Wilson 1, Opponents 1. **Play-offs – goals** (4): Boateng 1, Edwards 1, Harley 1, Stockley 1
**FA Cup goals** (8): Stockley 5, McAlinden 1, Moore-Taylor 1, Sweeney 1. **League Cup goals** (1): Holmes 1. **League Trophy goals** (4): Edwards 1, McAlinden 1, Reid 1, Sparkes 1
**Average home league attendance**: 4,005. **Player of Year**: Christy Pym

## FOREST GREEN ROVERS

Mark Cooper successfully reshaped his side in the winter transfer window and avoided an immediate return to the National League. The newcomers had struggled through the first part of the season, with a single win to show from the opening 13 matches – 4-3 at Yeovil after trailing 2-0 and 3-1. Then, after moving off bottom spot by beating Stevenage, Morecambe and Crewe in quick succession, they slipped back into trouble on the back of five successive defeats leading into the New Year. The manager made several new signings, offering much-needed support for leading scorer Christian Doidge. And a 5-2 win over Cambridge in which former sports teacher Dayle Grubb marked his full home debut with two goals, was one of four in succession at home which eased the pressure. There was still work to be done, but Doidge scored the only goal of the game against Cheltenham, then netted two more for a 4-1 win over Chesterfield which effectively ensured safety, while sending their opponents down.

Belford C .................. 2 (1)
Bennett D ......................33
Bray A ...................... 6 (5)
Brown R ............... 23 (10)
Bugiel O ................. 3 (16)
Campbell T ............. 3 (11)
Clements C ............ 11 (3)
Collins B.......................39
Collins L ................. 40 (3)
Cooper C................. 22 (3)
Doidge C................. 41 (1)
Evans C ..........................2
Fitzwater J............... 12 (2)
Gomes T..................... 3 (6)
Grubb D ................. 16 (5)
Gunning G.....................21
Hollis H .........................19
Iacovitti A................ 10 (4)
James L ..................... 9 (5)
Laird S.................... 28 (8)
Marsh-Brown K .......... 9 (5)
Monthe E .................. 9 (4)
Mullings S................. 2 (5)
Noble L...........................9
Osbourne I ....................35
Randall-Hurren W .......5 (2)
Rawson F ......................18
Reid R ......................20 (1)
Roberts M ...............11 (3)
Russell S.........................5
Simpson J .......................1
Stevens J ..................1 (8)
Traore D ..................17 (3)
Whittle A.....................- (2)
Wishart D...............20 (12)

**League goals** (54): Doidge 20, Reid 6, Grubb 5, Bugiel 3, Brown 2, Campbell 2, Collins L 2. Laird 2, Marsh-Brown 2, Bray 1, Clements 1, Cooper 1, Fitzwater 1, Gunning 1, Iacovitti 1, Mullings 1, Noble 1, Rawson 1, Opponents 1

**FA Cup goals** (5): Doidge 4, Laird 1. **League Cup goals**: None. **League Trophy goals** (5): Brown 1, Doidge 1, James 1, Stevens 1, Wishart 1

**Average home league attendance**: 2,772. **Player of Year**: Christian Doidge

## GRIMSBY TOWN

Penalties are a test of nerves for any player, even if there is little at stake. When your team face the prospect of returning to non-league football, they take on a whole new dimension. Such was the responsibility that Mitch Rose shouldered in the 88th minute of a match against relegation-rivals Chesterfield. Holding his nerve, Rose converted the winning spot-kick, did the same a week later in a 2-2 draw with Barnet, another side facing the drop, and completed a hat-trick with another for maximum points at Swindon. That gave Grimsby a five-point safety net and they finished off with two more wins, the latter against Forest Green featuring a hat-trick by JJ Hooper. They started the season with five players sent off in the first five league and cup games. There were three more dismissals in the New Year during a run of 12 matches without a victory which led to the dismissal of Russell Slade, manager for ten months. Former Burnley under-23 coach Michael Jolley replaced him three weeks later and saw that sequence extend to 20 games without success before wild celebrations greeted Rose's dramatic winner against Chesterfield. A failure to defend set pieces had proved a major factor in their struggles.

Berrett J ................. 29 (3)
Bolarinwa T................ 1 (2)
Cardwell H ................. 8 (8)
Clarke N ........................45
Clifton H.................... 7 (3)
Collins D........................40
Davies B .................. 28 (6)
Dembele S ............... 33 (3)
Dixon P..........................26
Fox A.............................10
Hall-Johnson R........... 8 (4)
Hooper JJ.............. 13 (18)
Jackson S................... 3 (2)
Jaiyesimi D............ 10 (20)
Jones S .................... 21 (4)
Kean J ............................3
Kelly S ....................... 3 (5)
Killip B ...................... 6 (1)
Matt J .................... 20 (14)
McAllister S......................1
McKeown J.....................37
McSheffrey G............. 2 (3)
Mills Z .....................24 (4)
Osborne J....................- (2)
Osborne K ..................9 (1)
Rose M ....................30 (3)
Suliman E...................1 (1)
Summerfield L..........36 (3)
Vernam C ...................7 (2)
Vernon S ...............15 (13)
Wilks M......................4 (2)
Woolford M..............26 (5)

**League goals** (42): Rose 8, Hooper 6, Jones 6, Collins 4, Dembele 4, Matt 4, Clarke 2, Davies 2, Woolford 2, Berrett 1, Jackson 1, Vernam 1, Vernon 1

**FA Cup goals**: None. **League Cup goals**: None. **League Trophy goals** (3): Cardwell 1, Hooper 1, Jaiyesimi 1

**Average home league attendance**: 4,658. **Player of Year**: James McKeown

## LINCOLN CITY

Another season to savour for Lincoln after winning the National League and reaching the last eight of the FA Cup. Losing to Exeter in the play-offs did not detract from the manner of their return to League Two after an absence of six years, with crowds averaging nearly 9,000 and a Wembley victory as a huge bonus. The Checkatrade Trophy may not be the most glamorous competition, but the club's rapidly-rising fortunes were again reflected in a following of 27,000 supporters for the 1-0 success against League One pacemakers Shrewsbury, courtesy of a 16th minute goal from Elliott Whitehouse. Lincoln ended a memorable 2017 by moving into a play-off place with 2-0 win at Yeovil, then into an automatic promotion spot by beating Stevenage 3-0. It was a brief stay and there was plenty more pressure in holding down a top-seven place. But a 4-2 victory at Coventry gave them breathing space during the run-in. Then, Tom Pett's first goal for the club on the last day of the regular season against Yeovil confirmed a semi-final against Exeter, who were 3-1 winners at home after a goalless first leg.

Allsop R......................16
Anderson H............ 23 (17)
Arnold N................. 15 (5)
Bostwick M...................44
Eardley N......................44
Farman P......................13
Frecklington L...............16
Ginnelly J.................. 8 (7)
Green M................. 43 (2)
Habergham S........... 32 (1)
Knott B...................... 9 (6)
Long S.................... 13 (4)
Maguire-Drew J........... 5 (6)
Palmer O.............. 10 (35)
Pett T....................... 4 (5)
Raggett S......................25
Rhead M................. 35 (6)
Dickie R.................. 17 (1)
Rowe D......................9 (3)
Stewart C...................2 (2)
Vickers J...................... 17
Waterfall L...............24 (6)
Wharton S...............13 (1)
Whitehouse E.........12 (20)
Williams J..................6 (5)
Wilson J.....................5 (3)
Woodyard A.................. 46

**Play-offs – appearances**: Allsop 2, Anderson 2, Bostwick 2, Eardley 2, Green 2, Rhead 2, Waterfall 2, Whitehouse 2, Woodyard 2, Wilson 2, Frecklington 1, Wharton 1, Palmer – (2), Pett – (2), Long – (1)
**League goals** (64): Green 13, Palmer 8, Rhead 8, Anderson 6, Bostwick 6, Frecklington 4, Ginnelly 2, Raggett 2, Waterfall 2, Wharton 2, Whitehouse 2, Woodyard 2, Eardley 1, Knott 1, Pett 1, Rowe 1, Wilson 1, Opponents 2. **Play-offs – goals** (1): Green 1
**FA Cup goals**: None. **League Cup goals** (1): Knott. **League Trophy goals** (17): Green 3, Palmer 3, Maguire-Drew 2, Whitehouse 2, Anderson 1, Ginnelly 1, Raggett 1, Rhead 1, Rowe 1, Waterfall 1, Opponents 1
**Average home league attendance**: 8,782. **Player of Year**: Neal Eardley

## LUTON TOWN

Luton returned to the third tier after a ten-year absence with a record-breaking goals tally. Manager Nathan Jones strengthened his strike force after losing in the previous season's play-offs – and the impact was immediate. James Collins, signed from Crawley, scored a hat-trick in the 8-2 opening day win over Yeovil. Luke Berry, from Cambridge, netted three as Stevenage were swept aside 7-1. Then, Danny Hylton got three and Olly Lee scored with a shot from 65 yards in a 7-0 victory over Cambridge. It was the first time a side had scored more than seven in three games before Christmas. Luton went top by beating Carlise in late November and stayed there for nearly four months until losing 2-1 at home to second-place Accrington, who went on to become champions. They clinched promotion, with two matches remaining after a 1-1 draw at Carlisle and finished runners-up, having chalked up 94 goals – more than any other side in the Football League. No fewer than 18 players contributed to the tally.

Berry L................... 31 (3)
Collins J................. 39 (3)
Cook J...................... 1 (9)
Cornick H............. 16 (21)
Cuthbert S.............. 20 (3)
D'Ath L...................... 3 (6)
Downes F................. 7 (3)
Famewo A................ 1 (2)
Gambin L................. 4 (9)
Hylton D................ 37 (2)
Jarvis A...................... - (1)
Jervis J...................... 2 (8)
Jones L....................... - (1)
Justin J.................. 10 (7)
Lee E.................... 16 (16)

| | | |
|---|---|---|
| Lee O ....38 | Rea G .... 39 (7) | Shinnie A.... 24 (4) |
| McCormack A.... 15 (1) | Ruddock P.... 17 (11) | Stacey J.... 40 (1) |
| Mullins J.... 14 (3) | Shea J....8 | Stech M....38 |
| Potts D....42 | Sheehan A....42 | Vassell I....2 |

**League goals** (94): Hylton 21, Collins 19, Lee E 10, Berry 7, Lee O 6, Potts 6, Cornick 5, Sheehan 3, Cuthbert 2, Justin 2, Mullins 2, Ruddock 2, Vassell 2, Gambin 1, McCormack 1, Rea 1, Shinnie 1, Stacey 1, Opponents 2

**FA Cup goals** (7): Hylton 2, Berry 1, Collins 1, Lee E 1, Lee O 1, Potts 1. **League Cup goals**: None. **League Trophy goals** (9): Shinnie 2, Cook 1, Cotter K 1, D'Ath 1, Gambin 1, Jarvis 1, Lee E 1, McQuoid J 1

**Average home league attendance**: 8,676. **Player of Year**: Alan Sheehan

## MANSFIELD TOWN

Mansfield failed to maintain a promotion push after a change of manager. They were within two points of a top-three place when Steve Evans left to take charge of Peterborough and was replaced immediately by Swindon's David Flitcroft. He had a tough baptism, with four his first six matches against promotion rivals and was still looking for his first win after two more games. It finally came when Mal Benning scored the only goal at Chesterfield. Then, two by substitute Lee Angol delivered a 3-2 success at Yeovil. That left his side needing to win the final game at home to Crawley, while relying on results elsewhere to go in their favour – a repeat of the previous season. Again, there was no joy. Mansfield were held to a 1-1 draw and the teams directly above them, Lincoln and Coventry, both got the point needed to make the play-offs. Evans had previously reshaped his squad during the summer and Flitcroft promised to do the same this time.

| | | |
|---|---|---|
| Anderson P.... 24 (9) | Hamilton C.... 28 (5) | Olejnik B....1 |
| Angol L.... 16 (13) | Hemmings K.... 36 (1) | Pearce K....36 (2) |
| Atkinson W.... 24 (15) | Hunt J....18 | Penney M....- (2) |
| Bennett R.... 34 (4) | King A.... 5 (2) | Potter A....16 (11) |
| Benning M.... 27 (1) | Logan C....45 | Rose D....35 (4) |
| Butcher C.... 10 (7) | MacDonald A.... 40 (1) | Spencer J....3 (15) |
| Byrom J.... 18 (1) | Mellis J.... 22 (8) | Sterling-James O....2 (11) |
| Diamond Z.... 18 (2) | Miller R.... - (8) | Thomas J....- (1) |
| Digby P.... 10 (5) | Mirfin D....12 | White H....25 (3) |

**League goals** (67): Hemmings 15, Rose 14, Angol 9, Potter 4, Diamond 3, MacDonald 3, Atkinson 2, Bennett 2, Hamilton 2, Anderson 1, Benning 1, Butcher 1, Byrom 1, Mellis 1, Miller 1, Mirfin 1, Pearce 1, Spencer 1, White 1, Opponents 3

**FA Cup goals** (7): Rose 3, Spencer 3, Pearce 1. **League Cup goals**: None. **League Trophy goals** (5): Angol 1, Butcher 1, Diamond 1, Hamilton 1, Potter 1

**Average home league attendance**: 4,309. **Player of Year**: Krystian Pearce

## MORECAMBE

Veteran goalkeeper Barry Roche played a key role as Morecambe preserved Football League status on a tense final day of the season. The 36-year-old Player of the Year, with more than 400 appearances under his belt in ten years at the club, made three top-drawer saves in a goalless draw away to promotion-chasing Coventry. It meant they survived on goal difference and Barnet, 3-0 winners over Chesterfield, dropped into the National League. The great escape came four days after the club were taken over by a London-based investment company. Morecambe struggled to stay out of the relegation zone for much of the campaign before two victories over promotion-minded teams provided breathing space. Kevin Ellison, another long-serving player, scored twice the day after his 39th birthday as Wycombe were defeated 4-2. Then, a 2-1 success against Exeter, took them eight points clear of trouble. But nine matches without a win, six without scoring, heightened fears of non-league football. They included a 1-0 defeat by Barnet in the last home fixture and meant a nail-biting finish.

| | | |
|---|---|---|
| Brough P ....................20 | Lavelle S ................ 26 (1) | Osborne E ................6 (5) |
| Campbell A........... 11 (14) | Lund M ..................... 8 (2) | Roche B.......................42 |
| Conlan L................ 25 (2) | McGowan A............ 38 (2) | Rose M ..................38 (4) |
| Ellison K............... 27 (13) | McGurk A............... 29 (5) | Thompson G..........26 (14) |
| Fleming A.............. 23 (9) | Muller M ................ 19 (1) | Turner R.....................1 (5) |
| Jordan L .................... - (1) | Nizic D...................... 4 (3) | Wildig A..................22 (9) |
| Kenyon A............... 33 (5) | Old S ...................... 40 (1) | Winnard D....................20 |
| Lang C.................. 14 (16) | Oliver V................ 24 (10) | Wylde G .................10 (5) |

**League goals** (41): Lang 10, Ellison 9, McGurk 5, Old 4, Oliver 3, Thompson 3, Rose 2, Wylde 2, Campbell 1, Lavelle 1, Wildig 1
**FA Cup goals** (3): Ellison 1, Fleming 1, Opponents 1. **League Cup goals** (3): Lavelle 1, Oliver 1, Rose 1. **League Trophy goals** (3): Osborne 1, Thompson 1, Opponents 1
**Average home league attendance**: 1,492. **Player of Year**: Barry Roche

## NEWPORT COUNTY

An FA Cup hangover forced Newport out of the promotion picture. They lost ground after threatening a major upset in a fourth round tie against Tottenham in front of a club record crowd for Rodney Parade of nearly 10,000. Padraig Amond's header put them ahead and the lead lasted until the 82nd minute when a goal by Harry Kane took the tie back to Wembley. The Premier League side were made to work for a 2-0 win in the replay and their manager Mauricio Pochettino felt Newport, who had knocked out Leeds in the previous round, were good enough to go up. But after closing to within two points of a play-off place, they went six games without winning, lost touch with the leading group and had to settle for a mid-table finish. Even so, it was a significant improvement on the previous season when escaping a return to non-league football in the final round of matches. On a pitch relaid after severe drainage problems, they had started with 24 points from 13 games, the best Football League haul since 1982.

| | | |
|---|---|---|
| Amond P................. 37 (6) | Jackson M .................. - (6) | Reid T.........................3 (4) |
| Barnum-Bobb J .......... - (1) | Jahraldo-Martin C......... - (4) | Reynolds L ................1 (9) |
| Bennett S ............... 21 (7) | Labadie J ................ 24 (1) | Rigg S........................9 (7) |
| Butler D................. 40 (4) | McCoulsky S............ 8 (19) | Sheehan J .................9 (4) |
| Cole R ...................... 2 (2) | Nouble F................. 38 (7) | Touray M ....................- (1) |
| Collins A................... 6 (4) | O'Brien M............... 26 (2) | Tozer B ....................33 (6) |
| Day J...........................46 | Osadebe E.................. - (3) | White B........................42 |
| Demetriou M ................46 | Owen-Evans T............ 3 (9) | Willmott R...............36 (3) |
| Dolan M................. 39 (1) | Pipe D .................... 33 (2) | |
| Hayes P ................. 3 (10) | Quigley J .................. 1 (1) | |

**League goals** (56): Amond 13, Nouble 9, Demetriou 7, McCoulsky 6, Dolan 3, Hayes 3, Labadie 3, Tozer 3, Bennett 2, Sheehan 2, Willmott 2, Butler 1, Cole 1, White 1
**FA Cup goals** (7): Labadie 2, McCoulsky 2, Amond 1, Nouble 1, Opponents 1. **League Cup goals** (3): McCoulsky 2, Labadie 1. **League Trophy goals** (2): McCoulsky 1, Reynolds 1
**Average home league attendance**: 3,489. **Player of Year**: Dan Butler

## NOTTS COUNTY

A season holding so much promise slipped away from Kevin Nolan's side and ended on a sour note. The manager was furious with refereeing decisions which went against them in both legs of the play-off semi-final against Coventry. Nolan disputed an 87th minute penalty which enabled Coventry to tie the first meeting at 1-1. In the return match at Meadow Lane, Jonathan Forte was denied an equaliser by a contentious offside flag which replays showed was incorrect. County, beaten 4-1 on the night, were left to reflect on surrendering a golden opportunity to gain automatic promotion. After winning 4-1 at Morecambe on Boxing Day, with two goals each from Jorge Grant and Lewis Alessandra, they had a seven-point lead over the fourth-place team. Inconsistency in the New Year then proved costly and it was not until the final month of the season that successive wins over Coventry, Colchester and Yeovil, with nine goals scored, restored some momentum. They left County just two points away from third place, but a stoppage-time winner conceded to Grimsby ended their hopes.

Alessandra L .......... 27 (12)
Ameobi S................. 26 (8)
Bennett M................. 1 (1)
Bird P......................... - (1)
Brisley S.................. 36 (1)
Collin A .........................30
Dickinson C.............. 23 (2)
Duffy R...........................43
Fitzsimons R ............ 16 (1)
Forte J................... 13 (17)
Grant J.................. 35 (10)
Hall B........................ 9 (2)
Hawkridge T ............ 29 (2)
Hewitt E.................. 35 (8)
Hodge E..................... - (1)
Hunt N..................... 10 (3)
Husin N .................. 10 (2)
Jones D.................... 23 (4)
Milsom R ................ 12 (5)
Noble L.................... 13 (5)
O'Connor M ...............1 (5)
Pindroch B .................- (1)
Saunders C..................- (3)
Smith A ....................- (17)
Stead J ...................38 (5)
Tootle M ........................36
Virtue M ....................9 (4)
Walker L.....................6 (5)
Yates R .........................25

**Play-offs – appearances**: Brisley 2, Collin 2, Duffy 2, Forte 2, Grant 2, Hewitt 2, Jones 2, Noble 2, Stead 2, Tootle 2, Alessandra 1 (1), Virtue 1, O'Connor – (2), Ameobi – (1), Smith - (1)
**League goals** (71): Grant 15, Stead 9, Alessandra 7, Forte 7, Ameobi 6, Hewitt 4, Jones 4, Hawkridge 3, Yates 3, Brisley 2, Duffy 2, Tootle 2, Bennett 1, Dickinson 1, Husin 1, Milsom 1, Noble 1, Opponents 2. **Play-offs – goals** (2): Forte 1, Grant 1
**FA Cup goals** (10): Stead 4, Grant 2, Yates 2, Duffy 1, Husin 1. **League Cup goals** (3): Brisley 1, Grant 1, Yates 1. **League Trophy goals** (4): Forte 2, Hollis 1, Smith 1
**Average home league attendance**: 7,911. **Player of Year**: Jorge Grant

## PORT VALE

Former long-serving defender Neil Aspin steered his side through the threat of a second successive relegation – and non-league football – amid a goalkeeping crisis and some wildly fluctuating form. Aspin left National League club Gateshead to replace Michael Brown as manager after a single victory in the opening eight matches left Vale bottom. Three straight wins over Cheltenham, Morecambe and Exeter, in which Tom Pope scored five goals, eased the pressure. And after beating leaders Luton 4-0, they had taken 26 points from 13 games. By that time, five different keepers had been used, bringing the total employed throughout 2017 to nine, including loanees brought in because of injuries. Vale were looking towards mid-table until form dipped alarmingly, with a barren run spanning 14 games. Relief came in the shape of a 2-1 victory over Chesterfield, despite the dismissal of Danny Pugh on the stroke of half-time. Antony Kay's header for a 1-0 win over promotion-chasing Lincoln then effectively ensured safety.

Anderson T .............. 18 (2)
Angus D..................... 2 (1)
Barnett T ................ 8 (17)
Benns H ..................... - (1)
Boot R...........................22
Calveley M .................. - (2)
Regis C....................... - (1)
Davis J .................... 16 (2)
Denton T................. 12 (3)
Evtimov D........................1
Forrester A................ 9 (4)
Gibbons J ............... 24 (6)
Gunning G .....................19
Hannant L.......................18
Harness M............... 26 (9)
Hornby S.................... 9 (2)
Howe C ...................... 1 (2)
Howkins K.......................10
Jules Z.............................2
Kay A...................... 32 (1)
Lainton R .........................6
Middleton H ............... 4 (2)
Montano C............... 21 (9)
Pope T............................41
Pugh D.................... 31 (2)
Pyke R ...................... 1 (6)
Raglan C ....................9 (1)
Reeves W ..................1 (2)
Roos K ..............................8
Smith N ..........................46
Stobbs J......................1 (4)
Tonge M ...................30 (3)
Turner D..................4 (13)
Whitfield B .............25 (12)
Wilson D ....................1 (7)
Wilson L......................6 (1)
Worrall D.................36 (4)
De Freitas A................6 (5)

**League goals** (49): Pope 17, Montano 4, Whitfield 4, Worrall 4, Kay 3, Tonge 3, Turner 3, Forrester 2, Pugh 2, Angus 1, Barnett 1, Hannant 1, Harness 1, Smith 1, Wilson D 1, Opponents 1
**FA Cup goals** (5): Pope 2, Gunning 1, Harness 1, Kay 1. **League Cup goals** (1): Tonge 1. **League Trophy goals** (6): Montano 2, Barnett 1, Forrester 1, Regis 1.Reeves 1
**Average home league attendance**: 4,583. **Player of Year**: Tom Pope

## STEVENAGE

A promising start to the season was undermined by a bleak run away from home and Stevenage spent the remainder of the season struggling to emerge from the bottom half of the table. They won half of the opening dozen fixtures to sit comfortably in the top-seven before a single goal defeat at Crewe was followed by a 7-1 drubbing by neighbours Luton. There were six more defeats in a row on their travels before the sequence was broken in a 1-1 draw at Morecambe, thanks to an 89th minute equaliser from Fraser Franks. A 5-1 win over Chesterfield and 4-1 victory over Cheltenham at the Lamex Stadium had helped balance things up, but not enough to prevent a change of manager, with Darren Sarll dismissed and Nuneaton's Dino Maamria, a former player and assistant manager at the club, replacing him. His side scored four more against Yeovil and Barnet and completed the home programme with Alex Revell's hat- trick to spoil Exeter's hopes of automatic promotion.

Amos L.................... 14 (2)
Beautyman H............ 8 (2)
Bowditch D............... 1 (4)
Conlon T................. 1 (11)
Franks F................ 22 (8)
Fryer J.........................28
Georgiou A................. - (3)
Goddard J.................. 9 (2)
Godden M.............. 35 (3)
Gorman D.............. 17 (7)
Gray J........................ - (8)
Henry R........................40
Iontton A..................... - (2)
Johnson R.......................1
Kennedy B ............ 24 (11)
King J.................... 29 (3)
King T...........................18
Lokko K ..................... - (2)
Martin J.........................39
McKee M ............... 19 (5)
Newton D............... 38 (7)
O'Donnell D................ - (2)
Pett T ..................... 23 (4)
Revell A........................12
Samuel A ................8 (14)
Sheaf B......................9 (1)
Slater L......................1 (1)
Smith J....................34 (2)
Toner K......................2 (4)
Vancooten T.............19 (3)
Whelpdale C............19 (8)
White J.......................- (3)
Wilkinson L .............23 (4)
Wilmot B......................10
Wootton K..................3 (5)

**League goals** (60): Newton 14, Godden 10, Kennedy 7, Pett 6, Revell 6, Smith 3, Amos 2, Bowditch 2, Gorman 2, Martin 2, Franks 1, McKee 1, Whelpdale 1, Wilkinson 1, Wootton 1, Opponents 1
**FA Cup goals** (10): Godden 4, Newton 2, Smith 2, Pett 1, Samuel 1. **League Cup goals**: None. **League Trophy goals** (5): Samuel 3, Beautyman 1, Wootton 1
**Average home league attendance**: 2,611. **Player of Year**: Danny Newton

## SWINDON TOWN

With little over a month of the season to go, Swindon were handily placed to secure a play-off spot. They had lost manager David Flitcroft to Mansfield, but a 3-1 victory over Cambridge left them within a point of the top-seven. It marked Phil Brown's first match in charge, his appointment to the end of the campaign coming two months after being sacked by Southend. Marc Richards, signed from Northampton in the January transfer window, scored twice, taking his tally to nine goals in ten matches for his new club. On paper, their remaining fixtures looked non-too daunting. But points were dropped points against Morecambe, Crawley, Yeovil and Newport, followed by a home defeat inflicted by struggling Grimsby with a penalty on the stroke of half-time. It was Swindon's seventh game without a victory and left them seven points adrift with two games to play, rendering a 3-0 win over champions Accington in the final match irrelevant. Brown was given the job on a two year contract.

Anderson K............. 36 (1)
Banks O.................. 16 (1)
Brophy J.................... 2 (4)
Charles-Cook R..............22
Conroy D.................... 6 (1)
Dunne J................... 37 (2)
Edwards J........................1
Elsnik T................... 18 (4)
Goddard J.................. 8 (5)
Gordon K.............. 12 (14)
Hussey C................ 17 (1)
Iandolo E.................. 7 (5)
Knoyle K................. 17 (1)
Lancashire O.................35
Linganzi A............... 19 (6)
McDermott D........... 7 (10)
McGivern R............... 3 (3)
Menayesse R........... 13 (1)
Moore S.........................10
Mullin P............... 20 (20)
Norris L.................. 30 (5)
Preston M.......................21
Purkiss B................38 (3)
Richards M..............18 (2)
Robertson C.............13 (5)
Romanski J................1 (1)
Smith H.....................7 (7)
Taylor M..................34 (4)
Thomas C...................- (2)
Twine S.....................3 (1)
Vigouroux L.................. 14
Woolery K..............21 (16)

**League goals** (67): Norris 13, Richards 11, Mullin 6, Taylor 6, Anderson 5, Woolery 4, Banks 3, Elsnik 3, Gordon 3, Linganzi 2, Preston 2, Smith 2, Goddard 1, Hussey 1, Iandolo 1, Lancashire 1, McDermott 1, Robertson 1, Opponents 1
**FA Cup goals** (7): Elsnik 2, Linganzi 2, Mullin 1, Smith 1, Taylor 1. **League Cup goals** (2): Lancashire 1, Mullin 1. **League Trophy goals** (7): Mullin 2, Goddard 1, Gordon 1, Norris 1, Preston 1, Woolery 1
**Average home league attendance**: 6,380. **Player of Year**: Matt Taylor

## WYCOMBE WANDERERS

Gareth Ainsworth led Wycombe into League One a year on from narrowly missing out on the chance of going up. They were two points away from a play-off place in 2017. This time, an automatic spot was theirs after an approach for Ainsworth, manager since 2012, from a Championship club thought to be Barnsley was rejected. It came in February when his side were in a rich vein of form, having won seven matches out of eight and drawn the other. The purple patch included a 3-2 success away to leaders Luton and a 4-3 win over Carlisle in which Paris Cowan-Hall and Marcus Bean, with his first goal for the club, scored in stoppage-time. A 4-0 home defeat by the eventual champions Accrington left Wycombe under pressure to hold on to third spot. But they came from behind to defeat relegated Chesterfield with goals by Nathan Tyson and Dominic Gape, his first of the season, while challengers Exeter and Notts County both lost. It gave them a four-point advantage with just one match left. Adebayo Akinfenwa scored 17 goals, along with several assists, while another highlight of the campaign was Craig Mackail-Smith's hat-trick in 11 second-half minutes against Crawley.

Akinfenwa A............ 41 (1)
Bean M.................... 23 (8)
Bloomfield M.......... 26 (11)
Brown S.........................46
Cowan-Hall P......... 22 (12)
De Havilland W........... 2 (1)
El-Abd A.........................36
Eze E..................... 16 (4)
Freeman N............ 10 (17)
Gape D.................... 34 (1)
Harriman M............. 17 (1)
Hayes P.................... 1 (1)
Jacobson J.....................46
Jombati S.......................20
Kashket S.................. 3 (6)
Mackail-Smith C..... 27 (14)
Ma-Makalamby Y.......... - (1)
McGinley N............... 7 (4)
O'Nien L................. 34 (1)
Saunders S.............. 16 (6)
Scarr D....................19 (3)
Southwell D...............3 (9)
Stewart A................16 (1)
Moore T........................ 13
Thompson C...............1 (6)
Tyson N..................22 (11)
Umerah J...................2 (4)
Williams J..................- (1)
Williams R..................3 (3)

**League goals** (79): Akinfenwa 17, Cowan-Hall 8, Mackail-Smith 8, Tyson 8, O'Nien 7, Jacobson 6, Eze 5, Bloomfield 3, Freeman 3, Bean 2, Umerah 2, El-Abd 1, Gape 1, Harriman 1, Jombati 1, Kashket 1, Saunders 1, Scarr 1, Stewart 1, Williams R 1, Opponents 1
**FA Cup goals** (6): Mackail-Smith 2, Akinfenwa 1, Freeman 1, O'Nien 1, Saunders 1. **League Cup goals**: None. **League Trophy goals** (3): De Havilland 1, Jombati 1, Southwell 1
**Average home league attendance**: 4,705. **Player of Year**: Adebayo Akinfenwa

## YEOVIL TOWN

There was no shortage of talking points, despite another season in the lower reaches of the table. Yeovil started with an 8-2 defeat at Luton, the first time an English league side had conceded that many on the opening day of the season since Wolves beat Manchester City 8-1 in 1962. They gave away three or more goals in seven other matches, while two of their players were sent off in three separate games. On the plus side, Yeovil chalked up six away from home for the first time in the Football League when Alex Fisher, Francois Zoko and Sam Surridge netted a brace each in the 6-2 defeat of promotion-casing Coventry. There were also three or more scored on seven other occasions. The victory over Coventry removed any lingering doubts about dropping into relegation trouble. With fixtures in hand on teams above them, Yeovil had the chance to go for a mid-table finish. Instead, they failed to win any of the final eight games and closed in 19th place, one better than in 2017.

Alfei D............................2
Bailey J..........................24
Barnes M.................. 1 (7)
Bird J......................... 9 (2)
Browne R.............. 16 (19)
Davies K.................... 1 (1)
Dickson R................ 35 (1)
Donnellan S....................11
Fiher A.................... 13 (4)
Gobern O.................. 7 (4)
Gray J...................... 21 (5)
Green J................. 18 (19)
James T.................. 37 (1)
Khan O................... 35 (3)
Krysiak A........................33
Maddison J................ 8 (2)
Mugabi B................ 19 (3)
Nelson Sid.....................12
Nelson Stuart...................5
Olomola C............... 18 (3)
Santos A..................6 (8)
Seager R....................2 (5)
Smith C..................15 (4)
Smith N...................30 (1)
Sowunmi O...............35 (1)
Surridge S..............21 (20)
Whelan C...................6 (1)
Wing L.....................18 (2)
Worthington M..........13 (2)
Zoko F.....................35 (2)

**League goals** (59): Zoko 13, Surridge 8, Olomola 7, Fisher 6, Khan 6, Browne 4, Gray 3, Wing 3, Green 2, Mugabi 2, Sowunmi 2, Bailey 1, Seager 1, Smith N 1
**FA Cup goals** (7): Khan 3, Green 2, Barnes 1, Zoko 1. **League Cup goals**: None. **League Trophy goals** (13): Browne 2, Surridge 2, Davies 1, Gray 1, James 1, Khan 1, Smith C 1, Smith N 1, Whelan 1, Zoko 1, Opponents 1
**Average home league attendance**: 2,941. **Player of Year**: Tom James

# LEAGUE CLUB MANAGERS 2018–19

Figure in brackets = number of managerial changes at club since the War. †Second spell at club

## PREMIER LEAGUE

| | | |
|---|---|---|
| Arsenal (12) | Unai Emery | May 2018 |
| Bournemouth (24) | Eddie Howe | October 2012 |
| Brighton (33) | Chris Hughton | December 2014 |
| Burnley (24) | Sean Dyche | October 2012 |
| Cardiff (31) | Neil Warnock | October 2016 |
| Chelsea (30) | Maurizio Sarri | July 2018 |
| Crystal Palace (43) | Roy Hodgson | September 2017 |
| Everton (20) | Marco Silva | June 2018 |
| Fulham (32) | Slavisa Jokanovic | December 2015 |
| Huddersfield (28) | David Wagner | November 2015 |
| Leicester (30) | Claude Puel | October 2017 |
| Liverpool (14) | Jurgen Klopp | October 2015 |
| Manchester City (30) | Pep Guardiola | May 2016 |
| Manchester Utd (11) | Jose Mourinho | May 2016 |
| Newcastle (27) | Rafael Benitez | March 2016 |
| Southampton (28) | Mark Hughes | March 2018 |
| Tottenham (23) | Mauricio Pochettino | May 2014 |
| Watford (36) | Javi Gracia | January 2018 |
| West Ham (16) | Manuel Pellegrini | May 2018 |
| Wolves (27) | Nuno Espirito Santo | May 2017 |

## CHAMPIONSHIP

| | | |
|---|---|---|
| Aston Villa (26) | Steve Bruce | October 2016 |
| Birmingham (29) | Garry Monk | March 2018 |
| Blackburn (31) | Tony Mowbray | February 2017 |
| Bolton (23) | Phil Parkinson | June 2016 |
| Brentford (33) | Dean Smith | November 2015 |
| Bristol City (26) | Lee Johnson | February 2016 |
| Derby (27) | Frank Lampard | June 2018 |
| Hull (30) | Nigel Adkins | December 2017 |
| Leeds (33) | Marcelo Bielsa | June 2018 |
| Middlesbrough (22) | Tony Pulis | December 2017 |
| Millwall (31) | Neil Harris | April 2015 |
| Ipswich (14) | Paul Hurst | May 2018 |
| Norwich (29) | Daniel Farke | May 2017 |
| Nottm Forest (25) | Aitor Karanka | January 2018 |
| Preston (29) | Alex Neil | July 2017 |
| QPR (35) | Steve McClaren | May 2018 |
| Reading (23) | Paul Clement | March 2018 |
| Rotherham (28) | Paul Warne | April 2017 |
| Sheffield Utd (38) | Chris Wilder | May 2016 |
| Sheffield Wed (30) | Jos Luhukay | January 2018 |
| Stoke (25) | Gary Rowett | May 2018 |
| Swansea (37) | Graham Potter | June 2018 |
| WBA (34) | Darren Moore | May 2018 |
| Wigan (24) | Paul Cook | June 2017 |

Number of changes since elected to Football League: Wigan 1978

## LEAGUE ONE

| | | |
|---|---|---|
| Accrington (4) | John Coleman | September 2014 |
| AFC Wimbledon (1) | Neal Ardley | October 2012 |
| Barnsley (27) | Daniel Stendel | June 2018 |
| Blackpool (31) | Gary Bowyer | June 2016 |

| | | |
|---|---|---|
| Bradford (36) | Michael Collins | June 2018 |
| Bristol Rov (-) | Darrell Clarke | March 2014 |
| Burton (3) | Nigel Clough | December 2015 |
| Charlton | | |
| Coventry (35) | Mark Robins | March 2017 |
| Doncaster (6) | Grant McCann | June 2018 |
| Fleetwood (5) | Joey Barton | June 2018 |
| Gillingham (26) | Steve Lovell | November 2017 |
| Luton (1) | Nathan Jones | January 2016 |
| Oxford (4) | Karl Robinson | March 2018 |
| Peterborough (31) | Steve Evans | February 2018 |
| Plymouth (34) | Derek Adams | June 2015 |
| Portsmouth (34) | Kenny Jackett | June 2017 |
| Rochdale (32) | Keith Hill | January 2013 |
| Scunthorpe (29) | Nick Daws | May 2018 |
| Shrewsbury (6) | John Askey | June 2018 |
| Southend (29) | Chris Powell | January 2018 |
| Sunderland (32) | Jack Ross | May 2018 |
| Walsall (36) | Dean Keates | March 2018 |
| Wycombe (10) | Gareth Ainsworth | November 2012 |

Number of changes since elected to Football League: Peterborough 1960, Wycombe 1993, Burton 2009, AFC Wimbledon 2011, Fleetwood 2012. Since returning: Doncaster 2003, Shrewsbury 2004, Accrington 2006, Oxford 2010, Luton 2014, Bristol Rov 2015

## LEAGUE TWO

| | | |
|---|---|---|
| Bury (28) | Ryan Lowe | May 2018 |
| Cambridge (2) | Joe Dunne | February 2018 |
| Carlisle (6) | John Sheridan | June 2018 |
| Cheltenham (-) | Gary Johnson | March 2015 |
| Colchester (28) | John McGreal | May 2016 |
| Crawley (7) | Harry Kewell | May 2017 |
| Crewe (22) | David Artell | January 2017 |
| Exeter (1) | Matt Taylor | June 2018 |
| Forest Green (-) | Mark Cooper | May 2016 |
| Grimsby (3) | Michael Jolley | March 2018 |
| Lincoln (-) | Danny Cowley | May 2016 |
| Macclesfield (1) | Mark Yates | June 2018 |
| Mansfield (3) | David Flitcroft | February 2018 |
| MK Dons (18) | Paul Tisdale | June 2018 |
| Morecambe (1) | Jim Bentley | May 2011 |
| Newport (5) | Mike Flynn | May 2017 |
| Northampton (35) | Dean Austin | May 2018 |
| Notts Co (43) | Kevin Nolan | January 2017 |
| Oldham (33) | Frankie Bunn | June 2018 |
| Port Vale (27) | Neil Aspin | October 2017 |
| Stevenage (5) | Dino Maamria | March 2018 |
| Swindon (32) | Phil Brown | March 2018 |
| Tranmere (-) | Micky Mellon | October 2016 |
| Yeovil (6) | Darren Way | December 2015 |

Number of changes since elected to Football League: Yeovil 2003, Morecambe 2007, Stevenage 2010, Crawley 2011, Forest Green 2017. Since returning: Colchester 1992, Carlisle 2005, Exeter 2008, Mansfield 2013, Newport 2013, Cambridge 2014, Cheltenham 2016, Grimsby 2016, Lincoln 2017, Macclesfield 2018, Tranmere 2018

# MANAGERIAL CHANGES 2017–18

## PREMIER LEAGUE

**Arsenal:** Out – Arsene Wenger (May 2018); In – Unai Emery
**Chelsea:** Out – Antonio Conte (Jul 2018); In – Maurizio Sarri
**Crystal Palace:** Out – Frank de Boer (Sep 2017); In – Roy Hodgson
**Everton:** Out – Ronald Koeman (Oct 2017); In – Sam Allardyce; Out (May 2018); In – Marco Silva
**Leicester:** Out – Craig Shakespeare (Oct 2017); In – Claude Puel
**Southampton:** Out – Mauricio Pellegrino (Mar 2018); In – Mark Hughes
**Stoke:** Out – Mark Hughes (Jan 2018); In – Paul Lambert; Out (May 2018); In – Gary Rowett
**Swansea:** Out – Paul Clement (Dec 2017); In – Carlos Carvalhal; Out (May 2018); In – Graham Potter
**Watford:** Out – Marco Silva (Jan 2018); In – Javi Gracia
**WBA:** Out – Tony Pulis (Nov 2017); In – Alan Pardew; Out (Apr 2018); In – Darren Moore
**West Ham:** Out – Slaven Bilic (Nov 2017; In – David Moyes; Out (May 2018); In – Manuel Pellegrini

## CHAMPIONSHIP

**Barnsley:** Out – Paul Heckingbottom (Feb 2018); In – Jose Morais; Out (May 2018); In – Daniel Stendel
**Birmingham:** Out: Harry Redknapp (Sep 2017); In – Steve Cotterill; Out (Mar 2018); In – Garry Monk
**Derby:** Out – Gary Rowett (May 2018); In – Frank Lampard
**Hull:** Out – Leonid Slutsky (Dec 2017); In – Nigel Adkins
**Ipswich:** Out – Mick McCarthy (Apr 2018); In – Paul Hurst
**Leeds:** Out – Thomas Christiansen (Feb 2018); In – Paul Heckingbottom; Out (Jun 2018); In – Marcelo Bielsa
**Middlesbrough:** Out – Garry Monk (Dec 2017); In – Tony Pulis
**Nottm Forest:** Out – Mark Warburton (Dec 2017); In – Aitor Karanka
**QPR:** Out – Ian Holloway (May 2018); In – Steve McClaren
**Reading:** Out – Jaap Stam (Mar 2018); In – Paul Clement
**Sheffield Wed:** Out – Carlos Carvalhal (Dec 2017); In – Jos Luhukay
**Sunderland:** Out – Simon Grayson (Oct 2017); In – Chris Coleman; Out (May 2018); In – Jack Ross

## LEAGUE ONE

**Bradford:** Out – Stuart McCall (Feb 2018); In – Simon Grayson; Out (May 2018); In – Michael Collins
**Bury:** Out – Lee Clark (Oct 2017); In – Chris Lucketti; Out (Jan 2018); In – Ryan Lowe (May 2018)
**Charlton:** Out – Karl Robinson (Mar 2018)
**Doncaster:** Out – Darren Ferguson (Jun 2018); In – Grant McCann
**Fleetwood:** Out – Uwe Rosler (Feb 2018); In – John Sheridan; Out (May 2018); In – Joey Barton
**Gillingham:** Out – Ady Pennock (Sept 2017); In – Steve Lovell
**MK Dons:** Out – Robbie Neilson (Jan 2018); In – Dan Micciche; Out (Apr 2018); In – Paul Tisdale
**Northampton:** Out- Justin Edinburgh (Aug 2017); In – Jimmy Floyd Hasselbaink; Out (Apr 2018); In – Dean Austin

**Oldham:** Out – John Sheridan (Sep 2017); In – Richie Wellens; Out (Jun 2018); In Frankie Bunn
**Oxford:** Out – Pep Clotet (Jan 2018); In – Karl Robinson
**Peterborough:** Out – Grant McCann (Feb 2018); In – Steve Evans
**Scunthorpe:** Out – Graham Alexander (Mar 2018): In – Nick Daws
**Shrewsbury:** Out – Paul Hurst (May 2018); In – John Askey
**Southend:** Out – Phil Brown (Jan 2018); In – Chris Powell
**Walsall:** Out – Jon Whitney (Mar 2018); In – Dean Keates

## LEAGUE TWO

**Barnet:** Out – Rossi Eames (Nov 2017); In – Mark McGhee; Out (Jan 2018); In – Graham Westley; Out (Mar 2018); In – Martin Allen; Out (May 2018); In – John Still
**Cambridge:** Out – Shaun Derry (Feb 2018); In – Joe Dunne
**Carlisle:** Out – Keith Curle (May 2018; In – John Sheridan
**Chesterfield:** Out – Gary Caldwell (Sep 2017); In – Jack Lester; Out (May 2018); In – Martin Allen
**Exeter:** Out – Paul Tisdale (Jun 2018); In – Matt Taylor
**Grimsby:** Out – Russell Slade (Feb 2018); In – Michael Jolley
**Mansfield:** Out – Steve Evans (Feb 2018); In – David Flitcroft
**Port Vale:** Out – Michael Brown (Sep 2017); In – Neil Aspin
**Stevenage:** Out – Darren Sarll (Mar 2018); In – Dino Maamria
**Swindon:** Out – David Flitcroft (Mar 2018); In – Phil Brown

# THE THINGS THEY SAY ...

'If I'd kicked my kid in the garden, I don't think he would fall like that' – **Sean Dyche**, Burnley manager, after his side conceded a controversial penalty to a theatrical tumble by Manchester City's Bernardo Silva.

'He's let his team down, his manager down and the supporters down. It was disgraceful for a player of his experience' – **Phil Neville**, *Match of the Day* analyst, after Christian Benteke insisted on taking a potentially match-winning penalty for Crystal Palace against Bournemouth and had it saved.

## EMERGENCY CALL

When Derby's Kelle Roos joined Plymouth on an emergency loan, he became the season's seventh goalkeeper to be used by the injury-hit League One club.

# EMIRATES FA CUP 2017–18

## FIRST ROUND

Delight turns to despair for Maidstone's Delano Sam-Yorke in their 4-2 win at Cheltenham. The striker puts his side on the way to victory, adds a second and is then shown a straight red card for a foul. Joe Pigott and Zavron Hines are also on the mark for Maidstone, one of four non-league sides delivering upsets away from home. Matt Paterson scores the only goal of the tie for Oxford City against Colchester; Woking embarrass Bury 3-0 in a replay with goals from Regan Charles-Cook, Inih Effiong and Jamie Philpot; ten-man Guiseley see off Accrington at the second time of asking, Jonny Maxted saving two spot-kicks in a penalty shoot-out after Chris M'Boungou is dismissed for a second yellow card. Boreham Wood use home advantage to beat EFL opposition for the first time, coming from behind to overcome Blackpool 2-1 with strikes from Blair Turgott and Dan Holman. The previous season's principal giant-killers both make early exits. Lincoln, now in the EFL, go down to AFC Wimbledon, while Sutton are beaten by Cambridge United. Three players record hat-tricks – Danny Lloyd for Peterborough at Tranmere, Matt Godden for Stevenage against Nantwich and Matthew Lench for Slough at Gainsborough.

AFC Fylde 4 Kidderminster 2
AFC Wimbledon 1 Lincoln 0
Blackburn 3 Barnet 1
Boreham Wood 2 Blackpool 1
Bradford 2 Chesterfield 0
Cambridge 1 Sutton 0
Carlisle 3 Oldham 2
Charlton 3 Truro 1
Cheltenham 2 Maidstone 4
Chorley 1 Fleetwood 2
Colchester 0 Oxford City 1
Coventry 2 Maidenhead 0
Crewe 2 Rotherham 1
Dartford 1 Swindon 5
Ebbsfleet 2 Doncaster 6
Exeter 3 Heybridge 1
Forest Green 1 Macclesfield 0
Gainsborough 0 Slough 6
Gateshead 2 Chelmsford 0
Gillingham 2 Leyton Orient 1
Guiseley 0 Accrington 0
Hereford 1 AFC Telford 0
Hyde 0 MK Dons 4
Leatherhead 1 Billericay 1
Luton 1 Portsmouth 0
Morecambe 3 Hartlepool 0
Newport 2 Walsall 1
Northampton 0 Scunthorpe 0
Notts Co 4 Bristol Rov 2
Peterborough 1 Tranmere 1
Plymouth 1 Grimsby 0
Port Vale 2 Oxford Utd 0
Rochdale 4 Bromley 0
Shaw Lane 1 Mansfield 3
Shrewsbury 5 Aldershot 0
Solihull 0 Wycombe 2
Stevenage 5 Nantwich 0
Wigan 2 Crawley 1
Woking 1 Bury 1
Yeovil 1 Southend 0

**Replays**

Accrington 1 Guiseley 1
(aet, Guiseley won 4-3 on pens)
Billericay 1 Leatherhead 3
Bury 0 Woking 3
Scunthorpe 1 Northampton 0
Tranmere 0 Peterborough 5

## SECOND ROUND

For the first time since 1951, not a single non-league team makes it beyond the second round. AFC Fylde come closest, leading Wigan 2-1 in a replay until the final ten minutes when two goals by Will Grigg put the League One leaders through. Hereford earn a second crack at Fleetwood. So do Woking against Peterborough. But both lose replays. Oxford City are denied one by a stoppage-time Jorge Grant goal which gives Notts County a 3-2 win. Guiseley's first appearance in the second round turns sour when Darren Holden and Chris M'Boungou are sent off in a 3-0 defeat by Mansfield. Jimmy Spencer scores all three goals, his first for the club. Blackburn also have two players dismissed, Rekeem Harper and Elliott Bennett, and surrender a 3-0 lead to Crewe. But they hold on for a replay and win it with the only goal.

AFC Fylde 1 Wigan 1
AFC Wimbledon 3 Charlton 1
Blackburn 3 Crewe 3
Bradford 3 Plymouth 1
Coventry 3 Boreham Wood 0
Doncaster 3 Scunthorpe 0
Fleetwood 1 Hereford 1
Forest Green 3 Exeter 3
Gateshead 0 Luton 5
Gillingham 1 Carlisle 1
Mansfield 3 Guiseley 0
MK Dons 4 Maidstone 1
Newport 2 Cambridge 0
Notts Co 3 Oxford City 2
Port Vale 1 Yeovil 1
Shrewsbury 2 Morecambe 0
Slough 0 Rochdale 4
Stevenage 5 Swindon 2
Woking 1 Peterborough 1
Wycombe 3 Leatherhead 1

**Replays**

Carlisle 3 Gillingham 1
Crewe 0 Blackburn 1
Exeter 2 Forest Green 1 (aet)
Hereford 0 Fleetwood 2
Peterborough 5 Woking 2
Wigan 3 AFC Fylde 2
Yeovil 3 Port Vale 2 (aet)

## THIRD ROUND

Coventry, winners in 1987, recapture some of that romance after sliding into League Two in recent seasons by beating Stoke 2-1 with goals from Jordan Willis and Jack Grimmer – a result followed by the sacking of the Premier League side's manager Mark Hughes. Wigan, who lifted the trophy in 2013, also have a taste of former glory. They are denied victory at Bournemouth by Steve Cook's stoppage-time equaliser, but make no mistake in the replay, goals by Sam Morsy, Dan Burn and Callum Elder delivering a 3-0 victory. There are also notable performances from three other lower-league teams. An own goal puts Newport on level terms with Leeds and an 89th minute header from substitute Shawn McCoulsky puts them through. Jack Marriott (2) and Ryan Tafazolli are on the mark for Peterborough, who win 3-1 at Villa Park, while Notts County's Jon Stead continues his run of scoring in every round with the only goal at Brentford. For the first time in 21 years at the club, Arsenal manager Arsene Wenger tastes defeat in the third round. A brace by full-back Eric Lichaj and penalties from Ben Brereton and Kieran Dowell enable Nottingham Forest, with caretaker Gary Brazil in charge following the dismissal of Mark Warburton, to knock out the holders 4-2. Virgil van Dijk, Liverpoool's £75m signing, makes a dream start with an 84th minute winner against Everton. Swansea's Jordan Ayew also makes headlines with a carbon-copy of Ricky Villa's immortal goal for Tottenham in the 1981 final, beating five defenders to put Swansea on the way to a 2-1 replay win over Wolves. The Video Assistant Referee system, used for the first time in English football, makes its mark in two other replays. Chelsea's Willian, Pedro and Alvaro Morata are booked for diving against Norwich, with Pedro and Morata sent off for second yellow cards. Norwich equalise in stoppage-time through Jamal Lewis, but lose on penalties. At Leicester, technology overturns an offside decision against Kelechi Iheanacho, allowing the second of his two goals against Fleetwood to stand. Iceland striker Jon Dadi Bodvarsson registers his first hat-trick in England football as Reading overcome Stevenage in another second meeting of teams.

Aston Villa 1 Peterborough 3
Birmingham 1 Burton 0
Blackburn 0 Hull 1
Bolton 1 Huddersfield 2
Bournemouth 2 Wigan 2
Brentford 0 Notts Co 1
Brighton 2 Crystal Palace 1
Cardiff 0 Mansfield 0
Carlisle 0 Sheffield Wed 0
Coventry 2 Stoke 1
Doncaster 0 Rochdale 1
Exeter 0 WBA 2
Fleetwood 0 Leicester 0
Fulham 0 Southampton 1
Ipswich 0 Sheffield Utd 1
Liverpool 2 Everton 1
Manchester City 4 Burnley 1
**Manchester Utd** 2 Derby 0
Middlesbrough 2 Sunderland 0
Millwall 4 Barnsley 1
Newcastle 3 Luton 1
Newport 2 Leeds 1
Norwich 0 **Chelsea** 0
Nottm Forest 4 Arsenal 2

QPR 0 MK Dons 1
Shrewsbury 0 West Ham 0
Stevenage 0 Reading 0
Tottenham 3 AFC Wimbledon 0
Watford 3 Bristol City 0
Wolves 0 Swansea 0
Wycombe 1 Preston 5
Yeovil 2 Bradford 0
**Replays**
**Chelsea** 1 Norwich 1
(aet, Chelsea won 5-3 on pens)
Leicester 2 Fleetwood 0
Mansfield 1 Cardiff 4
Reading 3 Stevenage 0
Sheffield Wed 2 Carlisle 0
Swansea 2 Wolves 1
West Ham 1 Shrewsbury 0 (aet)
Wigan 3 Bournemouth 0

## FOURTH ROUND

Two goals by Will Grigg, the second a penalty, give Wigan a second Premier League scalp – 2-0 against West Ham, who have Arthur Masuaku sent off for spitting at Nick Powell. Newport lead Tottenham through Padraig Amond's header and it needs an 82nd strike by Harry Kane to rescue his side. They win the replay 2-0 at Wembley after an own goal by Dan Butler. Two other lower division sides deliver notable performances. Rochdale, denied victory at Millwall by Ben Thompson's 90th minute equaliser, prevail in the replay with the only goal from captain Ian Henderson. Notts County hold Swansea thanks to Jon Stead's sixth goal in six games, but are overwhelmed 8-1 in the teams' second meeting. West Bromwich Albion, struggling in the Premier Division, surprise Liverpool at Anfield, with Jay Rodriguez on the mark twice in a 3-2 success.

Cardiff 0 Manchester City 2
**Chelsea** 3 Newcastle 0
Huddersfield 1 Birmingham 1
Hull 2 Nottm Forest 1
Liverpool 2 WBA 3
Middlesbrough 0- Brighton 1
Millwall 2 Rochdale 2
MK Dons 0 Coventry 1
Newport 1 Tottenham 1
Notts Co 1 Swansea 1
Peterborough 1 Leicester 5
Sheffield Utd 1 Preston 0
Sheffield Wed 3 Reading 1
Southampton 1 Watford 0
Wigan 2 West Ham 0
Yeovil 0 **Manchester Utd** 4
**Replays**
Birmingham 1 Huddersfield 4
Rochdale 1 Millwall 0
Swansea 8 Notts Co 1
Tottenham 2 Newport 0

## FIFTH ROUND

Manchester City's bid for four trophies is ended by Wigan, who complete a hat-trick of wins over Premier League opposition with a 79th minute goal by Will Grigg. It's a repeat of the club's 1-0 victory over City in the 2013 final. Rochdale, League One's bottom team, enjoy a moment in the spotlight. They trail Tottenham to an 88th minute penalty from Harry Kane, back at the ground where he made his professional debut while on loan with Leyton Orient in 2011. But substitute Steve Davies equalises in the third minute of added time for a replay, which Tottenham win 6-1, Fernando Llorente scoring a hat-trick in 12 second-half minutes. Coventry, the one remaining League Two side, go down 3-1 to Brighton, for whom January signings Jurgen Locadia and Leonardo Ulloa score for the first time. West Bromwich Albion's troubled week, in which their chairman and chief executive officer were sacked and four players allegendly stole a taxi while breaking a curfew at a training camp in Barcelona, ends with a 2-1 home defeat by Southampton. Swansea reach the quarter-finals for the first time since 1964 by beating Sheffield Wednesday 2-0 in a replay.

Brighton 3 Coventry 1
**Chelsea** 4 Hull 0
Huddersfield 0 **Manchester Utd** 2
Leicester 1 Sheffield Utd 0
Rochdale 2 Tottenham 2
Sheffield Wed 0 Swansea 0
WBA 1 Southampton 2
Wigan 1 Manchester City 0
**Replays**
Swansea 2 Sheffield Wed 0
Tottenham 6 Rochdale 1

## SIXTH ROUND

Wigan's run is ended by Southampton in Mark Hughes's first match as manager of the Premier League club. Pierre-Emile Hojbjerg and Cedric Soares score their first goals for the club and Manolo Gabbiadini has a penalty saved by Christian Walton. Four days after Chelsea are knocked out of the Champions League by Barcelona, an extra-time header by Pedro against Leicester keeps alive their chances of a trophy. Christian Eriksen scores twice in Tottenham's 3-0 success at Swansea, while Manchester United overcome Brighton 2-0.

Leicester 1 **Chelsea** 2 (aet)
**Manchester Utd** 2 Brighton 0
Swansea 0 Tottenham 3
Wigan 0 Southampton 2

## SEMI-FINALS (both at Wembley)

A brilliant individual goal by Olivier Giroud a minute into the second-half puts Chelsea on the way to the final. Alvaro Morata comes off the bench to replace him near the end and makes sure with a header. Tottenham lead through Dele Alli's strike, but suffer the club's eighth successive semi-final defeat in the competition when Alexis Sanchez scores his eighth goal for club and country in eight Wembley appearances and Ander Herrera nets Manchester United's winner.

**Chelsea** 2 Southampton 0
**Manchester Utd** 2 Tottenham 1

## FINAL

A palpable sense of uncertainty and relief accompanied Chelsea's Wembley victory. There were the usual celebrations by manager and players after Eden Hazard won and converted the decisive penalty on his 300th appearance for the club. But they were muted, certainly as far as Antonio Conte was concerned. And when it later emerged that owner Roman Abramovich missed the final because of unexplained delays in renewing his expired UK visa, the whole experience had seemed strangely surreal. Throughout the season, Conte was at loggerheads with the club's hierarchy over what he considered the failure to deliver the level of squad strengthening required to keep pace with their Premier League rivals. His dissatisfaction accompanied a poor title defence which ended 30 points behind Manchester City and without a Champions League place. So while there was satisfaction at ending with a trophy, as well as upstaging arch-rival Jose Mourinho, Conte faced as many questions afterwards about his future as he did about the club's eighth success in the competition. Hazard, wanted by Real Madrid and Paris Saint-Germain, was also the subject of renewed speculation about his future after a graceful performance in a modest final in which his side dictated the pattern of play in the first-half, then frustrated Manchester United's greater sense of urgency after the interval. For his part, Mourinho had to respond to accusations that negativity had made United a shadow of the team they once were. He insisted Chelsea were undeserving winners. The wider viewpoint seemed to be that his players had not done enough to win and whether that was down to him.

**CHELSEA 1 (Hazard 22 pen) MANCHESTER UNITED 0**
**Wembley (87,647); Saturday, May 19, 2018**

**Chelsea** (3-5-1-1): Courtois, Azpilicueta, Cahill (capt), Rudiger, Moses, Fabregas, Kante, Bakayoko, Alonso, Hazard (Willian 90), Giroud (Morata 89). **Subs not used**: Caballero, Barkley, Pedro, Zappacosta, Chalobah. **Booked**: Courtois. **Manager**: Antonio Conte
**Manchester United** (4-1-2-1-2): De Gea, Valencia, Smalling (capt), Jones (Mata 87), Young, Herrera, Matic, Pogba, Lingard (Martial 73), Sanchez, Rashford (Lukaku 73). **Subs not used**: Romero, Bailly, Darmian, McTominay. **Booked**: Jones, Valencia. **Manager**: Jose Mourinho
**Referee**: M Oliver (Northumberland). **Half-time**: 1-0

## HOW THEY REACHED THE FINAL

**Chelsea**
**Round 3**: 0-0 away to Norwich; 1-1 home to Norwich (Batshuayi) – aet, won 5-3 on pens
**Round 4**: 3-0 home to Newcastle (Batshuayi 2, Alonso)
**Round 5**: 4-0 home to Hull (Willian 2, Pedro, Giroud)
**Round 6**: 2-1 away to Leicester (Morata, Pedro) – aet
**Semi-finals**: 2-0 v Southampton (Giroud, Morata)

**Manchester Utd**
**Round 3**: 2-0 home to Derby (Lingard, Lukaku)
**Round 4**: 4-0 away to Yeovil (Rashford, Herrera, Lingard, Lukaku)
**Round 5**: 2-0 away to Huddersfield (Lukaku 2)
**Round 6**: 2-0 home to Brighton (Lukaku, Matic)
**Semi-finals**: 2-1 v Tottenham (Sanchez, Herrera)

**Leading scorers**: 7 Grigg (Wigan); 6 Henderson (Rochdale); 5 Lukaku (Manchester Utd), Marriott (Peterborough), Stockley (Exeter); 4 Doidge (Forest Green), Godden (Stevenage), Kane (Tottenham), Iheanacho (Leicester), Midson (Leatherhead), Danny Rowe (AFC Fylde), Tommy Rowe (Doncaster), Stead (Notts Co)

# FINAL FACTS AND FIGURES

- Chelsea moved level with Tottenham on eight FA Cup victories.

- The scoreline was a repeat of the first final at the new Wembley in 2007, decided by an extra-time goal from Didier Drogba.

- Antonio Conte won a domestic final for the first time as a manager, having lost with Juventus against Napoli in the 2012 Coppa Italia and with Chelsea against Arsenal in 2017.

- Jose Mourinho lost his first final in charge of an English club after winning four League Cups, one FA Cup and one Europa League with Chelsea and Manchester United.

- Chelsea's Olivier Giroud collected his fourth winners' medal, having won three with Arsenal. Nemanja Matic was a loser for the second successive year after Chelsea's defeat by Arsenal

- Eden Hazard's penalty was the first scored in the final, excluding shoot-outs, since Ruud van Nistelrooy's for Manchester United against Millwall in 2004.

- The video assistant referee system was employed in an FA Cup Final for the first time and. Michael Oliver it used to confirm confirmed that a goal by United's Alexis Sanchez was offside.

- Ray Wilkins's widow Jackie presented the trophy. The midfielder, who died the previous month, won it with Manchester United in 1983, scoring against Brighton. He also won it three as Chelsea's assistant manager.

# FA CUP FINAL SCORES & TEAMS

1872 **Wanderers 1** (Betts) Bowen, Alcock, Bonsor, Welch; Betts, Crake, Hooman, Lubbock, Thompson, Vidal, Wollaston. Note: Betts played under the pseudonym 'AH Chequer' on the day of the match **Royal Engineers 0** Capt Merriman; Capt Marindin; Lieut Addison, Lieut Cresswell, Lieut Mitchell, Lieut Renny-Tailyour, Lieut Rich, Lieut George Goodwyn, Lieut Muirhead, Lieut Cotter, Lieut Bogle

1873 **Wanderers 2** (Wollaston, Kinnaird) Bowen; Thompson, Welch, Kinnaird, Howell, Wollaston, Sturgis, Rev Stewart, Kenyon-Slaney, Kingsford, Bonsor **Oxford University 0** Kirke-Smith; Leach, Mackarness, Birley, Longman, Chappell-Maddison, Dixon, Paton, Vidal, Sumner, Ottaway. March 29; 3,000; A Stair

1874 **Oxford University 2** (Mackarness, Patton) Neapean; Mackarness, Birley, Green, Vidal, Ottaway, Benson, Patton, Rawson, Chappell-Maddison, Rev Johnson **Royal Engineers 0** Capt Merriman; Major Marindin, Lieut W Addison, Gerald Onslow, Lieut Oliver, Lieut Digby, Lieut Renny-Tailyour, Lieut Rawson, Lieut Blackman Lieut Wood, Lieut von Donop. March 14; 2,000; A Stair

1875 **Royal Engineers 1** (Renny-Tailyour) Capt Merriman; Lieut Sim, Lieut Onslow, Lieut (later Sir) Ruck, Lieut Von Donop, Lieut Wood, Lieut Rawson, Lieut Stafford, Capt Renny-Tailyour, Lieut Mein, Lieut Wingfield-Stratford **Old Etonians 1** (Bonsor) Thompson; Benson, Lubbock, Wilson, Kinnaird, (Sir) Stronge, Patton, Farmer, Bonsor, Ottaway, Kenyon-Slaney. March 13; 2,000; CW Alcock. aet **Replay – Royal Engineers 2** (Renny-Tailyour, Stafford) Capt Merriman; Lieut Sim, Lieut Onslow, Lieut (later Sir) Ruck, Lieut Von Donop, Lieut Wood, Lieut Rawson, Lieut Stafford, Capt Renny-Tailyour, Lieut Mein, Lieut Wingfield-Stratford **Old Etonians 0** Capt Drummond-Moray; Kinnaird, (Sir) Stronge, Hammond, Lubbock, Patton, Farrer, Bonsor, Lubbock, Wilson, Farmer. March 16; 3,000; CW Alcock

1876 **Wanderers 1** (Edwards) Greig; Stratford, Lindsay, Chappell-Maddison, Birley, Wollaston, C Heron, G Heron, Edwards, Kenrick, Hughes **Old Etonians 1** (Bonsor) Hogg; Rev Welldon, Lyttleton, Thompson, Kinnaird, Meysey, Kenyon-Slaney, Lyttleton, Sturgis, Bonsor, Allene. March 11; 3,500; WS Rawson aet **Replay – Wanderers 3** (Wollaston, Hughes 2) Greig, Stratford, Lindsay, Chappel-Maddison, Birley, Wollaston, C Heron, G Heron, Edwards, Kenrick, Hughes **Old Etonians 0** Hogg, Lubbock, Lyttleton, Farrer, Kinnaird, (Sir) Stronge, Kenyon-Slaney, Lyttleton, Sturgis, Bonsor, Allene. March 18; 1,500; WS Rawson

1877 **Wanderers 2** (Kenrick, Lindsay) Kinnaird; Birley, Denton, Green, Heron, Hughes, Kenrick, Lindsay, Stratford, Wace, Wollaston **Oxford University 1** (Kinnaird og) Allington; Bain, Dunnell, Rev Savory, Todd, Waddington, Rev Fernandez, Otter, Parry, Rawson. March 24; 3,000; SH Wright, aet

1878 **Wanderers 3** (Kinnaird, Kenrick 2) (Sir) Kirkpatrick; Stratford, Lindsay, Kinnaird, Green, Wollaston, Heron, Wylie, Wace, Denton, Kenrick **Royal Engineers 1** (Morris) Friend; Cowan, (Sir) Morris, Mayne, Heath, Haynes, Lindsay, Hedley, (Sir) Bond, Barnet, Ruck. March 23; 4,500; SR Bastard

1879 **Old Etonians 1** (Clerke) Hawtrey; Edward, Bury, Kinnaird, Lubbock, Clerke, Pares, Goodhart, Whitfield, Chevalier, Beaufoy **Clapham Rovers 0** Birkett; Ogilvie, Field, Bailey, Prinsep, Rawson, Stanley, Scott, Bevington, Growse, Keith-Falconer. March 29; 5,000; CW Alcock

1880 **Clapham Rovers 1** (Lloyd-Jones) Birkett; Ogilvie, Field, Weston, Bailey, Stanley, Brougham, Sparkes, Barry, Ram, Lloyd-Jones **Oxford University 0** Parr; Wilson, King, Phillips, Rogers, Heygate, Rev Childs, Eyre, (Dr) Crowdy, Hill, Lubbock. April 10; 6,000; Major Marindin

1881 **Old Carthusians 3** (Page, Wynyard, Parry) Gillett; Norris, (Sir) Colvin, Prinsep, (Sir) Vintcent, Hansell, Richards, Page, Wynyard, Parry, Todd **Old Etonians 0** Rawlinson; Foley, French, Kinnaird, Farrer, Macauley, Goodhart, Whitfield, Novelli, Anderson, Chevallier. April 9; 4,000; W Pierce-Dix

1882 **Old Etonians 1** (Macauley) Rawlinson; French, de Paravicini, Kinnaird, Foley, Novelli, Dunn, Macauley, Goodhart, Chevallier, Anderson **Blackburn Rov 0** Howarth; McIntyre, Suter, Hargreaves, Sharples, Hargreaves, Avery, Brown, Strachan, Douglas, Duckworth. March 25; 6,500; JC Clegg

1883 **Blackburn Olympic 2** (Matthews, Costley) Hacking; Ward, Warburton, Gibson, Astley, Hunter, Dewhurst, Matthews, Wilson, Costley, Yates **Old Etonians 1** (Goodhart) Rawlinson; French, de Paravicini, Kinnaird, Foley, Dunn, Bainbridge, Chevallier, Anderson, Goodhart, Macauley. March 31; 8,000; Major Marindin, aet

1884 **Blackburn Rov 2** (Sowerbutts, Forrest) Arthur; Suter, Beverley, McIntyre, Forrest, Hargreaves, Brown,

Inglis Sowerbutts, Douglas, Lofthouse **Queen's Park 1** (Christie) Gillespie; MacDonald, Arnott, Gow, Campbell, Allan, Harrower, (Dr) Smith, Anderson, Watt, Christie. March 29; 4,000; Major Marindin

**1885** **Blackburn Rov 2** (Forrest, Brown) Arthur; Turner, Suter, Haworth, McIntyre, Forrest, Sowerbutts, Lofthouse, Douglas, Brown, Fecitt **Queen's Park 0** Gillespie; Arnott, MacLeod, MacDonald, Campbell, Sellar, Anderson, McWhammel, Hamilton, Allan, Gray. April 4; 12,500; Major Marindin

**1886** **Blackburn Rov 0** Arthur; Turner, Suter, Heyes, Forrest, McIntyre, Douglas, Strachan, Sowerbutts, Fecitt, Brown **WBA 0** Roberts; Green, Bell, Horton, Perry, Timmins, Woodhall, Green, Bayliss, Loach, Bell. April 3; 15,000; Major Marindin **Replay – Blackburn Rov 2** (Sowerbutts, Brown) Arthur; Turner, Suter, Walton, Forrest, McIntyre, Douglas, Strachan, Sowerbutts, Fecitt, Brown **WBA 0** Roberts; Green, Bell, Horton, Perry, Timmins, Woodhall, Green, Bayliss, Loach, Bell. April 10; 12,000; Major Marindin

**1887** **Aston Villa 2** (Hodgetts, Hunter) Warner; Coulton, Simmonds, Yates, Dawson, Burton, Davis, Albert Brown, Hunter, Vaughton, Hodgetts **WBA 0** Roberts; Green, Aldridge, Horton, Perry, Timmins, Woodhall, Green, Bayliss, Paddock, Pearson. April 2; 15,500; Major Marindin

**1888** **WBA 2** (Bayliss), Woodhall) Roberts; Aldridge, Green, Horton, Perry, Timmins, Woodhall, Bassett, Bayliss, Wilson, Pearson **Preston 1** (Dewhurst) Mills-Roberts; Howarth, Holmes, Ross, Russell, Gordon, Ross, Goodall, Dewhurst, Drummond, Graham. March 24; 19,000; Major Marindin

**1889** **Preston 3** (Dewhurst, Ross, Thomson) Mills-Roberts; Howarth, Holmes, Drummond, Russell, Graham, Gordon, Goodall, Dewhurst, Thompson, Ross **Wolves 0** Baynton; Baugh, Mason, Fletcher, Allen, Lowder, Hunter, Wykes, Brodie, Wood, Knight. March 30; 22,000; Major Marindin

**1890** **Blackburn Rov 6** (Lofthouse, Jack Southworth, Walton, Townley 3) Horne; James Southworth, Forbes, Barton, Dewar, Forrest, Lofthouse, Campbell, Jack Southworth, Walton, Townley **Sheffield Wed 1** (Bennett) Smith; Morley, Brayshaw, Dungworth, Betts, Waller, Ingram, Woolhouse, Bennett, Mumford, Cawley. March 29; 20,000; Major Marindin

**1891** **Blackburn Rov 3** (Dewar, Jack Southworth, Townley) Pennington; Brandon, Forbes, Barton, Dewar, Forrest, Lofthouse, Walton, Southworth, Hall, Townley **Notts Co 1** (Oswald) Thraves; Ferguson, Hendry, Osborne, Calderhead, Shelton, McGregror, McInnes Oswald, Locker, Daft. March 21; 23,000; CJ Hughes

**1892** **WBA 3** (Geddes, Nicholls, Reynolds) Reader; Nicholson, McCulloch, Reynolds, Perry, Groves, Bassett, McLeod, Nicholls, Pearson, Geddes **Aston Villa 0** Warner; Evans, Cox, Devey, Cowan, Baird, Athersmith, Devey, Dickson, Hodgetts, Campbell. March 19; 32,810; JC Clegg

**1893** **Wolves 1** (Allen) Rose; Baugh, Swift, Malpass, Allen, Kinsey, Topham, Wykes, Butcher, Griffin, Wood **Everton 0** Williams; Kelso, Howarth, Boyle, Holt, Stewart, Latta, Gordon, Maxwell, Chadwick, Milward. March 25; 45,000; CJ Hughes

**1894** **Notts Co 4** (Watson, Logan 3) Toone; Harper, Hendry, Bramley, Calderhead, Shelton, Watson, Donnelly, Logan Bruce, Daft **Bolton 1** (Cassidy) Sutcliffe; Somerville, Jones , Gardiner, Paton, Hughes, Tannahill, Wilson, Cassidy, Bentley, Dickenson. March 31; 37,000; CJ Hughes

**1895** **Aston Villa 1** (Chatt) Wilkes; Spencer, Welford, Reynolds, Cowan, Russell, Athersmith Chatt, Devey, Hodgetts, Smith **WBA 0** Reader; Williams, Horton, Perry, Higgins, Taggart, Bassett, McLeod, Richards, Hutchinson, Banks. April 20; 42,560; J Lewis

**1896** **Sheffield Wed 2** (Spikesley 2) Massey; Earp, Langley, Brandon, Crawshaw, Petrie, Brash, Brady, Bell, Davis, Spikesley **Wolves 1** (Black) Tennant; Baugh, Dunn, Owen, Malpass, Griffiths, Tonks, Henderson, Beats, Wood, Black. April 18; 48,836; Lieut Simpson

**1897** **Aston Villa 3** (Campbell, Wheldon, Crabtree) Whitehouse; Spencer, Reynolds, Evans, Cowan, Crabtree, Athersmith, Devey, Campbell, Wheldon, Cowan **Everton 2** (Bell, Boyle) Menham; Meechan, Storrier, Boyle, Holt, Stewart, Taylor, Bell, Hartley, Chadwick, Milward. April 10; 65,891; J Lewis

**1898** **Nottm Forest 3** (Capes 2, McPherson) Allsop; Ritchie, Scott, Forman, McPherson, Wragg, McInnes, Richards, Benbow, Capes, Spouncer **Derby 1** (Bloomer) Fryer; Methven, Leiper, Cox, Goodall, Bloomer, Boag, Stevenson, McQueen. April 16; 62,017; J Lewis

**1899** **Sheffield Utd 4** (Bennett, Beers, Almond, Priest) Foulke; Thickett, Boyle, Johnson, Morren, Needham, Bennett, Beers, Hedley, Almond, Priest **Derby 1** (Boag) Fryer; Methven, Staley, Cox, Paterson, May, Arkesden, Bloomer, Boag, McDonald, Allen. April 15; 73,833; A Scragg

**1900 Bury 4** (McLuckie 2, Wood, Plant) Thompson; Darroch, Davidson, Pray, Leeming, Ross, Richards, Wood, McLuckie, Sagar, Plant **Southampton 0** Robinson; Meechan, Durber, Meston, Chadwick, Petrie, Turner, Yates, Farrell, Wood, Milward. April 21; 68,945; A Kingscott

**1901 Tottenham 2** (Brown 2) Clawley; Erentz, Tait, Morris, Hughes, Jones, Smith, Cameron, Brown, Copeland, Kirwan **Sheffield Utd 2** (Priest, Bennett) Foulke; Thickett, Boyle, Johnson, Morren, Needham, Bennett, Field, Hedley, Priest, Lipsham. April 20; 110,820; A Kingscott **Replay – Tottenham 3** (Cameron, Smith, Brown) Clawley; Erentz, Tait, Morris, Hughes, Jones, Smith, Cameron, Brown, Copeland, Kirwan. **Sheffield Utd 1** (Priest) Foulke; Thickett, Boyle, Johnson, Morren, Needham, Bennett, Field, Hedley, Priest, Lipsham. April 27; 20,470; A Kingscott

**1902 Sheffield Utd 1** (Common) Foulke; Thickett, Boyle, Needham, Wilkinson, Johnson, Bennett, Common, Hedley, Priest, Lipsham **Southampton 1** (Wood) Robinson; Fry, Molyneux, Meston, Bowman, Lee, Turner, Wood Brown, Chadwick, Turner. April 19; 76,914; T Kirkham. **Replay – Sheffield Utd 2** (Hedley, Barnes) Foulke; Thickett, Boyle, Needham, Wilkinson, Johnson, Barnes, Common, Hedley, Priest, Lipsham **Southampton 1** (Brown) Robinson; Fry, Molyneux, Meston, Bowman, Lee, Turner, Wood, Brown, Chadwick, Turner. April 26; 33,068; T Kirkham

**1903 Bury 6** (Leeming 2, Ross, Sagar, Wood, Plant) Monteith; Lindsey, McEwen, Johnston, Thorpe, Ross, Richards, Wood, Sagar Leeming, Plant **Derby 0** Fryer; Methven, Morris, Warren, Goodall, May, Warrington, York, Boag, Richards, Davis. April 18; 63,102; J Adams

**1904 Manchester City 1** (Meredith) Hillman; McMahon, Burgess, Frost, Hynds, Ashworth, Meredith, Livingstone, Gillespie, Turnbull, Booth **Bolton 0** Davies; Brown, Struthers, Clifford, Greenhalgh, Freebairn, Stokes, Marsh, Yenson, White, Taylor. April 23; 61,374; AJ Barker

**1905 Aston Villa 2** (Hampton 2) George; Spencer, Miles, Pearson, Leake, Windmill, Brawn, Garratty, Hampton, Bache, Hall **Newcastle 0** Lawrence; McCombie, Carr, Gardner, Aitken, McWilliam, Rutherford, Howie, Appleyard, Veitch, Gosnell. April 15; 101,117; PR Harrower

**1906 Everton 1** (Young) Scott; Crelley, W Balmer, Makepeace, Taylor, Abbott, Sharp, Bolton, Young, Settle, Hardman **Newcastle 0** Lawrence; McCombie, Carr, Gardner, Aitken, McWilliam, Rutherford, Howie, Orr, Veitch, Gosnell. April 21; 75,609; F Kirkham

**1907 Sheffield Wed 2** (Stewart, Simpson) Lyall; Layton, Burton, Brittleton, Crawshaw, Bartlett, Chapman, Bradshaw, Wilson, Stewart, Simpson **Everton 1** (Sharp) Scott; W Balmer, B Balmer, Makepeace, Taylor, Abbott, Sharp, Bolton, Young, Settle, Hardman. April 20; 84,594; N Whittaker

**1908 Wolves 3** (Hunt, Hedley, Harrison) Lunn; Jones, Collins, Rev Hunt, Wooldridge, Bishop, Harrison, Shelton, Hedley, Radford, Pedley **Newcastle 1** (Howie) Lawrence; McCracken, Pudan, Gardner, Veitch, McWilliam, Rutherford, Howie, Appleyard, Speedie, Wilson. April 25; 74,697; TP Campbell

**1909 Manchester Utd 1** (Sandy Turnbull) Moger; Stacey, Hayes, Duckworth, Roberts, Bell, Meredith, Halse, J Turnbull, S Turnbull, Wall **Bristol City 0** Clay; Annan, Cottle, Hanlin, Wedlock, Spear, Staniforth, Hardy, Gilligan, Burton, Hilton. April 24; 71,401; J Mason

**1910 Newcastle 1** (Rutherford) Lawrence; McCracken, Whitson, Veitch, Low, McWilliam, Rutherford, Howie, Higgins, Shepherd, Wilson **Barnsley 1** (Tufnell) Mearns; Downs, Ness, Glendinning, Boyle, Utley, Tufnell, Lillycrop, Gadsby, Forman, Bartrop. April 23; 77,747; JT Ibbotson **Replay – Newcastle 2** (Shepherd 2, 1pen) Lawrence; McCracken, Carr, Veitch, Low, McWilliam, Rutherford, Howie, Higgins, Shepherd, Wilson **Barnsley 0** Mearns; Downs, Ness, Glendinning, Boyle, Utley, Tufnell, Lillycrop, Gadsby, Forman, Bartrop. April 28; 69,000; JT Ibbotson.

**1911 Bradford City 0** Mellors; Campbell, Taylor, Robinson, Gildea, McDonald, Logan, Speirs, O'Rourke, Devine, Thompson **Newcastle 0** Lawrence; McCracken, Whitson, Veitch, Low, Willis, Rutherford, Jobey, Stewart, Higgins, Wilson. April 22; 69,068; JH Pearson **Replay – Bradford City 1** (Speirs) Mellors; Campbell, Taylor, Robinson, Torrance, McDonald, Logan, Speirs, O'Rourke, Devine, Thompson **Newcastle 0** Lawrence; McCracken, Whitson, Veitch, Low, Willis, Rutherford, Jobey, Stewart, Higgins, Wilson. April 26; 58,000; JH Pearson

**1912 Barnsley 0** Cooper; Downs, Taylor, Glendinning, Bratley, Utley, Bartrop, Tufnell, Lillycrop, Travers, Moore **WBA 0** Pearson; Cook, Pennington, Baddeley, Buck, McNeal, Jephcott, Wright, Pailor, Bowser, Shearman. April 20; 54,556; JR Shumacher **Replay – Barnsley 1** (Tufnell) Cooper; Downs, Taylor, Glendinning, Bratley, Utley, Bartrop, Harry, Lillycrop, Travers, Jimmy Moore **WBA 0** Pearson; Cook, Pennington, Baddeley, Buck, McNeal, Jephcott, Wright, Pailor, Bowser, Shearman. April 24; 38,555; JR Schumacher. aet

**1913 Aston Villa 1** (Barber) Hardy; Lyons, Weston, Barber, Harrop, Leach, Wallace, Halse, Hampton, Stephenson, Bache **Sunderland 0** Butler; Gladwin, Ness, Cuggy, Thomson, Low, Mordue, Buchan, Richardson, Holley, Martin. April 19; 120,081; A Adams

**1914 Burnley 1** (Freeman) Sewell; Bamford, Taylor, Halley, Boyle, Watson, Nesbit, Lindley, Freeman, Hodgson, Mosscrop **Liverpool 0** Campbell; Longworth, Pursell, Fairfoul, Ferguson, McKinley, Sheldon, Metcalfe, Miller, Lacey, Nicholl. April 25; 72,778; HS Bamlett

**1915 Sheffield Utd 3** (Simmons, Fazackerly, Kitchen) Gough; Cook, English, Sturgess, Brelsford, Utley, Simmons, Fazackerly, Kitchen, Masterman, Evans **Chelsea 0** Molyneux; Bettridge, Harrow, Taylor, Logan, Walker, Ford, Halse, Thomson, Croal, McNeil. April 24; 49,557; HH Taylor

**1920 Aston Villa 1** (Kirton) Hardy; Smart, Weston, Ducat, Barson, Moss, Wallace, Kirton, Walker, Stephenson, Dorrell **Huddersfield 0** Mutch; Wood, Bullock, Slade, Wilson, Watson, Richardson, Mann, Taylor, Swann, Islip. April 24; 50,018; JT Howcroft. aet

**1921 Tottenham 1** (Dimmock) Hunter; Clay, McDonald, Smith, Walters, Grimsdell, Banks, Seed, Cantrell, Bliss, Dimmock **Wolves 0** George; Woodward, Marshall, Gregory, Hodnett, Riley, Lea, Burrill, Edmonds, Potts, Brooks. April 23; 72,805; S Davies

**1922 Huddersfield 1** (Smith pen) Mutch; Wood, Wadsworth, Slade, Wilson, Watson, Richardson, Mann, Islip, Stephenson, Billy Smith **Preston 0** Mitchell; Hamilton, Doolan, Duxbury, McCall, Williamson, Rawlings, Jefferis, Roberts, Woodhouse, Quinn. April 29; 53,000; JWP Fowler

**1923 Bolton 2** (Jack, JR Smith) Pym; Haworth, Finney, Nuttall, Seddon, Jennings, Butler, Jack, JR Smith, Joe Smith, Vizard **West Ham 0** Hufton; Henderson, Young, Bishop, Kay, Tresadern, Richards, Brown, Watson, Moore, Ruffell. April 28; 126,047; DH Asson

**1924 Newcastle 2** (Harris, Seymour) Bradley; Hampson, Hudspeth, Mooney, Spencer, Gibson, Low, Cowan, Harris, McDonald, Seymour **Aston Villa 0** Jackson; Smart, Mort, Moss, Milne, Blackburn, York, Kirton, Capewell, Walker, Dorrell. April 26; 91,695; WE Russell

**1925 Sheffield Utd 1** (Tunstall) Sutcliffe; Cook, Milton, Pantling, King, Green, Mercer, Boyle, Johnson, Gillespie, Tunstall **Cardiff 0** Farquharson; Nelson, Blair, Wake, Keenor, Hardy, Davies, Gill, Nicholson, Beadles, Evans. April 25; 91,763; GN Watson

**1926 Bolton 1** (Jack) Pym; Haworth, Greenhalgh, Nuttall, Seddon, Jennings, Butler, JR Smith, Jack, Joe Smith, Vizard **Manchester City 0** Goodchild; Cookson, McCloy, Pringle, Cowan, McMullan, Austin, Browell, Roberts, Johnson, Hicks. April 24; 91,447; I Baker

**1927 Cardiff 1** (Ferguson) Farquharson; Nelson, Watson, Keenor, Sloan, Hardy, Curtis, Irving, Ferguson, Davies, McLachlan **Arsenal 0** Lewis; Parker, Kennedy, Baker, Butler, John, Hulme, Buchan, Brain, Blythe, Hoar. April 23; 91,206; WF Bunnell

**1928 Blackburn 3** (Roscamp 2, McLean) Crawford; Hutton, Jones, Healless, Rankin, Campbell, Thornewell, Puddefoot, Roscamp, McLean, Rigby **Huddersfield 1** (Jackson) Mercer; Goodall, Barkas, Redfern, Wilson, Steele, Jackson, Kelly, Brown, Stephenson, Smith. April 21; 92,041; TG Bryan

**1929 Bolton 2** (Butler, Blackmore) Pym; Haworth, Finney, Kean, Seddon, Nuttall, Butler, McClelland, Blackmore, Gibson, Cook **Portsmouth 0** Gilfillan; Mackie, Bell, Nichol, McIlwaine, Thackeray, Forward, Smith, Weddle, Watson, Cook. April 27; 92,576; A Josephs

**1930 Arsenal 2** (James, Lambert) Preedy; Parker, Hapgood, Baker, Seddon, John, Hulme, Jack, Lambert, James, Bastin **Huddersfield 0** Turner; Goodall, Spence, Naylor, Wilson, Campbell, Jackson, Kelly, Davies, Raw, Smith. April 26; 92,488; T Crew

**1931 WBA 2** (WG Richardson 2) Pearson; Shaw, Trentham, Magee, Bill Richardson, Edwards, Glidden, Carter, WG Richardson, Sandford, Wood **Birmingham 1** (Bradford) Hibbs; Liddell, Barkas, Cringan, Morrall, Leslie, Briggs, Crosbie, Bradford, Gregg, Curtis. April 25; 92,406; AH Kingscott

**1932 Newcastle 2** (Allen 2) McInroy; Nelson, Fairhurst, McKenzie, Davidson, Weaver, Boyd, Richardson, Allen, McMenemy, Lang **Arsenal 1** (John) Moss; Parker, Hapgood, Jones, Roberts, Male, Hulme, Jack, Lambert, Bastin, John. April 23; 92,298; WP Harper

**1933** **Everton 3** (Stein, Dean, Dunn) Sagar; Cook, Cresswell, Britton, White, Thomson, Geldard, Dunn, Dean, Johnson, Stein **Manchester City 0** Langford; Cann, Dale, Busby, Cowan, Bray, Toseland, Marshall, Herd, McMullan, Eric Brook. April 29; 92,950; E Wood

**1934** **Manchester City 2** (Tilson 2) Swift; Barnett, Dale, Busby, Cowan, Bray, Toseland, Marshall, Tilson, Herd, Brook **Portsmouth 1** (Rutherford) Gilfillan; Mackie, Smith, Nichol, Allen, Thackeray, Worrall, Smith, Weddle, Easson, Rutherford. April 28; 93,258; Stanley Rous

**1935** **Sheffield Wed 4** (Rimmer 2, Palethorpe, Hooper) Brown; Nibloe, Catlin, Sharp, Millership, Burrows, Hooper, Surtees, Palethorpe, Starling, Rimmer **WBA 2** (Boyes, Sandford) Pearson; Shaw, Trentham, Murphy, Bill Richardson, Edwards, Glidden, Carter, WG Richardson, Sandford, Wally. April 27; 93,204; AE Fogg

**1936** **Arsenal 1** (Drake) Wilson; Male, Hapgood, Crayston, Roberts, Copping, Hulme, Bowden, Drake, James, Bastin **Sheffield Utd 0** Smith; Hooper, Wilkinson, Jackson, Johnson, McPherson, Barton, Barclay, Dodds, Pickering, Williams. April 25; 93,384; H Nattrass

**1937** **Sunderland 3** (Gurney, Carter, Burbanks) Mapson; Gorman, Hall, Thomson, Johnston, McNab, Duns, Carter, Gurney, Gallacher, Burbanks **Preston 1** (Frank O'Donnell) Burns; Gallimore, Beattie, Shankly, Tremelling, Milne, Dougal, Beresford, O'Donnell, Fagan, O'Donnell. May 1; 93,495; RG Rudd

**1938** **Preston 1** (Mutch pen) Holdcroft; Gallimore, Beattie, Shankly, Smith, Batey, Watmough, Mutch, Maxwell, Beattie, O'Donnell **Huddersfield 0** Hesford; Craig, Mountford, Willingham, Young, Boot, Hulme, Issac, MacFadyen, Barclay, Beasley. April 30; 93,497; AJ Jewell. aet

**1939** **Portsmouth 4** (Parker 2, Barlow, Anderson) Walker; Morgan, Rochford, Guthrie, Rowe, Wharton, Worrall, McAlinden, Anderson, Barlow, Parker **Wolves 1** (Dorsett) Scott; Morris, Taylor, Galley, Cullis, Gardiner, Burton, McIntosh, Westcott, Dorsett, Maguire. April 29; 99,370; T Thompson

**1946** **Derby 4** (Stamps 2. Doherty, B Turner og) Woodley; Nicholas, Howe, Bullions, Leuty, Musson, Harrison, Carter, Stamps, Doherty, Duncan **Charlton Athletic 1** (B Turner) Bartram; Phipps, Shreeve, Turner, Oakes, Johnson, Fell, Brown, Turner, Welsh, Duffy. April 27; 98,000; ED Smith. aet

**1947** **Charlton Athletic 1** (Duffy) Bartram; Croker, Shreeve, Johnson, Phipps, Whittaker, Hurst, Dawson, Robinson, Welsh, Duffy **Burnley 0** Strong; Woodruff, Mather, Attwell, Brown, Bray, Chew, Morris, Harrison, Potts, Kippax. April 26; 99,000; JM Wiltshire. aet

**1948** **Manchester Utd 4** (Rowley 2, Pearson, Anderson) Crompton; Carey, Aston, Anderson, Chilton, Cockburn, Delaney, Morris, Rowley, Pearson, Mitten **Blackpool 2** (Shimwell pen, Mortensen) Robinson; Shimwell, Crosland, Johnston, Hayward, Kelly, Matthews, Munro, Mortensen, Dick, Rickett. April 24; 99,000; CJ Barrick

**1949** **Wolves 3** (Pye 2, Smyth) Williams; Pritchard, Springthorpe Crook, Shorthouse, Wright, Hancocks, Smyth, Pye, Dunn, Mullen **Leicester 1** (Griffiths) Bradley; Jelly, Scott, Harrison, Plummer, King, Griffiths, Lee, Harrison, Chisholm, Adam. April 30; 99,500; RA Mortimer

**1950** **Arsenal 2** (Lewis 2) Swindin; Scott, Barnes, Forbes, L Compton, Mercer, Cox, Logie, Goring, Lewis, D Compton **Liverpool 0** Sidlow; Lambert, Spicer, Taylor, Hughes, Jones, Payne, Baron, Stubbins, Fagan, Liddell. April 29; 100,000; H Pearce

**1951** **Newcastle 2** (Milburn 2) Fairbrother; Cowell, Corbett, Harvey, Brennan, Crowe, Walker, Taylor, Milburn, Jorge Robledo, Mitchell **Blackpool 0** Farm; Shimwell, Garrett, Johnston, Hayward, Kelly, Matthews, Mudie, Mortensen, Slater, Perry. April 28; 100,000; W Ling

**1952** **Newcastle 1** (G Robledo) Simpson; Cowell, McMichael, Harvey, Brennan, Eduardo Robledo, Walker, Foulkes, Milburn, Jorge Robledo, Mitchell **Arsenal 0** Swindin; Barnes, Smith, Forbes, Daniel Mercer, Cox, Logie, Holton, Lishman, Roper. May 3; 100,000; A Ellis

**1953** **Blackpool 4** (Mortensen 3, Perry) Farm; Shimwell, Garrett, Fenton, Johnston, Robinson, Matthews, Taylor, Mortensen, Mudie, Perry **Bolton 3** (Lofthouse, Moir, Bell) Hanson; Ball, Banks, Wheeler, Barrass, Bell, Holden, Moir, Lofthouse, Hassall, Langton. May 2; 100,000; M Griffiths

**1954** **WBA 3** (Allen 2 [1pen], Griffin) Sanders; Kennedy, Millard, Dudley, Dugdale, Barlow, Griffin, Ryan, Allen, Nicholls, Lee **Preston 2** (Morrison, Wayman) Thompson; Cunningham, Walton, Docherty, Marston, Forbes, Finney, Foster, Wayman, Baxter, Morrison. May 1; 100,000; A Luty

**1955** **Newcastle 3** (Milburn, Mitchell, Hannah) Simpson; Cowell, Batty, Scoular, Stokoe, Casey, White, Milburn, Keeble, Hannah, Mitchell **Manchester City 1** (Johnstone) Trautmann; Meadows, Little, Barnes, Ewing, Paul, Spurdle, Hayes, Revie, Johnstone, Fagan. May 7; 100,000; R Leafe

**1956** **Manchester City 3** (Hayes, Dyson, Johnstone) Trautmann; Leivers, Little, Barnes, Ewing, Paul, Johnstone, Hayes, Revie, Dyson, Clarke **Birmingham 1** (Kinsey) Merrick; Hall, Green, Newman, Smith, Boyd, Astall, Kinsey, Brown, Murphy, Govan. May 5; 100,000; A Bond

**1957** **Aston Villa 2** (McParland 2) Sims; Lynn, Aldis, Crowther, Dugdale, Saward, Smith, Sewell, Myerscough, Dixon, McParland **Manchester Utd 1** (Taylor) Wood; Foulkes, Byrne, Colman, Blanchflower, Edwards, Berry, Whelan, Taylor, Charlton, Pegg. May 4; 100,000; F Coultas

**1958** **Bolton 2** (Lofthouse 2) Hopkinson; Hartle, Banks, Hennin, Higgins, Edwards, Birch, Stevens, Lofthouse, Parry, Holden **Manchester Utd 0** Gregg; Foulkes, Greaves, Goodwin, Cope, Crowther, Dawson, Taylor, Charlton, Viollet, Webster. May 3; 100,000; J Sherlock

**1959** **Nottingham Forest 2** (Dwight, Wilson) Thomson; Whare, McDonald, Whitefoot, McKinlay, Burkitt, Dwight, Quigley, Wilson, Gray, Imlach **Luton Town 1** (Pacey) Baynham; McNally, Hawkes, Groves, Owen, Pacey, Bingham, Brown, Morton, Cummins, Gregory. May 2; 100,000; J Clough

**1960** **Wolves 3** (McGrath og, Deeley 2) Finlayson; Showell, Harris, Clamp, Slater, Flowers, Deeley, Stobart, Murray, Broadbent, Horne **Blackburn 0** Leyland; Bray, Whelan, Clayton, Woods, McGrath, Bimpson, Dobing, Dougan, Douglas, McLeod. May 7; 100,000; K Howley

**1961** **Tottenham 2** (Smith, Dyson) Brown; Baker, Henry, Blanchflower, Norman, Mackay, Jones, White, Smith, Allen, Dyson **Leicester 0** Banks; Chalmers, Norman, McLintock, King, Appleton, Riley, Walsh, McIlmoyle, Keyworth, Cheesebrough. May 6; 100,000; J Kelly

**1962** **Tottenham 3** (Greaves, Smith, Blanchflower pen) Brown; Baker, Henry, Blanchflower, Norman, Mackay, Medwin, White, Smith, Greaves, Jones **Burnley 1** (Robson) Blacklaw; Angus, Elder, Adamson, Cummings, Miller, Connelly, McIlroy, Pointer, Robson, Harris. May 5; 100,000; J Finney

**1963** **Manchester Utd 3** (Law, Herd 2) Gaskell; Dunne, Cantwell, Crerand, Foulkes, Setters, Giles, Quixall, Herd, Law, Charlton **Leicester 1** (Keyworth) Banks; Sjoberg, Norman, McLintock, King, Appleton, Riley, Cross, Keyworth, Gibson, Stringfellow. May 25; 100,000; K Aston

**1964** **West Ham 3** (Sissons, Hurst, Boyce) Standen; Bond, Burkett, Bovington, Brown, Moore, Brabrook, Boyce, Byrne, Hurst, Sissons **Preston 2** (Holden, Dawson) Kelly; Ross, Lawton, Smith, Singleton, Kendall, Wilson, Ashworth, Dawson, Spavin, Holden. May 2; 100,000; A Holland

**1965** **Liverpool 2** (Hunt, St John) Lawrence; Lawler, Byrne, Strong, Yeats, Stevenson, Callaghan, Hunt, St John, Smith, Thompson **Leeds 1** (Bremner) Sprake; Reaney, Bell, Bremner, Charlton, Hunter, Giles, Storrie, Peacock, Collins, Johanneson. May 1; 100,000; W Clements. aet

**1966** **Everton 3** (Trebilcock 2, Temple) West; Wright, Wilson, Gabriel, Labone, Harris, Scott, Trebilcock, Young, Harvey, Temple **Sheffield Wed 2** (McCalliog, Ford) Springett; Smith, Megson, Eustace, Ellis, Young, Pugh, Fantham, McCalliog, Ford, Quinn. May 14; 100,000; JK Taylor

**1967** **Tottenham 2** (Robertson, Saul) Jennings; Kinnear, Knowles, Mullery, England, Mackay, Robertson, Greaves, Gilzean, Venables, Saul. Unused sub: Jones **Chelsea 1** (Tambling) Bonetti; Allan Harris, McCreadie, Hollins, Hinton, Ron Harris, Cooke, Baldwin, Hateley, Tambling, Boyle. Unused sub: Kirkup. May 20; 100,000; K Dagnall

**1968** **WBA 1** (Astle) John Osborne; Fraser, Williams, Brown, Talbut, Kaye, Lovett, Collard, Astle Hope, Clark Sub: Clarke rep Kaye 91 **Everton 0** West; Wright, Wilson, Kendall, Labone, Harvey, Husband, Ball, Royle, Hurst, Morrissey. Unused sub: Kenyon. May 18; 100,000; L Callaghan. aet

**1969** **Manchester City 1** (Young) Dowd: Book, Pardoe, Doyle, Booth, Oakes, Summerbee, Bell, Lee, Young, Coleman. Unused sub: Connor **Leicester 0** Shilton; Rodrigues, Nish, Roberts, Woollett, Cross, Fern, Gibson, Lochhead, Clarke, Glover. Sub: Manley rep Glover 70. April 26; 100,000; G McCabe

**1970** **Chelsea 2** (Houseman, Hutchinson) Bonetti; Webb, McCreadie, Hollins, Dempsey, R Harris, Baldwin, Houseman, Osgood, Hutchinson, Cooke. Sub: Hinton rep Harris 91 **Leeds 2** (Charlton, Jones) Sprake; Madeley, Cooper, Bremner, Charlton, Hunter, Lorimer, Clarke, Jones, Giles, Gray Unusued sub: Bates. April 11; 100,000; E Jennings. aet **Replay – Chelsea 2** (Osgood, Webb) Bonetti, Webb,

McCreadie, Hollins, Dempsey, R Harris, Baldwin, Houseman, Osgood, Hutchinson, Cooke. Sub: Hinton rep Osgood 105 **Leeds 1** (Jones) Harvey; Madeley, Cooper, Bremner, Charlton, Hunter, Lorimer, Clarke, Jones, Giles, Gray Unusued sub: Bates. April 29; 62,078; E Jennings. aet

**1971** **Arsenal 2** (Kelly, George) Wilson; Rice, McNab, Storey, McLintock Simpson, Armstrong, Graham, Radford, Kennedy, George. Sub: Kelly rep Storey 70 **Liverpool 1** (Heighway) Clemence; Lawler, Lindsay, Smith, Lloyd, Hughes, Callaghan, Evans, Heighway, Toshack, Hall. Sub: Thompson rep Evans 70. May 8; 100,000; N Burtenshaw. aet

**1972** **Leeds 1** (Clarke) Harvey; Reaney, Madeley, Bremner, Charlton, Hunter, Lorimer, Clarke, Jones, Giles, Gray. Unused sub: Bates **Arsenal 0** Barnett; Rice, McNab, Storey, McLintock, Simpson, Armstrong, Ball, George, Radford, Graham. Sub: Kennedy rep Radford 80. May 6; 100,000; DW Smith

**1973** **Sunderland 1** (Porterfield) Montgomery; Malone, Guthrie, Horswill, Watson, Pitt, Kerr, Hughes, Halom, Porterfield, Tueart. Unused sub: Young **Leeds 0** Harvey; Reaney, Cherry, Bremner, Madeley, Hunter, Lorimer, Clarke, Jones, Giles, Gray. Sub: Yorath rep Gray 75. May 5; 100,000; K Burns

**1974** **Liverpool 3** (Keegan 2, Heighway) Clemence; Smith, Lindsay, Thompson, Cormack, Hughes, Keegan, Hall, Heighway, Toshack, Callaghan. Unused sub: Lawler **Newcastle 0** McFaul; Clark, Kennedy, McDermott, Howard, Moncur, Smith, Cassidy, Macdonald, Tudor, Hibbitt. Sub: Gibb rep Smith 70. May 4; 100,000; GC Kew

**1975** **West Ham 2** (Taylor 2) Day; McDowell, Taylor, Lock, Lampard, Bonds, Paddon, Brooking, Jennings, Taylor, Holland. Unused sub: Gould **Fulham 0** Mellor; Cutbush, Lacy, Moore, Fraser, Mullery, Conway, Slough, Mitchell, Busby, Barrett. Unused sub: Lloyd. May 3; 100,000; P Partridge

**1976** **Southampton 1** (Stokes) Turner; Rodrigues, Peach, Holmes, Blyth, Steele, Gilchrist, Channon, Osgood, McCalliog, Stokes. Unused sub: Fisher **Manchester Utd 0** Stepney; Forsyth, Houston, Daly, Greenhoff, Buchan, Coppell, McIlroy, Pearson, Macari, Hill. Sub: McCreery rep Hill 66. May 1; 100,000; C Thomas

**1977** **Manchester Utd 2** (Pearson, J Greenhoff) Stepney; Nicholl, Albiston, McIlroy, B Greenhoff, Buchan, Coppell, J Greenhoff, Pearson, Macari, Hill. Sub: McCreery rep Hill 81 **Liverpool 1** (Case) Clemence; Neal, Jones, Smith, Kennedy, Hughes, Keegan, Case, Heighway, Johnson, McDermott. Sub: Callaghan rep Johnson 64. May 21; 100,000; R Matthewson

**1978** **Ipswich Town 1** (Osborne) Cooper; Burley, Mills, Talbot, Hunter, Beattie, Osborne, Wark, Mariner, Geddis, Woods. Sub: Lambert rep Osborne 79 **Arsenal 0** Jennings; Rice, Nelson, Price, Young, O'Leary, Brady, Hudson, Macdonald, Stapleton, Sunderland. Sub: Rix rep Brady 65. May 6; 100,000; D Nippard

**1979** **Arsenal 3** (Talbot, Stapleton, Sunderland) Jennings; Rice, Nelson, Talbot, O'Leary, Young, Brady, Sunderland, Stapleton, Price, Rix. Sub: Walford rep Rix 83 **Manchester Utd 2** (McQueen, McIlroy) Bailey; Nicholl, Albiston, McIlroy, McQueen, Buchan, Coppell, J Greenhoff, Jordan, Macari, Thomas. Unused sub: Greenhoff. May 12; 100,000; R Challis

**1980** **West Ham 1** (Brooking) Parkes; Stewart, Lampard, Bonds, Martin, Devonshire, Allen, Pearson, Cross, Brooking, Pike. Unused sub: Brush **Arsenal 0** Jennings; Rice, Devine, Talbot, O'Leary, Young, Brady, Sunderland, Stapleton, Price, Rix. Sub: Nelson rep Devine 61. May 10; 100,000; G Courtney

**1981** **Tottenham 1** (Hutchinson og) Aleksic; Hughton, Miller, Roberts, Perryman, Villa, Ardiles, Archibald, Galvin, Hoddle, Crooks. Sub: Brooke rep Villa 68. **Manchester City 1** (Hutchinson) Corrigan; Ranson, McDonald, Reid, Power, Caton, Bennett, Gow, Mackenzie, Hutchison Reeves. Sub: Henry rep Hutchison 82. May 9; 100,000; K Hackett. aet **Replay – Tottenham 3** (Villa 2, Crooks) Aleksic; Hughton, Miller, Roberts, Perryman, Villa, Ardiles, Archibald, Galvin, Hoddle, Crooks. Unused sub: Brooke **Manchester City 2** (Mackenzie, Reeves pen) Corrigan; Ranson, McDonald, Reid, Power, Caton, Bennett, Gow, Mackenzie, Hutchison Reeves. Sub: Tueart rep McDonald 79. May 14; 92,000; K Hackett

**1982** **Tottenham 1** (Hoddle) Clemence; Hughton, Miller, Price, Hazard, Perryman, Roberts, Archibald, Galvin, Hoddle, Crooks. Sub: Brooke rep Hazard 104 **Queens Park Rangers 1** (Fenwick) Hucker; Fenwick, Gillard, Waddock, Hazell, Roeder, Currie, Flanagan, Allen, Stainrod, Gregory. Sub: Micklewhite rep Allen 50. May 22; 100,000; C White. aet **Replay – Tottenham 1** (Hoddle pen) Clemence; Hughton, Miller, Price, Hazard, Perryman, Roberts, Archibald, Galvin, Hoddle, Crooks. Sub: Brooke rep Hazard 67 **Queens Park Rangers 0** Hucker; Fenwick, Gillard, Waddock, Hazell, Neill, Currie, Flanagan, Micklewhite, Stainrod, Gregory. Sub: Burke rep Micklewhite 84. May 27; 90,000; C White

**1983** **Manchester Utd 2** (Stapleton, Wilkins) Bailey; Duxbury, Moran, McQueen, Albiston, Davies, Wilkins, Robson, Muhren, Stapleton, Whiteside. Unused sub: Grimes **Brighton 2** (Smith, Stevens) Moseley; Ramsey, Gary A Stevens, Pearce, Gatting, Smillie, Case, Grealish, Howlett, Robinson, Smith. Sub: Ryan rep Ramsey 56. May 21; 100,000; AW Grey, aet **Replay – Manchester Utd 4** (Robson 2, Whiteside, Muhren pen) Bailey; Duxbury, Moran, McQueen, Albiston, Davies, Wilkins, Robson, Muhren, Stapleton, Whiteside. Unused sub: Grimes **Brighton 0** Moseley; Gary A Stevens, Pearce, Foster, Gatting, Smillie, Case, Grealish, Howlett, Robinson, Smith. Sub: Ryan rep Howlett 74. May 26; 100,000; AW Grey

**1984** **Everton 2** (Sharp, Gray) Southall; Gary M Stevens, Bailey, Ratcliffe, Mountfield, Reid, Steven, Heath, Sharp, Gray, Richardson. Unused sub: Harper **Watford 0** Sherwood; Bardsley, Price, Taylor, Terry, Sinnott, Callaghan, Johnston, Reilly, Jackett, Barnes. Sub: Atkinson rep Price 58. May 19; 100,000; J Hunting

**1985** **Manchester Utd 1** (Whiteside) Bailey; Gidman, Albiston, Whiteside, McGrath, Moran, Robson, Strachan, Hughes, Stapleton, Olsen. Sub: Duxbury rep Albiston 91. Moran sent off 77. **Everton 0** Southall; Gary M Stevens, Van den Hauwe, Ratcliffe, Mountfield, Reid, Steven, Sharp, Gray, Bracewell, Sheedy. Unused sub: Harper. May 18; 100,000; P Willis. aet

**1986** **Liverpool 3** (Rush 2, Johnston) Grobbelaar; Lawrenson, Beglin, Nicol, Whelan, Hansen, Dalglish, Johnston, Rush, Molby, MacDonald. Unused sub: McMahon **Everton 1** (Lineker) Mimms; Gary M Stevens, Van den Hauwe, Ratcliffe, Mountfield, Reid, Steven, Lineker, Sharp, Bracewell, Sheedy. Sub: Heath rep Stevens 65. May 10; 98,000; A Robinson

**1987** **Coventry City 3** (Bennett, Houchen, Mabbutt og) Ogrizovic; Phillips, Downs, McGrath, Kilcline, Peake, Bennett, Gynn, Regis, Houchen, Pickering. Sub: Rodger rep Kilcline 88. Unused sub: Sedgley **Tottenham 2** (Allen, Mabbutt) Clemence; Hughton Thomas, Hodge, Gough, Mabbutt, C Allen, P Allen, Waddle, Hoddle, Ardiles. Subs: Gary A Stevens rep Ardiles 91; Claesen rep Hughton 97. May 16; 98,000; N Midgley. aet

**1988** **Wimbledon 1** (Sanchez) Beasant; Goodyear, Phelan, Jones, Young, Thorn, Gibson Cork, Fashanu, Sanchez, Wise. Subs: Cunningham rep Cork 56; Scales rep Gibson 63 **Liverpool 0** Grobbelaar; Gillespie, Ablett, Nicol, Spackman, Hansen, Beardsley, Aldridge, Houghton, Barnes, McMahon. Subs: Johnston rep Aldridge 63; Molby rep Spackman 72. May 14; 98,203; B Hill

**1989** **Liverpool 3** (Aldridge, Rush 2) Grobbelaar; Ablett, Staunton, Nichol, Whelan, Hansen, Beardsley, Aldridge Houghton, Barnes, McMahon. Subs: Rush rep Aldridge 72; Venison rep Staunton 91 **Everton 2** (McCall 2) Southall; McDonald, Van den Hauwe, Ratcliffe, Watson, Bracewell, Nevin, Trevor Steven, Cottee, Sharp, Sheedy. Subs: McCall rep Bracewell 58; Wilson rep Sheedy 77. May 20; 82,500; J Worrall. aet

**1990** **Manchester Utd 3** (Robson, Hughes 2) Leighton; Ince, Martin, Bruce, Phelan, Pallister, Robson, Webb, McClair, Hughes, Wallace. Subs: Blackmore rep Martin 88; Robins rep Pallister 93. **Crystal Palace 3** (O'Reilly, Wright 2) Martyn; Pemberton, Shaw, Gray, O'Reilly, Thorn, Barber, Thomas, Bright, Salako, Pardew. Subs: Wright rep Barber 69; Madden rep Gray 117. May 12; 80,000; A Gunn. aet **Replay – Manchester Utd 1** (Martin) Sealey; Ince, Martin, Bruce, Phelan, Pallister, Robson, Webb, McClair, Hughes, Wallace. Unused subs: Robins, Blackmore **Crystal Palace 0** Martyn; Pemberton, Shaw, Gray, O'Reilly, Thorn, Barber, Thomas, Bright, Salako, Pardew. Subs: Wright rep Barber 64; Madden rep Salako 79. May 17; 80,000; A Gunn

**1991** **Tottenham 2** (Stewart, Walker og) Thorstvedt; Edinburgh, Van den Hauwe, Sedgley, Howells, Mabbutt, Stewart, Gascoigne, Samways, Lineker, Allen. Subs: Nayim rep Gascoigne 18; Walsh rep Samways 82. **Nottingham Forest 1** (Pearce) Crossley; Charles, Pearce, Walker, Chettle, Keane, Crosby, Parker, Clough, Glover, Woan. Subs: Hodge rep Woan 62; Laws rep Glover 108. May 18; 80,000; R Milford. aet

**1992** **Liverpool 2** (Thomas, Rush) Grobbelaar; Jones, Burrows, Nicol, Molby, Wright, Saunders, Houghton, Rush, McManaman, Thomas. Unused subs: Marsh, Walters **Sunderland 0** Norman; Owers, Ball, Bennett, Rogan, Rush, Bracewell, Davenport, Armstrong, Byrne, Atkinson. Subs: Hardyman rep Rush 69; Hawke rep Armstrong 77. May 9; 80,000; P Don

**1993** **Arsenal 1** (Wright) Seaman; Dixon, Winterburn, Linighan, Adams, Jensen, Davis, Parlour, Merson, Campbell, Wright. Subs: Smith rep Parlour 66; O'Leary rep Wright 90. **Sheffield Wed 1** (Hirst) Woods; Nilsson Worthington, Palmer, Hirst, Anderson, Waddle, Warhurst, Bright, Sheridan, Harkes. Subs: Hyde rep Anderson 85; Bart-Williams rep Waddle 112. May 15; 79,347; K Barratt. aet **Replay – Arsenal**

**2** (Wright, Linighan) Seaman; Dixon, Winterburn, Linighan, Adams, Jensen, Davis, Smith, Merson, Campbell, Wright. Sub: O'Leary rep Wright 81. Unused sub: Selley **Sheffield Wed 1** (Waddle) Woods; Nilsson, Worthington, Palmer, Hirst, Wilson, Waddle, Warhurst, Bright, Sheridan, Harkes. Subs: Hyde rep Wilson 62; Bart-Williams rep Nilsson 118. May 20; 62,267; K Barratt. aet

**1994** **Manchester Utd 4** (Cantona 2 [2pens], Hughes, McClair) Schmeichel; Parker, Bruce, Pallister, Irwin, Kanchelskis, Keane, Ince, Giggs, Cantona, Hughes. Subs: Sharpe rep Irwin 84; McClair rep Kanchelskis 84. Unused sub: Walsh (gk) **Chelsea 0** Kharine; Clarke, Sinclair, Kjeldberg, Johnsen, Burley, Spencer, Newton, Stein, Peacock, Wise Substitutions Hoddle rep Burley 65; Cascarino rep Stein 78. Unused sub: Kevin Hitchcock (gk) May 14; 79,634; D Elleray

**1995** **Everton 1** (Rideout) Southall; Jackson, Hinchcliffe, Ablett, Watson, Parkinson, Unsworth, Horne, Stuart, Rideout, Limpar. Subs: Ferguson rep Rideout 51; Amokachi rep Limpar 69. Unused sub: Kearton (gk) **Manchester Utd 0** Schmeichel; Neville, Irwin, Bruce, Sharpe, Pallister, Keane, Ince, Brian McClair, Hughes, Butt. Subs: Giggs rep Bruce 46; Scholes rep Sharpe 72. Unused sub: Gary Walsh (gk) May 20; 79,592; G Ashby

**1996** **Manchester Utd 1** (Cantona) Schmeichel; Irwin, P Neville, May, Keane, Pallister, Cantona, Beckham, Cole, Butt, Giggs. Subs: Scholes rep Cole 65; G Neville rep Beckham 89. Unused sub: Sharpe **Liverpool 0** James; McAteer, Scales, Wright, Babb, Jones, McManaman, Barnes, Redknapp, Collymore, Fowler. Subs: Rush rep Collymore 74; Thomas rep Jones 85. Unused sub: Warner (gk) May 11; 79,007; D Gallagher

**1997** **Chelsea 2** (Di Matteo, Newton) Grodas; Petrescu, Minto, Sinclair, Lebouef, Clarke, Zola, Di Matteo, Newton, Hughes, Wise. Sub: Vialli rep Zola 89. Unused subs: Hitchcock (gk), Myers **Middlesbrough 0** Roberts; Blackmore, Fleming, Stamp, Pearson, Festa, Emerson, Mustoe, Ravanelli, Juninho, Hignett. Subs: Beck rep Ravanelli 24; Vickers rep Mustoe 29; Kinder, rep Hignett 74. May 17; 79,160; S Lodge

**1998** **Arsenal 2** (Overmars, Anelka) Seaman; Dixon, Winterburn, Vieira, Keown, Adams, Parlour, Anelka, Petit, Wreh, Overmars. Sub: Platt rep Wreh 63. Unused subs: Manninger (gk); Bould, Wright, Grimandi **Newcastle 0** Given; Pistone, Pearce, Batty, Dabizas, Howey, Lee, Barton, Shearer, Ketsbaia, Speed. Subs: Andersson rep Pearce 72; Watson rep Barton 77; Barnes rep Ketsbaia 85. Unused subs: Hislop (gk); Albert. May 16; 79,183; P Durkin

**1999** **Manchester Utd 2** (Sheringham, Scholes) Schmeichel; G Neville, Johnsen, May, P Neville, Beckham, Scholes, Keane, Giggs, Cole, Solskjaer. Subs: Sheringham rep Keane 9; Yorke rep Cole 61; Stam rep Scholes 77. Unused subs: Blomqvist, Van Der Gouw **Newcastle 0** Harper; Griffin, Charvet, Dabizas, Domi, Lee, Hamann, Speed, Solano, Ketsbaia, Shearer. Subs: Ferguson rep Hamann 46; Maric rep Solano 68; Glass rep Ketsbaia 79. Unused subs: Given (gk); Barton. May 22; 79,101; P Jones

**2000** **Chelsea 1** (Di Matteo) de Goey; Melchiot Desailly, Lebouef, Babayaro, Di Matteo, Wise, Deschamps, Poyet, Weah, Zola. Subs: Flo rep Weah 87; Morris rep Zola 90. Unused subs: Cudicini (gk), Terry , Harley **Aston Villa 0** James; Ehiogu, Southgate, Barry, Delaney, Taylor, Boateng, Merson, Wright, Dublin, Carbone. Subs: Stone rep Taylor 79; Joachim rep Carbone 79; Hendrie rep Wright 88. Unused subs: Enckelman (gk); Samuel May 20; 78,217; G Poll

**2001** **Liverpool 2** (Owen 2) Westerveld; Babbel, Henchoz, Hyypia, Carragher, Murphy, Hamann, Gerrard, Smicer, Heskey, Owen. Subs: McAllister rep Hamann 60; Fowler rep Smicer 77; Berger rep Murphy 77. Unused subs: Arphexad (gk); Vignal **Arsenal 1** (Ljungberg) Seaman; Dixon, Keown, Adams, Cole, Ljungberg, Grimandi, Vieira, Pires, Henry, Wiltord Subs: Parlour rep Wiltord 76; Kanu rep Ljungberg 85; Bergkamp rep Dixon 90. Unused subs: Manninger (gk); Lauren. May 12; 72,500; S Dunn

**2002** **Arsenal 2** (Parlour, Ljungberg) Seaman; Lauren, Campbell, Adams, Cole, Parlour, Wiltord, Vieira, Ljungberg, Bergkamp, Henry Subs: Edu rep Bergkamp 72; Kanu rep Henry 81; Keown rep Wiltord 90. Unused subs: Wright (gk); Dixon **Chelsea 0** Cudicini; Melchiot, Desailly, Gallas, Babayaro, Gronkjaer, Lampard, Petit, Le Saux, Floyd Hasselbaink, Gudjohnsen. Subs: Terry rep Babayaro 46; Zola rep Hasselbaink 68; Zenden rep Melchiot 77. Unused subs: de Goey (gk); Jokanovic. May 4; 73,963; M Riley

**2003** **Arsenal 1** (Pires) Seaman; Lauren, Luzhny, Keown, Cole, Ljungberg, Parlour, Gilberto, Pires, Bergkamp, Henry. Sub: Wiltord rep Bergkamp 77. Unused subs: Taylor (gk); Kanu, Toure, van Bronckhorst **Southampton 0** Niemi; Baird, Svensson, Lundekvam, Bridge, Telfer, Svensson, Oakley, Marsden, Beattie, Ormerod. Subs: Jones rep Niemi 66; Fernandes rep Baird 87; Tessem rep Svensson 75. Unused subs: Williams, Higginbotham. May 17; 73,726; G Barber

**2004** **Manchester Utd 3** (Van Nistelrooy [2, 1 pen], Ronaldo) Howard; G Neville, Brown, Silvestre, O'Shea, Fletcher, Keane, Ronaldo, Scholes, Giggs, Van Nistelrooy. Subs: Carroll rep Howard, Butt rep Fletcher, Solskjaer rep Ronaldo 84. Unused subs: P Neville, Djemba-Djemba **Millwall 0** Marshall; Elliott, Lawrence, Ward, Ryan, Wise, Ifill, Cahill, Livermore, Sweeney, Harris. Subs: Cogan rep Ryan, McCammon rep Harris 74 Weston rep Wise 88. Unused subs: Gueret (gk); Dunne. May 22; 71,350; J Winter

**2005** **Arsenal 0** Lehmann; Lauren, Toure, Senderos, Cole, Fabregas, Gilberto, Vieira, Pires, Reyes, Bergkamp Subs: Ljungberg rep Bergkamp 65, Van Persie rep Fabregas 86, Edu rep Pires 105. Unused subs: Almunia (gk); Campbell. Reyes sent off 90. **Manchester Utd 0** Carroll; Brown, Ferdinand, Silvestre, O'Shea, Fletcher, Keane, Scholes, Rooney, Van Nistelrooy, Ronaldo. Subs: Fortune rep O'Shea 77, Giggs rep Fletcher 91. Unused subs: Howard (gk); G Neville, Smith. **Arsenal** (Lauren, Ljungberg, van Persie, Cole, Vieira) beat Manchester Utd (van Nistelrooy, Scholes [missed], Ronaldo, Rooney, Keane) 5-4 on penalties

**2006** **Liverpool 3** (Gerrard 2, Cisse) Reina; Finnan, Carragher, Hyypiä, Riise, Gerrard, Xabi, Sissoko, Kewell, Cisse, Crouch. Subs: Morientes rep Kewell 48, Kromkamp rep Alonso 67, Hamman rep Crouch 71. Unused subs: Dudek (gk); Traoré **West Ham 3** (Ashton, Konchesky, Carragher (og)) Hislop; Scaloni, Ferdinand, Gabbidon, Konchesky, Benayoun, Fletcher, Reo-Coker, Etherington, Ashton, Harewood. Subs: Zamora rep Ashton 71, Dailly rep Fletcher, Sheringham rep Etherington 85. Unused subs: Walker (gk); Collins. **Liverpool** (Hamann, Hyypiä [missed], Gerrard, Riise) beat **West Ham** (Zamora [missed], Sheringham, Konchesky [missed], Ferdinand [missed]) 3-1 on penalties. May 13; 71,140; A Wiley

**2007** **Chelsea 1** (Drogba) Cech, Ferreira, Essien, Terry, Bridge, Mikel, Makelele, Lampard, Wright-Phillips, Drogba, J Cole Subs: Robben rep J Cole 45, Kalou rep Wright-Phillips 93, A Cole rep Robben 108. Unused subs: Cudicini (gk); Diarra. **Manchester Utd 0** Van der Sar, Brown, Ferdinand, Vidic, Heinze, Fletcher, Scholes, Carrick, Ronaldo, Rooney, Giggs Subs: Smith rep Fletcher 92, O'Shea rep Carrick, Solskjaer rep Giggs 112. Unused subs: Kuszczak (gk); Evra. May 19; 89,826; S Bennett

**2008 Portsmouth 1** (Kanu) James; Johnson, Campbell, Distin, Hreidarsson, Utaka, Muntari, Mendes, Diarra, Kranjcar, Kanu. Subs: Nugent rep Utaka 69, Diop rep Mendes 78, Baros rep Kanu 87. Unused subs: Ashdown (gk); Pamarot. **Cardiff 0** Enckelman; McNaughton, Johnson, Loovens, Capaldi, Whittingham, Rae, McPhail, Ledley, Hasselbaink, Parry. Subs: Ramsey rep Whittingham 62, Thompson rep Hasselbaink 70, Sinclair rep Rae 87. Unused subs: Oakes (gk); Purse. May 17; 89,874; M Dean

**2009 Chelsea 2** (Drogba, Lampard), Cech; Bosingwa, Alex, Terry, A Cole, Essien, Mikel, Lampard, Drogba, Anelka, Malouda. Subs: Ballack rep Essien 61. Unused subs: Hilario (gk), Ivanovic, Di Santo, Kalou, Belletti, Mancienne. **Everton** 1 (Saha) Howard; Hibbert, Yobo, Lescott, Baines, Osman, Neville, Cahill, Pienaar, Fellaini, Saha. Subs: Jacobsen rep Hibbert 46, Vaughan rep Saha 77, Gosling rep Osman 83. Unused subs: Nash, Castillo, Rodwell, Baxter. May 30; 89,391; H Webb

**2010 Chelsea 1** (Drogba) Cech; Ivanovic, Alex, Terry, A Cole, Lampard, Ballack, Malouda, Kalou, Drogba, Anelka. Subs: Belletti rep Ballack 44, J Cole rep Kalou 71, Sturridge rep Anelka 90. Unused subs: Hilario (gk), Zhirkov, Paulo Ferreira, Matic. **Portsmouth 0** James; Finnan, Mokoena, Rocha, Mullins, Dindane, Brown, Diop, Boateng, O'Hara, Piquionne. Subs: Utaka rep Boateng 73, Belhadj rep Mullins 81, Kanu rep Diop 81. Unused subs: Ashdown (gk), Vanden Borre, Hughes, Ben Haim. May 15; 88,335; C Foy

**2011 Manchester City 1** (Y Toure) Hart; Richards, Kompany, Lescott, Kolarov, De Jong, Barry, Silva, Y Toure, Balotelli, Tevez. Subs: Johnson rep Barry73, Zabaleta rep Tevez 87, Vieira rep Silva 90. Unused subs: Given (gk), Boyata, Milner, Dzeko. **Stoke 0** Sorensen; Wilkinson, Shawcross, Huth, Wilson, Pennant, Whelan, Delap, Etherington, Walters, Jones. Subs: Whitehead rep Etherington 62, Carew rep Delap 80, Pugh rep Whelan 84. Unused subs: Nash (gk), Collins, Faye, Diao. May 14; 88,643; M Atkinson

**2012 Chelsea 2** (Ramires, Drogba) Cech; Bosingwa, Ivanovic, Terry, Cole, Mikel, Lampard, Ramires, Mata, Kalou, Drogba. Subs: Meireles rep Ramires76, Malouda rep Mata 90. Unused subs: Turnbull (gk), Paulo Ferreira, Essien, Torres, Sturridge. **Liverpool 1** (Carroll) Reina; Johnson, Skrtel, Agger, Luis Enrique, Spearing, Bellamy, Henderson, Gerrard, Downing, Suarez. Subs Carroll rep Spearing 55, Kuyt rep Bellamy 78. Unused subs: Doni (gk), Carragher, Kelly, Shelvey, Rodriguez. May 5; 89,102; P Dowd

**2013 Wigan 1** (Watson) Robles; Boyce, Alcaraz, Scharner, McCarthy, McArthur, McManaman, Maloney, Gomez, Espinoza, Kone. Subs: Watson rep Gomez 81. Unused subs: Al Habsi (gk), Caldwell, Golobart, Fyvie, Henriquez, Di Santo. **Manchester City 0** Hart, Zabaleta, Kompany, Nastasic, Clichy, Toure, Barry, Silva, Tevez, Nasri, Aguero. Subs: Milner rep Nasri 54, Rodwell rep Tevez 69, Dzeko rep Barry 90. Unused subs: Pantilimon (gk), Lescott, Kolarov, Garcia. Sent off Zabaleta (84). May 11; 86,254; A Marriner

**2014 Arsenal 3** (Cazorla, Koscielny, Ramsey) Fabianski; Sagna, Koscielny, Mertesacker, Gibbs, Arteta, Ramsey, Cazorla, Ozil, Podolski, Giroud. Subs: Sanogo rep Podolski 61, Rosicky rep Cazorla 106, Wilshire rep Ozil 106. Unused subs: Szczesny (gk), Vermaelen, Monreal, Flamini. **Hull** 2 (Chester, Davies) McGregor; Davies, Bruce, Chester, Elmohamady, Livermore, Huddlestone, Meyler, Rosenior, Quinn, Fryatt. Subs: McShane rep Bruce 67, Aluko rep Quinn 71, Boyd rep Rosenior 102. Unused subs: Harper (gk), Figueroa, Koren, Sagbo. May 17; 89,345; L Probert. aet

**2015 Arsenal** 4 (Walcott, Sanchez, Mertesacker, Giroud) Szczesny; Bellerin, Koscielny, Mertesacker, Monreal, Coquelin, Cazorla, Ramsey, Ozil, A Sanchez, Walcott. Subs: Wilshere rep Ozil 77, Giroud rep Walcott 77, Oxlade-Chamberlain rep A Sanchez 90. Unused subs: Ospina (gk), Gibbs, Gabriel, Flamini. **Aston Villa** 0 Given; Hutton, Okore, Vlaar, Richardson, Cleverley, Westwood, Delph, N'Zogbia, Benteke, Grealish. Subs: Agbonlahor rep N'Zogbia 53, Bacuna rep Richardson 68, C Sanchez rep Westwood 71. Unused subs: Guzan (gk), Baker, Sinclair, Cole. May 30; 89,283; J Moss

**2016 Manchester Utd** 2 (Mata, Lingard) De Gea, Valencia, Smalling, Blind, Rojo, Carrick, Rooney, Fellaini, Mata, Martial, Rashford. Subs: Darmian rep Rojo 65, Young rep Rashford 71, Lingard rep Mata 90. Unused subs: Romero, Jones, Herrera, Schneiderlin. **Crystal Palace** 1 (Puncheon 78) Hennessey, Ward, Dann, Delaney, Souare, Cabaye, Jedinak, Zaha, McArthur, Bolasie, Wickham. Unused subs: Speroni, Adebayor, Sako, Kelly. May 21; 88,619; M Clattenburg

**2017 Arsenal** 2 (Sanchez, Ramsey) Ospina, Holding, Mertesacker, Monreal, Bellerin, Ramsey, Xhaka, Oxlade-Chamberlain, Sanchez, Ozil, Welbeck. Subs: Giroud rep Welbeck78, Coquelin rep Oxlade-Chamberlain 83, Elneny rep Sanchez 90. Unused subs: Cech (gk), Walcott, Iwobi, Lucas Perez. **Chelsea** 0 Courtois, Azpilicueta, Luiz, Cahill, Moses, Kante, Matic, Alonso, Pedro, Diego Costa, Hazard. Subs Fabregas rep Matic 62, Willian rep Pedro 72, Batshuayi rep Diego Costa 88. Unused subs: Begovic (gk), Terry, Zouma, Ake. May 27; 89,472; A Taylor

## VENUES

**Kennington Oval** 1872; **Lillie Bridge** 1873; **Kennington Oval** 1874 – 1892 (1886 replay at the **Racecourse Ground, Derby**); **Fallowfield**, Manchester, 1893; **Goodison Park** 1894; **Crystal Palace** 1895 – 1915 (1901 replay at **Burnden Park**; 1910 replay at **Goodison Park**; 1912 replay at **Bramall Lane**); **Old Trafford** 1915; **Stamford Bridge** 1920 – 1922; **Wembley** 1923 – 2000 (1970 replay at **Old Trafford**; all replays after 1981 at **Wembley**); **Millennium Stadium** 2001 – 2006; **Wembley** 2007 – 2018

## SUMMARY OF FA CUP WINS

| Club | Wins | Club | Wins | Club | Wins |
|---|---|---|---|---|---|
| Arsenal | 13 | Sheffield Wed | 3 | Clapham Rov | 1 |
| Manchester Utd | 12 | West Ham | 3 | Coventry | 1 |
| Tottenham | 8 | Bury | 2 | Derby | 1 |
| Chelsea | 8 | Nottm Forest | 2 | Huddersfield | 1 |
| Aston Villa | 7 | Old Etonians | 2 | Ipswich | 1 |
| Liverpool | 7 | Portsmouth | 2 | Leeds | 1 |
| Blackburn Rov | 6 | Preston | 2 | Notts Co | 1 |
| Newcastle | 6 | Sunderland | 2 | Old Carthusians | 1 |
| Everton | 5 | Barnsley | 1 | Oxford University | 1 |
| Manchester City | 5 | Blackburn Olympic | 1 | Royal Engineers | 1 |
| The Wanderers | 5 | Blackpool | 1 | Southampton | 1 |
| WBA | 5 | Bradford City | 1 | Wigan | 1 |
| Bolton | 4 | Burnley | 1 | Wimbledon | 1 |
| Sheffield Utd | 4 | Cardiff | 1 | | |
| Wolves | 4 | Charlton | 1 | | |

## APPEARANCES IN FINALS

**(Figures do not include replays)**

| | | | | | |
|---|---|---|---|---|---|
| Arsenal | 20 | The Wanderers* | 5 | Notts Co | 2 |
| Manchester Utd | 20 | West Ham | 5 | Queen's Park (Glasgow) | 2 |
| Liverpool | 14 | Derby | 4 | Blackburn Olympic* | 1 |
| Everton | 13 | Leeds | 4 | Bradford City* | 1 |
| Newcastle | 13 | Leicester | 4 | Brighton | 1 |
| Chelsea | 13 | Oxford University | 4 | Bristol City | 1 |
| Aston Villa | 11 | Royal Engineers | 4 | Coventry* | 1 |
| Manchester City | 10 | Southampton | 4 | Fulham | 1 |
| WBA | 10 | Sunderland | 4 | Hull | 1 |
| Tottenham | 9 | Blackpool | 3 | Ipswich* | 1 |
| Blackburn Rov | 8 | Burnley | 3 | Luton | 1 |
| Wolves | 8 | Cardiff | 3 | Middlesbrough | 1 |
| Bolton | 7 | Nottm Forest | 3 | Millwall | 1 |
| Preston | 7 | Barnsley | 2 | Old Carthusians* | 1 |
| Old Etonians | 6 | Birmingham | 2 | QPR | 1 |
| Sheffield Utd | 6 | Bury* | 2 | Stoke | 1 |
| Sheffield Wed | 6 | Charlton | 2 | Watford | 1 |
| Huddersfield | 5 | Clapham Rov | 2 | Wigan | 1 |
| Portsmouth | 5 | Crystal Palace | 2 | Wimbledon* | 1 |

(* Denotes undefeated)

## APPEARANCES IN SEMI-FINALS

**(Figures do not include replays)**

**30** Manchester Utd; **29** Arsenal; **26** Everton; **24** Liverpool; **23** Chelsea; **21** Aston Villa, Tottenham; **20** WBA; **18** Blackburn; **17** Newcastle; **16** Sheffield Wed; **14** Bolton, Sheffield Utd, Wolves; **13** Derby, Manchester City; **12** Nottm Forest, Southampton, Sunderland; **10** Preston; **9** Birmingham; **8** Burnley, Leeds; **7** Huddersfield, Leicester, Portsmouth, West Ham; **6** Fulham, Old Etonians, Oxford University, Watford; **5** Millwall, Notts Co, The Wanderers; **4** Cardiff, *Crystal Palace, Luton, Queen's Park (Glasgow), Royal Engineers, Stoke; **3** Barnsley, Blackpool, Clapham Rov, Ipswich, Middlesbrough, Norwich, Old Carthusians, Oldham, The Swifts; **2** Blackburn Olympic, Bristol City, Bury, Charlton, Grimsby, Hull, Reading, Swansea, Swindon, Wigan, Wimbledon; **1** Bradford City, Brighton, Cambridge University, Chesterfield, Coventry, Crewe, Darwen, Derby Junction, Marlow, Old Harrovians, Orient, Plymouth Argyle, Port Vale, QPR, Rangers (Glasgow), Shropshire Wand, Wycombe, York

(*A previous and different Crystal Palace club also reached the semi-final in season 1871–72)

# CARABAO EFL CUP 2017–18

## FIRST ROUND

Accrington 3 Preston 2
AFC Wimbledon 1 Brentford 3 (aet)
Barnsley 4 Morecambe 3
Birmingham 5 Crawley 1
Bradford 2 Doncaster 3
Bristol City 5 Plymouth 0
Bristol Rov 4 Cambridge 1
Bury 0 Sunderland 1
Cardiff 2 Portsmouth 1 (aet)
Colchester 1 Aston Villa 2
Coventry 1 Blackburn 3
Crewe 1 Bolton 2
Exeter 1 Charlton 2
Fleetwood 1 Carlisle 2 (aet)
Forest Green 0 MK Dons 1 (aet)
Grimsby 0 Derby 1
Leeds 4 Port Vale 1
Luton 0 Ipswich 2
Mansfield 0 Rochdale 1
Millwall 2 Stevenage 0
Norwich 3 Swindon 2
Nottm Forest 2 Shrewsbury 1
Oldham 2 Burton 3
Oxford 3 Cheltenham 4 (aet)
Peterborough 1 Barnet 3
QPR 1 Northampton 0
Reading 2 Gillingham 0
Rotherham 2 Lincoln 1
Scunthorpe 3 Notts Co 3
(aet, Scunthorpe won 6-5 on pens)
Sheffield Utd 3 Walsall 2
Sheffield Wed 4 Chesterfield 1
Southend 0 Newport 2
Wigan 2 Blackpool 1
Wolves 1 Yeovil 0
Wycombe 0 Fulham 2

## SECOND ROUND

Accrington 1 WBA 3
Aston Villa 4 Wigan 1
Barnsley 3 Derby 2
Birmingham 1 Bournemouth 2
Blackburn 0 Burnley 2
Bolton 3 Sheffield Wed 2
Brighton 1 Barnet 0
Cardiff 1 Burton 2
Carlisle 1 Sunderland 2
Cheltenham 0 West Ham 2
Crystal Palace 2 Ipswich 1
Doncaster 2 Hull 0
Fulham 0 Bristol Rov 1
Huddersfield 2 Rotherham 1
Leeds 5 Newport 1
Middlesbrough 3 Scunthorpe 0
MK Dons 1 Swansea 4
Newcastle 2 Nottm Forest 3 (aet)
Norwich 4 Charlton 1
QPR 1 Brentford 4
Reading 3 Millwall 1 (aet)
Sheffield Utd 1 Leicester 4
Southampton 0 Wolves 2
Stoke 4 Rochdale 0
Watford 2 Bristol City 3

## THIRD ROUND

**Arsenal** 1 Doncaster 0
Aston Villa 0 Middlesbrough 2
Bournemouth 1 Brighton 0 (aet)
Brentford 1 Norwich 3
Bristol City 2 Stoke 0
Burnley 2 Leeds 2
(aet, Leeds won 5-3 on pens)
Chelsea 5 Nottm Forest 1
Crystal Palace 1 Huddersfield 0
Everton 3 Sunderland 0
Leicester 2 Liverpool 0
Manchester Utd 4 Burton 1
Reading 0 Swansea 2
Tottenham 1 Barnsley 0
WBA1 **Manchester City** 2
West Ham 3 Bolton 0
Wolves 1 Bristol Rov 0 (aet)

## FOURTH ROUND

**Arsenal** 2 Norwich 1 (aet)
Bournemouth 3 Middlesbrough 1
Bristol City 4 Crystal Palace 1
Chelsea 2 Everton 1
Leicester 3 Leeds 1
**Manchester City** 0 Wolves 0
(aet, Manchester City won 4-1 on pens)
Swansea 0 Manchester Utd 2
Tottenham 2 West Ham 3

## FIFTH ROUND

**Arsenal** 1 West Ham 0
Bristol City 2 Manchester Utd 1
Chelsea 2 Bournemouth 1
Leicester 1 **Manchester City** 1
(aet, Manchester City won 4-3 on pens)

## SEMI-FINALS (two legs)

Chelsea 0 **Arsenal** 0
**Arsenal** 2 Chelsea 1
**Manchester City** 2 Bristol City 1
Bristol City 2 **Manchester City** 3

## FINAL

**ARSENAL 0 MANCHESTER CITY 3 (Aguero 18, Kompany 58, D Silva 65)**
**Wembley (85,671); Sunday, February 25, 2018**

**Arsenal** (3-4-2-1): Ospina, Chambers (Welbeck 65), Mustafi, Koscielny (capt), Bellerin, Ramsey (Iwobi 73), Xhaka, Monreal (Kolasinac 26), Ozil, Wilshere, Aubameyang. **Subs not used**: Cech, Elneny, Mertesacker, Maitland-Niles. **Booked**: Bellerin, Ramsey, Chambers, Wilshere. **Manager**: Arsene Wenger
**Manchester City** (4-3-3): Bravo, Walker, Kompany (capt), Otamendi, Danilo, Fernandinho, Gundogan, D Silva, De Bruyne, Aguero, Sane. **Subs not used:** Ederson, Stones, Laporte, Zinchenko. **Booked**: Kompany, Fernandinho. **Manager**: Pep Guardiola
**Referee**: C Pawson (South Yorks). **Half-time**: 0-1

Down the years, Wembley finals have witnessed many inspired, uplifting or emotional performances. A combination of all three qualities in a single match has been a rarity. So what Vincent Kompany delivered in the Carabao Cup Final will live long in the memory of an 85,000 crowd at the national stadium and the millions watching on television. Not just for a commanding display at the heart of Manchester City's defence, or the goal that tightened their grip on the trophy. More than anything, perhaps, was the unbridled joy the 31-year-old captain exuded after scoring it – galloping across the turf, arm aloft, roaring with delight to celebrate the way he had weathered a seemingly never-ending catalogue of injuries to return to the big stage. After leading his side to Premier League titles under Roberto Mancini in 2012 and Manuel Pellegrini in 2014, Kompany spent more time on the treatment table than on the pitch. Pep Guardiola regarded every game the Belgian could play as a bonus. Even so, the manager trusted him to perform and Kompany justified that faith with a man-of-the-match performance, typified also by the calm, controlled way he dealt with Pierre-Emerick Aubameyang in a race for the ball, brushing aside Arsenal's record-signing to extinguish a rare threat to the City goal. Sergio Aguero's opener and David Silva's clincher underlined their dominance, meant a third successive League Cup Final defeat for Arsene Wenger and exposed the season-long brittleness of his team.

# HOW THEY REACHED THE FINAL

## Arsenal

**Round 3**: 1-0 home to Doncaster (Walcott)
**Round 4**: 2-1 home to Norwich (Nketiah 2) – aet
**Round 5**: 1-0 home to West Ham (Welbeck)
**Semi-finals** v Chelsea – first leg, 0-0 away; second leg, 2-1 home (Rudiger og, Xhaka)

## Manchester City

**Round 3**: 2-1 away to WBA (Sane 2)
**Round 4**: 0-0 home to Wolves – aet, won 4-1 on pens
**Round 5**: 1-1 away to Leicester (Bernardo Silva) – aet, won 4-3 on pens
**Semi-finals** v Bristol City – first leg, 2-1 home (De Bruyne, Aguero); second leg, 3-2 away (Sane, Aguero, De Bruyne)

# LEAGUE CUP – COMPLETE RESULTS

## LEAGUE CUP FINALS

1961* Aston Villa beat Rotherham 3-2 on agg (0-2a, 3-0h)
1962 Norwich beat Rochdale 4-0 on agg (3-0a, 1-0h)
1963 Birmingham beat Aston Villa 3-1 o agg (3-1h, 0-0a)
1964 Leicester beat Stoke 4-3 on agg (1-1a, 3-2h)
1965 Chelsea beat Leicester 3-2 on agg (3-2h, 0-0a)
1966 WBA beat West Ham 5-3 on agg (1-2a, 4-1h)

## AT WEMBLEY

1967 QPR beat WBA (3-2)
1968 Leeds beat Arsenal (1-0)
1969* Swindon beat Arsenal (3-1)
1970* Man City beat WBA (2-1)
1971 Tottenham beat Aston Villa (2-0)
1972 Stoke beat Chelsea (2-1)
1973 Tottenham beat Norwich (1-0)
1974 Wolves beat Man City (2-1)
1975 Aston Villa beat Norwich (1-0)
1976 Man City beat Newcastle (2-1)
1977†* Aston Villa beat Everton (3-2 after 0-0 and 1-1 draws)
1978†† Nottm Forest beat Liverpool (1-0 after 0-0 draw)
1979 Nottm Forest beat Southampton (3-2)
1980 Wolves beat Nottm Forest (1-0)
1981††† Liverpool beat West Ham (2-1 after 1-1 draw)

## MILK CUP

1982* Liverpool beat Tottenham (3-1)
1983* Liverpool beat Man Utd (2-1)
1984** Liverpool beat Everton (1-0 after *0-0 draw)
1985 Norwich beat Sunderland (1-0)
1986 Oxford Utd beat QPR (3-0)

## LITTLEWOODS CUP

1987 Arsenal beat Liverpool (2-1)
1988 Luton beat Arsenal (3-2)
1989 Nottm Forest beat Luton (3-1)
1990 Nottm Forest beat Oldham (1-0)

## RUMBELOWS CUP

1991 Sheffield Wed beat Man Utd (1-0)
1992 Man Utd beat Nottm Forest (1-0)

## COCA-COLA CUP

1993 Arsenal beat Sheffield Wed (2-1)
1994 Aston Villa beat Man Utd (3-1)
1995 Liverpool beat Bolton (2-1)
1996 Aston Villa beat Leeds (3-0)
1997*** Leicester beat Middlesbrough (*1-0 after *1-1 draw)
1998 Chelsea beat Middlesbrough (2-0)

## WORTHINGTON CUP (at Millennium Stadium from 2001)

1999 Tottenham beat Leicester (1-0)
2000 Leicester beat Tranmere (2-1)
2001 Liverpool beat Birmingham (5-4 on pens after *1-1 draw)
2002 Blackburn beat Tottenham (2-1)
2003 Liverpool beat Man Utd (2-0)

## CARLING CUP (at Wembley from 2008)

2004 Middlesbrough beat Bolton (2-1)
2005* Chelsea beat Liverpool (3-2)

2006 Man Utd beat Wigan (4-0)
2007 Chelsea beat Arsenal (2-1)
2008* Tottenham beat Chelsea (2-1)
2009 Man Utd beat Tottenham (4-1 on pens after *0-0 draw)
2010 Man Utd beat Aston Villa (2-1)
2011 Birmingham beat Arsenal (2-1)
2012 Liverpool beat Cardiff (3-2 on pens after *2-2 draw)

## CAPITAL ONE CUP (at Wembley from 2013)

2013 Swansea beat Bradford (5-0)
2014 Manchester City beat Sunderland (3-1)
2015 Chelsea beat Tottenham (2-0)
2016 Manchester City beat Liverpool (3-1 on pens after *1-1 draw)

* After extra time. † First replay at Hillsborough, second replay at Old Trafford. †† Replayed at Old Trafford. ††† Replayed at Villa Park. ** Replayed at Maine Road. *** Replayed at Hillsborough

## EFL CUP (at Wembley from 2017)

2017 Manchester Utd beat Southampton (3-2)

## CARABAO CUP (at Wembley from 2018)

2018 Manchester City beat Arsenal (3-0)

## SUMMARY OF LEAGUE CUP WINNERS

| | | | | | |
|---|---|---|---|---|---|
| Liverpool | 8 | Arsenal | 2 | Oxford Utd | 1 |
| Aston Villa | 5 | Birmingham | 2 | QPR | 1 |
| Chelsea | 5 | Norwich | 2 | Sheffield Wed | 1 |
| Manchester City | 5 | Wolves | 2 | Stoke | 1 |
| Manchester Utd | 5 | Blackburn | 1 | Swansea | 1 |
| Nottm Forest | 4 | Leeds. | 1 | Swindon | 1 |
| Tottenham | 4 | Luton | 1 | WBA | 1 |
| Leicester | 3 | Middlesbrough | 1 | | |

## LEAGUE CUP FINAL APPEARANCES

**12** Liverpool; **9**, Manchester Utd; **8** Arsenal, Aston Villa, Chelsea, Tottenham; **6** Manchester City, Nottm Forest; **5** Leicester; **4** Norwich; **3** Birmingham, Middlesbrough, WBA; **2** Bolton, Everton, Leeds, Luton, QPR, Sheffield Wed, Southampton, Stoke, Sunderland, West Ham, Wolves; **1** Blackburn, Bradford, Cardiff, Newcastle, Oldham, Oxford Utd, Rochdale, Rotherham, Swansea, Swindon, Tranmere, Wigan (Figures do not include replays)

## LEAGUE CUP SEMI-FINAL APPEARANCES

**17** Liverpool; **16** Tottenham; **15** Arsenal, **14** Aston Villa; Manchester Utd; **13** Chelsea; **10** Manchester City; **9** West Ham; **6** Blackburn, Nottm Forest; **5** Birmingham, Everton, Leeds, Leicester, Middlesbrough, Norwich; **4** Bolton, Burnley, Crystal Palace, Ipswich, Sheffield Wed, Sunderland, WBA; **3** Bristol City, QPR, Southampton, Stoke, Swindon, Wolves; **2** Cardiff, Coventry, Derby, Luton, Oxford Utd, Plymouth, Sheffield Utd, Tranmere, Watford, Wimbledon; **1** Blackpool, Bradford, Bury, Carlisle, Chester, Huddersfield, Hull, Newcastle, Oldham, Peterborough, Rochdale, Rotherham, Shrewsbury, Stockport, Swansea, Walsall, Wigan, Wycombe (Figures do not include replays)

## THE THINGS THEY SAY...

'A storm has blown through us and we have struggled to cope. We have lost the trust of the public' – **Greg Clarke**, FA chairman, apologising for the governing body's handling of claims of discrimination against sacked England's women's manager Mark Sampson .

'The numbers are out of context with society. It is beyond rationality' – **Arsene Wenger** on Neymar's £198m transfer from Barcelona to Paris Saint-Germain.

'I was never motivated by money. I'm following my heart, looking for a new challenge and trophies' – **Neymar** on his reported salary of nearly £600,000 a week after tax.

# OTHER COMPETITIONS 2017–18

## FA COMMUNITY SHIELD

**ARSENAL 1 (Kolasinac 82) CHELSEA 1 (Moses 46)**
**(Arsenal won 4-1 on pens)**
**Wembley (83,325); Sunday, August 6, 2017**

**Arsenal** (3-4-3): Cech, Holding, Mertesacker (capt) (Kolasinac 33), Monreal, Bellerin, Elneny, Xhaka, Oxlade-Chamberlain, Welbeck (Nelson 88), Lacazette (Giroud 66), Iwobi (Walcott 67). **Subs not used**: Ospina, Maitland-Niles, Willock. **Booked**: Bellerin. **Manager**: Arsenal Wenger
**Chelsea** (3-4-3): Courtois, Azpilicueta, Luiz, Cahill (capt), Moses, Kante, Fabregas, Alonso (Rudiger 79), Pedro, Batshuayi (Morata 73), Willian (Musonda 83). **Subs not used**: Caballero, Christensen, Scott, Boga. **Booked**: Azpilicueta, Alonso, Willian. **Sent off**: Pedro (80). **Manager**: Antonio Conte
**Penalty shoot-out: Arsenal** – scored: Walcott, Monreal, Oxlade-Chamberlain, Giroud. **Chelsea** – scored: Cahill; missed, Courtois, Morata
**Referee:** R Madeley (West Yorks). **Half-time**: 0-0

# CHECKATRADE TROPHY

(Each team awarded one point for drawn group match after 90 minutes. Then penalties with winning team awarded one additional point. Group winners and runners-up through to knockout stage)

## GROUP STAGE – NORTH

### GROUP A

| | P | W | D | L | F | A | Pts |
|---|---|---|---|---|---|---|---|
| Fleetwood | 3 | 3 | 0 | 0 | 7 | 2 | 9 |
| Leicester U21 | 3 | 1 | 1 | 1 | 3 | 5 | 4 |
| Carlisle | 3 | 1 | 0 | 2 | 3 | 3 | 3 |
| Morecambe | 3 | 0 | 1 | 2 | 3 | 6 | 2 |

### GROUP B

| | | | | | | | |
|---|---|---|---|---|---|---|---|
| Blackpool | 3 | 2 | 1 | 0 | 7 | 3 | 7 |
| Accrington | 3 | 2 | 0 | 1 | 8 | 4 | 6 |
| Wigan | 3 | 1 | 1 | 1 | 5 | 6 | 5 |
| Middlesbrough U21 | 3 | 0 | 0 | 3 | 4 | 11 | 0 |

### GROUP C

| | | | | | | | |
|---|---|---|---|---|---|---|---|
| Rochdale | 3 | 1 | 2 | 0 | 5 | 1 | 6 |
| Bury | 3 | 2 | 0 | 1 | 4 | 5 | 6 |
| Blackburn | 3 | 1 | 1 | 1 | 2 | 2 | 4 |
| Stoke U21 | 3 | 0 | 1 | 2 | 1 | 4 | 2 |

### GROUP D

| | | | | | | | |
|---|---|---|---|---|---|---|---|
| Port Vale | 3 | 2 | 1 | 0 | 5 | 2 | 8 |
| Oldham | 3 | 2 | 1 | 0 | 5 | 1 | 7 |
| Newcastle U21 | 3 | 1 | 0 | 2 | 3 | 6 | 3 |
| Crewe | 3 | 0 | 0 | 3 | 3 | 7 | 0 |

### GROUP E

| | | | | | | | |
|---|---|---|---|---|---|---|---|
| Walsall | 3 | 2 | 1 | 0 | 6 | 3 | 7 |
| Shrewsbury | 3 | 2 | 0 | 1 | 6 | 3 | 6 |
| Coventry | 3 | 1 | 1 | 1 | 6 | 6 | 5 |
| WBA U21 | 3 | 0 | 0 | 3 | 2 | 8 | 0 |

### GROUP F

| | | | | | | | |
|---|---|---|---|---|---|---|---|
| Bradford | 3 | 2 | 0 | 1 | 6 | 6 | 6 |
| Chesterfield | 3 | 1 | 1 | 1 | 6 | 7 | 5 |
| Rotherham | 3 | 1 | 1 | 1 | 5 | 3 | 4 |
| Man City U21 | 3 | 0 | 2 | 1 | 4 | 5 | 3 |

### GROUP G

| | | | | | | | |
|---|---|---|---|---|---|---|---|
| Lincoln | 3 | 3 | 0 | 0 | 7 | 3 | 9 |
| Mansfield | 3 | 2 | 0 | 1 | 4 | 4 | 6 |
| Notts Co | 3 | 1 | 0 | 2 | 4 | 5 | 3 |
| Everton U21 | 3 | 0 | 0 | 3 | 2 | 5 | 0 |

### GROUP H

| | | | | | | | |
|---|---|---|---|---|---|---|---|
| Scunthorpe | 3 | 2 | 1 | 0 | 6 | 3 | 7 |
| Doncaster | 3 | 1 | 2 | 0 | 3 | 2 | 7 |
| Grimsby | 3 | 0 | 2 | 1 | 3 | 4 | 2 |
| Sunderland U21 | 3 | 0 | 1 | 2 | 2 | 5 | 2 |

## SOUTH

### GROUP A

| | | | | | | | |
|---|---|---|---|---|---|---|---|
| Portsmouth | 3 | 2 | 1 | 0 | 7 | 4 | 7 |
| Charlton | 3 | 2 | 0 | 1 | 5 | 3 | 6 |
| Fulham U21 | 3 | 1 | 1 | 1 | 8 | 7 | 5 |
| Crawley | 3 | 0 | 0 | 3 | 2 | 8 | 0 |

### GROUP B

| | | | | | | | |
|---|---|---|---|---|---|---|---|
| Gillingham | 3 | 3 | 0 | 0 | 10 | 6 | 9 |
| Southend | 3 | 2 | 0 | 1 | 4 | 2 | 6 |

| | | | | | | | |
|---|---|---|---|---|---|---|---|
| Colchester | 3 | 0 | 1 | 2 | 2 | 5 | 2 |
| Reading U21 | 3 | 0 | 1 | 2 | 7 | 10 | 1 |

**GROUP C**

| | | | | | | | |
|---|---|---|---|---|---|---|---|
| Swindon | 3 | 2 | 0 | 1 | 7 | 5 | 6 |
| West HamU21 | 3 | 2 | 0 | 1 | 6 | 5 | 6 |
| Bristol Rov | 3 | 1 | 0 | 2 | 8 | 8 | 3 |
| Wycombe | 3 | 1 | 0 | 2 | 3 | 6 | 3 |

**GROUP D**

| | | | | | | | |
|---|---|---|---|---|---|---|---|
| Yeovil | 3 | 2 | 1 | 0 | 6 | 3 | 7 |
| Chelsea U21 | 3 | 1 | 2 | 0 | 6 | 4 | 5 |
| Plymouth | 3 | 0 | 2 | 1 | 5 | 6 | 4 |
| Exeter | 3 | 0 | 1 | 2 | 4 | 8 | 1 |

**GROUP E**

| | | | | | | | |
|---|---|---|---|---|---|---|---|
| Swansea U21 | 3 | 3 | 0 | 0 | 6 | 2 | 9 |
| Forest Green | 3 | 2 | 0 | 1 | 4 | 3 | 6 |
| Cheltenham | 3 | 1 | 0 | 2 | 4 | 5 | 3 |
| Newport | 3 | 0 | 0 | 3 | 2 | 6 | 0 |

**GROUP F**

| | | | | | | | |
|---|---|---|---|---|---|---|---|
| AFC Wimbledon | 3 | 2 | 0 | 1 | 9 | 8 | 6 |
| Luton | 3 | 1 | 2 | 0 | 5 | 4 | 6 |
| Barnet | 3 | 1 | 1 | 1 | 6 | 6 | 4 |
| Tottenham U21 | 3 | 0 | 1 | 2 | 6 | 8 | 1 |

**GROUP G**

| | | | | | | | |
|---|---|---|---|---|---|---|---|
| MK Dons | 3 | 2 | 1 | 0 | 6 | 3 | 8 |
| Oxford | 3 | 1 | 1 | 1 | 11 | 8 | 4 |
| Stevenage | 3 | 1 | 1 | 1 | 5 | 7 | 4 |
| Brighton U21 | 3 | 0 | 1 | 2 | 3 | 7 | 2 |

**GROUP H**

| | | | | | | | |
|---|---|---|---|---|---|---|---|
| Peterborough | 3 | 2 | 1 | 0 | 5 | 1 | 7 |
| Northampton | 3 | 0 | 3 | 0 | 5 | 5 | 6 |
| Southampton U21 | 3 | 1 | 1 | 1 | 4 | 5 | 4 |
| Cambridge | 3 | 0 | 1 | 2 | 1 | 4 | 1 |

**SECOND ROUND**

**North**: Blackpool 1 Mansfield 1 (Blackpool won 5-4 on pens); Bradford 0 Oldham 1; Fleetwood 2 Chesterfield 0; Lincoln 3 Accrington 2; Port Vale 1 Shrewsbury 2; Rochdale 1 Doncaster 1 (Rochdale won 5-4 on pens); Scunthorpe 1 Leicester U21 2; Walsall 1 Bury 2
**South**: Gillingham 1 Oxford 2; Luton 4 West Ham U21 0; MK Dons 0 Chelsea U21 4; Peterborough 2 Southend 0; Portsmouth 2 Northampton 0; Swansea U21 2 Charlton 3; Swindon 0 Forest Green 1; Yeovil 2 AFC Wimbledon 0

**THIRD ROUND**

Bury 2 Fleetwood 3; Charlton 1 Oxford 1 (Oxford won 3-0 on pens); Luton 0 Peterborough 0 (Peterborough won 7-6 on pens); Oldham 4 Leicester U21 2; Portsmouth 1 Chelsea U21 2; Rochdale 0 Lincoln 1; Shrewsbury 0 Blackpool 0 (Shrewsbury won 4-2 on pens); Yeovil 2 Forest Green 0

**FOURTH ROUND**

Chelsea U21 3 Oxford 0; Lincoln 4 Peterborough 2; Shrewsbury 2 Oldham 1; Yeovil 3 Fleetwood 2

**SEMI-FINALS**

Lincoln 1 Chelsea U21 1 (Lincoln won 4-2 on pens); Shrewsbury 1 Yeovil 0

## FINAL

**Lincoln City 1 (Whitehouse 16) Shrewsbury Town 0**
**Wembley (41,261); Sunday, April 8, 2018**

**Lincoln City** (4-3-3): Allsop, Eardley, Bostwick, Waterfall (capt), Habergham, Whitehouse, Woodyard, Frecklinghton, Green (Long 90+5), Rhead (Palmer 64), Rowe (Anderson 64). **Subs not used**: Farman, Chapman, Stewart, O'Hare. **Booked**: Rhead, Frecklington. **Manager**: Danny Cowley
**Shrewsbury Town** (4-1-4-1): Henderson, Bolton, Nsiala, Sadler (capt), Beckles, B Morris (Rodman 67), Whalley (Gnahoua 86), Nolan, Godfrey, Thomas (Payne 75), C Morris. **Subs not used**: MacGillivray, John-Lewis, Lowe, Eisa. **Booked**: Nsiala, Nolan. **Manager**: Paul Hurst
**Referee**: G Ward (Surrey). **Half-time**: 1-0

# BUILDBASE FA TROPHY

**FIRST ROUND**: Billericay 3 Havant 1; Braintreet 0 Brackley 0; Blyth 1 AFC Telford 0; Chesham 0 Weston SM 2; Chester 2 AFC Fylde 2 (aet, Chester won 5-4 on pens, tie settled on the day); Chorley 1 Marine 3; Dartford 1 Boreham Wood 1; Dover 3 Eastbourne 0; East Thurrock 4 Aldershot 0; Ebbsfleet 2 Eastleigh 1; Halifax 1 Macclesfield 0; Hampton & Richmond 1 Heybridge 1; Haringey 1 Leyton Orient 2; Hartley Wintney 0 Bromley 2; Hendon 2 Bath 1; Hereford 3 Dagenham 2; Gateshead 2 Guiseley 1 (aet, tie settled on the day); Kiddderminster 2 York 1; Lancaster 1 Stockport 3; Leamington 0 Stourbridge 1; Nuneaton 0 Barrow 1; Solihull 2 Tranmere 0; Spennymoor 4 Gainsborough 4 (aet, Spennymoor won 5-3 on pens, tie settled on the day); Sutton 1 Truro 0; Taunton 1 Bognor Regis 4; Torquay 0 Maidstone 4; Warrington 0 Altrincham 0; Wealdstone 1 Wingate & Finchley 0; Whitehawk 1 St Albans 2; Woking 0 Maidenhead 2; Workington 1 Hartlepool 0; Wrexham 0 Harrogate 2. **Replays**: Brackley 2 Braintree 0; Heybridge 3 Hampton & Richmond 2; Boreham Wood 2 Dartford 2 (aet, Boreham Wood won 3-1 on pens); Altrincham 1 Warrington 2

**SECOND ROUND**: Billericay 3 Stourbridge 2; Blyth 1 Bromley 4; Bognor Regis 1 Leyton Orient 1; Brackley 0 Barrow 0; Dover 4 Marine 3; East Thurrock 1 Chester 0; Ebbsfleet 1 Warrington 1; Gateshead 3 Boreham Wood 3; Halifax 1 Maidenhead 4; Kidderminster 2 Stockport 2; Maidstone 2 Heybridge 1; St Albans 1 Harrogate 1; Spennymoor 2 Solihull 0; Sutton 3 Hendon 0; Wealdstone 1 Hereford 0; Weston SM 1 Workington 1. **Replays**: Barrow 0 Brackley 2; Boreham Wood 1 Gateshead 2; Harrogate 5 St Albans 0; Stockport 3 Kidderminster 0; Warrington 2 Ebbsfleet 0; Workington 2 Weston SM 1

**THIRD ROUND**: Brackley 3 Sutton 1; Dover 3 Leyton Orient 4; Harrogate 2 Billericay 2; Maidenhead 1 Stockport 1; Maidstone 2 Gateshead 2; Spennymoor 1 East Thurrock 1; Wealdstone 2 Warrington 1; Workington 1 Bromley 1. **Replays**: Billericay 3 Harrogate 2; Bromley 7 Workington 1; East Thurrock 2 Spennymoor 5; Gateshead 3 Maidstone 0; Stockport 3 Maidenhead 2 (aet)

**FOURTH ROUND**: Billericay 2 Wealdstone 5; Bromley 0 Spennymoor 0; Leyton Orient 3 Gateshead 3; Stockport 1 Brackley 1. **Replays**: Brackley 2 Stockport 1; Gateshead 3 Leyton Orient 2; Spennymoor 1 Bromley 2

**SEMI-FINALS: first leg**: Brackley 1 Wealdstone 0; Bromley 3 Gateshead 2. **Second leg**: Gateshead 1 Bromley 1 (Bromley won 4-3 on agg); Wealdstone 0 Brackley 2 (Brackley won 3-0 on agg)

## FINAL

**Brackley Town 1 (R Johnson 90+5 og) Bromley 1 (Bugiel 19) (aet, Brackley Town won 5-4 on pens)**

**Wembley (31,430); Sunday, May 20, 2018**

**Brackley:**: Lewis, Dean (capt), Gudger, Franklin (Myles 78), Lowe (Diggin 111), Byrne, Armson, A Walker, G Walker, Williams, Ndlovu (Brown 52). **Subs not used**: Graham, Streete. **Manager:** Kevin Wilkin

**Bromley**: Gregory, Higgs, Holland (capt), R Johnson, Sterling, Raymond, Sutherland, Porter (Rees 61), Dennis (Hanlan 68), Mekki (Chorley 71), Bugiel. **Subs not used**: Dunne, D Johnson. **Manager:** Neil Smith

**Referee**: C Kavanagh (Lancs), **Half-time**: 0-1

## WELSH CUP FINAL

**Connah's Quay** 4 (Bakare 23, Wilde 26, 41, Owens 90) **Aberystwyth Town** 1 (Wade 45) – Latham Park, Newtown

## FA VASE FINAL

**Thatcham Town** 1 (Cooper-Clark 24 pen) **Stockton Town** 0 – Wembley

## FA SUNDAY CUP FINAL

**Hardwick Social** (Stockton) 2 (Robinson og 107, Coleman 113) **Gym United** (Bury St Edmunds) 0 – aet, Bramall Lane, Sheffield

# FINALS – RESULTS

**Associated Members' Cup**

**1984** (Hull) Bournemouth 2 Hull 1

**Freight Rover Trophy – Wembley**

**1985** Wigan 3 Brentford 1
**1986** Bristol City 3 Bolton 0
**1987** Mansfield 1 Bristol City 1
(aet; Mansfield won 5-4 on pens)

**Sherpa Van Trophy – Wembley**

**1988** Wolves 2 Burnley 0
**1989** Bolton 4 Torquay 1

**Leyland Daf Cup – Wembley**

**1990** Tranmere 2 Bristol Rov 1
**1991** Birmingham 3 Tranmere 2

**Autoglass Trophy – Wembley**

**1992** Stoke 1 Stockport 0
**1993** Port Vale 2 Stockport 1
**1994** Huddersfield 1 Swansea 1
(aet; Swansea won 3-1 on pens)

**Auto Windscreens Shield – Wembley**

**1995** Birmingham 1 Carlisle 0
(Birmingham won in sudden-death overtime)
**1996** Rotherham 2 Shrewsbury 1
**1997** Carlisle 0 Colchester 0
(aet; Carlisle won 4-3 on pens)
**1998** Grimsby 2 Bournemouth 1
(Grimsby won with golden goal in extra-time)
**1999** Wigan 1 Millwall 0
**2000** Stoke 2 Bristol City 1

**LDV Vans Trophy – Millennium Stadium**

**2001** Port Vale 2 Brentford 1
**2002** Blackpool 4 Cambridge Utd 1
**2003** Bristol City 2 Carlisle 0
**2004** Blackpool 2 Southend 0
**2005** Wrexham 2 Southend 0

**Football League Trophy – Millennium Stadium**

**2006** Swansea 2 Carlisle 1

**Johnstone's Paint Trophy – Wembley**

**2007** Doncaster 3 Bristol Rov 2 (aet)
(Millennium Stadium)
**2008** MK Dons 2 Grimsby 0
**2009** Luton 3 Scunthorpe 2 (aet)
**2010** Southampton 4 Carlisle 1
**2011** Carlisle 1 Brentford 0
**2012** Chesterfield 2 Swindon 0
**2013** Crewe 2 Southend 0
**2014** Peterborough 3 Chesterfield 1
**2015** Bristol City 2 Walsall 0
**2016** Barnsley 3 Oxford 2

**Checkatrade Trophy – Wembley**

**2017** Coventry 2 Oxford 1
**2018** Lincoln 1 Shrewsbury 0

# FINALS – AT WEMBLEY

**Full Members' Cup (Discontinued after 1992)**

**1985–86** Chelsea 5 Man City 4
**1986–87** Blackburn 1 Charlton 0

**Simod Cup**

**1987–88** Reading 4 Luton 1
**1988–89** Nottm Forest 4 Everton 3

**Zenith Data Systems Cup**

**1989–90** Chelsea 1 Middlesbrough 0
**1990–91** Crystal Palace 4 Everton 1
**1991–92** Nottm Forest 3 Southampton 2

**Anglo-Italian Cup (Discontinued after 1996**

* Home club)
**1970** *Napoli 0 Swindon 3
**1971** *Bologna 1 Blackpool 2 (aet)
**1972** *AS Roma 3 Blackpool 1
**1973** *Fiorentina 1 Newcastle 2
**1993** Derby 1 Cremonese 3 (at Wembley)
**1994** Notts Co 0 Brescia 1 (at Wembley)
**1995** Ascoli 1 Notts Co 2 (at Wembley)
**1996** Port Vale 2 Genoa 5 (at Wembley)

**FA Vase**

**At Wembley (until 2000 and from 2007)**

**1975** Hoddesdon 2 Epsom & Ewell 1
**1976** Billericay 1 Stamford 0*
**1977** Billericay 2 Sheffield 1
(replay Nottingham after a 1-1 at Wembley)
**1978** Blue Star 2 Barton Rov 1
**1979** Billericay 4 Almondsbury Greenway 1
**1980** Stamford 2 Guisborough Town 0
**1981** Whickham 3 Willenhall 2*
**1982** Forest Green 3 Rainworth MF Welfare 0
**1983** VS Rugby 1 Halesowen 0
**1984** Stansted 3 Stamford 2
**1985** Halesowen 3 Fleetwood 1
**1986** Halesowen 3 Southall 0
**1987** St Helens 3 Warrington 2
**1988** Colne Dynamoes 1 Emley 0*
**1989** Tamworth 3 Sudbury 0 (replay Peterborough after a 1-1 at Wembley)
**1990** Yeading 1 Bridlington 0 (replay Leeds after 0-0 at Wembley)
**1991** Guiseley 3 Gresley Rov 1 (replay Bramall Lane Sheffield after a 4-4 at Wembley)
**1992** Wimborne 5 Guiseley 3
**1993** Bridlington 1 Tiverton 0
**1994** Diss 2 Taunton 1*

**1995** Arlesey 2 Oxford City 1
**1996** Brigg Town 3 Clitheroe 0
**1997** Whitby Town 3 North Ferriby 0
**1998** Tiverton 1 Tow Law 0
**1999** Tiverton 1 Bedlington 0
**2000** Deal 1 Chippenham 0
**2001** Taunton 2 Berkhamsted 1 (Villa Park)
**2002** Whitley Bay 1 Tiptree 0* (Villa Park)
**2003** Brigg 2 AFC Sudbury 1 (Upton Park)
**2004** Winchester 2 AFC Sudbury 0 (St Andrews)
**2005** Didcot 3 AFC Sudbury 2 (White Hart Lane)
**2006** Nantwich 3 Hillingdon 1 (St Andrews)
**2007** Truro 3 AFC Totton 1
**2008** Kirkham & Wesham (Fylde) 2 Lowestoft 1
**2009** Whitley Bay 2 Glossop 0
**2010** Whitley Bay 6 Wroxham1
**2011** Whitley Bay 3 Coalville 2
**2012** Dunston 2 West Auckland 0
**2013** Spennymoor 2 Tunbridge Wells 1
**2014** Sholing 1 West Auckland 0
**2015** North Shields 2 Glossop North End 1*
**2016** Morpeth 4 Hereford 1
**2017** South Shields 4 Cleethorpes 0
**2018** Thatcham 1 Stockton 0
* After extra-time

## FA Trophy Finals

**At Wembley**
**1970** Macclesfield 2 Telford 0
**1971** Telford 3 Hillingdon 2
**1972** Stafford 3 Barnet 0
**1973** Scarborough 2 Wigan 1*
**1974** Morecambe 2 Dartford 1
**1975** Matlock 4 Scarborough 0
**1976** Scarborough 3 Stafford 2*
**1977** Scarborough 2 Dag & Red 1
**1978** Altrincham 3 Leatherhead 1
**1979** Stafford 2 Kettering 0
**1980** Dag & Red 2 Mossley 1
**1981** Bishop's Stortford 1 Sutton 0
**1982** Enfield 1 Altrincham 0*
**1983** Telford 2 Northwich 1
**1984** Northwich 2 Bangor 1 (replay Stoke after a 1-1 at Wembley)
**1985** Wealdstone 2 Boston 1
**1986** Altrincham 1 Runcorn 0
**1987** Kidderminster 2 Burton 1 (replay WBA after a 0-0 at Wembley)
**1988** Enfield 3 Telford 2 (replay WBA after a 0-0 at Wembley)
**1989** Telford 1 Macclesfield 0*
**1990** Barrow 3 Leek 0
**1991** Wycombe 2 Kidderminster 1
**1992** Colchester 3 Witton 1
**1993** Wycombe 4 Runcorn 1
**1994** Woking 2 Runcorn 1
**1995** Woking 2 Kidderminster 1
**1996** Macclesfield 3 Northwich 1
**1997** Woking 1 Dag & Red & Redbridge 0*
**1998** Cheltenham 1 Southport 0
**1999** Kingstonian 1 Forest Green 0
**2000** Kingstonian 3 Kettering 2

**At Villa Park**
**2001** Canvey 1 Forest Green 0
**2002** Yeovil 2 Stevenage 0
**2003** Burscough 2 Tamworth 1
**2004** Hednesford 3 Canvey 2
**2005** Grays 1 Hucknall 1* (Grays won 6-5 on pens)

**At Upton Park**
**2006** Grays 2 Woking 0

**At Wembley**
**2007** Stevenage 3 Kidderminster 2
**2008** Ebbsfleet 1 Torquay 0
**2009** Stevenage 2 York 0
**2010** Barrow 2 Stevenage 1*
**2011** Darlington 1 Mansfield 0 *
**2012** York 2 Newport 0
**2013** Wrexham 1 Grimsby 1 * Wrexham won 4-1 on pens)
**2014** Cambridge Utd 4 Gosport 0
**2015** North Ferriby 3 Wrexham 3* (North Ferriby won 5-4 on pens)
**2016** Halifax 1 Grimsby 0
**2017** York 3 Macclesfield 2
**2018** Brackley 1 Bromley 1
(* Brackley won 5-4 on pens)
(*After extra-time)

## FA Youth Cup Winners

| Year | Winners | Runners-up | Agg |
|---|---|---|---|
| **1953** | Man Utd | Wolves | 9-3 |
| **1954** | Man Utd | Wolves | 5-4 |
| **1955** | Man Utd | WBA | 7-1 |
| **1956** | Man Utd | Chesterfield | 4-3 |
| **1957** | Man Utd | West Ham | 8-2 |
| **1958** | Wolves | Chelsea | 7-6 |
| **1959** | Blackburn | West Ham | 2-1 |
| **1960** | Chelsea | Preston | 5-2 |
| **1961** | Chelsea | Everton | 5-3 |
| **1962** | Newcastle | Wolves | 2-1 |
| **1963** | West Ham | Liverpool | 6-5 |
| **1964** | Man Utd | Swindon | 5-2 |
| **1965** | Everton | Arsenal | 3-2 |
| **1966** | Arsenal | Sunderland | 5-3 |
| **1967** | Sunderland | Birmingham | 2-0 |
| **1968** | Burnley | Coventry | 3-2 |

| | | | | | | | |
|---|---|---|---|---|---|---|---|
| **1969** | Sunderland | WBA | 6-3 | **1995** | Man Utd | Tottenham | †2-2 |
| **1970** | Tottenham | Coventry | 4-3 | **1996** | Liverpool | West Ham | 4-1 |
| **1971** | Arsenal | Cardiff | 2-0 | **1997** | Leeds | Crystal Palace | 3-1 |
| **1972** | Aston Villa | Liverpool | 5-2 | **1998** | Everton | Blackburn | 5-3 |
| **1973** | Ipswich | Bristol City | 4-1 | **1999** | West Ham | Coventry | 9-0 |
| **1974** | Tottenham | Huddersfield | 2-1 | **2000** | Arsenal | Coventry | 5-1 |
| **1975** | Ipswich | West Ham | 5-1 | **2001** | Arsenal | Blackburn | 6-3 |
| **1976** | WBA | Wolves | 5-0 | **2002** | Aston Villa | Everton | 4-2 |
| **1977** | Crystal Palace | Everton | 1-0 | **2003** | Man Utd | Middlesbrough | 3-1 |
| **1978** | Crystal Palace | Aston Villa | *1-0 | **2004** | Middlesbrough | Aston Villa | 4-0 |
| **1979** | Millwall | Man City | 2-0 | **2005** | Ipswich | Southampton | 3-2 |
| **1980** | Aston Villa | Man City | 3-2 | **2006** | Liverpool | Man City | 3-2 |
| **1981** | West Ham | Tottenham | 2-1 | **2007** | Liverpool | Man Utd | ††2-2 |
| **1982** | Watford | Man Utd | 7-6 | **2008** | Man City | Chelsea | 4-2 |
| **1983** | Norwich | Everton | 6-5 | **2009** | Arsenal | Liverpool | 6-2 |
| **1984** | Everton | Stoke | 4-2 | **2010** | Chelsea | Aston Villa | 3-2 |
| **1985** | Newcastle | Watford | 4-1 | **2011** | Man Utd | Sheffield Utd | 6-3 |
| **1986** | Man City | Man Utd | 3-1 | **2012** | Chelsea | Blackburn | 4-1 |
| **1987** | Coventry | Charlton | 2-1 | **2013** | Norwich | Chelsea | 4-2 |
| **1988** | Arsenal | Doncaster | 6-1 | **2014** | Chelsea | Fulham | 7-6 |
| **1989** | Watford | Man City | 2-1 | **2015** | Chelsea | Man City | 5-2 |
| **1990** | Tottenham | Middlesbrough | 3-2 | **2016** | Chelsea | Man City | 4-2 |
| **1991** | Millwall | Sheffield Wed | 3-0 | **2017** | Chelsea | Man City | 6-2 |
| **1992** | Man Utd | Crystal Palace | 6-3 | **2018** | Chelsea | Arsenal | 7-1 |
| **1993** | Leeds | Man Utd | 4-1 | | | | |
| **1994** | Arsenal | Millwall | 5-3 | | | | |

(*One match only; †Manchester Utd won 4-3 on pens, ††Liverpool won 4-3 on pens)

## CHARITY/COMMUNITY SHIELD RESULTS (POST WAR)

## [CHARITY SHIELD]

| Year | Winners | Runners-up | Score |
|---|---|---|---|
| 1948 | Arsenal | Manchester Utd | 4-3 |
| 1949 | Portsmouth | Wolves | *1-1 |
| 1950 | England World Cup XI | FA Canadian Tour Team | 4-2 |
| 1951 | Tottenham | Newcastle | 2-1 |
| 1952 | Manchester Utd | Newcastle | 4-2 |
| 1953 | Arsenal | Blackpool | 3-1 |
| 1954 | Wolves | WBA | *4-4 |
| 1955 | Chelsea | Newcastle | 3-0 |
| 1956 | Manchester Utd | Manchester City | 1-0 |
| 1957 | Manchester Utd | Aston Villa | 4-0 |
| 1958 | Bolton | Wolves | 4-1 |
| 1959 | Wolves | Nottm Forest | 3-1 |
| 1960 | Burnley | Wolves | *2-2 |
| 1961 | Tottenham | FA XI | 3-2 |
| 1962 | Tottenham | Ipswich Town | 5-1 |
| 1963 | Everton | Manchester Utd | 4-0 |
| 1964 | Liverpool | West Ham | *2-2 |
| 1965 | Manchester Utd | Liverpool | *2-2 |
| 1966 | Liverpool | Everton | 1-0 |
| 1967 | Manchester Utd | Tottenham | *3-3 |
| 1968 | Manchester City | WBA | 6-1 |
| 1969 | Leeds | Manchester City | 2-1 |
| 1970 | Everton | Chelsea | 2-1 |
| 1971 | Leicester | Liverpool | 1-0 |
| 1972 | Manchester City | Aston Villa | 1-0 |

# SCOTTISH TABLES 2017–2018

## LADBROKES PREMIERSHIP

| | | | Home | | | | | Away | | | | | | |
|---|---|---|---|---|---|---|---|---|---|---|---|---|---|---|
| | | P | W | D | L | F | A | W | D | L | F | A | Gd | Pts |
| 1 | Celtic | 38 | 11 | 7 | 1 | 38 | 9 | 13 | 3 | 3 | 35 | 16 | 48 | 82 |
| 2 | Aberdeen | 38 | 11 | 4 | 4 | 30 | 16 | 11 | 3 | 5 | 26 | 21 | 19 | 73 |
| 3 | Rangers | 38 | 10 | 2 | 7 | 32 | 20 | 11 | 5 | 3 | 44 | 30 | 26 | 70 |
| 4 | Hibernian | 38 | 11 | 4 | 4 | 39 | 27 | 7 | 9 | 3 | 23 | 19 | 16 | 67 |
| 5 | Kilmarnock | 38 | 9 | 3 | 7 | 27 | 26 | 7 | 8 | 4 | 22 | 21 | 2 | 59 |
| 6 | Hearts | 38 | 8 | 7 | 3 | 23 | 13 | 4 | 6 | 10 | 16 | 26 | 0 | 49 |
| 7 | Motherwell | 38 | 8 | 5 | 7 | 26 | 22 | 5 | 4 | 9 | 17 | 27 | -6 | 48 |
| 8 | St Johnstone | 38 | 5 | 7 | 7 | 17 | 27 | 7 | 3 | 9 | 25 | 26 | -11 | 46 |
| 9 | Dundee | 38 | 6 | 3 | 10 | 18 | 27 | 5 | 3 | 11 | 18 | 30 | -21 | 39 |
| 10 | Hamilton | 38 | 5 | 3 | 11 | 26 | 35 | 4 | 3 | 12 | 21 | 33 | -21 | 33 |
| 11 | Partick* | 38 | 6 | 4 | 9 | 20 | 24 | 2 | 5 | 12 | 11 | 37 | -30 | 33 |
| 12 | Ross | 38 | 3 | 7 | 9 | 23 | 29 | 3 | 4 | 12 | 17 | 33 | -22 | 29 |

*Also relegated

Celtic into Champions League first qualifying round; Rangers and Hibernian into Europa League first qualifying round, Aberdeen into second qualifying round

**Play-offs** (on agg) – **Quarter-final**: Dundee Utd 2 Dunfermline 1. **Semi-final**: Livingston 4 Dundee Utd 3. **Final**: Livingston 3 Partick 1

**Player of Year**: Scott Brown (Celtic). **Manager of Year**: Brendan Rodgers (Celtic)

**Team of Year**: McLaughlin (Hearts), Tavernier (Rangers), Berra (Hearts), McKenna (Aberdeen), Tierney (Celtic), Forrest (Celtic), McGinn (Hibernian), McGeouch (Hibernian), Brown (Celtic), Jones (Kilmarnock), Boyd (Kilmarnock)

**Leading league scorers**: 18 Boyd (Kilmarnock); 14 Morelos (Rangers); 13 Windass (Rangers); 12 Lafferty (Hearts); 11 Schalk (Ross Co); 10 Sinclair (Celtic); 9 Dembele (Celtic), Edouard (Celtic), Griffiths (Celtic), Kamberi (Hibernian), MacLean (St Johnstone), Rooney (Aberdeen)

## LADBROKES CHAMPIONSHIP

| | | | Home | | | | | Away | | | | | | |
|---|---|---|---|---|---|---|---|---|---|---|---|---|---|---|
| | | P | W | D | L | F | A | W | D | L | F | A | Gd | Pts |
| 1 | St Mirren | 36 | 14 | 2 | 2 | 37 | 12 | 9 | 3 | 6 | 26 | 24 | 27 | 74 |
| 2 | Livingston* | 36 | 8 | 7 | 3 | 26 | 16 | 9 | 4 | 5 | 30 | 21 | 19 | 62 |
| 3 | Dundee Utd | 36 | 12 | 3 | 3 | 30 | 16 | 6 | 4 | 8 | 22 | 26 | 10 | 61 |
| 4 | Dunfermline | 36 | 11 | 4 | 3 | 38 | 18 | 5 | 7 | 6 | 22 | 17 | 25 | 59 |
| 5 | Inverness | 36 | 9 | 5 | 4 | 31 | 17 | 7 | 4 | 7 | 22 | 20 | 16 | 57 |
| 6 | Queen of South | 36 | 5 | 7 | 6 | 26 | 26 | 9 | 3 | 6 | 33 | 27 | 6 | 52 |
| 7 | Morton | 36 | 7 | 3 | 8 | 23 | 22 | 6 | 8 | 4 | 24 | 18 | 7 | 50 |
| 8 | Falkirk | 36 | 7 | 6 | 5 | 27 | 22 | 5 | 5 | 8 | 18 | 27 | -4 | 47 |
| 9 | Dumbarton** | 36 | 4 | 3 | 11 | 13 | 32 | 3 | 6 | 9 | 14 | 31 | -36 | 30 |
| 10 | Brechin | 36 | 0 | 4 | 14 | 10 | 40 | 0 | 0 | 18 | 10 | 50 | -70 | 4 |

*Also promoted. **Also relegated

**Play-offs** (on agg) – **Semi-finals**: Dumbarton 3 Arbroath 2; Alloa 4 Raith 1. **Final**: Alloa 2 Dumbarton 1 (aet)

**Player of Year**: Lewis Morgan (St Mirren). **Manager of Year**: Jack Ross (St Mirren)

**Team of Year**: Alexander (Livingston), Williamson (Dunfermline), Halkett (Livingston), O'Ware (Morton), L Smith (St Mirren), C Smith (St Mirren), McGinn (St Mirren), Vigurs (Invernes), Reilly (St Mirren), Dobbie (Queen of South), Morgan (St Mirren)

**Leading league scorers**: 18 Dobbie (Queen of South); 15 McDonald (Dundee Utd); 14 Clark (Dunfermline), Morgan (St Mirren); 11 Reilly (St Mirren); 10 Higginbotham (Dunfermline), Smith (St Mirren)

## LADBROKES LEAGUE ONE

| | | Home | | | | | | Away | | | | | |
|---|---|---|---|---|---|---|---|---|---|---|---|---|---|
| | | P | W | D | L | F | A | W | D | L | F | A | Gd | Pts |
| 1 | Ayr | 36 | 11 | 2 | 5 | 43 | 20 | 13 | 2 | 3 | 49 | 22 | 50 | 76 |
| 2 | Raith | 36 | 15 | 3 | 0 | 36 | 9 | 7 | 6 | 5 | 32 | 23 | 36 | 75 |
| 3 | Alloa* | 36 | 10 | 4 | 4 | 32 | 24 | 7 | 5 | 6 | 24 | 19 | 13 | 60 |
| 4 | Arbroath | 36 | 7 | 5 | 6 | 30 | 25 | 10 | 3 | 5 | 40 | 26 | 19 | 59 |
| 5 | Stranraer | 36 | 9 | 1 | 8 | 32 | 35 | 7 | 4 | 7 | 26 | 31 | -8 | 53 |
| 6 | East Fife | 36 | 8 | 1 | 9 | 33 | 37 | 5 | 2 | 11 | 16 | 30 | -18 | 42 |
| 7 | Airdrieonians | 36 | 8 | 6 | 4 | 28 | 19 | 2 | 5 | 11 | 18 | 41 | -14 | 41 |
| 8 | Forfar | 36 | 6 | 3 | 9 | 20 | 30 | 5 | 2 | 11 | 20 | 35 | -25 | 38 |
| 9 | Queen's Park** | 36 | 2 | 7 | 9 | 22 | 41 | 5 | 3 | 10 | 20 | 31 | -30 | 31 |
| 10 | Albion | 36 | 3 | 3 | 12 | 22 | 40 | 5 | 3 | 10 | 35 | 40 | -23 | 30 |

*Also promoted. **Also relegated

**Play-offs** (on agg) – **Semi-finals**: Peterhead 4 Stirling 0; Stenhousemuir 3 Queen's Park 2; **Final**: Stenhousemuir 2 Peterhead 1
**Player of Year**: Lawrence Shankland (Ayr). **Manager of Year**: Ian McCall (Ayr)
**Team of Year**: Parry (Alloa), Taggart (Alloa), Davidson (Raith), O'Brien (Arbroath), Thomson (Raith), McDaid (Ayr), Vaughan (Raith), Flannigan (Alloa), Moffat (Ayr), Shankland (Ayr), Trouten (Albion)
**Leading league scorers**: 26 Shankland (Ayr); 20 Trouten (Albion); 19 Moore (Ayr); 16 Wallace (Arbroath); 15 Vaughan (Raith); 14 Duggan (East Fife); 11 Moffat (Ayr), Spence (Raith)

## LADBROKES LEAGUE TWO

| | | Home | | | | | | Away | | | | | |
|---|---|---|---|---|---|---|---|---|---|---|---|---|---|
| | | P | W | D | L | F | A | W | D | L | F | A | Gd | Pts |
| 1 | Montrose | 36 | 11 | 4 | 3 | 31 | 22 | 12 | 4 | 2 | 29 | 13 | 25 | 77 |
| 2 | Peterhead | 36 | 11 | 2 | 5 | 37 | 21 | 13 | 2 | 3 | 42 | 18 | 40 | 76 |
| 3 | Stirling | 36 | 8 | 4 | 6 | 30 | 24 | 8 | 3 | 7 | 31 | 28 | 9 | 55 |
| 4 | Stenhousemuir* | 36 | 9 | 1 | 8 | 32 | 26 | 6 | 8 | 4 | 24 | 21 | 9 | 54 |
| 5 | Clyde | 36 | 7 | 6 | 5 | 23 | 23 | 7 | 3 | 8 | 29 | 27 | 2 | 51 |
| 6 | Elgin | 36 | 10 | 4 | 4 | 31 | 16 | 4 | 3 | 11 | 23 | 45 | -7 | 49 |
| 7 | Annan | 36 | 6 | 8 | 4 | 24 | 17 | 6 | 3 | 9 | 25 | 24 | 8 | 47 |
| 8 | Berwick | 36 | 5 | 6 | 7 | 21 | 27 | 4 | 4 | 10 | 10 | 32 | -28 | 37 |
| 9 | Edinburgh City | 36 | 4 | 4 | 10 | 19 | 31 | 3 | 5 | 10 | 18 | 31 | -25 | 30 |
| 10 | Cowdenbeath | 36 | 3 | 3 | 12 | 12 | 35 | 1 | 7 | 10 | 11 | 21 | -33 | 22 |

*Also promoted

**Play-offs** (on agg); **Semi-final**: Cove 5 Spartans 2. **Final**: Cowdenbeath 3 Cove 2
**Player of Year**: Sean Dillon (Montrose). **Manager**: Stewart Petrie (Montrose)
**Team of Year**: Fleming (Peterhead), Brown (Peterhead), McCracken (Peterhead), Dillon (Montrose), Steeves (Montrose), Paton (Stenhousemuir), Reilly (Elgin), Gibson (Peterhead), McGuigan (Stenhousemuir), McAllister (Peterhead), D Smith (Stirling)
**Leading league scorers**: 25 Goodwillie (Clyde); 22 D Smith (Stirling); 20 McAllister (Peterhead), McGuigan (Stenhousemuir), 16 Henderson (Annan); 15 McLean (Peterhead); 12 A Smith (Annan)

# LADBROKES SCOTTISH LEAGUE RESULTS 2017–2018

## PREMIERSHIP

| | Aberdeen | Celtic | Dundee | Hamilton | Hearts | Hibernian | Kilmarnock | Motherwell | Partick | Rangers | Ross Co | St Johnstone |
|---|---|---|---|---|---|---|---|---|---|---|---|---|
| Aberdeen | – | 0-3 | 2-1 | 2-0 | 0-0 | 4-1 | 1-1 | 0-2 | 1-0 | 1-2 | 2-1 | 3-0 |
| | – | 0-2 | 1-0 | 3-0 | 2-0 | 0-0 | 3-1 | | | 1-1 | | 4-1 |
| Celtic | 3-0 | – | 1-0 | 3-1 | 4-1 | 2-2 | 1-1 | 5-1 | 2-0 | 0-0 | 4-0 | 1-1 |
| | 0-1 | – | 0-0 | | 3-1 | 1-0 | 0-0 | | | 5-0 | 3-0 | 0-0 |
| Dundee | 0-1 | 0-2 | – | 1-3 | 2-1 | 1-1 | 0-0 | 0-1 | 3-0 | 2-1 | 1-2 | 3-2 |
| | | | – | 1-0 | 1-1 | 0-1 | | 0-1 | 0-1 | | 1-4 | 0-4 |
| | | | | | | | | | | | | 2-1 |
| Hamilton | 2-2 | 1-4 | 3-0 | – | 1-2 | 1-1 | 1-2 | 1-2 | 0-0 | 1-4 | 3-2 | 0-1 |
| | | 1-2 | 1-2 | – | 0-3 | | | 2-0 | 2-1 | 3-5 | 2-0 | 1-2 |
| Hearts | 0-0 | 4-0 | 2-0 | 1-1 | – | 0-0 | 1-2 | 1-0 | 1-1 | 1-3 | 0-0 | 1-0 |
| | 2-0 | 1-3 | | | – | 2-1 | 1-1 | 1-1 | 3-0 | | | 1-0 |
| Hibernian | 0-1 | 2-2 | 2-1 | 1-3 | 1-0 | – | 1-1 | 2-2 | 3-1 | 1-2 | 2-1 | 1-2 |
| | 2-0 | 2-1 | | 3-1 | 2-0 | – | 5-3 | 2-1 | 2-0 | 5-5 | | |
| Kilmarnock | 1-3 | 0-2 | 1-1 | 2-2 | 0-1 | 0-3 | – | 1-0 | 5-1 | 2-1 | 0-2 | 1-2 |
| | 0-2 | 1-0 | 3-2 | 2-0 | 1-0 | 2-2 | – | | | | 3-2 | 2-0 |
| Motherwell | 0-1 | 1-1 | 1-1 | 1-3 | 2-1 | 0-1 | 2-0 | – | 3-0 | 1-2 | 2-0 | 2-0 |
| | 0-2 | 0-0 | 2-1 | 3-0 | | | 0-1 | – | 1-1 | 2-2 | 2-0 | 1-5 |
| Partick | 3-4 | 0-1 | 2-1 | 1-0 | 1-1 | 0-1 | 0-2 | 3-2 | – | 2-2 | 2-0 | 1-0 |
| | 0-0 | 1-2 | 1-2 | 2-1 | | | 0-1 | 0-1 | – | 0-2 | 1-1 | |
| Rangers | 3-0 | 0-2 | 4-1 | 0-2 | 0-0 | 2-3 | 1-1 | 2-0 | 3-0 | – | 2-1 | 1-3 |
| | 2-0 | 2-3 | 4-0 | | 2-0 | 1-2 | 0-1 | | | | | |
| | | | | | 2-1 | | 1-0 | | | | | |
| Ross Co | 1-2 | 0-1 | 0-2 | 2-1 | 1-2 | 0-1 | 2-2 | 3-2 | 1-1 | 1-3 | – | 1-1 |
| | 2-4 | | 0-1 | 2-2 | 1-1 | 1-1 | | 0-0 | 4-0 | 1-2 | | |
| St Johnstone | 0-3 | 0-4 | 0-2 | 2-1 | 0-0 | 1-1 | 1-2 | 4-1 | 1-0 | 0-3 | 0-0 | – |
| | | | | 1-0 | | 1-1 | | 0-0 | 1-3 | 1-4 | 2-0 | – |
| | | | | | | | | | 1-1 | | 1-1 | |

## CHAMPIONSHIP

| | Brechin | Dumbarton | Dundee Utd | Dunfermline | Falkirk | Inverness | Livingston | Morton | Queen of South | St Mirren |
|---|---|---|---|---|---|---|---|---|---|---|
| Brechin | – | 0-1 | 1-1 | 0-3 | 1-1 | 0-4 | 2-2 | 0-1 | 0-1 | 1-2 |
| | – | 1-3 | 0-5 | 0-3 | 0-1 | 2-3 | 0-2 | 1-1 | 1-5 | 0-1 |
| Dumbarton | 2-1 | – | 0-2 | 0-4 | 0-0 | 2-1 | 1-4 | 0-0 | 2-2 | 0-2 |
| | 1-0 | – | 3-2 | 0-1 | 2-5 | 0-1 | 0-3 | 0-1 | 0-1 | 0-2 |
| Dundee Utd | 1-0 | 1-1 | – | 2-1 | 3-0 | 0-2 | 3-0 | 2-1 | 2-1 | 2-1 |
| | 4-1 | 2-0 | – | 1-1 | 1-0 | 1-1 | 2-0 | 0-3 | 2-3 | 1-0 |
| Dunfermline | 2-1 | 2-2 | 1-3 | – | 3-1 | 5-1 | 3-1 | 1-1 | 2-5 | 3-0 |
| | 4-0 | 4-0 | 0-0 | – | 2-0 | 1-0 | 1-0 | 0-0 | 3-1 | 1-2 |
| Falkirk | 3-1 | 1-1 | 0-0 | 1-1 | – | 0-0 | 0-2 | 0-3 | 1-4 | 0-0 |
| | 3-0 | 0-0 | 6-1 | 1-2 | – | 3-1 | 1-3 | 3-1 | 3-2 | 1-0 |
| Inverness | 4-0 | 1-0 | 0-1 | 1-0 | 4-1 | – | 1-3 | 1-1 | 0-0 | 0-2 |
| | 4-0 | 5-1 | 1-0 | 2-2 | 1-0 | – | 1-1 | 0-2 | 3-1 | 2-2 |
| Livingston | 3-2 | 2-1 | 2-0 | 1-1 | 0-0 | 0-0 | – | 1-1 | 2-2 | 1-3 |
| | 3-0 | 2-0 | 2-1 | 0-0 | 0-0 | 0-1 | – | 3-2 | 0-1 | 4-1 |
| Morton | 4-1 | 1-1 | 0-2 | 3-2 | 0-1 | 1-0 | 0-1 | – | 1-2 | 4-1 |
| | 2-0 | 3-2 | 1-1 | 2-1 | 0-1 | 0-3 | 0-1 | – | 0-1 | 1-1 |
| Queen of South | 4-1 | 1-0 | 1-3 | 0-0 | 4-2 | 0-0 | 0-3 | 1-2 | – | 2-3 |
| | 3-1 | 0-0 | 3-0 | 0-0 | 2-2 | 0-2 | 3-3 | 1-1 | – | 1-3 |
| St Mirren | 2-1 | 0-1 | 3-0 | 1-0 | 3-1 | 4-2 | 3-1 | 2-2 | 3-1 | – |
| | 1-0 | 5-0 | 2-0 | 2-0 | 1-2 | 1-0 | 0-0 | 2-1 | 2-0 | – |

## LEAGUE ONE

| | Airdrieonians | Albion | Alloa | Arbroath | Ayr | East Fife | Forfar | Queen`s Park | Raith | Stranraer |
|---|---|---|---|---|---|---|---|---|---|---|
| Airdrieonians | – | 2-2 | 2-0 | 1-1 | 2-0 | 0-1 | 2-1 | 4-2 | 2-2 | 2-0 |
| | – | 2-0 | 2-2 | 0-0 | 1-2 | 0-0 | 1-2 | 2-1 | 1-2 | 2-1 |
| Albion | 1-2 | – | 0-2 | 1-2 | 1-5 | 3-2 | 3-4 | 0-1 | 2-1 | 0-4 |
| | 2-2 | – | 1-3 | 1-2 | 2-3 | 1-0 | 0-1 | 1-1 | 2-2 | 1-3 |
| Alloa | 1-0 | 2-5 | – | 5-3 | 1-2 | 4-1 | 2-1 | 1-0 | 1-1 | 1-0 |
| | 2-2 | 3-1 | – | 3-2 | 2-1 | 1-2 | 1-0 | 2-2 | 0-0 | 0-1 |
| Arbroath | 7-1 | 1-4 | 1-1 | – | 1-4 | 2-3 | 2-1 | 2-0 | 1-2 | 1-2 |
| | 2-0 | 1-0 | 0-0 | – | 1-1 | 1-1 | 2-0 | 2-1 | 1-1 | 2-3 |
| Ayr | 2-2 | 3-2 | 3-3 | 1-2 | – | 3-0 | 3-0 | 3-2 | 3-0 | 2-0 |
| | 3-0 | 2-0 | 1-2 | 1-2 | – | 3-0 | 2-3 | 4-0 | 3-0 | 1-2 |
| East Fife | 6-1 | 5-4 | 1-0 | 3-1 | 1-4 | – | 3-0 | 0-1 | 0-5 | 1-1 |
| | 2-1 | 2-0 | 2-1 | 0-5 | 2-3 | – | 1-2 | 0-2 | 2-3 | 2-3 |
| Forfar | 2-1 | 0-2 | 0-2 | 0-5 | 0-5 | 2-0 | – | 0-3 | 1-1 | 1-1 |
| | 0-1 | 4-2 | 0-1 | 0-1 | 0-2 | 2-0 | – | 1-1 | 2-1 | 5-1 |
| Queen`s Park | 1-1 | 2-5 | 0-4 | 0-2 | 0-2 | 2-1 | 1-1 | – | 0-5 | 2-2 |
| | 0-0 | 2-2 | 1-2 | 3-0 | 1-4 | 2-3 | 2-2 | – | 1-3 | 2-2 |
| Raith | 2-0 | 3-1 | 2-1 | 2-0 | 2-1 | 1-0 | 3-1 | 2-0 | – | 3-0 |
| | 2-1 | 2-0 | 0-0 | 2-2 | 1-1 | 2-0 | 2-1 | 2-0 | – | 3-0 |
| Stranraer | 3-1 | 2-2 | 2-0 | 2-6 | 3-4 | 1-0 | 3-0 | 3-0 | 1-0 | – |
| | 3-2 | 2-3 | 1-0 | 1-4 | 1-5 | 0-2 | 2-0 | 2-3 | 0-3 | – |

## LEAGUE TWO

| | Annan | Berwick | Clyde | Cowdenbeath | Edinburgh City | Elgin | Montrose | Peterhead | Stenhousemuir | Stirling |
|---|---|---|---|---|---|---|---|---|---|---|
| Annan | – | 0-0 | 0-0 | 1-0 | 2-1 | 2-0 | 0-1 | 1-2 | 1-1 | 1-1 |
| | – | 0-0 | 1-1 | 1-1 | 2-3 | 4-1 | 0-1 | 3-3 | 2-0 | 3-1 |
| Berwick | 1-5 | – | 3-1 | 1-0 | 1-1 | 3-2 | 0-1 | 2-3 | 0-0 | 1-0 |
| | 0-2 | – | 0-1 | 1-0 | 1-1 | 2-2 | 2-2 | 1-3 | 2-2 | 0-1 |
| Clyde | 2-1 | 0-0 | – | 1-1 | 2-3 | 2-4 | 0-0 | 1-4 | 1-1 | 1-1 |
| | 0-0 | 1-2 | – | 2-0 | 3-2 | 1-0 | 3-0 | 1-0 | 0-3 | 2-1 |
| Cowdenbeath | 1-1 | 0-1 | 0-3 | – | 1-0 | 1-3 | 1-3 | 0-4 | 1-1 | 0-3 |
| | 0-2 | 1-3 | 1-0 | – | 0-2 | 3-1 | 0-3 | 0-2 | 1-1 | 1-2 |
| Edinburgh City | 0-1 | 1-0 | 0-3 | 0-0 | – | 0-3 | 1-3 | 0-3 | 1-2 | 1-2 |
| | 3-2 | 3-0 | 1-3 | 1-1 | – | 4-0 | 0-2 | 0-0 | 1-4 | 2-2 |
| Elgin | 0-1 | 5-1 | 3-2 | 1-1 | 1-1 | – | 3-0 | 0-2 | 2-0 | 0-2 |
| | 2-1 | 3-0 | 2-1 | 1-0 | 1-1 | – | 2-2 | 0-1 | 2-0 | 3-0 |
| Montrose | 1-1 | 3-0 | 3-2 | 1-0 | 1-0 | 3-0 | – | 2-6 | 1-1 | 1-3 |
| | 2-1 | 1-0 | 1-3 | 1-1 | 3-0 | 1-1 | – | 3-2 | 1-0 | 2-1 |
| Peterhead | 1-0 | 0-2 | 2-1 | 3-2 | 3-0 | 3-0 | 1-1 | – | 2-3 | 2-4 |
| | 1-0 | 1-1 | 3-0 | 1-0 | 2-1 | 7-0 | 0-1 | – | 1-2 | 4-3 |
| Stenhousemuir | 1-3 | 3-0 | 1-1 | 1-0 | 3-0 | 4-1 | 0-1 | 3-1 | – | 2-3 |
| | 3-2 | 4-0 | 2-3 | 1-2 | 1-0 | 0-2 | 0-2 | 1-4 | – | 2-1 |
| Stirling | 3-2 | 4-0 | 2-3 | 1-0 | 2-0 | 2-2 | 0-1 | 0-1 | 1-2 | – |
| | 3-0 | 2-0 | 2-1 | 2-2 | 2-2 | 3-1 | 0-5 | 0-1 | 1-1 | – |

# HISTORIC DOUBLE TREBLE FOR CELTIC

Celtic became the first Scottish side to win back-to-back domestic trebles when beating Motherwell 2-0 in the Scottish FA Cup Final with goals by Callum McGregor and Olivier Ntcham. It followed their seventh consecutive title success and a League Cup victory, also against Motherwell by the same scoreline in the final. Celtic also swept the board for Player of the Year awards. Captain Scott Brown was the choice of both the PFA and football writers, while Kieran Tierney was voted best young player for the third year in a row. Brendan Rodgers was beaten to the Manager of the Year accolade which went to Jack Ross, who led St Mirren to the Championship title in his first full season at the club. Celtic set a British record of 63 games without defeat in domestic competitions when beating St Johnstone 4-0 to overtake the mark set by the club 101 years ago. They extended the run to 69 matches before a 4-0 Premiership defeat by Hearts.

## HOW CELTIC WON A SEVENTH SUCCESSIVE TITLE

### AUGUST 2017

**5** Celtic 4 (Griffiths 29, 63, Sinclair 51, McGregor 73) Hearts 1 (Goncalves 84). Att: 58,843
**11** Partick 0 Celtic 1 (Ntcham 25). Att: 8,041
**19** Kilmarnock 0 Celtic 2 (Forrest 40, McGregor 88). Att: 10,069
**26** Celtic 1 (McGregor 79) St Johnstone 1 (MacLean 39). Att: 58,446

### SEPTEMBER 2017

**8** Hamilton 1 (Gogic 86) Celtic 4 (Armstrong 17, Sinclair 29, 42, Edouard 65). Att: 5,208
**16** Celtic 4 (Rogic 13, Dembele 42, Forrest 52, 74) Ross Co 0. Att: 58,624
**23** Rangers 0 Celtic 2 (Rogic 50, Griffiths 65). Att: 50,116
**30** Celtic 2 (McGregor 15, 80) Hibernian 2 (McGinn 53, 77). Att: 59,259

### OCTOBER 2017

**14** Celtic 1 (Ntcham 61) Dundee 0. Att: 57,610
**25** Aberdeen 0 Celtic 3 (Tierney 13, Dembele 39, 63). Att: 20,528
**28** Celtic 1 (Griffiths 43) Kilmarnock 1 (Jones 60). Att: 58,060

### NOVEMBER 2017

**4** St Johnstone 0 Celtic 4 (Sinclair 28, Dembele 72, Anderson 75 og, Ntcham 89). Att: 6,800 (Celtic's 63rd domestic game without defeat – a British record)
**18** Ross Co 0 Celtic 1 (Griffiths 78). Att: 6,590
**29** Motherwell 1 (Lustig 78 og) Celtic 1 (Sinclair 88 pen). Att: 9,164

### DECEMBER 2017

**2** Celtic 5 (Edouard 16, 33, 85, Forrest 76, 88) Motherwell 1 (Frear 65). Att: 57,817
**10** Hibernian 2 (Ambrose 76, Shaw 79) Celtic 2 (Sinclair 60, 64). Att: 20,193
**13** Celtic 3 (Ntcham 12, Forrest 40, Sinclair 41) Hamilton 1 (Redmond 29). Att: 53,883
**17** Hearts 4 (Cochrane 26, Lafferty 35, Milinkovic 48, 76 pen) Celtic 0. Att: 18,555
**20** Celtic 2 (Armstrong 35, Tierney 67) Partick 0. Att: 54,187
**23** Celtic 3 (Lustig 40, Hayes 69, Ntcham 76) Aberdeen 0. Att: 58,975
**26** Dundee 0 Celtic 2 (Forrest 8, Griffiths 43). Att: 9,193
**30** Celtic 0 Rangers 0. Att: 59,004

## JANUARY 2018

**23** Partick 1 (Sammon 34 pen) Celtic 2 (Sinclair 55 pen, Griffiths 70). Att: 6,920
**27** Celtic 1 (Griffiths 27) Hibernian 0. Att: 58,998
**30** Celtic 3 (Edouard 3, Boyata 25, Dembele 36) Hearts 1 (Lafferty 67). Att: 56,296

## FEBRUARY 2018

**3** Kilmarnock 1 (Mulumbu 70) Celtic 0. Att: 10,702
**18** Celtic 0 St Johnstone 0. Att: 56,867
**25** Aberdeen 0 Celtic 2 (Dembele 37, Tierney 83). Att: 17,206

## MARCH 2018

**11** Rangers 2 (Windass 3, Candelas 26) Celtic 3 (Rogic 11, Dembele 45, Edouard 69). Att: 50,215
**18** Motherwell 0 Celtic 0. Att: 8,717
**31** Celtic 3 (Dembele 25 pen, Armstrong 48, Rogic 60) Ross Co 0. Att: 58,765

## APRIL 2018

**4** Celtic 0 Dundee 0. Att: 55,768
**8** Hamilton 1 (Bingham, 18) Celtic 2 (McGregor 3, Griffiths 46). Att: 4,851
**21** Hibernian 2 (Maclaren 24, Slivka 80) Celtic 1 (Edouard 87). Att: 19,886
**29** Celtic 5 (Edouard 14, 41, Forrest 45, Rogic 47, McGregor 53) Rangers 0. Att: 58,320 (Celtic clinched title)

## MAY 2018

**6** Hearts 1 (Lafferty 18) Celtic 3 (Boyata 21, Dembele 51, Sinclair 90+4). Att: 19,031
**9** Celtic 0 Kilmarnock 0. Att: 54,916
13 Celtic 0 Aberdeen 1 (Considine 47). Att: 58,388

## THE THINGS THEY SAY...

'We've been given a headache and now we have to find the aspirins to ease it' – **Roy Hodgson**, Crystal Palace's new manager, after seven successive goalless defeats to start the season.

'I do hope that you can give me one of the greatest memories of my life' – **Sir Bobby Charlton** tells Harry Kane he can fire England to World Cup success in Russia.

'It is so difficult to speak every day about Harry Kane, finding a different word to describe him' – **Mauricio Pochettino**, Tottenham manager, on another high-scoring season for his striker.

'The best part of the night was the view of the Pyrenees' – **Aidy Boothroyd**, England under-21 coach, after his side laboured to a 1-0 European Championship qualifying victory in Andorra.

'If the club think I've done something for them, then it's a fraction of what they've done for us as a family' – **Kenny Dalglish**, Liverpool legend, on the day Anfield's Centenary Stand was renamed in his honour.

That is as good as I have ever hit a football' – **Wayne Rooney** on his 60-yard goal for Everton against West Ham.

'I told him what I saw today was the best goalkeeper in the world' – **Jose Mourinho**, Manchester United manager, after David de Gea's man-of-the-match performance against Arsenal.

# SCOTTISH HONOURS LIST

## PREMIER DIVISION

| | *First* | *Pts* | *Second* | *Pts* | *Third* | *Pts* |
|---|---|---|---|---|---|---|
| 1975–6 | Rangers | 54 | Celtic | 48 | Hibernian | 43 |
| 1976–7 | Celtic | 55 | Rangers | 46 | Aberdeen | 43 |
| 1977–8 | Rangers | 55 | Aberdeen | 53 | Dundee Utd | 40 |
| 1978–9 | Celtic | 48 | Rangers | 45 | Dundee Utd | 44 |
| 1979–80 | Aberdeen | 48 | Celtic | 47 | St Mirren | 42 |
| 1980–81 | Celtic | 56 | Aberdeen | 49 | Rangers | 44 |
| 1981–2 | Celtic | 55 | Aberdeen | 53 | Rangers | 43 |
| 1982–3 | Dundee Utd | 56 | Celtic | 55 | Aberdeen | 55 |
| 1983–4 | Aberdeen | 57 | Celtic | 50 | Dundee Utd | 47 |
| 1984–5 | Aberdeen | 59 | Celtic | 52 | Dundee Utd | 47 |
| 1985–6 | *Celtic | 50 | Hearts | 50 | Dundee Utd | 47 |
| 1986–7 | Rangers | 69 | Celtic | 63 | Dundee Utd | 60 |
| 1987–8 | Celtic | 72 | Hearts | 62 | Rangers | 60 |
| 1988–9 | Rangers | 56 | Aberdeen | 50 | Celtic | 46 |
| 1989–90 | Rangers | 51 | Aberdeen | 44 | Hearts | 44 |
| 1990–1 | Rangers | 55 | Aberdeen | 53 | Celtic | 41 |
| 1991–2 | Rangers | 72 | Hearts | 63 | Celtic | 62 |
| 1992–3 | Rangers | 73 | Aberdeen | 64 | Celtic | 60 |
| 1993–4 | Rangers | 58 | Aberdeen | 55 | Motherwell | 54 |
| 1994–5 | Rangers | 69 | Motherwell | 54 | Hibernian | 53 |
| 1995–6 | Rangers | 87 | Celtic | 83 | Aberdeen | 55 |
| 1996–7 | Rangers | 80 | Celtic | 75 | Dundee Utd | 60 |
| 1997–8 | Celtic | 74 | Rangers | 72 | Hearts | 67 |

## PREMIER LEAGUE

| | *First* | *Pts* | *Second* | *Pts* | *Third* | *Pts* |
|---|---|---|---|---|---|---|
| 1998–99 | Rangers | 77 | Celtic | 71 | St Johnstone | 57 |
| 1999–2000 | Rangers | 90 | Celtic | 69 | Hearts | 54 |
| 2000–01 | Celtic | 97 | Rangers | 82 | Hibernian | 66 |
| 2001–02 | Celtic | 103 | Rangers | 85 | Livingston | 58 |
| 2002–03 | *Rangers | 97 | Celtic | 97 | Hearts | 63 |
| 2003–04 | Celtic | 98 | Rangers | 81 | Hearts | 68 |
| 2004–05 | Rangers | 93 | Celtic | 92 | Hibernian | 61 |
| 2005–06 | Celtic | 91 | Hearts | 74 | Rangers | 73 |
| 2006–07 | Celtic | 84 | Rangers | 72 | Aberdeen | 65 |
| 2007–08 | Celtic | 89 | Rangers | 86 | Motherwell | 60 |
| 2008–09 | Rangers | 86 | Celtic | 82 | Hearts | 59 |
| 2009–10 | Rangers | 87 | Celtic | 81 | Dundee Utd | 63 |
| 2010–11 | Rangers | 93 | Celtic | 92 | Hearts | 63 |
| 2011–12 | Celtic | 93 | **Rangers | 73 | Motherwell | 62 |
| 2012–13 | Celtic | 79 | Motherwell | 63 | St Johnstone | 56 |

Maximum points: 72 except 1986–8, 1991–4 (88), 1994–2000 (108), 2001–10 (114)
* Won on goal difference. **Deducted 10 pts for administration

## PREMIERSHIP

| | *First* | *Pts* | *Second* | *Pts* | *Third* | *Pts* |
|---|---|---|---|---|---|---|
| 2013–14 | Celtic | 99 | Motherwell | 70 | Aberdeen | 68 |
| 2014–15 | Celtic | 92 | Aberdeen | 75 | Inverness | 65 |
| 2015–16 | Celtic | 86 | Aberden | 71 | Hearts | 65 |
| 2016–17 | Celtic | 106 | Aberdeen | 76 | Rangers | 67 |
| 2017–18 | Celtic | 82 | Aberdeen | 73 | Rangers | 70 |

## FIRST DIVISION (Scottish Championship until 1975–76)

| | *First* | *Pts* | *Second* | *Pts* | *Third* | *Pts* |
|---|---|---|---|---|---|---|
| 1890–1a | ††Dumbarton | 29 | Rangers | 29 | Celtic | 24 |
| 1891–2b | Dumbarton | 37 | Celtic | 35 | Hearts | 30 |
| 1892–3a | Celtic | 29 | Rangers | 28 | St Mirren | 23 |
| 1893–4a | Celtic | 29 | Hearts | 26 | St Bernard's | 22 |
| 1894–5a | Hearts | 31 | Celtic | 26 | Rangers | 21 |
| 1895–6a | Celtic | 30 | Rangers | 26 | Hibernian | 24 |
| 1896–7a | Hearts | 28 | Hibernian | 26 | Rangers | 25 |
| 1897–8a | Celtic | 33 | Rangers | 29 | Hibernian | 22 |
| 1898–9a | Rangers | 36 | Hearts | 26 | Celtic | 24 |
| 1899–1900a | Rangers | 32 | Celtic | 25 | Hibernian | 24 |
| 1900–1c | Rangers | 35 | Celtic | 29 | Hibernian | 25 |
| 1901–2a | Rangers | 28 | Celtic | 26 | Hearts | 22 |
| 1902–3b | Hibernian | 37 | Dundee | 31 | Rangers | 29 |
| 1903–4d | Third Lanark | 43 | Hearts | 39 | Rangers | 38 |
| 1904–5a | †Celtic | 41 | Rangers | 41 | Third Lanark | 35 |
| 1905–6a | Celtic | 46 | Hearts | 39 | Rangers | 38 |
| 1906–7f | Celtic | 55 | Dundee | 48 | Rangers | 45 |
| 1907–8f | Celtic | 55 | Falkirk | 51 | Rangers | 50 |
| 1908–9f | Celtic | 51 | Dundee | 50 | Clyde | 48 |
| 1909–10f | Celtic | 54 | Falkirk | 52 | Rangers | 49 |
| 1910–11f | Rangers | 52 | Aberdeen | 48 | Falkirk | 44 |
| 1911–12f | Rangers | 51 | Celtic | 45 | Clyde | 42 |
| 1912–13f | Rangers | 53 | Celtic | 49 | Hearts | 41 |
| 1913–14g | Celtic | 65 | Rangers | 59 | Hearts | 54 |
| 1914–15g | Celtic | 65 | Hearts | 61 | Rangers | 50 |
| 1915–16g | Celtic | 67 | Rangers | 56 | Morton | 51 |
| 1916–17g | Celtic | 64 | Morton | 54 | Rangers | 53 |
| 1917–18f | Rangers | 56 | Celtic | 55 | Kilmarnock | 43 |
| 1918–19f | Celtic | 58 | Rangers | 57 | Morton | 47 |
| 1919–20h | Rangers | 71 | Celtic | 68 | Motherwell | 57 |
| 1920–1h | Rangers | 76 | Celtic | 66 | Hearts | 56 |
| 1921–2h | Celtic | 67 | Rangers | 66 | Raith | 56 |
| 1922–3g | Rangers | 55 | Airdrieonians | 50 | Celtic | 40 |
| 1923–4g | Rangers | 59 | Airdrieonians | 50 | Celtic | 41 |
| 1924–5g | Rangers | 60 | Airdrieonians | 57 | Hibernian | 52 |
| 1925–6g | Celtic | 58 | Airdrieonians | 50 | Hearts | 50 |
| 1926–7g | Rangers | 56 | Motherwell | 51 | Celtic | 49 |
| 1927–8g | Rangers | 60 | Celtic | 55 | Motherwell | 55 |
| 1928–9g | Rangers | 67 | Celtic | 51 | Motherwell | 50 |
| 1929–30g | Rangers | 60 | Motherwell | 55 | Aberdeen | 53 |
| 1930–1g | Rangers | 60 | Celtic | 58 | Motherwell | 56 |
| 1931–2g | Motherwell | 66 | Rangers | 61 | Celtic | 48 |
| 1932–3g | Rangers | 62 | Motherwell | 59 | Hearts | 50 |
| 1933–4g | Rangers | 66 | Motherwell | 62 | Celtic | 47 |
| 1934–5g | Rangers | 55 | Celtic | 52 | Hearts | 50 |
| 1935–6g | Celtic | 68 | Rangers | 61 | Aberdeen | 61 |
| 1936–7g | Rangers | 61 | Aberdeen | 54 | Celtic | 52 |
| 1937–8g | Celtic | 61 | Hearts | 58 | Rangers | 49 |
| 1938–9f | Rangers | 59 | Celtic | 48 | Aberdeen | 46 |
| 1946–7f | Rangers | 46 | Hibernian | 44 | Aberdeen | 39 |
| 1947–8g | Hibernian | 48 | Rangers | 46 | Partick | 46 |
| 1948–9i | Rangers | 46 | Dundee | 45 | Hibernian | 39 |
| 1949–50i | Rangers | 50 | Hibernian | 49 | Hearts | 43 |
| 1950–1i | Hibernian | 48 | Rangers | 38 | Dundee | 38 |
| 1951–2i | Hibernian | 45 | Rangers | 41 | East Fife | 37 |
| 1952–3i | *Rangers | 43 | Hibernian | 43 | East Fife | 39 |
| 1953–4i | Celtic | 43 | Hearts | 38 | Partick | 35 |

| | | | |
|---|---|---|---|
| 1954–5f | Aberdeen 49 | Celtic 46 | Rangers 41 |
| 1955–6f | Rangers 52 | Aberdeen 46 | Hearts 45 |
| 1956–7f | Rangers 55 | Hearts 53 | Kilmarnock 42 |
| 1957–8f | Hearts 62 | Rangers 49 | Celtic 46 |
| 1958–9f | Rangers 50 | Hearts 48 | Motherwell 44 |
| 1959–60f | Hearts 54 | Kilmarnock 50 | Rangers 42 |
| 1960–1f | Rangers 51 | Kilmarnock 50 | Third Lanark 42 |
| 1961–2f | Dundee 54 | Rangers 51 | Celtic 46 |
| 1962–3f | Rangers 57 | Kilmarnock 48 | Partick 46 |
| 1963–4f | Rangers 55 | Kilmarnock 49 | Celtic 47 |
| 1964–5f | *Kilmarnock 50 | Hearts 50 | Dunfermline 49 |
| 1965–6f | Celtic 57 | Rangers 55 | Kilmarnock 45 |
| 1966–7f | Celtic 58 | Rangers 55 | Clyde 46 |
| 1967–8f | Celtic 63 | Rangers 61 | Hibernian 45 |
| 1968–9f | Celtic 54 | Rangers 49 | Dunfermline 45 |
| 1969–70f | Celtic 57 | Rangers 45 | Hibernian 44 |
| 1970–1f | Celtic 56 | Aberdeen 54 | St Johnstone 44 |
| 1971–2f | Celtic 60 | Aberdeen 50 | Rangers 44 |
| 1972–3f | Celtic 57 | Rangers 56 | Hibernian 45 |
| 1973–4f | Celtic 53 | Hibernian 49 | Rangers 48 |
| 1974–5f | Rangers 56 | Hibernian 49 | Celtic 45 |

*Won on goal average †Won on deciding match ††Title shared. Competition suspended 1940–46 (Second World War)

## SCOTTISH TITLE WINS

| | | |
|---|---|---|
| Rangers *54 | Hibernian 4 | Kilmarnock 1 |
| Celtic 49 | Dumbarton *2 | Motherwell 1 |
| Aberdeen 4 | Dundee 1 | Third Lanark 1 |
| Hearts 4 | Dundee Utd 1 | (*Incl 1 shared) |

## FIRST DIVISION (Since formation of Premier Division)

| | First Pts | Second Pts | Third Pts |
|---|---|---|---|
| 1975–6d | Partick 41 | Kilmarnock 35 | Montrose 30 |
| 1976–7j | St Mirren 62 | Clydebank 58 | Dundee 51 |
| 1977–8j | *Morton 58 | Hearts 58 | Dundee 57 |
| 1978–9j | Dundee 55 | Kilmarnock 54 | Clydebank 54 |
| 1979–80j | Hearts 53 | Airdrieonians 51 | Ayr 44 |
| 1980–1j | Hibernian 57 | Dundee 52 | St Johnstone 51 |
| 1981–2j | Motherwell 61 | Kilmarnock 51 | Hearts 50 |
| 1982–3j | St Johnstone 55 | Hearts 54 | Clydebank 50 |
| 1983–4j | Morton 54 | Dumbarton 51 | Partick 46 |
| 1984–5j | Motherwell 50 | Clydebank 48 | Falkirk 45 |
| 1985–6j | Hamilton 56 | Falkirk 45 | Kilmarnock 44 |
| 1986–7k | Morton 57 | Dunfermline 56 | Dumbarton 53 |
| 1987–8k | Hamilton 56 | Meadowbank 52 | Clydebank 49 |
| 1988–9j | Dunfermline 54 | Falkirk 52 | Clydebank 48 |
| 1989–90j | St Johnstone 58 | Airdrieonians 54 | Clydebank 44 |
| 1990–1j | Falkirk 54 | Airdrieonians 53 | Dundee 52 |
| 1991–2k | Dundee 58 | Partick 57 | Hamilton 57 |
| 1992–3k | Raith 65 | Kilmarnock 54 | Dunfermline 52 |
| 1993–4k | Falkirk 66 | Dunfermline 65 | Airdrieonians 54 |
| 1994–5l | Raith 69 | Dunfermline 68 | Dundee 68 |
| 1995–6l | Dunfermline 71 | Dundee Utd 67 | Morton 67 |
| 1996–7l | St Johnstone 80 | Airdrieonians 60 | Dundee 58 |
| 1997–8l | Dundee 70 | Falkirk 65 | Raith 60 |
| 1998–9l | Hibernian 89 | Falkirk 66 | Ayr 62 |
| 1999–2000l | St Mirren 76 | Dunfermline 71 | Falkirk 68 |
| 2000–01l | Livingston 76 | Ayr 69 | Falkirk 56 |
| 2001–02l | Partick 66 | Airdie 56 | Ayr 52 |

| Season | First | Pts | Second | Pts | Third | Pts |
|---|---|---|---|---|---|---|
| 2002–03l | Falkirk | 81 | Clyde | 72 | St Johnstone | 67 |
| 2003–04l | Inverness | 70 | Clyde | 69 | St Johnstone | 57 |
| 2004–05l | Falkirk | 75 | St Mirren | 60 | Clyde | 60 |
| 2005–06l | St Mirren | 76 | St Johnstone | 66 | Hamilton | 59 |
| 2006–07l | Gretna | 66 | St Johnstone | 65 | Dundee | 53 |
| 2007–08l | Hamilton | 76 | Dundee | 69 | St Johnstone | 58 |
| 2008–09l | St Johnstone | 65 | Partick | 55 | Dunfermline | 51 |
| 2009–10l | Inverness | 73 | Dundee | 61 | Dunfermline | 58 |
| 2010–11l | Dunfermline | 70 | Raith | 60 | Falkirk | 58 |
| 2011–12l | Ross | 79 | Dundee | 55 | Falkirk | 52 |
| 2012–13l | Partick | 78 | Morton | 67 | Falkirk | 53 |

## CHAMPIONSHIP

| | *First* | *Pts* | *Second* | *Pts* | *Third* | *Pts* |
|---|---|---|---|---|---|---|
| 2013–14l | Dundee | 69 | Hamilton | 67 | Falkirk | 66 |
| 2014–15l | Hearts | 91 | Hibernian | 70 | Rangers | 67 |
| 2015–16l | Rangers | 81 | Falkirk | 70 | Hibernian | 70 |
| 2016–17l | Hibernian | 71 | Falkirk | 60 | Dundee Utd | 57 |
| 2017–18l | St Mirren | 74 | Livingston | 62 | Dundee Utd | 61 |

Maximum points: a, 36; b, 44; c,.40; d 52; e, 60; f, 68; g, 76; h, 84; i, 60; j, 78; k, 88; l, 108
*Won on goal difference

## SECOND DIVISION

| | *First* | *Pts* | *Second* | *Pts* | *Third* | *Pts* |
|---|---|---|---|---|---|---|
| 1921–2a | Alloa | 60 | Cowdenbeath | 47 | Armadale | 45 |
| 1922–3a | Queen's Park | 57 | Clydebank | 52 | St Johnstone | 50 |
| 1923–4a | St Johnstone | 56 | Cowdenbeath | 55 | Bathgate | 44 |
| 1924–5a | Dundee Utd | 50 | Clydebank | 48 | Clyde | 47 |
| 1925–6a | Dunfermline | 59 | Clyde | 53 | Ayr | 52 |
| 1926–7a | Bo'ness | 56 | Raith | 49 | Clydebank | 45 |
| 1927–8a | Ayr | 54 | Third Lanark | 45 | King'sPark | 44 |
| 1928–9b | Dundee Utd | 51 | Morton | 50 | Arbroath | 47 |
| 1929–30a | *LeithAthletic | 57 | East Fife | 57 | Albion | 54 |
| 1930–1a | Third Lanark | 61 | Dundee Utd | 50 | Dunfermline | 47 |
| 1931–2a | *E Stirling | 55 | St Johnstone | 55 | Stenhousemuir | 46 |
| 1932–3c | Hibernian | 55 | Queen of South | 49 | Dunfermline | 47 |
| 1933–4c | Albion | 45 | Dunfermline | 44 | Arbroath | 44 |
| 1934–5c | Third Lanark | 52 | Arbroath | 50 | St Bernard's | 47 |
| 1935–6c | Falkirk | 59 | St Mirren | 52 | Morton | 48 |
| 1936–7c | Ayr | 54 | Morton | 51 | St Bernard's | 48 |
| 1937–8c | Raith | 59 | Albion | 48 | Airdrieonians | 47 |
| 1938–9c | Cowdenbeath | 60 | Alloa | 48 | East Fife | 48 |
| 1946–7d | Dundee Utd | 45 | Airdrieonians | 42 | East Fife | 31 |
| 1947–8e | East Fife | 53 | Albion | 42 | Hamilton | 40 |
| 1948–9e | *Raith | 42 | Stirling | 42 | Airdrieonians | 41 |
| 1949–50e | Morton | 47 | Airdrieonians | 44 | St Johnstone | 36 |
| 1950–1e | *Queen of South | 45 | Stirling | 45 | Ayr | 36 |
| 1951–2e | Clyde | 44 | Falkirk | 43 | Ayr | 39 |
| 1952–3 | E Stirling | 44 | Hamilton | 43 | Queen's Park | 37 |
| 1953–4e | Motherwell | 45 | Kilmarnock | 42 | Third Lanark | 36 |
| 1954–5e | Airdrieonians | 46 | Dunfermline | 42 | Hamilton | 39 |
| 1955–6b | Queen's Park | 54 | Ayr | 51 | St Johnstone | 49 |
| 1956–7b | Clyde | 64 | Third Lanark | 51 | Cowdenbeath | 45 |
| 1957–8b | Stirling | 55 | Dunfermline | 53 | Arbroath | 47 |
| 1958–9b | Ayr | 60 | Arbroath | 51 | Stenhousemuir | 46 |
| 1959–60b | St Johnstone | 53 | Dundee Utd | 50 | Queen of South | 49 |
| 1960–1b | Stirling | 55 | Falkirk | 54 | Stenhousemuir | 50 |

| | | | |
|---|---|---|---|
| 1961–2b | Clyde 54 | Queen of South 53 | Morton 44 |
| 1962–3b | St Johnstone 55 | E Stirling 49 | Morton 48 |
| 1963–4b | Morton 67 | Clyde 53 | Arbroath 46 |
| 1964–5b | Stirling 59 | Hamilton 50 | Queen of South 45 |
| 1965–6b | Ayr 53 | Airdrieonians 50 | Queen of South 47 |
| 1966–7b | Morton 69 | Raith 58 | Arbroath 57 |
| 1967–8b | St Mirren 62 | Arbroath 53 | East Fife 49 |
| 1968–9b | Motherwell 64 | Ayr 53 | East Fife 48 |
| 1969–70b | Falkirk 56 | Cowdenbeath 55 | Queen of South 50 |
| 1970–1b | Partick 56 | East Fife 51 | Arbroath 46 |
| 1971–2b | *Dumbarton 52 | Arbroath 52 | Stirling 50 |
| 1972–3b | Clyde 56 | Dunfermline 52 | Raith 47 |
| 1973–4b | Airdrieonians 60 | Kilmarnock 58 | Hamilton 55 |
| 1974–5b | Falkirk 54 | Queen of South 53 | Montrose 53 |

## SECOND DIVISION (MODERN)

| | *First* Pts | *Second* Pts | *Third* Pts |
|---|---|---|---|
| 1975–6d | *Clydebank 40 | Raith 40 | Alloa 35 |
| 1976–7f | Stirling 55 | Alloa 51 | Dunfermline 50 |
| 1977–8f | *Clyde 53 | Raith 53 | Dunfermline 48 |
| 1978–9f | Berwick 54 | Dunfermline 52 | Falkirk 50 |
| 1979–80f | Falkirk 50 | E Stirling 49 | Forfar 46 |
| 1980–1f | Queen's Park 50 | Queen of South 46 | Cowdenbeath 45 |
| 1981–2f | Clyde 59 | Alloa 50 | Arbroath 50 |
| 1982–3f | Brechin 55 | Meadowbank 54 | Arbroath 49 |
| 1983–4f | Forfar 63 | East Fife 47 | Berwick 43 |
| 1984–5f | Montrose 53 | Alloa 50 | Dunfermline 49 |
| 1985–6f | Dunfermline 57 | Queen of South 55 | Meadowbank 49 |
| 1986–7f | Meadowbank 55 | Raith 52 | Stirling 52 |
| 1987–8f | Ayr 61 | St Johnstone 59 | Queen's Park 51 |
| 1988–9f | Albion 50 | Alloa 45 | Brechin 43 |
| 1989–90f | Brechin 49 | Kilmarnock 48 | Stirling 47 |
| 1990–1f | Stirling 54 | Montrose 46 | Cowdenbeath 45 |
| 1991–2f | Dumbarton 52 | Cowdenbeath 51 | Alloa 50 |
| 1992–3f | Clyde 54 | Brechin 53 | Stranraer 53 |
| 1993–4f | Stranraer 56 | Berwick 48 | Stenhousemuir 47 |
| 1994–5g | Morton 64 | Dumbarton 60 | Stirling 58 |
| 1995–6g | Stirling 81 | East Fife 67 | Berwick 60 |
| 1996–7g | Ayr 77 | Hamilton 74 | Livingston 64 |
| 1997–8g | Stranraer 61 | Clydebank 60 | Livingston 59 |
| 1998–9g | Livingston 77 | Inverness 72 | Clyde 53 |
| 1999–2000g | Clyde 65 | Alloa 64 | Ross Co 62 |
| 2000–01g | Partick 75 | Arbroath 58 | Berwick 54 |
| 2001–02g | Queen of South 67 | Alloa 59 | Forfar Athletic 53 |
| 2002–03g | Raith 59 | Brechin 55 | Airdrie 54 |
| 2003–04g | Airdrie 70 | Hamilton 62 | Dumbarton 60 |
| 2004–05g | Brechin 72 | Stranraer 63 | Morton 62 |
| 2005–06g | Gretna 88 | Morton 70 | Peterhead 57 |
| 2006–07g | Morton 77 | Stirling 69 | Raith 62 |
| 2007–08g | Ross 73 | Airdrie 66 | Raith 60 |
| 2008–09g | Raith 76 | Ayr 74 | Brechin 62 |
| 2009–10g | *Stirling 65 | Alloa 65 | Cowdenbeath 59 |
| 2010–11g | Livingston 82 | *Ayr 59 | Forfar 59 |
| 2011–12g | Cowdenbeath 71 | Arbroath 63 | Dumbarton 58 |
| 2012–13g | Queen of South 92 | Alloa 67 | Brechin 61 |

## LEAGUE ONE

| | First | Pts | Second | Pts | Third | Pts |
|---|---|---|---|---|---|---|
| 2013–14g | Rangers | 102 | Dunfermline | 63 | Stranraer | 51 |
| 2014–15g | Morton | 69 | Stranraer | 67 | Forfar | 66 |
| 2015–16g | Dunfermline | 79 | Ayr | 61 | Peterhead | 59 |
| 2016–17g | Livingston | 81 | Alloa | 62 | Aidrieonians | 52 |
| 2017–18g | Ayr | 76 | Raith | 75 | Alloa | 60 |

Maximum points: a, 76; b, 72; c, 68; d, 52e, 60; f, 78; g, 108 *Won on goal average/goal difference

## THIRD DIVISION (MODERN)

| | First | Pts | Second | Pts | Third | Pts |
|---|---|---|---|---|---|---|
| 1994–5 | Forfar | 80 | Montrose | 67 | Ross Co | 60 |
| 1995–6 | Livingston | 72 | Brechin | 63 | Caledonian Th | 57 |
| 1996–7 | Inverness | 76 | Forfar | 67 | Ross Co | 77 |
| 1997–8 | Alloa | 76 | Arbroath | 68 | Ross Co | 67 |
| 1998–9 | Ross Co | 77 | Stenhousemuir | 64 | Brechin | 59 |
| 1999–2000 | Queen's Park | 69 | Berwick | 66 | Forfar | 61 |
| 2000–01 | *Hamilton | 76 | Cowdenbeath | 76 | Brechin | 72 |
| 2001–02 | Brechin | 73 | Dumbarton | 61 | Albion | 59 |
| 2002–03 | Morton | 72 | East Fife | 71 | Albion | 70 |
| 2003–04 | Stranraer | 79 | Stirling | 77 | Gretna | 68 |
| 2004–05 | Gretna | 98 | Peterhead | 78 | Cowdenbeath | 51 |
| 2005–06 | *Cowdenbeath | 76 | Berwick | 76 | Stenhousemuir | 73 |
| 2006–07 | Berwick | 75 | Arbroath | 70 | Queen's Park | 68 |
| 2007–08 | East Fife | 88 | Stranraer | 65 | Montrose | 59 |
| 2008–09 | Dumbarton | 67 | Cowdenbeath | 63 | East Stirling | 61 |
| 2009–10 | Livingston | 78 | Forfar | 63 | East Stirling | 61 |
| 2010–11 | Arbroath | 66 | Albion | 61 | Queen's Park | 59 |
| 2011–12 | Alloa | 77 | Queen's Park | 63 | Stranraer | 58 |
| 2012–13 | Rangers | 83 | Peterhead | 59 | Queen's Park | 56 |

## LEAGUE TWO

| | First | Pts | Second | Pts | Third | Pts |
|---|---|---|---|---|---|---|
| 2013–14 | Peterhead | 76 | Annan | 63 | Stirling | 58 |
| 2014–15 | Albion | 71 | Queen's Park | 61 | Arbroath | 56 |
| 2015–16 | East Fife | 62 | Elgin | 59 | Clyde | 57 |
| 2016–17 | Arbroath | 66 | Forfar | 64 | Annan | 58 |
| 2017–18 | Montrose | 77 | Peterhead | 76 | Stirling | 55 |

Maximum points: 108 * Won on goal difference

## RELEGATED FROM PREMIER DIVISION/PREMIER LEAGUE/PREMIERSHIP

| | | | | |
|---|---|---|---|---|
| 1975–6 | Dundee, | St Johnstone | 1991–2 | St Mirren, Dunfermline |
| 1976–7 | Kilmarnock, | Hearts | 1992–3 | Falkirk, Airdrieonians |
| 1977–8 | Ayr, | Clydebank | 1993–4 | St J'stone, Raith, Dundee |
| 1978–9 | Hearts, | Motherwell | 1994–5 | Dundee Utd |
| 1979–80 | Dundee, | Hibernian | 1995–6 | Falkirk, Partick |
| 1980–1 | Kilmarnock, | Hearts | 1996–7 | Raith |
| 1981–2 | Partick, | Airdrieonians | 1997–8 | Hibernian |
| 1982–3 | Morton, | Kilmarnock | 1998–9 | Dunfermline |
| 1983–4 | St Johnstone, | Motherwell | 1999–2000 | No relegation |
| 1984–5 | Dumbarton, | Morton | 2000–01 | St Mirren |
| 1985–6 | No relegation | | 2001–02 | St Johnstone |
| 1986–7 | Clydebank, Hamilton | | 2002–03 | No relegation |
| 1987–8 | Falkirk, Dunfermline, Morton | | 2003–04 | Partick |
| 1988–9 | Hamilton | | 2004–05 | Dundee |
| 1989–90 | Dundee | | 2005–06 | Livingston |
| 1990–1 | No relegation | | 2006–07 | Dunfermline |

| | | | |
|---|---|---|---|
| 2007–08 | Gretna | 2014–15 | St Mirren |
| 2008–09 | Inverness | 2015–16 | Dundee Utd |
| 2009–10 | Falkirk | 2016–17 | Inverness |
| 2010–11 | Hamilton | 2017–18 | Partick, Ross Co |
| 2011–12 | Dunfermline, *Rangers | | |
| 2012–13 | Dundee | | |
| 2013–14 | Hibernian, **Hearts | | |

*Following administration, liquidationand new club formed. **Deducted 15 points for administration

## RELEGATED FROM FIRST DIVISION/CHAMPIONSHIP

| | | | |
|---|---|---|---|
| 1975–6 | Dunfermline, Clyde | 1996–7 | Clydebank, East Fife |
| 1976–7 | Raith, Falkirk | 1997–8 | Partick, Stirling |
| 1977–8 | Alloa, East Fife | 1998–9 | Hamilton, Stranraer |
| 1978–9 | Montrose, Queen of South | 1999–2000 | Clydebank |
| 1979–80 | Arbroath, Clyde | 2000–01 | Morton, Alloa |
| 1980–1 | Stirling, Berwick | 2001–02 | Raith |
| 1981–2 | E Stirling, Queen of South | 2002–03 | Alloa Athletic, Arbroath |
| 1982–3 | Dunfermline, Queen's Park | 2003–04 | Ayr, Brechin |
| 1983–4 | Raith, Alloa | 2004–05 | Partick, Raith |
| 1984–5 | Meadowbank, St Johnstone | 2005–06 | Brechin, Stranraer |
| 1985–6 | Ayr, Alloa | 2006–07 | Airdrie Utd, Ross Co |
| 1986–7 | Brechin, Montrose | 2007–08 | Stirling |
| 1987–8 | East Fife, Dumbarton | 2008–09 | *Livingston, Clyde |
| 1988–9 | Kilmarnock, Queen of South | 2009–10 | Airdrie, Ayr |
| 1989–90 | Albion, Alloa | 2010–11 | Cowdenbeath, Stirling |
| 1990–1 | Clyde, Brechin | 2011–12 | Ayr, Queen of South |
| 1991–2 | Montrose, Forfar | 2012–13 | Dunfermline, Airdrie |
| 1992–3 | Meadowbank, Cowdenbeath | 2013–14 | Morton |
| 1993–4 | Dumbarton, Stirling, Clyde, Morton, Brechin | 2014–15 | Cowdenbeath |
| | | 2015–16 | Livingston, Alloa |
| 1994–5 | Ayr, Stranraer | 2016–17 | Raith, Ayr |
| 1995–6 | Hamilton, Dumbarton | 2017–18 | Dumbarton, Brechin |

## RELEGATED FROM SECOND DIVISION/LEAGUE ONE

| | | | |
|---|---|---|---|
| 1993–4 | Alloa, Forfar, E Stirling, Montrose, Queen's Park, Arbroath, Albion, Cowdenbeath | 2004–05 | Arbroath, Berwick |
| | | 2005–06 | Dumbarton |
| | | 2006–07 | Stranraer, Forfar |
| | | 2007–08 | Cowdenbeath, Berwick |
| 1994–5 | Meadowbank, Brechin | 2008–09 | Queen's Park, Stranraer |
| 1995–6 | Forfar, Montrose | 2009–10 | Arbroath, Clyde |
| 1996–7 | Dumbarton, Berwick | 2010–11 | Alloa, Peterhead |
| 1997–8 | Stenhousemuir, Brechin | 2011–12 | Stirling |
| 1998–9 | East Fife, Forfar | 2012–13 | Albion |
| 1999–2000 | Hamilton | 2013–14 | East Fife, Arbroath |
| 2000–01 | Queen's Park, Stirling | 2014–15 | Stirling |
| 2001–02 | Morton | 2015–16 | Cowdenbeath, Forfar |
| 2002–03 | Stranraer, Cowdenbeath | 2016–17 | Peterhead, Stenhousemuir |
| 2003–04 | East Fife, Stenhousemuir | 2017–18 | Queen's Park, Albion |

## RELEGATED FROM LEAGUE TWO

| | |
|---|---|
| 2015–16 | East Stirling |

# SCOTTISH PREMIERSHIP 2017–2018

(appearances and scorers)

## ABERDEEN

Arnason K ............... 16 (5)
Ball D ..................... 9 (7)
Campbell D ................ - (1)
Christie R ............... 28 (4)
Considine A ............. 30 (2)
Cosgrove S ................ 4 (1)
Harvie D ..................... - (2)
Lewis J ........................31
Logan S ........................37
Mackay-Steven G ...... 22 (9)
May S ...................... 25 (4)
Maynard N .............. 2 (16)
McGinn N ................ 10 (1)
McKenna S ....................30
McLean K ......................37
Nwakali C .................. 3 (2)
O'Connor A .............. 37 (1)
Reynolds M ................ 6 (7)
Rogers D ....................2 (2)
Rooney A ................17 (19)
Ross F .......................1 (3)
Shinnie G ......................35
Stewart G ...............17 (13)
Storey M ......................- (1)
Tansey G .....................8 (1)
Woodman F .....................5
Wright S ...................6 (10)

**League goals** (56): Rooney 9, McLean 8, Mackay-Steven 5, May 5, Christie 4, Considine 4, Arnason 3, Stewart 3, Logan 2, McGinn 2, McKenna 2, O'Connor 2, Shinnie 2, Reynolds 1, Ross 1, Storey 1, Wright 1, Opponents 1. **Scottish Cup goals** (10): Mackay-Steven 3, Christie 2, McLean 2, Rooney 2, Shinnie 1. **League Cup goals** (1): McLean. **Europa League goals** (5): Christie 2, Mackay-Steven 1, Shinnie 1, Stewart 1. **Average home league attendance**: 15,775. **Player of Year**: Scott McKenna

## CELTIC

Ajer K ..................... 23 (1)
Armstrong S .......... 15 (12)
Bain S ............................7
Benyu K ..........................1
Biton N .................. 10 (4)
Boyata D .......................28
Brown S ........................34
Miller C ..........................3
Musonda C ................ 2 (2)
De Vries D ................. 5 (1)
Dembele M ............. 17 (8)
Edouard O ............. 12 (10)
Forrest J ................. 31 (4)
Gamboa C .......................2
Gordon C .......................26
Griffiths L .............. 11 (14)
Hayes J ..................... 6 (9)
Henderson E ............... - (1)
Henderson L ............... - (1)
Hendry J .................... 7 (4)
Johnston M ................ 1 (2)
Kouassi E .................. 5 (1)
Lustig M ..................25 (1)
McGregor C .............29 (7)
Ntcham O ................24 (5)
Ralston A .......................3
Roberts P ...................7 (5)
Rogic T ....................18 (5)
Simunovic J ..............13 (2)
Sinclair S ...............23 (12)
Tierney K .................30 (2)

**League goals** (73): Sinclair 10, Dembele 9, Edouard 9, Griffiths 9, Forrest 8, McGregor 7, Ntcham 5, Rogic 5, Armstrong 3, Tierney 3, Boyata 2, Hayes 1, Lustig 1, Opponents 1. **Scottish Cup goals** (17): Forrest 4, Dembele 3,Ntcham 3, Edouard 2, McGregor 2, Boyata 1, Rogic 1, Sinclair 1. **League Cup goals** (15): Dembele 3, Forrest 3, Griffiths 2, Lustig 2, Armstrong 1, McGregor 1, Ralston 1, Sinclair 1, Tierney 1. **Champions League goals** (5): Dembele 1, Griffiths 1, McGregor 1, Sinclair 1, Opponents 1. **Europa League goals** (1): McGregor 1. **Average home league attendance**: 57,775. **Player of Year**: Scott Brown

## DUNDEE

Allan S ...................... 8 (8)
Aurtenetxe J ............ 14 (2)
Bain S ..........................12
Caulker S ......................12
Curran J .................... 5 (3)
Deacon R ................ 25 (3)
El-Bakhtaoui F ....... 16 (12)
Etxabeguren J ............ - (1)
Ferie C ...................... 1 (1)
Haber M .................... 9 (2)
Hendry J ................. 23 (1)
Henvey M .................. - (4)
Holt K ..................... 22 (2)
Jefferies D ................. 1 (1)
Kamara G ......................37
Kerr C ..................... 27 (5)
Kusunga G ................ 7 (2)
Lambert J .................... - (1)
Leitch-Smith AJ ...... 14 (14)
McGowan P ............. 30 (4)
Meekings J .............. 21 (1)
Moussa S ................ 21 (5)
Murray S ................. 13 (1)
O'Dea D .................. 14 (2)
O'Hara M ................26 (6)
Parish E ........................25
Piggott J ......................- (1)
Scott C .........................- (3)
Spence L .................14 (4)
Vincent J ....................2 (1)
Waddell K ................10 (6)
Wighton C ..................5 (2)
Williams D ...................- (2)
Wolters R ....................4 (5)

**League goals** (36): Moussa 7, Leitch-Smith 6, O'Hara 4, El-Bakhtaoui 3, Murray 3, Waddell 3, Haber 2, Holt 2, Caulker 1, Deacon 1, Hendry 1, Henvey 1, Kusunga 1, McGowan 1. **Scottish Cup goals** (3): Allan 1, Leitch-Smith 1, O'Hara 1. **League Cup goals** (10): Moussa 5, El Bakhtaoui 2, Hendry 1, McGowan 1, O'Hara 1. **Average home league attendance**: 5,947. **Player of Year**: Glen Kamara

## HAMILTON ACADEMICAL

Biabi B.......... 3 (2)
Bingham R.......... 18 (14)
Boyd S.......... 7 (6)
Crawford A.......... 11 (3)
Cunningham R.......... - (6)
Docherty G..........21
Donati M.......... 6 (4)
Ferguson L.......... 12 (1)
Fulton R.......... 5 (1)
Gillespie G.......... 1 (2)
Gogic A.......... 15 (3)
Hughes R.......... 2 (1)
Imrie D.......... 33 (2)
Jamieson D.......... 1 (1)
Jenkins R.......... 9 (2)
Longridge L.......... 3 (6)
Lyon D.......... 21 (6)
MacKinnon D..........31
McMann S.......... 30 (4)
Miller M.......... 1 (5)
Ogboe M.......... 12 (4)
Ogkmpoe M.......... - (1)
Redmond D.......... 11 (14)
Rojano A.......... 14 (12)
Sarris G.......... 19 (2)
Scott C.......... 1 (1)
Skondras G.......... 20 (1)
Templeton D.......... 20 (7)
Tomas X.......... 36
Want S.......... 13
Woods G.......... 32
Van der Weg K.......... 10 (1)

**League goals** (47): Imrie 8, Templeton 8, Bingham 5, Docherty 3, Ogboe 3, Rojano 3, Skondras 3, Lyon 2, Redmond 2, Boyd 1, Crawford 1, Gogic 1, Longridge 1, MacKinnon 1, Sarris 1, Tomas 1, Opponents 3. **Scottish Cup goals**: None. **League Cup goals** (11): Boyd 2, Crawford 2, Want 2, Bingham 1, Donati 1, Longridge 1, MacKinnon 1, Templeton 1. **Average home league attendance**: 3,095

## HEART OF MIDLOTHIAN

Adao J.......... 9 (1)
Amankwaa D.......... 5 (6)
Djoum A.......... 15 (1)
Baur D.......... 1 (1)
Berra C..........37
Brandon J.......... 11 (1)
Callachan R.......... 18 (5)
Cochrane H.......... 14 (8)
Cowie D.......... 25 (3)
Currie R.......... - (1)
Esmael.......... 16 (4)
Godinho M..........5
Grzelak R.......... 9 (4)
Hamilton C..........1
Hamilton J..........5
Henderson E.......... 3 (9)
Hughes A.......... 17 (2)
Irving A.......... 2 (2)
Lafferty K.......... 30 (5)
Logan C..........1
Makovora L.......... - (1)
Martin M.......... - (1)
McDonald A.......... 5 (8)
McLaughlan J..........33
Milinkovic M.......... 15 (9)
Mitchell D..........9
Moore L.......... 10 (5)
Naismith S.......... 12 (2)
Nowak K.......... - (3)
Prince Bauben.......... 9 (8)
Randall C.......... 22 (2)
Sammon C.......... - (1)
Smith C.......... - (1)
Smith M.......... 29 (2)
Smith-Brown A.......... 1 (1)
Souttar J.......... 31
Stockton C.......... 4 (8)
Walker J.......... 14 (2)
Zanatta D.......... - (1)

**League goals** (39): Lafferty 12, Esmael 6, Milinkovic 6, Callachan 4, Naismith 4, Berra 2, Walker 2, Cochrane 1, Souttar 1, Zanatta 1. **Scottish Cup goals** (5): Lafferty 3, Cowie 1, Mitchell 1. **League Cup goals** (7): Lafferty 4, Berra 1, Cowie 1, Esmael 1. **Average home league attendance**: 18,429. **Player of Year**: Christophe Berra

## HIBERNIAN

Allan S..........12
Ambrose E.......... 37 (1)
Barker B.......... 17 (10)
Bartley M.......... 20 (6)
Bell C.......... 1 (1)
Boyle M..........34
Gray D.......... 6 (1)
Hanlon P..........36
Kamberi F..........14
Laidlaw R..........3
Maclaren J.......... 11 (4)
Marciano O..........34
Matulevicius D.......... - (12)
McGeouch D.......... 30 (5)
McGinn J..........35
McGregor D.......... 22 (2)
Murray F.......... - (2)
Murray S.......... 17 (5)
Porteous R.......... 2 (4)
Rherras F.......... - (1)
Shaw O.......... 5 (11)
Slivka V.......... 9 (13)
Stevenson L..........35
Stokes A.......... 15 (3)
Swanson D.......... 4 (13)
Whittaker S.......... 19 (7)

**League goals** (62): Kamberi 9, Maclaren 8, Stokes 7, Murray S 6, Boyle 5, McGinn 5, Shaw 4, Allan 3, Ambrose 2, Barker 2, Hanlon 2, Slivka 2, Whittaker 2, Porteous 1, Stevenson 1, Opponents 3. **Scottish Cup goals**: None. **League Cup goals** (23): Murray S 8, Stokes 4, Murray F 2, Porteous 2, Ambrose 1, Boyle 1, Graham 1, Matulevicius 1, McGinn 1, Shaw 1, Swanson 1
**Average home league attendance**: 18,123. **Player of Year**: Dylan McGeouch

## KILMARNOCK

Boyd K .................... 30 (4)
Boyd S .................... 10 (1)
Broadfoot K.............. 29 (1)
Brophy E................ 15 (13)
Burke C .................. 9 (11)
Cameron I .................. - (3)
Dicker G ................. 20 (1)
Erwin L................. 14 (20)
Fasan L ..........................3
Findlay S ................ 29 (3)
Frizzell A................. 10 (5)
Greer G ..........................20
Hawkshaw D.............. 2 (3)
Jones J.................... 28 (4)
Kiltie G ..................... 5 (4)
MacDonald J..................35
McKenzie R............. 21 (4)
Mulumbu Y.............. 16 (2)
O'Donnell S............. 35 (1)
Power A .................. 21 (3)
Samizadeh A ..............- (1)
Simpson A.................1 (3)
Smith S .........................3
Taylor G...................36 (2)
Thomas D..................7 (2)
Tshibola A .................9 (3)
Waters C ....................3 (2)
Wilson I......................7 (6)

**League goals** (49): Boyd K 18, Brophy 7, Erwin 5, Jones 4, Findlay 3, Frizzell 2, O'Donnell 2, Boyd S 1, Broadfoot 1, Burke 1, Greer 1, Mulumbu 1, Wilson 1, Opponents 2. **Scottish Cup goals** (7): Boyd K 2, O'Donnell 2, Brophy 1, Erwin 1, Tshibola 1. **League Cup goals** (9): Boyd K 3, McKenzie 2, Thomas 2, Burke 1, Erwin 1. **Average home league attendance**: 5,390. **Player of Year**: Alan Power

## MOTHERWELL

Aldred T .........................17
Bigirimana G.......... 11 (16)
Bowman R .............. 23 (9)
Brown L...................... - (1)
Cadden C................ 30 (3)
Campbell A ............. 25 (4)
Carson T........................33
Ciftci N..................... 8 (3)
Dunne C ........................34
Fisher A.................... 6 (5)
Frear E..................... 14 (9)
Griffiths R ................. 5 (1)
Grimshaw L ............. 11 (6)
Hammell S ................ 2 (2)
Hartley P.......................14
Hendrie S.................. 4 (2)
Heneghan B .....................4
Kipre C ................... 35 (1)
MacLean R................ 1 (7)
Maguire B ........................3
Main C.........................16
McHugh C...............33 (2)
Moult L...................13 (2)
Newell G ....................1 (7)
Petravicius D ...........2 (11)
Rose A.....................22 (6)
Scott J ......................- (2)
Tait R......................33 (1)
Tanner C ...............16 (10)
Turnbull D ....................2

**League goals** (43): Moult 8, Bowman 7, Tanner 6, Main 5, Ciftci 3, Campbell 2, Hartley 2, Rose 2, Aldred 1, Bigirmana 1, Dunne 1, Frear 1, Heneghan 1, Kipre 1, Tait 1, Opponents 2. **Scottish Cup goals** (9): Main 3, Tanner 2, Bowman 1, McHugh 1, Opponents 2. **League Cup goals** (20): Moult 6, Cadden 4, Bowman 2, Frear 2, Bigirimana 1, Dunne 1, Hartley 1, MacLean 1, Tait 1, Tanner 1. **Average home league attendance**: 5,448. **Player of Year**: Trevor Carson

## PARTICK THISTLE

Bannigan S ............... 4 (2)
Barton A ................. 27 (6)
Booth C .................. 11 (1)
Cargill B ........................16
Cerny T.........................34
Devine D.......................26
Doolan K................ 18 (15)
Dumbuya M ............... 4 (1)
Edwards R .............. 30 (6)
Elliott C ..........................17
Erskine C ................ 19 (9)
Fraser G ..................... - (5)
Keown N ........................30
Lawless S................ 21 (6)
McCarthy A............. 10 (5)
McGinn P................ 25 (1)
Nisbett K ................... - (6)
Nitriansky M............. 4 (3)
Osman A .................12 (1)
Penrice J.......................2
Sammon C ............21 (10)
Scully R .....................4 (2)
Spittal B .................24 (9)
Storey M .................24 (9)
Turnbull J.....................19
Woods M .................16 (2)

**League goals** (31): Sammon 7, Doolan 6, Erskine 5, Edwards 4, Spittal 4, Keown 2, Storey 2, Lawless 1. **Scottish Cup goals** (4): Sammon 3, Doolan 1. **League Cup goals** (13): Doolan 3, Lawless 3, Spittal 3, Erskine 2, Edwards 1, Elliott 1. **Average home league attendance**: 4,580. **Player of Year**: Chris Erskine

## RANGERS

Alnwick J ........................5
Barjonas J.................. 1 (4)
Bates D .................. 13 (2)
Bruno Alves ............ 17 (3)
Candeias D ............. 34 (3)
Cummings J.............. 6 (9)
Dalcio......................... - (1)
Docherty G................ 7 (4)
Dorrans G .....................16
Cardoso F ................. 9 (3)
Foderingham W .............33
Goss S ..................... 10 (3)
Halliday A ................. 5 (6)
Hardie R ..................... - (7)
Herrera E ................ 2 (17)
Hodson L .................... 5 (1)
Holt J...................... 23 (3)
Jack R ...........................17
John D.................... 25 (1)
Kranjcar N................. 4 (3)
Martin R.........................15
Miller K................... 15 (3)
Morelos A................29 (6)
Murphy J....................... 16
Nemane A ..................- (5)
O'Halloran M ..............- (1)
Pena C.......................6 (6)
McCrorie R ..............19 (2)
Rossiter J ..................1 (1)
Tavernier J................37 (1)
Wallace L ......................... 5
Wilson D .................12 (2)
Windass J.................31 (2)

**League goals** (76): Morelos 14, Windass 13, Tavernier 8, Candeias 6, Dorrans 5, Murphy 4, Pena 4, John 3, Miller 3, Wilson 3, Cummings 2, Goss 2, Holt 2, McCrorie 2, Bruno Alves 1, Bates 1, Herrera 1, Martin 1, Rossiter 1. **Scottish Cup goals** (13): Cummings 5, Windass 5, Morelos 2, Murphy 1. **League Cup goals** (9): Candelas 2, Morelos 2, Bruno Alves 1, Herrera 1, Miller 1, Pena 1, Tavernier 1. **Europa League goals** (1): Miller 1. **Average home league attendance**: 49,173. **Player of Year**: Daniel Candeias

## ROSS COUNTY

Chow T.................... 10 (4)
Curran C................ 20 (15)
Davies A ........................25
Dow R ..................... 4 (14)
Draper R.................. 25 (3)
Eagles C ................... 7 (1)
Effiong I ..........................2
Fontaine L .....................14
Fox S....................... 26 (1)
Fraser M ........................38
Gardyne M............... 28 (5)
Kait M ....................... 3 (3)
Kellior-Dunn D........ 18 (11)
Kelly S..................... 11 (2)
Lindsay J.................. 21 (5)
McCarey A............... 12 (2)
McKay B ................. 14 (9)
Melbourne M ....................6
Mikkelsen T............... 2 (7)
Naismith J............... 34 (1)
Ngog D.......................4 (6)
O'Brien J..................22 (3)
Routis C..................23 (3))
Schalk A ................19 (11)
Souttar H ................11 (2)
Tansey G ......................2 (1)
Tumility R .................1 (1)
Van der Weg K ..........16 (3)

**League goals** (40): Schalk 11, Curran 6, Gardyne 3, Kellior-Dunn 3, McKay 3, Lindsay 2, Mikkelsen 2, Naismith 2, Routis 2, Van der Weg 2, Chow 1, Davies 1, Draper 1, Ngog 1. **Scottish Cup goals**: None. **League Cup goals** (10): Curran 4, Mikkelsen 2, Schalk 2, Fraser 1, Opponents 1. **Average home league attendance**: 4,540

## ST JOHNSTONE

Alston B .................. 17 (7)
Anderson S ....................34
Clark Z ................... 16 (1)
Comrie A.......................12
Craig L .................. 17 (10)
Cummins G................ 6 (9)
Davidson M....................29
Easton B.................. 12 (1)
Foster R.................. 22 (2)
Gordon L................... 5 (2)
Hendry C .................. 1 (4)
Johnstone D ............ 8 (12)
Kane C..................... 10 (2)
Kerr J............................15
MacLean S .............. 26 (4)
Mannus A.......................22
McCann A ................. 1 (2)
McClean K ................. - (5)
McMillan D................ 2 (2)
Millar C.................... 13 (3)
O'Halloran M ........... 12 (4)
Paton P.................... 16 (1)
Robertson J .................- (2)
Scougall S................18 (6)
Shaughnessy J ..............38
Tanser S..................24 (5)
Thomson C .................- (4)
Watson K...................1 91)
Williams G................10 (1)
Willock M ..................6 (5)
Wotherspoon D........25 (10)

**League goals** (42): MacLean 9, Davidson 5, O'Halloran 5, Craig 3, Kane 3, Wotherspoon 3, Alston 2, Johnstone 2, McMillan 2, Anderson 1, Cummins 1, Kerr 1, Scougall 1, Shaughnessy 1, Willock 1, Opponents 2. **Scottish Cup goals** (4): Kane 3, McClean 1. **League Cup goals**: None. **Europa League goals** (1): Shaughnessy 1. **Average home league attendance**: 3,809. **Player of Year**: Joe Shaughnessy

# BETFRED SCOTTISH LEAGUE CUP 2017–18

(Each group team awarded three points for a win; one point for a drawn match after 90 minutes; then penalties with winners awarded one additional point. Group winners and four best runners-up through to knock-out stage to join four clubs competing in Europe – Celtic, Aberdeen, Rangers and St Johnsone)

**GROUP A**

| | P | W | D | L | F | A | Pts |
|---|---|---|---|---|---|---|---|
| Falkirk Q | 4 | 4 | 0 | 0 | 13 | 1 | 12 |
| Inverness | 4 | 2 | 1 | 1 | 5 | 3 | 8 |
| Stirling | 4 | 2 | 1 | 1 | 6 | 5 | 7 |
| Brechin | 4 | 0 | 1 | 3 | 1 | 9 | 2 |
| Forfar | 4 | 0 | 1 | 3 | 3 | 10 | 1 |

**GROUP B**

| | P | W | D | L | F | A | Pts |
|---|---|---|---|---|---|---|---|
| Dunfermline Q | 4 | 2 | 2 | 0 | 13 | 3 | 10 |
| Peterhead | 4 | 3 | 0 | 1 | 7 | 6 | 9 |
| Hearts | 4 | 2 | 1 | 1 | 7 | 4 | 7 |
| East Fife | 4 | 1 | 1 | 2 | 3 | 6 | 4 |
| Elgin | 4 | 0 | 0 | 4 | 2 | 13 | 0 |

**GROUP C**

| | P | W | D | L | F | A | Pts |
|---|---|---|---|---|---|---|---|
| Dundee Utd Q | 4 | 3 | 1 | 0 | 10 | 2 | 11 |
| Dundee Q | 4 | 3 | 1 | 0 | 8 | 2 | 10 |
| Raith | 4 | 2 | 0 | 2 | 9 | 5 | 6 |
| Cowdenbeath | 4 | 1 | 0 | 3 | 5 | 11 | 3 |
| Buckie | 4 | 0 | 0 | 4 | 3 | 15 | 0 |

**GROUP D**

| | P | W | D | L | F | A | Pts |
|---|---|---|---|---|---|---|---|
| Hibernian Q | 4 | 3 | 1 | 0 | 13 | 1 | 10 |
| Ross Co Q | 4 | 2 | 2 | 0 | 8 | 0 | 10 |
| Arbroath | 4 | 1 | 2 | 1 | 6 | 7 | 6 |
| Montrose | 4 | 1 | 0 | 3 | 2 | 15 | 3 |
| Alloa | 4 | 0 | 1 | 3 | 2 | 8 | 1 |

**GROUP E**

| | P | W | D | L | F | A | Pts |
|---|---|---|---|---|---|---|---|
| Ayr Q | 4 | 4 | 0 | 0 | 15 | 3 | 12 |
| Kilmarnock Q | 4 | 3 | 0 | 1 | 9 | 3 | 9 |
| Clyde | 4 | 2 | 0 | 2 | 7 | 11 | 6 |
| Annan | 4 | 0 | 1 | 3 | 2 | 10 | 2 |
| Dumbarton | 4 | 0 | 1 | 3 | 2 | 8 | 1 |

**GROUP F**

| | P | W | D | L | F | A | Pts |
|---|---|---|---|---|---|---|---|
| Motherwell Q | 4 | 4 | 0 | 0 | 12 | 2 | 12 |
| Morton | 4 | 2 | 1 | 1 | 8 | 6 | 8 |
| Queen's Park | 4 | 2 | 1 | 1 | 9 | 9 | 7 |
| Edinburgh City | 4 | 0 | 1 | 3 | 3 | 12 | 2 |
| Berwick | 4 | 0 | 1 | 3 | 4 | 7 | 1 |

**GROUP G**

| | P | W | D | L | F | A | Pts |
|---|---|---|---|---|---|---|---|
| Hamilton Q | 4 | 2 | 2 | 0 | 11 | 6 | 9 |
| Albion | 4 | 1 | 3 | 0 | 12 | 9 | 7 |
| Queen of South | 4 | 1 | 3 | 0 | 6 | 4 | 7 |
| East Kilbride | 4 | 1 | 1 | 2 | 5 | 9 | 5 |
| Stenhousemuir | 4 | 0 | 1 | 3 | 3 | 9 | 2 |

**GROUP H**

| | P | W | D | L | F | A | Pts |
|---|---|---|---|---|---|---|---|
| Livingston Q | 4 | 3 | 1 | 0 | 8 | 3 | 11 |
| Partick Q | 4 | 3 | 1 | 0 | 9 | 2 | 10 |
| St Mirren | 4 | 2 | 0 | 2 | 9 | 7 | 6 |
| Airdrieonians | 4 | 1 | 0 | 3 | 4 | 10 | 3 |
| Stranraer | 4 | 0 | 0 | 4 | 4 | 12 | 0 |

**SECOND ROUND**

Celtic 5 Kilmarnock 0; Dundee 2 Dundee Utd 1; Falkirk 1 Livingston 2 (aet); Hamilton 0 Aberdeen 1; Hibernian 5 Ayr 0; Rangers 6 Dunfermline 0; Ross Co 2 Motherwell 3 (aet); St Johnstone 0 Partick 3

**THIRD ROUND**

Dundee 0 Celtic 4; Hibernian 3 Livingston 2; Motherwell 3 Aberdeen 0; Partick 1 Rangers 3 (aet)

**SEMI-FINALS** (both at Hampden Park)

Hibernian 2 Celtic 4; Rangers 0 Motherwell 2

## FINAL

**MOTHERWELL 0 CELTIC 2 (Forrest 49, Dembele 60 pen)**

**Hampden Park (49,483); Sunday, November 26, 2017**

**Motherwell** (5-3-2): Carson, Cadden, Kipre, Hartley, Dunne, Tait, Grimshaw (Tanner 51), McHugh (capt), Rose (Frear 70), Bowman (Campbell 64), Moult. **Subs not used**: Griffiths, Hammell, Fisher, Petravicius. **Booked**: McHugh, Campbell. **Sent off**: Kipre (58). **Manager**: Stephen Robinson

**Celtic** (4-2-3-1): Gordon, Lustig, Boyata, Simunovic, Tierney, Armstrong, Brown (capt), Forrest (Roberts 78), McGregor (Rogic 89), Sinclair, Dembele (Griffiths 64). **Subs not used**: De Vries, Ntcham, Sviatchenko, Ajer. **Booked**: Dembele, Brown. **Manager**: Brendan Rodgers

**Referee**: C Thomson. **Half-time**: 0-0

# SCOTTISH LEAGUE CUP FINALS

**1946** Aberdeen beat Rangers (3-2)
**1947** Rangers beat Aberdeen (4-0)
**1948** East Fife beat Falkirk (4-1 after 0-0 draw)
**1949** Rangers beat Raith Rov (2-0)
**1950** East Fife beat Dunfermline Athletic (3-0)
**1951** Motherwell beat Hibernian (3-0)
**1952** Dundee beat Rangers (3-2)
**1953** Dundee beat Kilmarnock (2-0)
**1954** East Fife beat Partick (3-2)
**1955** Hearts beat Motherwell (4-2)
**1956** Aberdeen beat St Mirren (2-1)
**1957** Celtic beat Partick (3-0 after 0-0 draw)
**1958** Celtic beat Rangers (7-1)
**1959** Hearts beat Partick (5-1)
**1960** Hearts beat Third Lanark (2-1)
**1961** Rangers beat Kilmarnock (2-0)
**1962** Rangers beat Hearts (3-1 after 1-1 draw)
**1963** Hearts beat Kilmarnock (1-0)
**1964** Rangers beat Morton (5-0)
**1965** Rangers beat Celtic (2-1)
**1966** Celtic beat Rangers (2-1)
**1967** Celtic beat Rangers (1-0)
**1968** Celtic beat Dundee (5-3)
**1969** Celtic beat Hibernian (6-2)
**1970** Celtic beat St Johnstone (1-0)
**1971** Rangers beat Celtic (1-0)
**1972** Partick beat Celtic (4-1)
**1973** Hibernian beat Celtic (2-1)
**1974** Dundee beat Celtic (1-0)
**1975** Celtic beat Hibernian (6-3)
**1976** Rangers beat Celtic (1-0)
**1977†** Aberdeen beat Celtic (2-1)
**1978†** Rangers beat Celtic (2-1)
**1979** Rangers beat Aberdeen (2-1)
**1980** Dundee Utd beat Aberdeen (3-0 after 0-0 draw)
**1981** Dundee Utd beat Dundee (3-0)
**1982** Rangers beat Dundee Utd (2-1)
**1983** Celtic beat Rangers (2-1)
**1984†** Rangers beat Celtic (3-2)
**1985** Rangers beat Dundee Utd (1-0)
**1986** Aberdeen beat Hibernian (3-0)
**1987** Rangers beat Celtic (2-1)
**1988†** Rangers beat Aberdeen (5-3 on pens after 3-3 draw)
**1989** Rangers beat Aberdeen (3-2)
**1990†** Aberdeen beat Rangers (2-1)
**1991†** Rangers beat Celtic (2-1)
**1992** Hibernian beat Dunfermline Athletic (2-0)
**1993†** Rangers beat Aberdeen (2-1)
**1994** Rangers beat Hibernian (2-1)
**1995** Raith Rov beat Celtic (6-5 on pens after 2-2 draw)
**1996** Aberdeen beat Dundee (2-0)
**1997** Rangers beat Hearts (4-3)
**1998** Celtic beat Dundee Utd (3-0)
**1999** Rangers beat St Johnstone (2-1)
**2000** Celtic beat Aberdeen (2-0)
**2001** Celtic beat Kilmarnock (3-0)
**2002** Rangers beat Ayr (4-0)
**2003** Rangers beat Celtic (2-1)
**2004** Livingston beat Hibernian (2-0)
**2005** Rangers beat Motherwell (5-1)
**2006** Celtic beat Dunfermline Athletic (3-0)
**2007** Hibernian beat Kilmarnock (5-1)
**2008** Rangers beat Dundee Utd (3-2 on pens after 2-2 draw)
**2009†** Celtic beat Rangers (2-0)
**2010** Rangers beat St Mirren (1-0)
**2011†** Rangers beat Celtic (2-1)
**2012** Kilmarnock beat Celtic (1-0)
**2013** St Mirren beat Hearts (3-2)
**2014** Aberdeen beat Inverness Caledonian Thistle (4-2 on pens after 0-0 draw)
**2015** Celtic beat Dundee Utd (2-0)
**2016** Ross Co beat Hibernian (2-1)
**2017** Celtic beat Aberdeen (3-0)
**2018** Celtic beat Motherwell (2-0)

(† After extra time; Skol Cup 1985-93, Coca-Cola Cup 1995-97, Co-operative Insurance Cup 1999 onwards)

## SUMMARY OF SCOTTISH LEAGUE CUP WINNERS

Rangers........... 27
Celtic .............. 17
Aberdeen ........... 7
Hearts ............... 4
Dundee.............. 3
East Fife ................ 3
Hibernian................ 3
Dundee Utd ........... 2
Kilmarnock ............ 2
Livingston ............... 1
Motherwell............... 1
Partick .................... 1
Raith ...................... 1
Ross Co .................. 1
St Mirren ................. 1

# IRN-BRU SCOTTISH CHALLENGE CUP 2017–18

**First round**: Aberdeen U20 1 St Johnstone U20 0; Albion 0 Spartans 0 (aet, Albion won 5-4 on pens); Annan 3 Celtic U20 1; Buckie 2 Brechin 1; Clyde 2 Stranraer 3 (aet); Dumbarton 2 Rangers U20 1; Dundee U20 2 Alloa 4; Dundee Utd 2 Cowdenbeath 0; Dunfermline 2 Arbroath 0; East Fife 0 Peterhead 2; East Stirling1 Ayr 5; Formartine 2 Hearts U20 3 (aet); Hamilton U20 1 Edinburgh City 0; Hibernian U20 1 Elgin 2; Kilmarnock U20 0 Berwick 2; Morton 0 Livingston 2; Motherwell U20 2 Queen's Park 1; Partick U20 6 Stirling Univ 1; Queen of South 4 Airdrieonians 0; Raith 3 Brora 0; Ross Co U20 2 Forfar 1; St Mirren 2 East Kilbride 1; Stenhousemuir 0 Cove 2; Stirling 1 Montrose 3

**Second round:** Aberdeen U20 2 Inverness 4; Ayr 1 Montrose 1 (aet, Montrose won 6-5 on pens); Berwick 0 Queen of South 5; Buckie 0 Dunfermline 3; Crusaders 3 Motherwell U20 2; Dumbarton 2 Connah's Quay 1 (aet); Dundee Utd 3 Alloa 1; Elgin 2 Bray 1; Hamilton U20 1 Cove 3; New Saints 1 Livingston 1 (aet, New Saints won 6-5 on pens); Peterhead 2 Annan 0; Raith 4 Ross Co U20 0; Sligo 1 Falkirk 2; Spartans 1 Linfield 2; St Mirren 3 Hearts U20 1; Stranraer 2 Partick U20 0

**Third round**: Cove 0 Crusaders 3; Dundee Utd 1 Linfield 0; Falkirk 2 Dunfermline 0; Inverness 3 Peterhead 0; Montrose 1 Queen of South 3 (aet); St Mirren 1 Raith 3; New Saints 4 Elgin 0; Dumbarton 2 Stranraer 1

**Fourth round**: Dumbarton 2 Raith 0; Dundee Utd 1 Crusaders 2; Inverness 1 Falkirk 0; New Saints 0 Queen of South 0 (aet, New Saints won 4-3 on pens)

**Semi-finals**: Inverness 3 Crusaders 2; New Saints 1 Dumbarton 2

## FINAL

**DUMBARTON 0 INVERNESS CALEDONIAN THISTLE 1**
**McDiarmid Park, Perth (4,602); Saturday, March 24, 2018**

**Dumbarton** (4-2-1-3): Gallacher, Smith, Dowie (capt), Barr, McLaughlin, Carswell, Hutton, Handling, Walsh (Burt 81), C Gallagher (Stewart 74), Russell (Froxylias 68). **Subs not used**: Ewings, Wilson, G Gallagher, Hill. **Booked**: Dowie, McLaughlin, C Gallagher. **Manager**: Stevie Aitken

**Inverness Caledonian Thistle** (4-3-3): Ridgers, Seedorf, Warren (capt), Donaldson, Tremarco, Polworth, Vigurs, Chalmers, Oakley, Bell (Mackay 78), Mulraney (Doran 70). **Subs not used**: Esson, Calder, Elbouzedi, Trafford, Brown. **Scorer**: Tremarco (90+3). **Booked**: Donaldson, Tremarco. **Manager**: John Robetson

**Referee**: A Dallas. **Half-time**: 0-0

## DRONE STOPS PLAY

A drone interrupted the League Two match between Yeovil and Crawley last season. It flew over the Huish Park pitch, forcing referee Brett Huxtable to take the players off after 80 minutes. Play resumed 11 minutes later, with substitute Thomas Verheydt's header giving Crawley a 2-1 win over the nine-man home side who had two players sent off.

## MANAGER AND SON SENT OFF

Forest Green's Charlie Cooper and his father Mark, the club's manager, were both sent off in a 2-1 League Two defeat by Wycombe. The midfielder received a red card from referee Antony Coggins for a stamping offence and his father was sent to the stands for protesting at the decision.

# WILLIAM HILL SCOTTISH FA CUP 2017–18

## FIRST ROUND

Banks O'Dee 4 Huntly 0
Brora 5 Girvan 0
BSC Glasgow 1 Dalbeattie 0
Civil Service 2 Strathspey 1
Clachnacuddin 8 Fort William 0
Colville Park 2 Cumbernauld 1
Deveronvale 3 Hawick 1
Edinburgh Univ 2 Lossiemouth 1
Edusport Acad 1 Rothes Acad 1
Formartine 2 Turriff 1
Fraserburgh 2 Forres 1
Gala 0 Keith 2
Glenafton 4 Threave 0
Lothian 3 Iverurie 2
Nairn 1 Whitehill 0
Selkirk 4 Gretna 0
Wick 2 Stirling Univ 2

**Replays**

Rothes Acad 1 Edusport Acad 3
Stirling Univ 1 Wick 0

## SECOND ROUND

Banks O'Dee 2 Selkirk 0
Berwick 1 Annan 0
Buckie 6 BSC Glasgow 2
Civil Service 0 Brora 5
Cowdenbeath 0 East Kilbride 1
Deveronvale 0 Glenafton 2
Edinburgh City 0 Stenhousemuir 1
Edinburgh Univ 0 Fraserburgh 2
Elgin 3 Edusport Acad 1
Formartine 4 East Stirling 0
Keith 0 Clyde 3
Montrose 4 Stirling Univ 1
Nairn 1 Cove 2
Peterhead 9 Colville Park 0
Spartans 5 Clachnacuddin 0
Stirling 3 Lothian 5

## THIRD ROUND

Airdrieonians 2 Cove 3
Arbroath 3 Berwick 0
Banks O'Dee 2 Ayr 6
Buckie 2 Brechin 3
Clyde 0 East Fife 2
Dumbarton 1 Elgin 0
East Kilbride 3 Albion 4
Formartine 1 Forfar 0
Livingston 2 Glenafton 0
Lothian 1 St Mirren 7
Montrose 0 Queen of South 0
Peterhead 3 Raith 0
Queen's Park 1 Dunfermline 4
Spartans 1 Fraserburgh 2
Stenhousemuir 1 Alloa 2
Stranraer 0 Brora 1

**Replay**

Queen of South 2 Montrose 1

## FOURTH ROUND

Aberdeen 4 St Mirren 1
Albion 0 St Johnstone 4
Alloa 0 Dundee Utd 2
Ayr 4 Arbroath 1
**Celtic** 5 Brechin 0
Dundee 2 Inverness 2
Dunfermline 1 Morton 2
East Fife 0 Brora 1
Formartine 0 Cove 2
Fraserburgh 0 Rangers 3
Hearts 1 Hibernian 0
Kilmarnock 1 Ross Co 0
Livingston 0 Falkirk 1
**Motherwell** 2 Hamilton 0
Peterhead 2 Dumbarton 3
Queen of South 1 Partick 2

**Replay**

Inverness 0 Dundee 1

## FIFTH ROUND

Aberdeen 4 Dundee Utd 2
Ayr 1 Rangers 6
**Celtic** 3 Partick 2
Cove 1 Falkirk 3
Dundee 0 **Motherwell** 2
Hearts 3 St Johnstone 0
Kilmarnock 4 Brora 0
Morton 3 Dumbarton 0

## SIXTH ROUND

Aberdeen 1 Kilmarnock 1
**Celtic** 3 Morton 0
**Motherwell** 2 Hearts 1
Rangers 4 Falkirk 1

**Replay**
Kilmarnock 1 Aberdeen 1
(aet, Aberdeen won 3-2 on pens)

## SEMI-FINALS (both at Hampden Park)

**Celtic** 4 Rangers 0

**Motherwell** 3 Aberdeen 0

## FINAL

**CELTIC 2 (McGregor 11, Ntcham 24) MOTHERWELL 0**
**Hampden Park (49,967); Saturday, May 19, 2018**

**Celtic** (4-2-3-1): Gordon; Lustig, Boyata, Ajer (Simunovic 76), Tierney; Ntcham, Brown (capt); Forrest (Sinclair 90), Rogic (Armstrong 73), McGregor; Dembele. **Subs not used**: Bain, Roberts, L Griffiths, Kouassi. **Booked**: Boyata. **Manager**: Brendan Rodgers

**Motherwell** (3-5-2): Carson, Kipre, Aldred, Dunne, Cadden, Campbell (Frear 78), McHugh (capt) (Bigirimana 56), Grimshaw, Tait, Main, Bowman. **Subs not used**: R Griffiths, Hartley, Petravicius, Turnbull, Maguire. **Booked**: Tait, Grimshaw, Campbell. **Manager**: Stephen Robinson

**Referee**: K Clancy. **Half-time**: 2-0

# SCOTTISH FA CUP FINALS

**1874** Queen's Park beat Clydesdale (2-0)
**1875** Queen's Park beat Renton (3-0)
**1876** Queen's Park beat Third Lanark (2-0 after 1-1 draw)
**1877** Vale of Leven beat Rangers (3-2 after 0-0, 1-1 draws)
**1878** Vale of Leven beat Third Lanark (1-0)
**1879** Vale of Leven awarded Cup (Rangers withdrew after 1-1 draw)
**1880** Queen's Park beat Thornlibank (3-0)
**1881** Queen's Park beat Dumbarton (3-1)
**1882** Queen's Park beat Dumbarton (4-1 after 2-2 draw)
**1883** Dumbarton beat Vale of Leven (2-1 after 2-2 draw)
**1884** Queen's Park awarded Cup (Vale of Leven withdrew from Final)
**1885** Renton beat Vale of Leven (3-1 after 0-0 draw)
**1886** Queen's Park beat Renton (3-1)
**1887** Hibernian beat Dumbarton (2-1)
**1888** Renton beat Cambuslang (6-1)
**1889** Third Lanark beat Celtic (2-1)
**1890** Queen's Park beat Vale of Leven (2-1 after 1-1 draw)
**1891** Hearts beat Dumbarton (1-0)
**1892** Celtic beat Queen's Park (5-1)
**1893** Queen's Park beat Celtic (2-1)
**1894** Rangers beat Celtic (3-1)
**1895** St Bernard's beat Renton (2-1)
**1896** Hearts beat Hibernian (3-1)
**1897** Rangers beat Dumbarton (5-1)
**1898** Rangers beat Kilmarnock (2-0)
**1899** Celtic beat Rangers (2-0)
**1900** Celtic beat Queen's Park (4-3)
**1901** Hearts beat Celtic (4-3)
**1902** Hibernian beat Celtic (1-0)
**1903** Rangers beat Hearts (2-0 after 0-0, 1-1 draws)
**1904** Celtic beat Rangers (3-2)
**1905** Third Lanark beat Rangers (3-1 after 0-0 draw)
**1906** Hearts beat Third Lanark (1-0)
**1907** Celtic beat Hearts (3-0)
**1908** Celtic beat St Mirren (5-1)
**1909** Cup withheld because of riot after two drawn games in final between Celtic and Rangers (2-2, 1-1)
**1910** Dundee beat Clyde (2-1 after 2-2, 0-0 draws)
**1911** Celtic beat Hamilton (2-0 after 0-0 draw)
**1912** Celtic beat Clyde (2-0)
**1913** Falkirk beat Raith (2-0)
**1914** Celtic beat Hibernian (4-1 after 0-0 draw)
**1915–19** No competition (World War 1)
**1920** Kilmarnock beat Albion (3-2)
**1921** Partick beat Rangers (1-0)
**1922** Morton beat Rangers (1-0)
**1923** Celtic beat Hibernian (1-0)
**1924** Airdrieonians beat Hibernian (2-0)
**1925** Celtic beat Dundee (2-1)
**1926** St Mirren beat Celtic (2-0)
**1927** Celtic beat East Fife (3-1)
**1928** Rangers beat Celtic (4-0)
**1929** Kilmarnock beat Rangers (2-0)
**1930** Rangers beat Partick (2-1 after 0-0 draw)
**1931** Celtic beat Motherwell (4-2 after 2-2 draw)
**1932** Rangers beat Kilmarnock (3-0 after 1-1 draw)

**1933** Celtic beat Motherwell (1-0)
**1934** Rangers beat St Mirren (5-0)
**1935** Rangers beat Hamilton (2-1)
**1936** Rangers beat Third Lanark (1-0)
**1937** Celtic beat Aberdeen (2-1)
**1938** East Fife beat Kilmarnock (4-2 after 1-1 draw)
**1939** Clyde beat Motherwell (4-0)
**1940–6** No competition (World War 2)
**1947** Aberdeen beat Hibernian (2-1)
**1948†** Rangers beat Morton (1-0 after 1-1 draw)
**1949** Rangers beat Clyde (4-1)
**1950** Rangers beat East Fife (3-0)
**1951** Celtic beat Motherwell (1-0)
**1952** Motherwell beat Dundee (4-0)
**1953** Rangers beat Aberdeen (1-0 after 1-1 draw)
**1954** Celtic beat Aberdeen (2-1)
**1955** Clyde beat Celtic (1-0 after 1-1 draw)
**1956** Hearts beat Celtic (3-1)
**1957†** Falkirk beat Kilmarnock (2-1 after 1-1 draw)
**1958** Clyde beat Hibernian (1-0)
**1959** St Mirren beat Aberdeen (3-1)
**1960** Rangers beat Kilmarnock (2-0)
**1961** Dunfermline beat Celtic (2-0 after 0-0 draw)
**1962** Rangers beat St Mirren (2-0)
**1963** Rangers beat Celtic (3-0 after 1-1 draw)
**1964** Rangers beat Dundee (3-1)
**1965** Celtic beat Dunfermline (3-2)
**1966** Rangers beat Celtic (1-0 after 0-0 draw)
**1967** Celtic beat Aberdeen (2-0)
**1968** Dunfermline beat Hearts (3-1)
**1969** Celtic beat Rangers (4-0)
**1970** Aberdeen beat Celtic (3-1)
**1971** Celtic beat Rangers (2-1 after 1-1 draw)
**1972** Celtic beat Hibernian (6-1)
**1973** Rangers beat Celtic (3-2)
**1974** Celtic beat Dundee Utd (3-0)
**1975** Celtic beat Airdrieonians (3-1)
**1976** Rangers beat Hearts (3-1)
**1977** Celtic beat Rangers (1-0)
**1978** Rangers beat Aberdeen (2-1)
**1979†** Rangers beat Hibernian (3-2 after two 0-0 draws)
**1980†** Celtic beat Rangers (1-0)
**1981** Rangers beat Dundee Utd (4-1 after 0-0 draw)
**1982†** Aberdeen beat Rangers (4-1)
**1983†** Aberdeen beat Rangers (1-0)
**1984†** Aberdeen beat Celtic (2-1)
**1985** Celtic beat Dundee Utd (2-1)
**1986** Aberdeen beat Hearts (3-0)
**1987†** St Mirren beat Dundee Utd (1-0)
**1988** Celtic beat Dundee Utd (2-1)
**1989** Celtic beat Rangers (1-0)
**1990†** Aberdeen beat Celtic (9-8 on pens after 0-0 draw)
**1991†** Motherwell beat Dundee Utd (4-3)
**1992** Rangers beat Airdrieonians (2-1)
**1993** Rangers beat Aberdeen (2-1)
**1994** Dundee Utd beat Rangers (1-0)
**1995** Celtic beat Airdrieonians (1-0)
**1996** Rangers beat Hearts (5-1)
**1997** Kilmarnock beat Falkirk (1-0)
**1998** Hearts beat Rangers (2-1)
**1999** Rangers beat Celtic (1-0)
**2000** Rangers beat Aberdeen (4-0)
**2001** Celtic beat Hibernian (3-0)
**2002** Rangers beat Celtic (3-2)
**2003** Rangers beat Dundee (1-0)
**2004** Celtic beat Dunfermline (3-1)
**2005** Celtic beat Dundee Utd (1-0)
**2006†** Hearts beat Gretna (4-2 on pens after 1-1 draw)
**2007** Celtic beat Dunfermline (1-0)
**2008** Rangers beat Queen of the South (3-2)
**2009** Rangers beat Falkirk (1-0)
**2010** Dundee Utd beat Ross Co (3-0)
**2011** Celtic beat Motherwell (3-0)
**2012** Hearts beat Hibernian (5-1)
**2013** Celtic beat Hibernian (3-0)
**2014** St Johnstone beat Dundee Utd (2-0)
**2015** Inverness beat Falkirk (2-1)
**2016** Hibernian beat Rangers (3-2)
**2017** Celtic beat Aberdeen (2-1)
**2018** Celtic beat Motherwell (2-0)

† After extra time

## SUMMARY OF SCOTTISH CUP WINNERS

Celtic 38, Rangers 33, Queen's Park 10, Hearts 8, Aberdeen 7, Clyde 3, Hibernian 3, Kilmarnock 3, St Mirren 3, Vale of Leven 3, Dundee Utd 2, Dunfermline 2, Falkirk 2, Motherwell 2, Renton 2, Third Lanark 2, Airdrieonians 1, Dumbarton 1, Dundee 1, East Fife 1, Inverness 1, Morton 1, Partick 1, St Bernard's 1, St Johnstone 1

# VANARAMA NATIONAL LEAGUE 2017–2018

| | | Home | | | | | | Away | | | | | | |
|---|---|---|---|---|---|---|---|---|---|---|---|---|---|---|
| | | P | W | D | L | F | A | W | D | L | F | A | GD | PTS |
| 1 | Macclesfield | 46 | 13 | 7 | 3 | 31 | 19 | 14 | 4 | 5 | 36 | 27 | 21 | 92 |
| 2 | Tranmere* | 46 | 15 | 2 | 6 | 48 | 23 | 9 | 8 | 6 | 30 | 23 | 32 | 82 |
| 3 | Sutton | 46 | 12 | 6 | 5 | 36 | 28 | 11 | 4 | 8 | 31 | 25 | 14 | 79 |
| 4 | Boreham Wood | 46 | 12 | 5 | 6 | 33 | 25 | 8 | 10 | 5 | 31 | 22 | 17 | 75 |
| 5 | Aldershot | 46 | 11 | 7 | 5 | 35 | 23 | 9 | 8 | 6 | 29 | 29 | 12 | 75 |
| 6 | Ebbsfleet | 46 | 11 | 7 | 5 | 35 | 23 | 8 | 10 | 5 | 29 | 27 | 14 | 74 |
| 7 | Fylde | 46 | 11 | 9 | 3 | 51 | 27 | 9 | 4 | 10 | 31 | 29 | 26 | 73 |
| 8 | Dover | 46 | 12 | 5 | 6 | 32 | 17 | 8 | 8 | 7 | 30 | 27 | 18 | 73 |
| 9 | Bromley | 46 | 10 | 8 | 5 | 38 | 23 | 9 | 5 | 9 | 37 | 35 | 17 | 70 |
| 10 | Wrexham | 46 | 10 | 10 | 3 | 31 | 17 | 7 | 9 | 7 | 18 | 22 | 10 | 70 |
| 11 | Dagenham | 46 | 13 | 3 | 7 | 40 | 32 | 6 | 8 | 9 | 29 | 30 | 7 | 68 |
| 12 | Maidenhead | 46 | 11 | 6 | 6 | 36 | 26 | 6 | 7 | 10 | 29 | 40 | -1 | 64 |
| 13 | Leyton Orient | 46 | 8 | 6 | 9 | 33 | 26 | 8 | 6 | 9 | 25 | 30 | 2 | 60 |
| 14 | Eastleigh | 46 | 6 | 11 | 6 | 33 | 34 | 7 | 6 | 10 | 32 | 38 | -7 | 56 |
| 15 | Hartlepool | 46 | 7 | 6 | 10 | 24 | 26 | 7 | 8 | 8 | 29 | 37 | -10 | 56 |
| 16 | Halifax | 46 | 9 | 6 | 8 | 31 | 30 | 4 | 10 | 9 | 17 | 28 | -10 | 55 |
| 17 | Gateshead | 46 | 8 | 8 | 7 | 34 | 27 | 4 | 10 | 9 | 28 | 31 | 4 | 54 |
| 18 | Solihull | 46 | 8 | 7 | 8 | 28 | 30 | 6 | 5 | 12 | 21 | 30 | -11 | 54 |
| 19 | Maidstone | 46 | 6 | 9 | 8 | 25 | 31 | 7 | 6 | 10 | 27 | 33 | -12 | 54 |
| 20 | Barrow | 46 | 4 | 10 | 9 | 23 | 29 | 7 | 6 | 10 | 28 | 34 | -12 | 49 |
| 21 | Woking | 46 | 9 | 5 | 9 | 32 | 32 | 4 | 4 | 15 | 23 | 44 | -21 | 48 |
| 22 | Torquay | 46 | 5 | 6 | 12 | 26 | 36 | 5 | 6 | 12 | 19 | 37 | -28 | 42 |
| 23 | Chester | 46 | 5 | 5 | 13 | 20 | 37 | 3 | 8 | 12 | 22 | 42 | -37 | 37 |
| 24 | Guiseley | 46 | 3 | 9 | 11 | 21 | 33 | 4 | 3 | 16 | 23 | 56 | -45 | 33 |

*also promoted

**Player of Year**: Danny Rowe (AFC Fylde). **Manager of Year**: John Askew (Macclesfield)
**Leading league scorers**: 26 Cook (Tranmere); 24 Rowe (Fylde); 22 Andrade (Boreham Wood), Bonne (Leyton Orient); 20 Norwood (Tranmere); 18 Kedwell (Ebbsfleet); 16 Rees (Bromley), Bird (Dover)
**Team of Year**: Jalal (Macclesfield), Pearon (Wrexham), McNulty (Tranmere), Smith (Wrexham), Durrell (Macclesfield), Eastmond (Sutton), Whitaker (Macclesfield), Dennis (Bromley), Andrade (Boreham Wood), Rowe (Fylde), Cook (Tranmere)

## CHAMPIONS

| | |
|---|---|
| 1979–80 | Altrincham |
| 1980–81 | Altrincham |
| 1981–82 | Runcorn |
| 1982–83 | Enfield |
| 1983–84 | Maidstone |
| 1984–85 | Wealdstone |
| 1985–86 | Enfield |
| 1986–87* | Scarborough |
| 1987–88* | Lincoln |
| 1988–89* | Maidstone |
| 1989–90* | Darlington |
| 1990–91* | Barnet |
| 1991–92* | Colchester |
| 1992–93* | Wycombe |
| 1993–94 | Kidderminster |
| 1994–95 | Macclesfield |
| 1995–96 | Stevenage |
| 1996–97* | Macclesfield |
| 1997–98* | Halifax |
| 1998–99* | Cheltenham |
| 1999–2000* | Kidderminster |
| 2000–01* | Rushden |
| 2001–02* | Boston |
| 2002–03* | Yeovil |
| 2003–04* | Chester |
| 2004–05* | Barnet |
| 2005–06* | Accrington |
| 2006–07* | Dagenham |
| 2007–08* | Aldershot |
| 2008–09* | Burton |
| 2009–10* | Stevenage |
| 2010–11* | Crawley |
| 2011–2012* | Fleetwood |
| 2012–13* | Mansfield |
| 2013–14* | Luton |
| 2014–15* | Barnet |
| 2015–16* | Cheltenham |
| 2016–17* | Lincoln |
| 2017–18* | Macclesfield |

*Promoted to Football League

*Conference – Record attendance: 11,085 Bristol Rov v Alfreton, April 25, 2015*

# VANARAMA NATIONAL LEAGUE RESULTS 2017–2018

| | Aldershot | Barrow | Boreham Wood | Bromley | Chester | Dagenham | Dover | Ebbsfleet | Estleigh | Fylde | Gatehead | Guisley | Halifax | Hartlepool | Leyton Orient | Macclesfield | Maidstone | Maidenhead | Solihull | Sutton | Torquay | Tranmere | Woking | Wrexham |
|---|---|---|---|---|---|---|---|---|---|---|---|---|---|---|---|---|---|---|---|---|---|---|---|---|
| Aldershot | – | 1-1 | 2-0 | 1-1 | 1-2 | 1-1 | 0-2 | 0-0 | 0-2 | 2-1 | 1-0 | 6-0 | 0-1 | 2-1 | 2-2 | 1-2 | 1-1 | 1-0 | 1-0 | 2-2 | 3-2 | 2-1 | 3-1 | 2-0 |
| Barrow | 3-1 | – | 2-1 | 0-3 | 1-2 | 0-1 | 0-0 | 0-1 | 3-2 | 1-3 | 1-1 | 0-0 | 0-0 | 1-2 | 2-2 | 0-2 | 0-1 | 1-1 | 1-2 | 1-1 | 1-1 | 1-1 | 3-0 | 1-1 |
| Boreham Wood | 2-1 | 0-0 | – | 2-2 | 4-2 | 1-2 | 2-3 | 0-1 | 1-0 | 1-0 | 2-1 | 3-1 | 1-1 | 0-0 | 2-0 | 0-2 | 1-0 | 1-1 | 4-1 | 0-4 | 2-0 | 2-1 | 2-1 | 0-1 |
| Bromley | 0-2 | 0-0 | 3-2 | – | 1-1 | 3-1 | 2-2 | 4-2 | 0-0 | 0-1 | 0-0 | 2-1 | 3-0 | 2-0 | 6-1 | 1-1 | 2-2 | 2-3 | 1-0 | 0-1 | 3-1 | 0-1 | 2-0 | 1-1 |
| Chester | 0-0 | 3-2 | 1-2 | 3-2 | – | 0-4 | 0-2 | 1-1 | 3-1 | 1-1 | 1-3 | 0-2 | 0-0 | 1-1 | 0-1 | 0-2 | 1-3 | 2-0 | 1-0 | 2-3 | 0-2 | 0-2 | 0-2 | 0-1 |
| Dagenham | 0-2 | 2-1 | 2-3 | 5-1 | 3-2 | – | 1-0 | 3-3 | 1-2 | 2-0 | 3-1 | 3-2 | 3-1 | 4-2 | 0-0 | 1-0 | 2-1 | 1-0 | 1-3 | 1-2 | 1-0 | 0-4 | 1-1 | 0-1 |
| Dover | 1-2 | 1-1 | 0-1 | 1-2 | 4-0 | 1-0 | – | 1-1 | 2-0 | 0-1 | 3-2 | 2-1 | 0-0 | 4-0 | 1-0 | 2-0 | 2-2 | 1-1 | 1-0 | 0-1 | 1-0 | 0-1 | 3-1 | 1-0 |
| Ebbsfleet | 0-2 | 3-2 | 0-3 | 2-1 | 0-1 | 1-1 | 2-1 | – | 2-2 | 3-3 | 0-0 | 4-0 | 2-0 | 3-0 | 2-1 | 2-2 | 2-0 | 1-1 | 1-0 | 0-1 | 0-1 | 0-0 | 2-1 | 3-0 |
| Estleigh | 0-0 | 0-2 | 0-2 | 4-4 | 2-2 | 2-2 | 2-1 | 0-1 | – | 2-2 | 3-2 | 4-2 | 0-0 | 4-3 | 0-0 | 0-2 | 0-1 | 2-2 | 1-2 | 1-0 | 1-1 | 2-0 | 2-2 | 1-1 |
| Fylde | 7-1 | 1-0 | 2-2 | 2-2 | 1-1 | 2-2 | 3-1 | 1-1 | 2-2 | – | 0-0 | 2-1 | 2-0 | 3-3 | 0-1 | 6-0 | A-A | 1-4 | 1-1 | 2-1 | 2-0 | 5-2 | 1-2 | 2-0 |
| Gatehead | 0-1 | 1-2 | 1-1 | 1-2 | 3-2 | 0-0 | 0-0 | 2-5 | 2-0 | 1-2 | – | 1-0 | 0-0 | 2-2 | 1-3 | 3-0 | 2-1 | 7-1 | 2-2 | 0-2 | 3-0 | 1-0 | 1-1 | 0-0 |
| Guisley | 1-1 | 0-1 | 0-0 | 0-1 | 1-1 | 3-5 | 1-1 | 2-2 | 0-0 | 1-0 | 0-1 | – | 1-1 | 0-1 | 1-3 | 1-2 | 0-0 | 1-3 | 4-2 | 0-2 | 3-2 | 0-0 | 1-2 | 0-2 |
| Halifax | 0-2 | 0-1 | 2-1 | 2-1 | 4-0 | 2-1 | 1-2 | 1-2 | 3-3 | 2-1 | 2-2 | 2-0 | – | 2-0 | 1-2 | 1-4 | 0-2 | 3-2 | 0-0 | 2-1 | 1-1 | 0-2 | 0-0 | 0-0 |
| Hartlepool | 0-2 | 1-0 | 0-0 | 2-1 | 1-1 | 1-0 | 0-1 | 0-1 | 1-2 | 0-2 | 2-2 | 0-1 | 4-0 | – | 1-0 | 1-2 | 3-1 | 1-2 | 0-1 | 1-1 | 1-1 | 1-1 | 3-2 | 0-2 |
| Leyton Orient | 2-3 | 4-1 | 0-0 | 0-1 | 2-2 | 2-0 | 1-1 | 1-1 | 1-1 | 1-2 | 0-2 | 4-1 | 0-3 | 1-2 | – | 0-1 | 2-0 | 0-1 | 3-1 | 4-1 | 0-1 | 1-1 | 3-0 | 1-0 |
| Macclesfield | 2-0 | 3-1 | 0-0 | 0-0 | 1-0 | 2-0 | 1-0 | 1-0 | 1-2 | 2-1 | 1-0 | 2-1 | 2-1 | 1-1 | 1-1 | – | 1-4 | 1-0 | 0-0 | 1-0 | 1-1 | 2-2 | 1-3 | 4-1 |
| Maidstone | 1-1 | 0-1 | 0-4 | 0-2 | 1-0 | 0-0 | 2-2 | 1-2 | 2-3 | 1-0 | 2-2 | 1-1 | 0-0 | 1-2 | 0-2 | 2-2 | – | 1-1 | 1-1 | 1-0 | 1-0 | 2-3 | 3-1 | 2-1 |
| Maidenhead | 3-3 | 0-1 | 2-1 | 5-2 | 3-0 | 1-1 | 3-2 | 1-1 | 3-1 | 1-2 | 0-3 | 3-0 | 0-0 | 2-1 | 0-1 | 1-1 | 0-0 | – | 1-0 | A-A | 1-2 | 1-0 | 2-1 | 1-2 |
| Solihull | 0-0 | 3-3 | 0-0 | 2-0 | 2-0 | 2-2 | 3-2 | 1-3 | 1-4 | 0-4 | 1-1 | 3-1 | 0-1 | 1-2 | 1-0 | 0-1 | 1-0 | 3-1 | – | 0-2 | 1-1 | 0-2 | 3-0 | 0-0 |
| Sutton | 2-1 | 3-2 | 1-1 | 0-3 | 3-2 | 2-1 | 2-2 | 0-0 | 2-0 | 2-1 | 1-1 | 4-0 | 3-2 | 1-1 | 2-0 | 2-1 | 1-3 | 0-2 | 1-0 | – | 0-1 | 1-3 | 2-0 | 1-1 |
| Torquay | 0-0 | 3-1 | 2-4 | 0-4 | 1-1 | 0-3 | 0-2 | 1-1 | 1-2 | 1-3 | 1-1 | 3-4 | 1-0 | 0-2 | 3-0 | 0-1 | 0-1 | 4-0 | 1-2 | 2-3 | – | 0-0 | 2-1 | 0-0 |
| Tranmere | 2-0 | 1-0 | 2-2 | 1-0 | 0-0 | 2-0 | 0-1 | 3-0 | 3-1 | 4-1 | 4-2 | 4-0 | 4-2 | 1-2 | 2-1 | 1-4 | 4-0 | 3-2 | 1-2 | 0-1 | 3-0 | – | 3-1 | 0-1 |
| Woking | 1-2 | 1-2 | 0-0 | 0-2 | 1-0 | 1-0 | 1-2 | 1-0 | 2-1 | 1-0 | 2-1 | 2-3 | 1-3 | 1-1 | 0-2 | 2-3 | 4-4 | 1-1 | 2-1 | 2-0 | 4-1 | 0-1 | – | 2-2 |
| Wrexham | 2-2 | 3-3 | 0-1 | 2-0 | 2-0 | 1-2 | 0-0 | 2-0 | 2-1 | 0-0 | 1-0 | 1-1 | 1-1 | 0-0 | 2-2 | 0-1 | 1-0 | 2-0 | 1-0 | 1-1 | 4-0 | 2-2 | 1-0 | – |

## NATIONAL LEAGUE NORTH

| | P | W | D | L | F | A | GD | Pts |
|---|---|---|---|---|---|---|---|---|
| Salford | 42 | 28 | 7 | 7 | 80 | 45 | 35 | 91 |
| Harrogate* | 42 | 26 | 7 | 9 | 100 | 49 | 51 | 85 |
| Brackley | 42 | 23 | 11 | 8 | 72 | 37 | 35 | 80 |
| Kidderminster | 42 | 20 | 12 | 10 | 76 | 50 | 26 | 72 |
| Stockport | 42 | 20 | 9 | 13 | 75 | 57 | 18 | 69 |
| Chorley | 42 | 18 | 14 | 10 | 52 | 39 | 13 | 68 |
| Bradford PA | 42 | 18 | 9 | 15 | 66 | 56 | 10 | 63 |
| Spennymoor | 42 | 18 | 9 | 15 | 71 | 67 | 4 | 63 |
| Boston | 42 | 17 | 9 | 16 | 67 | 66 | 1 | 60 |
| Blyth | 42 | 19 | 2 | 21 | 76 | 69 | 7 | 59 |
| York | 42 | 16 | 10 | 16 | 65 | 62 | 3 | 58 |
| Darlington | 42 | 14 | 13 | 15 | 58 | 58 | 0 | 55 |
| Nuneaton | 42 | 14 | 13 | 15 | 50 | 57 | -7 | 55 |
| Telford | 42 | 16 | 5 | 21 | 55 | 69 | -14 | 53 |
| Southport | 42 | 14 | 8 | 20 | 60 | 72 | -12 | 50 |
| FC United | 42 | 14 | 8 | 20 | 58 | 72 | -14 | 50 |
| Alfreton | 42 | 14 | 7 | 21 | 67 | 71 | -4 | 49 |
| Curzon Ashton | 42 | 12 | 13 | 17 | 52 | 66 | -14 | 49 |
| Leamington | 42 | 13 | 10 | 19 | 51 | 65 | -14 | 49 |
| Gainsborough | 42 | 14 | 4 | 24 | 47 | 73 | -26 | 46 |
| Tamworth | 42 | 11 | 9 | 22 | 55 | 77 | -22 | 42 |
| North Ferriby | 42 | 4 | 9 | 29 | 25 | 101 | -76 | 21 |

*Also promoted. **Play-off Final**: Harrogate 3 Brackley 0

## NATIONAL LEAGUE SOUTH

| | P | W | D | L | F | A | GD | Pts |
|---|---|---|---|---|---|---|---|---|
| Havant | 42 | 25 | 11 | 6 | 70 | 30 | 40 | 86 |
| Dartford | 42 | 26 | 8 | 8 | 81 | 44 | 37 | 86 |
| Chelmsford | 42 | 21 | 11 | 10 | 68 | 45 | 23 | 74 |
| Hampton & R | 42 | 18 | 18 | 6 | 58 | 37 | 21 | 72 |
| Hemel Hempstead | 42 | 19 | 13 | 10 | 71 | 51 | 20 | 70 |
| Braintree* | 42 | 19 | 13 | 10 | 73 | 55 | 18 | 69 |
| Truro | 42 | 20 | 9 | 13 | 71 | 55 | 16 | 69 |
| St Albans | 42 | 19 | 8 | 15 | 71 | 58 | 13 | 65 |
| Bath | 42 | 17 | 12 | 13 | 64 | 48 | 16 | 63 |
| Welling | 42 | 17 | 10 | 15 | 68 | 59 | 9 | 61 |
| Wealdstone | 42 | 16 | 11 | 15 | 64 | 62 | 2 | 59 |
| Weston SM | 42 | 16 | 7 | 19 | 66 | 73 | -7 | 55 |
| Chippenham | 42 | 15 | 9 | 18 | 64 | 70 | -6 | 54 |
| Gloucester | 42 | 15 | 8 | 19 | 56 | 70 | -14 | 53 |
| East Thurrock | 42 | 13 | 11 | 18 | 68 | 84 | -16 | 50 |
| Oxford City | 42 | 13 | 10 | 19 | 60 | 69 | -9 | 49 |
| Concord | 42 | 12 | 10 | 20 | 46 | 62 | -16 | 46 |
| Eastbourne | 42 | 13 | 7 | 22 | 57 | 80 | -23 | 46 |
| Hungerford | 42 | 12 | 7 | 23 | 45 | 68 | -23 | 43 |
| Poole | 42 | 11 | 9 | 22 | 47 | 73 | -26 | 42 |
| Whitehawk | 42 | 8 | 10 | 24 | 51 | 89 | -38 | 34 |
| Bognor Regis | 42 | 5 | 12 | 25 | 41 | 78 | -37 | 27 |

*Also promoted. **Play-off Final:** Braintree 1 Hampton & R 1 (aet, Braintree won 4-3 on penalties. Braintree deducted 1 pt

# OTHER LEAGUES 2017–18

## JD WELSH PREMIER

| | P | W | D | L | F | A | GD | Pts |
|---|---|---|---|---|---|---|---|---|
| New Saints | 32 | 23 | 5 | 4 | 83 | 32 | 51 | 74 |
| Bangor* | 32 | 19 | 3 | 10 | 49 | 32 | 17 | 60 |
| Connah's Quay | 32 | 17 | 6 | 9 | 46 | 29 | 17 | 57 |
| Bala | 32 | 15 | 4 | 13 | 37 | 48 | -11 | 49 |
| Cefn Druids | 32 | 12 | 8 | 12 | 38 | 41 | -3 | 44 |
| Cardiff Met | 32 | 12 | 7 | 13 | 46 | 41 | 5 | 43 |
| Barry | 32 | 16 | 5 | 11 | 39 | 31 | 8 | 53 |
| Newtown | 32 | 12 | 4 | 16 | 52 | 55 | -3 | 40 |
| Aberystwyth | 32 | 10 | 7 | 15 | 47 | 56 | -9 | 37 |
| Llandudno | 32 | 9 | 9 | 14 | 39 | 44 | -5 | 36 |
| Carmarthen | 32 | 8 | 5 | 19 | 35 | 62 | -27 | 29 |
| Prestatyn | 32 | 4 | 7 | 21 | 27 | 67 | -40 | 19 |

*Bangor relegated for financial reasons. **Cup Final**: New Saints 1 Cardiff Met 0

## BOSTIK PREMIER

| | P | W | D | L | F | A | GD | Pts |
|---|---|---|---|---|---|---|---|---|
| Billericay | 46 | 30 | 9 | 7 | 110 | 50 | 60 | 99 |
| Dulwich Hamlet* | 46 | 28 | 11 | 7 | 91 | 41 | 50 | 95 |
| Hendon | 46 | 25 | 10 | 11 | 96 | 59 | 37 | 85 |
| Folkestone | 46 | 25 | 10 | 11 | 104 | 71 | 33 | 85 |
| Leiston | 46 | 23 | 10 | 13 | 82 | 53 | 29 | 79 |
| Leatherhead | 46 | 24 | 7 | 15 | 68 | 49 | 19 | 79 |
| Margate | 46 | 20 | 17 | 9 | 77 | 53 | 24 | 77 |
| Staines | 46 | 21 | 12 | 13 | 106 | 83 | 23 | 75 |
| Wingate & F | 46 | 20 | 9 | 17 | 63 | 71 | -8 | 69 |
| Met Police | 46 | 19 | 12 | 15 | 76 | 71 | 5 | 66 |
| Tonbridge | 46 | 19 | 7 | 20 | 58 | 63 | -5 | 64 |
| Harrow | 46 | 19 | 6 | 21 | 69 | 76 | -7 | 63 |
| Kingstonian | 46 | 18 | 5 | 23 | 57 | 70 | -13 | 59 |
| Dorking | 46 | 16 | 10 | 20 | 77 | 80 | -3 | 58 |
| Thurrock | 46 | 17 | 6 | 23 | 68 | 79 | -11 | 57 |
| Worthing | 46 | 15 | 12 | 19 | 71 | 84 | -13 | 57 |
| Enfield | 46 | 14 | 14 | 18 | 72 | 80 | -8 | 56 |
| Merstham | 46 | 15 | 11 | 20 | 69 | 80 | -11 | 56 |
| Needham Market | 46 | 13 | 10 | 23 | 65 | 84 | -19 | 49 |
| Brightlingsea | 46 | 13 | 9 | 24 | 67 | 89 | -22 | 48 |
| Harlow | 46 | 13 | 8 | 25 | 55 | 88 | -33 | 47 |
| Lowestoft | 46 | 12 | 7 | 27 | 52 | 92 | -40 | 43 |
| Burgess Hill | 46 | 9 | 9 | 28 | 64 | 102 | -38 | 36 |
| Tooting & M | 46 | 9 | 9 | 28 | 52 | 101 | -49 | 36 |

*Also promoted. Met Police deducted 3 pts. **Play-off Final**: Dulwich Hamlet 1 Hendon 1 (aet, Dulwich Hamlet won 4-3 on pens)

## EVOSTICK NORTH

| | P | W | D | L | F | A | GD | Pts |
|---|---|---|---|---|---|---|---|---|
| Altrincham | 46 | 28 | 11 | 7 | 101 | 42 | 59 | 95 |
| Ashton* | 46 | 23 | 13 | 10 | 85 | 59 | 26 | 82 |
| Warrington | 46 | 23 | 13 | 10 | 72 | 49 | 23 | 82 |
| Grantham | 46 | 24 | 9 | 13 | 90 | 55 | 35 | 81 |
| Farsley | 46 | 23 | 11 | 12 | 87 | 69 | 18 | 80 |
| Shaw Lane | 46 | 25 | 7 | 14 | 79 | 62 | 17 | 79 |
| Witton | 46 | 19 | 13 | 14 | 83 | 63 | 20 | 70 |
| Rushall | 46 | 19 | 9 | 18 | 73 | 79 | -6 | 66 |
| Buxton | 46 | 17 | 13 | 16 | 71 | 66 | 5 | 64 |
| Barwell | 46 | 17 | 13 | 16 | 65 | 67 | -2 | 64 |
| Stourbridge | 46 | 16 | 14 | 16 | 67 | 56 | 11 | 62 |
| Workington | 46 | 18 | 8 | 20 | 72 | 69 | 3 | 62 |
| Mickleover | 46 | 16 | 13 | 17 | 68 | 60 | 8 | 61 |
| Stafford | 46 | 16 | 13 | 17 | 54 | 58 | -4 | 61 |
| Matlock | 46 | 18 | 6 | 22 | 69 | 75 | -6 | 60 |
| Nantwich | 46 | 16 | 9 | 21 | 62 | 72 | -10 | 57 |
| Hednesford | 46 | 15 | 12 | 19 | 60 | 79 | -19 | 57 |
| Lancaster | 46 | 14 | 13 | 19 | 66 | 72 | -6 | 55 |
| Marine | 46 | 14 | 11 | 21 | 67 | 78 | -11 | 53 |
| Coalville | 46 | 15 | 7 | 24 | 70 | 92 | -22 | 52 |
| Whitby | 46 | 12 | 14 | 20 | 60 | 82 | -22 | 50 |
| Stalybridge | 46 | 14 | 6 | 26 | 57 | 90 | -33 | 48 |
| Halesowen | 46 | 13 | 10 | 23 | 48 | 76 | -28 | 45 |
| Sutton Coldfield | 46 | 10 | 6 | 30 | 52 | 108 | -56 | 35 |

*Also promoted. Halesowen deducted 4 pts; Shaw Lane deducted 3 pts; Sutton Coldfield deducted 1 pt. **Play-off Final**: Ashton 2 Grantham 0

## EVOSTICK SOUTH

| | P | W | D | L | F | A | GD | Pts |
|---|---|---|---|---|---|---|---|---|
| Hereford | 46 | 36 | 5 | 5 | 111 | 33 | 78 | 113 |
| King's Lynn | 46 | 30 | 10 | 6 | 99 | 39 | 60 | 100 |
| Slough* | 46 | 30 | 9 | 7 | 111 | 49 | 62 | 99 |
| Kettering | 46 | 30 | 7 | 9 | 122 | 56 | 66 | 97 |
| Weymouth | 46 | 30 | 7 | 9 | 103 | 48 | 55 | 97 |
| Tiverton | 46 | 24 | 6 | 16 | 78 | 69 | 9 | 78 |
| Royston | 46 | 24 | 5 | 17 | 84 | 65 | 19 | 77 |
| Chesham | 46 | 21 | 11 | 14 | 85 | 61 | 24 | 74 |
| Banbury | 46 | 19 | 15 | 12 | 90 | 59 | 31 | 72 |
| Basingstoke | 46 | 21 | 8 | 17 | 92 | 72 | 20 | 71 |
| Hitchin | 46 | 19 | 9 | 18 | 67 | 66 | 1 | 66 |
| St Neots | 46 | 17 | 13 | 16 | 79 | 79 | 0 | 64 |
| Frome | 46 | 18 | 7 | 21 | 78 | 96 | -18 | 61 |
| Redditch | 46 | 15 | 10 | 21 | 73 | 73 | 0 | 55 |
| Stratford | 46 | 15 | 10 | 21 | 68 | 81 | -13 | 55 |
| Biggleswade | 46 | 14 | 11 | 21 | 52 | 63 | -11 | 53 |
| Merthyr | 46 | 13 | 14 | 19 | 76 | 98 | -22 | 53 |
| Bishop's Stortford | 46 | 14 | 10 | 22 | 74 | 79 | -5 | 52 |
| Dorchester | 46 | 13 | 12 | 21 | 62 | 83 | -21 | 51 |
| Farnborough | 46 | 15 | 6 | 25 | 82 | 120 | -38 | 51 |
| King's Langley | 46 | 8 | 14 | 24 | 63 | 98 | -35 | 38 |
| St Ives | 46 | 8 | 9 | 29 | 54 | 105 | -51 | 33 |
| Gosport | 46 | 5 | 5 | 36 | 41 | 142 | -101 | 20 |
| Dunstable | 46 | 4 | 5 | 37 | 27 | 137 | -110 | 17 |

*Also promoted. **Play-off Final**: Slough 2 King's Lynn 1

## PRESS AND JOURNAL HIGHLAND LEAGUE

| | P | W | D | L | F | A | GD | Pts |
|---|---|---|---|---|---|---|---|---|
| Cove | 34 | 29 | 3 | 2 | 127 | 22 | 105 | 90 |
| Formartine | 34 | 26 | 1 | 7 | 124 | 41 | 83 | 79 |
| Inverurie | 34 | 25 | 3 | 6 | 104 | 37 | 67 | 78 |
| Fraserburgh | 34 | 23 | 4 | 7 | 101 | 38 | 63 | 73 |
| Forres | 34 | 23 | 4 | 7 | 88 | 45 | 43 | 73 |
| Brora | 34 | 20 | 3 | 11 | 87 | 39 | 48 | 63 |
| Buckie | 34 | 15 | 6 | 13 | 80 | 56 | 24 | 51 |
| Deveronvale | 34 | 16 | 3 | 15 | 73 | 76 | -3 | 51 |
| Nairn | 34 | 16 | 3 | 15 | 61 | 71 | -10 | 51 |
| Rothes | 34 | 15 | 4 | 15 | 77 | 70 | 7 | 49 |
| Huntly | 34 | 15 | 4 | 15 | 66 | 81 | -15 | 49 |
| Wick | 34 | 12 | 10 | 12 | 67 | 54 | 13 | 46 |
| Clachnacuddin | 34 | 11 | 8 | 15 | 54 | 69 | -15 | 41 |
| Turriff | 34 | 11 | 4 | 19 | 54 | 70 | -16 | 37 |
| Keith | 34 | 4 | 4 | 26 | 45 | 104 | -59 | 16 |
| Lossiemouth | 34 | 4 | 3 | 27 | 41 | 125 | -84 | 15 |
| Strathspey | 34 | 4 | 2 | 28 | 26 | 124 | -98 | 14 |
| Fort William | 34 | 0 | 5 | 29 | 31 | 184 | -153 | 5 |

**Cup Final**: Formartine 2 Fraserburgh 1. **Inter-league play-off**: Cove 5 Spartans 2 (4-0, 1-2)

## FERRARI PACKING LOWLAND LEAGUE

| | P | W | D | L | F | A | GD | Pts |
|---|---|---|---|---|---|---|---|---|
| Spartans | 30 | 23 | 4 | 3 | 64 | 17 | 47 | 73 |
| East Kilbride | 30 | 22 | 5 | 3 | 76 | 23 | 53 | 71 |
| BSC | 30 | 20 | 5 | 5 | 71 | 27 | 44 | 65 |
| East Stirling | 30 | 15 | 3 | 12 | 67 | 31 | 36 | 64 |
| Selkirk | 30 | 15 | 3 | 12 | 63 | 50 | 13 | 48 |
| Cumbernauld | 30 | 11 | 8 | 11 | 53 | 54 | -1 | 41 |
| Civil Service | 30 | 11 | 7 | 12 | 47 | 44 | 3 | 40 |
| Gretna | 30 | 12 | 4 | 14 | 50 | 56 | -6 | 40 |
| Univ Stirling | 30 | 11 | 5 | 14 | 45 | 49 | -4 | 38 |
| Edusport Acad | 30 | 9 | 7 | 14 | 46 | 49 | -3 | 34 |
| Edinburgh Univ | 30 | 9 | 7 | 14 | 40 | 45 | -5 | 34 |
| Whitehill | 30 | 11 | 1 | 18 | 50 | 66 | -16 | 34 |
| Gala | 30 | 8 | 7 | 15 | 43 | 63 | -20 | 31 |
| Dallbeattie | 30 | 7 | 8 | 15 | 46 | 65 | -19 | 29 |
| Vale of Leithen | 30 | 8 | 5 | 17 | 44 | 76 | -32 | 29 |
| Hawick | 30 | 1 | 3 | 26 | 18 | 108 | -90 | 6 |

**Cup Final**: Cumbernauld 3 Selkirk 1

## PREMIER LEAGUE UNDER 23

### DIVISION ONE

| | P | W | D | L | F | A | GD | Pts |
|---|---|---|---|---|---|---|---|---|
| Arsenal | 22 | 13 | 3 | 6 | 48 | 32 | 16 | 42 |
| Liverpool | 22 | 13 | 1 | 8 | 43 | 27 | 16 | 40 |
| Leicester | 22 | 11 | 6 | 5 | 36 | 20 | 16 | 39 |
| Swansea | 22 | 11 | 4 | 7 | 40 | 31 | 9 | 37 |
| West Ham | 22 | 9 | 4 | 9 | 30 | 32 | -2 | 31 |
| Manchester City | 22 | 8 | 6 | 8 | 41 | 31 | 10 | 30 |
| Everton | 22 | 9 | 3 | 10 | 32 | 36 | -4 | 30 |
| Chelsea | 22 | 8 | 5 | 9 | 34 | 35 | -1 | 29 |
| Tottenham | 22 | 7 | 5 | 10 | 38 | 48 | -10 | 26 |
| Derby | 22 | 7 | 3 | 12 | 32 | 44 | -12 | 24 |
| Sunderland | 22 | 6 | 4 | 12 | 19 | 39 | -20 | 22 |
| Manchester Utd | 22 | 4 | 8 | 10 | 22 | 40 | -18 | 20 |

### DIVISION TWO

| | P | W | D | L | F | A | GD | Pts |
|---|---|---|---|---|---|---|---|---|
| Blackburn | 22 | 15 | 4 | 3 | 47 | 20 | 27 | 49 |
| Aston Villa | 22 | 14 | 0 | 8 | 51 | 30 | 21 | 42 |
| Brighton* | 22 | 11 | 7 | 4 | 46 | 25 | 21 | 40 |
| Middlesbrough | 22 | 11 | 4 | 7 | 41 | 36 | 5 | 37 |
| Reading | 22 | 10 | 4 | 8 | 38 | 44 | -6 | 34 |
| Southampton | 22 | 10 | 3 | 9 | 41 | 37 | 4 | 33 |
| Norwich | 22 | 9 | 5 | 8 | 33 | 33 | 0 | 32 |
| Fulham | 22 | 9 | 3 | 10 | 38 | 37 | 1 | 30 |
| Wolves | 22 | 8 | 4 | 10 | 30 | 41 | -11 | 28 |
| Newcastle | 22 | 6 | 3 | 13 | 29 | 45 | -16 | 21 |
| Stoke | 22 | 6 | 2 | 14 | 31 | 46 | -15 | 20 |
| WBA | 22 | 2 | 3 | 17 | 20 | 48 | -28 | 9 |

*Also promoted. **Play-off Final**: Aston Villa 0 Brighton 2

# THE THINGS THEY SAY ...

'I'm prouder than the proudest man from Proudsville' – **Sean Dyche**, Burnley manager, after his side reached as high as fourth during the Premier League season.

'I don't know what you mean by 'parking the bus.' I don't know who created this, but it's not a lot to do with football' – **Arsene Wenger** dismissing the game's latest terminology.

'It's about working harder, doing more training, finding little percentages' – **Harry Kane**, Tottenham striker, on how to follow his Premier League record of 39 goals in 2017.

'We're in a dogfight and you don't go into a dogfight with kittens' – **Chris Coleman** on tackling Sunderland's relegation struggle.

'They deserve to go to Wembley for a replay. Sometimes I miss this type of football because it's the reality of the game. It's pure passion' – **Mauricio Pochettino**, Tottenham manager, after his side were held 1-1 by Newport in the FA Cup fourth round.

# WOMEN'S FOOTBALL 2017–18

Fran Kirby rounded off a season of club success and individual honours with a new three-year contract at Chelsea. The 25-year-old England forward helped her club complete a domestic double and reach the semi-finals of the Champions League. She was also named Player of the Year by the PFA and football writers. Chelsea maintained their unbeaten Super League record by coming from 2-0 down to beat Liverpool 3-2 in the final match with two goals from South Korean international Ji So-Yun and one from Eni Aluko. They defeated Arsenal 3-1 in the FA Cup Final, with Kirby on the mark, alongside two from Switzerland's Ramona Bachmann, in front of a record Wembley crowd for the competition of 45,423. In Europe, their team overcame Montpellier 5-1 on aggregate in the quarter-finals, but lost 5-1 to Wolfsburg in the last four. Manchester City went through with a 7-3 victory over the Swedish side Linkoping, then went down 1-0 over the two legs of their semi-final to the eventual winners Lyon. Arsenal lifted the League Cup for a record fifth time, beating Manchester City 1-0 in the final with a goal from Holland's Vivianne Miedema.

## SUPER LEAGUE 1

| | P | W | D | L | F | A | GD | Pts |
|---|---|---|---|---|---|---|---|---|
| Chelsea | 18 | 13 | 5 | 0 | 44 | 13 | 31 | 44 |
| Manchester City | 18 | 12 | 2 | 4 | 51 | 17 | 34 | 38 |
| Arsenal | 18 | 11 | 4 | 3 | 38 | 18 | 20 | 37 |
| Reading | 18 | 9 | 5 | 4 | 40 | 18 | 22 | 32 |
| Birmingham | 18 | 9 | 3 | 6 | 30 | 18 | 12 | 30 |
| Liverpool | 18 | 9 | 1 | 8 | 30 | 27 | 3 | 28 |
| Sunderland | 18 | 5 | 1 | 12 | 15 | 40 | -25 | 16 |
| Bristol City | 18 | 5 | 1 | 12 | 13 | 47 | -34 | 16 |
| Everton | 18 | 4 | 2 | 12 | 19 | 30 | -11 | 14 |
| Yeovil | 18 | 0 | 2 | 16 | 2 | 54 | -52 | 2 |

## SUPER LEAGUE 2

| | P | W | D | L | F | A | GD | Pts |
|---|---|---|---|---|---|---|---|---|
| Doncaster | 18 | 15 | 2 | 1 | 52 | 15 | 37 | 47 |
| Brighton | 18 | 12 | 1 | 5 | 35 | 26 | 9 | 37 |
| Millwall* | 18 | 12 | 3 | 3 | 40 | 23 | 17 | 36 |
| Durham | 18 | 11 | 2 | 5 | 44 | 26 | 18 | 35 |
| Sheffield FC | 18 | 9 | 1 | 8 | 40 | 31 | 9 | 28 |
| London Bees | 18 | 6 | 5 | 7 | 29 | 32 | -3 | 23 |
| Tottenham | 18 | 6 | 4 | 8 | 32 | 34 | -2 | 22 |
| Oxford Utd | 18 | 3 | 3 | 12 | 24 | 41 | -17 | 12 |
| Aston Villa | 18 | 3 | 2 | 13 | 21 | 40 | -19 | 11 |
| Watford | 18 | 1 | 1 | 16 | 8 | 57 | -49 | 4 |

*Deducted 3 pts

## PREMIER LEAGUE – NORTH

| | P | W | D | L | F | A | GD | Pts |
|---|---|---|---|---|---|---|---|---|
| Blackburn | 22 | 18 | 2 | 2 | 68 | 17 | 51 | 56 |
| Leicester | 22 | 14 | 4 | 4 | 68 | 32 | 36 | 46 |
| Middlesbrough | 22 | 14 | 0 | 8 | 63 | 52 | 11 | 42 |
| Stoke | 22 | 12 | 4 | 6 | 52 | 38 | 14 | 40 |
| Fylde | 22 | 10 | 6 | 6 | 35 | 35 | 0 | 36 |
| Huddersfield | 22 | 10 | 5 | 7 | 45 | 27 | 18 | 35 |
| Derby | 22 | 7 | 5 | 10 | 27 | 37 | -10 | 26 |
| Bradford City | 22 | 7 | 4 | 11 | 40 | 45 | -5 | 25 |
| Nottm Forest | 22 | 5 | 4 | 13 | 23 | 57 | -34 | 19 |

| | | | | | | | |
|---|---|---|---|---|---|---|---|
| Guiseley | 22 | 4 | 5 | 13 | 33 | 56 | -23 | 17 |
| Wolves | 22 | 4 | 5 | 13 | 30 | 56 | -26 | 17 |
| WBA | 22 | 4 | 2 | 16 | 27 | 59 | -32 | 14 |

## PREMIER LEAGUE – SOUTH

| | | | | | | | | |
|---|---|---|---|---|---|---|---|---|
| Charlton | 22 | 20 | 0 | 2 | 98 | 13 | 85 | 60 |
| Basildon | 22 | 17 | 1 | 4 | 51 | 24 | 27 | 52 |
| Crystal Palace | 22 | 16 | 2 | 4 | 59 | 15 | 44 | 50 |
| Coventry Utd | 22 | 14 | 2 | 6 | 69 | 20 | 49 | 44 |
| Lewes | 22 | 14 | 2 | 6 | 45 | 25 | 20 | 44 |
| Portsmouth | 22 | 12 | 1 | 9 | 44 | 35 | 9 | 37 |
| West Ham | 22 | 9 | 2 | 11 | 57 | 42 | 15 | 29 |
| Chichester | 22 | 8 | 4 | 10 | 43 | 48 | -5 | 28 |
| Gillingham | 22 | 5 | 2 | 15 | 24 | 53 | -29 | 17 |
| Cardiff | 22 | 4 | 4 | 14 | 40 | 69 | -29 | 16 |
| QPR | 22 | 2 | 2 | 18 | 17 | 94 | -77 | 8 |
| Swindon | 22 | 0 | 0 | 22 | 10 | 119 | -109 | 0 |

**Championship play-off**: Charlton 2 Blackburn 1. **League Cup Final**: Blackburn 3 Leicester 1

# WORLD CUP 2019 QUALIFYING

(Seven group winners to finals; four best runners-up into play-offs)

## GROUP ONE

| | P | W | D | L | F | A | Pts |
|---|---|---|---|---|---|---|---|
| **Wales** | 7 | 5 | 2 | 0 | 7 | 0 | 17 |
| **England** | 6 | 5 | 1 | 0 | 20 | 1 | 16 |
| Russia | 6 | 2 | 1 | 3 | 10 | 13 | 7 |
| Kazakhstan | 6 | 1 | 0 | 5 | 2 | 12 | 3 |
| Bosnia-Herz | 7 | 1 | 0 | 6 | 3 | 16 | 3 |

## GROUP TWO

| | | | | | | | |
|---|---|---|---|---|---|---|---|
| Switzerland | 6 | 6 | 0 | 0 | 20 | 3 | 18 |
| **Scotland** | 6 | 5 | 0 | 1 | 15 | 5 | 15 |
| Poland | 6 | 2 | 1 | 3 | 12 | 11 | 7 |
| Albania | 7 | 1 | 1 | 5 | 5 | 20 | 4 |
| Belarus | 7 | 1 | 0 | 6 | 4 | 17 | 3 |

## GROUP THREE

| | | | | | | | |
|---|---|---|---|---|---|---|---|
| Holland | 7 | 6 | 1 | 0 | 21 | 0 | 19 |
| Norway | 6 | 5 | 0 | 1 | 16 | 3 | 15 |
| **Rep of Ireland** | 7 | 3 | 1 | 3 | 6 | 6 | 10 |
| **N Ireland** | 6 | 1 | 0 | 5 | 4 | 22 | 3 |
| Slovakia | 5 | 0 | 0 | 5 | 3 | 18 | 0 |

# IRISH FOOTBALL 2017–18

## SSE AIRTRICITY LEAGUE OF IRELAND

### PREMIER DIVISION

| | P | W | D | L | F | A | Pts |
|---|---|---|---|---|---|---|---|
| Cork City | 33 | 24 | 4 | 5 | 67 | 23 | 76 |
| Dundalk | 33 | 22 | 3 | 8 | 72 | 24 | 69 |
| Shamrock | 33 | 17 | 3 | 13 | 49 | 41 | 54 |
| Derry City | 33 | 14 | 9 | 10 | 49 | 40 | 51 |
| Bohemians | 33 | 14 | 5 | 14 | 36 | 40 | 47 |
| Bray Wdrs | 33 | 13 | 7 | 13 | 55 | 52 | 46 |
| Limerick | 33 | 10 | 10 | 13 | 41 | 51 | 40 |
| St Patrick's | 33 | 9 | 12 | 12 | 45 | 52 | 39 |
| Sligo Rov | 33 | 8 | 15 | 10 | 33 | 44 | 39 |
| Galway | 33 | 7 | 14 | 12 | 45 | 50 | 35 |
| Finn Harps | 33 | 9 | 3 | 21 | 35 | 67 | 30 |
| Drogheda | 33 | 5 | 7 | 21 | 22 | 65 | 22 |

**Leading scorer**: 20 Seán Maguire (Cork City). **Player of Year**: Seán Maguire. **Young Player of Year**: Trevor Clarke (Shamrock Rov). **Goalkeeper of Year**: Mark McNulty (Cork City). **Personality of Year**: John Caulfield (Cork City)

### FIRST DIVISION

| | P | W | D | L | F | A | Pts |
|---|---|---|---|---|---|---|---|
| Waterford | 28 | 17 | 8 | 3 | 47 | 17 | 59 |
| Cobh | 28 | 16 | 3 | 9 | 37 | 28 | 51 |
| UCD | 28 | 13 | 8 | 7 | 42 | 23 | 47 |
| Shelbourne | 28 | 11 | 7 | 10 | 37 | 32 | 40 |
| Longford | 28 | 10 | 8 | 10 | 34 | 26 | 38 |
| Cabinteely | 28 | 10 | 8 | 10 | 41 | 37 | 38 |
| Wexford FC | 28 | 4 | 7 | 17 | 16 | 41 | 19 |
| Athlone | 28 | 4 | 5 | 19 | 29 | 79 | 17 |

**Leading scorer**: 17 George Kelly (UCD). **Player of the Year**: Kieran Marty Waters (Cabinteely)

## DAILY MAIL CUP FINAL

**Cork City** 1 (Campion) **Dundalk** 1 (Vemmelund) – aet, Cork City won 5-3 on pens. Aviva Stadium, November 5, 2017

**Cork City**: McNulty, Beattie, Bennett, Delaney, Griffin, McCormack, Morrissey (Bolger), Keohane (Sadlier), Buckley (Campion), Dooley, Sheppard

**Dundalk**: Rogers, Gannon, Gartland (Hoare), Vemmelund, Massey, O'Donnell, Benson, McGrath (Connolly), McEleney (Mountney), Duffy, McMillan

**Referee**: P McLaughlin (Donegal)

## EA SPORTS LEAGUE CUP FINAL

**Dundalk** 3 (McMillan, McEleney, Stewart) **Shamrock Rov** 0. Tallaght Stadium, Dublin, September 16, 2017.

## DANSKE BANK PREMIERSHIP

| | P | W | D | L | F | A | Pts |
|---|---|---|---|---|---|---|---|
| Crusaders | 38 | 28 | 7 | 3 | 106 | 38 | 91 |
| Coleraine | 38 | 26 | 11 | 1 | 76 | 31 | 89 |
| Glenavon | 38 | 19 | 12 | 7 | 85 | 52 | 69 |
| Linfield | 38 | 20 | 7 | 11 | 72 | 45 | 67 |
| Cliftonville | 38 | 20 | 5 | 13 | 68 | 45 | 65 |
| Ballymena | 38 | 14 | 6 | 18 | 53 | 65 | 48 |
| Glentoran | 38 | 14 | 9 | 15 | 52 | 52 | 51 |
| Dungannon | 38 | 13 | 6 | 19 | 42 | 62 | 45 |
| Ards | 38 | 12 | 4 | 22 | 42 | 74 | 40 |
| Warrenpoint | 38 | 8 | 6 | 24 | 52 | 86 | 30 |
| Carrick | 38 | 6 | 5 | 27 | 31 | 78 | 23 |
| Ballinamallard | 38 | 5 | 8 | 25 | 38 | 89 | 23 |

**Leading scorer**: 22 Joe Gormley (Cliftonville). **Manager of Year**: Oran Kearney (Coleraine). **Player of Year**: Gavin Whyte (Crusaders). **Young Player of Year**: Gavin Whyte. **Goalkeeper of Year**: Chris Jones (Coleraine)

## BLUEFIN SPORT CHAMPIONSHIP - DIVISION ONE

| | P | W | D | L | F | A | Pts |
|---|---|---|---|---|---|---|---|
| Institute | 32 | 21 | 5 | 6 | 55 | 36 | 68 |
| Newry City | 32 | 17 | 8 | 7 | 58 | 31 | 59 |
| H&W | 32 | 16 | 8 | 8 | 54 | 42 | 56 |
| Portadown | 32 | 14 | 9 | 9 | 61 | 36 | 51 |
| Ballyclare | 32 | 15 | 3 | 14 | 56 | 52 | 48 |
| Loughall | 32 | 12 | 2 | 18 | 45 | 59 | 38 |
| Larne | 32 | 12 | 11 | 9 | 59 | 47 | 47 |
| PSNI | 32 | 11 | 8 | 13 | 55 | 50 | 41 |
| Limavady | 32 | 10 | 7 | 15 | 52 | 58 | 37 |
| Knockbreda | 32 | 9 | 9 | 14 | 50 | 54 | 36 |
| Dergview | 32 | 9 | 9 | 14 | 49 | 59 | 36 |
| Lurgan Celtic | 32 | 3 | 7 | 22 | 32 | 102 | 16 |

**Leading scorer**: 18 Mark McCabe (Newry City). **Player of Year**: Michael McCrudden (Institute)

## TENNENT'S IRISH CUP FINAL

**Coleraine** 3 (McCauley, Burns, Bradley) **Cliftonville** 1 (Donnelly). Windsor Park, May 6, 2018

**Coleraine**: Johns, Mullan, Harkin, McCauley (Smith), Bradley, McConaghie, Lyons, O'Donnell, Traynor, McGonigle (Burns), Dooley (Parkhill)

**Cliftonville**: Neeson, Ives (Grimes), Breen (Harkin), Harney, Curran (Garrett), Bagnall, Gormley, J Donnelly, Cosgrove, McDonald, R Donnelly

**Referee**: A Hunter (Maguiresbridge)

## BETMCLEAN LEAGUE CUP FINAL

**Dungannon Swifts** 3 (Mayse 2, Burke), **Ballymena Utd** 1 (Owens).Windsor Park, February 18, 2018

## TOALS COUNTY ANTRIM SHIELD FINAL

**Ballymena Utd** 2 (McMurray, Friel), **Crusaders** 4 (Beverland, Owens, Caddell, Heatley). Showgrounds, Ballymena, January 23, 2018

# UEFA CHAMPIONS LEAGUE 2017–18

## FIRST QUALIFYING ROUND, FIRST LEG

**Linfield** 1 (J Stewart 89) La Fiorita 0. Att: 2,839. **New Saints** 1 (Quigley 44) Europa FC 2 (Quillo 8, Gomez 78). Att: 1,148

## FIRST QUALIFYING ROUND, SECOND LEG

Europa FC 1 (Walker 53 pen) **New Saints** 3 (Fletcher 37, Quigley 41, 104). Att: 261 (aet, New Saints won 4-3 on agg)). La Fiorita 0 **Linfield** 0. Att: 911 (Linfield won 1-0 on agg)

## FIRST QUALIFYING ROUND, ON AGGREGATE

Alashkert 2 Santa Coloma 1; Hibernians 3 Tallinna Infonet 0; Vikingur 6 Trepca 2

## SECOND QUALIFYING ROUND, FIRST LEG

**Dundalk** 1 (McMillan 18) Rosenborg 1 (Reginiussen 44). Att: 3,050. **Linfield** 0 **Celtic** 2 (Sinclair 18, Rogic 23). Att: 6,359. Rijeka 2 (Misic 4, Matei 69) **New Saints** 0. Att: 5,883

## SECOND QUALIFYING ROUND, SECOND LEG

**Celtic** 4 (Sinclair 5, 54, Rogic 48, Armstrong 90) **Linfield** 0. Att: 58,075 (Celtic won 6-0 on agg). **New Saints** 1 (Cieslewicz 69) Rijeka 5 (Matei 41, Gavranovic 54, 79, Gorgon 61, Ristovski 64). Att: 1,150 (Rijeka won 7-1 on agg). Rosenborg 2 (De Lanlay 43, Vilhjalmsson 98) **Dundalk** 1 (Gartland 12). Att: 14,817 (aet, Rosenborg won 3-2 on agg)

## SECOND QUALIFYING ROUND ON AGGREGATE

Apoel Nicosia 2 Dudelange 0; Astana 2 Spartaks Jurmala 1; BATE Borisov 4 Alashkert 2; Copenhagen 4 Zilina 3; Hafnarfjordur 3 Vikingur 1; Hapoel Beer Sheva 5 Honved 3; Legia Warsaw 9 Mariehamn 0; Ludogrets 5 Zalgiris 3; Maribor 3 Zrinjski 2; Partizan Belgrade 2 Buducnost Podgorica 0; Qarabag 6 Samtredia 0; Salzburg 6 Hibernians 0; Sheriff Tiraspol 2 Kukesi 2 (Sheriff Tiraspol won on away goal); Vardar 4 Malmo 2

## THIRD QUALIFYING ROUND, FIRST LEG

**Celtic** 0 Rosenborg 0. Att: 49,172

## THIRD QUALIFYING ROUND, SECOND LEG

Rosenborg 0 **Celtic** 1 (Forrest 69). Att: 20,974 (Celtic won 1-0 on agg)

## THIRD QUALIFYING ROUND, ON AGGREGATE

Apoel Nicosia 4 Viitorul 1; Astana 3 Legia Warsaw 2; Basaksehir 5 Club Bruges 3; Copenhagen 4 Vardar 2; CSKA Moscow 3 AEK Athens 0; Hapoel Beer Sheva 3 Ludogorest 3 (Hapoel Beer Sheva won on away goal); Maribor 2 Hafnarfjordur 0; Nice 3 Ajax 3 (Nice won on away goals); Olympiacos 5 Partizan Belgrade 3; Qarabag 2 Sheriff Tiraspol 1; Rijeka 1 Salzburg 1 (Rijeka won on away goal); Slavia Prague 2 BATE Borisov 2 (Slavia Prague won on away goal); Steaua Bucharest 6 Viktoria Plzen 3; Young Boys 3 Dynamo Kiev 3 (Young Boys won on away goal)

## PLAY-OFFS, FIRST LEG

**Celtic** 5 (Postnikov 32 og, Sinclair 42, 60, Forrest 79, Shitov 88 og) Astana 0. Att: 54,016. Hoffenheim 1 (Uth 87) **Liverpool** 2 (Alexander-Arnold 35, Nordveit 77 og). Att: 25,568

## PLAY-OFFS, SECOND LEG

Astana 4 (Ajker 26 og, Muzhikov 48, Twumasi 49, 69) **Celtic** 3 (Sinclair 33, Ntcham 80, Griffiths 90). Att: 19,075 (Celtic won 8-4 on agg). **Liverpool** 4 (Emre Can 10, 21, Salah 19, Firmino 63) Hoffenheim 2 (Uth 28, Wagner 79). Att: 51,808 (Liverpool won 6-3 on agg)

## PLAY-OFFS, ON AGGREGATE

Apoel Nicosia 2 Slavia Prague 0; CSKA Moscow 3 Young Boys 0; Maribor 2 Hapoel Beer Sheva 2 (Maribor won on away goal); Napoli 4 Nice 0; Olympiacos 3 Rijeka 1; Qarabag 2 Copenhagen 2 (Qarabag won on away goal); Sevilla 4 Basaksehir 3; Sporting Lisbon 5 Steaua Bucharest 1

## GROUP A

**September 12, 2017**
**Benfica** 1 (Seferovic 50) **CSKA Moscow** 2 (Vitinho 64 pen, Zhamaletdinov 71). Att: 38,323
**Manchester Utd** 3 (Fellaini 35, Lukaku 53, Rashford 84) **Basle** 0. Att: 73,854
**Manchester Utd** (4-2-3-1): De Gea, Young, Lindelof, Smalling, Blind, Matic, Pogba (Fellaini 19), Mata (Rashford 77), Mkhitaryan, Martial (Lingard 69), Lukaku. **Booked**: Young, Blind

**September 27, 2017**
**Basle** 5 (Lang 2, Oberlin 20, 69, Van Wolfswinkel 59 pen, Riveros 76) **Benfica** 0. Att: 34,111
**CSKA Moscow** 1 (Kuchaev 90) **Manchester Utd** 4 (Lukaku 4, 26, Martial 19 pen, Mkhitaryan 57). Att: 29,073
**Manchester Utd** (3-4-3): De Gea, Bailly, Lindelof, Smalling, Young (Darmian 67), Matic, Herrera, Blind, Mkhitaryan (Lingard 60), Lukaku, Martial (Rashford 72)

**October 18, 2017**
**Benfica** 0 **Manchester Utd** 1 (Rashford 64). Att: 57,684
**Manchester Utd** (4-2-3-1): De Gea, Valencia, Lindelof, Smalling, Blind, Matic, Herrera, Mata (Lingard 83), Mkhitaryan (McTominay 90+2), Rashford (Martial 76), Lukaku. **Booked**: Valencia, Lingard
**CSKA Moscow** 0 **Basle** 2 (Xhaka 29, Oberlin 90). Att: 27,996

**October 31, 2017**
**Basle** 1 (Zuffi 32) **CSKA Moscow** 2 (Dzagoev 65, Wernbloom 79). Att: 33,303
**Manchester Utd** 2 (Svilar 45 og, Blind 78 pen) **Benfica** 0. Att: 74,437
**Manchester Utd** (4-2-3-1): De Gea, Darmian, Bailly, Smalling, Blind, Matic, McTominay, Mata (Herrera 68), Lingard (Mkhitaryan 46), Martial (Rashford 75), Lukaku. **Booked**: Bailly, Lingard

**November 22, 2017**
**Basle** 1 (Lang 89) **Manchester Utd** 0. Att: 36,000
**Manchester Utd** (4-2-3-1): Romero, Darmian, Smalling, Rojo, Blind, Fellaini, Herrera, Lingard (Rashford 63), Pogba (Matic 66), Martial (Ibrahimovic 74), Lukaku. **Booked**: Darmian
**CSKA Moscow** 2 (Schennikov 13, Jardel 57 og) **Benfica** 0. Att: 27,709

**December 5, 2017**
**Benfica** 0 **Basle** 2 (Elyounoussi 6, Oberlin 66). Att: 22,470
**Manchester Utd** 2 (Lukaku 65, Rashford 66) **CSKA Moscow** 1 (Vitinho 45). Att: 74,669
**Manchester Utd** (5-3-2): Romero, Valencia (Tuanzebe 72), Lindelof, Smalling, Blind, Shaw, Herrera (McTominay 67), Pogba, Mata, Rashford, Lukaku (Martial 74). **Booked**: McTominay

| | P | W | D | L | F | A | Pts |
|---|---|---|---|---|---|---|---|
| **Manchester Utd** Q | 6 | 5 | 0 | 1 | 12 | 3 | 15 |
| Basle Q | 6 | 4 | 0 | 2 | 11 | 5 | 12 |
| CSKA Moscow | 6 | 3 | 0 | 3 | 8 | 10 | 9 |
| Benfica | 6 | 0 | 0 | 6 | 1 | 14 | 0 |

## GROUP B

**September 12, 2017**
**Bayern Munich** 3 (Lewandowski 12 pen, Thiago Alcantara 65, Kimmich 90) **Anderlecht** 0. Att: 70,000
**Celtic** 0 **Paris SG** 5 (Neymar 19, Mbappe 34, Cavani 40 pen, 85, Lustig 83 og). Att: 57,562
**Celtic** (4-2-3-1): Gordon, Ralston, Lustig, Simunovic, Tierney, Ntcham, Brown, Roberts (Forrest 77), Armstrong (Rogic 46), Sinclair, Griffiths (Edouard 69). **Booked**: Simunovic, Ralston

**September 27, 2017**
**Anderlecht** 0 **Celtic** 3 (Griffiths 38, Mbodji 50 og, Sinclair 90+3). Att: 19,896
**Celtic** (4-2-3-1) Gordon, Lustig, Boyata, Simunovic, Tierney, Ntcham, Brown (Bitton 69), Roberts (Forrest 77), Rogic (McGregor 64), Sinclair; Griffiths
**Paris SG** 3 (Dani Alves 2, Cavani 31, Neymar 63) **Bayern Munich** 0. Att: 46,252

**October 18, 2017**
**Anderlecht** 0 **Paris SG** 4 (Mbappe 3, Cavani 44, Neymar 61, Di Maria 88). Att: 19,108
**Bayern Munich** 3 (Muller 17, Kimmich 29, Hummels 51) **Celtic** 0. Att: 70,000
**Celtic** (4-2-3-1): Gordon, Gamboa, Lustig, Boyata, Tierney, Ntcham, Brown, Roberts (Forrest 78), Armstrong (Rogic 65), Sinclair, Griffiths (Dembele 65). **Booked**: Roberts

**October 31, 2017**
**Celtic** 1 (McGregor 74) **Bayern Munich** 2 (Coman 22, Javi Martinez 77). Att: 58,269
**Celtic** (4-2-3-1): Gordon, Lustig, Boyata, Bitton, Tierney, Brown, Armstrong (Griffiths 78), Forrest, McGregor, Sinclair (Rogic 64), Dembele
**Paris SG** 5 (Verratti 30, Neymar 45, Kurzawa 53, 72, 78) **Anderlecht** 0. Att: 46,403

**November 22, 2017**
**Anderlecht** 1 (Hanni 63) **Bayern Munich** 2 (Lewandowski 51, Tolisso 77). Att: 19,753
**Paris SG** 7 (Neymar 9, 22, Cavani 28, 79, Mbappe 35, Verratti 75, Dani Alves 80) **Celtic** 1 (Dembele 2). Att: 46,288
**Celtic** (3-5-2): Gordon, Lustig (Bitton 13), Boyata, Tierney, Simunovic, Brown, Forrest, McGregor, Rogic, Ntcham (Eboue 69), Dembele (Griffiths 77). **Booked**: Bitton, Simunovic

**December 5, 2017**
**Bayern Munich** 3 (Lewandowski 8, Tolisso 37, 69) **Paris SG** 1 (Mbappe 50). Att: 70,000
**Celtic** 0 **Anderlecht** 1 (Simunovic 62 og). Att: 57,931
**Celtic** (4-2-3-1): Gordon, Lustig, Simunovic, Boyata, Tierney, Brown, McGregor, Forrest, Armstrong (Ntcham 46), Sinclair (Rogic 46), Dembele (Edouard 74). **Booked**: Ntcham

| | P | W | D | L | F | A | Pts |
|---|---|---|---|---|---|---|---|
| Paris SG Q | 6 | 5 | 0 | 1 | 25 | 4 | 15 |
| Bayern Munich Q | 6 | 5 | 0 | 1 | 13 | 6 | 15 |
| **Celtic** | 6 | 1 | 0 | 5 | 5 | 18 | 3 |
| Anderlecht | 6 | 1 | 0 | 5 | 2 | 17 | 3 |

## GROUP C

**September 12, 2017**
**Chelsea** 6 (Pedro 5, Zappacosta 30, Azpilicueta 55, Bakayoko 71, Batshuayi 76, Medvedev

82 og) **Qarabag** 0. Att: 41,150
**Chelsea** (3-4-2-1): Courtois, Azpilicueta (Rudiger 74), Christensen, Cahill, Zappacosta, Fabregas, Kante (Bakayoko 63), Alonso, William, Pedro (Hazard 58), Batshuayi. **Booked**: Cahill
**Roma** 0 **Atletico Madrid** 0. Att: 36,064

**September 27, 2017**
**Atletico Madrid** 1 (Griezmann 40 pen) **Chelsea** 2 (Morata 60, Batshuayi 90+4). Att: 60,643
**Chelsea** (3-4-2-1): Courtois, Azpilicueta, Luiz, Cahill, Moses, Kante, Bakayoko, Alonso, Fabregas (Christensen 86), Hazard (Willian 82), Morata (Batshuayi 82). **Booked**: Luiz
**Qarabag** 1 (Pedro Henrique 28) **Roma** 2 (Manolas 7, Dzeko 15). Att: 67,200

**October 18, 2017**
**Chelsea** 3 (Luiz 11, Hazard 37, 75) **Roma** 3 (Kolarov 40, Dzeko 64, 70). Att: 41,105
**Chelsea** (3-5-2): Courtois, Azpilicueta, Christensen, Cahill, Zappacosta (Rudiger 73), Fabregas, Luiz (Pedro 56), Bakayoko, Alonso, Hazard (Willian 80), Morata. **Booked**: Bakayoko
**Qarabag** 0 **Atletico Madrid** 0. Att: 47,923

**October 31, 2017**
**Atletico Madrid** 1 (Thomas 56) **Qarabag** 1 (Michel 40). Att: 55,893
**Roma** 3 (El Shaarawy 1, 36, Perotti 63) **Chelsea** 0. Att: 55,036
**Chelsea** (3-4-3): Courtois, Cahill (Willian 56), Luiz, Rudiger, Azpilicueta, Fabregas (Drinkwater 71), Bakayoko, Alonso, Pedro, Morata (Batshuayi 75), Hazard

**November 22, 2017**
**Atletico Madrid** 2 (Griezmann 69, Gameiro 85) **Roma** 0. Att: 56,253
**Qarabag** 0 **Chelsea** 4 (Hazard 21 pen, Willian 36, 85, Fabregas 72 pen). Att: 67,100
**Chelsea** (3-4-3): Courtois, Azpilicueta, Luiz, Rudiger, Zappacosta, Fabregas, Kante (Drinkwater 75), Alonso (Cahill 58), Pedro, Hazard (Morata 65), Willian. **Booked**: Alonso

**December 5, 2017**
**Chelsea** 1 (Savic 75 og) **Atletico Madrid** 1 (Saul 56). Att: 40,875
**Chelsea** (3-5-2): Courtois, Azpilicueta, Christensen, Cahill, Moses, Fabregas, Kante, Bakayoko (Pedro 64), Zappacosta (Willian 73), Morata (Batshuayi 81), Hazard. **Booked**: Zappacosta
**Roma** 1 (Perotti 54) **Qarabag** 0. Att: 34,258

| | P | W | D | L | F | A | Pts |
|---|---|---|---|---|---|---|---|
| Roma Q | 6 | 3 | 2 | 1 | 9 | 6 | 11 |
| **Chelsea Q** | 6 | 3 | 2 | 1 | 16 | 8 | 11 |
| Atletico Madrid | 6 | 1 | 4 | 1 | 5 | 4 | 7 |
| Qarabag | 6 | 0 | 2 | 4 | 2 | 14 | 2 |

## GROUP D

**September 12, 2017**
**Barcelona** 3 (Messi 45, 69, Rakitic 56) **Juventus** 0. Att: 78,658
**Olympiacos** 2 (Pardo 89, 90+3) **Sporting Lisbon** 3 (Doumbia 2, Gelson Martins 13, Bruno Fernandes 43). Att: 30,168

**September 27, 2017**
**Juventus** 2 (Higuain 69, Mandzukic 80) **Olympiacos** 0. Att: 33,460
**Sporting Lisbon** 0 **Barcelona** 1 (Coates 49 og). Att: 48, 575

**October 18, 2017**
**Barcelona** 3 (Nikolaou 18 og, Messi 61, Digne 64) **Olympiacos** 1 (Nikolaou 89). Att: 55,026

**Juventus** 2 (Pjanic 29, Mandzukic 84) **Sporting Lisbon** 1 (Alex Sandro 12 og). Att: 36,288

**October 31, 2017**
**Olympiacos** 0 **Barcelona** 0. Att: 31,600
**Sporting Lisbon** 1 (Bruno Cesar 21) **Juventus** 1 (Higuain 79). Att: 48,442

**November 22, 2017**
**Juventus** 0 **Barcelona** 0. Att: 40,876
**Sporting Lisbon** 3 (Bas Dost 40, 66, Bruno Cesar 44) **Olympiacos** 1 (Odjidja-Ofoe 86). Att: 42,528

**December 5, 2017**
**Barcelona** 2 (Alcacer 59, Mathieu 90+1 og) **Sporting Lisbon** 0. Att: 48,336
**Olympiacos** 0 **Juventus** 2 (Cuadrado 15, Bernardeschi 89). Att: 29,567

| | P | W | D | L | F | A | Pts |
|---|---|---|---|---|---|---|---|
| Barcelona Q | 6 | 4 | 2 | 0 | 9 | 1 | 14 |
| Juventus Q | 6 | 3 | 2 | 1 | 7 | 5 | 11 |
| Sporting Lisbon | 6 | 2 | 1 | 3 | 8 | 9 | 7 |
| Olympiacos | 6 | 0 | 1 | 5 | 4 | 13 | 1 |

## GROUP E

**September 13, 2017**
**Liverpool** 2 (Firmino 21, Salah 37) **Sevilla** 2 (Ben Yedder 5, Correa 72). Att: 52,332
**Liverpool** (4-3-3): Karius, Gomez, Lovren, Matip, Moreno, Wijnaldum, Henderson, Emre Can (Coutinho 76), Salah (Oxlade-Chamberlain 89), Firmino, Mane (Sturridge 84). **Booked**: Moreno, Gomez. **Sent off**: Gomez (94)
**Maribor** 1 (Bohar 85) **Spartak Moscow** 1 (Samedov 60). Att: 12,566

**September 26, 2017**
**Sevilla** 3 (Ben Yedder 27, 38, 83 pen) **Maribor** 0. Att: 34,705
**Spartak Moscow** 1 (Fernando 23) **Liverpool** 1 (Coutinho 31). Att: 43,376
**Liverpool** (4-3-3): Karius, Alexander-Arnold, Lovren, Matip, Moreno, Emre Can (Wijnaldum 73), Henderson, Coutinho, Salah, Firmino, Mane (Sturridge 70). **Booked**: Emre Can, Firmino

**October 17, 2017**
**Maribor** 0 **Liverpool** 7 (Firmino 4, 54, Coutinho 13, Salah 19, 39, Oxlade-Chamberlain 86, Alexander-Arnold 90). Att: 12,508
**Liverpool** (4-3-3): Karius, Alexander-Arnold, Matip, Lovren, Moreno, Wijnaldum (Solanke 76), Milner, Emre Can, Firmino (Sturridge 68), Salah (Oxlade-Chamberlain 57), Coutinho
**Spartak Moscow** 5 (Promes 18, 90, Melgarejo 58, Glushakov 67, Luiz Adriano 74) **Sevilla** 1 (Kjaer 30). Att: 44,307

**November 1, 2017**
**Liverpool** 3 (Salah 49, Emre Can 64, Sturridge 90) **Maribor** 0. Att: 47,957
**Liverpool** (4-3-3): Karius, Alexander-Arnold, Matip, Klavan, Moreno, Emre Can, Milner, Wijnaldum (Henderson 17), Salah (Sturridge 74), Firmino (Grujic 85), Oxlade-Chamberlain
**Sevilla** 2 (Lenglet 30, Banega 59) **Spartak Moscow** 1 (Ze Luis). Att: 38,002

**November 21, 2017**
**Sevilla** 3 (Ben Yedder 51, 61 pen, Pizarro 90+3) **Liverpool** 3 (Firmino 2, 30, Mane 22). Att: 39,495
**Liverpool** (4-3-3): Karius, Gomez, Lovren, Klavan, Moreno (Milner 63), Wijnaldum Henderson, Coutinho (Emre Can 63), Salah (Oxlade-Chamberlain 87), Firmino, Mane. **Booked**: Henderson, Moreno, Emre Can
**Spartak Moscow** 1 (Ze Luis 82) **Maribor** 1 (Mesanovic 90+2). Att: 42,920

**December 6, 2017**
**Liverpool** 7 (Coutinho 4 pen, 15, 50, Firmino 18, Mane 47, 76, Salah 85) **Spartak Moscow** 0. Att: 48,775
**Liverpool** (4-3-3): Karius, Gomez, Lovren (Alexander-Arnold 60), Klavan, Moreno (Milner 46), Coutinho, Emre Can, Wijnaldum, Salah, Firmino (Sturridge 72) Mane. **Booked**: Emre Can
**Maribor** 1 (Tavares 10) **Sevilla** 1 (Ganso 75). Att: 11,976

| | P | W | D | L | F | A | Pts |
|---|---|---|---|---|---|---|---|
| **Liverpool** Q | 6 | 3 | 3 | 0 | 23 | 6 | 12 |
| Sevilla Q | 6 | 2 | 3 | 1 | 12 | 12 | 9 |
| Spartak Moscow | 6 | 1 | 3 | 2 | 9 | 13 | 6 |
| Maribor | 6 | 0 | 3 | 3 | 3 | 16 | 3 |

## GROUP F

**September 13, 2017**
**Feyenoord** 0 **Manchester City** 4 (Stones 2, 63, Aguero 10, Gabriel Jesus 25). Att: 43,500
**Manchester City** (4-1-2-3): Ederson, Walker, Stones, Otamendi, Mendy, Fernandinho (Sane 72), De Bruyne, D Silva (Delph 67), Bernardo Silva 7, Aguero (Sterling 60), Gabriel Jesus. **Booked**: De Bruyne
**Shakhtar Donetsk** 2 (Taison 15, Ferreyra 58) **Napoli** 1 (Milik 72 pen). Att: 32,679

**September 26, 2017**
**Manchester City** 2 (De Bruyne 48, Sterling 90) **Shakhtar Donetsk** 0. Att: 45,310
**Manchester City** (4-3-3): Ederson, Walker, Stones, Otamendi, Delph, De Bruyne, Fernandinho, D Silva (Gundogan 81), Gabriel Jesus (Sterling 54), Aguero (Bernardo Silva 85), Sane
**Napoli** 3 (Insigne 7, Mertens 49, Callejon 69) **Feyenoord** 1 (Amrabat 90+3). Att: 22,577

**October 17, 2017**
**Feyenoord** 1 (Berghuis 8) **Shakhtar Donetsk** 2 (Bernard 24, 54). Att: 43,500
**Manchester City** 2 (Sterling 9, Gabriel Jesus 13) **Napoli** 1 (Diawara 73 pen). Att: 48,520
**Manchester City** (4-3-3): Ederson, Walker, Stones, Otamendi, Delph, Fernandinho, D Silva (Gundogan 76), De Bruyne, Sterling (Bernardo Silva 70), Gabriel Jesus (Danilo 87), Sane. **Booked**: Walker, De Bruyne, Fernandinho

**November 1, 2017**
**Napoli** 2 (Insigne 21, Jorginho 62 pen) **Manchester City** 4 (Otamendi 34, Stones 48, Aguero 69, Sterling 90+2). Att: 44,483
**Manchester City** (4-3-3): Ederson, Danilo, Stones, Otamendi, Delph, De Bruyne, Fernandinho, Gundogan (D Silva 71), Sterling, Aguero (Bernardo Silva 76), Sane (Gabriel Jesus 90). **Booked**: Otamendi
**Shakhtar Donetsk** 3 (Ferreyra 15, Marios 17, 68) **Feyenoord** 1 (Jorgensen 13). Att: 24,570

**November 21, 2017**
**Manchester City** 1 (Sterling 88) **Feyenoord** 0. Att: 43,548
**Manchester City** (3-4-3): Ederson, Walker, Mangala, Otamendi, Danilo, Gundogan, Toure (Foden 75), De Bruyne (Gabriel Jesus 63), Bernardo Silva, Aguero, Sterling (Diaz 90). **Booked**: Mangala, De Bruyne, Danilo
**Napoli** 3 (Insigne 56, Zielinski 81, Mertens 84) **Shakhtar Donetsk** 0. Att: 10,573

**December 6, 2017**
**Feyenoord** 2 (Jorgensen 33, St Juste 90+1) **Napoli** 1 (Zielinski 2). Att: 36,500
**Shakhtar Donetsk** 2 (Bernard 26, Ismaily 32) **Manchester City** 1 (Aguero 90+2 pen). Att: 33,154
**Manchester City** (3-4-3): Ederson, Adarabioyo, Fernandinho (Aguero 70), Mangala, Danilo, Toure, Gundogan, Foden, Silva, Gabriel Jesus, Sane (Diaz 62). **Booked**: Danilo, Gundogan

| | P | W | D | L | F | A | Pts |
|---|---|---|---|---|---|---|---|
| **Manchester City** Q | 6 | 5 | 0 | 1 | 14 | 5 | 15 |
| Shakhtar Donetsk Q | 6 | 4 | 0 | 2 | 9 | 9 | 12 |
| Napoli | 6 | 2 | 0 | 4 | 11 | 11 | 6 |
| Feyenoord | 6 | 1 | 0 | 5 | 5 | 14 | 3 |

## GROUP G

**September 13, 2017**
**Leipzig** 1 (Forsberg 33) **Monaco** 1 (Tielemens 34). Att: 40,068
**Porto** 1 (Tosic 21 og) **Besiktas** 3 (Anderson Talisca 14, Cenk Tosun 28, Babel 86). Att: 42,429

**September 26, 2017**
**Besiktas** 2 (Babel 11, Anderson Talisca 43) **Leipzig** 0. Att: 36,641
**Monaco** 0 **Porto** 3 (Aboubakar 32, 69, Layun 89). Att: 11,703

**October 17, 2017**
**Monaco** 1 (Falcao 30) **Besiktas** 2 (Cenk Tosun 34, 55). Att: 7,403
**Leipzig** 3 (Orban 8, Forsberg 37, Augustin 40) **Porto** 2 (Aboubakar 18, Marcano 44). Att: 41,496

**November 1, 2017**
**Besiktas** 1 (Cenk Tosun 54 pen) **Monaco** 1 (Lopes 45). Att: 39,346
**Porto** 3 (Herrera 83, Danilo Pereira 61, Maxi Pereira 90) **Leipzig** 1 (Werner 48). Att: 41,616

**November 21, 2017**
**Besiktas** 1 (Anderson Talisca 41) **Porto** 1 (Felipe 29). Att: 36,919
**Monaco** 1 (Falcao 43) **Leipzig** 4 (Jemerson 6 og, Werner 9, 31 pen, Keita 45). Att: 9,029

**December 6, 2017**
**Leipzig** 1 (Keita 87) **Besiktas** 2 (Negredo 10 pen, Anderson Talisca 90). Att: 42,558
**Porto** 5 (Aboubakar 9, 33, Brahimi 45, Alex Telles 65, Tiquinho Soares 88) **Monaco** 2 (Glik 61 pen, Falcao 78). Att: 42,509

| | P | W | D | L | F | A | Pts |
|---|---|---|---|---|---|---|---|
| Besiktas Q | 6 | 4 | 2 | 0 | 11 | 5 | 14 |
| Porto Q | 6 | 3 | 1 | 2 | 15 | 13 | 10 |
| Leipzig | 6 | 2 | 1 | 3 | 10 | 13 | 7 |
| Monaco | 6 | 0 | 2 | 4 | 6 | 16 | 2 |

## GROUP H

**September 13, 2017**
**Real Madrid** 3 (Ronaldo 12, 51 pen, Sergio Ramos 61) **Apoel Nicosia** 0. Att: 71,060
**Tottenham** 3 (Son Heung-Min 4, Kane 15, 60) **Borussia Dortmund** 1 (Yarmolenko 11). Att: 67,343
**Tottenham** (3-4-2-1): Lloris, Alderweireld, Sanchez, Vertonghen, Aurier, Dembele, Dier, Davies, Son Heung-Min (Sissoko 83), Eriksen, Kane (Llorente 87). **Booked**: Dier, Vertonghen. **Sent off**: Vertonghen (90+2)

**September 26, 2017**
**Apoel Nicosia** 0 **Tottenham** 3 (Kane 39, 62, 67). Att: 16,234
**Tottenham** (3-4-2-1): Lloris, Alderweireld, Sanchez, Davies, Aurier (Llorente 57), Dier, Winks, Trippier, Sissoko (Georgiou 84), Son Heung-Min, Kane (Nkoudou 75). **Booked**: Winks
**Borussia Dortmund** 1 (Aubameyang 54) **Real Madrid** 3 (Bale 18, Ronaldo 49, 79). Att: 65,849

**October 17, 2017**
**Apoel Nicosia** 1 (Pote 62) **Borussia Dortmund** 1 (Papastathopoulos 68). Att: 15,406
**Real Madrid** 1 (Ronaldo 43 pen) **Tottenham** 1 (Varane 28 og). Att: 76,589
**Tottenham** (5-3-2): Lloris, Aurier, Sanchez, Dier, Alderweireld, Vertonghen, Sissoko (Son Heung-Min 89), Winks, Eriksen, Llorente (Rose 80), Kane. **Booked**: Aurier

**November 1, 2017**
**Borussia Dortmund** 1 (Guerreiro 29) **Apoel Nicosia** 1 (Pote 51). Att: 64,500
**Tottenham** 3 (Alli 27, 56, Eriksen 65) **Real Madrid** 1 (Ronaldo 80). Att: 83,782
**Tottenham** (3-4-2-1): Lloris, Alderweireld (Sissoko 24), Sanchez, Vertonghen, Trippier, Eriksen, Winks (Dembele 66), Dier, Davies, Alli, Kane (Llorente 79). **Booked**: Dembele

**November 21, 2017**
**Apoel Nicosia** 0 **Real Madrid** 6 (Modric 23, Benzema 39, 45, Nacho 41, Ronaldo 49, 54). Att: 19,705
**Borussia Dortmund** 1 (Aubameyang 31) **Tottenham** 2 (Kane 49, Son Heung-Min 76). Att: 65,849
**Tottenham** (3-5-2): Lloris, Dier, Sanchez, Vertonghen, Aurier, Eriksen (Sissoko 85), Winks, Alli (Dembele 81), Rose, Son Heung-Min, Kane (Llorente 86)

**December 6, 2017**
**Real Madrid** 3 (Borja Mayoral 8, Ronaldo 12, Lucas 81) **Borussia Dortmund** 2 (Aubameyang 44, 49). Att: 73,323
**Tottenham** 3 (Llorente 20, Son Heung-Min 37, N'Koudou 80) **Apoel Nicosia** 0. Att: 42,679
**Tottenham** (4-2-3-1): Vorm, Aurier, Foyth, Sanchez, Rose (Walker-Peters 70), Sissoko, Winks, N'Koudou, Alli (Sterling 88), Son Heung-Min (Dembele 65), Llorente. **Booked**: Aurier, Rose

| | P | W | D | L | F | A | Pts |
|---|---|---|---|---|---|---|---|
| **Tottenham** Q | 6 | 5 | 1 | 0 | 15 | 4 | 16 |
| Real Madrid Q | 6 | 4 | 1 | 1 | 17 | 7 | 13 |
| Borussia Dortmund | 6 | 0 | 2 | 4 | 7 | 13 | 2 |
| Apoel Nicosia | 6 | 0 | 2 | 4 | 2 | 17 | 2 |

## ROUND OF 16, FIRST LEG

**February 13, 2018**
**Basle** 0 **Manchester City** 4 (Gundogan 14, 53, Bernardo Silva 18, Aguero 23). Att: 36,000
**Manchester City** (4-3-3): Ederson, Walker, Kompany, Otamendi, Delph, De Bruyne (D Silva 62), Fernandinho, Gundogan, Berrnardo Silva, Aguero (Danilo 86), Sterling (Sane 57). **Booked**: Fernandinho, Gundogan
**Juventus** 2 (Higuain 2, 9 pen) **Tottenham** 2 (Kane 35, Eriksen 71). Att: 41,232
**Tottenham** (4-2-3-1): Lloris, Aurier, Sanchez, Vertonghen, Davies, Dier, Dembele, Eriksen (Wanyama 90+2), Alli (Son Heung-Min 83), Lamela (Lucas Moura 89), Kane. **Booked**: Davies, Aurier

**February 14, 2018**
**Real Madrid** 3 (Ronaldo 45 pen, 83, Marcelo 86) **Paris SG** 1 (Rabiot 33). Att: 78,158
**Porto** 0 **Liverpool** 5 (Mane 25, 53, 85, Salah 30, Firmino 70). Att: 47,718
**Liverpool** (4-3-3): Karius, Alexander-Arnold (Gomez 79), Van Dijk, Lovren, Robertson, Wijnaldum, Henderson (Matip 75), Milner, Salah, Firmino (Ings 80), Mane

**February 20, 2018**
**Bayern Munich** 5 (Muller 43, 66, Coman 52, Lewandowski 79, 88) **Besiktas** 0. Att: 70,000
**Chelsea** 1 (Willian 62) **Barcelona** 1 (Messi 75). Att: 37,741
**Chelsea** (3-4-3): Courtois, Azpilicueta, Christensen, Rudiger, Moses, Fabregas (Drinkwater 84), Kante, Alonso, Willian, Pedro (Morata 83), Hazard. **Booked**: Rudiger

**February 21, 2018**
**Sevilla** 0 **Manchester Utd** 0. Att: 39,725
**Manchester Utd** (4-3-3): De Gea, Valencia, Smalling, Lindelof, Young, Herrera (Pogba 17), Matic, McTominay, Mata (Martial 80), Lukaku, Sanchez (Rashford 75). **Booked**: Sanchez
**Shakhtar Donetsk** 2 (Ferreyra 52, Fred 71) **Roma** 1 (Under 41). Att: 35,124

**ROUND OF 16, SECOND LEG**
**March 6, 2018**
**Liverpool** 0 **Porto** 0. Att: 48,768 (Liverpool won 5-0 on agg)
**Liverpool** (4-3-3): Karius, Gomez, Matip, Lovren, Moreno, Emre Can (Klavan 80), Henderson, Milner, Lallana, Firmino (Ings 62), Mane (Salah 74). **Booked**: Henderson
**Paris SG** 1 (Cavani 71) **Real Madrid** 2 (Ronaldo 51, Casemiro 80). Att: 46,585 (Real Madrid won 5-2 on agg)

**March 7, 2018**
**Manchester City** 1 (Gabriel Jesus 8) **Basle** 2 (Elyounoussi 17, Lang 71). Att: 49,411 (Manchester City won 5-2 on agg)
**Manchester City** (4-3-3): Bravo, Danilo, Stones, Laporte, Zinchenko, Gundogan (Diaz 66), Toure, Foden (Adarabioyo 89), Bernardo Silva, Gabriel Jesus, Sane
**Tottenham** 1 (Son Heung-Min 39) **Juventus** 2 (Higuain 64, Dybala 67). Att: 84,010 (Juventus won 4-3 on agg)
**Tottenham** (4-3-3): Lloris, Trippier, Sanchez, Vertonghen, Davies, Dembele, Dier (Lamela 74), Eriksen, Alli (Llorente 86), Kane, Son Heung-Min. **Booked**: Vertonghen, Alli, Dembele

**March 13, 2018**
**Manchester Utd** 1 (Lukaku 84) **Sevilla** 2 (Ben Yedder 74, 78). Att: 74,909 (Sevilla won 2-1 on agg)
**Manchester Utd** (4-2-3-1): De Gea, Valencia (Mata 77), Bailly, Smalling, Young, Matic, Fellaini (Pogba 60), Lingard (Martial 77), Sanchez, Rashford, Lukaku. **Booked**: Rashford
**Roma** 1 (Dzeko 52) **Shakhtar Donetsk** 0. Att: 47,693 (agg 2-2, Roma won on away goal)

**March 14, 2018**
**Barcelona** 3 (Messi 3, 63, Dembele 20) **Chelsea** 0. Att: 97,183 (Barcelona won 4-1 on agg)
**Chelsea** (3-4-3): Courtois, Azpilicueta, Christensen, Rudiger, Moses, Fabregas, Kante, Alonso, Willian, Giroud, Hazard. **Booked**: Willian, Giroud, Alonso
**Besiktas** 1 (Vagner Love 58) **Bayern Munich** 3 (Thiago Alcantara 18, Gonul 46 og, Wagner 84). Att: 36,885 (Bayern Munich won 8-1 on agg)

## QUARTER-FINALS, FIRST LEG

**April 3, 2018**
**Juventus** 0 **Real Madrid** 3 (Ronaldo 3, 64, Marcelo 72). Att: 40,849
**Sevilla** 1 (Sarabia 32) **Bayern Munich** 2 (Jesus Navas 38 og, Thiago Alcantara 68). Att: 40,635

**April 4, 2018**
**Barcelona** 4 (De Rossi 39 og, Manolas 57 og, Pique 59, Suarez 87) **Roma** 1 (Dzeko 80). Att: 90,106
**Liverpool** 3 (Salah 12, Oxlade-Chamberlain 20, Mane 31) **Manchester City 0**. Att: 50,685
**Liverpool** (4-3-3): Karius, Alexander-Arnold, Lovren, Van Dijk, Robertson, Oxlade-Chamberlain (Moreno 85), Henderson, Milner, Salah (Wijnaldum 53), Firmino (Solanke 71), Mane. **Booked**: Henderson
**Manchester City** (4-3-3): Ederson, Walker, Otamendi, Kompany, Laporte, De Bruyne, Fernandinho, D Silva, Gundogan (Sterling 57), Gabriel Jesus, Sane. **Booked**: Otamendi, Gabriel Jesus, De Bruyne, Sterling

## QUARTER-FINALS, SECOND LEG

**April 10, 2018**
**Manchester City** 1 (Gabriel Jesus 2) **Liverpool** 2 (Salah 56, Firmino 77). Att: 53,461 (Liverpool won 5-1 on agg)
**Manchester City** (3-1-4-2): Ederson, Walker, Otamendi, Laporte, Fernandinho, Bernardo Silva (Gundogan 74), De Bruyne, D Silva (Aguero 66), Sane, Sterling, Gabriel Jesus. **Booked**: Ederson, Bernardo Silva
**Liverpool** (4-3-3): Karius, Alexander-Arnold (Clyne 84), Lovren, Van Dijk, Robertson, Oxlade-Chamberlain, Wijnaldum, Milner, Salah (Ings 89), Firmino (Klavan 81), Mane. **Booked**: Mane, Alexander-Arnold, Firmino, Van Dijk
**Roma** 3 (Dzeko 6, De Rossi 58 pen, Manolas 82) **Barcelona** 0. Att: 56,580 (agg 4-4, Roma won on away goal)

**April 11, 2018**
**Bayern Munich** 0 **Sevilla** 0. Att: 70,000 (Bayern Munich won 2-1 on agg)
**Real Madrid** 1 (Ronaldo 90+7 pen) **Juventus** 3 (Mandzukic 2, 37, Matuidi 61). Att: 75,796 (Real Madrid won 4-3 on agg)

## SEMI-FINALS, FIRST LEG

**April 24, 2018**
**Liverpool** 5 (Salah 36, 45, Mane 56, Firmino 61, 69) **Roma** 2 (Dzeko 81, Perotti 85 pen). Att: 51,236
**Liverpool** (4-3-3): Karius, Alexander-Arnold, Lovren, Van Dijk, Robertson, Oxlade-Chamberlain (Wijnaldum 18), Henderson, Milner, Salah (Ings 75), Firmino (Klavan 90+3), Mane. **Booked**: Alexander-Arnold, Lovren, Milner

**April 25, 2018**
**Bayern Munich** 1 (Kimmich 28) **Real Madrid** 2 (Marcelo 44, Marco Asensio 57). Att: 70,000

## SEMI-FINALS, SECOND LEG

**May 1, 2018**
**Real Madrid** 2 (Benzema 11, 46) **Bayern Munich** 2 (Kimmich 3, Rodriguez 63). Att: 77,459 (Real Madrid won 4-3 on agg)

**May 2, 2018**
**Roma** 4 (Milner 16 og, Dzeko 52, Nainggolan 87, 90 pen) **Liverpool** 2 (Mane 9, Wijnaldum 26). Att: 61,889 (Liverpool won 7-6 on agg)
**Liverpool** (4-3-3): Karius, Alexander-Arnold (Clyne 87), Lovren, Van Dijk, obertson,Wijnaldum, Henderson, Milner, Salah, Firmino (Solanke 87), Mane (Klavan 83). **Booked**: Lovren, Robertson, Solanke

## FINAL

**REAL MADRID 3 (Benzema 51, Bale 64, 83) LIVERPOOL 1 (Mane 55)**
**Olimpiyskiy Stadium, Kiev (61,561), Saturday, May 26, 2018**

**Real Madrid** (4-3-1-2): Navas, Daniel Carvajal (Nacho 37), Varane, Sergio Ramos (capt), Marcelo, Modric, Casemiro, Kroos, Isco (Bale 61), Ronaldo, Benzema (Marco Asensio 89). **Subs not used**: Casilla, Hernandez, Lucas Vasquz, Kovacic. **Coach**: Zinedine Zidane
**Liverpool** (4-3-3): Karius, Alexander-Arnold, Lovren, Van Dijk, Robertson, Wijnaldum, Henderson (capt), Milner (Emre Can 83), Salah (Lallana 30), Firmino, Mane. **Subs not used**: Mignolet, Clyne, Klavan, Moreno, Solanke. **Booked**: Mane. **Manager**: Jurgen Klopp
**Referee**: M Mazic (Serbia). **Half-time**: 0-0

It had all the makings of a shoot-out between Cristiano Ronaldo and Mohamed Salah, two players going head-to-head after each scoring 44 goals in all competitions during the season. It turned out to be a one-sided duel between an unhappy substitute and a goalkeeper whose world collapsed after two glaring mistakes handed Real Madrid their third successive triumph. Rarely has the final of Europe's premier club competition encompassed so much individual delight and despair as that experienced by Gareth Bale's mood-changing, match-winning goals and the two blunders committed by Loris Karius. Liverpool argued, justifiably, that the shoulder injury Sergio Ramos inflicted on Salah was a game-changer, coming as it did nearly half-an-hour into a match in which they had been the better and more threatening side. Sadly, they could have no complaint about what happened next. As captain Jordan Henderson insisted: 'We win as a team and lose as a team.' That offered no comfort or consolation to Karius, who conceded gifts to Karim Benzema and then Bale, along with the Welshman's spectacular midair volley for Real's second which he could do nothing about. Was it better than his coach Zinedine Zidane's acrobatic volley for Real in the 2002 final against Bayer Leverkusen at Hampden Park? That will be the subject of discussion for years to come. Of more immediate importance was Bale's future, following his admission that he was devastated not to start the match and needed to be playing week in and week out. Was he using this performance to put pressure on the club's management, or as a 'come and get me' plea to other big clubs?

**Leading scores** (from group stage): 15 Ronaldo (Real Madrid); 10 Firmino (Liverpool), Mane (Liverpool), Salah (Liverpool); 8 Dzeko (Roma), Ben Yedder (Sevilla); 7 Cavani (Paris SG), Kane (Tottenham); 6 Messi (Barcelona), Neymar (Paris SG)

# CHAMPIONS LEAGUE/EUROPEAN CUP FINAL FACTS AND FIGURES

- Real Madrid became the first club to win three straight titles twice. They have now been successful 13 times.

- Zinedine Zidane set a record as a coach with three victories in a row. Liverpool's Bob Paisley won three in 1977, 1978 and 1981; Carlo Ancelotti had three with AC Milan in 2003 and 2007 and with Real in 2014.

- Real had the same starting line-up they fielded against Juventus in Cardiff in 2017. For every member of Liverpool's squad it was a new experience.

- Liverpool scored a record 47 goals in the tournament, including two play-off matches. There were 7-0 group wins over Maribor and Spartak Moscow.

- Liverpool were the first team to have three players score ten or more goals from the group stage onwards – Roberto Firmino, Sadio Mane and Mohamed Salah.

- Jurgen Klopp has lost six of seven major finals as a manager, his one success coming with Borussia Dortmund in the German Cup in 2012.

# EUROPEAN CUP/CHAMPIONS LEAGUE FINALS

**1956** Real Madrid 4 Reims 3 (Paris)
**1957** Real Madrid 2 Fiorentina 0 (Madrid)
**1958†** Real Madrid 3 AC Milan 2 (Brussels)
**1959** Real Madrid 2 Reims 0 (Stuttgart)
**1960** Real Madrid 7 Eintracht Frankfurt 3 (Glasgow)

| | |
|---|---|
| **1961** | Benfica 3 Barcelona 2 (Berne) |
| **1962** | Benfica 5 Real Madrid 3 (Amsterdam) |
| **1963** | AC Milan 2 Benfica 1 (Wembley) |
| **1964** | Inter Milan 3 Real Madrid 1 (Vienna) |
| **1965** | Inter Milan 1 Benfica 0 (Milan) |
| **1966** | Real Madrid 2 Partizan Belgrade 1 (Brussels) |
| **1967** | Celtic 2 Inter Milan 1 (Lisbon) |
| **1968†** | Manchester Utd 4 Benfica 1 (Wembley) |
| **1969** | AC Milan 4 Ajax 1 (Madrid) |
| **1970†** | Feyenoord 2 Celtic 1 (Milan) |
| **1971** | Ajax 2 Panathinaikos 0 (Wembley) |
| **1972** | Ajax 2 Inter Milan 0 (Rotterdam) |
| **1973** | Ajax 1 Juventus 0 (Belgrade) |
| **1974** | Bayern Munich 4 Atletico Madrid 0 (replay Brussels after a 1-1 draw Brussels) |
| **1975** | Bayern Munich 2 Leeds Utd 0 (Paris) |
| **1976** | Bayern Munich 1 St. Etienne 0 (Glasgow) |
| **1977** | Liverpool 3 Borussia Moenchengladbach 1 (Rome) |
| **1978** | Liverpool 1 Brugge 0 (Wembley) |
| **1979** | Nottm Forest 1 Malmo 0 (Munich) |
| **1980** | Nottm Forest 1 Hamburg 0 (Madrid) |
| **1981** | Liverpool 1 Real Madrid 0 (Paris) |
| **1982** | Aston Villa 1 Bayern Munich 0 (Rotterdam) |
| **1983** | SV Hamburg 1 Juventus 0 (Athens) |
| **1984†** | Liverpool 1 AS Roma 1 (Liverpool won 4-2 on penalties) (Rome) |
| **1985** | Juventus 1 Liverpool 0 (Brussels) |
| **1986†** | Steaua Bucharest 0 Barcelona 0 (Steaua won 2-0 on penalties) (Seville) |
| **1987** | Porto 2 Bayern Munich 1 (Vienna) |
| **1988†** | PSV Eindhoven 0 Benfica 0 (PSV won 6-5 on penalties) (Stuttgart) |
| **1989** | AC Milan 4 Steaua Bucharest 0 (Barcelona) |
| **1990** | AC Milan 1 Benfica 0 (Vienna) |
| **1991†** | Red Star Belgrade 0 Marseille 0 (Red Star won 5-3 on penalties) (Bari) |
| **1992** | Barcelona 1 Sampdoria 0 (Wembley) |
| **1993** | Marseille 1 AC Milan 0 (Munich) |
| **1994** | AC Milan 4 Barcelona 0 (Athens) |
| **1995** | Ajax 1 AC Milan 0 (Vienna) |
| **1996†** | Juventus 1 Ajax 1 (Juventus won 4-2 on penalties) (Rome) |
| **1997** | Borussia Dortmund 3 Juventus 1 (Munich) |
| **1998** | Real Madrid 1 Juventus 0 (Amsterdam) |
| **1999** | Manchester Utd 2 Bayern Munich 1 (Barcelona) |
| **2000** | Real Madrid 3 Valencia 0 (Paris) |
| **2001** | Bayern Munich 1 Valencia 1 (Bayern Munich won 5-4 on penalties) (Milan) |
| **2002** | Real Madrid 2 Bayer Leverkusen 1 (Glasgow) |
| **2003†** | AC Milan 0 Juventus 0 (AC Milan won 3-2 on penalties) (Manchester) |
| **2004** | FC Porto 3 Monaco 0 (Gelsenkirchen) |
| **2005†** | Liverpool 3 AC Milan 3 (Liverpool won 3-2 on penalties) (Istanbul) |
| **2006** | Barcelona 2 Arsenal 1 (Paris) |
| **2007** | AC Milan 2 Liverpool 1 (Athens) |
| **2008†** | Manchester Utd 1 Chelsea 1 (Manchester Utd won 6-5 on penalties) (Moscow) |
| **2009** | Barcelona 2 Manchester Utd 0 (Rome) |
| **2010** | Inter Milan 2 Bayern Munich 0 (Madrid) |
| **2011** | Barcelona 3 Manchester Utd 1 (Wembley) |
| **2012†** | Chelsea 1 Bayern Munich 1 (Chelsea won 4-3 on pens) (Munich) |
| **2013** | Bayern Munich 3 Borussia Dortmund 1 (Wembley) |
| **2014†** | Real Madrid 4 Atletico Madrid 1 (Lisbon) |
| **2015** | Barcelona 3 Juventus 1 (Berlin) |
| **2016** | Real Madrid 1 Atletico Madrid 1 (Real Madrid won 5-3 on pens) (Milan) |
| **2017** | Real Madrid 4 Juventus 1 (Cardiff) |
| **2018** | Real Madrid 3 Liverpool 1 (Kiev)† aet |

● Champions League since 1993. † after extra time

# UEFA EUROPA LEAGUE 2017–18

## FIRST QUALIFYING ROUND (selected results)

### FIRST LEG

**Bala** 1 (Venables 61) Vaduz 2 (Zarate 21, Brunner 29). Att: 803. **Connah's Quay** 1 (Woolfe 40) HJK Helsinki 0. Att: 472. **Crusaders** 3 (Lowry 27, Carvill 35, Owens 55) Liepaja 1 (Karasaukis 62). Att: 1,375. Haugesund 7 (Tronstad 8, Abdi 33, Hajradinovic 42, Ideki 49, Shuaibu 52, Huseklepp 61, Buduson 71) **Coleraine** 0. Att: 2,523
Levadia Tallinn 0 **Cork** 2 (Buckley 43, Beattie 82). Att: 1,504. Lyngby 1 (Blume 13) **Bangor** 0. Att: 2,574. Odd 3 (Mladenovic 1, Broberg 53, Haugen 90+2) **Ballymena** 0. Att: 2,969. Midtjylland 6 (Dal Hende 4, Riis 15, Poulsen 44 pen, Kroon 58, 62, Kraev 84) **Derry** 1 (Curtis 66). Att: 5,122
**Rangers** 1 (Miller 37) Niederkorn 0. Att: 48,861. Stjarnan 0 **Shamrock Rov** 1 (Shaw 38). Att: 1,020. **St Johnstone** 1 (Shaughnessy 32) Trakai 2 (Maksimov 13, Silenas 36). Att: 5,636

### SECOND LEG

**Ballymena** 0 Odd 2 (Millar 79 og, Haugen 88). Att: 1,792 (Odd won 5-0 on agg). **Bangor** 0 Lyngby 3 (Larsen 3, 44, Kjaer 88). Att: 1,089 (Lyngby won 4-0 on agg). **Coleraine** 0 Haugesund 0. Att: 944 (Haugesund won 7-0 on agg). **Cork** 4 (Sheppard 28, Maguire 46, 86, 90) Levadia Tallinn 2 (Kobzar 15, Andreev 59). Att: 6,314 (Cork won 6-2 on agg)
**Derry** 1 (McEneff 41) Midtjylland 4 (Onuachu 7, 39, 69, Wikheim 59). Att: 467 (Midtjylland won 10-2 on agg). HJK Helsinki 3 (Yaghoubi 11, Pelvas 32, 55) **Connah's Quay** 0. Att: 6,103 (HJK Helsinki won 3-1 on agg). Liepaja 2 (Eristavi 33 pen, Karasaukis 90+4) **Crusaders** 0. Att: 2,310 (agg 3-3, Liepaja won on away goal). Niederkorn 2 (Francoise 66, Thill 75) **Rangers** 0. Att: 5,534 (Niederkorn won 2-1 on agg)
**Shamrock Rov** 1 (Burke 20) Stjarnan 0. Att: 3,352 (Shamrock Rov won 2-0 on agg). Trakai 1 (Maksimov 88) **St Johnstone** 0. Att: 2,100 (Trakai won 3-1 on agg). Vaduz 3 (Turkes 22, 39, Mathys 43) **Bala** 0. Att: 621 (Vaduz won 5-1 on agg)

## SECOND QUALIFYING ROUND (selected results)

### FIRST LEG

**Aberdeen** 1 (Christie 17) Siroki Brijeg 1 (Markovic 69). Att: 17,067. **Cork** 0 AEK Larnaca 1 (Truyois 70). Att: 6,441. **Shamrock Rov** 2 (Burke 48, 90+2) Mlada Boleslav 3 (Mebrahtu 35, 63, Chramostra 89). Att: 3,160

### SECOND LEG

AEK Larnaca 1 (Pintado 34) **Cork** 0. Att: 3,771 (AEK Larnaca won 2-0 on agg). Mlada Boleslav 2 (Chramostra 9, Mebrahtu 31) **Shamrov Rov** 0. Att: 4,727 (Mlada Boleslav won 5-2 on agg). Siroki Brijeg 0 **Aberdeen** 2 (Stewart 71, Mackay-Steven 77). Att: 4,800 (Aberdeen won 3-1 on agg)

## THIRD QUALYFING ROUND (selected results)

### FIRST LEG

**Aberdeen** 2 (Christie 4, Shinnie 78) Apollon Limassol 1 (Santana 59). Att: 20,085. **Everton** 1 (Baines 65) Ruzomberok 0. Att: 32,124

### SECOND LEG

Apollon Limassol 2 (Schembri 17, Zelaya 88) **Aberdeen** 0. Att: 6,250 (Apollon Limassol won 3-2 on agg). Ruzomberok 0 **Everton** 1 (Calvert-Lewin 80). Att: 4,752 (Everton won 2-0 on agg)

## PLAY-OFFS, FIRST LEG

**Everton** 2 (Keane 30, Gueye 45) **Hajduk Split** 0. Att: 34,977

## PLAY-OFFS, SECOND LEG

Hajduk Split 1 (Radosevic 43) **Everton** 1 (Sigurdsson 46). Att: 31,645 (Everton won 3-1 on agg)

## PLAY-OFFS, ON AGGREGATE

AC Milan 7 Shkendija Tetovo 0; AEK Athens 3 Club Bruges 0; Apollon Limassol 4 Midtjylland 3; Athletic Bilbao 4 Panathinaikos 2; Austria Vienna 2 Osijek 2 (Austria Vienna won on away goals); BATE Borisov 3 Oleksandriya 2; Braga 5 Hafnarfjordur 3; Dynamo Kiev 3 Maritimo 1; Ludogorets 2 Suduva 0; Maccabi Tel Aviv 3 Altach 2; Marseille 4 Domzale 1; Ostersunds 3 PAOK Salonika 3 (Ostersunds won on away goal)

Partizan Belgrade 4 Videoton 0; Rosenborg 4 Ajax 2; Red Star Belgrade 4 Krasnodar 4 (Red Star Belgrade won on away goals); Salzburg 7 Viitorul 1; Sheriff Tiraspol 1 Legia Warsaw 1 (Sheriff Tiraspol won on away goal); Skenderbeu 1 Dinamo Zagreb 1 (Skenderbeu won on away goal); Vardar 2 Fenerbahce 1; Viktoria Plzen 3 AEK Larnaca 1; Zenit St Petersburg 2 Utrecht 1

# GROUP STAGE

## GROUP A

**Match-day 1**: Slavia Prague 1 (Necid 12) Maccabi Tel Aviv 0. Att: 13,035. Villarreal 3 (Sansone 16, Bakambu 75, Cheryshev 77) Astana 1 (Logvinenko 68). Att: 18,144
**Match-day 2**: Astana 1 (Tomasov 42) Slavia Prague 1 (Ngadeu-Ngadjui 18). Att: 17,215. Maccabi Tel Aviv 0 Villarreal 0. Att: 11,865
**Match-day 3**: Astana 4 (Twumasi 33 pen, 42, Kabananga 47, 52) Maccabi Tel Aviv 0. Att: 10,350. Villarrel 2 (Munoz 41, Bacca 44) Slavia Prague 2 (Necid 18, Danny 30). Att: 15,634
**Match-day 4**: Maccabi Tel Aviv 0 Astana 1 (Twumasi 57). Att: 7,934. Slavia Prague 0 Villarreal 2 (Bacca 15, Deli 89 og). Att: 18,403
**Match-day 5**: Astana 2 (Kabananga 22, Twumasi 88) Villarreal 3 (Raba 39, Bakambu 65, 83). Att: 29,800. Maccabi Tel Aviv 0 Slavia Prague 2 (Husbauer 45, 54). Att: 6,874
**Match-day 6**: Slavia Prague 0 Astana 1 (Anicic 38). Att: 14,198. Villarreal 0 Maccabi Tel Aviv 1 (Blackman 60). Att: 12,613

| | P | W | D | L | F | A | Pts |
|---|---|---|---|---|---|---|---|
| Villarreal Q | 6 | 3 | 2 | 1 | 10 | 6 | 11 |
| Astana Q | 6 | 3 | 1 | 2 | 10 | 7 | 10 |
| Slavia Prague | 6 | 2 | 2 | 2 | 6 | 6 | 8 |
| Maccabi Tel Aviv | 6 | 1 | 1 | 4 | 1 | 8 | 4 |

## GROUP B

**Match-day 1**: Dynamo Kiev 3 (Sydorchuk 47, Moraes 50, Mbokani 65 pen) Skenderbeu 1 (Muzaka 39). Att: 24,883. Young Boys 1 (Jankovic 11) Partizan Belgrade 1 (Fassnacht 14). Att: 13,604
**Match-day 2**: Partizan Belgrade 2 (Ozegovic 34, Tawamba 42) Dynamo Kiev 3 (Moraes 54 pen, 84, Buyalskiy 68). Played behind closed doors – previous crowd trouble. Skenderbeu 1 (Sowe 65) Young Boys 1 (Assale 72). Att: 3,300
**Match-day 3**: Dynamo Kiev 2 (Mbokani 34, Morozyuk 49) Young Boys 2 (Assale 17, 39). Att: 21,700. Skenderbeu 0 Partizan Belgrade 0. Att: 6,300
**Match-day 4**: Partizan Belgrade 2 (Tosic 39, Tawamba 66) Skenderbeu 0. Att: 12,659. Young Boys 0 Dynamo Kiev 1 (Buyalskiy 70). Att: 10,077
**Match-day 5**: Partizan Belgrade 2 (Tawanba 12, Ozegovic 53) Young Boys 1 (Ngamaleu 25).

Att: 20,568. Skenderbeu 3 (Lilaj 18, Adeniyi 52, Sowe 56) Dynamo Kiev 2 (Tsygankov 16, Rusyn 90+1). Played behind closed doors – previous crowd trouble

**Match-day 6**: Dynamo Kiev 4 (Morozyuk 6, Moraes 28, 31, 77 pen) Partizan Belgrade 1 (Jevtovic 45). Att: 14,678. Young Boys 2 (Hoarau 55, Assale 90+5) Skenderbeu 1 (Gavazaj 51). Att: 8,029

| | P | W | D | L | F | A | Pts |
|---|---|---|---|---|---|---|---|
| Dynamo Kiev Q | 6 | 4 | 1 | 1 | 15 | 9 | 13 |
| Partizan Belgrade Q | 6 | 2 | 2 | 2 | 8 | 9 | 8 |
| Young Boys | 6 | 1 | 3 | 2 | 7 | 8 | 6 |
| Skenderbeu | 6 | 1 | 2 | 3 | 6 | 10 | 5 |

## GROUP C

**Match-day 1**: Basaksehir 0 Ludogorets 0. Att: 6,804. Hoffenheim 1 (Wagner 24) Braga 2 (Joao Carlos 45, Sousa 50). Att: 15,714

**Match-day 2**: Braga 2 (Hassan 26, Fransergio 89) Basaksehir 1 (Belozoglu 28). Att: 10,376. Ludogorets 2 (Dyakov 46, Lukoki 72) Hoffenheim 1 (Kaderabek 2). Att: 6,155

**Match-day 3**: Braga 0 Ludogorets 2 (Moti 25, Raul Silva 56 og). Att: 8,623. Hoffenheim 3 (Hubner 52, Amiri 59, Schulz 75) Basaksehir 1 (Napoleoni 90+3). Att: 21,167

**Match-day 4**: Basaksehir 1 (Grillitsch 47) Hoffenheim 1 (Visca 90+3). Att: 5,214. Ludogorets 1 (Marcelinho 68) Braga 1 (Fransergio 83). Att: 7,544

**Match-day 5**: Braga 3 (Goiano 1, Fransergio 81, 90+3) Hoffenheim 1 (Uth 74). Att: 10,054 Ludogorets 1 (Marcelinho 65) Basaksehir 2 (Visca 20, Frei 27). Att: 7,520

**Match-day 6**: Basaksehir 2 (Visca 10, Belozoglu 77 pen) Braga 1 (Raul Silva 55): Att: 5,241. Hoffenheim 1 (Ochs 25) Ludogorets 1 (Wanderson 62). Att: 7,814

| | P | W | D | L | F | A | Pts |
|---|---|---|---|---|---|---|---|
| Braga Q | 6 | 3 | 1 | 2 | 9 | 8 | 10 |
| Ludogorets Q | 6 | 2 | 3 | 1 | 7 | 5 | 9 |
| Basaksehir | 6 | 2 | 2 | 2 | 7 | 8 | 8 |
| Hoffenheim | 6 | 1 | 2 | 3 | 8 | 10 | 5 |

## GROUP D

**Match-day 1**: Austria Vienna 1 (Barkovic 47) AC Milan 5 (Calhanoglu 7, Andre Silva 10, 20, 56, Suso 63). Att: 31,409. Rijeka 1 (Elez 29) AEK Athens 2 (Mantalos 16, Christodoulopoulos 62). Att: 5,932

**Match-day 2**: AC Milan 3 (Andre Silva 14, Musacchio 53, Cutrone 90+4) Rijeka 2 (Acosty 84, Elez 90 pen). Att: 23,917. AEK Athens 2 (Livaja 28, 90) Austria Vienna 2 (Monschein 43, Tajouri 49). Att: 16,954

**Match-day 3**: AC Milan 0 AEK Athen 0. Att: 20,812. Austria Vienna 1 (Friesenbichler 90) Rijeka 3 (Gavranovic 21, 31, Kvrzic 90+2). Att: 20,602

**Match-day 4**: AEK Athens 0 AC Milan 0. Att: 40,538. Rijeka 1 (Pavicic 61) Austria Vienna 4 (Prokop 41, 62, Serbest 73, Monschein 83). Att: 7,912

**Match-day 5**: AC Milan 5 (Rodriguez 27, Andre Silva 36, 70, Cutrone 42, 90+3) Austria Vienna 1 (Monschein 21). Att: 17,932. AEK Athens 2 (Araujo 45, Christodoulopoulos 55) Rijeka 2 (Gorgon 8, 26). Att: 17,100

**Match-day 6**: Austria Vienna 0 AEK Athens 0. Att: 23,133. Rijeka 2 (Puljic 7, Gavranovic 47). AC Milan 0. Att: 8,021

| | P | W | D | L | F | A | Pts |
|---|---|---|---|---|---|---|---|
| AC Milan Q | 6 | 3 | 2 | 1 | 13 | 6 | 11 |
| AEK Athens Q | 6 | 1 | 5 | 0 | 6 | 5 | 8 |
| Rijeka | 6 | 2 | 1 | 3 | 11 | 12 | 7 |
| Austria Vienna | 6 | 1 | 2 | 3 | 9 | 16 | 5 |

## GROUP E

**Match-day 1**: Apollon Limassol 1 (Sardinero 90+3) Lyon 1 (Depay 53 pen). Att: 5,134. Atalanta 3 (Masiello 27, Gomez 41, Cristante 44) **Everton** 0. Att: 14,890
**Match-day 2**: **Everton** 2 (Rooney 21, Vlasic 66) Apollon Limassol 2 (Sardinero 12, Yuste 87). Att: 27,034. Lyon 1 (Traore 45) Atalanta 1 (Gomez 57). Att: 27,715
**Match-day 3**: Atalanta 3 (Ilicic 12, Petagna 64, Freuler 66) Apollon Limassol 1 (Schembri 59). Att: 13,803. **Everton** 1 (Williams 69) Lyon 2 (Fekir 6 pen, Traore 76). Att: 27,194
**Match-day 4**: Apollon Limassol 1 (Zelaya 90+4) Atalanta 1 (Ilicic 35 pen). Att: 5,658. Lyon 3 (Traore 68, Aouar 76, Depay 88) **Everton** 0. Att: 48,103
**Match-day 5**: **Everton** 1 (Sandro 71) Atalanta 5 (Cristante 13, 64, Gosens 86, Cornelius 90+4). Att: 17,431. Lyon 4 (Diakhaby 29, Fekir 32, Mariano 67, Maolida 90) Apollon Limassol 0. Att: 26,972
**Match-day 6**: Apollon Limassol 0 **Everton** 3 (Lookman 21, 28, Vlasic 87). Att: 2,355. Atalanta 1 (Petagna 10) Lyon 0. Att: 14,500

| | P | W | D | L | F | A | Pts |
|---|---|---|---|---|---|---|---|
| Atalanta Q | 6 | 4 | 2 | 0 | 14 | 4 | 14 |
| Lyon Q | 6 | 3 | 2 | 1 | 11 | 4 | 11 |
| **Everton** | 6 | 1 | 1 | 4 | 7 | 15 | 4 |
| Apollon Limassol | 6 | 0 | 3 | 3 | 5 | 14 | 3 |

## GROUP F

**Match-day 1**: Copenhagen 0 Lokomotiv Moscow 0. Att: 17,285. Fastav Zlin 0 Sheriff Tiraspol 0. Att: 4,499
**Match-day 2**: Lokomotiv Moscow 3 (Ferando 2 pen, 6, 17) Fastav Zlin 0. Att: 10,065. Sheriff Tiraspol 0 Copenhagen 0. Att: 5,070
**Match-day 3**: Fastav Zlin 1 (Diop 11) Copenhagen 1 (Ankersen 19). Att: 6,345. Sheriff Tiraspol 1 (Badibanga 31) Lokomotiv Moscow 1 (Miranchuk 17). Att: 10,511
**Match-day 4**: Copenhagen 3 (Luftner 40, Verbic 49, 90+2) Fastav Zlin 0. Att: 16,189. Lokomotiv Moscow 1 (Farfan 26) Sheriff Tiraspol 2 (Badibanga 41, Brezovec 58). Att: 10,118
**Match-day 5**: Lokomotiv Moscow 2 (Farfan 17, 51) Copenhagen 1 (Verbic 31). Att: 10,696. Sheriff Tiraspol 1 (Jairo 11) Fastav Zlin 0. Att: 5,486
**Match-day 6**: Copenhagen 2 (Sotiriou 56, Luftner 59) Sheriff Tiraspol 0. Att: 14,246. Fastav Zlin 0 Lokomotiv Moscow 2 (Miranchuk 70, Farfan 75). Att: 4,682

| | P | W | D | L | F | A | Pts |
|---|---|---|---|---|---|---|---|
| Lokomotiv Moscow Q | 6 | 3 | 2 | 1 | 9 | 4 | 11 |
| Copenhagen Q | 6 | 2 | 3 | 1 | 7 | 3 | 9 |
| Sheriff Tiraspol | 6 | 2 | 3 | 1 | 4 | 4 | 9 |
| Fastav Zlin | 6 | 0 | 2 | 4 | 1 | 10 | 2 |

## GROUP G

**Match-day 1**: Hapoel Beer Sheva 2 (Einbinder 2, Tzedek 60 pen) Lugano 1 (Tzedek 67 og). Att: 14,752. Steaua Bucharest 3 (Budescu 21 pen, 44, Alibec 73) Viktoria Plzen 0. Att: 20,714
**Match-day 2**: Lugano 1 (Bottani 14) Steaua Bucharest 2 (Budescu 58, Maranhao 64). Att: 2,680. Viktoria Plzen 3 (Petrzela 29, Kopic 76, Bakos 89) Hapoel Beer Sheva 1 (Nwakaeme 68). Att: 10,314
**Match-day 3**: Hapoel Beer Sheva 1 (Cuenca 87) Steaua Bucharest 2 (Gnohere 70, 75). Att: 15,117. Lugano 3 (Bottani 63, Carlinhos 69, Gerndt 88), Viktoria Plzen 2 (Krmencik 76, Bakos 90). Att: 2,530
**Match-day 4**: Steaua Bucharest 1 (Coman 31) Hapoel Beer Sheva 1 (Ben Sahar 37). Att: 27,134. Viktoria Plzen 4 (Krmencik 4, 19, Horava 45, Cermak 55) Lugano 1 (Mariani 15). Att: 9,483

**Match-day 5**: Lugano 1 (Carlinhos 50) Hapoel Beer Sheva 0. Att: 3,011. Viktoria Plzen 2 (Petrzela 49, Kopic 76) Steaua Bucharest 0. Att: 10,197
**Match-day 6**: Hapoel Beer Sheva 0 Viktoria Plzen 2 (Hejda 29, Horava 83). Att: 10,542. Steaua Bucharest 1 (Gnohere 60) Lugano 2 (Daprela 3, Vecsei 32). Att: 13,231

| | P | W | D | L | F | A | Pts |
|---|---|---|---|---|---|---|---|
| Viktoria Plzen Q | 6 | 4 | 0 | 2 | 13 | 8 | 12 |
| Steaua Bucharest Q | 6 | 3 | 1 | 2 | 9 | 7 | 10 |
| Lugano | 6 | 3 | 0 | 3 | 9 | 11 | 9 |
| Hapoel Beer Sheva | 6 | 1 | 1 | 4 | 5 | 10 | 4 |

## GROUP H

**Match-day 1**: **Arsenal** 3 (Kolasinac 49, Sanchez 67, Bellerin 82) Cologne 1 (Cordoba 9). Att: 59,359. Red Star Belgrade 1 (Radonjic 54) BATE Borisov 1 (Signevich 72). Att: 40,284
**Match-day 2**: BATE Borisov 2 (Ivanic 28, Gordeichuk 67) **Arsenal** 4 (Walcott 9, 22, Holding 25, Giroud 49 pen). Att: 13,100. Cologne 0 Red Star Belgrade 1 (Boakye 30). Att: 45,300
**Match-day 3**: BATE Borisov 1 (Rios 55) Cologne 0. Att: 11,783. Red Star Belgrade 0 **Arsenal** 1 (Giroud 85). Att: 50,327
**Match-day 4**: **Arsenal** 0 Red Star Belgrade 0. Att: 58,285. Cologne 5 (Zoller 16, Osako 54, 82, Guirassy 63, Jojic 90) BATE Borisov 2 (Milunovic 31, Signevich 33). Att: 45,200
**Match-day 5**: BATE Borisov 0 Red Star Belgrade 0. Att: 12,009. Cologne 1 (Guirassy 62 pen) **Arsenal** 0. Att: 45,300
**Match-day 6**: **Arsenal** 6 (Debuchy 11, Walcott 37, Wilshere 43, Polyakov 52 og, Giroud 64 pen, Elneny 74) BATE Borisov 0. Att: 54,648. Red Star Belgrade 1 (Srnic 22) Cologne 0. Att: 51,364

| | P | W | D | L | F | A | Pts |
|---|---|---|---|---|---|---|---|
| **Arsenal** Q | 6 | 4 | 1 | 1 | 14 | 4 | 13 |
| Red Star Belgrade Q | 6 | 2 | 3 | 1 | 3 | 2 | 9 |
| Cologne | 6 | 2 | 0 | 4 | 7 | 8 | 6 |
| BATE Borisov | 6 | 1 | 2 | 3 | 6 | 16 | 5 |

## GROUP I

**Match-day 1**: Marseille 1 (Rami 48) Konyaspor 0. Att: 8,549. Guimaraes 1 (Pedrao 25) Salzburg 1 (Berish 45). Att: 13,972
**Match-day 2**: Konyaspor 2 (Araz 24, Milosevic 48) Guimaraes 1 (Hurtado 74). Att: 21,116. Salzburg 1 (Dabbur 73) Marseille 0. Att: 11,832
**Match-day 3**: Konyaspor 0 Salzburg 2 (Gulbrandsen 5, Dabbur 80). Att: 23,354. Marseille 2 (Ocampos 28, Lopez 76) Guimaraes 1 (Martins 17). Att: 13,359
**Match-day 4**: Guimaraes 1 (Hurtado 80) Marseille 0. Att: 14,181. Salzburg 0 Konyaspor 0. Att: 8,773
**Match-day 5**: Konyaspor 1 (Skubic 82 pen) Marseille 1 (Moke 90+3 og). Att: 18,000. Salzburg 3 (Dabbur 26, Ulmer 45, Hee-chan Hwang 67). Att: 6,474
**Match-day 6**: Guimaraes 1 (Turan 77 og) Konyaspor 1 (Bourabia 15). Att: 9,040. Marseille 0 Salzburg 0. Att: 23,865

| | P | W | D | L | F | A | Pts |
|---|---|---|---|---|---|---|---|
| Salzburg Q | 6 | 3 | 3 | 0 | 7 | 1 | 12 |
| Marseille Q | 6 | 2 | 2 | 2 | 4 | 4 | 8 |
| Konyaspor | 6 | 1 | 3 | 2 | 4 | 6 | 6 |
| Guimaraes | 6 | 1 | 2 | 3 | 5 | 9 | 5 |

## GROUP J

**Match-day 1**: Hertha Berlin 0 Athletic Bilbao 0. Att: 28,832. Zorya Lugansk 0 Ostersunds 2 (Ghoddas 50, Gero 90+4). Att: 5,097

**Match-day 2**: Athletic Bilbao 0 Zorya Lugansk 1 (Kharatin 26). Att: 32,462. Ostersunds 1 (Nouri 22 pen) Hertha Berlin 0. Att: 8,009

**Match-day 3**: Ostersunds 2 (Gero 52, Edwards 64) Athletic Bilbao 2 (Aduriz 14, Wiliams 89). Att: 7,870. Zorya Lugansk 2 (Da Silva 42, Svatok 79) Hertha Berlin 1 (Selke 56). Att: 9,521

**Match-day 4**: Athletic Bilbao 1 (Adruriz 70) Ostersunds 0. Att: 32,354. Hertha Berlin 2 (Selke 16, 73) Zorya Lugansk 0. Att: 20,358

**Match-day 5**: Athletic Bilbao 3 (Aduriz 35 pen, 66 pen, Williams 82) Hertha Berlin 2 (Leckie 26, Selke 36). Att: 38,928. Ostersunds 2 (Grechyshkin 40 og, Ghoddos 78) Zorya Lugansk 0. Att: 7,754

**Match-day 6**: Hertha Berlin 1 (Pekarik 61) Ostersunds 1 (Papagiannopoulos 58). Att: 15,686. Zorya Lugansk 0 Athletic Bilbao 2 (Aduriz 70, Raul Garcia 86). Att: 8,428

| | P | W | D | L | F | A | Pts |
|---|---|---|---|---|---|---|---|
| Athletic Bilbao Q | 6 | 3 | 2 | 1 | 8 | 5 | 11 |
| Ostersunds Q | 6 | 3 | 2 | 1 | 8 | 4 | 11 |
| Zorya Lugansk | 6 | 2 | 0 | 4 | 3 | 9 | 6 |
| Hertha Berlin | 6 | 1 | 2 | 3 | 6 | 7 | 5 |

## GROUP K

**Match-day 1**: Vitesse Arnhem 2 (Matavz 33, Linssen 57) Lazio 3 (Parolo 51, Immobile 67, Murgia 75). Att: 19,867. Zulte-Waregem 1 (Iseka 46) Nice 5 (Plea 16, 20, Dante 28, Saint-Maximin 69, Balotelli 74). Att: 9,072

**Match-day 2**: Lazio 2 (Caicedo 18, Immobile 90) Zulte-Waregem 0. Played behind closed doors – previous crowd trouble. Nice 3 (Plea 16, 82, Saint-Maximin 45) Vitesse Arnhem 0. Att: 15,006

**Match-day 3**: Nice 1 (Balotelli 4) Lazio 3 (Caicedo 5, Milinkovic-Savic 65, 89). Att: 21,386. Zulte-Waregam 1 (Kashia 23 og) Vitesse Arnhem 1 (Bruns 27). Att: 9,488

**Match-day 4**: Lazio 1 (Le Marchand 90+2 og) Nice 0. Att: 21,327. Vitesse Arnhem 0 Zulte-Waregem 2 (Baudry 3, Kaya 70). Att: 17,906

**Match-day 5**: Lazio 1 (Luis Alberto 42) Vitesse Arnhem 1 (Linssen 13). Att: 8,226. Nice 3 (Balotelli 5 pen, 31, Tameze 86) Zulte-Waregen 1 (Hamalainen 81). Att: 20,274

**Match-day 6**: Vitesse Arnhem 1 (Castiagnos 85) Nice 0. Att: 17,564. Zulte-Waregem 3 (De Pauw 6, Haylen 60, Iseka 83) Lazio 2 (Caicedo 67, Lucas Leiva 76). Att: 8,845

| | P | W | D | L | F | A | Pts |
|---|---|---|---|---|---|---|---|
| Lazio Q | 6 | 4 | 1 | 1 | 12 | 7 | 13 |
| Nice Q | 6 | 3 | 0 | 3 | 12 | 7 | 9 |
| Zulte Waregem | 6 | 2 | 1 | 3 | 8 | 13 | 7 |
| Vitesse Arnhem | 6 | 1 | 2 | 3 | 5 | 10 | 5 |

## GROUP L

**Match-day 1**: Real Sociedad 4 (Llorente 9, 77, Zurutuza 10, Skjelvik 41) Rosenborg 0. Att: 21,479. Vardar 0 Zenit St Petersburg 5 (Kokorin 6, 21, Dzyuba 39, Ivanovic 66, Rigoni 89). Att: 11,118

**Match-day 2**: Rosenborg 3 (Bendtner 25 pen, Konradsen 56, Hedenstad 68) Vardar 1 (Juan Felip 90+1). Att: 16,038. Zenit St Petersburg 3 (Rigoni 5, Kokorin 24, 60) Real Sociedad 1 (Llorente 41). Att: 50,487

**Match-day 3**: Vardar 0 Real Sociedad 6 (Oyarzabal 12, Willian Jose 34, 42, 55, 59, De la Bella 90). Att: 20,368. Zenit St Petersburg 3 (Rigoni 1, 68, 75) Rosenborg 1 (Helland 88). Att: 46,211

**Match-day 4**: Real Sociedad 3 (Juanmi 31, De la Bella 69, Bautista 81) Varda 0. Att: 17,242. Rosenborg 1 (Bendtner 55 pen) Zenit St Petersburg 1 (Kokorin 90+3). Att: 18,597
**Match-day 5**: Rosenborg 0 Real Sociedad 1 (Oyarzabal 90). Att: 18,307. Zenit St Petersburg 2 (Poloz 16, Rigoni 43) Vardar 1 (Blazevski 90+3). Att: 38,196
**Match-day 6**: Real Sociedad 1 (Jose 58) Zenit St Petersburg 3 (Erokhin 35, Ivanovic 64, Paredes 85). Att: 20,609. Vardar 1 (Ytalo 9) Rosenborg 1 (Bendtner 45 pen). Att: 7,839

| | P | W | D | L | F | A | Pts |
|---|---|---|---|---|---|---|---|
| Zenit St Petersburg Q | 6 | 5 | 1 | 0 | 17 | 5 | 16 |
| Real Sociedad Q | 6 | 4 | 0 | 2 | 16 | 6 | 12 |
| Rosenborg | 6 | 1 | 2 | 3 | 6 | 11 | 5 |
| Vardar | 6 | 0 | 1 | 5 | 3 | 20 | 1 |

## ROUND OF 32, FIRST LEG

AEK Athens 1 (Ajdarevic 80) Dynamo Kiev 1 (Tsygankov 19). Att: 30,518. Astana 1 (Tomasov 7) Sporting Lisbon 3 (Bruno Fernandes 48 pen, Martins 50, Doumbia 56), Att: 29,737. Borussia Dortmund 3 (Schurrle 30, Batshuayi 65, 90+1) Atalanta 2 (Ilicic 51, 56). Att: 62,501. **Celtic** 1 (McGregor 78) Zenit St Petersburg 0. Att: 56,743
Copenhagen 1 (Fischer 15) Atletico Madrid 4 (Saul 21, Gameiro 37, Griezmann 71, Vitolo 77). Att: 34,912. Ludogorets 0 AC Milan 3 (Cutrone 45, Rodriguez 64, Borini 90+2). Att: 12,512; Lyon 3 (Ndombele 46, Fekir 49, Depay 82) Villarreal 1 (Fornals 63). Att: 46,846. Marseille 3 (Germain 4, 69, Thavin 74) Braga 0. Att: 21,731
Napoli 1 (Ounas 52) Leipzig 3 (Werner 61, 90+3, Bruma 74). Att: 14,554. Nice 2 (Balotelli 4, 28) Lokomotiv Moscow 3 (Manuel Fernandes 45 pen, 69, 77). Att: 16,918. Ostersunds 0 **Arsenal** 3 (Monreal 14, Papaglannopoulos 24 og, Ozil 58). Att: 8,008. Partizan Belgrade 1 (Tawamba 58) Viktoria Plzen 1 (Reznik 81). Att: 21,568
Real Sociedad 2 (Odriozola 57, Januzaj 80) Salzburg 2 (Oyarzabal 27 og, Minamino 90+4). Att: 21,543. Red Star Belgrade 0 CSKA Moscow 0. Att: 35,642. Steaua Bucharest 1 (Gnohere 29) Lazio 0. Att: 33,455. Spartak Mosow 1 (Luiz Adriano 60) Athletic Bilbao 3 (Aduriz 22, 39, Kutepov 45 og). Att: 43,145

## ROUND OF 32, SECOND LEG

AC Milan 1 (Borini 21) Ludogorets 0. Att: 17,453 (AC Milan won 4-0 on agg). **Arsenal** 1 (Kolasinac 47) Ostersunds 2 (Alesh 22, Sema 24). Att: 58,405 (Arsenal won 4-2 on agg). Atalanta 1 (Toloi 11) Borussia Dortmund 1 (Schmelzer 83). Att: 17,492 (Borussia Dortmund won 4-3 on agg). Athletic Bilbao 1 (Etxeita 57) Spartak Moscow 2 (Luiz Adriano 44, Melgarejo 85). Att: 36,873 (Athletic Bilbao won 4-3 on agg)
Atletico Madrid 1 (Gameiro 7) Copenhagen 0. Att: 44,035 (Atletico Madrid won 5-1 on agg) Braga 1 (Horta 31) Marseille 0. Att: 9,016 (Marseille won 3-1 on agg). CSKA Moscow 1 (Dzagoev 45) Red Star Belgrade 0. Att: 18,753 (CSKA Moscow won 1-0 on agg). Dynamo Kiev 0 AEK Athens 0. Att: 27,024 (agg 1-1, Dynamo Kiev won on away goal)
Lazio 5 (Immobile 7, 43, 71, Bastos 35, Felipe Anderson 51) Steaua Bucharest 1 (Gnohere 82). Att: 27,597 (Lazio won 5-2 on agg). Lokomotiv Moscow 1 (Denisov 30) Nice 0. Att: 18,104 (Lokomotiv Moscow won 4-2 on agg). Leipzig 0 Napoli 2 (Zielinski 32, Insigne 86). Att: 36,163 (agg 3-3, Leipzig won on away goals). Salzburg 2 (Dabbur 10, Berisha 74 pen) Real Sociedad 1 (Navas 28). Att: 13,912 (Salzburg won 4-3 on agg)
Sporting Lisbon 3 (Bas Dost 3, Bruno Fernandes 53, 63) Astana 3 (Tomasov 37, Twumasi 80, Shomko 90+4). Att: 30,456 (Sporting Lisbon won 6-4 on agg). Viktoria Plzen 2 (Krmencik 67, Cermak 90+4) Partizan Belgrade 0. Att: 10,185 (Viktoria Plzen won 3-1 on agg). Villarreal 0 Lyon 1 (Traore 85). Att: 17,028 (Lyon won 4-1 on agg). Zenit St Petersburg 3 (Ivanovic 8, Kuzyaev 27, Kokorin 61) **Celtic** 0. Att: 50,492 (Zenit St Petersburg won 3-1 on agg)

## ROUND OF 16, FIRST LEG

AC Milan 0 **Arsenal** 2 (Mkhitaryan 15, Ramsey 45). Att: 72,821. Atletico Madrid 3 (Saul 22, Diego Costa 47, Koke 90) Lokomotiv Moscow 0. Att: 40,767. Borussia Dortmund 1 (Schurrle 62) Salzburg 2 (Berisha 49 pen, 56). Att: 53,700, CSKA Moscow 0 Lyon 1 (Marcelo 68). Att: 13,990

Lazio 2 (Immobile 54, Anderson 62) Dynamo Kiev 2 (Tsygankov 52, Moraes 79). Att: 21,562. Leipzig 2 (Bruma 56, Werner 77) Zenit St Petersburg 1 (Criscito 86). Att: 19,877. Marseille 3 (Ocampos 1, 57, Payet 14) Athletic Bilbao 1 (Aduriz 45 pen). Att: 37,657. Sporting Lisbon 2 (Krmencik 67, Cermak 90+4) Vikoria Plzen 0. Att: 10,185

## ROUND OF 16, SECOND LEG

**Arsenal** 3 (Welbeck 39 pen, 87, Xhaka 71) AC Milan 1 (Calhanoglu 35). Att: 58,973 (Arsenal won 5-1 on agg); Athletic Bilbao 1 (Williams 74) Marseille 2 (Payet 38 pen, Ocampos 52). Att: 40,586 (Marseille won 5-2 on agg). Dynamo Kiev 0 Lazio 2 (Lucas 23, De Vrij 83). Att: 52,639 (Lazio won 4-2 on agg). Lokomotiv Moscow 1 (Rybus 20) Atletico Madrid 5 (Correa 16, Saul 47, Torres 65 pen, 70, Griezmann 85). Att: 22,041 (Atletico Madrid won 8-1 on agg)

Lyon 2 (Cornet 58, Mariano 71) CSKA Moscow 3 (Golovin 39, Musa 61, Wernbloom 65). Att: 38,622 (agg 3-3, CSKA Moscow won on away goals). Salzburg 0 Borussia Dortmund 0. Att: 29,520 (Salzburg won 2-1 on agg). Viktoria Plzen 2 (Bakos 7, 65) Sporting Lisbon 1 (Battaglia 105). Att: 9,370 (aet, Sporting Lisbon won 3-2 on agg). Zenit St Petersburg 1 (Driussi 45) Leipzig 1 (Augustin 22). Att: 44,062 (Leipzig won 3-2 on agg)

## QUARTER-FINALS, FIRST LEG

**Arsenal** 4 (Ramsey 9, 28, Lacazette 23 pen, 35) CSKA Moscow 1 (Golovin 15). Att: 58,285. Atletico Madrid 2 (Koke 1, Griezmann 40) Sporting Lisbon 0. Att: 53,301. Lazio 4 (Lulic 8, Parolo 49, Anderson 74, Immobile 76) Salzburg 2 (Berisha 30 pen, Minamino 71). Att: 42,538. Leipzig 1 (Werner 45) Marseille 0. Att: 34,043

## QUARTER-FINALS, SECOND LEG

CSKA Moscow 2 (Chalov 39, Nababkin 50) **Arsenal** 2 (Welbeck 75, Ramsey 90+2). Att: 29,284. (Arsenal won 6-3 on agg). Marseille 5 (Ilsanker 6 og, Sarr 10, Thavin 38, Payet 60, Sakai 90+4) Leipzig 2 ( Bruma 2, Augustin 55). Att: 61,882 (Marseille won 5-3 on agg). Salzburg 4 (Dabbur 56, Haidara 72, Hwang 74, Lainer 76) Lazio 1 (Immobile 55). Att: 29,520 (Salzburg won 6-5 on agg). Sporting Lisbon 1 (Montero 28) Atletico Madrid 0. Att: 28,437 (Atletico Madrid won 2-1 on agg)

## SEMI-FINALS, FIRST LEG

**Arsenal** 1 (Lacazette 61) Atletico Madrid 1 (Griezmann 82). Att: 59,066. Marseille 2 (Thauvin 15, N'Jie 63) Salzburg 0. Att: 62,312

## SEMI-FINALS, SECOND LEG

Atletico Madrid 1 (Diego Costa 45) **Arsenal** 0. Att: 64,196 (Atletico Madrid won 2-1 on agg); Salzburg 2 (Haidara 53, Sarr 65 og) Marseille 1 (Rolando 116)). Att: 29,250 (aet, Marseille won 3-2 on agg)

## FINAL

**MARSEILLE 0 ATLETICO MADRID 3 (Griezmann 21, 49, Gabi 89)**
**Groupama Stadium, Lyon (55,768); Wednesday, May 16, 2018**

**Marseille** (4-2-3-1): Mandanda, Sarr, Rami, Luiz Gustavo, Amavi, Zambo Anguissa, Sanson,

Thauvin, Payet (capt) (Lopez 32), Ocampos (N'Jie 55), Germain (Mitroglou 74). **Subs not used**: Pele, Sakai, Kamara, Rolando. **Booked**: Amavi, Luiz Gustavo, N'Jie. **Coach**: Rudi Garcia
**Atletico Madrid** (4-4-2): Oblak, Vrsalijko (Juanfran 46), Gimenez, Godin, Lucas Hernandez, Correa (Thomas 88), Gabi (capt), Saul, Koke, Griezmann (Torres 90), Diego Costa, **Subs not used**: Werner, Filipe Luis, Savic, Gameiro. **Booked**: Vrsalijko, Lucas Hernandez. **Coach**: Diego Simeone
**Referee**: B Kuipers (Holland). **Half-time**: 0-1

**Leading scorers**: 8 Aduriz (Athletic Bilbao), Immobile (Lazio); 7 Moraes (Dynamo Kiev); 6 Andre Silva (AC Milan), Balotelli (Nice), Griezmann (Atletico Madrid), Kokorin (Zenit St Petersburg), Fernandes (Lokomotiv Moscow), Rigoni (Zenit St Petersburg)

# FIFA CLUB WORLD CUP – UNITED ARAB EMIRATES 2017

## QUALIFYING MATCHES

Al Jazira1(UAE) 1 (Ali Ahmed 52) Urawa Reds (Japan) 0. Att: 15,593. Pachuca (Mexico) 1 (Guzman 112) Wydad Casablanca (Morocco) 0. Att: 12,488 (aet)

## SEMI-FINALS

Al Jazira 1 (Da Silva 41) Real Madrid 2 (Ronaldo 53, Bale 81). Att: 36,650. Gremio (Brazil) 1 (Everton 95) Pachuca 0. Att: 6,428 (aet)

## FINAL

**REAL MADRID 1 (Ronaldo 53) GREMIO 0**
**Sports City, Abu Dhabi (41,094); Saturday, December 16, 2017**

**Real Madrid** (4-3-1-2): Navas, Daniel Carvajal, Varane, Sergio Ramos (capt), Marcelo, Modric, Casemiro, Kroos, Isco (Lucas Vazquez 73), Benzema (Bale 80), Ronaldo. **Booked**: Casemiro. **Coach**: Zinedine Zidane
**Gremio** (4-2-3-1): Marcelo Grohe, Edilson, Geromel (capt), Kannemann, Bruno Cortez, Jailson, Michel (Maicon 84), Ramiro (Everton 71), Barrios (Jael 63), Fernandinho, Luan. **Coach**: Renato Gaucho
**Referee**: C Ramos (Mexico). **Half-time**: 0-0

# EUROPEAN SUPER CUP 2017

**Real Madrid 2 (Casemiro 24, Isco 52) Manchester United 1 (Lukaku 62)**
**Telekom Arena, Skopje (30,421); Tuesday, August 8, 2017**

**Real Madrid** (4-3-1-2): Navas, Daniel Carvajal, Varane, Sergio Ramos (capt), Marcelo, Modric, Casemiro, Kroos, Isco (Lucas Vazquez 75), Bale (Marco Asensio 74), Benzema (Ronaldo 82). **Subs not used:** Kiko Casilla, Nacho, Hernandez, Kovacic. **Booked**: Daniel Carvajal, Sergio Ramos. **Coach**: Zinedine Zidane
**Manchester United** (3-5-1-1): De Gea, Lindelof, Smalling, Darmian, Valencia, Matic, Herrera (Fellaini 56), Pogba, Lingard (Rashford 46), Mkhitaryan, Lukaku. **Subs not used**: Romero, Blind, Carrick (capt), Mata, Martial. **Scorer**: Lukaku (62). **Booked**: Lingard, Rashford **Manager**: Jose Mourinho
**Referee**: G Rocchi (Italy). **Half-time**: 1-0

# UEFA CUP FINALS

**1972** Tottenham beat Wolves 3-2 on agg (2-1a, 1-1h)
**1973** Liverpool beat Borussia Moenchengladbach 3-2 on agg (3-0h, 0-2a)
**1974** Feyenoord beat Tottenham 4-2 on agg (2-2a, 2-0h)
**1975** Borussia Moenchengladbach beat Twente Enschede 5-1 on agg (0-0h, 5-1a)
**1976** Liverpool beat Brugge 4-3 on agg (3-2h, 1-1a)
**1977** Juventus beat Atletico Bilbao on away goals after 2-2 agg (1-0h, 1-2a)
**1978** PSV Eindhoven beat Bastia 3-0 on agg (0-0a, 3-0h)
**1979** Borussia Moenchengladbach beat Red Star Belgrade 2-1 on agg (1-1a, 1-0h)
**1980** Eintracht Frankfurt beat Borussia Moenchengladbach on away goals after 3-3 agg (2-3a, 1-0h)
**1981** Ipswich Town beat AZ 67 Alkmaar 5-4 on agg (3-0h, 2-4a)
**1982** IFK Gothenburg beat SV Hamburg 4-0 on agg (1-0h, 3-0a)
**1983** Anderlecht beat Benfica 2-1 on agg (1-0h, 1-1a)
**1984** Tottenham beat Anderlecht 4-3 on penalties after 2-2 agg (1-1a, 1-1h)
**1985** Real Madrid beat Videoton 3-1 on agg (3-0a, 0-1h)
**1986** Real Madrid beat Cologne 5-3 on agg (5-1h, 0-2a)
**1987** IFK Gothenburg beat Dundee Utd 2-1 on agg (1-0h, 1-1a)
**1988** Bayer Leverkusen beat Espanol 3-2 on penalties after 3-3 agg (0-3a, 3-0h)
**1989** Napoli beat VfB Stuttgart 5-4 on agg (2-1h, 3-3a)
**1990** Juventus beat Fiorentina 3-1 on agg (3-1h, 0-0a)
**1991** Inter Milan beat AS Roma 2-1 on agg (2-0h, 0-1a)
**1992** Ajax beat Torino on away goals after 2-2 agg (2-2a, 0-0h)
**1993** Juventus beat Borussia Dortmund 6-1 on agg (3-1a, 3-0h)
**1994** Inter Milan beat Salzburg 2-0 on agg (1-0a, 1-0h)
**1995** Parma beat Juventus 2-1 on agg (1-0h, 1-1a)
**1996** Bayern Munich beat Bordeaux 5-1 on agg (2-0h, 3-1a)
**1997** FC Schalke beat Inter Milan 4-1 on penalties after 1-1 agg (1-0h, 0-1a)
**1998** Inter Milan beat Lazio 3-0 (one match) – Paris
**1999** Parma beat Marseille 3-0 (one match) – Moscow
**2000** Galatasaray beat Arsenal 4-1 on penalties after 0-0 (one match) – Copenhagen
**2001** Liverpool beat Alaves 5-4 on golden goal (one match) – Dortmund
**2002** Feyenoord beat Borussia Dortmund 3-2 (one match) – Rotterdam
**2003** FC Porto beat Celtic 3-2 on silver goal (one match) – Seville
**2004** Valencia beat Marseille 2-0 (one match) – Gothenburg
**2005** CSKA Moscow beat Sporting Lisbon 3-1 (one match) – Lisbon
**2006** Sevilla beat Middlesbrough 4-0 (one match) – Eindhoven
**2007** Sevilla beat Espanyol 3-1 on penalties after 2-2 (one match) – Hampden Park
**2008** Zenit St Petersburg beat Rangers 2-0 (one match) – City of Manchester Stadium
**2009†** Shakhtar Donetsk beat Werder Bremen 2-1 (one match) – Istanbul

# EUROPA LEAGUE FINALS

**2010†** Atletico Madrid beat Fulham 2-1 (one match) – Hamburg
**2011** Porto beat Braga 1-0 (one match) – Dublin
**2012** Atletico Madrid beat Athletic Bilbao 3-0 (one match) – Bucharest
**2013** Chelsea beat Benfica 2-1 (one match) – Amsterdam
**2014** Sevilla beat Benfica 4-2 on penalties after 0-0 (one match) – Turin
**2015** Sevilla beat Dnipro 3-2 (one match) – Warsaw
**2016** Sevilla beat Liverpool 3-1 (one match) – Basle
**2017** Manchester Utd beat Ajax 2-0 (one match) – Stockholm
**2018** Atletico Madrid beat Marseille 3-0 (one match) – Lyon
(† After extra-time)

# FAIRS CUP FINALS

**(As UEFA Cup previously known)**

**1958** Barcelona beat London 8-2 on agg (2-2a, 6-0h)
**1960** Barcelona beat Birmingham 4-1 on agg (0-0a, 4-1h)
**1961** AS Roma beat Birmingham City 4-2 on agg (2-2a, 2-0h)
**1962** Valencia beat Barcelona 7-3 on agg (6-2h, 1-1a)
**1963** Valencia beat Dynamo Zagreb 4-1 on agg (2-1a, 2-0h)
**1964** Real Zaragoza beat Valencia 2-1 (Barcelona)
**1965** Ferencvaros beat Juventus 1-0 (Turin)
**1966** Barcelona beat Real Zaragoza 4-3 on agg (0-1h, 4-2a)
**1967** Dinamo Zagreb beat Leeds Utd 2-0 on agg (2-0h, 0-0a)
**1968** Leeds Utd beat Ferencvaros 1-0 on agg (1-0h, 0-0a)
**1969** Newcastle Utd beat Ujpest Dozsa 6-2 on agg (3-0h, 3-2a)
**1970** Arsenal beat Anderlecht 4-3 on agg (1-3a, 3-0h)
**1971** Leeds Utd beat Juventus on away goals after 3-3 agg (2-2a, 1-1h)

# CUP-WINNERS' CUP FINALS

**1961** Fiorentina beat Rangers 4-1 on agg (2-0 Glasgow first leg, 2-1 Florence second leg)
**1962** Atletico Madrid beat Fiorentina 3-0 (replay Stuttgart, after a 1-1 draw, Glasgow)
**1963** Tottenham beat Atletico Madrid 5-1 (Rotterdam)
**1964** Sporting Lisbon beat MTK Budapest 1-0 (replay Antwerp, after a 3-3 draw, Brussels)
**1965** West Ham Utd beat Munich 1860 2-0 (Wembley)
**1966†** Borussia Dortmund beat Liverpool 2-1 (Glasgow)
**1967†** Bayern Munich beat Rangers 1-0 (Nuremberg)
**1968** AC Milan beat SV Hamburg 2-0 (Rotterdam)
**1969** Slovan Bratislava beat Barcelona 3-2 (Basle)
**1970** Manchester City beat Gornik Zabrze 2-1 (Vienna)
**1971†** Chelsea beat Real Madrid 2-1 (replay Athens, after a 1-1 draw, Athens)
**1972** Rangers beat Moscow Dynamo 3-2 (Barcelona)
**1973** AC Milan beat Leeds Utd 1-0 (Salonika)
**1974** Magdeburg beat AC Milan 2-0 (Rotterdam)
**1975** Dynamo Kiev beat Ferencvaros 3-0 (Basle)
**1976** Anderlecht beat West Ham Utd 4-2 (Brussels)
**1977** SV Hamburg beat Anderlecht 2-0 (Amsterdam)
**1978** Anderlecht beat Austria WAC 4-0 (Paris)
**1979†** Barcelona beat Fortuna Dusseldorf 4-3 (Basle)
**1980†** Valencia beat Arsenal 5-4 on penalties after a 0-0 draw (Brussels)
**1981** Dinamo Tbilisi beat Carl Zeiss Jena 2-1 (Dusseldorf)
**1982** Barcelona beat Standard Liege 2-1 (Barcelona)
**1983†** Aberdeen beat Real Madrid 2-1 (Gothenburg)
**1984** Juventus beat Porto 2-1 (Basle)
**1985** Everton beat Rapid Vienna 3-1 (Rotterdam)
**1986** Dynamo Kiev beat Atletico Madrid 3-0 (Lyon)
**1987** Ajax beat Lokomotiv Leipzig 1-0 (Athens)
**1988** Mechelen beat Ajax 1-0 (Strasbourg)
**1989** Barcelona beat Sampdoria 2-0 (Berne)
**1990** Sampdoria beat Anderlecht 2-0 (Gothenburg)
**1991** Manchester Utd beat Barcelona 2-1 (Rotterdam)
**1992** Werder Bremen beat Monaco 2-0 (Lisbon)
**1993** Parma beat Royal Antwerp 3-1 (Wembley)

**1994** Arsenal beat Parma 1-0 (Copenhagen)
**1995†** Real Zaragoza beat Arsenal 2-1 (Paris)
**1996** Paris St Germain beat Rapid Vienna 1-0 (Brussels)
**1997** Barcelona beat Paris St Germain 1-0 (Rotterdam)
**1998** Chelsea beat VfB Stuttgart 1-0 (Stockholm)
**1999** Lazio beat Real Mallorca 2-1 (Villa Park, Birmingham)
(† After extra time)

# EUROPEAN SUPER CUP RESULTS

**1972*** Ajax beat Rangers 6-3 on agg (3-1, 3-2)
**1973** Ajax beat AC Milan 6-1 on agg (0-1, 6-0)
**1974** Bayern Munich and Magdeburg did not play
**1975** Dynamo Kiev beat Bayern Munich 3-0 on agg (1-0, 2-0)
**1976** Anderlecht beat Bayern Munich 5-3 on agg (1-2, 4-1)
**1977** Liverpool beat Hamburg 7-1 on agg (1-1, 6-0)
**1978** Anderlecht beat Liverpool 4-3 on agg (3-1, 1-2)
**1979** Nottm Forest beat Barcelona 2-1 on agg (1-0, 1-1)
**1980** Valencia beat Nottm Forest on away goal after 2-2 agg (1-2, 1-0)
**1981** Liverpool and Dinamo Tbilisi did not play
**1982** Aston Villa beat Barcelona 3-1 on agg (0-1, 3-0 aet)
**1983** Aberdeen beat Hamburg 2-0 on agg (0-0, 2-0)
**1984** Juventus beat Liverpool 2-0 – one match (Turin)
**1985** Juventus and Everton did not play
**1986** Steaua Bucharest beat Dynamo Kiev 1-0 – one match (Monaco)
**1987** Porto beat Ajax 2-0 on agg (1-0, 1-0)
**1988** Mechelen beat PSV Eindhoven 3-1 on agg (3-0, 0-1)
**1989** AC Milan beat Barcelona 2-1 on agg (1-1, 1-0)
**1990** AC Milan beat Sampdoria 3-1 on agg (1-1, 2-0)
**1991** Manchester Utd beat Red Star Belgrade 1-0 – one match (Old Trafford)
**1992** Barcelona beat Werder Bremen 3-2 on agg (1-1, 2-1)
**1993** Parma beat AC Milan 2-1 on agg (0-1, 2-0 aet)
**1994** AC Milan beat Arsenal 2-0 on agg (0-0, 2-0)
**1995** Ajax beat Real Zaragoza 5-1 on agg (1-1, 4-0)
**1996** Juventus beat Paris St Germain 9-2 on agg (6-1, 3-1)
**1997** Barcelona beat Borussia Dortmund 3-1 on agg (2-0, 1-1)
**1998** Chelsea beat Real Madrid 1-0 (Monaco)
**1999** Lazio beat Manchester Utd 1-0 (Monaco)
**2000** Galatasaray beat Real Madrid 2-1 – aet, golden goal (Monaco)
**2001** Liverpool beat Bayern Munich 3-2 (Monaco)
**2002** Real Madrid beat Feyenoord 3-1 (Monaco)
**2003** AC Milan beat Porto 1-0 (Monaco)
**2004** Valencia beat Porto 2-1 (Monaco)
**2005** Liverpool beat CSKA Moscow 3-1 – aet (Monaco)
**2006** Sevilla beat Barcelona 3-0 (Monaco)
**2007** AC Milan beat Sevilla 3-1 (Monaco)
**2008** Zenit St Petersburg beat Manchester Utd 2-1 (Monaco)
**2009** Barcelona beat Shakhtar Donetsk 1-0 – aet (Monaco)
**2010** Atletico Madrid beat Inter Milan 2-0 (Monaco)
**2011** Barcelona beat Porto 2-0 (Monaco)
**2012** Atletico Madrid beat Chelsea 4-1 (Monaco)
**2013** Bayern Munich beat Chelsea 5-4 on pens, aet – 2-2 (Prague)
**2014** Real Madrid beat Sevilla 2-0 (Cardiff)

**2015** Barcelona beat Sevilla 5-4 – aet (Tbilisi)
**2016** Real Madrid beat Sevilla 3-2 – aet (Trondheim)
**2017** Real Madrid beat Manchester Utd 2-1 (Skopje)
*not recognised by UEFA; from 1998 one match

# INTER-CONTINENTAL CUP

| *Year* | *Winners* | *Runners-up* | *Score* |
|---|---|---|---|
| **1960** | Real Madrid (Spa) | Penarol (Uru) | 0-0 5-1 |
| **1961** | Penarol (Uru) | Benfica (Por) | 0-1 2-1 5-0 |
| **1962** | Santos (Bra) | Benfica (Por) | 3-2 5-2 |
| **1963** | Santos (Bra) | AC Milan (Ita) | 2-4 4-2 1-0 |
| **1964** | Inter Milan (Ita) | Independiente (Arg) | 0-1 2-0 1-0 |
| **1965** | Inter Milan (Ita) | Independiente (Arg) | 3-0 0-0 |
| **1966** | Penarol (Uru) | Real Madrid (Spa) | 2-0 2-0 |
| **1967** | Racing (Arg) | Celtic | 0-1 2-1 1-0 |
| **1968** | Estudiantes (Arg) | Manchester Utd | 1-0 1-1 |
| **1969** | AC Milan (Ita) | Estudiantes (Arg) | 3-0 1-2 |
| **1970** | Feyenoord (Hol) | Estudiantes (Arg) | 2-2 1-0 |
| **1971** | Nacional (Uru) | Panathanaikos (Gre) | *1-1 2-1 |
| **1972** | Ajax (Hol) | Independiente (Arg) | 1-1 3-0 |
| **1973** | Independiente (Arg) | Juventus* (Ita) | 1-0 # |
| **1974** | Atletico Madrid (Spa)* | Independiente (Arg) | 0-1 2-0 |
| **1975** | Not played | | |
| **1976** | Bayern Munich (WGer) | Cruzeiro (Bra) | 2-0 0-0 |
| **1977** | Boca Juniors (Arg) | Borussia Mönchengladbach* (WGer) | 2-2 3-0 |
| **1978** | Not played | | |
| **1979** | Olimpia Asuncion (Par) | Malmö* (Swe) | 1-0 2-1 |
| **1980** | Nacional (Arg) | Nott'm Forest | 1-0 |
| **1981** | Flamengo (Bra) | Liverpool | 3-0 |
| **1982** | Penarol (Uru) | Aston Villa | 2-0 |
| **1983** | Porto Alegre (Bra) | SV Hamburg (WGer) | 2-1 |
| **1984** | Independiente (Arg) | Liverpool | 1-0 |
| **1985** | Juventus (Ita) | Argentinos Juniors (Arg) | 2-2 (aet) |
| | | *(Juventus won 4-2 on penalties)* | |
| **1986** | River Plate (Arg) | Steaua Bucharest (Rom) | 1-0 |
| **1987** | Porto (Por) | Penarol (Uru) | 2-1 (aet) |
| **1988** | Nacional (Uru) | PSV Eindhoven (Hol) | 1-1 (aet) |
| | | *(Nacional won 7-6 on penalties)* | |
| **1989** | AC Milan (Ita) | Nacional (Col) | 1-0 (aet) |
| **1990** | AC Milan (Ita) | Olimpia Asuncion (Par) | 3-0 |
| **1991** | Red Star (Yug) | Colo Colo (Chi) | 3-0 |
| **1992** | Sao Paulo (Bra) | Barcelona (Spa) | 2-1 |
| **1993** | Sao Paulo (Bra) | AC Milan (Ita) | 3-2 |
| **1994** | Velez Sarsfield (Arg) | AC Milan (Ita) | 2-0 |
| **1995** | Ajax (Hol) | Gremio (Bra) | 0-0 (aet) |
| | | *(Ajax won 4-3 on penalties)* | |
| **1996** | Juventus (Ita) | River Plate (Arg) | 1-0 |
| **1997** | Borussia Dortmund (Ger) | Cruzeiro (Arg) | 2-0 |
| **1998** | Real Madrid (Spa) | Vasco da Gama (Bra) | 2-1 |
| **1999** | Manchester Utd | Palmeiras (Bra) | 1-0 |
| **2000** | Boca Juniors (Arg) | Real Madrid (Spa) | 2-1 |
| **2001** | Bayern Munich (Ger) | Boca Juniors (Arg) | 1-0 |

| | | | |
|---|---|---|---|
| **2002** | Real Madrid (Spa) | Olimpia Ascuncion (Par) | 2-0 |
| **2003** | Boca Juniors (Arg) | AC Milan (Ita) | 1-1 |
| | (Boca Juniors won 3-1 on penalties) | | |
| **2004** | FC Porto (Por) | Caldas (Col) | 0-0 |

*(FC Porto won 8-7 on penalties)*

Played as a single match in Japan since 1980

* European Cup runners-up # One match only

Summary: 43 contests; South America 22 wins, Europe 23 wins

# CLUB WORLD CHAMPIONSHIP

| | | |
|---|---|---|
| **2005** | Sao Paulo (Bra) beat Liverpool | 1-0 |
| **2006** | Internacional (Bra) beat Barcelona (Spa) | 1-0 |
| **2007** | AC Milan (Ita) beat Boca Juniors (Arg) | 4-2 |

# CLUB WORLD CUP

| | | |
|---|---|---|
| **2008** | Manchester Utd beat Liga de Quito (Ecu) | 1-0 |
| **2009** | Barcelona beat Estudiantes (Arg) | 2-1 (aet) |
| **2010** | Inter Milan (Ita) beat TP Mazembe (DR Congo) | 3-0 |
| **2011** | Barcelona beat Santos (Bra) | 4-0 |
| **2012** | Corinthians (Bra) beat Chelsea | 1-0 |
| **2013** | Bayern Munich (Ger) beat Raja Casablanca (Mar) | 2-0 |
| **2014** | Real Madrid (Spa) beat San Lorenzo (Arg) | 2-0 |
| **2015** | Barcelona beat River Plate (Arg) | 3-0 |
| **2016** | Real Madrid beat Kashima Antlers (Jap) | 4-2 (aet) |
| **2017** | Real Madrid beat Gremio (Bra) | 1-0 |

## RECORD-BREAKER CALLS IT A DAY

Non-league football's record-breaking veteran retired at the end of last season after 1,277 matches spanning 30 years. Goalkeeper Paul Bastock called it a day at 47 when helping Wisbech Town finish runners-up in the United Counties Premier Division. After winning the FA Youth Cup with Coventry in 1987, he joined the first of his 19 clubs in the lower reaches of the English game. More than half of his games were in two spells with Boston United over the course of 13 years. Former England goalkeeper Peter Shilton holds the record for first-class club appearances with 1,249.

## HAT-TRICKS AT THE DOUBLE

Chelmsford City striker Scott Fenwick scored a hat-trick of penalties in successive National League South matches last season. The first came on his 28th birthday in a 4-2 win over Whitehawk. Five days later, he scored all four goals in victory over East Thurrock by the same scoreline, the final three from the spot. Fenwick was on the books of Newcastle, Sunderland and Middlesbrough as a youngster and had two seasons with Hartlepool in League Two.

# EUROPEAN TABLES 2017–2018

## FRANCE – LIGUE 1

| | P | W | D | L | F | A | GD | Pts |
|---|---|---|---|---|---|---|---|---|
| Paris SG | 38 | 29 | 6 | 3 | 108 | 29 | 79 | 93 |
| Monaco | 38 | 24 | 8 | 6 | 85 | 45 | 40 | 80 |
| Lyon | 38 | 23 | 9 | 6 | 87 | 43 | 44 | 78 |
| Marseille | 38 | 22 | 11 | 5 | 80 | 47 | 33 | 77 |
| Rennes | 38 | 16 | 10 | 12 | 50 | 44 | 6 | 58 |
| Bordeaux | 38 | 16 | 7 | 15 | 53 | 48 | 5 | 55 |
| St Etienne | 38 | 15 | 10 | 13 | 47 | 50 | -3 | 55 |
| Nice | 38 | 15 | 9 | 14 | 53 | 52 | 1 | 54 |
| Nantes | 38 | 14 | 10 | 14 | 36 | 41 | -5 | 52 |
| Montpellier | 38 | 11 | 18 | 9 | 36 | 33 | 3 | 51 |
| Dijon | 38 | 13 | 9 | 16 | 55 | 73 | -18 | 48 |
| Guingamp | 38 | 12 | 11 | 15 | 48 | 59 | -11 | 47 |
| Amiens | 38 | 12 | 9 | 17 | 37 | 42 | -5 | 45 |
| Angers | 38 | 9 | 14 | 15 | 42 | 52 | -10 | 41 |
| Strasbourg | 38 | 9 | 11 | 18 | 44 | 67 | -23 | 38 |
| Caen | 38 | 10 | 8 | 20 | 27 | 52 | -25 | 38 |
| Lille | 38 | 10 | 8 | 20 | 41 | 67 | -26 | 38 |
| Toulouse | 38 | 9 | 10 | 19 | 38 | 54 | -16 | 37 |
| Troyes | 38 | 9 | 6 | 23 | 32 | 59 | -27 | 33 |
| Metz | 38 | 6 | 8 | 24 | 34 | 76 | -42 | 26 |

**Leading league scorers**: 28 Cavani (Paris SG); 22 Thauvin (Marseille); 19 Depay (Lyon), Neymar (Paris SG); 18 Balotelli (Nice), Diaz (Lyon), Falcao (Monaco), Fekir (Lyon); 17 Ekambi (Angers); 16 Plea (Nice)

**Cup Final**: Paris SG 2 (Lo Celso 26, Cavani 74 pen) Les Herbiers 0

## HOLLAND – EREDIVISIE

| | P | W | D | L | F | A | GD | Pts |
|---|---|---|---|---|---|---|---|---|
| PSV Eindhoven | 34 | 26 | 5 | 3 | 87 | 39 | 48 | 83 |
| Ajax | 34 | 25 | 4 | 5 | 89 | 33 | 56 | 79 |
| Alkmaar | 34 | 22 | 5 | 7 | 72 | 38 | 34 | 71 |
| Feyenoord | 34 | 20 | 6 | 8 | 76 | 39 | 37 | 66 |
| Utrecht | 34 | 14 | 12 | 8 | 58 | 53 | 5 | 54 |
| Vitesse | 34 | 13 | 10 | 11 | 63 | 47 | 16 | 49 |
| Den Haag | 34 | 13 | 8 | 13 | 45 | 53 | -8 | 47 |
| Heerenveen | 34 | 12 | 10 | 12 | 48 | 53 | -5 | 46 |
| Zwolle | 34 | 12 | 8 | 14 | 42 | 54 | -12 | 44 |
| Heracles | 34 | 11 | 9 | 14 | 50 | 64 | -14 | 42 |
| Excelsior | 34 | 11 | 7 | 16 | 41 | 56 | -15 | 40 |
| Groningen | 34 | 8 | 14 | 12 | 50 | 50 | 0 | 38 |
| Willem | 34 | 10 | 7 | 17 | 50 | 63 | -13 | 37 |
| Breda | 34 | 9 | 7 | 18 | 41 | 57 | -16 | 34 |
| Venlo | 34 | 7 | 13 | 14 | 35 | 54 | -19 | 34 |
| Roda | 34 | 8 | 6 | 20 | 42 | 69 | -27 | 30 |
| Sparta Rotterdam | 34 | 7 | 6 | 21 | 34 | 75 | -41 | 27 |
| Twente | 34 | 5 | 9 | 20 | 37 | 63 | -26 | 24 |

**Leading league scorers**: 21 Jahanbakhsh (Alkmaar 21); 19 Johnsen (Den Haag); 18 Berghuis (Feyenoord), Weghorst (Alkmaar); 17 Lozano (PSV Eindhoven); 16 Sol (Willem); 15 Linssen (Vitesse); 14 Neres (Ajax), Matavz (Vitesse), Van Ginkel (PSV Eindhoven)

**Cup Final**: Feyenoord 3 (Jorgensen 28, Van Persie 57, Toornstra 90+3) Alkmaar 0

## GERMANY – BUNDESLIGA

| | P | W | D | L | F | A | GD | Pts |
|---|---|---|---|---|---|---|---|---|
| Bayern Munich | 34 | 27 | 3 | 4 | 92 | 28 | 64 | 84 |
| Schalke | 34 | 18 | 9 | 7 | 53 | 37 | 16 | 63 |
| Hoffenheim | 34 | 15 | 10 | 9 | 66 | 48 | 18 | 55 |
| Borussia Dortmund | 34 | 15 | 10 | 9 | 64 | 47 | 17 | 55 |
| Bayer Leverkusen | 34 | 15 | 10 | 9 | 58 | 44 | 14 | 55 |
| Leipzig | 34 | 15 | 8 | 11 | 57 | 53 | 4 | 53 |
| Stuttgart | 34 | 15 | 6 | 13 | 36 | 36 | 0 | 51 |
| Eintracht Frankfurt | 34 | 14 | 7 | 13 | 45 | 45 | 0 | 49 |
| Borussia M'gladbach | 34 | 13 | 8 | 13 | 47 | 52 | -5 | 47 |
| Hertha Berlin | 34 | 10 | 13 | 11 | 43 | 46 | -3 | 43 |
| Werder Bremen | 34 | 10 | 12 | 12 | 37 | 40 | -3 | 42 |
| Augsburg | 34 | 10 | 11 | 13 | 43 | 46 | -3 | 41 |
| Hannover | 34 | 10 | 9 | 15 | 44 | 54 | -10 | 39 |
| Mainz | 34 | 9 | 9 | 16 | 38 | 52 | -14 | 36 |
| Freiburg | 34 | 8 | 12 | 14 | 32 | 56 | -24 | 36 |
| Wolfsburg | 34 | 6 | 15 | 13 | 36 | 48 | -12 | 33 |
| Hamburg | 34 | 8 | 7 | 19 | 29 | 53 | -24 | 31 |
| Cologne | 34 | 5 | 7 | 22 | 35 | 70 | -35 | 22 |

**Leading league scorers**: 29 Lewandowski (Bayern Munich); 15 Petersen (Freiburg); 14 Fullkrug (Hannover), Uth (Hoffenheim), Volland (Bayer Leverkusen); 13 Aubameyang (Borussia Dortmund), Gregoritsch (Augsburg), Kramaric (Hoffenheim), Werner (Leipzig)
**Cup Final**: Eintracht Frankfurt 3 (Rebic 11, 82, Gacinovic 90+6) Bayern Munich 1 (Lewandowski 53)

## ITALY – SERIE A

| | P | W | D | L | F | A | GD | Pts |
|---|---|---|---|---|---|---|---|---|
| Juventus | 38 | 30 | 5 | 3 | 86 | 24 | 62 | 95 |
| Napoli | 38 | 28 | 7 | 3 | 77 | 29 | 48 | 91 |
| Roma | 38 | 23 | 8 | 7 | 61 | 28 | 33 | 77 |
| Inter Milan | 38 | 20 | 12 | 6 | 66 | 30 | 36 | 72 |
| Lazio | 38 | 21 | 9 | 8 | 89 | 49 | 40 | 72 |
| AC Milan | 38 | 18 | 10 | 10 | 56 | 42 | 14 | 64 |
| Atalanta | 38 | 16 | 12 | 10 | 57 | 39 | 18 | 60 |
| Fiorentina | 38 | 16 | 9 | 13 | 54 | 46 | 8 | 57 |
| Torino | 38 | 13 | 15 | 10 | 54 | 46 | 8 | 54 |
| Sampdoria | 38 | 16 | 6 | 16 | 56 | 60 | -4 | 54 |
| Sassuolo | 38 | 11 | 10 | 17 | 29 | 59 | -30 | 43 |
| Genoa | 38 | 11 | 8 | 19 | 33 | 43 | -10 | 41 |
| Chievo | 38 | 10 | 10 | 18 | 36 | 59 | -23 | 40 |
| Udinese | 38 | 12 | 4 | 22 | 48 | 63 | -15 | 40 |
| Bologna | 38 | 11 | 6 | 21 | 40 | 52 | -12 | 39 |
| Cagliari | 38 | 11 | 6 | 21 | 33 | 61 | -28 | 39 |
| SPAL | 38 | 8 | 14 | 16 | 39 | 59 | -20 | 38 |
| Crotone | 38 | 9 | 8 | 21 | 40 | 66 | -26 | 35 |
| Verona | 38 | 7 | 4 | 27 | 30 | 78 | -48 | 25 |
| Benevento | 38 | 6 | 3 | 29 | 33 | 84 | -51 | 21 |

**Leading league scorers**: 29 Icardi (Inter Milan), Immobile (Lazio); 22 Dybala (Juventus); 19 Quagliarella (Sampdoria); 18 Mertens (Napoli); 16 Dzeko (Roma), Higuain (Juventus); 14 Simeone (Fiorentina); 12 Falque (Torino), Inglese (Chievo), Lasagna (Udinese), Milinkovic-Savic (Lazio)
**Cup Final**: Juventus 4 (Benatia 56, 64, Douglas Costa 61, Kalinic 76 og) AC Milan 0

## PORTUGAL – PRIMEIRA LIGA

| | P | W | D | L | F | A | GD | Pts |
|---|---|---|---|---|---|---|---|---|
| Porto | 34 | 28 | 4 | 2 | 82 | 18 | 64 | 88 |
| Benfica | 34 | 25 | 6 | 3 | 80 | 22 | 58 | 81 |
| Sporting Lisbon | 34 | 24 | 6 | 4 | 63 | 24 | 39 | 78 |
| Sporting Braga | 34 | 24 | 3 | 7 | 74 | 29 | 45 | 75 |
| Rio Ave | 34 | 15 | 6 | 13 | 40 | 42 | -2 | 51 |
| Chaves | 34 | 13 | 8 | 13 | 47 | 55 | -8 | 47 |
| Maritimo | 34 | 13 | 8 | 13 | 36 | 49 | -13 | 47 |
| Boavista | 34 | 13 | 6 | 15 | 35 | 44 | -9 | 45 |
| Guimaraes | 34 | 13 | 4 | 17 | 45 | 56 | -11 | 43 |
| Portimonense | 34 | 10 | 8 | 16 | 52 | 60 | -8 | 38 |
| Tondela | 34 | 10 | 8 | 16 | 41 | 50 | -9 | 38 |
| Belenenses | 34 | 9 | 10 | 15 | 33 | 46 | -13 | 37 |
| Aves | 34 | 9 | 7 | 18 | 36 | 51 | -15 | 34 |
| Setubal | 34 | 7 | 11 | 16 | 39 | 62 | -23 | 32 |
| Morierense | 34 | 8 | 8 | 18 | 29 | 50 | -21 | 32 |
| Feirense | 34 | 9 | 4 | 21 | 32 | 48 | -16 | 31 |
| Pacos Ferreira | 34 | 7 | 9 | 18 | 33 | 59 | -26 | 30 |
| Estoril | 34 | 8 | 6 | 20 | 29 | 61 | -32 | 30 |

**Leading league scorers**: 34 Jonas (Benfica); 27 Bas Dost (Sporting Lisbon); 21 Marega (Porto); 15 Aboubakar (Porto), Fabricio (Portimonense), Raphinha (Guimaraes); 13 Paulino (Sporting Braga); 11 Bruno Fernandes (Sporting Lisbon), Horta (Sporting Braga), Hurtado (Guimaraes), Oliveira (Chaves)
**Cup Final**: Aves 2 (Guedes 16, 75) Sporting Lisbon 1 (Montero 85)

## SPAIN – LA LIGA

| | P | W | D | L | F | A | GD | Pts |
|---|---|---|---|---|---|---|---|---|
| Barcelona | 38 | 28 | 9 | 1 | 99 | 29 | 70 | 93 |
| Atletico Madrid | 38 | 23 | 10 | 5 | 58 | 22 | 36 | 79 |
| Real Madrid | 38 | 22 | 10 | 6 | 94 | 44 | 50 | 76 |
| Valencia | 38 | 22 | 7 | 9 | 65 | 38 | 27 | 73 |
| Villarreal | 38 | 18 | 7 | 13 | 57 | 50 | 7 | 61 |
| Real Betis | 38 | 18 | 6 | 14 | 60 | 61 | -1 | 60 |
| Sevilla | 38 | 17 | 7 | 14 | 49 | 58 | -9 | 58 |
| Getafe | 38 | 15 | 10 | 13 | 42 | 33 | 9 | 55 |
| Eibar | 38 | 14 | 9 | 15 | 44 | 50 | -6 | 51 |
| Girona | 38 | 14 | 9 | 15 | 50 | 59 | -9 | 51 |
| Real Sociedad | 38 | 14 | 7 | 17 | 66 | 59 | 7 | 49 |
| Celta Vigo | 38 | 13 | 10 | 15 | 59 | 60 | -1 | 49 |
| Espanyol | 38 | 12 | 13 | 13 | 36 | 42 | -6 | 49 |
| Alaves | 38 | 15 | 2 | 21 | 40 | 50 | -10 | 47 |
| Levante | 38 | 11 | 13 | 14 | 44 | 58 | -14 | 46 |
| Athletic Bilbao | 38 | 10 | 13 | 15 | 41 | 49 | -8 | 43 |
| Leganes | 38 | 12 | 7 | 19 | 34 | 51 | -17 | 43 |
| Deportivo | 38 | 6 | 11 | 21 | 38 | 76 | -38 | 29 |
| La Palmas | 38 | 5 | 7 | 26 | 24 | 74 | -50 | 22 |
| Malaga | 38 | 5 | 5 | 28 | 24 | 61 | -37 | 20 |

**Leading league scorers**: 34 Messi (Barcelona); 26 Ronaldo (Real Madrid); 25 Suarez (Barcelona); 22 Aspas (Celta Vigo); 21 Stuani (Girona); 19 Griezmann (Atletico Madrid); 17 Gomez (Celta Vigo); 16 Bale (Real Madrid), Moreno (Espanyol), Rodrigo (Valencia)
**Cup Final**: Barcelona 5 (Suarez 14, 40, Messi 31, Iniesta 52, Coutinho 69 pen) Seville 0

# BRITISH AND IRISH INTERNATIONALS 2017–18

(*denotes new cap)

# WORLD CUP QUALIFIERS

## GROUP C

**SAN MARINO 0 NORTHERN IRELAND 3**
**Serravalle (2,544); Friday, September 1, 2017**

**San Marino** (4-5-1): A Simoncini, D Simoncini (Gasperoni 76), Bonini, Cervellini, Grandoni, Biordi (Vitaioli 57), Battistini, Berardi (Golinucci 81), Rinaldi, Palazzi, Bernardi. **Booked**: Bernadi, D Simoncini, Biordi, Bonini
**Northern Ireland** (4-4-2): McGovern, C McLaughlin, Hughes, J Evans, Brunt, Magennis, Norwood, Davis, Dallas (McGinn 80), Washington (C Evans 78), K Lafferty (Ferguson 61).
**Scorers**: Magennis (70, 75), Davis (79 pen)
**Referee**: E Jorgji (Albania). **Half-time**: 0-0

**NORTHERN IRELAND 2 CZECH REPUBLIC 0**
**Windsor Park (18,167); Monday September 4, 2017**

**Northern Ireland** (4-1-4-1): McGovern, C McLaughlin, Hughes, J Evans, Brunt, Norwood, Magennis (Ferguson 84), Davis, C Evans, Dallas (K Lafferty 74), Washington (Hodson 58).
**Scorers**: J Evans (28), Brunt (41). **Booked**: J Evans
**Czech Republic** (3-4-3): Vaclik, Suchy, Kalas, Novak (Dockal 66), Boril, Soucek, Darida, Gebre Selassie, Krejci (Kliment 55), Krmencik. Jankto (Husbauer 55). **Booked**: Kalas, Husbauer
**Referee**: D Orsato (Italy). **Half-time**: 2-0

**NORTHERN IRELAND 1 GERMANY 3**
**Windsor Park (18,104); Thursday, October 5, 2017**

**Northern Ireland** (5-4-1): McGovern, Hodson (Dallas 46), J Evans (*Saville 80), McAuley, C McLaughlin, Brunt, Magennis, C Evans, Davis, Norwood, K Lafferty (Washington 68). **Scorer**: Magennis (90+3)
**Germany** (4-2-3-1): Ter Stegen, Kimmich, Boateng, Hummels, Plattenhardt, Rudy, Kroos, Draxler (Sane 71), Muller (Stindl 83), Goretzka (Emre Can 66), Wagner. **Scorers**: Rudy (2), Wagner (21), Kimmich (86)
**Referee**: D Makkelie (Holland). **Half-time**: 0-2

**NORWAY 1 NORTHERN IRELAND 0**
**Oslo (10,244); Sunday, October 8, 2017**

**Norway** (4-4-2): Nyland, Svensson, Nordveit, Reginiussen, Meling, M Elyounoussi (T Elyounoussi 72), Henriksen (Seinaes 83), Berge, Johansen (Linnes 87), Soderlund, Sorloth.
**Scorer**: Brunt (71 og)
**Northern Ireland** (4-5-1): McGovern, C McLaughlin, McAuley, J Evans, Brunt, Magennis, C Evans (Ferguson 79), Norwood (Saville 46), Davis, Dallas, Washington (K Lafferty 69).
**Booked**: Brunt
**Referee**: S Boyko (Ukraine). **Half-time**: 0-0

## GROUP D

**WALES 1 AUSTRIA 0**
**Cardiff City Stadium (32,633); Saturday, September 2, 2017**

**Wales** (3-4-2-1): Hennessey, Chester, A Williams, B Davies, Gunter, Ramsey, Edwards,

Richards (King 46), Bale, Lawrence (*Woodburn 69), Vokes (Robson-Kanu 69). **Scorer**: Woodburn (74). **Booked**: Chester
**Austria** (4-2-3-1): Lindner, Lainer, Dragovic, Prodl (Danso 27), Hinteregger, Baumgartlinger, Ilsanker, Sabitzer (Gregoritsch 79), Alaba, Arnautovic, Harnik (Janko 81). **Booked**: Prodl, Baumgartlinger
**Referee**: O Hategan (Romania). **Half-time**: 0-0

### GEORGIA 1 REPUBLIC OF IRELAND 1
**Tbilisi (19,669); Saturday, September 2, 2017**

**Georgia** (4-2-3-1): Makaridze, Kashia, Kverkvelia, Kakabadze, Navalovsky, Ananidze, Kazaishvili (Khocholava 90), Kvekveskiri, Gviliia, Jighouri (Chanturia 75), Kvilitaia (Merebashvili 85). **Scorer**: Kazaishvili (34). **Booked**: Kvekeskiri, Jighauri
**Republic of Ireland** (4-2-3-1): Randolph, Christie, Duffy, Clark, Ward, Whelan (Murphy 79), Arter (McGeady 62), Walters, Brady, McClean, S Long. **Scorer**: Duffy (4). **Booked**: McClean
**Referee**: I Kruzliak (Slovakia). **Half-time**: 1-1

### MOLDOVA 0 WALES 2
**Chisinau (10,272); Tuesday, September 5, 2017**

**Moldova** (4-2-3-1): Cebanu, Bordian, Posmac, Epureanu, Rozgoniuc, Anton, Ionita (Bugaev 85), Graur (Ambros 85), Pascenco (Cojocari 70), Dedov, Ginsari. **Booked**: Epureanu, Dedov, Graur
**Wales** (4-2-3-1): Hennessey, Gunter, Chester, A Williams, B Davies, Allen, King (Vokes 67), Bale, Ramsey, Lawrence (Woodburn 60), Robson-Kanu (Edwards 88). **Scorers**: Robson-Kanu (80), Ramsey (90+3). **Booked**: King, Robson-Kanu
**Referee**: P Raczkowski (Poland). **Half-time**: 0-0

### REPUBLIC OF IRELAND 0 SERBIA 1
**Aviva Stadium (50,153); Tuesday, September 5, 2017**

**Republic of Ireland** (4-1-3-2): Randolph, Christie, Duffy, Clark, Ward (O'Dowda 72), Meyler (Hourihane 79), Brady, Hoolahan (Murphy 62), McClean, Walters, S Long. **Booked**: Brady, McClean
**Serbia** (3-4-2-1): Stojkovic, Ivanovic, Maksimovic, Vukovic, Rukavina, Milivojevic, Matic, Kolarov, Tadic (Gudlj 81), Kostic (S Mitrovic 72), A Mitrovic (Prijovic 79). **Scorer**: Kolarov (55). **Booked**: Rukavina, Stojkovic. **Sent off**: Maksimovic (68)
**Referee**: C Cakir (Turkey). **Half-time**: 0-0

### GEORGIA 0 WALES 1
**Tbilisi (22,290): Friday, October 6, 2017**

**Georgia** (4-3-2-1): Loria, Kababadze, Kverkvelia, Kashia, Navalovski, Merebashvili, Kverkveskiri (Jighouri 76), Kazaishvili, Kankava, Gvilia (Khocholava 89), Kvilitaia (Skhirtladze 76)
**Wales** (4-3-2-1): Hennessey, Gunter, Chester, A Williams, B Davies, King, Allen, Ledley (Edwards 81), Lawrence (Woodburn 90+1), Ramsey, Vokes (Robson-Kanu 74). **Scorer**: Lawrence (49). **Booked**: Lawrence
**Referee**: J Gil (Spain). **Half-time**: 0-0

### REPUBLIC OF IRELAND 2 MOLDOVA 0
**Aviva Stadium (50,560); Friday, October 6, 2017**

**Republic of Ireland** (4-1-3-2): Randolph, Christie, Duffy, Clark, Ward, Meyler, Hendrick, Hoolahan (McGeady 78), O'Dowda, S Long (Maguire 83), Murphy (Arter 78). **Scorer**: Murphy (2, 19). **Booked**: Arter
**Moldova** (4-1-4-1): Cebanu, Bordian, Racu, Epureanu, Rozgoniuc, Anton, Platica (Ambrosat 79), Gatcan, Ionita, Dedov (Cociuc 55), Ginsari. **Booked**: Rozgoniuc. **Sent off**: Gatcan (90+2)
**Referee**: B Nijhuis (Holland). **Half-time**: 2-0

### WALES 0 REPUBLIC OF IRELAND 1
**Cardiff City Stadium (32,711); Monday, October 9, 2017**

**Wales** (4-2-3-1): Hennessey, Gunter, Chester, A Williams, B Davies, King (Woodburn 65), Allen

(J Williams 37), Ledley, Lawrence, Ramsey, Robson-Kanu (Vokes 71). **Booked**: Allen
**Republic of Ireland** (4-4-2): Randolph, Christie, Duffy, Clark, Ward, Arter (Whelan 78), Brady, Meyler, Hendrick, McClean, Murphy (K Long 90+2). **Scorer**: McClean (57). **Booked**: Murphy, Clark, Randolph, McClean, Meyler
**Referee**: D Skomina (Slovenia). **Half-time**: 0-0

## GROUP F

**MALTA 0 ENGLAND 4**
**Ta'Qali (16,994); Friday, September 1, 2017**

**Malta** (5-3-2): Hogg, Borg, Magri, Agius, Muscat, Zerafa (Camilleri 75), Kristensen, R Fenech (P Fenech 83), Pisani, Schembri (Mifsud 86), Farrugia
**England** (4-2-3-1): Hart, Walker, Jones, Cahill, Bertrand, Henderson, Livermore, Sterling (Rashford 46), Alli (Vardy 70), Oxlade-Chamberlain (Welbeck 76), Kane. **Scorers**: Kane (53, 90+2), Bertrand (86), Welbeck 90+1)
**Referee**: A Dias Soares (Portugal). **Half-time**: 0-0

**LITHUANIA 0 SCOTLAND 3**
**Vilnius (5,067); Friday, September 1, 2017**

**Lithuania** (4-4-2): Setkus, Borovskij, Freidgeimas, Kijanskas, Vaitkunas, Zulpa (Spalvis 68), Kuklys, Slivka, Novikas, Cernych (Verbickas 79), Sernas (Matulevicius 82). **Booked**: Cernych
**Scotland** (4-2-3-1): Gordon, Tierney, Berra, Mulgrew, Robertson, Brown, McArthur, Forrest (Ritchie 65), Armstrong (McGinn 84), Phillips, Griffiths (C Martin 79). **Scorers**: Armstrong (25), Robertson (31), McArthur (72). **Booked**: Mulgrew
**Referee**: C Del Cerro Grande (Spain). **Half-time**: 0-2

**ENGLAND 2 SLOVAKIA 1**
**Wembley (67,823); Monday, September 4, 2017**

**England** (4-4-1-1): Hart, Walker, Jones, Cahill, Bertrand, Rashford (Welbeck 83), Henderson, Dier, Oxlade-Chamberlain (Sterling 83), Alli (Livermore 90), Kane. **Scorers**: Dier (37), Rashford (59)
**Slovakia** (4-1-3-1): Dubravka, Pekarik, Skrtel, Durica, Hubocan, Skriniar, Lobotka, Weiss (Rusnak 69), Hamsik (Duda 79), Mak, Nemec (Duris 69). **Scorer**: Lobotka (3). **Booked**: Skriniar
**Referee**: C Turpin (France). **Half-time**: 1-1

**SCOTLAND 2 MALTA 0**
**Hampden Park (26,371); Monday, September 4, 2017**

**Scotland** (4-2-3-1): Gordon, Tierney, Berra, Mulgrew (Hanley 56), Robertson, Brown, McArthur (Morrison 46), Forrest, Armstrong, Phillips, Griffiths (C Martin 70). **Scorers**: Berra (9), Griffiths (49)
**Malta** (3-5-2): Hogg, Borg (A Muscat 86), Magri, Agius, Z Muscat, Zerafa. Kristensen (P Fenech 85), R Fenech, Pisani, Schembri (Gambin 71), Effiong. **Booked**: R Fenech
**Referee**: J Kehlet (Denmark). **Half-time**: 1-0

**ENGLAND 1 SLOVENIA 0**
**Wembley (61,598); Thursday, October 5, 2017**

**England** (4-2-3-1): Hart, Walker, Stones, Cahill, Bertrand, Henderson, Dier, Oxlade-Chamberlain (Lingard 64), Sterling (Keane 86), Rashford, Kane. **Scorer**: Kane (90+4). **Booked**: Stones
**Serbia** (4-4-2): Oblak, Struna, Mevlja, Cesar, Jokic, Verbic, Rotman (Matavz 79), Krhin, Bezjak (Repas 72), Sporar (Birsa 55), Ilicic. **Booked**: Krhin, Mevlja, Rotman, Struna, Birsa
**Referee**: F Zwayer (Germany). **Half-time**: 0-0

**SCOTLAND 1 SLOVAKIA 0**
**Hampden Park (46,773); Thursday, October 5, 2017**

**Scotland** (4-1-4-1): Gordon, Tierney (Anya 82), Berra, Mulgrew, Robertson, D Fletcher (McArthur 78), Forrest (C Martin 60), Bannan. Morrison, Phillips, Griffiths. **Scorer**: Skrtel (89 og). **Booked**: Morrison, Bannan
**Slovakia** (4-3-2-1): Dubravka, Pecarik, Durica, Skrtel, Hubocan, Lobotka, Gregus, Kucka (Gyomber 80), Hamsik (Duda 80), Mak, Nemec (Weiss 79). **Booked**: Mak, Hamsik, Kucka. **Sent off**: Mak (23)
**Referee**: M Mazic (Serbia). **Half-time**: 0-0

**LITHUANIA 0 ENGLAND 1**
**Vilnius (5,067); Sunday, October 8, 2017**
**Lithuania** (4-1-4-1): Setkus, Borovskis, Klimavicius, Girdvainis, Andriuskevicius, Zulpa, Novikovas, Verbickas, Cernych, Slivka (Chvedukas 90+1), Sernas (Matulevicius 76). **Booked**: Slivka
**England** (3-4-2-1): Butland, Keane, Stones, *Maguire, Trippier, Henderson, *Winks, Cresswell, Alli (Lingard 81), Rashford (Sturridge 72), Kane. **Scorer**: Kane (27 pen)
**Referee**: O Grinfeld (Israel). **Half-time**: 0-1

**SLOVENIA 2 SCOTLAND 2**
**Ljubljana (11,123); Sunday, October 8, 2017**
**Serbia** (4-4-1-1): Oblak, Struna (Skubic 46), Mevlja, Cesar, Jokic, Kurtic, Rotman, Repas (Bezjak 46), Verbic, Ilicic, Matavz (Vetrih 89). **Scorer**: Bezjak (52, 72). **Booked**: Rotman. Verbic, Cesar. **Sent off**: Cesar (90+2)
**Scotland** (4-4-2): Gordon, Tierney (S Fletcher 80), Berra, Mulgrew, Robertson, Phillips, McArthur (Snodgrass 79), D Fletcher, Bannan, C Martin (Anya 52), Griffiths. **Scorers**: Griffiths (32), Snodgrass (88). **Booked**: Tierney, McArthur, Mulgrew, Berra
**Referee**: J Eriksson (Sweden). **Half-time**: 0-1

## PLAY-OFFS

**NORTHERN IRELAND 0 SWITZERLAND 1**
**First leg: Windsor Park (18,269); Thursday, November 9, 2017**
**Northern Ireland** (4-5-1): McGovern, C McLaughlin, McAuley, J Evans, Brunt, Magennis, Norwood, Davis, C Evans (Saville 66), Dallas (Ward 52), K Lafferty (Washington 78). **Booked**: C Evans
**Switzerland** (4-2-3-1): Sommer, Lichtsteiner, Schar, Akanji, Rodriguez, Zakaria, Xhaka, Shaqiri, Dzemaili (Frei 83), Zuber (Mehmedi 87), Seferovic (Embolo 77). **Scorer**: Rodriguez (58 pen). **Booked**: Schar
**Referee**: O Hategan (Romania). **Half-time**: 0-0

**DENMARK 0 REPUBLIC OF IRELAND 0**
**First leg: Copenhagen (36,189); Saturday, November 11, 2017**
**Denmark** (4-2-3-1): Schmeichel, Ankeresen, Kjaer, Bjelland, Larsen, Kvist, Delaney, Cornelius (Poulsen 64), Eriksen, Sisto (Bendtner 73) Jorgensen
**Republic of Ireland** (4-4-2): Randolph, Christie, Duffy, Clark, Ward, Arter (Whelan 88), Hendrick (Hourihane 90+3), O'Dowda, Brady, McClean, Murphy (S Long 74).
**Referee**: M Mazic (Serbia)

**SWITZERLAND 0 NORTHERN IRELAND 0 (Switzerland won 1-0 on agg)**
**Second leg: Basle (36,210); Sunday, November 12, 2017**
**Switzerland** (4-2-3-1): Sommer, Lichtsteiner, Schar, Akanji, Rodriguez, Zakaria, Xhaka, Shaqiri (Freuler 80), Dzemaili (Mehmedi 61), Zuber, Seferovic (Embolo 86). **Booked**: Seferovic
**Northern Ireland** (4-5-1): McGovern, Hughes, J Evans, McAuley, Brunt, Ward (*Jones 74), Norwood (Magennis 75), Davis, Saville, Dallas, Washington (McNair 82). **Booked**: Brunt, J Evans
**Referee**: F Brych (Germany)

**REPUBLIC OF IRELAND 1 DENMARK 5 (Denmark won 5-1 on agg)**
**Second leg: Aviva Stadium (50,060); Tuesday, November 14, 2017**
**Republic of Ireland** (4-2-3-1): Randolph, Christie, Duffy, Clark (S Long 70), Ward, Meyler

(Hoolahan 46), Arter (McGeady 46)), Hendrick, Brady, McClean, Murphy. **Scorer**: Duffy (6)
**Denmark** (4-2-3-1): Schmeichel, Christensen, Kjaer, Bjelland, Larsen (Ankersen 53) Kvist, Delaney, Poulsen (Cornelius 69), Eriksen, Sisto, Jorgensen (Bendtner 83). **Scorers**: Christie (29 og), Eriksen (32, 63, 73), Bendtner (90 pen)
**Referee**: S Marciniak (Poland). **Half-time**: 1-2

# FRIENDLY INTERNATIONALS

**SCOTLAND 0 HOLLAND 1**

**Pittodrie, Aberdeen (17,883); Thursday, November 9, 2017**

**Scotland** (4-2-3-1): Gordon, *Jack, Berra (Mulgrew 46), Tierney, Robertson, McLean, McGinn, Forrest (Fraser 71), *McGregor (*Cummings 86), *Christie, Phillips. **Booked**: McGinn
**Holland** (4-3-3): Cillessen, Fosu-Mensah (Veltman 71), Van Dijk, Rekik, Ake, Wijnaldum, Blind, Strootman, Promes (Berghuis 76), Babel, Depay. **Scorer**: Depay (40). **Booked**: Strootman
**Referee**: R Buquet (France). **Half-time**: 0-1

**ENGLAND 0 GERMANY 0**

**Wembley (81,382); Friday, November 10, 2017**

**England** (3-5-2): *Pickford, Jones (*Gomez 25), Stones, Maguire, Trippier (Walker 71), Livermore (*Cork 86), Dier, *Loftus-Cheek, Rose (Bertrand 71), *Abraham (Rashford 60), Vardy (Lingard 86). **Booked**: Livermore
**Germany** (3-4-3): Ter Stegen, Ginter, Hummels, Rudiger, Kimmich, Gundogan (Rudy 86), Ozil, Halstenberg, Draxler (Emre Can 67), Werner (Wagner 73), Sane (Brandt 87)
**Referee**: P Raczkowski (Poland)

**FRANCE 2 WALES 0**

**Paris (60,000); Friday, November 10, 2017**

**France** (4-2-3-1): Mandana, Jallet (Pavard 46), Koscielny, Umtiti, Kurzawa, Tolisso (N'Zonzi 46), Matuidi, Griezmann (Fekir 63), Mbappe (Thauvin 84), Coman (Martial 73), Giroud (Lacazette 73). **Scorers**: Griezmann (18), Giroud (71)
**Wales** (3-4-2-1): Hennessey, Chester, A Williams, B Davies (Woodburn 63), Gunter, Allen, Ledley (*Ampadu 64), Taylor, King (*Brooks 64), Ramsey, Vokes (Lawrence 83). **Booked**: Allen
**Referee**: J Sousa (Portugal). **Half-time**: 1-0

**ENGLAND 0 BRAZIL 0**

**Wembley (84,545); Tuesday, November 14, 2017**

**England** (3-4-1-2): Hart, Gomez, Stones, McGuire, Walker, Dier, Livermore (Rose 89), Bertrand (Young 80), Loftus-Cheek (Lingard 35), Vardy (*Solanke 75), Rashford (Abraham 75). **Booked**: Livermore
**Brazil** (4-3-3): Alisson, Dani Alves, Miranda, Marquinhos, Marcelo, Casemiro, Augusto (Fernandinho 67), Paulinho, Coutinho (Willian 67), Gabriel Jesus (Firmino 75), Neymar. **Booked**: Dani Alves
**Referee:** A Dias Soares (Portugal)

**WALES 1 PANAMA 1**

**Cardiff City Stadium (13,747); Tuesday, November 14, 2017**

**Wales** (4-2-3-1): Ward, Gunter, Chester, Davies (*Lockyer 46), Taylor, Ampadu (Crofts 67), Edwards (*Evans 62), Brooks (*Watkins 71), Lawrence, Woodburn (*Hedges 71), Vokes (Bradshaw 46). **Scorer**: Lawrence (75). **Booked**: Ampadu, Crofts, Lawrence, Gunter
**Panama** (4-4-2): Penedo, Murillo, Baloy, Escobar, Ovalle, Cooper, M Vargas (Buitrago 71), Heraldez, Avila (J Vargas 67), Perez, Torres. **Scorer**: Cooper (90+3). **Booked**: Cooper
**Referee**: B Vertenten (Belgium). **Half-time**: 0-0

**CHINA 0 WALES 6 (China Cup)**

**Nanning (36,533); Thursday, March 22, 2018**

**China** (4-2-3-1): Yan Junling, Wang Shenchao (Lu Xuepeng 46), He Guan (Liu Yiming 46),

Feng Xiaoting (Deng Hanwen 71), Zheng Zheng, Hao Junmin, Huang Bowen (He Chao 46), Wu Lei, Wei Shihao, Gao Lin (Yu Hanchao 46), Yu Dabao (Zhao Xuri 46)
**Wales** (3-4-2-1); Hennessey, Chester (Lockyer 71), A Williams, Davies (*Mepham 71), Gunter, King, Allen (Evans 63), John, Bale (Woodburn 63), Wilson (Watkins 73), Vokes (Bradshaw 63). **Scorers**: Bale (2, 21, 62), Vokes (38, 58), Wilson (45)
**Referee**: M Yaacob (Malaysia). **Half-time**: 0-4
(Gareth Bale becomes Wales's all-time leading scorer with 29 goals)

**HOLLAND 0 ENGLAND 1**
**Amsterdam (51,500): Friday, March 23, 2018**

**Holland** (3-4-3): Zoet, De Ligt, De Vrij (Weghorst 89), Van Dijk, Hateboer, Wijnaldum, Strootman (Van de Beek 90), Van Aanholt, Promes (Propper 66), Bas Dost (Babel 66), Depay
**England** (3-5-1-1): Pickford, Walker, Stones, Gomez (Maguire 10) (Dier 89), Trippier, Henderson, Oxlade-Chamberlain, Lingard (Alli 68), Rose (Young 71), Sterling (Welbeck 68), Rashford (Vardy 68). **Scorer**: Lingard (59)
**Referee**: J Gil Manzano (Spain). **Half-time**: 0-0

**SCOTLAND 0 COSTA RICA 1**
**Hampden Park (20,488); Friday, March 23, 2018**

**Scotland** (5-4-1): A McGregor, Paterson, Hanley, Mulgrew (McGinn 81), *McKenna, Robertson, Ritchie (*Murphy 86), *McTominay (Armstrong 57), *McDonald, Cairney (C McGregor 57), *McBurnie (Phillips 76)
**Costa Rica** (5-4-1): Navas, Acosta, Gonzalez, Duarte, Gamboa (Smith 74), Oviedo (Calvo 77), Borges, Guzman (Tejeda 55), Ruiz, Colindres (Wallace 63), Urena. **Scorer**: Urena (14)
**Referee**: T Stieler (Germany). **Half-time**: 0-1

**TURKEY 1 REPUBLIC OF IRELAND 0**
**Antalya (32,000): Friday, March 23, 2018**

**Turkey** (4-2-3-1): Babacan, Gonul, Aziz (Ayhan 82), Soyuncu, Kaldirim, Topal, Yokuslu, Yazici (Potuk 87), Akbaba (Malli 69), Calhanoglu (Kahveci 80), Tosun (Unal 64). **Scorer**: Topal (51). **Booked**: Soyuncu
**Republic of Ireland** (3-5-2): Doyle, Duffy, *Rice, K Long, Coleman (Doherty 63), Hourihane (Clark 68), Browne (Meyler 69), Hendrick (Judge 80), McClean, *Hogan (Horgan 75), Maguire (S Long 62). **Booked**: Browne
**Referee**: S Vincic (Slovenia). **Half-time**: 0-0

**NORTHERN IRELAND 2 SOUTH KOREA 1**
**Windsor Park (18,103): Saturday, March 24, 2018**

**Northern Ireland** (4-3-3): *Carson, Hughes (McLaughlin 18), McAuley, J Evans (Cathcart 68), *Lewis, C Evans (Boyce 62), Norwood (McNair 72), Saville, Ward (Washington 62), Magennis, Jones (*Smyth 82). **Scorers**: Kim Min-jae (20 og), Smyth (86)
**South Korea** (4-3-3): Kim Seung-gyu, Lee Yong, Jang Hyun-soo, Kim Min-jae, Kim Jin-su (Kim Min-woo 35), Park Joo-ho (Lee Chang-min 68), Ki Sung-yeung (Jung Woo-young 67), Lee Jae-sung, Kwon Chang-hoon (Hwang Hee-chan 62), Kim Shin-wook, Son Heung-min (Yeom Ki-hun 75). **Scorer**: Kwon Chang-hoon (7)
**Referee**: R Madden (England). **Half-time**: 1-1

**WALES 0 URUGUAY 1 (China Cup)**
**Nanning (41,016); Monday, March 26, 2018**

**Wales** (3-4-2-1); Hennessey, Chester (Lockyer 75), A Williams, Davies (Hedges 90), Gunter (Matthews 79), King, Allen, John (*Roberts 60), Bale, Wilson (Evans 72), Vokes (*Bodin 67)
**Booked**: Allen
**Uruguay** (4-4-2): Muslera, Valera, Giminez (Coates 8), Godlin, Laxalt, Nandez (Stuani 85), Bentancur (Silva 78), Vecino, Rodriguez (Torreira 70), Suarez, Cavani (Gomez 90+3). **Scorer**: Cavani (49)
**Referee**: S Ahmad Falahi (Qatar). **Half-time**: 0-0

## ENGLAND 1 ITALY 1

**Wembley (82,598); Tuesday, March 27, 2018**

**England** (3-5-1-1): Butland, Walker, Stones (Henderson 73), *Tarkowski, Dier, Trippier (Rose 60), Oxlade-Chamberlain (Lallana 60), Lingard (*L Cook 71), Young, Sterling, Vardy (Rashford 70). **Scorer**: Vardy (26). **Booked**: Oxlade-Chamberlain, Walker, Young

**Italy** (4-3-3): Donnarumma, Zappacosta, Rugani, Bonucci, De Sciglio, Pellegrini (Gagliardini 79), Jorginho, Parolo, Candreva (Chiesa 56), Immobile (Belotti 64), Insigne. **Scorer**: Insigne (87 pen).

**Referee**: D Aytekin (Germany). **Half-time**: 1-0

## HUNGARY 0 SCOTLAND 1

**Budapest (9,000): Tuesday, March 27, 2018**

**Hungary** (3-4-3): Gulacsi, Fiola, Otigba, Lovrencsics, Hangya (Szabo 46), Pinter (Elek 46), Kleinheister (Patkai 67), Dzsudzsak (Nemeth 58), Varga (Nikolics 83), Guzmics, Szalai (Bode 77). **Booked**: Szalai, Elek, Otigba

**Scotland** (3-4-2-1): A McGregor, *Hendry, Mulgrew, McKenna, Fraser (Paterson 81), McGinn, Armstrong (McLean 70), Robertson (*Douglas 66), Forrest (Christie 77), C McGregor (Cummings 90+2), Phillips (McBurnie 83). **Scorer**: Phillips (48). **Booked**: C McGregor, Mulgrew, McGinn

**Referee**: H Lechner (Austria). **Half-time**: 0-0

## FRANCE 2 REPUBLIC OF IRELAND 0

**Paris (72,000); Monday, May 28, 2018**

**France** (4-3-1-2): Mandanda, Sidibe (Pavard 83), Rami, Umtiti (Kimpembe 64), Mendy (Hernandez 63), Tolisso (Pogba 77), Nzonzi, Matuidi, Fekir (Griezmann 64), Giroud, Mbappe (Dembele 77). **Scorers**: Giroud (41), Fekir (44)

**Republic of Ireland** (4-5-1): Doyle, Coleman, Duffy, K Long (*S Williams), *D Williams (Doherty 82), Walters (Meyler 59), Browne (Arter 59), Rice, O'Dowda (*Burke 70), McClean, S Long (Judge 70). **Booked**: McClean, Arter

**Referee**: G Kabakov (Bulgaria). **Half-time**: 2-0

## MEXICO 0 WALES 0

**Pasadena, USA (82,395); Tuesday, May 29, 2018**

**Mexico** (4-3-3): Jose Corona, Alvarez, Ayala, Alanis (Salcedo 46), Gallardo, Herrera (J dos Santos 61), Molina (Dammat 46), Gutierrez (Fabian 74), Jesus Corona (G dos Santos 69), Hernandez (Peralta 59), Aquino. **Booked**: Gutierrez

**Wales** (4-2-3-1): Hennessey, Gunter (Roberts 46), A Williams (Lockyer 21), Mepham, Davies, King, Ledley (John 46), Wilson (Thomas 64), Ramsey, Lawrence (Smith 81), Vokes (Brooks 46). **Booked**: Ramsey

**Referee**: A Villarreal (USA)

## PERU 2 SCOTLAND 0

**Lima (40,000): Wednesday, May 30, 2018**

**Peru** (4-3-3): Carvallo, Advincula (Corzo 87), Ramos, Rodriguez, Trauco, Flores, Tapia (Cartagena 84),Yotun (Ruidiaz 69), Carrillo (Polo 69), Farfan (Hurtado 81), Cueva (Aquino 80). **Scorers**: Cueva (37 pen), Farfan (47)

**Scotland** (4-1-4-1): *Archer, *O'Donnell, Mulgrew, McKenna, *Stevenson, *McGeouch (*Shinnie 76), McLean (*Cadden 87), McTominay, McGinn (Paterson 63), Murphy (McBurnie 63), Phillips (*Morgan 72)

**Referee**: F Guerrero (Mexico). **Half-time**: 1-0

## PANAMA 0 NORTHERN IRELAND 0

**Panama City (26,000); Wednesday, May 30, 2018**

**Panama** (4-1-4-1): Calderon, Baloy (Torres 76), Machado, Ovalle, Escobar, Gomez (Pimentel 46), Cooper (Camargo 46), Godoy (Avila 46), Barcenas, Rodriguez (Nurse 60), Tejada (Perez 46).

**Northern Ireland** (4-4-2): Carson (*Peacock-Farrell 46), Hughes, McAuley, J Evans, Cathcart, C Evans (*Thompson 82), Ferguson (Smyth 72), Dallas (Hodson 59), McNair, Boyce (R McLaughlin 72), Magennis (*Lavery 88)
**Referee**: H Bejarano (Costa Rica)

**ENGLAND 2 NIGERIA 1**
**Wembley (70,025); Saturday, June 2, 2018**

**England** (3-1-4-2): Pickford, Walker, Stones, Cahill, Dier, Trippier, Lingard (Loftus-Cheek 67), Alli (Delph 81), Young (Rose 67), Kane (Welbeck 73), Sterling (Rashford 73). **Scorers**: Cahill (7), Kane (39). **Booked**: Sterling
**Nigeria** (4-2-3-1): Uzoho, Shehu (Ebuehi 46), Troost-Ekong, Balogun (Omeruo 46), Idowu, Onazi (Etebo 46), Mikel (Ogu 46), Iwobi, Obinna, Moses (Musa 63), Ighalo (Iheanacho 77). **Scorer**: Iwobi (47). **Booked**: Musa
**Referee**: M Guida (Italy). **Half-time**: 2-0

**REPUBLIC OF IRELAND 2 USA 1**
**Aviva Stadium (32,300); Saturday, June 2, 2018**

**Republic of Ireland** (3-5-2): Doyle; Duffy (*Stevens 77), O'Shea (*Lenihan 35), K Long; Coleman, Hendrick (Arter 83), Rice, O'Dowda (Judge 89), McClean; Burke (Horgan 58), Walters. **Scorers**: Burke (57), Judge (89)
**USA** (4-1-4-1): Hamid; Yedlin (Moore 70), Carter-Vickers (Parker 61), Miazga, Villafana, Trapp, Weah, Adams, McKennie (Corona 81), Rubin (De la Torre 77); Wood (Sargent 70). **Booked**: Carter-Vickers, Adams, Corona
**Referee**: A Dallas (Scotland). **Half-time**: 0-1

**MEXICO 1 SCOTLAND 0**
**Mexico City (70,993); Sunday, June 3, 2018**

**Mexico** (4-2-3-1): Ochoa, Alvarez, Ayala, Salcedo, Gallardo, Layun, Herrera (Fabian 58), Vela (Aquino 63), G dos Santos (J dos Santos 57), Lozano (Jesus Corona 73), Jimenez (Peralta 57). **Scorer**: G dos Santos (13)
**Scotland**: *McLaughlin (*Bain 46), O'Donnell, Hendry, McKenna, Shinnie, McGeouch, McLean (Cadden 55), Russell, Paterson (Mulgrew 55), Christie (McGinn 55), McBurnie (Morgan 80)
**Referee**: H Bejarano (Costa Rica). **Half-time**: 1-0

**COSTA RICA 3 NORTHERN IRELAND 0**
**San Jose (35,100); Sunday, June 3, 2018**

**Costa Rica** (5-4-1): Navas (Moreira 35), Gamboa (Smith 64), Acosta, Gonzales (Waston 73), Duarte (Calvo 46), Oviedo, Campbell, Borges (Tejeda 46), Guzman, Colindres, Venegas (Matarrita 70). **Scorers**: Venega (30), Campbell (46), Calvo (66)
**Northern Ireland** (4-1-4-1): Carson (*Hazard 73), Hodson (C McLaughlin 39), Cathcart (McCullough 73), McAuley, Hughes, J. Evans, Boyce (McCartan 39), McNair, C. Evans (Thompson 85), Dallas Magennis (R McLaughlin 60)
**Referee**: F Guerro (Mexico). **Half-time**: 1-0

**ENGLAND 2 COSTA RICA 0**
**Elland Road, Leeds (36,104); Thursday, June 7, 2018**

**England** (3-5-2): Butland (*Pope 65), Jones (Cahill 64), Stones, Maguire, *Alexander-Arnold (Tripper 65), Loftus-Cheek (Lingard 79), Henderson (Alli 64), Delph, Rose, Rashford, Vardy (Welbeck 61). **Scorers**: Rashford (13), Welbeck (76)
**Costa Rica** (5-4-1): Navas, Gamboa (Smith 72), Waston, Gonzalez, Calvo, Oviedo (Matarrita 60), Venegas (Bolanos 61), Guzman (Tejeda 69), Borges, Campbell, Urena. **Booked**: Matarrita, Gonzalez
**Referee**: H Kimura (Japan). **Half-time**: 1-0

# OTHER BRITISH & IRISH INTERNATIONAL RESULTS

## ENGLAND

### v ALBANIA

| | | E | A |
|---|---|---|---|
| 1989 | Tirana (WC) | 2 | 0 |
| 1989 | Wembley (WC) | 5 | 0 |
| 2001 | Tirana (WC) | 3 | 1 |
| 2001 | Newcastle (WC) | 2 | 0 |

### v ALGERIA

| | | E | A |
|---|---|---|---|
| 2010 | Cape Town (WC) | 0 | 0 |

### v ANDORRA

| | | E | A |
|---|---|---|---|
| 2006 | Old Trafford (EC) | 5 | 0 |
| 2007 | Barcelona (EC) | 3 | 0 |
| 2008 | Barcelona (WC) | 2 | 0 |
| 2009 | Wembley (WC) | 6 | 0 |

### v ARGENTINA

| | | E | A |
|---|---|---|---|
| 1951 | Wembley | 2 | 1 |
| 1953* | Buenos Aires | 0 | 0 |
| 1962 | Rancagua (WC) | 3 | 1 |
| 1964 | Rio de Janeiro | 0 | 1 |
| 1966 | Wembley (WC) | 1 | 0 |
| 1974 | Wembley | 2 | 2 |
| 1977 | Buenos Aires | 1 | 1 |
| 1980 | Wembley | 3 | 1 |
| 1986 | Mexico City (WC) | 1 | 2 |
| 1991 | Wembley | 2 | 2 |
| 1998† | St Etienne (WC) | 2 | 2 |
| 2000 | Wembley | 0 | 0 |
| 2002 | Sapporo (WC) | 1 | 0 |
| 2005 | Geneva | 3 | 2 |

(*Abandoned after 21 mins – rain)
(† England lost 3-4 on pens)

### v AUSTRALIA

| | | E | A |
|---|---|---|---|
| 1980 | Sydney | 2 | 1 |
| 1983 | Sydney | 0 | 0 |
| 1983 | Brisbane | 1 | 0 |
| 1983 | Melbourne | 1 | 1 |
| 1991 | Sydney | 1 | 0 |
| 2003 | West Ham | 1 | 3 |
| 2016 | Sunderland | 2 | 1 |

### v AUSTRIA

| | | E | A |
|---|---|---|---|
| 1908 | Vienna | 6 | 1 |
| 1908 | Vienna | 11 | 1 |
| 1909 | Vienna | 8 | 1 |
| 1930 | Vienna | 0 | 0 |
| 1932 | Stamford Bridge | 4 | 3 |
| 1936 | Vienna | 1 | 2 |
| 1951 | Wembley | 2 | 2 |
| 1952 | Vienna | 3 | 2 |
| 1958 | Boras (WC) | 2 | 2 |
| 1961 | Vienna | 1 | 3 |
| 1962 | Wembley | 3 | 1 |
| 1965 | Wembley | 2 | 3 |
| 1967 | Vienna | 1 | 0 |
| 1973 | Wembley | 7 | 0 |
| 1979 | Vienna | 3 | 4 |
| 2004 | Vienna (WC) | 2 | 2 |
| 2005 | Old Trafford (WC) | 1 | 0 |
| 2007 | Vienna | 1 | 0 |

### v AZERBAIJAN

| | | E | A |
|---|---|---|---|
| 2004 | Baku (WC) | 1 | 0 |
| 2005 | Newcastle (WC) | 2 | 0 |

### v BELARUS

| | | E | B |
|---|---|---|---|
| 2008 | Minsk (WC) | 3 | 1 |
| 2009 | Wembley (WC) | 3 | 0 |

### v BELGIUM

| | | E | B |
|---|---|---|---|
| 1921 | Brussels | 2 | 0 |
| 1923 | Highbury | 6 | 1 |
| 1923 | Antwerp | 2 | 2 |
| 1924 | West Bromwich | 4 | 0 |
| 1926 | Antwerp | 5 | 3 |
| 1927 | Brussels | 9 | 1 |
| 1928 | Antwerp | 3 | 1 |
| 1929 | Brussels | 5 | 1 |
| 1931 | Brussels | 4 | 1 |
| 1936 | Brussels | 2 | 3 |
| 1947 | Brussels | 5 | 2 |
| 1950 | Brussels | 4 | 1 |
| 1952 | Wembley | 5 | 0 |
| 1954 | Basle (WC) | 4 | 4 |
| 1964 | Wembley | 2 | 2 |
| 1970 | Brussels | 3 | 1 |
| 1980 | Turin (EC) | 1 | 1 |
| 1990 | Bologna (WC) | 1 | 0 |
| 1998* | Casablanca | 0 | 0 |
| 1999 | Sunderland | 2 | 1 |
| 2012 | Wembley | 1 | 0 |
| 2018 | Kaliningrad (WC) | 0 | 1 |
| 2018 | St Petersburg (WC) | 0 | 2 |

(*England lost 3-4 on pens)

### v BOHEMIA

| | | E | B |
|---|---|---|---|
| 1908 | Prague | 4 | 0 |

### v BRAZIL

| | | E | B |
|---|---|---|---|
| 1956 | Wembley | 4 | 2 |
| 1958 | Gothenburg (WC) | 0 | 0 |
| 1959 | Rio de Janeiro | 0 | 2 |
| 1962 | Vina del Mar (WC) | 1 | 3 |
| 1963 | Wembley | 1 | 1 |
| 1964 | Rio de Janeiro | 1 | 5 |
| 1969 | Rio de Janeiro | 1 | 2 |
| 1970 | Guadalajara (WC) | 0 | 1 |
| 1976 | Los Angeles | 0 | 1 |
| 1977 | Rio de Janeiro | 0 | 0 |
| 1978 | Wembley | 1 | 1 |
| 1981 | Wembley | 0 | 1 |
| 1984 | Rio de Janeiro | 2 | 0 |
| 1987 | Wembley | 1 | 1 |
| 1990 | Wembley | 1 | 0 |
| 1992 | Wembley | 1 | 1 |
| 1993 | Washington | 1 | 1 |
| 1995 | Wembley | 1 | 3 |
| 1997 | Paris (TF) | 0 | 1 |

| | | | |
|---|---|---|---|
| 2000 | Wembley | 1 | 1 |
| 2002 | Shizuoka (WC) | 1 | 2 |
| 2007 | Wembley | 1 | 1 |
| 2009 | Doha | 0 | 1 |
| 2013 | Wembley | 2 | 1 |
| 2013 | Rio de Janeiro | 2 | 2 |
| 2017 | Wembley | 0 | 0 |

**v BULGARIA**

| | | *E* | *B* |
|---|---|---|---|
| 1962 | Rancagua (WC) | 0 | 0 |
| 1968 | Wembley | 1 | 1 |
| 1974 | Sofia | 1 | 0 |
| 1979 | Sofia (EC) | 3 | 0 |
| 1979 | Wembley (EC) | 2 | 0 |
| 1996 | Wembley | 1 | 0 |
| 1998 | Wembley (EC) | 0 | 0 |
| 1999 | Sofia (EC) | 1 | 1 |
| 2010 | Wembley (EC) | 4 | 0 |
| 2011 | Sofia (EC) | 3 | 0 |

**v CAMEROON**

| | | *E* | *C* |
|---|---|---|---|
| 1990 | Naples (WC) | 3 | 2 |
| 1991 | Wembley | 2 | 0 |
| 1997 | Wembley | 2 | 0 |
| 2002 | Kobe (Japan) | 2 | 2 |

**v CANADA**

| | | *E* | *C* |
|---|---|---|---|
| 1986 | Vancouver | 1 | 0 |

**v CHILE**

| | | *E* | *C* |
|---|---|---|---|
| 1950 | Rio de Janeiro (WC) | 2 | 0 |
| 1953 | Santiago | 2 | 1 |
| 1984 | Santiago | 0 | 0 |
| 1989 | Wembley | 0 | 0 |
| 1998 | Wembley | 0 | 2 |
| 2013 | Wembley | 0 | 2 |

**v CHINA**

| | | *E* | *C* |
|---|---|---|---|
| 1996 | Beijing | 3 | 0 |

**v CIS**
(formerly Soviet Union)

| | | *E* | *CIS* |
|---|---|---|---|
| 1992 | Moscow | 2 | 2 |

**v COLOMBIA**

| | | *E* | *C* |
|---|---|---|---|
| 1970 | Bogota | 4 | 0 |
| 1988 | Wembley | 1 | 1 |
| 1995 | Wembley | 0 | 0 |
| 1998 | Lens (WC) | 2 | 0 |
| 2005 | New York | 3 | 2 |
| 2018† | Moscow (WC) | 1 | 1 |

(† England won 4-3 on pens)

**v COSTA RICA**

| | | *E* | *CR* |
|---|---|---|---|
| 2014 | Belo Horizonte (WC) | 0 | 0 |
| 2018 | Leeds | 2 | 0 |

**v CROATIA**

| | | *E* | *C* |
|---|---|---|---|
| 1995 | Wembley | 0 | 0 |
| 2003 | Ipswich | 3 | 1 |
| 2004 | Lisbon (EC) | 4 | 2 |
| 2006 | Zagreb (EC) | 0 | 2 |
| 2007 | Wembley (EC) | 2 | 3 |
| 2008 | Zagreb (WC) | 4 | 1 |
| 2009 | Wembley (WC) | 5 | 1 |
| 2018 | Moscow (WC) | 1 | 2 |

**v CYPRUS**

| | | *E* | *C* |
|---|---|---|---|
| 1975 | Wembley (EC) | 5 | 0 |
| 1975 | Limassol (EC) | 1 | 0 |

**v CZECH REPUBLIC**

| | | *E* | *C* |
|---|---|---|---|
| 1998 | Wembley | 2 | 0 |
| 2008 | Wembley | 2 | 2 |

**v CZECHOSLOVAKIA**

| | | *E* | *C* |
|---|---|---|---|
| 1934 | Prague | 1 | 2 |
| 1937 | White Hart Lane | 5 | 4 |
| 1963 | Bratislava | 4 | 2 |
| 1966 | Wembley | 0 | 0 |
| 1970 | Guadalajara (WC) | 1 | 0 |
| 1973 | Prague | 1 | 1 |
| 1974 | Wembley (EC) | 3 | 0 |
| 1975* | Bratislava (EC) | 1 | 2 |
| 1978 | Wembley (EC) | 1 | 0 |
| 1982 | Bilbao (WC) | 2 | 0 |
| 1990 | Wembley | 4 | 2 |
| 1992 | Prague | 2 | 2 |

(* Aband 0-0, 17 mins prev day – fog)

**v DENMARK**

| | | *E* | *D* |
|---|---|---|---|
| 1948 | Copenhagen | 0 | 0 |
| 1955 | Copenhagen | 5 | 1 |
| 1956 | W'hampton (WC) | 5 | 2 |
| 1957 | Copenhagen (WC) | 4 | 1 |
| 1966 | Copenhagen | 2 | 0 |
| 1978 | Copenhagen (EC) | 4 | 3 |
| 1979 | Wembley (EC) | 1 | 0 |
| 1982 | Copenhagen (EC) | 2 | 2 |
| 1983 | Wembley (EC) | 0 | 1 |
| 1988 | Wembley | 1 | 0 |
| 1989 | Copenhagen | 1 | 1 |
| 1990 | Wembley | 1 | 0 |
| 1992 | Malmo (EC) | 0 | 0 |
| 1994 | Wembley | 1 | 0 |
| 2002 | Niigata (WC) | 3 | 0 |
| 2003 | Old Trafford | 2 | 3 |
| 2005 | Copenhagen | 1 | 4 |
| 2011 | Copenhagen | 2 | 1 |
| 2014 | Wembley | 1 | 0 |

**v EAST GERMANY**

| | | *E* | *EG* |
|---|---|---|---|
| 1963 | Leipzig | 2 | 1 |
| 1970 | Wembley | 3 | 1 |
| 1974 | Leipzig | 1 | 1 |
| 1984 | Wembley | 1 | 0 |

**v ECUADOR**

| | | *E* | *Ec* |
|---|---|---|---|
| 1970 | Quito | 2 | 0 |
| 2006 | Stuttgart (WC) | 1 | 0 |
| 2014 | Miami | 2 | 2 |

**v EGYPT**

| | | *E* | *Eg* |
|---|---|---|---|
| 1986 | Cairo | 4 | 0 |

| | | | |
|---|---|---|---|
| 1990 | Cagliari (WC) | 1 | 0 |
| 2010 | Wembley | 3 | 1 |

### v ESTONIA

| | | *E* | *Est* |
|---|---|---|---|
| 2007 | Tallinn (EC) | 3 | 0 |
| 2007 | Wembley (EC) | 3 | 0 |
| 2014 | Tallinn (EC) | 1 | 0 |
| 2015 | Wembley (EC) | 2 | 0 |

### v FIFA

| | | *E* | *F* |
|---|---|---|---|
| 1938 | Highbury | 3 | 0 |
| 1953 | Wembley | 4 | 4 |
| 1963 | Wembley | 2 | 1 |

### v FINLAND

| | | *E* | *F* |
|---|---|---|---|
| 1937 | Helsinki | 8 | 0 |
| 1956 | Helsinki | 5 | 1 |
| 1966 | Helsinki | 3 | 0 |
| 1976 | Helsinki (WC) | 4 | 1 |
| 1976 | Wembley (WC) | 2 | 1 |
| 1982 | Helsinki | 4 | 1 |
| 1984 | Wembley (WC) | 5 | 0 |
| 1985 | Helsinki (WC) | 1 | 1 |
| 1992 | Helsinki | 2 | 1 |
| 2000 | Helsinki (WC) | 0 | 0 |
| 2001 | Liverpool (WC) | 2 | 1 |

### v FRANCE

| | | *E* | *F* |
|---|---|---|---|
| 1923 | Paris | 4 | 1 |
| 1924 | Paris | 3 | 1 |
| 1925 | Paris | 3 | 2 |
| 1927 | Paris | 6 | 0 |
| 1928 | Paris | 5 | 1 |
| 1929 | Paris | 4 | 1 |
| 1931 | Paris | 2 | 5 |
| 1933 | White Hart Lane | 4 | 1 |
| 1938 | Paris | 4 | 2 |
| 1947 | Highbury | 3 | 0 |
| 1949 | Paris | 3 | 1 |
| 1951 | Highbury | 2 | 2 |
| 1955 | Paris | 0 | 1 |
| 1957 | Wembley | 4 | 0 |
| 1962 | Hillsborough (EC) | 1 | 1 |
| 1963 | Paris (EC) | 2 | 5 |
| 1966 | Wembley (WC) | 2 | 0 |
| 1969 | Wembley | 5 | 0 |
| 1982 | Bilbao (WC) | 3 | 1 |
| 1984 | Paris | 0 | 2 |
| 1992 | Wembley | 2 | 0 |
| 1992 | Malmo (EC) | 0 | 0 |
| 1997 | Montpellier (TF) | 1 | 0 |
| 1999 | Wembley | 0 | 2 |
| 2000 | Paris | 1 | 1 |
| 2004 | Lisbon (EC) | 1 | 2 |
| 2008 | Paris | 0 | 1 |
| 2010 | Wembley | 1 | 2 |
| 2012 | Donetsk (EC) | 1 | 1 |
| 2015 | Wembley | 2 | 0 |
| 2017 | Paris | 2 | 3 |

### v GEORGIA

| | | *E* | *G* |
|---|---|---|---|
| 1996 | Tbilisi (WC) | 2 | 0 |
| 1997 | Wembley (WC) | 2 | 0 |

### v GERMANY/WEST GERMANY

| | | *E* | *G* |
|---|---|---|---|
| 1930 | Berlin | 3 | 3 |
| 1935 | White Hart Lane | 3 | 0 |
| 1938 | Berlin | 6 | 3 |
| 1954 | Wembley | 3 | 1 |
| 1956 | Berlin | 3 | 1 |
| 1965 | Nuremberg | 1 | 0 |
| 1966 | Wembley | 1 | 0 |
| 1966 | Wembley (WCF) | 4 | 2 |
| 1968 | Hanover | 0 | 1 |
| 1970 | Leon (WC) | 2 | 3 |
| 1972 | Wembley (EC) | 1 | 3 |
| 1972 | Berlin (EC) | 0 | 0 |
| 1975 | Wembley | 2 | 0 |
| 1978 | Munich | 1 | 2 |
| 1982 | Madrid (WC) | 0 | 0 |
| 1982 | Wembley | 1 | 2 |
| 1985 | Mexico City | 3 | 0 |
| 1987 | Dusseldorf | 1 | 3 |
| 1990* | Turin (WC) | 1 | 1 |
| 1991 | Wembley | 0 | 1 |
| 1993 | Detroit | 1 | 2 |
| 1996† | Wembley (EC) | 1 | 1 |
| 2000 | Charleroi (EC) | 1 | 0 |
| 2000 | Wembley (WC) | 0 | 1 |
| 2001 | Munich (WC) | 5 | 1 |
| 2007 | Wembley | 1 | 2 |
| 2008 | Berlin | 2 | 1 |
| 2010 | Bloemfontein (WC) | 1 | 4 |
| 2012 | Donetsk (EC) | 1 | 1 |
| 2013 | Wembley | 0 | 1 |
| 2016 | Berlin | 3 | 2 |
| 2017 | Dortmund | 0 | 1 |
| 2017 | Wembley | 0 | 0 |

(*England lost 3-4 on pens)
(† England lost 5-6 on pens)

### v GHANA

| | | *E* | *G* |
|---|---|---|---|
| 2011 | Wembley | 1 | 1 |

### v GREECE

| | | *E* | *G* |
|---|---|---|---|
| 1971 | Wembley (EC) | 3 | 0 |
| 1971 | Athens (EC) | 2 | 0 |
| 1982 | Salonika (EC) | 3 | 0 |
| 1983 | Wembley (EC) | 0 | 0 |
| 1989 | Athens | 2 | 1 |
| 1994 | Wembley | 5 | 0 |
| 2001 | Athens (WC) | 2 | 0 |
| 2001 | Old Trafford (WC) | 2 | 2 |
| 2006 | Old Trafford | 4 | 0 |

### v HOLLAND

| | | *E* | *H* |
|---|---|---|---|
| 1935 | Amsterdam | 1 | 0 |
| 1946 | Huddersfield | 8 | 2 |
| 1964 | Amsterdam | 1 | 1 |
| 1969 | Amsterdam | 1 | 0 |
| 1970 | Wembley | 0 | 0 |
| 1977 | Wembley | 0 | 2 |
| 1982 | Wembley | 2 | 0 |
| 1988 | Wembley | 2 | 2 |
| 1988 | Dusseldorf (EC) | 1 | 3 |
| 1990 | Cagliari (WC) | 0 | 0 |

| | | | |
|---|---|---|---|
| 1993 | Wembley (WC) | 2 | 2 |
| 1993 | Rotterdam (WC) | 0 | 2 |
| 1996 | Wembley (EC) | 4 | 1 |
| 2001 | White Hart Lane | 0 | 2 |
| 2002 | Amsterdam | 1 | 1 |
| 2005 | Villa Park | 0 | 0 |
| 2006 | Amsterdam | 1 | 1 |
| 2009 | Amsterdam | 2 | 2 |
| 2012 | Wembley | 2 | 3 |
| 2016 | Wembley | 1 | 2 |
| 2018 | Amsterdam | 1 | 0 |

### v HONDURAS

| | | E | H |
|---|---|---|---|
| 2014 | Miami | 0 | 0 |

### v HUNGARY

| | | E | H |
|---|---|---|---|
| 1908 | Budapest | 7 | 0 |
| 1909 | Budapest | 4 | 2 |
| 1909 | Budapest | 8 | 2 |
| 1934 | Budapest | 1 | 2 |
| 1936 | Highbury | 6 | 2 |
| 1953 | Wembley | 3 | 6 |
| 1954 | Budapest | 1 | 7 |
| 1960 | Budapest | 0 | 2 |
| 1962 | Rancagua (WC) | 1 | 2 |
| 1965 | Wembley | 1 | 0 |
| 1978 | Wembley | 4 | 1 |
| 1981 | Budapest (WC) | 3 | 1 |
| 1981 | Wembley (WC) | 1 | 0 |
| 1983 | Wembley (EC) | 2 | 0 |
| 1983 | Budapest (EC) | 3 | 0 |
| 1988 | Budapest | 0 | 0 |
| 1990 | Wembley | 1 | 0 |
| 1992 | Budapest | 1 | 0 |
| 1996 | Wembley | 3 | 0 |
| 1999 | Budapest | 1 | 1 |
| 2006 | Old Trafford | 3 | 1 |
| 2010 | Wembley | 2 | 1 |

### v ICELAND

| | | E | I |
|---|---|---|---|
| 1982 | Reykjavik | 1 | 1 |
| 2004 | City of Manchester | 6 | 1 |
| 2016 | Nice (EC) | 1 | 2 |

### v ISRAEL

| | | E | I |
|---|---|---|---|
| 1986 | Tel Aviv | 2 | 1 |
| 1988 | Tel Aviv | 0 | 0 |
| 2006 | Tel Aviv (EC) | 0 | 0 |
| 2007 | Wembley (EC) | 3 | 0 |

### v ITALY

| | | E | I |
|---|---|---|---|
| 1933 | Rome | 1 | 1 |
| 1934 | Highbury | 3 | 2 |
| 1939 | Milan | 2 | 2 |
| 1948 | Turin | 4 | 0 |
| 1949 | White Hart Lane | 2 | 0 |
| 1952 | Florence | 1 | 1 |
| 1959 | Wembley | 2 | 2 |
| 1961 | Rome | 3 | 2 |
| 1973 | Turin | 0 | 2 |
| 1973 | Wembley | 0 | 1 |
| 1976 | New York | 3 | 2 |
| 1976 | Rome (WC) | 0 | 2 |
| 1977 | Wembley (WC) | 2 | 0 |
| 1980 | Turin (EC) | 0 | 1 |
| 1985 | Mexico City | 1 | 2 |
| 1989 | Wembley | 0 | 0 |
| 1990 | Bari (WC) | 1 | 2 |
| 1996 | Wembley (WC) | 0 | 1 |
| 1997 | Nantes (TF) | 2 | 0 |
| 1997 | Rome (WC) | 0 | 0 |
| 2000 | Turin | 0 | 1 |
| 2002 | Leeds | 1 | 2 |
| 2012* | Kiev (EC) | 0 | 0 |
| 2012 | Berne | 2 | 1 |
| 2014 | Manaus (WC) | 1 | 2 |
| 2015 | Turin | 1 | 1 |
| 2018 | Wembley | 1 | 1 |

(*England lost 2-4 on pens)

### v JAMAICA

| | | E | J |
|---|---|---|---|
| 2006 | Old Trafford | 6 | 0 |

### v JAPAN

| | | E | J |
|---|---|---|---|
| 1995 | Wembley | 2 | 1 |
| 2004 | City of Manchester | 1 | 1 |
| 2010 | Graz | 2 | 1 |

### v KAZAKHSTAN

| | | E | K |
|---|---|---|---|
| 2008 | Wembley (WC) | 5 | 1 |
| 2009 | Almaty (WC) | 4 | 0 |

### v KUWAIT

| | | E | K |
|---|---|---|---|
| 1982 | Bilbao (WC) | 1 | 0 |

### v LIECHTENSTEIN

| | | E | L |
|---|---|---|---|
| 2003 | Vaduz (EC) | 2 | 0 |
| 2003 | Old Trafford (EC) | 2 | 0 |

### v LITHUANIA

| | | E | L |
|---|---|---|---|
| 2015 | Wembley (EC) | 4 | 0 |
| 2015 | Vilnius (EC) | 3 | 0 |
| 2017 | Wembley (WC) | 2 | 0 |
| 2017 | Vilnius (WC) | 1 | 0 |

### v LUXEMBOURG

| | | E | L |
|---|---|---|---|
| 1927 | Luxembourg | 5 | 2 |
| 1960 | Luxembourg (WC) | 9 | 0 |
| 1961 | Highbury (WC) | 4 | 1 |
| 1977 | Wembley (WC) | 5 | 0 |
| 1977 | Luxembourg (WC) | 2 | 0 |
| 1982 | Wembley (EC) | 9 | 0 |
| 1983 | Luxembourg (EC) | 4 | 0 |
| 1998 | Luxembourg (EC) | 3 | 0 |
| 1999 | Wembley (EC) | 6 | 0 |

### v MACEDONIA

| | | E | M |
|---|---|---|---|
| 2002 | Southampton (EC) | 2 | 2 |
| 2003 | Skopje (EC) | 2 | 1 |
| 2006 | Skopje (EC) | 1 | 0 |
| 2006 | Old Trafford (EC) | 0 | 0 |

### v MALAYSIA

| | | E | M |
|---|---|---|---|
| 1991 | Kuala Lumpur | 4 | 2 |

## v MALTA

| | | E | M |
|---|---|---|---|
| 1971 | Valletta (EC) | 1 | 0 |
| 1971 | Wembley (EC) | 5 | 0 |
| 2000 | Valletta | 2 | 1 |
| 2016 | Wembley (WC) | 2 | 0 |
| 2017 | Ta'Qali (WC) | 4 | 0 |

## v MEXICO

| | | E | M |
|---|---|---|---|
| 1959 | Mexico City | 1 | 2 |
| 1961 | Wembley | 8 | 0 |
| 1966 | Wembley (WC) | 2 | 0 |
| 1969 | Mexico City | 0 | 0 |
| 1985 | Mexico City | 0 | 1 |
| 1986 | Los Angeles | 3 | 0 |
| 1997 | Wembley | 2 | 0 |
| 2001 | Derby | 4 | 0 |
| 2010 | Wembley | 3 | 1 |

## v MOLDOVA

| | | E | M |
|---|---|---|---|
| 1996 | Kishinev | 3 | 0 |
| 1997 | Wembley (WC) | 4 | 0 |
| 2012 | Chisinu (WC) | 5 | 0 |
| 2013 | Wembley (WC) | 4 | 0 |

## v MONTENEGRO

| | | E | M |
|---|---|---|---|
| 2010 | Wembley (EC) | 0 | 0 |
| 2011 | Podgorica (EC) | 2 | 2 |
| 2013 | Podgorica (WC) | 1 | 1 |
| 2013 | Wembley (WC) | 4 | 1 |

## v MOROCCO

| | | E | M |
|---|---|---|---|
| 1986 | Monterrey (WC) | 0 | 0 |
| 1998 | Casablanca | 1 | 0 |

## v NEW ZEALAND

| | | E | NZ |
|---|---|---|---|
| 1991 | Auckland | 1 | 0 |
| 1991 | Wellington | 2 | 0 |

## v NIGERIA

| | | E | NZ |
|---|---|---|---|
| 1994 | Wembley | 1 | 0 |
| 2002 | Osaka (WC) | 0 | 0 |
| 2018 | Wembley | 2 | 1 |

## v NORWAY

| | | E | NZ |
|---|---|---|---|
| 1937 | Oslo | 6 | 0 |
| 1938 | Newcastle | 4 | 0 |
| 1949 | Oslo | 4 | 1 |
| 1966 | Oslo | 6 | 1 |
| 1980 | Wembley (WC) | 4 | 0 |
| 1981 | Oslo (WC) | 1 | 2 |
| 1992 | Wembley (WC) | 1 | 1 |
| 1993 | Oslo (WC) | 0 | 2 |
| 1994 | Wembley | 0 | 0 |
| 1995 | Oslo | 0 | 0 |
| 2012 | Oslo | 1 | 0 |
| 2014 | Wembley | 1 | 0 |

## v PANAMA

| | | E | P |
|---|---|---|---|
| 2018 | Nizhny Novgorod (WC) | 6 | 1 |

## v PARAGUAY

| | | E | P |
|---|---|---|---|
| 1986 | Mexico City (WC) | 3 | 0 |
| 2002 | Anfield | 4 | 0 |
| 2006 | Frankfurt (WC) | 1 | 0 |

## v PERU

| | | E | P |
|---|---|---|---|
| 1959 | Lima | 1 | 4 |
| 1961 | Lima | 4 | 0 |
| 2014 | Wembley | 3 | 0 |

## v POLAND

| | | E | P |
|---|---|---|---|
| 1966 | Goodison Park | 1 | 1 |
| 1966 | Chorzow | 1 | 0 |
| 1973 | Chorzow (WC) | 0 | 2 |
| 1973 | Wembley (WC) | 1 | 1 |
| 1986 | Monterrey (WC) | 3 | 0 |
| 1989 | Wembley (WC) | 3 | 0 |
| 1989 | Katowice (WC) | 0 | 0 |
| 1990 | Wembley (EC) | 2 | 0 |
| 1991 | Poznan (EC) | 1 | 1 |
| 1993 | Chorzow (WC) | 1 | 1 |
| 1993 | Wembley (WC) | 3 | 0 |
| 1996 | Wembley (WC) | 2 | 1 |
| 1997 | Katowice (WC) | 2 | 0 |
| 1999 | Wembley (EC) | 3 | 1 |
| 1999 | Warsaw (EC) | 0 | 0 |
| 2004 | Katowice (WC) | 2 | 1 |
| 2005 | Old Trafford (WC) | 2 | 1 |
| 2012 | Warsaw (WC) | 1 | 1 |
| 2013 | Wembley (WC) | 2 | 0 |

## v PORTUGAL

| | | E | P |
|---|---|---|---|
| 1947 | Lisbon | 10 | 0 |
| 1950 | Lisbon | 5 | 3 |
| 1951 | Goodison Park | 5 | 2 |
| 1955 | Oporto | 1 | 3 |
| 1958 | Wembley | 2 | 1 |
| 1961 | Lisbon (WC) | 1 | 1 |
| 1961 | Wembley (WC) | 2 | 0 |
| 1964 | Lisbon | 4 | 3 |
| 1964 | Sao Paulo | 1 | 1 |
| 1966 | Wembley (WC) | 2 | 1 |
| 1969 | Wembley | 1 | 0 |
| 1974 | Lisbon | 0 | 0 |
| 1974 | Wembley (EC) | 0 | 0 |
| 1975 | Lisbon (EC) | 1 | 1 |
| 1986 | Monterrey (WC) | 0 | 1 |
| 1995 | Wembley | 1 | 1 |
| 1998 | Wembley | 3 | 0 |
| 2000 | Eindhoven (EC) | 2 | 3 |
| 2002 | Villa Park | 1 | 1 |
| 2004 | Faro | 1 | 1 |
| 2004* | Lisbon (EC) | 2 | 2 |
| 2006† | Gelsenkirchen (WC) | 0 | 0 |
| 2016 | Wembley | 1 | 0 |

(† England lost 1–3 on pens)
(*England lost 5–6 on pens)

## v REPUBLIC OF IRELAND

| | | E | RoI |
|---|---|---|---|
| 1946 | Dublin | 1 | 0 |
| 1949 | Goodison Park | 0 | 2 |
| 1957 | Wembley (WC) | 5 | 1 |
| 1957 | Dublin (WC) | 1 | 1 |
| 1964 | Dublin | 3 | 1 |

| | | | |
|---|---|---|---|
| 1977 | Wembley | 1 | 1 |
| 1978 | Dublin (EC) | 1 | 1 |
| 1980 | Wembley (EC) | 2 | 0 |
| 1985 | Wembley | 2 | 1 |
| 1988 | Stuttgart (EC) | 0 | 1 |
| 1990 | Cagliari (WC) | 1 | 1 |
| 1990 | Dublin (EC) | 1 | 1 |
| 1991 | Wembley (EC) | 1 | 1 |
| 1995* | Dublin | 0 | 1 |
| 2013 | Wembley | 1 | 1 |
| 2015 | Dublin | 0 | 0 |

(*Abandoned 27 mins – crowd riot)

## v ROMANIA

| | | E | R |
|---|---|---|---|
| 1939 | Bucharest | 2 | 0 |
| 1968 | Bucharest | 0 | 0 |
| 1969 | Wembley | 1 | 1 |
| 1970 | Guadalajara (WC) | 1 | 0 |
| 1980 | Bucharest (WC) | 1 | 2 |
| 1981 | Wembley (WC) | 0 | 0 |
| 1985 | Bucharest (WC) | 0 | 0 |
| 1985 | Wembley (WC) | 1 | 1 |
| 1994 | Wembley | 1 | 1 |
| 1998 | Toulouse (WC) | 1 | 2 |
| 2000 | Charleroi (EC) | 2 | 3 |

## v RUSSIA

| | | E | R |
|---|---|---|---|
| 2007 | Wembley (EC) | 3 | 0 |
| 2007 | Moscow (EC) | 1 | 2 |
| 2016 | Marseille (EC) | 1 | 1 |

## v SAN MARINO

| | | E | SM |
|---|---|---|---|
| 1992 | Wembley (WC) | 6 | 0 |
| 1993 | Bologna (WC) | 7 | 1 |
| 2012 | Wembley (WC) | 5 | 0 |
| 2013 | Serravalle (WC) | 8 | 0 |
| 2014 | Wembley (EC) | 5 | 0 |
| 2015 | Serravalle (EC) | 6 | 0 |

## v SAUDI ARABIA

| | | E | SA |
|---|---|---|---|
| 1988 | Riyadh | 1 | 1 |
| 1998 | Wembley | 0 | 0 |

## v SERBIA-MONTENEGRO

| | | E | S-M |
|---|---|---|---|
| 2003 | Leicester | 2 | 1 |

## v SLOVAKIA

| | | E | S |
|---|---|---|---|
| 2002 | Bratislava (EC) | 2 | 1 |
| 2003 | Middlesbrough (EC) | 2 | 1 |
| 2009 | Wembley | 4 | 0 |
| 2016 | St Etienne (EC) | 0 | 0 |
| 2016 | Trnava (WC) | 1 | 0 |
| 2017 | Wembley (WC) | 2 | 1 |

## v SLOVENIA

| | | E | S |
|---|---|---|---|
| 2009 | Wembley | 2 | 1 |
| 2010 | Port Elizabeth (WC) | 1 | 0 |
| 2014 | Wembley (EC) | 3 | 1 |
| 2015 | Ljubljana (EC) | 3 | 2 |
| 2016 | Ljubljana (WC) | 0 | 0 |
| 2017 | Wembley (WC) | 1 | 0 |

## v SOUTH AFRICA

| | | E | SA |
|---|---|---|---|
| 1997 | Old Trafford | 2 | 1 |
| 2003 | Durban | 2 | 1 |

## v SOUTH KOREA

| | | E | SK |
|---|---|---|---|
| 2002 | Seoguipo | 1 | 1 |

## v SOVIET UNION (see also CIS)

| | | E | SU |
|---|---|---|---|
| 1958 | Moscow | 1 | 1 |
| 1958 | Gothenburg (WC) | 2 | 2 |
| 1958 | Gothenburg (WC) | 0 | 1 |
| 1958 | Wembley | 5 | 0 |
| 1967 | Wembley | 2 | 2 |
| 1968 | Rome (EC) | 2 | 0 |
| 1973 | Moscow | 2 | 1 |
| 1984 | Wembley | 0 | 2 |
| 1986 | Tbilisi | 1 | 0 |
| 1988 | Frankfurt (EC) | 1 | 3 |
| 1991 | Wembley | 3 | 1 |

## v SPAIN

| | | E | S |
|---|---|---|---|
| 1929 | Madrid | 3 | 4 |
| 1931 | Highbury | 7 | 1 |
| 1950 | Rio de Janeiro (WC) | 0 | 1 |
| 1955 | Madrid | 1 | 1 |
| 1955 | Wembley | 4 | 1 |
| 1960 | Madrid | 0 | 3 |
| 1960 | Wembley | 4 | 2 |
| 1965 | Madrid | 2 | 0 |
| 1967 | Wembley | 2 | 0 |
| 1968 | Wembley (EC) | 1 | 0 |
| 1968 | Madrid (EC) | 2 | 1 |
| 1980 | Barcelona | 2 | 0 |
| 1980 | Naples (EC) | 2 | 1 |
| 1981 | Wembley | 1 | 2 |
| 1982 | Madrid (WC) | 0 | 0 |
| 1987 | Madrid | 4 | 2 |
| 1992 | Santander | 0 | 1 |
| 1996* | Wembley (EC) | 0 | 0 |
| 2001 | Villa Park | 3 | 0 |
| 2004 | Madrid | 0 | 1 |
| 2007 | Old Trafford | 0 | 1 |
| 2009 | Seville | 0 | 2 |
| 2011 | Wembley | 1 | 0 |
| 2015 | Alicante | 0 | 2 |
| 2016 | Wembley | 2 | 2 |

(*England won 4-2 on pens)

## v SWEDEN

| | | E | S |
|---|---|---|---|
| 1923 | Stockholm | 4 | 2 |
| 1923 | Stockholm | 3 | 1 |
| 1937 | Stockholm | 4 | 0 |
| 1948 | Highbury | 4 | 2 |
| 1949 | Stockholm | 1 | 3 |
| 1956 | Stockholm | 0 | 0 |
| 1959 | Wembley | 2 | 3 |
| 1965 | Gothenburg | 2 | 1 |
| 1968 | Wembley | 3 | 1 |
| 1979 | Stockholm | 0 | 0 |
| 1986 | Stockholm | 0 | 1 |
| 1988 | Wembley (WC) | 0 | 0 |
| 1989 | Stockholm (WC) | 0 | 0 |
| 1992 | Stockholm (EC) | 1 | 2 |

| | | | |
|---|---|---|---|
| 1995 | Leeds | 3 | 3 |
| 1998 | Stockholm (EC) | 1 | 2 |
| 1999 | Wembley (EC) | 0 | 0 |
| 2001 | Old Trafford | 1 | 1 |
| 2002 | Saitama (WC) | 1 | 1 |
| 2004 | Gothenburg | 0 | 1 |
| 2006 | Cologne (WC) | 2 | 2 |
| 2011 | Wembley | 1 | 0 |
| 2012 | Kiev (EC) | 3 | 2 |
| 2012 | Stockholm | 2 | 4 |
| 2018 | Samara (WC) | 2 | 0 |

### v SWITZERLAND

| | | *E* | *S* |
|---|---|---|---|
| 1933 | Berne | 4 | 0 |
| 1938 | Zurich | 1 | 2 |
| 1947 | Zurich | 0 | 1 |
| 1949 | Highbury | 6 | 0 |
| 1952 | Zurich | 3 | 0 |
| 1954 | Berne (WC) | 2 | 0 |
| 1962 | Wembley | 3 | 1 |
| 1963 | Basle | 8 | 1 |
| 1971 | Basle (EC) | 3 | 2 |
| 1971 | Wembley (EC) | 1 | 1 |
| 1975 | Basle | 2 | 1 |
| 1977 | Wembley | 0 | 0 |
| 1980 | Wembley (WC) | 2 | 1 |
| 1981 | Basle (WC) | 1 | 2 |
| 1988 | Lausanne | 1 | 0 |
| 1995 | Wembley | 3 | 1 |
| 1996 | Wembley (EC) | 1 | 1 |
| 1998 | Berne | 1 | 1 |
| 2004 | Coimbra (EC) | 3 | 0 |
| 2008 | Wembley | 2 | 1 |
| 2010 | Basle (EC) | 3 | 1 |
| 2011 | Wembley (EC) | 2 | 2 |
| 2014 | Basle (EC) | 2 | 0 |
| 2015 | Wembley (EC) | 2 | 0 |

### v TRINIDAD & TOBAGO

| | | *E* | *T* |
|---|---|---|---|
| 2006 | Nuremberg (WC) | 2 | 0 |
| 2008 | Port of Spain | 3 | 0 |

### v TUNISIA

| | | *E* | *T* |
|---|---|---|---|
| 1990 | Tunis | 1 | 1 |
| 1998 | Marseille (WC) | 2 | 0 |
| 2018 | Volgograd (WC) | 2 | 1 |

### v TURKEY

| | | *E* | *T* |
|---|---|---|---|
| 1984 | Istanbul (WC) | 8 | 0 |
| 1985 | Wembley (WC) | 5 | 0 |
| 1987 | Izmir (EC) | 0 | 0 |
| 1987 | Wembley (EC) | 8 | 0 |
| 1991 | Izmir (EC) | 1 | 0 |
| 1991 | Wembley (EC) | 1 | 0 |
| 1992 | Wembley (WC) | 4 | 0 |
| 1993 | Izmir (WC) | 2 | 0 |
| 2003 | Sunderland (EC) | 2 | 0 |
| 2003 | Istanbul (EC) | 0 | 0 |
| 2016 | Etihad Stadium | 2 | 1 |

### v UKRAINE

| | | *E* | *U* |
|---|---|---|---|
| 2000 | Wembley | 2 | 0 |
| 2004 | Newcastle | 3 | 0 |
| 2009 | Wembley (WC) | 2 | 1 |
| 2009 | Dnipropetrovski (WC) | 0 | 1 |
| 2012 | Donetsk (EC) | 1 | 0 |
| 2012 | Wembley (WC) | 1 | 1 |
| 2013 | Kiev (WC) | 0 | 0 |

### v URUGUAY

| | | *E* | *U* |
|---|---|---|---|
| 1953 | Montevideo | 1 | 2 |
| 1954 | Basle (WC) | 2 | 4 |
| 1964 | Wembley | 2 | 1 |
| 1966 | Wembley (WC) | 0 | 0 |
| 1969 | Montevideo | 2 | 1 |
| 1977 | Montevideo | 0 | 0 |
| 1984 | Montevideo | 0 | 2 |
| 1990 | Wembley | 1 | 2 |
| 1995 | Wembley | 0 | 0 |
| 2006 | Anfield | 2 | 1 |
| 2014 | Sao Paulo (WC) | 1 | 2 |

### v USA

| | | *E* | *USA* |
|---|---|---|---|
| 1950 | Belo Horizonte (WC) | 0 | 1 |
| 1953 | New York | 6 | 3 |
| 1959 | Los Angeles | 8 | 1 |
| 1964 | New York | 10 | 0 |
| 1985 | Los Angeles | 5 | 0 |
| 1993 | Boston | 0 | 2 |
| 1994 | Wembley | 2 | 0 |
| 2005 | Chicago | 2 | 1 |
| 2008 | Wembley | 2 | 0 |
| 2010 | Rustenburg (WC) | 1 | 1 |

### v YUGOSLAVIA

| | | *E* | *Y* |
|---|---|---|---|
| 1939 | Belgrade | 1 | 2 |
| 1950 | Highbury | 2 | 2 |
| 1954 | Belgrade | 0 | 1 |
| 1956 | Wembley | 3 | 0 |
| 1958 | Belgrade | 0 | 5 |
| 1960 | Wembley | 3 | 3 |
| 1965 | Belgrade | 1 | 1 |
| 1966 | Wembley | 2 | 0 |
| 1968 | Florence (EC) | 0 | 1 |
| 1972 | Wembley | 1 | 1 |
| 1974 | Belgrade | 2 | 2 |
| 1986 | Wembley (EC) | 2 | 0 |
| 1987 | Belgrade (EC) | 4 | 1 |
| 1989 | Wembley | 2 | 1 |
| 1937 | Stockholm | 4 | 0 |
| 1948 | Highbury | 4 | 2 |
| 1949 | Stockholm | 1 | 3 |
| 1956 | Stockholm | 0 | 0 |
| 1959 | Wembley | 2 | 3 |
| 1965 | Gothenburg | 2 | 1 |
| 1968 | Wembley | 3 | 1 |
| 1979 | Stockholm | 0 | 0 |
| 1986 | Stockholm | 0 | 1 |
| 1988 | Wembley (WC) | 0 | 0 |
| 1989 | Stockholm (WC) | 0 | 0 |
| 1992 | Stockholm (EC) | 1 | 2 |
| 1995 | Leeds | 3 | 3 |
| 1998 | Stockholm (EC) | 1 | 2 |
| 1999 | Wembley (EC) | 0 | 0 |
| 2001 | Old Trafford | 1 | 1 |
| 2002 | Saitama (WC) | 1 | 1 |
| 2004 | Gothenburg | 0 | 1 |
| 2006 | Cologne (WC) | 2 | 2 |

**ENGLAND'S RECORD** England's first international was a 0-0 draw against Scotland in Glasgow, on the West of Scotland cricket ground, Partick, on November 30, 1872 Their complete record at the start of 2018–19 is:

| *P* | *W* | *D* | *L* | *F* | *A* |
|---|---|---|---|---|---|
| 985 | 559 | 240 | 186 | 2151 | 969 |

# ENGLAND'S 'B' TEAM RESULTS

England scores first

| | | | |
|---|---|---|---|
| 1949 | Finland (A) | 4 | 0 |
| 1949 | Holland (A) | 4 | 0 |
| 1950 | Italy (A) | 0 | 5 |
| 1950 | Holland (H) | 1 | 0 |
| 1950 | Holland (A) | 0 | 3 |
| 1950 | Luxembourg (A) | 2 | 1 |
| 1950 | Switzerland (H) | 5 | 0 |
| 1952 | Holland (A) | 1 | 0 |
| 1952 | France (A) | 1 | 7 |
| 1953 | Scotland (A) | 2 | 2 |
| 1954 | Scotland (H) | 1 | 1 |
| 1954 | Germany (A) | 4 | 0 |
| 1954 | Yugoslavia (A) | 1 | 2 |
| 1954 | Switzerland (A) | 0 | 2 |
| 1955 | Germany (H) | 1 | 1 |
| 1955 | Yugoslavia (H) | 5 | 1 |
| 1956 | Switzerland (H) | 4 | 1 |
| 1956 | Scotland (A) | 2 | 2 |
| 1957 | Scotland (H) | 4 | 1 |
| 1978 | W Germany (A) | 2 | 1 |
| 1978 | Czechoslovakia (A) | 1 | 0 |
| 1978 | Singapore (A) | 8 | 0 |
| 1978 | Malaysia (A) | 1 | 1 |
| 1978 | N Zealand (A) | 4 | 0 |
| 1978 | N Zealand (A) | 3 | 1 |
| 1978 | N Zealand (A) | 4 | 0 |
| 1979 | Austria (A) | 1 | 0 |
| 1979 | N Zealand (H) | 4 | 1 |
| 1980 | USA (H) | 1 | 0 |
| 1980 | Spain (H) | 1 | 0 |
| 1980 | Australia (H) | 1 | 0 |
| 1981 | Spain (A) | 2 | 3 |
| 1984 | N Zealand (H) | 2 | 0 |
| 1987 | Malta (A) | 2 | 0 |
| 1989 | Switzerland (A) | 2 | 0 |
| 1989 | Iceland (A) | 2 | 0 |
| 1989 | Norway (A) | 1 | 0 |
| 1989 | Italy (H) | 1 | 1 |
| 1989 | Yugoslavia (H) | 2 | 1 |
| 1990 | Rep of Ireland (A) | 1 | 4 |
| 1990 | Czechoslovakia (H) | 2 | 0 |
| 1990 | Algeria (A) | 0 | 0 |
| 1991 | Wales (A) | 1 | 0 |
| 1991 | Iceland (H) | 1 | 0 |
| 1991 | Switzerland (H) | 2 | 1 |
| 1991 | Spanish XI (A) | 1 | 0 |
| 1992 | France (H) | 3 | 0 |
| 1992 | Czechoslovakia (A) | 1 | 0 |
| 1992 | CIS (A) | 1 | 1 |
| 1994 | N Ireland (H) | 4 | 2 |
| 1995 | Rep of Ireland (H) | 2 | 0 |
| 1998 | Chile (H) | 1 | 2 |
| 1998 | Russia (H) | 4 | 1 |
| 2006 | Belarus (H) | 1 | 2 |
| 2007 | Albania | 3 | 1 |

# GREAT BRITAIN v REST OF EUROPE (FIFA)

| | | *GB* | *RofE* |
|---|---|---|---|
| 1947 | Glasgow | 6 | 1 |
| 1955 | Belfast | 1 | 4 |

# SCOTLAND

**v ARGENTINA**

| | | *S* | *A* |
|---|---|---|---|
| 1977 | Buenos Aires | 1 | 1 |
| 1979 | Glasgow | 1 | 3 |
| 1990 | Glasgow | 1 | 0 |
| 2008 | Glasgow | 0 | 1 |

**v AUSTRALIA**

| | | *S* | *A* |
|---|---|---|---|
| 1985* | Glasgow (WC) | 2 | 0 |
| 1985* | Melbourne (WC) | 0 | 0 |
| 1996 | Glasgow | 1 | 0 |
| 2000 | Glasgow | 0 | 2 |
| 2012 | Edinburgh | 3 | 1 |

(* World Cup play-off)

**v AUSTRIA**

| | | *S* | *A* |
|---|---|---|---|
| 1931 | Vienna | 0 | 5 |
| 1933 | Glasgow | 2 | 2 |
| 1937 | Vienna | 1 | 1 |
| 1950 | Glasgow | 0 | 1 |
| 1951 | Vienna | 0 | 4 |
| 1954 | Zurich (WC) | 0 | 1 |
| 1955 | Vienna | 4 | 1 |
| 1956 | Glasgow | 1 | 1 |
| 1960 | Vienna | 1 | 4 |
| 1963* | Glasgow | 4 | 1 |
| 1968 | Glasgow (WC) | 2 | 1 |
| 1969 | Vienna (WC) | 0 | 2 |
| 1978 | Vienna (EC) | 2 | 3 |
| 1979 | Glasgow (EC) | 1 | 1 |
| 1994 | Vienna | 2 | 1 |
| 1996 | Vienna (WC) | 0 | 0 |
| 1997 | Glasgow (WC) | 2 | 0 |

(* Abandoned after 79 minutes)

| | | | |
|---|---|---|---|
| 2003 | Glasgow | 0 | 2 |
| 2005 | Graz | 2 | 2 |
| 2007 | Vienna | 1 | 0 |

### v BELARUS

| | | S | B |
|---|---|---|---|
| 1997 | Minsk (WC) | 1 | 0 |
| 1997 | Aberdeen (WC) | 4 | 1 |
| 2005 | Minsk (WC) | 0 | 0 |
| 2005 | Glasgow (WC) | 0 | 1 |

### v BELGIUM

| | | S | B |
|---|---|---|---|
| 1947 | Brussels | 1 | 2 |
| 1948 | Glasgow | 2 | 0 |
| 1951 | Brussels | 5 | 0 |
| 1971 | Liege (EC) | 0 | 3 |
| 1971 | Aberdeen (EC) | 1 | 0 |
| 1974 | Brugge | 1 | 2 |
| 1979 | Brussels (EC) | 0 | 2 |
| 1979 | Glasgow (EC) | 1 | 3 |
| 1982 | Brussels (EC) | 2 | 3 |
| 1983 | Glasgow (EC) | 1 | 1 |
| 1987 | Brussels (EC) | 1 | 4 |
| 1987 | Glasgow (EC) | 2 | 0 |
| 2001 | Glasgow (WC) | 2 | 2 |
| 2001 | Brussels (WC) | 0 | 2 |
| 2012 | Brussels (WC) | 0 | 2 |
| 2013 | Glasgow (WC) | 0 | 2 |

### v BOSNIA

| | | S | B |
|---|---|---|---|
| 1999 | Sarajevo (EC) | 2 | 1 |
| 1999 | Glasgow (EC) | 1 | 0 |

### v BRAZIL

| | | S | B |
|---|---|---|---|
| 1966 | Glasgow | 1 | 1 |
| 1972 | Rio de Janeiro | 0 | 1 |
| 1973 | Glasgow | 0 | 1 |
| 1974 | Frankfurt (WC) | 0 | 0 |
| 1977 | Rio de Janeiro | 0 | 2 |
| 1982 | Seville (WC) | 1 | 4 |
| 1987 | Glasgow | 0 | 2 |
| 1990 | Turin (WC) | 0 | 1 |
| 1998 | St Denis (WC) | 1 | 2 |
| 2011 | Arsenal | 0 | 2 |

### v BULGARIA

| | | S | B |
|---|---|---|---|
| 1978 | Glasgow | 2 | 1 |
| 1986 | Glasgow (EC) | 0 | 0 |
| 1987 | Sofia (EC) | 1 | 0 |
| 1990 | Sofia (EC) | 1 | 1 |
| 1991 | Glasgow (EC) | 1 | 1 |
| 2006 | Kobe | 5 | 1 |

### v CANADA

| | | S | C |
|---|---|---|---|
| 1983 | Vancouver | 2 | 0 |
| 1983 | Edmonton | 3 | 0 |
| 1983 | Toronto | 2 | 0 |
| 1992 | Toronto | 3 | 1 |
| 2002 | Edinburgh | 3 | 1 |
| 2017 | Edinburgh | 1 | 1 |

### v CHILE

| | | S | C |
|---|---|---|---|
| 1977 | Santiago | 4 | 2 |
| 1989 | Glasgow | 2 | 0 |

### v CIS (formerly Soviet Union)

| | | S | C |
|---|---|---|---|
| 1992 | Norrkoping (EC) | 3 | 0 |

### v COLOMBIA

| | | S | C |
|---|---|---|---|
| 1988 | Glasgow | 0 | 0 |
| 1996 | Miami | 0 | 1 |
| 1998 | New York | 2 | 2 |

### v COSTA RICA

| | | S | C |
|---|---|---|---|
| 1990 | Genoa (WC) | 0 | 1 |
| 2018 | Glasgow | 0 | 1 |

### v CROATIA

| | | S | C |
|---|---|---|---|
| 2000 | Zagreb (WC) | 1 | 1 |
| 2001 | Glasgow (WC) | 0 | 0 |
| 2008 | Glasgow | 1 | 1 |
| 2013 | Zagreb (WC) | 1 | 0 |
| 2013 | Glasgow (WC) | 2 | 0 |

### v CYPRUS

| | | S | C |
|---|---|---|---|
| 1968 | Nicosia (WC) | 5 | 0 |
| 1969 | Glasgow (WC) | 8 | 0 |
| 1989 | Limassol (WC) | 3 | 2 |
| 1989 | Glasgow (WC) | 2 | 1 |
| 2011 | Larnaca | 2 | 1 |

### v CZECH REPUBLIC

| | | S | C |
|---|---|---|---|
| 1999 | Glasgow (EC) | 1 | 2 |
| 1999 | Prague (EC) | 2 | 3 |
| 2008 | Prague | 1 | 3 |
| 2010 | Glasgow | 1 | 0 |
| 2010 | Prague (EC) | 0 | 1 |
| 2011 | Glasgow (EC) | 2 | 2 |
| 2016 | Prague | 1 | 0 |

### v CZECHOSLOVAKIA

| | | S | C |
|---|---|---|---|
| 1937 | Prague | 3 | 1 |
| 1937 | Glasgow | 5 | 0 |
| 1961 | Bratislava (WC) | 0 | 4 |
| 1961 | Glasgow (WC) | 3 | 2 |
| 1961* | Brussels (WC) | 2 | 4 |
| 1972 | Porto Alegre | 0 | 0 |
| 1973 | Glasgow (WC) | 2 | 1 |
| 1973 | Bratislava (WC) | 0 | 1 |
| 1976 | Prague (WC) | 0 | 2 |
| 1977 | Glasgow (WC) | 3 | 1 |

(*World Cup play-off)

### v DENMARK

| | | S | D |
|---|---|---|---|
| 1951 | Glasgow | 3 | 1 |
| 1952 | Copenhagen | 2 | 1 |
| 1968 | Copenhagen | 1 | 0 |
| 1970 | Glasgow (EC) | 1 | 0 |
| 1971 | Copenhagen (EC) | 0 | 1 |
| 1972 | Copenhagen (WC) | 4 | 1 |
| 1972 | Glasgow (WC) | 2 | 0 |
| 1975 | Copenhagen (EC) | 1 | 0 |
| 1975 | Glasgow (EC) | 3 | 1 |
| 1986 | Neza (WC) | 0 | 1 |
| 1996 | Copenhagen | 0 | 2 |
| 1998 | Glasgow | 0 | 1 |
| 2002 | Glasgow | 0 | 1 |
| 2004 | Copenhagen | 0 | 1 |
| 2011 | Glasgow | 2 | 1 |
| 2016 | Glasgow | 1 | 0 |

## v EAST GERMANY

| | | S | EG |
|---|---|---|---|
| 1974 | Glasgow | 3 | 0 |
| 1977 | East Berlin | 0 | 1 |
| 1982 | Glasgow (EC) | 2 | 0 |
| 1983 | Halle (EC) | 1 | 2 |
| 1986 | Glasgow | 0 | 0 |
| 1990 | Glasgow | 0 | 1 |

## v ECUADOR

| | | S | E |
|---|---|---|---|
| 1995 | Toyama, Japan | 2 | 1 |

## v EGYPT

| | | S | E |
|---|---|---|---|
| 1990 | Aberdeen | 1 | 3 |

## v ESTONIA

| | | S | E |
|---|---|---|---|
| 1993 | Tallinn (WC) | 3 | 0 |
| 1993 | Aberdeen | 3 | 1 |
| 1996 | Tallinn (WC) | *No result | |
| 1997 | Monaco (WC) | 0 | 0 |
| 1997 | Kilmarnock (WC) | 2 | 0 |
| 1998 | Edinburgh (EC) | 3 | 2 |
| 1999 | Tallinn (EC) | 0 | 0 |
| (* Estonia absent) | | | |
| 2004 | Tallinn | 1 | 0 |
| 2013 | Aberdeen | 1 | 0 |

## v FAROE ISLANDS

| | | S | F |
|---|---|---|---|
| 1994 | Glasgow (EC) | 5 | 1 |
| 1995 | Toftir (EC) | 2 | 0 |
| 1998 | Aberdeen (EC) | 2 | 1 |
| 1999 | Toftir (EC) | 1 | 1 |
| 2002 | Toftir (EC) | 2 | 2 |
| 2003 | Glasgow (EC) | 3 | 1 |
| 2006 | Glasgow (EC) | 6 | 0 |
| 2007 | Toftir (EC) | 2 | 0 |
| 2010 | Aberdeen | 3 | 0 |

## v FINLAND

| | | S | F |
|---|---|---|---|
| 1954 | Helsinki | 2 | 1 |
| 1964 | Glasgow (WC) | 3 | 1 |
| 1965 | Helsinki (WC) | 2 | 1 |
| 1976 | Glasgow | 6 | 0 |
| 1992 | Glasgow | 1 | 1 |
| 1994 | Helsinki (EC) | 2 | 0 |
| 1995 | Glasgow (EC) | 1 | 0 |
| 1998 | Edinburgh | 1 | 1 |

## v FRANCE

| | | S | F |
|---|---|---|---|
| 1930 | Paris | 2 | 0 |
| 1932 | Paris | 3 | 1 |
| 1948 | Paris | 0 | 3 |
| 1949 | Glasgow | 2 | 0 |
| 1950 | Paris | 1 | 0 |
| 1951 | Glasgow | 1 | 0 |
| 1958 | Orebro (WC) | 1 | 2 |
| 1984 | Marseilles | 0 | 2 |
| 1989 | Glasgow (WC) | 2 | 0 |
| 1990 | Paris (WC) | 0 | 3 |
| 1997 | St Etienne | 1 | 2 |
| 2000 | Glasgow | 0 | 2 |
| 2002 | Paris | 0 | 5 |
| 2006 | Glasgow (EC) | 1 | 0 |
| 2007 | Paris (EC) | 1 | 0 |
| 2016 | Metz | 0 | 3 |

## v GEORGIA

| | | S | G |
|---|---|---|---|
| 2007 | Glasgow (EC) | 2 | 1 |
| 2007 | Tbilisi (EC) | 0 | 2 |
| 2014 | Glasgow (EC) | 1 | 0 |
| 2015 | Tbilisi (EC) | 0 | 1 |

## v GERMANY/WEST GERMANY

| | | S | G |
|---|---|---|---|
| 1929 | Berlin | 1 | 1 |
| 1936 | Glasgow | 2 | 0 |
| 1957 | Stuttgart | 3 | 1 |
| 1959 | Glasgow | 3 | 2 |
| 1964 | Hanover | 2 | 2 |
| 1969 | Glasgow (WC) | 1 | 1 |
| 1969 | Hamburg (WC) | 2 | 3 |
| 1973 | Glasgow | 1 | 1 |
| 1974 | Frankfurt | 1 | 2 |
| 1986 | Queretaro (WC) | 1 | 2 |
| 1992 | Norrkoping (EC) | 0 | 2 |
| 1993 | Glasgow | 0 | 1 |
| 1999 | Bremen | 1 | 0 |
| 2003 | Glasgow (EC) | 1 | 1 |
| 2003 | Dortmund (EC) | 1 | 2 |
| 2014 | Dortmund (EC) | 1 | 2 |
| 2015 | Glasgow (EC) | 2 | 3 |

## v GIBRALTAR

| | | S | G |
|---|---|---|---|
| 2015 | Glasgow (EC) | 6 | 1 |
| 2015 | Faro (EC) | 6 | 0 |

## v GREECE

| | | S | G |
|---|---|---|---|
| 1994 | Athens (EC) | 0 | 1 |
| 1995 | Glasgow | 1 | 0 |

## v HOLLAND

| | | S | H |
|---|---|---|---|
| 1929 | Amsterdam | 2 | 0 |
| 1938 | Amsterdam | 3 | 1 |
| 1959 | Amsterdam | 2 | 1 |
| 1966 | Glasgow | 0 | 3 |
| 1968 | Amsterdam | 0 | 0 |
| 1971 | Amsterdam | 1 | 2 |
| 1978 | Mendoza (WC) | 3 | 2 |
| 1982 | Glasgow | 2 | 1 |
| 1986 | Eindhoven | 0 | 0 |
| 1992 | Gothenburg (EC) | 0 | 1 |
| 1994 | Glasgow | 0 | 1 |
| 1994 | Utrecht | 1 | 3 |
| 1996 | Birmingham (EC) | 0 | 0 |
| 2000 | Arnhem | 0 | 0 |
| 2003* | Glasgow (EC) | 1 | 0 |
| 2003* | Amsterdam (EC) | 0 | 6 |
| 2009 | Amsterdam (WC) | 0 | 3 |
| 2009 | Glasgow (WC) | 0 | 1 |
| 2017 | Aberdeen | 0 | 1 |
| (*Qual Round play-off) | | | |

## v HUNGARY

| | | S | H |
|---|---|---|---|
| 1938 | Glasgow | 3 | 1 |
| 1955 | Glasgow | 2 | 4 |

| | | | |
|---|---|---|---|
| 1955 | Budapest | 1 | 3 |
| 1958 | Glasgow | 1 | 1 |
| 1960 | Budapest | 3 | 3 |
| 1980 | Budapest | 1 | 3 |
| 1987 | Glasgow | 2 | 0 |
| 2004 | Glasgow | 0 | 3 |
| 2018 | Budapest | 1 | 0 |

### v ICELAND

| | | *S* | *I* |
|---|---|---|---|
| 1984 | Glasgow (WC) | 3 | 0 |
| 1985 | Reykjavik (WC) | 1 | 0 |
| 2002 | Reykjavik (EC) | 2 | 0 |
| 2003 | Glasgow (EC) | 2 | 1 |
| 2008 | Reykjavik (WC) | 2 | 1 |
| 2009 | Glasgow (WC) | 2 | 1 |

### v IRAN

| | | *S* | *I* |
|---|---|---|---|
| 1978 | Cordoba (WC) | 1 | 1 |

### v ISRAEL

| | | *S* | *I* |
|---|---|---|---|
| 1981 | Tel Aviv (WC) | 1 | 0 |
| 1981 | Glasgow (WC) | 3 | 1 |
| 1986 | Tel Aviv | 1 | 0 |

### v ITALY

| | | *S* | *I* |
|---|---|---|---|
| 1931 | Rome | 0 | 3 |
| 1965 | Glasgow (WC) | 1 | 0 |
| 1965 | Naples (WC) | 0 | 3 |
| 1988 | Perugia | 0 | 2 |
| 1992 | Glasgow (WC) | 0 | 0 |
| 1993 | Rome (WC) | 1 | 3 |
| 2005 | Milan (WC) | 0 | 2 |
| 2005 | Glasgow (WC) | 1 | 1 |
| 2007 | Bari (EC) | 0 | 2 |
| 2007 | Glasgow (EC) | 1 | 2 |
| 2016 | Ta'Qali | 0 | 1 |

### v JAPAN

| | | *S* | *J* |
|---|---|---|---|
| 1995 | Hiroshima | 0 | 0 |
| 2006 | Saitama | 0 | 0 |
| 2009 | Yokohama | 0 | 2 |

### v LATVIA

| | | *S* | *L* |
|---|---|---|---|
| 1996 | Riga (WC) | 2 | 0 |
| 1997 | Glasgow (WC) | 2 | 0 |
| 2000 | Riga (WC) | 1 | 0 |
| 2001 | Glasgow (WC) | 2 | 1 |

### v LIECHTENSTEIN

| | | *S* | *L* |
|---|---|---|---|
| 2010 | Glasgow (EC) | 2 | 1 |
| 2011 | Vaduz (EC) | 1 | 0 |

### v LITHUANIA

| | | *S* | *L* |
|---|---|---|---|
| 1998 | Vilnius (EC) | 0 | 0 |
| 1999 | Glasgow (EC) | 3 | 0 |
| 2003 | Kaunus (EC) | 0 | 1 |
| 2003 | Glasgow (EC) | 1 | 0 |
| 2006 | Kaunas (EC) | 2 | 1 |
| 2007 | Glasgow (EC) | 3 | 1 |
| 2010 | Kaunas (EC) | 0 | 0 |
| 2011 | Glasgow (EC) | 1 | 0 |
| 2016 | Glasgow (WC) | 1 | 1 |
| 2017 | Vilnius (WC) | 3 | 0 |

### v LUXEMBOURG

| | | *S* | *L* |
|---|---|---|---|
| 1947 | Luxembourg | 6 | 0 |
| 1986 | Glasgow (EC) | 3 | 0 |
| 1987 | Esch (EC) | 0 | 0 |
| 2012 | Josy Barthel | 2 | 1 |

### v MACEDONIA

| | | *S* | *M* |
|---|---|---|---|
| 2008 | Skopje (WC) | 0 | 1 |
| 2009 | Glasgow (WC) | 2 | 0 |
| 2012 | Glasgow (WC) | 1 | 1 |
| 2013 | Skopje (WC) | 2 | 1 |

### v MALTA

| | | *S* | *M* |
|---|---|---|---|
| 1988 | Valletta | 1 | 1 |
| 1990 | Valletta | 2 | 1 |
| 1993 | Glasgow (WC) | 3 | 0 |
| 1993 | Valletta (WC) | 2 | 0 |
| 1997 | Valletta | 3 | 2 |
| 2016 | Ta'Qali (WC) | 5 | 1 |
| 2017 | Glasgow (WC) | 2 | 0 |

### v MEXICO

| | | *S* | *M* |
|---|---|---|---|
| 2018 | Mexico City | 0 | 1 |

### v MOLDOVA

| | | *S* | *M* |
|---|---|---|---|
| 2004 | Chisinau (WC) | 1 | 1 |
| 2005 | Glasgow (WC) | 2 | 0 |

### v MOROCCO

| | | *S* | *M* |
|---|---|---|---|
| 1998 | St Etienne (WC) | 0 | 3 |

### v NEW ZEALAND

| | | *S* | *NZ* |
|---|---|---|---|
| 1982 | Malaga (WC) | 5 | 2 |
| 2003 | Edinburgh | 1 | 1 |

### v NIGERIA

| | | *S* | *N* |
|---|---|---|---|
| 2002 | Aberdeen | 1 | 2 |
| 2014 | Fulham | 2 | 2 |

### v NORWAY

| | | *S* | *N* |
|---|---|---|---|
| 1929 | Bergen | 7 | 3 |
| 1954 | Glasgow | 1 | 0 |
| 1954 | Oslo | 1 | 1 |
| 1963 | Bergen | 3 | 4 |
| 1963 | Glasgow | 6 | 1 |
| 1974 | Oslo | 2 | 1 |
| 1978 | Glasgow (EC) | 3 | 2 |
| 1979 | Oslo (EC) | 4 | 0 |
| 1988 | Oslo (WC) | 2 | 1 |
| 1989 | Glasgow (WC) | 1 | 1 |
| 1992 | Oslo | 0 | 0 |
| 1998 | Bordeaux (WC) | 1 | 1 |
| 2003 | Oslo | 0 | 0 |
| 2004 | Glasgow (WC) | 0 | 1 |
| 2005 | Oslo (WC) | 2 | 1 |
| 2008 | Glasgow (WC) | 0 | 0 |
| 2009 | Oslo (WC) | 0 | 4 |
| 2013 | Molde | 1 | 0 |

### v PARAGUAY

| | | *S* | *P* |
|---|---|---|---|
| 1958 | Norrkoping (WC) | 2 | 3 |

## v PERU

| | | S | P |
|---|---|---|---|
| 1972 | Glasgow | 2 | 0 |
| 1978 | Cordoba (WC) | 1 | 3 |
| 1979 | Glasgow | 1 | 1 |
| 2018 | Lima | 0 | 2 |

## v POLAND

| | | S | P |
|---|---|---|---|
| 1958 | Warsaw | 2 | 1 |
| 1960 | Glasgow | 2 | 3 |
| 1965 | Chorzow (WC) | 1 | 1 |
| 1965 | Glasgow (WC) | 1 | 2 |
| 1980 | Poznan | 0 | 1 |
| 1990 | Glasgow | 1 | 1 |
| 2001 | Bydgoszcz | 1 | 1 |
| 2014 | Warsaw | 1 | 0 |
| 2014 | Warsaw (EC) | 2 | 2 |
| 2015 | Glasgow (EC) | 2 | 2 |

## v PORTUGAL

| | | S | P |
|---|---|---|---|
| 1950 | Lisbon | 2 | 2 |
| 1955 | Glasgow | 3 | 0 |
| 1959 | Lisbon | 0 | 1 |
| 1966 | Glasgow | 0 | 1 |
| 1971 | Lisbon (EC) | 0 | 2 |
| 1971 | Glasgow (EC) | 2 | 1 |
| 1975 | Glasgow | 1 | 0 |
| 1978 | Lisbon (EC) | 0 | 1 |
| 1980 | Glasgow (EC) | 4 | 1 |
| 1980 | Glasgow (WC) | 0 | 0 |
| 1981 | Lisbon (WC) | 1 | 2 |
| 1992 | Glasgow (WC) | 0 | 0 |
| 1993 | Lisbon (WC) | 0 | 5 |
| 2002 | Braga | 0 | 2 |

## v QATAR

| | | S | Q |
|---|---|---|---|
| 2015 | Edinburgh | 1 | 0 |

## v REPUBLIC OF IRELAND

| | | S | RoI |
|---|---|---|---|
| 1961 | Glasgow (WC) | 4 | 1 |
| 1961 | Dublin (WC) | 3 | 0 |
| 1963 | Dublin | 0 | 1 |
| 1969 | Dublin | 1 | 1 |
| 1986 | Dublin (EC) | 0 | 0 |
| 1987 | Glasgow (EC) | 0 | 1 |
| 2000 | Dublin | 2 | 1 |
| 2003 | Glasgow (EC) | 0 | 2 |
| 2011 | Dublin (CC) | 0 | 1 |
| 2014 | Glasgow (EC) | 1 | 0 |
| 2015 | Dublin (EC) | 1 | 1 |

## v ROMANIA

| | | S | R |
|---|---|---|---|
| 1975 | Bucharest (EC) | 1 | 1 |
| 1975 | Glasgow (EC) | 1 | 1 |
| 1986 | Glasgow | 3 | 0 |
| 1990 | Glasgow (EC) | 2 | 1 |
| 1991 | Bucharest (EC) | 0 | 1 |
| 2004 | Glasgow | 1 | 2 |

## v RUSSIA

| | | S | R |
|---|---|---|---|
| 1994 | Glasgow (EC) | 1 | 1 |
| 1995 | Moscow (EC) | 0 | 0 |

## v SAN MARINO

| | | S | SM |
|---|---|---|---|
| 1991 | Serravalle (EC) | 2 | 0 |
| 1991 | Glasgow (EC) | 4 | 0 |
| 1995 | Serravalle (EC) | 2 | 0 |
| 1995 | Glasgow (EC) | 5 | 0 |
| 2000 | Serravalle (WC) | 2 | 0 |
| 2001 | Glasgow (WC) | 4 | 0 |

## v SAUDI ARABIA

| | | S | SA |
|---|---|---|---|
| 1988 | Riyadh | 2 | 2 |

## v SERBIA

| | | S | Se |
|---|---|---|---|
| 2012 | Glasgow (WC) | 0 | 0 |
| 2013 | Novi Sad (WC) | 0 | 2 |

## v SLOVAKIA

| | | S | Sl |
|---|---|---|---|
| 2016 | Trnava (WC) | 0 | 3 |
| 2017 | Glasgow (WC) | 1 | 0 |

## v SLOVENIA

| | | S | SL |
|---|---|---|---|
| 2004 | Glasgow (WC) | 0 | 0 |
| 2005 | Celje (WC) | 3 | 0 |
| 2012 | Koper | 1 | 1 |
| 2017 | Glasgow (WC) | 1 | 0 |
| 2017 | Ljubljana (WC) | 2 | 2 |

## v SOUTH AFRICA

| | | S | SA |
|---|---|---|---|
| 2002 | Hong Kong | 0 | 2 |
| 2007 | Aberdeen | 1 | 0 |

## v SOUTH KOREA

| | | S | SK |
|---|---|---|---|
| 2002 | Busan | 1 | 4 |

## v SOVIET UNION (see also CIS and RUSSIA)

| | | S | SU |
|---|---|---|---|
| 1967 | Glasgow | 0 | 2 |
| 1971 | Moscow | 0 | 1 |
| 1982 | Malaga (WC) | 2 | 2 |
| 1991 | Glasgow | 0 | 1 |

## v SPAIN

| | | S | Sp |
|---|---|---|---|
| 1957 | Glasgow (WC) | 4 | 2 |
| 1957 | Madrid (WC) | 1 | 4 |
| 1963 | Madrid | 6 | 2 |
| 1965 | Glasgow | 0 | 0 |
| 1975 | Glasgow (EC) | 1 | 2 |
| 1975 | Valencia (EC) | 1 | 1 |
| 1982 | Valencia | 0 | 3 |
| 1985 | Glasgow (WC) | 3 | 1 |
| 1985 | Seville (WC) | 0 | 1 |
| 1988 | Madrid | 0 | 0 |
| 2004* | Valencia | 1 | 1 |
| (*Abandoned after 59 mins – floodlight failure) | | | |
| 2010 | Glasgow (EC) | 2 | 3 |
| 2011 | Alicante (EC) | 1 | 3 |

## v SWEDEN

| | | S | Swe |
|---|---|---|---|
| 1952 | Stockholm | 1 | 3 |
| 1953 | Glasgow | 1 | 2 |
| 1975 | Gothenburg | 1 | 1 |
| 1977 | Glasgow | 3 | 1 |
| 1980 | Stockholm (WC) | 1 | 0 |

| | | | |
|---|---|---|---|
| 1981 | Glasgow (WC) | 2 | 0 |
| 1990 | Genoa (WC) | 2 | 1 |
| 1995 | Solna | 0 | 2 |
| 1996 | Glasgow (WC) | 1 | 0 |
| 1997 | Gothenburg (WC) | 1 | 2 |
| 2004 | Edinburgh | 1 | 4 |
| 2010 | Stockholm | 0 | 3 |

### v SWITZERLAND

| | | *S* | *Sw* |
|---|---|---|---|
| 1931 | Geneva | 3 | 2 |
| 1948 | Berne | 1 | 2 |
| 1950 | Glasgow | 3 | 1 |
| 1957 | Basle (WC) | 2 | 1 |
| 1957 | Glasgow (WC) | 3 | 2 |
| 1973 | Berne | 0 | 1 |
| 1976 | Glasgow | 1 | 0 |
| 1982 | Berne (EC) | 0 | 2 |
| 1983 | Glasgow (EC) | 2 | 2 |
| 1990 | Glasgow (EC) | 2 | 1 |
| 1991 | Berne (EC) | 2 | 2 |
| 1992 | Berne (WC) | 1 | 3 |
| 1993 | Aberdeen (WC) | 1 | 1 |
| 1996 | Birmingham (EC) | 1 | 0 |
| 2006 | Glasgow | 1 | 3 |

### v TRINIDAD & TOBAGO

| | | *S* | *T* |
|---|---|---|---|
| 2004 | Hibernian | 4 | 1 |

### v TURKEY

| | | *S* | *T* |
|---|---|---|---|
| 1960 | Ankara | 2 | 4 |

### v UKRAINE

| | | *S* | *U* |
|---|---|---|---|
| 2006 | Kiev (EC) | 0 | 2 |
| 2007 | Glasgow (EC) | 3 | 1 |

### v USA

| | | *S* | *USA* |
|---|---|---|---|
| 1952 | Glasgow | 6 | 0 |
| 1992 | Denver | 1 | 0 |
| 1996 | New Britain, Conn | 1 | 2 |
| 1998 | Washington | 0 | 0 |
| 2005 | Glasgow | 1 | 1 |
| 2012 | Jacksonville | 1 | 5 |
| 2013 | Glasgow | 0 | 0 |

### v URUGUAY

| | | *S* | *U* |
|---|---|---|---|
| 1954 | Basle (WC) | 0 | 7 |
| 1962 | Glasgow | 2 | 3 |
| 1983 | Glasgow | 2 | 0 |
| 1986 | Neza (WC) | 0 | 0 |

### v YUGOSLAVIA

| | | *S* | *Y* |
|---|---|---|---|
| 1955 | Belgrade | 2 | 2 |
| 1956 | Glasgow | 2 | 0 |
| 1958 | Vaasteras (WC) | 1 | 1 |
| 1972 | Belo Horizonte | 2 | 2 |
| 1974 | Frankfurt (WC) | 1 | 1 |
| 1984 | Glasgow | 6 | 1 |
| 1988 | Glasgow (WC) | 1 | 1 |
| 1989 | Zagreb (WC) | 1 | 3 |

### v ZAIRE

| | | *S* | *Z* |
|---|---|---|---|
| 1974 | Dortmund (WC) | 2 | 0 |

# WALES

### v ALBANIA

| | | *W* | *A* |
|---|---|---|---|
| 1994 | Cardiff (EC) | 2 | 0 |
| 1995 | Tirana (EC) | 1 | 1 |

### v ANDORRA

| | | *W* | *A* |
|---|---|---|---|
| 2014 | La Vella (EC) | 2 | 1 |
| 2015 | Cardiff (EC) | 2 | 0 |

### v ARGENTINA

| | | *W* | *A* |
|---|---|---|---|
| 1992 | Gifu (Japan) | 0 | 1 |
| 2002 | Cardiff | 1 | 1 |

### v ARMENIA

| | | *W* | *A* |
|---|---|---|---|
| 2001 | Yerevan (WC) | 2 | 2 |
| 2001 | Cardiff (WC) | 0 | 0 |

### v AUSTRALIA

| | | *W* | *A* |
|---|---|---|---|
| 2011 | Cardiff | 1 | 2 |

### v AUSTRIA

| | | *W* | *A* |
|---|---|---|---|
| 1954 | Vienna | 0 | 2 |
| 1955 | Wrexham | 1 | 2 |
| 1975 | Vienna (EC) | 1 | 2 |
| 1975 | Wrexham (EC) | 1 | 0 |
| 1992 | Vienna | 1 | 1 |
| 2005 | Cardiff | 0 | 2 |
| 2005 | Vienna | 0 | 1 |
| 2013 | Swansea | 2 | 1 |
| 2016 | Vienna (WC) | 2 | 2 |
| 2017 | Cardiff (WC) | 1 | 0 |

### v AZERBAIJAN

| | | *W* | *A* |
|---|---|---|---|
| 2002 | Baku (EC) | 2 | 0 |
| 2003 | Cardiff (EC) | 4 | 0 |
| 2004 | Baku (WC) | 1 | 1 |
| 2005 | Cardiff (WC) | 2 | 0 |
| 2008 | Cardiff (WC) | 1 | 0 |
| 2009 | Baku (WC) | 1 | 0 |

### v BELARUS

| | | *W* | *B* |
|---|---|---|---|
| 1998 | Cardiff (EC) | 3 | 2 |
| 1999 | Minsk (EC) | 2 | 1 |
| 2000 | Minsk (WC) | 1 | 2 |
| 2001 | Cardiff (WC) | 1 | 0 |

### v BELGIUM

| | | *W* | *B* |
|---|---|---|---|
| 1949 | Liege | 1 | 3 |
| 1949 | Cardiff | 5 | 1 |
| 1990 | Cardiff (EC) | 3 | 1 |
| 1991 | Brussels (EC) | 1 | 1 |
| 1992 | Brussels (WC) | 0 | 2 |
| 1993 | Cardiff (WC) | 2 | 0 |
| 1997 | Cardiff (WC) | 1 | 2 |
| 1997 | Brussels (WC) | 2 | 3 |

| | | | |
|---|---|---|---|
| 2012 | Cardiff (WC) | 0 | 2 |
| 2013 | Brussels (WC) | 1 | 1 |
| 2014 | Brussels (EC) | 0 | 0 |
| 2015 | Cardiff (EC) | 1 | 0 |
| 2016 | Lille (EC) | 3 | 1 |

**v BOSNIA-HERZEGOVINA**

| | | *W* | *B-H* |
|---|---|---|---|
| 2003 | Cardiff | 2 | 2 |
| 2012 | Llanelli | 0 | 2 |
| 2014 | Cardiff (EC) | 0 | 0 |
| 2015 | Zenica (EC) | 0 | 2 |

**v BRAZIL**

| | | *W* | *B* |
|---|---|---|---|
| 1958 | Gothenburg (WC) | 0 | 1 |
| 1962 | Rio de Janeiro | 1 | 3 |
| 1962 | Sao Paulo | 1 | 3 |
| 1966 | Rio de Janeiro | 1 | 3 |
| 1966 | Belo Horizonte | 0 | 1 |
| 1983 | Cardiff | 1 | 1 |
| 1991 | Cardiff | 1 | 0 |
| 1997 | Brasilia | 0 | 3 |
| 2000 | Cardiff | 0 | 3 |
| 2006 | White Hart Lane | 0 | 2 |

**v BULGARIA**

| | | *W* | *B* |
|---|---|---|---|
| 1983 | Wrexham (EC) | 1 | 0 |
| 1983 | Sofia (EC) | 0 | 1 |
| 1994 | Cardiff (EC) | 0 | 3 |
| 1995 | Sofia (EC) | 1 | 3 |
| 2006 | Swansea | 0 | 0 |
| 2007 | Bourgas | 1 | 0 |
| 2010 | Cardiff (EC) | 0 | 1 |
| 2011 | Sofia (EC) | 1 | 0 |

**v CANADA**

| | | *W* | *C* |
|---|---|---|---|
| 1986 | Toronto | 0 | 2 |
| 1986 | Vancouver | 3 | 0 |
| 2004 | Wrexham | 1 | 0 |

**v CHILE**

| | | *W* | *C* |
|---|---|---|---|
| 1966 | Santiago | 0 | 2 |

**v CHINA**

| | | *W* | *C* |
|---|---|---|---|
| 2018 | Nanning | 6 | 0 |

**v COSTA RICA**

| | | *W* | *C* |
|---|---|---|---|
| 1990 | Cardiff | 1 | 0 |
| 2012 | Cardiff | 0 | 1 |

**v CROATIA**

| | | *W* | *C* |
|---|---|---|---|
| 2002 | Varazdin | 1 | 1 |
| 2010 | Osijek | 0 | 2 |
| 2012 | Osijek (WC) | 0 | 2 |
| 2013 | Swansea (WC) | 1 | 2 |

**v CYPRUS**

| | | *W* | *C* |
|---|---|---|---|
| 1992 | Limassol (WC) | 1 | 0 |
| 1993 | Cardiff (WC) | 2 | 0 |
| 2005 | Limassol | 0 | 1 |
| 2006 | Cardiff (EC) | 3 | 1 |
| 2007 | Nicosia (EC) | 1 | 3 |
| 2014 | Cardiff (EC) | 2 | 1 |
| 2015 | Nicosia | 1 | 0 |

**v CZECHOSLOVAKIA (see also RCS)**

| | | *W* | *C* |
|---|---|---|---|
| 1957 | Cardiff (WC) | 1 | 0 |
| 1957 | Prague (WC) | 0 | 2 |
| 1971 | Swansea (EC) | 1 | 3 |
| 1971 | Prague (EC) | 0 | 1 |
| 1977 | Wrexham (WC) | 3 | 0 |
| 1977 | Prague (WC) | 0 | 1 |
| 1980 | Cardiff (WC) | 1 | 0 |
| 1981 | Prague (WC) | 0 | 2 |
| 1987 | Wrexham (EC) | 1 | 1 |
| 1987 | Prague (EC) | 0 | 2 |

**v CZECH REPUBLIC**

| | | *W* | *CR* |
|---|---|---|---|
| 2002 | Cardiff | 0 | 0 |
| 2006 | Teplice (EC) | 1 | 2 |
| 2007 | Cardiff (EC) | 0 | 0 |

**v DENMARK**

| | | *W* | *D* |
|---|---|---|---|
| 1964 | Copenhagen (WC) | 0 | 1 |
| 1965 | Wrexham (WC) | 4 | 2 |
| 1987 | Cardiff (EC) | 1 | 0 |
| 1987 | Copenhagen (EC) | 0 | 1 |
| 1990 | Copenhagen | 0 | 1 |
| 1998 | Copenhagen (EC) | 2 | 1 |
| 1999 | Anfield (EC) | 0 | 2 |
| 2008 | Copenhagen | 1 | 0 |

**v EAST GERMANY**

| | | *W* | *EG* |
|---|---|---|---|
| 1957 | Leipzig (WC) | 1 | 2 |
| 1957 | Cardiff (WC) | 4 | 1 |
| 1969 | Dresden (WC) | 1 | 2 |
| 1969 | Cardiff (WC) | 1 | 3 |

**v ESTONIA**

| | | *W* | *E* |
|---|---|---|---|
| 1994 | Tallinn | 2 | 1 |
| 2009 | Llanelli | 1 | 0 |

**v FAROE ISLANDS**

| | | *W* | *FI* |
|---|---|---|---|
| 1992 | Cardiff (WC) | 6 | 0 |
| 1993 | Toftir (WC) | 3 | 0 |

**v FINLAND**

| | | *W* | *F* |
|---|---|---|---|
| 1971 | Helsinki (EC) | 1 | 0 |
| 1971 | Swansea (EC) | 3 | 0 |
| 1986 | Helsinki (EC) | 1 | 1 |
| 1987 | Wrexham (EC) | 4 | 0 |
| 1988 | Swansea (WC) | 2 | 2 |
| 1989 | Helsinki (WC) | 0 | 1 |
| 2000 | Cardiff | 1 | 2 |
| 2002 | Helsinki (EC) | 2 | 0 |
| 2003 | Cardiff (EC) | 1 | 1 |
| 2009 | Cardiff (WC) | 0 | 2 |
| 2009 | Helsinki (WC) | 1 | 2 |
| 2013 | Cardiff | 1 | 1 |

**v FRANCE**

| | | *W* | *F* |
|---|---|---|---|
| 1933 | Paris | 1 | 1 |
| 1939 | Paris | 1 | 2 |
| 1953 | Paris | 1 | 6 |
| 1982 | Toulouse | 1 | 0 |
| 2017 | Paris | 0 | 2 |

### v GEORGIA

| | | W | G |
|---|---|---|---|
| 1994 | Tbilisi (EC) | 0 | 5 |
| 1995 | Cardiff (EC) | 0 | 1 |
| 2008 | Swansea | 1 | 2 |
| 2016 | Cardiff (WC) | 1 | 1 |
| 2017 | Tbilisi (WC) | 1 | 0 |

### v GERMANY/WEST GERMANY

| | | W | G |
|---|---|---|---|
| 1968 | Cardiff | 1 | 1 |
| 1969 | Frankfurt | 1 | 1 |
| 1977 | Cardiff | 0 | 2 |
| 1977 | Dortmund | 1 | 1 |
| 1979 | Wrexham (EC) | 0 | 2 |
| 1979 | Cologne (EC) | 1 | 5 |
| 1989 | Cardiff (WC) | 0 | 0 |
| 1989 | Cologne (WC) | 1 | 2 |
| 1991 | Cardiff (EC) | 1 | 0 |
| 1991 | Nuremberg (EC) | 1 | 4 |
| 1995 | Dusseldorf (EC) | 1 | 1 |
| 1995 | Cardiff (EC) | 1 | 2 |
| 2002 | Cardiff | 1 | 0 |
| 2007 | Cardiff (EC) | 0 | 2 |
| 2007 | Frankfurt (EC) | 0 | 0 |
| 2008 | Moenchengladbach (WC) | 0 | 1 |
| 2009 | Cardiff (WC) | 0 | 2 |

### v GREECE

| | | W | G |
|---|---|---|---|
| 1964 | Athens (WC) | 0 | 2 |
| 1965 | Cardiff (WC) | 4 | 1 |

### v HOLLAND

| | | W | H |
|---|---|---|---|
| 1988 | Amsterdam (WC) | 0 | 1 |
| 1989 | Wrexham (WC) | 1 | 2 |
| 1992 | Utrecht | 0 | 4 |
| 1996 | Cardiff (WC) | 1 | 3 |
| 1996 | Eindhoven (WC) | 1 | 7 |
| 2008 | Rotterdam | 0 | 2 |
| 2014 | Amsterdam | 0 | 2 |
| 2015 | Cardiff | 2 | 3 |

### v HUNGARY

| | | W | H |
|---|---|---|---|
| 1958 | Sanviken (WC) | 1 | 1 |
| 1958 | Stockholm (WC) | 2 | 1 |
| 1961 | Budapest | 2 | 3 |
| 1963 | Budapest (EC) | 1 | 3 |
| 1963 | Cardiff (EC) | 1 | 1 |
| 1974 | Cardiff (EC) | 2 | 0 |
| 1975 | Budapest (EC) | 2 | 1 |
| 1986 | Cardiff | 0 | 3 |
| 2004 | Budapest | 2 | 1 |
| 2005 | Cardiff | 2 | 0 |

### v ICELAND

| | | W | I |
|---|---|---|---|
| 1980 | Reykjavik (WC) | 4 | 0 |
| 1981 | Swansea (WC) | 2 | 2 |
| 1984 | Reykjavik (WC) | 0 | 1 |
| 1984 | Cardiff (WC) | 2 | 1 |
| 1991 | Cardiff | 1 | 0 |
| 2008 | Reykjavik | 1 | 0 |
| 2014 | Cardiff | 3 | 1 |

### v IRAN

| | | W | I |
|---|---|---|---|
| 1978 | Tehran | 1 | 0 |

### v ISRAEL

| | | W | I |
|---|---|---|---|
| 1958 | Tel Aviv (WC) | 2 | 0 |
| 1958 | Cardiff (WC) | 2 | 0 |
| 1984 | Tel Aviv | 0 | 0 |
| 1989 | Tel Aviv | 3 | 3 |
| 2015 | Haifa (EC) | 3 | 0 |
| 2015 | Cardiff (EC) | 0 | 0 |

### v ITALY

| | | W | I |
|---|---|---|---|
| 1965 | Florence | 1 | 4 |
| 1968 | Cardiff (WC) | 0 | 1 |
| 1969 | Rome (WC) | 1 | 4 |
| 1988 | Brescia | 1 | 0 |
| 1996 | Terni | 0 | 3 |
| 1998 | Anfield (EC) | 0 | 2 |
| 1999 | Bologna (EC) | 0 | 4 |
| 2002 | Cardiff (EC) | 2 | 1 |
| 2003 | Milan (EC) | 0 | 4 |

### v JAMAICA

| | | W | J |
|---|---|---|---|
| 1998 | Cardiff | 0 | 0 |

### v JAPAN

| | | W | J |
|---|---|---|---|
| 1992 | Matsuyama | 1 | 0 |

### v KUWAIT

| | | W | K |
|---|---|---|---|
| 1977 | Wrexham | 0 | 0 |
| 1977 | Kuwait City | 0 | 0 |

### v LATVIA

| | | W | L |
|---|---|---|---|
| 2004 | Riga | 2 | 0 |

### v LIECHTENSTEIN

| | | W | L |
|---|---|---|---|
| 2006 | Wrexham | 4 | 0 |
| 2008 | Cardfiff (WC) | 2 | 0 |
| 2009 | Vaduz (WC) | 2 | 0 |

### v LUXEMBOURG

| | | W | L |
|---|---|---|---|
| 1974 | Swansea (EC) | 5 | 0 |
| 1975 | Luxembourg (EC) | 3 | 1 |
| 1990 | Luxembourg (EC) | 1 | 0 |
| 1991 | Luxembourg (EC) | 1 | 0 |
| 2008 | Luxembourg | 2 | 0 |
| 2010 | Llanelli | 5 | 1 |

### v MACEDONIA

| | | W | M |
|---|---|---|---|
| 2013 | Skopje (WC) | 1 | 2 |
| 2013 | Cardiff (WC) | 1 | 0 |

### v MALTA

| | | W | M |
|---|---|---|---|
| 1978 | Wrexham (EC) | 7 | 0 |
| 1979 | Valletta (EC) | 2 | 0 |
| 1988 | Valletta | 3 | 2 |
| 1998 | Valletta | 3 | 0 |

### v MEXICO

| | | W | M |
|---|---|---|---|
| 1958 | Stockholm (WC) | 1 | 1 |
| 1962 | Mexico City | 1 | 2 |
| 2012 | New York | 0 | 2 |
| 2018 | Pasadena | 0 | 0 |

## v MOLDOVA

| | | W | M |
|---|---|---|---|
| 1994 | Kishinev (EC) | 2 | 3 |
| 1995 | Cardiff (EC) | 1 | 0 |
| 2016 | Cardiff (WC) | 4 | 0 |
| 2017 | Chisinau (WC) | 2 | 0 |

## v MONTENEGRO

| | | W | M |
|---|---|---|---|
| 2009 | Podgorica | 1 | 2 |
| 2010 | Podgorica (EC) | 0 | 1 |
| 2011 | Cardiff (EC) | 2 | 1 |

## v NEW ZEALAND

| | | W | NZ |
|---|---|---|---|
| 2007 | Wrexham | 2 | 2 |

## v NORWAY

| | | W | N |
|---|---|---|---|
| 1982 | Swansea (EC) | 1 | 0 |
| 1983 | Oslo (EC) | 0 | 0 |
| 1984 | Trondheim | 0 | 1 |
| 1985 | Wrexham | 1 | 1 |
| 1985 | Bergen | 2 | 4 |
| 1994 | Cardiff | 1 | 3 |
| 2000 | Cardiff (WC) | 1 | 1 |
| 2001 | Oslo (WC) | 2 | 3 |
| 2004 | Oslo | 0 | 0 |
| 2008 | Wrexham | 3 | 0 |
| 2011 | Cardiff | 4 | 1 |

## v PANAMA

| | | W | P |
|---|---|---|---|
| 2017 | Cardiff | 1 | 1 |

## v PARAGUAY

| | | W | P |
|---|---|---|---|
| 2006 | Cardiff | 0 | 0 |

## v POLAND

| | | W | P |
|---|---|---|---|
| 1973 | Cardiff (WC) | 2 | 0 |
| 1973 | Katowice (WC) | 0 | 3 |
| 1991 | Radom | 0 | 0 |
| 2000 | Warsaw (WC) | 0 | 0 |
| 2001 | Cardiff (WC) | 1 | 2 |
| 2004 | Cardiff (WC) | 2 | 3 |
| 2005 | Warsaw (WC) | 0 | 1 |
| 2009 | Vila-Real (Por) | 0 | 1 |

## v PORTUGAL

| | | W | P |
|---|---|---|---|
| 1949 | Lisbon | 2 | 3 |
| 1951 | Cardiff | 2 | 1 |
| 2000 | Chaves | 0 | 3 |
| 2016 | Lyon (EC) | 0 | 2 |

## v QATAR

| | | W | Q |
|---|---|---|---|
| 2000 | Doha | 1 | 0 |

## v RCS (formerly Czechoslovakia)

| | | W | RCS |
|---|---|---|---|
| 1993 | Ostrava (WC) | 1 | 1 |
| 1993 | Cardiff (WC) | 2 | 2 |

## v REPUBLIC OF IRELAND

| | | W | RI |
|---|---|---|---|
| 1960 | Dublin | 3 | 2 |
| 1979 | Swansea | 2 | 1 |
| 1981 | Dublin | 3 | 1 |
| 1986 | Dublin | 1 | 0 |
| 1990 | Dublin | 0 | 1 |
| 1991 | Wrexham | 0 | 3 |
| 1992 | Dublin | 1 | 0 |
| 1993 | Dublin | 1 | 2 |
| 1997 | Cardiff | 0 | 0 |
| 2007 | Dublin (EC) | 0 | 1 |
| 2007 | Cardiff (EC) | 2 | 2 |
| 2011 | Dublin (CC) | 0 | 3 |
| 2013 | Cardiff | 0 | 0 |
| 2017 | Dublin (WC) | 0 | 0 |
| 2017 | Cardiff (WC) | 0 | 1 |

## v REST OF UNITED KINGDOM

| | | W | UK |
|---|---|---|---|
| 1951 | Cardiff | 3 | 2 |
| 1969 | Cardiff | 0 | 1 |

## v ROMANIA

| | | W | R |
|---|---|---|---|
| 1970 | Cardiff (EC) | 0 | 0 |
| 1971 | Bucharest (EC) | 0 | 2 |
| 1983 | Wrexham | 5 | 0 |
| 1992 | Bucharest (WC) | 1 | 5 |
| 1993 | Cardiff (WC) | 1 | 2 |

## v RUSSIA (See also Soviet Union)

| | | W | R |
|---|---|---|---|
| 2003* | Moscow (EC) | 0 | 0 |
| 2003* | Cardiff (EC) | 0 | 1 |
| 2008 | Moscow (WC) | 1 | 2 |
| 2009 | Cardiff (WC) | 1 | 3 |
| 2016 | Toulouse (EC) | 3 | 0 |

(*Qual Round play-offs)

## v SAN MARINO

| | | W | SM |
|---|---|---|---|
| 1996 | Serravalle (WC) | 5 | 0 |
| 1996 | Cardiff (WC) | 6 | 0 |
| 2007 | Cardiff (EC) | 3 | 0 |
| 2007 | Serravalle (EC) | 2 | 1 |

## v SAUDI ARABIA

| | | W | SA |
|---|---|---|---|
| 1986 | Dahran | 2 | 1 |

## v SERBIA

| | | W | S |
|---|---|---|---|
| 2012 | Novi Sad (WC) | 1 | 6 |
| 2013 | Cardiff (WC) | 0 | 3 |
| 2016 | Cardiff (WC) | 1 | 1 |
| 2017 | Belgrade (WC) | 1 | 1 |

## v SERBIA & MONTENEGRO

| | | W | S |
|---|---|---|---|
| 2003 | Belgrade (EC) | 0 | 1 |
| 2003 | Cardiff (EC) | 2 | 3 |

## v SLOVAKIA

| | | W | S |
|---|---|---|---|
| 2006 | Cardiff (EC) | 1 | 5 |
| 2007 | Trnava (EC) | 5 | 2 |
| 2016 | Bordeaux (EC) | 2 | 1 |

## v SLOVENIA

| | | W | S |
|---|---|---|---|
| 2005 | Swansea | 0 | 0 |

## v SOVIET UNION (See also Russia)

| | | W | SU |
|---|---|---|---|
| 1965 | Moscow (WC) | 1 | 2 |
| 1965 | Cardiff (WC) | 2 | 1 |
| 1981 | Wrexham (WC) | 0 | 0 |
| 1981 | Tbilisi (WC) | 0 | 3 |
| 1987 | Swansea | 0 | 0 |

### v SPAIN

| | | W | S |
|---|---|---|---|
| 1961 | Cardiff (WC) | 1 | 2 |
| 1961 | Madrid (WC) | 1 | 1 |
| 1982 | Valencia | 1 | 1 |
| 1984 | Seville (WC) | 0 | 3 |
| 1985 | Wrexham (WC) | 3 | 0 |

### v SWEDEN

| | | W | S |
|---|---|---|---|
| 1958 | Stockholm (WC) | 0 | 0 |
| 1988 | Stockholm | 1 | 4 |
| 1989 | Wrexham | 0 | 2 |
| 1990 | Stockholm | 2 | 4 |
| 1994 | Wrexham | 0 | 2 |
| 2010 | Swansea | 0 | 1 |
| 2016 | Stockholm | 0 | 3 |

### v SWITZERLAND

| | | W | S |
|---|---|---|---|
| 1949 | Berne | 0 | 4 |
| 1951 | Wrexham | 3 | 2 |
| 1996 | Lugano | 0 | 2 |
| 1999 | Zurich (EC) | 0 | 2 |
| 1999 | Wrexham (EC) | 0 | 2 |
| 2010 | Basle (EC) | 1 | 4 |
| 2011 | Swansea (EC) | 2 | 0 |

### v TRINIDAD & TOBAGO

| | | W | T |
|---|---|---|---|
| 2006 | Graz | 2 | 1 |

### v TUNISIA

| | | W | T |
|---|---|---|---|
| 1998 | Tunis | 0 | 4 |

### v TURKEY

| | | W | T |
|---|---|---|---|
| 1978 | Wrexham (EC) | 1 | 0 |
| 1979 | Izmir (EC) | 0 | 1 |
| 1980 | Cardiff (WC) | 4 | 0 |
| 1981 | Ankara (WC) | 1 | 0 |
| 1996 | Cardiff (WC) | 0 | 0 |
| 1997 | Istanbul (WC) | 4 | 6 |

### v UKRAINE

| | | W | U |
|---|---|---|---|
| 2001 | Cardiff (WC) | 1 | 1 |
| 2001 | Kiev (WC) | 1 | 1 |
| 2015 | Kiev | 0 | 1 |

### v URUGUAY

| | | W | U |
|---|---|---|---|
| 1986 | Wrexham | 0 | 0 |
| 2018 | Nanning | 0 | 1 |

### v USA

| | | W | USA |
|---|---|---|---|
| 2003 | San Jose | 0 | 2 |

### v YUGOSLAVIA

| | | W | Y |
|---|---|---|---|
| 1953 | Belgrade | 2 | 5 |
| 1954 | Cardiff | 1 | 3 |
| 1976 | Zagreb (EC) | 0 | 2 |
| 1976 | Cardiff (EC) | 1 | 1 |
| 1982 | Titograd (EC) | 4 | 4 |
| 1983 | Cardiff (EC) | 1 | 1 |
| 1988 | Swansea | 1 | 2 |

# NORTHERN IRELAND

### v ALBANIA

| | | NI | A |
|---|---|---|---|
| 1965 | Belfast (WC) | 4 | 1 |
| 1965 | Tirana (WC) | 1 | 1 |
| 1983 | Tirana (EC) | 0 | 0 |
| 1983 | Belfast (EC) | 1 | 0 |
| 1992 | Belfast (WC) | 3 | 0 |
| 1993 | Tirana (WC) | 2 | 1 |
| 1996 | Belfast (WC) | 2 | 0 |
| 1997 | Zurich (WC) | 0 | 1 |
| 2010 | Tirana | 0 | 1 |

### v ALGERIA

| | | NI | A |
|---|---|---|---|
| 1986 | Guadalajara (WC) | 1 | 1 |

### v ARGENTINA

| | | NI | A |
|---|---|---|---|
| 1958 | Halmstad (WC) | 1 | 3 |

### v ARMENIA

| | | NI | A |
|---|---|---|---|
| 1996 | Belfast (WC) | 1 | 1 |
| 1997 | Yerevan (WC) | 0 | 0 |
| 2003 | Yerevan (EC) | 0 | 1 |
| 2003 | Belfast (EC) | 0 | 1 |

### v AUSTRALIA

| | | NI | A |
|---|---|---|---|
| 1980 | Sydney | 2 | 1 |
| 1980 | Melbourne | 1 | 1 |
| 1980 | Adelaide | 2 | 1 |

### v AUSTRIA

| | | NI | A |
|---|---|---|---|
| 1982 | Madrid (WC) | 2 | 2 |
| 1982 | Vienna (EC) | 0 | 2 |
| 1983 | Belfast (EC) | 3 | 1 |
| 1990 | Vienna (EC) | 0 | 0 |
| 1991 | Belfast (EC) | 2 | 1 |
| 1994 | Vienna (EC) | 2 | 1 |
| 1995 | Belfast (EC) | 5 | 3 |
| 2004 | Belfast (WC) | 3 | 3 |
| 2005 | Vienna (WC) | 0 | 2 |

### v AZERBAIJAN

| | | NI | A |
|---|---|---|---|
| 2004 | Baku (WC) | 0 | 0 |
| 2005 | Belfast (WC) | 2 | 0 |
| 2012 | Belfast (WC) | 1 | 1 |
| 2013 | Baku (WC) | 0 | 2 |
| 2016 | Belfast (WC) | 4 | 0 |
| 2017 | Baku (WC) | 1 | 0 |

### v BARBADOS

| | | NI | B |
|---|---|---|---|
| 2004 | Bridgetown | 1 | 1 |

### v BELARUS

| | | NI | B |
|---|---|---|---|
| 2016 | Belfast | 3 | 0 |

### v BELGIUM

| | | NI | B |
|---|---|---|---|
| 1976 | Liege (WC) | 0 | 2 |

| | | | |
|---|---|---|---|
| 1977 | Belfast (WC) | 3 | 0 |
| 1997 | Belfast | 3 | 0 |

**v BRAZIL**

| | | *NI* | *B* |
|---|---|---|---|
| 1986 | Guadalajara (WC) | 0 | 3 |

**v BULGARIA**

| | | *NI* | *B* |
|---|---|---|---|
| 1972 | Sofia (WC) | 0 | 3 |
| 1973 | Sheffield (WC) | 0 | 0 |
| 1978 | Sofia (EC) | 2 | 0 |
| 1979 | Belfast (EC) | 2 | 0 |
| 2001 | Sofia (WC) | 3 | 4 |
| 2001 | Belfast (WC) | 0 | 1 |
| 2008 | Belfast | 0 | 1 |

**v CANADA**

| | | *NI* | *C* |
|---|---|---|---|
| 1995 | Edmonton | 0 | 2 |
| 1999 | Belfast | 1 | 1 |
| 2005 | Belfast | 0 | 1 |

**v CHILE**

| | | *NI* | *C* |
|---|---|---|---|
| 1989 | Belfast | 0 | 1 |
| 1995 | Edmonton, Canada | 0 | 2 |
| 2010 | Chillan | 0 | 1 |
| 2014 | Valparaiso | 0 | 2 |

**v COLOMBIA**

| | | *NI* | *C* |
|---|---|---|---|
| 1994 | Boston, USA | 0 | 2 |

**v COSTA RICA**

| | | *NI* | *CR* |
|---|---|---|---|
| 2018 | San Jose | 0 | 3 |

**v CROATIA**

| | | *NI* | *C* |
|---|---|---|---|
| 2016 | Belfast | 0 | 3 |

**v CYPRUS**

| | | *NI* | *C* |
|---|---|---|---|
| 1971 | Nicosia (EC) | 3 | 0 |
| 1971 | Belfast (EC) | 5 | 0 |
| 1973 | Nicosia (WC) | 0 | 1 |
| 1973 | Fulham (WC) | 3 | 0 |
| 2002 | Belfast | 0 | 0 |
| 2014 | Nicosia | 0 | 0 |

**v CZECHOSLOVAKIA/CZECH REP**

| | | *NI* | *C* |
|---|---|---|---|
| 1958 | Halmstad (WC) | 1 | 0 |
| 1958 | Malmo (WC) | 2 | 1 |
| 2001 | Belfast (WC) | 0 | 1 |
| 2001 | Teplice (WC) | 1 | 3 |
| 2008 | Belfast (WC) | 0 | 0 |
| 2009 | Prague (WC) | 0 | 0 |
| 2016 | Prague (WC) | 0 | 0 |
| 2017 | Belfast (WC) | 2 | 0 |

**v DENMARK**

| | | *NI* | *D* |
|---|---|---|---|
| 1978 | Belfast (EC) | 2 | 1 |
| 1979 | Copenhagen (EC) | 0 | 4 |
| 1986 | Belfast | 1 | 1 |
| 1990 | Belfast (EC) | 1 | 1 |
| 1991 | Odense (EC) | 1 | 2 |
| 1992 | Belfast (WC) | 0 | 1 |
| 1993 | Copenhagen (WC) | 0 | 1 |
| 2000 | Belfast (WC) | 1 | 1 |
| 2001 | Copenhagen (WC) | 1 | 1 |
| 2006 | Copenhagen (EC) | 0 | 0 |
| 2007 | Belfast (EC) | 2 | 1 |

**v ESTONIA**

| | | *NI* | *E* |
|---|---|---|---|
| 2004 | Tallinn | 1 | 0 |
| 2006 | Belfast | 1 | 0 |
| 2011 | Tallinn (EC) | 1 | 4 |
| 2011 | Belfast (EC) | 1 | 2 |

**v FAROE ISLANDS**

| | | *NI* | *FI* |
|---|---|---|---|
| 1991 | Belfast (EC) | 1 | 1 |
| 1991 | Landskrona, Sw (EC) | 5 | 0 |
| 2010 | Toftir (EC) | 1 | 1 |
| 2011 | Belfast (EC) | 4 | 0 |
| 2014 | Belfast (EC) | 2 | 0 |
| 2015 | Torshavn (EC) | 3 | 1 |

**v FINLAND**

| | | *NI* | *F* |
|---|---|---|---|
| 1984 | Pori (WC) | 0 | 1 |
| 1984 | Belfast (WC) | 2 | 1 |
| 1998 | Belfast (EC) | 1 | 0 |
| 1999 | Helsinki (EC) | 1 | 4 |
| 2003 | Belfast | 0 | 1 |
| 2006 | Helsinki | 2 | 1 |
| 2012 | Belfast | 3 | 3 |
| 2015 | Belfast (EC) | 2 | 1 |
| 2015 | Helsinki (EC) | 1 | 1 |

**v FRANCE**

| | | *NI* | *F* |
|---|---|---|---|
| 1951 | Belfast | 2 | 2 |
| 1952 | Paris | 1 | 3 |
| 1958 | Norrkoping (WC) | 0 | 4 |
| 1982 | Paris | 0 | 4 |
| 1982 | Madrid (WC) | 1 | 4 |
| 1986 | Paris | 0 | 0 |
| 1988 | Belfast | 0 | 0 |
| 1999 | Belfast | 0 | 1 |

**v GEORGIA**

| | | *NI* | *G* |
|---|---|---|---|
| 2008 | Belfast | 4 | 1 |

**v GERMANY/WEST GERMANY**

| | | *NI* | *G* |
|---|---|---|---|
| 1958 | Malmo (WC) | 2 | 2 |
| 1960 | Belfast (WC) | 3 | 4 |
| 1961 | Berlin (WC) | 1 | 2 |
| 1966 | Belfast | 0 | 2 |
| 1977 | Cologne | 0 | 5 |
| 1982 | Belfast (EC) | 1 | 0 |
| 1983 | Hamburg (EC) | 1 | 0 |
| 1992 | Bremen | 1 | 1 |
| 1996 | Belfast | 1 | 1 |
| 1997 | Nuremberg (WC) | 1 | 1 |
| 1997 | Belfast (WC) | 1 | 3 |
| 1999 | Belfast (EC) | 0 | 3 |
| 1999 | Dortmund (EC) | 0 | 4 |
| 2005 | Belfast | 1 | 4 |
| 2016 | Paris (EC) | 0 | 1 |
| 2016 | Hannover (WC) | 0 | 2 |
| 2017 | Belfast (WC) | 1 | 3 |

**v GREECE**

| | | *NI* | *G* |
|---|---|---|---|
| 1961 | Athens (WC) | 1 | 2 |

| | | | |
|---|---|---|---|
| 1961 | Belfast (WC) | 2 | 0 |
| 1988 | Athens | 2 | 3 |
| 2003 | Belfast (EC) | 0 | 2 |
| 2003 | Athens (EC) | 0 | 1 |
| 2014 | Piraeus (EC) | 2 | 0 |
| 2015 | Belfast (EC) | 3 | 1 |

**v HOLLAND**

| | | *NI* | *H* |
|---|---|---|---|
| 1962 | Rotterdam | 0 | 4 |
| 1965 | Belfast (WC) | 2 | 1 |
| 1965 | Rotterdam (WC) | 0 | 0 |
| 1976 | Rotterdam (WC) | 2 | 2 |
| 1977 | Belfast (WC) | 0 | 1 |
| 2012 | Amsterdam | 0 | 6 |

**v HONDURAS**

| | | *NI* | *H* |
|---|---|---|---|
| 1982 | Zaragoza (WC) | 1 | 1 |

**v HUNGARY**

| | | *NI* | *H* |
|---|---|---|---|
| 1988 | Budapest (WC) | 0 | 1 |
| 1989 | Belfast (WC) | 1 | 2 |
| 2000 | Belfast | 0 | 1 |
| 2008 | Belfast | 0 | 2 |
| 2014 | Budapest (EC) | 2 | 1 |
| 2015 | Belfast (EC) | 1 | 1 |

**v ICELAND**

| | | *NI* | *I* |
|---|---|---|---|
| 1977 | Reykjavik (WC) | 0 | 1 |
| 1977 | Belfast (WC) | 2 | 0 |
| 2000 | Reykjavik (WC) | 0 | 1 |
| 2001 | Belfast (WC) | 3 | 0 |
| 2006 | Belfast (EC) | 0 | 3 |
| 2007 | Reykjavik (EC) | 1 | 2 |

**v ISRAEL**

| | | *NI* | *I* |
|---|---|---|---|
| 1968 | Jaffa | 3 | 2 |
| 1976 | Tel Aviv | 1 | 1 |
| 1980 | Tel Aviv (WC) | 0 | 0 |
| 1981 | Belfast (WC) | 1 | 0 |
| 1984 | Belfast | 3 | 0 |
| 1987 | Tel Aviv | 1 | 1 |
| 2009 | Belfast | 1 | 1 |
| 2013 | Belfast (WC) | 0 | 2 |
| 2013 | Ramat Gan (WC) | 1 | 1 |

**v ITALY**

| | | *NI* | *I* |
|---|---|---|---|
| 1957 | Rome (WC) | 0 | 1 |
| 1957 | Belfast | 2 | 2 |
| 1958 | Belfast (WC) | 2 | 1 |
| 1961 | Bologna | 2 | 3 |
| 1997 | Palermo | 0 | 2 |
| 2003 | Campobasso | 0 | 2 |
| 2009 | Pisa | 0 | 3 |
| 2010 | Belfast (EC) | 0 | 0 |
| 2011 | Pescara (EC) | 0 | 3 |

**v LATVIA**

| | | *NI* | *L* |
|---|---|---|---|
| 1993 | Riga (WC) | 2 | 1 |
| 1993 | Belfast (WC) | 2 | 0 |
| 1995 | Riga (EC) | 1 | 0 |
| 1995 | Belfast (EC) | 1 | 2 |
| 2006 | Belfast (EC) | 1 | 0 |
| 2007 | Riga (EC) | 0 | 1 |
| 2015 | Belfast | 1 | 0 |

**v LIECHTENSTEIN**

| | | *NI* | *L* |
|---|---|---|---|
| 1994 | Belfast (EC) | 4 | 1 |
| 1995 | Eschen (EC) | 4 | 0 |
| 2002 | Vaduz | 0 | 0 |
| 2007 | Vaduz (EC) | 4 | 1 |
| 2007 | Belfast (EC) | 3 | 1 |

**v LITHUANIA**

| | | *NI* | *L* |
|---|---|---|---|
| 1992 | Belfast (WC) | 2 | 2 |

**v LUXEMBOURG**

| | | *NI* | *L* |
|---|---|---|---|
| 2000 | Luxembourg | 3 | 1 |
| 2012 | Belfast (WC) | 1 | 1 |
| 2013 | Luxembourg (WC) | 2 | 3 |

**v MALTA**

| | | *NI* | *M* |
|---|---|---|---|
| 1988 | Belfast (WC) | 3 | 0 |
| 1989 | Valletta (WC) | 2 | 0 |
| 2000 | Ta'Qali | 3 | 0 |
| 2000 | Belfast (WC) | 1 | 0 |
| 2001 | Valletta (WC) | 1 | 0 |
| 2005 | Valletta | 1 | 1 |
| 2013 | Ta'Qali | 0 | 0 |

**v MEXICO**

| | | *NI* | *M* |
|---|---|---|---|
| 1966 | Belfast | 4 | 1 |
| 1994 | Miami | 0 | 3 |

**v MOLDOVA**

| | | *NI* | *M* |
|---|---|---|---|
| 1998 | Belfast (EC) | 2 | 2 |
| 1999 | Kishinev (EC) | 0 | 0 |

**v MONTENEGRO**

| | | *W* | *M* |
|---|---|---|---|
| 2010 | Podgorica | 0 | 2 |

**v MOROCCO**

| | | *NI* | *M* |
|---|---|---|---|
| 1986 | Belfast | 2 | 1 |
| 2010 | Belfast | 1 | 1 |

**v NEW ZEALAND**

| | | *NI* | *NZ* |
|---|---|---|---|
| 2017 | Belfast | 1 | 0 |

**v NORWAY**

| | | *NI* | *N* |
|---|---|---|---|
| 1974 | Oslo (EC) | 1 | 2 |
| 1975 | Belfast (EC) | 3 | 0 |
| 1990 | Belfast | 2 | 3 |
| 1996 | Belfast | 0 | 2 |
| 2001 | Belfast | 0 | 4 |
| 2004 | Belfast | 1 | 4 |
| 2012 | Belfast | 0 | 3 |
| 2017 | Belfast (WC) | 2 | 0 |
| 2017 | Oslo (WC) | 0 | 1 |

**v PANAMA**

| | | *NI* | *P* |
|---|---|---|---|
| 2018 | Panama City | 0 | 0 |

**v POLAND**

| | | NI | P |
|---|---|---|---|
| 1962 | Katowice (EC) | 2 | 0 |
| 1962 | Belfast (EC) | 2 | 0 |
| 1988 | Belfast | 1 | 1 |
| 1991 | Belfast | 3 | 1 |
| 2002 | Limassol (Cyprus) | 1 | 4 |
| 2004 | Belfast (WC) | 0 | 3 |
| 2005 | Warsaw (WC) | 0 | 1 |
| 2009 | Belfast (WC) | 3 | 2 |
| 2009 | Chorzow (WC) | 1 | 1 |
| 2016 | Nice (EC) | 0 | 1 |

**v PORTUGAL**

| | | NI | P |
|---|---|---|---|
| 1957 | Lisbon (WC) | 1 | 1 |
| 1957 | Belfast (WC) | 3 | 0 |
| 1973 | Coventry (WC) | 1 | 1 |
| 1973 | Lisbon (WC) | 1 | 1 |
| 1980 | Lisbon (WC) | 0 | 1 |
| 1981 | Belfast (WC) | 1 | 0 |
| 1994 | Belfast (EC) | 1 | 2 |
| 1995 | Oporto (EC) | 1 | 1 |
| 1997 | Belfast (WC) | 0 | 0 |
| 1997 | Lisbon (WC) | 0 | 1 |
| 2005 | Belfast | 1 | 1 |
| 2012 | Porto (WC) | 1 | 1 |
| 2013 | Belfast (WC) | 2 | 4 |

**v QATAR**

| | | NI | Q |
|---|---|---|---|
| 2015 | Crewe | 1 | 1 |

**v REPUBLIC OF IRELAND**

| | | NI | RI |
|---|---|---|---|
| 1978 | Dublin (EC) | 0 | 0 |
| 1979 | Belfast (EC) | 1 | 0 |
| 1988 | Belfast (WC) | 0 | 0 |
| 1989 | Dublin (WC) | 0 | 3 |
| 1993 | Dublin (WC) | 0 | 3 |
| 1993 | Belfast (WC) | 1 | 1 |
| 1994 | Belfast (EC) | 0 | 4 |
| 1995 | Dublin (EC) | 1 | 1 |
| 1999 | Dublin | 1 | 0 |
| 2011 | Dublin (CC) | 0 | 5 |

**v ROMANIA**

| | | NI | R |
|---|---|---|---|
| 1984 | Belfast (WC) | 3 | 2 |
| 1985 | Bucharest (WC) | 1 | 0 |
| 1994 | Belfast | 2 | 0 |
| 2006 | Chicago | 0 | 2 |
| 2014 | Bucharest (EC) | 0 | 2 |
| 2015 | Belfast (EC) | 0 | 0 |

**v RUSSIA**

| | | NI | R |
|---|---|---|---|
| 2012 | Moscow (WC) | 0 | 2 |
| 2013 | Belfast (WC) | 1 | 0 |

**v SAN MARINO**

| | | NI | SM |
|---|---|---|---|
| 2008 | Belfast (WC) | 4 | 0 |
| 2009 | Serravalle (WC) | 3 | 0 |
| 2016 | Belfast (WC) | 4 | 0 |
| 2017 | Serravalle (WC) | 3 | 0 |

**v SERBIA & MONTENEGRO**

| | | NI | S |
|---|---|---|---|
| 2004 | Belfast | 1 | 1 |

**v SERBIA**

| | | NI | S |
|---|---|---|---|
| 2009 | Belfast | 0 | 1 |
| 2011 | Belgrade (EC) | 1 | 2 |
| 2011 | Belfast (EC) | 0 | 1 |

**v SLOVAKIA**

| | | NI | S |
|---|---|---|---|
| 1998 | Belfast | 1 | 0 |
| 2008 | Bratislava (WC) | 1 | 2 |
| 2009 | Belfast (WC) | 0 | 2 |
| 2016 | Trnava | 0 | 0 |

**v SLOVENIA**

| | | NI | S |
|---|---|---|---|
| 2008 | Maribor (WC) | 0 | 2 |
| 2009 | Belfast (WC) | 1 | 0 |
| 2010 | Maribor (EC) | 1 | 0 |
| 2011 | Belfast (EC) | 0 | 0 |
| 2016 | Belfast | 1 | 0 |

**v SOUTH KOREA**

| | | NI | SK |
|---|---|---|---|
| 2018 | Belfast | 2 | 1 |

**v SOVIET UNION**

| | | NI | SU |
|---|---|---|---|
| 1969 | Belfast (WC) | 0 | 0 |
| 1969 | Moscow (WC) | 0 | 2 |
| 1971 | Moscow (EC) | 0 | 1 |
| 1971 | Belfast (EC) | 1 | 1 |

**v SPAIN**

| | | NI | S |
|---|---|---|---|
| 1958 | Madrid | 2 | 6 |
| 1963 | Bilbao | 1 | 1 |
| 1963 | Belfast | 0 | 1 |
| 1970 | Seville (EC) | 0 | 3 |
| 1972 | Hull (EC) | 1 | 1 |
| 1982 | Valencia (WC) | 1 | 0 |
| 1985 | Palma, Majorca | 0 | 0 |
| 1986 | Guadalajara (WC) | 1 | 2 |
| 1988 | Seville (WC) | 0 | 4 |
| 1989 | Belfast (WC) | 0 | 2 |
| 1992 | Belfast (WC) | 0 | 0 |
| 1993 | Seville (WC) | 1 | 3 |
| 1998 | Santander | 1 | 4 |
| 2002 | Belfast | 0 | 5 |
| 2002 | Albacete (EC) | 0 | 3 |
| 2003 | Belfast (EC) | 0 | 0 |
| 2006 | Belfast (EC) | 3 | 2 |
| 2007 | Las Palmas (EC) | 0 | 1 |

**v ST KITTS & NEVIS**

| | | NI | SK |
|---|---|---|---|
| 2004 | Basseterre | 2 | 0 |

**v SWEDEN**

| | | NI | S |
|---|---|---|---|
| 1974 | Solna (EC) | 2 | 0 |
| 1975 | Belfast (EC) | 1 | 2 |
| 1980 | Belfast (WC) | 3 | 0 |
| 1981 | Stockholm (WC) | 0 | 1 |
| 1996 | Belfast | 1 | 2 |
| 2007 | Belfast (EC) | 2 | 1 |
| 2007 | Stockholm (EC) | 1 | 1 |

**v SWITZERLAND**

| | | NI | S |
|---|---|---|---|
| 1964 | Belfast (WC) | 1 | 0 |

| | | | |
|---|---|---|---|
| 1964 | Lausanne (WC) | 1 | 2 |
| 1998 | Belfast | 1 | 0 |
| 2004 | Zurich | 0 | 0 |
| 2010 | Basle (EC) | 1 | 4 |
| 2017 | Belfast (WC) | 0 | 1 |
| 2017 | Basle (WC) | 0 | 0 |

**v THAILAND**

| | | NI | T |
|---|---|---|---|
| 1997 | Bangkok | 0 | 0 |

**v TRINIDAD & TOBAGO**

| | | NI | T |
|---|---|---|---|
| 2004 | Port of Spain | 3 | 0 |

**v TURKEY**

| | | NI | T |
|---|---|---|---|
| 1968 | Belfast (WC) | 4 | 1 |
| 1968 | Istanbul (WC) | 3 | 0 |
| 1983 | Belfast (EC) | 2 | 1 |
| 1983 | Ankara (EC) | 0 | 1 |
| 1985 | Belfast (WC) | 2 | 0 |
| 1985 | Izmir (WC) | 0 | 0 |
| 1986 | Izmir (EC) | 0 | 0 |
| 1987 | Belfast (EC) | 1 | 0 |
| 1998 | Istanbul (EC) | 0 | 3 |
| 1999 | Belfast (EC) | 0 | 3 |
| 2010 | Connecticut | 0 | 2 |
| 2013 | Adana | 0 | 1 |

**v UKRAINE**

| | | NI | U |
|---|---|---|---|
| 1996 | Belfast (WC) | 0 | 1 |
| 1997 | Kiev (WC) | 1 | 2 |
| 2002 | Belfast (EC) | 0 | 0 |
| 2003 | Donetsk (EC) | 0 | 0 |
| 2016 | Lyon (EC) | 2 | 0 |

**v URUGUAY**

| | | NI | U |
|---|---|---|---|
| 1964 | Belfast | 3 | 0 |
| 1990 | Belfast | 1 | 0 |
| 2006 | New Jersey | 0 | 1 |
| 2014 | Montevideo | 0 | 1 |

**v YUGOSLAVIA**

| | | NI | Y |
|---|---|---|---|
| 1975 | Belfast (EC) | 1 | 0 |
| 1975 | Belgrade (EC) | 0 | 1 |
| 1982 | Zaragoza (WC) | 0 | 0 |
| 1987 | Belfast (EC) | 1 | 2 |
| 1987 | Sarajevo (EC) | 0 | 3 |
| 1990 | Belfast (EC) | 0 | 2 |
| 1991 | Belgrade (EC) | 1 | 4 |
| 2000 | Belfast | 1 | 2 |

# REPUBLIC OF IRELAND

**v ALBANIA**

| | | RI | A |
|---|---|---|---|
| 1992 | Dublin (WC) | 2 | 0 |
| 1993 | Tirana (WC) | 2 | 1 |
| 2003 | Tirana (EC) | 0 | 0 |
| 2003 | Dublin (EC) | 2 | 1 |

**v ALGERIA**

| | | RI | A |
|---|---|---|---|
| 1982 | Algiers | 0 | 2 |
| 2010 | Dublin | 3 | 0 |

**v ANDORRA**

| | | RI | A |
|---|---|---|---|
| 2001 | Barcelona (WC) | 3 | 0 |
| 2001 | Dublin (WC) | 3 | 1 |
| 2010 | Dublin (EC) | 3 | 1 |
| 2011 | La Vella (EC) | 2 | 0 |

**v ARGENTINA**

| | | RI | A |
|---|---|---|---|
| 1951 | Dublin | 0 | 1 |
| 1979* | Dublin | 0 | 0 |
| 1980 | Dublin | 0 | 1 |
| 1998 | Dublin | 0 | 2 |
| 2010 | Dublin | 0 | 1 |

(*Not regarded as full Int)

**v ARMENIA**

| | | RI | A |
|---|---|---|---|
| 2010 | Yerevan (EC) | 1 | 0 |
| 2011 | Dublin (EC) | 2 | 1 |

**v AUSTRALIA**

| | | RI | A |
|---|---|---|---|
| 2003 | Dublin | 2 | 1 |
| 2009 | Limerick | 0 | 3 |

**v AUSTRIA**

| | | RI | A |
|---|---|---|---|
| 1952 | Vienna | 0 | 6 |
| 1953 | Dublin | 4 | 0 |
| 1958 | Vienna | 1 | 3 |
| 1962 | Dublin | 2 | 3 |
| 1963 | Vienna (EC) | 0 | 0 |
| 1963 | Dublin (EC) | 3 | 2 |
| 1966 | Vienna | 0 | 1 |
| 1968 | Dublin | 2 | 2 |
| 1971 | Dublin (EC) | 1 | 4 |
| 1971 | Linz (EC) | 0 | 6 |
| 1995 | Dublin (EC) | 1 | 3 |
| 1995 | Vienna (EC) | 1 | 3 |
| 2013 | Dublin (WC) | 2 | 2 |
| 2013 | Vienna (WC) | 0 | 1 |
| 2016 | Vienna (WC) | 1 | 0 |
| 2017 | Dublin (WC | 1 | 1 |

**v BELARUS**

| | | RI | B |
|---|---|---|---|
| 2016 | Cork | 1 | 2 |

**v BELGIUM**

| | | RI | B |
|---|---|---|---|
| 1928 | Liege | 4 | 2 |
| 1929 | Dublin | 4 | 0 |
| 1930 | Brussels | 3 | 1 |
| 1934 | Dublin (WC) | 4 | 4 |
| 1949 | Dublin | 0 | 2 |
| 1950 | Brussels | 1 | 5 |
| 1965 | Dublin | 0 | 2 |
| 1966 | Liege | 3 | 2 |
| 1980 | Dublin (WC) | 1 | 1 |
| 1981 | Brussels (WC) | 0 | 1 |
| 1986 | Brussels (EC) | 2 | 2 |

| | | | |
|---|---|---|---|
| 1987 | Dublin (EC) | 0 | 0 |
| 1997* | Dublin (WC) | 1 | 1 |
| 1997* | Brussels (WC) | 1 | 2 |
| 2016 | Bordeaux (EC) | 0 | 3 |

(*World Cup play-off)

### v BOLIVIA

| | | *RI* | *B* |
|---|---|---|---|
| 1994 | Dublin | 1 | 0 |
| 1996 | East Rutherford, NJ | 3 | 0 |
| 2007 | Boston | 1 | 1 |

### v BOSNIA HERZEGOVINA

| | | *RI* | *B-H* |
|---|---|---|---|
| 2012 | Dublin | 1 | 0 |
| 2015 | Zenica (EC) | 1 | 1 |
| 2015 | Dublin (EC) | 2 | 0 |

### v BRAZIL

| | | *RI* | *B* |
|---|---|---|---|
| 1974 | Rio de Janeiro | 1 | 2 |
| 1982 | Uberlandia | 0 | 7 |
| 1987 | Dublin | 1 | 0 |
| 2004 | Dublin | 0 | 0 |
| 2008 | Dublin | 0 | 1 |
| 2010 | Arsenal | 0 | 2 |

### v BULGARIA

| | | *RI* | *B* |
|---|---|---|---|
| 1977 | Sofia (WC) | 1 | 2 |
| 1977 | Dublin (WC) | 0 | 0 |
| 1979 | Sofia (EC) | 0 | 1 |
| 1979 | Dublin (EC) | 3 | 0 |
| 1987 | Sofia (EC) | 1 | 2 |
| 1987 | Dublin (EC) | 2 | 0 |
| 2004 | Dublin | 1 | 1 |
| 2009 | Dublin (WC) | 1 | 1 |
| 2009 | Sofia (WC) | 1 | 1 |

### v CAMEROON

| | | *RI* | *C* |
|---|---|---|---|
| 2002 | Niigata (WC) | 1 | 1 |

### v CANADA

| | | *RI* | *C* |
|---|---|---|---|
| 2003 | Dublin | 3 | 0 |

### v CHILE

| | | *RI* | *C* |
|---|---|---|---|
| 1960 | Dublin | 2 | 0 |
| 1972 | Recife | 1 | 2 |
| 1974 | Santiago | 2 | 1 |
| 1982 | Santiago | 0 | 1 |
| 1991 | Dublin | 1 | 1 |
| 2006 | Dublin | 0 | 1 |

### v CHINA

| | | *RI* | *C* |
|---|---|---|---|
| 1984 | Sapporo | 1 | 0 |
| 2005 | Dublin | 1 | 0 |

### v COLOMBIA

| | | *RI* | *C* |
|---|---|---|---|
| 2008 | Fulham | 1 | 0 |

### v COSTA RICA

| | | *RI* | *CR* |
|---|---|---|---|
| 2014 | Chester, USA | 1 | 1 |

### v CROATIA

| | | *RI* | *C* |
|---|---|---|---|
| 1996 | Dublin | 2 | 2 |
| 1998 | Dublin (EC) | 2 | 0 |
| 1999 | Zagreb (EC) | 0 | 1 |
| 2001 | Dublin | 2 | 2 |
| 2004 | Dublin | 1 | 0 |
| 2011 | Dublin | 0 | 0 |
| 2012 | Poznan (EC) | 1 | 3 |

### v CYPRUS

| | | *RI* | *C* |
|---|---|---|---|
| 1980 | Nicosia (WC) | 3 | 2 |
| 1980 | Dublin (WC) | 6 | 0 |
| 2001 | Nicosia (WC) | 4 | 0 |
| 2001 | Dublin (WC) | 4 | 0 |
| 2004 | Dublin (WC) | 3 | 0 |
| 2005 | Nicosia (WC) | 1 | 0 |
| 2006 | Nicosia (EC) | 2 | 5 |
| 2007 | Dublin (EC) | 1 | 1 |
| 2008 | Dublin (WC) | 1 | 0 |
| 2009 | Nicosia (WC) | 2 | 1 |

### v CZECHOSLOVAKIA/CZECH REP

| | | *RI* | *C* |
|---|---|---|---|
| 1938 | Prague | 2 | 2 |
| 1959 | Dublin (EC) | 2 | 0 |
| 1959 | Bratislava (EC) | 0 | 4 |
| 1961 | Dublin (WC) | 1 | 3 |
| 1961 | Prague (WC) | 1 | 7 |
| 1967 | Dublin (EC) | 0 | 2 |
| 1967 | Prague (EC) | 2 | 1 |
| 1969 | Dublin (WC) | 1 | 2 |
| 1969 | Prague (WC) | 0 | 3 |
| 1979 | Prague | 1 | 4 |
| 1981 | Dublin | 3 | 1 |
| 1986 | Reykjavik | 1 | 0 |
| 1994 | Dublin | 1 | 3 |
| 1996 | Prague | 0 | 2 |
| 1998 | Olomouc | 1 | 2 |
| 2000 | Dublin | 3 | 2 |
| 2004 | Dublin | 2 | 1 |
| 2006 | Dublin (EC) | 1 | 1 |
| 2007 | Prague (EC) | 0 | 1 |
| 2012 | Dublin | 1 | 1 |

### v DENMARK

| | | *RI* | *D* |
|---|---|---|---|
| 1956 | Dublin (WC) | 2 | 1 |
| 1957 | Copenhagen (WC) | 2 | 0 |
| 1968* | Dublin (WC) | 1 | 1 |
| 1969 | Copenhagen (WC) | 0 | 2 |
| 1969 | Dublin (WC) | 1 | 1 |
| 1978 | Copenhagen (EC) | 3 | 3 |
| 1979 | Dublin (EC) | 2 | 0 |
| 1984 | Copenhagen (WC) | 0 | 3 |
| 1985 | Dublin (WC) | 1 | 4 |
| 1992 | Copenhagen (WC) | 0 | 0 |
| 1993 | Dublin (WC) | 1 | 1 |
| 2002 | Dublin | 3 | 0 |

(*Abandoned after 51 mins – fog)

| | | | |
|---|---|---|---|
| 2007 | Aarhus | 4 | 0 |
| 2017 | Copenhagen (WC) | 0 | 0 |
| 2017 | Dublin (WC) | 1 | 5 |

### v ECUADOR

| | | *RI* | *E* |
|---|---|---|---|
| 1972 | Natal | 3 | 2 |
| 2007 | New York | 1 | 1 |

## v EGYPT

| | | RI | E |
|---|---|---|---|
| 1990 | Palermo (WC) | 0 | 0 |

## v ESTONIA

| | | RI | E |
|---|---|---|---|
| 2000 | Dublin (WC) | 2 | 0 |
| 2001 | Tallinn (WC) | 2 | 0 |
| 2011 | Tallinn (EC) | 4 | 0 |
| 2011 | Dublin (EC) | 1 | 1 |

## v FAROE ISLANDS

| | | RI | F |
|---|---|---|---|
| 2004 | Dublin (WC) | 2 | 0 |
| 2005 | Torshavn (WC) | 2 | 0 |
| 2012 | Torshavn (WC) | 4 | 1 |
| 2013 | Dublin (WC) | 3 | 0 |

## v FINLAND

| | | RI | F |
|---|---|---|---|
| 1949 | Dublin (WC) | 3 | 0 |
| 1949 | Helsinki (WC) | 1 | 1 |
| 1990 | Dublin | 1 | 1 |
| 2000 | Dublin | 3 | 0 |
| 2002 | Helsinki | 3 | 0 |

## v FRANCE

| | | RI | F |
|---|---|---|---|
| 1937 | Paris | 2 | 0 |
| 1952 | Dublin | 1 | 1 |
| 1953 | Dublin (WC) | 3 | 5 |
| 1953 | Paris (WC) | 0 | 1 |
| 1972 | Dublin (WC) | 2 | 1 |
| 1973 | Paris (WC) | 1 | 1 |
| 1976 | Paris (WC) | 0 | 2 |
| 1977 | Dublin (WC) | 1 | 0 |
| 1980 | Paris (WC) | 0 | 2 |
| 1981 | Dublin (WC) | 3 | 2 |
| 1989 | Dublin | 0 | 0 |
| 2004 | Paris (WC) | 0 | 0 |
| 2005 | Dublin (WC) | 0 | 1 |
| 2009 | Dublin (WC) | 0 | 1 |
| 2009 | Paris (WC) | 1 | 1 |
| 2016 | Lyon (EC) | 1 | 2 |
| 2018 | Paris | 0 | 2 |

## v GEORGIA

| | | RI | G |
|---|---|---|---|
| 2002 | Tbilisi (EC) | 2 | 1 |
| 2003 | Dublin (EC) | 2 | 0 |
| 2008 | Mainz (WC) | 2 | 1 |
| 2009 | Dublin (WC) | 2 | 1 |
| 2013 | Dublin | 4 | 0 |
| 2014 | Tbilisi (EC) | 2 | 1 |
| 2015 | Dublin (EC) | 1 | 0 |
| 2016 | Dublin (WC) | 1 | 0 |
| 2017 | Tbilisi (WC) | 1 | 1 |

## v GERMANY/WEST GERMANY

| | | RI | G |
|---|---|---|---|
| 1935 | Dortmund | 1 | 3 |
| 1936 | Dublin | 5 | 2 |
| 1939 | Bremen | 1 | 1 |
| 1951 | Dublin | 3 | 2 |
| 1952 | Cologne | 0 | 3 |
| 1955 | Hamburg | 1 | 2 |
| 1956 | Dublin | 3 | 0 |
| 1960 | Dusseldorf | 1 | 0 |
| 1966 | Dublin | 0 | 4 |
| 1970 | Berlin | 1 | 2 |
| 1975* | Dublin | 1 | 0 |
| 1979 | Dublin | 1 | 3 |
| 1981 | Bremen | 0 | 3 |
| 1989 | Dublin | 1 | 1 |
| 1994 | Hanover | 2 | 0 |
| 2002 | Ibaraki (WC) | 1 | 1 |
| 2006 | Stuttgart (EC) | 0 | 1 |
| 2007 | Dublin (EC) | 0 | 0 |
| 2012 | Dublin (WC) | 1 | 6 |
| 2013 | Cologne (WC) | 0 | 3 |
| 2014 | Gelsenkirchen (EC) | 1 | 1 |
| 2015 | Dublin (EC) | 1 | 0 |

(*v W Germany 'B')

## v GIBRALTAR

| | | RI | G |
|---|---|---|---|
| 2014 | Dublin (EC) | 7 | 0 |
| 2015 | Faro (EC) | 4 | 0 |

## v GREECE

| | | RI | G |
|---|---|---|---|
| 2000 | Dublin | 0 | 1 |
| 2002 | Athens | 0 | 0 |
| 2012 | Dublin | 0 | 1 |

## v HOLLAND

| | | RI | H |
|---|---|---|---|
| 1932 | Amsterdam | 2 | 0 |
| 1934 | Amsterdam | 2 | 5 |
| 1935 | Dublin | 3 | 5 |
| 1955 | Dublin | 1 | 0 |
| 1956 | Rotterdam | 4 | 1 |
| 1980 | Dublin (WC) | 2 | 1 |
| 1981 | Rotterdam (WC) | 2 | 2 |
| 1982 | Rotterdam (EC) | 1 | 2 |
| 1983 | Dublin (EC) | 2 | 3 |
| 1988 | Gelsenkirchen (EC) | 0 | 1 |
| 1990 | Palermo (WC) | 1 | 1 |
| 1994 | Tilburg | 1 | 0 |
| 1994 | Orlando (WC) | 0 | 2 |
| 1995* | Liverpool (EC) | 0 | 2 |
| 1996 | Rotterdam | 1 | 3 |
| (*Qual Round play-off) | | | |
| 2000 | Amsterdam (WC) | 2 | 2 |
| 2001 | Dublin (WC) | 1 | 0 |
| 2004 | Amsterdam | 1 | 0 |
| 2006 | Dublin | 0 | 4 |
| 2016 | Dublin | 1 | 1 |

## v HUNGARY

| | | RI | H |
|---|---|---|---|
| 1934 | Dublin | 2 | 4 |
| 1936 | Budapest | 3 | 3 |
| 1936 | Dublin | 2 | 3 |
| 1939 | Cork | 2 | 2 |
| 1939 | Budapest | 2 | 2 |
| 1969 | Dublin (WC) | 1 | 2 |
| 1969 | Budapest (WC) | 0 | 4 |
| 1989 | Budapest (WC) | 0 | 0 |
| 1989 | Dublin (WC) | 2 | 0 |
| 1992 | Gyor | 2 | 1 |
| 2012 | Budapest | 0 | 0 |

## v ICELAND

| | | RI | I |
|---|---|---|---|
| 1962 | Dublin (EC) | 4 | 2 |

| | | | |
|---|---|---|---|
| 1962 | Reykjavik (EC) | 1 | 1 |
| 1982 | Dublin (EC) | 2 | 0 |
| 1983 | Reykjavik (EC) | 3 | 0 |
| 1986 | Reykjavik | 2 | 1 |
| 1996 | Dublin (WC) | 0 | 0 |
| 1997 | Reykjavik (WC) | 4 | 2 |
| 2017 | Dublin | 0 | 1 |

**v IRAN**

| | | RI | I |
|---|---|---|---|
| 1972 | Recife | 2 | 1 |
| 2001* | Dublin (WC) | 2 | 0 |
| 2001* | Tehran (WC) | 0 | 1 |

(*Qual Round play-off)

**v ISRAEL**

| | | RI | I |
|---|---|---|---|
| 1984 | Tel Aviv | 0 | 3 |
| 1985 | Tel Aviv | 0 | 0 |
| 1987 | Dublin | 5 | 0 |
| 2005 | Tel Aviv (WC) | 1 | 1 |
| 2005 | Dublin (WC) | 2 | 2 |

**v ITALY**

| | | RI | I |
|---|---|---|---|
| 1926 | Turin | 0 | 3 |
| 1927 | Dublin | 1 | 2 |
| 1970 | Florence (EC) | 0 | 3 |
| 1971 | Dublin (EC) | 1 | 2 |
| 1985 | Dublin | 1 | 2 |
| 1990 | Rome (WC) | 0 | 1 |
| 1992 | Boston, USA | 0 | 2 |
| 1994 | New York (WC) | 1 | 0 |
| 2005 | Dublin | 1 | 2 |
| 2009 | Bari (WC) | 1 | 1 |
| 2009 | Dublin (WC) | 2 | 2 |
| 2011 | Liege | 2 | 0 |
| 2012 | Poznan (EC) | 0 | 2 |
| 2014 | Fulham | 0 | 0 |
| 2016 | Lille (EC) | 1 | 0 |

**v JAMAICA**

| | | RI | J |
|---|---|---|---|
| 2004 | Charlton | 1 | 0 |

**v KAZAKHSTAN**

| | | RI | K |
|---|---|---|---|
| 2012 | Astana (WC) | 2 | 1 |
| 2013 | Dublin (WC) | 3 | 1 |

**v LATVIA**

| | | RI | L |
|---|---|---|---|
| 1992 | Dublin (WC) | 4 | 0 |
| 1993 | Riga (WC) | 2 | 0 |
| 1994 | Riga (EC) | 3 | 0 |
| 1995 | Dublin (EC) | 2 | 1 |
| 2013 | Dublin | 3 | 0 |

**v LIECHTENSTEIN**

| | | RI | L |
|---|---|---|---|
| 1994 | Dublin (EC) | 4 | 0 |
| 1995 | Eschen (EC) | 0 | 0 |
| 1996 | Eschen (WC) | 5 | 0 |
| 1997 | Dublin (WC) | 5 | 0 |

**v LITHUANIA**

| | | RI | L |
|---|---|---|---|
| 1993 | Vilnius (WC) | 1 | 0 |
| 1993 | Dublin (WC) | 2 | 0 |
| 1997 | Dublin (WC) | 0 | 0 |
| 1997 | Zalgiris (WC) | 2 | 1 |

**v LUXEMBOURG**

| | | RI | L |
|---|---|---|---|
| 1936 | Luxembourg | 5 | 1 |
| 1953 | Dublin (WC) | 4 | 0 |
| 1954 | Luxembourg (WC) | 1 | 0 |
| 1987 | Luxembourg (EC) | 2 | 0 |
| 1987 | Luxembourg (EC) | 2 | 1 |

**v MACEDONIA**

| | | RI | M |
|---|---|---|---|
| 1996 | Dublin (WC) | 3 | 0 |
| 1997 | Skopje (WC) | 2 | 3 |
| 1999 | Dublin (EC) | 1 | 0 |
| 1999 | Skopje (EC) | 1 | 1 |
| 2011 | Dublin (EC) | 2 | 1 |
| 2011 | Skopje (EC) | 2 | 0 |

**v MALTA**

| | | RI | M |
|---|---|---|---|
| 1983 | Valletta (EC) | 1 | 0 |
| 1983 | Dublin (EC) | 8 | 0 |
| 1989 | Dublin (WC) | 2 | 0 |
| 1989 | Valletta (WC) | 2 | 0 |
| 1990 | Valletta | 3 | 0 |
| 1998 | Dublin (EC) | 1 | 0 |
| 1999 | Valletta (EC) | 3 | 2 |

**v MEXICO**

| | | RI | M |
|---|---|---|---|
| 1984 | Dublin | 0 | 0 |
| 1994 | Orlando (WC) | 1 | 2 |
| 1996 | New Jersey | 2 | 2 |
| 1998 | Dublin | 0 | 0 |
| 2000 | Chicago | 2 | 2 |
| 2017 | New Jersey | 1 | 3 |

**v MOLDOVA**

| | | RI | M |
|---|---|---|---|
| 2016 | Chisinau (WC) | 3 | 1 |
| 2017 | Dublin (WC) | 2 | 0 |

**v MONTENEGRO**

| | | RI | M |
|---|---|---|---|
| 2008 | Podgorica (WC) | 0 | 0 |
| 2009 | Dublin (WC) | 0 | 0 |

**v MOROCCO**

| | | RI | M |
|---|---|---|---|
| 1990 | Dublin | 1 | 0 |

**v NIGERIA**

| | | RI | N |
|---|---|---|---|
| 2002 | Dublin | 1 | 2 |
| 2004 | Charlton | 0 | 3 |
| 2009 | Fulham | 1 | 1 |

**v NORWAY**

| | | RI | N |
|---|---|---|---|
| 1937 | Oslo (WC) | 2 | 3 |
| 1937 | Dublin (WC) | 3 | 3 |
| 1950 | Dublin | 2 | 2 |
| 1951 | Oslo | 3 | 2 |
| 1954 | Dublin | 2 | 1 |
| 1955 | Oslo | 3 | 1 |
| 1960 | Dublin | 3 | 1 |
| 1964 | Oslo | 4 | 1 |
| 1973 | Oslo | 1 | 1 |
| 1976 | Dublin | 3 | 0 |
| 1978 | Oslo | 0 | 0 |
| 1984 | Oslo (WC) | 0 | 1 |

| | | | |
|---|---|---|---|
| 1985 | Dublin (WC) | 0 | 0 |
| 1988 | Oslo | 0 | 0 |
| 1994 | New York (WC) | 0 | 0 |
| 2003 | Dublin | 1 | 0 |
| 2008 | Oslo | 1 | 1 |
| 2010 | Dublin | 1 | 2 |

**v OMAN**

| | | RI | O |
|---|---|---|---|
| 2012 | Fulham | 4 | 1 |
| 2014 | Dublin | 2 | 0 |
| 2016 | Dublin | 4 | 0 |

**v PARAGUAY**

| | | RI | P |
|---|---|---|---|
| 1999 | Dublin | 2 | 0 |
| 2010 | Dublin | 2 | 1 |

**v POLAND**

| | | RI | P |
|---|---|---|---|
| 1938 | Warsaw | 0 | 6 |
| 1938 | Dublin | 3 | 2 |
| 1958 | Katowice | 2 | 2 |
| 1958 | Dublin | 2 | 2 |
| 1964 | Cracow | 1 | 3 |
| 1964 | Dublin | 3 | 2 |
| 1968 | Dublin | 2 | 2 |
| 1968 | Katowice | 0 | 1 |
| 1970 | Dublin | 1 | 2 |
| 1970 | Poznan | 0 | 2 |
| 1973 | Wroclaw | 0 | 2 |
| 1973 | Dublin | 1 | 0 |
| 1976 | Poznan | 2 | 0 |
| 1977 | Dublin | 0 | 0 |
| 1978 | Lodz | 0 | 3 |
| 1981 | Bydgoszcz | 0 | 3 |
| 1984 | Dublin | 0 | 0 |
| 1986 | Warsaw | 0 | 1 |
| 1988 | Dublin | 3 | 1 |
| 1991 | Dublin (EC) | 0 | 0 |
| 1991 | Poznan (EC) | 3 | 3 |
| 2004 | Bydgoszcz | 0 | 0 |
| 2008 | Dublin | 2 | 3 |
| 2013 | Dublin | 2 | 0 |
| 2013 | Poznan | 0 | 0 |
| 2015 | Dublin (EC) | 1 | 1 |
| 2015 | Warsaw (EC) | 1 | 2 |

**v PORTUGAL**

| | | RI | P |
|---|---|---|---|
| 1946 | Lisbon | 1 | 3 |
| 1947 | Dublin | 0 | 2 |
| 1948 | Lisbon | 0 | 2 |
| 1949 | Dublin | 1 | 0 |
| 1972 | Recife | 1 | 2 |
| 1992 | Boston, USA | 2 | 0 |
| 1995 | Dublin (EC) | 1 | 0 |
| 1995 | Lisbon (EC) | 0 | 3 |
| 1996 | Dublin | 0 | 1 |
| 2000 | Lisbon (WC) | 1 | 1 |
| 2001 | Dublin (WC) | 1 | 1 |
| 2005 | Dublin | 1 | 0 |
| 2014 | East Rutherford, USA | 1 | 5 |

**v ROMANIA**

| | | RI | R |
|---|---|---|---|
| 1988 | Dublin | 2 | 0 |
| 1990* | Genoa | 0 | 0 |
| 1997 | Bucharest (WC) | 0 | 1 |
| 1997 | Dublin (WC) | 1 | 1 |
| 2004 | Dublin | 1 | 0 |

(*Rep won 5-4 on pens)

**v RUSSIA (See also Soviet Union)**

| | | RI | R |
|---|---|---|---|
| 1994 | Dublin | 0 | 0 |
| 1996 | Dublin | 0 | 2 |
| 2002 | Dublin | 2 | 0 |
| 2002 | Moscow (EC) | 2 | 4 |
| 2003 | Dublin (EC) | 1 | 1 |
| 2010 | Dublin (EC) | 2 | 3 |
| 2011 | Moscow (EC) | 0 | 0 |

**v SAN MARINO**

| | | RI | SM |
|---|---|---|---|
| 2006 | Dublin (EC) | 5 | 0 |
| 2007 | Rimini (EC) | 2 | 1 |

**v SAUDI ARABIA**

| | | RI | SA |
|---|---|---|---|
| 2002 | Yokohama (WC) | 3 | 0 |

**v SERBIA**

| | | RI | S |
|---|---|---|---|
| 2008 | Dublin | 1 | 1 |
| 2012 | Belgrade | 0 | 0 |
| 2014 | Dublin | 1 | 2 |
| 2016 | Belgrade (WC) | 2 | 2 |
| 2017 | Dublin (WC) | 0 | 1 |

**v SLOVAKIA**

| | | RI | S |
|---|---|---|---|
| 2007 | Dublin (EC) | 1 | 0 |
| 2007 | Bratislava (EC) | 2 | 2 |
| 2010 | Zilina (EC) | 1 | 1 |
| 2011 | Dublin (EC) | 0 | 0 |
| 2016 | Dublin | 2 | 2 |

**v SOUTH AFRICA**

| | | RI | SA |
|---|---|---|---|
| 2000 | New Jersey | 2 | 1 |
| 2009 | Limerick | 1 | 0 |

**v SOVIET UNION** (See also Russia)

| | | RI | SU |
|---|---|---|---|
| 1972 | Dublin (WC) | 1 | 2 |
| 1973 | Moscow (WC) | 0 | 1 |
| 1974 | Dublin (EC) | 3 | 0 |
| 1975 | Kiev (EC) | 1 | 2 |
| 1984 | Dublin (WC) | 1 | 0 |
| 1985 | Moscow (WC) | 0 | 2 |
| 1988 | Hanover (EC) | 1 | 1 |
| 1990 | Dublin | 1 | 0 |

**v SPAIN**

| | | RI | S |
|---|---|---|---|
| 1931 | Barcelona | 1 | 1 |
| 1931 | Dublin | 0 | 5 |
| 1946 | Madrid | 1 | 0 |
| 1947 | Dublin | 3 | 2 |
| 1948 | Barcelona | 1 | 2 |
| 1949 | Dublin | 1 | 4 |
| 1952 | Madrid | 0 | 6 |
| 1955 | Dublin | 2 | 2 |
| 1964 | Seville (EC) | 1 | 5 |
| 1964 | Dublin (EC) | 0 | 2 |

| | | | |
|---|---|---|---|
| 1965 | Dublin (WC) | 1 | 0 |
| 1965 | Seville (WC) | 1 | 4 |
| 1965 | Paris (WC) | 0 | 1 |
| 1966 | Dublin (EC) | 0 | 0 |
| 1966 | Valencia (EC) | 0 | 2 |
| 1977 | Dublin | 0 | 1 |
| 1982 | Dublin (EC) | 3 | 3 |
| 1983 | Zaragoza (EC) | 0 | 2 |
| 1985 | Cork | 0 | 0 |
| 1988 | Seville (WC) | 0 | 2 |
| 1989 | Dublin (WC) | 1 | 0 |
| 1992 | Seville (WC) | 0 | 0 |
| 1993 | Dublin (WC) | 1 | 3 |
| 2002* | Suwon (WC) | 1 | 1 |
| (*Rep lost 3-2 on pens) | | | |
| 2012 | Gdansk (EC) | 0 | 4 |
| 2013 | New York | 0 | 2 |

**v SWEDEN**

| | | RI | S |
|---|---|---|---|
| 1949 | Stockholm (WC) | 1 | 3 |
| 1949 | Dublin (WC) | 1 | 3 |
| 1959 | Dublin | 3 | 2 |
| 1960 | Malmo | 1 | 4 |
| 1970 | Dublin (EC) | 1 | 1 |
| 1970 | Malmo (EC) | 0 | 1 |
| 1999 | Dublin | 2 | 0 |
| 2006 | Dublin | 3 | 0 |
| 2013 | Stockholm (WC) | 0 | 0 |
| 2013 | Dublin (WC) | 1 | 2 |
| 2016 | Paris (EC) | 1 | 1 |

**v SWITZERLAND**

| | | RI | S |
|---|---|---|---|
| 1935 | Basle | 0 | 1 |
| 1936 | Dublin | 1 | 0 |
| 1937 | Berne | 1 | 0 |
| 1938 | Dublin | 4 | 0 |
| 1948 | Dublin | 0 | 1 |
| 1975 | Dublin (EC) | 2 | 1 |
| 1975 | Berne (EC) | 0 | 1 |
| 1980 | Dublin | 2 | 0 |
| 1985 | Dublin (WC) | 3 | 0 |
| 1985 | Berne (WC) | 0 | 0 |
| 1992 | Dublin | 2 | 1 |
| 2002 | Dublin (EC) | 1 | 2 |
| 2003 | Basle (EC) | 0 | 2 |
| 2004 | Basle (WC) | 1 | 1 |
| 2005 | Dublin (WC) | 0 | 0 |
| 2016 | Dublin | 1 | 0 |

**v TRINIDAD & TOBAGO**

| | | RI | T&T |
|---|---|---|---|
| 1982 | Port of Spain | 1 | 2 |

**v TUNISIA**

| | | RI | T |
|---|---|---|---|
| 1988 | Dublin | 4 | 0 |

**v TURKEY**

| | | RI | T |
|---|---|---|---|
| 1966 | Dublin (EC) | 2 | 1 |
| 1967 | Ankara (EC) | 1 | 2 |
| 1974 | Izmir (EC) | 1 | 1 |
| 1975 | Dublin (EC) | 4 | 0 |
| 1976 | Ankara | 3 | 3 |
| 1978 | Dublin | 4 | 2 |
| 1990 | Izmir | 0 | 0 |
| 1990 | Dublin (EC) | 5 | 0 |
| 1991 | Istanbul (EC) | 3 | 1 |
| 1999 | Dublin (EC) | 1 | 1 |
| 1999 | Bursa (EC) | 0 | 0 |
| 2003 | Dublin | 2 | 2 |
| 2014 | Dublin | 1 | 2 |
| 2018 | Antalya | 0 | 1 |

**v URUGUAY**

| | | RI | U |
|---|---|---|---|
| 1974 | Montevideo | 0 | 2 |
| 1986 | Dublin | 1 | 1 |
| 2011 | Dublin | 2 | 3 |
| 2017 | Dublin | 3 | 1 |

**v USA**

| | | RI | USA |
|---|---|---|---|
| 1979 | Dublin | 3 | 2 |
| 1991 | Boston | 1 | 1 |
| 1992 | Dublin | 4 | 1 |
| 1992 | Washington | 1 | 3 |
| 1996 | Boston | 1 | 2 |
| 2000 | Foxboro | 1 | 1 |
| 2002 | Dublin | 2 | 1 |
| 2014 | Dublin | 4 | 1 |
| 2018 | Dublin | 2 | 1 |

**v YUGOSLAVIA**

| | | RI | Y |
|---|---|---|---|
| 1955 | Dublin | 1 | 4 |
| 1988 | Dublin | 2 | 0 |
| 1998 | Belgrade (EC) | 0 | 1 |
| 1999 | Dublin (EC) | 2 | 1 |

## NEVER-SAY-DIE SALFORD

A remarkable comeback helped Salford City, the club established by former Manchester Unite players Ryan Giggs, Gary Neville, Phil Neville, Paul Scholes and Nicky Butt, to their thir promotion in four seasons. Trailing 4-0 at Kiddermister, they gained a point with goals by Jos Askew (80), Nick Haughton (89), Mani Dieseruvwe (90+3) and Tom Walker (90+6). Salfor reached the National League, one step below the Football League.

# BRITISH AND IRISH INTERNATIONAL APPEARANCES SINCE THE WAR (1946–2018)

(As start of season 2018-19; in year shown 2018 = season 2017-18.
*Also a pre-war international player. Totals include appearances as substitute)

## ENGLAND

Agbonlahor G (Aston Villa, 2009–10) 3
Abraham T (Chelsea 2018) 2
A'Court A (Liverpool, 1958–59) 5
Adams T (Arsenal, 1987–2001) 66
Alexander-Arnold (Liverpool 2018) 2
Alli D (Tottenham, 2016–18) 30
Allen A (Stoke, 1960) 3
Allen C (QPR, Tottenham, 1984–88) 5
Allen R (WBA, 1952–55) 5
Anderson S (Sunderland, 1962) 2
Anderson V (Nottm Forest, Arsenal, Manchester Utd, 1979–88) 30
Anderton D (Tottenham, 1994–2002) 30
Angus J (Burnley, 1961) 1
Armfield J (Blackpool, 1959–66) 43
Armstrong D (Middlesbrough, Southampton, 1980–4) 3
Armstrong K (Chelsea, 1955) 1
Ashton D (West Ham, 2008) 1
Astall G (Birmingham, 1956) 2
Astle J (WBA, 1969–70) 5
Aston J (Manchester Utd, 1949–51) 17
Atyeo J (Bristol City, 1956–57) 6

Bailey G (Manchester Utd, 1985) 2
Bailey M (Charlton, 1964–5) 2
Baily E (Tottenham, 1950–3) 9
Baines L (Everton, 2010–15) 30
Baker J (Hibernian, Arsenal, 1960–6) 8
Ball A (Blackpool, Everton, Arsenal, 1965–75) 72
Ball M (Everton, 2001) 1
Banks G (Leicester, Stoke, 1963–72) 73
Banks T (Bolton, 1958–59) 6
Bardsley D (QPR, 1993) 2
Barham M (Norwich, 1983) 2
Barkley R (Everton, 2014–16) 22
Barlow R (WBA, 1955) 1
Barmby N (Tottenham, Middlesbrough, Everton, Liverpool, 1995–2002) 23
Barnes J (Watford, Liverpool, 1983–96) 79
Barnes P (Manchester City, WBA, Leeds, 1978–82) 22
Barrass M (Bolton, 1952–53) 3
Barrett E (Oldham, Aston Villa, 1991–93) 3
Barry G (Aston Villa, Manchester City, 2000–12) 53
Barton J (Manchester City, 2007) 1
Barton W (Wimbledon, Newcastle, 1995) 3
Batty D (Leeds, Blackburn, Newcastle, Leeds, 1991–2000) 42
Baynham R (Luton, 1956) 3
Beardsley P (Newcastle, Liverpool, Newcastle, 1986–96) 59
Beasant D (Chelsea, 1990) 2
Beattie J (Southampton, 2003–04) 5
Beattie K (Ipswich, 1975–58) 9
Beckham D (Manchester Utd, Real Madrid, LA Galaxy, AC Milan 1997–2010) 115
Bell C (Manchester City, 1968–76) 48
Bent D (Charlton, Tottenham Sunderland, Aston Villa, 2006–12) 13
Bentley D (Blackburn, 2008–09) 7
Bentley R (Chelsea, 1949–55) 12
Berry J (Manchester Utd, 1953–56) 4
Bertrand R (Chelsea, Southampton, 2013–18) 19
Birtles G (Nottm Forest, 1980–81) 3
Blissett L (Watford, AC Milan, 1983–84) 14
Blockley J (Arsenal, 1973) 1
Blunstone F (Chelsea, 1955–57) 5
Bonetti P (Chelsea, 1966–70) 7
Bothroyd J (Cardiff, 2011) 1
Bould S (Arsenal, 1994) 2
Bowles S (QPR, 1974–77) 5
Bowyer L (Leeds, 2003) 1
Boyer P (Norwich, 1976) 1
Brabrook P (Chelsea, 1958–60) 3
Bracewell P (Everton, 1985–86) 3
Bradford G (Bristol Rov, 1956) 1
Bradley W (Manchester Utd, 1959) 3
Bridge W (Southampton, Chelsea, Manchester City 2002–10) 36
Bridges B (Chelsea, 1965–66) 4
Broadbent P (Wolves, 1958–60) 7
Broadis I (Manchester City, Newcastle, 1952–54) 14
Brooking T (West Ham, 1974–82) 47
Brooks J (Tottenham, 1957) 3
Brown A (WBA, 1971) 1
Brown K (West Ham, 1960) 1
Brown W (Manchester Utd, 1999–2010) 23
Bull S (Wolves, 1989–91) 13
Butcher T (Ipswich, Rangers, 1980–90) 77
Butland J (Birmingham, Stoke, 2013–18) 8
Butt N (Manchester Utd, Newcastle, 1997–2005) 39
Byrne G (Liverpool, 1963–66) 2
Byrne J (Crystal Palace, West Ham, 1962–65) 11
Byrne R (Manchester Utd, 1954–58) 33

Cahill G (Bolton, Chelsea, 2011–18) 61
Callaghan I (Liverpool, 1966–78) 4
Campbell F (Sunderland, 2012) 1
Campbell S (Tottenham, Arsenal, Portsmouth, 1996–2008) 73
Carragher J (Liverpool, 1999–2010) 38
Carrick M (West Ham, Tottenham, Manchester Utd, 2001–16) 34
Carroll A (Newcastle, Liverpool 2011– 13) 9
Carson S (Liverpool, Aston Villa WBA, Bursaspor 2008–12) 4

| | |
|---|---|
| *Carter H (Derby, 1947) | 7 |
| Caulker S (Tottenham, 2013) | 1 |
| Chamberlain M (Stoke, 1983–85) | 8 |
| Chambers C (Arsenal, 2015) | 3 |
| Channon M (Southampton, Manchester City, 1973–78) | 46 |
| Charles G (Nottm Forest, 1991) | 2 |
| Charlton, J (Leeds, 1965–70) | 35 |
| Charlton, R (Manchester Utd, 1958–70) | 106 |
| Charnley R (Blackpool, 1963) | 1 |
| Cherry T (Leeds, 1976–80) | 27 |
| Chilton A (Manchester Utd, 1951–52) | 2 |
| Chivers M (Tottenham, 1971–74) | 24 |
| Clamp E (Wolves, 1958) | 4 |
| Clapton D (Arsenal, 1959) | 1 |
| Clarke A (Leeds, 1970–6) | 19 |
| Clarke H (Tottenham, 1954) | 1 |
| Clayton R (Blackburn, 1956–60) | 35 |
| Clemence R (Liverpool, Tottenham, 1973–84) | 61 |
| Clement D (QPR, 1976–7) | 5 |
| Cleverley T (Manchester Utd, 2013–14) | 13 |
| Clough B (Middlesbrough, 1960) | 2 |
| Clough N (Nottm Forest, Liverpool, 1989–93) | 14 |
| Clyne N (Southampton, Liverpool, 2015–17) | 14 |
| Coates R (Burnley, Tottenham, 1970–71) | 4 |
| Cockburn H (Manchester Utd, 1947–52) | 13 |
| Cohen G (Fulham, 1964–68) | 37 |
| Cole Andy (Manchester Utd, 1995–2002) | 15 |
| Cole Ashley (Arsenal, Chelsea, 2001–14) | 107 |
| Cole C (West Ham, 2009–10) | 7 |
| Cole J (West Ham, Chelsea, 2001–10) | 56 |
| Collymore S (Nottm Forest, Aston Villa, 1995–97) | 3 |
| Compton L (Arsenal, 1951) | 2 |
| Connelly J (Burnley, Manchester Utd, 1960–66) | 20 |
| Cook L (Bournemouth, 2018) | 1 |
| Cooper C (Nottm Forest, 1995) | 2 |
| Cooper T (Leeds, 1969–75) | 20 |
| Coppell S (Manchester Utd, 1978–83) | 42 |
| Cork J (Burnley 2018) | 1 |
| Corrigan J (Manchester City, 1976–82) | 9 |
| Cottee T (West Ham, Everton, 1987–89) | 7 |
| Cowans G (Aston Villa, Bari, Aston Villa, 1983–91) | 10 |
| Crawford R (Ipswich, 1962) | 2 |
| Cresswell A (West Ham, 2017–18) | 3 |
| Crouch P (Southampton, Liverpool, Portsmouth, Tottenham, 2005–11) | 42 |
| Crowe C (Wolves, 1963) | 1 |
| Cunningham L (WBA, Real Madrid, 1979–81) | 6 |
| Curle K (Manchester City, 1992) | 3 |
| Currie A (Sheffield Utd, Leeds, 1972–79) | 17 |
| | |
| Daley T (Aston Villa, 1992) | 7 |
| Davenport P (Nottm Forest, 1985) | 1 |
| Davies K (Bolton, 2011) | 1 |
| Dawson M (Tottenham 2011) | 4 |
| Deane B (Sheffield Utd, 1991–93) | 3 |
| Deeley N (Wolves, 1959) | 2 |
| Defoe J (Tottenham, Portsmouth, Tottenham, Sunderland, 2004–17) | 57 |
| Delph F (Aston Villa, Manchester City, 2015–18) | 15 |
| Devonshire A (West Ham, 1980–84) | 8 |
| Dickinson J (Portsmouth, 1949–57) | 48 |
| Dier E (Tottenham, 2016–18) | 32 |
| Ditchburn E (Tottenham, 1949–57) | 6 |
| Dixon K (Chelsea, 1985–87) | 8 |
| Dixon L (Arsenal, 1990–99) | 22 |
| Dobson M (Burnley, Everton, 1974–75) | 5 |
| Dorigo T (Chelsea, Leeds, 1990–94) | 15 |
| Douglas B (Blackburn, 1959–63) | 36 |
| Downing S (Middlesbrough, Aston Villa, Liverpool, West Ham, 2005–15) | 35 |
| Doyle M (Manchester City, 1976–77) | 5 |
| Drinkwater D (Leicester, 2016) | 3 |
| Dublin D (Coventry, Aston Villa, 1998–99) | 4 |
| Dunn D (Blackburn, 2003) | 1 |
| Duxbury, M (Manchester Utd, 1984–85) | 10 |
| Dyer K (Newcastle, West Ham, 2000–08) | 33 |
| | |
| Eastham G (Arsenal, 1963–66) | 19 |
| Eckersley W (Blackburn, 1950–54) | 17 |
| Edwards, D (Manchester Utd, 1955–58) | 18 |
| Ehiogu U (Aston Villa, Middlesbrough, 1996–2002) | 4 |
| Ellerington W (Southampton, 1949) | 2 |
| Elliott W (Burnley, 1952–53) | 5 |
| | |
| Fantham J (Sheffield Wed, 1962) | 1 |
| Fashanu J (Wimbledon, 1989) | 2 |
| Fenwick T (QPR, 1984–88) | 20 |
| Ferdinand L (QPR, Newcastle, Tottenham, 1993–98) | 17 |
| Ferdinand R (West Ham, Leeds, Manchester Utd, 1997–2011) | 81 |
| Finney T (Preston, 1947–59) | 76 |
| Flanagan J (Liverpool, 2014) | 1 |
| Flowers R (Wolves, 1955–66) | 49 |
| Flowers T (Southampton, Blackburn, 1993–98) | 11 |
| Forster F (Celtic, Southampton, 2014–16) | 6 |
| Foster B (Manchester Utd, Birmingham, WBA, 2007–14) | 8 |
| Foster S (Brighton, 1982) | 3 |
| Foulkes W (Manchester Utd, 1955) | 1 |
| Fowler R (Liverpool, Leeds, 1996–2002) | 26 |
| Francis G (QPR, 1975–76) | 12 |
| Francis T (Birmingham, Nottm Forest, Man City, Sampdoria, 1977–86) | 52 |
| Franklin N (Stoke, 1947–50) | 27 |
| Froggatt J (Portsmouth, 1950–53) | 13 |
| Froggatt R (Sheffield Wed, 1953) | 4 |
| | |
| Gardner A (Tottenham, 2004) | 1 |
| Garrett T (Blackpool, 1952–54) | 3 |
| Gascoigne P (Tottenham, Lazio, Rangers, Middlesbrough, 1989–98) | 57 |
| Gates E (Ipswich, 1981) | 2 |
| George C (Derby, 1977) | 1 |
| Gerrard S (Liverpool, 2000–14) | 114 |
| Gibbs K (Arsenal, 2011–16) | 10 |
| Gidman J (Aston Villa, 1977) | 1 |
| Gillard I (QPR, 1975–76) | 3 |
| Goddard P (West Ham, 1982) | 1 |

Gomez J (Liverpool, 2018) 3
Grainger C (Sheffield Utd, Sunderland, 1956–57) 7
Gray A (Crystal Palace, 1992) 1
Gray M (Sunderland, 1999) 3
Greaves J (Chelsea, Tottenham, 1959–67) 57
Green R (Norwich, West Ham 2005–12) 12
Greenhoff B (Manchester Utd, Leeds, 1976–80) 18
Gregory J (QPR, 1983–84) 6
Guppy S (Leicester, 2000) 1

Hagan J (Sheffield Utd, 1949) 1
Haines J (WBA, 1949) 1
Hall J (Birmingham, 1956–57) 17
Hancocks J (Wolves, 1949–50) 3
Hardwick G (Middlesbrough, 1947–48) 13
Harford M (Luton, 1988–89) 2
Hargreaves O (Bayern Munich, Manchester Utd, 2002–08) 42
Harris G (Burnley, 1966) 1
Harris P (Portsmouth, 1950–54) 2
Hart J (Manchester City, 2010–18) 75
Harvey C (Everton, 1971) 1
Hassall H (Huddersfield, Bolton, 1951–54) 5
Hateley M (Portsmouth, AC Milan, Monaco, Rangers, 1984–92) 32
Haynes J (Fulham, 1955–62) 56
Heaton T (Burnley, 2016–17) 3
Hector K (Derby, 1974) 2
Hellawell M (Birmingham, 1963) 2
Henderson J (Sunderland, Liverpool, 2011–18) 44
Hendrie L (Aston Villa, 1999) 1
Henry R (Tottenham, 1963) 1
Heskey E (Leicester, Liverpool, Birmingham, Wigan, Aston Villa 1999–2010) 62
Hill F (Bolton, 1963) 2
Hill G (Manchester Utd, 1976–78) 6
Hill R (Luton, 1983–86) 3
Hinchcliffe A (Everton, Sheffield Wed, 1997–99) 7
Hinton A (Wolves, Nottm Forest, 1963–65) 3
Hirst D (Sheffield Wed, 1991–92) 3
Hitchens G (Aston Villa, Inter Milan, 1961–62) 7
Hoddle G (Tottenham, Monaco, 1980–88) 53
Hodge S (Aston Villa, Tottenham, Nottm Forest, 1986–91) 24
Hodgkinson A (Sheffield Utd, 1957–61) 5
Holden D (Bolton, 1959) 5
Holliday E (Middlesbrough, 1960) 3
Hollins J (Chelsea, 1967) 1
Hopkinson E (Bolton, 1958–60) 14
Howe D (WBA, 1958–60) 23
Howe J (Derby, 1948–49) 3
Howey S (Newcastle, 1995–96) 4
Huddlestone T (Tottenham, 2010–13) 4
Hudson A (Stoke, 1975) 2
Hughes E (Liverpool, Wolves, 1970–80) 62
Hughes L (Liverpool, 1950) 3
Hunt R (Liverpool, 1962–69) 34
Hunt S (WBA, 1984) 2
Hunter N (Leeds, 1966–75) 28
Hurst G (West Ham, 1966–72) 49

Ince P (Manchester Utd, Inter Milan, Liver-ool, Middlesbrough, 1993–2000) 53
Ings D (Liverpool 2016) 1
Jagielka P (Everton, 2008–17) 40
James D (Liverpool, Aston Villa, West Ham, Manchester City, Portsmouth, 1997–2010) 53
Jarvis M (Wolves, 2011) 1
Jeffers F (Arsenal, 2003) 1
Jenas J (Newcastle, Tottenham, 2003–10) 21
Jenkinson C (Arsenal, 2013) 1
Jezzard B (Fulham, 1954–56) 2
Johnson A (Crystal Palace, Everton, 2005–08) 8
Johnson A (Manchester City, 2010–13) 12
Johnson D (Ipswich, Liverpool, 1975–80) 8
Johnson G (Chelsea, Portsmouth, Liverpool, 2004–14) 54
Johnson S (Derby, 2001) 1
Johnston H (Blackpool, 1947–54) 10
Jones M (Leeds, Sheffield Utd, 1965–70) 3
Jones P (Manchester Utd, 2012–18) 27
Jones R (Liverpool, 1992–95) 8
Jones W H (Liverpool, 1950) 2

Kane H (Tottenham) 2005–18) 30
Kay A (Everton, 1963) 1
Keane M (Burnley, Everton, 2017–18) 4
Keegan K (Liverpool, Hamburg, Southampton, 1973–82) 63
Kelly, M (Liverpool, 2012) 1
Kennedy A (Liverpool, 1984) 2
Kennedy R (Liverpool, 1976–80) 17
Keown M (Everton, Arsenal, 1992–2002) 43
Kevan D (WBA, 1957–61) 14
Kidd B (Manchester Utd, 1970) 2
King L (Tottenham, 2002–10) 21
Kirkland C (Liverpool, 2007) 1
Knight Z (Fulham, 2005) 2
Knowles C (Tottenham, 1968) 4
Konchesky P (Charlton, 2003–06) 2

Labone B (Everton, 1963–70) 26
Lallana A (Southampton, Liverpool, 2014–18) 34
Lambert R (Southampton, Liverpool, 2014–15) 11
Lampard F Snr (West Ham, 1973–80) 2
Lampard F Jnr (West Ham, Chelsea, 2000–14) 106
Langley J (Fulham, 1958) 3
Langton R (Blackburn, Preston, Bolton, 1947–51) 11
Latchford R (Everton, 1978–9) 12
Lawler C (Liverpool, 1971–72) 4
*Lawton T (Chelsea, Notts Co, 1947–49) 15
Lee F (Manchester City, 1969–72) 27
Lee J (Derby, 1951) 1
Lee R (Newcastle, 1995–99) 21
Lee S (Liverpool, 1983–84) 14
Lennon A (Tottenham, 2006–13) 21
Le Saux G (Blackburn, Chelsea, 1994–2001) 36
Lescott J (Everton, Manchester City, 2008–13) 26
Le Tissier M (Southampton, 1994–97) 8
Lindsay A (Liverpool, 1974) 4

Lineker G (Leicester, Everton, Barcelona, Tottenham, 1985–92) 80
Lingard J (Manchester Utd, 2017–18) 18
Little B (Aston Villa, 1975) 1
Livermore J (Tottenham, WBA, 2013–18) 7
Lloyd L (Liverpool, Nottm Forest, 1971–80) 4
Lofthouse N (Bolton, 1951–59) 33
Loftus-Cheek R (Chelsea 2018) 8
Lowe E (Aston Villa, 1947) 3

Mabbutt G (Tottenham, 1983–92) 16
Macdonald M (Newcastle, 1972–76) 14
Madeley P (Leeds, 1971–77) 24
Maguire H (Leicester, 2018) 12
Mannion W (Middlesbrough, 1947–52) 26
Mariner P (Ipswich, Arsenal, 1977–85) 35
Marsh R (QPR, Manchester City, 1972–73) 9
Mason R (Tottenham, 2015) 1
Martin A (West Ham, 1981–87) 17
Martyn N (Crystal Palace, Leeds, 1992–2002) 23
Marwood B (Arsenal, 1989) 1
Matthews R (Coventry, 1956–57) 5
*Matthews S (Stoke, Blackpool, 1947–57) 37
McCann G (Sunderland, 2001) 1
McDermott T (Liverpool, 1978–82) 25
McDonald C (Burnley, 1958–59) 8
McFarland R (Derby, 1971–77) 28
McGarry W (Huddersfield, 1954–56) 4
McGuinness W (Manchester Utd, 1959) 2
McMahon S (Liverpool, 1988–91) 17
McManaman S (Liverpool, Real Madrid, 1995–2002) 37
McNab R (Arsenal, 1969) 4
McNeil M (Middlesbrough, 1961–62) 9
Meadows J (Manchester City, 1955) 1
Medley L (Tottenham, 1951–52) 6
Melia J (Liverpool, 1963) 2
Merrick G (Birmingham, 1952–54) 23
Merson P (Arsenal, Middlesbrough, Aston Villa, 1992–99) 21
Metcalfe V (Huddersfield, 1951) 2
Milburn J (Newcastle, 1949–56) 13
Miller B (Burnley, 1961) 1
Mills D (Leeds, 2001–04) 19
Mills M (Ipswich, 1973–82) 42
Milne G (Liverpool, 1963–65) 14
Milner J (Aston Villa, Manchester City, Liverpool, 2010–16) 61
Milton A (Arsenal, 1952) 1
Moore R (West Ham, 1962–74) 108
Morley A (Aston Villa, 1982–83) 6
Morris J (Derby, 1949–50) 3
Mortensen S (Blackpool, 1947–54) 25
Mozley B (Derby, 1950) 3
Mullen J (Wolves, 1947–54) 12
Mullery A (Tottenham, 1965–72) 35
Murphy D (Liverpool, 2002–04) 9

Neal P (Liverpool, 1976–84) 50
Neville G (Manchester Utd, 1995–2009) 85
Neville P (Manchester Utd, Everton, 1996–2008) 59
Newton K (Blackburn, Everton, 1966–70) 27
Nicholls J (WBA, 1954) 2
Nicholson W (Tottenham, 1951) 1
Nish D (Derby, 1973–74) 5
Norman M (Tottenham, 1962–5) 23
Nugent D (Preston, 2007) 1

O'Grady M (Huddersfield, Leeds, 1963–9) 2
Osgood P (Chelsea, 1970–74) 4
Osman L (Everton, 2013) 2
Osman R (Ipswich, 1980–84) 11
Owen M (Liverpool, Real Madrid, Newcastle, 1998–2008) 89
Owen S (Luton, 1954) 3
Oxlade-Chamberlain A (Arsenal, Liverpool, 2012–18) 32

Paine T (Southampton, 1963–66) 19
Pallister G (Middlesbrough, Manchester Utd 1988–97) 22
Palmer C (Sheffield Wed, 1992–94) 18
Parker P (QPR, Manchester Utd, 1989–94) 19
Parker S (Charlton, Chelsea, Newcastle, West Ham, Tottenham, 2004–13) 18
Parkes P (QPR, 1974) 1
Parlour R (Arsenal, 1999–2001) 10
Parry R (Bolton, 1960) 2
Peacock A (Middlesbrough, Leeds, 1962–66) 6
Pearce S (Nottm Forest, West Ham, 1987–2000) 78
Pearson Stan (Manchester Utd, 1948–52) 8
Pearson Stuart (Manchester Utd, 1976–78) 15
Pegg D (Manchester Utd, 1957) 1
Pejic M (Stoke, 1974) 4
Perry W (Blackpool, 1956) 3
Perryman S (Tottenham, 1982) 1
Peters M (West Ham, Tottenham, 1966–74) 67
Phelan M (Manchester Utd, 1990) 1
Phillips K (Sunderland, 1999–2002) 8
Phillips L (Portsmouth, 1952–55) 3
Pickering F (Everton, 1964–65) 3
Pickering N (Sunderland, 1983) 1
Pickford J (Everton, 2018) 10
Pilkington B (Burnley, 1955) 1
Platt D (Aston Villa, Bari, Juventus, Sampdoria, Arsenal, 1990–96) 62
Pointer R (Burnley, 1962) 3
Pope N (Burnley, 2018) 1
Powell C (Charlton, 2001–02) 5
Pye J (Wolves, 1950) 1

Quixall A (Sheffield Wed, 1954–55) 5

Radford J (Arsenal, 1969–72) 2
Ramsey A (Southampton, Tottenham, 1949–54) 32
Rashford M (Manchester Utd, 2016–18) 25
Reaney P (Leeds, 1969–71) 3
Redknapp J (Liverpool, 1996–2000) 17
Redmond N (Southampton 2017)
Reeves K (Norwich, Manchester City, 1980) 2

Redmond N (Southampton, 2017) 1
Regis C (WBA, Coventry, 1982–88) 5
Reid P (Everton, 1985–88) 13
Revie D (Manchester City, 1955–57) 6
Richards, J (Wolves, 1973) 1
Richards M (Manchester City, 2007–12) 13
Richardson K (Aston Villa, 1994) 1
Richardson K (Manchester Utd, 2005–07) 8
Rickaby S (WBA, 1954) 1
Ricketts M (Bolton, 2002) 1
Rimmer J (Arsenal, 1976) 1
Ripley S (Blackburn, 1994–97) 2
Rix G (Arsenal, 1981–84) 17
Robb G (Tottenham, 1954) 1
Roberts G (Tottenham, 1983–84) 6
Robinson P (Leeds, Tottenham, 2003–08) 41
Robson B (WBA, Manchester Utd, 1980–92) 90
Robson R (WBA, 1958–62) 20
Rocastle D (Arsenal, 1989–92) 14
Rodriguez J (Southampton, 2014) 1
Rodwell J (Everton, Manchester City, 2012–13) 3
Rooney W (Everton, Manchester Utd, 2003–17) 119
Rose D (Tottenham, 2016–18) 23
Rowley J (Manchester Utd, 1949–52) 6
Royle J (Everton, Manchester City, 1971–77) 6
Ruddock N (Liverpool, 1995) 1
Ruddy J (Norwich, 2013) 1

Sadler D (Manchester Utd, 1968–71) 4
Salako J (Crystal Palace, 1991–92) 5
Sansom K (Crystal Palace, Arsenal, 1979–88) 86
Scales J (Liverpool, 1995) 3
Scholes P (Manchester Utd, 1997–2004) 66
Scott L (Arsenal, 1947–49) 17
Seaman D (QPR, Arsenal, 1989–2003) 75
Sewell J (Sheffield Wed, 1952–54) 6
Shackleton L (Sunderland, 1949–55) 5
Sharpe L (Manchester Utd, 1991–94) 8
Shaw G (Sheffield Utd, 1959–63) 5
Shaw L (Southampton, Manchester Utd, 2014–17) 7
Shawcross, R (Stoke, 2013) 1
Shearer A (Southampton, Blackburn, Newcastle, 1992–2000) 63
Shellito K (Chelsea, 1963) 1
Shelvey J (Liverpool, Swansea, 2013–16) 6
Sheringham E (Tottenham, Manchester Utd, Tottenham, 1993–2002) 51
Sherwood T (Tottenham, 1999) 3
Shilton P (Leicester, Stoke, Nottm Forest, Southampton, Derby, 1971–90) 125
Shimwell E (Blackpool, 1949) 1
Shorey N (Reading, 2007) 2
Sillett P (Chelsea, 1955) 3
Sinclair T (West Ham, Manchester City, 2002–04) 12
Sinton A (QPR, Sheffield Wed, 1992–94) 12
Slater W (Wolves, 1955–60) 12
Smalling C (Manchester Utd, 2012–17) 31
Smith A (Arsenal, 1989–92) 13
Smith A (Leeds, Manchester Utd, Newcastle, 2001–08) 19
Smith L (Arsenal, 1951–53) 6
Smith R (Tottenham, 1961–64) 15
Smith T (Birmingham, 1960) 2
Smith T (Liverpool, 1971) 1
Solanke D (Liverpool, 2018) 1
Southgate G (Aston Villa, Middlesbrough, 1996–2004) 57
Spink N (Aston Villa, 1983) 1
Springett R (Sheffield Wed, 1960–66) 33
Staniforth R (Huddersfield, 1954–55) 8
Statham D (WBA, 1983) 3
Stein B (Luton, 1984) 1
Stepney A (Manchester Utd, 1968) 1
Sterland M (Sheffield Wed, 1989) 1
Sterling R (Liverpool, Manchester City, 2013–18) 44
Steven T (Everton, Rangers, Marseille, 1985–92) 36
Stevens G (Everton, Rangers, 1985–92) 46
Stevens G (Tottenham, 1985–86) 7
Stewart P (Tottenham, 1992) 3
Stiles N (Manchester Utd, 1965–70) 28
Stone S (Nottm Forest, 1996) 9
Stones J (Everton, Manchester City, 2014–18) 33
Storey P (Arsenal, 1971–73) 19
Storey–Moore I (Nottm Forest, 1970) 1
Streten B (Luton, 1950) 1
Sturridge D (Chelsea, Liverpool, 2012–18) 26
Summerbee M (Manchester City, 1968–73) 8
Sunderland, A (Arsenal, 1980) 1
Sutton C (Blackburn, 1997) 1
Swan P (Sheffield Wed, 1960–62) 19
Swift F (Manchester City, 1947–79) 19

Talbot B (Ipswich, Arsenal, 1977–80) 6
Tambling R (Chelsea, 1963–66) 3
Tarkowski J (Burnley, 2018) 1
Taylor E (Blackpool, 1954) 1
Taylor J (Fulham, 1951) 2
Taylor P (Liverpool, 1948) 3
Taylor P (Crystal Palace, 1976) 4
Taylor T (Manchester Utd, 1953–58) 19
Temple D (Everton, 1965) 1
Terry J (Chelsea, 2003–13) 78
Thomas D (QPR, 1975–76) 8
Thomas D (Coventry, 1983) 2
Thomas G (Crystal Palace, 1991–92) 9
Thomas M (Arsenal, 1989–90) 2
Thompson A (Celtic, 2004) 1
Thompson Peter (Liverpool, 1964–70) 16
Thompson Phil (Liverpool, 1976–83) 42
Thompson T (Aston Villa, Preston, 1952–57) 2
Thomson R (Wolves, 1964–65) 8
Todd C (Derby, 1972–77) 27
Towers A (Sunderland, 1978) 3
Townsend A (Tottenham, Newcastle, Crystal Palace, 2014–17) 13
Tripper K (Tottenham, 2017–18) 13
Tueart D (Manchester City, 1975–77) 6

Ufton D (Charlton, 1954) 1
Unsworth D (Everton, 1995) 1
Upson M (Birmingham, West Ham, 2003–10) 21

Vardy (Leicester, 2015–18) 26
Vassell D (Aston Villa, 2002–04) 22
Venables T (Chelsea, 1965) 2
Venison B (Newcastle, 1995) 2
Viljoen C (Ipswich, 1975) 2
Viollet D (Manchester Utd, 1960) 2
Waddle C (Newcastle, Tottenham, Marseille, 1985–92) 62
Waiters A (Blackpool, 1964–65) 5
Walcott T (Arsenal, 2006–17) 47
Walker D (Nottm Forest, Sampdoria, Sheffield Wed, 1989–94) 59
Walker I (Tottenham, Leicester, 1996–2004) 4
Walker K (Tottenham, Manchester City, 2012–18) 40
Wallace D (Southampton, 1986) 1
Walsh P (Luton, 1983–4) 5
Walters M (Rangers, 1991) 1
Ward P (Brighton, 1980) 1
Ward T (Derby, 1948) 2
Ward-Prowse J (Southampton, 2017) 1
Warnock S (Blackburn, Aston Villa, 2008–11) 2
Watson D (Sunderland, Manchester City, Werder Bremen, Southampton, Stoke, 1974–82) 65
Watson D (Norwich, Everton, 1984–8) 12
Watson W (Sunderland, 1950–1) 4
Webb N (Nottm Forest, Manchester Utd, 1988–92) 26
Welbeck D (Manchester Utd, Arsenal, 2011–18) 40
Weller K (Leicester, 1974) 4
West G (Everton, 1969) 3
Wheeler J (Bolton, 1955) 1
White D (Manchester City, 1993) 1
Whitworth S (Leicester, 1975–76) 7
Whymark T (Ipswich, 1978) 1
Wignall F (Nottm Forest, 1965) 2
Wilcox J (Blackburn, Leeds, 1996–2000) 3
Wilkins R (Chelsea, Manchester Utd, AC Milan, 1976–87) 84
Williams B (Wolves, 1949–56) 24
Williams S (Southampton, 1983–85) 6
Willis A (Tottenham, 1952) 1
Wilshaw D (Wolves, 1954–57) 12
Wilshere J (Arsenal, 2011–16) 34
Wilson R (Huddersfield, Everton, 1960–8) 63
Winks H (Tottenham, 2018) 1
Winterburn N (Arsenal, 1990–93) 2
Wise D (Chelsea, 1991–2001) 21
Withe P (Aston Villa, 1981–85) 11
Wood R (Manchester Utd, 1955–56) 3
Woodcock A (Nottm Forest, Cologne, Arsenal, 1977–86) 42
Woodgate J (Leeds, Newcastle, Middlesbrough, Tottenham, 1999–2008) 8
Woods C (Norwich, Rangers, Sheffield Wed, 1984–93) 43
Worthington F (Leicester, 1974–75) 8
Wright I (Crystal Palace, Arsenal, West Ham, 1991–99) 33
Wright M (Southampton, Derby, Liverpool, 1984–96) 45
Wright R (Ipswich, Arsenal, 2000–02) 2
Wright T (Everton, 1968–70) 11
Wright W (Wolves, 1947–59) 105
Wright-Phillips S (Manchester City, Chelsea, Manchester City, 2005–11) 36

Young A (Aston Villa, Manchester Utd, 2008–18) 39
Young G (Sheffield Wed, 1965) 1
Young L (Charlton, 2005) 7

Zaha W (Manchester Utd, 2013–14) 2
Zamora R (Fulham, 2011–12) 2

## SCOTLAND

Adam C (Rangers, Blackpool, Liverpool, Stoke, 2007–15) 26
Aird J (Burnley, 1954) 4
Aitken G (East Fife, 1949–54) 8
Aitken R (Celtic, Newcastle, St Mirren, 1980–92) 57
Albiston A (Manchester Utd, 1982–6) 14
Alexander G (Preston, Burnley, 2002–10) 40
Alexander N (Cardiff, 2006) 2
Allan T (Dundee, 1974) 2
Anderson J (Leicester, 1954) 1
Anderson R (Aberdeen, Sunderland, 2003–08) 11
Anya I (Watford, Derby, 2014–18) 29
Archer J (Millwall, 2018) 1
Archibald S (Aberdeen, Tottenham, Barcelona, 1980–86) 27
Armstrong S (Celtic, 2017–18) 6
Auld B (Celtic, 1959–60) 3

Bain S (Celtic, 2018) 1
Baird H (Airdrie, 1956) 1
Baird S (Rangers, 1957–58) 7
Bannan B (Aston Villa, Crystal Palace, Sheffield Wed, 2011–18) 27
Bannon E (Dundee Utd, 1980–86) 11
Bardsley P (Sunderland, 2011–14) 13
Barr D (Falkirk, 2009) 1
Bauld W (Hearts, 1950) 3
Baxter J (Rangers, Sunderland, 1961–68) 34
Beattie C (Celtic, WBA, 2006–08) 7
Bell C (Kilmarnock, 2011) 1
Bell W (Leeds, 1966) 2
Bernard P (Oldham, 1995) 2
Berra C (Hearts, Wolves, Ipswich, Hearts, 2008–18) 41
Bett J (Rangers, Lokeren, Aberdeen, 1982–90) 26
Black E (Metz, 1988) 2
Black I (Southampton, 1948) 1
Black I (Rangers, 2013) 1

| | |
|---|---|
| Blacklaw A (Burnley, 1963–66) | 3 |
| Blackley J (Hibernian, 1974–77) | 7 |
| Blair J (Blackpool, 1947) | 1 |
| Blyth J (Coventry, 1978) | 2 |
| Bone J (Norwich, 1972–73) | 2 |
| Booth S (Aberdeen, Borussia Dortmund, Twente Enschede 1993–2002) | 22 |
| Bowman D (Dundee Utd, 1992–94) | 6 |
| Boyd G (Peterborough, Hull, 2013–14) | 2 |
| Boyd K (Rangers, Middlesbrough, 2006–11) | 18 |
| Boyd T (Motherwell, Chelsea, Celtic, 1991–2002) | 72 |
| Brand R (Rangers, 1961–62) | 8 |
| Brazil A (Ipswich, Tottenham, 1980–83) | 13 |
| Bremner D (Hibernian, 1976) | 1 |
| Bremner W (Leeds, 1965–76) | 54 |
| Brennan F (Newcastle, 1947–54) | 7 |
| Bridcutt L (Brighton, Sunderland, 2013–16) | 2 |
| Broadfoot K (Rangers, 2009–11) | 4 |
| Brogan J (Celtic, 1971) | 4 |
| Brown A (East Fife, Blackpool, 1950–54) | 13 |
| Brown H (Partick, 1947) | 3 |
| Brown J (Sheffield Utd, 1975) | 1 |
| Brown R (Rangers, 1947–52) | 3 |
| Brown S (Hibernian, Celtic, 2007–18) | 55 |
| Brown W (Dundee, Tottenham, 1958–66) | 28 |
| Brownlie J (Hibernian, 1971–76) | 7 |
| Bryson C (Kilmarnock, Derby, 2011–16) | 3 |
| Buchan M (Aberdeen, Manchester Utd, 1972–8) | 34 |
| Buckley P (Aberdeen, 1954–55) | 3 |
| Burchill M (Celtic, 2000) | 6 |
| Burke C (Rangers, Birmingham, 2006–14) | 7 |
| Burke O (Nottm Forest, Leipzig, 2016–17) | 5 |
| Burley C (Chelsea, Celtic, Derby, 1995–2003) | 46 |
| Burley G (Ipswich, 1979–82) | 11 |
| Burns F (Manchester Utd, 1970) | 1 |
| Burns K (Birmingham, Nottm Forest, 1974–81) | 20 |
| Burns T (Celtic, 1981–88) | 8 |
| Cadden C (Motherwell, 2018) | 2 |
| Caddis P (Birmingham, 2016) | 1 |
| Cairney T (Fulham, 2017) | 2 |
| Calderwood C (Tottenham, Aston Villa, 1995–2000) | 36 |
| Caldow E (Rangers, 1957–63) | 40 |
| Cairney T (Fulham, 2017–18) | 2 |
| Caldwell G (Newcastle, Sunderland, Hibernian, Wigan, 2002–13) | 55 |
| Caldwell S (Newcastle, Sunderland, Celtic, Wigan, 2001–11) | 12 |
| Callaghan T (Dunfermline, 1970) | 2 |
| Cameron C (Hearts, Wolves, 1999–2005) | 28 |
| Campbell R (Falkirk, Chelsea, 1947–50) | 5 |
| Campbell W (Morton, 1947–48) | 5 |
| Canero P (Leicester, 2004) | 1 |
| Carr W (Coventry, 1970–73) | 6 |
| Chalmers S (Celtic, 1965–67) | 5 |
| Christie R (Celtic, 2018) | 3 |
| Clark J (Celtic, 1966–67) | 4 |
| Clark R (Aberdeen, 1968–73) | 17 |
| Clarke S (Chelsea, 1988–94) | 6 |
| Clarkson D (Motherwell, 2008–09) | 2 |
| Collins J (Hibernian, Celtic, Monaco, Everton, 1988–2000) | 58 |
| Collins R (Celtic, Everton, Leeds, 1951–65) | 31 |
| Colquhoun E (Sheffield Utd, 1972–73) | 9 |
| Colquhoun J (Hearts, 1988) | 2 |
| Combe J (Hibernian, 1948) | 3 |
| Commons K (Derby, Celtic, 2009–13) | 12 |
| Conn A (Hearts, 1956) | 1 |
| Conn A (Tottenham, 1975) | 2 |
| Connachan E (Dunfermline, 1962) | 2 |
| Connelly G (Celtic, 1974) | 2 |
| Connolly J (Everton, 1973) | 1 |
| Connor R (Dundee, Aberdeen, 1986–91) | 4 |
| Conway C (Dundee Utd, Cardiff, 2010–14) | 7 |
| Cooke C (Dundee, Chelsea, 1966–75) | 16 |
| Cooper D (Rangers, Motherwell, 1980–90) | 22 |
| Cormack P (Hibernian, 1966–72) | 9 |
| Cowan J (Morton, 1948–52) | 25 |
| Cowie D (Dundee, 1953–58) | 20 |
| Cowie D (Watford, 2010–12) | 10 |
| Cox C (Hearts, 1948) | 1 |
| Cox S (Rangers, 1948–54) | 25 |
| Craig JP (Celtic, 1968) | 1 |
| Craig J (Celtic, 1977) | 1 |
| Craig T (Newcastle, 1976) | 1 |
| Crainey S (Celtic, Southampton, Blackpool, 2002–12) | 12 |
| Crawford S (Raith, Dunfermline, Plymouth Argyle, 1995–2005) | 25 |
| Crerand P (Celtic, Manchester Utd, 1961–66) | 16 |
| Cropley A (Hibernian, 1972) | 2 |
| Cruickshank J (Hearts, 1964–76) | 6 |
| Cullen M (Luton, 1956) | 1 |
| Cumming J (Hearts, 1955–60) | 9 |
| Cummings J (Nottm Forest, 2018) | 2 |
| Cummings W (Chelsea, 2002) | 1 |
| Cunningham W (Preston, 1954–55) | 8 |
| Curran H (Wolves, 1970–71) | 5 |
| Dailly C (Derby, Blackburn, West Ham, 1997–2008) | 67 |
| Dalglish K (Celtic, Liverpool, 1972–87) | 102 |
| Davidson C (Blackburn, Leicester, Preston, 1999–2010) | 19 |
| Davidson M (St Johnstone, 2013) | 1` |
| Davidson J (Partick, 1954–55) | 8 |
| Dawson A (Rangers, 1980–83) | 5 |
| Deans J (Celtic, 1975) | 2 |
| *Delaney J (Manchester Utd, 1947–48) | 4 |
| Devlin P (Birmingham, 2003–04) | 10 |
| Dick J (West Ham, 1959) | 1 |
| Dickov P (Manchester City, Leicester, Blackburn, 2001–05) | 10 |
| Dickson W (Kilmarnock, 1970–71) | 5 |
| Dixon P (Huddersfield, 2013) | 3 |
| Dobie S (WBA, 2002–03) | 6 |
| Docherty T (Preston, Arsenal, 1952–59) | 25 |

Dodds D (Dundee Utd, 1984) 2
Dodds W (Aberdeen, Dundee Utd, Rangers, 1997–2002) 26
Donachie W (Manchester City, 1972–79) 35
Donnelly S (Celtic, 1997–99) 10
Dorrans G (WBA, Norwich, 2010–16) 12
Dougall C (Birmingham, 1947) 1
Dougan R (Hearts, 1950) 1
Douglas B (Wolves, 2018) 1
Douglas R (Celtic, Leicester, 2002–06) 19
Doyle J (Ayr, 1976) 1
Duncan A (Hibernian, 1975–76) 6
Duncan D (East Fife, 1948) 3
Duncanson J (Rangers, 1947) 1
Durie G (Chelsea, Tottenham, Rangers, 1988–98) 43
Durrant I (Rangers, Kilmarnock, 1988–2000) 20
Elliott M (Leicester, 1997–2002) 18
Evans A (Aston Villa, 1982) 4
Evans R (Celtic, Chelsea, 1949–60) 48
Ewing T (Partick, 1958) 2

Farm G (Blackpool, 1953–59) 10
Ferguson B (Rangers, Blackburn, Rangers, 1999–2009) 45
Ferguson D (Dundee Utd, Everton, 1992–97) 7
Ferguson D (Rangers, 1988) 2
Ferguson I (Rangers, 1989–97) 9
Ferguson R (Kilmarnock, 1966–67) 7
Fernie W (Celtic, 1954–58) 12
Flavell R (Airdrie, 1947) 2
Fleck R (Norwich, 1990–91) 4
Fleming C (East Fife, 1954) 1
Fletcher D (Manchester Utd, WBA, 2004–18) 80
Fletcher S (Hibernian, Burnley, Wolves, Sunderland, Sheffield Wed, 2008–18) 31
Forbes A (Sheffield Utd, Arsenal, 1947–52) 14
Ford D (Hearts, 1974) 3
Forrest J (Motherwell, 1958) 1
Forrest J (Rangers, Aberdeen, 1966–71) 5
Forrest J (Celtic, 2011–18) 22
Forsyth A (Partick, Manchester Utd, 1972–76) 10
Forsyth C (Kilmarnock, 1964) 4
Forsyth C (Derby, 2014–15) 4
Forsyth T (Motherwell, Rangers, 1971–78) 22
Fox D (Burnley, Southampton, 2010–13) 4
Fraser D (WBA, 1968–69) 2
Fraser R (Bournemouth, 2017–18) 3
Fraser W (Sunderland, 1955) 2
Freedman D (Crystal Palace, 2002) 2

Gabriel J (Everton, 1961–64) 2
Gallacher K (Dundee Utd, Coventry, Blackburn, Newcastle, 1988–2001) 53
Gallacher P (Dundee Utd, 2003–04) 8
Gallagher P (Blackburn, 2004) 1
Galloway M (Celtic, 1992) 1
Gardiner I (Motherwell, 1958) 1
Gemmell T (St Mirren, 1955) 2
Gemmell T (Celtic, 1966–71) 18
Gemmill A (Derby, Nottm Forest, Birmingham, 1971–81) 43
Gemmill S (Nottm Forest, Everton, 1995–2003) 26
Gibson D (Leicester, 1963–65) 7
Gilks M (Blackpool, 2013–14) 3
Gillespie G (Liverpool, 1988–91) 13
Gilzean A (Dundee, Tottenham, 1964–71) 22
Glass S (Newcastle Utd 1999) 1
Glavin R (Celtic, 1977) 1
Glen A (Aberdeen, 1956) 2
Goodwillie D (Dundee Utd, Blackburn, 2011–12) 3
Goram A (Oldham, Hibernian, Rangers, 1986–98) 43
Gordon C (Hearts, Sunderland, Celtic, 2004–18) 52
Gough R (Dundee Utd, Tottenham, Rangers, 1983–93) 61
Gould J (Celtic, 2000–01) 2
Govan J (Hibernian, 1948–49) 6
Graham A (Leeds, 1978–81) 10
Graham G (Arsenal, Manchester Utd, 1972–73) 12
Gray A (Aston Villa, Wolves, Everton, 1976–85) 20
Gray A (Bradford City, 2003) 2
Gray E (Leeds, 1969–77) 12
Gray F (Leeds, Nottm Forest, 1976–83) 32
Grant J (Hibernian, 1958) 2
Grant P (Celtic, 1989) 2
Green A (Blackpool, Newcastle, 1971–72) 6
Greer G (Brighton, 2014–16) 11
Greig J (Rangers, 1964–76) 44
Griffiths L (Wolves, Celtic, 2013–18) 17
Gunn B (Norwich, 1990–94) 6

Haddock H (Clyde, 1955–58) 6
Haffey F (Celtic, 1960–61) 2
Hamilton A (Dundee, 1962–66) 24
Hamilton G (Aberdeen, 1947–54) 5
Hamilton W (Hibernian, 1965) 1
Hammell S (Motherwell, 2005) 1
Hanley G (Blackburn, Newcastle, Norwich, 2011–18) 29
Hansen A (Liverpool, 1979–87) 26
Hansen J (Partick, 1972) 2
Harper J (Aberdeen, Hibernian, 1973–78) 4
Hartford A (WBA, Manchester City, Everton, 1972–82) 50
Hartley P (Hearts, Celtic, Bristol City, 2005–10) 25
Harvey D (Leeds, 1973–77) 16
Haughney M (Celtic, 1954) 1
Hay D (Celtic, 1970–74) 27
Hegarty P (Dundee Utd, 1979–83) 8
Henderson J (Portsmouth, Arsenal, 1953–59) 7
Henderson W (Rangers, 1963–71) 29
Hendry C (Blackburn, Rangers, Coventry, Bolton, 1994–2001) 51
Hendry J (Celtic, 2018) 2

Herd D (Arsenal, 1959–61) 5
Herd G (Clyde, 1958–61) 5
Herriot J (Birmingham, 1969–70) 8
Hewie J (Charlton, 1956–60) 19
Holt D (Hearts, 1963–64) 5
Holt G (Kilmarnock, Norwich, 2001–05) 10
Holton J (Manchester Utd, 1973–75) 15
Hope R (WBA, 1968–69) 2
Hopkin D (Crystal Palace, Leeds, 1997–2000) 7
Houliston W (Queen of the South, 1949) 3
Houston S (Manchester Utd, 1976) 1
Howie H (Hibernian, 1949) 1
Hughes J (Celtic, 1965–70) 8
Hughes R (Portsmouth, 2004–06) 5
Hughes S (Norwich, 2010) 1
Hughes W (Sunderland, 1975) 1
Humphries W (Motherwell, 1952) 1
Hunter A (Kilmarnock, Celtic, 1972–74) 4
Hunter W (Motherwell, 1960–61) 3
Husband J (Partick, 1947) 1
Hutchison D (Everton, Sunderland, West Ham, 1999–2004) 26
Hutchison T (Coventry, 1974–76) 17
Hutton A (Rangers, Tottenham, Aston Villa, 2007–16) 50

Imlach S (Nottm Forest, 1958) 4
Irvine B (Aberdeen, 1991–94) 9
Iwelumo C (Wolves, Burnley, 2009–11) 4

Jack R (Rangers, 2018) 1
Jackson C (Rangers, 1975–77) 8
Jackson D (Hibernian, Celtic, 1995–99) 28
Jardine A (Rangers, 1971–80) 38
Jarvie A (Airdrie, 1971) 3
Jess E (Aberdeen, Coventry, Aberdeen, 1993–99) 18
Johnston A (Sunderland, Rangers, Middlesbrough, 1999–2003) 18
Johnston L (Clyde, 1948) 2
Johnston M (Watford, Celtic, Nantes, Rangers, 1984–92) 38
Johnston W (Rangers, WBA, 1966–78) 21
Johnstone D (Rangers, 1973–80) 14
Johnstone J (Celtic, 1965–75) 23
Johnstone R (Hibernian, Manchester City, 1951–56) 17
Jordan J (Leeds, Manchester Utd, AC Milan, 1973–82) 52

Kelly H (Blackpool, 1952) 1
Kelly J (Barnsley, 1949) 2
Kelly L (Kilmarnock, 2013) 1
Kennedy J (Celtic, 1964–65) 6
Kennedy J (Celtic, 2004) 1
Kennedy S (Rangers, 1975) 5
Kennedy S (Aberdeen, 1978–82) 8
Kenneth G (Dundee Utd, 2011) 2
Kerr A (Partick, 1955) 2
Kerr B (Newcastle, 2003–04) 3
Kingsley S (Swansea, 2016) 1
Kyle K (Sunderland, Kilmarnock, 2002–10) 10

Lambert P (Motherwell, Borussia Dortmund, Celtic, 1995–2003) 40
Law D (Huddersfield, Manchester City, Torino, Manchester Utd, 1959–74) 55
Lawrence T (Liverpool, 1963–69) 3
Leggat G (Aberdeen, Fulham, 1956–60) 18
Leighton J (Aberdeen, Manchester Utd, Hibernian, Aberdeen, 1983–99) 91
Lennox R (Celtic, 1967–70) 10
Leslie L (Airdrie, 1961) 5
Levein C (Hearts, 1990–95) 16
Liddell W (Liverpool, 1947–55) 28
Linwood A (Clyde, 1950) 1
Little R (Rangers, 1953) 1
Logie J (Arsenal, 1953) 1
Long H (Clyde, 1947) 1
Lorimer P (Leeds, 1970–76) 21
Macari L (Celtic, Manchester Utd, 1972–78) 24
Macaulay A (Brentford, Arsenal, 1947–48) 7
MacDonald A (Rangers, 1976) 1
MacDougall E (Norwich, 1975–76) 7
Mackail-Smith C (Peterborough, Brighton 2011–12) 7
MacKay D (Celtic, 1959–62) 14
Mackay D (Hearts, Tottenham, 1957–66) 22
Mackay G (Hearts, 1988) 4
Mackay M (Norwich, 2004–05) 5
Mackay-Steven G (Dundee Utd, 2014) 1
MacKenzie J (Partick, 1954–56) 9
Mackie J (QPR, 2011–13) 9
MacLeod J (Hibernian, 1961) 4
MacLeod M (Celtic, Borussia Dortmund, Hibernian, 1985–91) 20
Maguire C (Aberdeen, 2011) 2
Maloney S (Celtic, Aston Villa, Celtic, Wigan, Chicago, Hull, 2006–16) 47
Malpas M (Dundee Utd, 1984–93) 55
Marshall D (Celtic, Cardiff, Hull, 2005–17) 27
Marshall G (Celtic, 1992) 1
Martin B (Motherwell, 1995) 2
Martin C (Derby, 2014–18) 17
Martin F (Aberdeen, 1954–55) 6
Martin N (Hibernian, Sunderland, 1965–66) 3
Martin R (Norwich, 2011–17) 29
Martis J (Motherwell, 1961) 1
Mason J (Third Lanark 1949–51) 7
Masson D (QPR, Derby, 1976–78) 17
Mathers D (Partick, 1954) 1
Matteo D (Leeds, 2001–02) 6
May S (Sheffield Wed, 2015) 1
McAllister B (Wimbledon, 1997) 3
McAllister G (Leicester, Leeds, Coventry, 1990–99) 57
McAllister J (Livingston, 2004) 1
McArthur J (Wigan, Crystal Palace, 2011–18) 32
McAvennie F (West Ham, Celtic, 1986–88) 5
McBride J (Celtic, 1967) 2
McBurnie O (Swansea, 2018) 4
McCall S (Everton, Rangers, 1990–98) 40
McCalliog J (Sheffield Wed, Wolves, 1967–71) 5
McCann N (Hearts, Rangers, Southampton, 1999–2006) 26

McCann R (Motherwell, 1959–61) 5
McClair B (Celtic, Manchester Utd, 1987–93) 30
McCloy P (Rangers, 1973) 4
McCoist A (Rangers, Kilmarnock, 1986–99) 61
McColl I (Rangers, 1950–58) 14
McCormack R (Motherwell, Cardiff, Leeds, Fulham, 2008–16) 13
McCreadie E (Chelsea, 1965–9) 23
McCulloch L (Wigan, Rangers, 2005–11) 18
McDonald J (Sunderland, 1956) 2
McDonald K (Fulham, 2018) 1
McEveley, J (Derby, 2008) 3
McFadden J (Motherwell, Everton, Birmingham, 2002–11) 48
McFarlane W (Hearts, 1947) 1
McGarr E (Aberdeen, 1970) 2
McGarvey F (Liverpool, Celtic, 1979–84) 7
McGeouch D (Hibernian, 2018) 2
McGhee M (Aberdeen, 1983–84) 4
McGinlay J (Bolton, 1995–97) 13
McGinn J (Hibernian, 2016–18) 9
McGrain D (Celtic, 1973–82) 62
McGregor A (Rangers, Besiktas, Hull, 2007–18) 38
McGregor C (Celtic, 2018) 3
McGrory J (Kilmarnock, 1965–66) 3
McInally A (Aston Villa, Bayern Munich, 1989–90) 8
McInally J (Dundee Utd, 1987–93) 10
McInnes D (WBA, 2003) 2
McKay B (Rangers, 2016) 1
McKean R (Rangers, 1976) 1
McKenna S (Aberdeen, 2018) 4
McKimmie S (Aberdeen, 1989–96) 40
McKinlay T (Celtic, 1996–98) 22
McKinlay W (Dundee Utd, Blackburn, 1994–99) 29
McKinnon R (Rangers, 1966–71) 28
McKinnon R (Motherwell, 1994–95) 3
McLaren A (Preston, 1947–48) 4
McLaren A (Hearts, Rangers, 1992–96) 24
McLaren A (Kilmarnock, 2001) 1
McLaughlin J (Hearts, 2018) 1
McLean G (Dundee, 1968) 1
McLean K (Aberdeen, Norwich, 2016–18) 5
McLean T (Kilmarnock, Rangers, 1969–71) 6
McLeish A (Aberdeen, 1980–93) 77
McLintock F (Leicester, Arsenal, 1963–71) 9
McManus S (Celtic, Middlesbrough, 2007–11) 26
McMillan I (Airdrie, 1952–61) 6
McNamara J (Celtic, Wolves, 1997–2006) 33
McNamee D (Livingston, 2004–06) 4
McNaught W (Raith, 1951–55) 5
McNaughton K (Aberdeen, Cardiff, 2002–08) 4
McNeill W (Celtic, 1961–72) 29
McPhail J (Celtic, 1950–54) 5
McPherson D (Hearts, Rangers, 1989–93) 27
McQueen G (Leeds, Manchester Utd, 1974–81) 30
McStay P (Celtic, 1984–97) 76
McSwegan G (Hearts, 2000) 2
McTominay S (Manchester Utd, 2018) 2
Millar J (Rangers, 1963) 2
Miller C (Dundee Utd, 2001) 1
Miller K (Rangers, Wolves, Celtic, Derby, Rangers, Bursaspor, Cardiff, Vancouver, 2001–14) 69
Miller L (Dundee Utd, Aberdeen 2006–10) 3
Miller W (Celtic, 1946–47) 6
Miller W (Aberdeen, 1975–90) 65
Mitchell R (Newcastle, 1951) 2
Mochan N (Celtic, 1954) 3
Moir W (Bolton, 1950) 1
Moncur R (Newcastle, 1968–72) 16
Morgan L (Celtic, 2018) 2
Morgan W (Burnley, Manchester Utd, 1968–74) 21
Morris H (East Fife, 1950) 1
Morrison J (WBA, 2008–18) 46
Mudie J (Blackpool, 1957–58) 17
Mulgrew C (Celtic, Blackburn, 2012–18) 36
Mulhall G (Aberdeen, Sunderland, 1960–64) 3
Munro F (Wolves, 1971–75) 9
Munro I (St Mirren, 1979–80) 7
Murdoch R (Celtic, 1966–70) 12
Murphy J (Brighton, 2018) 2
Murray I (Hibernian, Rangers, 2003–06) 6
Murray J (Hearts, 1958) 5
Murray S (Aberdeen, 1972) 1
Murty G (Reading, 2004–08) 4

Naismith S (Kilmarnock, Rangers, Everton, Norwich, 2007–17) 45
Narey D (Dundee Utd, 1977–89) 35
Naysmith G (Hearts, Everton, Sheffield Utd, 2000–09) 46
Neilson R (Hearts, 2007) 1
Nevin P (Chelsea, Everton, Tranmere, 1987–96) 28
Nicholas C (Celtic, Arsenal, Aberdeen, 1983–89) 20
Nicholson B (Dunfermline, 2001–05) 3
Nicol S (Liverpool, 1985–92) 27
O'Connor G (Hibernian, Lokomotiv Moscow, Birmingham, 2002–10) 16
O'Donnell P (Motherwell, 1994) 1
O'Donnell S (Kilmarnock, 2018) 2
O'Hare J (Derby, 1970–72) 13
O'Neil B (Celtic, VfL Wolfsburg, Derby, Preston, 1996–2006) 7
O'Neil J (Hibernian, 2001) 1
Ormond W (Hibernian, 1954–59) 6
Orr T (Morton, 1952) 2

Parker A (Falkirk, Everton, 1955–56) 15
Parlane D (Rangers, 1973–77) 12
Paterson C (Hearts, Cardiff, 2016–18) 9

Paton A (Motherwell, 1952) 2
Pearson S (Motherwell, Celtic, Derby, 2004–07) 10
Pearson T (Newcastle, 1947) 2
Penman A (Dundee, 1966) 1
Pettigrew W (Motherwell, 1976–77) 5
Phillips M (Blackpool, QPR, WBA, 2012–18) 12
Plenderleith J (Manchester City, 1961) 1
Pressley S (Hearts, 2000–07) 32
Provan D (Rangers, 1964–66) 5
Provan D (Celtic, 1980–82) 10

Quashie N (Portsmouth, Southampton, WBA, 2004–07) 14
Quinn P (Motherwell, 1961–62) 4

Rae G (Dundee, Rangers, Cardiff, 2001–09) 14
Redpath W (Motherwell, 1949–52) 9
Reilly L (Hibernian, 1949–57) 38
Rhodes J (Huddersfield, Blackburn, Sheffield Wed, 2012–17) 14
Ring T (Clyde, 1953–58) 12
Rioch B (Derby, Everton, 1975–78) 24
Riordan D (Hibernian, 2006–10) 3
Ritchie M (Bournemouth, Newcastle, 2015–18) 16
Ritchie P (Hearts, Bolton, 1999–2000) 7
Ritchie W (Rangers, 1962) 1
Robb D (Aberdeen, 1971) 5
Robertson A (Clyde, 1955) 5
Robertson A (Dundee Utd, Hull, Liverpool, 2014–18) 22
Robertson D (Rangers, 1992–94) 3
Robertson H (Dundee, 1962) 1
Robertson J (Tottenham, 1964) 1
Robertson J (Nottm Forest, Derby, 1978–84) 28
Robertson J (Hearts, 1991–96) 16
Robertson S (Dundee Utd, 2009–11) 2
Robinson R (Dundee, 1974–75) 4
Robson B (Celtic, Middlesbrough, 2008–12) 17
Ross M (Rangers, 2002–04) 13
Rough A (Partick, Hibernian, 1976–86) 53
Rougvie D (Aberdeen, 1984) 1
Russell J (Derby, Kansas City, 2015–18) 5
Rutherford E (Rangers, 1948) 1

Saunders S (Motherwell, 2011) 1
Schaedler E (Hibernian, 1974) 1
Scott A (Rangers, Everton, 1957–66) 16
Scott J (Hibernian, 1966) 1
Scott J (Dundee, 1971) 2
Scoular J (Portsmouth, 1951–53) 9
Severin S (Hearts, Aberdeen, 2002–07) 15
Sharp G (Everton, 1985–88) 12
Shaw D (Hibernian, 1947–49) 8
Shaw J (Rangers, 1947) 4
Shearer D (Aberdeen, 1994–96) 7
Shearer R (Rangers, 1961) 4
Shinnie A (Inverness, 2013) 1
Shinnie G (Aberdeen, 2018) 2
Simpson N (Aberdeen, 1983–88) 5
Simpson R (Celtic, 1967–69) 5
Sinclair J (Leicester, 1966) 1

Smith D (Aberdeen, Rangers, 1966–68) 2
Smith G (Hibernian, 1947–57) 18
Smith H (Hearts, 1988–92) 3
Smith JE (Celtic, 1959) 2
Smith J (Aberdeen, Newcastle, 1968–74) 4
Smith J (Celtic, 2003) 2
Snodgrass R (Leeds, Norwich, West Ham, 2011–18) 25
Souness G (Middlesbrough, Liverpool, Sampdoria, Rangers, 1975–86) 54
Speedie D (Chelsea, Coventry, 1985–89) 10
Spencer J (Chelsea, QPR, 1995–97) 14
Stanton P (Hibernian, 1966–74) 16
Steel W (Morton, Derby, Dundee, 1947–53) 30
Stein C (Rangers, Coventry, 1969–73) 21
Stephen J (Bradford Park Avenue, 1947–48) 2
Stevenson L (Hibernian, 2018) 1
Stewart D (Leeds, 1978) 1
Stewart J (Kilmarnock, Middlesbrough, 1977–79) 2
Stewart M (Manchester Utd, Hearts 2002–09) 4
Stewart R (West Ham, 1981–7) 10
St John I (Motherwell, Liverpool, 1959–65) 21
Stockdale R (Middlesbrough, 2002–03) 5
Strachan G (Aberdeen, Manchester Utd, Leeds, 1980–92) 50
Sturrock P (Dundee Utd, 1981–87) 20
Sullivan N (Wimbledon, Tottenham, 1997–2003) 28
Teale G (Wigan, Derby, 2006–09) 13
Telfer P (Coventry, 2000) 1
Telfer W (St Mirren, 1954) 1
Thomson K (Rangers, Middlesbrough, 2009–11) 3
Thompson S (Dundee Utd, Rangers, 2002–05) 16
Thomson W (St Mirren, 1980–84) 7
Thornton W (Rangers, 1947–52) 7
Tierney K (Celtic, 2016–18) 9
Toner W (Kilmarnock, 1959) 2
Turnbull E (Hibernian, 1948–58) 8

Ure I (Dundee, Arsenal, 1962–68) 11

Waddell W (Rangers, 1947–55) 17
Walker A (Celtic, 1988–95) 3
Walker N (Hearts, 1993–96) 2
Wallace I (Coventry, 1978–79) 3
Wallace L (Hearts, Rangers, 2010–17) 10
Wallace R (Preston, 2010) 1
Wallace W (Hearts, Celtic, 1965–69) 7
Wardhaugh J (Hearts, 1955–57) 2
Wark J (Ipswich, Liverpool, 1979–85) 29
Watson J (Motherwell, Huddersfield, 1948–54) 2
Watson R (Motherwell, 1971) 1
Watt T (Charlton, 2016) 1
Webster A (Hearts, Rangers, Hearts, 2003–13) 28

Weir A (Motherwell, 1959–60) 6
Weir D (Hearts, Everton, Rangers, 1997–2011) 69
Weir P (St Mirren, Aberdeen, 1980–84) 6
White J (Falkirk, Tottenham, 1959–64) 22
Whittaker S (Rangers, Norwich, 2010–16) 31
Whyte D (Celtic, Middlesbrough, Aberdeen, 1988–99) 12
Wilkie L (Dundee, 2002–03) 11
Williams G (Nottm Forest, 2002–03) 5
Wilson A (Portsmouth, 1954) 1
Wilson D (Liverpool, 2011–12) 5
Wilson D (Rangers, 1961–65) 22
Wilson I (Leicester, Everton, 1987–8) 5
Wilson M (Celtic, 2011) 1
Wilson P (Celtic, 1975) 1
Wilson R (Arsenal, 1972) 2
Wood G (Everton, Arsenal, 1978–82) 4
Woodburn W (Rangers, 1947–52) 24
Wright K (Hibernian, 1992) 1
Wright S (Aberdeen, 1993) 2
Wright T (Sunderland, 1953) 3

Yeats R (Liverpool, 1965–66) 2
Yorston H (Aberdeen, 1955) 1
Young A (Hearts, Everton, 1960–66) 8
Young G (Rangers, 1947–57) 53
Younger T (Hibernian, Liverpool, 1955–58) 24

## WALES

Aizlewood M (Charlton, Leeds, Bradford City, Bristol City, Cardiff, 1986–95) 39
Allchurch I (Swansea City, Newcastle, Cardiff, 1951–66) 68
Allchurch L (Swansea City, Sheffield Utd, 1955–64) 11
Allen B (Coventry, 1951) 2
Allen J (Swansea, Liverpool, Stoke, 2009–18) 43
Allen M (Watford, Norwich, Millwall, Newcastle, 1986–94) 14
Ampadu E (Chelsea, 2018) 2

Baker C (Cardiff, 1958–62) 7
Baker W (Cardiff, 1948) 1
Bale G (Southampton, Tottenham, Real Madrid, 2006–18) 70
Barnard D (Barnsley, Grimsby, 1998–2004) 24
Barnes W (Arsenal, 1948–55) 22
Bellamy C (Norwich, Coventry, Newcastle, Blackburn, Liverpool, West Ham, Manchester City, Liverpool, Cardiff, 1998–2014) 78
Berry G (Wolves, Stoke, 1979–83) 5
Blackmore C (Manchester Utd, Middlesbrough, 1985–97) 39
Blake D (Cardiff, Crystal Palace, 2011–13) 14
Blake N (Sheffield Utd, Bolton, Blackburn, Wolves, 1994–2004) 29
Bodin B (Preston, 2018) 1
Bodin P (Swindon, Crystal Palace, Swindon, 1990–95) 23
Bowen D (Arsenal, 1955–59) 19
Bowen J (Swansea City, Birmingham, 1994–97) 2
Bowen M (Tottenham, Norwich, West Ham, 1986–97) 41
Boyle T (Crystal Palace, 1981) 2
Bradley M (Walsall, 2010) 1
Bradshaw T (Walsall, Barnsley, 2016–18) 3
Brooks D (Sheffield Utd 2018) 3
Brown J (Gillingham, Blackburn, Aberdeen, 2006–12) 3
Browning M (Bristol Rov, Huddersfield, 1996–97) 5
Burgess R (Tottenham, 1947–54) 32
Burton A (Norwich, Newcastle, 1963–72) 9

Cartwright L (Coventry, Wrexham, 1974–79) 7
Charles Jeremy (Swansea City, QPR, Oxford Utd, 1981–87) 19
Charles John (Leeds, Juventus, Cardiff, 1950–65) 38
Charles M (Swansea City, Arsenal, Cardiff, 1955–63) 31
Chester J (Hull, WBA, Aston Villa, 2014–18) 31
Church S (Reading, Nottm Forest, Charlton, MK Dons 2009–16) 38
Clarke R (Manchester City, 1949–56) 22
Coleman C (Crystal Palace, Blackburn, Fulham, 1992–2002) 32
Collins D (Sunderland, Stoke, 2005–11) 12
Collins J (Cardiff, West Ham, Aston Villa, West Ham, 2004–17) 50
Collison J (West Ham, 2008–14) 17
Cornforth J (Swansea City, 1995) 2
Cotterill D (Bristol City, Wigan, Sheffield Utd, Swansea, Doncaster, Birmingham, 2006–17) 24
Coyne D (Tranmere, Grimsby, Leicester, Burnley, Tranmere, 1996–2008) 16
Crofts A (Gillingham, Brighton, Norwich, Brighton, Scunthorpe, 2006–18) 29
Crossley M (Nottm Forest, Middlesbrough, Fulham, 1997–2005) 8
Crowe V (Aston Villa, 1959–63) 16
Curtis A (Swansea City, Leeds, Southampton, Cardiff, 1976–87) 35

Daniel R (Arsenal, Sunderland, 1951–57) 21
Davies A (Manchester Utd, Newcastle, Swansea City, Bradford City, 1983–90) 13
Davies A (Yeovil 2006) 1
Davies B (Swansea, Tottenham, 2013–18) 39
Davies C (Charlton, 1972) 1
Davies C (Oxford, Verona, Oldham, Barnsley, Bolton, 2006–14) 7
Davies D (Everton, Wrexham, Swansea City 1975–83) 52
Davies ER (Newcastle, 1953–58) 6
Davies G (Fulham, Chelsea, Manchester City, 1980–86) 16
Davies RT (Norwich, Southampton, Portsmouth, 1964–74) 29
Davies RW (Bolton, Newcastle, Man Utd, Man City, Blackpool, 1964–74) 34
Davies S (Manchester Utd, 1996) 1

Davies S (Tottenham, Everton, Fulham, 2001–10) 58
Davis G (Wrexham, 1978) 3
Deacy N (PSV Eindhoven, Beringen, 1977–79) 12
Delaney M (Aston Villa, 2000–07) 36
Derrett S (Cardiff, 1969–71) 4
Dibble A (Luton, Manchester City, 1986–89) 3
Dorman A (St Mirren, Crystal Palace, 2010–11) 3
Dummett P (Newcastle, 2014–16) 2
Duffy R (Portsmouth, 2006–08) 13
Durban A (Derby, 1966–72) 27
Dwyer P (Cardiff, 1978–80) 10

Eardley N (Oldham, Blackpool, 2008–11) 16
Earnshaw R (Cardiff, WBA, Norwich, Derby, Nottm Forest, Cardiff, 2002–13) 59
Easter J (Wycombe, Crystal Palace, Millwall, 2007–14) 12
Eastwood F (Wolves, Coventry, 2008–11) 11
Edwards C (Swansea City, 1996) 1
Edwards D (Luton, Wolves, Reading, 2007–18) 43
Edwards, G (Birmingham, Cardiff, 1947–50) 12
Edwards, I (Chester, Wrexham, 1978–80) 4
Edwards, L (Charlton, 1957) 2
Edwards, R (Bristol City, 1997–98) 4
Edwards, R (Aston Villa, Wolves, 2003–07) 15
Emmanuel W (Bristol City, 1973) 2
England M (Blackburn, Tottenham, 1962–75) 44
Evans B (Swansea City, Hereford, 1972–74) 7
Evans C (Manchester City, Sheffield Utd, 2008–11) 13
Evans I (Crystal Palace, 1976–78) 13
Evans L (Wolves, Sheffield Utd, 2018) 3
Evans P (Brentford, Bradford City, 2002–03) 2
Evans R (Swansea City, 1964) 1
Evans S (Wrexham, 2007–09) 7

Felgate D (Lincoln, 1984) 1
Fletcher C (Bournemouth, West Ham, Crystal Palace, 2004–09) 36
Flynn B (Burnley, Leeds, 1975–84) 66
Fon Williams O (Inverness, 2016) 1
Ford T (Swansea City, Sunderland, Aston Villa, Cardiff, 1947–57) 38
Foulkes W (Newcastle, 1952–54) 11
Freestone R (Swansea City, 2000–03) 1

Gabbidon D (Cardiff, West Ham, QPR, Crystal Palace, 2002–14) 49
Garner G (Leyton Orient, 2006) 1
Giggs R (Manchester Utd, 1992–2007) 64
Giles D (Swansea City, Crystal Palace, 1980–83) 12
Godfrey B (Preston, 1964–65) 3
Goss J (Norwich, 1991–96) 9
Green C (Birmingham, 1965–69) 15
Green R (Wolves, 1998) 2
Griffiths A (Wrexham, 1971–77) 17
Griffiths H (Swansea City, 1953) 1
Griffiths M (Leicester, 1947–54) 11
Gunter C (Cardiff, Tottenham, Nottm Forest, Reading, 2007–18) 88

Hall G (Chelsea, 1988–92) 9
Harrington A (Cardiff, 1956–62) 11
Harris C (Leeds, 1976–82) 24
Harris W (Middlesbrough, 1954–58) 6
Hartson J (Arsenal, West Ham, Wimbledon, Coventry, Celtic, 1995–2006) 51
Haworth S (Cardiff, Coventry, 1997–8) 5
Hedges R (Barnsley, 2018) 2
Henley A (Blackburn, 2016) 2
Hennessey T (Birmingham, Nottm Forest, Derby, 1962–73) 39
Hennessey W (Wolves, Crystal Palace, 2007–18) 76
Hewitt R (Cardiff, 1958) 5
Hill M (Ipswich, 1972) 2
Hockey T (Sheffield Utd, Norwich, Aston Villa, 1972–74) 9
Hodges G (Wimbledon, Newcastle, Watford, Sheffield Utd, 1984–96) 18
Holden A (Chester, 1984) 1
Hole B (Cardiff, Blackburn, Aston Villa, Swansea City, 1963–71) 30
Hollins D (Newcastle, 1962–66) 11
Hopkins J (Fulham, Crystal Palace, 1983–90) 16
Hopkins M (Tottenham, 1956–63) 34
Horne B (Portsmouth, Southampton, Everton, Birmingham, 1988–97) 59
Howells R (Cardiff, 1954) 2
Hughes C (Luton, Wimbledon, 1992–97) 8
Hughes I (Luton, 1951) 4
Hughes M (Manchester Utd, Barcelona, Bayern Munich, Manchester Utd, Chelsea, Southampton, 1984–99) 72
*Hughes W (Birmingham, 1947) 3
Hughes WA (Blackburn, 1949) 5
Humphreys J (Everton, 1947) 1
Huws E (Manchester City, Wigan, Cardiff , 2014–17) 11

Isgrove L (Southampton, 2016) 1

Jackett K (Watford, 1983–88) 31
James EG (Blackpool, 1966–71) 9
James L (Burnley, Derby, QPR, Swansea City, Sunderland, 1972–83) 54
James R (Swansea, Stoke, QPR, Leicester, Swansea, 1979–88) 47
Jarvis A (Hull, 1967) 3
Jenkins S (Swansea, Huddersfield, 1996–2002) 16
John D (Cardiff, Rangers, 2014–18) 5
Johnson A (Nottm Forest, WBA, 1999–2005) 15
Johnson M (Swansea, 1964) 1
Jones A (Port Vale, Charlton, 1987–90) 6
Jones Barrie (Swansea, Plymouth Argyle, Cardiff, 1963–9) 15

*Jones Bryn (Arsenal, 1947–9) 4
Jones C (Swansea, Tottenham, Fulham, 1954–69) 59
Jones D (Norwich, 1976–80) 8
Jones E (Swansea, Tottenham, 1947–9) 4
Jones J (Liverpool, Wrexham, Chelsea, Huddersfield, 1976–86) 72
Jones K (Aston Villa, 1950) 1
Jones L (Liverpool, Tranmere, 1997) 2
Jones M (Leeds, Leicester, 2000–03) 13
Jones M (Wrexham, 2007–08) 2
Jones P (Stockport, Southampton, Wolves, Millwall, QPR, 1997–2007) 50
Jones R (Sheffield Wed, 1994) 1
*Jones TG (Everton, 1946–49) 13
Jones V (Wimbledon, 1995–97) 9
Jones W (Bristol Rov, 1971) 1

Kelsey J (Arsenal, 1954–62) 41
King A (Leicester 2009–18) 47
King J (Swansea, 1955) 1
Kinsey N (Norwich, Birmingham, 1951–56) 7
Knill A (Swansea, 1989) 1
Koumas J (Tranmere, WBA, Wigan, 2001–09) 34
Krzywicki R (WBA, Huddersfield, 1970–72) 8

Lambert R (Liverpool, 1947–9) 5
Law B (QPR, 1990) 1
Lawrence T (Leicester, Derby, 2016–18) 13
Ledley J (Cardiff, Celtic, Crystal Palace, Derby) 77
Lea C (Ipswich, 1965) 2
Leek K (Leicester, Newcastle, Birmingham, Northampton, 1961–65) 13
Legg A (Birmingham, Cardiff, 1996–2001) 6
Lever A (Leicester, 1953) 1
Lewis D (Swansea, 1983) 1
Llewellyn C (Norwich, Wrexham, 1998–2007) 6
Lloyd B (Wrexham, 1976) 3
Lockyer T (Bristol Rov, 2018) 3
Lovell S (Crystal Palace, Millwall, 1982–86) 6
Lowndes S (Newport, Millwall, Brighton, Barnsley, 1983–88) 10
Lowrie G (Coventry, Newcastle, 1948–49) 4
Lucas M (Leyton Orient, 1962–63) 4
Lucas W (Swansea, 1949–51) 7
Lynch J (Huddersfield, 2013) 1

MacDonald S (Swansea, Bournemouth 2011–2015) 2
Maguire G (Portsmouth, 1990–92) 7
Mahoney J (Stoke, Middlesbrough, Swansea, 1968–83) 51
Mardon P (WBA, 1996) 1
Margetson M (Cardiff, 2004) 1
Marriott A (Wrexham, 1996–98) 5
Marustik C (Swansea, 1982–83) 6
Matthews A (Cardiff, Celtic, Sunderland, 2011–18) 14
Medwin T (Swansea, Tottenham, 1953–63) 30
Melville A (Swansea, Oxford Utd, Sunderland, Fulham, West Ham, 1990–2005) 65
Mepham C (Brentford, 2018) 2
Mielczarek R (Rotherham, 1971) 1
Millington A (WBA, Peterborough, Swansea, 1963–72) 21
Moore G (Cardiff, Chelsea, Manchester Utd, Northampton, Charlton, 1960–71) 21
Morgan C (MK Dons, Peterborough, Preston, 2007–11) 23
Morison S (Millwall, Norwich, 2011–13) 20
Morris W (Burnley, 1947–52) 5
Myhill B (Hull, WBA, 2008–14) 20

Nardiello D (Coventry, 1978) 2
Nardiello D (Barnsley, 2007–08) 1
Neilson A (Newcastle, Southampton, 1992–97) 5
Nicholas P (Crystal Palace, Arsenal, Crystal Palace, Luton, Aberdeen, Chelsea, Watford, 1979–92) 73
Niedzwiecki E (Chelsea, 1985–88) 2
Nogan L (Watford, Reading, 1991–96) 2
Norman T (Hull, 1986–88) 5
Nurse M (Swansea, Middlesbrough, 1960–63) 12
Nyatanga L (Derby, Bristol City, 2006–11) 34

O'Sullivan P (Brighton, 1973–78) 3
Oster J (Everton, Sunderland, 1997–2005) 13

Page M (Birmingham, 1971–79) 28
Page R (Watford, Sheffield Utd, Cardiff, Coventry, 1997–2006) 41
Palmer D (Swansea, 1957) 3
Parry J (Swansea, 1951) 1
Parry P (Cardiff, 2004–07) 12
Partridge D (Motherwell, Bristol City, 2005–06) 7
Pascoe C (Swansea, Sunderland, 1984–92) 10
Paul R (Swansea, Manchester City, 1949–56) 33
Pembridge M (Luton, Derby, Sheffield Wed, Benfica, Everton, Fulham, 1992–2005) 54
Perry J (Cardiff, 1994) 1
Phillips D (Plymouth Argyle, Manchester City, Coventry, Norwich, Nottm Forest, 1984–96) 62
Phillips J (Chelsea, 1973–78) 4
Phillips L (Cardiff, Aston Villa, Swansea, Charlton, 1971–82) 58
Pipe D (Coventry, 2003) 1
Pontin K (Cardiff, 1980) 2
Powell A (Leeds, Everton, Birmingham, 1947–51) 8
Powell D (Wrexham, Sheffield Utd, 1968–71) 11
Powell I (QPR, Aston Villa, 1947–51) 8
Price L (Ipswich, Derby, Crystal Palace, 2006–13) 11
Price P (Luton, Tottenham, 1980–84) 25

Pring K (Rotherham, 1966–67) 3
Pritchard H (Bristol City, 1985) 1

Ramsey A (Arsenal, 2009–18) 53
Rankmore F (Peterborough, 1966) 1
Ratcliffe K (Everton, Cardiff, 1981–93) 59
Ready K (QPR, 1997–98) 5
Reece G (Sheffield Utd, Cardiff, 1966–75) 29
Reed W (Ipswich, 1955) 2
Rees A (Birmingham, 1984) 1
Rees J (Luton, 1992) 1
Rees R (Coventry, WBA, Nottm Forest, 1965–72) 39
Rees W (Cardiff, Tottenham, 1949–50) 4
Ribeiro C (Bristol City, 2010–11) 2
Richards A (Swansea, Fulham, Cardiff, 2012–18) 13
Richards, S (Cardiff, 1947) 1
Ricketts S (Swansea, Hull, Bolton, Wolves, 2005–14) 52
Roberts A (QPR, 1993–97) 2
Roberts C (Swansea, 2018) 2
Roberts D (Oxford Utd, Hull, 1973–78) 17
Roberts G (Tranmere 2000–06) 9
Roberts I (Watford, Huddersfield, Leicester, Norwich, 1990–2002) 15
Roberts J (Arsenal, Birmingham, 1971–76) 22
Roberts J (Bolton, 1949) 1
Roberts N (Wrexham, Wigan, 2000–04) 4
Roberts P (Portsmouth, 1974) 4
Roberts S (Wrexham, 2005) 1
Robinson C (Wolves, Portsmouth, Sunderland, Norwich, Toronto 2000–08) 52
Robinson J (Charlton, 1996–2002) 30
Robson-Kanu H (Reading, WBA, 2010–18) 44
Rodrigues P (Cardiff, Leicester, City Sheffield Wed, 1965–74) 40
Rogan A (Celtic, Sunderland, Millwall, 1988–97) 18
Rouse V (Crystal Palace, 1959) 1
Rowley T (Tranmere, 1959) 1
Rush I (Liverpool, Juventus, Liverpool, 1980–96) 73

Saunders D (Brighton, Oxford Utd, Derby, Liverpool, Aston Villa, Galatasaray, Nottm Forest, Sheffield Utd, Benfica, Bradford City, 1986–2001) 75
Savage R (Crewe, Leicester, Birmingham, 1996–2005) 39
Sayer P (Cardiff, 1977–8) 7
Scrine F (Swansea, 1950) 2
Sear C (Manchester City, 1963) 1
Sherwood A (Cardiff, Newport, 1947–57) 41
Shortt W (Plymouth Argyle, 1947–53) 12
Showers D (Cardiff, 1975) 2
Sidlow C (Liverpool, 1947–50) 7
Slatter N (Bristol Rov, Oxford Utd, 1983–89) 22
Smallman D (Wrexham, Everton, 1974–6) 7
Smith M (Manchester City, 2018) 1
Southall N (Everton, 1982–97) 92
Speed G (Leeds, Everton, Newcastle, 1990–2004) 85
Sprake G (Leeds, Birmingham, 1964–75) 37
Stansfield F (Cardiff, 1949) 1
Stevenson B (Leeds, Birmingham, 1978–82) 15
Stevenson N (Swansea, 1982–83) 4
Stitfall R (Cardiff, 1953–57) 2
Stock B (Doncaster, 2010–11) 3
Sullivan D (Cardiff, 1953–60) 17
Symons K (Portsmouth, Manchester City, Fulham, Crystal Palace, 1992–2004) 37

Tapscott D (Arsenal, Cardiff, 1954–59) 14
Taylor G (Crystal Palace, Sheffield Utd, Burnley, Nottm Forest, 1996–2005) 15
Taylor J (Reading, 2015) 1
Taylor N (Wrexham, Swansea, Aston Villa, 2010–18) 41
Thatcher B (Leicester, Manchester City, 2004–05) 7
Thomas D (Swansea, 1957–58) 2
Thomas G (Leicester, 2018) 1
Thomas M (Wrexham, Manchester Utd, Everton, Brighton, Stoke, Chelsea, WBA, 1977–86) 51
Thomas M (Newcastle, 1987) 1
Thomas R (Swindon, Derby, Cardiff, 1967–78) 50
Thomas S (Fulham, 1948–49) 4
Toshack J (Cardiff, Liverpool, Swansea, 1969–80) 40
Trollope P (Derby, Fulham, Northampton, 1997–2003) 9
Tudur Jones O (Swansea, Norwich, Hibernian, 2008–14) 7

Van den Hauwe P (Everton, 1985–89) 13
Vaughan D (Crewe, Real Sociedad, Blackpool, Sunderland, Nottm Forest, 20013–16) 42
Vaughan N (Newport, Cardiff, 1983–85) 10
Vearncombe G (Cardiff, 1958–61) 2
Vernon R (Blackburn, Everton, Stoke, 1957–68) 32
Villars A (Cardiff, 1974) 3
Vokes S (Wolves, Burnley, 2008–18) 59

Walley T (Watford, 1971) 1
Walsh I (Crystal Palace, 1980–82) 18
Ward D (Bristol Rov, Cardiff, 1959–62) 2
Ward D (Notts Co, Nottm Forest, 2000–04) 5
Ward D (Liverpool, 2016–18) 4
Watkins M (Norwich, 2018) 2
Webster C (Manchester Utd, 1957–58) 4
Weston R (Arsenal, Cardiff, 2000–05) 7
Williams A (Stockport, Swansea, Everton, 2008–18) 79
Williams A (Reading, Wolves, Reading, 1994–2003) 13
Williams A (Southampton, 1997–98) 2
Williams D (Norwich, 1986–87) 5
Williams G (Cardiff, 1951) 1
Williams G (Derby, Ipswich, 1988–96) 13

Williams G (West Ham, 2006) 2
Williams G (Fulham, 2014–16) 7
Williams GE (WBA, 1960–69) 26
Williams GG (Swansea, 1961–62) 5
Williams HJ (Swansea, 1965–72) 3
Williams HT (Newport, Leeds, 1949–50) 4
Williams J (Crystal Palace, 2013–18) 18
Williams S (WBA, Southampton, 1954–66) 43
Wilson H (Liverpool, 2014–18) 4
Wilson J (Bristol City, 2014) 1
Witcomb D (WBA, Sheffield Wed, 1947) 3
Woosnam P (Leyton Orient, West Ham, Aston Villa, 1959–63) 17
Woodburn B (Liverpool, 2018) 7
Yorath T (Leeds, Coventry, Tottenham, Vancouver Whitecaps 1970–81) 59
Young E (Wimbledon, Crystal Palace, Wolves, 1990–96) 21

## NORTHERN IRELAND

Aherne T (Belfast Celtic, Luton, 1947–50) 4
Anderson T (Manchester Utd, Swindon, Peterborough, 1973–79) 22
Armstrong G (Tottenham, Watford, Real Mallorca, WBA, 1977–86) 63

Baird C (Southampton, Fulham, Burnley, WBA, Derby, 2003–16) 79
Barr H (Linfield, Coventry, 1962–63) 3
Barton A (Preston, 2011) 1
Best G (Manchester Utd, Fulham, 1964–77) 37
Bingham W (Sunderland, Luton, Everton, Port Vale, 1951–64) 56
Black K (Luton, Nottm Forest, 1988–94) 30
Blair R (Oldham, 1975–76) 5
Blanchflower RD (Barnsley, Aston Villa, Tottenham, 1950–63) 56
Blanchflower J (Manchester Utd, 1954–58) 12
Blayney A (Doncaster, Linfield, 2006–11) 5
Bowler G (Hull, 1950) 3
Boyce L (Werder Bremen, Ross Co, 2011–18) 13
Braithwaite R (Linfield, Middlesbrough, 1962–65) 10
Braniff K (Portadown, 2010) 2
Brennan R (Luton, Birmingham, Fulham, 1949–51) 5
Briggs W (Manchester Utd, Swansea, 1962–65) 2
Brotherston N (Blackburn, 1980–85) 27
Bruce A (Hull, 2013–14) 2
Bruce W (Glentoran, 1961–67) 2
Brunt C (Sheffield Wed, WBA, 2005–18) 65
Bryan, M (Watford, 2010) 2

Camp L (Nottm Forest, 2011–13) 9
Campbell D (Nottm Forest, Charlton, 1987–88) 10
Campbell J (Fulham, 1951) 2
Campbell R (Crusaders, 1963–65) 2
Campbell R (Bradford City, 1982) 2
Campbell W (Dundee, 1968–70) 6
Capaldi A (Plymouth Argyle, Cardiff, 2004–08) 22
Carey J (Manchester Utd, 1947–49) 7
Carroll R (Wigan, Manchester Utd, West Ham, Olympiacos, Notts Co, Linfield, 1997–2017) 45
Carson J (Ipswich, 2011–13) 4
Carson S (Coleraine, 2009) 1
Carson T (Motherwell, 2018) 3
Casey T (Newcastle, Portsmouth, 1955–59) 12
Casement C (Ipswich, 2009) 1
Caskey W (Derby, Tulsa, Roughnecks, 1979–82) 7
Cassidy T (Newcastle, Burnley, 1971–82) 24
Cathcart C (Blackpool, Watford, 2011–18) 36
Caughey M (Linfield, 1986) 2
Clarke C (Bournemouth, Southampton, QPR, Portsmouth, 1986–93) 38
Cleary J (Glentoran, 1982–85) 5
Clements D (Coventry, Sheffield Wed, Everton, New York Cosmos, 1965–76) 48
Clingan S (Nottm Forest, Norwich, Coventry, Kilmarnock, 2006–15) 39
Clyde, M (Wolves, 2005) 3
Coates C (Crusaders, 2009–11) 6
Cochrane A (Coleraine, Burnley, Middlesbrough, Gillingham, 1976–84) 26
Cochrane D (Leeds, 1947–50) 10
Connell T (Coleraine, 1978) 1
Coote A (Norwich, 1999–2000) 6
Cowan J (Newcastle, 1970) 1
Coyle F (Coleraine, Nottm Forest, 1956–58) 4
Coyle L (Derry City, 1989) 1
Coyle R (Sheffield Wed, 1973–74) 5
Craig D (Newcastle, 1967–75) 25
Craigan S (Partick, Motherwell, 2003–11) 54
Crossan E (Blackburn, 1950–55) 3
Crossan J (Sparta Rotterdam, Sunderland, Manchester City, Middlesbrough, 1960–68) 24
Cunningham W (St Mirren, Leicester, Dunfermline, 1951–62) 30
Cush W (Glenavon, Leeds, Portadown, 1951–62) 26

Dallas S (Crusaders, Brentford, Leeds, 2011–18) 30
D'Arcy S (Chelsea, Brentford, 1952–53) 5
Davis S (Aston Villa, Fulham, Rangers, Southampton, 2005–18) 101
Davison A (Bolton, Bradford City, Grimsby, 1996–97) 3
Dennison R (Wolves, 1988–97) 18
Devine J (Glentoran, 1990) 1
Dickson D (Coleraine, 1970–73) 4
Dickson T (Linfield, 1957) 1
Dickson W (Chelsea, Arsenal, 1951–55) 12
Doherty L (Linfield, 1985–88) 2
*Doherty P (Derby, Huddersfield, Doncaster, 1946–50) 6

Doherty T (Bristol City, 2003–05) 9
Donaghy M (Luton, Manchester Utd, Chelsea, 1980–94) 91
Donnelly L (Fulham, 2014) 1
Donnelly M (Crusaders, 2009) 1
Dougan D (Portsmouth, Blackburn, Aston Villa, Leicester, Wolves, 1958–73) 43
Douglas J (Belfast Celtic, 1947) 1
Dowd H (Glenavon, 1974) 3
Dowie I (Luton, Southampton, Crystal Palace, West Ham, QPR, 1990–2000) 59
Duff M (Cheltenham, Burnley, 2002–12) 24
Dunlop G (Linfield, 1985–90) 4

Eglington T (Everton, 1947–49) 6
Elder A (Burnley, Stoke, 1960–70) 40
Elliott S (Motherwell, Hull, 2001–08) 38
Evans C (Manchester Utd, Hull, Blackburn, 2009–18) 47
Evans J (Manchester Utd, WBA, 2007–18) 70

Farrell P (Everton, 1947–49) 7
Feeney J (Linfield, Swansea, 1947–50) 2
Feeney W (Glentoran, 1976) 1
Feeney W (Bournemouth, Luton, Cardiff, Oldham, Plymouth 2002–12) 46
Ferguson G (Linfield, 1999–2001) 5
Ferguson S (Newcastle, Millwall, 2009–18) 35
Ferguson W (Linfield, 1966–67) 2
Ferris R (Birmingham, 1950–52) 3
Fettis A (Hull, Nottm Forest, Blackburn, 1992–99) 25
Finney T (Sunderland, Cambridge Utd, 1975–80) 14
Flanagan T (Burton, 2017) 1
Fleming G (Nottm Forest, Manchester City, Barnsley, 1987–95) 31
Forde J (Ards, 1959–61) 4

Gallogly C (Huddersfield, 1951) 2
Garrett R (Stoke, Linfield, 2009–11) 5
Gaston R (Coleraine, 1969) 1
Gault M (Linfield, 2008) 1
Gillespie K (Manchester Utd, Newcastle, Blackburn, Leicester, Sheffield Utd, 1995–2009) 86
Gorman J (Wolves, 2010–12) 9
Gorman W (Brentford, 1947–48) 4
Graham W (Doncaster, 1951–99) 14
Gray P (Luton, Sunderland, Nancy, Burnley, Oxford Utd, 1993–2001) 25
Gregg H (Doncaster, Manchester Utd, 1954–64) 25
Griffin D (St Johnstone, Dundee Utd, Stockport, 1996–2004) 29
Grigg W (Walsall, Brentford, Wigan, 2012–17) 10

Hamill R (Glentoran, 1999) 1
Hamilton B (Linfield, Ipswich, Everton, Millwall, Swindon, 1969–80) 50
Hamilton G (Glentoran, Portadown, 2003–08) 5
Hamilton W (QPR, Burnley, Oxford Utd, 1978–86) 41
Harkin J (Southport, Shrewsbury,1968–70) 5
Harvey M (Sunderland, 1961–71) 34
Hatton S (Linfield, 1963) 2
Hazard C (Celtic, 2018) 1
Healy D (Manchester Utd, Preston, Leeds, Fulham, Sunderland, Rangers, Bury, 2000–13) 95
Healy F (Coleraine, Glentoran, 1982–83) 4
Hegan D (WBA, Wolves, 1970–73) 7
Hill C (Sheffield Utd, Leicester, Trelleborg, Northampton, 1990–99) 27
Hill J (Norwich, Everton, 1959–64) 7
Hinton E (Fulham, Millwall, 1947–51) 7
Hodson L (Watford, MK Dons, Rangers, 2011–18) 24
Holmes S (Wrexham, 2002) 1
Horlock K (Swindon, Manchester City, 1995–2003) 32
Hughes A (Newcastle, Aston Villa, Fulham, QPR, Brighton, Melbourne, Hearts, 1997–2018) 112
Hughes J (Lincoln, 2006) 2
Hughes M (Oldham, 2006) 2
Hughes M (Manchester City, Strasbourg, West Ham, Wimbledon, Crystal Palace, 1992–2005) 71
Hughes P (Bury, 1987) 3
Hughes W (Bolton, 1951) 1
Humphries W (Ards, Coventry, Swansea, 1962–65) 14
Hunter A (Blackburn, Ipswich, 1970–80) 53
Hunter B (Wrexham, Reading, 1995–2000) 15
Hunter V (Coleraine, 1962) 2
Ingham M (Sunderland, Wrexham, 2005–07) 3
Irvine R (Linfield, Stoke, 1962–5) 8
Irvine W (Burnley, Preston, Brighton, 1963–72) 23

Jackson T (Everton, Nottm Forest, Manchester Utd, 1969–77) 35
Jamison J (Glentoran, 1976) 1
Jenkins I (Chester, Dundee Utd, 1997–2000) 6
Jennings P (Watford, Tottenham, Arsenal, Tottenham, 1964–86) 119
Johnson D (Blackburn, Birmingham, 1999–2010) 56
Johnston W (Glenavon, Oldham, 1962–66) 2
Jones J (Glenavon, 1956–57) 3
Jones J (Kilmarnock, 2018) 2
Jones S (Crewe, Burnley, 2003–08) 29
Keane T (Swansea, 1949) 1
Kee P (Oxford Utd, Ards, 1990–95) 9
Keith R (Newcastle, 1958–62) 23
Kelly H (Fulham, Southampton, 1950–51) 4
Kelly P (Barnsley, 1950) 1
Kennedy P (Watford, Wigan, 1999–2004) 20
Kirk A (Hearts, Boston, Northampton, Dunfermline, 2000–10) 11

Lafferty D (Burnley, 2012–16) 13
Lafferty K (Burnley, Rangers, Sion, Palermo, Norwich, Hearts, 2006–18) 67
Lavery S (Everton, 2018) 1
Lawrie J (Port Vale, 2009–10) 3
Lawther W (Sunderland, Blackburn, 1960–62) 4

Lennon N (Crewe, Leicester, Celtic, 1994–2002) 40
Lewis J (Norwich, 2018) 1
Little A (Rangers, 2009–13) 9
Lockhart N (Linfield, Coventry, Aston Villa, 1947–56) 8
Lomas S (Manchester City, West Ham, 1994–2003) 45
Lund M (Rochdale, 2017) 3
Lutton B (Wolves, West Ham, 1970–4) 6

Magennis J (Cardiff, Aberdeen, Kilmarnock, Charlton, 2010–18) 38
Magill E (Arsenal, Brighton, 1962–66) 26
Magilton J (Oxford Utd, Southampton, Sheffield Wed, Ipswich, 1991–2002) 52
Mannus A (Linfield, St Johnstone, 2004–17) 9
Martin C (Glentoran, Leeds, Aston Villa, 1947–50) 6
McAdams W (Manchester City, Bolton, Leeds, 1954–62) 15
*McAlinden J (Portsmouth, Southend, 1947–49) 2
McArdle R (Rochdale, Aberdeen, Bradford, 2010–14) 7
McAuley G (Lincoln, Leicester, Ipswich, WBA, 2005–18) 79
McBride S (Glenavon, 1991–92) 4
McCabe J (Leeds, 1949–54) 6
McCann G (West Ham, Cheltenham, Barnsley, Scunthorpe, Peterborough, 2002–12) 39
McCartan S (Accrington, Bradford, 2017–18) 2
McCarthy J (Port Vale, Birmingham, 1996–2001) 18
McCartney G (Sunderland, West Ham) Sunderland 2002–10) 34
McCavana T (Coleraine, 1954–55) 3
McCleary J (Cliftonville, 1955) 1
McClelland J (Arsenal, Fulham, 1961–67) 6
McClelland J (Mansfield, Rangers, Watford, Leeds, 1980–90) 53
McCourt F (Manchester City, 1952–53) 6
McCourt P (Rochdale, Celtic, Barnsley, Brighton, Luton, 2002–16) 18
McCoy R (Coleraine, 1987) 1
McCreery D (Manchester Utd, QPR, Tulsa, Newcastle, 1976–90) 67
McCrory S (Southend, 1958) 1
McCullough L (Doncaster, 2014–18) 6
McCullough W (Arsenal, Millwall, 1961–67) 10
McCurdy C (Linfield, 1980) 1
McDonald A (QPR, 1986–96) 52
McElhinney G (Bolton, 1984–85) 6
McEvilly L (Rochdale, 2002) 1
McFaul W (Linfield, Newcastle, 1967–74) 6
McGarry J (Cliftonville, 1951) 3
McGaughey M (Linfield, 1985) 1
McGibbon P (Manchester Utd, Wigan, 1995–2000) 7
McGinn N (Derry, Celtic, Aberdeen, Gwangjiu, 2009–18) 53
McGivern R (Manchester City, Hibernian, Port Vale, Shrewsbury, 2009–17) 24
McGovern M (Ross Co, Hamilton, Norwich, 2010–18) 28
McGrath C (Tottenham, Manchester Utd 1974–79) 21
McIlroy J (Burnley, Stoke, 1952–66) 55
McIlroy S (Manchester Utd, Stoke, Manchester City, 1972–87) 88
McKay W (Inverness, Wigan, 2013–16) 11
McKeag W (Glentoran, 1968) 2
McKenna J (Huddersfield, 1950–52) 7
McKenzie R (Airdrie, 1967) 1
McKinney W (Falkirk, 1966) 1
McKnight A (Celtic, West Ham, 1988–89) 10
McLaughlin C (Preston, Fleetwood, Millwall, 2012–18) 33
McLaughlin J (Shrewsbury, Swansea, 1962–66) 12
McLaughlin R (Liverpool, Oldham, 2014–18) 5
McLean B (Motherwell, 2006) 1
McMahon G (Tottenham, Stoke, 1995–98) 17
McMichael A (Newcastle, 1950–60) 40
McMillan S (Manchester Utd, 1963) 2
McMordie A (Middlesbrough, 1969–73) 21
McMorran E (Belfast Celtic, Barnsley, Doncaster, 1947–57) 15
McNair P (Manchester Utd, Sunderland, 2015–18) 20
McNally B (Shrewsbury, 1987–88) 5
McPake J (Coventry, 2012) 1
McParland P (Aston Villa, Wolves, 1954–62) 34
McQuoid J (Millwall, 2011–12) 5
McVeigh P (Tottenham, Norwich, 1999–2005) 20
Montgomery F (Coleraine, 1955) 1
Moore C (Glentoran, 1949) 1
Moreland V (Derby, 1979–80) 6
Morgan S (Port Vale, Aston Villa, Brighton, Sparta Rotterdam, 1972–99) 18
Morrow S (Arsenal, QPR, 1990–2000) 39
Mulgrew J (Linfield, 2010) 2
Mullan G (Glentoran, 1983) 4
Mulryne P (Manchester Utd, Norwich, 1997–2005) 27
Murdock C (Preston, Hibernian, Crewe, Rotherham, 2000–06) 34

Napier R (Bolton, 1966) 1
Neill T (Arsenal, Hull, 1961–73) 59
Nelson S (Arsenal, Brighton, 1970–82) 51
Nicholl C (Aston Villa, Southampton, Grimsby, 1975–83) 51
Nicholl J (Manchester Utd, Toronto, Sunderland, Rangers, WBA, 1976–86) 73
Nicholson J (Manchester Utd, Huddersfield, 1961–72) 41
Nolan I (Sheffield Wed, Bradford City, Wigan, 1997–2002) 18
Norwood O (Manchester Utd, Huddersfield, Reading, Brighton, 2011–18) 53

O'Boyle G (Dunfermline, St Johnstone, 1994–99) 13
O'Connor M (Crewe, Scunthorpe, Rotherham, 2008–14) 11

O'Doherty A (Coleraine, 1970) 2
O'Driscoll J (Swansea, 1949) 3
O'Kane W (Nottm Forest, 1970–75) 20
O'Neill C (Motherwell, 1989–91) 3
O'Neill J (Sunderland, 1962) 1
O'Neill J (Leicester, 1980–86) 39
O'Neill M (Distillery, Nottm Forest, Norwich, Manchester City, Notts Co, 1972–85) 64
O'Neill M (Newcastle, Dundee Utd, Hibernian, Coventry, 1989–97) 31
Owens J (Crusaders, 2011) 1

Parke J (Linfield, Hibernian, Sunderland, 1964–68) 14
Paterson M (Scunthorpe, Burnley, Huddersfield, 2008–14) 22
Paton P (Dundee Utd, St Johnstone, 2014–17) 4
Patterson D (Crystal Palace, Luton, Dundee Utd, 1994–99) 17
Patterson R (Coleraine, Plymouth, 2010–11) 5
Peacock R (Celtic, Coleraine, 1952–62) 31
Peacock-Farrell B (Leeds, 2018) 1
Penney S (Brighton, 1985–89) 17
Platt J (Middlesbrough, Ballymena, Coleraine, 1976–86) 23
Quinn J (Blackburn, Swindon, Leicester, Bradford City, West Ham, Bournemouth, Reading, 1985–96) 46
Quinn SJ (Blackpool, WBA, Willem 11, Sheffield Wed, Peterborough, Northampton, 1996–2007) 50

Rafferty P (Linfield, 1979) 1
Ramsey P (Leicester, 1984–89) 14
Reeves B (MK Dons, 2015) 2
Rice P (Arsenal, 1969–80) 49
Robinson S (Bournemouth, Luton, 1997–2008) 7
Rogan A (Celtic, Sunderland, Millwall, 1988–97) 18
Ross W (Newcastle, 1969) 1
Rowland K (West Ham, QPR, 1994–99) 19
Russell A (Linfield, 1947) 1
Ryan R (WBA, 1950) 1

Sanchez L (Wimbledon, 1987–89) 3
Saville G (Millwall, 2018) 5
Scott J (Grimsby, 1958) 2
Scott P (Everton, York, Aldershot, 1976–79) 10
Sharkey P (Ipswich, 1976) 1
Shields J (Southampton, 1957) 1
Shiels D (Hibernian, Doncaster, Kilmarnock, Rangers, 2006–13) 14
Simpson W (Rangers, 1951–59) 12
Sloan D (Oxford Utd, 1969–71) 2
Sloan J (Arsenal, 1947) 1
Sloan T (Manchester Utd, 1979) 3
Smith A (Glentoran, Preston, 2003–05) 18
Smith M (Peterborough, 2016) 1
Smyth P (QPR, 2018) 2
Smyth S (Wolves, Stoke, 1948–52) 9
Smyth W (Distillery, 1949–54) 4
Sonner D (Ipswich, Sheffield Wed, Birmingham, Nottm Forest, Peterborough, 1997–2005) 13
Spence D (Bury, Blackpool, Southend, 1975–82) 29
Sproule I (Hibernian, 2006–08) 11
*Stevenson A (Everton, 1947–48) 3
Steele J (New York Bulls, 2014) 3
Stewart A (Glentoran, Derby, 1967–69) 7
Stewart D (Hull, 1978) 1
Stewart I (QPR, Newcastle, 1982–87) 31
Stewart T (Linfield, 1961) 1
Taggart G (Barnsley, Bolton, Leicester, 1990–2003) 51
Taylor M (Fulham, Birmingham, 1999–2012) 88
Thompson A (Watford, 2011) 2
Thompson, J (Rangers, 2018) 2
Thompson P (Linfield, 2006–08) 8
Todd S (Burnley, Sheffield Wed, 1966–71) 11
Toner C (Leyton Orient, 2003) 2
Trainor D (Crusaders, 1967) 1
Tuffey J (Partick, Inverness, 2009–11) 8
Tully C (Celtic, 1949–59) 10
Uprichard W (Swindon, Portsmouth, 1952–59) 18
Vernon J (Belfast Celtic, WBA, 1947–52) 17

Walker J (Doncaster, 1955) 1
Walsh D (WBA, 1947–50) 9
Walsh W (Manchester City, 1948–49) 5
Ward J (Derby Nottm Forest, 2012–18) 33
Washington C (QPR, 2016–18) 17
Watson P (Distillery, 1971) 1
Webb S (Ross Co, 2006–07) 4
Welsh E (Carlisle, 1966–67) 4
Whiteside N (Manchester Utd, Everton, 1982–90) 38
Whitley Jeff (Manchester City, Sunderland, Cardiff, 1997–2006) 20
Whitley Jim (Manchester City, 1998–2000) 3
Williams M (Chesterfield, Watford, Wimbledon, Stoke, Wimbledon, MK Dons, 1999–2005) 36
Williams M (Chesterfield, Watford Wimbledon, Stoke, Wimbledon MK Dons 1999–2005) 36
Williams P (WBA, 1991) 1
Wilson D (Brighton, Luton, Sheffield Wed, 1987–92) 24
Wilson K (Ipswich, Chelsea, Notts Co, Walsall, 1987–95) 42
Wilson S (Glenavon, Falkirk, Dundee, 1962–68) 12
Winchester C (Oldham, 2011) 1
Wood T (Walsall, 1996) 1
Worthington N (Sheffield Wed, Leeds, Stoke, 1984–97) 66
Wright T (Newcastle, Nottm Forest, Reading, Manchester City, 1989–2000) 31

## REPUBLIC OF IRELAND

Aherne T (Belfast Celtic, Luton, 1946–54) 16
Aldridge J (Oxford Utd, Liverpool, Real Sociedad, Tranmere, 1986–97) 69
Ambrose P (Shamrock R, 1955–64) 5
Anderson J (Preston, Newcastle, 1980–89) 16
Andrews K (Blackburn, WBA, 2009–13) 35
Arter H (Bournemouth, 2015–18) 13

Babb P (Coventry, Liverpool, Sunderland, 1994–2003) 35
Bailham E (Shamrock R, 1964) 1
Barber E (Bohemians, Birmingham, 1966) 2
Barrett G (Arsenal, Coventry, 2003–05) 6
Beglin J (Liverpool, 1984–87) 15
Bennett A (Reading, 2007) 2
Best L (Coventry, 2009–10) 7
Braddish S (Dundalk, 1978) 2
Branagan K (Bolton, 1997) 1
Bonner P (Celtic, 1981–96) 80
Boyle A (Preston, 2017) 1
Brady L (Arsenal, Juventus, Sampdoria, Inter-Milan, Ascoli, West Ham, 1975–90) 72
Brady R (QPR, 1964) 6
Brady R (Manchester Utd, Hull, Burnley, 2013–18) 39
Breen G (Birmingham, Coventry, West Ham, Sunderland, 1996–2006) 63
*Breen T (Shamrock R, 1947) 3
Brennan F (Drumcondra, 1965) 1
Brennan S (Manchester Utd, Waterford, 1965–71) 19
Browne A (Preston, 2017–18) 3
Browne W (Bohemians, 1964) 3
Bruce A (Ipswich, 2007–09) 2
Buckley L (Shamrock R, Waregem, 1984–85) 2
Burke F (Cork Ath, 1952) 1
Burke G (Shamrock Rov, 2018) 2
Butler P (Sunderland, 2000) 1
Butler T (Sunderland, 2003) 2
Byrne A (Southampton, 1970–74) 14
Byrne J (Shelbourne, 2004–06) 2
Byrne J (QPR, Le Havre, Brighton, Sunderland, Millwall, 1985–93) 23
Byrne P (Shamrock R, 1984–86) 8

Campbell A (Santander, 1985) 3
Campbell N (St Patrick's Ath, Fortuna Cologne, 1971–77) 11
Cantwell N (West Ham, Manchester Utd, 1954–67) 36
Carey B (Manchester Utd, Leicester, 1992–94) 3
*Carey J (Manchester Utd, 1946–53) 21
Carolan J (Manchester Utd, 1960) 2
Carr S (Tottenham, Newcastle, 1999–2008) 43
Carroll B (Shelbourne, 1949–50) 2
Carroll T (Ipswich, 1968–73) 17
Carsley L (Derby, Blackburn, Coventry, Everton, 1997–2008) 39
Cascarino A (Gillingham, Millwall, Aston Villa, Chelsea, Marseille, Nancy, 1986–2000) 88
Chandler J (Leeds, 1980) 2
Christie C (Derby, Middlesbrough, 2015–18) 17
Clark C (Aston Villa, Newcastle, 2011–18) 31
Clarke C (Stoke, 2004) 2
Clarke J (Drogheda, 1978) 1
Clarke K (Drumcondra, 1948) 2
Clarke M (Shamrock R, 1950) 1
Clinton T (Everton, 1951–54) 3
Coad P (Shamrock R, 1947–52) 11
Coffey T (Drumcondra, 1950) 1
Colfer M (Shelbourne, 1950–51) 2
Coleman S (Everton, 2011–18) 46
Colgan N (Hibernian, 2002–07) 9
Conmy O (Peterborough, 1965–70) 5
Connolly D (Watford, Feyenoord, Excelsior Feyenoord, Wimbledon, West Ham, Wigan, 1996–2006) 41
Conroy G (Stoke, 1970–77) 27
Conway J (Fulham, Manchester City, 1967–77) 20
Corr P (Everton, 1949–50) 4
Courtney E (Cork Utd, 1946) 1
Cox S (WBA, Nottm Forest, 2011–14) 30
Coyle O (Bolton, 1994) 1
Coyne T (Celtic, Tranmere, Motherwell, 1992–98) 22
Crowe G (Bohemians, 2003) 2
Cummins G (Luton, 1954–61) 19
Cuneen T (Limerick, 1951) 1
Cunningham G (Man City, Bristol City, 2010–13) 4
Cunningham K (Wimbledon, Birmingham, 1996–2006) 72
Curtis D (Shelbourne, Bristol City, Ipswich, Exeter, 1956–63) 17
Cusack S (Limerick, 1953) 1

Daish L (Cambridge Utd, Coventry, 1992–96) 5
Daly G (Manchester Utd, Derby, Coventry, Birmingham, Shrewsbury, 1973–87) 48
Daly M (Wolves, 1978) 2
Daly P (Shamrock R, 1950) 1
Deacy E (Aston Villa, 1982) 4
Delaney D (QPR, Ipswich, Crystal Palace, 2008–14) 9
Delap R (Derby, Southampton, 1998–2004) 11
De Mange K (Liverpool, Hull, 1987–89) 2
Dempsey J (Fulham, Chelsea, 1967–72) 19
Dennehy J (Cork Hibernian, Nottm Forest, Walsall, 1972–77) 11
Desmond P (Middlesbrough, 1950) 4
Devine J (Arsenal, 1980–85) 13
Doherty G (Tottenham, Norwich, 2000–06) 34
Doherty M (Wolves, 2018) 2
Donovan D (Everton, 1955–57) 5

Donovan T (Aston Villa, 1980) 2
Douglas J (Blackburn, Leeds, 2004–08) 8
Doyle C (Shelbourne, 1959) 1
Doyle C (Birmingham, Bradford, 2007–18) 4
Doyle K (Reading Wolves, Colorado, 2006–17) 63
Doyle M (Coventry, 2004) 1
Duff D (Blackburn, Chelsea, Newcastle, Fulham, 1998–2012) 100
Duffy B (Shamrock R, 1950) 1
Duffy S (Everton, Blackburn, Brighton, 2014–18) 20
Dunne A (Manchester Utd, Bolton,1962–76) 33
Dunne J (Fulham, 1971) 1
Dunne P (Manchester Utd, 1965–67) 5
Dunne R (Everton, Manchester City, Aston Villa, 2000–14) 80
Dunne S (Luton, 1953–60) 15
Dunne T (St Patrick's, 1956–57) 3
Dunning P (Shelbourne, 1971) 2
Dunphy E (York, Millwall, 1966–71) 23
Dwyer N (West Ham, Swansea, 1960–65) 14

Eccles P (Shamrock R, 1986) 1
Egan J (Brentford, 2017) 2
Eglington T (Shamrock R, Everton, 1946–56) 24
Elliot R (Newcastle, 2014–16) 4
Elliott S (Sunderland, 2005–07) 9
Evans M (Southampton, 1997) 1

Fagan E (Shamrock R, 1973) 1
Fagan F (Manchester City, Derby, 1955–61) 8
Fahey K (Birmingham, 2010–13) 16
Fairclough M (Dundalk, 1982) 2
Fallon S (Celtic, 1951–55) 8
Farrell P (Shamrock R, Everton, 1946–57) 28
Farrelly G (Aston Villa, Everton, Bolton, 1996–2000) 6
Finnan S (Fulham, Liverpool, Espanyol 2000–09) 53
Finucane A (Limerick, 1967–72) 11
Fitzgerald F (Waterford, 1955–6) 2
Fitzgerald P (Leeds, 1961–2) 5
Fitzpatrick K (Limerick, 1970) 1
Fitzsimons A (Middlesbrough, Lincoln, 1950–59) 26
Fleming C (Middlesbrough, 1996–8) 10
Fogarty A (Sunderland, Hartlepool Utd, 1960–64) 11
Folan C (Hull, 2009–10) 7
Foley D (Watford, 2000–01) 6
Foley K (Wolves, 2009–11) 8
Foley T (Northampton, 1964–67) 9
Fullam J (Preston, Shamrock R, 1961–70) 11
Forde D (Millwall, 2011–16) 24
Fullam J (Preston, Shamrock, 1961–70) 11

Gallagher C (Celtic, 1967) 2
Gallagher M (Hibernian, 1954) 1
Galvin A (Tottenham, Sheffield Wed, Swindon, 1983–90) 29
Gamble J (Cork City, 2007) 2
Gannon E (Notts Co, Sheffield Wed, Shelbourne, 1949–55) 14
Gannon M (Shelbourne, 1972) 1
Gavin J (Norwich, Tottenham, Norwich, 1950–57) 7
Gibbons A (St Patrick's Ath, 1952–56) 4
Gibson D (Manchester Utd, Everton, 2008–16) 27
Gilbert R (Shamrock R, 1966) 1
Giles C (Doncaster, 1951) 1
Giles J (Manchester Utd, Leeds, WBA, Shamrock R, 1960–79) 59
Given S (Blackburn, Newcastle, Manchester City, Aston Villa, Stoke, 1996–2016) 134
Givens D (Manchester Utd, Luton, QPR, Birmingham, Neuchatel, 1969–82) 56
Gleeson S (Wolves, Birmingham, 2007–17) 4
Glynn D (Drumcondra, 1952–55) 2
Godwin T (Shamrock R, Leicester, Bournemouth, 1949–58) 13
Goodman J (Wimbledon, 1997) 4
Goodwin J (Stockport, 2003) 1
*Gorman W (Brentford, 1947) 2
Grealish A (Orient Luton, Brighton, WBA, 1976–86) 45
Green P (Derby, Leeds, 2010–14) 22
Gregg E (Bohemians, 1978–80) 8
Grimes A (Manchester Utd, Coventry, Luton, 1978–88) 18

Hale A (Aston Villa, Doncaster, Waterford, 1962–72) 14
Hamilton T (Shamrock R, 1959) 2
Hand E (Portsmouth, 1969–76) 20
Harte I (Leeds, Levante, 1996–2007) 64
Hartnett J (Middlesbrough, 1949–54) 2
Haverty J (Arsenal, Blackburn, Millwall, Celtic, Bristol Rov, Shelbourne, 1956–67) 32
Hayes A (Southampton, 1979) 1
Hayes J (Aberdeen, 2016–17) 4
*Hayes W (Huddersfield, 1947) 2
Hayes W (Limerick, 1949) 1
Healey R (Cardiff, 1977–80) 2
Healy C (Celtic, Sunderland, 2002–04) 13
Heighway S (Liverpool, Minnesota, 1971–82) 34
Henderson B (Drumcondra, 1948) 2
Henderson W (Brighton, Preston, 2006–08) 6
Hendrick J (Derby, Burnley, 2013–18) 39
Hennessy J (Shelbourne, St Patrick's Ath, 1956–69) 5
Herrick J (Cork Hibernian, Shamrock R, 1972–73) 3
Higgins J (Birmingham, 1951) 1
Hogan S (Aston Villa, 2018) 1
Holland M (Ipswich, Charlton, 2000–06) 49
Holmes J (Coventry, Tottenham, Vancouver W'caps, 1971–81) 30
Hoolahan W (Blackpool, Norwich, 2008–18) 43
Horgan D (Preston, 2017–18) 4
Houghton R (Oxford Utd, Liverpool, Aston Villa, Crystal Palace, Reading, 1986–97) 73

Hourihane C (Aston Villa, 2017–18) 5
Howlett G (Brighton, 1984) 1
Hughton C (Tottenham, West Ham, 1980–92) 53
Hunt N (Reading, 2009) 2
Hunt S (Reading, Hull, Wolves, 2007–12) 39
Hurley C (Millwall, Sunderland, Bolton, 1957–69) 40

Ireland S (Manchester City, 2006–08) 6
Irwin D (Manchester Utd, 1991–2000) 56

Judge A (Brentford, 2016–18) 4

Kavanagh G (Stoke, Cardiff, Wigan, 1998–2007) 16
Keane, R (Wolves, Coventry, Inter Milan, Leeds Tottenham, Liverpool, LA Galaxy, 1998–2017) 146
Keane R (Nottm Forest, Manchester Utd, 1991–2006) 67
Keane T (Swansea, 1949) 4
Kearin M (Shamrock R, 1972) 1
Kearns F (West Ham, 1954) 1
Kearns M (Oxford Utd, Walsall, Wolves, 1970–80) 18
Kelly A (Sheffield Utd, Blackburn, 1993–2002) 34
Kelly D (Walsall, West Ham, Leicester, Newcastle, Wolves, Sunderland, Tranmere, 1988–98) 26
Kelly G (Leeds, 1994–2003) 52
Kelly JA (Drumcondra, Preston, 1957–73) 47
Kelly M (Portsmouth, 1988–91) 4
Kelly N (Nottm Forest, 1954) 1
Kelly P (Wolves, 1961–62) 5
Kelly S (Tottenham, Birmingham, Fulham, Reading, 2006–14) 39
Kenna J (Blackburn, 1995–2000) 27
Kennedy M (Portsmouth, 1986) 2
Kennedy M (Liverpool, Wimbledon, Manchester City, Wolves, 1996–2004) 35
Kenny P (Sheffield Utd, 2004–07) 7
Keogh A (Wolves, Millwall, 2007–14) 30
Keogh J (Shamrock R, 1966) 1
Keogh R (Derby 2013–17 17
Keogh S (Shamrock R, 1959) 1
Kernaghan A (Middlesbrough, Manchester City, 1993–96) 22
Kiely D (Charlton, WBA, 2000–09) 11
Kiernan F (Shamrock R, Southampton, 1951–2) 5
Kilbane K (WBA, Sunderland, Everton, Wigan, Hull, 1997–2011) 110
Kinnear J (Tottenham, Brighton, 1967–76) 26
Kinsella M (Charlton, Aston Villa, WBA, 1998–2004) 48

Langan D (Derby, Birmingham, Oxford Utd, 1978–88) 26
Lapira J (Notre Dame, 2007) 1
Lawler R (Fulham, 1953–56) 8
Lawlor J (Drumcondra, Doncaster, 1949–51) 3
Lawlor M (Shamrock R, 1971–73) 
Lawrence L (Stoke, Portsmouth, 2009–11) 
Lawrenson M (Preston, Brighton, Liverpool, 1977–88) 3[illegible]
Lee A (Rotherham, Cardiff, Ipswich, 2003–07) 1[illegible]
Leech M (Shamrock R, 1969–73) 8
Lenihan D (Blackburn, 2018) 1
Long K (Burnley, 2017–18) 7
Long S (Reading, WBA, Hull, Southampton, 2007–18) 80
Lowry D (St Patrick's Ath, 1962) 1

McAlinden J (Portsmouth, 1946) 2
McAteer J (Bolton, Liverpool, Blackburn, Sunderland, 1994–2004) 52
McCann J (Shamrock R, 1957) 1
McCarthy J (Wigan, Everton, 2011–17) 41
McCarthy M (Manchester City, Celtic, Lyon, Millwall, 1984–92) 57
McClean J (Sunderland, Wigan, WBA, 2012–18) 60
McConville T (Dundalk, Waterford, 1972–73) 6
McDonagh J (Everton, Bolton, Sunderland, Notts Co, 1981–86) 25
McDonagh J (Shamrock R, 1984–85) 3
McEvoy A (Blackburn, 1961–67) 17
McGeady A (Celtic, Spartak Moscow, Everton, Sunderland, 2004–18) 93
McGee P (QPR, Preston, 1978–81) 15
McGoldrick E (Crystal Palace, Arsenal, 1992–95) 15
McGoldrick D (Ipswich, 2015–17) 6
McGowan D (West Ham, 1949) 3
McGowan J (Cork Utd, 1947) 1
McGrath M (Blackburn, Bradford PA, 1958–66) 22
McGrath P (Manchester Utd, Aston Villa, Derby, 1985–97) 83
Macken J (Manchester City, 2005) 1
Mackey G (Shamrock R, 1957) 3
McLoughlin A (Swindon, Southampton, Portsmouth, 1990–2000) 42
McMillan W (Belfast Celtic, 1946) 2
McNally B (Luton, 1959–63) 3
McPhail S (Leeds, 2000–04) 10
McShane P (WBA, Sunderland, Hull, Reading, 2006–16) 33
Macken A (Derby, 1977) 1
Madden P (Yeovil, 2014) 1
Maguire S (Preston, 2018) 2
Mahon A (Tranmere, 2000) 2
Malone G (Shelbourne, 1949) 1
Mancini T (QPR, Arsenal, 1974–75) 5
Martin C (Glentoran, Leeds, Aston Villa, 1946–56) 30
Martin M (Bohemians, Manchester Utd, 1972–83) 52
Maybury, A (Leeds, Hearts, Leicester, 1998–2005) 10
Meagan M (Everton, Huddersfield, Drogheda, 1961–70) 17
Meyler D (Sunderland, Hull, 2013–18) 25
Miller L (Celtic, Manchester Utd, Sunderland, QPR 2004–10) 21
Milligan M (Oldham, 1992) 1



oney J (Shamrock R, 1965) 2
ore A (Middlesbrough, 1996–97) 8
ran K (Manchester Utd, Sporting Gijon, Blackburn, 1980–94) 71
roney T (West Ham, 1948–54) 12
rris C (Celtic, Middlesbrough, 1988–93) 35
rrison C (Crystal Palace, Birmingham, Crystal Palace, 2002–07) 36
oulson G (Lincoln, 1948–49) 3
ucklan C (Drogheda, 1978) 1
ulligan P (Shamrock R, Chelsea, Crystal Palace, WBA, Shamrock R, 1969–80) 50
unroe L (Shamrock R, 1954) 1
urphy A (Clyde, 1956) 1
urphy B (Bohemians, 1986) 1
urphy D (Sunderland, Ipswich, Newcastle, Nottm Forest, 2007–18) 33
Murphy J (Crystal Palace, 1980) 3
Murphy J (Scunthorpe, 2009–10) 2
Murphy J (WBA, 2004) 1
Murphy P (Carlisle, 2007) 1
Murray T (Dundalk, 1950) 1

Newman W (Shelbourne, 1969) 1
Nolan E (Preston, 2009–10) 3
Nolan R (Shamrock R, 1957–63) 10

O'Brien Alan (Newcastle, 2007) 5
O'Brien Andy (Newcastle, Portsmouth, 2001–07) 26
O'Brien F (Philadelphia Forest, 1980) 3
O'Brien J (Bolton, West Ham, 2006–13) 5
O'Brien L (Shamrock R, Manchester Utd, Newcastle, Tranmere, 1986–97)
O'Brien R (Notts [illegible]
O'Byrne [illegible]

O'Regan [illegible]
O'Reilly J (Cork Utd, 1946)
O'Shea J (Manchester Utd, Sunderland, 2002–18)

Pearce A (Reading, Derby, 2013–17
Peyton G (Fulham, Bournemouth, Everton, 1977–92)
Peyton N (Shamrock R, Leeds, 1957–61)
Phelan T (Wimbledon, Manchester City, Chelsea, Everton, Fulham, 1992–2000)
Pilkington A (Norwich, Cardiff, 2014–16
Potter D (Wolves, 2007–08)
Quinn A (Sheffield Wed, Sheffield Utd, 2003–07)
Quinn B (Coventry, 2000)
Quinn N (Arsenal, Manchester City, Sunderland, 1986–2002)
Quinn S (Hull, Reading, 2013–17)

Randolph D (Motherwell, West Ham, Middlesbrough, 2013–18)
Reid A (Nottm Forest, Tottenham, Charlton, Sunderland, Nottm Forest, 2004–14)
Reid S (Millwall, Blackburn, 2002–09)
Rice D (West Ham, 2018)
Richardson D (Shamrock R, Gillingham, 1972–80)
Ringstead A (Sheffield Utd, 1951–59)
Robinson M (Brighton, Liverpool, QPR, 1981–86)

16
…Co, 1976–77) 5
…amrock R, 1949) 1
…oke, 1979–82) 6
…h, Portsmouth,
21
…007) 2
…ohemians, 1967–71) 2
…R, 1950) 4
…ndalk,
…73) 7
…istol City, 2016–18) 10
…nto,
…K, 2010–14) 20
…a, 1949) 3
…m, 1982) 3
…Ham, Preston, 1952–59) 9
…K (Arsenal, 1947) 3
…(Bohemians, 1947) 1
…(Aston Villa, 2007) 2
…K (Rotherham, 1988) 1
…(Bournemouth, Leeds, 2016–17 7
…E (Everton, Port Vale, 1981–85) 5
…D (Arsenal, 1977–93) 68
…P (Shamrock R, 1980–1) 7
…mrock R, 1962–72) 20
…1952–59) 17
…) 1
…ddlesbrough,
13

24

Roche P (Shelbourne, Manchester Utd, 1972–76) 8
Rogers E (Blackburn, Charlton, 1968–73) 19
Rowlands M (QPR, 2004–10) 5
Ryan G (Derby, Brighton, 1978–85) 18
Ryan R (WBA, Derby, 1950–56) 16

Sadlier R (Millwall, 2002) 1
Sammon C (Derby, 2013–14) 9
Savage D (Millwall, 1996) 5
Saward P (Millwall, Aston Villa, Huddersfield, 1954–63) 18
Scannell T (Southend, 1954) 1
Scully P (Arsenal, 1989) 1
Sheedy K (Everton, Newcastle, 1984–93) 46
Sheridan C (Celtic, CSKA Sofia, 2010–11) 3
Sheridan J (Leeds, Sheffield Wed, 1988–96) 34
Slaven B (Middlesbrough, 1990–93) 7
Sloan P (Arsenal, 1946) 2
Smyth M (Shamrock R, 1969) 1
St Ledger S (Preston, Leicester, 2009–14) 37
Stapleton F (Arsenal, Manchester Utd, Ajax Derby, Le Havre, Blackburn, 1977–90) 71
Staunton S (Liverpool, Aston Villa, Liverpool, Crystal Palace, Aston Villa, 1989–2002) 102

Lofthouse
Shearer 30
Lampard Frank jnr 29
Platt 27
Robson B 26
Hurst 24
Mortensen 23
Crouch 22
Channon 21
Gerrard 21
Keegan 21
Defoe 20
Peters 20
Kane 19
Haynes 18
Hunt R 18
Beckham 17
Lawton 16
Taylor T 16
Woodcock 16
Welbeck 16
Scholes 14
Chivers 13
Mariner 13
Smith R 13
Francis T 12
Barnes J 11
Douglas 11
Mannion 11
Sheringham 11

Bentley 9
Hateley 9
Wright I 9
Ball 8
Broadis 8
Byrne J 8
Hoddle 8
Kevan 8
Sturridge 8
Walcott 8
Anderton 7
Connelly 7
Coppell 7
Fowler 7
Heskey 7
Paine 7
Vardy 7
Young A 7
Charlton J 6
Macdonald 6
Mullen 6
Oxlade-Chamberlain 6
Rowley 6
Terry 6
Vassell 6
Waddle 6
Wright-Phillips S 6
Adams 5

Neal
Pearce
Pearson Stan
Pearson Stuart
Pickering F
Barmby
Barnes P
Bent
Bull
Dixon K
Hassall
Revie
Robson R
Steven
Watson Dave (Sunderland)
Alli
Baker
Blissett
Butcher
Currie
Dier 3
Elliott 3
Francis G 3
Grainger 3
Jaglelka 3
Kennedy R
Lallana

Lambert ........................... 3
McDermott ........................... 3
McManaman ........................... 3
Matthews S ........................... 3
Merson ........................... 3
Morris ........................... 3
O'Grady ........................... 3
Peacock ........................... 3
Ramsey ........................... 3
Rashford ........................... 3
Sewell ........................... 3
Townsend ........................... 3
Webb ........................... 3
Wilkins ........................... 3
Wright W ........................... 3
Allen R ........................... 2
Anderson ........................... 2
Barkley ........................... 2
Barry ........................... 2
Bradley ........................... 2
Broadbent ........................... 2
Brooks ........................... 2
Carroll ........................... 2
Cowans ........................... 2
Eastham ........................... 2
Ferdinand R ........................... 2
Froggatt J ........................... 2
Froggatt R ........................... 2
Haines ........................... 2
Hancocks ........................... 2
Hunter ........................... 2
Ince ........................... 2
Johnson A ........................... 2
Keown ........................... 2
Lee R ........................... 2
Lee S ........................... 2
Lingard ........................... 2
Moore ........................... 2
Perry ........................... 2
Pointer ........................... 2
Richardson ........................... 2
Royle ........................... 2
Smith A (1989–92) ........................... 2
Southgate ........................... 2
Sterling ........................... 2
Stone ........................... 2
Stones ........................... 2
Taylor P ........................... 2
Tueart ........................... 2
Upson ........................... 2
Wignall ........................... 2
Wilshere ........................... 2
Worthington ........................... 2
A'Court ........................... 1
Astall ........................... 1
Baines ........................... 1
Beattie K ........................... 1
Bertrand ........................... 1
Bowles ........................... 1
Bradford ........................... 1
Bridge ........................... 1
Bridges ........................... 1
Brown ........................... 1
Campbell ........................... 1
Caulker ........................... 1
Chamberlain ........................... 1
Cole Andy ........................... 1
Crawford ........................... 1
Dixon L ........................... 1
Ehiogu ........................... 1
Goddard ........................... 1
Hirst ........................... 1
Hughes E ........................... 1
Jeffers ........................... 1
Jenas ........................... 1
Johnson G ........................... 1
Kay ........................... 1
Kidd ........................... 1
King ........................... 1
Langton ........................... 1
Lawler ........................... 1
Lee J ........................... 1
Lescott ........................... 1
Le Saux ........................... 1
Mabbutt ........................... 1
Maguire ........................... 1
Marsh ........................... 1
Medley ........................... 1
Melia ........................... 1
Milner ........................... 1
Mullery ........................... 1
Murphy ........................... 1
Nicholls ........................... 1
Nicholson ........................... 1
Nugent ........................... 1
Palmer ........................... 1
Parry ........................... 1
Redknapp ........................... 1
Richards ........................... 1
Sansom ........................... 1
Shackleton ........................... 1
Smalling ........................... 1
Smith A (2001–5) ........................... 1
Stiles ........................... 1
Summerbee ........................... 1
Tambling ........................... 1
Thompson Phil ........................... 1
Trippier ........................... 1
Viollet ........................... 1
Wallace ........................... 1
Walsh ........................... 1
Weller ........................... 1
Wise ........................... 1
Withe ........................... 1
Wright M ........................... 1

**SCOTLAND**

Dalglish ........................... 30
Law ........................... 30
Reilly ........................... 22
McCoist ........................... 19
Miller K ........................... 18
McFadden ........................... 15
Johnston M ........................... 14
Collins J ........................... 12
Gilzean ........................... 12
Steel ........................... 12
Jordan ........................... 11
Collins R ........................... 10
Johnstone R ........................... 10
Wilson D ........................... 10
Fletcher S ........................... 9
Gallacher ........................... 9
McStay ........................... 9
Mudie ........................... 9
St John ........................... 9
Stein ........................... 9
Brand ........................... 8
Gemmill A ........................... 8
Leggat ........................... 8
Robertson J (1978–84) ........................... 8
Boyd K ........................... 7
Dodds ........................... 7
Durie ........................... 7
Gray A ........................... 7
Maloney ........................... 7
Naismith ........................... 7
Snodgrass ........................... 7
Wark ........................... 7
Booth ........................... 6
Brown A ........................... 6
Cooper ........................... 6
Dailly ........................... 6
Gough ........................... 6
Hutchison D ........................... 6
Liddell ........................... 6
Murdoch ........................... 6
Rioch ........................... 6
Waddell ........................... 6
Fletcher D ........................... 5
Hartford ........................... 5
Henderson W ........................... 5
Macari ........................... 5
Masson ........................... 5
McAllister G ........................... 5
McQueen ........................... 5
Nevin ........................... 5
Nicholas ........................... 5
O'Hare ........................... 5
Scott A ........................... 5
Strachan ........................... 5
Young A ........................... 5
Archibald ........................... 4
Berra ........................... 4
Brown S ........................... 4
Caldow ........................... 4
Crawford ........................... 4

Griffiths ............................ 4
Hamilton ............................ 4
Jackson D ............................ 4
Johnstone J ............................ 4
Lorimer ............................ 4
Mackay D ............................ 4
Mason ............................ 4
McArthur ............................ 4
McGinlay ............................ 4
McKinlay W ............................ 4
McLaren ............................ 4
O'Connor ............................ 4
Smith G ............................ 4
Souness ............................ 4
Anya ............................ 3
Baxter ............................ 3
Bremner W ............................ 3
Burley C ............................ 3
Chalmers ............................ 3
Ferguson B ............................ 3
Gibson ............................ 3
Graham G ............................ 3
Gray E ............................ 3
Greig ............................ 3
Hendry ............................ 3
Herd D ............................ 3
Lennox ............................ 3
MacDougall ............................ 3
McCann ............................ 3
McInally A ............................ 3
McNeill ............................ 3
McPhail ............................ 3
Martin C ............................ 3
Morris ............................ 3
Morrison ............................ 3
Rhodes ............................ 3
Ritchie M ............................ 3
Robertson J (1991–5) ............................ 3
Sturrock ............................ 3
Thompson ............................ 3
White ............................ 3
Baird S ............................ 2
Bauld ............................ 2
Burke ............................ 2
Caldwell G ............................ 2
Cameron ............................ 2
Commons ............................ 2
Flavell ............................ 2
Fleming ............................ 2
Graham A ............................ 2
Harper ............................ 2
Hewie ............................ 2
Holton ............................ 2
Hopkin ............................ 2
Houliston ............................ 2
Jess ............................ 2
Johnston A ............................ 2
Johnstone D ............................ 2
Mackie ............................ 2
McClair ............................ 2
McCormack ............................ 2
McGhee ............................ 2
McMillan ............................ 2
McManus ............................ 2
Mulgrew ............................ 2
Ormond ............................ 2
Pettigrew ............................ 2
Ring ............................ 2
Robertson A (1955) ............................ 2
Robertson A (2014–16) ............................ 2
Shearer D ............................ 2
Aitken R ............................ 1
Armstrong ............................ 1
Bannon ............................ 1
Beattie ............................ 1
Bett ............................ 1
Bone ............................ 1
Boyd T ............................ 1
Brazil ............................ 1
Broadfoot ............................ 1
Buckley ............................ 1
Burns ............................ 1
Calderwood ............................ 1
Campbell R ............................ 1
Clarkson ............................ 1
Combe ............................ 1
Conn A (1956) ............................ 1
Craig J ............................ 1
Curran ............................ 1
Davidson ............................ 1
Dickov ............................ 1
Dobie ............................ 1
Docherty ............................ 1
Duncan D ............................ 1
Elliott ............................ 1
Fernie ............................ 1
Freedman ............................ 1
Goodwillie ............................ 1
Gray F ............................ 1
Gemmill S ............................ 1
Gemmell T (1966–71) ............................ 1
Gemmell T (1955) ............................ 1
Hanley ............................ 1
Hartley ............................ 1
Henderson J ............................ 1
Herd G ............................ 1
Holt ............................ 1
Howie ............................ 1
Hughes J ............................ 1
Hunter W ............................ 1
Hutchison T ............................ 1
Jackson C ............................ 1
Jardine ............................ 1
Johnston L ............................ 1
Kyle ............................ 1
Lambert ............................ 1
Linwood ............................ 1
Mackail-Smith ............................ 1
Mackay G ............................ 1
MacLeod ............................ 1
MacKenzie ............................ 1
McAvennie ............................ 1
McCall ............................ 1
McCalliog ............................ 1
McCulloch ............................ 1
McKimmie ............................ 1
McKinnon ............................ 1
McLean ............................ 1
McLintock ............................ 1
McSwegan ............................ 1
Miller W ............................ 1
Mitchell ............................ 1
Morgan ............................ 1
Mulhall ............................ 1
Murray J ............................ 1
Narey ............................ 1
Naysmith ............................ 1
Orr ............................ 1
Parlane ............................ 1
Phillips ............................ 1
Provan D (1980–82) ............................ 1
Quashie ............................ 1
Ritchie P ............................ 1
Sharp ............................ 1
Stewart R ............................ 1
Thornton ............................ 1
Wallace I ............................ 1
Webster ............................ 1
Weir A ............................ 1
Weir D ............................ 1
Wilkie ............................ 1
Wilson Danny ............................ 1

## WALES

Bale ............................ 29
Rush ............................ 28
Allchurch I ............................ 23
Ford ............................ 23
Saunders ............................ 22
Bellamy ............................ 19
Earnshaw ............................ 16
Hughes M ............................ 16
Jones C ............................ 16
Charles John ............................ 15
Hartson ............................ 14
Ramsey ............................ 13
Toshack ............................ 13
Giggs ............................ 12
James L ............................ 10
Koumas ............................ 10
Vokes ............................ 10
Davies RT ............................ 9
Vernon ............................ 8
Flynn ............................ 7
James R ............................ 7
Speed ............................ 7
Walsh I ............................ 7

Charles M ........................6
Curtis A ............................6
Davies RW ........................6
Davies S ...........................6
Griffiths A ........................6
Medwin ..............................6
Pembridge .........................6
Clarke R ............................5
Leek ...................................5
Blake ..................................4
Coleman .............................4
Deacy .................................4
Eastwood ............................4
Edwards I ...........................4
England .............................4
Ledley ................................4
Robson-Kanu ......................4
Tapscott .............................4
Thomas M ..........................4
Allen M ..............................3
Bodin .................................3
Bowen M ............................3
Church ...............................3
Collins J .............................3
Edwards D .........................3
Melville ..............................3
Palmer D ............................3
Rees R ...............................3
Robinson J .........................3
Woosnam ...........................3
Allen J ...............................2
Cotterill .............................2
Davies G ............................2
Durban A ...........................2
Dwyer ................................2
Edwards G .........................2
Evans C .............................2
Giles D ..............................2
Godfrey ..............................2
Griffiths M .........................2
Hodges ..............................2
Horne .................................2
Jones Barrie .......................2
Jones Bryn .........................2
King ...................................2
Lawrence ............................2
Lowrie ................................2
Nicholas .............................2
Phillips D ...........................2
Reece G .............................2
Savage ...............................2
Slatter ...............................2
Symons ..............................2
Taylor N .............................2
Williams Ashley ..................2
Yorath ................................2
Barnes ...............................1
Blackmore ..........................1
Blake ..................................1
Bowen D ............................1
Boyle T ...............................1
Burgess R ...........................1
Charles Jeremy ...................1
Evans I ...............................1
Fletcher ..............................1
Foulkes ...............................1
Harris C ..............................1
Hewitt R .............................1
Hockey ...............................1
Huws ..................................1
Jones A ...............................1
Jones D ..............................1
Jones J ...............................1
Krzywicki ...........................1
Llewellyn ............................1
Lovell .................................1
Mahoney .............................1
Moore G .............................1
Morison ..............................1
O'Sullivan ...........................1
Parry ..................................1
Paul ....................................1
Powell A .............................1
Powell D .............................1
Price P ................................1
Roberts P ............................1
Robinson C .........................1
Smallman ............................1
Vaughan ..............................1
Williams Adrian ...................1
Williams GE .........................1
Williams GG .........................1
Wilson H ..............................1
Woodburn ............................1
Young ..................................1

## N IRELAND

Healy ................................36
Lafferty K ..........................20
Clarke ...............................13
Armstrong .........................12
Dowie ...............................12
Quinn JM ..........................12
Bingham ............................10
Crossan J ..........................10
McIlroy J ...........................10
McParland .........................10
Best ....................................9
Davis ...................................9
McAuley ..............................9
Whiteside ............................9
Dougan ................................8
Irvine W ...............................8
O'Neill M (1972–85) .............8
McAdams .............................7
Taggart G .............................7
Wilson S ...............................7
Gray .....................................6
McLaughlin ..........................6
Nicholson J ..........................6
Wilson K ..............................6
Cush ....................................5
Feeney (2002–9)) .................5
Hamilton W ..........................5
Hughes M ............................5
Magilton ..............................5
McIlroy S .............................5
Simpson ..............................5
Smyth S ...............................5
Walsh D ...............................5
Anderson T ..........................4
Elliott ...................................4
Hamilton B ...........................4
McCann ...............................4
Magennis .............................4
McGrath ..............................4
McMorran ............................4
O'Neill M (1989–96) .............4
Quinn SJ ..............................4
Ward ....................................4
Brotherston ..........................3
Brunt ....................................3
Harvey M .............................3
Lockhart ...............................3
Lomas ..................................3
McDonald .............................3
McGinn ................................3
McMordie .............................3
Morgan S ..............................3
Mulryne ................................3
Nicholl C ...............................3
Paterson ...............................3
Spence D ..............................3
Tully .....................................3
Washington ...........................3
Whitley (1997–2006) .............3
Blanchflower D .....................2
Casey ....................................2
Cathcart ................................2
Clements ...............................2
Doherty P ..............................2
Evans J .................................2
Finney ...................................2
Gillespie ................................2
Harkin ...................................2
Lennon ..................................2
McCourt ................................2
McMahon ..............................2
Neill W ..................................2
O'Neill J ................................2
Peacock ................................2
Penney ..................................2
Stewart I ...............................2
Barr ......................................1
Black .....................................1
Blanchflower J .......................1
Boyce ....................................1

Brennan....1
Campbell W....1
Caskey....1
Cassidy....1
Cochrane T....1
Crossan E....1
Dallas....1
D'Arcy....1
Doherty L....1
Elder....1
Evans C....1
Ferguson S....1
Ferguson W....1
Ferris....1
Griffin....1
Grigg....1
Hill C....1
Hughes....1
Humphries....1
Hunter A....1
Hunter B....1
Johnston....1
Jones J....1
Jones, S....1
McCartney....1
McClelland (1961)....1
McCrory....1
McCurdy....1
McGarry....1
McLaughlin C....1
Moreland....1
Morrow....1
Murdock....1
Nelson....1
Nicholl J....1
O'Boyle....1
O'Kane....1
Patterson D....1
Patterson R....1
Rowland....1
Shiels....1
Smyth P....1
Sproule....1
Stevenson....1
Thompson....1
Walker....1
Welsh....1
Williams....1
Wilson D....1

## REP OF IRELAND

Keane Robbie....68
Quinn N....21
Stapleton....20
Aldridge....19
Cascarino....19
Givens....19
Long....16
Cantwell....14
Doyle....14
Walters....14
Daly....13
Harte....12
McClean....10
Brady L....9
Connolly....9
Keane Roy....9
Kelly D....9
Morrison....9
Sheedy....9
Curtis....8
Duff....8
Dunne R....8
Grealish....8
Kilbane....8
McGrath P....8
Staunton....8
Brady R....7
Breen G....7
Fitzsimons....7
Ringstead....7
Townsend....7
Coyne....6
Houghton....6
McEvoy....6
Martin C....6
Moran....6
Cummins....5
Fagan F....5
Giles....5
Holland....5
Lawrenson....5
McGeady....5
Rogers....5
Sheridan....5
Treacy....5
Walsh D....5
Walters....5
Byrne J....4
Cox....4
Doherty....4
Ireland....4
Irwin....4
McGee....4
Martin M....4
O'Neill K....4
Reid A....4
Robinson....4
Tuohy....4
Andrews....3
Carey J....3
Coad....3
Conway....3
Duffy....3
Fahey....3
Farrell....3
Fogarty....3
Haverty....3
Hoolahan....3
Kennedy Mark....3
Kinsella....3
McAteer....3
Murphy D....3
O'Shea....3
Ryan R....3
St Ledger S....3
Waddock....3
Walsh M....3
Ward....3
Whelan R....3
Barrett....2
Clark....2
Conroy....2
Christie....2
Dennehy....2
Eglington....2
Fallon....2
Finnan....2
Fitzgerald P....2
Foley....2
Gavin....2
Hale....2
Hand....2
Hurley....2
Kelly G....2
Keogh A....2
Lawrence....2
Leech....2
McCarthy....2
McLoughlin....2
O'Connor (1968–73....2
O'Farrell....2
Pearce....2
Reid S....2
Whelan G....2
Ambrose....1
Anderson....1
Burke G....1
Carroll....1
Coleman....1
Dempsey....1
Elliott....1
Fitzgerald F....1
Fullam....1
Galvin....1
Gibson....1
Gleeson....1
Glynn....1
Gibson....1
Green....1
Grimes....1
Healy....1
Hendrick....1
Holmes....1
Hughton....1
Hunt S....1
Judge....1

Mooney J (Shamrock R, 1965) 2
Moore A (Middlesbrough, 1996–97) 8
Moran K (Manchester Utd, Sporting Gijon, Blackburn, 1980–94) 71
Moroney T (West Ham, 1948–54) 12
Morris C (Celtic, Middlesbrough, 1988–93) 35
Morrison C (Crystal Palace, Birmingham, Crystal Palace, 2002–07) 36
Moulson G (Lincoln, 1948–49) 3
Mucklan C (Drogheda, 1978) 1
Mulligan P (Shamrock R, Chelsea, Crystal Palace, WBA, Shamrock R, 1969–80) 50
Munroe L (Shamrock R, 1954) 1
Murphy A (Clyde, 1956) 1
Murphy B (Bohemians, 1986) 1
Murphy D (Sunderland, Ipswich, Newcastle, Nottm Forest, 2007–18) 33
Murphy J (Crystal Palace, 1980) 3
Murphy J (Scunthorpe, 2009–10) 2
Murphy J (WBA, 2004) 1
Murphy P (Carlisle, 2007) 1
Murray T (Dundalk, 1950) 1

Newman W (Shelbourne, 1969) 1
Nolan E (Preston, 2009–10) 3
Nolan R (Shamrock R, 1957–63) 10

O'Brien Alan (Newcastle, 2007) 5
O'Brien Andy (Newcastle, Portsmouth, 2001–07) 26
O'Brien F (Philadelphia Forest, 1980) 3
O'Brien J (Bolton, West Ham, 2006–13) 5
O'Brien L (Shamrock R, Manchester Utd, Newcastle, Tranmere, 1986–97) 16
O'Brien R (Notts Co, 1976–77) 5
O'Byrne L (Shamrock R, 1949) 1
O'Callaghan B (Stoke, 1979–82) 6
O'Callaghan K (Ipswich, Portsmouth, 1981–87) 21
O'Cearuill J (Arsenal, 2007) 2
O'Connell A (Dundalk, Bohemians, 1967–71) 2
O'Connor T (Shamrock R, 1950) 4
O'Connor T (Fulham, Dundalk, Bohemians, 1968–73) 7
O'Dowda C (Oxford, Bristol City, 2016–18) 10
O'Dea D (Celtic, Toronto, Metalurh Donetsk, 2010–14) 20
O'Driscoll J (Swansea, 1949) 3
O'Driscoll S (Fulham, 1982) 3
O'Farrell F (West Ham, Preston, 1952–59) 9
*O'Flanagan Dr K (Arsenal, 1947) 3
O'Flanagan M (Bohemians, 1947) 1
O'Halloran S (Aston Villa, 2007) 2
O'Hanlon K (Rotherham, 1988) 1
O'Kane E (Bournemouth, Leeds, 2016–17 7
O'Keefe E (Everton, Port Vale, 1981–85) 5
O'Leary D (Arsenal, 1977–93) 68
O'Leary P (Shamrock R, 1980–1) 7
O'Neill F (Shamrock R, 1962–72) 20
O'Neill J (Everton, 1952–59) 17
O'Neill J (Preston, 1961) 1
O'Neill K (Norwich, Middlesbrough, 1996–2000) 13
O'Regan K (Brighton, 1984–85) 4
O'Reilly J (Cork Utd, 1946) 2
O'Shea J (Manchester Utd, Sunderland, 2002–18) 118

Pearce A (Reading, Derby, 2013–17) 9
Peyton G (Fulham, Bournemouth, Everton, 1977–92) 33
Peyton N (Shamrock R, Leeds, 1957–61) 6
Phelan T (Wimbledon, Manchester City, Chelsea, Everton, Fulham, 1992–2000) 42
Pilkington A (Norwich, Cardiff, 2014–16) 9
Potter D (Wolves, 2007–08) 5
Quinn A (Sheffield Wed, Sheffield Utd, 2003–07) 7
Quinn B (Coventry, 2000) 4
Quinn N (Arsenal, Manchester City, Sunderland, 1986–2002) 92
Quinn S (Hull, Reading, 2013–17) 18

Randolph D (Motherwell, West Ham, Middlesbrough, 2013–18) 28
Reid A (Nottm Forest, Tottenham, Charlton, Sunderland, Nottm Forest, 2004–14) 29
Reid S (Millwall, Blackburn, 2002–09) 23
Rice D (West Ham, 2018) 3
Richardson D (Shamrock R, Gillingham, 1972–80) 3
Ringstead A (Sheffield Utd, 1951–59) 20
Robinson M (Brighton, Liverpool, QPR, 1981–86) 24
Roche P (Shelbourne, Manchester Utd, 1972–76) 8
Rogers E (Blackburn, Charlton, 1968–73) 19
Rowlands M (QPR, 2004–10) 5
Ryan G (Derby, Brighton, 1978–85) 18
Ryan R (WBA, Derby, 1950–56) 16

Sadlier R (Millwall, 2002) 1
Sammon C (Derby, 2013–14) 9
Savage D (Millwall, 1996) 5
Saward P (Millwall, Aston Villa, Huddersfield, 1954–63) 18
Scannell T (Southend, 1954) 1
Scully P (Arsenal, 1989) 1
Sheedy K (Everton, Newcastle, 1984–93) 46
Sheridan C (Celtic, CSKA Sofia, 2010–11) 3
Sheridan J (Leeds, Sheffield Wed, 1988–96) 34
Slaven B (Middlesbrough, 1990–93) 7
Sloan P (Arsenal, 1946) 2
Smyth M (Shamrock R, 1969) 1
St Ledger S (Preston, Leicester, 2009–14) 37
Stapleton F (Arsenal, Manchester Utd, Ajax Derby, Le Havre, Blackburn, 1977–90) 71
Staunton S (Liverpool, Aston Villa, Liverpool, Crystal Palace, Aston Villa, 1989–2002) 102

| Player | Caps |
|---|---|
| Stevens E (Sheffield Utd, 2018) | 1 |
| *Stevenson A (Everton, 1947–49) | 6 |
| Stokes A (Sunderland, Celtic, 2007–15) | 9 |
| Strahan F (Shelbourne, 1964–65) | 5 |
| Swan M (Drumcondra, 1960) | 1 |
| Synnott N (Shamrock R, 1978–79) | 3 |
| Taylor T (Waterford, 1959) | 1 |
| Thomas P (Waterford, 1974) | 2 |
| Thompson J (Nottm Forest, 2004) | 1 |
| Townsend A (Norwich, Chelsea, Aston Villa, Middlesbrough, 1989–97) | 70 |
| Traynor T (Southampton, 1954–64) | 8 |
| Treacy K (Preston, Burnley 2011–12) | 6 |
| Treacy R (WBA, Charlton, Swindon, Preston, Shamrock R, 1966–80) | 42 |
| Tuohy L (Shamrock R, Newcastle, Shamrock R, 1956–65) | 8 |
| Turner A (Celtic, 1963) | 2 |
| Vernon J (Belfast Celtic, 1946) | 2 |
| Waddock G (QPR, Millwall, 1980–90) | 21 |
| Walsh D (WBA, Aston Villa, 1946–54) | 20 |
| Walsh J (Limerick, 1982) | 1 |
| Walsh M (Blackpool, Everton, QPR, Porto, 1976–85) | 21 |
| Walsh M (Everton, Norwich, 1982–83) | 4 |
| Walsh W (Manchester City, 1947–50) | 9 |
| Walters J (Stoke, Burnley, 2011–18) | 53 |
| Ward S (Wolves, Burnley, 2011–18) | 49 |
| Waters J (Grimsby, 1977–80) | 2 |
| Westwood K (Coventry, Sunderland, Sheffield Wed, 2009–17) | 21 |
| Whelan G (Stoke, Aston Villa 2009–18) | 84 |
| Whelan R (St Patrick's Ath, 1964) | 2 |
| Whelan R (Liverpool, Southend, 1981–95) | 53 |
| Whelan L (Manchester Utd, 1956–57) | 4 |
| Whittaker R (Chelsea, 1959) | 1 |
| Williams D (Blackburn, 2018) | 1 |
| Williams S (Millwall, 2018) | 1 |
| Wilson M (Stoke, Bournemouth, 2011–17) | 25 |

# INTERNATIONAL GOALSCORERS 1946–2018

(start of season 2018–19)

## ENGLAND

Rooney ....................53
Charlton R ....................49
Lineker ....................48
Greaves ....................44
Owen ....................40
Finney ....................30
Lofthouse ....................30
Shearer ....................30
Lampard Frank jnr ....................29
Platt ....................27
Robson B ....................26
Hurst ....................24
Mortensen ....................23
Crouch ....................22
Channon ....................21
Gerrard ....................21
Keegan ....................21
Defoe ....................20
Peters ....................20
Kane ....................19
Haynes ....................18
Hunt R ....................18
Beckham ....................17
Lawton ....................16
Taylor T ....................16
Woodcock ....................16
Welbeck ....................16
Scholes ....................14
Chivers ....................13
Mariner ....................13
Smith R ....................13
Francis T ....................12
Barnes J ....................11
Douglas ....................11
Mannion ....................11
Sheringham ....................11
Clarke A ....................10
Cole J ....................10
Flowers R ....................10
Gascoigne ....................10
Lee F ....................10
Milburn ....................10
Wilshaw ....................10
Beardsley ....................9
Bell ....................9
Bentley ....................9
Hateley ....................9
Wright I ....................9
Ball ....................8
Broadis ....................8
Byrne J ....................8
Hoddle ....................8
Kevan ....................8
Sturridge ....................8
Walcott ....................8
Anderton ....................7
Connelly ....................7
Coppell ....................7
Fowler ....................7
Heskey ....................7
Paine ....................7
Vardy ....................7
Young A ....................7
Charlton J ....................6
Macdonald ....................6
Mullen ....................6
Oxlade-Chamberlain ....................6
Rowley ....................6
Terry ....................6
Vassell ....................6
Waddle ....................6
Wright-Phillips S ....................6
Adams ....................5
Atyeo ....................5
Baily ....................5
Brooking ....................5
Cahill ....................5
Carter ....................5
Edwards ....................5
Ferdinand L ....................5
Hitchens ....................5
Johnson D ....................5
Latchford ....................5
Neal ....................5
Pearce ....................5
Pearson Stan ....................5
Pearson Stuart ....................5
Pickering F ....................5
Barmby ....................4
Barnes P ....................4
Bent ....................4
Bull ....................4
Dixon K ....................4
Hassall ....................4
Revie ....................4
Robson R ....................4
Steven ....................4
Watson Dave (Sunderland) ....4
Alli ....................3
Baker ....................3
Blissett ....................3
Butcher ....................3
Currie ....................3
Dier ....................3
Elliott ....................3
Francis G ....................3
Grainger ....................3
Jagielka ....................3
Kennedy R ....................3
Lallana ....................3

Lambert 3
McDermott 3
McManaman 3
Matthews S 3
Merson 3
Morris 3
O'Grady 3
Peacock 3
Ramsey 3
Rashford 3
Sewell 3
Townsend 3
Webb 3
Wilkins 3
Wright W 3
Allen R 2
Anderson 2
Barkley 2
Barry 2
Bradley 2
Broadbent 2
Brooks 2
Carroll 2
Cowans 2
Eastham 2
Ferdinand R 2
Froggatt J 2
Froggatt R 2
Haines 2
Hancocks 2
Hunter 2
Ince 2
Johnson A 2
Keown 2
Lee R 2
Lee S 2
Lingard 2
Moore 2
Perry 2
Pointer 2
Richardson 2
Royle 2
Smith A (1989–92) 2
Southgate 2
Sterling 2
Stone 2
Stones 2
Taylor P 2
Tueart 2
Upson 2
Wignall 2
Wilshere 2
Worthington 2
A'Court 1
Astall 1
Baines 1
Beattie K 1
Bertrand 1
Bowles 1
Bradford 1
Bridge 1
Bridges 1
Brown 1
Campbell 1
Caulker 1
Chamberlain 1
Cole Andy 1
Crawford 1
Dixon L 1
Ehiogu 1
Goddard 1
Hirst 1
Hughes E 1
Jeffers 1
Jenas 1
Johnson G 1
Kay 1
Kidd 1
King 1
Langton 1
Lawler 1
Lee J 1
Lescott 1
Le Saux 1
Mabbutt 1
Maguire 1
Marsh 1
Medley 1
Melia 1
Milner 1
Mullery 1
Murphy 1
Nicholls 1
Nicholson 1
Nugent 1
Palmer 1
Parry 1
Redknapp 1
Richards 1
Sansom 1
Shackleton 1
Smalling 1
Smith A (2001–5) 1
Stiles 1
Summerbee 1
Tambling 1
Thompson Phil 1
Trippier 1
Viollet 1
Wallace 1
Walsh 1
Weller 1
Wise 1
Withe 1
Wright M 1

**SCOTLAND**

Dalglish 30
Law 30
Reilly 22
McCoist 19
Miller K 18
McFadden 15
Johnston M 14
Collins J 12
Gilzean 12
Steel 12
Jordan 11
Collins R 10
Johnstone R 10
Wilson D 10
Fletcher S 9
Gallacher 9
McStay 9
Mudie 9
St John 9
Stein 9
Brand 8
Gemmill A 8
Leggat 8
Robertson J (1978–84) 8
Boyd K 7
Dodds 7
Durie 7
Gray A 7
Maloney 7
Naismith 7
Snodgrass 7
Wark 7
Booth 6
Brown A 6
Cooper 6
Dailly 6
Gough 6
Hutchison D 6
Liddell 6
Murdoch 6
Rioch 6
Waddell 6
Fletcher D 5
Hartford 5
Henderson W 5
Macari 5
Masson 5
McAllister G 5
McQueen 5
Nevin 5
Nicholas 5
O'Hare 5
Scott A 5
Strachan 5
Young A 5
Archibald 4
Berra 4
Brown S 4
Caldow 4
Crawford 4

Griffiths 4
Hamilton 4
Jackson D 4
Johnstone J 4
Lorimer 4
Mackay D 4
Mason 4
McArthur 4
McGinlay 4
McKinlay W 4
McLaren 4
O'Connor 4
Smith G 4
Souness 4
Anya 3
Baxter 3
Bremner W 3
Burley C 3
Chalmers 3
Ferguson B 3
Gibson 3
Graham G 3
Gray E 3
Greig 3
Hendry 3
Herd D 3
Lennox 3
MacDougall 3
McCann 3
McInally A 3
McNeill 3
McPhail 3
Martin C 3
Morris 3
Morrison 3
Rhodes 3
Ritchie M 3
Robertson J (1991–5) 3
Sturrock 3
Thompson 3
White 3
Baird S 2
Bauld 2
Burke 2
Caldwell G 2
Cameron 2
Commons 2
Flavell 2
Fleming 2
Graham A 2
Harper 2
Hewie 2
Holton 2
Hopkin 2
Houliston 2
Jess 2
Johnston A 2
Johnstone D 2
Mackie 2
McClair 2
McCormack 2
McGhee 2
McMillan 2
McManus 2
Mulgrew 2
Ormond 2
Pettigrew 2
Ring 2
Robertson A (1955) 2
Robertson A (2014–16) 2
Shearer D 2
Aitken R 1
Armstrong 1
Bannon 1
Beattie 1
Bett 1
Bone 1
Boyd T 1
Brazil 1
Broadfoot 1
Buckley 1
Burns 1
Calderwood 1
Campbell R 1
Clarkson 1
Combe 1
Conn A (1956) 1
Craig J 1
Curran 1
Davidson 1
Dickov 1
Dobie 1
Docherty 1
Duncan D 1
Elliott 1
Fernie 1
Freedman 1
Goodwillie 1
Gray F 1
Gemmill S 1
Gemmell T (1966–71) 1
Gemmell T (1955) 1
Hanley 1
Hartley 1
Henderson J 1
Herd G 1
Holt 1
Howie 1
Hughes J 1
Hunter W 1
Hutchison T 1
Jackson C 1
Jardine 1
Johnston L 1
Kyle 1
Lambert 1
Linwood 1
Mackail-Smith 1
Mackay G 1
MacLeod 1
MacKenzie 1
McAvennie 1
McCall 1
McCalliog 1
McCulloch 1
McKimmie 1
McKinnon 1
McLean 1
McLintock 1
McSwegan 1
Miller W 1
Mitchell 1
Morgan 1
Mulhall 1
Murray J 1
Narey 1
Naysmith 1
Orr 1
Parlane 1
Phillips 1
Provan D (1980–82) 1
Quashie 1
Ritchie P 1
Sharp 1
Stewart R 1
Thornton 1
Wallace I 1
Webster 1
Weir A 1
Weir D 1
Wilkie 1
Wilson Danny 1

## WALES

Bale 29
Rush 28
Allchurch I 23
Ford 23
Saunders 22
Bellamy 19
Earnshaw 16
Hughes M 16
Jones C 16
Charles John 15
Hartson 14
Ramsey 13
Toshack 13
Giggs 12
James L 10
Koumas 10
Vokes 10
Davies RT 9
Vernon 8
Flynn 7
James R 7
Speed 7
Walsh I 7

Charles M ........................6
Curtis A ..........................6
Davies RW ........................6
Davies S ..........................6
Griffiths A ........................6
Medwin .............................6
Pembridge .........................6
Clarke R ...........................5
Leek ................................5
Blake ...............................4
Coleman ............................4
Deacy ...............................4
Eastwood ...........................4
Edwards I ..........................4
England .............................4
Ledley ..............................4
Robson-Kanu .......................4
Tapscott ............................4
Thomas M ...........................4
Allen M .............................3
Bodin ...............................3
Bowen M ............................3
Church ..............................3
Collins J ............................3
Edwards D ..........................3
Melville ..............................3
Palmer D ............................3
Rees R ..............................3
Robinson J ..........................3
Woosnam ...........................3
Allen J ..............................2
Cotterill .............................2
Davies G ............................2
Durban A ............................2
Dwyer ...............................2
Edwards G ..........................2
Evans C .............................2
Giles D ..............................2
Godfrey .............................2
Griffiths M ..........................2
Hodges ..............................2
Horne ...............................2
Jones Barrie ........................2
Jones Bryn ..........................2
King .................................2
Lawrence ...........................2
Lowrie ...............................2
Nicholas .............................2
Phillips D ...........................2
Reece G .............................2
Savage ..............................2
Slatter ...............................2
Symons .............................2
Taylor N .............................2
Williams Ashley .....................2
Yorath ...............................2
Barnes ...............................1
Blackmore ..........................1
Blake ................................1
Bowen D ............................1
Boyle T ..............................1
Burgess R ...........................1
Charles Jeremy .....................1
Evans I ..............................1
Fletcher .............................1
Foulkes ..............................1
Harris C .............................1
Hewitt R .............................1
Hockey ..............................1
Huws ................................1
Jones A ..............................1
Jones D ..............................1
Jones J ..............................1
Krzywicki ...........................1
Llewellyn ............................1
Lovell ................................1
Mahoney ............................1
Moore G .............................1
Morison .............................1
O'Sullivan ...........................1
Parry ................................1
Paul .................................1
Powell A .............................1
Powell D .............................1
Price P ...............................1
Roberts P ............................1
Robinson C ..........................1
Smallman ............................1
Vaughan .............................1
Williams Adrian .....................1
Williams GE .........................1
Williams GG .........................1
Wilson H .............................1
Woodburn ...........................1
Young ...............................1

## N IRELAND

Healy ..............................36
Lafferty K ..........................20
Clarke ..............................13
Armstrong ..........................12
Dowie ..............................12
Quinn JM ...........................12
Bingham ............................10
Crossan J ...........................10
McIlroy J ...........................10
McParland ..........................10
Best .................................9
Davis ................................9
McAuley .............................9
Whiteside ............................9
Dougan ..............................8
Irvine W .............................8
O'Neill M (1972–85) ................8
McAdams ............................7
Taggart G ...........................7
Wilson S .............................7
Gray .................................6
McLaughlin ..........................6
Nicholson J ..........................6
Wilson K .............................6
Cush .................................5
Feeney (2002–9)) ....................5
Hamilton W ..........................5
Hughes M ............................5
Magilton .............................5
McIlroy S .............................5
Simpson .............................5
Smyth S ..............................5
Walsh D ..............................5
Anderson T ..........................4
Elliott ................................4
Hamilton B ...........................4
McCann ..............................4
Magennis .............................4
McGrath .............................4
McMorran ...........................4
O'Neill M (1989–96) ................4
Quinn SJ .............................4
Ward .................................4
Brotherston ..........................3
Brunt ................................3
Harvey M ............................3
Lockhart .............................3
Lomas ...............................3
McDonald ............................3
McGinn ..............................3
McMordie ............................3
Morgan S .............................3
Mulryne ..............................3
Nicholl C .............................3
Paterson .............................3
Spence D .............................3
Tully .................................3
Washington ..........................3
Whitley (1997–2006) ................3
Blanchflower D ......................2
Casey ................................2
Cathcart ..............................2
Clements .............................2
Doherty P ............................2
Evans J ...............................2
Finney ...............................2
Gillespie .............................2
Harkin ...............................2
Lennon ...............................2
McCourt ..............................2
McMahon ............................2
Neill W ...............................2
O'Neill J .............................2
Peacock ..............................2
Penney ...............................2
Stewart I .............................2
Barr .................................1
Black ................................1
Blanchflower J ......................1
Boyce ................................1

Brennan.............................1
Campbell W ......................1
Caskey ..............................1
Cassidy .............................1
Cochrane T .......................1
Crossan E .........................1
Dallas.................................1
D'Arcy ...............................1
Doherty L ..........................1
Elder .................................1
Evans C .............................1
Ferguson S.........................1
Ferguson W .......................1
Ferris ................................1
Griffin ...............................1
Grigg .................................1
Hill C ................................1
Hughes..............................1
Humphries ........................1
Hunter A ...........................1
Hunter B ...........................1
Johnston............................1
Jones J ..............................1
Jones, S.............................1
McCartney .........................1
McClelland (1961) ..............1
McCrory.............................1
McCurdy............................1
McGarry.............................1
McLaughlin C......................1
Moreland ...........................1
Morrow .............................1
Murdock ............................1
Nelson ..............................1
Nicholl J ............................1
O'Boyle..............................1
O'Kane ..............................1
Patterson D .......................1
Patterson R........................1
Rowland ............................1
Shiels.................................1
Smyth P .............................1
Sproule...............................1
Stevenson ..........................1
Thompson ..........................1
Walker ..............................1
Welsh ................................1
Williams ............................1
Wilson D ...........................1

## REP OF IRELAND

Keane Robbie...................68
Quinn N ..........................21
Stapleton .........................20
Aldridge ...........................19
Cascarino .........................19
Givens ..............................19
Long.................................16
Cantwell ...........................14
Doyle................................14
Walters .............................14
Daly .................................13
Harte ...............................12
McClean ...........................10
Brady L...............................9
Connolly .............................9
Keane Roy ..........................9
Kelly D ...............................9
Morrison .............................9
Sheedy ...............................9
Curtis .................................8
Duff ...................................8
Dunne R .............................8
Grealish..............................8
Kilbane...............................8
McGrath P ..........................8
Staunton .............................8
Brady R ..............................7
Breen G...............................7
Fitzsimons ..........................7
Ringstead ...........................7
Townsend ...........................7
Coyne ................................6
Houghton ...........................6
McEvoy...............................6
Martin C .............................6
Moran ................................6
Cummins ............................5
Fagan F ..............................5
Giles ..................................5
Holland ..............................5
Lawrenson ..........................5
McGeady ............................5
Rogers ...............................5
Sheridan.............................5
Treacy ...............................5
Walsh D..............................5
Walters ..............................5
Byrne J ...............................4
Cox ....................................4
Doherty...............................4
Ireland ...............................4
Irwin ..................................4
McGee ...............................4
Martin M ............................4
O'Neill K ............................4
Reid A ...............................4
Robinson ...........................4
Tuohy ................................4
Andrews..............................3
Carey J ...............................3
Coad ..................................3
Conway ..............................3
Duffy .................................3
Fahey .................................3
Farrell ...............................3
Fogarty ..............................3
Haverty ..............................3
Hoolahan ............................3
Kennedy Mark .....................3
Kinsella ..............................3
McAteer...............................3
Murphy D.............................3
O'Shea ...............................3
Ryan R ...............................3
St Ledger S..........................3
Waddock..............................3
Walsh M .............................3
Ward ..................................3
Whelan R ............................3
Barrett ...............................2
Clark ..................................2
Conroy ...............................2
Christie...............................2
Dennehy .............................2
Eglington ............................2
Fallon ................................2
Finnan ...............................2
Fitzgerald P ........................2
Foley .................................2
Gavin .................................2
Hale ..................................2
Hand ..................................2
Hurley ................................2
Kelly G ...............................2
Keogh A..............................2
Lawrence ............................2
Leech .................................2
McCarthy ............................2
McLoughlin .........................2
O'Connor (1968–73..............2
O'Farrell .............................2
Pearce.................................2
Reid S .................................2
Whelan G.............................2
Ambrose ..............................1
Anderson ............................1
Burke G...............................1
Carroll ...............................1
Coleman ..............................1
Dempsey .............................1
Elliott ................................1
Fitzgerald F ........................1
Fullam ................................1
Galvin ................................1
Gibson................................1
Gleeson ..............................1
Glynn .................................1
Gibson.................................1
Green .................................1
Grimes ...............................1
Healy .................................1
Hendrick..............................1
Holmes ...............................1
Hughton ..............................1
Hunt S ................................1
Judge .................................1

| | | | | | |
|---|---|---|---|---|---|
| Kavanagh | 1 | Mooney | 1 | O'Leary | 1 |
| Keogh R | 1 | Moroney | 1 | O'Neill F | 1 |
| Kernaghan | 1 | Mulligan | 1 | O'Reilly J | 1 |
| Mancini | 1 | O'Brien A | 1 | Pilkington | 1 |
| McCann | 1 | O'Dea | 1 | Ryan G | 1 |
| McPhail | 1 | O'Callaghan K | 1 | Slaven | 1 |
| Miller | 1 | O'Keefe | 1 | Sloan | 1 |

# HOME INTERNATIONAL RESULTS

Note: In the results that follow, WC = World Cup, EC = European Championship, CC = Carling Cup
TF = Tournoi de France For Northern Ireland read Ireland before 1921

## ENGLAND V SCOTLAND

Played 114; England won 48; Scotland 41; drawn 25 Goals: England 203, Scotland 174

| | | *E* | *S* |
|---|---|---|---|
| 1872 | Glasgow | 0 | 0 |
| 1873 | The Oval | 4 | 2 |
| 1874 | Glasgow | 1 | 2 |
| 1875 | The Oval | 2 | 2 |
| 1876 | Glasgow | 0 | 3 |
| 1877 | The Oval | 1 | 3 |
| 1878 | Glasgow | 2 | 7 |
| 1879 | The Oval | 5 | 4 |
| 1880 | Glasgow | 4 | 5 |
| 1881 | The Oval | 1 | 6 |
| 1882 | Glasgow | 1 | 5 |
| 1883 | Sheffield | 2 | 3 |
| 1884 | Glasgow | 0 | 1 |
| 1885 | The Oval | 1 | 1 |
| 1886 | Glasgow | 1 | 1 |
| 1887 | Blackburn | 2 | 3 |
| 1888 | Glasgow | 5 | 0 |
| 1889 | The Oval | 2 | 3 |
| 1890 | Glasgow | 1 | 1 |
| 1891 | Blackburn | 2 | 1 |
| 1892 | Glasgow | 4 | 1 |
| 1893 | Richmond | 5 | 2 |
| 1894 | Glasgow | 2 | 2 |
| 1895 | Goodison Park | 3 | 0 |
| 1896 | Glasgow | 1 | 2 |
| 1897 | Crystal Palace | 1 | 2 |
| 1898 | Glasgow | 3 | 1 |
| 1899 | Birmingham | 2 | 1 |
| 1900 | Glasgow | 1 | 4 |
| 1901 | Crystal Palace | 2 | 2 |
| 1902 | Birmingham | 2 | 2 |
| 1903 | Sheffield | 1 | 2 |
| 1904 | Glasgow | 1 | 0 |
| 1905 | Crystal Palace | 1 | 0 |
| 1906 | Glasgow | 1 | 2 |
| 1907 | Newcastle | 1 | 1 |
| 1908 | Glasgow | 1 | 1 |
| 1909 | Crystal Palace | 2 | 0 |
| 1910 | Glasgow | 0 | 2 |
| 1911 | Goodison Park | 1 | 1 |
| 1912 | Glasgow | 1 | 1 |
| 1913 | Stamford Bridge | 1 | 0 |
| 1914 | Glasgow | 1 | 3 |
| 1920 | Sheffield | 5 | 4 |
| 1921 | Glasgow | 0 | 3 |
| 1922 | Birmingham | 0 | 1 |
| 1923 | Glasgow | 2 | 2 |
| 1924 | Wembley | 1 | 1 |
| 1925 | Glasgow | 0 | 2 |
| 1926 | Manchester | 0 | 1 |
| 1927 | Glasgow | 2 | 1 |
| 1928 | Wembley | 1 | 5 |
| 1929 | Glasgow | 0 | 1 |
| 1930 | Wembley | 5 | 2 |
| 1931 | Glasgow | 0 | 2 |
| 1932 | Wembley | 3 | 0 |
| 1933 | Glasgow | 1 | 2 |
| 1934 | Wembley | 3 | 0 |
| 1935 | Glasgow | 0 | 2 |
| 1936 | Wembley | 1 | 1 |
| 1937 | Glasgow | 1 | 3 |
| 1938 | Wembley | 0 | 1 |
| 1939 | Glasgow | 2 | 1 |
| 1947 | Wembley | 1 | 1 |
| 1948 | Glasgow | 2 | 0 |
| 1949 | Wembley | 1 | 3 |
| 1950 | Glasgow (WC) | 1 | 0 |
| 1951 | Wembley | 2 | 3 |
| 1952 | Glasgow | 2 | 1 |
| 1953 | Wembley | 2 | 2 |
| 1954 | Glasgow (WC) | 4 | 2 |
| 1955 | Wembley | 7 | 2 |
| 1956 | Glasgow | 1 | 1 |
| 1957 | Wembley | 2 | 1 |
| 1958 | Glasgow | 4 | 0 |
| 1959 | Wembley | 1 | 0 |
| 1960 | Glasgow | 1 | 1 |
| 1961 | Wembley | 9 | 3 |
| 1962 | Glasgow | 0 | 2 |
| 1963 | Wembley | 1 | 2 |
| 1964 | Glasgow | 0 | 1 |
| 1965 | Wembley | 2 | 2 |
| 1966 | Glasgow | 4 | 3 |
| 1967 | Wembley (EC) | 2 | 3 |
| 1968 | Glasgow (EC) | 1 | 1 |
| 1969 | Wembley | 4 | 1 |
| 1970 | Glasgow | 0 | 0 |
| 1971 | Wembley | 3 | 1 |
| 1972 | Glasgow | 1 | 0 |
| 1973 | Glasgow | 5 | 0 |
| 1973 | Wembley | 1 | 0 |
| 1974 | Glasgow | 0 | 2 |
| 1975 | Wembley | 5 | 1 |
| 1976 | Glasgow | 1 | 2 |
| 1977 | Wembley | 1 | 2 |
| 1978 | Glasgow | 1 | 0 |
| 1979 | Wembley | 3 | 1 |

| | | | |
|---|---|---|---|
| 1980 | Glasgow | 2 | 0 |
| 1981 | Wembley | 0 | 1 |
| 1982 | Glasgow | 1 | 0 |
| 1983 | Wembley | 2 | 0 |
| 1984 | Glasgow | 1 | 1 |
| 1985 | Glasgow | 0 | 1 |
| 1986 | Wembley | 2 | 1 |
| 1987 | Glasgow | 0 | 0 |
| 1988 | Wembley | 1 | 0 |
| 1989 | Glasgow | 2 | 0 |
| 1996 | Wembley (EC) | 2 | 0 |
| 1999 | Glasgow (EC) | 2 | 0 |
| 1999 | Wembley (EC) | 0 | 1 |
| 2013 | Wembley | 3 | 2 |
| 2014 | Glasgow | 3 | 1 |
| 2016 | Wembley (WC) | 3 | 0 |
| 2017 | Glasgow (WC) | 2 | 2 |

## ENGLAND v WALES

Played 102; England won 67; Wales 14; drawn 21; Goals: England 247 Wales 91

| | | E | W |
|---|---|---|---|
| 1879 | The Oval | 2 | 1 |
| 1880 | Wrexham | 3 | 2 |
| 1881 | Blackburn | 0 | 1 |
| 1882 | Wrexham | 3 | 5 |
| 1883 | The Oval | 5 | 0 |
| 1884 | Wrexham | 4 | 0 |
| 1885 | Blackburn | 1 | 1 |
| 1886 | Wrexham | 3 | 1 |
| 1887 | The Oval | 4 | 0 |
| 1888 | Crewe | 5 | 1 |
| 1889 | Stoke | 4 | 1 |
| 1890 | Wrexham | 3 | 1 |
| 1891 | Sunderland | 4 | 1 |
| 1892 | Wrexham | 2 | 0 |
| 1893 | Stoke | 6 | 0 |
| 1894 | Wrexham | 5 | 1 |
| 1895 | Queens Club, London | 1 | 1 |
| 1896 | Cardiff | 9 | 1 |
| 1897 | Bramall Lane | 4 | 0 |
| 1898 | Wrexham | 3 | 0 |
| 1899 | Bristol | 4 | 0 |
| 1900 | Cardiff | 1 | 1 |
| 1901 | Newcastle | 6 | 0 |
| 1902 | Wrexham | 0 | 0 |
| 1903 | Portsmouth | 2 | 1 |
| 1904 | Wrexham | 2 | 2 |
| 1905 | Anfield | 3 | 1 |
| 1906 | Cardiff | 1 | 0 |
| 1907 | Fulham | 1 | 1 |
| 1908 | Wrexham | 7 | 1 |
| 1909 | Nottingham | 2 | 0 |
| 1910 | Cardiff | 1 | 0 |
| 1911 | Millwall | 3 | 0 |
| 1912 | Wrexham | 2 | 0 |
| 1913 | Bristol | 4 | 3 |
| 1914 | Cardiff | 2 | 0 |
| 1920 | Highbury | 1 | 2 |
| 1921 | Cardiff | 0 | 0 |
| 1922 | Anfield | 1 | 0 |
| 1923 | Cardiff | 2 | 2 |
| 1924 | Blackburn | 1 | 2 |
| 1925 | Swansea | 2 | 1 |
| 1926 | Selhurst Park | 1 | 3 |
| 1927 | Wrexham | 3 | 3 |
| 1927 | Burnley | 1 | 2 |
| 1928 | Swansea | 3 | 2 |
| 1929 | Stamford Bridge | 6 | 0 |
| 1930 | Wrexham | 4 | 0 |
| 1931 | Anfield | 3 | 1 |
| 1932 | Wrexham | 0 | 0 |
| 1933 | Newcastle | 1 | 2 |
| 1934 | Cardiff | 4 | 0 |
| 1935 | Wolverhampton | 1 | 2 |
| 1936 | Cardiff | 1 | 2 |
| 1937 | Middlesbrough | 2 | 1 |
| 1938 | Cardiff | 2 | 4 |
| 1946 | Maine Road | 3 | 0 |
| 1947 | Cardiff | 3 | 0 |
| 1948 | Villa Park | 1 | 0 |
| 1949 | Cardiff (WC) | 4 | 1 |
| 1950 | Sunderland | 4 | 2 |
| 1951 | Cardiff | 1 | 1 |
| 1952 | Wembley | 5 | 2 |
| 1953 | Cardiff (WC) | 4 | 1 |
| 1954 | Wembley | 3 | 2 |
| 1955 | Cardiff | 1 | 2 |
| 1956 | Wembley | 3 | 1 |
| 1957 | Cardiff | 4 | 0 |
| 1958 | Villa Park | 2 | 2 |
| 1959 | Cardiff | 1 | 1 |
| 1960 | Wembley | 5 | 1 |
| 1961 | Cardiff | 1 | 1 |
| 1962 | Wembley | 4 | 0 |
| 1963 | Cardiff | 4 | 0 |
| 1964 | Wembley | 2 | 1 |
| 1965 | Cardiff | 0 | 0 |
| 1966 | Wembley (EC) | 5 | 1 |
| 1967 | Cardiff (EC) | 3 | 0 |
| 1969 | Wembley | 2 | 1 |
| 1970 | Cardiff | 1 | 1 |
| 1971 | Wembley | 0 | 0 |
| 1972 | Cardiff | 3 | 0 |
| 1972 | Cardiff (WC) | 1 | 0 |
| 1973 | Wembley (WC) | 1 | 1 |
| 1973 | Wembley | 3 | 0 |
| 1974 | Cardiff | 2 | 0 |
| 1975 | Wembley | 2 | 2 |
| 1976 | Wrexham | 2 | 1 |
| 1976 | Cardiff | 1 | 0 |
| 1977 | Wembley | 0 | 1 |
| 1978 | Cardiff | 3 | 1 |
| 1979 | Wembley | 0 | 0 |
| 1980 | Wrexham | 1 | 4 |
| 1981 | Wembley | 0 | 0 |
| 1982 | Cardiff | 1 | 0 |
| 1983 | Wembley | 2 | 1 |
| 1984 | Wrexham | 0 | 1 |
| 2004 | Old Trafford (WC) | 2 | 0 |
| 2005 | Cardiff (WC) | 1 | 0 |
| 2011 | Cardiff (EC) | 2 | 0 |
| 2011 | Wembley (EC) | 1 | 0 |
| 2016 | Lens (EC) | 2 | 1 |

## ENGLAND v N IRELAND

Played 98; England won 75; Ireland 7; drawn 16 Goals: England 323, Ireland 81

| Year | Venue | E | I |
|---|---|---|---|
| 1882 | Belfast | 13 | 0 |
| 1883 | Aigburth, Liverpool | 7 | 0 |
| 1884 | Belfast | 8 | 1 |
| 1885 | Whalley Range | 4 | 0 |
| 1886 | Belfast | 6 | 1 |
| 1887 | Bramall Lane | 7 | 0 |
| 1888 | Belfast | 5 | 1 |
| 1889 | Goodison Park | 6 | 1 |
| 1890 | Belfast | 9 | 1 |
| 1891 | Wolverhampton | 6 | 1 |
| 1892 | Belfast | 2 | 0 |
| 1893 | Perry Barr | 6 | 1 |
| 1894 | Belfast | 2 | 2 |
| 1895 | Derby | 9 | 0 |
| 1896 | Belfast | 2 | 0 |
| 1897 | Nottingham | 6 | 0 |
| 1898 | Belfast | 3 | 2 |
| 1899 | Sunderland | 13 | 2 |
| 1900 | Dublin | 2 | 0 |
| 1901 | Southampton | 3 | 0 |
| 1902 | Belfast | 1 | 0 |
| 1903 | Wolverhampton | 4 | 0 |
| 1904 | Belfast | 3 | 1 |
| 1905 | Middlesbrough | 1 | 1 |
| 1906 | Belfast | 5 | 0 |
| 1907 | Goodison Park | 1 | 0 |
| 1908 | Belfast | 3 | 1 |
| 1909 | Bradford PA | 4 | 0 |
| 1910 | Belfast | 1 | 1 |
| 1911 | Derby | 2 | 1 |
| 1912 | Dublin | 6 | 1 |
| 1913 | Belfast | 1 | 2 |
| 1914 | Middlesbrough | 0 | 3 |
| 1919 | Belfast | 1 | 1 |
| 1920 | Sunderland | 2 | 0 |
| 1921 | Belfast | 1 | 1 |
| 1922 | West Bromwich | 2 | 0 |
| 1923 | Belfast | 1 | 2 |
| 1924 | Goodison Park | 3 | 1 |
| 1925 | Belfast | 0 | 0 |
| 1926 | Anfield | 3 | 3 |
| 1927 | Belfast | 0 | 2 |
| 1928 | Goodison Park | 2 | 1 |
| 1929 | Belfast | 3 | 0 |
| 1930 | Bramall Lane | 5 | 1 |
| 1931 | Belfast | 6 | 2 |
| 1932 | Blackpool | 1 | 0 |
| 1933 | Belfast | 3 | 0 |
| 1935 | Goodison Park | 2 | 1 |
| 1935 | Belfast | 3 | 1 |
| 1936 | Stoke | 3 | 1 |
| 1937 | Belfast | 5 | 1 |
| 1938 | Old Trafford | 7 | 0 |
| 1946 | Belfast | 7 | 2 |
| 1947 | Goodison Park | 2 | 2 |
| 1948 | Belfast | 6 | 2 |
| 1949 | Maine Road (WC) | 9 | 2 |
| 1950 | Belfast | 4 | 1 |
| 1951 | Villa Park | 2 | 0 |
| 1952 | Belfast | 2 | 2 |
| 1953 | Goodison Park (WC) | 3 | 1 |
| 1954 | Belfast | 2 | 0 |
| 1955 | Wembley | 3 | 0 |
| 1956 | Belfast | 1 | 1 |
| 1957 | Wembley | 2 | 3 |
| 1958 | Belfast | 3 | 3 |
| 1959 | Wembley | 2 | 1 |
| 1960 | Belfast | 5 | 2 |
| 1961 | Wembley | 1 | 1 |
| 1962 | Belfast | 3 | 1 |
| 1963 | Wembley | 8 | 3 |
| 1964 | Belfast | 4 | 3 |
| 1965 | Wembley | 2 | 1 |
| 1966 | Belfast (EC) | 2 | 0 |
| 1967 | Wembley (EC) | 2 | 0 |
| 1969 | Belfast | 3 | 1 |
| 1970 | Wembley | 3 | 1 |
| 1971 | Belfast | 1 | 0 |
| 1972 | Wembley | 0 | 1 |
| 1973 | *Goodison Park | 2 | 1 |
| 1974 | Wembley | 1 | 0 |
| 1975 | Belfast | 0 | 0 |
| 1976 | Wembley | 4 | 0 |
| 1977 | Belfast | 2 | 1 |
| 1978 | Wembley | 1 | 0 |
| 1979 | Wembley (EC) | 4 | 0 |
| 1979 | Belfast | 2 | 0 |
| 1979 | Belfast (EC) | 5 | 1 |
| 1980 | Wembley | 1 | 1 |
| 1982 | Wembley | 4 | 0 |
| 1983 | Belfast | 0 | 0 |
| 1984 | Wembley | 1 | 0 |
| 1985 | Belfast (WC) | 1 | 0 |
| 1985 | Wembley (WC) | 0 | 0 |
| 1986 | Wembley (EC) | 3 | 0 |
| 1987 | Belfast (EC) | 2 | 0 |
| 2005 | Old Trafford (WC) | 4 | 0 |
| 2005 | Belfast (WC) | 0 | 1 |

(*Switched from Belfast because of political situation)

## SCOTLAND v WALES

Played 107; Scotland won 61; Wales 23; drawn 23; Goals: Scotland 243, Wales 124

| Year | Venue | S | W |
|---|---|---|---|
| 1876 | Glasgow | 4 | 0 |
| 1877 | Wrexham | 2 | 0 |
| 1878 | Glasgow | 9 | 0 |
| 1879 | Wrexham | 3 | 0 |
| 1880 | Glasgow | 5 | 1 |
| 1881 | Wrexham | 5 | 1 |
| 1882 | Glasgow | 5 | 0 |
| 1883 | Wrexham | 3 | 0 |
| 1884 | Glasgow | 4 | 1 |
| 1885 | Wrexham | 8 | 1 |

| | | | |
|---|---|---|---|
| 1886 | Glasgow | 4 | 1 |
| 1887 | Wrexham | 2 | 0 |
| 1888 | Edinburgh | 5 | 1 |
| 1889 | Wrexham | 0 | 0 |
| 1890 | Paisley | 5 | 0 |
| 1891 | Wrexham | 4 | 3 |
| 1892 | Edinburgh | 6 | 1 |
| 1893 | Wrexham | 8 | 0 |
| 1894 | Kilmarnock | 5 | 2 |
| 1895 | Wrexham | 2 | 2 |
| 1896 | Dundee | 4 | 0 |
| 1897 | Wrexham | 2 | 2 |
| 1898 | Motherwell | 5 | 2 |
| 1899 | Wrexham | 6 | 0 |
| 1900 | Aberdeen | 5 | 2 |
| 1901 | Wrexham | 1 | 1 |
| 1902 | Greenock | 5 | 1 |
| 1903 | Cardiff | 1 | 0 |
| 1904 | Dundee | 1 | 1 |
| 1905 | Wrexham | 1 | 3 |
| 1906 | Edinburgh | 0 | 2 |
| 1907 | Wrexham | 0 | 1 |
| 1908 | Dundee | 2 | 1 |
| 1909 | Wrexham | 2 | 3 |
| 1910 | Kilmarnock | 1 | 0 |
| 1911 | Cardiff | 2 | 2 |
| 1912 | Tynecastle | 1 | 0 |
| 1913 | Wrexham | 0 | 0 |
| 1914 | Glasgow | 0 | 0 |
| 1920 | Cardiff | 1 | 1 |
| 1921 | Aberdeen | 2 | 1 |
| 1922 | Wrexham | 1 | 2 |
| 1923 | Paisley | 2 | 0 |
| 1924 | Cardiff | 0 | 2 |
| 1925 | Tynecastle | 3 | 1 |
| 1926 | Cardiff | 3 | 0 |
| 1927 | Glasgow | 3 | 0 |
| 1928 | Wrexham | 2 | 2 |
| 1929 | Glasgow | 4 | 2 |
| 1930 | Cardiff | 4 | 2 |
| 1931 | Glasgow | 1 | 1 |
| 1932 | Wrexham | 3 | 2 |
| 1933 | Edinburgh | 2 | 5 |
| 1934 | Cardiff | 2 | 3 |
| 1935 | Aberdeen | 3 | 2 |
| 1936 | Cardiff | 1 | 1 |
| 1937 | Dundee | 1 | 2 |
| 1938 | Cardiff | 1 | 2 |
| 1939 | Edinburgh | 3 | 2 |
| 1946 | Wrexham | 1 | 3 |
| 1947 | Glasgow | 1 | 2 |
| 1948 | Cardiff (WC) | 3 | 1 |
| 1949 | Glasgow | 2 | 0 |
| 1950 | Cardiff | 3 | 1 |
| 1951 | Glasgow | 0 | 1 |
| 1952 | Cardiff (WC) | 2 | 1 |
| 1953 | Glasgow | 3 | 3 |
| 1954 | Cardiff | 1 | 0 |
| 1955 | Glasgow | 2 | 0 |
| 1956 | Cardiff | 2 | 2 |
| 1957 | Glasgow | 1 | 1 |
| 1958 | Cardiff | 3 | 0 |
| 1959 | Glasgow | 1 | 1 |
| 1960 | Cardiff | 0 | 2 |
| 1961 | Glasgow | 2 | 0 |
| 1962 | Cardiff | 3 | 2 |
| 1963 | Glasgow | 2 | 1 |
| 1964 | Cardiff | 2 | 3 |
| 1965 | Glasgow (EC) | 4 | 1 |
| 1966 | Cardiff (EC) | 1 | 1 |
| 1967 | Glasgow | 3 | 2 |
| 1969 | Wrexham | 5 | 3 |
| 1970 | Glasgow | 0 | 0 |
| 1971 | Cardiff | 0 | 0 |
| 1972 | Glasgow | 1 | 0 |
| 1973 | Wrexham | 2 | 0 |
| 1974 | Glasgow | 2 | 0 |
| 1975 | Cardiff | 2 | 2 |
| 1976 | Glasgow | 3 | 1 |
| 1977 | Glasgow (WC) | 1 | 0 |
| 1977 | Wrexham | 0 | 0 |
| 1977 | Anfield (WC) | 2 | 0 |
| 1978 | Glasgow | 1 | 1 |
| 1979 | Cardiff | 0 | 3 |
| 1980 | Glasgow | 1 | 0 |
| 1981 | Swansea | 0 | 2 |
| 1982 | Glasgow | 1 | 0 |
| 1983 | Cardiff | 2 | 0 |
| 1984 | Glasgow | 2 | 1 |
| 1985 | Glasgow (WC) | 0 | 1 |
| 1985 | Cardiff (WC) | 1 | 1 |
| 1997 | Kilmarnock | 0 | 1 |
| 2004 | Cardiff | 0 | 4 |
| 2009 | Cardiff | 0 | 3 |
| 2011 | Dublin (CC) | 3 | 1 |
| 2012 | Cardiff (WC) | 1 | 2 |
| 2013 | Glasgow (WC | 1 | 2 |

## SCOTLAND v NORTHERN IRELAND

Played 96; Scotland won 64; Northern Ireland 15; drawn 17; Goals: Scotland 258, Northern Ireland 80

| | | | |
|---|---|---|---|
| 1884 | Belfast | 5 | 0 |
| 1885 | Glasgow | 8 | 2 |
| 1886 | Belfast | 7 | 2 |
| 1887 | Belfast | 4 | 1 |
| 1888 | Belfast | 10 | 2 |
| 1889 | Glasgow | 7 | 0 |
| 1890 | Belfast | 4 | 1 |
| 1891 | Glasgow | 2 | 1 |
| 1892 | Belfast | 3 | 2 |
| 1893 | Glasgow | 6 | 1 |
| 1894 | Belfast | 2 | 1 |
| 1895 | Glasgow | 3 | 1 |
| 1896 | Belfast | 3 | 3 |
| 1897 | Glasgow | 5 | 1 |
| 1898 | Belfast | 3 | 0 |
| 1899 | Glasgow | 9 | 1 |
| 1900 | Belfast | 3 | 0 |
| 1901 | Glasgow | 11 | 0 |
| 1902 | Belfast | 5 | 1 |
| 1902 | Belfast | 3 | 0 |
| 1903 | Glasgow | 0 | 2 |
| 1904 | Dublin | 1 | 1 |

| | | | |
|---|---|---|---|
| 1905 | Glasgow | 4 | 0 |
| 1906 | Dublin | 1 | 0 |
| 1907 | Glasgow | 3 | 0 |
| 1908 | Dublin | 5 | 0 |
| 1909 | Glasgow | 5 | 0 |
| 1910 | Belfast | 0 | 1 |
| 1911 | Glasgow | 2 | 0 |
| 1912 | Belfast | 4 | 1 |
| 1913 | Dublin | 2 | 1 |
| 1914 | Belfast | 1 | 1 |
| 1920 | Glasgow | 3 | 0 |
| 1921 | Belfast | 2 | 0 |
| 1922 | Glasgow | 2 | 1 |
| 1923 | Belfast | 1 | 0 |
| 1924 | Glasgow | 2 | 0 |
| 1925 | Belfast | 3 | 0 |
| 1926 | Glasgow | 4 | 0 |
| 1927 | Belfast | 2 | 0 |
| 1928 | Glasgow | 0 | 1 |
| 1929 | Belfast | 7 | 3 |
| 1930 | Glasgow | 3 | 1 |
| 1931 | Belfast | 0 | 0 |
| 1932 | Glasgow | 3 | 1 |
| 1933 | Belfast | 4 | 0 |
| 1934 | Glasgow | 1 | 2 |
| 1935 | Belfast | 1 | 2 |
| 1936 | Edinburgh | 2 | 1 |
| 1937 | Belfast | 3 | 1 |
| 1938 | Aberdeen | 1 | 1 |
| 1939 | Belfast | 2 | 0 |
| 1946 | Glasgow | 0 | 0 |
| 1947 | Belfast | 0 | 2 |
| 1948 | Glasgow | 3 | 2 |
| 1949 | Belfast | 8 | 2 |
| 1950 | Glasgow | 6 | 1 |
| 1951 | Belfast | 3 | 0 |
| 1952 | Glasgow | 1 | 1 |
| 1953 | Belfast | 3 | 1 |
| 1954 | Glasgow | 2 | 2 |
| 1955 | Belfast | 1 | 2 |
| 1956 | Glasgow | 1 | 0 |
| 1957 | Belfast | 1 | 1 |
| 1958 | Glasgow | 2 | 2 |
| 1959 | Belfast | 4 | 0 |
| 1960 | Glasgow | 5 | 1 |
| 1961 | Belfast | 6 | 1 |
| 1962 | Glasgow | 5 | 1 |
| 1963 | Belfast | 1 | 2 |
| 1964 | Glasgow | 3 | 2 |
| 1965 | Belfast | 2 | 3 |
| 1966 | Glasgow | 2 | 1 |
| 1967 | Belfast | 0 | 1 |
| 1969 | Glasgow | 1 | 1 |
| 1970 | Belfast | 1 | 0 |
| 1971 | Glasgow | 0 | 1 |
| 1972 | Glasgow | 2 | 0 |
| 1973 | Glasgow | 1 | 2 |
| 1974 | Glasgow | 0 | 1 |
| 1975 | Glasgow | 3 | 0 |
| 1976 | Glasgow | 3 | 0 |
| 1977 | Glasgow | 3 | 0 |
| 1978 | Glasgow | 1 | 1 |
| 1979 | Glasgow | 1 | 0 |
| 1980 | Belfast | 0 | 1 |
| 1981 | Glasgow (WC) | 1 | 1 |
| 1981 | Glasgow | 2 | 0 |
| 1981 | Belfast (WC) | 0 | 0 |
| 1982 | Belfast | 1 | 1 |
| 1983 | Glasgow | 0 | 0 |
| 1984 | Belfast | 0 | 2 |
| 1992 | Glasgow | 1 | 0 |
| 2008 | Glasgow | 0 | 0 |
| 2011 | Dublin (CC) | 3 | 0 |
| 2015 | Glasgow | 1 | 0 |

## WALES v NORTHERN IRELAND

Played 97; Wales won 45; Northern Ireland won 27; drawn 25; Goals: Wales 191 Northern Ireland 132

| | | W | I |
|---|---|---|---|
| 1882 | Wrexham | 7 | 1 |
| 1883 | Belfast | 1 | 1 |
| 1884 | Wrexham | 6 | 0 |
| 1885 | Belfast | 8 | 2 |
| 1886 | Wrexham | 5 | 0 |
| 1887 | Belfast | 1 | 4 |
| 1888 | Wrexham | 11 | 0 |
| 1889 | Belfast | 3 | 1 |
| 1890 | Shrewsbury | 5 | 2 |
| 1891 | Belfast | 2 | 7 |
| 1892 | Bangor | 1 | 1 |
| 1893 | Belfast | 3 | 4 |
| 1894 | Swansea | 4 | 1 |
| 1895 | Belfast | 2 | 2 |
| 1896 | Wrexham | 6 | 1 |
| 1897 | Belfast | 3 | 4 |
| 1898 | Llandudno | 0 | 1 |
| 1899 | Belfast | 0 | 1 |
| 1900 | Llandudno | 2 | 0 |
| 1901 | Belfast | 1 | 0 |
| 1902 | Cardiff | 0 | 3 |
| 1903 | Belfast | 0 | 2 |
| 1904 | Bangor | 0 | 1 |
| 1905 | Belfast | 2 | 2 |
| 1906 | Wrexham | 4 | 4 |
| 1907 | Belfast | 3 | 2 |
| 1908 | Aberdare | 0 | 1 |
| 1909 | Belfast | 3 | 2 |
| 1910 | Wrexham | 4 | 1 |
| 1911 | Belfast | 2 | 1 |
| 1912 | Cardiff | 2 | 3 |
| 1913 | Belfast | 1 | 0 |
| 1914 | Wrexham | 1 | 2 |
| 1920 | Belfast | 2 | 2 |
| 1921 | Swansea | 2 | 1 |
| 1922 | Belfast | 1 | 1 |
| 1923 | Wrexham | 0 | 3 |
| 1924 | Belfast | 1 | 0 |
| 1925 | Wrexham | 0 | 0 |
| 1926 | Belfast | 0 | 3 |
| 1927 | Cardiff | 2 | 2 |
| 1928 | Belfast | 2 | 1 |
| 1929 | Wrexham | 2 | 2 |
| 1930 | Belfast | 0 | 7 |

| | | | |
|---|---|---|---|
| 1931 | Wrexham | 3 | 2 |
| 1932 | Belfast | 0 | 4 |
| 1933 | Wrexham | 4 | 1 |
| 1934 | Belfast | 1 | 1 |
| 1935 | Wrexham | 3 | 1 |
| 1936 | Belfast | 2 | 3 |
| 1937 | Wrexham | 4 | 1 |
| 1938 | Belfast | 0 | 1 |
| 1939 | Wrexham | 3 | 1 |
| 1947 | Belfast | 1 | 2 |
| 1948 | Wrexham | 2 | 0 |
| 1949 | Belfast | 2 | 0 |
| 1950 | Wrexham (WC) | 0 | 0 |
| 1951 | Belfast | 2 | 1 |
| 1952 | Swansea | 3 | 0 |
| 1953 | Belfast | 3 | 2 |
| 1954 | Wrexham (WC) | 1 | 2 |
| 1955 | Belfast | 3 | 2 |
| 1956 | Cardiff | 1 | 1 |
| 1957 | Belfast | 0 | 0 |
| 1958 | Cardiff | 1 | 1 |
| 1959 | Belfast | 1 | 4 |
| 1960 | Wrexham | 3 | 2 |
| 1961 | Belfast | 5 | 1 |
| 1962 | Cardiff | 4 | 0 |
| 1963 | Belfast | 4 | 1 |
| 1964 | Swansea | 2 | 3 |
| 1965 | Belfast | 5 | 0 |
| 1966 | Cardiff | 1 | 4 |
| 1967 | Belfast (EC) | 0 | 0 |
| 1968 | Wrexham (EC) | 2 | 0 |
| 1969 | Belfast | 0 | 0 |
| 1970 | Swansea | 1 | 0 |
| 1971 | Belfast | 0 | 1 |
| 1972 | Wrexham | 0 | 0 |
| 1973 | *Goodison Park | 0 | 1 |
| 1974 | Wrexham | 1 | 0 |
| 1975 | Belfast | 0 | 1 |
| 1976 | Swansea | 1 | 0 |
| 1977 | Belfast | 1 | 1 |
| 1978 | Wrexham | 1 | 0 |
| 1979 | Belfast | 1 | 1 |
| 1980 | Cardiff | 0 | 1 |
| 1982 | Wrexham | 3 | 0 |
| 1983 | Belfast | 1 | 0 |
| 1984 | Swansea | 1 | 1 |
| 2004 | Cardiff (WC) | 2 | 2 |
| 2005 | Belfast (WC) | 3 | 2 |
| 2007 | Belfast | 0 | 0 |
| 2008 | Glasgow | 0 | 0 |
| 2011 | Dublin (CC) | 2 | 0 |
| 2016 | Cardiff | 1 | 1 |
| 2016 | Paris (EC) | 1 | 0 |

(*Switched from Belfast because of political situation)

# THE THINGS THEY SAY...

'If I say what I think I would pay the biggest fine in world football' – **Jurgen Klopp**, Liverpool manager, on the decision to award Tottenham a stoppage-time, point-saving penalty at Anfield.

'It's going to be a new dawn for the club' – **Shaun Derry**, Cambridge manager, on businessman Paul Barry becoming owner.

'Cambridge United can confirm that Shaun Derry will be leaving the club by mutual consent' – club statement the following day issued minutes after a goalless draw with Lincoln.

'I've been called many things in my career, but never a peacemaker' – **Peter Reid**, Wigan coach, who stepped in to separate managers Pep Guardiola and Paul Cook during Wigan's shock FA Cup win over Manchester City.

'Antonio Conte summed it up by saying "You always have a bag packed." I've got a bag-and-a-half packed' – **Alan Pardew** before his sacking as West Bromwich Albion manager.

'This is not pressure. Pressure is in Syria and Afghanistan, those kind of situations' – **Carlos Carvalhal** putting Swansea's bid to escape relegation into perspective.

'Some of the aggression was so strong it went back to the bad old days of 25 years ago' – **Sir Trevor Brooking** on the violence and abuse which broke out at London Stadium during West Ham's 3-0 defeat by Burnley and left the club legend sitting alone in the directors' box.

# UEFA NATIONS LEAGUE 2018–19

International football in Europe will have a new look in the new season. Most friendlies are being replaced by the UEFA Nations League featuring the four home countries, along with the Republic of Ireland and 50 other teams. The governing body's aim is to have more meaningful competition in the years when there is no World Cup or European Championship. Home and away games will be played between September and November 2018, with the top-seeded league, which includes England, producing four section winners to go through to the final stages from June 5-9, 2019. There will be two semi-finals, a third-place match and a final, all to be staged by one country, still to be chosen. Wales, Northern Ireland and the Republic compete in the second-seeded league and Scotland in the third. The three winners of each of B, C and D groups will be promoted; the bottom-placed sides in A, B and C relegated. This means that qualifying for Euro 2020 starts in March 2019, instead of following on from the World Cup in Russia. Four countries will qualify via the Nations League, along with the winners and runners-up of the standard ten groups. The Euro finals will also have a new look, with 12 different countries staging matches. Wembley's allocation has been increased from three to seven games because Belgium's proposed new national stadium in Brussels never got off the ground. In addition to both semi-finals and the final, Wembley will now host three group fixtures and one in the last 16. Hampden Park and Dublin's Aviva Stadium both have three group games and one in the last 16. Other countries involved are Azerbaijan (Baku), Denmark (Copenhagen), Germany (Munich), Holland (Amsterdam), Hungary (Budapest), Italy (Rome), Romania (Bucharest), Russia (St Petersburg) and Spain (Bilbao). There will be no automatic qualification. Draw for qualifying is on December 2, 2018.

## NATIONS LEAGUE LINE-UP

**LEAGUE A**
**Group 1:** France, Germany, Holland. **Group 2**: Belgium, Iceland, Switzerland. **Group 3**: Italy, Poland, Portugal. **Group 4**: England, Croatia, Spain

**LEAGUE B**
**Group 1**: Czech Republic, Slovakia, Ukraine. **Group 2**: Russia, Sweden, Turkey. **Group 3**: Austria, Bosnia Herzegovina, Northern Ireland. **Group 4**: Denmark, Republic of Ireland, Wales

**LEAGUE C**
**Group 1**: Albania, Israel, Scotland. **Group 2**: Estonia, Finland, Greece, Hungary. **Group 3**: Bulgaria, Cyprus, Norway, Slovenia. **Group 4**: Lithuania, Montenegro, Romania, Serbia.

**LEAGUE D**
**Group 1**: Andorra, Georgia, Kazakhstan, Latvia. **Group 2**: Belarus, Luxembourg, Moldova, San Marino. **Group 3**: Azerbaijan, Faroe Islands, Kosovo, Malta. **Group 4**: Armenia, Gibraltar, Liechtenstein, Macedonia

# BRITISH AND IRISH UNDER-21 INTERNATIONALS 2017–18

## EUROPEAN CHAMPIONSHIP 2019 QUALIFYING

### GROUP TWO

**NORTHERN IRELAND 1 ALBANIA 0**
**Mourneview Park, Lurgan (234); August 31, 2017**

**Northern Ireland**: Mitchell, Donnelly, Dummigan, Johnson, McDermott, Gorman, Thompson, B Doherty, Dunwoody (Kennedy 63), Parkhouse (McGonigle 77), Smyth. **Booked**: Johnson, McDermott, Gorman

**Scorer – Northern Ireland**: Donnelly (90+5). **Half-time**: 0-0

**SLOVAKIA 1 NORTHERN IRELAND 0**
**Senica (2,339); September 5, 2017**

**Northern Ireland**: Mitchell, Donnelly, Dummigan, Johnson, Hall, Gorman (Gordon 57), Kennedy, Thompson, B Doherty (McDonagh 78), Owens, Smyth (Parkhouse 78). **Booked**: Donnelly, Gorman, Thompson, Doherty

**Scorer – Slovakia**: Benes (61). **Half-time**: 0-0

**NORTHERN IRELAND 4 ESTONIA 2**
**Mourneview Park, Lurgan (463); October 10, 2017**

**Northern Ireland**: Mitchell, Donnelly, Dummigan, Johnson, B Doherty, Gorman (Paul 58) Thompson (Owens 81), Sykes, McDonagh, Parkhouse, Kennedy (Smyth 75). **Booked**: Donnelly, Parkhouse

**Scorers – Northern Ireland**: Johnson (2), Gorman (43), Sykes (61), Igonen (75 og). **Estonia**: Lilvak (11), Sappinen (20). **Half-time**: 2-2

**ALBANIA 1 NORTHERN IRELAND 1**
**Tirana (1,250); November 10, 2017**

**Northern Ireland**: Mitchell, Donnelly, Dummigan, Johnson, J Doherty (B Doherty 67), Gorman McDonagh, Thompson (McGonigle 86), Sykes, Parkhouse, Smyth (Lavery 75). **Booked**: Sykes, Gorman, Johnson, Smyth, McDonagh

**Scorers – Albania**: Ramadani (83). **Northern Ireland**: Lavery (89). **Half-time**: 0-0

**NORTHERN IRELAND 3 SPAIN 5**
**Shamrock Park, Portadown (2,309); March 22, 2018**

**Northern Ireland**: Mitchell, Dummigan (Paul 44), McDermott, Donnelly, Hall, Johnson, Thompson, Sykes, Whyte (Kennedy 70), Smyth, Lavery (McDonagh 80). **Booked**: Thompson, Smyth

**Scorers – Northern Ireland**: Donnelly (30 pen, 45), Lavery (68). **Spain**: Oyarzabal (15, 44), Mayoral (47, 75, 84). **Half-time**: 2-2

**NORTHERN IRELAND 0 ICELAND 0**
**Coleraine Showgrounds (1,088); March 26, 2018**

**Northern Ireland**: Peacock-Farrell, McDonagh, Hall, Donnelly, Johnson, Thompson, Burns, Gorman, Whyte, Lavery, Kennedy (Sykes 82). **Booked**: Kennedy, Gorman, Thompson

### GROUP FOUR

**HOLLAND 1 ENGLAND 1**
**Doetinchem (5,211); September 1, 2017**

**England**: Gunn, Kenny, Gomez, Fry, Chilwell, Cook, Onomah, Lookman, Solanke (Palmer, 71), Dowell (Gray 71), Calvert-Lewin (Abraham 76). **Booked**: Gomez

**Scorers – Holland**: Ramselaar (31). **England**: Calvert-Lewin (20). **Half-time**: 1-1

**ENGLAND 3 LATVIA 0**
**Vitality Stadium, Bournemouth (8,514); September 5, 2017**

**England**: Woodman, Alexander-Arnold, Gomez, Tomori, Walker-Peters, Davies, Cook, Ojo (Lookman 59), Palmer (Solanke 70), Gray, Abraham (Calvert-Lewin 68). **Booked**: Walker-Peters
**Scorers – England**: Gray (13), Abraham (35), Palmer (70). **Half-time**: 2-0

**SCOTLAND 2 HOLLAND 0**
**Paisley Stadium (2,474); September 5, 2017**

**Scotland**: Fulton, Ralston, Taylor, Souttar, McKenna, Wilson, Burke (Archibald 85), Morgan, Mallan (Wright 80), Thomas (McCrorie 72), Cadden. **Booked**: Mallan
**Scorers – Scotland**: Burke (62), Mallan (79). **Half-time**: 0-0

**ENGLAND 3 SCOTLAND 1**
**Riverside Stadium, Middlesbrough (20,126); October 6, 2017**

**England**: Gunn, Alexander-Arnold, Gomez, Fry, Walker-Peters, Cook, Onomah, Gray (Kenny 70), Solanke (Lookman 83), Calvert-Lewin, Abraham (Harrison 89)
**Scotland**: Fulton, Smith, Taylor, Souttar, McKenna, Burke (McBurnie 46), Morgan, Mallan (Docherty 82), Thomas (Williamson 67), Cadden, Campbell
**Scorers – England**: Onomah (14), Abraham (49 pen), Solanke (79). **Scotland**: Cadden (78). **Half-time**: 1-0

**ANDORRA 0 ENGLAND 1**
**La Vella (457); October 10, 2017**

**England**: Gunn, Kenny, Tomori, Worrall, Walker-Peters, Lookman, Maitland-Niles (Cook 76), Davies, Harrison (Gray 71), Calvert-Lewin (Solanke 79), Dowell. **Booked**: Maitland-Niles
**Scorer – England**: Davies (53). **Half-time**: 0-0

**LATVIA 0 SCOTLAND 2**
**Liepaja (826); October 10, 2017**

**Scotland**: Fulton, Smith, Taylor, Souttar, McKenna, Burke (Williamson 79), McBurnie (Hardie 85) Morgan, Thomas (McCrorie 66), Cadden, Campbell. **Booked**: Campbell, Burke
**Scorers– Scotland**: Burke (16), McBurnie (19). **Half-time**: 0-2

**UKRAINE 0 ENGLAND 2**
**Kiev (2,520); November 10, 2017**

**England**: Gunn, Kenny, Tomori, Worrall, Walker-Peters, Cook, Maitland-Niles (Tuanzebe 56), Gray, Lookman, Dowell (Calvert-Lewin 56), Solanke (Maddison 81). **Booked**: Cook
**Scorers – England**: Solanke (16), Lukianchuk (62 og). **Half-time**: 0-1

**SCOTLAND 1 LATVIA 1**
**McDiarmid Park, Perth (1,449); November 10, 2017**

**Scotland**: Fulton, Smith (Hardie 64), Taylor, Souttar (McCrorie 68), McKenna, McBurnie, Morgan, Wright (Thomas 86), Mallan, Cadden, Campbell. **Booked**: McKenna, McBurnie
**Scorers – Scotland**: Hardie (90+3 pen). **Latvia**: Ukldrikis (45). **Half-time**: 0-1

**SCOTLAND 0 UKRAINE 2**
**McDiarmid Park, Perth (1,138); November 14, 2017**

**Scotland**: Fulton, Smith (Hardie 71), Taylor, McCrorie, McKenna, McBurnie (Wright 7), Morgan, Thomas (Williamson 55), Mallan, Cadden, Campbell. **Booked**: McKenna
**Scorers – Ukraine**: Boryachuck (45), Kovalenk (90+4)

**ANDORRA 1 SCOTLAND 1**
**La Vella (554); March 23, 2018**

**Scotland**: Fulton, Cadden, Souttar, Kerr, Taylor, Campbell, Burke (Wright 81), Docherty (Brophy 53), Mallan (Smith 61), Morgan, Hardie. **Booked**: Souttar, Smith
**Scorers – Andorra**: Fernandez (77 pen). **Scotland**: Morgan (90+1). **Half-time**: 0-0

**ENGLAND 2 UKRAINE 1**
**Bramall Lane, Sheffield (22,601); March 27, 2018**

**England**: Gunn, Kenny, Fry, Worrall, Chilwell, Gray (Lookman 73), Davies, Onomah, Sessegnon, Maddison (Solanke 77), Calvert-Lewin (Maitland-Niles 90+1). **Booked**: Onomah
**Scorers – England**: Calvert-Lewin (41), Solanke (88). **Ukraine**: Shaparenko (83). **Half-time**: 1-0

## GROUP FIVE

**AZERBAIJAN 1 REPUBLIC OF IRELAND 3**
**Baku (213); September 5, 2017**

**Republic of Ireland**: O'Hara, Kane (Delaney 90+2), Whelan, Donnellan, Sweeney, Cullen, Rice, Charsley (Kinsella 90+3), Grego-Cox (Quigley 88), Manning, Curtis. **Booked**: Sweeney
**Scorers – Azerbaijan**: Medetov (12). **Republic of Ireland**: Manning (9, 37), Grego-Cox (51). **Half-time**: 1-2

**REPUBLIC OF IRELAND 0 NORWAY 0**
**Tallaght Stadium, Dublin (803); October 5, 2017**

**Republic of Ireland**: O'Hara, Kane, Whelan, Donnellan, Sweeney, Cullen, Rice, Charsley, Grego-Cox, Manning (Ronan 87), Curtis. **Booked**: Curtis

**REPUBLIC OF IRELAND 4 ISRAEL 0**
**Tallaght Stadium, Dublin (371); October 9, 2017**

**Republic of Ireland**: O'Hara, Kane, Whelan, Donnellan, Sweeney, Cullen, Rice (Shaughnessy 77), Charsley (Quigley 80), Grego-Cox (Mulraney 69), Manning, Curtis. **Booked**: Whelan, Rice
**Scorers – Republic of Ireland**: Grego-Cox (1, 38 pen, 51), Charsley (35). **Half-time**: 3-0

**NORWAY 2 REPUBLIC OF IRELAND 1**
**Drammen (876); November 14, 2017**

**Republic of Ireland**: O'Hara, Kane, Whelan, Donnellan, Sweeney, Cullen, Rice, Charsley, Curtis, Manning (Ronan 85), Mulraney. **Booked**: Curtis, Sweeney, O'Hara
**Scorers – Norway**: Odegaard (18), Fossum (90+1). **Republic of Ireland**: Mulraney (32). **Half-time**: 1-1

**REPUBLIC OF IRELAND 1 AZERBAIJAN 0**
**Tallaght Stadium, Dublin (500); March 27, 2018**

**Republic of Ireland**: O'Hara, Kane, (Ronan Hale 82), Donnellan, Sweeney, Whelan, Cullen, Rice, Manning, Mulraney (Shodipo 56), Grego-Cox, Curtis (Quigley, 89). **Booked**: Manning, Donnellan
**Scorer – Republic of Ireland**: Donnellan (90-9). **Half-time**: 0-0

## GROUP EIGHT

**SWITZERLAND 0 WALES 3**
**Biel-Bienne (412); September 1, 2017**

**Wales**: Pilling, Coxe, Abbruzzese, Poole, Rodon, Mepham, Thomas, Smith, Roberts (Harris 83), Brooks (Evans 90+2), James (Broadhead 65). **Booked**: Thomas, Coxe, Brooks
**Scorers – Wales**: Roberts (7), Brooks (27), Thomas (90+1). **Half-time**: 0-2

**PORTUGAL 2 WALES 0**
**Chaves (7,111); September 5, 2017**

**Wales**: Pilling, Coxe, Abbruzzese, Poole, Rodon, Mepham, Thomas, Smith (Evans 59), Roberts (Broadhead 67), Brooks, James (Harris 46). **Booked**: Mepham. **Sent off**: Mepham (82)
**Scorers – Portugal**: Neves (25), Guedes (41). **Half-time**: 2-0

**LIECHTENSTEIN 1 WALES 3**
**Eschen (278); October 5, 2017**

**Wales**: Pilling, Coxe, Abbruzzese, Poole, Rodon, Harries, Thomas, Smith (Evans 85), Roberts, Broadhead (Harris 74), Morrell (Matondo 85). **Booked**: Harries

**Scorers – Liechtenstein**: Kardesoglu (57). **Wales**: Thomas (24, 31 pen), Smith (52). **Half-time**: 0-2

**WALES 0 BOSNIA-HERZEGOVINA 4**
**Bangor University Stadium (1,041); November 10, 2017**

**Wales**: Pilling, Poole, Dasilva (Norrington-Davies 46), Coxe, Rodon, Mepham, Thomas (Matondo 62), Wilson, Smith, Roberts, Harris (Broadhead 72). **Booked**: Rodon, Coxe, Smith
**Scorers – Bosnia-Herzegovina**: Gojak (26, 51), Cavar (71), Menado (77): **Half-time**: 0-1

**WALES 0 ROMANIA 0**
**Bangor University Stadium (916); November 14, 2017**

**Wales**: Pilling, Harries, Poole, Coxe, Mepham, Norrington-Davies, Thomas, Wilson, Evans (Smith 90+1), Roberts, Harris (Matondo 79). **Booked**: Roberts, Norrington-Davies, Evans

**BOSNIA-HERZEGOVINA 1 WALES 0**
**Zenica (810); March 23, 2018**

**Wales**: Pilling, Coxe, Poole, Rodon, Harries, Thomas (Matondo 79), Evans, Harris, Brooks, Morrell (James 64), Lewis. **Booked**: Harries, Brooks
**Scorer – Bosnia-Herzegovina**: Todorovic (65). **Half-time**: 0-0

## QUALIFYING TABLES

(Group winners qualify for finals; four best runners-up to two play-off matches to determine two more finalists; Italy qualify as joint hosts. San Marino, the other joint hosts, do not qualify automatically)

### GROUP 1

| | P | W | D | L | F | A | Pts |
|---|---|---|---|---|---|---|---|
| Greece | 7 | 6 | 1 | 0 | 22 | 2 | 19 |
| Croatia | 7 | 5 | 1 | 1 | 21 | 5 | 16 |
| Belarus | 6 | 3 | 1 | 2 | 8 | 6 | 10 |
| Czech Rep | 6 | 3 | 1 | 2 | 10 | 12 | 10 |
| Moldova | 7 | 1 | 0 | 6 | 5 | 20 | 3 |
| San Marino | 7 | 0 | 0 | 7 | 1 | 22 | 0 |

### GROUP 2

| | P | W | D | L | F | A | Pts |
|---|---|---|---|---|---|---|---|
| Spain | 6 | 6 | 0 | 0 | 19 | 6 | 18 |
| Slovakia | 7 | 4 | 0 | 3 | 12 | 15 | 12 |
| **Northern Ireland** | 7 | 3 | 2 | 2 | 11 | 10 | 11 |
| Iceland | 6 | 2 | 2 | 2 | 7 | 6 | 8 |
| Albania | 7 | 1 | 3 | 3 | 7 | 11 | 6 |
| Estonia | 7 | 0 | 1 | 6 | 7 | 15 | 1 |

### GROUP 3

| | P | W | D | L | F | A | Pts |
|---|---|---|---|---|---|---|---|
| Poland | 6 | 4 | 2 | 0 | 14 | 6 | 14 |
| Denmark | 6 | 4 | 1 | 1 | 22 | 7 | 13 |
| Georgia | 7 | 2 | 2 | 3 | 9 | 15 | 8 |
| Finland | 5 | 1 | 3 | 1 | 8 | 11 | 6 |
| Faroe Is | 6 | 1 | 2 | 3 | 6 | 11 | 5 |
| Lithuania | 6 | 1 | 0 | 5 | 3 | 12 | 3 |

### GROUP 4

| | P | W | D | L | F | A | Pts |
|---|---|---|---|---|---|---|---|
| **England** | 6 | 5 | 1 | 0 | 12 | 3 | 16 |
| Holland | 6 | 3 | 2 | 1 | 14 | 4 | 11 |
| **Scotland** | 6 | 2 | 2 | 2 | 7 | 7 | 8 |
| Ukraine | 6 | 2 | 2 | 2 | 11 | 6 | 8 |
| Latvia | 6 | 0 | 3 | 3 | 2 | 10 | 3 |
| Andorra | 6 | 0 | 2 | 4 | 1 | 17 | 2 |

### GROUP 5

| | P | W | D | L | F | A | Pts |
|---|---|---|---|---|---|---|---|
| Germany | 7 | 5 | 1 | 1 | 23 | 6 | 16 |
| **Rep of Ireland** | 6 | 4 | 1 | 1 | 10 | 3 | 13 |
| Kosovo | 8 | 3 | 2 | 3 | 8 | 8 | 11 |
| Norway | 7 | 3 | 2 | 2 | 10 | 9 | 11 |
| Israel | 7 | 2 | 1 | 4 | 10 | 16 | 7 |
| Azerbaijan | 7 | 0 | 1 | 6 | 3 | 22 | 1 |

### GROUP 6

| | P | W | D | L | F | A | Pts |
|---|---|---|---|---|---|---|---|
| Belgium | 7 | 5 | 2 | 0 | 13 | 5 | 17 |
| Sweden | 6 | 4 | 2 | 0 | 14 | 4 | 14 |
| Hungary | 6 | 3 | 2 | 1 | 10 | 6 | 11 |
| Turkey | 7 | 2 | 2 | 3 | 7 | 9 | 8 |
| Cyprus | 8 | 2 | 0 | 6 | 7 | 18 | 6 |
| Malta | 6 | 0 | 0 | 6 | 5 | 14 | 0 |

### GROUP 7

| | P | W | D | L | F | A | Pts |
|---|---|---|---|---|---|---|---|
| Serbia | 6 | 6 | 0 | 0 | 19 | 3 | 18 |
| Russia | 7 | 5 | 1 | 1 | 17 | 7 | 16 |
| Austria | 6 | 4 | 0 | 2 | 15 | 4 | 12 |
| Armenia | 7 | 2 | 1 | 4 | 5 | 11 | 7 |
| Macedonia | 6 | 1 | 0 | 5 | 6 | 13 | 3 |
| Gibraltar | 8 | 1 | 0 | 7 | 1 | 25 | 3 |

## GROUP 8

| | | | | | | | |
|---|---|---|---|---|---|---|---|
| Bosnia-Herz | 7 | 5 | 0 | 2 | 19 | 5 | 15 |
| Portugal | 6 | 4 | 1 | 1 | 17 | 7 | 13 |
| Romania | 6 | 3 | 3 | 0 | 9 | 3 | 12 |
| Switzerland | 7 | 2 | 1 | 4 | 7 | 12 | 7 |
| **Wales** | 6 | 2 | 1 | 3 | 6 | 8 | 7 |
| Liechtenstein | 6 | 0 | 0 | 6 | 1 | 24 | 0 |

## GROUP 9

| | | | | | | | |
|---|---|---|---|---|---|---|---|
| France | 7 | 7 | 0 | 0 | 20 | 5 | 21 |
| Slovenia | 6 | 3 | 1 | 2 | 10 | 9 | 10 |
| Kazakhstan | 7 | 2 | 3 | 2 | 11 | 11 | 9 |
| Bulgaria | 6 | 2 | 2 | 2 | 9 | 8 | 8 |
| Luxembourg | 7 | 1 | 1 | 5 | 6 | 16 | 4 |
| Montenegro | 7 | 1 | 1 | 5 | 7 | 14 | 4 |

# TOULON TREBLE FOR ENGLAND

England's under-21 side displayed commendable powers of recovery to win the Toulon Tournament for the third successive year. They came from behind to defeat China 2-1 in the opening group match with goals from Middlesbrough's Dael Fry and Chelsea's Tammy Abraham. In the semi-finals, two by Eddie Nketiah (Arsenal) followed an equaliser from Callum Connolly (Everton) after Celtic's Michael Johnston put Scotland ahead. England also trailed to a second-minute Mexico goal in the final. But Fry took advantage of a goalkeeping mistake to level and Nketiah set up Everton's Kieran Dowell for the winner.

### GROUP A

| | P | W | D | L | F | A | Pts |
|---|---|---|---|---|---|---|---|
| Mexico Q | 3 | 2 | 1 | 0 | 7 | 2 | 7 |
| England Q | 3 | 2 | 1 | 0 | 6 | 1 | 7 |
| China | 3 | 0 | 1 | 2 | 3 | 6 | 1 |
| Qatar | 3 | 0 | 1 | 2 | 2 | 9 | 1 |

**Match-day 1**: England 2 (Fry 57, Abraham 85) China 1 (Yan Dinghao 20). **Match-day 2**: England 0 Mexico 0. **Match-day 3**: England 4 (Al Hamawende 38 og, Vieira 58, Abraham, 61, Armstrong 72) Qatar 0

### GROUP B

| | | | | | | | |
|---|---|---|---|---|---|---|---|
| Scotland Q | 3 | 2 | 1 | 0 | 4 | 2 | 7 |
| France | 3 | 2 | 0 | 1 | 6 | 2 | 6 |
| Togo | 3 | 1 | 1 | 1 | 3 | 4 | 4 |
| South Korea | 3 | 0 | 0 | 3 | 3 | 8 | 0 |

**Match-day 1**: Scotland 1 (Hornby 18) Togo 1 (Wogodo 3). **Match-day 2**: Scotland 1 (Burke 35) France 0. **Match-day 3**: Scotland 2 (Gilmour 2, Burke 8) South Korea 1 (Lee Kangin 76)

### GROUP C

| | | | | | | | |
|---|---|---|---|---|---|---|---|
| Turkey Q | 3 | 2 | 0 | 1 | 4 | 3 | 6 |
| Canada | 3 | 1 | 2 | 0 | 2 | 1 | 5 |
| Japan | 3 | 1 | 1 | 1 | 5 | 5 | 4 |
| Portugal | 3 | 0 | 1 | 2 | 3 | 5 | 1 |

**Semi-finals**: England 3 (Connolly 46, Nketiah 50, 69) Scotland 1 (Johnston 30). Mexico 3 Turkey 1. **Third-place match**: Scotland 0 Turkey 0 (Turkey won 5-3 on pens)

### FINAL

**ENGLAND 2 MEXICO 1 (June 9, 2018)**

**England** (3-4-2-1): Woodman, Kenny, Fry, Clarke-Salter, Connolly (Tomori 86), Cook (capt), Vieira (Choudhury 56), Dasilva, Dowell, Nketiah (Armstrong 76), Abraham (Nmecha 79). **Manager**: Aidy Boothroyd
**Scorers – England**: Fry (32), Dowell (36). **Mexico**: Alvarado (2). **Half-time**: 2-1

**England squad**: Ramsdale (Bournemouth), Woodman (Newcastle); Clarke-Salter (Chelsea), Connolly (Everton), Dasilva (Chelsea), Fry (Middlesbrough), Kenny (Everton), Konsa (Charlton), Pearce (Leeds), Tomori (Chelsea); Cook (Bournemouth), Choudhury (Leicester), Davies (Everton), Dowell (Everton), Vieira (Leeds); Abraham (Chelsea), Armstrong (Newcastle), Nketiah (Arsenal), Nmecha (Manchester City)

# FRIENDLY INTERNATIONALS

**REPUBLIC OF IRELAND 3 ICELAND 1**
**Tallaght Stadium, Dublin (400); March 22, 2018**

**Republic of Ireland**: Bossin, Kinsella, Kane (Doyle-Hayes 85), Sweeney (Delaney 46), Whelan (Dunne 72), Cullen, Dimaio, Quigley (Ronan Hale 68), Manning, Curtis, Rory Hale (Shodipo, 46)
**Scorers – Republic of Ireland**: Rory Hale (1), Manning (40), Ronan Hale (89). **Iceland**: Ljubicic (67)

**ENGLAND 2 ROMANIA 1 (Cyrille Regis international)**
**Molineux Stadium, Wolverhampton (15,314); March 24, 2018**

**England**: Henderson, Alexander-Arnold, Tomori, Clarke-Salter, Walker-Peters, Ejaria, Maitland-Niles (Onomah 70), Dowell (Maddison 84), Lookman, Gray (Kenny 58), Abraham (Calvert-Lewin 84)
**Scorers – England**: Gray (8), Clarke-Salter (72). **Romania**: Costache (79). **Half-time**: 1-0

# ANOTHER WORLD CUP FOR ENGLAND YOUNGSTERS

England retrieved a 2-0 deficit in the final to win another age-group World Cup. Four months after the under-20 side's success in South Korea, the under-17 team defeated Spain 5-2 in India with a strong second-half performance. In front of a crowd of more than 66,000, they pulled a goal back just before the interval through Rhian Brewster, then dominated with two from Phil Foden and one each by Morgan Gibbs-White and Marc Guehi. Manchester City's Foden was named the tournament's best player and Liverpool striker Brewster won the Golden Boot award with eight goals, including hat-tricks in quarter-final and semi-final victories.

**ENGLAND'S GROUP**

| | P | W | D | L | F | A | Pts |
|---|---|---|---|---|---|---|---|
| England | 3 | 3 | 0 | 0 | 11 | 2 | 9 |
| Iraq | 3 | 1 | 1 | 1 | 4 | 5 | 4 |
| Mexico | 3 | 0 | 2 | 1 | 3 | 4 | 2 |
| Chile | 3 | 0 | 1 | 2 | 0 | 7 | 1 |

**Match-day 1**: England 4 (Hudson-Odoi 5, Sancho 51, 60, Gomes 81) Chile 0. Att: 46,154 (Kolkata). **Match-day 2**: England 3 (Brewster 39, Foden 48, Sancho 55 pen) Mexico 2 (Lainez 65, 72). Att: 48,620 (Kolkata). **Match-day 3**: England 4 (Gomes 11, Smith Rowe 57, Loader 59, 71) Iraq 0. Att: 56,372 (Kolkata)

## KNOCKOUT STAGE

**Last 16**: England 0 Japan 0. Att: 53,302 (Kolkata) - England won 5-3 on pens. Brazil 3 Honduras 0, Germany 4 Colombia 0, Ghana 2 Niger 0, Iran 2 Mexico 1, Mali 5 Iraq 1, Spain 2 France 1, USA 5 Paraguay 0
**Quarter-finals**: England 4 (Brewster 11, 14, 90+6 pen, Gibbs-White 64) USA 1 (Sargent 72). Att: 16,148 (Goa). Brazil 2 Germany 1, Mali 2 Ghana 1, Spain 3 Iran 1
**Semi-finals**: England 3 (Brewster 10, 39, 77) Brazil 1 (Wesley 21). Att: 63,881 (Kolkata). Spain 3 Mali 1

## FINAL

**ENGLAND 5 SPAIN 2**
**Kolkata (66,684); Saturday, October 28, 2017**

**England** (4-2-3-1): Anderson, S Sessegnon, Latibeaudiere, Guehi, Panzo, Oakley-Boothe (Gomes 90), McEachran (Gallagher 87), Foden, Gibbs-White (Kirby 81), Hudson-Odoi, Brewster. **Booked**: Brewster. **Manager**: Steve Cooper
**Scorers – England**: Brewster (44), Gibbs-White (58), Foden (69, 88), Guehi (84). **Spain**: Gomez (10, 31). **Half-time**: 1-2

**England squad**: Anderson (Manchester City), Bursik (Stoke), Crellin (Fleetwood); Eyoma (Tottenham), Gibson (Everton), Guehi (Chelsea), Latibeaudiere (Manchester City), Panzo (Chelsea), S Sessegnon (Fulham); Gallagher (Chelsea), Gibbs-White (Wolves), Gomes (Manchester Utd), Kirby (Crystal Palace), McEachran (Chelsea), Oakley-Boothe (Tottenham); Brewster (Liverpool), Foden (Manchester City), Hudson-Odoi (Chelsea), Loader (Reading), Sancho (Borussia Dortmund), Smith Rowe (Arsenal)

# PENALTY WOE FOR ENGLAND AND THE IRISH

A new England under-17 team under manager Steve Cooper were knocked out of the European Championship 6-5 on penalties after a goalless semi-final against Holland. The Republic of Ireland also went out on spot-kicks, in a controversial ending to their quarter-final against the Dutch. Jimmy Corcoran saved the fifth penalty he faced, but received a second yellow card for moving off his line and was sent off, having also been cautioned during the match. Defender Oisin McEntee, taking the goalkeeper's jersey, was beaten by the retaken penalty, giving Holland a 5-4 win. Martin O'Neill, the senior Republic manager who watched the match with his assistant Roy Keane, confronted Czech Republic referee Zbynek Proske on the pitch afterwards. Holland also won the final of the tournament, held in England, on penalties after a 2-2 draw with Italy.

**ENGLAND'S GROUP**

| | P | W | D | L | F | A | Pts |
|---|---|---|---|---|---|---|---|
| Italy | 3 | 2 | 0 | 1 | 5 | 2 | 6 |
| England | 3 | 2 | 0 | 1 | 4 | 3 | 6 |
| Switzerland | 3 | 2 | 0 | 1 | 4 | 2 | 6 |
| Israel | 3 | 0 | 0 | 3 | 1 | 7 | 0 |

**Match-day 1**: England 2 (Doyle 29 pen, Daly 66) Israel 1 (Lugassy 41 pen). Att: 6,102 (Chesterfield). **Match-day 2**: England 2 (Appiah 68, Doyle 74 pen) Italy 1 (Riccardi 13). Att: 7,159 (Walsall). **Match-day** 3: England 0 Switzerland 1 (Mambimbi 41). Att: 6,146 (Rotherham)

**REPUBLIC OF IRELAND'S GROUP**

| | P | W | D | L | F | A | Pts |
|---|---|---|---|---|---|---|---|
| Belgium | 3 | 3 | 0 | 0 | 7 | 0 | 9 |
| Rep of Ireland | 3 | 2 | 0 | 1 | 3 | 2 | 6 |
| Bosnia-Herz | 3 | 1 | 0 | 2 | 3 | 8 | 3 |
| Denmark | 3 | 0 | 0 | 3 | 2 | 5 | 0 |

**Match-day 1**: Republic of Ireland 0 Belgium 2 (Sidibe 34, Vertessen 73). Att: 824 (Loughborough). **Match-day 2**: Republic of Ireland 1 (Parrott 5) Denmark 0. Att: 481 (St George's Park). **Match-day 3**: Republic of Ireland 2 (Parrott 69, Idah 89) Bosnia-Herzegovina 0. Att: 406 (St George's Park)

## KNOCKOUT STAGE

**Quarter-finals**: England 2 (Duncan 14, Amaechi 54) Norway 0. Att: 5,102 (Burton). Republic of Ireland 1 (Parrott 69) Holland 1 (Van Gelderen 67). Att: 673 (Chesterfield) – Holland won 5-4 on pens. Belgium 2 Spain 1, Italy 1 Sweden 0

**Semi-finals**: England 0 Holland 0. Att: 7,952 (Chesterfield) – Holland won 6-5 on pens. Italy 2 Belgium 1

**Final (May 20, 2018)**: Holland 2 Italy 2. Att: 4,612 (Rotherham) – Holland won 4-1 on pens

## VARDY OUT OF TOUCH

Jamie Vardy offered plenty of running when he came on as a 68th minute substitute in England's friendly international against Holland. But that was all the Leicester striker managed when replacing Marcus Rashford in the Amsterdam Arena. Vardy did not touch the ball once as England successfully defended the 1-0 lead established by Jesse Lingard.

# TRANSFER TRAIL

| Player | From | To | Date | £ |
|---|---|---|---|---|
| Philippe Coutinho | Liverpool | Barcelona | 1/18 | 142,000,000 |
| Paul Pogba | Juventus | Manchester Utd | 8/16 | 89,300,000 |
| Gareth Bale | Tottenham | Real Madrid | 8/13 | 85,300,000 |
| Cristiano Ronaldo | Manchester Utd | Real Madrid | 7/09 | 80,000,000 |
| Romelu Lukaku | Everton | Manchester Utd | 7/17 | 75,000,000 |
| Virgil van Dijk | Southampton | Liverpool | 1/18 | 75,000,000 |
| Luis Suarez | Liverpool | Barcelona | 7/14 | 65,000,000 |
| Riyad Mahrez | Leicester | Manchester City | 7/18 | 60,000,000 |
| Angel di Maria | Real Madrid | Manchester Utd | 8/14 | 59,700,000 |
| Alvaro Morata | Real Madrid | Chelsea | 7/17 | 57,200,000 |
| Diego Costa | Chelsea | Atletico Madrid | 1/18 | 57,000,000 |
| Aymeric Laporte | Athletic Bilbao | Manchester City | 1/18 | 57,000,000 |
| Pierre-Emerick Aubameyang | Borussia Dortmund | Arsenal | 1/18 | 56,000,000 |
| Kevin De Bruyne | Wolfsburg | Manchester City | 8/15 | 54,500,000 |
| Oscar | Chelsea | Shanghai Shenhua | 1/17 | 52,000,000 |
| Benjamin Mendy | Monaco | Manchester City | 7/17 | 52,000,000 |
| Fred | Shaktar Donetsk | Manchester Utd | 6/18 | 52,000,000 |
| Fernando Torres | Liverpool | Chelsea | 1/11 | 50,000,000 |
| David Luiz | Chelsea | Paris SG | 6/14 | 50,000,000 |
| Jorginho | Napoli | Chelsea | 7/18 | 50,000,000 |
| Raheem Sterling | Liverpool | Manchester City | 7/15 | 49,000,000 |
| Naby Keita | Leipzig | Liverpool | 7/18 | 48,000,000 |
| John Stones | Everton | Manchester City | 8/16 | 47,500,000 |
| Alexandre Lacazette | Lyon | Arsenal | 7/17 | 46,500,000 |
| Gylfi Sigurdsson | Swansea | Everton | 8/17 | 45,000,000 |
| Kyle Walker | Tottenham | Manchester City | 7/17 | 45,000,000 |
| Angel di Maria | Manchester Utd | Paris SG | 8/15 | 44,300,000 |
| Fabinho | Monaco | Liverpool | 5/8 | 43,700,000 |
| Bernardo Silva | Monaco | Manchester City | 6/17 | 43,000,000 |
| Mesut Ozil | Real Madrid | Arsenal | 9/13 | 42,400,000 |
| Davinson Sanchez | Ajax | Tottenham | 8/17 | 42,000,000 |
| Nemanja Matic | Chelsea | Manchester Utd | 7/17 | 40,000,000 |
| Tiemoue Bakayoko | Monaco | Chelsea | 7/17 | 39,700,000 |
| Sergio Aguero | Atletico Madrid | Manchester City | 7/11 | 38,500,000 |
| Juan Mata | Chelsea | Manchester Utd | 1/14 | 37,100,000 |
| Leroy Sane | Schalke | Manchester City | 7/16 | 37,000,000 |
| Anthony Martial | Monaco | Manchester Utd | 9/15 | 36,000,000 |
| Felipe Anderson | Lazio | West Ham | 7/18 | 36,000,000 |
| Andy Carroll | Newcastle | Liverpool | 1/11 | 35,000,000 |
| Cesc Fabregas | Arsenal | Barcelona | 8/11 | 35,000,000 |
| Alexis Sanchez | Barcelona | Arsenal | 7/14 | 35,000,000 |
| Granit Xhaka | Borussia M'gladbach | Arsenal | 6/16 | 35,000,000 |
| Shkodran Mustafi | Valencia | Arsenal | 8/16 | 35,000,000 |
| Alex Oxlade-Chamberlain | Arsenal | Liverpool | 8/17 | 35,000,000 |
| Danny Drinkwater | Leicester | Chelsea | 8/17 | 35,000,000 |
| Ederson | Benfica | Manchester City | 6/17 | 34,900,000 |
| Mohamed Salah | Roma | Liverpool | 7/17 | 34,300,000 |
| Sadio Mane | Southampton | Liverpool | 6/16 | 34,000,000 |
| Michy Batshuayi | Marseille | Chelsea | 7/16 | 33,000,000 |
| Robinho | Real Madrid | Manchester City | 9/08 | 32,500,000 |
| Christian Benteke | Aston Villa | Liverpool | 7/15 | 32,500,000 |

| | | | | |
|---|---|---|---|---|
| Eden Hazard | Lille | Chelsea | 6/12 | 32,000,000 |
| Diego Costa | Atletico Madrid | Chelsea | 7/14 | 32,000,000 |
| N'Golo Kante | Leicester | Chelsea | 7/16 | 32,000,000 |
| David Luiz | Paris SG | Chelsea | 8/16 | 32,000,000 |
| Eliaquim Mangala | Porto | Manchester City | 8/14 | 31,900,000 |
| Dimitar Berbatov | Tottenham | Manchester Utd | 9/08 | 30,750,000 |
| Victor Lindelof | Benfica | Manchester Utd | 6/17 | 30,700,000 |
| Andriy Shevchenko | AC Milan | Chelsea | 5/06 | 30,800,000 |
| Xabi Alonso | Liverpool | Real Madrid | 8/09 | 30,000,000 |
| Fernandinho | Shakhtar Donetsk | Manchester City | 6/13 | 30,000,000 |
| Willian | Anzhi Makhachkala | Chelsea | 8/13 | 30,000,000 |
| Erik Lamela | Roma | Tottenham | 8/13 | 30,000,000 |
| Luke Shaw | Southampton | Manchester Utd | 6/14 | 30,000,000 |
| Eric Bailly | Villarreal | Manchester Utd | 6/16 | 30,000,000 |
| Moussa Sissoko | Newcastle | Tottenham, | 8/16 | 30,000,000 |
| Islam Slimani | Sporting Lisbon | Leicester | 8/16 | 29,700,000 |
| Rio Ferdinand | Leeds | Manchester Utd | 7/02 | 29,100,000 |
| Antonio Rudiger | Roma | Chelsea | 7/17 | 29,000,000 |
| Ander Herrara | Athletic Bilbao | Manchester Utd | 6/14 | 28,800,000 |
| Nicolas Otamendi | Valencia | Manchester City | 8/15 | 28,500,000 |
| Juan Sebastian Veron | Lazio | Manchester Utd | 7/01 | 28,100,000 |
| Yaya Toure | Barcelona | Manchester City | 7/10 | 28,000,000 |
| Romelu Lukaku | Chelsea | Everton | 7/14 | 28,000,000 |
| Wilfried Bony | Swansea | Manchester City | 1/15 | 28,000,000 |
| Roberto Firmino | Hoffenheim | Liverpool | 6/15 | 28,000,000 |
| Marouane Fellaini | Everton | Manchester Utd | 9/13 | 27,500,000 |
| Wayne Rooney | Everton | Manchester Utd | 8/04 | 27,000,000 |
| Edin Dzeko | Wolfsburg | Manchester City | 1/11 | 27,000,000 |
| Luka Modric | Tottenham | Real Madrid | 8/12 | 27,000,000 |
| Cesc Fabregas | Barcelona | Chelsea | 6/14 | 27,000,000 |
| Gabriel Jesus | Palmeiras | Manchester City | 7/16 | 27,000,000 |
| Christian Benteke | Liverpool | Crystal Palace | 8/16 | 27,000,000 |
| Cenk Tosun | Besiktas | Everton | 1/18 | 27,000,000 |
| Danilo | Real Madrid | Manchester City | 7/17 | 26,500,000 |
| Roberto Soldado | Valencia | Tottenham | 8/13 | 26,000,000 |
| Henrikh Mkhitaryan | Borussua Dortmund | Manchester Utd | 7/16 | 26,000,000 |
| Mamadou Sakho | Liverpool | Crystal Palace | 8/17 | 26,000,000 |
| Marc Overmars | Arsenal | Barcelona | 7/00 | 25,000,000 |
| Carlos Tevez | Manchester Utd | Manchester City | 7/09 | 25,000,000 |
| Emmanuel Adebayor | Arsenal | Manchester City | 7/09 | 25,000,000 |
| Samir Nasri | Arsenal | Manchester City | 8/11 | 25,000,000 |
| Oscar | Internacional | Chelsea | 7/12 | 25,000,000 |
| Adam Lallana | Southampton | Liverpool | 7/14 | 25,000,000 |
| Memphis Depay | PSV Eindhoven | Manchester Utd | 6/15 | 25,000,000 |
| Morgan Schneiderlin | Southampton | Manchester Utd | 7/15 | 25,000,000 |
| Ramires | Chelsea | Jiangsu Suning | 2/16 | 25,000,000 |
| Georginio Wijnaldum | Newcastle | Liverpool | 7/16 | 25,000,000 |
| Yannick Bolasie | Crystal Palace | Everton | 8/16 | 25,000,000 |
| Jordan Pickford | Sunderland | Everton | 6/17 | 25,000,000 |
| Michael Keane | Burnley | Everton | 7/17 | 25,000,000 |
| Kelechi Iheanacho | Manchester City | Leicester | 7/17 | 25,000,000 |
| Theo Walcott | Arsenal | Everton | 1/18 | 25,000,000 |
| Davide Zappacosta | Torino | Chelsea | 8/17 | 25,000,000 |
| Jean Michael Seri | Nice | Fulham | 7/18 | 25,000,000 |

| | | | | |
|---|---|---|---|---|
| Arjen Robben | Chelsea | Real Madrid | 8/07 | 24,500,000 |
| Michael Essien | Lyon | Chelsea | 8/05 | 24,400,000 |
| David Silva | Valencia | Manchester City | 7/10 | 24,000,000 |
| James Milner | Aston Villa | Manchester City | 8/10 | 24,000,000 |
| Mario Balotelli | Inter Milan | Manchester City | 8/10 | 24,000,000 |
| Robin van Persie | Arsenal | Manchester Utd | 8/12 | 24,000,000 |
| Marko Arnautovic | Stoke | West Ham | 7/17 | 24,000,000 |
| Alvaro Negredo | Manchester City | Valencia | 7/15 | 23,800,000 |
| Davy Klaassen | Ajax | Everton | 6/17 | 23,600,000 |
| Juan Mata | Valencia | Chelsea | 8/11 | 23,500,000 |
| David Beckham | Manchester Utd | Real Madrid | 7/03 | 23,300,000 |
| Juan Cuadrado | Fiorentina | Chelsea | 2/15 | 23,300,000 |
| Didier Drogba | Marseille | Chelsea | 7/04 | 23,200,000 |
| Andre Schurrle | Chelsea | Wolfsburg | 2/15 | 23,000,000 |
| Marcos Alonso | Fiorentina | Chelsea | 8/16 | 23,000,000 |
| Luis Suarez | Ajax | Liverpool | 1/11 | 22,700,000 |
| Serge Aurier | Paris SG | Tottenham | 8/17 | 23,000,000 |
| Lucas Moura | Paris SG | Tottenham | 1/18 | 23,000,000 |
| Nicolas Anelka | Arsenal | Real Madrid | 8/99 | 22,300,000 |
| Fernando Torres | Atletico Madrid | Liverpool | 7/07 | 22,000,000 |
| Joloen Lescott | Everton | Manchester City | 8/09 | 22,000,000 |
| Stevan Jovetic | Fiorentina | Manchester City | 7/13 | 22,000,000 |
| Adrien Silva | Sporting Lisbon | Leicester | 1/18 | 22,000,000 |
| Issa Diop | Toulouse | West Ham | 6/18 | 22,000,000 |
| James Maddison | Norwich | Leicester | 6/18 | 22,000,000 |
| Son Heung-min | Bayer Leverkusen | Tottenham | 8/15 | 21,900,000 |
| Baba Rahman | Augsburg | Chelsea | 8/15 | 21,700,000 |
| David Luiz | Benfica | Chelsea | 1/11 | 21,300,000 |
| Shaun Wright-Phillips | Manchester City | Chelsea | 7/05 | 21,000,000 |
| Nemanja Matic | Benfica | Chelsea | 01/14 | 21,000,000 |
| Pedro | Barcelona | Chelsea | 8/15 | 21,000,000 |
| Ilkay Gundogan | Borussia Dortmund | Manchester City | 6/16 | 21,000,000 |
| Andre Ayew | Swansea | West Ham | 8/16 | 20,500,000 |
| Morgan Schneiderlin | Manchester Utd | Everton | 1/17 | 20,000,000 |
| Lassana Diarra | Portsmouth | Real Madrid | 12/08 | 20,000,000 |
| Alberto Aquilani | Roma | Liverpool | 8/09 | 20,000,000 |
| Stewart Downing | Aston Villa | Liverpool | 7/11 | 20,000,000 |
| Lazar Markovic | Benfica | Liverpool | 7/14 | 20,000,000 |
| Dejan Lovren | Southampton | Liverpool | 7/14 | 20,000,000 |
| Odion Ighalo | Watford | Changchun Yatai | 1/17 | 20,000,000 |
| Nathan Ake | Chelsea | Bournemouth | 6/17 | 20,000,000 |

## BRITISH RECORD TRANSFERS FROM FIRST £1,000 DEAL

| Player | From | To | Date | £ |
|---|---|---|---|---|
| Alf Common | Sunderland | Middlesbrough | 2/1905 | 1,000 |
| Syd Puddefoot | West Ham | Falkirk | 2/22 | 5,000 |
| Warney Cresswell | South Shields | Sunderland | 3/22 | 5,500 |
| Bob Kelly | Burnley | Sunderland | 12/25 | 6,500 |
| David Jack | Bolton | Arsenal | 10/28 | 10,890 |
| Bryn Jones | Wolves | Arsenal | 8/38 | 14,500 |
| Billy Steel | Morton | Derby | 9/47 | 15,000 |
| Tommy Lawton | Chelsea | Notts Co | 11/47 | 20,000 |
| Len Shackleton | Newcastle | Sunderland | 2/48 | 20,500 |
| Johnny Morris | Manchester Utd | Derby | 2/49 | 24,000 |

| | | | | |
|---|---|---|---|---|
| Eddie Quigley | Sheffield Wed | Preston | 12/49 | 26,500 |
| Trevor Ford | Aston Villa | Sunderland | 10/50 | 30,000 |
| Jackie Sewell | Notts Co | Sheffield Wed | 3/51 | 34,500 |
| Eddie Firmani | Charlton | Sampdoria | 7/55 | 35,000 |
| John Charles | Leeds | Juventus | 4/57 | 65,000 |
| Denis Law | Manchester City | Torino | 6/61 | 100,000 |
| Denis Law | Torino | Manchester Utd | 7/62 | 115,000 |
| Allan Clarke | Fulham | Leicester | 6/68 | 150,000 |
| Allan Clarke | Leicester | Leeds | 6/69 | 165,000 |
| Martin Peters | West Ham | Tottenham | 3/70 | 200,000 |
| Alan Ball | Everton | Arsenal | 12/71 | 220,000 |
| David Nish | Leicester | Derby | 8/72 | 250,000 |
| Bob Latchford | Birmingham | Everton | 2/74 | 350,000 |
| Graeme Souness | Middlesbrough | Liverpool | 1/78 | 352,000 |
| Kevin Keegan | Liverpool | Hamburg | 6/77 | 500,000 |
| David Mills | Middlesbrough | WBA | 1/79 | 516,000 |
| Trevor Francis | Birmingham | Nottm Forest | 2/79 | 1,180,000 |
| Steve Daley | Wolves | Manchester City | 9/79 | 1,450,000 |
| Andy Gray | Aston Villa | Wolves | 9/79 | 1,469,000 |
| Bryan Robson | WBA | Manchester Utd | 10/81 | 1,500,000 |
| Ray Wilkins | Manchester Utd | AC Milan | 5/84 | 1,500,000 |
| Mark Hughes | Manchester Utd | Barcelona | 5/86 | 2,300,000 |
| Ian Rush | Liverpool | Juventus | 6/87 | 3,200,000 |
| Chris Waddle | Tottenham | Marseille | 7/89 | 4,250,000 |
| David Platt | Aston Villa | Bari | 7/91 | 5,500,000 |
| Paul Gascoigne | Tottenham | Lazio | 6/92 | 5,500,000 |
| Andy Cole | Newcastle | Manchester Utd | 1/95 | 7,000,000 |
| Dennis Bergkamp | Inter Milan | Arsenal | 6/95 | 7,500,000 |
| Stan Collymore | Nottm Forest | Liverpool | 6/95 | 8,500,000 |
| Alan Shearer | Blackburn | Newcastle | 7/96 | 15,000,000 |
| Nicolas Anelka | Arsenal | Real Madrid | 8/99 | 22,500,000 |
| Juan Sebastian Veron | Lazio | Manchester Utd | 7/01 | 28,100,000 |
| Rio Ferdinand | Leeds | Manchester Utd | 7/02 | 29,100,000 |
| Andriy Shevchenko | AC Milan | Chelsea | 5/06 | 30,800,000 |
| Robinho | Real Madrid | Manchester City | 9/08 | 32,500,000 |
| Cristiano Ronaldo | Manchester Utd | Real Madrid | 7/09 | 80,000,000 |
| Gareth Bale | Tottenham | Real Madrid | 9/13 | 85,300,000 |
| Paul Pogba | Juventus | Manchester Utd | 8/16 | 89.300,000 |
| Philippe Coutinho | Liverpool | Barcelona | 1/18 | 142,000,000 |

• World's first £1m transfer: GuiseppeSavoldi, Bologna to Napoli, July 1975

## TOP FOREIGN SIGNINGS

| Player | From | To | Date | £ |
|---|---|---|---|---|
| Neymar | Barcelona | Paris SG | 8/17 | 198,000,000 |
| Kylian Mbappe | Monaco | Paris SG | 8/17 | 165,700,000 |
| Ousmane Dembele | Borussia Dortmund | Barcelona | 8/17 | 134,000,000 |
| Christiano Ronaldo | Real Madrid | Juventus | 7/18 | 99,200,000 |
| Gonzalo Higuain | Napoli | Juventus | 7/16 | 75,300,000 |
| Zlatan Ibrahimovic | Inter Milan | Barcelona | 7/09 | 60,300,000 |
| James Rodriguez | Monaco | Real Madrid | 7/14 | 60,000,000 |
| Kaka | AC Milan | Real Madrid | 6/08 | 56,000,000 |
| Edinson Cavani | Napoli | Paris SG | 7/13 | 53,000,000 |
| Thomas Lemar | Monaco | Atletico Madrid | 6/18 | 52,700,000 |
| Radamel Falcao | Atletico Madrid | Monaco | 6/13 | 51,000,000 |

| | | | | |
|---|---|---|---|---|
| Neymar | Santos | Barcelona | 6/13 | 48,600,000 |
| Zinedine Zidane | Juventus | Real Madrid | 7/01 | 47,200,000 |
| Hulk | Zenit St Petersburg | Shanghai SIPG | 7/16 | 46,100,000 |
| Vinicius Junior | Flamengo | Real Madrid | 7/18 | 39,600,000 |
| James Rodriguez | Porto | Monaco | 5/13 | 38,500,000 |
| Alex Teixeira | Shekhtar Donetsk | Jiangsu Suning | 2/16 | 38,400,000 |
| Joao Mario | Sporting Lisbon | Inter Milan | 8/16 | 38,400,000 |
| Luis Figo | Barcelona | Real Madrid | 7/00 | 37,200,000 |
| Javier Pastore | Palermo | Paris SG | 8/11 | 36,600,000 |
| Corentin Tolisso | Lyon | Bayern Munich | 6/17 | 36,500,000 |
| Joao Cancelo | Valencia | Juventus | 7/18 | 36,300,000 |
| Karim Benzema | Lyon | Real Madrid | 7/09 | 35,800,000 |
| Julian Draxler | Wolfsburg | Paris SG | 1/17 | 35,500,000 |
| Douglas Costa | Bayern Munich | Juventus | 6/18 | 35,200,000 |
| Hernan Crespo | Parma | Lazio | 7/00 | 35,000,000 |
| Radamel Falcao | Porto | Atletico Madrid | 8/11 | 34,700,000 |
| Gonzalo Higuain | Real Madrid | Napoli | 7/13 | 34,500,000 |
| David Villa | Valencia | Barcelona | 5/10 | 34,000,000 |
| Thiago Silva | AC Milan | Paris SG | 7/12 | 34,000,000 |
| Lucas Moura | Sao Paulo | Paris SG | 1/13 | 34,000,000 |
| Asier Illarramendi | Real Sociedad | Real Madrid | 7/13 | 34,000,000 |
| Ronaldo | Inter Milan | Real Madrid | 8/02 | 33,000,000 |
| Gianluigi Buffon | Parma | Juventus | 7/01 | 32,600,000 |
| Axel Witsel | Benfica | Zenit St Petersburg | 8/12 | 32,500,000 |
| Hulk | Porto | Zenit St Petersburg | 8/12 | 32,000,000 |
| Javi Martinez | Athletic Bilbao | Bayern Munich | 8/12 | 31,600,000 |
| Mario Gotze | Borussia Dortmund | Bayern Munich | 6/13 | 31,500,000 |
| Christian Vieri | Lazio | Inter Milan | 6/99 | 31,000,000 |
| Jackson Martinez | Atletico Madrid | Guangzhou Evergrande | 2/16 | 31,000,000 |
| Alessandro Nesta | Lazio | AC Milan | 8/02 | 30,200,000 |

## WORLD'S MOST EXPENSIVE TEENAGER

**£165,700,000:** Kylian Mbappe, 19, Monaco to Paris SG, August 2017

## WORLD RECORD FOR 16-YEAR-OLD

**£39,600,000**: Vinicius Junior, Flamengo to Real Madrid, July 2018

## RECORD TRIBUNAL FEE

£6.5m: Danny Ings, Burnley to Liverpool, Jun 2016

## RECORD FEE BETWEEN SCOTTISH CLUBS

**£4.4m**: Scott Brown, Hibernian to Celtic, May 2007

## RECORD NON-LEAGUE FEE

**£1m:** Jamie Vardy, Fleetwood to Leicester, May 2012

## RECORD FEE BETWEEN NON-LEAGUE CLUBS

**£275,000:** Richard Brodie, York to Crawley, Aug 2010

# MILESTONES

**1848:** First code of rules compiled at Cambridge University.
**1857:** Sheffield FC, world's oldest football club, formed.
**1862:** Notts Co (oldest League club) formed.
**1863:** Football Association founded – their first rules of game agreed.
**1871:** FA Cup introduced.
**1872:** First official International: Scotland 0 England 0. Corner-kick introduced.
**1873:** Scottish FA formed; Scottish Cup introduced.
**1874:** Shinguards introduced.
**1875:** Crossbar introduced (replacing tape).
**1876:** FA of Wales formed.
**1877:** Welsh Cup introduced.
**1878:** Referee's whistle first used.
**1880:** Irish FA founded; Irish Cup introduced.
**1883:** Two-handed throw-in introduced.
**1885:** Record first-class score (Arbroath 36 Bon Accord 0 – Scottish Cup). Professionalism legalised.
**1886:** International Board formed.
**1887:** Record FA Cup score (Preston 26 Hyde 0).
**1888:** Football League founded by William McGregor. First matches on Sept 8.
**1889** Preston win Cup and League (first club to complete Double).
**1890:** Scottish League and Irish League formed.
**1891:** Goal-nets introduced. Penalty-kick introduced.
**1892:** Inter-League games began. Football League Second Division formed.
**1893:** FA Amateur Cup launched.
**1894:** Southern League formed.
**1895:** FA Cup stolen from Birmingham shop window – never recovered.
**1897:** First Players' Union formed. Aston Villa win Cup and League.
**1898:** Promotion and relegation introduced.
**1901:** Maximum wage rule in force (£4 a week). Tottenham first professional club to take FA Cup south. First six-figure attendance (110,802) at FA Cup Final.
**1902:** Ibrox Park disaster (25 killed). Welsh League formed.
**1904:** FIFA founded (7 member countries).
**1905:** First £1,000 transfer (Alf Common, Sunderland to Middlesbrough).
**1907:** Players' Union revived.
**1908:** Transfer fee limit (£350) fixed in January and withdrawn in April.
**1911:** New FA Cup trophy – in use to 1991. Transfer deadline introduced.
**1914:** King George V first reigning monarch to attend FA Cup Final.
**1916:** Entertainment Tax introduced.
**1919:** League extended to 44 clubs.
**1920:** Third Division (South) formed.
**1921:** Third Division (North) formed.
**1922:** Scottish League (Div II) introduced.
**1923:** Beginning of football pools. First Wembley Cup Final.
**1924:** First International at Wembley (England 1 Scotland 1). Rule change allows goals to be scored direct from corner-kicks.
**1925:** New offside law.
**1926:** Huddersfield complete first League Championship hat-trick.
**1927:** First League match broadcast (radio): Arsenal v Sheffield United. First radio broadcast of Cup Final (winners Cardiff City). Charles Clegg, president of FA, becomes first knight of football.
**1928:** First £10,000 transfer – David Jack (Bolton to Arsenal). WR ('Dixie') Dean (Everton) creates League record – 60 goals in season. Britain withdraws from FIFA

elected president of Football League. Death of Sir Stanley Rous (91). 100th edition of News of the World Football Annual. League Cup sponsored for next three years by Littlewoods (£2m). Football League voting majority (for rule changes) reduced from three-quarters to two-thirds. Wales move HQ from Wrexham to Cardiff after 110 years. Two substitutes in FA Cup and League (Littlewoods) Cup. Two-season League/TV deal (£6.2m):- BBC and ITV each show seven live League matches per season, League Cup semi-finals and Final. Football League sponsored by Today newspaper. Luton first club to ban all visiting supporters; as sequel are themselves banned from League Cup. Oldham and Preston install artificial pitches, making four in Football League (following QPR and Luton).

**1987:** League introduce play-off matches to decide final promotion/relegation places in all divisions. Re-election abolished – bottom club in Div 4 replaced by winners of GM Vauxhall Conference. Two substitutes approved for Football League 1987–8. Red and yellow disciplinary cards (scrapped 1981) re-introduced by League and FA Football League sponsored by Barclays. First Div reduced to 21 clubs.

**1988:** Football League Centenary. First Division reduced to 20 clubs.

**1989:** Soccer gets £74m TV deal: £44m over 4 years, ITV; £30m over 5 years, BBC/BSB. But it costs Philip Carter the League Presidency. Ted Croker retires as FA chief executive; successor Graham Kelly, from Football League. Hillsborough disaster: 95 die at FA Cup semi-final (Liverpool v Nottm Forest). Arsenal win closest-ever Championship with last kick. Peter Shilton sets England record with 109 caps.

**1990:** Nottm Forest win last Littlewoods Cup Final. Both FA Cup semi-finals played on Sunday and televised live. Play-off finals move to Wembley; Swindon win place in Div 1, then relegated back to Div 2 (breach of financial regulations) – Sunderland promoted instead. England reach World Cup semi-final in Italy and win FIFA Fair Play Award. Peter Shilton retires as England goalkeeper with 125 caps (world record). Graham Taylor (Aston Villa) succeeds Bobby Robson as England manager. International Board amend offside law (player 'level' no longer offside). FIFA make "professional foul" a sending-off offence. English clubs back in Europe (Manchester United and Aston Villa) after 5-year exile.

**1991:** First FA Cup semi-final at Wembley (Tottenham 3 Arsenal 1). Bert Millichip (FA chairman) and Philip Carter (Everton chairman) knighted. End of artificial pitches in Div 1 (Luton, Oldham). Scottish League reverts to 12-12-14 format (as in 1987–8). Penalty shoot-out introduced to decide FA Cup ties level after one replay.

**1992:** FA launch Premier League (22 clubs). Football League reduced to three divisions (71 clubs). Record TV-sport deal: BSkyB/BBC to pay £304m for 5-year coverage of Premier League. ITV do £40m, 4-year deal with Football League. Channel 4 show Italian football live (Sundays). FIFA approve new back-pass rule (goalkeeper must not handle ball kicked to him by team-mate). New League of Wales formed. Record all-British transfer, £3.3m: Alan Shearer (Southampton to Blackburn). Charlton return to The Valley after 7-year absence.

**1993:** Barclays end 6-year sponsorship of Football League. For first time both FA Cup semi-finals at Wembley (Sat, Sun). Arsenal first club to complete League Cup/FA Cup double. Rangers pull off Scotland's domestic treble for fifth time. FA in record British sports sponsorship deal (£12m over 4 years) with brewers Bass for FA Carling Premiership, from Aug. Brian Clough retires after 18 years as Nottm Forest manager; as does Jim McLean (21 years manager of Dundee Utd). Football League agree 3-year, £3m sponsorship with Endsleigh Insurance. Premier League introduce squad numbers with players' names on shirts. Record British transfer: Duncan Ferguson, Dundee Utd to Rangers (£4m). Record English-club signing: Roy Keane, Nottm Forest to Manchester United (£3.75m). Graham Taylor resigns as England manager after World Cup exit (Nov). Death of Bobby Moore (51), England World Cup winning captain 1966.

**1994:** Death of Sir Matt Busby. Terry Venables appointed England coach. Manchester United complete the Double. Last artificial pitch in English football goes – Preston revert to grass, summer 1994. Bobby Charlton knighted. Scottish League format changes to four divisions of ten clubs. Record British transfer: Chris Sutton, Norwich to Blackburn (£5m). FA announce first sponsorship of FA Cup – Littlewoods Pools (4-year, £14m deal, plus £6m for Charity Shield). Death of Billy Wright.

**1995:** New record British transfer: Andy Cole, Newcastle to Manchester United (£7m). First England match abandoned through crowd trouble (v Republic of Ireland, Dublin). Blackburn Champions for first time since 1914. Premiership reduced to 20 clubs. British transfer record broken again: Stan Collymore, Nottm Forest to Liverpool (£8.5m). Starting season 1995–6, teams allowed to use 3 substitutes per match, not necessarily including a goalkeeper. European Court of Justice upholds Bosman ruling, barring transfer fees for players out of contract and removing limit on number of foreign players clubs can field.

**1996:** Death of Bob Paisley (77), ex-Liverpool, most successful manager in English Football. FA appoint Chelsea manager Glenn Hoddle to succeed Terry Venables as England coach after Euro 96. Manchester United first English club to achieve Double twice (and in 3 seasons). Football League completes £125m, 5-year TV deal with BSkyB starting 1996–7. England stage European Championship, reach semi-finals, lose on pens to tournament winners Germany. Keith Wiseman succeeds Sir Bert Millichip as FA Chairman. Linesmen become known as 'referees' assistants'. Alan Shearer football's first £15m player (Blackburn to Newcastle). Nigeria first African country to win Olympic soccer. Nationwide Building Society sponsor Football League in initial 3-year deal worth £5.25m Peter Shilton first player to make 1000 League appearances.

**1997:** Howard Wilkinson appointed English football's first technical director. England's first home defeat in World Cup (0-1 v Italy). Ruud Gullit (Chelsea) first foreign coach to win FA Cup. Rangers equal Celtic's record of 9 successive League titles. Manchester United win Premier League for fourth time in 5 seasons. New record World Cup score: Iran 17, Maldives 0 (qualifying round). Season 1997–8 starts Premiership's record £36m, 4-year sponsorship extension with brewers Bass (Carling).

**1998:** In French manager Arsene Wenger's second season at Highbury, Arsenal become second English club to complete the Double twice. Chelsea also win two trophies under new player-manager Gianluca Vialli (Coca-Cola Cup, Cup Winners' Cup). In breakaway from Scottish League, top ten clubs form new Premiership under SFA, starting season 1998–9. Football League celebrates its 100th season, 1998–9. New FA Cup sponsors – French insurance giants AXA (25m, 4-year deal). League Cup becomes Worthington Cup in £23m, 5-year contract with brewers Bass. Nationwide Building Society's sponsorship of Football League extended to season 2000–1.

**1999:** FA buy Wembley Stadium (£103m) for £320m, plan rebuilding (Aug 2000–March 2003) as new national stadium (Lottery Sports fund contributes £110m) Scotland's new Premier League takes 3-week mid-season break in January. Sky screen Oxford Utd v Sunderland (Div 1) as first pay-per-view match on TV. FA sack England coach Glenn Hoddle; Fulham's Kevin Keegan replaces him at £1m a year until 2003. Sir Alf Ramsey, England's World Cup-winning manager, dies aged 79. With effect 1999, FA Cup Final to be decided on day (via penalties, if necessary). Hampden Park re-opens for Scottish Cup Final after £63m refit. Alex Ferguson knighted after Manchester United complete Premiership, FA Cup, European Cup treble. Starting season 1999–2000, UEFA increase Champions League from 24 to 32 clubs. End of Cup-Winners' Cup (merged into 121-club UEFA Cup). FA allow holders Manchester United to withdraw from FA Cup to participate in FIFA's inaugural World Club Championship in Brazil in January. Chelsea first British club to field an all-foreign line-up – at Southampton (Prem). FA vote in favour of streamlined 14-man board of directors to replace its 92-member council.

**2000:** Scot Adam Crozier takes over as FA chief executive. Wales move to Cardiff's £125m Millennium Stadium (v Finland). Brent Council approve plans for new £475m Wembley Stadium (completion target spring 2003); demolition of old stadium to begin after England v Germany (World Cup qual.). Fulham Ladies become Britain's first female professional team. FA Premiership and Nationwide League to introduce (season 2000–01) rule whereby referees advance free-kick by 10 yards and caution player who shows dissent, delays kick or fails to retreat 10 yards. Scottish football increased to 42 League clubs in 2000–01 (12 in Premier League and 3 divisions of ten; Peterhead and Elgin elected from Highland League). France win European Championship – first time a major international tournament has been jointly hosted (Holland/ Belgium). England's £10m bid to stage 2006 World Cup fails; vote goes to Germany. England manager Kevin Keegan resigns after 1-0 World Cup defeat by Germany in Wembley's last International. Lazio's Swedish coach Sven-Goran Eriksson agrees to become England head coach.

**2001:** Scottish Premier League experiment with split into two 5-game mini leagues (6 clubs in each) after 33 matches completed. New transfer system agreed by FIFA/UEFA is ratified. Barclaycard begin £48m, 3-year sponsorship of the Premiership, and Nationwide's contract with the Football League is extended by a further 3 years (£12m). ITV, after winning auction against BBC's Match of the Day, begin £183m, 3-season contract for highlights of Premiership matches; BSkyB's live coverage (66 matches per season) for next 3 years will cost £1.1bn. BBC and BSkyB pay £400m (3-year contract) for live coverage of FA Cup and England home matches. ITV and Ondigital pay £315m to screen Nationwide League and Worthington Cup matches. In new charter for referees, top men can earn up to £60,000 a season in Premiership. Real Madrid break world transfer record, buying Zinedine Zidane from Juventus for £47.2m. FA introduce prize money, round by round, in FA Cup.

**2002:** Scotland appoint their first foreign manager, Germany's former national coach Bertie Vogts replacing Craig Brown. Collapse of ITV Digital deal, with Football League owed £178m, threatens lower-division clubs. Arsenal complete Premiership/FA Cup Double for second time in 5 seasons, third time in all. Newcastle manager Bobby Robson knighted in Queen's Jubilee Honours. New record British transfer and world record for defender, £29.1m Rio Ferdinand (Leeds to Manchester United). Transfer window introduced to British football. FA Charity Shield renamed FA Community Shield. After 2-year delay, demolition of Wembley Stadium begins. October: Adam Crozier, FA chief executive, resigns.

**2003:** FA Cup draw (from 4th Round) reverts to Monday lunchtime. Scottish Premier League decide to end mid-winter shut-down. Mark Palios appointed FA chief executive. For first time, two Football League clubs demoted (replaced by two from Conference). Ban lifted on loan transfers between Premiership clubs. July: David Beckham becomes record British export (Manchester United to Real Madrid, £23.3m). Biggest takeover in British football history – Russian oil magnate Roman Abramovich buys control of Chelsea for £150m Wimbledon leave rented home at Selhurst Park, become England's first franchised club in 68-mile move to Milton Keynes.

**2004:** Arsenal first club to win Premiership with unbeaten record and only the third in English football history to stay undefeated through League season. Trevor Brooking knighted in Queen's Birthday Honours. Wimbledon change name to Milton Keynes Dons. Greece beat hosts Portugal to win European Championship as biggest outsiders (80-1 at start) ever to succeed in major international tournament. New contracts – Premiership in £57m deal with Barclays, seasons 2004–07. Coca-Cola replace Nationwide as Football League sponsors (£15m over 3 years), rebranding Div 1 as Football League Championship, with 2nd and 3rd Divisions, becoming Leagues 1 and 2. All-time League record of 49 unbeaten Premiership matches set by Arsenal. Under new League rule, Wrexham forfeit 10 points for going into administration.

**2005:** Brian Barwick, controller of ITV Sport, becomes FA chief executive. Foreign managers take all major trophies for English clubs: Chelsea, in Centenary year, win Premiership (record 95 points) and League Cup in Jose Mourinho's first season; Arsene Wenger's Arsenal win FA Cup in Final's first penalty shoot-out; under new manager Rafael Benitez, Liverpool lift European Cup on penalties after trailing 0-3 in Champions League Final. Wigan, a League club only since 1978, promoted to Premiership. In new record British-club take-over, American tycoon Malcolm Glazer buys Manchester United for £790m Tributes are paid world-wide to George Best, who dies aged 59.

**2006:** Steve Staunton succeeds Brian Kerr as Republic of Ireland manager. Chelsea post record losses of £140m. Sven-Goran Eriksson agrees a settlement to step down as England coach. Steve McClaren replaces him. The Premier League announce a new 3-year TV deal worth £1.7 billion under which Sky lose their monopoly of coverage. Chelsea smash the British transfer record, paying £30.8m for Andriy Shevchenko. Clydesdale Bank replace Bank of Scotland as sponsor of the SPL.

**2007:** Michel Platini becomes the new president of UEFA. Walter Smith resigns as Scotland manager to return to Rangers and is replaced by Alex McLeish. The new £800m Wembley Stadium is finally completed. The BBC and Sky lose TV rights for England's home matches and FA Cup ties to ITV and Setanta. World Cup-winner Alan Ball dies aged 61. Lawrie Sanchez resigns as Northern Ireland manager to take over at Fulham. Nigel Worthington succeeds him. Lord Stevens names five clubs in his final report into alleged transfer irregularities. Steve McClaren is sacked after England fail to qualify for the European Championship Finals and is replaced by Fabio Capello. The Republic of Ireland's Steve Staunton also goes. Scotland's Alex McLeish resigns to become Birmingham manager.

**2008:** The Republic of Ireland follow England's lead in appointing an Italian coach – Giovanni Trapattoni. George Burley leaves Southampton to become Scotland manager. Manchester United beat Chelsea in the first all-English Champions League Final. Manchester City smash the British transfer record when signing Robinho from Real Madrid for £32.5m.

**2009**: Sky secure the rights to five of the six Premier League packages from 2010–13 with a bid of £1.6bn. Reading's David Beckham breaks Bobby Moore's record number of caps for an England outfield player with his 109th appearance. A British league record for not conceding a goal ends on 1,311 minutes for Manchester United's Edwin van der Sar. AC Milan's Kaka moves to Real Madrid for a world record fee of £56m. Nine days later, Manchester United agree to sell Cristiano Ronaldo to Real for £80m. Sir Bobby Robson dies aged 76 after a long battle with cancer. Shay Given and Kevin Kilbane win their 100th caps for the Republic of Ireland. The Premier League vote for clubs to have eight home-grown players in their squads. George Burley is sacked as Scotland manager and replaced by Craig Levein.

**2010**: npower succeed Coca-Cola as sponsors of the Football League. Portsmouth become the first Premier League club to go into administration. Chelsea achieve the club's first League and FA Cup double. Lord Triesman resigns as chairman of the FA and of England's 2018 World Cup bid. John Toshack resigns as Wales manager and is replaced by former captain Gary Speed. England are humiliated in the vote for the 2018 World Cup which goes to Russia, with the 2022 tournament awarded to Qatar.

**2011:** Seven club managers are sacked in a week. The transfer record between British clubs is broken twice in a day, with Liverpool buying Newcastle's Andy Carroll for £35m and selling Fernando Torres to Chelsea for £50m. Vauxhall replace Nationwide as sponsors of England and the other home nations. John Terry is restored as England captain. Football League clubs vote to reduce the number of substitutes from seven to five. Nigel Worthington steps down as Northern Ireland manager and is succeeded by Michael O'Neill. Sir Alex Ferguson completes 25 years as Manchester United manager. Manchester City post record annual losses of nearly £195m. Huddersfield set a Football League record of 43 successive unbeaten league games. Football mourns Gary Speed after the Wales manager is found dead at his home.

**2012:** Chris Coleman is appointed the new Wales manager. Fabio Capello resigns as manager after John Terry is stripped of the England captaincy for the second time. Roy Hodgson takes over. Rangers are forced into liquidation by crippling debts and a newly-formed club are demoted from the Scottish Premier League to Division Three. Manchester City become champions for the first time since 1968 after the tightest finish to a Premier League season. Chelsea win a penalty shoot-out against Bayern Munich in the

Champions League Final. Capital One replace Carling as League Cup sponsors. Steven Gerrard (England) and Damien Duff (Republic of Ireland) win their 100th caps. The FA's new £120m National Football Centre at Burton upon Trent is opened. Scotland manager Craig Levein is sacked.

**2013:** Gordon Strachan is appointed Scotland manager. FIFA and the Premier League announce the introduction of goal-line technology. Energy company npower end their sponsorship of the Football League and are succeeded by Sky Bet. Sir Alex Ferguson announces he is retiring after 26 years as Manchester United manager. Wigan become the first club to lift the FA Cup and be relegated in the same season. Chelsea win the Europa League. Ashley Cole and Frank Lampard win their 100th England caps. Robbie Keane becomes the most capped player in the British Isles on his 126th appearance for the Republic of Ireland. Scottish Football League clubs agree to merge with the Scottish Premier League. Greg Dyke succeeds David Bernstein as FA chairman. Real Madrid sign Tottenham's Gareth Bale for a world record £85.3m. Giovanni Trapatonni is replaced as Republic of Ireland manager by Martin O'Neill.

**2014**: Sir Tom Finney, one of the finest British players of all-time, dies aged 91. England experience their worst-ever World Cup, finishing bottom the group with a single point. Germany deliver one of the most remarkable scorelines in World Cup history – 7-1 against Brazil in the semi-finals. Manchester United announce a world-record kit sponsorship with adidas worth £750m. United break the incoming British transfer record by paying £59.7m for Real Madrid's Angel di Maria, part of a record £835m spending by Premier League clubs in the summer transfer window. England's Wayne Rooney and the Republic of Ireland's John O'Shea win their 100th caps.

**2015**: The Premier League sell live TV rights for 2016-19 to Sky and BT for a record £5.13bn. Bournemouth, a club on the brink of folding in 2008, win promotion to the Premier League. FIFA president Sepp Blatter resigns as a bribery and corruption scandal engulfs the world governing body. Blatter and suspended UEFA president Michel Platini are banned for eight years, reduced on appeal to six years.

**2016**: An inquest jury rules that the 96 Liverpool fans who died in the Hillsborough disaster of 1989 were unlawfully killed. Leicester, 5,000-1 outsiders become Premier League champions in one of the game's biggest-ever surprises. Aaron Hughes wins his 100th cap for Northern Ireland. FA Cup quarter-final replays are scrapped. England manager Roy Hodgson resigns. He is replaced by Sam Allardyce, who is forced out after one match for 'inappropriate conduct' and succeeded by Gareth Southgate. Manchester United sign Paul Pogba for a world record £89.3m.

**2017** Paris Saint-Germain sign Barcelona's Neymar for a world record £198m. Managers Gordon Strachan (Scotland) and Chris Coleman (Wales) resign. Steven Davis reaches a century of Northern Ireland caps. Manchester United win the Europa League. Celtic are champions without losing a game. Arsenal win a record 13th FA Cup, Arsene Wenger for a record seventh time. Wayne Rooney retires from international football as England's record scorer with 53 goals.

**2018** Manchester City become the first English champions to total 100 points. Celtic are the first in Scotland to win back-to-back domestic trebles. Alex McLeish (Scotland) and Ryan Giggs (Wales) are appointed. Arsene Wenger leaves Arsenal after 22 years as manager.

# FINAL WHISTLE – OBITUARIES 2017–18

## JULY 2017

**JIMMY WHITE**, 75, made his league debut with Bournemouth, aged 15 years and 321 days, against Port Vale in 1958 and remains the youngest to do so in their history. The England youth international had two spells at the club, returning after playing for Portsmouth and then Gillingham, where he was converted from centre-forward to centre-half. He ended his career at Cambridge United.

**DAVIE LAING**, 92, played more than 300 matches for Hearts between 1946–54. The wing-half then helped Clyde win the Scottish Cup 1-0 in a replay against Celtic. He also had spells with Hibernian and Gillingham.

**JOE WALTERS**, 82, was a Scottish Cup winner with Clyde, who defeated Hibernian 1-0 in the 1958 final. The wing-half spent six years at the club, making 230 appearances, and also played for Albion.

## AUGUST 2017

**BILL GREEN**, 66, served a dozen clubs as player, manager and scout during nearly half a century in league football. He joined the final one, Southampton, in 2011 and had spent six years there as senior recruitment officer. Green, a centre-half, started at Hartlepool, led Carlisle into the old First Division in 1974 and scored their first goal in the top-flight on the opening day of the season against Chelsea at Stamford Bridge. He also had spells with West Ham, Peterborough, Chesterfield and Doncaster, then managed Scunthorpe. That was followed by scouting appointments at Wigan, Leicester, Sheffield Wednesday and Derby.

**DAVE CALDWELL**, 85, won league and cup honours with Aberdeen. He played left-back in the title-winning side of 1954–55 when they finished three points ahead of Celtic. The following year, Aberdeen defeated St Mirren 2-1 in the Scottish League Cup Final. Caldwell also had spells with Rotherham and Toronto City in Canada.

**MIKE DEAKIN**, 83, scored 62 goals in 150 appearances during five years with Crystal Palace – 27 of them in the 1958–59 Fourth Division season. The centre-forward later played for Northampton and Aldershot.

**DUNCAN RUSSELL**, 59, had six months as manager of Mansfield in the 2010–11 National League season, taking his side to the FA Trophy Final at Wembley, where they lost 1-0 to Darlington in extra-time. He previously coached at Blackburn, Derby, Wolves, MK Dons and Walsall.

**JOHN OGSTON**, 78, made his debut for Aberdeen against Rangers in 1958 and went on to make 230 appearances for his home-town club. They included three successive seasons without missing a match. The Scottish under-23 goalkeeper played just one game in three years after moving to Liverpool, then played for Doncaster.

**ALAN BOSWELL**, 74, was a goalkeeper whose career spanned 479 games – nearly half of them for Shrewsbury between 1963–68. He also served Walsall, Wolves, Bolton and Port Vale.

## SEPTEMBER 2017

**PAUL WILSON**, 66, won league and cup honours with Celtic – and made his mark in international football. Appearing as a substitute for Scotland in a European Championship qualifier against Spain in Valencia in 1975, he became the first Asian to represent any of the home nations at senior level. It was the one cap gained by the Bangalore-born player, whose Scottish father was based in India with the RAF. Wilson joined Celtic in 1967 and during 11 years at the club won two league titles and two Scottish Cups, scoring twice in the 3-1 win over Airdrie in the 1975 final, days after his mother died. He was also on the mark as Celtic defeated Hibernian 6-3 to lift the previous year's League Cup. After 217 appearances and 55 goals for the club, Wilson played for Motherwell and Partick.

**FREDDY SHEPHERD**, 75, was a pivotal figure in Newcastle's rise in the 1990s. He played a key role in appointing Kevin Keegan as manager and signing Alan Shearer from Blackburn for a then world-record fee of £15m. A director of the club from 1992, he served as vice-chairman to Sir John Hall as the club finished Premier League runners-up to Manchester United in 1996 and 1997. He was then chairman for ten years until selling his stake to current owner Mike Ashley in June 2007. In 2016, his family paid for a £250,000 statue of Shearer at St James' Park.

**DEREK WILKINSON**, 82, spent 12 years with Sheffield Wednesday and was a key figure in the 1958–59 Division Two title-winning side when they finished two points ahead of Fulham. Two seasons later, he helped them finish runners-up to Tottenham in the top division. The right-winger scored 57 goals in 231 appearances for the club before he was forced to retire at 29 with a persistent groin injury in 1965.

**JOHN WORSDALE**, 68, came through the youth ranks at home-town club Stoke and made his senior debut against Arsenal in 1968. The right-winger played three more games for the club, then had three seasons with Lincoln before going into non-league football.

## OCTOBER 2017

**IAN MCNEILL**, 85, played an influential role in Chelsea's revival in the early 1980s when they climbed from near the bottom of the old Second Division to the upper reaches of the top-flight. As manager John Neal's right-hand man, he recruited several little-known players who went on to become major names at Stamford Bridge, including Kerry Dixon, Pat Nevin and Gordon Durie. And when Neal suffered poor health, McNeill's importance grew alongside coach John Hollins. He returned to management in his own right at Shrewsbury in 1987, having previously taken Wigan into the Football League a decade earlier and managed Ross County in Scotland. McNeill, who also discovered Jimmy Floyd Hasselbaink when scouting for Leeds, was an inside-forward for Aberdeen, Leicester, Brighton and Southend in his playing days.

**LES MUTRIE**, 65, holds an unrivalled place in Hull's record books, having scored in nine successive games during the 1981–82 season. The sequence included four goals in a 5-2 win over Hartlepool. He was part of the side that won promotion from Division Four the following season and in 132 games for the club netted 50 goals. The centre-forward, signed from Blyth Spartans for £30,000, also played for Carlisle, Hartlepool, Doncaster and Colchester.

**GEOFF DUNFORD**, 66, had a 28-year involvement with Bristol Rovers and was chairman between 2004 and 2007. The businessman succeeded his father Denis, with whom he had saved the club in 1986 by the move from Eastville Stadium to ground-share with Bath City at Twerton Park. Geoff Dunford stepped down from the board in 2014 and was made a life-president.

**DICK HEWITT**, 74, won promotion from Division Four with Barnsley (1968) and York (1971). The inside-forward was previously with Huddersfield and Bradford City. He also played in Scarborough's FA Trophy-winning team of 1973 against Wigan at Wembley.

**BRIAN RILEY**, 80, signed for his home-town club Bolton in 1954 and made eight first-team appearances. The outside-left was an unused member of the squad that won the FA Cup by beating Manchester United 2-0 in 1958. He was forced to retire with an injury sustained while playing for Buxton.

**JIMMY REID**, 81, was a 5ft 4in inside-forward who had two spells with Dundee United in the 1950s. In between, he was with Bury and Stockport. Reid later played for East Fife, Arbroath and Brechin.

## NOVEMBER 2017

**ALLAN HARRIS**, 74, played alongside younger brother Ron for Chelsea in the 1967 FA Cup Final won 2-1 by Tottenham. The full-back had two spells at Stamford Bridge and also played for Coventry, Queens Park Rangers, Plymouth and Cambridge. Later, he was assistant manager to Terry Venables at QPR, following Venables to Barcelona where they won La Liga in 1985 and reached the European Cup Final the following year, losing to Steaua Bucharest on penalties. He had a brief spell in charge of Espanyol, then managed Al-Ahly in Egypt and was head coach of the Malaysia national side.

**DERMOT DRUMMY**, 56, served Chelsea as Academy boss, reserve team manager and international head coach. He left the club in April 2016 for his first managerial appointment, at Crawley, where he had 13 months before being sacked. Drummy spent most of his playing career in non-league football after brief spells with Arsenal and Blackpool.

## DECEMBER 2017

**WILLIE PENMAN**, 78, helped Newcastle win the Second Division title under Joe Harvey in the 1964–65 season when they finished a point ahead of Northampton. The inside-forward had three years at the club after signing from Rangers. He went on to play for Swindon, Walsall, Dundalk and Seattle, then managed Cheltenham in 1973.

**JOHN FAULKNER**, 69, impressed Don Revie playing for Sutton United in an FA Cup tie against his side in 1970 and was signed by the Leeds manager. The centre-half made only a handful of appearances before moving to Luton, where he played 209 league games. After four years in the United States, Faulkner rejoined Luton as a coach. He also had a spell as assistant manager at Norwich.

**CYRIL BEAVON**, 80, made more than 500 appearances for Oxford United after signing from Wolves in 1959. The full-back, an England youth international, played every game in their Southern League title-winning season of 1961–62, after which the club were elected to the Football League. Beavon left after ten years for Banbury, before retiring through injury. Son Stuart senior played for Tottenham, Notts County and Reading, while grandson Stuart junior was a Checkatrade Trophy winner with Coventry in 2017.

**JACKIE MOONEY**, 79, scored on his debut for the Republic of Ireland against Poland at Dalymount Park in 1964. It was a successful year for the inside-right, who was influential in Shamrock Rovers winning the League of Ireland title and FAI Cup. He was awarded a second cap, against Belgium, in 1965.

**STEVE PIPER**, 64, came through the youth ranks at Brighton and made 162 senior appearances for his home-town club between 1972–77. The central-defender also played for Portsmouth before moving into non-league football.

**IAN TWITCHIN**, 65, made 435 appearances for Torquay, his only Football League club, between 1970–81. The England youth international made his debut as an 18-year-old right-winger and also played at full-back. He later played and managed in non-league football.

## JANUARY 2018

**CYRILLE REGIS**, 59, exerted a massive influence on English football during a career spanning more than 600 games for club and country. He was a centre-forward of raw power and spectacular goals, but admired even more as a pioneer for black players. Overcoming years of racist abuse from supporters, he proved the inspiration for many youngsters to take up the sport and his death from a heart attack was mourned throughout the game. Regis did it the hard way, coming through the Isthmian League at Hayes before being signed by West Bromwich Albion manager Ronnie Allen in 1977. Alongside Laurie Cunningham and Brendon Batson, he changed the face of football, with Allen's successor, Ron Atkinson,

**JOE SCOTT**, 88, scored 16 goals in 29 games in his first season after joining Middlesborough from Luton in 1954. He spent nearly five years at the club before moving to Hartlepool, then playing for York.

## FEBRUARY 2018

**LIAM MILLER**, 36, played for 12 clubs in six countries and won 21 caps for the Republic of Ireland. After coming through the youth ranks at Celtic, he was part of their Scottish Premier League title-winning squad in 2004. The midfielder helped Sunderland to promotion to the Premier League in 2007, along with spells at Manchester United, Leeds, Queens Park Rangers and Hibernian. Abroad, he played for Australian teams in Perth, Brisbane and Melbourne, Wilmington in the United States and Aarhus in Denmark. Miller, who died of cancer, also served his home-town club Cork. He scored a European under-16 title winner with the Republic, progressing to the senior international side for whom he scored one goal, against Sweden in 2006.

**KIERON DURKAN**, 44, scored two memorable goals in Wrexham's FA Cup run during the 1994–95 season. He was on the mark as they defeated Ipswich, from the Premiership, 2-1, then opened the scoring in a fourth-round tie against Manchester United at Old Trafford which his side lost 5-2. The Republic of Ireland under-21 midfielder helped Stockport finish Division Two runners-up in 1997, following a £100,000 move, and Macclesfield to second place in Division Three a year later. He also played for York on loan, Rochdale and Swansea.

**DICK SCOTT**, 76, was a League Cup winner with Norwich, playing in both legs of the 1962 final when they defeated Rochdale 3-0 and 1-0. The right-half had five years at the club, then played for Cardiff, Scunthorpe and Lincoln.

**BILLY WILSON**, 71, made 247 league appearances for Blackburn between 1964–72. He joined Portsmouth for a £15,000 fee, played 216 games in seven years and was inducted into the club's Hall of Fame.

**JOHN MUIR**, 70, signed for St Johnstone in 1969 after scoring 28 goals in 57 appearances for Alloa. His first three seasons were dogged by injury, but he then reproduced some of that scoring form with tallies of 14, 14 and 16. Muir rejoined Alloa in 1976.

## MARCH 2018

**KEN MULHEARN**, 72, joined Joe Mercer's Manchester City from Stockport as cover for goalkeeper Harry Dowd in September 1967. Two days later, Dowd was injured and Mulhearn played for the rest of the season in which City became champions, two points ahead of Manchester United and three clear of Liverpool. He lost his place the following season and, with the emergence of Joe Corrigan, moved to Shrewsbury, making 432 appearances for the club over the next decade. It included two promotions – Division Four runners-up in 1975 and Third Division champions four years later. Dowd finished his career at Crewe.

**BOBBY FERGUSON**, 80, was Bobby Robson's first-team coach when Ipswich won the UEFA Cup in 1981, beating Alkmaar 5-4 on aggregate in the two-leg final. He became manager when Robson took the England job the following season and was in charge until 1987 when his contract was not renewed. Ferguson later coached Sunderland, after former Ipswich player Terry Butcher was appointed manager, and had a spell at Birmingham under Dave Mackay. His playing career, at full-back, took in Newcastle, Derby, Cardiff and Newport.

**DEREK SAUNDERS**, 90, was an ever-present in Chelsea's first League Championship-winning team in season 1954–55 when they finished four points ahead of both Wolves and Portsmouth. The red-haired left-half joined the club as an England amateur international from Walthamstow Avenue, with whom he won the FA Amateur Cup 1952. In six seasons at Stamford Bridge, he made 222 appearances before retiring to join the coaching staff.

**JOHN KURILA**, 76, helped Colchester deliver one of the FA Cup's biggest-ever giant-killing performances. The Glasgow-born wing-half's Fourth Division side upset all the odds by beating Don Revie's Leeds 3-2 in a fifth round tie watched by a 16,000 crowd at their old Layer Road ground in 1971. Kurila had another season to remember earlier in his career, playing for Northampton in their one season in the old First Division. He also had spells with Celtic, Bristol City, Southend and Lincoln.

**FRANK HODGETTS**, 93, holds a unique place in the history of West Bromwich Albion – as the youngest-ever to represent the club and, at the time of his death, their oldest surviving player. The left-winger signed as war was breaking out in 1939. The following year, he made his debut, aged 16 years and 26 days, against Notts County. After 178 appearances, including war-time football, he moved to Millwall in 1949, returning in 1958 to spend four years coaching Albion's youngsters.

**GEORGE MEEK**, 84, played a key role as Leeds returned to the top division, after a decade's absence, in the 1955–56 season. The winger's crosses set up numerous goals for John Charles, who netted 28 in the final 28 matches to clinch the runners-up spot behind Sheffield Wednesday. Meek, at 5ft 3in the club's smallest-ever player, made 200 appearances after signing from Hamilton. He then had spells with Walsall and Leicester.

**ARTHUR STEWART**, 76, won seven Northern Ireland caps, four of them with Derby after Brian Clough signed him in 1967. The wing-half spent two-and-half seasons at the club after winning league and cup honours with Glentoran. He also played for home-town side Ballymena and New Jersey and Detroit in America. Stewart later managed Ballymena and Glentoran.

**COLIN HARPER**, 71, helped Ipswich become Second Division champions, under Bill McGarry, in the 1967–68 season when they finished a point ahead of Queens Park Rangers and Blackpool. The left-back then played under McGarry's successor, Bobby Robson, spending 11 years at the club. He also had loan spells at Grimsby and Cambridge United, followed by time at Port Vale and the Irish side Waterford.

**JOHN MOLYNEUX**, 87, made 249 appearances for Liverpool after signing from Chester in 1955. The England youth international right-back spent seven years at Anfield before returning to Chester, for whom he played a total of 245 games.

**RON MAILER**, 85, captained Dunfermline to their first Scottish Cup win in 1961. Jock Stein's team defeated Celtic 2-0 in the final after their first meeting finished goalless. Mailer, a wing-half, made 325 appearances for the club, either side of a brief spell with Darlington, and was awarded a testimonial in 1965.

**WALLY GOULD**, 79, was Brighton's leading marksman in their Fourth Division championship-winning season of 1964–65. He scored 21 goals, one of them in a 3-1 victory over Darlington which clinched the title in front of a crowd of 31,000 at the old Goldstone Ground. The right-winger joined the club after spells with Sheffield United and York and later played, coached and managed in South Africa. After returning home, he coached at Stoke.

**ALEX RENNIE**, 69, joined St Johnstone from Stirling Albion and made 254 appearances in central defence and midfield between 1967–75. He returned to the club as manager, winning the Division One title in the 1982–83 season. His career also embraced playing for Dundee United, coaching Hearts and managing Stenhousemuir.

## APRIL 2018

**RAY WILKINS**, 61, was an accomplished midfielder for club and country whose nickname 'Butch' was at odds with the style and vision of his play. Mature beyond his years, he became Chelsea's youngest-ever captain at 18, spending six years at Stamford Bridge before joining Manchester United for £825,000. There, he won the FA Cup in 1983, scoring one of the great Wembley final goals with a curling left-footed shot in the first drawn match against Brighton. Wilkins then took his talents abroad, to AC Milan and Paris Saint-Germain, before a move to Rangers which brought Scottish titles in 1989 and 1990 and a League Cup winners' medal. After that, he played for Queens Park Rangers, Crystal Palace, Wycombe, Hibernian, Millwall and finally Leyton Orient. The first of 84 games for England, ten as captain, came against Italy in 1976. The second of two World Cups, Mexico in 1986, brought a sending-off in a group match against Morocco for throwing the ball away – England's first dismissal in the tournament. Wilkins went on to manage Queens Park Rangers and Fulham, was twice assistant manager at Chelsea and had his final appointment at Aston Villa under Tim Sherwood. Wilkins, awarded an MBE in 1993, became a respected media pundit and was analysing a game a week before suffering a heart attack.

**ROY BENTLEY**, 93, was the last surviving member of England's 1950 World Cup squad. He made his debut in 1949 and scored nine goals in 12 appearances – one of which was in the shock defeat by the United States in a qualifying match. The centre-forward captained Chelsea to their first top-flight title in the 1954–55 season and scored 150 goals in 367 appearances for the club. Bentley, who served in the Royal Navy during World War Two, began his career with spells at home-town clubs Bristol City and Bristol Rovers. He also played for Newcastle, Fulham and Queens Park Rangers before retiring at 38 and moving into management with Reading and Swansea.

**GEORGE MULHALL**, 81, played every match as Sunderland reached the old First Division by finishing runners-up to Leeds in the 1963–64 season. The sequence formed part of 114 successive appearances following a move from Aberdeen, where he had spent almost a decade. Mulhall, who won two of his three Scottish caps while at Roker Park, scored 67 goals in 289 appearances for the club. The outside-left also played in Canada and South Africa and in Scotland, for Morton. He managed Bradford City and Bolton, then led Halifax back into the Football League.

**JOHN LAMBIE**, 77, had four separate spells as manager of Partick Thistle between 1988–2005, twice taking the club into Scotland's top division. With Hamilton, he won promotion and supervised a shock Scottish Cup win over Rangers. He also managed Falkirk. Lambie was a full-back for Falkirk and St Johnstone, reached the 1970 League Cup Final with the Perth side (0-1 v Celtic), helped them finish third in the league and shared their European debut in the UEFA Cup.

**RON COOPER**, 79, played in the Peterborough team that defeated Arsenal 2-1 on the way to reaching the quarter-finals of the FA Cup in 1965. The right-back played for the club for ten years and had a testimonial against Brian Clough's Derby in which the manager also made an appearance and scored a goal.

**BARRIE WILLIAMS**, 79, was Sutton United's manager in their famous 2-1 FA Cup third round win over Premier League Coventry at the club's Gander Green Lane ground in 1989. He spent a decade at the non-league side and also managed the England women's team.

**EDDIE BLACKBURN**, 61, was a goalkeeper who played for Hull, York and Hartlepool. He finished his career with the Sweden club Halmstads, having to retire with an ankle injury.

**DICK BATE**, 71, spent more than 40 years as a coach, technical director, academy manager and consultant with a wide range of clubs. They included Burnley, Watford, Leeds, Sheffield Wednesday, Lincoln and Notts County. He also worked for the FA and had a brief spell as Southend manager.

## MAY 2018

**RAY WILSON**, 83, was a World Cup and FA Cup winner within two months in 1966. At 31, the left-back was the oldest member of the England side that defeated West Germany 4-2 in the final at Wembley. Wilson, arguably the world's finest in his position, played in all their previous matches against Uruguay, Mexico and France at the group stage, Argentina in the quarter-finals and Portugal in the semi-finals. Four years earlier, in Chile, he was also an ever-present against Hungary, Argentina and Bulgaria in group games and in the 3-1 defeat by Brazil in the last eight. He won 63 caps, the first against Scotland in 1960. Wilson, christened Ramon, had returned to the old national stadium after helping Everton beat Sheffield Wednesday 3-2 in the FA Cup after being two goals down. Two years later, he was in the final again, this time a 1-0 defeat by West Bromwich Albion. His club career flourished at Huddersfield after manager Bill Shankly advised that full-back was his best position after spells in a forward role and central defence. He made 283 appearances after joining the club at 17, played 154 times for Everton, moved on to Oldham, then finished at Bradford, where he was also briefly manager. Wilson opened an undertaker's business in Huddersfield and was later awarded an MBE. He was diagnosed with Alzheimer's disease in 2004.

**NEALE COOPER**, 54, won the European Cup-Winners' Cup with Aberdeen in 1983 when Sir Alex Ferguson's team defeated Real Madrid 2-1 after extra-time in the final in Gothenburg. Later that year, they beat Hamburg 2-0 over two legs in the European Super Cup. Cooper gained league winners' medals in 1984 and 1985, lifted the Scottish Cup four times in five years and the League Cup once. The midfielder went on to have injury-hit spells with Aston Villa, Rangers and Reading, along with a return to Aberdeen and time spent at Dunfermline and Ross County. As a manager, he led Ross to successive promotions, then took charge of Hartlepool and Peterhead. Cooper died after being found injured outside his home. Among the condolences was one from Real Madrid

**GRAHAM LOVETT**, 70, joined West Bromwich Albion straight from school and made his debut aged 17 against Chelsea in 1964. Lovett played in the first leg of their League Cup Final win over West Ham two years later, but his career was interrupted by serious injuries in two car crashes. The first left him with a broken neck, amid fears he would never play again. He came back and manager Alan Ashman showed faith in the wing-half with a place in the 1968 FA Cup Final team against Everton – only his ninth appearance of that season. Lovett was given the job of stopping the runs of World Cup-winning left-back Ray Wilson and his side won 1-0. The following year, he sustained a collapsed lung, broken ribs and a broken thigh bone, was unable to recapture his previous form when returning and after a spell on loan at Southampton was released by Albion in the summer of 1972.

**JLLOYD SAMUEL**, 37, was an England under-21 international who won two senior caps with Trinidad and Tobago, where he was born. The defender made 199 appearances for Aston Villa between 1998-2007, playing every match in the 2003-04 season when Villa finished sixth in the Premier League. He had four years at Bolton, loan spells with Gillingham and Cardiff and also played club football in Iran. He died in a car crash in Cheshire.

**CLIFF JACKSON**, 76, scored the goal which clinched promotion for Crystal Palace to the top-flight for the first time in 1969. It came against Fulham, gave Palace the runners-up spot to Derby and came in a season when he was leading scorer with 17 in league and cup after being converted from a left-winger to centre-forward. The England schoolboy international joined Palace from Plymouth, having previously helped home-town club Swindon to promotion to Division Two in 1963. He finished his career at Torquay.

**ARTHUR FITZSIMONS**, 88, made his international debut for the Republic of Ireland against Finland in 1969 and went on to win 26 caps, scoring seven goals. He spent a large part of his club career at Middlesbrough, where he played alongside Wilf Mannion and Brian Clough. After 231 appearances and 51 goals, the inside-forward moved to Lincoln, then joined Mansfield. He also served Irish clubs Shelbourne, Crusaders and Drogheda and managed Drogheda and Shamrock Rovers.

**KEN HODGKISSON**, 85, helped Walsall rise from the Fourth Division to Division Two with back-to-back promotions in 1960 and 1961. The inside-forward made 352 appearances and scored 56 goals in 11 seasons at the club after starting his career with West Bromwich Albion. He returned to Albion in 1981 and had four years as youth team manager.

**TOMMY MCGHEE**, 89, was Portsmouth's oldest surviving player. The England amateur international left the Royal Navy to sign professional forms in 1954, made his debut in a 5-0 win over Everton and helped the club to third place behind Chelsea and Wolves. McGhee, a right-back, had five seasons in the top-flight before joining Reading, then playing non-league football.

**PHIL MCKNIGHT**, 93, joined Chelsea from the Scottish club Alloa in 1947 and spent seven years at the club, primarily as a back-up wing-half. After 33 appearances, he moved to Leyton Orient, where he played more than 200 games.

**FRANNY FIRTH**, 61, was part of Huddersfield's academy team that reached the 1974 FA Youth Cup Final, losing 2-1 on aggregate to Tottenham. The winger went on to play for the club's senior side until sustaining a broken leg in 1976. After recovering, he played for Halifax and Bury.

## JUNE 2018

**STAN ANDERSON**, 84, is the only player to have captained the three big north-east teams. He became a legend at Sunderland with 447 appearances in 11 years, a rare home-grown player in the 'Bank of England' side of the 1950s. Anderson helped them reach two FA Cup semi-finals and had his finest day in that competition, scoring both goals in a man-of-the-match performance against Arsenal in a third round tie. The wing-half led Newcastle to the Second Division title in the 1964-65 season, then joined Middlesbrough, where he later became manager. He won two England caps, against Austria and Scotland, and was part of the 1962 World Cup squad in Chile. He also holds an unwanted record as the first player in an England shirt to be sent off – against Bulgaria in an under-23 international in Sofia in 1957. Anderson took Middlesbrough back to Division Two in his first season as manager. He was in charge for seven years from 1966 and also managed AEK Athens in Greece, Queens Park Rangers, Doncaster and Bolton.

**ERNIE HUNT**, 75, will be remembered for scoring the 'donkey kick' free-kick for Coventry which won the BBC's Goal of the Season award for 1970-71. Willie Carr gripped the ball between his heels in the match against Everton, flicked it up and Hunt scored with a volley. The manoeuvre was outlawed by the FA at the end of that campaign. The inside-forward, an England under-23 international, spent five years at Coventry, having started his career with home-town club Swindon, where he was leading scorer for four successive seasons. He also played for Wolves, Everton, Doncaster and Bristol City.

**JOHN SHEPHERD**, 86, made headlines as a 20-year-old in 1952 when scoring four goals against Leyton Orient in his first away match for Millwall – an achievement which has never been bettered in the Football League. Eighteen months earlier, he was in quarantine in hospital with polio and doctors feared he would never walk again. The centre-forward finished his debut season as leading marksman with 21 goals in 22 appearances. He also topped the scoring charts, with 24, in 1957, the year in which Millwall knocked Newcastle out of the FA Cup in front of a crowd of more than 45,000 at The Den. Shepherd went on to play for Brighton and Gillingham.

**HAROLD DAVIS**, 85, overcame severe injuries in the Korean War to win trophies with Rangers and gain a place in the Ibrox Hall of Fame. Serving with the Black Watch, he came under heavy machine gun fire and spent almost two years recovering in hospital. That he was able to lead a normal life after that was remarkable enough. To have the football career he did spoke volumes for his strength of character. Davis, a right-half, joined Rangers from East Fife in 1956 and in eight years at the club they were champions four times, won two League Cups, the Scottish Cup and were the first British side to reach a European final – the 1961 Cup-Winners' Cup which Fiorentina won 4-1 on aggregate. He finished his career with Partick, then managed Queen of the South and was assistant manager at Dundee.

**GARETH WILLIAMS**, 76, joined Cardiff after being spotted playing local football and was captain during six years at the club. He joined Bolton for £45,000 in 1967, proving a mainstay in midfield during some testing seasons which ended with relegation to the third tier for the first time in the club's history. Williams then played for a further two seasons at Bury.

**RON HEALEY**, 65, was a Republic of Ireland international goalkeeper who helped Cardiff to promotion to the old Second Division in season 1975-76. He made more than 200 appearances for the club before a pelvic injury cut short his career at 30. Previously he was understudy to Joe Corrigan at Manchester and had spells at Coventry and Preston. Healey, who collapsed while out cycling, won two international caps.

**JOHN RITCHIE**, 70, kept goal for Bradford City from 1971-73 in between serving three Scottish clubs. He had two spells with Brechin and also played for Dundee United and Cowdenbeath. Ritchie returned to Brechin as manager and led them to the Division Two title in 1990.

**GORAN BUNJEVCEVIC**, 45, joined Tottenham from Red Star Belgrade for £1.4m in 2001 and made 58 appearances in five injury-dogged years at the club. The Serbian defender, who won 16 caps with the old Yugoslavia, later played for De Haag in Holland.

## JULY 2018

**ALAN GILZEAN**, 79, achieved legendary status with clubs in Scotland and England as a prolific scorer and major trophy winner. He fired Dundee to the title in 1961-2, ahead of Rangers and Celtic, and the following season scored hat-tricks against Cologne and Sporting Club of Portugal on the way to the European Cup semi-finals. Gilzean scored a club-record 169 goals in 190 games before joining Tottenham for a then Scottish record fee of £72,500. In a decade at White Hart Lane, he formed dynamic partnerships with Jimmy Greaves and later Martin Chivers, winning the FA Cup against Chelsea in 1967, two League Cups and the 1972 UEFA Cup in an all-English final against Wolves. There were 133 goals in 439 games for Spurs, along with a dozen in 22 appearances for Scotland. Gilzean finished his career with three months in South Africa and had a year as manager of non-league Stevenage.

# THE THINGS THEY SAY...

'It was a moment of madness. I lost my head. You can't behave like that. There is no excuse. I brought it on myself' – **Jamie Carragher**, Sky pundit and former Liverpool stalwart, after being caught on camera spitting through his car window at a man goading him over Liverpool's defeat by Manchester United.

'We must never take it for granted or think we have a divine right to be here. We have to earn that right every single day' – **Eddie Howe**, Bournemouth manager, on the demands on his players to stay in the Premier League.

'It shows the state of our society that when people are generous we are surprised' – **Arsene Wenger** after Pierre-Emerick Aubameyang passed up the chance of a hat-trick against Stoke by handing the ball over to team-mate Alexandre Lacazette.

'I'm out of here' – **Mick McCarthy**, Ipswich manager, walks away from the club, earlier than planned, after more protests from fans.

'Wooooow really' – **Mohamed Salah**, Liverpool goal ace, reacting to the Premier League's decision to uphold Tottenham's appeal for Harry Kane, not Christian Eriksen, to be awarded their second goal in a 2-1 win at Stoke to boost his chances of winning the Golden Boot award.

# RECORDS SECTION

**Compiled by Albert Sewell**

**INDEX**


*Goalscoring* ....................349
*Attendances* ....................371
*International Records* ............373
*Famous Club Feats* ................378
*League Records* ....................381
*FA Cup Records* ....................392
*League Cup Records* .............402
*Discipline* ............................402
*Managers* ....................................410
*Wembley Stadium* .........................417
*Football Tragedies* .........................419
*Great Service* .............................. 423
*Penalties* .................................... 425
*Scottish Records* .......................... 429
*Miscellaneous* ............................. 433


## GOALSCORING

(†Football League pre-1992–93)

**Highest:** Arbroath 36 Bon Accord (Aberdeen) 0 in Scottish Cup 1, Sep 12, 1885. On same day, also in Scottish Cup 1, Dundee Harp beat Aberdeen Rov 35-0.

**Internationals:** France 0 England 15 in Paris, 1906 (Amateur); Ireland 0 England 13 in Belfast Feb 18, 1882 (record in UK); England 9 Scotland 3 at Wembley, Apr 15, 1961; Biggest England win at Wembley: 9-0 v Luxembourg (Euro Champ), Dec 15, 1982.

**Other record wins: Scotland:** 11-0 v Ireland (Glasgow, Feb 23, 1901); **Northern Ireland:** 7-0 v Wales (Belfast, Feb 1, 1930); **Wales:** 11-0 v Ireland (Wrexham, Mar 3, 1888); **Rep of Ireland:** 8-0 v Malta (Euro Champ, Dublin, Nov 16, 1983).

**Record international defeats: England:** 1-7 v Hungary (Budapest, May 23, 1954); **Scotland:** 3-9 v England (Wembley, Apr 15, 1961); **Ireland:** 0-13 v England (Belfast, Feb 18, 1882); **Wales:** 0-9 v Scotland (Glasgow, Mar 23, 1878); **Rep of Ireland:** 0-7 v Brazil (Uberlandia, May 27, 1982).

**World Cup: Qualifying round** – Australia 31 American Samoa 0, world record international score (Apr 11, 2001); Australia 22 Tonga 0 (Apr 9, 2001); Iran 19 Guam 0 (Nov 25, 2000); Maldives 0 Iran 17 (Jun 2, 1997). **Finals – highest scores:** Hungary 10 El Salvador 1 (Spain, Jun 15, 1982); Hungary 9 S Korea 0 (Switzerland, Jun 17, 1954); Yugoslavia 9 Zaire 0 (W Germany, Jun 18, 1974).

**European Championship: Qualifying round – highest scorers:** San Marino 0 Germany 13 (Serravalle, Sep 6, 2006). **Finals – highest score:** Holland 6 Yugoslavia 1 (quarter-final, Rotterdam, Jun 25, 2000).

**Biggest England U-21 win:** 9-0 v San Marino (Shrewsbury, Nov 19, 2013).

**FA Cup:** Preston 26 Hyde 0 1st round, Oct 15, 1887.

**League Cup:** West Ham 10 Bury 0 (2nd round, 2nd leg, Oct 25, 1983); Liverpool 10 Fulham 0 (2nd round, 1st leg, Sep 23, 1986). **Record aggregates:** Liverpool 13 Fulham 2 (10-0h, 3-2a), Sep 23, Oct 7, 1986; West Ham 12 Bury 1 (2-1a, 10-0h), Oct 4, 25, 1983; Liverpool 11 Exeter 0 (5-0h, 6-0a), Oct 7, 28, 1981.

**League Cup – most goals in one match: 12** Reading 5 Arsenal 7 aet (4th round, Oct 30, 2012). Dagenham & Redbridge 6 Brentford 6 aet (Brentford won 4-2 on pens; 1st round, Aug 12, 2014

**Premier League** (beginning 1992–93): Manchester Utd 9 Ipswich 0, Mar 4, 1995. **Record away win:** Nottm Forest 1 Manchester Utd 8 Feb 6, 1999.

**Highest aggregate scores in Premier League – 11:** Portsmouth 7 Reading 4, Sep 29, 2007; **10:** Tottenham 6 Reading 4, Dec 29, 2007; Tottenham 9 Wigan 1, Nov 22, 2009; Manchester Utd 8 Arsenal 2, Aug 28, 2011; Arsenal 7 Newcastle 3, Dec 29, 2012; WBA 5 Manchester Utd 5, May 19, 2013.

**†Football League (First Division):** Aston Villa 12 Accrington 2, Mar 12, 1892; Tottenham 10 Everton 4, Oct 11, 1958 (highest Div 1 aggregate that century); WBA 12 Darwen 0, Apr 4, 1892; Nottm Forest 12 Leicester Fosse 0, Apr 21, 1909. **Record away win:** Newcastle 1 Sunderland 9, Dec 5, 1908; Cardiff 1 Wolves 9, Sep 3, 1955; Wolves 0 WBA 8, Dec 27, 1893.

**New First Division** (beginning 1992–93): Bolton 7 Swindon 0, Mar 8, 1997; Sunderland 7 Oxford Utd 0, Sep 19, 1998. **Record away win:** Stoke 0 Birmingham 7, Jan 10, 1998; Oxford Utd 0 Birmingham 7, Dec 12, 1998. **Record aggregate:** Grimsby 6 Burnley 5, Oct 29, 2002; Burnley 4 Watford 7, Apr 5, 2003.

**Championship (beginning 2004–05):** Birmingham 0 Bournemouth 8, Oct 25, 2014. **Record away win:** Birmingham 0 Bournemouth 8, Oct 25, 2014. **Record aggregate:** Leeds 4 Preston 6, Sep 29, 2010; Leeds 3 Nottm Forest 7, Mar 20, 2012; Bristol City 5 Hull 5, Apr 21, 2018.

**†Second Division:** Newcastle 13 Newport Co 0, Oct 5, 1946; Small Heath 12 Walsall Town Swifts 0, Dec 17, 1892; Darwen 12 Walsall 0, Dec 26, 1896; Woolwich Arsenal 12 Loughborough 0, Mar 12, 1900; Small Heath 12 Doncaster 0, Apr 11, 1903. **Record away win:** *Burslem Port Vale 0 Sheffield Utd 10, Dec 10, 1892. **Record aggregate:** Manchester City 11 Lincoln 3, Mar 23, 1895.

**New Second Division** (beginning 1992–93): Hartlepool 1 Plymouth Argyle 8, May 7, 1994; Hartlepool 8 Grimsby 1, Sep 12, 2003.

**New League 1 (beginning 2004–05):** MK Dons 7 Oldham 0, Dec 20, 2014; Oxford 0 Wigan 7, Dec 23, 2017. **Record aggregate:** Hartlepool 4 Wrexham 6, Mar 5, 2005; Wolves 6 Rotherham 4, Apr 18, 2014; Bristol City 8 Walsall 2, May 3, 2015.

**†Third Division:** Gillingham 10 Chesterfield 0, Sep 5, 1987; Tranmere 9 Accrington 0, Apr 18, 1959; Brentford 9 Wrexham 0, Oct 15, 1963. **Record away win:** Halifax 0 Fulham 8, Sep 16, 1969. **Record aggregate:** Doncaster 7 Reading 5, Sep 25, 1982.

**New Third Division** (beginning 1992–93): Barnet 1 Peterborough 9, Sep 5, 1998. **Record aggregate:** Hull 7 Swansea 4, Aug 30, 1997.

**New League 2 (beginning 2004–05):** Peterborough 7 Brentford 0, Nov 24, 2007 Shrewsbury 7 Gillingham 0, Sep 13, 2008; Crewe 7 Barnet 0, Aug 21, 2010; Crewe 8 Cheltenham 1, Apr 2, 2011; Cambridge 7 Morecambe 0, Apr 19, 2016; Luton 7 Cambridge 0, Nov 18, 2017.

**Record away win:** Boston 0 Grimsby 6, Feb 3, 2007; Macclesfield 0 Darlington 6, Aug 30, 2008; Lincoln 0 Rotherham 6, Mar 25, 2011. **Record aggregate:** Burton 5 Cheltenham 6, Mar 13, 2010; Accrington 7 Gillingham 4, Oct 2, 2010.

**†Third Division (North):** Stockport 13 Halifax 0 (still joint biggest win in Football League – see Div 2) Jan 6, 1934; Tranmere 13 Oldham 4, Dec 26, 1935. (17 is highest Football League aggregate score). **Record away win:** Accrington 0 Barnsley 9, Feb 3, 1934.

**†Third Division (South):** Luton 12 Bristol Rov 0, Apr 13, 1936; Bristol City 9 Gillingham 4, Jan 15, 1927; Gillingham 9 Exeter 4, Jan 7, 1951. **Record away win:** Northampton 0 Walsall 8, Apr 8, 1947.

**†Fourth Division:** Oldham 11 Southport 0, Dec 26, 1962. **Record away win:** Crewe 1 Rotherham 8, Sep 8, 1973. **Record aggregate:** Hartlepool 10 Barrow 1, Apr 4, 1959; Crystal Palace 9 Accrington 2, Aug 20, 1960; Wrexham 10 Hartlepool 1, Mar 3, 1962; Oldham 11 Southport 0, Dec 26, 1962; Torquay 8 Newport 3, Oct 19, 1963; Shrewsbury 7 Doncaster 4, Feb 1, 1975; Barnet 4 Crewe 7, Aug 17, 1991.

**Scottish Premier – Highest aggregate: 12:** Motherwell 6 Hibernian 6, May 5, 2010; **11:** Celtic 8 Hamilton 3, Jan 3, 1987; Motherwell 5 Aberdeen 6, Oct 20, 1999. **Other highest team scores:** Aberdeen 8 Motherwell 0 (Mar 26, 1979); Hamilton 0 Celtic 8 (Nov 5, 1988); Celtic 9 Aberdeen 0 (Nov 6, 2010).

**Scottish League Div 1:** Celtic 11 Dundee 0, Oct 26, 1895. **Record away win:** Hibs 11 *Airdrie 1, Oct 24, 1959.

**Scottish League Div 2:** Airdrieonians 15 Dundee Wanderers 1, Dec 1, 1894 (biggest win in history of League football in Britain).

**Record modern Scottish League aggregate: 12** – Brechin 5 Cowdenbeath 7, Div 2, Jan 18, 2003.

**Record British score since 1900:** Stirling 20 Selkirk 0 (Scottish Cup 1, Dec 8, 1984). Winger Davie Thompson (7 goals) was one of 9 Stirling players to score.

## LEAGUE GOALS – BEST IN SEASON (Before restructure in 1992)

| Div | | Goals | Games |
|---|---|---|---|
| 1 | WR (Dixie) Dean, Everton, 1927–28 | 60 | 39 |
| 2 | George Camsell, Middlesbrough, 1926–27 | 59 | 37 |

| | | | |
|---|---|---|---|
| **3(S)** | Joe Payne, Luton, 1936–37 | 55 | 39 |
| **3(N)** | Ted Harston, Mansfield, 1936–37 | 55 | 41 |
| **3** | Derek Reeves, Southampton, 1959–60 | 39 | 46 |
| **4** | Terry Bly, Peterborough, 1960–61 | 52 | 46 |

**(Since restructure in 1992)**

| Div | | Goals | Games |
|---|---|---|---|
| **1** | Guy Whittingham, Portsmouth, 1992–93 | 42 | 46 |
| **2** | Jimmy Quinn, Reading, 1993–94 | 35 | 46 |
| **3** | Andy Morrell, Wrexham, 2002–03 | 34 | 45 |

**Premier League – BEST IN SEASON**

Andy Cole **34 goals** (Newcastle – 40 games, 1993–94); Alan Shearer **34 goals** (Blackburn – 42 games, 1994–95).

## FOOTBALL LEAGUE – BEST MATCH HAULS

*(Before restructure in 1992)*

| Div | Goals | |
|---|---|---|
| **1** | Ted Drake (Arsenal), away to Aston Villa, Dec 14, 1935 | **7** |
| | James Ross (Preston) v Stoke, Oct 6, 1888 | **7** |
| **2** | *Neville (Tim) Coleman (Stoke) v Lincoln, Feb 23, 1957 | **7** |
| | Tommy Briggs (Blackburn) v Bristol Rov, Feb 5, 1955 | **7** |
| **3(S)** | Joe Payne (Luton) v Bristol Rov, Apr 13, 1936 | **10** |
| **3(N)** | Robert ('Bunny') Bell (Tranmere) v Oldham, Dec 26, 1935 he also missed a penalty | **9** |
| **3** | Barrie Thomas (Scunthorpe) v Luton, Apr 24, 1965 | **5** |
| | Keith East (Swindon) v Mansfield, Nov 20, 1965 | **5** |
| | Steve Earle (Fulham) v Halifax, Sep 16, 1969 | **5** |
| | Alf Wood (Shrewsbury) v Blackburn, Oct 2, 1971 | **5** |
| | Tony Caldwell (Bolton) v Walsall, Sep 10, 1983 | **5** |
| | Andy Jones (Port Vale) v Newport Co., May 4, 1987 | **5** |
| **4** | Bert Lister (Oldham) v Southport, Dec 26, 1962 | **6** |

*Scored from the wing

(Since restructure in 1992)

Div Goals

**1** **4** in match – John Durnin (Oxford Utd v Luton, 1992–93); Guy Whittingham (Portsmouth v Bristol Rov 1992–93); Craig Russell (Sunderland v Millwall, 1995–96); David Connolly (Wolves at Bristol City 1998–99); Darren Byfield (Rotherham at Millwall, 2002–03); David Connolly (Wimbledon at Bradford City, 2002–03); Marlon Harewood (Nottm Forest v Stoke, 2002–03); Michael Chopra (Watford at Burnley, 2002–03); Robert Earnshaw (Cardiff v Gillingham, 2003–04). **25** in match – Paul Barnes (Burnley v Stockport, 1996–97); Robert Taylor (all 5, Gillingham at Burnley, 1998–99); Lee Jones (all 5, Wrexham v Cambridge Utd, 2001–02).

**3** **5** in match – Tony Naylor (Crewe v Colchester, 1992–93); Steve Butler (Cambridge Utd v Exeter, 1993–4); Guiliano Grazioli (Peterborough at Barnet, 1998–99).

**Champ** **4** in match – Garath McCleary (Nottm Forest at Leeds 2011–12); Nikola Zigic (Birmingham at Leeds 2011–12; Craig Davies (Barnsley at Birmingham 2012–13; Ross McCormack (Leeds at Charlton 2013–14), Jesse Lingard (Birmingham v Sheffield Wed 2013–14); Odion Ighalo (Watford v Blackpool, 2014-15); ; Leon Clarke (all 4, Sheffield Utd v Hull, 2017–18).

**Lge 1** **4** in match – Jordan Rhodes (all 4, Huddersfield at Sheffield Wed, 2011–12); Ellis Harrison (Bristol Rov v Northampton, 2016–17); James Vaughan (Bury v Peterborough, 2016–17).

**5** in match – Juan Ugarte (Wrexham at Hartlepool, 2004–05); Jordan Rhodes (Huddersfield at Wycombe, 2011–12).

**Last player to score 6 in English League match**: Geoff Hurst (West Ham 8 Sunderland 0, Div 1 Oct 19,1968.

## PREMIER LEAGUE – BEST MATCH HAULS

**5 goals** in match: Andy Cole (Manchester Utd v Ipswich, Mar 4, 1995); Alan Shearer (Newcastle v Sheffield Wed, Sep 19, 1999); Jermain Defoe (Tottenham v Wigan, Nov 22, 2009); Dimitar Berbatov (Manchester Utd v Blackburn, Nov 27, 2010), Sergio Aguero (Manchester City v Newcastle, Oct 3, 2015).

## SCOTTISH LEAGUE

| Div | | Goals |
|---|---|---|
| **Prem** | Gary Hooper (Celtic) v Hearts, May 13, 2012 | 5 |
| | Kris Boyd (Rangers) v Dundee Utd, Dec 30, 2009 | 5 |
| | Kris Boyd (Kilmarnock) v Dundee Utd, Sep 25, 2004 | 5 |
| | Kenny Miller (Rangers) v St Mirren, Nov 4, 2000 | 5 |
| | Marco Negri (Rangers) v Dundee Utd, Aug. 23, 1997 | 5 |
| | Paul Sturrock (Dundee Utd) v Morton, Nov 17, 1984 | 5 |
| 1 | Jimmy McGrory (Celtic) v Dunfermline, Jan 14, 1928 | 8 |
| 1 | Owen McNally (Arthurlie) v Armadale, Oct 1, 1927 | 8 |
| 2 | Jim Dyet (King's Park) v Forfar, Jan 2, 1930 on his debut for the club | 8 |
| 2 | John Calder (Morton) v Raith, Apr 18, 1936 | 8 |
| 2 | Norman Haywood (Raith) v Brechin, Aug. 20, 1937 | 8 |

### SCOTTISH LEAGUE – BEST IN SEASON

| | | |
|---|---|---|
| **Prem** | Brian McClair (Celtic, 1986–87) | **35** |
| | Henrik Larsson (Celtic, 2000–01) | **35** |
| 1 | William McFadyen (Motherwell, 1931–32) | **53** |
| 2 | *Jimmy Smith (Ayr, 1927–28 – 38 appearances) | **66** |
| | (*British record) | |

## CUP FOOTBALL

**Scottish Cup:** John Petrie (Arbroath) v Bon Accord, at Arbroath, 1st round, Sep 12, 1885 **13**

**FA Cup:** Ted MacDougall (Bournemouth) v Margate, 1st round, Nov 20,1971 **9**

**FA Cup Final:** Billy Townley (Blackburn) v Sheffield Wed, at Kennington Oval, 1890; Jimmy Logan (Notts Co) v Bolton, at Everton, 1894; Stan Mortensen (Blackpool) v Bolton, at Wembley, 1953 **3**

**League Cup:** Frank Bunn (Oldham) v Scarborough (3rd round), Oct 25, 1989 **6**

**Scottish League Cup:** Willie Penman (Raith) v Stirling, Sep 18, 1948 **6**

**Scottish Cup:** Most goals in match since war: 10 by **Gerry Baker** (St Mirren) in 15-0 win (1st round) v Glasgow Univ, Jan 30, 1960; 9 by his brother **Joe Baker** (Hibernian) in 15-1 win (2nd round) v Peebles, Feb 11, 1961.

## AGGREGATE LEAGUE SCORING RECORDS

| | Goals |
|---|---|
| *Arthur Rowley (1947–65, WBA, Fulham, Leicester, Shrewsbury) | **434** |
| †Jimmy McGrory (1922–38, Celtic, Clydebank) | **410** |
| Hughie Gallacher (1921–39, Airdrieonians, Newcastle, Chelsea, Derby, Notts Co, Grimsby, Gateshead) | **387** |
| William ('Dixie') Dean (1923–37, Tranmere, Everton, Notts Co) | **379** |
| Hugh Ferguson (1916–30, Motherwell, Cardiff, Dundee) | **362** |
| • Jimmy Greaves (1957–71, Chelsea, Tottenham, West Ham) | **357** |
| Steve Bloomer (1892–1914, Derby, Middlesbrough, Derby) | **352** |
| George Camsell (1923–39, Durham City, Middlesbrough) | **348** |

Dave Halliday (1920–35, St Mirren, Dundee, Sunderland, Arsenal, Manchester City, Clapton Orient) **338**
John Aldridge (1979–98, Newport, Oxford Utd, Liverpool, Tranmere) ................ **329**
Harry Bedford (1919–34), Nottm Forest, Blackpool, Derby, Newcastle, Sunderland, Bradford PA, Chesterfield ................ **326**
John Atyeo (1951–66, Bristol City) ................ **315**
Joe Smith (1908–29, Bolton, Stockport) ................ **315**
Victor Watson (1920–36, West Ham, Southampton) ................ **312**
Harry Johnson (1919–36, Sheffield Utd, Mansfield) ................ **309**
Bob McPhail (1923–1939, Airdrie, Rangers) ................ **306**

(***Rowley** scored 4 for WBA, 27 for Fulham, 251 for Leicester, 152 for Shrewsbury.

- **Greaves'** 357 is record top-division total (he also scored 9 League goals for AC Milan). **Aldridge** also scored 33 League goals for Real Sociedad. †**McGrory** scored 397 for Celtic, 13 for Clydebank).

**Most League goals for one club: 349 – Dixie Dean** (Everton 1925–37); **326 – George Camsell** (Middlesbrough 1925–39); **315 – John Atyeo** (Bristol City 1951–66); **306 – Vic Watson** (West Ham 1920–35); **291 – Steve Bloomer** (Derby 1892–1906, 1910–14); **259 – Arthur Chandler** (Leicester 1923–35); **255 – Nat Lofthouse** (Bolton 1946–61); **251 – Arthur Rowley** (Leicester 1950–58).

**More than 500 goals: Jimmy McGrory** (Celtic, Clydebank and Scotland) scored a total of **550** goals in his first-class career (1922–38).

**More than 1,000 goals:** Brazil's **Pele** is reputedly the game's all-time highest scorer with **1,283** goals in 1,365 matches (1956–77), but many of them were scored in friendlies for his club, Santos. He scored his 1,000th goal, a penalty, against Vasco da Gama in the Maracana Stadium, Rio, on Nov 19, 1969. • Pele (born Oct 23, 1940) played regularly for Santos from the age of 16. During his career, he was sent off only once. He played 95 'A' internationals for Brazil and in their World Cup-winning teams in 1958 and 1970. † Pele (Edson Arantes do Nascimento) was subsequently Brazil's Minister for Sport. He never played at Wembley, apart from being filmed there scoring a goal for a commercial. Aged 57, Pele received an 'honorary knighthood' (Knight Commander of the British Empire) from the Queen at Buckingham Palace on Dec 3, 1997.

**Romario** (retired Apr, 2008, aged 42) scored more than 1,000 goals for Vasco da Gama, Barcelona, PSV Eindhoven, Valencia and Brazil (56 in 73 internationals).

## MOST LEAGUE GOALS IN SEASON: DEAN'S 60

**WR ('Dixie') Dean,** Everton centre-forward, created a League scoring record in 1927–28 with 60 in 39 First Division matches. He also scored three in FA Cup ties, and 19 in representative games, totalling 82 for the season.

**George Camsell,** of Middlesbrough, previously held the record with 59 goals in 37 Second Division matches in 1926–27, his total for the season being 75.

## SHEARER'S RECORD 'FIRST'

**Alan Shearer** (Blackburn) is the only player to score more than 30 top-division goals in 3 successive seasons since the War: 31 in 1993–94, 34 in 1994–95, 31 in 1995–96.

**Thierry Henry** (Arsenal) is the first player to score more than 20 Premiership goals in five consecutive seasons (2002–06). **David Halliday** (Sunderland) topped 30 First Division goals in 4 consecutive seasons with totals of 38, 36, 36 and 49 from 1925–26 to 1928–29.

## MOST GOALS IN A MATCH

**Sep 12, 1885: John Petrie** set the all-time British individual record for a first-class match when, in Arbroath's 36-0 win against Bon Accord (Scottish Cup 1), he scored **13.**

**Apr 13, 1936: Joe Payne** set the still-existing individual record on his debut as a centre-forward, for Luton v Bristol Rov (Div 3 South). In a 12-0 win he scored **10.**

## ROWLEY'S ALL-TIME RECORD

**Arthur Rowley** is English football's top club scorer with a total of 464 goals for WBA, Fulham, Leicester and Shrewsbury (1947–65). There were 434 in the League, 26 FA Cup, 4 League Cup.

**Jimmy Greaves** is second with a total of 420 goals for Chelsea, AC Milan, Tottenham and West Ham, made up of 366 League, 35 FA Cup, 10 League Cup and 9 in Europe. He also scored nine goals for AC Milan.

**John Aldridge** retired as a player at the end of season 1997–98 with a career total of 329 League goals for Newport, Oxford Utd, Liverpool and Tranmere (1979–98). In all competitions for those clubs he scored 410 in 737 appearances. He also scored 45 in 63 games for Real Sociedad.

## MOST GOALS IN INTERNATIONAL MATCHES

**13** by **Archie Thompson** for Australia v American Samoa in World Cup (Oceania Group qualifier) at Coff's Harbour, New South Wales, Apr 11, 2001. Result: 31-0.

**7** by **Stanley Harris** for England v France in Amateur International in Paris, Nov 1, 1906. Result: 15-0.

**6** by **Nat Lofthouse** for Football League v Irish League, at Wolverhampton, Sep 24, 1952. Result: 7-1.

**Joe Bambrick** for Northern Ireland against Wales (7-0) in Belfast, Feb 1, 1930 – a record for a Home Nations International.

**WC Jordan** in Amateur International for England v France, at Park Royal, Mar 23, 1908. Result: 12-0.

**Vivian Woodward** for England v Holland in Amateur International, at Chelsea, Dec 11,1909. Result: 9-1.

**5** by **Howard Vaughton** for England v Ireland (Belfast) Feb 18, 1882. Result: 13-0.

**Steve Bloomer** for England v Wales (Cardiff) Mar 16, 1896. Result: 9-1.

**Hughie Gallacher** for Scotland against Ireland (Belfast), Feb 23, 1929. Result: 7-3.

**Willie Hall** for England v Northern Ireland, at Old Trafford, Nov 16, 1938. Five in succession (first three in 3·5 mins – fastest international hat-trick). Result: 7-0.

**Malcolm Macdonald** for England v Cyprus (Wembley) Apr 16, 1975. Result: 5-0.

**Hughie Gallacher** for Scottish League against Irish League (Belfast) Nov 11, 1925. Result: 7-3.

**Barney Battles** for Scottish League against Irish League (Firhill Park, Glasgow) Oct 31, 1928. Result: 8-2.

**Bobby Flavell** for Scottish League against Irish League (Belfast) Apr 30, 1947. Result: 7-4.

**Joe Bradford** for Football League v Irish League (Everton) Sep 25, 1929. Result: 7-2.

**Albert Stubbins** for Football League v Irish League (Blackpool) Oct 18, 1950. Result: 6-3.

**Brian Clough** for Football League v Irish League (Belfast) Sep 23, 1959. Result: 5-0.

## LAST ENGLAND PLAYER TO SCORE ...

**3 goals:** Harry Kane v Panama (6-1) World Cup finals, Nizhny Novgorod, June 24, 2018.
**4 goals:** Ian Wright v San Marino (7-1), World Cup qual, Bologna, Nov 17, 1993.
**5 goals:** Malcolm Macdonald v Cyprus (5-0), Euro Champ qual, Wembley, Apr 16, 1975.

## INTERNATIONAL TOP SHOTS

| | | Goals | Games |
|---|---|---|---|
| **England** | Wayne Rooney (2003–2017) | 53 | 119 |
| **N Ireland** | David Healy (2000–13) | 36 | 95 |
| **Scotland** | Denis Law (1958–74) | 30 | 55 |
| | Kenny Dalglish (1971–86) | 30 | 102 |
| **Wales** | Gareth Bale (2006-18) | 29 | 70 |
| **Rep of Ire** | Robbie Keane (1998–2017) | 68 | 146 |

## ENGLAND'S TOP MARKSMEN

(As at start of season 2018–19)

| | Goals | Games |
|---|---|---|
| Wayne Rooney (2003–17) | 53 | 119 |
| Bobby Charlton (1958–70) | 49 | 106 |
| Gary Lineker (1984–92) | 48 | 80 |
| Jimmy Greaves (1959–67) | 44 | 57 |
| Michael Owen (1998–2008) | 40 | 89 |
| Tom Finney (1946–58) | 30 | 76 |
| Nat Lofthouse (1950–58) | 30 | 33 |
| Alan Shearer (1992–2000) | 30 | 63 |
| Vivian Woodward (1903–11) | 29 | 23 |
| Frank Lampard (2003–14) | 29 | 106 |
| Steve Bloomer (1895–1907) | 28 | 23 |
| David Platt (1989–96) | 27 | 62 |
| Bryan Robson (1979–91) | 26 | 90 |
| Geoff Hurst (1966–72) | 24 | 49 |
| Stan Mortensen (1947–53) | 23 | 25 |
| Tommy Lawton (1938–48) | 22 | 23 |
| Peter Crouch (2005–11) | 22 | 42 |
| Mike Channon (1972–77) | 21 | 46 |
| Kevin Keegan (1972–82) | 21 | 63 |

## ROONEY'S ENGLAND RECORD

**Wayne Rooney** reached 50 international goals with a penalty against Switzerland at Wembley on September 8, 2015 to become England's record scorer, surpassing Bobby Charlton's mark. Charlton's record was set in 106 games, Rooney's tally in 107.

## CONSECUTIVE GOALS FOR ENGLAND

**Steve Bloomer** scored in **10** consecutive appearances (19 goals) between Mar 1895 and Mar 1899.
**Jimmy Greaves** scored 11 goals in five consecutive matches from the start of season 1960–61.
**Paul Mariner** scored in five consecutive appearances (7 goals) between Nov 1981 and Jun 1982.
**Wayne Rooney** scored in five consecutive appearances (6 goals) between Oct 2012 and Mar 2013.

## ENGLAND'S TOP FINAL SERIES MARKSMAN

**Gary Lineker** with 6 goals at 1986 World Cup in Mexico.

## ENGLAND TOP SCORERS IN COMPETITIVE INTERNATIONALS

**Michael Owen** 26 goals in 53 matches; **Gary Lineker** 22 in 39; **Alan Shearer** 20 in 31.

## MOST ENGLAND GOALS IN SEASON

**13 – Jimmy Greaves** (1960–61 in 9 matches); **12 – Dixie Dean** (1926–27 in 6 matches); **10 – Gary Lineker** (1990–91 in 10 matches); **10 – Wayne Rooney** – (2008–09 in 9 matches).

## MOST ENGLAND HAT-TRICKS

**Jimmy Greaves** 6; **Gary Lineker** 5, **Bobby Charlton** 4, **Vivian Woodward** 4, **Stan Mortensen** 3.

## MOST GOALS FOR ENGLAND U-21s

**13** – Alan Shearer (11 apps) Francis Jeffers (13 apps).

## GOLDEN GOAL DECIDERS

The Football League, in an experiment to avoid penalty shoot-outs, introduced a new golden goal system in the 1994–95 **Auto Windscreens Shield** to decide matches in the knock-out stages of the competition in which scores were level after 90 minutes. The first goal scored in overtime ended play.

**Iain Dunn** (Huddersfield) became the first player in British football to settle a match by this sudden-death method. His 107th-minute goal beat Lincoln 3-2 on Nov 30, 1994, and to mark his 'moment in history' he was presented with a golden football trophy.

The AWS Final of 1995 was decided when Paul Tait headed the only goal for Birmingham against Carlisle 13 minutes into overtime – the first time a match at Wembley had been decided by the 'golden goal' formula.

First major international tournament match to be decided by sudden death was the Final of the **1996 European Championship** at Wembley in which Germany beat Czech Rep 2-1 by **Oliver Bierhoff's** goal in the 95th minute.

In the **1998 World Cup Finals** (2nd round), host country France beat Paraguay 1-0 with **Laurent Blanc's** goal (114).

France won the **2000 European Championship** with golden goals in the semi-final, 2-1 v Portugal (Zinedine Zidane pen, 117), and in the Final, 2-1 v Italy (David Trezeguet, 103).

**Galatasaray** (Turkey) won the **European Super Cup** 2-1 against Real Madrid (Monaco, Aug 25, 2000) with a 103rd minute golden goal, a penalty.

**Liverpool** won the **UEFA Cup** 5-4 against Alaves with a 117th-min golden goal, an own goal, in the Final in Dortmund (May 19, 2001).

In the **2002 World Cup Finals**, 3 matches were decided by Golden Goals: in the 2nd round Senegal beat Sweden 2-1 (Henri Camara, 104) and South Korea beat Italy 2-1 (Ahn Jung-hwan, 117); in the quarter-final, Turkey beat Senegal 1-0 (Ilhan Mansiz, 94).

**France** won the 2003 **FIFA Confederations Cup Final** against Cameroon (Paris, Jun 29) with a 97th-minute golden goal by Thierry Henry.

**Doncaster** won promotion to Football League with a 110th-minute golden goal winner (3-2) in the Conference Play-off Final against Dagenham at Stoke (May 10, 2003).

**Germany** won the **Women's World Cup Final** 2-1 v Sweden (Los Angeles, Oct 12, 2003) with a 98th-minute golden goal.

## GOLD TURNS TO SILVER

Starting with the 2003 Finals of the UEFA Cup and Champions League/European Cup, UEFA introduced a new rule by which a silver goal could decide the winners if the scores were level after 90 minutes.

Team leading after 15 minutes' extra time win match. If sides level, a second period of 15 minutes to be played. If still no winner, result to be decided by penalty shoot-out.

UEFA said the change was made because the golden goal put too much pressure on referees and prompted teams to play negative football.

Although both 2003 European Finals went to extra-time, neither was decided by a silver goal. The new rule applied in the 2004 European Championship Finals, and Greece won their semi-final against the Czech Republic in the 105th minute.

The **International Board** decided (Feb 28 2004) that the golden/silver goal rule was 'unfair' and that from July 1 competitive international matches level after extra-time would, when necessary, be settled on penalties.

## PREMIER LEAGUE TOP SHOTS (1992–2018)

| | | | |
|---|---|---|---|
| Alan Shearer | 260 | Les Ferdinand | 149 |
| Wayne Rooney | 208 | Teddy Sheringham | 146 |
| Andy Cole | 187 | Robin van Persie | 144 |
| Frank Lampard | 177 | Sergio Aguero | 143 |
| Thierry Henry | 175 | Jimmy Floyd Hasselbaink | 127 |
| Robbie Fowler | 163 | Robbie Keane | 126 |
| Jermain Defoe | 162 | Nicolas Anelka | 125 |
| Michael Owen | 150 | Dwight Yorke | 123 |

| | | | |
|---|---|---|---|
| Steven Gerrard | 120 | Harry Kane | 108 |
| Ian Wright | 113 | Paul Scholes | 107 |
| Dion Dublin | 111 | Darren Bent | 106 |
| Emile Heskey | 110 | Didier Drogba | 104 |
| Ryan Giggs | 109 | Romelu Lukaku | 101 |
| Peter Crouch | 108 | Matt Le Tissier | 100 |

## LEAGUE GOAL RECORDS

The highest goal-scoring aggregates in the Football League, Premier and Scottish League are:

**For**

| | *Goals* | *Games* | *Club* | *Season* |
|---|---|---|---|---|
| **Prem** | 106 | 38 | Manchester City | 2017–18 |
| **Div 1** | 128 | 42 | Aston Villa | 1930–31 |
| **New Div 1** | 108 | 46 | Manchester City | 2001–02 |
| **New Champ** | 99 | 46 | Reading | 2005–06 |
| **Div 2** | 122 | 42 | Middlesbrough | 1926–27 |
| **New Div 2** | 89 | 46 | Millwall | 2000–01 |
| **New Lge 1** | 106 | 46 | Peterborough | 2010–11 |
| **Div 3(S)** | 127 | 42 | Millwall | 1927–28 |
| **Div 3(N)** | 128 | 42 | Bradford City | 1928–29 |
| **Div 3** | 111 | 46 | QPR | 1961–62 |
| **New Div 3** | 96 | 46 | Luton | 2001–02 |
| **New Lge 2** | 96 | 46 | Notts Co | 2009–10 |
| **Div 4** | 134 | 46 | Peterborough | 1960–61 |
| **Scot Prem** | 105 | 38 | Celtic | 2003–04 |
| **Scot L 1** | 132 | 34 | Hearts | 1957–58 |
| **Scot L 2** | 142 | 34 | Raith Rov | 1937–38 |
| **Scot L 3 (Modern)** | 130 | 36 | Gretna | 2004–05 |

**Against**

| | *Goals* | *Games* | *Club* | *Season* |
|---|---|---|---|---|
| **Prem** | 100 | 42 | Swindon | 1993–94 |
| **Div 1** | 125 | 42 | Blackpool | 1930–31 |
| **New Div 1** | 102 | 46 | Stockport | 2001–02 |
| **New Champ** | 86 | 46 | Crewe | 2004–05 |
| **Div 2** | 141 | 34 | Darwen | 1898–99 |
| **New Div 2** | 102 | 46 | Chester | 1992–93 |
| **New Lge 1** | 98 | 46 | Stockport | 2004–05 |
| **Div 3(S)** | 135 | 42 | Merthyr T | 1929–30 |
| **Div 3(N)** | 136 | 42 | Nelson | 1927–28 |
| **Div 3** | 123 | 46 | Accrington Stanley | 1959–60 |
| **New Div 3** | 113 | 46 | Doncaster | 1997–98 |
| **New Lge 2** | 96 | 46 | Stockport | 2010–11 |
| **Div 4** | 109 | 46 | Hartlepool Utd | 1959–60 |
| **Scot Prem** | 100 | 36 | Morton | 1984–85 |
| **Scot Prem** | 100 | 44 | Morton | 1987–88 |
| **Scot L 1** | 137 | 38 | Leith A | 1931–32 |
| **Scot L 2** | 146 | 38 | Edinburgh City | 1931–32 |
| **Scot L 3 (Modern)** | 118 | 36 | East Stirling | 2003–04 |

## BEST DEFENSIVE RECORDS

**Denotes under old offside law*

| *Div* | *Goals Agst* | *Games* | *Club* | *Season* |
|---|---|---|---|---|
| **Prem** | 15 | 38 | Chelsea | 2004–05 |
| **1** | 16 | 42 | Liverpool | 1978–79 |
| **1** | *15 | 22 | Preston | 1888–89 |

| | | | | |
|---|---|---|---|---|
| **New Div 1** | 28 | 46 | Sunderland | 1998–99 |
| **New Champ** | 30 | 46 | Preston | 2005–06 |
| **2** | 18 | 28 | Liverpool | 1893–94 |
| **2** | *22 | 34 | Sheffield Wed | 1899–1900 |
| **2** | 24 | 42 | Birmingham | 1947–48 |
| **2** | 24 | 42 | Crystal Palace | 1978–79 |
| **New Div 2** | 25 | 46 | Wigan | 2002–03 |
| **New Lge 1** | 32 | 46 | Nottm Forest | 2007–08 |
| **3(S)** | *21 | 42 | Southampton | 1921–22 |
| **3(S)** | 30 | 42 | Cardiff | 1946–47 |
| **3(N)** | *21 | 38 | Stockport | 1921–22 |
| **3(N)** | 21 | 46 | Port Vale | 1953–54 |
| **3** | 30 | 46 | Middlesbrough | 1986–87 |
| **New Div 3** | 20 | 46 | Gillingham | 1995–96 |
| **New Lge 2** | 31 | 46 | Notts Co | 2009–10 |
| **4** | 25 | 46 | Lincoln | 1980–81 |

## SCOTTISH LEAGUE

| *Div* | *Goals Agst* | *Games* | *Club* | *Season* |
|---|---|---|---|---|
| **Prem** | 17 | 38 | Celtic | 2014–15 |
| **1** | *12 | 22 | Dundee | 1902–03 |
| **1** | *14 | 38 | Celtic | 1913–14 |
| **2** | 20 | 38 | Morton | 1966–67 |
| **2** | *29 | 38 | Clydebank | 1922–23 |
| **2** | 29 | 36 | East Fife | 1995–96 |
| **New Div 3** | 21 | 36 | Brechin | 1995–96 |

## TOP SCORERS (LEAGUE ONLY)

| | | *Goals* | *Div* |
|---|---|---|---|
| **2017–18** | Mohamed Salah (Liverpool) | 32 | Prem |
| **2016–17** | Billy Sharp (Sheffield Utd) | 30 | Lge 1 |
| **2015–16** | Matt Taylor (Bristol Rov) | 27 | Lge 2 |
| **2014–15** | Daryl Murphy (Ipswich) | 27 | Champ |
| **2013–14** | Luis Suarez (Liverpool) | 31 | Prem |
| **2012–13** | Tom Pope (Port Vale) | 31 | Lge 2 |
| **2011–12** | Jordan Rhodes (Huddersfield) | 36 | Lge 1 |
| **2010–11** | Clayton Donaldson (Crewe) | 28 | Lge 2 |
| **2009–10** | Rickie Lambert (Southampton ) | 31 | Lge 1 |
| **2008– 09** | Simon Cox (Swindon) | | |
| | Rickie Lambert (Bristol Rov) | 29 | Lge 1 |
| **2007–08** | Cristiano Ronaldo (Manchester Utd) | 31 | Prem |
| **2006–07** | Billy Sharp (Scunthorpe) | 30 | Lge 1 |
| **2005–06** | Thierry Henry (Arsenal) | 27 | Prem |
| **2004–05** | Stuart Elliott (Hull) | 27 | 1 |
| | Phil Jevons (Yeovil) | 27 | 2 |
| | Dean Windass (Bradford City) | 27 | 1 |
| **2003–04** | Thierry Henry (Arsenal) | 30 | Prem |
| **2002–03** | Andy Morrell (Wrexham) | 34 | 3 |
| **2001–02** | Shaun Goater (Manchester City) | 28 | 1 |
| | Bobby Zamora (Brighton) | 28 | 2 |
| **2000–01** | Bobby Zamora (Brighton) | 28 | 3 |
| **1999–00** | Kevin Phillips (Sunderland) | 30 | Prem |
| **1998–99** | Lee Hughes (WBA) | 31 | 1 |
| **1997–98** | Pierre van Hooijdonk (Nottm Forest) | 29 | 1 |
| | Kevin Phillips (Sunderland) | 29 | 1 |

| | | | |
|---|---|---|---|
| **1996–97** | Graeme Jones (Wigan) | 31 | 3 |
| **1995–96** | Alan Shearer (Blackburn) | 31 | Prem |
| **1994–95** | Alan Shearer (Blackburn) | 34 | Prem |
| **1993–94** | Jimmy Quinn (Reading) | 35 | 2 |
| **1992–93** | Guy Whittingham (Portsmouth) | 42 | 1 |
| **1991–92** | Ian Wright (Crystal Palace 5, Arsenal 24) | 29 | 1 |
| **1990–91** | Teddy Sheringham (Millwall) | 33 | 2 |
| **1989–90** | Mick Quinn (Newcastle) | 32 | 2 |
| **1988–89** | Steve Bull (Wolves) | 37 | 3 |
| **1987–88** | Steve Bull (Wolves) | 34 | 4 |
| **1986–87** | Clive Allen (Tottenham) | 33 | 1 |
| **1985–86** | Gary Lineker (Everton) | 30 | 1 |
| **1984–85** | Tommy Tynan (Plymouth Argyle) | 31 | 3 |
| | John Clayton (Tranmere) | 31 | 4 |
| **1983–84** | Trevor Senior (Reading) | 36 | 4 |
| **1982–83** | Luther Blissett (Watford) | 27 | 1 |
| **1981–82** | Keith Edwards (Hull 1, Sheffield Utd 35) | 36 | 4 |
| **1980–81** | Tony Kellow (Exeter) | 25 | 3 |
| **1979–80** | Clive Allen (Queens Park Rangers) | 28 | 2 |
| **1978–79** | Ross Jenkins (Watford) | 29 | 3 |
| **1977–78** | Steve Phillips (Brentford) | 32 | 4 |
| | Alan Curtis (Swansea City) | 32 | 4 |
| **1976–77** | Peter Ward (Brighton) | 32 | 3 |
| **1975–76** | Dixie McNeil (Hereford) | 35 | 3 |
| **1974–75** | Dixie McNeil (Hereford) | 31 | 3 |
| **1973–74** | Brian Yeo (Gillingham) | 31 | 4 |
| **1972–73** | Bryan (Pop) Robson (West Ham) | 28 | 1 |
| **1971–72** | Ted MacDougall (Bournemouth) | 35 | 3 |
| **1970–71** | Ted MacDougall (Bournemouth) | 42 | 4 |
| **1969–70** | Albert Kinsey (Wrexham) | 27 | 4 |
| **1968–69** | Jimmy Greaves (Tottenham) | 27 | 1 |
| **1967–68** | George Best (Manchester Utd) | 28 | 1 |
| | Ron Davies (Southampton) | 28 | 1 |
| **1966–67** | Ron Davies (Southampton) | 37 | 1 |
| **1965–66** | Kevin Hector (Bradford PA) | 44 | 4 |
| **1964–65** | Alick Jeffrey (Doncaster) | 36 | 4 |
| **1963–64** | Hugh McIlmoyle (Carlisle) | 39 | 4 |
| **1962–63** | Jimmy Greaves (Tottenham) | 37 | 1 |
| **1961–62** | Roger Hunt (Liverpool) | 41 | 2 |
| **1960–61** | Terry Bly (Peterborough) | 52 | 4 |

## 100 LEAGUE GOALS IN SEASON

**Manchester City,** First Div Champions in 2001–02, scored 108 goals.

**Bolton,** First Div Champions in 1996–97, reached 100 goals, the first side to complete a century in League football since 103 by **Northampton** (Div 4 Champions) in 1986–87.

Last League Champions to reach 100 League goals: **Manchester City** (106 in 2017–18). Last century of goals in the top division: 111 by runners-up **Tottenham** in 1962–63.

Clubs to score a century of Premier League goals in season: **Manchester City** 106 in 2017-18, **Chelsea** 103 in 2009–10, Manchester City (102) and Liverpool (101) in 2013–14.

**Wolves** topped 100 goals in four successive First Division seasons (1957–58, 1958–59, 1959–60, 1960–61).

In **1930–31,** the top three all scored a century of League goals: 1 Arsenal (127), 2 Aston Villa (128), 3 Sheffield Wed (102).

Latest team to score a century of League goals: Peterborough with 106 in 2010–11 (Lge 1).

## 100 GOALS AGAINST

**Swindon,** relegated with 100 goals against in 1993–94, were the first top-division club to concede a century of League goals since **Ipswich** (121) went down in 1964. Most goals conceded in the top division: 125 by **Blackpool** in 1930–31, but they avoided relegation.

## MOST LEAGUE GOALS ON ONE DAY

A record of 209 goals in the four divisions of the Football League (43 matches) was set on **Jan 2, 1932:** 56 in Div 1, 53 in Div 2, 57 in Div 3 South and 43 in Div 3 North.

There were two 10-goal aggregates: Bradford City 9, Barnsley 1 in Div 2 and Coventry City 5, Fulham 5 in Div 3 South.

That total of 209 League goals on one day was equalled on **Feb 1, 1936** (44 matches): 46 in Div 1, 46 in Div 2, 49 in Div 3 South and 69 in Div 3 North. Two matches in the Northern Section produced 23 of the goals: Chester 12, York 0 and Crewe 5, Chesterfield 6.

## MOST GOALS IN TOP DIV ON ONE DAY

This record has stood since **Dec 26, 1963,** when 66 goals were scored in the ten First Division matches played.

## MOST PREMIER LEAGUE GOALS ON ONE DAY

**47**, in nine matches on **May 8, 1993** (last day of season). For the first time, all 20 clubs scored in the Premier League programme over the weekend of Nov 27-28, 2010.

## FEWEST PREMIER LEAGUE GOALS IN ONE WEEK-END

**10,** in **10** matches on **Nov 24/25, 2001**.

## FEWEST FIRST DIV GOALS ON ONE DAY

For full/near full programme: **Ten goals**, all by home clubs, in ten matches on Apr 28, 1923 (day of Wembley's first FA Cup Final).

## SCORER OF LEAGUE'S FIRST GOAL

Kenny Davenport (2 mins) for Bolton v Derby, Sep 8, 1888.

## VARDY'S RECORD

**Jamie Vardy** set a Premier League record by scoring in 11 consecutive matches for Leicester (Aug-Nov 2015). The all-time top division record of scoring in 12 successive games was set by **Jimmy Dunne** for Sheffield Utd in the old First Division in season 1931-32. **Stan Mortensen** scored in 15 successive matches for Blackpool (First Division) in season 1950-51, but that sequence included two injury breaks.

## LUTON GOAL FEAST

Luton set a Football League record in season 2017–18 by scoring seven or more goals in three games before Christmas – beating Yeovil 8-2 on the opening day of the season, Stevenage 7-1 and Cambridge 7-0.

## SCORERS FOR 7 PREMIER LEAGUE CLUBS

**Craig Bellamy** (Coventry, Newcastle, Blackburn, Liverpool, West Ham, Manchester City, Cardiff).

## SCORERS FOR 6 PREMIER LEAGUE CLUBS

**Les Ferdinand** (QPR, Newcastle, Tottenham, West Ham, Leicester, Bolton); **Andy Cole** (Newcastle, Manchester Utd, Blackburn, Fulham, Manchester City, Portsmouth); **Marcus Bent** (Crystal Palace, Ipswich, Leicester, Everton, Charlton, Wigan); **Nick Barmby** (Tottenham, Middlesbrough, Everton, Liverpool, Leeds, Hull); **Peter Crouch** (Tottenham, Aston Villa, Southampton, Liverpool, Portsmouth, Stoke); **Robbie Keane** (Coventry, Leeds, Tottenham, Liverpool, West Ham, Aston Villa); **Nicolas Anelka** (Arsenal, Liverpool, Manchester City, Bolton, Chelsea, WBA); **Darren Bent** (Ipswich, Charlton, Tottenham, Sunderland, Aston Villa, Fulham).

## SCORERS FOR 5 PREMIER LEAGUE CLUBS

**Stan Collymore** (Nottm Forest, Liverpool, Aston Villa, Leicester, Bradford); **Mark Hughes** (Manchester Utd, Chelsea, Southampton, Everton, Blackburn); **Benito Carbone** (Sheffield Wed, Aston Villa, Bradford, Derby, Middlesbrough); **Ashley Ward** (Norwich, Derby, Barnsley, Blackburn Bradford); **Teddy Sheringham** (Nottm Forest, Tottenham, Manchester Utd, Portsmouth, West Ham); **Chris Sutton** (Norwich, Blackburn, Chelsea, Birmingham, Aston Villa).

## SCORERS IN MOST CONSECUTIVE LEAGUE MATCHES

**Arsenal** broke the record by scoring in 55 successive Premiership fixtures: the last match in season 2000–01, then all 38 games in winning the title in 2001–02, and the first 16 in season 2002–03. The sequence ended with a 2-0 defeat away to Manchester Utd on December 7, 2002.

**Chesterfield** previously held the record, having scored in 46 consecutive matches in Div 3 (North), starting on Christmas Day, 1929 and ending on December 27, 1930.

## SIX-OUT-OF-SIX HEADERS

When **Oxford Utd** beat Shrewsbury 6-0 (Div 2) on Apr 23, 1996, all six goals were headers.

## ALL–ROUND MARKSMEN

**Alan Cork** scored in four divisions of the Football League and in the Premier League in his 18-season career with Wimbledon, Sheffield Utd and Fulham (1977–95).

**Brett Ormerod** scored in all four divisions (2, 1, Champ and Prem Lge) for Blackpool in two spells (1997–2002, 2008–11). **Grant Holt** (Sheffield Wed, Rochdale, Nottm Forest, Shrewsbury, Norwich) has scored in four Football League divisions and in the Premier League.

## CROUCH AHEAD OF THE GAME

Peter Crouch holds the record for most headed goals in the Premier League with a total of 53, ahead of Alan Shearer (46) and Dion Dublin (45).

## MOST CUP GOALS

**FA Cup – most goals in one season: 20** by **Jimmy Ross** (Preston, runners-up 1887–88); 15 by **Alex (Sandy) Brown** (Tottenham, winners 1900–01).

**Most FA Cup goals in individual careers: 49** by **Harry Cursham** (Notts Co 1877–89); 20th century: **44** by **Ian Rush** (39 for Liverpool, 4 for Chester, 1 for Newcastle 1979–98). **Denis Law** was the previous highest FA Cup scorer in the 20th century with 41 goals for Huddersfield Town, Manchester City and Manchester Utd (1957–74).

**Most FA Cup Final goals by individual: 5** by **Ian Rush** for Liverpool (2 in 1986, 2 in 1989, 1 in 1992).

## HOTTEST CUP HOT-SHOT

**Geoff Hurst** scored 21 cup goals in season 1965–66: 11 League Cup, 4 FA Cup and 2 Cup-Winners' Cup for West Ham, and 4 in the World Cup for England.

## SCORERS IN EVERY ROUND

Twelve players have scored in every round of the FA Cup in one season, from opening to Final inclusive: **Archie Hunter** (Aston Villa, winners 1887); **Sandy Brown** (Tottenham, winners 1901); **Harry Hampton** (Aston Villa, winners 1905); **Harold Blackmore** (Bolton, winners 1929); **Ellis Rimmer** (Sheffield Wed, winners 1935); **Frank O'Donnell** (Preston, beaten 1937); **Stan Mortensen** (Blackpool, beaten 1948); **Jackie Milburn** (Newcastle, winners 1951); **Nat Lofthouse** (Bolton, beaten 1953); **Charlie Wayman** (Preston, beaten 1954); **Jeff Astle** (WBA, winners 1968); **Peter Osgood** (Chelsea, winners 1970).

Blackmore and the next seven completed their 'set' in the Final at Wembley; Osgood did so in the Final replay at Old Trafford.

Only player to score in every **Football League Cup** round possible in one season**: Tony Brown** for WBA, winners 1965–66, with 9 goals in 10 games (after bye in Round 1).

## TEN IN A ROW

**Dixie McNeill** scored for Wrexham in ten successive FA Cup rounds (18 goals): 11 in Rounds 1-6, 1977–78; 3 in Rounds 3-4, 1978–79; 4 in Rounds 3-4, 1979–80.

**Stan Mortensen** (Blackpool) scored 25 goals in 16 FA Cup rounds out of 17 (1946–51).

## TOP MATCH HAULS IN FA CUP

**Ted MacDougall** scored nine goals, a record for the competition proper, in the FA Cup first round on Nov 20, 1971, when Bournemouth beat Margate 11-0. On Nov 23, 1970 he had scored six in an 8-1 first round replay against Oxford City.

Other six-goal FA Cup scorers include **George Hilsdon** (Chelsea v Worksop, 9-1, 1907–08), **Ronnie Rooke** (Fulham v Bury, 6-0, 1938–39), **Harold Atkinson** (Tranmere v Ashington, 8-1, 1952–53), **George Best** (Manchester Utd v Northampton 1969–70, 8-2 away), **Duane Darby** (Hull v Whitby, 8-4, 1996–97).

**Denis Law** scored all six for Manchester City at Luton (6-2) in an FA Cup 4th round tie on Jan 28, 1961, but none of them counted – the match was abandoned (69 mins) because of a waterlogged pitch. He also scored City's goal when the match was played again, but they lost 3-1.

**Tony Philliskirk** scored **five** when Peterborough beat Kingstonian 9-1 in an FA Cup 1st round replay on Nov 25, 1992, but had them wiped from the records.

With the score at 3-0, the Kingstonian goalkeeper was concussed by a coin thrown from the crowd and unable to play on. The FA ordered the match to be replayed at Peterborough behind closed doors, and Kingstonian lost 1-0.

- Two players have scored **ten goals** in FA Cup preliminary round matches: **Chris Marron** for South Shields against Radcliffe in Sep 1947; **Paul Jackson** when Sheffield-based club Stocksbridge Park Steels beat Oldham Town 17-1 on Aug 31, 2002. He scored 5 in each half and all ten with his feet – goal times 6, 10, 22, 30, 34, 68, 73, 75, 79, 84 mins.

## QUICKEST GOALS AND RAPID SCORING

A goal in **4 sec** was claimed by **Jim Fryatt,** for Bradford PA v Tranmere (Div 4, Apr 25, 1965), and by **Gerry Allen** for Whitstable v Danson (Kent League, Mar 3,1989). **Damian Mori** scored in **4 sec** for Adelaide v Sydney (Australian National League, December 6, 1995).

Goals after **6 sec – Albert Mundy** for Aldershot v Hartlepool, Oct 25, 1958; **Barrie Jones** for Notts Co v Torquay, Mar 31, 1962; **Keith Smith** for Crystal Palace v Derby, Dec 12, 1964.

**9.6 sec** by **John Hewitt** for Aberdeen at Motherwell, 3rd round, Jan 23, 1982 (fastest goal in Scottish Cup history).

**Colin Cowperthwaite** reputedly scored in **3.5 sec** for Barrow v Kettering (Alliance Premier League) on Dec 8, 1979, but the timing was unofficial.

**Phil Starbuck** for Huddersfield **3 sec** after entering the field as 54th min substitute at home to Wigan (Div 2) on Easter Monday, Apr 12, 1993. Corner was delayed, awaiting his arrival and he scored with a header.

**Malcolm Macdonald** after **5 sec** (officially timed) in Newcastle's 7-3 win in a pre-season friendly at St Johnstone on Jul 29, 1972.

**World's fastest goal: 2.8 sec,** direct from kick-off, Argentinian **Ricardo Olivera** for Rio Negro v Soriano (Uruguayan League), December 26, 1998.

**Fastest international goal: 7 sec, Christian Benteke** for Belgium v Gibraltar (World Cup qual, Faro), Oct 10, 2016.

**Fastest England goals: 17 sec, Tommy Lawton** v Portugal in Lisbon, May 25, 1947. **27 sec, Bryan Robson** v France in World Cup at Bilbao, Spain on Jun 16, 1982; **37 sec, Gareth Southgate** v South Africa in Durban, May 22, 2003; **30 sec, Jack Cock** v Ireland, Belfast, Oct 25, 1919; **30 sec, Bill Nicholson** v Portugal at Goodison Park, May 19, 1951. **38 sec, Bryan Robson** v Yugoslavia at Wembley, Dec 13, 1989; **42 sec, Gary Lineker** v Malaysia in Kuala Lumpur, Jun 12, 1991.

**Fastest international goal by substitute: 5 sec, John Jensen** for Denmark v Belgium (Euro Champ), Oct 12, 1994.

**Fastest goal by England substitute: 10 sec, Teddy Sheringham** v Greece (World Cup qualifier) at Old Trafford, Oct 6, 2001.

**Fastest FA Cup goal: 4 sec, Gareth Morris** (Ashton Utd) v Skelmersdale, 1st qual round, Sep 15, 2001.

**Fastest FA Cup goal (comp proper): 9.7 sec, Jimmy Kebe** for Reading v WBA, 5th Round, Feb 13, 2010.

**Fastest FA Cup Final goal: 25 sec, Louis Saha** for Everton v Chelsea at Wembley, May 30, 2009.

**Fastest goal by substitute in FA Cup Final: 96 sec, Teddy Sheringham** for Manchester Utd v Newcastle at Wembley, May 22, 1999.

**Fastest League Cup Final goal: 45 sec, John Arne Riise** for Liverpool v Chelsea, 2005.

**Fastest goal on full League debut: 7.7 sec, Freddy Eastwood** for Southend v Swansea (Lge 2), Oct 16, 2004. He went on to score hat-trick in 4-2 win.

**Fastest goal in cup final: 4.07 sec, 14-year-old Owen Price** for Ernest Bevin College, Tooting, beaten 3-1 by Barking Abbey in Heinz Ketchup Cup Final at Arsenal on May 18, 2000. Owen, on Tottenham's books, scored from inside his own half when the ball was played back to him from kick-off.

**Fastest Premier League goals: 10 sec, Ledley King** for Tottenham away to Bradford, Dec 9, 2000; **10.4 sec, Alan Shearer for** Newcastle v Manchester City, Jan 18, 2003: **11 sec, Mark Viduka** for Leeds v Charlton, Mar 17, 2001, **Christian Eriksen** for Tottenham v Manchester Utd, Jan 31, 2018; **12.5 sec. James Beattie** for Southampton at Chelsea, Aug 28, 2004; **13 sec, Chris Sutton** for Blackburn at Everton, Apr 1, 1995; **13 sec, Dwight Yorke** for Aston Villa at Coventry, Sep 30, 1995; **13 sec Asmir Begovic** (goalkeeper) for Stoke v Southampton, Nov 2, 2013; **13 sec Jay Rodriguez** for Southampton at Chelsea, Dec 1, 2013.

**Fastest top-division goal: 7 sec, Bobby Langton** for Preston v Manchester City (Div 1), Aug 25, 1948.

**Fastest goal in Champions League: 10 sec, Roy Makaay** for Bayern Munich v Real Madrid (1st ko rd), Mar 7, 2007.

**Fastest Premier League goal by substitute: 9 sec, Shaun Goater,** Manchester City's equaliser away to Manchester Utd (1-1), Feb 9, 2003. In Dec, 2011, Wigan's **Ben Watson** was brought off the bench to take a penalty against Stoke and scored.

**Fastest goal on Premier League debut: 36 sec, Thievy Bifouma** on as sub for WBA away to Crystal Palace, Feb 8, 2014.

**Fastest Scottish Premiership goal: 10 sec, Kris Boyd** for Kilmarnock v Ross Co, Jan 28, 2017.

**Fastest-ever hat-trick: 90 sec,** credited to 18-year-old **Tommy Ross** playing in a Highland match for Ross County against Nairn County on Nov 28, 1964.

**Fastest goal by goalkeeper in professional football: 13 sec, Asmir Begovic** for Stoke v Southampton (Prem Lge), Nov 2, 2013.

**Fastest goal in Olympic Games: 14 sec, Neymar** for Brazil in semi-finals v Honduras, Aug 17, 2016, Rio de Janeiro.

**Fastest goal in women's football: 7 sec, Angie Harriott** for Launton v Thame (Southern League, Prem Div), season 1998–99.

**Fastest hat-trick in League history: 2 min 20 sec**, Bournemouth's 84th-minute substitute **James Hayter** in 6-0 home win v Wrexham (Div 2) on Feb 24, 2004 (goal times 86, 87, 88 mins).

**Fastest First Division hat-tricks since war: Graham Leggat,** 3 goals in 3 minutes (first half) when Fulham beat Ipswich 10-1 on Boxing Day, 1963; **Nigel Clough**, 3 goals in **4 minutes** (81, 82, 85 pen) when Nottm Forest beat QPR 4-0 on Dec 13, 1987.

**Fastest Premier League hat-trick: 2 min 56 sec** (13, 14, 16) by **Sadio Mane** in Southampton 6, Aston Villa 1 on May 16, 2015.

**Fastest international hat-trick: 2 min 35 sec,** Abdul Hamid Bassiouny for Egypt in 8-2 win over Namibia in Abdallah, Libya, (African World Cup qual), Jul 13, 2001.

**Fastest international hat-trick in British matches: 3.5 min, Willie Hall** for England v N Ireland at Old Trafford, Manchester, Nov 16, 1938. (Hall scored 5 in 7-0 win); **3min 30 sec, Arif Erdem** for Turkey v N Ireland, European Championship qualifier, at Windsor Park, Belfast, on Sep 4, 1999.

**Fastest FA Cup hat-tricks: In 3 min, Billy Best** for Southend v Brentford (2nd round, Dec 7, 1968); **2 min 20 sec, Andy Locke** for Nantwich v Droylsden (1st Qual round, Sep 9, 1995).

**Fastest Scottish hat-trick: 2 min 30 sec, Ian St John** for Motherwell away to Hibernian (Scottish League Cup), Aug 15, 1959.

**Fastest hat-trick of headers: Dixie Dean's** 5 goals in Everton's 7-2 win at home to Chelsea (Div 1) on Nov 14, 1931 included 3 headers between **5th** and **15th-min.**

**Scored first kick: Billy Foulkes** (Newcastle) for Wales v England at Cardiff, Oct 20, 1951, in his first international match.

**Preston** scored six goals in **7 min** in record 26-0 FA Cup 1st round win v Hyde, Oct 15, 1887.

**Notts Co** scored six second-half goals in **12 min** (Tommy Lawton 3, Jackie Sewell 3) when beating Exeter 9-0 (Div 3 South) at Meadow Lane on Oct 16, 1948.

**Arsenal** scored six in **18 min** (71-89 mins) in 7-1 home win (Div 1) v Sheffield Wed, Feb 15, 1992.

**Tranmere** scored six in first **19 min** when beating Oldham 13-4 (Div 3 North), December 26, 1935.

**Sunderland** scored eight in **28 min** at Newcastle (9-1 Div 1), December 5, 1908. Newcastle went on to win the title.

**Southend** scored all seven goals in **29 min** in 7-0 win at home to Torquay (Leyland Daf Cup, Southern quarter-final), Feb 26, 1991. Score was 0-0 until 55th minute.

**Plymouth** scored five in first **18 min** in 7-0 home win v Chesterfield (Div 2), Jan 3, 2004.

**Five in 20 min: Frank Keetley** in Lincoln's 9-1 win over Halifax in Div 3 (North), Jan 16, 1932; **Brian Dear** for West Ham v WBA (6-1, Div 1) Apr 16, 1965. **Kevin Hector** for Bradford PA v Barnsley (7-2, Div 4), Nov 20, 1965.

**Four in 5 min: John McIntyre** for Blackburn v Everton (Div 1), Sep 16, 1922; **WG (Billy) Richardson** for WBA v West Ham (Div 1), Nov 7, 1931.

**Three in 2·5 min: Jimmy Scarth** for Gillingham v Leyton Orient (Div 3S), Nov 1, 1952.

**Three in three minutes: Billy Lane** for Watford v Clapton Orient (Div 3S), December 20, 1933; **Johnny Hartburn** for Leyton Orient v Shrewsbury (Div 3S), Jan 22, 1955; **Gary Roberts** for Brentford v Newport, (Freight Rover Trophy, South Final), May 17, 1985; **Gary Shaw** for Shrewsbury v Bradford City (Div 3), December 22, 1990.

**Two in 9 sec: Jamie Bates** with last kick of first half, **Jermaine McSporran** 9 sec into second half when Wycombe beat Peterborough 2-0 at home (Div 2) on Sep 23, 2000.

**Premier League – fastest scoring: Four goals in 4 min 44 sec, Tottenham** home to Southampton on Sunday, Feb 7, 1993.

**Premiership – fast scoring away:** When **Aston Villa** won 5-0 at Leicester (Jan 31, 2004), all goals scored in **18 second-half min** (50-68).

**Four in 13 min by Premier League sub: Ole Gunnar Solskjaer for** Manchester Utd away to Nottm Forest, Feb 6, 1999.

**Five in 9 mins by substitute: Robert Lewandowski** for Bayern Munich v Wolfsburg (5-1, Bundesliga), Sep 22, 2015.

## FASTEST GOALS IN WORLD CUP FINAL SERIES

**10.8 sec, Hakan Sukur** for Turkey against South Korea in 3rd/4th-place match at Taegu, Jun 29, 2002; **15 sec, Vaclav Masek** for Czechoslovakia v Mexico (in Vina, Chile, 1962); **27 sec, Bryan Robson** for England v France (in Bilbao, Spain, 1982).

## TOP MATCH SCORES SINCE WAR

**By English clubs:** 13-0 by Newcastle v Newport (Div 2, Oct 1946); 13-2 by Tottenham v Crewe (FA Cup 4th. Rd replay, Feb 1960); 13-0 by Chelsea v Jeunesse Hautcharage, Lux. (Cup-Winners' Cup 1st round, 2nd leg, Sep 1971).

**By Scottish club:** 20-0 by Stirling v Selkirk (E. of Scotland League) in Scottish Cup 1st round. (Dec 1984). That is the highest score in British first-class football since Preston beat Hyde 26-0 in FA Cup, Oct 1887.

## MOST GOALS IN CALENDAR YEAR

**88** by **Lionel Messi** in 2012 (76 Barcelona, 12 Argentina).

## ROONEY'S DOUBLE TOP

Wayne Rooney ended season 2016–17 as top scorer for England (53) and Manchester Utd (253).

## PREMIER LEAGUE LONGEST-RANGE GOALS BY OUTFIELD PLAYERS

**66 yards: Charlie Adam** (Stoke at Chelsea, Apr 4, 2015)
**64 yards: Xabi Alonso** (Liverpool v Newcastle, Sep 20, 2006)
**62 yards: Maynor Figueroa** (Wigan at Stoke, Dec 12, 2009)
**60 yards: Wayne Rooney** (Everton v West Ham, Nov 29, 2017)
**59 yards: David Beckham** (Manchester Utd at Wimbledon, Aug 17, 1996)
**55 yards: Wayne Rooney** (Manchester Utd at West Ham, Mar 22, 2014)

## GOALS BY GOALKEEPERS

*(Long clearances unless stated)*

**Pat Jennings** for Tottenham v Manchester Utd (goalkeeper Alex Stepney), Aug 12, 1967 (FA Charity Shield).

**Peter Shilton** for Leicester v Southampton (Campbell Forsyth), Oct 14, 1967 (Div 1).

**Ray Cashley** for Bristol City v Hull (Jeff Wealands), Sep 18, 1973 (Div 2).

**Steve Sherwood** for Watford v Coventry (Raddy Avramovic), Jan 14, 1984 (Div 1).

**Steve Ogrizovic** for Coventry v Sheffield Wed (Martin Hodge), Oct 25, 1986 (Div 1).

**Andy Goram** for Hibernian v Morton (David Wylie), May 7, 1988 (Scot Prem Div).

**Andy McLean**, on Irish League debut, for Cliftonville v Linfield (George Dunlop), Aug 20, 1988.

**Alan Paterson** for Glentoran v Linfield (George Dunlop), Nov 30, 1988 (Irish League Cup Final – only instance of goalkeeper scoring winner in a senior cup final in UK).

**Ray Charles** for East Fife v Stranraer (Bernard Duffy), Feb 28, 1990 (Scot Div 2).

**Iain Hesford** for Maidstone v Hereford (Tony Elliott), Nov 2, 1991 (Div 4).

**Chris Mackenzie** for Hereford v Barnet (Mark Taylor), Aug 12, 1995 (Div 3).

**Peter Schmeichel** for Manchester Utd v Rotor Volgograd, Sep 26, 1995 (header, UEFA Cup 1).

**Mark Bosnich** (Aston Villa) for Australia v Solomon Islands, Jun 11, 1997 (penalty in World Cup qual – 13-0).

**Peter Keen** for Carlisle away to Blackpool (goalkeeper John Kennedy), Oct 24, 2000 (Div 3).

**Steve Mildenhall** for Notts Co v Mansfield (Kevin Pilkington), Aug 21, 2001 (free-kick inside own half, League Cup 1).

**Peter Schmeichel** for Aston Villa v Everton (Paul Gerrard), Oct 20, 2001 (volley, first goalkeeper to score in Premiership).

**Mart Poom** for Sunderland v Derby (Andy Oakes), Sep 20, 2003 (header, Div 1).

**Brad Friedel** for Blackburn v Charlton (Dean Kiely), Feb 21, 2004 (shot, Prem).

**Paul Robinson** for Leeds v Swindon (Rhys Evans), Sep 24, 2003 (header, League Cup 2).

**Andy Lonergan** for Preston v Leicester (Kevin Pressman), Oct 2, 2004 (Champ).

**Matt Glennon** for St Johnstone away to Ross Co (Joe Malin), Mar 11, 2006 (shot, Scot Div 1).

**Gavin Ward** for Tranmere v Leyton Orient (Glenn Morris), Sep 2, 2006 (free-kick Lge 1).

**Mark Crossley** for Sheffield Wed v Southampton (Kelvin Davis), Dec 23, 2006 (header, Champ).

**Paul Robinson** for Tottenham v Watford (Ben Foster), Mar 17, 2007 (Prem).

**Adam Federici** for Reading v Cardiff (Peter Enckelman), Dec 28, 2008 (shot, Champ).

**Chris Weale** for Yeovil v Hereford (Peter Gulacsi), Apr 21, 2009 (header, Lge 1).

**Scott Flinders** for Hartlepool v Bournemouth (Shwan Jalal), Apr 30, 2011 (header, Lge 1).

**Iain Turner** for Preston v Notts Co (Stuart Nelson), Aug 27 2011 (shot, Lge 1).

**Andy Leishman** for Auchinleck v Threave (Vinnie Parker), Oct 22, 2011 (Scot Cup 2).

**Tim Howard** for Everton v Bolton (Adam Bogdan), Jan 4, 2012 (Prem).

**Asmir Begovic** for Stoke v Southampton (Artur Boruc), Nov 2, 2013 (Prem).

**Mark Oxley** for Hibernian v Livingston (Darren Jamieson), Aug 9, 2014 (Scot Champ).

**Jesse Joronen** for Stevenage v Wycombe (Matt Ingram), Oct 17, 2015 (Lge 2).

**Barry Roche** for Morecambe v Portsmouth (Ryan Fulton), Feb 2, 2016 (header, Lge 2).

## MORE GOALKEEPING HEADLINES

**Arthur Wilkie**, sustained a hand injury in Reading's Div 3 match against Halifax on Aug 31, 1962, then played as a forward and scored twice in a 4-2 win.

**Alex Stepney** was Manchester Utd's joint top scorer for two months in season 1973–74 with two penalties.

**Dundee Utd** goalkeeper Hamish McAlpine scored three penalties in a ten-month period between 1976–77, two against Hibernian, home and away, and one against Rangers at Ibrox.

**Alan Fettis** scored twice for Hull in 1994–95 Div 2 season, as a substitute in 3-1 home win over Oxford Utd (Dec 17) and, when selected outfield, with last-minute winner (2-1) against Blackpool on May 6.

**Roger Freestone** scored for Swansea with a penalty at Oxford Utd (Div 2, Apr 30, 1995) and twice from the spot the following season against Shrewsbury (Aug 12) and Chesterfield (Aug 26).

**Jimmy Glass,** on loan from Swindon, kept Carlisle in the Football League on May 8, 1999. With ten seconds of stoppage-time left, he went upfield for a corner and scored the winner against Plymouth that sent Scarborough down to the Conference instead.

**Paul Smith,** Nottm Forest goalkeeper, was allowed to run through Leicester's defence unchallenged and score direct from the kick-off of a Carling Cup second round second match on Sep 18, 2007. It replicated the 1-0 score by which Forest had led at half-time when the original match was abandoned after Leicester defender Clive Clarke suffered a heart attack. Leicester won the tie 3-2.

**Tony Roberts** (Dagenham), is the only known goalkeeper to score from open play in the FA Cup, his last-minute goal at Basingstoke in the fourth qualifying round on Oct 27, 2001 earning a 2-2 draw. Dagenham won the replay 3-0 and went on to reach the third round proper.

The only known instance in first-class football in Britain of a goalkeeper scoring direct from a goal-kick was in a First Division match at Roker Park on Apr 14, 1900. The kick by Manchester City's **Charlie Williams** was caught in a strong wind and Sunderland keeper J. E Doig fumbled the ball over his line.

**Jose Luis Chilavert,** Paraguay's international goalkeeper, scored a hat-trick of penalties when his club Velez Sarsfield beat Ferro Carril Oeste 6-1 in the Argentine League on Nov 28, 1999. In all, he scored 8 goals in 72 internationals. He also scored with a free-kick from just inside his own half for Velez Sarsfield against River Plate on Sep 20, 2000.

**Most goals by a goalkeeper in a League season:** 5 (all penalties) by **Arthur Birch** for Chesterfield (Div 3 North), 1923–24.

When Brazilian goalkeeper **Rogerio Ceni** (37) converted a free-kick for Sao Paulo's winner (2-1) v Corinthians in a championship match on Mar 27, 2011, it was his 100th goal (56 free-kicks, 44 pens) in a 20-season career.

## OWN GOALS

**Most by player in one season:** 5 by **Robert Stuart** (Middlesbrough) in 1934–35.

**Three in match by one team:** Sheffield Wed's **Vince Kenny, Norman Curtis** and **Eddie Gannon** in 5-4 defeat at home to WBA (Div 1) on Dec 26, 1952; Rochdale's **George Underwood, Kenny Boyle** and **Danny Murphy** in 7-2 defeat at Carlisle (Div 3 North), Dec 25, 1954; Sunderland's **Stephen Wright** and **Michael Proctor** (2) at home to Charlton (1-3, Prem), Feb 1, 2003; Brighton's **Liam Bridcutt** (2) and **Lewis Dunk** in 6-1 FA Cup 5th rd defeat at Liverpool, Feb 19, 2012.; Sunderland's **Santiago Vergini, Liam Bridcutt** and **Patrick van Aanholt** in 8-0 defeat at Southampton (Prem), Oct 18, 2014.

**One-man show: Chris Nicholl** (Aston Villa) scored all four goals in 2-2 draw away to Leicester (Div 1), Mar 20, 1976 – two for his own side and two own goals.

**Fastest own goals: 8 sec** by **Pat Kruse** of Torquay, for Cambridge Utd (Div 4), Jan 3, 1977; in First Division, **16 sec** by **Steve Bould** (Arsenal) away to Sheffield Wed, Feb 17, 1990.

**Late own-goal man: Frank Sinclair** (Leicester) put through his own goal in the 90th minute of Premiership matches away to Arsenal (L1-2) and at home to Chelsea (2-2) in Aug 1999.

**Half an own goal each:** Chelsea's second goal in a 3-1 home win against Leicester on December 18, 1954 was uniquely recorded as 'shared own goal'. Leicester defenders **Stan Milburn** and **Jack Froggatt**, both lunging at the ball in an attempt to clear, connected simultaneously and sent it rocketing into the net.

**Match of 149 own goals:** When Adama, Champions of Malagasy (formerly Madagascar) won a League match 149-0 on Oct 31, 2002, all 149 were own goals scored by opponents

## TON UP – BOTH ENDS

**Manchester City** are the only club to score and concede a century of League goals in the same season. When finishing fifth in the 1957–58 season, they scored 104 and gave away 100.

## TOURNAMENT TOP SHOTS

Most individual goals in a World Cup Final series: 13 by **Just Fontaine** for France, in Sweden 1958. Most in European Championship Finals: 9 by **Michel Platini** for France, in France 1984.

## MOST GOALS ON CLUB DEBUT

**Jim Dyet** scored eight in King's Park's 12-2 win against Forfar (Scottish Div 2, Jan 2, 1930). **Len Shackleton** scored six times in Newcastle's 13-0 win v Newport (Div 2, Oct 5, 1946) in the week he joined them from Bradford Park Avenue.

## MOST GOALS ON LEAGUE DEBUT

Five by **George Hilsdon,** for Chelsea (9-2) v Glossop, Div 2, Sep 1, 1906. **Alan Shearer,** with three goals for Southampton (4-2) v Arsenal, Apr 9, 1988, became, at 17, the youngest player to score a First Division hat-trick on his full debut.

## FOUR-GOAL SUBSTITUTE

**James Collins** (Swindon), sub from 60th minute, scored 4 in 5-0 home win v Portsmouth (Lge 1) on Jan 1, 2013.

## CLEAN-SHEET RECORDS

On the way to promotion from Div 3 in season 1995–96, Gillingham's ever-present goalkeeper **Jim Stannard** set a clean-sheet record. In 46 matches. He achieved 29 shut-outs (17 at home, 12 away), beating the 28 by **Ray Clemence** for Liverpool (42 matches in Div 1, 1978–79) and the previous best in a 46-match programme of 28 by Port Vale (Div 3 North, 1953–54). In conceding only 20 League goals in 1995–96, Gillingham created a defensive record for the lower divisions.

**Chris Woods,** Rangers' England goalkeeper, set a British record in season 1986–87 by going 1,196 minutes without conceding a goal. The sequence began in the UEFA Cup match against Borussia Moenchengladbach on Nov 26, 1986 and ended when Rangers were sensationally beaten 1-0 at home by Hamilton in the Scottish Cup 3rd round on Jan 31, 1987 with a 70th-minute goal by **Adrian Sprott.** The previous British record of 1,156 minutes without a goal conceded was held by Aberdeen goalkeeper **Bobby Clark** (season 1970–01).

Manchester Utd set a new Premier League clean-sheet record of 1,333 minutes (including 14 successive match shut-outs) in season 2008–09 (Nov 15–Feb 21). **Edwin van der Sar's** personal British league record of 1,311 minutes without conceding ended when United won 2-1 at Newcastle on Mar 4, 2009.

Most clean sheets in season in top English division: **28** by **Liverpool** (42 matches) in 1978–79; **25** by **Chelsea** (38 matches) in 2004–05.

There have been three instances of clubs keeping 11 consecutive clean sheets in the Football League: **Millwall** (Div 3 South, 1925–26), **York** (Div 3, 1973–74) and **Reading** (Div 4, 1978–79). In his sequence, Reading goalkeeper **Steve Death** set the existing League shut-out record of 1,103 minutes.

**Sasa Ilic** remained unbeaten for over 14 hours with 9 successive shut-outs (7 in Div 1, 2 in play-offs) to equal a Charlton club record in Apr/May 1998. He had 12 clean sheets in 17 first team games after winning promotion from the reserves with 6 successive clean sheets.

**Sebastiano Rossi** kept a clean sheet in 8 successive away matches for AC Milan (Nov 1993–Apr 1994).

A world record of 1,275 minutes without conceding a goal was set in 1990–01 by **Abel Resino,** the Atletico Madrid goalkeeper. He was finally beaten by Sporting Gijon's Enrique in Atletico's 3-1 win on Mar 19, 1991.

In international football, the record is held by **Dino Zoff** with a shut-out for Italy (Sep 1972 to Jun 1974) lasting 1,142 minutes.

## LOW SCORING

**Fewest goals by any club in season** in Football League: 18 by **Loughborough** (Div 2, 34 matches, 1899–1900); in 38 matches 20 by **Derby** (Prem Lge, 2007–08); in 42 matches, 24 by **Watford** (Div 2, 1971–72) and by **Stoke** (Div 1, 1984–85)); in 46-match programme, 27 by **Stockport** (Div 3, 1969–70).

**Arsenal** were the lowest Premier League scorers in its opening season (1992–93) with 40 goals in 42 matches, but won both domestic cup competitions. In subsequent seasons the lowest Premier League scorers were **Ipswich** (35) in 1993–94, **Crystal Palace** (34) in 1994–95, **Manchester City** (33) in 1995–96 and **Leeds** (28) in 1996–97 until **Sunderland** set the Premiership's new fewest-goals record with only 21 in 2002–03. Then, in 2007–08, **Derby** scored just 20.

## LONG TIME NO SCORE

**The world international non-scoring record** was set by **Northern Ireland** when they played 13 matches and 1,298 minutes without a goal. The sequence began against Poland on Feb 13, 2002 and ended 2 years and 5 days later when David Healy scored against Norway (1-4) in Belfast on Feb 18, 2004.

**Longest non-scoring sequences in Football League:** 11 matches by **Coventry** in 1919–20 (Div 2); 11 matches in 1992–93 (Div 2) by **Hartlepool,** who after beating Crystal Palace 1-0 in the FA Cup 3rd round on Jan 2, went 13 games and 2 months without scoring (11 League, 1 FA Cup, 1 Autoglass Trophy). The sequence ended after 1,227 blank minutes with a 1-1 draw at Blackpool (League) on Mar 6.

In the Premier League (Oct–Jan season 1994–95) **Crystal Palace** failed to score in nine consecutive matches.

The British non-scoring club record is held by **Stirling:** 14 consecutive matches (13 League, 1 Scottish Cup) and 1,292 minutes play, from Jan 31 1981 until Aug 8, 1981 (when they lost 4-1 to Falkirk in the League Cup).

In season 1971–72, **Mansfield** did not score in any of their first nine home games in Div 3. They were relegated on goal difference of minus two.

## FA CUP CLEAN SHEETS

Most consecutive FA Cup matches without conceding a goal: 11 by **Bradford City.** The sequence spanned 8 rounds, from 3rd in 1910–11 to 4th. Round replay in 1911–12, and included winning the Cup in 1911.

## GOALS THAT WERE WRONGLY GIVEN

**Tottenham's** last-minute winner at home to Huddersfield (Div 1) on Apr 2, 1952: Eddie Baily's corner-kick struck referee WR Barnes in the back, and the ball rebounded to Baily, who crossed for Len Duquemin to head into the net. Baily had infringed the Laws by playing the ball twice, but the result (1-0) stood. Those two points helped Spurs to finish Championship runners-up; Huddersfield were relegated.

The second goal (66 mins) in **Chelsea**'s 2-1 home win v Ipswich (Div 1) on Sep 26, 1970: Alan Hudson's shot hit the stanchion on the outside of goal and the ball rebounded on to the pitch. But instead of the goal-kick, referee Roy Capey gave a goal, on a linesman's confirmation. TV pictures proved otherwise. The Football League quoted from the Laws of the Game: 'The referee's decision on all matters is final.'

When **Watford's** John Eustace and **Reading's** Noel Hunt challenged for a 13th minute corner at Vicarage Road on Sep 20, 2008, the ball was clearly diverted wide. But referee Stuart Attwell signalled for a goal on the instruction on his assistant and it went down officially as a Eustace own goal. The Championship match ended 2-2.

**Sunderland's** 1-0 Premier League win over **Liverpool** on Oct 17, 2009 was decided by one of the most bizarre goals in football history when Darren Bent's shot struck a red beach ball thrown from the crowd and wrong-footed goalkeeper Jose Reina. Referee Mike Jones wrongly allowed it to stand. The Laws of the Game state: 'An outside agent interfering with play should result in play being stopped and restarted with a drop ball.'

**Blackburn's** 59th minute equaliser (2-2) in 3-3 draw away to Wigan (Prem) on Nov 19, 2011 was illegal. Morten Gamst Pedersen played the ball to himself from a corner and crossed for Junior Hoilett to net.

**The Republic of Ireland** were deprived of the chance of a World Cup place in the second leg of their play-off with France on Nov 18, 2009. They were leading 1-0 in Paris when Thierry Henry blatantly handled before setting up William Gallas to equalise in extra-time time and give his side a 2-1 aggregate victory. The FA of Ireland's call for a replay was rejected by FIFA.

• The most notorious goal in World Cup history was fisted in by Diego Maradona in **Argentina's** 2-1 quarter-final win over England in Mexico City on Jun 22, 1986.

# ATTENDANCES

## GREATEST WORLD CROWDS

**World Cup,** Maracana Stadium, Rio de Janeiro, Jul 16, 1950. Final match (Brazil v Uruguay) attendance 199,850; receipts £125,000.

**Total attendance** in three matches (including play-off) between Santos (Brazil) and AC Milan for the Inter-Continental Cup (World Club Championship) 1963, exceeded 375,000.

## BRITISH RECORD CROWDS

**Most to pay:** 149,547, Scotland v England, at Hampden Park, Glasgow, Apr 17, 1937. This was the first all-ticket match in Scotland (receipts £24,000).

**At Scottish FA Cup Final:** 146,433, Celtic v Aberdeen, at Hampden Park, Apr 24, 1937. Estimated another 20,000 shut out.

**For British club match** (apart from a Cup Final): 143,470, Rangers v Hibernian, at Hampden Park, Mar 27, 1948 (Scottish Cup semi-final).

**FA Cup Final:** 126,047, Bolton v West Ham, Apr 28, 1923. Estimated 150,000 in ground at opening of Wembley Stadium.

**New Wembley**: 89,874, FA Cup Final, Cardiff v Portsmouth, May 17, 2008.

**World Cup Qualifying ties:** 120,000, Cameroon v Morocco, Yaounde, Nov 29, 1981; 107,580, Scotland v Poland, Hampden Park, Oct 13, 1965.

**European Cup:** 135,826, Celtic v Leeds (semi-final, 2nd leg) at Hampden Park, Apr 15, 1970.

**European Cup Final:** 127,621, Real Madrid v Eintracht Frankfurt, at Hampden Park, May 18, 1960.

**European Cup-Winners' Cup Final:** 100,000, West Ham v TSV Munich, at Wembley, May 19, 1965.

**Scottish League:** 118,567, Rangers v Celtic, Jan 2, 1939.

**Scottish League Cup Final:** 107,609, Celtic v Rangers, at Hampden Park, Oct 23, 1965.

**Football League old format: First Div:** 83,260, Manchester Utd v Arsenal, Jan 17, 1948 (at Maine Road); **Div 2** 70,302 Tottenham v Southampton, Feb 25, 1950; **Div 3S:** 51,621, Cardiff v Bristol City, Apr 7, 1947; **Div 3N:** 49,655, Hull v Rotherham, Dec 25, 1948; **Div 3:** 49,309, Sheffield Wed v Sheffield Utd, Dec 26, 1979; **Div 4:** 37,774, Crystal Palace v Millwall, Mar 31, 1961.

**Premier League:** 83,222, Tottenham v Arsenal (Wembley), Feb 10, 2018

**Football League – New Div 1:** 41,214, Sunderland v Stoke, Apr 25, 1998; **New Div2:** 32,471, Manchester City v York, May 8, 1999; **New Div 3:** 22,319, Hull v Hartlepool Utd, Dec 26, 2002. **New Champs:** 52,181, Newcastle v Ipswich, Apr 24, 2010; **New Lge 1:** 38,256, Leeds v Gillingham, May 3, 2008; **New Lge 2**: 28,343, Coventry v Accrington, Feb 10, 2018.

**In English Provinces:** 84,569, Manchester City v Stoke (FA Cup 6), Mar 3, 1934.

**Record for Under-21 International:** 55,700, England v Italy, first match at New Wembley, Mar 24, 2007.

**Record for friendly match:** 104,679, Rangers v Eintracht Frankfurt, at Hampden Park, Glasgow, Oct 17, 1961.

**FA Youth Cup:** 38,187, Arsenal v Manchester Utd, at Emirates Stadium, Mar 14, 2007.

**Record Football League aggregate (season):** 41,271,414 (1948–49) – 88 clubs.

**Record Football League aggregate (single day):** 1,269,934, December 27, 1949, previous day, 1,226,098.

**Record average home League attendance for season:** 75,691 by Manchester Utd in 2007–08.

**Long-ago League attendance aggregates:** 10,929,000 in 1906–07 (40 clubs); 28,132,933 in 1937–38 (88 clubs).

**Last 1m crowd aggregate, League (single day):** 1,007,200, December 27, 1971.

**Record Amateur match attendance:** 100,000 for FA Amateur Cup Final, Pegasus v Harwich & Parkeston at Wembley, Apr 11, 1953.

**Record Cup-tie aggregate:** 265,199, at two matches between Rangers and Morton, in Scottish Cup Final, 1947–48.

**Abandoned match attendance records:** In England – 63,480 at Newcastle v Swansea City FA Cup 3rd round, Jan 10, 1953, abandoned 8 mins (0-0), fog.

**In Scotland:** 94,596 at Scotland v Austria (4-1), Hampden Park, May 8, 1963. Referee Jim Finney ended play (79 minutes) after Austria had two players sent off and one carried off.

**Colchester's** record crowd (19,072) was for the FA Cup 1st round tie v Reading on Nov 27, 1948, abandoned 35 minutes (0-0), fog.

## SMALLEST CROWDS

**Smallest League attendances:** 450 Rochdale v Cambridge Utd (Div 3, Feb 5, 1974); 469, Thames v Luton (Div 3 South, December 6, 1930).

Only 13 people paid to watch Stockport v Leicester (Div 2, May 7, 1921) at Old Trafford, but up to 2,000 stayed behind after Manchester Utd v Derby earlier in the day. Stockport's ground was closed.

**Lowest Premier League crowd:** 3,039 for Wimbledon v Everton, Jan 26, 1993 (smallest top-division attendance since War).

**Lowest Saturday post-war top-division crowd:** 3,231 for Wimbledon v Luton, Sep 7, 1991 (Div 1).

**Lowest Football League crowds, new format – Div 1:** 849 for Wimbledon v Rotherham, (Div 1) Oct 29, 2002 (smallest attendance in top two divisions since War); 1,054 Wimbledon v Wigan (Div 1), Sep 13, 2003 in club's last home match when sharing Selhurst Park; **Div 2:** 1,077, Hartlepool Utd v Cardiff, Mar 22, 1994; **Div 3:** 739, Doncaster v Barnet, Mar 3, 1998.

**Lowest top-division crowd at a major ground since the war:** 4,554 for Arsenal v Leeds (May 5, 1966) – fixture clashed with live TV coverage of Cup-Winners' Cup Final (Liverpool v Borussia Dortmund).

**Smallest League Cup attendances:** 612, Halifax v Tranmere (1st round, 2nd leg) Sep 6, 2000; 664, Wimbledon v Rotherham (3rd round), Nov 5, 2002.

**Smallest League Cup attendance at top-division ground:** 1,987 for Wimbledon v Bolton (2nd Round, 2nd Leg) Oct 6, 1992.

**Smallest Wembley crowds for England matches:** 15,628 v Chile (Rous Cup, May 23, 1989 – affected by Tube strike); 20,038 v Colombia (Friendly, Sep 6, 1995); 21,432 v Czech. (Friendly, Apr 25, 1990); 21,142 v Japan (Umbro Cup, Jun 3, 1995); 23,600 v Wales (British Championship, Feb 23, 1983); 23,659 v Greece (Friendly, May 17, 1994); 23,951 v East Germany (Friendly, Sep 12, 1984); 24,000 v N Ireland (British Championship, Apr 4, 1984); 25,756 v Colombia (Rous Cup, May 24, 1988); 25,837 v Denmark (Friendly, Sep 14, 1988).

**Smallest international modern crowds:** 221 for Poland v N Ireland (4-1, friendly) at Limassol, Cyprus, on Feb 13, 2002. Played at neutral venue at Poland's World Cup training base. 265 (all from N Ireland) at their Euro Champ qual against Serbia in Belgrade on Mar 25, 2011. Serbia ordered by UEFA to play behind closed doors because of previous crowd trouble.

**Smallest international modern crowds at home:** N Ireland: 2,500 v Chile (Belfast, May 26, 1989 – clashed with ITV live screening of Liverpool v Arsenal Championship decider); Scotland: 7,843 v N Ireland (Hampden Park, May 6, 1969); Wales: 2,315 v N Ireland (Wrexham, May 27, 1982).

**Smallest attendance for post-war England match:** 2,378 v San Marino (World Cup) at Bologna (Nov 17, 1993). Tie clashed with Italy v Portugal (World Cup) shown live on Italian TV.

**Lowest England attendance at New Wembley:** 40,181 v Norway (friendly), Sep 3, 2014

**Smallest paid attendance for British first-class match:** 29 for Clydebank v East Stirling, CIS Scottish League Cup 1st round, Jul 31, 1999. Played at Morton's Cappielow Park ground, shared by Clydebank. Match clashed with the Tall Ships Race which attracted 200,000 to the area.

## FA CUP CROWD RECORD (OUTSIDE FINAL)

The first FA Cup-tie shown on closed-circuit TV (5th round, Saturday, Mar 11, 1967, kick-off 7pm) drew a total of 105,000 spectators to Goodison Park and Anfield. At Goodison, 64,851 watched the match 'for real', while 40,149 saw the TV version on eight giant screens at Anfield. Everton beat Liverpool 1-0.

## LOWEST SEMI-FINAL CROWD

**The smallest** FA Cup semi-final attendance since the War was 17,987 for the Manchester Utd–Crystal Palace replay at Villa Park on Apr 12, 1995. Palace supporters largely boycotted tie after a fan died in car-park clash outside pub in Walsall before first match.

**Previous lowest:** 25,963 for Wimbledon v Luton, at Tottenham on Apr 9, 1988.

**Lowest quarter-final crowd since the war:** 8,735 for Chesterfield v Wrexham on Mar 9, 1997.

**Smallest FA Cup 3rd round attendances for matches between League clubs:** 1,833 for Chester v Bournemouth (at Macclesfield) Jan 5, 1991; 1,966 for Aldershot v Oxford Utd, Jan 10, 1987.

## PRE-WEMBLEY CUP FINAL CROWDS

### AT CRYSTAL PALACE

| | | | | | |
|---|---|---|---|---|---|
| 1895 | 42,560 | 1902 | 48,036 | 1908 | 74,967 |
| 1896 | 48,036 | Replay | 33,050 | 1909 | 67,651 |
| 1897 | 65,891 | 1903 | 64,000 | 1910 | 76,980 |
| 1898 | 62,017 | 1904 | 61,734 | 1911 | 69,098 |
| 1899 | 73,833 | 1905 | 101,117 | 1912 | 54,434 |
| 1900 | 68,945 | 1906 | 75,609 | 1913 | 120,028 |
| 1901 | 110,802 | 1907 | 84,584 | 1914 | 72,778 |

### AT OLD TRAFFORD

1915 50,000

### AT STAMFORD BRIDGE

| | | | | | |
|---|---|---|---|---|---|
| 1920 | 50,018 | 1921 | 72,805 | 1922 | 53,000 |

**England women's record crowd:** 45,619 v Germany, 0-3 (Wembley, Nov 23, 2014) – Karen Carney's 100th cap.

# INTERNATIONAL RECORDS

## MOST APPEARANCES

**Peter Shilton,** England goalkeeper, then aged 40, retired from international football after the 1990 World Cup Finals with the European record number of caps – 125. Previous record (119) was set by **Pat Jennings,** Northern Ireland's goalkeeper from 1964–86, who retired on his 41st birthday during the 1986 World Cup in Mexico. Shilton's England career spanned 20 seasons from his debut against East Germany at Wembley on Nov 25, 1970.

Nine players have completed a century of appearances in full international matches for England. **Billy Wright** of Wolves, was the first, retiring in 1959 with a total of 105 caps. **Bobby Charlton,** of Manchester Utd, beat Wright's record in the World Cup match against West Germany in Leon, Mexico, in Jun 1970 and **Bobby Moore,** of West Ham, overtook Charlton's 106 caps against Italy in Turin, in Jun 1973. Moore played 108 times for England, a record that stood until **Shilton** reached 109 against Denmark in Copenhagen (Jun 7, 1989). In season 2008–09, **David Beckham** (LA Galaxy/AC Milan) overtook Moore as England's most-capped outfield player. In the vastly different selection processes of their eras, Moore played 108 full games for his country, whereas Beckham's total of 115 to the end of season 2009–10, included 58 part matches, 14 as substitute and 44 times substituted. **Steven Gerrard** won his 100th cap against Sweden in Stockholm on Nov 14, 2012 and **Ashley Cole** reached 100 appearances against Brazil at Wembley on Feb 6, 2013. **Frank Lampard** played his 100th game against

Ukraine in Kiev (World Cup qual) on Sep 10, 2013. **Wayne Rooney**'s 100th appearance was against Slovenia at Wembley (Euro Champ qual) on Nov 15, 2014.

**Robbie Keane** won his 126th Republic of Ireland cap, overtaking Shay Given's record, In a World Cup qualifier against the Faroe Islands on Jun 7, 2013. Keane scored all his team's three goals in a 3-0 win.

**Kenny Dalglish** became Scotland's first 100-cap international v Romania (Hampden Park, Mar 26, 1986).

**World's most-capped player: Ahmed Hassan,** 184 for Egypt (1995–2012).

**Most-capped European player: Vitalijs Astafjevs,** 167 for Latvia (1992–2010).

**Most-capped European goalkeeper: Thomas Ravelli**, 143 Internationals for Sweden (1981–97).

**Gillian Coultard, (Doncaster Belles),** England Women's captain, received a special presentation from Geoff Hurst to mark 100 caps when England beat Holland 1-0 at Upton Park on Oct 30, 1997. She made her international debut at 18 in May 1981, and retired at the end of season 1999–2000 with a record 119 caps (30 goals).

## BRITAIN'S MOST-CAPPED PLAYERS

(As at start of season 2018–19)

**England**

| | |
|---|---|
| Peter Shilton | 125 |
| Wayne Rooney | 119 |
| David Beckham | 115 |
| Steven Gerrard | 114 |
| Bobby Moore | 108 |
| Ashley Cole | 107 |
| Bobby Charlton | 106 |
| Frank Lampard | 106 |
| Billy Wright | 105 |

**Scotland**

| | |
|---|---|
| Kenny Dalglish | 102 |
| Jim Leighton | 91 |
| Darren Fletcher | 80 |
| Alex McLeish | 77 |
| Paul McStay | 76 |
| Tommy Boyd | 72 |

**Wales**

| | |
|---|---|
| Neville Southall | 92 |
| Chris Gunter | 88 |
| Gary Speed | 85 |
| Ashley Williams | 79 |
| Craig Bellamy | 78 |
| Joe Ledley | 77 |

**Northern Ireland**

| | |
|---|---|
| Pat Jennings | 119 |
| Aaron Hughes | 112 |
| Steven Davis | 101 |
| David Healy | 95 |
| Mal Donaghy | 91 |
| Sammy McIlroy | 88 |
| Maik Taylor | 88 |

**Republic of Ireland**

| | |
|---|---|
| Robbie Keane | 146 |
| Shay Given | 134 |
| John O'Shea | 118 |
| Kevin Kilbane | 110 |
| Steve Staunton | 102 |
| Damien Duff | 100 |

## ENGLAND'S MOST-CAPPED PLAYER (either gender)

**Fara Williams** (Liverpool midfielder) with 155 appearances for the England's women's team to end of season 2015–16.

## MOST ENGLAND CAPS IN ROW

**Most consecutive international appearances:** 70 by **Billy Wright,** for England from Oct 1951 to May 1959. He played 105 of England's first 108 post-war matches.

**England captains most times: Billy Wright** and **Bobby Moore,** 90 each.

**England captains – 4 in match** (v Serbia & Montenegro at Leicester Jun 3, 2003): **Michael Owen** was captain for the first half and after the interval the armband passed to **Emile Heskey** (for 15 minutes), **Phil Neville** (26 minutes) and substitute **Jamie Carragher** (9 minutes, including time added).

## MOST SUCCESSIVE ENGLAND WINS

10 (Jun 1908–Jun 1909. Modern: 8 (Oct 2005–Jun 2006).

## ENGLAND'S LONGEST UNBEATEN RUN

19 matches (16 wins, 3 draws), Nov 1965–Nov 1966.

## ENGLAND'S TALLEST

At **6ft 7in, Peter Crouch** became England's tallest-ever international when he made his debut against Colombia in New Jersey, USA on May 31, 2005.

## MOST PLAYERS FROM ONE CLUB IN ENGLAND SIDES

**Arsenal** supplied seven men (a record) to the England team v Italy at Highbury on Nov 14, 1934. They were: Frank Moss, George Male, Eddie Hapgood, Wilf Copping, Ray Bowden, Ted Drake and Cliff Bastin. In addition, Arsenal's Tom Whittaker was England's trainer.

Since then until 2001, the most players from one club in an England team was six from **Liverpool** against Switzerland at Wembley in Sep 1977. The side also included a Liverpool old boy, Kevin Keegan (Hamburg).

Seven **Arsenal** men took part in the England – France (0-2) match at Wembley on Feb 10, 1999. Goalkeeper David Seaman and defenders Lee Dixon, Tony Adams and Martin Keown lined up for England. Nicolas Anelka (2 goals) and Emmanuel Petit started the match for France and Patrick Vieira replaced Anelka.

**Manchester Utd** equalled Arsenal's 1934 record by providing England with seven players in the World Cup qualifier away to Albania on Mar 28, 2001. Five started the match – David Beckham (captain), Gary Neville, Paul Scholes, Nicky Butt and Andy Cole – and two went on as substitutes: Wes Brown and Teddy Sheringham.

## INTERNATIONAL SUBS RECORDS

**Malta** substituted all 11 players in their 1-2 home defeat against England on Jun 3, 2000. Six substitutes by England took the total replacements in the match to 17, then an international record.

Most substitutions in match by **England:** 11 in second half by Sven-Goran Eriksson against Holland at Tottenham on Aug 15, 2001; 11 against Italy at Leeds on Mar 27, 2002; Italy sent on 8 players from the bench – the total of 19 substitutions was then a record for an England match; 11 against Australia at Upton Park on Feb 12, 2003 (entire England team changed at half-time); 11 against Iceland at City of Manchester Stadium on Jun 5, 2004.

Forty three players, a record for an England match, were used in the international against Serbia & Montenegro at Leicester on Jun 3, 2003. England sent on 10 substitutes in the second half and their opponents changed all 11 players.

The **Republic of Ireland** sent on 12 second-half substitutes, using 23 players in all, when they beat Russia 2-0 in a friendly international in Dublin on Feb 13, 2002.

**First England substitute:** Wolves winger **Jimmy Mullen** replaced injured Jackie Milburn (15 mins) away to Belgium on May 18, 1950. He scored in a 4-1 win.

## ENGLAND'S WORLD CUP-WINNERS

At Wembley, Jul 30, 1966, 4-2 v West Germany (2-2 after 90 mins), scorers Hurst 3, Peters. Team: Banks; Cohen, Wilson, Stiles, Jack Charlton, Moore (capt), Ball, Hurst, Bobby Charlton, Hunt, Peters. Manager **Alf Ramsey** fielded that same eleven in six successive matches (an England record): the World Cup quarter-final, semi-final and Final, and the first three games of the following season. England wore red shirts in the Final and The Queen presented the Cup to Bobby Moore. The players each received a £1,000 bonus, plus £60 World Cup Final appearance money, all less tax, and Ramsey a £6,000 bonus from the FA The match was shown live on TV (in black and white).

England's non-playing 'reserves' – there were no substitutes – also received the £1,000 bonus, but no medals. That remained the case until FIFA finally decided that non-playing members and staff of World Cup-winning squads should be given replica medals. England's 'forgotten heroes' received theirs at a reception in Downing Street on June 10, 2009 and were later guests of honour at the World Cup qualifier against Andorra at Wembley. The 11 'reserves' were: Springett, Bonetti, Armfield, Byrne, Flowers, Hunter, Paine, Connelly, Callaghan, Greaves, Eastham. Jimmy Greaves played in all three group games, against Uruguay, Mexico and France. John Connelly was in the team against Uruguay, Terry Paine against Mexico and Ian Callaghan against France.

## BRAZIL'S RECORD RUN

**Brazil** hold the record for the longest unbeaten sequence in international football: 45 matches from 1993–97. The previous record of 31 was held by Hungary between Jun 1950 and Jul 1954.

## ENGLAND MATCHES ABANDONED

May 17, 1953 v **Argentina** (Friendly, Buenos Aires) after 23 mins (0-0) – rain.

Oct 29, 1975 v **Czechoslovakia** (Euro Champ qual, Bratislava) after 17 mins (0-0) – fog. Played next day.

Feb 15, 1995 v **Rep of Ireland** (Friendly, Dublin) after 27 mins (1-0) – crowd disturbance.

## ENGLAND POSTPONEMENTS

Nov 21, 1979 v **Bulgaria** (Euro Champ qual, Wembley, postponed for 24 hours – fog; Aug 10, 2011 v **Holland** (friendly), Wembley, postponed after rioting in London.

Oct 16, 2012 v **Poland** (World Cup qual, Warsaw) postponed to next day – pitch waterlogged.

The friendly against **Honduras** (Miami, Jun 7, 2014) was suspended midway through the first half for 44 minutes – thunderstorm.

## ENGLAND UNDER COVER

England played indoors for the first time when they beat Argentina 1-0 in the World Cup at the Sapporo Dome, Japan, on Jun 7, 2002.

## ALL-SEATED INTERNATIONALS

The first **all-seated crowd** (30,000) for a full international in Britain saw **Wales** and **West Germany** draw 0-0 at Cardiff Arms Park on May 31, 1989. The terraces were closed.

**England's** first all-seated international at Wembley was against Yugoslavia (2-1) on December 13, 1989 (attendance 34,796). The terracing behind the goals was closed for conversion to seating.

The first **full-house all-seated** international at Wembley was for England v Brazil (1-0) on Mar 28, 1990, when a capacity 80,000 crowd paid record British receipts of £1,200,000.

## MOST NEW CAPS IN ENGLAND TEAM

**6, by Sir Alf Ramsey** (v Portugal, Apr 3, 1974) and **by Sven-Goran Eriksson** (v Australia, Feb 12, 2003; 5 at half-time when 11 changes made).

## PLAYED FOR MORE THAN ONE COUNTRY

Multi-nationals in senior international football include: **Johnny Carey** (1938–53) – caps Rep of Ireland 29, N Ireland 7; **Ferenc Puskas** (1945–62) – caps Hungary 84, Spain 4; **Alfredo di Stefano** (1950–56) – caps Argentina 7, Spain 31; **Ladislav Kubala** (1948–58) – caps, Hungary 3, Czechoslovakia 11, Spain 19, only player to win full international honours with 3 countries. Kubala also played in a fourth international team, scoring twice for FIFA v England at Wembley in 1953. Eleven players, including **Carey**, appeared for both N Ireland and the Republic of Ireland in seasons directly after the last war.

**Cecil Moore,** capped by N Ireland in 1949 when with Glentoran, played for USA v England in 1953.

**Hawley Edwards** played for England v Scotland in 1874 and for Wales v Scotland in 1876.

**Jack Reynolds** (Distillery and WBA) played for both Ireland (5 times) and England (8) in the 1890s.

**Bobby Evans** (Sheffield Utd) had played 10 times for Wales when capped for England, in 1910–11. He was born in Chester of Welsh parents.

In recent years, several players have represented USSR and one or other of the breakaway republics. The same applies to Yugoslavia and its component states. **Josip Weber** played for Croatia in 1992 and made a 5-goal debut for Belgium in 1994.

## THREE-GENERATION INTERNATIONAL FAMILY

When Bournemouth striker **Warren Feeney** was capped away to Liechtenstein on Mar 27, 2002, he became the third generation of his family to play for Northern Ireland. He followed in the footsteps of his grandfather James (capped twice in 1950) and father Warren snr. (1 in 1976).

## FATHERS & SONS CAPPED BY ENGLAND

**George Eastham senior** (pre-war) and **George Eastham junior**; **Brian Clough** and **Nigel Clough**; **Frank Lampard snr** and **Frank Lampard jnr; Mark Chamberlain** and **Alex Oxlade-Chamberlain.**

## FATHER & SON SAME-DAY CAPS

**Iceland** made father-and-son international history when they beat Estonia 3-0 in Tallin on Apr 24, 1996. **Arnor Gudjohnsen** (35) started the match and was replaced (62 mins) by his 17-year-old son **Eidur.**

## LONGEST UNBEATEN START TO ENGLAND CAREER

**Steven Gerrard**, 21 matches (W16, D5) 2000–03.

## SUCCESSIVE ENGLAND HAT-TRICKS

The last player to score a hat-trick in consecutive England matches was **Dixie Dean** on the summer tour in May 1927, against Belgium (9-1) and Luxembourg (5-2).

## SCORED ON ENGLAND DEBUT

**Marcus Rashford**, against Australia on May 27, 2016, joined a list which includes **Stanley Matthews, Tom Finney, Jimmy Greaves, Bobby Charlton, Alan Shearer** and **Rickie Lambert**.

## MOST GOALS BY PLAYER v ENGLAND

**4** by **Zlatan Ibrahimovic** (Sweden 4 England 2, Stockholm, Nov 14, 2012).

## POST-WAR HAT-TRICKS v ENGLAND

Nov 25, 1953, **Nandor Hidegkuti** (England 3, Hungary 6, Wembley); May 11, 1958, **Aleksandar Petakovic** (Yugoslavia 5, England 0, Belgrade); May 17, 1959, **Juan Seminario** (Peru 4, England 1, Lima); Jun 15, 1988, **Marco van Basten** (Holland 3, England 1, European Championship, Dusseldorf). Six other players scored hat-tricks against England (1878–1930).

## NO-SAVE GOALKEEPERS

**Chris Woods** did not have one save to make when England beat San Marino 6-0 (World Cup) at Wembley on Feb 17, 1993. He touched the ball only six times.

**Gordon Banks** had a similar no-save experience when England beat Malta 5-0 (European Championship) at Wembley on May 12, 1971. Malta did not force a goal-kick or corner, and the four times Banks touched the ball were all from back passes.

**Robert Green** was also idle in the 6-0 World Cup qualifying win over Andorra at Wembley on Jun 10, 2009.

**Joe Hart** was untroubled in England's 5-0 win over San Marino in a World Cup qualifier at Wembley on Oct 12, 2012.

## WORLD/EURO MEMBERS

**FIFA** has 209 member countries, **UEFA** 55

## NEW FIFA PRESIDENT

The 18-year reign of FIFA president **Sepp Blatter** ended in December 2015 amid widespread allegations of corruption. He was replaced in February 2016 by Gianni Infantino, a 45-year-old Swiss-Italian lawyer, who was previously general secretary of UEFA. Under new rules, he will serve four years.

## FIFA WORLD YOUTH CUP (UNDER-20)

**Finals: 1977** (Tunis) Soviet Union 2 Mexico 2 (Soviet won 9-8 on pens.); **1979** (Tokyo) Argentina 3 Soviet Union 1; **1981** (Sydney) W Germany 4 Qatar 0; **1983** (Mexico City) Brazil 1 Argentina 0; **1985** (Moscow) Brazil 1 Spain 0; **1987** (Santiago) Yugoslavia 1 W Germany 1 (Yugoslavia won 5-4 on pens.); **1989** (Riyadh) Portugal 2 Nigeria 0; **1991** (Lisbon) Portugal 0 Brazil 0 (Portugal won 4-2 on pens.); **1993** (Sydney) Brazil 2 Ghana 1; **1995** (Qatar) Argentina 2 Brazil 0; **1997** (Kuala Lumpur) Argentina 2 Uruguay 1; **1999** (Lagos) Spain 4 Japan 0; **2001** (Buenos Aires) Argentina 3 Ghana 0; **2003** (Dubai) Brazil 1 Spain 0; **2005** (Utrecht) Argentina 2 Nigeria 1; **2007** (Toronto) Argentina 2 Czech Republic 1; **2009** (Cairo)

Ghana 0 Brazil 0 (aet, Ghana won 4-3 on pens); **2011** (Bogota) Brazil 3 Portugal 2 (aet); **2013** (Istanbul) France 0 Uruguay 0 (aet, France won 4-1 on pens), **2015** (Auckland) Serbia 2 Brazil 1 (aet); **2017** (Suwon) England 1 Venezuela 0.

# FAMOUS CLUB FEATS

**Manchester City** won the 2017–18 Premier League title under Pep Guardiola in record style. They became England's first champions to total 100 points and had the longest winning streak, 18 matches, in top-flight history. There were other new Premier League marks for goals scored (106), goal difference (79), overall wins (32), away victories (16), and for a 19-point gap to second-place.

**Arsenal** created an all-time English League record sequence of 49 unbeaten Premiership matches (W36, D13), spanning 3 seasons, from May 7, 2003 until losing 2-0 away to Manchester Utd on Oct 24, 2004. It included all 38 games in season 2003–04.

**The Double:** There have been 11 instances of a club winning the Football League/Premier League title and the FA Cup in the same season. **Preston** 1888–89; **Aston Villa** 1896–97; **Tottenham** 1960–61; **Arsenal** 1970–71, 1997–98, 2001–02; **Liverpool** 1985–86; **Manchester Utd** 1993–94, 1995–96, 1998–99; **Chelsea** 2009–10.

**The Treble: Liverpool** were the first English club to win three major competitions in one season when in 1983–84, Joe Fagan's first season as manager, they were League Champions, League Cup winners and European Cup winners.

Sir Alex Ferguson's **Manchester Utd** achieved an even more prestigious treble in 1998–99, completing the domestic double of Premiership and FA Cup and then winning the European Cup. In season 2008–09, they completed another major triple success – Premier League, Carling Cup and World Club Cup.

**Liverpool** completed a unique treble by an English club with three cup successes under Gerard Houllier in season 2000–01: the League Cup, FA Cup and UEFA Cup.

**Liverpool** the first English club to win five major trophies in one calendar year (Feb– Aug 2001): League Cup, FA Cup, UEFA Cup, Charity Shield, UEFA Super Cup.

As Champions in season 2001–02, **Arsenal** set a Premiership record by winning the last 13 matches. They were the first top-division club since Preston in the League's inaugural season (1888–89) to maintain an unbeaten away record.

(See Scottish section for treble feats by Rangers and Celtic).

**Record Home Runs: Liverpool** went 85 competitive first-team games unbeaten at home between losing 2-3 to Birmingham on Jan 21, 1978 and 1-2 to Leicester on Jan 31, 1981. They comprised 63 in the League, 9 League Cup, 7 in European competition and 6 FA Cup.

**Chelsea** hold the record unbeaten home League sequence of 86 matches (W62, D24) between losing 1-2 to Arsenal, Feb 21, 2004, and 0-1 to Liverpool, Oct 26, 2008.

**Third to First: Charlton,** in 1936, became the first club to advance from the Third to First Division in successive seasons. **Queens Park Rangers** were the second club to achieve the feat in 1968, and **Oxford Utd** did it in 1984 and 1985 as Champions of each division. Subsequently, **Derby** (1987), **Middlesbrough** (1988), **Sheffield Utd** (1990) and **Notts Co** (1991) climbed from Third Division to First in consecutive seasons.

**Watford** won successive promotions from the modern Second Division to the Premier League in 1997–98, 1998–99. **Manchester City** equalled the feat in 1998–99, 1999–2000. **Norwich** climbed from League 1 to the Premier League in seasons 2009–10, 2010–11. **Southampton** did the same in 2010–11 and 2011–12.

**Fourth to First: Northampton** , in 1965 became the first club to rise from the Fourth to the First Division. **Swansea** climbed from the Fourth Division to the First (three promotions in four seasons), 1977–78 to 1980–81. **Wimbledon** repeated the feat, 1982–83 to 1985–86 **Watford** did it in five seasons, 1977–8 to 1981–82. **Carlisle** climbed from Fourth Division to First, 1964–74.

**Non-League to First:** When **Wimbledon** finished third in the Second Division in 1986, they completed the phenomenal rise from non-League football (Southern League) to the First Division in nine years. Two years later they won the FA Cup.

**Tottenham,** in 1960–61, not only carried off the First Division Championship and the FA Cup for the first time that century but set up other records by opening with 11 successive wins, registering most First Division wins (31), most away wins in the League's history (16), and equalling Arsenal's First Division records of 66 points and 33 away points. They already held the Second Division record of 70 points (1919–20).

**Arsenal,** in 1993, became the first club to win both English domestic cup competitions (FA Cup and League Cup) in the same season. **Liverpool** repeated the feat in 2001. **Chelsea** did it in 2007.

**Chelsea** achieved the FA Cup/Champions League double in May 2012.

**Preston,** in season 1888–89, won the first League Championship without losing a match and the FA Cup without having a goal scored against them. Only other English clubs to remain unbeaten through a League season were **Liverpool** (Div 2 Champions in 1893–94) and **Arsenal** (Premiership Champions 2003–04).

**Bury**, in 1903, also won the FA Cup without conceding a goal.

**Everton** won Div 2, Div 1 and the FA Cup in successive seasons, 1930–31, 1931–32, 1932–33.

**Wolves** won the League Championship in 1958 and 1959 and the FA Cup in 1960.

**Liverpool** won the title in 1964, the FA Cup in 1965 and the title again in 1966. In 1978 they became the first British club to win the European Cup in successive seasons. Nottm Forest repeated the feat in 1979 and 1980.

**Liverpool** won the League Championship six times in eight seasons (1976–83) under **Bob Paisley's** management.

Sir Alex Ferguson's **Manchester Utd** won the Premier League in 13 of its 21 seasons (1992–2013). They were runners-up five times and third three times.

## FA CUP/PROMOTION DOUBLE

**WBA** are the only club to achieve this feat in the same season (1930–31).

## COVENTRY UNIQUE

**Coventry** are the only club to have played in the Premier League, all four previous divisions of the Football League, in both sections (North and South) of the old Third Division and in the modern Championship.

## FAMOUS UPS & DOWNS

**Sunderland:** Relegated in 1958 after maintaining First Division status since their election to the Football League in 1890. They dropped into Division 3 for the first time in 1987.

**Aston Villa:** Relegated with Preston to the Third Division in 1970.

**Arsenal up:** When the League was extended in 1919, Woolwich Arsenal (sixth in Division Two in 1914–15, last season before the war) were elected to Division One. Arsenal have been in the top division ever since.

**Tottenham down:** At that same meeting in 1919 Chelsea (due for relegation) retained their place in Division One but the bottom club (Tottenham) had to go down to Division Two.

**Preston** and **Burnley down**: Preston, the first League Champions in season 1888–89, dropped into the Fourth Division in 1985. So did Burnley, also among the League's original members in 1888. In 1986, Preston had to apply for re-election.

**Wolves' fall:** Wolves, another of the Football League's original members, completed the fall from First Division to Fourth in successive seasons (1984–85–86).

**Lincoln out:** Lincoln became the first club to suffer automatic demotion from the Football League when they finished bottom of Div 4, on goal difference, in season 1986–87. They were replaced by Scarborough, champions of the GM Vauxhall Conference. Lincoln regained their place a year later.

**Swindon up and down:** In the 1990 play-offs, Swindon won promotion to the First Division for the first time, but remained in the Second Division because of financial irregularities.

## MOST CHAMPIONSHIP WINS

**Manchester Utd** have been champions of England a record 20 times (7 Football League, 13 Premier League).

## LONGEST CURRENT MEMBERS OF TOP DIVISION

**Arsenal** (since 1919), **Everton** (1954), **Liverpool** (1962), **Manchester Utd** (1975).

## CHAMPIONS: FEWEST PLAYERS

**Liverpool** used only **14** players (five ever-present) when they won the League Championship in season 1965–66. **Aston Villa** also called on no more than 14 players to win the title in 1980–81, with seven ever-present.

## UNBEATEN CHAMPIONS

Only two clubs have become Champions of England with an unbeaten record: **Preston** as the Football League's first winners in 1888–89 (22 matches) and **Arsenal**, Premiership winners in 2003–04 (38 matches).

## LEAGUE HAT-TRICKS

**Huddersfield** created a record in 1924–25–26 by winning the League Championship three years in succession.

**Arsenal** equalled this hat-trick in 1933–34–35, **Liverpool** in 1982–83–84 and **Manchester Utd** in 1999–2000–01. Sir Alex Ferguson's side became the first to complete two hat-tricks (2007–08–09).

## 'SUPER DOUBLE' WINNERS

Since the War, there have been three instances of players appearing in and then managing FA Cup and Championship-winning teams:

**Joe Mercer:** Player in Arsenal Championship teams 1948, 1953 and in their 1950 FA Cup side; manager of Manchester City when they won Championship 1968, FA Cup 1969.

**Kenny Dalglish:** Player in Liverpool Championship-winning teams 1979, 1980, 1982, 1983, 1984, player-manager 1986, 1988, 1990: player-manager when Liverpool won FA Cup (to complete Double) 1986; manager of Blackburn, Champions 1995.

**George Graham:** Played in Arsenal's Double-winning team in 1971, and as manager took them to Championship success in 1989 and 1991 and the FA Cup – League Cup double in 1993.

## ORIGINAL TWELVE

The original 12 members of the Football League (formed in 1888) were: **Accrington, Aston Villa, Blackburn, Bolton, Burnley, Derby, Everton, Notts Co, Preston, Stoke, WBA** and **Wolves.**

Results on the opening day (Sep 8, 1888): Bolton 3, Derby 6; Everton 2, Accrington 1; Preston 5, Burnley 2; Stoke 0, WBA 2; Wolves 1, Aston Villa 1. Preston had the biggest first-day crowd: 6,000. Blackburn and Notts Co did not play that day. They kicked off a week later (Sep 15) – Blackburn 5, Accrington 5; Everton 2, Notts Co 1.

Accrington FC resigned from the league in 1893 and later folded. A new club, Accrington Stanley, were members of the league from 1921 until 1962 when financial problems forced their demise. The current Accrington Stanley were formed in 1968 and gained league status in 2007.

## FASTEST CLIMBS

Three promotions in four seasons by two clubs – **Swansea City**: 1978 third in Div 4; 1979 third in Div 3; 1981 third in Div 2; **Wimbledon:** 1983 Champions of Div 4; 1984 second in Div 3; 1986 third in Div 2.

## MERSEYSIDE RECORD

**Liverpool** is the only city to have staged top-division football – through Everton and/or Liverpool – **in every season** since League football began in 1888.

## EARLIEST PROMOTIONS TO TOP DIVISION POST-WAR

Mar 23, 1974, **Middlesbrough;** Mar 25, 2006, **Reading.**

## EARLIEST RELEGATIONS POST-WAR

From top division: **QPR** went down from the old First Division on Mar 29, 1969; **Derby** went down from the Premier League on Mar 29, 2008, with 6 matches still to play. From modern First Division: **Stockport** on Mar 16, 2002, with 7 matches still to play; **Wimbledon** on Apr 6, 2004, with 7 matches to play.

# LEAGUE RECORDS

## CHAMPIONS OF ENGLAND 1888–2018

**Football League and Premier league**

Manchester Utd 20, Liverpool 18, Arsenal 13, Everton 9, Aston Villa 7, Chelsea 6, Sunderland 6, Manchester City 5, Newcastle 4, Sheffield Wed 4, Blackburn 3, Huddersfield 3, Leeds 3, Wolves 3, Burnley 2, Derby 2, Portsmouth 2, Preston 2, Tottenham 2, Ipswich 1, Leicester 1, Nottm Forest 1, Sheffield Utd 1, WBA 1

## DOUBLE CHAMPIONS

**Nine men have played in and managed League Championship-winning teams:**

**Ted Drake** Player – Arsenal 1934, 1935, 1938. Manager – Chelsea 1955.
**Bill Nicholson** Player – Tottenham 1951. Manager – Tottenham 1961.
**Alf Ramsey** Player – Tottenham 1951. Manager – Ipswich 1962.
**Joe Mercer** Player – Everton 1939, Arsenal 1948, 1953. Manager – Manchester City 1968.
**Dave Mackay** Player – Tottenham 1961. Manager – Derby 1975.
**Bob Paisley** Player – Liverpool 1947. Manager – Liverpool 1976, 1977, 1979, 1980, 1982, 1983.
**Howard Kendall** Player – Everton 1970. Manager – Everton 1985, 1987.
**Kenny Dalglish** Player – Liverpool 1979, 1980, 1982, 1983, 1984. Player-manager – Liverpool 1986, 1988, 1990. Manager – Blackburn 1995.
**George Graham** Player – Arsenal 1971. Manager – Arsenal 1989, 1991.

## CANTONA'S FOUR-TIMER

**Eric Cantona** played in four successive Championship-winning teams: Marseille 1990–01, Leeds 1991–92, Manchester Utd 1992–93 and 1993–94.

## ARRIVALS AND DEPARTURES

The following are the Football League arrivals and departures since 1923:

| Year | In | Out |
|---|---|---|
| **1923** | Doncaster | Stalybridge Celtic |
| | New Brighton | |
| **1927** | Torquay | Aberdare Athletic |
| **1928** | Carlisle | Durham |
| **1929** | York | Ashington |
| **1930** | Thames | Merthyr Tydfil |
| **1931** | Mansfield | Newport Co |
| | Chester | Nelson |
| **1932** | Aldershot | Thames |
| | Newport Co | Wigan Borough |
| **1938** | Ipswich | Gillingham |
| **1950** | Colchester, Gillingham | |
| | Scunthorpe, Shrewsbury | |
| **1951** | Workington | New Brighton |
| **1960** | Peterborough | Gateshead |

| | | |
|---|---|---|
| **1962** | Oxford Utd | Accrington (resigned) |
| **1970** | Cambridge Utd | Bradford PA |
| **1972** | Hereford | Barrow |
| **1977** | Wimbledon | Workington |
| **1978** | Wigan | Southport |
| **1987** | Scarborough | Lincoln |
| **1988** | Lincoln | Newport Co |
| **1989** | Maidstone | Darlington |
| **1990** | Darlington | Colchester |
| **1991** | Barnet | |
| **1992** | Colchester | Aldershot, Maidstone (resigned) |
| **1993** | Wycombe | Halifax |
| **1997** | Macclesfield | Hereford |
| **1998** | Halifax | Doncaster |
| **1999** | Cheltenham | Scarborough |
| **2000** | Kidderminster | Chester |
| **2001** | Rushden | Barnet |
| **2002** | Boston | Halifax |
| **2003** | Yeovil, Doncaster | Exeter, Shrewsbury |
| **2004** | Chester, Shrewsbury | Carlisle, York |
| **2005** | Barnet, Carlisle | Kidderminster, Cambridge Utd |
| **2006** | Accrington, Hereford | Oxford Utd, Rushden & Diamonds |
| **2007** | Dagenham, Morecambe | Torquay, Boston |
| **2008** | Aldershot, Exeter | Wrexham, Mansfield |
| **2009** | Burton, Torquay | Chester, Luton |
| **2010** | Stevenage, Oxford Utd | Grimsby, Darlington |
| **2011** | Crawley, AFC Wimbledon | Lincoln, Stockport |
| **2012** | Fleetwood, York | Hereford, Macclesfield |
| **2013** | Mansfield, Newport | Barnet, Aldershot |
| **2014** | Luton, Cambridge Utd | Bristol Rov, Torquay |
| **2015** | Barnet, Bristol Rov | Cheltenham, Tranmere |
| **2016** | Cheltenham, Grimsby | Dagenham & Redbridge, York |
| **2017** | Lincoln, Forest Green | Hartlepool, Leyton Orient |
| **2018** | Macclesfield, Tranmere | Barnet, Chesterfield |

Leeds City were expelled from Div 2 in Oct, 1919; Port Vale took over their fixtures.

## EXTENSIONS TO FOOTBALL LEAGUE

| **Clubs** | **Season** | **Clubs** | **Season** |
|---|---|---|---|
| 12 to 14 | 1891–92 | 44 to 66† | 1920–21 |
| 14 to 28* | 1892–93 | 66 to 86† | 1921–22 |
| 28 to 31 | 1893–94 | 86 to 88 | 1923–24 |
| 31 to 32 | 1894–95 | 88 to 92 | 1950–51 |
| 32 to 36 | 1898–99 | 92 to 93 | 1991–92 |
| 36 to 40 | 1905–06 | (Reverted to 92 when Aldershot closed, Mar 1992) | |

*Second Division formed. † Third Division (South) formed from Southern League clubs.
†Third Division (North) formed.

Football League reduced to 70 clubs and three divisions on the formation of the FA Premier League in 1992; increased to 72 season 1994–95, when Premier League reduced to 20 clubs.

## RECORD RUNS

**Arsenal** hold the record unbeaten sequence in the English League – 49 Premiership matches (36 wins, 13 draws) from May 7, 2003 until Oct 24, 2004 when beaten 2-0 away to Manchester Utd. The record previously belonged to **Nottm Forest** – 42 First Division matches (21 wins, 21 draws) from Nov 19, 1977 until beaten 2-0 at Liverpool on December 9, 1978.

**Huddersfield** set a new Football League record of 43 League 1 matches unbeaten from Jan 1,

2011 until Nov 28, 2011 when losing 2-0 at Charlton.

**Best debuts: Ipswich** won the First Division at their first attempt in 1961–62.

**Peterborough** in their first season in the Football League (1960–01) not only won the Fourth Division but set the all-time scoring record for the League of 134 goals. **Hereford** were promoted from the Fourth Division in their first League season, 1972–73.

**Wycombe** were promoted from the Third Division (via the play-offs) in their first League season, 1993–94. **Stevenage** were promoted from League 2 (via the play-offs) in their first League season, 2010–11. **Crawley** gained automatic promotion in their first season in 2011–12.

**Record winning sequence in a season:** 18 consecutive League victories by Manchester City, 2017–18, longest in English top-flight football.

**Best winning start to League season:** 13 successive victories in Div 3 by **Reading,** season 1985–86.

**Best starts in 'old' First Division:** 11 consecutive victories by **Tottenham** in 1960–61; 10 by **Manchester Utd in** 1985–86. In 'new' First Division, 11 consecutive wins by **Newcastle** in 1992–93 and by **Fulham** in 2000–01.

**Longest unbeaten sequence (all competitions):** 40 by **Nottm Forest,** Mar–December 1978. It comprised 21 wins, 19 draws (in 29 League matches, 6 League Cup, 4 European Cup, 1 Charity Shield).

**Longest unbeaten starts to League season:** 38 matches (26 wins, 12 draws) in **Arsenal's** undefeated Premiership season, 2003–04; 29 matches – **Leeds,** Div 1 1973–74 (19 wins, 10 draws); **Liverpool**, Div 1 1987–88 (22 wins, 7 draws).

**Most consecutive League matches unbeaten in a season:** 38 **Arsenal** Premiership season 2003–04 (see above); 33 **Reading** (25 wins, 8 draws) 2005–06.

**Longest winning sequence in Div 1:** 13 matches by **Tottenham** – last two of season 1959–60, first 11 of 1960–61.

**Longest unbeaten home League sequence in top division:** 86 matches (62 wins, 24 draws) by **Chelsea** (Mar 2004–Oct 2008).

**League's longest winning sequence with clean sheets:** 9 matches by **Stockport** (Lge 2, 2006–07 season).

**Premier League – best starts to season: Arsenal,** 38 games, 2003–04; **Manchester City,** 14 games, 2011–12.

**Best winning start to Premiership season:** 9 consecutive victories by **Chelsea** in 2005–06.

**Premier League – most consecutive home wins:** 20 by **Manchester City** (last 5 season 2010–11, first 15 season 2011–12).

**Most consecutive away League wins in top flight:** 11 by **Chelsea** (3 at end 2007–08 season, 8 in 2008–09).

**Premier League – longest unbeaten away run:** 27 matches (W17, D10) by **Arsenal** (Apr 5, 2003–Sep 25, 2004).

**Record home-win sequences: Bradford Park Avenue** won 25 successive home games in Div 3 North – the last 18 in 1926–27 and the first 7 the following season. Longest run of home wins in the top division is 21 by **Liverpool** – the last 9 of 1971–72 and the first 12 of 1972–73.

**British record for successive League wins:** 25 by **Celtic** (Scottish Premier League), 2003–04.

## WORST SEQUENCES

**Derby** experienced the longest run without a win in League history in season 2007–08 – 32 games from Sep 22 to the end of the campaign (25 lost, 7 drawn). They finished bottom by a 24-pt margin. The sequence increased to 36 matches (28 lost, 8 drawn) at the start of the following season.

**Cambridge Utd** had the previous worst of 31 in 1983–84 (21 lost, 10 drawn). They were bottom of Div 2.

**Longest sequence without home win**: Sunderland, in the Championship, went an English record 21 games in all competitions without a victory in front of their own supporters (Dec 2016-Nov 2017).

**Worst losing start to a League season :** 12 consecutive defeats by **Manchester Utd** (Div 1), 1930–31.

**Worst Premier League start: QPR** 16 matches without win (7 draws, 9 defeats), 2012–13.

**Premier League – most consecutive defeats:** 20 **Sunderland** last 15 matches, 2002–03, first five matches 2005–06.

**Longest non-winning start to League season: 25** matches (4 draws, 21 defeats) by **Newport,** Div 4. Worst no-win League starts since then: 16 matches by **Burnley** (9 draws, 7 defeats in Div 2, 1979–80); 16 by **Hull** (10 draws, 6 defeats in Div 2, 1989–90); 16 by **Sheffield Utd** (4 draws, 12 defeats in Div 1, 1990–91).

**Most League defeats in season:** 34 by **Doncaster** (Div 3) 1997–98.

**Fewest League wins in season:** 1 by **Loughborough** (Div 2, season 1899–1900). They lost 27, drew 6, goals 18-100 and dropped out of the League. (See also Scottish section). 1 by **Derby** (Prem Lge, 2007–08). They lost 29, drew 8, goals 20-89.

**Most consecutive League defeats in season:** 18 by **Darwen** (Div 1, 1898–99); 17 by **Rochdale** (Div 3 North, 1931–32).

**Fewest home League wins in season:** 1 by **Loughborough** (Div 2, 1899–1900), **Notts Co** (Div 1, 1904–05), **Woolwich Arsenal** (Div 1, 1912–13), **Blackpool** (Div 1, 1966–67), **Rochdale** (Div 3, 1973–74), **Sunderland** (Prem Lge, 2005–06); **Derby** (Prem Lge, 2007–08).

**Most home League defeats in season:** 18 by **Cambridge Utd** (Div 3, 1984–85).

**Away League defeats record:** 24 in row by **Crewe** (Div 2) – all 15 in 1894–95 followed by 9 in 1895–96; by **Nelson** (Div 3 North) – 3 in Apr 1930 followed by all 21 in season 1930–31. They then dropped out of the League.

**Biggest defeat in Champions' season:** During **Newcastle's** title-winning season in 1908–09, they were beaten 9-1 at home by Sunderland on December 5.

## WORST START BY EVENTUAL CHAMPIONS

**Sunderland** took only 2 points from their first 7 matches in season 1912–13 (2 draws, 5 defeats). They won 25 of the remaining 31 games to clinch their fifth League title.

## DISMAL DERBY

**Derby** were relegated in season 2007–08 as the worst-ever team in the Premier League: fewest wins (1), fewest points (11); fewest goals (20), first club to go down in March (29th).

## UNBEATEN LEAGUE SEASON

Only three clubs have completed an English League season unbeaten: **Preston** (22 matches in 1888–89, the League's first season), **Liverpool** (28 matches in Div 2, 1893–94) and **Arsenal** (38 matches in Premiership, 2003–04).

## 100 PER CENT HOME RECORDS

Six clubs have won every home League match in a season: **Sunderland** (13 matches)' in 1891–92 and four teams in the old Second Division: **Liverpool** (14) in 1893–94, **Bury** (15) in 1894–95, **Sheffield Wed** (17) in 1899–1900 and **Small Heath,** subsequently **Birmingham** (17) in 1902–03. The last club to do it, **Brentford,** won all 21 home games in Div 3 South in 1929–30. **Rotherham** just failed to equal that record in 1946–47. They won their first 20 home matches in Div 3 North, then drew the last 3-3 v Rochdale.

## BEST HOME LEAGUE RECORDS IN TOP FLIGHT

**Sunderland,** 1891–92 (P13, W13); **Newcastle,** 1906–07 (P19, W18, D1); **Chelsea,** 2005–06 (P19, W18, D1); **Manchester Utd,** 2010–11 (P19, W18, D1); **Manchester City,** 2011–12 (P19, W18, D1).

## MOST CONSECUTIVE CLEAN SHEETS

**Premier League** – 14: **Manchester Utd** (2008–09); **Football League** – 11: **Millwall** (Div 3 South 1925–26); **York** (Div 3 1973–74); **Reading** (Div 4, 1978–79).

## WORST HOME RUNS

**Most consecutive home League defeats:** 14 **Rochdale** (Div 3 North) seasons 1931–32 and 1932–33; 10 **Birmingham** (Div 1) 1985–86; 9 **Darwen** (Div 2) 1897–98; 9 **Watford** (Div 2) 1971–72.

Between Nov 1958 and Oct 1959 **Portsmouth** drew 2 and lost 14 out of 16 consecutive home games.

**West Ham** did not win in the Premiership at Upton Park in season 2002–03 until the 13th home match on Jan 29.

## MOST AWAY WINS IN SEASON

**Doncaster** won 18 of their 21 away League fixtures when winning Div 3 North in 1946–47.

## AWAY WINS RECORD

**Most consecutive away League wins:** 11 **Chelsea** (Prem Lge) – 8 at start of 2008–09 after ending previous season with 3.

## 100 PER CENT HOME WINS ON ONE DAY

**Div 1** – All 11 home teams won on Feb 13, 1926 and on Dec 10, 1955. **Div 2** – All 12 home teams won on Nov 26, 1988. **Div 3**, all 12 home teams won in the week-end programme of Oct 18–19, 1968.

## NO HOME WINS IN DIV ON ONE DAY

**Div 1** – 8 away wins, 3 draws in 11 matches on Sep 6, 1986. **Div 2** – 7 away wins, 4 draws in 11 matches on Dec 26, 1987. **Premier League** – 6 away wins, 5 draws in 11 matches on Dec 26, 1994.

The week-end **Premiership** programme on Dec 7–8–9, 1996 produced no home win in the ten games (4 aways, 6 draws). There was again no home victory (3 away wins, 7 draws) in the week-end **Premiership** fixtures on Sep 23–24, 2000.

## MOST DRAWS IN A SEASON (FOOTBALL LEAGUE)

23 by **Norwich** (Div 1, 1978–79), **Exeter** (Div 4, 1986–87). **Cardiff** and **Hartlepool** (both Div 3, 1997–98). **Norwich** played 42 matches, the others 46.

## MOST DRAWS IN PREMIER LEAGUE SEASON

18 (in 42 matches) by **Manchester City** (1993–94), **Sheffield Utd** (1993–94), **Southampton** (1994–95).

## MOST DRAWS IN ONE DIV ON ONE DAY

On Sep 18, 1948 **nine** out of 11 First Division matches were drawn.

## MOST DRAWS IN PREMIER DIV PROGRAMME

Over the week-ends of December 2–3–4, 1995, and Sep 23–24, 2000, **seven** out of the ten matches finished level.

## FEWEST DRAWS IN SEASON

In 46 matches: 3 by **Reading** (Div 3 South, 1951–52); **Bradford Park Avenue** (Div 3 North, 1956–57); **Tranmere** (Div 4, 1984–85); **Southend** (Div 3, 2002–03); in 42 matches: 2 by **Reading** (Div 3 South, 1935–36); **Stockport** (Div 3 North, 1946–47); in 38 matches: 2 by **Sunderland** (Div 1, 1908–09).

## HIGHEST-SCORING DRAWS IN LEAGUE

**Leicester** 6, **Arsenal** 6 (Div 1 Apr 21, 1930); **Charlton** 6, **Middlesbrough** 6 (Div 2. Oct 22, 1960)

Latest **6-6** draw in first-class football was between **Tranmere** and **Newcastle** in the Zenith Data Systems Cup 1st round on Oct 1, 1991. The score went from 3-3 at 90 minutes to 6-6 after extra time, and Tranmere won 3-2 on penalties. In Scotland: **Queen of the South** 6, **Falkirk** 6 (Div 1, Sep 20, 1947).

Most recent **5-5** draws in top division: **Southampton** v **Coventry** (Div 1, May 4, 1982); **QPR** v **Newcastle** (Div 1, Sep 22, 1984); **WBA** v **Manchester Utd** (Prem Lge, May 19, 2013).

## DRAWS RECORDS

**Most consecutive drawn matches in Football League:** 8 by **Torquay** (Div 3, 1969–70), **Middlesbrough** (Div 2, 1970–71), **Peterborough** (Div 4, 1971–72), **Birmingham** (Div 3 (1990–91), **Southampton** (Champ, 2005–06), **Chesterfield** (Lge 1, 2005–06), **Swansea** (Champ, 2008–09).

**Longest sequence of draws by the same score:** six 1-1 results by **QPR** in season 1957–58. **Tranmere** became the first club to play **five consecutive 0-0 League draws**, in season 1997–98.

## IDENTICAL RECORDS

There is only **one instance** of two clubs in one division finishing a season with identical records. In 1907–08, **Blackburn** and **Woolwich Arsenal** were bracketed equal 14th in the First Division with these figures: P38, W12, D12, L14, Goals 51-63, Pts. 36.

The total of **1195 goals** scored in the Premier League in season 1993–94 was repeated in 1994–95.

## DEAD LEVEL

**Millwall's** record in Division Two in season 1973–74 was P42, W14, D14, L14, F51, A51, Pts 42.

## CHAMPIONS OF ALL DIVISIONS

**Wolves, Burnley** and **Preston** are the only clubs to have won titles in the old Divisions 1, 2, 3 and 4. Wolves also won the Third Division North and the new Championship.

## POINTS DEDUCTIONS

**2000–01: Chesterfield** 9 for breach of transfer regulations and falsifying gate receipts.
**2002–03: Boston** 4 for contractual irregularities.
**2004–05: Wrexham, Cambridge Utd** 10 for administration.
**2005–06: Rotherham** 10 for administration.
**2006–07: Leeds, Boston** 10 for administration; **Bury** 1 for unregistered player.
**2007–08: Leeds** 15 over insolvency rules; **Bournemouth, Luton, Rotherham** 10 for administration.
**2008–09: Luton** 20 for failing Insolvency rules, 10 over payments to agents; **Bournemouth, Rotherham** 17 for breaking administration rules; **Southampton, Stockport** 10 for administration – **Southampton** with effect from season 2009–10 **Crystal Palace** 1 for ineligible player.
**2009–10: Portsmouth** 9, **Crystal Palace** 10 for administration; **Hartlepool** 3 for ineligible player.
**2010–11: Plymouth** 10 for administration; **Hereford** 3, **Torquay** 1, each for ineligible player
**2011–12: Portsmouth** and **Port Vale** both 10 for administration – Portsmouth from following season.
**2013–14: Coventry** 10 for administration; **AFC Wimbledon** 3 for ineligible player.
**2014–15: Rotherham** 3 for ineligible player.
**2015–16: Bury** 3 for ineligible player.

Among previous points penalties imposed:
**Nov 1990: Arsenal** 2, **Manchester Utd** 1 following mass players' brawl at Old Trafford.
**Dec 1996: Brighton** 2 for pitch invasions by fans.
**Jan 1997: Middlesbrough** 3 for refusing to play Premiership match at Blackburn because of injuries and illness.
**Jun 1994: Tottenham** 12 (reduced to 6) and banned from following season's FA Cup for making illegal payments to players. On appeal, points deduction annulled and club re-instated in Cup.

## NIGHTMARE STARTS

**Most goals conceded by a goalkeeper on League debut:** 13 by **Steve Milton** when Halifax lost 13-0 at Stockport (Div 3 North) on Jan 6, 1934.

**Post-war:** 11 by Crewe's new goalkeeper **Dennis Murray** (Div 3 North) on Sep 29, 1951, when Lincoln won 11-1.

## RELEGATION ODD SPOTS

None of the Barclays Premiership relegation places in season 2004–05 were decided until the last day (Sunday, May 15). **WBA (**bottom at kick-off) survived with a 2-0 home win against Portsmouth, and the three relegated clubs were **Southampton** (1-2 v Manchester Utd), **Norwich** (0-6 at Fulham) and **Crystal Palace** (2-2 at Charlton).

In season 1937–38, **Manchester City** were the highest-scoring team in the First Division with 80 goals (3 more than Champions Arsenal), but they finished in 21st place and were relegated – a year after winning the title. They scored more goals than they conceded (77).

That season produced the **closest relegation battle** in top-division history, with only 4 points spanning the bottom 11 clubs in Div 1. **WBA** went down with **Manchester City**.

Twelve years earlier, in 1925–26, City went down to Division 2 despite totalling 89 goals – still the most scored in any division by a relegated team. Manchester City also scored 31 FA Cup goals that season, but lost the Final 1-0 to Bolton Wanderers.

**Cardiff** were relegated from Div 1 in season 1928–29, despite conceding fewest goals in the division (59). They also scored fewest (43).

On their way to relegation from the First Division in season 1984–85, **Stoke** twice lost ten matches in a row.

## RELEGATION TREBLES

Two Football League clubs have been relegated three seasons in succession. **Bristol City** fell from First Division to Fourth in 1980–81–82 and **Wolves** did the same in 1984–85–86.

## OLDEST CLUBS

Oldest Association Football Club is **Sheffield FC** (formed in 1857). The oldest Football League clubs are **Notts Co,** 1862; **Nottm Forest,** 1865; and **Sheffield Wed,** 1866.

## FOUR DIVISIONS

In **May, 1957**, the Football League decided to re-group the two sections of the Third Division into Third and Fourth Divisions in **season 1958–59**.

The Football League was reduced to three divisions on the formation of the Premier League in **1992**.

In season 2004–05, under new sponsors Coca-Cola, the titles of First, Second and Third Divisions were changed to League Championship, League One and League Two.

## THREE UP – THREE DOWN

The Football League annual general meeting of Jun 1973 agreed to adopt the promotion and relegation system of three up and three down.

The **new system** came into effect in **season 1973–74** and applied only to the first three divisions; four clubs were still relegated from the Third and four promoted from the Fourth.

It was the first change in the promotion and relegation system for the top two divisions in 81 years.

## MOST LEAGUE APPEARANCES

Players with more than 700 English League apps (as at end of season 2017–18)

**1005** Peter Shilton 1966–97 (286 Leicester, 110 Stoke, 202 Nottm Forest, 188 Southampton, 175 Derby, 34 Plymouth Argyle, 1 Bolton, 9 Leyton Orient).

**931** Tony Ford 1975–2002 (423 Grimsby, 9 Sunderland, 112 Stoke, 114 WBA, 5 Bradford City, 76 Scunthorpe, 103 Mansfield, 89 Rochdale).

**840** Graham Alexander 1991–2012 (159 Scunthorpe, 152 Luton, 372 Preston, 157 Burnley)

**824** Terry Paine 1956–77 (713 Southampton, 111 Hereford).

**795** Tommy Hutchison 1968–91 (165 Blackpool, 314 Coventry City, 46 Manchester City, 92 Burnley, 178 Swansea). In addition, 68 Scottish League apps for Alloa 1965–68, giving career League app total of 863.

**790** Neil Redfearn 1982–2004 (35 Bolton, 100 Lincoln, 46 Doncaster, 57 Crystal Palace, 24 Watford, 62 Oldham, 292 Barnsley, 30 Charlton, 17 Bradford City, 22

Wigan, 42 Halifax, 54 Boston, 9 Rochdale).

**782** Robbie James 1973–94 (484 Swansea, 48 Stoke, 87 QPR, 23 Leicester, 89 Bradford City, 51 Cardiff).

**777** Alan Oakes 1959–84 (565 Manchester City, 211 Chester, 1 Port Vale).

**773** Dave Beasant 1980–2003 (340 Wimbledon, 20 Newcastle, 6 Grimsby, 4 Wolves, 133 Chelsea, 88 Southampton, 139 Nottm F, 27 Portsmouth, 16 Brighton).

**770** John Trollope 1960–80 (all for Swindon, record total for one club).

**769** David James 1990–2012 (89 Watford, 214 Liverpool, 67 Aston Villa, 91 West Ham, 93 Manchester City, 134 Portsmouth, 81 Bristol City).

**764** Jimmy Dickinson 1946–65 (all for Portsmouth).

**761** Roy Sproson 1950–72 (all for Port Vale).

**760** Mick Tait 1974–97 (64 Oxford Utd, 106 Carlisle, 33 Hull, 240 Portsmouth, 99 Reading, 79 Darlington, 139 Hartlepool Utd).

**758** Billy Bonds 1964–88 (95 Charlton, 663 West Ham).

**758** Ray Clemence 1966–88 (48 Scunthorpe, 470 Liverpool, 240 Tottenham).

**757** Pat Jennings 1963–86 (48 Watford, 472 Tottenham, 237 Arsenal).

**757** Frank Worthington 1966–88 (171 Huddersfield Town, 210 Leicester, 84 Bolton, 75 Birmingham, 32 Leeds, 19 Sunderland, 34 Southampton, 31 Brighton, 59 Tranmere, 23 Preston, 19 Stockport).

**755** Wayne Allison 1986–2008 (84 Halifax, 7 Watford, 195 Bristol City, 103 Swindon, 76 Huddersfield, 102 Tranmere, 73 Sheffield Utd, 115 Chesterfield).

**749** Ernie Moss 1968–88 (469 Chesterfield, 35 Peterborough, 57 Mansfield, 74 Port Vale, 11 Lincoln, 44 Doncaster, 26 Stockport, 23 Scarborough, 10 Rochdale).

**746** Les Chapman 1966–88 (263 Oldham, 133 Huddersfield Town, 70 Stockport, 139 Bradford City, 88 Rochdale, 53 Preston).

**744** Asa Hartford 1967–90 (214 WBA, 260 Manchester City, 3 Nottm Forest, 81 Everton, 28 Norwich, 81 Bolton, 45 Stockport, 7 Oldham, 25 Shrewsbury).

**743** Alan Ball 1963–84 (146 Blackpool, 208 Everton, 177 Arsenal, 195 Southampton, 17 Bristol Rov).

**743** John Hollins 1963–84 (465 Chelsea, 151 QPR, 127 Arsenal).

**743** Phil Parkes 1968–91 (52 Walsall, 344 QPR, 344 West Ham, 3 Ipswich).

**737** Steve Bruce 1979–99 (205 Gillingham, 141 Norwich, 309 Manchester Utd 72 Birmingham, 10 Sheffield Utd).

**734** Teddy Sheringham 1983–2007 (220 Millwall, 5 Aldershot, 42 Nottm Forest, 104 Manchester Utd, 236 Tottenham, 32 Portsmouth, 76 West Ham, 19 Colchester)

**732** Mick Mills 1966–88 (591 Ipswich, 103 Southampton, 38 Stoke).

**731** Ian Callaghan 1959–81 (640 Liverpool, 76 Swansea, 15 Crewe).

**731** David Seaman 1982–2003 (91 Peterborough, 75 Birmingham, 141 QPR, 405 Arsenal, 19 Manchester City).

**725** Steve Perryman 1969–90 (655 Tottenham, 17 Oxford Utd, 53 Brentford).

**722** Martin Peters 1961–81 (302 West Ham, 189 Tottenham, 207 Norwich, 24 Sheffield Utd).

**718** Mike Channon 1966–86 (511 Southampton, 72 Manchester City, 4 Newcastle, 9 Bristol Rov, 88 Norwich, 34 Portsmouth).

**716** Ron Harris 1961–83 (655 Chelsea, 61 Brentford).

**716** Mike Summerbee 1959–79 (218 Swindon, 357 Manchester City, 51 Burnley, 3 Blackpool, 87 Stockport).

**714** Glenn Cockerill 1976–98 (186 Lincoln, 26 Swindon, 62 Sheffield Utd, 387 Southampton, 90 Leyton Orient, 40 Fulham, 23 Brentford).

**705** Keith Curle 1981–2003 (32 Bristol Rov, 16 Torquay, 121 Bristol City, 40 Reading, 93 Wimbledon, 171 Manchester City, 150 Wolves, 57 Sheffield Utd, 11 Barnsley, 14 Mansfield.

**705** Phil Neal 1968–89 (186 Northampton, 455 Liverpool, 64 Bolton).

**705** John Wile 1968–86 (205 Peterborough, 500 WBA).

**701** Neville Southall 1980–2000 (39 Bury, 578 Everton, 9 Port Vale, 9 Southend, 12 Stoke, 53 Torquay, 1 Bradford City).

- **Stanley Matthews** made 701 League apps 1932–65 (322 Stoke, 379 Blackpool), incl. 3 for Stoke at start of 1939–40 before season abandoned (war).
- Goalkeeper **John Burridge** made a total of 771 League appearances in a 28-season career in English and Scottish football (1968–96). He played 691 games for 15 English clubs (Workington, Blackpool, Aston Villa, Southend, Crystal Palace, QPR, Wolves, Derby, Sheffield Utd, Southampton, Newcastle, Scarborough, Lincoln, Manchester City and Darlington) and 80 for 5 Scottish clubs (Hibernian, Aberdeen, Dumbarton, Falkirk and Queen of the South).

## LONGEST LEAGUE APPEARANCE SEQUENCE

**Harold Bell,** centre-half of Tranmere, was ever-present for the first nine post-war seasons (1946–55), achieving a League record of 401 consecutive matches. Counting FA Cup and other games, his run of successive appearances totalled 459.

The longest League sequence since Bell's was 394 appearances by goalkeeper **Dave Beasant** for Wimbledon, Newcastle and Chelsea. His nine-year run began on Aug 29, 1981 and was ended by a broken finger sustained in Chelsea's League Cup-tie against Portsmouth on Oct 31, 1990. Beasant's 394 consecutive League games comprised 304 for Wimbledon (1981–88), 20 for Newcastle (1988–89) and 70 for Chelsea (1989–90).

**Phil Neal** made 366 consecutive First Division appearances for Liverpool between December 1974 and Sep 1983, a remarkable sequence for an outfield player in top-division football.

## MOST CONSECUTIVE PREMIER LEAGUE APPEARANCES

310 by goalkeeper **Brad Friedel** (152 Blackburn, 114 Aston Villa, 44 Tottenham, May 2004–Oct 2012). He played in 8 **ever-present seasons** (2004–12, Blackburn 4, Villa 3, Tottenham 1).

## EVER-PRESENT DEFENCE

The **entire defence** of **Huddersfield** played in all 42 Second Division matches in season 1952–53, namely, Bill Wheeler (goal), Ron Staniforth and Laurie Kelly (full-backs), Bill McGarry, Don McEvoy and Len Quested (half-backs). In addition, Vic Metcalfe played in all 42 League matches at outside-left.

## FIRST SUBSTITUTE USED IN LEAGUE

**Keith Peacock** (Charlton), away to Bolton (Div 2) on Aug 21, 1965.

## FROM PROMOTION TO CHAMPIONS

Clubs who have become Champions of England a year after winning promotion: **Liverpool** 1905, 1906; **Everton** 1931, 1932; **Tottenham** 1950, 1951; **Ipswich** 1961, 1962; **Nottm Forest** 1977, 1978. The first four were placed top in both seasons: Forest finished third and first.

## PREMIERSHIP'S FIRST MULTI-NATIONAL LINE-UP

**Chelsea** made history on December 26, 1999 when starting their Premiership match at Southampton without a single British player in the side.

**Fulham's Unique XI**: In the Worthington Cup 3rd round at home to Bury on Nov 6, 2002, Fulham fielded 11 players of 11 different nationalities. Ten were full Internationals, with Lee Clark an England U–21 cap.

On Feb 14, 2005 **Arsenal** became the first English club to select an all-foreign match squad when Arsene Wenger named 16 non-British players at home to Crystal Palace (Premiership).

**Fifteen nations** were represented at Fratton Park on Dec 30, 2009 (Portsmouth 1 Arsenal 4) when, for the first time in Premier League history, not one Englishman started the match. The line-up comprised seven Frenchmen, two Algerians and one from each of 13 other countries.

Players from 22 nationalities (subs included) were involved in the Blackburn–WBA match at Ewood Park on Jan 23, 2011.

## PREMIER LEAGUE'S FIRST ALL-ENGLAND LINE-UP

On Feb 27, 1999 **Aston Villa** (at home to Coventry) fielded the first all-English line up seen in the Premier League (starting 11 plus 3 subs).

## ENTIRE HOME-GROWN TEAM

**Crewe Alexandra's** starting 11 in the 2-0 home win against Walsall (Lge 1) on Apr 27, 2013 all graduated from the club's academy.

## THREE-NATION CHAMPIONS

**David Beckham** won a title in four countries: with Manchester Utd six times (1996–97–99–2000–01–03), Real Madrid (2007), LA Galaxy (2011 and Paris St Germain (2013).

**Trevor Steven** earned eight Championship medals in three countries: two with Everton (1985, 1987); five with Rangers (1990, 1991, 1993, 1994, 1995) and one with Marseille in 1992.

## LEEDS NO WIN AWAY

**Leeds,** in 1992–93, provided the first instance of a club failing to win an away League match as reigning Champions.

## PIONEERS IN 1888 AND 1992

Three clubs among the twelve who formed the Football League in 1888 were also founder members of the Premier League: **Aston Villa, Blackburn** and **Everton.**

## CHAMPIONS (MODERN) WITH TWO CLUBS – PLAYERS

**Francis Lee** (Manchester City 1968, Derby 1975); **Ray Kennedy** (Arsenal 1971, Liverpool 1979, 1980, 1982); **Archie Gemmill** (Derby 1972, 1975, Nottm Forest 1978); **John McGovern** (Derby 1972, Nottm Forest 1978) **Larry Lloyd** (Liverpool 1973, Nottm Forest 1978); **Peter Withe** (Nottm Forest 1978, Aston Villa 1981); **John Lukic** (Arsenal 1989, Leeds 1992); **Kevin Richardson** (Everton 1985, Arsenal 1989); **Eric Cantona (**Leeds 1992, Manchester Utd 1993, 1994, 1996, 1997); **David Batty** (Leeds 1992, Blackburn 1995), **Bobby Mimms** (Everton 1987, Blackburn 1995), **Henning Berg** (Blackburn 1995, Manchester Utd 1999, 2000); **Nicolas Anelka** (Arsenal 1998, Chelsea 2010); **Ashley Cole** (Arsenal 2002, 2004, Chelsea 2010); **Gael Clichy** (Arsenal 2004, Manchester City 2012); **Kolo Toure** (Arsenal 2004, Manchester City 2012); **Carlos Tevez** (Manchester Utd 2008, 2009, Manchester City 2012).

## TITLE TURNABOUTS

In Jan 1996, **Newcastle** led the Premier League by 13 points. They finished runners-up to Manchester Utd.

At Christmas 1997, **Arsenal** were 13 points behind leaders Manchester Utd and still 11 points behind at the beginning of Mar 1998. But a run of 10 wins took the title to Highbury.

On Mar 2, 2003, **Arsenal,** with 9 games left, went 8 points clear of Manchester Utd, who had a match in hand. United won the Championship by 5 points.

In Mar 2002, **Wolves** were in second (automatic promotion) place in Nationwide Div 1, 11 points ahead of WBA, who had 2 games in hand. They were overtaken by Albion on the run-in, finished third, then failed in the play-offs. A year later they won promotion to the Premiership via the play-offs.

## CLUB CLOSURES

Four clubs have left the Football League in mid-season: **Leeds City** (expelled Oct 1919); **Wigan Borough** (Oct 1931, debts of £20,000); **Accrington Stanley** (Mar 1962, debts £62,000); **Aldershot** (Mar 1992, debts £1.2m). **Maidstone,** with debts of £650,000, closed Aug 1992, on the eve of the season.

## FOUR-DIVISION MEN

In season 1986–87, goalkeeper **Eric Nixon,** became the first player to appear in **all four divisions** of the Football League **in one season**. He served two clubs in Div 1: Manchester City (5 League games) and Southampton (4); in Div 2 Bradford City (3); in Div 3 Carlisle (16); and in Div 4 Wolves (16). Total appearances: 44.

**Harvey McCreadie,** a teenage forward, played in four divisions over two seasons inside a calendar year – from Accrington (Div 3) to Luton (Div 1) in Jan 1960, to Div 2 with Luton later that season and to Wrexham (Div 4) in Nov.

**Tony Cottee** played in all four divisions in season 2000–01, for Leicester (Premiership), Norwich (Div 1), Barnet (Div 3, player-manager) and Millwall (Div 2).

## FATHERS AND SONS

When player-manager **Ian** (39) and **Gary** (18) **Bowyer** appeared together in the **Hereford** side at Scunthorpe (Div 4, Apr 21, 1990), they provided the first instance of father and son playing in the same team in a Football League match for 39 years. Ian played as substitute, and Gary scored Hereford's injury-time equaliser in a 3-3 draw.

**Alec** (39) and **David** (17) **Herd** were among previous father-and-son duos in league football – for Stockport, 2-0 winners at Hartlepool (Div 3 North) on May 5, 1951.

When Preston won 2-1 at Bury in Div 3 on Jan 13, 1990, the opposing goalkeepers were brothers: **Alan Kelly** (21) for Preston and **Gary** (23) for Bury. Their father, **Alan** (who kept goal for Preston in the 1964 FA Cup Final and won 47 Rep of Ireland caps) flew from America to watch the sons he taught to keep goal line up on opposite sides.

Other examples: **Bill Dodgin Snr** (manager, Bristol Rov) faced son **Bill Jnr** (manager of Fulham) four times between 1969 and 1971. On Apr 16, 2013 (Lge 1), Oldham, under **Lee Johnson,** won 1-0 at home to Yeovil, managed by his father **Gary.**

**George Eastham Snr** (manager) and son **George Eastham Jnr** were inside-forward partners for Ards in the Irish League in season 1954–55.

## FATHER AND SON REFEREE PLAY-OFF FINALS

Father and son refereed two of the 2009 Play-off Finals. **Clive Oliver**, 46, took charge of Shrewsbury v Gillingham (Lge 2) and **Michael Oliver,** 26, refereed Millwall v Scunthorpe (Lge 1) the following day.

## FATHER AND SON BOTH CHAMPIONS

**John Aston snr** won a Championship medal with Manchester Utd in 1952 and **John Aston jnr** did so with the club in 1967. **Ian Wright** won the Premier League title with Arsenal in 1998 and **Shaun Wright-Phillips** won with Chelsea in 2006.

## FATHER AND SON RIVAL MANAGERS

When **Bill Dodgin snr** took Bristol Rov to Fulham for an FA Cup 1st Round tie in Nov 1971, the opposing manager was his son, **Bill jnr.** Rovers won 2-1. Oldham's new manager, **Lee Johnson**, faced his father **Gary's** Yeovil in a Lge 1 match in April, 2013. Oldham won 1-0.

## FATHER AND SON ON OPPOSITE SIDES

It happened for the first time in FA Cup history (1st Qual Round on Sep 14, 1996) when 21-year-old **Nick Scaife** (Bishop Auckland) faced his father **Bobby** (41), who played for Pickering. Both were in midfield. Home side Bishops won 3-1.

## THREE BROTHERS IN SAME SIDE

Southampton provided the first instance for 65 years of three brothers appearing together in a Div 1 side when **Danny Wallace** (24) and his 19-year-old twin brothers **Rodney** and **Ray** played against Sheffield Wed on Oct 22, 1988. In all, they made 25 appearances together for Southampton until Sep 1989.

A previous instance in Div 1 was provided by the Middlesbrough trio, **William, John** and **George Carr** with 24 League appearances together from Jan 1920 to Oct 1923.

The **Tonner** brothers, **Sam, James** and **Jack,** played together in 13 Second Division matches for Clapton Orient in season 1919–20.

Brothers **David, Donald** and **Robert Jack** played together in Plymouth's League side in 1920.

## TWIN TEAM-MATES (see also Wallace twins above)

Twin brothers **David** and **Peter Jackson** played together for three League clubs (Wrexham, Bradford City and Tranmere) from 1954–62. The **Morgan** twins, **Ian** and **Roger**, played regularly in the QPR forward line from 1964–68. WBA's **Adam** and **James Chambers,** 18, were the first twins to represent England (v Cameroon in World Youth Championship, Apr 1999). They first played together in Albion's senior team, aged 19, in the League Cup 2nd. Round against Derby in Sep 2000. Brazilian identical twins **Rafael** and **Fabio Da Silva** (18) made first team debuts at full-back for Manchester Utd in season 2008– 09. Swedish twins **Martin** and **Marcus Olsson** played together for Blackburn in season 2011–12. **Josh** and **Jacob Murphy**, 19, played for Norwich in season 2013–2014.

## SIR TOM DOES THE HONOURS

**Sir Tom Finney,** England and Preston legend, opened the Football League's new headquarters on their return to Preston on Feb 23, 1999. Preston had been the League's original base for 70 years before the move to Lytham St Annes in 1959.

## SHORTENED MATCHES

The 0-0 score in the **Bradford City v Lincoln** Third Division fixture on May 11, 1985, abandoned through fire after 40 minutes, was subsequently confirmed as a result. It is the shortest officially- completed League match on record, and was the fourth of only five instances in Football League history of the score of an unfinished match being allowed to stand.

The other occasions: **Middlesbrough 4, Oldham 1** (Div 1, Apr 3, 1915), abandoned after 55 minutes when Oldham defender Billy Cook refused to leave the field after being sent off; **Barrow 7, Gillingham 0** (Div 4, Oct 9, 1961), abandoned after 75 minutes because of bad light, the match having started late because of Gillingham's delayed arrival.

A crucial **Manchester** derby (Div 1) was abandoned after 85 minutes, and the result stood, on Apr 27, 1974, when a pitch invasion at Old Trafford followed the only goal, scored for City by Denis Law, which relegated United, Law's former club.

The only instance of a first-class match in England being abandoned **'through shortage of players'** occurred in the First Division at Bramall Lane on Mar 16, 2002. Referee Eddie Wolstenholme halted play after 82 minutes because **Sheffield Utd** were reduced to 6 players against **WBA.** They had had 3 men sent off (goalkeeper and 2 substitutes), and with all 3 substitutes used and 2 players injured, were left with fewer than the required minimum of 7 on the field. Promotion contenders WBA were leading 3-0, and the League ordered the result to stand.

The last 60 seconds of **Birmingham v Stoke** (Div 3, 1-1, on Feb 29, 1992) were played behind locked doors. The ground had been cleared after a pitch invasion.

A First Division fixture, **Sheffield Wed v Aston Villa** (Nov 26, 1898), was abandoned through bad light after 79 mins with Wednesday leading 3-1. The Football League ruled that the match should be completed, and the remaining 10.5 minutes were played four months later (Mar 13, 1899), when Wednesday added another goal to make the result 4-1.

# FA CUP RECORDS

(See also Goalscoring section)

## CHIEF WINNERS

**13** Arsenal; **12** Manchester Utd; **8** Tottenham, Chelsea; **7** Aston Villa, Liverpool; **6** Blackburn, Newcastle.

**Three times in succession:** The Wanderers (1876–77–78) and Blackburn (1884–85–86).

**Trophy handed back:** The FA Cup became the Wanderers' absolute property in 1878, but they handed it back to the Association on condition that it was not to be won outright by any club.

**In successive years by professional clubs:** Blackburn (1890 and 1891); Newcastle (1951 and 1952); Tottenham (1961 and 1962); Tottenham (1981 and 1982); Arsenal (2002 and 2003); Chelsea (2009–10).

**Record Final-tie score:** Bury 6, Derby 0 (1903).

**Most FA Cup Final wins at Wembley:** Arsenal 10, Manchester Utd 10, Chelsea 7, Tottenham 6, Liverpool 5, Newcastle 5.

## SECOND DIVISION WINNERS

**Notts Co** (1894), **Wolves** (1908), **Barnsley** (1912), **WBA** (1931), **Sunderland** (1973), **Southampton** (1976), **West Ham** (1980). When **Tottenham** won the Cup in 1901 they were a Southern League club.

## 'OUTSIDE' SEMI-FINALISTS

**Sheffield Utd, in 2014,** became the ninth team from outside the top two divisions to reach the semi-finals, following **Millwall** (1937), **Port Vale** (1954), **York** (1955), **Norwich** (1959), **Crystal Palace** (1976), **Plymouth** (1984), **Chesterfield** (1997) and **Wycombe** (2001). None reached the Final.

## FOURTH DIVISION QUARTER-FINALISTS

**Oxford Utd** (1964), **Colchester** (1971), **Bradford City** (1976), **Cambridge Utd** (1990).

## FOURTH ROUND – NO REPLAYS

No replays were necessary in the 16 fourth round ties in January 2008 (7 home wins, 9 away). This had not happened for 51 years, since 8 home and 8 away wins in season 1956–57.

## FIVE TROPHIES

The trophy which Arsenal won in 2014 was the fifth in FA Cup history. These were its predecessors:

**1872–95:** First Cup stolen from shop in Birmingham while held by Aston Villa. Never seen again.

**1910:** Second trophy presented to Lord Kinnaird on completing 21 years as FA president.

**1911–91:** Third trophy used until replaced ('battered and fragile') after 80 years' service.

**1992–2013** Fourth FA Cup lasted 21 years – now retained at FA headquarters at Wembley Stadium.

Traditionally, the Cup stays with the holders until returned to the FA in March.

## FINALISTS RELEGATED

Six clubs have reached the FA Cup Final and been relegated. The first five all lost at Wembley – **Manchester City** 1926, **Leicester** 1969, **Brighton** 1983, **Middlesbrough** 1997 and **Portsmouth** 2010. **Wigan,** Cup winners for the first time in 2013, were relegated from the Premier League three days later.

## FA CUP – TOP SHOCKS

(2018 = season 2017–18; rounds shown in brackets; R = replay)

| | | | | |
|---|---|---|---|---|
| **1922 (1)** | Everton | 0 | Crystal Palace | 6 |
| **1933 (3)** | Walsall | 2 | Arsenal | 0 |
| **1939 (F)** | Portsmouth | 4 | Wolves | 1 |
| **1948 (3)** | Arsenal | 0 | Bradford PA | 1 |
| **1948 (3)** | Colchester | 1 | Huddersfield | 0 |
| **1949 (4)** | Yeovil | 2 | Sunderland | 1 |
| **1954 (4)** | Arsenal | 1 | Norwich | 2 |
| **1955 (5)** | York | 2 | Tottenham | 1 |
| **1957 (4)** | Wolves | 0 | Bournemouth | 1 |

| | | | | |
|---|---|---|---|---|
| **1957 (5)** | Bournemouth | 3 | Tottenham | 1 |
| **1958 (4)** | Newcastle | 1 | Scunthorpe | 3 |
| **1959 (3)** | Norwich | 3 | Manchester Utd | 0 |
| **1959 (3)** | Worcester | 2 | Liverpool | 1 |
| **1961 (3)** | Chelsea | 1 | Crewe | 2 |
| **1964 (3)** | Newcastle | 1 | Bedford | 2 |
| **1965 (4)** | Peterborough | 2 | Arsenal | 1 |
| **1971 (5)** | Colchester | 3 | Leeds | 2 |
| **1972 (3)** | Hereford | 2 | Newcastle | 1R |
| **1973 (F)** | Sunderland | 1 | Leeds | 0 |
| **1975 (3)** | Burnley | 0 | Wimbledon | 1 |
| **1976 (F)** | Southampton | 1 | Manchester Utd | 0 |
| **1978 (F)** | Ipswich | 1 | Arsenal | 0 |
| **1980 (3)** | Chelsea | 0 | Wigan | 1 |
| **1980 (3)** | Halifax | 1 | Manchester City | 0 |
| **1980 (F)** | West Ham | 1 | Arsenal | 0 |
| **1981 (4)** | Exeter | 4 | Newcastle | 0R |
| **1984 (3)** | Bournemouth | 2 | Manchester Utd | 0 |
| **1985 (4)** | York | 1 | Arsenal | 0 |
| **1986 (3)** | Birmingham | 1 | Altrincham | 2 |
| **1988 (F)** | Wimbledon | 1 | Liverpool | 0 |
| **1989 (3)** | Sutton | 2 | Coventry | 1 |
| **1991 (3)** | WBA | 2 | Woking | 4 |
| **1992 (3)** | Wrexham | 2 | Arsenal | 1 |
| **1994 (3)** | Liverpool | 0 | Bristol City | 1R |
| **1994 (3)** | Birmingham | 1 | Kidderminster | 2 |
| **1997 (5)** | Chesterfield | 1 | Nottm Forest | 0 |
| **2001 (4)** | Everton | 0 | Tranmere | 3 |
| **2003 (3)** | Shrewsbury | 2 | Everton | 1 |
| **2005 (3)** | Oldham | 1 | Manchester City | 0 |
| **2008 (6)** | Barnsley | 1 | Chelsea | 0 |
| **2009 (2)** | Histon | 1 | Leeds | 0 |
| **2010 (4)** | Liverpool | 1 | Reading | 2R |
| **2011 (3)** | Stevenage | 3 | Newcastle | 1 |
| **2012 (3)** | Macclesfield | 2 | Cardiff | 1 |
| **2013 (4)** | Norwich | 0 | Luton | 1 |
| **2013 (4)** | Oldham | 3 | Liverpool | 2 |
| **2013 (F)** | Wigan | 1 | Manchester City | 0 |
| **2014 (3)** | Rochdale | 2 | Leeds | 0 |
| **2015 (4)** | Chelsea | 2 | Bradford City | 4 |
| **2015 (5)** | Bradford City | 2 | Sunderland | 0 |
| **2016 (3)** | Oxford | 3 | Swansea | 2 |
| **2017 (5)** | Burnley | 0 | Lincoln | 1 |
| **2018 (5)** | Wigan | 1 | Manchester City | 0 |

## YEOVIL TOP GIANT-KILLERS

**Yeovil's** victories over Colchester and Blackpool in season 2000–01 gave them a total of 20 FA Cup wins against League opponents. They set another non-League record by reaching the third round 13 times.

This was Yeovil's triumphant (non-League) Cup record against League clubs: 1924–25 Bournemouth 3-2; 1934–35 Crystal Palace 3-0, Exeter 4-1; 1938–39 Brighton 2-1; 1948–49 Bury 3-1, Sunderland 2-1; 1958–59 Southend 1-0; 1960–61 Walsall 1-0; 1963–64 Southend 1-0, Crystal Palace 3-1; 1970–71 Bournemouth 1-0; 1972–73 Brentford 2-1; 1987–88 Cambridge Utd 1-0; 1991–92 Walsall 1-0; 1992–93 Torquay 5-2, Hereford 2-1; 1993–94 Fulham 1-0; 1998–99 Northampton 2-0; 2000–01 Colchester 5-1, Blackpool 1-0.

## NON-LEAGUE BEST

Since League football began in 1888, three non-League clubs have reached the FA Cup Final. **Sheffield Wed** (Football Alliance) were runners-up in 1890, as were **Southampton** (Southern League) in 1900 and 1902. **Tottenham** won the Cup as a Southern League team in 1901.

**Lincoln** won 1-0 at Burnley on Feb 18, 2017, to become the first non-league club to reach the last eight in 103 years. Two non-league sides – **Lincoln** and **Sutton** – had reached the last 16 for the first time.

Otherwise, the furthest progress by non-League clubs has been to the 5th round on 7 occasions: **Colchester** 1948, **Yeovil** 1949, **Blyth** 1978, **Telford** 1985, **Kidderminster** 1994, **Crawley** 2011, **Luton** 2013.

Greatest number of non-League sides to reach the **3rd round** is **8** in 2009: **Barrow, Blyth, Eastwood, Forest Green, Histon, Kettering, Kidderminster** and **Torquay.**

Most to reach **Round 4: 3** in 1957 (**Rhyl, New Brighton, Peterborough**) and 1975 (**Leatherhead, Stafford** and **Wimbledon**).

Five non-League clubs reaching **round 3** in 2001 was a Conference record. They were **Chester, Yeovil, Dagenham, Morecambe** and **Kingstonian**.

In season 2002–03, **Team Bath** became the first University-based side to reach the FA Cup 1st Round since **Oxford University** (Finalists in 1880).

## NON-LEAGUE 'LAST TIMES'

Last time no non-League club reached round 3: 1951. Last time only one did so: 1969 (**Kettering**).

## TOP-DIVISION SCALPS

Victories in FA Cup by non-League clubs over top-division teams since 1900 include: 1900–01 (Final, replay): **Tottenham** 3 Sheffield Utd 1 (Tottenham then in Southern League); 1919–20 **Cardiff** 2, Oldham 0; Sheffield Wed 0, **Darlington** 2; 1923–24 **Corinthians** 1, Blackburn 0; 1947–48 **Colchester** 1, Huddersfield 0; 1948–9 **Yeovil** 2, Sunderland 1; 1971–72 **Hereford** 2, Newcastle 1; 1974–75 Burnley 0, **Wimbledon** 1; 1985–86 Birmingham 1, **Altrincham** 2; 1988–89 **Sutton** 2, Coventry 1; 2012–13 Norwich 0, **Luton** 1, 2016–17 Burnley 0 **Lincoln** 1.

## MOST WINNING MEDALS

**Ashley Cole** has won the trophy seven times, with (Arsenal 2002–03–05) and Chelsea (2007–09–10–12). **The Hon Arthur Kinnaird** (The Wanderers and Old Etonians), **Charles Wollaston** (The Wanderers) and **Jimmy Forrest** (Blackburn) each earned five winners' medals. Kinnaird, later president of the FA, played in nine of the first 12 FA Cup Finals, and was on the winning side three times for The Wanderers, in 1873 (captain), 1877, 1878 (captain), and twice as captain of Old Etonians (1879, 1882).

## MANAGERS' MEDALS BACKDATED

In 2010, the FA agreed to award Cup Final medals to all living managers who took their teams to the Final before 1996 (when medals were first given to Wembley team bosses). Lawrie McMenemy had campaigned for the award since Southampton's victory in 1976.

## MOST WINNERS' MEDALS AT WEMBLEY

**4 – Mark Hughes** (3 for Manchester Utd, 1 for Chelsea), **Petr Cech, Frank Lampard, John Terry, Didier Drogba, Ashley Cole** (all Chelsea), **Olivier Giroud** (3 for Arsenal, 1 for Chelsea).

**3 – Dick Pym** (3 clean sheets in Finals), **Bob Haworth, Jimmy Seddon, Harry Nuttall, Billy Butler** (all Bolton); **David Jack** (2 Bolton, 1 Arsenal); **Bob Cowell, Jack Milburn, Bobby Mitchell** (all Newcastle); **Dave Mackay** (Tottenham); **Frank Stapleton** (1 Arsenal, 2 Manchester Utd); **Bryan Robson** (3 times winning captain), **Arthur Albiston, Gary Pallister** (all Manchester Utd); **Bruce Grobbelaar, Steve Nicol, Ian Rush** (all Liverpool); **Roy Keane, Peter Schmeichel, Ryan Giggs** (all Manchester Utd); **Dennis Wise** (1 Wimbledon, 2 Chelsea).

Arsenal's **David Seaman** and **Ray Parlour** have each earned 4 winners' medals (2 at Wembley, 2 at Cardiff) as have Manchester Utd's **Roy Keane** and **Ryan Giggs** (3 at Wembley, 1 at Cardiff).

## MOST WEMBLEY FINALS

Nine players appeared in five FA Cup Finals at Wembley, replays excluded:

- **Joe Hulme** (Arsenal: 1927 lost, 1930 won, 1932 lost, 1936 won; Huddersfield: 1938 lost).
- **Johnny Giles** (Manchester Utd: 1963 won; Leeds: 1965 lost, 1970 drew at Wembley, lost replay at Old Trafford, 1972 won, 1973 lost).
- **Pat Rice** (all for Arsenal: 1971 won, 1972 lost, 1978 lost, 1979 won, 1980 lost).
- **Frank Stapleton** (Arsenal: 1978 lost, 1979 won, 1980 lost; Manchester Utd; 1983 won, 1985 won).
- **Ray Clemence** (Liverpool: 1971 lost, 1974 won, 1977 lost; Tottenham: 1982 won, 1987 lost).
- **Mark Hughes** (Manchester Utd: 1985 won, 1990 won, 1994 won, 1995 lost; Chelsea: 1997 won).
- **John Barnes** (Watford: 1984 lost; Liverpool: 1988 lost, 1989 won, 1996 lost; Newcastle: 1998 sub, lost): – first player to lose Wembley FA Cup Finals with three different clubs.
- **Roy Keane** (Nottm Forest: 1991 lost; Manchester Utd: 1994 won, 1995 lost, 1996 won, 1999 won).
- **Ryan Giggs** (Manchester Utd: 1994 won, 1995 lost, 1996 won, 1999 won, 2007 lost).
- Clemence, Hughes and Stapleton also played in a replay, making six actual FA Cup Final appearances for each of them.
- **Glenn Hoddle** also made six appearances at Wembley: 5 for Tottenham (incl. 2 replays), in 1981 won, 1982 won and 1987 lost, and 1 for Chelsea as sub in 1994 lost.
- **Paul Bracewell** played in four FA Cup Finals without being on the winning side – for Everton 1985, 1986, 1989, Sunderland 1992.

## MOST WEMBLEY/CARDIFF FINAL APPEARANCES

**8** by **Ashley Cole** (Arsenal: 2001 lost; 2002 won; 2003 won; 2005 won; Chelsea: 2007 won; 2009 won; 2010 won, 2012 won).

**7** by **Roy Keane** (Nottm Forest: 1991 lost; Manchester Utd: 1994 won; 1995 lost; 1996 won; 1999 won; 2004 won; 2005 lost).

**7** by **Ryan Giggs** (Manchester Utd): 1994 won; 1995 lost; 1996 won; 1999 won; 2004 won; 2005 lost; 2007 lost.

**6** by **Paul Scholes** (Manchester Utd): 1995 lost; 1996 won; 1999 won; 2004 won; 2005 lost; 2007 lost.

**5** by **David Seaman** and **Ray Parlour** (Arsenal): 1993 won; 1998 won; 2001 lost; 2002 won; 2003 won; **Dennis Wise** (Wimbledon 1988 won; Chelsea 1994 lost; 1997 won; 2000 won; Millwall 2004 lost); Patrick Vieira (Arsenal): 1998 won; 2001 lost; 2002 won; 2005 won; (Manchester City) 2011 won.

## BIGGEST FA CUP SCORE AT WEMBLEY

5-0 by Stoke v Bolton (semi-final, Apr 17, 2011.

## WINNING GOALKEEPER-CAPTAINS

1988 **Dave Beasant** (Wimbledon); 2003 **David Seaman** (Arsenal).

## MOST WINNING MANAGERS

**7 Arsene Wenger** (Arsenal) 1998, 2002, 2003, 2005, 2014, 2015, 2017; **6 George Ramsay** (Aston Villa) 1887, 1895, 1897, 1905, 1913, 1920; **5 Sir Alex Ferguson** (Manchester Utd) 1990, 1994, 1996, 1999, 2004.

## PLAYER-MANAGERS IN FINAL

**Kenny Dalglish** (Liverpool, 1986); **Glenn Hoddle** (Chelsea, 1994); **Dennis Wise** (Millwall, 2004).

## DEBUTS IN FINAL

**Alan Davies** (Manchester Utd v Brighton, 1983); **Chris Baird** (Southampton v Arsenal, 2003); **Curtis Weston** (Millwall sub v Manchester Utd, 2004).

## SEMI-FINALS AT WEMBLEY

**1991** Tottenham 3 Arsenal 1; **1993** Sheffield Wed 2 Sheffield Utd 1, Arsenal 1 Tottenham 0; **1994** Chelsea 2 Luton 0, Manchester Utd 1 Oldham 1; **2000** Aston Villa beat Bolton 4-1 on pens (after 0-0), Chelsea 2 Newcastle 1; **2008** Portsmouth 1 WBA 0, Cardiff 1 Barnsley 0; **2009** Chelsea 2 Arsenal 1, Everton beat Manchester Utd 4-2 on pens (after 0-0); **2010** Chelsea 3 Aston Villa 0, Portsmouth 2 Tottenham 0; **2011** Manchester City 1 Manchester Utd 0, Stoke 5 Bolton 0; **2012** Liverpool 2 Everton 1, Chelsea 5 Tottenham 1; **2013** Wigan 2 Millwall 0, Manchester City 2 Chelsea 1; **2014** Arsenal beat Wigan 4-2 on pens (after 1-1), Hull 5 Sheffield Utd 3; **2015** Arsenal 2 Reading 1, Aston Villa 2 Liverpool 1; **2016** Manchester Utd 2 Everton 1, Crystal Palace 2 Watford 1; **2017** Arsenal 2 Manchester City 1, Chelsea 4 Tottenham 2; **2018** Chelsea 2 Southampton 0, Manchester Utd 2 Tottenham 1.

## CHELSEA'S FA CUP MILESTONES

Their victory over Liverpool in the 2012 Final set the following records:

Captain **John Terry** first player to lift the trophy four times for one club; **Didier Drogba** first to score in four Finals; **Ashley Cole** first to earn seven winner's medals (Arsenal 3, Chelsea 4); **Roberto Di Matteo** first to score for and manage the same winning club (player for Chelsea 1997, 2000, interim manager 2012).

Chelsea's four triumphs in six seasons (2007–12) the best winning sequence since Wanderers won five of the first seven competitions (1872–78) and Blackburn won five out of eight (1884–91).

## FIRST ENTRANTS (1871–72)

Barnes, Civil Service, Crystal Palace, Clapham Rov, Donnington School (Spalding), Hampstead Heathens, Harrow Chequers, Hitchin, Maidenhead, Marlow, Queen's Park (Glasgow), Reigate Priory, Royal Engineers, Upton Park and Wanderers. Total 15.

## LAST ALL-ENGLISH WINNERS

**Manchester City,** in 1969, were the last club to win the final with a team of all English players.

## FA CUP FIRSTS

**Out of country:** Cardiff, by defeating Arsenal 1-0 in the 1927 Final at Wembley, became the first and only club to take the FA Cup out of England.

**All-English Winning XI:** First club to win the FA Cup with all-English XI: Blackburn Olympic in 1883. Others since: WBA in 1888 and 1931, Bolton (1958), Manchester City (1969), West Ham (1964 and 1975).

**Non-English Winning XI:** Liverpool in 1986 (Mark Lawrenson, born Preston, was a Rep of Ireland player).

**Won both Cups: Old Carthusians** won the FA Cup in 1881 and the FA Amateur Cup in 1894 and 1897. **Wimbledon** won Amateur Cup in 1963, FA Cup in 1988.

## MOST GAMES NEEDED TO WIN

**Barnsley** played a record 12 matches (20 hours' football) to win the FA Cup in season 1911–12. All six replays (one in round 1, three in round 4 and one in each of semi-final and Final) were brought about by goalless draws.

**Arsenal** played 11 FA Cup games when winning the trophy in 1979. Five of them were in the 3rd round against Sheffield Wed.

## LONGEST TIES

**6 matches:** (11 hours): Alvechurch v Oxford City (4th qual round, 1971–72). Alvechurch won 1-0.

**5 matches:** (9 hours, 22 mins – record for competition proper): Stoke v Bury (3rd round, 1954–55). Stoke won 3-2.

**5 matches:** Chelsea v Burnley (4th round, 1955–56). Chelsea won 2-0.

**5 matches:** Hull v Darlington (2nd round, 1960–61). Hull won 3-0.

**5 matches:** Arsenal v Sheffield Wed (3rd round, 1978–79). Arsenal won 2-0.

**Other marathons** (qualifying comp, all 5 matches, 9 hours): Barrow v Gillingham (last qual round, 1924–25) – winners Barrow; Leyton v Ilford (3rd qual round, 1924–25) – winners Leyton; Falmouth v Bideford (3rd qual round, 1973–74) – winners Bideford.

**End of Cup Final replays:** The FA decided that, with effect from 1999, there would be no Cup Final replays. In the event of a draw after extra-time, the match would be decided on penalties. This happened for the first time in 2005, when Arsenal beat Manchester Utd 5-4 on penalties after a 0-0 draw. A year later, Liverpool beat West Ham 3-1 on penalties after a 3-3 draw.

**FA Cup marathons** ended in season 1991–92, when the penalty shoot-out was introduced to decide ties still level after one replay and extra-time.

In 1932–33 **Brighton** (Div 3 South) played 11 FA Cup games, including replays, and scored 43 goals, without getting past round 5. They forgot to claim exemption and had to play from 1st qual round.

## LONGEST ROUND

The longest round in FA Cup history was the **3rd round** in **1962–63**. It took 66 days to complete, lasting from Jan 5 to Mar 11, and included 261 postponements because of bad weather.

## LONGEST UNBEATEN RUN

**23 matches by Blackburn** In winning the Cup in three consecutive years (1884–05–06), they won 21 ties (one in a replay), and their first Cup defeat in four seasons was in a first round replay of the next competition.

## RE-STAGED TIES

**Sixth round,** Mar 9, 1974: Newcastle 4, Nottm Forest 3. Match declared void by FA and ordered to be replayed following a pitch invasion after Newcastle had a player sent off. Forest claimed the hold-up caused the game to change its pattern. The tie went to two further matches at Goodison Park (0-0, then 1-0 to Newcastle).

**Third round,** Jan 5, 1985: Burton 1, Leicester 6 (at Derby). Burton goalkeeper Paul Evans was hit on the head by a missile thrown from the crowd and continued in a daze. The FA ordered the tie to be played again, behind closed doors at Coventry (Leicester won 1-0).

**First round replay**, Nov 25, 1992: Peterborough 9 (Tony Philliskirk 5), Kingstonian 1. Match expunged from records because, at 3-0 after 57 mins, Kingstonian were reduced to ten men when goalkeeper Adrian Blake was concussed by a 50 pence coin thrown from the crowd. The tie was re-staged on the same ground behind closed doors (Peterborough won 1-0).

**Fifth round:** Within an hour of holders Arsenal beating Sheffield Utd 2-1 at Highbury on Feb 13, 1999, the FA took the unprecedented step of declaring the match void because an unwritten rule of sportsmanship had been broken. With United's Lee Morris lying injured, their goalkeeper Alan Kelly kicked the ball into touch. Play resumed with Arsenal's Ray Parlour throwing it in the direction of Kelly, but Nwankwo Kanu took possession and centred for Marc Overmars to score the 'winning' goal. After four minutes of protests by manager Steve Bruce and his players, referee Peter Jones confirmed the goal. Both managers absolved Kanu of cheating but Arsenal's Arsene Wenger offered to replay the match. With the FA immediately approving, it was re-staged at Highbury ten days later (ticket prices halved) and Arsenal again won 2-1.

## PRIZE FUND

The makeover of the FA Cup competition took off in 2001–02 with the introduction of round-by-round prize-money.

## FA CUP FOLLIES

**1999–2000** The FA broke with tradition by deciding the 3rd round be moved from its regular Jan date and staged before Christmas. Criticism was strong, gates poor and the 3rd round in 2000–01 reverted to the New Year. By allowing the holders Manchester Utd to withdraw from the 1999–2000 competition in order to play in FIFA's inaugural World Club Championship in Brazil in Jan, the FA were left with an odd number of clubs in the 3rd round. Their solution was a 'lucky losers' draw among clubs knocked out in round 2. Darlington, beaten at Gillingham, won it to re-enter the competition, then lost 2-1 away to Aston Villa.

## HAT-TRICKS IN FINAL

There have been three in the history of the competition: **Billy Townley** (Blackburn, 1890), **Jimmy Logan** (Notts Co, 1894) and **Stan Mortensen** (Blackpool, 1953).

## MOST APPEARANCES

**88** by **Ian Callaghan** (79 for Liverpool, 7 for Swansea City, 2 for Crewe); **87** by **John Barnes** (31 for Watford, **51** for Liverpool, 5 for Newcastle); **86** by **Stanley Matthews** (37 for Stoke, 49 for Blackpool); **84** by **Bobby Charlton** (80 for Manchester Utd, 4 for Preston); **84** by **Pat Jennings** (3 for Watford, 43 for Tottenham, 38 for Arsenal); **84** by **Peter Shilton** for seven clubs (30 for Leicester, 7 for Stoke, **18** for Nottm Forest, 17 for Southampton, 10 for Derby, 1 for Plymouth Argyle, 1 for Leyton Orient); **82** by **David Seaman** (5 for Peterborough, 5 for Birmingham, 17 for QPR, 54 for Arsenal, 1 for Manchester City).

## THREE-CLUB FINALISTS

Five players have appeared in the FA Cup Final for three clubs: **Harold Halse** for Manchester Utd (1909), Aston Villa (1913) and Chelsea (1915); **Ernie Taylor** for Newcastle (1951), Blackpool (1953) and Manchester Utd (1958); **John Barnes** for Watford (1984), Liverpool (1988, 1989, 1996) and Newcastle (1998); **Dennis Wise** for Wimbledon (1988), Chelsea (1994, 1997, 2000), Millwall (2004); **David James** for Liverpool (1996), Aston Villa (2000) and Portsmouth (2008, 2010).

## CUP MAN WITH TWO CLUBS IN SAME SEASON

**Stan Crowther**, who played for Aston Villa against Manchester Utd in the 1957 FA Cup Final, appeared for both Villa and United in the 1957–58 competition. United signed him directly after the Munich air crash and, in the circumstances, he was given dispensation to play for them in the Cup, including the Final.

## CAPTAIN'S CUP DOUBLE

**Martin Buchan** is the only player to have captained Scottish and English FA Cup-winning teams – Aberdeen in 1970 and Manchester Utd in 1977.

## MEDALS BEFORE AND AFTER

Two players appeared in FA Cup Final teams before and after the Second World War: **Raich Carter** was twice a winner (Sunderland 1937, Derby 1946) and **Willie Fagan** twice on the losing side (Preston 1937, Liverpool 1950).

## DELANEY'S COLLECTION

Scotland winger **Jimmy Delaney** uniquely earned Scottish, English, Northern Ireland and Republic of Ireland Cup medals. He was a winner with Celtic (1937), Manchester Utd (1948) and Derry City (1954) and a runner-up with Cork City (1956).

## STARS WHO MISSED OUT

Internationals who never won an FA Cup winner's medal include: Tommy Lawton, Tom Finney, Johnny Haynes, Gordon Banks, George Best, Terry Butcher, Peter Shilton, Martin Peters, Nobby Stiles, Alan Ball, Malcolm Macdonald, Alan Shearer, Matthew Le Tissier, Stuart Pearce, Des Walker, Phil Neal, Ledley King.

## CUP WINNERS AT NO COST

Not one member of **Bolton**'s 1958 FA Cup-winning team cost the club a transfer fee. Each joined the club for a £10 signing-on fee.

## 11-NATIONS LINE-UP

**Liverpool** fielded a team of 11 different nationalities in the FA Cup 3rd round at Yeovil on Jan 4, 2004.

## HIGH-SCORING SEMI-FINALS

The **record team score** in FA Cup semi-finals is **6**: 1891–92 WBA 6, Nottm Forest 2; 1907–08 Newcastle 6, Fulham 0; 1933–34 Manchester City 6, Aston Villa 1.

Most goals in semi-finals (aggregate): 17 in 1892 (4 matches) and 1899 (5 matches). In modern times: 15 in 1958 (3 matches, including Manchester Utd 5, Fulham 3 – highest-scoring semi-final since last war); 16 in 1989–90 (Crystal Palace 4, Liverpool 3; Manchester Utd v Oldham 3-3, 2-1. All **16 goals** in those three matches were scored by **different players**.

Stoke's win against Bolton at Wembley in 2011 was the first 5-0 semi-final result since Wolves beat Grimsby at Old Trafford in 1939. In 2014, Hull defeated Sheffield Utd 5-3.

Last hat-trick in an FA Cup semi-final was scored by **Alex Dawson** for Manchester Utd in 5-3 replay win against Fulham at Highbury in 1958.

## SEMI-FINAL VENUES

Villa Park has staged more such matches (55 including replays) than any other ground. Next is Hillsborough (33).

## ONE IN A HUNDRED

The 2008 semi-finals included only one top-division club, Portsmouth, for the first time in 100 years – since Newcastle in 1908.

## FOUR SPECIAL AWAYS

For the only time in FA Cup history, **all four quarter-finals** in season 1986–87 were won by the away team.

## DRAWS RECORD

In season 1985–86, **seven** of the eight 5th round ties went to replays – a record for that stage of the competition.

## SHOCK FOR TOP CLUBS

The fourth round on Jan 24, 2015 produced an astonishing set of home defeats for leading clubs. The top three in the Premier League, Chelsea, Manchester City and Southampton were all knocked out and sixth-place Tottenham also lost at home. Odds against this happening were put at 3825-1.

## LUCK OF THE DRAW

In the FA Cup on Jan 11, 1947, eight of **London**'s ten Football League clubs involved in the 3rd round were drawn at home (including Chelsea v Arsenal). Only Crystal Palace played outside the capital (at Newcastle).

In the 3rd round in Jan 1992, Charlton were the only London club drawn at home (against Barnet), but the venue of the Farnborough v West Ham tie was reversed on police instruction. So Upton Park staged Cup ties on successive days, with West Ham at home on the Saturday and Charlton (who shared the ground) on Sunday.

**Arsenal** were drawn away in every round on the way to reaching the Finals of 1971 and 1972. **Manchester Utd** won the Cup in 1990 without playing once at home.

The 1999 finalists, **Manchester Utd** and **Newcastle,** were both drawn at home every time in Rounds 3–6.

On their way to the semi-finals of both domestic Cup competitions in season 2002–03, **Sheffield Utd** were drawn at home ten times out of ten and won all ten matches – six in the League's Worthington Cup and four in the FA Cup.

On their way to winning the Cup in 2014, **Arsenal** did not play once outside London. Home draws in rounds 3, 4, 5 and 6 were followed by the semi-final at Wembley.

## ALL TOP-DIVISION VICTIMS

The only instance of an FA Cup-winning club meeting top-division opponents in every round was provided by Manchester Utd in 1947–48. They beat Aston Villa, Liverpool, Charlton, Preston, then Derby in the semi-final and Blackpool in the Final.

In contrast, these clubs have reached the Final without playing top-division opponents on the way: West Ham (1923), Bolton (1926), Blackpool (1948), Bolton (1953), Millwall (2004).

## WON CUP WITHOUT CONCEDING GOAL

1873 **The Wanderers** (1 match; as holders, exempt until Final); 1889 **Preston** (5 matches); 1903 **Bury** (5 matches). In 1966 **Everton** reached Final without conceding a goal (7 matches), then beat Sheffield Wed 3-2 at Wembley.

## HOME ADVANTAGE

For the first time in FA Cup history, all eight ties in the 1992–93 5th round were won (no replays) by the **clubs drawn at home.** Only other instance of eight home wins at the last 16 stage was in 1889–90, in what was then the 2nd round.

## NORTH-EAST WIPE-OUT

For the first time in 54 years, since the 4th round in Jan, 1957, the North-East's 'big three' were knocked out on the same date, Jan 8, 2011 (3rd round). All lost to lower-division opponents – **Newcastle** 3-1 at Stevenage, **Sunderland** 2-1 at home to Notts County and **Middlesbrough** 2-1 at Burton.

## FEWEST TOP-DIVISION CLUBS IN LAST 16 (5th ROUND)

**5** in 1958; **6** in 1927, 1970, 1982; **7** in 1994, 2003; **8** in 2002, 2004.

## SIXTH-ROUND ELITE

For the first time in FA Cup 6th round history, dating from 1926 when the format of the competition changed, all **eight quarter-finalists** in 1995–96 were from the top division.

## SEMI-FINAL – DOUBLE DERBIES

There have been three instances of both FA Cup semi-finals in the same year being local derbies: **1950** Liverpool beat Everton 2-0 (Maine Road), Arsenal beat Chelsea 1-0 after 2-2 draw (both at Tottenham); **1993** Arsenal beat Tottenham 1-0 (Wembley), Sheffield Wed beat Sheffield Utd 2-1 (Wembley); **2012** Liverpool beat Everton 2-1 (Wembley), Chelsea beat Tottenham 5-1 (Wembley).

## TOP CLUB DISTINCTION

Since the Football League began in 1888, there has never been an FA Cup Final in which **neither club** represented the top division.

## CLUBS THROWN OUT

**Bury** expelled (Dec 2006) for fielding an ineligible player in 3-1 2nd rd replay win at Chester. **Droylsden** expelled for fielding a suspended player in 2-1 2nd rd replay win at home to Chesterfield (Dec 2008).

## SPURS OUT – AND IN

**Tottenham** were banned, pre-season, from the 1994–95 competition because of financial irregularities, but were re-admitted on appeal and reached the semi-finals.

## FATHER & SON FA CUP WINNERS

**Peter Boyle** (Sheffield Utd 1899, 1902) and **Tommy Boyle** (Sheffield Utd 1925); **Harry Johnson Snr** (Sheffield Utd 1899, 1902) and **Harry Johnson Jnr** (Sheffield Utd 1925); **Jimmy Dunn Snr** (Everton 1933) and **Jimmy Dunn Jnr** (Wolves 1949); **Alec Herd** (Manchester City 1934) and **David Herd** (Manchester Utd 1963); **Frank Lampard Snr** (West Ham 1975, 1980) and **Frank Lampard Jnr** (Chelsea 2007, 2009, 2010, 2012).

### BROTHERS IN FA CUP FINAL TEAMS (modern times)

1950 **Denis and Leslie Compton** (Arsenal); 1952 **George and Ted Robledo** (Newcastle); 1967 **Ron and Allan Harris** (Chelsea); 1977 **Jimmy and Brian Greenhoff** (Manchester Utd); 1996 and 1999 **Gary and Phil Neville** (Manchester Utd).

### FA CUP SPONSORS

**Littlewoods Pools** became the first sponsors of the FA Cup in season 1994–95 in a £14m, 4-year deal. French insurance giants **AXA** took over (season 1998–99) in a sponsorship worth £25m over 4 years. German energy company **E.ON** agreed a 4-year deal worth £32m from season 2006–07 and extended it for a year to 2011. American beer company **Budweiser** began a three-year sponsorship worth £24m in season 2011–12. The **Emirates** airline became the first title sponsor (2015-18) in a reported £30m deal with the FA.

### FIRST GOALKEEPER-SUBSTITUTE IN FINAL

**Paul Jones** (Southampton), who replaced injured Antti Niemi against Arsenal in 2003.

## LEAGUE CUP RECORDS

*(See also Goalscoring section)*

**Most winning managers: 4** Brian Clough (Nottm Forest), Sir Alex Ferguson (Manchester Utd), Jose Mourinho (3 Chelsea, 1 Manchester Utd).

**Highest scores:** West Ham 10-0 v Bury (2nd round, 2nd leg 1983–84; agg 12-1); Liverpool 10-0 v Fulham (2nd round, 1st leg 1986–87; agg 13-2).

**Most League Cup goals** (career): 49 Geoff Hurst (43 West Ham, 6 Stoke, 1960–75); 49 Ian Rush (48 Liverpool, 1 Newcastle, 1981–98).

**Highest scorer** (season): 12 Clive Allen (Tottenham 1986–87 in 9 apps).

**Most goals in match:** 6 Frank Bunn (Oldham v Scarborough, 3rd round, 1989–90).

**Most winners' medals:** 5 Ian Rush (Liverpool).

**Most appearances in Final:** 6 Kenny Dalglish (Liverpool 1978–87), Ian Rush (Liverpool 1981–95). Emile Heskey (Leicester 1997, 1999, 2000), Liverpool (2001, 2003), Aston Villa (2010)

**Biggest Final win:** Swansea City 5 Bradford City 0 (2013).

**League Cup sponsors:** Milk Cup 1981–86, Littlewoods Cup 1987–90, Rumbelows Cup 1991–92, Coca-Cola Cup 1993–98. Worthington Cup 1999–2003, Carling Cup 2003–12; Capital One Cup from season 2012–16.

**Up for the cup, then down:** In 2011, Birmingham became only the second club to win a major trophy (the Carling Cup) and be relegated from the top division. It previously happened to Norwich in 1985 when they went down from the old First Division after winning the Milk Cup.

**Liverpool's League Cup records:** Winners a record 8 times. **Ian Rush** only player to win 5 times. Rush also first to play in 8 winning teams in Cup Finals **at Wembley**, all with Liverpool (FA Cup 1986–89–92; League Cup 1981–82–83–84–95).

**Britain's first under-cover Cup Final:** Worthington Cup Final between Blackburn and Tottenham at Cardiff's Millennium Stadium on Sunday, Feb 24, 2002. With rain forecast, the retractable roof was closed on the morning of the match.

**Record penalty shoot-out:** Liverpool beat Middlesbrough 14-13 (3rd round, Sep 23, 2014) after 2-2. Derby beat Carlisle 14-13 (2nd round, Aug 23, 2016) after 1-1.

## DISCIPLINE

### SENDINGS-OFF

Season 2003–04 set an **all-time record** of 504 players sent off in English domestic football competitions. There were 58 in the Premiership, 390 Nationwide League, 28 FA Cup (excluding non-League dismissals), 22 League Cup, 2 in Nationwide play-offs, 4 in LDV Vans Trophy.

**Most sendings-off in Premier League programme** (10 matches): 9 (8 Sat, 1 Sun, Oct 31–Nov 1, 2009).

The 58 Premiership red cards was 13 fewer than the record English **top-division** total of 71 in 2002–03. **Bolton** were the only club in the English divisions without a player sent off in any first-team competition that season.

**Worst day** for dismissals in English football was Boxing Day, 2007, with **20 red cards** (5 Premier League and 15 Coca-Cola League). Three players, Chelsea's Ashley Cole and Ricardo Carvalho and Aston Villa's Zat Knight were sent off in a 4-4 draw at Stamford Bridge. Luton had three men dismissed in their game at Bristol Rov, but still managed a 1-1 draw.

Previous worst day was Dec 13, 2003, with **19 red cards** (2 Premiership and the 17 Nationwide League).

In the entire first season of post-war League football (1946–47) only 12 players were sent off, followed by 14 in 1949–50, and the total League dismissals for the first nine seasons after the War was 104.

The worst pre-War total was 28 in each of seasons 1921–22 and 1922–23.

## ENGLAND SENDINGS-OFF

In a total of 15 England dismissals, David Beckham and Wayne Rooney have been red-carded twice. Beckham and Steven Gerrard are the only England captains to be sent off and Robert Green the only goalkeeper.

| | | |
|---|---|---|
| Jun 5, 1968 | **Alan Mullery** | v Yugoslavia (Florence, Euro Champ) |
| Jun 6, 1973 | **Alan Ball** | v Poland (Chorzow, World Cup qual) |
| Jun 12, 1977 | **Trevor Cherry** | v Argentina (Buenos Aires, friendly) |
| Jun 6, 1986 | **Ray Wilkins** | v Morocco (Monterrey, World Cup Finals) |
| Jun 30, 1998 | **David Beckham** | v Argentina (St Etienne, World Cup Finals) |
| Sep 5, 1998 | **Paul Ince** | v Sweden (Stockholm, Euro Champ qual) |
| Jun 5, 1999 | **Paul Scholes** | v Sweden (Wembley, Euro Champ qual) |
| Sep 8, 1999 | **David Batty** | v Poland (Warsaw, Euro Champ qual) |
| Oct 16, 2002 | **Alan Smith** | v Macedonia (Southampton, Euro Champ qual) |
| Oct 8, 2005 | **David Beckham** | v Austria (Old Trafford, World Cup qual) |
| Jul 1, 2006 | **Wayne Rooney** | v Portugal (Gelsenkirchen, World Cup Finals) |
| Oct 10, 2009 | **Robert Green** | v Ukraine (Dnipropetrovsk, World Cup qual) |
| Oct 7, 2011 | **Wayne Rooney** | v Montenegro (Podgorica, Euro Champ qual) |
| Sep 11, 2012 | **Steven Gerrard** | v Ukraine (Wembley, World Cup qual) |
| Jun 4, 2014 | **Raheem Sterling** | v Ecuador (Miami, friendly) |

**Other countries:** Most recent sendings-off of players representing other Home Countries:
**N Ireland – Chris Baird** (European Champ qual v Hungary, Belfast, Sep 7, 2015).
**Scotland – Charlie Mulgrew** (European Champ qual v Germany, Dortmund, Sep 7, 2014).
**Wales – Neil Taylor** (World Cup qual v Republic of Ireland, Dublin, Mar 24, 2017).
**Rep of Ireland – Shane Duffy** (European Champ v France, Lyon, June 26, 2016).
**England dismissals at other levels:**

**U-23: Stan Anderson** (v Bulgaria, Sofia, May 19, 1957); **Alan Ball** (v Austria, Vienna, Jun 2, 1965); **Kevin Keegan** (v E Germany, Magdeburg, Jun 1, 1972); **Steve Perryman** (v Portugal, Lisbon, Nov 19, 1974).

**U-21: Sammy Lee** (v Hungary, Keszthely, Jun 5, 1981); **Mark Hateley** (v Scotland, Hampden Park, Apr 19, 1982); **Paul Elliott** (v Denmark, Maine Road, Manchester, Mar 26, 1986); **Tony Cottee** (v W Germany, Ludenscheid, Sep 8, 1987); **Julian Dicks** (v Mexico, Toulon, France, Jun 12, 1988); **Jason Dodd** (v Mexico, Toulon, May 29, 1991; 3 Mexico players also sent off in that match); **Matthew Jackson** (v France, Toulon, May 28, 1992); **Robbie Fowler** (v Austria, Kafkenberg, Oct 11, 1994); **Alan Thompson** (v Portugal, Oporto, Sep 2, 1995); **Terry Cooke** (v Portugal, Toulon, May 30, 1996); **Ben Thatcher** (v Italy, Rieti, Oct 10, 1997); **John Curtis** (v Greece, Heraklion, Nov 13, 1997); **Jody Morris** (v Luxembourg, Grevenmacher, Oct 13,

1998); **Stephen Wright** (v Germany, Derby, Oct 6, 2000); **Alan Smith** (v Finland, Valkeakoski, Oct 10, 2000); **Luke Young** and **John Terry** (v Greece, Athens, Jun 5, 2001); **Shola Ameobi** (v Portugal, Rio Maior, Mar 28, 2003); **Jermaine Pennant** (v Croatia, Upton Park, Aug 19, 2003); **Glen Johnson** (v Turkey, Istanbul, Oct 10, 2003); **Nigel Reo-Coker** (v Azerbaijan, Baku, Oct 12, 2004); **Glen Johnson** (v Spain, Henares, Nov 16, 2004); **Steven Taylor** (v Germany, Leverkusen, Oct 10, 2006); **Tom Huddlestone** (v Serbia & Montenegro, Nijmegen, Jun 17, 2007); **Tom Huddlestone** (v Wales, Villa Park, Oct 14, 2008); **Michael Mancienne** (v Finland, Halmstad, Jun 15, 2009); **Fraizer Campbell** (v Sweden, Gothenburg, Jun 26, 2009); **Ben Mee** (v Italy, Empoli, Feb 8, 2011); **Danny Rose** (v Serbia, Krusevac, Oct 16, 2012); **Andre Wisdom** (v Finland, Tampere, Sep 9, 2013); **Jack Stephens** (v Bosnia-Herz, Sarajevo, Nov 12, 2015; **Jordon Ibe** (vSwitzerland, Thun, Mar 26, 2016.

**England 'B'** (1): **Neil Webb** (v Algeria, Algiers, Dec 11, 1990).

## MOST DISMISSALS IN INTERNATIONAL MATCHES

**19** (10 Chile, 9 Uruguay), Jun 25, 1975; **6** (2 Mexico, 4 Argentina), 1956; **6** (5 Ecuador, 1 Uruguay), Jan 4, 1977 (4 Ecuadorians sent off in 78th min, match abandoned, 1-1); **5** (Holland 3, Brazil 2), Jun 6, 1999 in Goianio, Brazil.

## INTERNATIONAL STOPPED THROUGH DEPLETED SIDE

Portugal v Angola (5-1), friendly international in Lisbon on Nov 14, 2001, abandoned (68 mins) because Angola were down to 6 players (4 sent off, 1 carried off, no substitutes left).

## MOST 'CARDS' IN WORLD CUP FINALS MATCH

**20** in Portugal v Holland quarter-final, Nuremberg, Jun 25, 2006 (9 yellow, 2 red, Portugal; 7 yellow, 2 red, Holland).

## FIVE OFF IN ONE MATCH

For the first time since League football began in 1888, five players were sent off in one match (two Chesterfield, three Plymouth) in Div 2 at Saltergate on **Feb 22, 1997.** Four were dismissed (two from each side) in a goalmouth brawl in the last minute. Five were sent off on Dec 2, 1997 (4 Bristol Rov, 1 Wigan) in Div 2 match at Wigan, four in the 45th minute. The third instance occurred at Exeter on **Nov 23, 2002** in Div 3 (three Exeter, two Cambridge United) all in the last minute. On **Mar 27, 2012** (Lge 2) three Bradford players and two from Crawley were shown red cards in the dressing rooms after a brawl at the final whistle at Valley Parade.

Matches with **four** Football League club players being sent off in one match:

**Jan 8, 1955:** Crewe v Bradford City (Div 3 North), two players from each side.

**Dec 13, 1986:** Sheffield Utd (1 player) v Portsmouth (3) in Div 2.

**Aug 18, 1987:** Port Vale v Northampton (Littlewoods Cup 1st Round, 1st Leg), two players from each side.

**Dec 12, 1987:** Brentford v Mansfield (Div 3), two players from each side.

**Sep 6, 1992:** First instance in British first-class football of four players from one side being sent off in one match. Hereford's seven survivors, away to Northampton (Div 3), held out for a 1-1 draw.

**Mar 1, 1977:** Norwich v Huddersfield (Div 1), two from each side.

**Oct 4, 1977:** Shrewsbury (1 player), Rotherham (3) in Div 3.

**Aug 22, 1998:** Gillingham v Bristol Rov (Div 2), two from each side, all after injury-time brawl.

**Mar 16, 2001:** Bristol City v Millwall (Div 2), two from each side.

**Aug 17, 2002:** Lincoln (1 player), Carlisle (3) in Div 3.

**Aug 26, 2002:** Wycombe v QPR (Div 2), two from each side.

**Nov 1, 2005:** Burnley (1 player) v Millwall (3) in Championship.

**Nov 24, 2007:** Swindon v Bristol Rov (Lge 1), two from each side.

**Mar 4, 2008:** Hull v Burnley (Champ) two from each side.

Four Stranraer players were sent off away to Airdrie (Scottish Div 1) on Dec 3, 1994, and that Scottish record was equalled when four Hearts men were ordered off away to Rangers (Prem

Div) on Sep 14, 1996. Albion had four players sent off (3 in last 8 mins) away to Queen's Park (Scottish Div 3) on Aug 23, 1997.

In the **Island Games** in Guernsey (Jul 2003), five players (all from Rhodes) were sent off against Guernsey for violent conduct and the match was abandoned by referee Wendy Toms.

**Most dismissals one team, one match:** Five players of America Tres Rios in first ten minutes after disputed goal by opponents Itaperuna in Brazilian cup match in Rio de Janeiro on Nov 23, 1991. Tie then abandoned and awarded to Itaperuna.

**Eight dismissals in one match:** Four on each side in South American Super Cup quarter-final (Gremio, Brazil v Penarol, Uruguay) in Oct 1993.

**Five dismissals in one season** – Dave Caldwell (2 with Chesterfield, 3 with Torquay) in 1987–88.

**First instance of four dismissals in Scottish match:** three Rangers players (all English – Terry Hurlock, Mark Walters, Mark Hateley) and Celtic's Peter Grant in Scottish Cup quarter-final at Parkhead on Mar 17, 1991 (Celtic won 2-0).

**Four players** (3 Hamilton, 1 Airdrie) were sent off in Scottish Div 1 match on Oct 30, 1993.

**Four players** (3 Ayr, 1 Stranraer) were sent off in Scottish Div 1 match on Aug 27, 1994.

In Scottish Cup first round replays on Dec 16, 1996, there were two instances of three players of one side sent off: Albion Rov (away to Forfar) and Huntly (away to Clyde).

## FASTEST SENDINGS-OFF

**World record – 10 sec: Giuseppe Lorenzo** (Bologna) for striking opponent in Italian League match v Parma, Dec 9, 1990. Goalkeeper **Preston Edwards** (Ebbsfleet) for bringing down opponent and conceding penalty in Blue Square Premier League South match v Farnborough, Feb 5, 2011.

**World record (non-professional) – 3 sec: David Pratt** (Chippenham) at Bashley (British Gas Southern Premier League, Dec 27, 2008).

**Domestic – 13 sec: Kevin Pressman** (Sheffield Wed goalkeeper at Wolves, Div 1, Sunday, Aug 14, 2000); **15 sec: Simon Rea** (Peterborough at Cardiff, Div 2, Nov 2, 2002). **19 sec: Mark Smith** (Crewe goalkeeper at Darlington, Div 3, Mar 12, 1994). **Premier League – 72 sec: Tim Flowers** (Blackburn goalkeeper v Leeds Utd, Feb 1, 1995).

**In World Cup – 55 sec: Jose Batista** (Uruguay v Scotland at Neza, Mexico, Jun 13, 1986).

**In European competition – 90 sec: Sergei Dirkach** (Dynamo Moscow v Ghent UEFA Cup 3rd round, 2nd leg, Dec 11, 1991).

**Fastest FA Cup dismissal – 52 sec: Ian Culverhouse** (Swindon defender, deliberate hand-ball on goal-line, away to Everton, 3rd Round, Sunday Jan 5, 1997).

**Fastest League Cup dismissal – 33 sec: Jason Crowe** (Arsenal substitute v Birmingham, 3rd Round, Oct 14, 1997). Also fastest sending off on debut.

**Fastest Sending-off of substitute – 0 sec: Walter Boyd** (Swansea City) for striking opponent before ball in play after he went on (83 mins) at home to Darlington, Div 3, Nov 23, 1999. **15 secs: Keith Gillespie** (Sheffield Utd) for striking an opponent at Reading (Premiership), Jan 20, 2007. **90 sec: Andreas Johansson** (Wigan), without kicking a ball, for shirt-pulling (penalty) away to Arsenal (Premiership), May 7, 2006.

## MOST SENDINGS-OFF IN CAREER

21 **Willie Johnston** , 1964–82 (Rangers 7, WBA 6, Vancouver Whitecaps 4, Hearts 3, Scotland 1)
21 **Roy McDonough**, 1980–95 (13 in Football League – Birmingham, Walsall, Chelsea, Colchester, Southend, Exeter, Cambridge Utd plus 8 non-league)
13 **Steve Walsh** (Wigan, Leicester, Norwich, Coventry)
13 **Martin Keown** (Arsenal, Aston Villa, Everton)
13 **Alan Smith** (Leeds, Manchester Utd, Newcastle, England U–21, England)
12 **Dennis Wise** (Wimbledon, Chelsea, Leicester, Millwall)
12 **Vinnie Jones** (Wimbledon, Leeds, Sheffield Utd, Chelsea, QPR)
12 **Mark Dennis** (Birmingham, Southampton, QPR)
12 **Roy Keane** (Manchester Utd, Rep of Ireland)
10 **Patrick Vieira** (Arsenal)
10 **Paul Scholes** (Manchester Utd, England)

**Most Premier League sendings-off:** Patrick Vieira 9, Duncan Ferguson 8, Richard Dunne 8,

Vinnie Jones 7, Roy Keane 7, Alan Smith 7. Lee Cattermole 7.

- **Carlton Palmer** holds the unique record of having been sent off with each of his five Premiership clubs: Sheffield Wed, Leeds, Southampton, Nottm Forest and Coventry.

## FA CUP FINAL SENDINGS-OFF

**Kevin Moran** (Manchester Utd) v Everton, Wembley, 1985; **Jose Antonio Reyes** (Arsenal) v Manchester Utd, Cardiff, 2005; **Pablo Zabaleta** (Manchester City) v Wigan, Wembley 2013; **Chris Smalling** (Manchester Utd) v Crystal Palace , Wembley, 2016; **Victor Moses** (Chelsea) v Arsenal, Wembley, 2017

## WEMBLEY SENDINGS-OFF

**Aug 1948** **Branko Stankovic** (Yugoslavia) v Sweden, Olympic Games
**Jul 1966** **Antonio Rattin** (Argentina captain) v England, World cup quarter-final
**Aug 1974** **Billy Bremner** (Leeds) and **Kevin Keegan** (Liverpool), Charity Shield
**Mar 1977** **Gilbert Dresch** (Luxembourg) v England, World Cup
**May 1985** **Kevin Moran** (Manchester Utd) v Everton, FA Cup Final
**Apr 1993** **Lee Dixon** (Arsenal) v Tottenham, FA Cup semi-final
**May 1993** **Peter Swan** (Port Vale) v WBA, Div 2 Play-off Final
**Mar 1994** **Andrei Kanchelskis** (Manchester Utd) v Aston Villa, League Cup Final
**May 1994** **Mike Wallace, Chris Beaumont** (Stockport) v Burnley, Div 2 Play-off Final
**Jun 1995** **Tetsuji Hashiratani** (Japan) v England, Umbro Cup
**May 1997** **Brian Statham** (Brentford) v Crewe, Div 2 Play-off Final
**Apr 1998** **Capucho** (Portugal) v England, friendly
**Nov 1998** **Ray Parlour** (Arsenal) and **Tony Vareilles** (Lens), Champions League
**Mar 1999** **Justin Edinburgh** (Tottenham) v Leicester, League Cup Final
**Jun 1999** **Paul Scholes** (England) v Sweden, European Championship qual
**Feb 2000** **Clint Hill** (Tranmere) v Leicester, League Cup Final
**Apr 2000** **Mark Delaney** (Aston Villa) v Bolton, FA Cup semi-final
**May 2000** **Kevin Sharp** (Wigan) v Gillingham, Div 2 Play-off Final
**Aug 2000** **Roy Keane** (Manchester Utd captain) v Chelsea, Charity Shield
**May 2007** **Marc Tierney** (Shrewsbury) v Bristol Rov, Lge 2 Play-off Final
**May 2007** **Matt Gill** (Exeter) v Morecambe, Conf Play-off Final
**May 2009** **Jamie Ward** (Sheffield Utd) and **Lee Hendrie** (Sheffield Utd) v Burnley, Champ Play-off Final (Hendrie after final whistle)
**May 2009** **Phil Bolland** (Cambridge Utd) v Torquay, Blue Square Prem Lge Play-off Final
**May 2010** **Robin Hulbert** (Barrow) and **David Bridges** (Stevenage), FA Trophy Final
**Apr 2011** **Paul Scholes** (Manchester Utd ) v Manchester City, FA Cup semi-final
**Apr 2011** **Toumani Diagouraga** (Brentford) v Carlisle, Johnstone's Paint Trophy Final
**Sep 2012** **Steven Gerrard** (England) v Ukraine, World Cup qual
**Feb 2013** **Matt Duke** (Bradford) v Swansea, League Cup Final
**May 2013** **Pablo Zabaleta** (Manchester City) v Wigan, FA Cup Final
**Mar 2014** **Joe Newell** (Peterborough) v Chesterfield, Johnstone's Paint Trophy Final
**May 2014** **Gary O'Neil** (QPR) v Derby, Champ Play-off Final
**May 2016** **Chris Smalling** (Manchester Utd) v Crystal Palace, FA Cup Final
**May 2017** **Victor Moses** (Chelsea) v Arsenal, FA Cup Final
**Aug 2017** **Pedro** (Chelsea) v Arsenal, Community Shield
**Sep 2017** **Jan Vertonghen** (Tottenham) v Borussia Dortmund, Champions League
**May 2018** **Liam Ridehalgh** (Tranmere) v Boreham Wood, National League Play-off Final – after 48 secs
**May 2018** **Denis Odoi** (Fulham) v Aston Villa, Championship Play-off Final

## WEMBLEY'S SUSPENDED CAPTAINS

Suspension prevented four **club captains** playing at Wembley in modern finals, in successive years. Three were in FA Cup Finals – **Glenn Roeder** (QPR, 1982), **Steve Foster** (Brighton, 1983), **Wilf**

**Rostron** (Watford, 1984). Sunderland's **Shaun Elliott** was banned from the 1985 Milk Cup Final. Roeder was banned from QPR's 1982 Cup Final replay against Tottenham, and Foster was ruled out of the first match in Brighton's 1983 Final against Manchester Utd.

## RED CARD FOR KICKING BALL-BOY

Chelsea's **Eden Hazard** was sent off (80 mins) in the League Cup semi-final, second leg at Swansea on Jan 23, 2013 for kicking a 17-year-old ball-boy who refused to hand over the ball that had gone out of play. The FA suspended Hazard for three matches.

## BOOKINGS RECORDS

Most players of one Football League club booked in one match is **TEN** – members of the Mansfield team away to Crystal Palace in FA Cup third round, Jan 1963. Most yellow cards for one team in Premier League match – **9** for Tottenham away to Chelsea, May 2, 2016.

**Fastest bookings** – 3 seconds after kick-off, **Vinnie Jones** (Chelsea, home to Sheffield Utd, FA Cup fifth round, Feb 15, 1992); 5 seconds after kick-off: **Vinnie Jones** (Sheffield Utd, away to Manchester City, Div 1, Jan 19, 1991). He was sent-off (54 mins) for second bookable offence.

## FIGHTING TEAM-MATES

Charlton's **Mike Flanagan** and **Derek Hales** were sent off for fighting each other five minutes from end of FA Cup 3rd round tie at home to Southern League Maidstone on Jan 9, 1979.

Bradford City's **Andy Myers** and **Stuart McCall** had a fight during the 1-6 Premiership defeat at Leeds on Sunday, May 13, 2001.

On Sep 28, 1994 the Scottish FA suspended Hearts players **Graeme Hogg** and **Craig Levein** for ten matches for fighting each other in a pre-season 'friendly' v Raith.

Blackburn's England players **Graeme Le Saux** and **David Batty** clashed away to Spartak Moscow (Champions League) on Nov 22, 1995. Neither was sent off.

Newcastle United's England Internationals **Lee Bowyer** and **Kieron Dyer** were sent off for fighting each other at home to Aston Villa (Premiership on Apr 2, 2005).

Arsenal's **Emmanuel Adebayor** and **Nicklas Bendtner** clashed during the 5-1 Carling Cup semi-final 2nd leg defeat at Tottenham on Jan 22, 2008. Neither was sent off; each fined by their club.

Stoke's **Richardo Fuller** was sent off for slapping his captain, Andy Griffin, at West Ham in the Premier League on Dec 28, 2008.

Preston's **Jermaine Beckford** and **Eoin Doyle** clashed in the Championship game against Sheffield Wednesday on Dec 3, 2016, and were sent off.

St Johnstone's **Richard Foster** and **Danny Swanson** were dismissed for brawling in the Scottish Premiership match with Hamilton on Apr 1, 2017.

## FOOTBALL'S FIRST BETTING SCANDAL

A Football League investigation into the First Division match which ended Manchester Utd 2, Liverpool 0 at Old Trafford on Good Friday, Apr 2, 1915 proved that the result had been 'squared' by certain players betting on the outcome. Four members of each team were suspended for life, but some of the bans were lifted when League football resumed in 1919 in recognition of the players' war service.

## PLAYERS JAILED

**Ten professional footballers** found guilty of conspiracy to fraud by 'fixing' matches for betting purposes were given prison sentences at Nottingham Assizes on Jan 26, 1965.

**Jimmy Gauld** (Mansfield), described as the central figure, was given four years. Among the others sentenced, **Tony Kay** (Sheffield Wed, Everton & England), **Peter Swan** (Sheffield Wed & England) and **David 'Bronco' Layne** (Sheffield Wed) were suspended from football for life by the FA.

## DRUGS BANS

**Abel Xavier** (Middlesbrough) was the first Premiership player found to have taken a performance-enchancing drug. He was banned by UEFA for 18 months in Nov 2005 after testing positive for an anabolic steroid. The ban was reduced to a year in Jul 2006 by the Court of Arbitration for Sport. **Paddy Kenny** (Sheffield Utd goalkeeper) was suspended by an FA commission for 9 months from July, 2009 for failing a drugs test the previous May. Kolo Toure (Manchester City) received a 6-month ban in May 2011 for a doping offence. It was backdated to Mar 2.

## LONG SUSPENSIONS

The longest suspension (8 months) in modern times for a player in British football was imposed on two Manchester Utd players. First was **Eric Cantona** following his attack on a spectator as he left the pitch after being sent off at Crystal Palace (Prem League) on Jan 25, 1995. The club immediately suspended him to the end of the season and fined him 2 weeks' wages (est £20,000). Then, on a disrepute charge, the FA fined him £10,000 (Feb 1995) and extended the ban to Sep 30 (which FIFA confirmed as world-wide). A subsequent 2-weeks' jail sentence on Cantona for assault was altered, on appeal, to 120 hours' community service, which took the form of coaching schoolboys in the Manchester area.

On **Dec 19, 2003** an FA Commission, held at Bolton, suspended **Rio Ferdinand** from football for 8 months (plus £50,000 fine) for failing to take a random drug test at the club's training ground on Sep 23. The ban operated from Jan 12, 2004.

**Aug 1974: Kevin Keegan** (Liverpool) and **Billy Bremner** (Leeds) both suspended for 10 matches and fined £500 after being sent off in FA Charity Shield at Wembley.

**Jan 1988: Mark Dennis** (QPR) given 8-match ban after 11th sending-off of his career.

**Oct 1988: Paul Davis** (Arsenal) banned for 9 matches for breaking the jaw of Southampton's Glenn Cockerill.

**Oct 1998: Paolo Di Canio** (Sheff Wed) banned for 11 matches and fined £10,000 for pushing referee Paul Alcock after being sent off at home to Arsenal (Prem), Sep 26.

**Mar 2005: David Prutton** (Southampton) banned for 10 matches (plus 1 for red card) and fined £6,000 by FA for shoving referee Alan Wiley when sent off at home to Arsenal (Prem), Feb 26.

**Aug 2006: Ben Thatcher** (Manchester City) banned for 8 matches for elbowing Pedro Mendes (Portsmouth).

**Sep 2008: Joey Barton** (Newcastle) banned for 12 matches (6 suspended) and fined £25,000 by FA for training ground assault on former Manchester City team-mate Ousmane Dabo.

**May 2012: Joey Barton** (QPR) suspended for 12 matches and fined £75,000 for violent conduct when sent off against Manchester City on final day of Premier League season.

**Mar 2014: Joss Labadie** (Torquay) banned for 10 matches and fined £2,000 for biting Chesterfield's Ollie Banks (Lge 2) on Feb 15, 2014.

**Seven-month ban: Frank Barson**, 37-year-old Watford centre-half, sent off at home to Fulham (Div 3 South) on Sep 29, 1928, was suspended by the FA for the remainder of the season.

**Twelve-month ban:** Oldham full-back **Billy Cook** was given a 12-month suspension for refusing to leave the field when sent off at Middlesbrough (Div 1), on Apr 3, 1915. The referee abandoned the match with 35 minutes still to play, and the score (4-1 to Middlesbrough) was ordered to stand.

**Long Scottish bans: Sep 1954: Willie Woodburn**, Rangers and Scotland centre-half, suspended for rest of career after fifth sending-off in 6 years.

**Billy McLafferty,** Stenhousemuir striker, was banned (Apr 14) for 8 and a half months, to Jan 1, 1993, and fined £250 for failing to appear at a disciplinary hearing after being sent off against Arbroath on Feb 1.

**Twelve-match ban:** On May 12, 1994 Scottish FA suspended Rangers forward **Duncan Ferguson** for 12 matches for violent conduct v Raith on Apr 16. On Oct 11, 1995, Ferguson (then with Everton) sent to jail for 3 months for the assault (served 44 days); Feb 1, 1996 Scottish judge quashed 7 matches that remained of SFA ban on Ferguson.

On Sep 29, 2001 the SFA imposed a **17-match suspension** on Forfar's former Scottish international **Dave Bowman** for persistent foul and abusive language when sent off against Stranraer on Sep 22. As his misconduct continued, he was shown **5 red cards** by the referee.

On Apr 3, 2009, captain **Barry Ferguson** and goalkeeper **Allan McGregor** were banned for life from playing for Scotland for gestures towards photographers while on the bench for a World Cup qualifier against Iceland.

On Dec 20, 2011 Liverpool and Uruguay striker **Luis Suarez** was given an 8-match ban and fined £40,000 by the FA for making 'racially offensive comments' to Patrice Evra of Manchester Utd (Prem Lge, Oct 15).

On Apr 25, 2013 **Luis Suarez** was given a 10-match suspension by the FA for 'violent conduct' – biting Chelsea defender Branislav Ivanovic, Prem Lge, Apr 21. The Liverpool player was also fined £200,000 by Liverpool. His ban covered the last 4 games of that season and the first 6 of 2013–14. On Jun 26, 2014, Suarez, while still a Liverpool player, received the most severe punishment in World Cup history – a four-month ban from 'all football activities' and £66,000 fine from FIFA for biting Giorgio Chiellini during Uruguay's group game against Italy.

On Nov 4, 2016 Rochdale's **Calvin Andrew** was banned by the FA for 12 matches – reduced to 9 on appeal – for elbowing Peter Clarke (Oldham) in the face.

On Apr 16, 2017 **Joey Barton** was banned by the FA for 18 months and fined £30,000 for breaching betting rules. The Burnley player admitted placing 1,260 bets on matches.

## TOP FINES

**Clubs: £49,000,000** (World record) Manchester City: May 2014 for breaking UEFA Financial Fair Play rules **(£32,600,000** suspended subject to City meeting certain conditions over two seasons). **£40m** Queens Park Rangers: Oct 2017, breaking Financial Fair Play rules - club continue to appeal; **£7.6m** Bournemouth: May 2016, for breaking Financial Fair Play rules; **£5,500,000** West Ham: Apr 2007, for breaches of regulations involving 'dishonesty and deceit' over Argentine signings Carlos Tevez and Javier Mascherano; **£3.95m**: Watford: Aug 2017, forged banking letter; **£1,500,000** (increased from original £600,000) Tottenham: Dec 1994, financial irregularities; £875,000 QPR: May 2011 for breaching rules when signing Argentine Alejandro Faurlin; **£375,000** (reduced to £290,000 on appeal) Chelsea: May 2016, players brawl v Tottenham; **£300,000** (reduced to £75,000 on appeal) Chelsea: Jun 2005, illegal approach to Arsenal's Ashley Cole; **£300,000** (plus 2-year ban on signing academy players, part suspended) Manchester City: May 2017, approaching young players; **£225,000** (reduced to £175,000 on appeal) Tottenham: May 2016, players brawl v Chelsea; **£200,000** Aston Villa: May 2015 for fans' pitch invasion after FA Cup quarter-final v WBA; **£175,000** Arsenal: Oct 2003, players' brawl v Manchester Utd; **£150,000** Leeds: Mar 2000, players' brawl v Tottenham; **£150,000** Tottenham: Mar 2000, players brawl v Leeds; **£145,000** Hull: Feb 2015, breaching Financial Fair Play rules; **£115,000** West Ham: Aug 2009, crowd misconduct at Carling Cup; v Millwall; **£105,000** Chelsea: Jan 1991, irregular payments; **£100,000** Boston Utd: Jul 2002, contract irregularities; **£100,000** Arsenal and Chelsea: Mar 2007 for mass brawl after Carling Cup Final; **£100,000** (including suspended fine) Blackburn: Aug 2007, poor disciplinary record; **£100,000** Sunderland: May 2014, breaching agents' regulations; **£100,000** Reading: Aug 2015, pitch invasion, FA Cup tie v Bradford (reduced to £40,000 on appeal); **£100,000** Chelsea: Dec 2016, players brawl v Manchester City; **£100,000** (plus 2-year ban on signing academy players, part suspended) Liverpool: Apr 2017, approaching young player; **£90,000** Brighton: Feb 2015, breaching rules on agents; **£71,000** West Ham: Feb 2015 for playing Diafra Sakho in FA Cup 4th round tie against Bristol City after declaring him unfit for Senegal's Africa Cup of Nations squad; **£65,000** Chelsea: Jan 2016, players brawl v WBA; **£62,000** Macclesfield: Dec 2005, funding of a stand at club's ground.

**Players: £220,000 (plus 4-match ban)** John Terry (Chelsea): Sep 2012, racially abusing Anton Ferdinand (QPR); **£150,000** Roy Keane (Manchester Utd): Oct 2002, disrepute offence over autobiography; **£100,000** (reduced to £75,000 on appeal) Ashley Cole (Arsenal): Jun 2005, illegal approach by Chelsea; **£100,000** (plus 5-match ban) Jonjo Shelvey (Newcastle): Dec 2016, racially abusing Romain Saiss (Wolves); **£90,000** Ashley Cole (Chelsea): Oct 2012, offensive Tweet against FA; **£80,000 (plus 5-match ban)** Nicolas Anelka (WBA): Feb 2014, celebrating goal at West Ham with racially-offensive 'quenelle' gesture; **£75,000 (plus 12-match ban)** Joey Barton (QPR): May 2012, violent conduct v Manchester City; **£60,000 (plus 3-match ban)** John Obi Mikel (Chelsea): Dec 2012, abusing referee Mark Clattenburg after Prem Lge v Manchester Utd); **£60,000** Dexter Blackstock (Nottm Forest): May 2014, breaching betting rules; **£50,000** Cameron Jerome (Stoke): Aug 2013, breaching FA betting rules; **£50,000** Benoit Assou-Ekotto (Tottenham): Sep 2014, publicly backing Nicolas Anelka's controversial 'quenelle' gesture; **£45,000** Patrick Vieira (Arsenal): Oct 1999, tunnel incidents v West Ham; **£45,000** Rio Ferdinand (Manchester Utd): Aug 2012, improper comments about Ashley Cole on Twitter; **£40,000** Lauren (Arsenal): Oct 2003, players' fracas v Manchester Utd; **£40,000 (plus 8-match ban)** Luis Suarez (Liverpool): Dec 2011, racially abusing Patrice Evra (Manchester Utd); **£40,000 (plus 3-match ban)** Dani Osvaldo (Southampton): Jan 2014, violent conduct, touchline Newcastle; **£40,000** Bacary Sagna (Manchester City): Jan 2017, questioning integrity of referee Lee Mason; **£40,000 (plus 3-mtch ban)** Arsene Wenger (Arsenal): Jan 2018, abuse towards referee Mike Dean v WBA.

*In eight seasons with Arsenal (1996–2004) **Patrick Vieira** was fined a total of £122,000 by the FA for disciplinary offences.

**Managers: £200,000** (reduced to £75,000 on appeal) Jose Mourinho (Chelsea): Jun 2005, illegal approach to Arsenal's Ashley Cole; **£60,000 (plus 7-match ban)** Alan Pardew (Newcastle): head-butting Hull player David Meyler (also fined £100,000 by club); **£58,000** Jose Mourinho (Manchester Utd): Nov 2016, misconduct involving referees Mark Clattenburg and Anthony Taylor; **£50,000** Jose Mourinho (Chelsea): Oct 2015, accusing referees of bias; **£40,000 (plus 1 match stadium ban)** Jose Mourinho (Chelsea): Nov 2015, abusive behaviour towards referee Jon Moss v West Ham, **£40,000 (plus 3-match Euro ban)** Arsene Wenger (Arsenal): Jan 2018, abuse towards referee Mike Dean v WBA; **£33,000 (plus 3-match Euro ban**) Arsene Wenger: Mar 2012, criticising referee after Champions League defeat by AC Milan; **£30,000** Sir Alex Ferguson (Manchester Utd): Mar 2011 criticising referee Martin Atkinson v Chelsea; **£30,000 (plus 6-match ban ( (plus 6-match ban reduced to 4 on appeal)**; Rui Faria (Chelsea assistant): May 2014, confronting match officials v Sunderland.

- Jonathan Barnett, Ashley Cole's agent was fined **£100,000** in Sep 2006 for his role in the 'tapping up' affair involving the player and Chelsea.
- Gillingham and club chairman Paul Scally each fined £75,000 in Jul 2015 for 'racial victimisation' towards player Mark McCammon. Club fine reduced to £50,000 on appeal.
- Leyton Orient owner Francesco Becchetti fined £40,000 and given six-match stadium ban in Jan 2016 for violent conduct towards assistant manager Andy Hessenthaler.

***£68,000** FA: May 2003, pitch invasions and racist chanting by fans during England v Turkey, Sunderland.

**£50,000** FA: Dec 2014, for Wigan owner-chairman Dave Whelan, plus six-week ban from all football activity, for remarks about Jewish and Chinese people in newspaper interview.

***£250,000** FA: Dec 2016, for Leeds owner Massimo Cellino, plus 18-month ban, for breaking agent regulations (reduced to £100,000 and one year on appeal). Club fined £250,000 (reduced to £200,000 on appeal). Agent Derek Day fined £75,000 and banned for 18 months (11 months suspended).

# MANAGERS

## INTERNATIONAL RECORDS

(As at start of season 2018–19)

| | P | W | D | L | F | A |
|---|---|---|---|---|---|---|
| **Gareth Southgate** (England appointed Sep 2016 | 25 | 13 | 7 | 5 | 39 | 19 |
| **Alex McLeish** (Scotland – appointed Feb 2018) | 4 | 1 | 0 | 3 | 1 | 4 |
| **Ryan Giggs** (Wales – appointed Jan 2018) | 3 | 1 | 1 | 1 | 6 | 1 |
| **Michael O'Neill** (Northern Ireland – appointed Oct 2011) | 56 | 19 | 16 | 21 | 57 | 61 |
| **Martin O'Neill** (Republic of Ireland – appointed Nov 2013) | 49 | 19 | 16 | 14 | 66 | 50 |
| **COMPLETED RECORDS** | | | | | | |
| **Gordon Strachan** (Scotland – Jan 2013-Oct 2017) | 40 | 20 | 9 | 11 | 61 | 41 |
| **Malkay Mackay** (Scotland, caretaker Nov 2017) | 1 | 0 | 0 | 1 | 0 | 1 |
| **Chris Coleman** (Wales – Jan 2012-Nov 2017) | 49 | 19 | 13 | 17 | 53 | 56 |

## ENGLAND MANAGERS

| | | P | W | D | L |
|---|---|---|---|---|---|
| 1946–62 | **Walter Winterbottom** | 139 | 78 | 33 | 28 |

| | | | | | |
|---|---|---|---|---|---|
| 1963–74 | **Sir Alf Ramsey** | 113 | 69 | 27 | 17 |
| 1974 | **Joe Mercer**, caretaker | 7 | 3 | 3 | 1 |
| 1974–77 | **Don Revie** | 29 | 14 | 8 | 7 |
| 1977–82 | **Ron Greenwood** | 55 | 33 | 12 | 10 |
| 1982–90 | **Bobby Robson** | 95 | 47 | 30 | 18 |
| 1990–93 | **Graham Taylor** | 38 | 18 | 13 | 7 |
| 1994–96 | **Terry Venables** | 23 | 11 | 11 | 1 |
| 1996–99 | **Glenn Hoddle** | 28 | 17 | 6 | 5 |
| 1999 | **Howard Wilkinson**, caretaker | 1 | 0 | 0 | 1 |
| 1999–2000 | **Kevin Keegan** | 18 | 7 | 7 | 4 |
| 2000 | **Howard Wilkinson**, caretaker | 1 | 0 | 1 | 0 |
| 2000 | **Peter Taylor**, caretaker | 1 | 0 | 0 | 1 |
| 2001–06 | **Sven–Goran Eriksson** | 67 | 40 | 17 | 10 |
| 2006–07 | **Steve McClaren** | 18 | 9 | 4 | 5 |
| 2007–12 | **Fabio Capello** | 42 | 28 | 8 | 6 |
| 2012 | **Stuart Pearce**, caretaker | 1 | 0 | 0 | 1 |
| 2012–16 | **Roy Hodgson** | 56 | 33 | 15 | 8 |
| 2016 | **Sam Allardyce** | 1 | 1 | 0 | 0 |

## INTERNATIONAL MANAGER CHANGES

**England: Walter Winterbottom** 1946–62 (initially coach); **Alf Ramsey** (Feb 1963–May 1974); **Joe Mercer** (caretaker May 1974); **Don Revie** (Jul 1974–Jul 1977); **Ron Greenwood** (Aug 1977–Jul 1982); **Bobby Robson** (Jul 1982–Jul 1990); **Graham Taylor** (Jul 1990–Nov 1993); **Terry Venables**, coach (Jan 1994–Jun 1996); **Glenn Hoddle**, coach (Jun 1996–Feb 1999); **Howard Wilkinson** (caretaker Feb 1999); **Kevin Keegan coach** (Feb 1999–Oct 2000); **Howard Wilkinson** (caretaker Oct 2000); **Peter Taylor** (caretaker Nov 2000); **Sven–Goran Eriksson** (Jan 2001–Aug 2006); **Steve McClaren** (Aug 2006–Nov 2007); **Fabio Capello** (Dec 2007–Feb 2012); **Roy Hodgson** (May 2012– Jun 2016); **Sam Allardyce** (Jul-Sep 2016); **Gareth Southgate** (Sep-Nov 2016 interim, then permanent appointment).

**Scotland (modern): Bobby Brown** (Feb 1967–Jul 1971); **Tommy Docherty** (Sep 1971–Dec 1972); **Willie Ormond** (Jan 1973–May 1977); **Ally MacLeod** (May 1977–Sep 1978); **Jock Stein** (Oct 1978–Sep 1985); **Alex Ferguson** (caretaker Oct 1985–Jun 1986); **Andy Roxburgh**, coach (Jul 1986–Sep 1993); **Craig Brown** (Sep 1993–Oct 2001); **Berti Vogts** (Feb 2002–Oct 2004); **Walter Smith** (Dec 2004–Jan 2007); **Alex McLeish** (Jan 2007–Nov 2007); **George Burley** (Jan 2008–Nov 2009); **Craig Levein** (Dec 2009–Nov 2012); **Billy Stark** (caretaker Nov–Dec 2012); **Gordon Strachan** (Jan 2013-Oct 2017); **Malky Mackay**, (caretaker Nov 2017); **Alex McLeish** (since Feb 2018).

**Northern Ireland (modern): Peter Doherty** (1951–62); **Bertie Peacock** (1962–67); **Billy Bingham** (1967–Aug 1971); **Terry Neill** (Aug 1971–Mar 1975); **Dave Clements** (player-manager Mar 1975–1976); **Danny Blanchflower** (Jun 1976–Nov 1979); **Billy Bingham** (Feb 1980–Nov 1993); **Bryan Hamilton** Feb 1994–Feb 1998); **Lawrie McMenemy** (Feb 1998–Nov 1999); **Sammy McIlroy** (Jan 2000–Oct 2003); **Lawrie Sanchez** (Jan 2004–May 2007); **Nigel Worthington** (May 2007–Oct 2011); **Michael O'Neill** (since Oct 2011).

**Wales (modern): Mike Smith** (Jul 1974–Dec 1979); **Mike England** (Mar 1980–Feb 1988); **David Williams** (caretaker Mar 1988); **Terry Yorath** (Apr 1988–Nov 1993); **John Toshack** (Mar 1994, one match); **Mike Smith** (Mar 1994–Jun 1995); **Bobby Gould** (Aug 1995–Jun 1999); **Mark Hughes** (Aug 1999 – Oct 2004); **John Toshack** (Nov 2004–Sep 2010); Brian Flynn (caretaker Sep–Dec 2010); **Gary Speed** (Dec 2010–Nov 2011); **Chris Coleman** (Jan 2012-Nov 2017); **Ryan Giggs** (since Jan 2018)

**Republic of Ireland (modern): Liam Tuohy** (Sep 1971–Nov 1972); **Johnny Giles** (Oct 1973–Apr 1980, initially player–manager); **Eoin Hand** (Jun 1980–Nov 1985); **Jack Charlton** (Feb 1986–Dec 1995); **Mick McCarthy** (Feb 1996–Oct 2002); **Brian Kerr** (Jan 2003–Oct 2005); **Steve Staunton** (Jan 2006–Oct 2007); **Giovanni Trapattoni** (May 2008–Sep 2013); **Martin O'Neill** (since Nov 2013).

## WORLD CUP-WINNING MANAGERS

1930 Uruguay (Alberto Suppici); 1934 and 1938 Italy (Vittorio Pozzo); 1950 Uruguay (Juan Lopez Fontana); 1954 West Germany (Sepp Herberger); 1958 Brazil (Vicente Feola); 1962 Brazil (Aymore Moreira); 1966 England (Sir Alf Ramsey); 1970 Brazil (Mario Zagallo); 1974 West Germany (Helmut Schon); 1978 Argentina (Cesar Luis Menotti); 1982 Italy (Enzo Bearzot); 1986 Argentina (Carlos Bilardo); 1990 West Germany (Franz Beckenbauer); 1994 Brazil (Carlos Alberto Parreira); 1998 France (Aimee Etienne Jacquet); 2002 Brazil (Luiz Felipe Scolari); 2006 Italy (Marcello Lippi); 2010 Spain (Vicente Del Bosque); 2014 Germany (Joachim Low); 2018 France (Didier Deschamps).

Each of the 21 winning teams had a manager/coach of that country's nationality.

## YOUNGEST LEAGUE MANAGERS

**Ivor Broadis**, 23, appointed player-manager of Carlisle, Aug 1946; **Chris Brass**, 27, appointed player-manager of York, Jun 2003; **Terry Neill**, 28, appointed player manager of Hull, Jun 1970; **Graham Taylor**, 28, appointed manager of Lincoln, Dec 1972.

## LONGEST-SERVING LEAGUE MANAGERS – ONE CLUB

**Fred Everiss**, secretary–manager of WBA for 46 years (1902–48); **George Ramsay**, secretary–manager of Aston Villa for 42 years (1884–1926); **John Addenbrooke**, Wolves, for 37 years (1885–1922). Since last war: **Sir Alex Ferguson** at Manchester Utd for 27 seasons (1986–2013); **Sir Matt Busby**, in charge of Manchester Utd for 25 seasons (1945–69, 1970–71; **Dario Gradi** at Crewe for 26 years (1983–2007, 2009–11); **Jimmy Seed** at Charlton for 23 years (1933–56); **Brian Clough** at Nottm Forest for 18 years (1975–93); **Arsene Wenger** at Arsenal for 22 years (1996-2018).

## LAST ENGLISH MANAGER TO WIN CHAMPIONSHIP

**Howard Wilkinson** (Leeds), season 1991–92.

## 1,000-TIME MANAGERS

Seven have managed in more than **1,000 English League games**: Alec Stock, Brian Clough, Jim Smith, Graham Taylor, Dario Gradi, Sir Alex Ferguson and Tony Pulis.

Sir Matt Busby, Dave Bassett, Lennie Lawrence, Alan Buckley, Denis Smith, Joe Royle, Ron Atkinson, Brian Horton, Neil Warnock, Harry Redknapp, Graham Turner, Steve Coppell, Roy Hodgson, Arsene Wenger, Len Ashurst, Lawrie McMenemy, Sir Bobby Robson, Danny Wilson and Tony Pulis have each managed more than **1,000 matches in all first class competitions**.

## SHORT-TERM MANAGERS

| Departed | | |
|---|---|---|
| 3 days | Bill Lambton (Scunthorpe) | Apr 1959 |
| 6 days | Tommy McLean (Raith Rov) | Sep 1996 |
| 7 days | Tim Ward (Exeter) | Mar 1953 |
| 7 days | Kevin Cullis (Swansea City) | Feb 1996 |
| 8 days | Billy McKinlay (Watford) | Oct 2014 |
| 10 days | Dave Cowling (Doncaster) | Oct 1997 |
| 10 days | Peter Cormack (Cowdenbeath) | Dec 2000 |
| 13 days | Johnny Cochrane (Reading) | Apr 1939 |
| 13 days | Micky Adams (Swansea City) | Oct 1997 |
| 16 days | Jimmy McIlroy (Bolton) | Nov 1970 |
| 19 days | Martin Allen (Barnet) | Apr 2011 |
| 20 days | Paul Went (Leyton Orient) | Oct 1981 |
| 27 days | Malcolm Crosby (Oxford Utd) | Jan 1998 |
| 27 days | Oscar Garcia (Watford) | Sep 2014 |
| 28 days | Tommy Docherty (QPR) | Dec 1968 |
| 28 days | Paul Hart (QPR) | Jan 2010 |
| 32 days | Steve Coppell (Manchester City) | Nov 1996 |

| | | |
|---|---|---|
| 32 days | Darko Milanic (Leeds) | Oct 2014 |
| 34 days | Niall Quinn (Sunderland) | Aug 2006 |
| 36 days | Steve Claridge (Millwall) | Jul 2005 |
| 39 days | Paul Gascoigne (Kettering) | Dec 2005 |
| 39 days | Kenny Jackett (Rotherham) | Nov 2016 |
| 40 days | Alex McLeish (Nottm Forest) | Feb 2013 |
| 41 days | Steve Wicks (Lincoln) | Oct 1995 |
| 41 days | Les Reed (Charlton) | Dec 2006 |
| 43 days | Mauro Milanese (Leyton Orient) | Dec 2014 |
| 44 days | Brian Clough (Leeds) | Sep 1974 |
| 44 days | Jock Stein (Leeds) | Oct 1978 |
| 45 days | Paul Murray (Hartlepool) | Dec 2014 |
| 48 days | John Toshack (Wales) | Mar 1994 |
| 48 days | David Platt (Sampdoria coach) | Feb 1999 |
| 49 days | Brian Little (Wolves) | Oct 1986 |
| 49 days | Terry Fenwick (Northampton) | Feb 2003 |
| 52 days | Alberto Cavasin (Leyton Orient) | Nov 2016 |
| 54 days | Craig Levein (Raith Rov) | Oct 1996 |
| 54 days | Chris Lucketti (Bury) | Jan 2018 |
| 56 days | Martin Ling (Swindon) | Dec 2015 |
| 57 days | Henning Berg (Blackburn) | Dec 2012 |
| 59 days | Kevin Nugent (Barnet) | Apr 2017 |
| 61 days | Bill McGarry (Wolves) | Nov 1985 |

- In May 1984, Crystal Palace named **Dave Bassett** as manager, but he changed his mind four days later, without signing the contract, and returned to Wimbledon.
- In May 2007, **Leroy Rosenior** was reportedly appointed manager of Torquay after relegation and sacked ten minutes later when the club came under new ownership.
- **Brian Laws** lost his job at Scunthorpe on Mar 25, 2004 and was reinstated three weeks later.
- In an angry outburst after a play-off defeat in May 1992, Barnet chairman Stan Flashman sacked manager **Barry Fry** and re-instated him a day later.

## EARLY-SEASON MANAGER SACKINGS

**2012:** Andy Thorn (Coventry) 8 days; John Sheridan (Chesterfield) 10 days; **2011:** Jim Jefferies (Hearts) 9 days; **2010** Kevin Blackwell (Sheffield Utd) 8 days; **2009** Bryan Gunn (Norwich) 6 days; **2007:** Neil McDonald (Carlisle) 2 days; Martin Allen (Leicester) 18 days; **2004:** Paul Sturrock (Southampton) 9 days; **2004:** Sir Bobby Robson (Newcastle) 16 days; **2003:** Glenn Roeder (West Ham) 15 days; **2000:** Alan Buckley (Grimsby) 10 days; **1997:** Kerry Dixon (Doncaster) 12 days; **1996:** Sammy Chung (Doncaster) on morning of season's opening League match; **1996:** Alan Ball (Manchester City) 12 days; **1994:** Kenny Hibbitt (Walsall) and Kenny Swain (Wigan) 20 days; **1993:** Peter Reid (Manchester City) 12 days; **1991:** Don Mackay (Blackburn) 14 days; **1989:** Mick Jones (Peterborough) 12 days; **1980:** Bill McGarry (Newcastle) 13 days; **1979:** Dennis Butler (Port Vale) 12 days; **1977:** George Petchey (Leyton O) 13 days; **1977:** Willie Bell (Birmingham) 16 days; **1971:** Len Richley (Darlington) 12 days.

## FOUR GAMES AND OUT

Frank de Boer was sacked as Crystal Palace manager after his first four Premier League matches at the start of the 2017–18 season – the competition's shortest reign in terms of games.

## BRUCE'S FOUR-TIMER

**Steve Bruce** is the only manager to win four promotions to the Premier League – with Birmingham in 2002 and 2007 and with Hull in 2013 and 2016.

## RECORD START FOR MANAGER

**Russ Wilcox**, appointed by Scunthorpe in Nov 2013, remained unbeaten in his first 28 league matches (14 won, 14 drawn) and took the club to promotion from League Two. It was the most successful start to a managerial career In English football, beating the record of 23 unbeaten games by Preston's William Sudell in 1889.

## RECORD TOP DIVISION START

Arsenal were unbeaten in 17 league matches from the start of season 1947-48 under new manager **Tom Whittaker**.

## SACKED, REINSTATED, FINISHED

**Brian McDermott** was sacked as Leeds manager on Jan 31, 2014. The following day, he was reinstated. At the end of the season, with the club under new ownership, he left by 'mutual consent.'

## CARETAKER SUPREME

As Chelsea's season collapsed, Andre Villas-Boas was sacked in March 2012 after eight months as manager, 2012. Roberto Di Matteo was appointed caretaker and by the season's end his team had won the FA Cup and the Champions League.

## MANAGER DOUBLES

Four managers have won the League Championship with different clubs: **Tom Watson**, secretary–manager with Sunderland (1892–93–95) and **Liverpool** (1901); **Herbert Chapman** with Huddersfield (1923–24, 1924–25) and Arsenal (1930–31, 1932–33); **Brian Clough** with Derby (1971–72) and Nottm Forest (1977–78); **Kenny Dalglish** with Liverpool (1985–86, 1987–88, 1989–90) and Blackburn (1994–95).

Managers to win the FA Cup with different clubs: **Billy Walker** (Sheffield Wed 1935, Nottm Forest 1959); **Herbert Chapman** (Huddersfield 1922, Arsenal 1930).

**Kenny Dalglish** (Liverpool) and **George Graham** (Arsenal) completed the Championship/FA Cup double as both player and manager with a single club. **Joe Mercer** won the title as a player with Everton, the title twice and FA Cup as a player with Arsenal and both competitions as manager of Manchester City.

## CHAIRMAN–MANAGER

On Dec 20, 1988, after two years on the board, Dundee Utd manager **Jim McLean** was elected chairman, too. McLean, Scotland's longest-serving manager (appointed on Nov 24, 1971), resigned at end of season 1992–93 (remained chairman).

**Ron Noades** was chairman-manager of Brentford from Jul 1998–Mar 2001. **John Reames** did both jobs at Lincoln from Nov 1998–Apr 2000)

**Niall Quinn** did both jobs for five weeks in 2006 before appointing Roy Keane as manager of Sunderland.

## TOP DIVISION PLAYER–MANAGERS

**Les Allen** (QPR 1968–69); **Johnny Giles** (WBA 1976–77); **Howard Kendall** (Everton 1981–82); **Kenny Dalglish** (Liverpool, 1985–90); **Trevor Francis** (QPR, 1988–89); **Terry Butcher** (Coventry, 1990–91), **Peter Reid** (Manchester City, 1990–93), **Trevor Francis** (Sheffield Wed, 1991–94), **Glenn Hoddle**, (Chelsea, 1993–95), **Bryan Robson** (Middlesbrough, 1994–97), **Ray Wilkins** (QPR, 1994–96), **Ruud Gullit** (Chelsea, 1996–98), **Gianluca Vialli** (Chelsea, 1998–2000).

## FIRST FOREIGN MANAGER IN ENGLISH LEAGUE

Uruguayan **Danny Bergara** (Rochdale 1988–89).

## COACHING KINGS OF EUROPE

Five coaches have won the European Cup/Champions League with two different clubs: **Ernst Happel** with Feyenoord (1970) and Hamburg (1983); **Ottmar Hitzfeld** with Borussia Dortmund (1997) and Bayern Munich (2001); **Jose Mourinho** with Porto (2004) and Inter Milan (2010); **Jupp Heynckes** with Real Madrid (1998) and Bayern Munich (2013); **Carlo Ancelotti** with AC Milan (2003, 2007) and Real Madrid (2014).

## FOREIGN TRIUMPH

Former Dutch star **Ruud Gullit** became the first foreign manager to win a major English competition when Chelsea took the FA Cup in 1997.

**Arsene Wenger** and **Gerard Houllier** became the first foreign managers to receive recognition when they were awarded honorary OBEs in the Queen's Birthday Honours in Jun 2003 'for their contribution to English football and Franco–British relations'.

## MANAGERS OF POST-WAR CHAMPIONS (*Double winners)

**1947** George Kay (Liverpool); **1948** Tom Whittaker (Arsenal); **1949** Bob Jackson (Portsmouth).

**1950** Bob Jackson (Portsmouth); **1951** Arthur Rowe (Tottenham); **1952** Matt Busby (Manchester Utd); **1953** Tom Whittaker (Arsenal); **1954** Stan Cullis (Wolves); **1955** Ted Drake (Chelsea); **1956** Matt Busby (Manchester Utd); **1957** Matt Busby (Manchester Utd); **1958** Stan Cullis (Wolves); **1959** Stan Cullis (Wolves).

**1960** Harry Potts (Burnley); **1961** *Bill Nicholson (Tottenham); **1962** Alf Ramsey (Ipswich); **1963** Harry Catterick (Everton); **1964** Bill Shankly (Liverpool); **1965** Matt Busby (Manchester Utd); **1966** Bill Shankly (Liverpool); **1967** Matt Busby (Manchester Utd); **1968** Joe Mercer (Manchester City); **1969** Don Revie (Leeds).

**1970** Harry Catterick (Everton); **1971** *Bertie Mee (Arsenal); **1972** Brian Clough (Derby); **1973** Bill Shankly (Liverpool); **1974** Don Revie (Leeds); **1975** Dave Mackay (Derby); **1976** Bob Paisley (Liverpool); **1977** Bob Paisley (Liverpool); **1978** Brian Clough (Nottm Forest); **1979** Bob Paisley (Liverpool).

**1980** Bob Paisley (Liverpool); **1981** Ron Saunders (Aston Villa); **1982** Bob Paisley (Liverpool); **1983** Bob Paisley (Liverpool); **1984** Joe Fagan (Liverpool); **1985** Howard Kendall (Everton); **1986** *Kenny Dalglish (Liverpool – player/manager); **1987** Howard Kendall (Everton); **1988** Kenny Dalglish (Liverpool – player/manager); **1989** George Graham (Arsenal).

**1990** Kenny Dalglish (Liverpool); **1991** George Graham (Arsenal); **1992** Howard Wilkinson (Leeds); **1993** Alex Ferguson (Manchester Utd); **1994** *Alex Ferguson (Manchester Utd); **1995** Kenny Dalglish (Blackburn); **1996** *Alex Ferguson (Manchester Utd); **1997** Alex Ferguson (Manchester Utd); **1998** *Arsene Wenger (Arsenal); **1999** *Alex Ferguson (Manchester Utd).

**2000** Sir Alex Ferguson (Manchester Utd); **2001** Sir Alex Ferguson (Manchester Utd); **2002** *Arsene Wenger (Arsenal); **2003** Sir Alex Ferguson (Manchester Utd); **2004** Arsene Wenger (Arsenal); **2005** Jose Mourinho (Chelsea); **2006** Jose Mourinho (Chelsea); **2007** Sir Alex Ferguson (Manchester Utd); **2008** Sir Alex Ferguson (Manchester Utd); **2009** Sir Alex Ferguson (Manchester Utd); **2010** *Carlo Ancelotti (Chelsea); **2011** Sir Alex Ferguson (Manchester Utd); **2012** Roberto Mancini (Manchester City); **2013** Sir Alex Ferguson (Manchester Utd); **2014** Manuel Pellegrini (Manchester City); **2015** Jose Mourinho (Chelsea) **2016** Claudio Ranieri (Leicester); **2017** Antonio Conte (Chelsea); **2018** Pep Guardiola (Manchester City).

## WORLD NO 1 MANAGER

When **Sir Alex Ferguson**, 71, retired in May 2013, he ended the most successful managerial career in the game's history. He took Manchester United to a total of 38 prizes – 13 Premier League titles, 5 FA Cup triumphs, 4 League Cups, 10 Charity/Community Shields (1 shared), 2 Champions League wins, 1 Cup-Winners' Cup, 1 FIFA Club World Cup, 1 Inter-Continental Cup and 1 UEFA Super Cup. Having played centre-forward for Rangers, the Glaswegian managed 3 Scottish clubs, East Stirling, St Mirren and then Aberdeen, where he broke the Celtic/Rangers duopoly with 9 successes: 3 League Championships, 4 Scottish Cups, 1 League Cup and 1 UEFA Cup. Appointed at Old Trafford in November 1986, when replacing Ron Atkinson, he did not win a prize there until his fourth season (FA Cup 1990), but thereafter the club's trophy cabinet glittered with silverware. His total of 1,500 matches in charge ended with a 5-5 draw away to West Bromwich Albion. The longest-serving manager in the club's history, he constructed 4 triumphant teams. Sir Alex was knighted in 1999 and in 2012 he received the FIFA award for services to football. On retirement from management, he became a director and club ambassador. United maintained the dynasty of long-serving Scottish managers (Sir Matt Busby for 24 seasons) by appointing David Moyes, who had been in charge at Everton for 11 years.

## WENGER'S LEGACY

**Arsene Wenger** was a virtually unknown French manager when taking over Arsenal in 1996. He left 22 years later as the most successful in the club's history. Wenger led them to three Premier League titles, including the unbeaten season in 2003-04 achieved by the team known as the 'Invincibles.' There were seven FA Cup successes, one in 2002 when Arsenal completed the Double. He was also closely involved in planning the move from Highbury to the Emirates Stadium in 2006.

## THE PROMOTION MAN

**Neil Warnock** set a record of eight promotions when he took Cardiff back to the Premier League in 2018. In 38 years as a manager, he was also successful with Scarborough, Notts County twice, Plymouth, Huddersfield, Sheffield United and Queens Park Rangers. Warnock's achievements were marked by a special award from the League Managers' Association.

## MANAGERS' EURO TREBLES

Two managers have won the European Cup/Champions League three times. **Bob Paisley** did it with Liverpool (1977,78, 81).

**Carlo Ancelotti's** successes were with AC Milan in 2003 and 2007 and with Real Madrid in 2014.

## WINNER MOURINHO

In winning the Premier League and League Cup in 2015, Jose Mourinho embellished his reputation as Chelsea's most successful manager. Those achievements took his total of honours in two spells at the club to 8: 3 Premier League, 3 League Cup, 1 FA Cup, 1 Community Shield. Joining from Portuguese champions Porto, Mourinho was initially with Chelsea from June 2004 to September 2007. He then successfulty coached Inter Milan and Real Madrid before returning to Stamford Bridge in June 2013. His Premier League triumph in 2015 was his eighth title In 11 years in four countries (England 3, Portugal 2, Italy 2, Spain 1). In his first season with Manchester Utd (2016–17), he won three trophies – League Cup, Europa League and Community Shield.

## WENGER'S CUP AGAIN

Arsenal's win against Aston Villa in the 2015 Final was a record 12th success for them in the FA Cup and a sixth triumph in the competition for manager Arsene Wenger, equalling the record of George Ramsay for Villa (1887-1920). With his sixth victory in seven Finals, Wenger made history as the first manager to win the Cup in successive seasons twice (previously in 2002 and 2003). He won it for a record seventh time – in eight finals – in 2017.

## RECORD MANAGER FEE

Chelsea paid Porto a record £13.25m compensation when they appointed **Andre Villas-Boas** as manager in June 2011. He lasted less than nine months at Stamford Bridge.

## FATHER AND SON MANAGERS WITH SAME CLUB

**Fulham:** Bill Dodgin Snr 1949–53; Bill Dodgin Jnr 1968–72. **Brentford:** Bill Dodgin Snr 1953–57; Bill Dodgin Jnr 1976–80. **Bournemouth:** John Bond 1970–73; Kevin Bond 2006–08. **Derby:** Brian Clough 1967–73; Nigel Clough 2009–2013. **Bristol City:** Gary Johnson 2005–10; Lee Johnson 2016-present.

## SIR BOBBY'S HAT-TRICK

**Sir Bobby Robson**, born and brought up in County Durham, achieved a unique hat-trick when he received the Freedom of Durham in Dec 2008. He had already been awarded the Freedom of Ipswich and Newcastle. He died in July 2009 and had an express loco named after him on the East Coast to London line.

## MANAGERS WITH MOST FA CUP SUCCESSES

**7 Arsene Wenger** (Arsenal); **6 George Ramsay** (Aston Villa); **5 Sir Alex Ferguson** (Manchester Utd); **3 Charles Foweraker** (Bolton), **John Nicholson** (Sheffield Utd), **Bill Nicholson** (Tottenham).

## RELEGATION 'DOUBLES'

Managers associated with two clubs relegated in same season: **John Bond** in 1985–86 (Swansea City and Birmingham); **Ron Saunders** in 1985–86 (WBA – and their reserve team – and Birmingham); **Bob Stokoe** in 1986–87 (Carlisle and Sunderland); **Billy McNeill** in 1986–87 (Manchester City and Aston Villa); **Dave Bassett** in 1987–88 (Watford and Sheffield Utd); **Mick Mills** in 1989–90 (Stoke and Colchester); **Gary Johnson** in 2014-15 (Yeovil and Cheltenham)

## THREE FA CUP DEFEATS IN ONE SEASON

Manager **Michael Appleton** suffered three FA Cup defeats in season 2012-13, with Portsmouth (v Notts Co, 1st rd); Blackpool (v Fulham, 3rd rd); Blackburn (v Millwall, 6th rd).

# WEMBLEY STADIUM

## NEW WEMBLEY

A new era for English football began in March 2007 with the completion of the new national stadium. The 90,000-seater arena was hailed as one of the world's finest – but came at a price. Costs soared, the project fell well behind schedule and disputes involving the FA, builders Multiplex and the Government were rife. The old stadium, opened in 1923, cost £750,000. The new one, originally priced at £326m in 2000, ended up at around £800m. The first international after completion was an Under-21 match between England and Italy. The FA Cup Final returned to its spiritual home after being staged at the Millennium Stadium in Cardiff for six seasons. Then, England's senior team were back for a friendly against Brazil.

## DROGBA'S WEMBLEY RECORD

**Didier Drogba**'s FA Cup goal for Chelsea against Liverpool in May 2012 meant that he had scored in all his 8 competitive appearances for the club at Wembley. (7 wins, 1 defeat). They came in: 2007 FA Cup Final (1-0 v Manchester Utd); 2008 League Cup Final (1-2 v Tottenham); 2009 FA Cup semi-final (2-1 v Arsenal); 2009 FA Cup Final (2-1 v Everton); 2010 FA Cup semi-final (3-0 v Aston Villa); 2010 FA Cup Final (1-0 v Portsmouth); 2012 FA Cup semi-final (5-1 v Tottenham); 2012 FA Cup Final (2-1 v Liverpool).

## INVASION DAY

Memorable scenes were witnessed at the first **FA Cup Final at Wembley**, Apr 28, 1923, between **Bolton** and **West Ham**. An accurate return of the attendance could not be made owing to thousands breaking in, but there were probably more than 200,000 spectators present. The match was delayed for 40 minutes by the crowd invading the pitch. Official attendance was 126,047. Gate receipts totalled £27,776. The two clubs and the FA each received £6,365 and the FA refunded £2,797 to ticket-holders who were unable to get to their seats. Cup Final admission has since been by ticket only.

## REDUCED CAPACITY

Capacity of the all-seated Wembley Stadium was 78,000. The last 100,000 attendance was for the 1985 FA Cup Final between Manchester Utd and Everton. Crowd record for New Wembley: 89,874 for 2008 FA Cup Final (Portsmouth v Cardiff).

## WEMBLEY'S FIRST UNDER LIGHTS

**Nov 30, 1955** (England 4, Spain 1), when the floodlights were switched on after 73 minutes (afternoon match played in damp, foggy conditions).

**First Wembley international played throughout under lights:** England 8, N Ireland 3 on evening of Nov 20, 1963 (att: 55,000).

## MOST WEMBLEY APPEARANCES

**59** by **Tony Adams** (35 England, 24 Arsenal); 57 by **Peter Shilton** (52 England, 3 Nottm Forest, 1 Leicester, 1 Football League X1).

## WEMBLEY HAT-TRICKS

Three players have scored hat-tricks in major finals at Wembley: **Stan Mortensen** for Blackpool v Bolton (FA Cup Final, 1953), **Geoff Hurst** for England v West Germany (World Cup Final, 1966) and **David Speedie** for Chelsea v Manchester City (Full Members Cup, 1985).

## ENGLAND'S WEMBLEY DEFEATS

England have lost 25 matches to foreign opponents at Wembley:

| | | | |
|---|---|---|---|
| **Nov 1953** | 3-6 v Hungary | **Jun 1995** | 1-3 v Brazil |
| **Oct 1959** | 2-3 v Sweden | **Feb 1997** | 0-1 v Italy |
| **Oct 1965** | 2-3 v Austria | **Feb 1998** | 0-2 v Chile |
| **Apr 1972** | 1-3 v W Germany | **Feb 1999** | 0-2 v France |
| **Nov 1973** | 0-1 v Italy | **Oct 2000** | 0-1 v Germany |
| **Feb 1977** | 0-2 v Holland | **Aug 2007** | 1-2 v Germany |
| **Mar 1981** | 1-2 v Spain | **Nov 2007** | 2-3 v Croatia |
| **May 1981** | 0-1 v Brazil | **Nov 2010** | 1-2 v France |
| **Oct 1982** | 1-2 v W Germany | **Feb 2012** | 2-3 v Holland |
| **Sep 1983** | 0-1 v Denmark | **Nov 2013** | 0-2 v Chile |
| **Jun 1984** | 0-2 v Russia | **Nov 2013** | 0-1 v Germany |
| **May 1990** | 1-2 v Uruguay | **Mar 2016** | 1-2 v Holland |
| **Sep 1991** | 0-1 v Germany | | |

A further defeat came in **Euro 96**. After drawing the semi-final with Germany 1-1, England went out 6-5 on penalties.

## FASTEST GOALS AT WEMBLEY

In first-class matches: **25 sec** by **Louis Saha** for Everton in 2009 FA Cup Final against Chelsea; **38 sec** by **Bryan Robson** for England's against Yugoslavia in 1989; **42 sec** by **Roberto Di Matteo** for Chelsea in 1997 FA Cup Final v Middlesbrough; **44 sec** by **Bryan Robson** for England v Northern Ireland in 1982.

Fastest goal in **any** match at Wembley: **20 sec** by **Maurice Cox** for Cambridge University against Oxford in 1979.

## FOUR WEMBLEY HEADERS

When **Wimbledon** beat Sutton 4-2 in the FA Amateur Cup Final at Wembley on May 4, 1963, Irish centre-forward **Eddie Reynolds** headed all four goals.

## WEMBLEY ONE-SEASON DOUBLES

In 1989, **Nottm Forest** became the first club to win two Wembley Finals in the same season (Littlewoods Cup and Simod Cup).

In 1993, **Arsenal** made history there as the first club to win the League (Coca-Cola) Cup and the FA Cup in the same season. They beat Sheffield Wed 2-1 in both finals.

In 2012, **York** won twice at Wembley in nine days at the end of the season, beating Newport 2-0 in the FA Trophy Final and Luton 2-1 in the Conference Play-off Final to return to the Football League.

## SUDDEN-DEATH DECIDERS

First Wembley Final decided on sudden death (first goal scored in overtime): Apr 23, 1995 – **Birmingham** beat Carlisle (1-0, Paul Tait 103 mins) to win Auto Windscreens Shield.

First instance of a golden goal deciding a major international tournament was at Wembley on Jun 30, 1996, when **Germany** beat the Czech Republic 2-1 in the European Championship Final with Oliver Bierhoff's goal in the 95th minute.

**WEMBLEY'S MOST ONE-SIDED FINAL** (in major domestic cups)

**Swansea** 5 **Bradford City** 0 (League Cup, Feb 24, 2013).

# FOOTBALL TRAGEDIES

## DAYS OF TRAGEDY – CLUBS

Season 1988–89 brought the worst disaster in the history of British sport, with the death of 96 Liverpool supporters (200 injured) at the **FA Cup semi-final** against Nottm Forest at **Hillsborough, Sheffield**, on Saturday, Apr 15. The tragedy built up in the minutes preceding kick-off, when thousands surged into the ground at the Leppings Lane end. Many were crushed in the tunnel between entrance and terracing, but most of the victims were trapped inside the perimeter fencing behind the goal. The match was abandoned without score after six minutes' play. The dead included seven women and girls, two teenage sisters and two teenage brothers. The youngest victim was a boy of ten, the oldest 67-year-old Gerard Baron, whose brother Kevin played for Liverpool in the 1950 Cup Final. (*Total became 96 in Mar 1993, when Tony Bland died after being in a coma for nearly four years). A two-year inquest at Warrington ended on April 26, 2016 with the verdict that the 96 were 'unlawfully killed.' It cleared Liverpool fans of any blame and ruled that South Yorkshire Police and South Yorkshire Ambulance Service 'caused or contributed' to the loss of life.

The two worst disasters in one season in British soccer history occurred at the end of 1984–85. On May 11, the last Saturday of the League season, 56 people (two of them visiting supporters) were burned to death – and more than 200 taken to hospital – when fire destroyed the main stand at the **Bradford City–Lincoln** match at Valley Parade.

The wooden, 77-year-old stand was full for City's last fixture before which, amid scenes of celebration, the club had been presented with the Third Division Championship trophy. The fire broke out just before half-time and, within five minutes, the entire stand was engulfed.

### Heysel Tragedy

Eighteen days later, on May 29, at the European Cup Final between **Liverpool** and **Juventus** at the Heysel Stadium, Brussels, 39 spectators (31 of them Italian) were crushed or trampled to death and 437 injured. The disaster occurred an hour before the scheduled kick-off when Liverpool supporters charged a Juventus section of the crowd at one end of the stadium, and a retaining wall collapsed. The sequel was a 5-year ban by UEFA on English clubs generally in European competition, with a 6-year ban on Liverpool.

On May 26 1985 ten people were trampled to death and 29 seriously injured in a crowd panic on the way into the **Olympic Stadium, Mexico City** for the Mexican Cup Final between local clubs National University and America.

More than 100 people died and 300 were injured in a football disaster at **Nepal's national stadium** in Katmandu in Mar 1988. There was a stampede when a violent hailstorm broke over the capital. Spectators rushed for cover, but the stadium exits were locked, and hundreds were trampled in the crush.

In South Africa, on Jan 13 1991 40 black fans were trampled to death (50 injured) as they tried to escape from fighting that broke out at a match in the gold-mining town of Orkney, 80 miles from Johannesburg. The friendly, between top teams **Kaiser Chiefs** and **Orlando Pirates**, attracted a packed crowd of 20,000. Violence erupted after the referee allowed Kaiser Chiefs a disputed second-half goal to lead 1-0.

Disaster struck at the French Cup semi-final (May 5, 1992), with the death of 15 spectators and 1,300 injured when a temporary metal stand collapsed in the Corsican town of Bastia. The tie between Second Division **Bastia** and French Champions **Marseille** was cancelled. Monaco, who won the other semi-final, were allowed to compete in the next season's Cup-Winners' Cup.

A total of 318 died and 500 were seriously injured when the crowd rioted over a disallowed goal at the National Stadium in Lima, Peru, on May 24, 1964. **Peru** and **Argentina** were competing to play in the Olympic Games in Tokyo.

That remained **sport's heaviest death** toll until Oct 20, 1982, when (it was revealed only in Jul 1989) 340 Soviet fans were killed in Moscow's Lenin Stadium at the UEFA Cup second round first leg match between **Moscow Spartak** and **Haarlem** (Holland). They were crushed on an open stairway when a last-minute Spartak goal sent departing spectators surging back into the ground.

Among other crowd disasters abroad: Jun, 1968 – 74 died in Argentina. Panic broke out at the end of a goalless match between River Plate and Boca Juniors at Nunez, Buenos Aires, when Boca supporters threw lighted newspaper torches on to fans in the tiers below.

Feb 1974 – 49 killed in **Egypt** in crush of fans clamouring to see Zamalek play Dukla Prague.

Sep 1971 – 44 died in **Turkey**, when fighting among spectators over a disallowed goal (Kayseri v Siwas) led to a platform collapsing.

The then worst disaster in the history of British football, in terms of loss of life, occurred at Glasgow Rangers' ground at **Ibrox Park**, Jan 2 1971. Sixty-six people were trampled to death (100 injured) as they tumbled down Stairway 13 just before the end of the **Rangers v Celtic** New Year's match. That disaster led to the 1975 Safety of Sports Grounds legislation.

The Ibrox tragedy eclipsed even the Bolton disaster in which 33 were killed and about 500 injured when a wall and crowd barriers collapsed near a corner-flag at the **Bolton v Stoke** FA Cup sixth round tie on Mar 9 1946. The match was completed after half an hour's stoppage.

In a previous crowd disaster at **Ibrox** on Apr 5, 1902, part of the terracing collapsed during the Scotland v England international and 25 people were killed. The match, held up for 20 minutes, ended 1-1, but was never counted as an official international.

Eight leading players and three officials of **Manchester Utd** and eight newspaper representatives were among the 23 who perished in the air crash at **Munich** on Feb 6, 1958, during take-off following a European Cup-tie in Belgrade. The players were Roger Byrne, Geoffrey Bent, Eddie Colman, Duncan Edwards, Mark Jones, David Pegg, Tommy Taylor and Liam Whelan, and the officials were Walter Crickmer (secretary), Tom Curry (trainer) and Herbert Whalley (coach). The newspaper representatives were Alf Clarke, Don Davies, George Follows, Tom Jackson, Archie Ledbrooke, Henry Rose, Eric Thompson and Frank Swift (former England goalkeeper of Manchester City).

On May 14, 1949, the entire team of Italian Champions **Torino**, 8 of them Internationals, were killed when the aircraft taking them home from a match against Benfica in Lisbon crashed at Superga, near Turin. The total death toll of 28 included all the club's reserve players, the manager, trainer and coach.

On Feb 8, 1981, 24 spectators died and more than 100 were injured at a match in **Greece**. They were trampled as thousands of the 40,000 crowd tried to rush out of the stadium at Piraeus after Olympiacos beat AEK Athens 6-0.

On Nov 17, 1982, 24 people (12 of them children) were killed and 250 injured when fans stampeded at the end of a match at the Pascual Guerrero stadium in **Cali, Colombia**. Drunken spectators hurled fire crackers and broken bottles from the higher stands on to people below and started a rush to the exits.

On Dec 9, 1987, the 18-strong team squad of **Alianza Lima**, one of Peru's top clubs, were wiped out, together with 8 officials and several youth players, when a military aircraft taking them home from Puccalpa crashed into the sea off Ventillana, ten miles from Lima. The only survivor among 43 on board was a member of the crew.

On Apr 28, 1993, 18 members of **Zambia's international squad** and 5 ZFA officials died when the aircraft carrying them to a World Cup qualifying tie against Senegal crashed into the Atlantic soon after take-off from Libreville, Gabon.

On Oct 16 1996, 81 fans were crushed to death and 147 seriously injured in the '**Guatemala Disaster**' at the World Cup qualifier against Costa Rica in Mateo Flores stadium. The tragedy happened an hour before kick-off, allegedly caused by ticket forgery and overcrowding – 60,000 were reported in the 45,000-capacity ground – and safety problems related to perimeter fencing.

On Jul 9, 1996, 8 people died, 39 injured in riot after derby match between **Libya's two top clubs** in Tripoli. Al-Ahli had beaten Al-Ittihad 1-0 by a controversial goal.

On Apr 6, 1997, 5 spectators were crushed to death at **Nigeria's national stadium** in Lagos after the 2-1 World Cup qualifying victory over Guinea. Only two of five gates were reported open as the 40,000 crowd tried to leave the ground.

It was reported from the **Congo** (Oct 29, 1998) that a bolt of lightning struck a village match, killing all 11 members of the home team Benatshadi, but leaving the opposing players from Basangana unscathed. It was believed the surviving team wore better-insulated boots.

On Jan 10, 1999, eight fans died and 13 were injured in a stampede at **Egypt's Alexandria Stadium**. Some 25,000 spectators had pushed into the ground. Despite the tragedy, the cup-tie between Al-Ittihad and Al-Koroum was completed.

Three people suffocated and several were seriously injured when thousands of fans forced their way into **Liberia's national stadium** in Monrovia at a goalless World Cup qualifying match against Chad on Apr 23, 2000. The stadium (capacity 33,000) was reported 'heavily overcrowded'.

On Jul 9, 2000, 12 spectators died from crush injuries when police fired tear gas into the 50,000 crowd after South Africa scored their second goal in a World Cup group qualifier against Zimbabwe in **Harare**. A stampede broke out as fans scrambled to leave the national stadium. Players of both teams lay face down on the pitch as fumes swept over them. FIFA launched an investigation and decided that the result would stand, with South Africa leading 2-0 at the time of the 84th-minute abandonment.

On Apr 11, 2001, at one of the biggest matches of the South African season, 43 died and 155 were injured in a crush at **Ellis Park, Johannesburg**. After tearing down a fence, thousands of fans surged into a stadium already packed to its 60,000 capacity for the Premiership derby between top Soweto teams Kaizer Chiefs and Orlando Pirates. The match was abandoned at 1-1 after 33 minutes. In Jan 1991, 40 died in a crowd crush at a friendly between the same clubs at Orkney, 80 miles from Johannesburg.

On Apr 29, 2001, seven people were trampled to death and 51 injured when a riot broke out at a match between two of Congo's biggest clubs, Lupopo and Mazembe at **Lubumbashi**, southern Congo.

On May 6, 2001, two spectators were killed in Iran and hundreds were injured when a glass fibre roof collapsed at the over-crowded Mottaqi Stadium at Sari for the match between Pirouzi and Shemshak Noshahr.

On May 9, 2001, in Africa's worst football disaster, 123 died and 93 were injured in a stampede at the national stadium in **Accra, Ghana**. Home team Hearts of Oak were leading 2-1 against Asante Kotoko five minutes from time, when Asanti fans started hurling bottles on to the pitch. Police fired tear gas into the stands, and the crowd panicked in a rush for the exits, which were locked. It took the death toll at three big matches in Africa in Apr/May to 173.

On Aug 12, 2001, two players were killed by lightning and ten severely burned at a **Guatemala** Third Division match between Deportivo Culquimulilla and Pueblo Nuevo Vinas.

On Nov 1, 2002, two players died from injuries after lightning struck Deportivo Cali's training ground in **Colombia**.

On Mar 12 2004, five people were killed and more than 100 injured when spectators stampeded shortly before the Syrian Championship fixture between Al-Jihad and Al-Fatwa in **Qameshli**, Northern Syria. The match was cancelled.

On Oct 10, 2004, three spectators died in a crush at the African Zone World Cup qualifier between **Guinea** and **Morocco** (1-1) at Conakry, Guinea.

On Mar 25, 2005, five were killed as 100,000 left the Azadi Stadium, **Tehran**, after Iran's World Cup qualifying win (2-1) against Japan.

On Jun 2, 2007, 12 spectators were killed and 46 injured in a crush at the Chillabombwe Stadium, **Zambia**, after an African Nations Cup qualifier against Congo.

On Mar 29, 2009, 19 people died and 139 were injured after a wall collapsed at the Ivory Coast stadium in **Abidjan** before a World Cup qualifier against Malawi. The match went ahead, Ivory Coast winning 5-0 with two goals from Chelsea's Didier Drogba. The tragedy meant that, in 13 years, crowd disasters at club and internationals at ten different grounds across Africa had claimed the lives of 283 people.

On Jan 8, 2010, terrorists at **Cabinda**, Angola machine-gunned the Togo team buses travelling to the Africa Cup of Nations. They killed a driver, an assistant coach and a media officer and injured several players. The team were ordered by their Government to withdraw from the tournament.

On Oct 23, 2010, seven fans were trampled to death when thousands tried to force their way into the Nyayo National Stadium in **Nairobi** at a Kenya Premier League match between the Gor Mahia and AFC Leopards clubs.

On Feb 1, 2012, 74 died and nearly 250 were injured in a crowd riot at the end of the Al-Masry v Al-Ahly match in **Port Said** – the worst disaster in Egyptian sport.

On Nov 28, 2016, 71 died in the worst air crash in world football history when a charter flight carrying players, officials and staff of leading Brazilian club Chapecoense from **Bolivia** to **Colombia** hit a mountain ridge at 8,500 feet. The victims included 65 people from the club.

## DAYS OF TRAGEDY – PERSONAL

**Sam Wynne**, Bury right-back, collapsed five minutes before half-time in the First Division match away to Sheffield Utd on Apr 30, 1927, and died in the dressing-room.

**John Thomson**, Celtic and Scotland goalkeeper, sustained a fractured skull when diving at an opponent's feet in the Rangers v Celtic League match on Sep 5, 1931, and died the same evening.

**Sim Raleigh** (Gillingham), injured in a clash of heads at home to Brighton (Div 3 South) on Dec 1, 1934, continued to play but collapsed in second half and died in hospital the same night.

**James Thorpe**, Sunderland goalkeeper, was injured during the First Division match at home to Chelsea on Feb 1, 1936 and died in a diabetic coma three days later.

**Derek Dooley**, Sheffield Wed centre-forward and top scorer in 1951–52 in the Football League with 46 goals in 30 matches, broke a leg in the League match at Preston on Feb 14, 1953, and, after complications set in, had to lose the limb by amputation.

**John White**, Tottenham's Scottish international forward, was killed by lightning on a golf course at Enfield, North London in Jul, 1964.

**Tony Allden**, Highgate centre-half, was struck by lightning during an Amateur Cup quarter-final with Enfield on Feb 25, 1967. He died the following day. Four other players were also struck but recovered.

**Roy Harper** died while refereeing the York v Halifax (Div 4) match on May 5, 1969.

**Jim Finn** collapsed and died from a heart attack while refereeing Exeter v Stockport (Div 4) on Sep 16, 1972.

Scotland manager **Jock Stein**, 62, collapsed and died at the end of the Wales-Scotland World Cup qualifying match (1-1) at Ninian Park, Cardiff on Sep 10, 1985.

**David Longhurst**, York forward, died after being carried off two minutes before half-time in the Fourth Division fixture at home to Lincoln on Sep 8, 1990. The match was abandoned (0-0). The inquest revealed that Longhurst suffered from a rare heart condition.

**Mike North** collapsed while refereeing Southend v Mansfield (Div 3) on Apr 16, 2001 and died shortly afterwards. The match was abandoned and re-staged on May 8, with the receipts donated to his family.

**Marc-Vivien Foe**, on his 63rd appearance in Cameroon's midfield, collapsed unchallenged in the centre circle after 72 minutes of the FIFA Confederations Cup semi-final against Colombia in Lyon, France, on Jun 26, 2003, and despite the efforts of the stadium medical staff he could not be revived. He had been on loan to Manchester City from Olympique Lyonnais in season 2002–03, and poignantly scored the club's last goal at Maine Road.

**Paul Sykes**, Folkestone Invicta (Ryman League) striker, died on the pitch during the Kent Senior Cup semi-final against Margate on Apr 12, 2005. He collapsed after an innocuous off-the-ball incident.

**Craig Gowans**, Falkirk apprentice, was killed at the club's training ground on Jul 8, 2005 when he came into contact with power lines.

**Peter Wilson**, Mansfield goalkeeping coach, died of a heart attack after collapsing during the warm-up of the League Two game away to Shrewsbury on Nov 19, 2005.

**Matt Gadsby**, Hinckley defender, collapsed and died while playing in a Conference North match at Harrogate on Sep 9, 2006.

**Phil O'Donnell**, 35-year-old Motherwell captain and Scotland midfield player, collapsed when about to be substituted near the end of the SPL home game against Dundee Utd on Dec 29, 2007 and died shortly afterwards in hospital.

# GREAT SERVICE

'For services to Association Football', **Stanley Matthews** (Stoke, Blackpool and England), already a CBE, became the first professional footballer to receive a knighthood. This was bestowed in 1965, his last season. Before he retired and five days after his 50th birthday, he played for Stoke to set a record as the oldest First Division footballer (v Fulham, Feb 6, 1965).

Over a brilliant span of 33 years, he played in 886 first-class matches, including 54 full Internationals (plus 31 in war time), 701 League games (including 3 at start of season 1939–40, which was abandoned on the outbreak of war) and 86 FA Cup-ties, and scored 95 goals. He was never booked in his career.

Sir Stanley died on Feb 23, 2000, three weeks after his 85th birthday. His ashes were buried under the centre circle of Stoke's Britannia Stadium. After spending a number of years in Toronto, he made his home back in the Potteries in 1989, having previously returned to his home town, Hanley in Oct, 1987 to unveil a life-size bronze statue of himself. The inscription reads: 'Sir Stanley Matthews, CBE. Born Hanley, 1 Feb 1915.

His name is symbolic of the beauty of the game, his fame timeless and international, his sportsmanship and modesty universally acclaimed. A magical player, of the people, for the people.' On his home-coming in 1989, Sir Stanley was made President of Stoke, the club he joined as a boy of 15 and served as a player for 20 years between 1931 and 1965, on either side of his spell with Blackpool.

In Jul 1992 FIFA honoured him with their 'Gold merit award' for outstanding services to the game.

Former England goalkeeper **Peter Shilton** has made more first-class appearances (1,387) than any other footballer in British history. He played his 1,000th. League game in Leyton Orient's 2-0 home win against Brighton on Dec 22, 1996 and made 9 appearances for Orient in his final season. He retired from international football after the 1990 World Cup in Italy with 125 caps, then a world record. Shilton kept a record 60 clean sheets for England.

Shilton's career spanned 32 seasons, 20 of them on the international stage. He made his League debut for Leicester in May 1966, two months before England won the World Cup.

His 1,387 first-class appearances comprise a record 1,005 in the Football League, 125 Internationals, 102 League Cup, 86 FA Cup, 13 for England U-23s, 4 for the Football League and 52 other matches (European Cup, UEFA Cup, World Club Championship, Charity Shield, European Super Cup, Full Members' Cup, Play-offs, Screen Sports Super Cup, Anglo-Italian Cup, Texaco Cup, Simod Cup, Zenith Data Systems Cup and Autoglass Trophy).

Shilton appeared 57 times at Wembley, 52 for England, 2 League Cup Finals, 1 FA Cup Final, 1 Charity Shield match, and 1 for the Football League. He passed a century of League appearances with each of his first five clubs: Leicester (286), Stoke (110), Nottm Forest (202), Southampton (188) and Derby (175) and subsequently played for Plymouth, Bolton and Leyton Orient.

He was awarded the MBE and OBE for services to football. At the Football League Awards ceremony in March 2013, he received the League's Contribution award.

Six other British footballers have made more than 1,000 first-class appearances:

**Ray Clemence**, formerly with Tottenham, Liverpool and England, retired through injury in season 1987–88 after a goalkeeping career of 1,119 matches starting in 1965–66.

Clemence played 50 times for his first club, Scunthorpe; 665 for Liverpool; 337 for Tottenham; his 67 representative games included 61 England caps.

A third great British goalkeeper, **Pat Jennings**, ended his career (1963–86) with a total of 1,098 first-class matches for Watford, Tottenham, Arsenal and N Ireland. They were made up of 757 in the Football League, 119 full Internationals, 84 FA Cup appearances, 72 League/ Milk Cup, 55 European club matches, 2 Charity Shield, 3 Other Internationals, 1 Under-23 cap, 2 Texaco Cup, 2 Anglo-Italian Cup and 1 Super Cup. Jennings played his 119th and final international on his 41st birthday, Jun 12, 1986, against Brazil in Guadalajara in the Mexico World Cup.

Yet another outstanding 'keeper, **David Seaman**, passed the 1,000 appearances milestone for clubs and country in season 2002–03, reaching 1,004 when aged 39, he captained Arsenal to FA Cup triumph against Southampton.

With Arsenal, Seaman won 3 Championship medals, the FA Cup 4 times, the Double twice, the League Cup and Cup-Winners' Cup once each. After 13 seasons at Highbury, he joined Manchester City (Jun 2003) on a free transfer. He played 26 matches for City before a shoulder injury forced his retirement in Jan 2004, aged 40.

Seaman's 22-season career composed 1,046 first-class matches: 955 club apps (Peterborough 106, Birmingham 84, QPR 175, Arsenal 564, Manchester City 26); 75 senior caps for England, 6 'B' caps and 10 at U-21 level.

Defender **Graeme Armstrong**, 42-year-old commercial manager for an Edinburgh whisky company and part-time assistant-manager and captain of Scottish Third Division club Stenhousemuir, made the 1000th first team appearance of his career in the Scottish Cup 3rd Round against Rangers at Ibrox on Jan 23, 1999. He was presented with the Man of the Match award before kick-off.

Against East Stirling on Boxing Day, he had played his 864th League game, breaking the British record for an outfield player set by another Scot, Tommy Hutchison, with Alloa, Blackpool, Coventry, Manchester City, Burnley and Swansea City.

Armstrong's 24-year career, spent in the lower divisions of the Scottish League, began as a 1-match trialist with Meadowbank Thistle in 1975 and continued via Stirling Albion, Berwick Rangers, Meadowbank and, from 1992, Stenhousemuir.

**Tony Ford** became the first English outfield player to reach 1000 senior appearances in Rochdale's 1-0 win at Carlisle (Auto Windscreens Shield) on Mar 7, 2000. Grimsby-born, he began his 26-season midfield career with Grimsby and played for 7 other League clubs: Sunderland (loan), Stoke, WBA, Bradford City (loan), Scunthorpe, Mansfield and Rochdale. He retired, aged 42, in 2001 with a career record of 1072 appearances (121 goals) and his total of 931 League games is exceeded only by Peter Shilton's 1005.

On Apr 16, 2011, **Graham Alexander** reached 1,000 appearances when he came on as a sub for Burnley at home to Swansea. Alexander, 40, ended a 22-year career with the equaliser for Preston against Charlton (2-2, Lge 1) on Apr 28, 2012 – his 1,023rd appearance. He also played for Luton and Scunthorpe and was capped 40 times by Scotland.

## RECORD FOR BARRY

Gareth Barry surpassed Ryan Giggs's record of 632 Premier League appearances in West Bromwich Albion's 2-0 defeat by Arsenal in the 2017–18 season.

## GIGGS RECORD COLLECTION

**Ryan Giggs** (Manchester Utd) has collected the most individual honours in English football with a total of 34 prizes. They comprise: 13 Premier League titles, 4 FA Cups, 3 League Cups, 2 European Cups, 1 UEFA Super Cup, 1 Inter-Continental Cup, 1 World Club Cup, 9 Charity Shields/ Community Shields. One-club man Giggs played 24 seasons for United, making a record 963 appearances. He won 64 Wales caps and on retiring as a player, aged 40, in May 2014, became the club's assistant manager. He ended a 29-year association with the club in June 2016.

## KNIGHTS OF SOCCER

Players, managers and administrators who have been honoured for their services to football: **Charles Clegg** (1927), **Stanley Rous** (1949), **Stanley Matthews** (1965), **Alf Ramsey** (1967), **Matt Busby** (1968), **Walter Winterbottom** (1978) **Bert Millichip** (1991), **Bobby Charlton** (1994), **Tom Finney** (1998), **Geoff Hurst** (1998), **Alex Ferguson** (1999), **Bobby Robson** (2002), **Trevor Brooking** (2004), **Dave Richards** (2006), **Doug Ellis** (2011), **Kenny Dalglish** (2018).

- On Nov 6, 2014, **Karren Brady**, vice-chairman of West Ham, was elevated to the Lords as Karren, Baroness Brady, OBE, of Knightsbridge, life peer

# PENALTIES

The **penalty-kick** was introduced to the game, following a proposal to the Irish FA in 1890 by William McCrum, son of the High Sheriff for Co Omagh, and approved by the International Football Board on Jun 2, 1891.

First penalty scored in a first-class match in England was by John Heath, for Wolves v Accrington Stanley (5-0 in Div 1, Sep 14, 1891).

The greatest influence of the penalty has come since the 1970s, with the introduction of the shoot-out to settle deadlocked ties in various competitions.

Manchester Utd were the first club to win a competitive match in British football via a shoot-out (4-3 away to Hull, Watney Cup semi-final, Aug 5, 1970); in that penalty contest, George Best was the first player to score, Denis Law the first to miss.

The shoot-out was adopted by FIFA and UEFA the same year (1970).

In season 1991–92, penalty shoot-outs were introduced to decide FA Cup ties still level after one replay and extra time.

Wembley saw its first penalty contest in the 1974 Charity Shield. Since then many major matches across the world have been settled in this way, including:

**1976** **European Championship Final (Belgrade):** Czechoslovakia beat West Germany 5-3 (after 2-2)
**1980** **Cup-Winners' Cup Final (Brussels):** Valencia beat Arsenal 5-4 (after 0-0)
**1984** **European Cup Final (Rome):** Liverpool beat Roma 4-2 (after 1-1)
**1984** **UEFA Cup Final:** Tottenham (home) beat Anderlecht 4-3 (2-2 agg)
**1986** **European Cup Final (Seville):** Steaua Bucharest beat Barcelona 2-0 (after 0-0).
**1987** **Freight Rover Trophy Final (Wembley):** Mansfield beat Bristol City 5-4 (after 1-1)
**1987** **Scottish League Cup Final (Hampden Park):** Rangers beat Aberdeen 5-3 (after 3-3)
**1988** **European Cup Final (Stuttgart):** PSV Eindhoven beat Benfica 6-5 (after 0-0)
**1988** **UEFA Cup Final:** Bayer Leverkusen (home) beat Espanyol 3-2 after 3-3 (0-3a, 3-0h)
**1990** **Scottish Cup Final (Hampden Park):** Aberdeen beat Celtic 9-8 (after 0-0)
**1991** **European Cup Final (Bari):** Red Star Belgrade beat Marseille 5-3 (after 0-0)
**1991** **Div 4 Play-off Final (Wembley):** Torquay beat Blackpool 5-4 (after 2-2)
**1992** **Div 4 Play-off Final (Wembley):** Blackpool beat Scunthorpe 4-3 (after 1-1)
**1993** **Div 3 Play-off Final(Wembley):** York beat Crewe 5-3 (after 1-1)
**1994** **Autoglass Trophy Final (Wembley):** Swansea City beat Huddersfield 3-1 (after 1-1)
**1994** **World Cup Final (Los Angeles):** Brazil beat Italy 3-2 (after 0-0)
**1994** **Scottish League Cup Final (Ibrox Park):** Raith beat Celtic 6-5 (after 2-2)
**1995** **Copa America Final (Montevideo):** Uruguay beat Brazil 5-3 (after 1-1)
**1996** **European Cup Final (Rome):** Juventus beat Ajax 4-2 (after 1-1)
**1996** **European U-21 Champ Final (Barcelona):** Italy beat Spain 4-2 (after 1-1)
**1997** **Auto Windscreens Shield Final (Wembley):** Carlisle beat Colchester 4-3 (after 0-0)
**1997** **UEFA Cup Final:** FC Schalke beat Inter Milan 4-1 (after 1-1 agg)
**1998** **Div 1 Play-off Final (Wembley):** Charlton beat Sunderland 7-6 (after 4-4)
**1999** **Div 2 Play-off Final (Wembley):** Manchester City beat Gillingham 3-1 (after 2-2)
**1999** **Women's World Cup Final (Pasedena):** USA beat China 5-4 (after 0-0)
**2000** **African Nations Cup Final (Lagos):** Cameroon beat Nigeria 4-3 (after 0-0)
**2000** **UEFA Cup Final (Copenhagen):** Galatasaray beat Arsenal 4-1 (after 0-0)
**2000** **Olympic Final (Sydney):** Cameroon beat Spain 5-3 (after 2-2)
**2001** **League Cup Final (Millennium Stadium):** Liverpool beat Birmingham 5-4 (after 1-1)
**2001** **Champions League Final (Milan):** Bayern Munich beat Valencia 5-4 (after 1-1)
**2002** **Euro U-21 Champ Final (Basle):** Czech Republic beat France 3-1 (after 0-0)
**2002** **Div 1 Play-off Final (Millennium Stadium):** Birmingham beat Norwich 4-2 (after 1-1)
**2003** **Champions League Final (Old Trafford):** AC Milan beat Juventus 3-2 (after 0-0)

2004 **Div 3 Play-off Final (Millennium Stadium):** Huddersfield beat Mansfield 4-1 (after 0-0)
2004 **Copa America Final (Lima):** Brazil beat Argentina 4-2 (after 2-2)
2005 **FA Cup Final (Millennium Stadium):** Arsenal beat Manchester Utd 5-4 (after 0-0)
2005 **Champions League Final (Istanbul):** Liverpool beat AC Milan 3-2 (after 3-3)
2006 **African Cup of Nations Final (Cairo):** Egypt beat Ivory Coast 4-2 (after 0-0)
2006 **FA Cup Final (Millennium Stadium):** Liverpool beat West Ham 3-1 (after 3-3)
2006 **Scottish Cup Final (Hampden Park):** Hearts beat Gretna 4-2 (after 1-1)
2006 **Lge 1 Play-off Final (Millennium Stadium):** Barnsley beat Swansea City 4-3 (after 2-2)
2006 **World Cup Final (Berlin):** Italy beat France 5-3 (after 1-1)
2007 **UEFA Cup Final (Hampden Park):** Sevilla beat Espanyol 3-1 (after 2-2)
2008 **Champions League Final (Moscow):** Manchester Utd beat Chelsea 6-5 (after 1-1)
2008 **Scottish League Cup Final (Hampden Park):** Rangers beat Dundee Utd 3-2 (after 2-2)
2009 **League Cup Final (Wembley):** Manchester Utd beat Tottenham 4-1 (after 0-0)
2011 **Women's World Cup Final (Frankfurt):** Japan beat USA 3-1 (after 2-2)
2012 **League Cup Final (Wembley):** Liverpool beat Cardiff 3-2 (after 2-2)
2012 **Champions League Final (Munich):** Chelsea beat Bayern Munich 4-3 (after 1-1)
2012 **Lge 1 Play-off Final (Wembley):** Huddersfield beat Sheffield Utd 8-7 (after 0-0)
2012 **Africa Cup of Nations Final (Gabon):** Zambia beat Ivory Coast 8-7 (after 0-0)
2013 **FA Trophy Final (Wembley):** Wrexham beat Grimsby 4-1 (after 1-1)
2013 **European Super Cup (Prague):** Bayern Munich beat Chelsea 5-4 (after 2-2)
2014 **Scottish League Cup Final (Celtic Park):** Aberdeen beat Inverness 4-2 (after 0-0)
2014 **Lge 1 Play-off Final (Wembley):** Rotherheam beat Leyton Orient 4-3 (after 2-2)
2014 **Europa Lge Final (Turin):** Sevilla beat Benfica 4-2 (after 0-0)
2015 **Africa Cup of Nations Final (Equ Guinea):** Ivory Coast beat Ghana 9-8 (after 0-0)
2015 **Conference Play-off Final (Wembley):** Bristol Rov beat Grimsby 5-3 (after 1-1)
2015 **Lge 2 Play-off Final (Wembley):** Southend beat Wycombe 7-6 (after 1-1)
2015 **FA Trophy Final (Wembley)** North Ferriby beat Wrexham 5-4 (after3-3)
2015 **Euro U-21 Champ Final (Prague):** Sweden beat Portugal 4-3 (after 0-0)
2015 **Copa America Final (Santiago):** Chile beat Argentina 4-1 (after 0-0)
2016 **League Cup Final (Wembley):** Manchester City beat Liverpool 3-1 (after 1-1)
2016 **Champions League Final (Milan):** Real Madrid beat Atletico Madrid 5-3 (after 1-1)
2016 **Olympic Men's Final (Rio de Janeiro):** Brazil beat Germany 5-4 (after 1-1)
2017 **Champ Play-off Final (Wembley):** Huddersfield beat Reading 4-3 (after 0-0)
2017 **Community Shield (Wembley):** Arsenal beat Chelsea 4-1 (after 1-1)

In South America in 1992, in a 26-shot competition, **Newell's Old Boys** beat America 11-10 in the Copa Libertadores.

Longest-recorded penalty contest in first-class matches was in Argentina in 1988 – from 44 shots, **Argentinos Juniors** beat Racing Club 20-19. Genclerbirligi beat Galatasaray 17-16 in a Turkish Cup-tie in 1996. Only one penalty was missed.

Highest-scoring shoot-outs in international football: **North Korea** beat Hong Kong 11-10 (after 3-3 draw) in an Asian Cup match in 1975; and **Ivory Coast** beat Ghana 11-10 (after 0-0 draw) in African Nations Cup Final, 1992.

Most penalties needed to settle an adult game in Britain: **44** in Norfolk Primary Cup 4th round replay, Dec 2000. Aston Village side **Freethorpe** beat Foulsham 20-19 (5 kicks missed). All 22 players took 2 penalties each, watched by a crowd of 20. The sides had drawn 2-2, 4-4 in a tie of 51 goals.

**Penalty that took 24 days:** That was how long elapsed between the award and the taking of a penalty in an Argentine Second Division match between **Atalanta** and Defensores in 2003. A riot ended the original match with 5 minutes left. The game resumed behind closed doors with the penalty that caused the abandonment. Lucas Ferreiro scored it to give Atalanta a 1-0 win.

## INTERNATIONAL PENALTIES, MISSED

Four penalties out of five were missed when **Colombia** beat Argentina 3-0 in a Copa America group tie in Paraguay in Jul 1999. Martin Palmermo missed three for Argentina and

Colombia's Hamilton Ricard had one spot-kick saved.

In the European Championship semi-final against Italy in Amsterdam on Jun 29, 2000, **Holland** missed five penalties – two in normal time, three in the penalty contest which Italy won 3-1 (after 0-0). Dutch captain Frank de Boer missed twice from the spot.

## ENGLAND'S SHOOT-OUT RECORD

England have been beaten in eight out of 11 penalty shoot-outs in major tournaments:

**1990** (World Cup semi-final, Turin) 3-4 v West Germany after 1-1.
**1996** (Euro Champ quarter-final, Wembley) 4-2 v Spain after 0-0.
**1996** (Euro Champ semi-final, Wembley) 5-6 v Germany after 1-1.
**1998** (World Cup 2nd round., St Etienne) 3-4 v Argentina after 2-2.
**2004** (Euro Champ quarter-final, Lisbon) 5-6 v Portugal after 2-2.
**2006** (World Cup quarter-final, Gelsenkirchen) 1-3 v Portugal after 0-0.
**2007** (Euro U-21 Champ semi-final, Heerenveen) 12-13 v Holland after 1-1.
**2009** (Euro U-21 Champ semi-final, Gothenburg) 5-4 v Sweden after 3-3.
**2012** (Euro Champ quarter-final, Kiev) 2-4 v Italy after 0-0.
**2017** (Euro-21 Champ semi-final, Tychy) 3-4 v Germany after 2-2.
**2018** (World Cup round of 16, Moscow) 4-3 v Colombia after 1-1.

## FA CUP SHOOT-OUTS

**First penalty contest** in the FA Cup took place in 1972. In the days of the play-off for third place, the match was delayed until the eve of the following season when losing semi-finalists Birmingham and Stoke met at St Andrew's on Aug 5. The score was 0-0 and Birmingham won 4-3 on penalties.

**Highest-scoring:** Preliminary round replay (Aug 30, 2005): Tunbridge Wells beat Littlehampton 16-15 after 40 spot-kicks (9 missed).

**Competition proper: Scunthorpe beat** Worcester 14-13 in 2nd round replay (Dec 17, 2014) after 1-1 (32 kicks).

**Shoot-out abandoned:** The FA Cup 1st round replay between Oxford City and Wycombe at Wycombe on Nov 9, 1999 was abandoned (1-1) after extra-time. As the penalty shoot-out was about to begin, a fire broke out under a stand. Wycombe won the second replay 1-0 at Oxford Utd's ground.

**First FA Cup Final** to be decided by shoot-out was in 2005 (May 21), when Arsenal beat Manchester Utd 5-4 on penalties at Cardiff's Millennium Stadium (0-0 after extra time). A year later (May 13) Liverpool beat West Ham 3-1 (3-3 after extra-time).

## MARATHON SHOOT-OUT BETWEEN LEAGUE CLUBS

Highest recorded score in shoot-out between league clubs: Dagenham & Redbridge 14-13 against Leyton Orient (after 1-1) in Johnstone's Paint Trophy southern section on Sep 7, 2011

## SHOOT-OUT RECORD WINNERS AND LOSERS

When **Bradford** beat Arsenal 3-2 on penalties in a League Cup fifth round tie, it was the club's ninth successive shoot-out victory in FA Cup, League Cup and Johnstone's Paint Trophy ties between Oct 2009 and Dec 2012.

**Tottenham**'s 4-1 spot-kick failure against Basel in the last 16 of the Europa League was their seventh successive defeat in shoot-outs from Mar 1996 to Apr 2013 (FA Cup, League Cup, UEFA Cup, Europa League)

## MISSED CUP FINAL PENALTIES

**John Aldridge** (Liverpool) became the first player to miss a penalty in an FA Cup Final at Wembley when Dave Beasant saved his shot in 1988 to help Wimbledon to a shock 1-0 win. Seven penalties before had been scored in the Final at Wembley.

Previously, **Charlie Wallace**, of Aston Villa, had failed from the spot in the 1913 Final against Sunderland at Crystal Palace, which his team won 1-0

**Gary Lineker** (Tottenham) had his penalty saved by Nottm Forest's Mark Crossley in the 1991 FA Cup Final.

For the first time, two spot-kicks were missed in an FA Cup Final. In 2010, Petr Cech saved from Portsmouth's **Kevin-Prince Boateng** while Chelsea's **Frank Lampard** put his kick wide.

Another miss at Wembley was by Arsenal's **Nigel Winterburn**, Luton's Andy Dibble saving his spot-kick in the 1988 Littlewoods Cup Final, when a goal would have put Arsenal 3-1 ahead. Instead, they lost 3-2.

Winterburn was the third player to fail with a League Cup Final penalty at Wembley, following **Ray Graydon** (Aston Villa) against Norwich in 1975 and **Clive Walker** (Sunderland), who shot wide in the 1985 Milk Cup Final, also against Norwich who won 1-0. Graydon had his penalty saved by Kevin Keelan, but scored from the rebound and won the cup for Aston Villa (1-0).

Derby's Martin Taylor saved a penalty from **Eligio Nicolini** in the Anglo-Italian Cup Final at Wembley on Mar 27, 1993, but Cremonese won 3-1.

## LEAGUE PENALTIES RECORD

Most penalties in Football League match: Five – 4 to Crystal Palace (3 missed), 1 to Brighton (scored) in Div 2 match at Selhurst Park on Mar 27 (Easter Monday), 1989. Crystal Palace won 2-1. Three of the penalties were awarded in a 5-minute spell. The match also produced 5 bookings and a sending-off. Other teams missing 3 penalties in a match: Burnley v Grimsby (Div 2), Feb 13, 1909; Manchester City v Newcastle (Div 1), Jan 17, 1912.

## HOTTEST MODERN SPOT-SHOTS

**Matthew Le Tissier** ended his career in season 2001–02 with the distinction of having netted 48 out of 49 first-team penalties for Southampton. He scored the last 27 after his only miss when Nottm Forest keeper Mark Crossley saved in a Premier League match at The Dell on Mar 24, 1993.

**Graham Alexander** scored 78 out of 84 penalties in a 22-year career (Scunthorpe, Luton, Preston twice and Burnley) which ended in 2012.

## SPOT-KICK HAT-TRICKS

Right-back **Joe Willetts** scored three penalties when Hartlepool beat Darlington 6-1 (Div 3N) on Good Friday 1951.

Danish international **Jan Molby**'s only hat-trick in English football, for Liverpool in a 3-1 win at home to Coventry (Littlewoods Cup, 4th round replay, Nov 26, 1986) comprised three goals from the penalty spot.

It was the first such hat-trick in a major match for two years – since **Andy Blair** scored three penalties for Sheffield Wed against Luton (Milk Cup 4th round, Nov 20 1984).

Portsmouth's **Kevin Dillon** scored a penalty hat-trick in the Full Members Cup (2nd round) at home to Millwall (3-2) on Nov 4, 1986.

**Alan Slough** scored a hat-trick of penalties in an away game, but was on the losing side, when Peterborough were beaten 4-3 at Chester (Div 3, Apr 29, 1978).

**Josh Wright**'s three penalties in the space of 11 minutes enabled Gillingham to come from 2-0 down to defeat his former club Scunthorpe 3-2 in League One on Mar 11, 2017

Penalty hat-tricks in **international football: Dimitris Saravakos** (in 9 mins) for Greece v Egypt in 1990. He scored 5 goals in match. **Henrik Larsson**, among his 4 goals in Sweden's 6-0 home win v Moldova in World Cup qualifying match, Jun 6, 2001.

## MOST PENALTY GOALS (LEAGUE) IN SEASON

13 out of 13 by **Francis Lee** for Manchester City (Div 1) in 1971–72. His goal total for the season was 33. In season 1988–89, **Graham Roberts** scored 12 League penalties for Second Division Champions Chelsea. In season 2004–05, **Andrew Johnson** scored 11 Premiership penalties for Crystal Palace, who were relegated.

## PENALTY-SAVE SEQUENCES

Ipswich goalkeeper **Paul Cooper** saved eight of the ten penalties he faced in 1979–80. **Roy**

**Brown** (Notts Co) saved six in a row in season 1972–73.

**Andy Lomas**, goalkeeper for Chesham (Diadora League) claimed a record eighth **consecutive** penalty saves – three at the end of season 1991–92 and five in 1992–93.

**Mark Bosnich** (Aston Villa) saved five in two consecutive matches in 1993–94: three in Coca-Cola Cup semi-final penalty shoot-out v Tranmere (Feb 26), then two in Premiership at Tottenham (Mar 2).

## MISSED PENALTIES SEQUENCE

Against Wolves in Div 2 on Sep 28, 1991, **Southend** missed their seventh successive penalty (five of them the previous season).

# SCOTTISH RECORDS

*(See also under 'Goals' & 'Discipline')*

## CELTIC SUPREME

In winning the Treble for the fourth time in 2016–17, **Celtic** rewrote the Scottish records. In the first season under **Brendan Rodgers**, previously Liverpool manager, they did not lose a domestic match, the first to stay unbeaten in the league since Rangers in 1899. They set new records for points (106), goals (106), victories (34) and for a 30-point winning margin. In 2017–18, Celtic became the first in Scotland to win back-to-back domestic trebles and stretched an unbeaten run to a British record 69 games in domestic competitions. The club have now been champions 49 times, won the SFA Cup 38 times and the League Cup on 17 occasions. Their 25 consecutive victories in season 2003–04 also represents a British best, while the 1966–67 record was the most successful by a British side in one season. They won the Treble and became the first to win the European Cup. Under Jock Stein, there were nine titles in a row (1966–74).

## RANGERS' MANY RECORDS

**Rangers**' record-breaking feats include:

**League Champions:** 54 times (once joint holders) – world record.

**Winning every match** in Scottish League (18 games, 1898–99 season).

**Major hat-tricks:** Rangers have completed the domestic treble (League Championship, League Cup and Scottish FA Cup) a record seven times (1948–49, 1963–64, 1975–76, 1977–78, 1992–93, 1998–99, 2002–03).

**League & Cup double:** 17 times.

**Nine successive Championships** (1989–97). Four men played in all nine sides: Richard Gough, Ally McCoist, Ian Ferguson and Ian Durrant.

**115 major trophies:** Championships 54, Scottish Cup 33, League Cup 27, Cup-Winners' Cup 1.

## UNBEATEN SCOTTISH CHAMPIONS

**Celtic** and **Rangers** have each won the Scottish Championship with an unbeaten record: Celtic in 1897–98 (P18, W15, D3), Rangers in 1898–99 (P18, W18).

## FORSTER'S SHUT-OUT RECORD

Celtic goalkeeper **Fraser Forster** set a record in Scottish top-flight football by not conceding a goal for 1,256 consecutive minutes in season 2013–14.

## TRIO OF TOP CLUBS MISSING

Three of Scotland's leading clubs were missing from the 2014-15 Premiership season. With **Hearts** finishing bottom and **Rangers** still working their way back through the divisions after being demoted, they were joined in the second tier by **Hibernian**, who lost the play-off final on penalties to Hamilton.

## SCOTTISH CUP HAT-TRICKS

**Aberdeen**'s feat of winning the Scottish FA Cup in 1982–83–84 made them only the third club to achieve that particular hat-trick. **Queen's Park** did it twice (1874–75–76 and 1880–81–82), and **Rangers** have won the Scottish Cup three years in succession on three occasions: 1934–35–36, 1948–49–50 and 1962–63–64.

## SCOTTISH CUP FINAL DISMISSALS

Five players have been sent off in the Scottish FA Cup Final: **Jock Buchanan** (Rangers v Kilmarnock, 1929); **Roy Aitken** (Celtic v Aberdeen, 1984); **Walter Kidd** (Hearts captain v Aberdeen, 1986); **Paul Hartley** (Hearts v Gretna, 2006); **Pa Kujabi** (Hibernian v Hearts, 2012); **Carl Tremarco** (Inverness v Falkirk, 2015).

## HIGHEST-SCORING SHOOT-OUT

In Scottish football's highest-scoring penalty shoot-out, **Stirling Albion** beat junior club Hurlford 13-12 after 28 spot-kicks in a third round replay. The tie, on Nov 8, 2014, had ended 2-2 after extra-time.

## RECORD SEQUENCES

**Celtic** hold Britain's League record of 62 matches undefeated, from Nov 13, 1915 to Apr 21, 1917, when Kilmarnock won 2-0 at Parkhead. They won 49, drew 13 (111 points) and scored 126 goals to 26.

**Greenock Morton in** 1963–64 accumulated 67 points out of 72 and scored 135 goals.

**Queen's Park** did not have a goal scored against them during the first seven seasons of their existence (1867–74, before the Scottish League was formed).

## EARLIEST PROMOTIONS IN SCOTLAND

**Dundee** promoted from Div 2, Feb 1, 1947; **Greenock Morton** promoted from Div 2, Mar 2, 1964; **Gretna** promoted from Div 3, Mar 5, 2005; **Hearts** promoted from Championship, Mar 21, 2015.

## WORST HOME SEQUENCE

After gaining promotion to Div 1 in 1992, **Cowdenbeath** went a record 38 consecutive home League matches without a win. They ended the sequence (drew 8, lost 30) when beating Arbroath 1-0 on Apr 2, 1994, watched by a crowd of 225.

## ALLY'S RECORDS

**Ally McCoist** became the first player to complete 200 goals in the Premier Division when he scored Rangers' winner (2-1) at Falkirk on Dec 12, 1992. His first was against Celtic in Sep 1983, and he reached 100 against Dundee on Boxing Day 1987.

When McCoist scored twice at home to Hibernian (4-3) on Dec 7, 1996, he became Scotland's record post-war League marksman, beating Gordon Wallace's 264.

Originally with St Johnstone (1978–81), he spent two seasons with Sunderland (1981–83), then joined Rangers for £200,000 in Jun 1983.

In 15 seasons at Ibrox, he scored 355 goals for Rangers (250 League), and helped them win 10 Championships (9 in succession), 3 Scottish Cups and earned a record 9 League Cup winner's medals. He won the European Golden Boot in consecutive seasons (1991–92, 1992–93).

His 9 Premier League goals in three seasons for Kilmarnock gave him a career total of 281 Scottish League goals when he retired at the end of 2000–01. McCoist succeeded Walter Smith as manager of Rangers in May 2011.

## SCOTLAND'S MOST SUCCESSFUL MANAGER

**Bill Struth**, 30 trophies for Rangers, 1920–54 (18 Championships, 10 Scottish Cups, 2 League Cups.

## SMITH'S IBROX HONOURS

**Walter Smith**, who retired in May, 2011, won a total of 21 trophies in two spells as Rangers manager (10 League titles, 5 Scottish Cups, 6 League Cups).

## RANGERS PUNISHED

In April 2012, **Rangers** (in administration) were fined £160,000 by the Scottish FA and given a 12-month transfer ban on charges relating to their finances. The ban was later overturned in court. The club had debts estimated at around £135m and on June 12, 2012 were forced into liquidation. A new company emerged, but Rangers were voted out of the Scottish Premier League and demoted to Division Three for the start of the 2012-13 season. They returned to the top division in 2016 via three promotions in four seasons.

## FIVE IN A MATCH

**Paul Sturrock** set an individual scoring record for the Scottish Premier Division with 5 goals in Dundee Utd's 7-0 win at home to Morton on Nov 17, 1984. **Marco Negri** equalled the feat with all 5 when Rangers beat Dundee Utd 5-1 at Ibrox (Premier Division) on Aug 23, 1997, and **Kenny Miller** scored 5 in Rangers' 7-1 win at home to St Mirren on Nov 4, 2000. **Kris Boyd** scored all Kilmarnock's goals in a 5-2 SPL win at home to Dundee Utd on Sep 25, 2004. **Boyd** scored another 5 when Rangers beat Dundee Utd 7-1 on Dec 30, 2009. That took his total of SPL goals to a record 160. **Gary Hooper** netted all Celtic's goals in 5-0 SPL win against Hearts on May 13, 2012

## NEGRI'S TEN-TIMER

**Marco Negri** scored in Rangers' first ten League matches (23 goals) in season 1997–98, a Premier Division record. The previous best was 8 by **Ally MacLeod** for Hibernian in 1978.

## DOUBLE SCOTTISH FINAL

Rangers v Celtic drew **129,643** and **120,073** people to the Scottish Cup Final and replay at Hampden Park, Glasgow, in 1963. Receipts for the two matches totalled £50,500.

## MOST SCOTTISH CHAMPIONSHIP MEDALS

**13** by **Sandy Archibald** (Rangers, 1918–34). Post-war record: 10 by **Bobby Lennox** (Celtic, 1966–79).

**Alan Morton** won **nine** Scottish Championship medals with Rangers in 1921–23–24–25–27–28–29–30–31. **Ally McCoist** played in the Rangers side that won nine successive League titles (1989–97).

Between 1927 and 1939 **Bob McPhail** helped Rangers win nine Championships, finish second twice and third once. He scored 236 League goals but was never top scorer in a single season.

## TOP SCOTTISH LEAGUE SCORERS IN SEASON

**Raith Rovers** (Div 2) 142 goals in 1937–38; **Morton** (Div 2) 135 goals in 1963–64; **Hearts** (Div 1) 132 goals in 1957–58; **Falkirk** (Div 2) 132 goals in 1935–36; **Gretna** (Div 3) 130 goals in 2004–05.

## SCOTTISH CUP – NO DECISION

The **Scottish FA** withheld their Cup and medals in 1908–09 after Rangers and Celtic played two drawn games in the Final. Spectators rioted.

## FEWEST LEAGUE WINS IN SEASON

**In modern times:** 1 win by **Ayr** (34 matches, Div 1, 1966–67); **Forfar** (38 matches, Div 2, 1973–74); **Clydebank** (36 matches, Div 1, 1999–2000).

**Vale of Leven** provided the only instance of a British team failing to win a single match in a league season (Div 1, 18 games,1891–92).

## HAMPDEN'S £63M REDEVELOPMENT

On completion of redevelopment costing £63m **Hampden Park**, home of Scottish football and the oldest first-class stadium in the world, was re-opened full scale for the Rangers-Celtic Cup Final on May 29, 1999.

Work on the 'new Hampden' (capacity 52,000) began in 1992. The North and East stands were restructured (£12m); a new South stand and improved West stand cost £51m. The Millennium Commission contributed £23m and the Lottery Sports Fund provided a grant of £3.75m.

## FIRST FOR INVERNESS

**Inverness Caledonian Thistle** won the Scottish Cup for the Highlands for the first time when beating Falkirk 2-1 in the Final on May 30, 2015.

## FASTEST GOALS IN SPL

10.4 sec by **Kris Boyd** for Kilmarnock in 3-2 win over Ross Co, Jan 28, 2017; 12.1 sec by **Kris Commons** for Celtic in 4-3 win over Aberdeen, Mar 16, 2013; 12.4 sec by **Anthony Stokes** for Hibernian in 4-1 home defeat by Rangers, Dec 27, 2009.

## YOUNGEST SCORER IN SPL

**Fraser Fyvie**, aged 16 years and 306 days, for Aberdeen v Hearts (3-0) on Jan 27, 2010.

## 12 GOALS SHARED

There was a record aggregate score for the SPL on May 5, 2010, when **Motherwell** came from 6-2 down to draw 6-6 with **Hibernian**.

## 25-POINT DEDUCTION

Dundee were deducted 25 points by the Scottish Football League in November 2010 for going into administration for the second time. It left the club on minus 11 points, but they still managed to finish in mid-table in Division One.

## GREAT SCOTS

In Feb 1988, the Scottish FA launched a national **Hall of Fame**, initially comprising the first 11 Scots to make 50 international appearances, to be joined by all future players to reach that number of caps. Each member receives a gold medal, invitation for life at all Scotland's home matches, and has his portrait hung at Scottish FA headquarters in Glasgow.

## MORE CLUBS IN 2000

The **Scottish Premier League** increased from 10 to 12 clubs in season 2000–01. The **Scottish Football League** admitted two new clubs – Peterhead and Elgin City from the Highland League – to provide three divisions of 10 in 2000–01.

## FIRST FOR EDINBURGH CITY

In May 2016, **Edinburgh City** became the first club to be promoted to Scottish League Two through the pyramid system with a 2-1 aggregate play-off aggregate win over East Stirling, whose 61 years in senior football came to an end.

## NOTABLE SCOTTISH 'FIRSTS'

- The father of League football was a Scot, **William McGregor**, a draper in Birmingham. The 12-club Football League kicked off in Sep 1888, and McGregor was its first president.
- **Hibernian** were the first British club to play in the European Cup, by invitation. They reached the semi-final when it began in 1955–56.
- **Celtic** were Britain's first winners of the European Cup, in 1967.
- Scotland's First Division became the **Premier Division** in season 1975–76.
- Football's **first international** was staged at the West of Scotland cricket ground, Partick, on Nov 30, 1872: Scotland 0, England 0.

- Scotland introduced its **League Cup** in 1945–46, the first season after the war. It was another 15 years before the Football League Cup was launched.
- Scotland pioneered the use in British football of **two subs** per team in League and Cup matches.
- The world's **record football score** belongs to Scotland: Arbroath 36, Bon Accord 0 (Scottish Cup 1st rd) on Sep 12, 1885.
- The Scottish FA introduced the penalty **shoot-out** to their Cup Final in 1990.
- On Jan 22, 1994 all six matches in the **Scottish Premier Division** ended as draws.
- Scotland's new Premier League introduced a **3-week shut-down** in Jan 1999 – first instance of British football adopting the winter break system that operates in a number of European countries. The SPL ended its New Year closure after 2003. The break returned from season 2016–17.
- **Rangers** made history at home to St Johnstone (Premier League, 0-0, Mar 4, 2000) when fielding a team entirely without Scottish players.
- **John Fleck**, aged 16 years, 274 days, became the youngest player in a Scottish FA Cup Final when he came on as a substitute for Rangers in their 3-2 win over Queen of the South at Hampden Park on May 24, 2008

## SCOTTISH CUP SHOCK RESULTS

| | | |
|---|---|---|
| **1885–86** | (1) | Arbroath 36 Bon Accord 0 |
| **1921–22** | (F) | Morton 1 Rangers 0 |
| **1937–38** | (F) | East Fife 4 Kilmarnock 2 (replay, after 1-1) |
| **1960–61** | (F) | Dunfermline 2 Celtic 0 (replay, after 0-0) |
| **1966–67** | (1) | Berwick 1 Rangers 0 |
| **1979–80** | (3) | Hamilton 2 Keith 3 |
| **1984–85** | (1) | Stirling 20 Selkirk 0 |
| **1984–85** | (3) | Inverness 3 Kilmarnock 0 |
| **1986–87** | (3) | Rangers 0 Hamilton 1 |
| **1994–95** | (4) | Stenhousemuir 2 Aberdeen 0 |
| **1998–99** | (3) | Aberdeen 0 Livingston 1 |
| **1999–2000** | (3) | Celtic 1 Inverness 3 |
| **2003–04** | (5) | Inverness 1 Celtic 0 |
| **2005–06** | (3) | Clyde 2 Celtic 1 |
| **2008–09** | (6) | St Mirren 1 Celtic 0 |
| **2009–10** | (SF) | Ross Co 2 Celtic 0 |
| **2013–14** | (4) | Albion 1 Motherwell 0 |

**Scottish League (Coca-Cola) Cup Final**
**1994–95** Raith 2, Celtic 2 (Raith won 6-5 on pens)

**Europa League first qualifying round**
**2017–18** Progres Niederkorn (Luxembourg) 2 Rangers 1 (on agg)

# MISCELLANEOUS

## NATIONAL ASSOCIATIONS FORMED

| | |
|---|---|
| FA | **1863** |
| FA of Wales | **1876** |
| Scottish FA | **1873** |
| Irish FA | **1904** |
| Federation of International Football Associations (FIFA) | **1904** |

## NATIONAL & INTERNATIONAL COMPETITIONS LAUNCHED

| | |
|---|---|
| FA Cup | **1871** |
| Welsh Cup | **1877** |

| | |
|---|---|
| Scottish Cup | **1873** |
| Irish Cup | **1880** |
| Football League | **1888** |
| Premier League | **1992** |
| Scottish League | **1890** |
| Scottish Premier League | **1998** |
| Scottish League Cup | **1945** |
| Football League Cup | **1960** |
| Home International Championship | **1883–84** |
| World Cup | **1930** |
| European Championship | **1958** |
| European Cup | **1955** |
| Fairs/UEFA Cup | **1955** |
| Cup-Winners' Cup | **1960** |
| European Champions League | **1992** |
| Olympic Games Tournament, at Shepherd's Bush | **1908** |

## INNOVATIONS

**Size of Ball:** Fixed in **1872**.

**Shinguards:** Introduced and registered by Sam Weller Widdowson (Nottm Forest & England) in **1874**.

**Referee's whistle:** First used on Nottm Forest's ground in **1878**.

**Professionalism:** Legalised in England in the summer of **1885** as a result of agitation by Lancashire clubs.

**Goal-nets:** Invented and patented in **1890** by Mr JA Brodie of Liverpool. They were first used in the North v South match in Jan, **1891**.

**Referees and linesmen:** Replaced umpires and referees in Jan, **1891**.

**Penalty-kick:** Introduced at Irish FA's request in the season **1891–92**. The penalty law ordering the goalkeeper to remain on the goal-line came into force in Sep, **1905**, and the order to stand on his goal-line until the ball is kicked arrived in **1929–30**.

**White ball:** First came into official use in **1951**.

**Floodlighting:** First FA Cup-tie (replay), Kidderminster Harriers v Brierley Hill Alliance, **1955**. First Football League match: Portsmouth v Newcastle (Div 1), **1956**.

**Heated pitch** to beat frost tried by Everton at Goodison Park in **1958**.

**First soccer closed-circuit TV:** At Coventry ground in Oct **1965** (10,000 fans saw their team win at Cardiff, 120 miles away).

**Substitutes** (one per team) were first allowed in Football League matches at the start of season **1965–66**. Three substitutes (one a goalkeeper) allowed, two of which could be used, in Premier League matches, **1992–93**. The Football League introduced three substitutes for **1993–94**.

**Three points for a win:** Introduced by the Football League in **1981–82**, by FIFA in World Cup games in **1994**, and by the Scottish League in the same year.

**Offside law amended**, player 'level' no longer offside, and 'professional foul' made sending-off offence, **1990**.

**Penalty shoot-outs** introduced to decide FA Cup ties level after one replay and extra time, **1991–92**.

**New back-pass rule:** goalkeeper must not handle ball kicked to him by team-mate, **1992**.

**Linesmen** became 'referees' assistants', **1998**.

**Goalkeepers** not to hold ball longer than 6 seconds, **2000**.

**Free-kicks** advanced by ten yards against opponents failing to retreat, **2000**. This experimental rule in England was scrapped in 2005).

## YOUNGEST AND OLDEST

**Youngest Caps**

| | |
|---|---|
| **Harry Wilson** (Wales v Belgium, Oct 15, 2013) | **16 years 207 days** |

**Norman Whiteside** (N Ireland v Yugoslavia, Jun 17, 1982) **17 years 41 days**
**Theo Walcott** (England v Hungary, May 30, 2006) **17 years 75 days**
**Johnny Lambie** (Scotland v Ireland, Mar 20, 1886) **17 years 92 days**
**Jimmy Holmes** (Rep of Ireland v Austria, May 30, 1971) **17 years 200 days**

**Youngest England scorer:** Wayne Rooney (17 years, 317 days) v Macedonia, Skopje, Sep 6, 2003.

**Youngest scorer on England debut**: Marcus Rashford (18 years, 208 days) v Australia, Sunderland, May 27, 2016.

**Youngest England hat-trick scorer:** Theo Walcott (19 years, 178 days) v Croatia, Zagreb, Sep 10, 2008.

**Youngest England captains:** Bobby Moore (v Czech., Bratislava, May 29, 1963), 22 years, 47 days; Michael Owen (v Paraguay, Anfield, Apr 17, 2002), 22 years, 117 days.

**Youngest England goalkeeper:** Jack Butland (19 years, 158 days) v Italy, Bern, Aug 15, 2012

**Youngest England players to reach 50 caps:** Michael Owen (23 years, 6 months) v Slovakia at Middlesbrough, Jun 11, 2003; Bobby Moore (25 years, 7 months) v Wales at Wembley, Nov 16, 1966.

**Youngest player in World Cup Final:** Pele (Brazil) aged 17 years, 237 days v Sweden in Stockholm, Jun 12, 1958.

**Youngest player to appear in World Cup Finals:** Norman Whiteside (N Ireland v Yugoslavia in Spain – Jun 17, 1982, age 17 years and 42 days.

**Youngest First Division player:** Derek Forster (Sunderland goalkeeper v Leicester, Aug 22, 1964) aged 15 years, 185 days.

**Youngest First Division scorer:** At 16 years and 57 days, schoolboy Jason Dozzell (substitute after 30 minutes for Ipswich at home to Coventry on Feb 4, 1984). Ipswich won 3-1 and Dozzell scored their third goal.

**Youngest Premier League player:** Matthew Briggs (Fulham sub at Middlesbrough, May 13, 2007) aged 16 years and 65 days.

**Youngest Premier League scorer:** James Vaughan (Everton, home to Crystal Palace, Apr 10, 2005), 16 years, 271 days.

**Youngest Premier League captain:** Lee Cattermole (Middlesbrough away to Fulham, May 7, 2006) aged 18 years, 47 days.

**Youngest player sent off in Premier League:** Wayne Rooney (Everton, away to Birmingham, Dec 26, 2002) aged 17 years, 59 days.

**Youngest First Division hat-trick scorer:** Alan Shearer, aged 17 years, 240 days, in Southampton's 4-2 home win v Arsenal (Apr 9, 1988) on his full debut. Previously, Jimmy Greaves (17 years, 309 days) with 4 goals for Chelsea at home to Portsmouth (7-4), Christmas Day, 1957.

**Youngest to complete 100 Football League goals:** Jimmy Greaves (20 years, 261 days) when he did so for Chelsea v Manchester City, Nov 19, 1960.

**Youngest players in Football League:** Reuben Noble-Lazarus (Barnsley 84th minute sub at Ipswich, Sep 30, 2008, Champ) aged 15 years, 45 days; Mason Bennett (Derby at Middlesbrough, Champ, Oct 22, 2011) aged 15 years, 99 days; Albert Geldard (Bradford PA v Millwall, Div 2, Sep 16, 1929) aged 15 years, 158 days; Ken Roberts (Wrexham v Bradford Park Avenue, Div 3 North, Sep 1, 1951) also 15 years, 158 days.

**Youngest Football League scorer:** Ronnie Dix (for Bristol Rov v Norwich, Div 3 South, Mar 3, 1928) aged 15 years, 180 days.

**Youngest player in Scottish League:** Goalkeeper Ronnie Simpson (Queens Park) aged 15 in 1946.

**Youngest player in FA Cup:** Andy Awford, Worcester City's England Schoolboy defender, aged 15 years, 88 days when he substituted in second half away to Boreham Wood (3rd qual round) on Oct 10, 1987.

**Youngest player in FA Cup proper:** Luke Freeman, Gillingham substitute striker (15 years, 233 days) away to Barnet in 1st round, Nov 10, 2007.

**Youngest FA Cup scorer:** Sean Cato (16 years, 25 days), second half sub in Barrow Town's 7-2 win away to Rothwell Town (prelim rd), Sep 3, 2011.

**Youngest Wembley Cup Final captain:** Barry Venison (Sunderland v Norwich, Milk Cup Final, Mar 24, 1985 – replacing suspended captain Shaun Elliott) – aged 20 years, 220 days.

**Youngest FA Cup-winning captain:** Bobby Moore (West Ham, 1964, v Preston), aged 23 years, 20 days.

**Youngest FA Cup Final captain:** David Nish aged 21 years and 212 days old when he captained Leicester against Manchester City at Wembley on Apr 26, 1969.

**Youngest FA Cup Final player:** Curtis Weston (Millwall sub last 3 mins v Manchester Utd, 2004) aged 17 years, 119 days.

**Youngest FA Cup Final scorer:** Norman Whiteside (Manchester Utd v Brighton, 1983 replay, Wembley), aged 18 years, 19 days.

**Youngest FA Cup Final managers:** Stan Cullis, Wolves (32) v Leicester, 1949; Steve Coppell, Crystal Palace (34) v Manchester Utd, 1990; Ruud Gullit, Chelsea (34) v Middlesbrough, 1997.

**Youngest player in Football League Cup:** Chris Coward (Stockport) sub v Sheffield Wed, 2nd Round, Aug 23, 2005, aged 16 years and 31 days.

**Youngest Wembley scorer:** Norman Whiteside (Manchester Utd v Liverpool, Milk Cup Final, Mar 26, 1983) aged 17 years, 324 days.

**Youngest Wembley Cup Final goalkeeper:** Chris Woods (18 years, 125 days) for Nottm Forest v Liverpool, League Cup Final on Mar 18, 1978.

**Youngest Wembley FA Cup Final goalkeeper:** Peter Shilton (19 years, 219 days) for Leicester v Manchester City, Apr 26, 1969.

**Youngest senior international at Wembley:** Salomon Olembe (sub for Cameroon v England, Nov 15, 1997), aged 16 years, 342 days.

**Youngest winning manager at Wembley:** Stan Cullis, aged 32 years, 187 days, as manager of Wolves, FA Cup winners on April 30 1949.

**Youngest scorer in full international:** Mohamed Kallon (Sierra Leone v Congo, African Nations Cup, Apr 22, 1995), reported as aged 15 years, 192 days.

**Youngest English player to start a Champions League game**: Phil Foden (Manchester City v Shakhtar Donetsk, Dec 6, 2017) aged 17 years, 192 days

**Youngest English scorer in Champions League:** Alex Oxlade-Chamberlain (Arsenal v Olympiacos, Sep 28, 2011) aged 18 years 1 month, 13 days

**Youngest player sent off in World Cup Final series:** Rigobert Song (Cameroon v Brazil, in USA, Jun 1994) aged 17 years, 358 days.

**Youngest FA Cup Final referee:** Kevin Howley, of Middlesbrough, aged 35 when in charge of Wolves v Blackburn, 1960.

**Youngest player in England U-23 team:** Duncan Edwards (v Italy, Bologna, Jan 20, 1954), aged 17 years, 112 days.

**Youngest player in England U-21 team:** Theo Walcott (v Moldova, Ipswich, Aug 15, 2006), aged 17 years, 152 days.

**Youngest player in Scotland U-21 team:** Christian Dailly (v Romania, Hampden Park, Sep 11, 1990), aged 16 years, 330 days.

**Youngest player in senior football:** Cameron Campbell Buchanan, Scottish-born outside right, aged 14 years, 57 days when he played for Wolves v WBA in War-time League match, Sep 26, 1942.

**Youngest player in peace-time senior match:** Eamon Collins (Blackpool v Kilmarnock, Anglo-Scottish Cup quarter-final 1st leg, Sep 9, 1980) aged 14 years, 323 days.

**World's youngest player in top division match:** Centre-forward Fernando Rafael Garcia, aged 13, played for 23 minutes for Peruvian club Juan Aurich in 3-1 win against Estudiantes on May 19, 2001.

**Oldest player to appear in Football League:** New Brighton manager Neil McBain (51 years, 120 days) as emergency goalkeeper away to Hartlepool (Div 3 North, Mar 15, 1947).

**Other oldest post-war League players:** Sir Stanley Matthews (Stoke, 1965, 50 years, 5 days); Peter Shilton (Leyton Orient 1997, 47 years, 126 days); Kevin Poole (Burton, 2010, 46 years, 291 days); Dave Beasant (Brighton 2003, 44 years, 46 days); Alf Wood (Coventry, 1958, 43 years, 199 days); Tommy Hutchison (Swansea City, 1991, 43 years, 172 days).

**Oldest Football League debutant:** Andy Cunningham, for Newcastle at Leicester (Div 1) on Feb 2, 1929, aged 38 years, 2 days.

**Oldest post-war debut in English League:** Defender David Donaldson (35 years, 7 months, 23 days) for Wimbledon on entry to Football League (Div 4) away to Halifax, Aug 20, 1977.

**Oldest player to appear in First Division:** Sir Stanley Matthews (Stoke v Fulham, Feb 6, 1965), aged 50 years, 5 days – on that his last League appearance, the only 50-year-old ever to play in the top division.

**Oldest players in Premier League:** Goalkeepers John Burridge (Manchester City v QPR, May 14, 1995), 43 years, 5 months, 11 days; Alec Chamberlain (Watford v Newcastle, May 13, 2007) 42 years, 11 months, 23 days; Steve Ogrizovic (Coventry v Sheffield Wed, May 6, 2000), 42 years, 7 months, 24 days; Brad Friedel (Tottenham v Newcastle, Nov 10, 2013) 42 years, 4 months, 22 days; Neville Southall (Bradford City v Leeds, Mar 12, 2000), 41 years, 5 months, 26 days. Outfield: Teddy Sheringham (West Ham v Manchester City, Dec 30, 2006), 40 years, 8 months, 28 days; Ryan Giggs (Manchester Utd v Hull, May 6, 2014), 40 years, 5 months, 7 days; Gordon Strachan (Coventry City v Derby, May 3, 1997), 40 years, 2 months, 24 days.

**Oldest player for British professional club:** John Ryan (owner-chairman of Conference club Doncaster, played as substitute for last minute in 4-2 win at Hereford on Apr 26, 2003), aged 52 years, 11 months, 3 weeks.

**Oldest FA Cup Final player:** Walter (Billy) Hampson (Newcastle v Aston Villa on Apr 26, 1924), aged 41 years, 257 days.

**Oldest captain and goalkeeper in FA Cup Final:** David James (Portsmouth v Chelsea, May 15, 2010) aged 39 years, 287 days.

**Oldest FA Cup Final scorers:** Bert Turner (Charlton v Derby, Apr 27, 1946) aged 36 years, 312 days. Scored for both sides. Teddy Sheringham (West Ham v Liverpool, May 13, 2006) aged 40 years, 41 days. Scored in penalty shoot-out.

**Oldest FA Cup-winning team:** Arsenal 1950 (average age 31 years, 2 months). Eight of the players were over 30, with the three oldest centre-half Leslie Compton 37, and skipper Joe Mercer and goalkeeper George Swindin, both 35.

**Oldest World Cup-winning captain:** Dino Zoff, Italy's goalkeeper v W Germany in 1982 Final, aged 40 years, 92 days.

**Oldest player capped by England:** Stanley Matthews (v Denmark, Copenhagen, May 15, 1957), aged 42 years, 103 days.

**Oldest England scorer:** Stanley Matthews (v N Ireland, Belfast, Oct 6, 1956), aged 41 years, 248 days.

**Oldest British international player:** Billy Meredith (Wales v England at Highbury, Mar 15, 1920), aged 45 years, 229 days.

**Oldest 'new caps':** Goalkeeper Alexander Morten, aged 41 years, 113 days when earning his only England Cap against Scotland on Mar 8, 1873; Arsenal centre-half Leslie Compton, at 38 years, 64 days when he made his England debut in 4-2 win against Wales at Sunderland on Nov 15, 1950. **For Scotland:** Goalkeeper Ronnie Simpson (Celtic) at 36 years, 186 days v England at Wembley, Apr 15, 1967.

**Oldest scorer in Wembley Final**: Chris Swailes, 45, for Morpeth in 4-1 win over Hereford (FA Vase), May 22, 2016.

**Longest Football League career:** This spanned 32 years and 10 months, by Stanley Matthews (Stoke, Blackpool, Stoke) from Mar 19, 1932 until Feb 6, 1965.

**Shortest FA Cup-winning captain:** 5ft 4in – Bobby Kerr (Sunderland v Leeds, 1973).

## KANTE'S PEAK

**N'Golo Kante** became the first player in English football to win back-to-back titles with different clubs while playing a full season with each – Leicester (2015-16), Chelsea (2016–17).

## SHIRT NUMBERING

**Numbering players** in Football League matches was made compulsory in 1939. Players wore numbered shirts (1-22) in the FA Cup Final as an experiment in 1933 (Everton 1-11 v Manchester City 12-22).

**Squad numbers** for players were introduced by the Premier League at the start of season 1993–94. They were optional in the Football League until made compulsory in 1999–2000.

**Names on shirts:** For first time, players wore names as well as numbers on shirts in League Cup and FA Cup Finals, 1993.

## SUBSTITUTES

In **1965**, the Football League, by 39 votes to 10, agreed that **one substitute** be allowed for an injured player at any time during a League match. First substitute used in Football League: Keith Peacock (Charlton), away to Bolton in Div 2, Aug 21, 1965.

**Two substitutes** per team were approved for the League (Littlewoods) Cup and FA Cup in season 1986–87 and two were permitted in the Football League for the first time in 1987–88.

**Three substitutes** (one a goalkeeper), two of which could be used, introduced by the Premier League for 1992–93. The Football League followed suit for 1993–94.

**Three substitutes** (one a goalkeeper) were allowed at the World Cup Finals for the first time at US '94.

**Three substitutes** (any position) introduced by Premier League and Football League in 1995–96.

**Five named substitutes** (three of which could be used) introduced in Premier League in 1996–97, in FA Cup in 1997–98, League Cup in 1998–99 and Football League in 1999–2000.

**Seven named substitutes for** Premier League, FA Cup and League Cup in 2008–09. Still only three to be used. Football League adopted this rule for 2009–10, reverted to five in 2011–12 and went back to seven for the 2012–13 season.

**First substitute to score in FA Cup Final:** Eddie Kelly (Arsenal v Liverpool, 1971). The **first recorded use** of a substitute was in 1889 (Wales v Scotland at Wrexham on Apr 15) when Sam Gillam arrived late – although he was a Wrexham player – and Allen Pugh (Rhostellyn) was allowed to keep goal until he turned up. The match ended 0-0.

When **Dickie Roose**, the Welsh goalkeeper, was injured against England at Wrexham, Mar 16, 1908, **Dai Davies** (Bolton) was allowed to take his place as substitute. Thus Wales used 12 players. England won 7-1.

## END OF WAGE LIMIT

**Freedom from the maximum wage system** – in force since the formation of the Football League in 1888 – was secured by the Professional Footballers' Association in 1961. About this time Italian clubs renewed overtures for the transfer of British stars and Fulham's **Johnny Haynes** became the first British player to earn £100 a week.

## THE BOSMAN RULING

On Dec 15, 1995 the **European Court of Justice** ruled that clubs had no right to transfer fees for out-of-contract players, and the outcome of the 'Bosman case' irrevocably changed football's player-club relationship. It began in 1990, when the contract of 26-year-old **Jean-Marc Bosman**, a midfield player with FC Liege, Belgium, expired. French club Dunkirk wanted him but were unwilling to pay the £500,000 transfer fee, so Bosman was compelled to remain with Liege. He responded with a lawsuit against his club and UEFA on the grounds of 'restriction of trade', and after five years at various court levels the European Court of Justice ruled not only in favour of Bosman but of all professional footballers.

The end of restrictive labour practices revolutionised the system. It led to a proliferation of transfers, rocketed the salaries of elite players who, backed by an increasing army of agents, found themselves in a vastly improved bargaining position as they moved from team to team, league to league, nation to nation. Removing the limit on the number of foreigners clubs could field brought an increasing ratio of such signings, not least in England and Scotland.

Bosman's one-man stand opened the way for footballers to become millionaires, but ended his own career. All he received for his legal conflict was 16 million Belgian francs (£312,000) in compensation, a testimonial of poor reward and martyrdom as the man who did most to change the face of football.

By 2011, he was living on Belgian state benefits, saying: 'I have made the world of football rich and shifted the power from clubs to players. Now I find myself with nothing.'

## INTERNATIONAL SHOCK RESULTS

**1950** USA 1 England 0 (World Cup).
**1953** England 3 Hungary 6 (friendly).
**1954** Hungary 7 England 1 ( friendly)

**1966** North Korea 1 Italy 0 (World Cup).
**1982** Spain 0, Northern Ireland 1; Algeria 2, West Germany 1 (World Cup).
**1990** Cameroon 1 Argentina 0; Scotland 0 Costa Rica 1; Sweden 1 Costa Rica 2 (World Cup).
**1990** Faroe Islands 1 Austria 0 (European Champ qual).
**1992** Denmark 2 Germany 0 (European Champ Final).
**1993** USA 2 England 0 (US Cup tournament).
**1993** Argentina 0 Colombia 5 (World Cup qual).
**1993** France 2 Israel 3 (World Cup qual).
**1994** Bulgaria 2 Germany 1 (World Cup).
**1994** Moldova 3 Wales 2; Georgia 5 Wales 0 (European Champ qual).
**1995** Belarus 1 Holland 0 (European Champ qual).
**1996** Nigeria 4 Brazil 3 (Olympics).
**1998** USA 1 Brazil 0 (Concacaf Gold Cup).
**1998** Croatia 3 Germany 0 (World Cup).
**2000** Scotland 0 Australia 2 (friendly).
**2001** Australia 1 France 0; Australia 1, Brazil 0 (Confederations Cup).
**2001** Honduras 2 Brazil 0 (Copa America).
**2001** Germany 1 England 5 (World Cup qual).
**2002** France 0 Senegal 1; South Korea 2 Italy 1 (World Cup).
**2003:** England 1 Australia 3 (friendly)
**2004:** Portugal 0 Greece 1 (European Champ Final).
**2005:** Northern Ireland 1 England 0 (World Cup qual).
**2014:** Holland 5 Spain 1 (World Cup).
**2014:** Brazil 1 Germany 7 (World Cup).
**2016** England 1 Iceland 2 (European Champ)
**2018** South Korea 2 Germany 0 (World Cup)

## GREAT RECOVERIES – DOMESTIC FOOTBALL

On Dec 21, 1957, **Charlton** were losing 5-1 against Huddersfield (Div 2) at The Valley with only 28 minutes left, and from the 15th minute, had been reduced to ten men by injury, but they won 7-6, with left-winger Johnny Summers scoring five goals. **Huddersfield** (managed by Bill Shankly) remain the only team to score six times in a League match and lose. On Boxing Day, 1927 in Div 3 South, **Northampton** won 6-5 at home to Luton after being 1-5 down at half-time.
Season 2010–11 produced a Premier League record for **Newcastle**, who came from 4-0 down at home to Arsenal to draw 4-4. Previous instance of a team retrieving a four-goal deficit in the top division to draw was in 1984 when Newcastle trailed at QPR in a game which ended 5-5.
In the 2012-13 League Cup, **Arsenal** were 0-4 down in a fourth round tie at Reading, levelled at 4-4 and went on to win 7-5 in extra-time.

## MATCHES OFF

**Worst day for postponements:** Feb 9, 1963, when 57 League fixtures in England and Scotland were frozen off. Only 7 Football League matches took place, and the entire Scottish programme was wiped out.
**Other weather-hit days:**
Jan 12, 1963 and Feb 2, 1963 – on both those Saturdays, only 4 out of 44 Football League matches were played.
Jan 1, 1979 – 43 out of 46 Football League fixtures postponed.
Jan 17, 1987 – 37 of 45 scheduled Football League fixtures postponed; only 2 Scottish matches survived.
Feb 8–9, 1991 – only 4 of the week-end's 44 Barclays League matches survived the freeze-up (4 of the postponements were on Friday night). In addition, 11 Scottish League matches were off.
Jan 27, 1996 – 44 Cup and League matches in England and Scotland were frozen off.
On the weekend of Jan 9, 10, 11, 2010, 46 League and Cup matches in England and Scotland were victims of the weather. On the weekend of Dec 18-21, 2010, 49 matches were

frozen off in England and Scotland.

**Fewest matches left on one day** by postponements was during the Second World War – Feb 3, 1940 when, because of snow, ice and fog only one out of 56 regional league fixtures took place. It resulted Plymouth Argyle 10, Bristol City 3.

The Scottish Cup second round tie between Inverness Thistle and Falkirk in season 1978–79 was **postponed 29 times** because of snow and ice. First put off on Jan 6, it was eventually played on Feb 22. Falkirk won 4-0.

**Pools Panel's busiest days:** Jan 17, 1987 and Feb 9, 1991 – on both dates they gave their verdict on 48 postponed coupon matches.

## FEWEST 'GAMES OFF'

**Season 1947–48** was the best since the war for English League fixtures being played to schedule. Only six were postponed.

## LONGEST SEASON

**The latest that League football** has been played in a season was **Jun 7, 1947** (six weeks after the FA Cup Final). The season was extended because of mass postponements caused by bad weather in mid-winter.

**The latest the FA Cup competition** has been completed was in season 2014–15 when Arsenal beat Aston Villa 4-0 in the Final on May 30, kick-off 5.30pm

**Worst winter hold-up was in season 1962–63**. The Big Freeze began on Boxing Day and lasted until Mar, with nearly 500 first-class matches postponed. The FA Cup 3rd round was the longest on record – it began with only three out of 32 ties playable on Jan 5 and ended 66 days and 261 postponements later on Mar 11. The Lincoln–Coventry tie was put off 15 times. The Pools Panel was launched that winter, on Jan 26, 1963.

## HOTTEST DAYS

The Nationwide League kicked off season 2003–04 on Aug 9 with pitch temperatures of 102 degrees recorded at Luton v Rushden and Bradford v Norwich. On the following day, there was a pitch temperature of 100 degrees for the Community Shield match between Manchester Utd and Arsenal at Cardiff's Millennium Stadium. Wembley's pitch-side thermometer registered 107 degrees for the 2009 Chelsea–Everton FA Cup Final.

## FOOTBALL LEAGUE NAME CHANGE

From the start of the 2016-17 season, the Football League was renamed the English Football League, as part of a corporate and competition rebranding.

## FOOTBALL ASSOCIATION SECRETARIES/CHIEF EXECUTIVES

**1863–66 Ebenezer Morley**; 1866–68 **Robert Willis**; 1868–70 **RG Graham**; 1870–95 **Charles Alcock** (paid from 1887); 1895–1934 **Sir Frederick Wall**; 1934–62 **Sir Stanley Rous**; 1962–73 **Denis Follows**; 1973–89 **Ted Croker** (latterly chief executive); 1989–99 **Graham Kelly** (chief executive); 2000–02 **Adam Crozier** (chief executive); 2003–04 **Mark Palios** (chief executive); 2005–08: **Brian Barwick** (chief executive); 2009–10 **Ian Watmore** (chief executive); 2010-15 **Alex Horne** (chief executive); 2015 **Martin Glenn** (chief executive).

## FOOTBALL'S SPONSORS

**Football League:** Canon 1983–86; Today Newspaper 1986–87; Barclays 1987–93; Endsleigh Insurance 1993–96; Nationwide Building Society 1996–2004; Coca-Cola 2004–10; npower 2010–14; Sky Bet from 2014.

**League Cup:** Milk Cup 1982–86; Littlewoods 1987–90; Rumbelows 1991–92; Coca-Cola 1993–98; Worthington 1998–2003; Carling 2003–12; Capital One 2012–16; Carabao from 2017.

**Premier League:** Carling 1993–2001; Barclaycard 2001–04; Barclays 2004–16.

**FA Cup:** Littlewoods 1994–98; AXA 1998–2002; E.ON 2006–11; Budweiser 2011–15; Emirates (title sponsor) from 2015.

## NEW HOMES FOR CLUBS

Newly-constructed League grounds in England since the war: 1946 Hull (Boothferry Park); 1950 Port Vale (Vale Park); 1955 Southend (Roots Hall); 1988 Scunthorpe (Glanford Park); 1990 Walsall (Bescot Stadium); 1990 Wycombe (Adams Park); 1992 Chester (Deva Stadium); 1993 Millwall (New Den); 1994 Huddersfield (McAlpine Stadium); 1994 Northampton (Sixfields Stadium); 1995 Middlesbrough (Riverside Stadium); 1997 Bolton (Reebok Stadium); 1997 Derby (Pride Park); 1997 Stoke (Britannia Stadium); 1997 Sunderland (Stadium of Light); 1998 Reading (Madejski Stadium); 1999 Wigan (JJB Stadium); 2001 Southampton (St Mary's Stadium); 2001 Oxford Utd (Kassam Stadium); 2002 Leicester (Walkers Stadium); 2002 Hull (Kingston Communications Stadium); 2003 Manchester City (City of Manchester Stadium); 2003 Darlington (New Stadium); 2005 Coventry (Ricoh Arena); Swansea (Stadium of Swansea, Morfa); 2006 Arsenal (Emirates Stadium); 2007 Milton Keynes Dons (Stadium: MK); Shrewsbury (New Meadow); 2008 Colchester (Community Stadium); 2009 Cardiff City Stadium; 2010 Chesterfield (b2net Stadium), Morecambe (Globe Arena); 2011 Brighton (American Express Stadium); 2012 Rotherham (New York Stadium). 2016 West Ham (Olympic Stadium).

## NATIONAL FOOTBALL CENTRE

The FA's new £120m centre at St George's Park, Burton upon Trent, was opened on Oct 9, 20012 by the Duke of Cambridge, president of the FA. The site covers 330 acres, has 12 full-size pitches (5 with undersoil heating and floodlighting). There are 5 gyms, a 90-seat lecture theatre, a hydrotherapy unit with swimming pool for the treatment of injuries and two hotels. It is the base for England teams, men and women, at all levels.

## GROUND-SHARING

**Manchester Utd** played their home matches at **Manchester City's** Maine Road ground for 8 years after Old Trafford was bomb-damaged in Aug 1941. **Crystal Palace** and **Charlton** shared Selhurst Park (1985–91); **Bristol Rov** and **Bath City** (Twerton Park, Bath, 1986–96); **Partick Thistle** and **Clyde** (Firhill Park, Glasgow, 1986–91; in seasons 1990–01, 1991–92 **Chester** shared **Macclesfield**'s ground (Moss Rose).

**Crystal Palace** and **Wimbledon** shared Selhurst Park, from season 1991–92, when **Charlton** (tenants) moved to rent Upton Park from **West Ham**, until 2003 when Wimbledon relocated to Milton Keynes. **Clyde** moved to Douglas Park, **Hamilton Academical's** home, in 1991–92. **Stirling Albion** shared **Stenhousemuir**'s ground, Ochilview Park, in 1992–93. In 1993–94, **Clyde** shared **Partick**'s home until moving to Cumbernauld. In 1994–95, **Celtic** shared Hampden Park with **Queen's Park** (while Celtic Park was redeveloped); **Hamilton** shared **Partick**'s ground. **Airdrie** shared **Clyde**'s Broadwood Stadium. **Bristol Rov** left **Bath City**'s ground at the start of season 1996–97, sharing Bristol Rugby Club's Memorial Ground. **Clydebank** shared **Dumbarton**'s Boghead Park from 1996–97 until renting **Greenock Morton**'s Cappielow Park in season 1999–2000. **Brighton** shared **Gillingham**'s ground in seasons 1997–98, 1998–99. **Fulham** shared **QPR**'s home at Loftus Road in seasons 2002–03, 2003–04, returning to Craven Cottage in Aug 2004. **Coventry** played home fixtures at Northampton in season 2013–14, returning to their own ground, the Ricoh Arena, in Sept 2014.

**Inverness Caledonian Thistle** moved to share **Aberdeen**'s Pittodrie Stadium in 2004–05 after being promoted to the SPL; **Gretna's** home matches on arrival in the SPL in 2007–08 were held at Motherwell and Livingston. Stenhousemuir (owners) share Ochilview with East Stirling (tenants).

## ARTIFICIAL TURF

**QPR** were the first British club to install an artificial pitch, in 1981. They were followed by **Luton** in 1985, and **Oldham** and **Preston** in **1986**. QPR reverted to grass in 1988, as did Luton and promoted Oldham in season 1991–92 (when artificial pitches were banned in Div 1). **Preston** were the last Football League club playing 'on plastic' in 1993–94, and their Deepdale ground was restored to grass for the start of 1994–95.

**Stirling** were the **first Scottish club** to play on plastic, in season 1987–88.

## DOUBLE RUNNERS-UP

There have been nine instances of clubs finishing runner-up in **both the League Championship** and **FA Cup** in the same season: 1928 Huddersfield; 1932 Arsenal; 1939 Wolves; 1962 Burnley; 1965 and 1970 Leeds; 1986 Everton; 1995 Manchester Utd; 2001 Arsenal.

## CORNER-KICK RECORDS

Not a single corner-kick was recorded when **Newcastle** drew 0-0 at home to **Portsmouth** (Div 1) on Dec 5, 1931.

The record for **most corners** in a match for one side is believed to be **Sheffield Utd's 28** to **West Ham's 1** in Div 2 at Bramall Lane on Oct 14, 1989. For all their pressure, Sheffield Utd lost 2-0.

**Nottm Forest** led **Southampton** 22-2 on corners (Premier League, Nov 28, 1992) but lost the match 1-2.

**Tommy Higginson** (Brentford, 1960s) once passed back to his own goalkeeper from a corner kick.

When **Wigan** won 4-0 at home to Cardiff (Div 2) on Feb 16, 2002, all four goals were headed in from corners taken by N Ireland international **Peter Kennedy**.

**Steve Staunton** (Rep of Ireland) is believed to be the only player to score direct from a corner in **two** Internationals.

In the 2012 Champions League Final, **Bayern Munich** forced 20 corners without scoring, while **Chelsea** scored from their only one.

## SACKED AT HALF-TIME

**Leyton Orient** sacked **Terry Howard** on his 397th appearance for the club – at half-time in a Second Division home defeat against Blackpool (Feb 7, 1995) for 'an unacceptable performance'. He was fined two weeks' wages, given a free transfer and moved to Wycombe.

Bobby Gould resigned as **Peterborough**'s head coach at half-time in their 1-0 defeat in the LDV Vans Trophy 1st round at Bristol City on Sep 29, 2004.

**Harald Schumacher**, former Germany goalkeeper, was sacked as Fortuna Koln coach when they were two down at half-time against Waldhof Mannheim (Dec 15, 1999). They lost 5-1.

## MOST GAMES BY 'KEEPER FOR ONE CLUB

**Alan Knight** made 683 League appearances for Portsmouth, over 23 seasons (1978–2000), a record for a goalkeeper at one club. The previous holder was Peter Bonetti with 600 League games for Chelsea (20 seasons, 1960–79).

## PLAYED TWO GAMES ON SAME DAY

**Jack Kelsey** played full-length matches for both club and country on Wednesday Nov 26, 1958. In the afternoon he kept goal for Wales in a 2-2 draw against England at Villa Park, and he then drove to Highbury to help Arsenal win 3-1 in a prestigious floodlit friendly against Juventus.

On the same day, winger **Danny Clapton** played for England (against Wales and Kelsey) and then in part of Arsenal's match against Juventus.

On Nov 11, 1987, **Mark Hughes** played for Wales against Czechoslovakia (European Championship) in Prague, then flew to Munich and went on as substitute that night in a winning Bayern Munich team, to whom he was on loan from Barcelona.

On Feb 16, 1993 goalkeeper **Scott Howie** played in Scotland's 3-0 U-21 win v Malta at Tannadice Park, Dundee (ko 1.30pm) and the same evening played in Clyde's 2-1 home win v Queen of South (Div 2).

Ryman League **Hornchurch**, faced by end-of-season fixture congestion, played **two matches** on the same night (May 1, 2001). They lost 2-1 at home to Ware and drew 2-2 at Clapton.

## RECORD LOSS

**Manchester City** made a record loss of £194.9m in the 2010–11 financial year.

## FIRST 'MATCH OF THE DAY'

**BBC TV (recorded highlights):** Liverpool 3, Arsenal 2 on Aug 22, 1964. **First complete match to be televised:** Arsenal 3, Everton 2 on Aug 29, 1936. **First League match televised in colour:** Liverpool 2, West Ham 0 on Nov 15, 1969.

## 'MATCH OF THE DAY' – BIGGEST SCORES

**Football League:** Tottenham 9, Bristol Rov 0 (Div 2, 1977–78). **Premier League:** Nottm Forest 1, Manchester Utd 8 (1998–99); Portsmouth 7 Reading 4 (2007–08).

## FIRST COMMENTARY ON RADIO

**Arsenal 1 Sheffield Utd 1** (Div 1) broadcast on BBC, Jan 22, 1927.

## OLYMPIC FOOTBALL WINNERS

**1908** Great Britain (in London); **1912** Great Britain (Stockholm); **1920** Belgium (Antwerp); **1924** Uruguay (Paris); **1928** Uruguay (Amsterdam); **1932** No soccer in Los Angeles Olympics; **1936** Italy (Berlin); **1948** Sweden (London); **1952** Hungary (Helsinki); **1956** USSR (Melbourne); **1960** Yugoslavia (Rome); **1964** Hungary (Tokyo); **1968** Hungary (Mexico City); **1972** Poland (Munich); **1976** E Germany (Montreal); **1980** Czechoslovakia (Moscow); **1984** France (Los Angeles); **1988** USSR (Seoul); **1992** Spain (Barcelona); **1996** Nigeria (Atlanta); **2000** Cameroon (Sydney); **2004** Argentina (Athens); **2008** Argentina (Beijing); **2012** Mexico (Wembley); **2016** Brazil (Rio de Janeiro).

**Highest scorer in Final tournament:** Ferenc Bene (Hungary) 12 goals, 1964.

**Record crowd for Olympic Soccer Final:** 108,800 (France v Brazil, Los Angeles 1984).

## MOST AMATEUR CUP WINS

**Bishop Auckland** set the FA Amateur Cup record with 10 wins, and in 1957 became the only club to carry off the trophy in three successive seasons. The competition was discontinued after the Final on Apr 20, 1974. (Bishop's Stortford 4, Ilford 1, at Wembley).

## FOOTBALL FOUNDATION

This was formed (May 2000) to replace the **Football Trust**, which had been in existence since 1975 as an initiative of the Pools companies to provide financial support at all levels, from schools football to safety and ground improvement work throughout the game.

## SEVEN-FIGURE TESTIMONIALS

The first was **Sir Alex Ferguson**'s at Old Trafford on Oct 11, 1999, when a full-house of 54,842 saw a Rest of the World team beat Manchester Utd 4-2. United's manager pledged that a large percentage of the estimated £1m receipts would go to charity.

Estimated receipts of £1m and over came from testimonials for **Denis Irwin** (Manchester Utd) against Manchester City at Old Trafford on Aug 16, 2000 (45,158); **Tom Boyd** (Celtic) against Manchester Utd at Celtic Park on May 15, 2001 (57,000) and **Ryan Giggs** (Manchester Utd) against Celtic on Aug 1, 2001 (66,967).

**Tony Adams**' second testimonial (1-1 v Celtic on May 13, 2002) two nights after Arsenal completed the Double, was watched by 38,021 spectators at Highbury. Of £1m receipts, he donated £500,000 to Sporting Chance, the charity that helps sportsmen/women with drink, drug, gambling problems.

Sunderland and a Republic of Ireland XI drew 0-0 in front of 35,702 at the Stadium of Light on May 14, 2002. The beneficiary, **Niall Quinn**, donated his testimonial proceeds, estimated at £1m, to children's hospitals in Sunderland and Dublin, and to homeless children in Africa and Asia.

A record testimonial crowd of 69,591 for **Roy Keane** at Old Trafford on May 9, 2006 netted more than £2m for charities in Dublin, Cork and Manchester. Manchester Utd beat Celtic 1-0, with Keane playing for both teams.

**Alan Shearer**'s testimonial on May 11, 2006, watched by a crowd of 52,275 at St James' Park, raised more than £1m. The club's record scorer, in his farewell match, came off the bench in stoppage time to score the penalty that gave Newcastle a 3-2 win over Celtic. Total proceeds from his testimonial events, £1.64m, were donated to 14 charities in the north-east.

**Ole Gunnar Solskjaer**, who retired after 12 years as a Manchester Utd player, had a crowd of 68,868, for his testimonial on Aug 2, 2008 (United 1 Espanyol 0). He donated the estimated receipts of £2m to charity, including the opening of a dozen schools In Africa.

Liverpool's **Jamie Carragher** had his testimonial against Everton (4-1) on Sep 4, 2010. It was watched by a crowd of 35,631 and raised an estimated £1m for his foundation, which supports community projects on Merseyside.

**Gary Neville** donated receipts of around £1m from his testimonial against Juventus (2-1) in front of 42,000 on May 24, 2011, to charities and building a Supporters' Centre near Old Trafford.

**Paul Scholes** had a crowd of 75,000 for his testimonial, Manchester United against New York Cosmos, on Aug 5, 2011. Receipts were £1.5m.

**Steven Gerrard**, Liverpool captain, donated £500,000 from his testimonial to the local Alder Hey Children's Hospital after a match against Olympiacos was watched by a crowd of 44,362 on Aug 3, 2013. Gerrard chose the Greek champions because he scored a special goal against them in the season Liverpool won the 2005 Champions League.

**Wayne Rooney**'s match against Everton on Aug 3, 2016, raised £1.2m, which the Manchester United captain donated to local children's charities.

## WHAT IT USED TO COST

**Minimum admission** to League football was one shilling in 1939 After the war, it was increased to 1s 3d in 1946; 1s 6d in 1951; 1s 9d in 1952; 2s in 1955; 2s 6d; in 1960; 4s in 1965; 5s in 1968; 6s in 1970; and 8s (40p) in 1972 After that, the fixed minimum charge was dropped.

Wembley's first Cup Final programme in 1923 cost three pence (1¼p in today's money). The programme for the 'farewell' FA Cup Final in May, 2000 was priced £10.

FA Cup Final ticket prices in 2011 reached record levels – £115, £85, £65 and £45.

## WHAT THEY USED TO EARN

In the 1930s, First Division players were on £8 a week (£6 in close season) plus bonuses of £2 win, £1 draw. The maximum wage went up to £12 when football resumed post-war in 1946 and had reached £20 by the time the limit was abolished in 1961.

## EUROPEAN TROPHY WINNERS

**European Cup/Champions League: 13** Real Madrid; **7** AC Milan; **5** Liverpool, Barcelona, Bayern Munich; **4** Ajax; **3** Inter Milan, Manchester Utd; **2** Benfica, Juventus, Nottm Forest, Porto; **1** Aston Villa, Borussia Dortmund, Celtic, Chelsea, Feyenoord, Hamburg, Marseille, PSV Eindhoven, Red Star Belgrade, Steaua Bucharest

**Cup-Winners' Cup: 4** Barcelona; **2** Anderlecht, Chelsea, Dynamo Kiev, AC Milan; **1** Aberdeen, Ajax, Arsenal, Atletico Madrid, Bayern Munich, Borussia Dortmund, Dynamo Tbilisi, Everton, Fiorentina, Hamburg, Juventus, Lazio, Magdeburg, Manchester City, Manchester Utd, Mechelen, Paris St Germain, Parma, Rangers, Real Zaragoza, Sampdoria, Slovan Bratislava, Sporting Lisbon, Tottenham, Valencia, Werder Bremen, West Ham.

**UEFA Cup: 3** Barcelona, Inter Milan, Juventus, Liverpool, Valencia; **2** Borussia Moenchengladbach, Feyenoord, Gothenburg, Leeds, Parma, Real Madrid, Sevilla, Tottenham; **1** Anderlecht, Ajax, Arsenal, Bayer Leverkusen, Bayern Munich, CSKA Moscow, Dynamo Zagreb, Eintracht Frankfurt, Ferencvaros, Galatasaray, Ipswich, Napoli, Newcastle, Porto, PSV Eindhoven, Real Zaragoza, Roma, Schalke, Shakhtar Donetsk, Zenit St Petersburg.

**Europa League: 3** Sevilla, Atletico Madrid; **1** Chelsea, Manchester Utd, Porto.

- The Champions League was introduced into the European Cup in 1992–93 to counter the threat of a European Super League. The UEFA Cup became the Europa League, with a new format, in season 2009–10.

## BRITAIN'S 35 TROPHIES IN EUROPE

| Euro Cup/Champs Lge (13) | Cup-Winners' Cup (10) | Fairs/UEFA Cup/Europa Lge (12) |
|---|---|---|

| | | |
|---|---|---|
| 1967 Celtic | 1963 Tottenham | 1968 Leeds |
| 1968 Manchester Utd | 1965 West Ham | 1969 Newcastle |
| 1977 Liverpool | 1970 Manchester City | 1970 Arsenal |
| 1978 Liverpool | 1971 Chelsea | 1971 Leeds |
| 1979 Nottm Forest | 1972 Rangers | 1972 Tottenham |
| 1980 Nottm Forest | 1983 Aberdeen | 1973 Liverpool |
| 1981 Liverpool | 1985 Everton | 1976 Liverpool |
| 1982 Aston Villa | 1991 Manchester Utd | 1981 Ipswich |
| 1984 Liverpool | 1994 Arsenal | 1984 Tottenham |
| 1999 Manchester Utd | 1998 Chelsea | 2001 Liverpool |
| 2005 Liverpool | | 2013 Chelsea |
| 2008 Manchester Utd | | 2017 Manchester Utd |
| 2012 Chelsea | | |

## ENGLAND'S EUROPEAN RECORD

Manchester Utd, Chelsea, Arsenal and Liverpool all reached the Champions League quarter-finals in season 2007–08 – the first time one country had provided four of the last eight. For the first time, England supplied both finalists in 2008 (Manchester Utd and Chelsea) and have provided three semi-finalists in 2007–08–09).

## END OF CUP-WINNERS' CUP

The **European Cup-Winners' Cup**, inaugurated in 1960–61, terminated with the 1999 Final. The competition merged into a revamped **UEFA Cup**.

From its inception in 1955, the **European Cup** comprised only championship-winning clubs until 1998–99, when selected runners-up were introduced. Further expansion came in 1999–2000 with the inclusion of clubs finishing third in certain leagues and fourth in 2002.

## EUROPEAN CLUB COMPETITIONS – SCORING RECORDS

**European Cup – record aggregate:** 18-0 by Benfica v Dudelange (Lux) (8-0a, 10-0h), prelim rd, 1965–66.

**Record single-match score:** 11-0 by Dinamo Bucharest v Crusaders (rd 1, 2nd leg, 1973-74 (agg 12-0).

**Champions League – record single-match score:** Liverpool 8-0 v Besiktas, Group A qual (Nov 6, 2007).

**Highest match aggregate:** 13 – Bayern Munich 12 Sporting Lisbon 1 (5-0 away, 7-1 at home, 1st ko rd, 2008–09)

**Cup-Winners' Cup – *record aggregate:** 21-0 by Chelsea v Jeunesse Hautcharage (Lux) (8-0a, 13-0h), 1st rd, 1971–72.

**Record single-match score:** 16-1 by Sporting Lisbon v Apoel Nicosia, 2nd round, 1st leg, 1963–64 (aggregate was 18-1).

**UEFA Cup (prev Fairs Cup) – *Record aggregate:** 21-0 by Feyenoord v US Rumelange (Lux) (9-0h, 12-0a), 1st round, 1972–73.

**Record single-match score:** 14-0 by Ajax Amsterdam v Red Boys (Lux) 1st rd, 2nd leg, 1984–85 (aggregate also 14-0).

**Record British score in Europe:** 13-0 by **Chelsea** at home to Jeunesse Hautcharage (Lux) in Cup-Winners' Cup 1st round, 2nd leg, 1971–72. Chelsea's overall 21-0 win in that tie is highest aggregate by British club in Europe.

**Individual scoring record for European tie (over two legs): 10 goals** (6 home, 4 away) by **Kiril Milanov** for Levski Spartak in 19-3 agg win Cup-Winners' Cup 1st round v Lahden Reipas, 1976–77. Next highest: **8 goals** by **Jose Altafini** for AC Milan v US Luxembourg (European Cup, prelim round, 1962–63, agg 14-0) and by **Peter Osgood** for Chelsea v Jeunesse Hautcharage (Cup-Winners' Cup, 1st round 1971–72, agg 21-0). Altafini and Osgood each scored 5 goals at home, 3 away.

**Individual single-match scoring record** in European competition: **6** by **Mascarenhas** for Sporting Lisbon in 16-1 Cup-Winner's Cup 2nd round, 1st leg win v Apoel, 1963–64; and by **Lothar**

**Emmerich** for Borussia Dortmund in 8-0 CWC 1st round, 2nd leg win v Floriana 1965–66; and by **Kiril Milanov** for Levski Spartak in 12-2 CWC 1st round, 1st leg win v Lahden Reipas, 1976–77.

**Most goals in single European campaign: 15** by **Jurgen Klinsmann** for Bayern Munich (UEFA Cup 1995–96).

**Most goals by British player in European competition: 30** by **Peter Lorimer** (Leeds, in 9 campaigns).

**Most individual goals in Champions League match: 5** by **Lionel Messi** (Barcelona) in 7-1 win at home to Bayer Leverkusen in round of 16 second leg, 2011–12.

**Most European Cup goals by individual player: 49** by **Alfredo di Stefano** in 58 apps for Real Madrid (1955–64).

(*Joint record European aggregate)

**First European treble: Clarence Seedorf** became the first player to win the European Cup with three clubs: Ajax in 1995, Real Madrid in 1998 and AC Milan in 2003.

## EUROPEAN FOOTBALL – BIG RECOVERIES

In the most astonishing Final in the history of the European Cup/Champions League, **Liverpool** became the first club to win it from a 3-0 deficit when they beat AC Milan 3-2 on penalties after a 3-3 draw in Istanbul on May 25, 2005. Liverpool's fifth triumph in the competition meant that they would keep the trophy.

The following season, **Middlesbrough** twice recovered from three-goal aggregate deficits in the **UEFA Cup**, beating Basel 4-3 in the quarter finals and Steaua Bucharest by the same scoreline in the semi-finals. In 2010, **Fulham** beat Juventus 5-4 after trailing 1-4 on aggregate in the second leg of their Europa League, Round of 16 match at Craven Cottage.

Two Scottish clubs have won a European tie from a 3-goal, first leg deficit: **Kilmarnock** 0-3, 5-1 v Eintracht Frankfurt (Fairs Cup 1st round, 1964–65); **Hibernian** 1-4, 5-0 v Napoli (Fairs Cup 2nd Round, 1967–68).

English clubs have three times gone out of the **UEFA Cup** after leading 3-0 from the first leg: 1975–76 (2nd Rd) **Ipswich** lost 3-4 on agg to Bruges; 1976–77 (quarter-final) **QPR** lost on penalties to AEK Athens after 3-3 agg; 1977–78 (3rd round) **Ipswich** lost on penalties to Barcelona after 3-3 agg.

On Oct 16, 2012, Sweden recovered from 0-4 down to draw 4-4 with Germany (World Cup qual) in Berlin.

- In the **1966 World Cup quarter-final** (Jul 23) at Goodison Park, North Korea led Portugal 3-0, but Eusebio scored 4 times to give **Portugal** a 5-3 win.

## RONALDO'S EURO CENTURY

**Cristiano Ronaldo** became the first player to reach a century of goals in European club competitions when scoring twice for Real Madrid away to Bayern Munich on Apr 12, 2017. He reached the hundred in 143 matches (84 for Real, 16 for Manchester Utd) in the Champions League (97), UEFA Super Cup (2) and Champions League qualifying round (1).

## RECORD COMEBACK

The greatest turnaround in Champions League history took place in a round of 16 match on Mar 8, 2017. **Barcelona**, 0-4 down to Paris St Germain, won the return leg 6-1, scoring three goals in the last seven minutes.

## HEAVIEST ENGLISH-CLUB DEFEATS IN EUROPE

(Single-leg scores)

**Champions League**: Porto 5 Leicester 0 (group, Dec 6, 2016)

**European Cup:** Artmedia Bratislava 5, **Celtic** 0 (2nd qual round), Jul 2005 (agg 5-4); Ajax 5, **Liverpool** 1 (2nd round), Dec 1966 (agg 7-3); Real Madrid 5, **Derby** 1 (2nd round), Nov 1975 (agg 6-5).

**Cup-Winners' Cup:** Sporting Lisbon 5, **Manchester Utd** 0 (quarter-final), Mar 1964 (agg 6-4).

**Fairs/UEFA Cup:** Bayern Munich 6, **Coventry** 1 (2nd round), Oct 1970 (agg 7-3). **Combined London** team lost 6-0 (agg 8-2) in first Fairs Cup Final in 1958. Barcelona 5, **Chelsea** 0 in Fairs Cup semi-final play-off, 1966, in Barcelona (after 2-2 agg).

## SHOCK ENGLISH CLUB DEFEATS

**1968–69** (Eur Cup, 1st round): **Manchester City** beaten by Fenerbahce, 1-2 agg.
**1971–72** (CWC, 2nd round): **Chelsea** beaten by Atvidaberg on away goals.
**1993–94** (Eur Cup, 2nd round): **Manchester Utd** beaten by Galatasaray on away goals.
**1994–95** (UEFA Cup, 1st round): **Blackburn** beaten by Trelleborgs, 2-3 agg.
**2000–01** (UEFA Cup, 1st round): **Chelsea** beaten by St Gallen, Switz 1-2 agg.

## PFA FAIR PLAY AWARD (Bobby Moore Trophy from 1993)

| | | | |
|---|---|---|---|
| 1988 | Liverpool | 2003 | Crewe |
| 1989 | Liverpool | 2004 | Crewe |
| 1990 | Liverpool | 2005 | Crewe |
| 1991 | Nottm Forest | 2006 | Crewe |
| 1992 | Portsmouth | 2007 | Crewe |
| 1993 | Norwich | 2008 | Crewe |
| 1994 | Crewe | 2009 | Stockport |
| 1995 | Crewe | 2010 | Rochdale |
| 1996 | Crewe | 2011 | Rochdale |
| 1997 | Crewe | 2012 | Chesterfield |
| 1998 | Cambridge Utd | 2013 | Crewe |
| 1999 | Grimsby | 2014 | Exeter |
| 2000 | Crewe | 2015 | Exeter |
| 2001 | Hull | 2016 | Walsall |
| 2002 | Crewe | 2017 | Bradford City |

## RECORD MEDAL SALES

At Sotherby's in London on Nov 11, 2014, the FA Cup winner's medal which **Sir Stanley Matthews** earned with Blackpool in 1953 was sold for £220,000 – the most expensive medal in British sporting history. At the same auction, **Ray Wilson's** 1966 World Cup winner's medal fetched £136,000, while **Jimmy Greaves**, who was left out of the winning England team, received £44,000 for the medal the FA belatedly awarded him in 2009

**West Ham** bought (Jun 2000) the late **Bobby Moore**'s collection of medals and trophies for £1.8m at Christie's auction. It was put up for sale by his first wife Tina and included his World Cup-winner's medal.

A No. 6 duplicate red shirt made for England captain **Bobby Moore** for the 1966 World Cup Final fetched £44,000 at an auction at Wolves' ground in Sep, 1999. Moore kept the shirt he wore in that Final and gave the replica to England physio Harold Shepherdson.

**Sir Geoff Hurst**'s 1966 World Cup-winning shirt fetched a record £91,750 at Christie's in Sep, 2000. His World Cup Final cap fetched £37,600 and his Man of the Match trophy £18,800. Proceeds totalling £274,410 from the 129 lots went to Hurst's three daughters and charities of his choice, including the Bobby Moore Imperial Cancer Research Fund.

In Aug, 2001, Sir Geoff sold his World Cup-winner's medal to his former club West Ham Utd (for their museum) at a reported £150,000.

'The **Billy Wright** Collection' – caps, medals and other memorabilia from his illustrious career – fetched over £100,000 at Christie's in Nov, 1996.

At the sale in Oct 1993, trophies, caps and medals earned by **Ray Kennedy**, former England, Arsenal and Liverpool player, fetched a then record total of £88,407. Kennedy, suffering from Parkinson's Disease, received £73,000 after commission. The PFA paid £31,080 for a total of 60 lots – including a record £16,000 for his 1977 European Cup winner's medal – to be exhibited at their Manchester museum. An anonymous English collector paid £17,000 for the medal and plaque commemorating Kennedy's part in the Arsenal Double in 1971.

Previous record for one player's medals, shirts etc collection: £30,000 (**Bill Foulkes**, Manchester Utd in 1992). The sale of **Dixie Dean**'s medals etc in 1991 realised £28,000.

In Mar, 2001, **Gordon Banks**' 1966 World Cup-winner's medal fetched a new record £124,750. TV's Nick Hancock, a Stoke fan, paid £23,500 for **Sir Stanley Matthews's** 1953 FA Cup-winner's medal. He also bought one of Matthews's England caps for £3,525 and paid £2,350 for a Stoke Div 2 Championship medal (1963).

**Dave Mackay's** 1961 League Championship and FA Cup winner's medals sold for £18,000 at Sotherby's. Tottenham bought them for their museum.

A selection of England World Cup-winning manager **Sir Alf Ramsey**'s memorabilia – England caps, championship medals with Ipswich etc. – fetched more than £80,000 at Christie's. They were offered for sale by his family, and his former clubs Tottenham and Ipswich were among the buyers.

**Ray Wilson**'s 1966 England World Cup-winning shirt fetched £80,750. Also in Mar, 2002, the No. 10 shirt worn by **Pele** in Brazil's World Cup triumph in 1970 was sold for a record £157,750 at Christies. It went to an anonymous telephone bidder.

In Oct, 2003, **George Best**'s European Footballer of the Year (1968) trophy was sold to an anonymous British bidder for £167,250 at Bonham's. It was the then most expensive item of sporting memorabilia ever auctioned in Britain.

England captain **Bobby Moore**'s 1970 World Cup shirt, which he swapped with Pele after Brazil's 1-0 win in Mexico, was sold for £60,000 at Christie's in Mar, 2004.

Sep, 2004: England shirt worn by tearful **Paul Gascoigne** in 1990 World Cup semi-final v Germany sold at Christie's for £28,680. At same auction, shirt worn by Brazil's **Pele** in 1958 World Cup Final in Sweden sold for £70,505.

May, 2005: The **second FA Cup** (which was presented to winning teams from 1896 to 1909) was bought for £420,000 at Christie's by Birmingham chairman David Gold, a world record for an item of football memorabilia. It was presented to the National Football Museum, Preston. At the same auction, the World Cup-winner's medal earned by England's **Alan Ball** in 1966 was sold for £164,800.

Oct, 2005: At auction at Bonham's, the medals and other memorabilia of Hungary and Real Madrid legend **Ferenc Puskas** were sold for £85,000 to help pay for hospital treatment.

Nov, 2006: A ball used in the 2006 World Cup Final and signed by the winning **Italy** team was sold for £1.2m (a world record for football memorabilia) at a charity auction in Qatar. It was bought by the Qatar Sports Academy.

Feb, 2010: A pair of boots worn by **Sir Stanley Matthews** in the 1953 FA Cup Final was sold at Bonham's for £38,400.

Oct, 2010: Trophies and memorabilia belonging to **George Best** were sold at Bonham's for £193,440. His 1968 European Cup winner's medal fetched £156,000.

Oct–Nov 2010: **Nobby Stiles** sold his 1966 World Cup winner's medal at an Edinburgh auction for a record £188,200. His old club, Manchester Utd, also paid £48,300 for his 1968 European Cup medal to go to the club's museum at Old Trafford. In London, the shirt worn by Stiles in the 1966 World Cup Final went for £75,000. A total of 45 items netted £424,438. **George Cohen** and **Martin Peters** had previously sold their medals from 1966.

Oct 2011: **Terry Paine** (who did not play in the Final) sold his 1966 World Cup medal for £27,500 at auction.

Mar 2013: **Norman Hunter** (Leeds and England) sold his honours' collection on line for nearly £100,000

Nov 2013: A collection of **Nat Lofthouse's** career memorabilia was sold at auction for £100,000. Bolton Council paid £75,000 for items including his 1958 FA Cup winner's medal to go on show at the local museum.

## LONGEST UNBEATEN CUP RUN

**Liverpool** established the longest unbeaten Cup sequence by a Football League club: 25 successive rounds in the League/Milk Cup between semi-final defeat by Nottm Forest (1-2 agg) in 1980 and defeat at Tottenham (0-1) in the third round on Oct 31, 1984. During this period Liverpool won the tournament in four successive seasons, a feat no other Football League club has achieved in any competition.

## BIG HALF-TIME SCORES

**Tottenham 10, Crewe 1** (FA Cup 4th round replay, Feb 3, 1960; result 13-2); Tranmere 8,

Oldham 1 (Div 3N., Dec 26, 1935; result 13-4); **Chester City 8, York 0** (Div 3N., Feb 1, 1936; result 12-0; believed to be record half-time scores in League football).

Nine goals were scored in the first half – **Burnley 4, Watford 5** in Div 1 on Apr 5, 2003. Result: 4-7.

**Stirling Albion led Selkirk 15-0** at half-time (result 20-0) in the Scottish Cup 1st round, Dec 8, 1984.

World record half-time score: **16-0** when **Australia** beat **American Samoa** 31-0 (another world record) in the World Cup Oceania qualifying group at Coff's Harbour, New South Wales, on Apr 11 2001.

- On Mar 4 1933 **Coventry** beat QPR (Div 3 South) 7-0, having led by that score at half-time. This repeated the half-time situation in Bristol City's 7-0 win over Grimsby on Dec 26, 1914.

## TOP SECOND-HALF TEAM

Most goals scored by a team in one half of a League match is **11. Stockport** led Halifax 2-0 at half-time in Div 3 North on Jan 6 1934 and won 13-0.

## FIVE NOT ENOUGH

Last team to score **5** in League match and lose: **Burton**, beaten 6-5 by Cheltenham (Lge 2, Mar 13, 2010).

## LONG SERVICE WITH ONE CLUB

**Bill Nicholson**, OBE, was associated with Tottenham for 67 years – as a wing-half (1938–55), then the club's most successful manager (1958–74) with 8 major prizes, subsequently chief advisor and scout. He became club president, and an honorary freeman of the borough, had an executive suite named after him at the club, and the stretch of roadway from Tottenham High Road to the main gates has the nameplate Bill Nicholson Way. He died, aged 85, in Oct 2004.

**Ted Bates**, the Grand Old Man of Southampton with 66 years of unbroken service to the club, was awarded the Freedom of the City in Apr, 2001. He joined Saints as an inside-forward from Norwich in 1937, made 260 peace-time appearances for the club, became reserve-team trainer in 1953 and manager at The Dell for 18 years (1955–73), taking Southampton into the top division in 1966. He was subsequently chief executive, director and club president. He died in Oct 2003, aged 85.

**Bob Paisley** was associated with Liverpool for 57 years from 1939, when he joined them from Bishop Auckland, until he died in Feb 1996. He served as player, trainer, coach, assistant-manager, manager, director and vice-president. He was Liverpool's most successful manager, winning 13 major trophies for the club (1974–83).

**Dario Gradi**, MBE, stepped down after completing 24 seasons and more than 1,000 matches as manager of Crewe (appointed Jun 1983). Never a League player, he previously managed Wimbledon and Crystal Palace. At Crewe, his policy of finding and grooming young talent has earned the club more than £20m in transfer fees. He stayed with Crewe as technical director, and twice took charge of team affairs again following the departure of the managers who succeeded him, Steve Holland and Gudjon Thordarson.

**Ronnie Moran**, who joined Liverpool in as a player 1952, retired from the Anfield coaching staff in season 1998–99.

**Ernie Gregory** served West Ham for 52 years as goalkeeper and coach. He joined them as boy of 14 from school in 1935, retired in May 1987.

**Ryan Giggs** played 24 seasons for Manchester Utd (1990-2014), then became assistant manager under Louis van Gaal.

**Ted Sagar**, Everton goalkeeper, 23 years at Goodison Park (1929–52, but only 16 League seasons because of war).

**Alan Knight**, goalkeeper, played 23 seasons (1977–2000) for his only club, Portsmouth.

**Sam Bartram** was recognised as one of the finest goalkeepers never to play for England, apart from unofficial wartime games. He was with Charlton from 1934–56

**Jack Charlton,** England World Cup winner, served Leeds from 1952–73.

**Roy Sproson**, defender, played 21 League seasons for his only club, Port Vale (1950–71).

**John Terry** had a 22-year association with Chelsea from 1994–2017.

## TIGHT AT HOME

Fewest home goals conceded in League season (modern times): 4 by **Liverpool** (Div 1, 1978–9); 4 by **Manchester Utd** (Premier League, 1994–95) – both in 21 matches.

## VARSITY MATCH

First played in 1873, this is the game's second oldest contest (after the FA Cup). Played 134, Oxford 53 wins, Cambridge 49, Draws 32. Goals: Oxford 217, Cambridge 207. Latest result: Oxford 3 Cambridge 0, March 25, 2018, The Hive, Barnet.

## TRANSFER WINDOW

This was introduced to Britain in Sep 2002 via FIFA regulations to bring uniformity across Europe (the rule previously applied in a number of other countries).

The transfer of contracted players is restricted to two periods: Jun 1–Aug 31 and Jan 1–31).

On appeal, Football League clubs continued to sign/sell players (excluding deals with Premiership clubs).

## PROGRAMME PIONEERS

**Chelsea** pioneered football's magazine-style programme by introducing a 16-page issue for the First Division match against Portsmouth on Christnmas Day 1948. It cost sixpence (2.5p). A penny programme from the 1909 FA Cup Final fetched £23,500 at a London auction in May, 2012.

## FOOTBALL POOLS

Littlewoods launched them in 1923 with capital of £100. Coupons (4,000 of them) were first issued outside Manchester United's ground, the original 35 investors staking a total of £4 7s 6d (pay-out £2 12s). Vernons joined Littlewoods as leading promoters. The Treble Chance, leading to bonanza dividends, was introduced in 1946 and the Pools Panel began in January 1963 to counter mass fixture postponements caused by the Big Freeze winter.

But business was hard hit by the launch of the National Lottery in 1994. Dividends slumped, the work-force was cut severely and in June 2000 the Liverpool-based Moores family sold Littlewoods Pools in a £161m deal. After 85 years, the name Littlewoods disappeared from Pools betting in August 2008. The New Football Pools was formed. Vernons and Zetters continued to operate in their own name under the ownership of Sportech. The record prize remains the £2,924,622 paid to a syndicate in Worsley, Manchester, in November 1994.

## WORLD'S OLDEST FOOTBALL ANNUAL

Now in its 132nd edition, this publication began as the 16-page Athletic News Football Supplement & Club Directory in 1887. From the long-established Athletic News, it became the Sunday Chronicle Annual in 1946, the Empire News in 1956, the News of the World & Empire News in 1961 and the News of the World Annual from 1965 until becoming the Nationwide Annual in 2008.

# PREMIER LEAGUE CLUB DETAILS AND SQUADS 2018–19

(at time of going to press)

## ARSENAL

**Ground**: Emirates Stadium, Highbury, London, N5 IBU
**Telephone**: 0207 619 5000. **Club nickname**: Gunners
**Capacity**: 59,867. **Colours**: Red and white. **Main sponsor**: Emirates
**Record transfer fee**: £56.1m to Borussia Dortmund for Pierre-Emerick Aubameyang, Jan 20018
**Record fee received**: £35m from Barcelona for Cesc Fabregas, Aug 2011; £35m from Liverpool for Alex Oxlade-Chamberlain, 8/17
**Record attendance**: Highbury: 73,295 v Sunderland (Div 1) Mar 9, 1935. Emirates Stadium: 60,161 v Manchester Utd (Prem Lge) Nov 3, 2007. Wembley: 73,707 v Lens (Champ Lge) Nov 25, 1998
**League Championship**: Winners 1930–31, 1932–33, 1933–34, 1934–35, 1937–38, 1947–48, 1952–53, 1970–71, 1988–89, 1990–91, 1997–98, 2001–02, 2003–04
**FA Cup**: Winners 1930, 1936, 1950, 1971, 1979, 1993, 1998, 2002, 2003, 2005, 2014, 2015, 2017
**League Cup**: Winners 1987, 1993
**European competitions**: Winners Fairs Cup 1969–70; Cup-Winners' Cup 1993–94
**Finishing positions in Premier League**: 1992–93 10th, 1993–94 4th, 1994–95 12th, 1995–96 5th, 1996–97 3rd, 1997–98 1st, 1998–99 2nd, 1999–2000 2nd, 2000–01 2nd, 2001–02 1st, 2002–03 2nd, 2003–04 1st, 2004–05 2nd, 2005–06 4th, 2006–07 4th, 2007–08 3rd, 2008–09 4th, 2009–10 3rd, 2010–11 4th, 2011–12 3rd, 2012–13 4th, 2013–14 4th,2014–15 3rd, 2015–16 2nd, 2016–17 5th, 2017–18 6th
**Biggest win**: 12-0 v Loughborough (Div 2) Mar 12, 1900
**Biggest defeat**: 0-8 v Loughborough (Div 2) Dec 12, 1896
**Highest League scorer in a season**: Ted Drake 42 (1934–35)
**Most League goals in aggregate**: Thierry Henry 175 (1999–2007) (2012)
**Longest unbeaten League sequence**: 49 matches (2003–04)
**Longest sequence without a League win**: 23 matches (1912–13)
**Most capped player**: Thierry Henry (France) 81

| Name | Height ft in | Previous club | Birthplace | Birthdate |
|---|---|---|---|---|
| **Goalkeepers** | | | | |
| Cech, Petr | 6.5 | Chelsea | Plzen, Cz | 20.05.82 |
| Leno, Bernd | 6.3 | Bayer Leverkusen | Bietighem-Bissingen, Ger | 04.03.92 |
| Martinez, Damian | 6.4 | Independiente | Mar del Plata, Arg | 02.09.92 |
| Ospina, David | 6.0 | Nice | Medellin, Col | 31.08.88 |
| **Defenders** | | | | |
| Bellerin, Hector | 5.10 | Barcelona | Barcelona, Sp | 19.03.95 |
| Chambers, Calum | 6.0 | Southampton | Petersfield | 20.01.95 |
| Holding, Rob | 6.0 | Bolton | Tameside | 12.09.95 |
| Jenkinson, Carl | 6.1 | Charlton | Harlow | 08.02.92 |
| Kolasinac, Sead | 6.0 | Schalke | Karlsruhe, Ger | 20.06.93 |
| Koscielny, Laurent | 6.1 | Lorient | Tulle, Fr | 10.09.85 |
| Lichtsteiner, Stephan | 6.0 | Juventus | Adligenswil, Switz | 16.01.84 |
| Mavropanos, Konstantinos | 6.4 | Giannina | Athens, Gre | 11.12.97 |
| Monreal, Nacho | 5.10 | Malaga | Pamplona, Sp | 26.02.86 |
| Mustafi, Shkodran | 6.1 | Valencia | Bad Hersfeld, Ger | 17.04.92 |
| Papastathopoulos, Sokratis | 6.1 | Borussia Dortmund | Kalamata, Gre | 09.06.88 |
| **Midfielders** | | | | |
| Elneny, Mohamed | 5.11 | Basle | El-Mahalla, Egy | 11.07.92 |

| | | | | |
|---|---|---|---|---|
| Guendouzi, Matteo | 6.1 | Lorient | Poissy, Fr | 14.04.99 |
| Maitland-Niles, Ainsley | 5.10 | – | Goodmayes | 29.08.97 |
| Mkhitaryan, Henrikh | 5.10 | Manchester Utd | Yerevan, Arm | 21.01.89 |
| Ozil, Mesut | 5.11 | Real Madrid | Gelsenkirchen, Ger | 15.10.88 |
| Ramsey, Aaron | 5.11 | Cardiff | Caerphilly | 26.12.90 |
| Torreira, Lucas | 5.6 | Sampdoria | Fray Bentos, Uru | 11.02.96 |
| Xhaka, Granit | 6.1 | Borussia M'gladbach | Basle, Swi | 27.09.92 |
| **Forwards** | | | | |
| Akpom, Chuba | 6.0 | Southend | Canning Town | 09.10.95 |
| Aubameyang, Pierre-Emerick | 6.2 | Borussia Dortmund | Laval, Fr | 18.06.89 |
| Campbell, Joel | 5.10 | Saprissa | San Jose, CRica | 26.06.92 |
| Iwobi, Alex | 5.11 | – | Lagos, Nig | 03.05.96 |
| Lacazette, Alexandre | 5.9 | Lyon | Lyon, Fr | 28.05.91 |
| Lucas Perez | 6.0 | Deportivo La Coruna | La Coruna, Sp | 10.09.88 |
| Nelson, Reiss | 5.9 | – | Elephant and Castle | 10.12.99 |
| Welbeck, Danny | 5.10 | Manchester Utd | Manchester | 26.11.90 |

## BOURNEMOUTH

**Ground**: Vitality Stadium, Dean Court, Bournemouth BH7 7AF
**Telephone**: 0344 576 1910. **Club nickname**: Cherries
**Capacity**: 11,360. **Colours**: Red and black. **Main sponsor**: M88
**Record transfer fee**: £20m to Chelsea for Nathan Ake, Jun 2017
**Record fee received**: £10m from Wolves for Benik Afobe, Jun 2018
**Record attendance**: 28,799 v Manchester Utd (FA Cup 6) Mar 2, 1957
**FA Cup**: Sixth round 1957
**League Cup**: Fifth round 2014
**Finishing position in Premier League:** 2015–16 16th, 2016–17 9th, 2017–18 12th
**Biggest win**: 8-0 v Birmingham (Champ) Oct 15, 2014. Also: 11-0 v Margate (FA Cup 1) Nov20, 1971
**Biggest defeat**: 0-9 v Lincoln (Div 3) Dec 18, 1982
**Highest League scorer in a season**: Ted MacDougall 42 (1970–71)
**Most League goals in aggregate**: Ron Eyre 202 (1924–33)
**Longest unbeaten League sequence**: 18 (1982)
**Longest sequence without a League win**: 14 (1974)

| | | | | |
|---|---|---|---|---|
| **Goalkeepers** | | | | |
| Begovic, Asmir | 6.5 | Chelsea | Trebinje, Bos | 20.06.87 |
| Boruc, Artur | 6.4 | Southampton | Siedice, Pol | 20.02.80 |
| **Defenders** | | | | |
| Ake, Nathan | 5.11 | Chelsea | The Hague, Hol | 18.02.95 |
| Cook, Steve | 6.1 | Brighton | Hastings | 19.04.91 |
| Daniels, Charlie | 5.10 | Leyton Orient | Harlow | 07.09.86 |
| Francis, Simon | 6.0 | Charlton | Nottingham | 16.02.85 |
| Mings, Tyrone | 6.3 | Ipswich | Bath | 13.03.93 |
| Simpson, Jack | 5.10 | – | Weymouth | 08.01.97 |
| Smith, Adam | 5.11 | Tottenham | Leystonstone | 29.04.91 |
| Smith, Brad | 5.10 | Liverpool | Penrith, Aus | 09.04.94 |
| **Midfielders** | | | | |
| Arter, Harry | 5.9 | Woking | Eltham | 28.12.89 |
| Brooks, David | 5.8 | Sheffield Utd | Warrington | 08.07.97 |
| Cook, Lewis | 5.9 | Leeds | Leeds | 03.02.97 |
| Fraser, Ryan | 5.4 | Aberdeen | Aberdeen | 24.02.94 |
| Gosling, Dan | 5.10 | Newcastle | Brixham | 02.02.90 |
| Hyndman, Emerson | 5.8 | Fulham | Dallas, US | 09.04.96 |

| | | | | |
|---|---|---|---|---|
| Ibe, Jordon | 5.7 | Liverpool | Bermondsey | 08.12.95 |
| Mahoney, Connor | 5.9 | Blackburn | Blackburn | 12.02.97 |
| Pugh, Marc | 5.11 | Hereford | Bacup | 02.04.87 |
| Stanislas, Junior | 6.0 | Burnley | Eltham | 26.11.89 |
| Surman, Andrew | 5.11 | Norwich | Johannesburg, SA | 20.08.86 |
| **Forwards** | | | | |
| Defoe, Jermain | 5.8 | Sunderland | Beckton | 07.10.82 |
| King, Josh | 5.11 | Blackburn | Oslo, Nor | 15.01.92 |
| Mousset, Lys | 6.0 | Le Havre | Montivilliers, Fr | 08.12.96 |
| Wilson, Callum | 5.11 | Coventry | Coventry | 27.02.92 |

## BRIGHTON AND HOVE ALBION

**Ground**: American Express Community Stadium, Village Way, Brighton BN1 9BL
**Telephone**: 01273 878288. **Club nickname**: Seagulls
**Capacity**: 30,666. **Colours**: Blue and white. **Main sponsor**: American Express
**Record transfer fee**: £14.1m to PSV Eindhoven for Jurgen Locadia, Jan 2018
**Record fee received:** £1.5m from Tottenham for Bobby Zamora, Jul 2003; from Celtic for Adam Virgo, Jul 2005; from Norwich for Elliott Bennett, Jun 2011
**Record attendance**: Goldstone Ground: 36,747 v Fulham (Div 2) Dec 27, 1958; Withdean Stadium: 8,729 v Manchester City (League Cup 2) Sep 24, 2008; Amex Stadium: 30,634 v Liverpool (Prem Lge) Dec 2, 2017
**League Championship**: 13th1981–92
**FA Cup**: Runners-up 1983
**League Cup**: Fifth round 1979
**Finishing position in Premier League: 2017–18 15th**
**Biggest win**: 10-1 v Wisbech (FA Cup 1) Nov 13, 1965
**Biggest defeat**: 0-9 v Middlesbrough (Div 2) Aug 23, 1958
**Highest League scorer in a season**: Peter Ward 32 (1976–77)
**Most League goals in aggregate**: Tommy Cook 114 (1922–29)
**Longest unbeaten League sequence**: 22 matches (2015)
**Longest sequence without a League win**: 15matches (1972–73)
**Most capped player**: Gerry Ryan (Republic of Ireland) 17, Steve Penney (Northern Ireland) 17

| | | | | |
|---|---|---|---|---|
| **Goalkeepers** | | | | |
| Maenpaa, Niki | 6.3 | Venlo | Espoo, Fin | 23.01.85 |
| Ryan, Mathew | 6.1 | Valencia | Plumpton, Aus | 08.04.92 |
| **Defenders** | | | | |
| Balogun, Leon | 6.3 | Mainz | Berlin, Ger | 28.06,88 |
| Bernardo | 6.1 | Leipzig | Sao Paulo, Bra | 14.05.95 |
| Bong, Gaetan | 6.2 | Wigan | Sakbayeme, Cam | 25.04.88 |
| Bruno | 5.11 | Valencia | El Masnou, Sp | 01.10.80 |
| Duffy, Shane | 6.4 | Blackburn | Derry | 01.01.92 |
| Dunk, Lewis | 6.4 | – | Brighton | 1.11.91 |
| Schelotto, Ezequiel | 6.2 | Sporting Lisbon | Buenos Aires, Arg | 23.05.89 |
| Suttner, Markus | 5.10 | Ingolstadt | Hollabrunn, Aut | 16.04.87 |
| **Midfielders** | | | | |
| Ahannach, Soufyan | 5.8 | Almere City | Amsterdan, Hol | 09.09.95 |
| Gross, Pascal | 6.0 | Ingolstadt | Mannheim, Ger | 15.06.91 |
| Izquierdo, Jose | 5.8 | Club Bruges | Pereira, Col | 07.07.92 |
| Kayal, Beram | 5.10 | Celtic | Jadeidi, Isr | 02.05.88 |
| Knockaert, Anthony | 5.8 | Standard Liege | Roubaix, Fr | 20.11.91 |
| March, Solly | 5.11 | – | Eastbourne | 20.07.94 |
| Norwood, Oliver | 5.11 | Reading | Burnley | 12.04.91 |
| Propper, Davy | 6.1 | PSV Eindhoven | Arnhem, Hol | 02.09.91 |

| | | | | |
|---|---|---|---|---|
| Skalak, Jiri | 5.9 | Mlada Boleslav | Pardubice, Cz | 12.03.92 |
| Stephens, Dale | 5.7 | Charlton | Bolton | 12.06.89 |
| Towell, Richie | 5.8 | Dundalk | Dublin, Ire | 17.07.91 |
| **Forwards** | | | | |
| Andone, Florin | 5.11 | Dep La Coruna | Botosani, Rom | 11.04.93 |
| Baldock, Sam | 5.8 | Bristol City | Bedford | 15.03.89 |
| Gyokeres, Viktor | 6.2 | Brommapojkarna | Sweden | 04.06.98 |
| Hemed, Tomer | 6.0 | Almeria Kiryat | Tivon, Isr | 02.05.87 |
| Locadia, Jurgen | 6.1 | PSV Eindhoven | Emmen, Hol | 07.11.93 |
| Murray, Glenn | 6.1 | Bournemouth | Maryport | 25.09.83 |

## BURNLEY

**Ground:** Turf Moor, Harry Potts Way, Burnlety BB10 4BX
**Telephone**: 0871 221 1882. **Club nickname**: Clarets
**Capacity**: 21,944. **Colours**: Claret and blue. **Main sponsor**: Dafabet
**Record transfer fee**: £15m to Leeds for Chris Wood, Aug 2017
**Record fee received**: £25m from Everton for Michael Keane, Jul 2017
**Record attendance**: 54,775 v Huddersfield (FA Cup 3) Feb 23, 1924
**League Championship: Winners** 1920–21, 1959–60
**FA Cup**: Winners 1914
**League Cup**: Semi-finals 1961, 1969, 1983, 2009
**European competitions**: European Cup quarter-finals 1960–61
**Finishing positions in Premier League**: 2014–15 19th, 2016–17 16th, 2017–18 7th
**Biggest win**: 9-0 v Darwen (Div 1) Jan 9, 1892, v Crystal Palace (FA Cup 2) Feb 10, 1909, v New Brighton (FA Cup 4) Jan 26, 1957, v Penrith (FA Cup 1) Nov 17, 1984
**Biggest defeat**: 0-10 v Aston Villa (Div 1) Aug 29, 1925, v Sheffield Utd (Div 1) Jan 19, 1929
**Highest League scorer in a season**: George Beel 35 (1927–28
**Highest League scorer in aggregate**: George Beel 178 (1923–32
**Longest unbeaten League sequence**: 30 matches (1920–21)
**Longest sequence without a League win**: 24 matches (1979)
**Most capped player**: Jimmy McIlroy (Northern Ireland) 51

| | | | | |
|---|---|---|---|---|
| **Goalkeepers** | | | | |
| Heaton, Tom | 6.1 | Bristol City | Chester | 15.04.86 |
| Lindegaard, Anders | 6.4 | Preston | Odense, Den | 13.04.84 |
| Pope, Nick | 6.3 | Charlton | Cambridge | 19.04.92 |
| **Defenders** | | | | |
| Bardsley, Phil | 5.11 | Stoke | Salford | 28.06.85 |
| Darikwa, Tendayi | 6.2 | Chesterfield | Nottingham | 13.12.91 |
| Long, Kevin | 6.2 | Cork | Cork, Ire | 18.08.90 |
| Lowton, Matthew | 5.11 | Aston Villa | Chesterfield | 09.06.89 |
| Mee, Ben | 5.11 | Manchester City | Sale | 23.09.89 |
| Taylor, Charlie | 5.9 | Leeds | York | 18.09.93 |
| Ward, Stephen | 5.11 | Wolves | Dublin, Ire | 20.08.85 |
| **Midfielders** | | | | |
| Brady, Robbie | 5.10 | Norwich | Dublin, Ire | 14.01.92 |
| Cork, Jack | 6.1 | Swansea | Carshalton | 25.06.89 |
| Defour, Steven | 5.9 | Anderlecht | Mechelen, Bel | 15.04.88 |
| Gudmundsson, Johann Berg | 6.1 | Charlton | Reykjavik, Ice | 27.10.90 |
| Hendrick, Jeff | 6.1 | Derby | Dublin, Ire | 31.01.92 |
| Lennon, Aaron | 5.5 | Everton | Leeds | 16.04.87 |
| O'Neill, Aiden | 5.10 | Brisbane | Brisbane, Aus | 04.07.98 |
| Tarkowski, James | 6.1 | Brentford | Manchester | 19.11.92 |
| Westwood, Ashley | 5.7 | Aston Villa | Nantwich | 01.04.90 |

**Forwards**

| | | | | |
|---|---|---|---|---|
| Agyei, Dan | 6.0 | AFC Wimbledon | Kingston upon Thames | 01.06.97 |
| Barnes, Ashley | 6.0 | Brighton | Bath | 31.10.89 |
| Lennon, Aaron | 5.5 | Everton | Leeds | 16.04.87 |
| Vokes, Sam | 5.11 | Wolves | Lymington | 21.10.89 |
| Walters, Jon | 6.0 | Stoke | Birkenhead | 20.09.83 |
| Wells, Nahki | 5.7 | Huddersfield | Hamilton, Berm | 01.06.90 |
| Wood, Chris | 6.3 | Leeds | Auckland, NZ | 07.12.91 |

## CARDIFF CITY

**Ground**: Cardiff City Stadium, Leckwith Road, Cardiff CF11 8AZ
**Telephone**: 0845 365 1115. **Club nickname**: Bluebirds
**Capacity**: 33,300. **Colours**: Blue. **Main sponsor**: Tourism Malaysia
**Record transfer fee:** £11m to Sevilla for Gary Medel, Aug 2013
**Record fee received:** £10 from Inter Milan for Gary Medel, Aug 2014
**Record attendance**: Ninian Park: 62,634 Wales v England, Oct 17, 1959; Club: 57,893 v Arsenal (Div 1) Apr 22, 1953, Cardiff City Stadium: 33,280 (Wales v Belgium) Jun 12, 2015. Club: 32,478 v Reading (Champ) May 6, 2018
**League Championship:** Runners-up 1923–24
**FA Cup:** Winners 1927
**League Cup:** Runners-up 2012
**European competitions:** Cup Winners' Cup semi-finals 1967–68
**Finishing position in Premier League:** 2013–14 20th
**Biggest win:** 9-2 v Thames (Div 3 south) Feb 6, 1932. Also: 8-0 v Enfield (FA Cup 1) Nov 28, 1931
**Biggest defeat:** 2-11 v Sheffield Utd (Div 1) Jan 1, 1926
**Highest League scorer in a season:** Robert Earnshaw 31 (2002–03)
**Most League goals in aggregate:** Len Davies 128 (1920–31)
**Longest unbeaten League sequence:** 21 matches (1946–47)
**Longest sequence without a League win:** 15 matches (1936–37)
**Most capped player:** Alf Sherwood (Wales) 39

| | | | | |
|---|---|---|---|---|
| **Goalkeepers** | | | | |
| Etheridge, Neil | 6.3 | Walsall | Enfield | 07.02.90 |
| Murphy, Brian | 6.1 | Portsmouth | Waterford, Ire | 07.05.83 |
| Smithies, Alex | 6.3 | QPR | Huddersfield | 05.03.90 |
| **Defenders** | | | | |
| Bamba, Sol | 6.3 | Leeds | Ivry-sur-Seine, Fr | 13.01.85 |
| Bennett, Joe | 5.10 | Aston Villa | Rochdale | 28.03.90 |
| Connolly, Matthew | 6.2 | QPR | Barnet | 24.09.87 |
| Cunningham, Greg | 6.0 | Preston | Carnmore, Ire | 31.01.91 |
| Halford, Greg | 6.4 | Rotherham | Chelmsford | 08.12.84 |
| Manga, Bruno | 6.1 | Lorient | Libreville, Gab | 16.07.88 |
| Morrison, Sean | 6.1 | Reading | Plymouth | 08.01.91 |
| Paterson, Callum | 6.0 | Hearts | London | 13.10.94 |
| Peltier, Lee | 5.11 | Huddersfield | Liverpool | 11.12.86 |
| Richards, Jazz | 6.1 | Fulham | Swansea | 12.04.91 |
| **Midfielders** | | | | |
| Damour, Loic | 5.11 | Bourg-Peronnas | Chantilly, Fr | 08.01.91 |
| Gunnarsson, Aron | 5.11 | Coventry | Akureyri, Ice | 22.04.89 |
| Harris, Kadeem | 5.9 | Wycombe | Westminster | 08.06.93 |
| Hoilett, Junior | 5.8 | QPR | Brampton, Can | 05.06.90 |
| Kennedy, Matthew | 5.9 | Everton | Dundonald | 01.11.94 |
| Mendez-Laing, Nathaniel | 5.10 | Rochdale | Birmingham | 15.04.92 |

| | | | | |
|---|---|---|---|---|
| Murphy, Josh | 5.9 | Norwich | Wembley | 24.02.95 |
| O'Keefe, Stuart | 5.8 | Crystal Palace | Norwich | 04.03.91 |
| Pilkington, Anthony | 6.0 | Norwich | Blackburn | 06.06.88 |
| Ralls, Joe | 6.0 | – | Aldershot | 13.10.93 |
| Reid, Bobby | 5.7 | Bristol City | Bristol | 02.02.93 |
| **Forwards** | | | | |
| Bogle, Omar | 6.3 | Wigan | Birmingham | 26.07.92 |
| Gounongbe, Frederic | 6.3 | Westerlo | Brussels, Bel | 01.05.88 |
| Healey, Rhys | 5.11 | Connah's Quay | Manchester | 06.12.94 |
| Madine, Gary | 6.3 | Bolton | Gateshead | 24.08.90 |
| Tomlin, Lee | 5.11 | Bristol City | Leicester | 12.01.89 |
| Ward, Danny | 5.11 | Rotherham | Bradford | 09.12.90 |
| Zohore, Kenneth | 6.3 | Kortrijk | Copenhagen, Den | 31.01.94 |

## CHELSEA

**Ground**: Stamford Bridge Stadium, London SW6 1HS
**Telephone**: 0871 984 1905. **Club nickname**: Blues
**Capacity**: 41,631. **Colours**: Blue. **Main sponsor**: Yokohama Tyres
**Record transfer fee**: £57.2m to Real Madrid for Alvaro Morata, Jul 2017
**Record fee received**: £57m from Atletico Madrid for Diego Costa, Jan 2018
**Record attendance**: 82,905 v Arsenal (Div 1) Oct 12, 1935
**League Championship**: Winners 1954–55, 2004–05, 2005–06, 2009–10, 2014–15, 2016–17
**FA Cup**: Winners 1970, 1997, 2000, 2007, 2009, 2010, 2012, 2018
**League Cup**: Winners 1965, 1998, 2005, 2007, 2015
**European competitions**: Winners Champions League 2011–12; Cup-Winners' Cup 1970–71, 1997–98; Europa League 2012–13; European Super Cup 1998
**Finishing positions in Premier League**: 1992–93 11th, 1993–94 14th, 1994–95 11th, 1995–96 11th, 1996–97 6th, 1997–98 4th, 1998–99 3rd, 1999–2000 5th, 2000–01 6th, 2001–02 6th, 2002–03 4th, 2003–04 2nd, 2004–05 1st, 2005–06 1st, 2006–07 2nd, 2007–08 2nd, 2008–09 3rd, 2009–10 1st, 2010–11 2nd, 2011–12 6th, 2012–13 3rd, 2013–14 3rd, 2014–15 1st, 2015–16 10th, 2016–17 1st, 2017–18 5th
**Biggest win**: 8-0 v Aston Villa (Prem Lge) Dec 23, 2012. Also: 13-0 v Jeunesse Hautcharage, (Cup-Winners' Cup 1) Sep 29, 1971
**Biggest defeat**: 1-8 v Wolves (Div 1) Sep 26, 1953; 0-7 v Leeds (Div 1) Oct 7, 1967, v Nottm Forest (Div 1) Apr 20, 1991
**Highest League scorer in a season**: Jimmy Greaves 41 (1960–61)
**Most League goals in aggregate**: Bobby Tambling 164 (1958–70)
**Longest unbeaten League sequence**: 40 matches (2004–05)
**Longest sequence without a League win**: 21 matches (1987–88)
**Most capped player**: Frank Lampard (England) 104

| | | | | |
|---|---|---|---|---|
| **Goalkeepers** | | | | |
| Caballero, Willy | 6.1 | Manchester City | Santa Elena, Arg | 28.09.81 |
| Courtois, Thibaut | 6.6 | Genk | Bree, Bel | 11.05.92 |
| Eduardo | 6.2 | Dinamo Zagreb | Mirandela, Port | 19.09.82 |
| **Defenders** | | | | |
| Aina, Ola | 5.9 | – | Southwark | 08.10.96 |
| Alonso, Marcos | 6.2 | Fiorentina | Madrid, Sp | 28.12.90 |
| Azpilicueta, Cesar | 5.10 | Marseille | Pamplona, Sp | 28.08.89 |
| Cahill, Gary | 6.2 | Bolton | Sheffield | 19.12.85 |
| Christensen, Andreas | 6.2 | Brondby | Lillerod, Den | 10.04.96 |
| Hector, Michael | 6.4 | Reading | East Ham | 19.07.92 |
| Luiz, David | 6.3 | Paris SG | Diadema, Br | 22.04.87 |
| Palmieri, Emerson | 5.9 | Roma | Santos, Br | 03.08.94 |

| | | | | |
|---|---|---|---|---|
| Rudiger, Antonio | 6.3 | Roma | Berlin, Ger | 03.03.93 |
| Zappacosta, Davide | 6.1 | Torino | Sora, It | 11.06.92 |
| Zouma, Kurt | 6.3 | St Etienne | Lyon, Fr | 27.10.94 |
| **Midfielders** | | | | |
| Bakayoko, Tiemoue | 6.1 | Monaco | Paris, Fr | 17.08.94 |
| Barkley, Ross | 6.2 | Everton | Liverpool | 05.12.93 |
| Drinkwater, Danny | 5.10 | Leicester | Manchester | 05.03.90 |
| Fabregas, Cesc | 5.11 | Barcelona | Arenys de Mar,Sp | 04.05.87 |
| Hazard, Eden | 5.8 | Lille | La Louviere, Bel | 07.01.91 |
| Jorginho | 5.11 | Napoli | Imbituba, Bra | 20.12.91 |
| Kante, N'Golo | 5.7 | Leicester | Paris, Fr | 29.03.91 |
| Musconda, Charly | 5.8 | Anderlecht | Brussels, Bel | 15.10.96 |
| Moses, Victor | 5.10 | Wigan | Lagos, Nig | 12.12.90 |
| Pedro | 5.6 | Barcelona | Santa Cruz, Ten | 28.07.87 |
| Willian | 5.9 | Anzhi Makhachkala | Ribeirao Pires, Br | 09.08.88 |
| **Forwards** | | | | |
| Batshuayi, Michy | 6.0 | Marseille | Brussels, Bel | 02.10.93 |
| Giroud, Olivier | 6.4 | Arsenal | Chambery, Fr | 30.09.86 |
| Hudson-Odoi, Callum | 6.0 | – | Wandsworth | 07.11.00 |
| Morata, Alvaro | 6.2 | Real Madrid | Madrid, Sp | 23.10.92 |

## CRYSTAL PALACE

**Ground**: Selhurst Park, Whitehorse Lane, London SE25, 6PU
**Telephone**: 0208 768 6000. **Club nickname**: Eagles
**Capacity**: 25,456. **Colours**: Red and blue. **Main sponsor**: ManBetX
**Record transfer fee**: £27m to Liverpool for Christian Benteke, Aug 2016
**Record fee received**: £25m from Everton for Yannick Bolasie, Aug 2016
**Record attendance**: 51,482 v Burnley (Div 2), May 11, 1979
**League Championship**: 3rd 1990–91
**FA Cup**: Runners-up 1990, 2016
**League Cup**: Semi-finals 1993, 1995, 2001, 2012
**Finishing positions in Premier League**: 1992–93 20th, 1994–95 19th, 1997–98 20th, 2004–05 18th, 2013–14 11th, 2014–15 10th, 2015–16 15th, 2016–17 14th, 2017–18 11th
**Biggest win**: 9-0 v Barrow (Div 4) Oct 10, 1959
**Biggest defeat**: 0-9 v Liverpool (Div 1) Sep 12, 1989. Also: 0-9 v Burnley (FA Cup 2 rep) Feb 10, 1909
**Highest League scorer in a season**: Peter Simpson 46 (1930–31)
**Most League goals in aggregate**: Peter Simpson 153 (1930–36)
**Longest unbeaten League sequence**: 18 matches (1969)
**Longest sequence with a League win**: 20 matches (1962)
**Most capped player**: Mile Jedinak (Australia) 37

| | | | | |
|---|---|---|---|---|
| **Goalkeepers** | | | | |
| Guaita, Vicente | 6.3 | Getafe | Torrente, Sp | 10.01.87 |
| Hennessey, Wayne | 6.5 | Wolves | Bangor, Wal | 24.01.87 |
| Speroni, Julian | 6.1 | Dundee | Buenos Aires, Arg | 18.05.79 |
| **Defenders** | | | | |
| Dann, Scott | 6.2 | Blackburn | Liverpool | 14.02.87 |
| Jach, Jaroslaw | 6.3 | Zaglebie Lubin | Bielawa, Pol | 17.02.94 |
| Kelly, Martin | 6.3 | Liverpool | Whiston | 27.04.90 |
| Riedewald, Jairo | 6.0 | Ajax | Haarlem, Hol | 09.09.96 |
| Sakho, Mamadou | 6.2 | Liverpool | Paris, Fr | 13.02.90 |
| Schlupp, Jeffrey | 5.8 | Leicester | Hamburg, Ger | 23.12.92 |
| Souare, Pape | 5.10 | Lille | Mbao, Sen | 06.06.90 |

| | | | | |
|---|---|---|---|---|
| Tomkins, James | 6.3 | West Ham | Basildon | 29.03.89 |
| Van Aanholt, Patrick | 5.9 | Sunderland | Hertogenbosch, Hol | 29.08.90 |
| Wan-Bissaka, Aaron | 6.0 | – | Croydon | 26.11.97 |
| **Midfielders** | | | | |
| Kaikai, Sullay | 6.0 | – | Southwark | 26.08.95 |
| Loftus-Cheek, Ruben | 6.3 | Chelsea (loan) | Lewisham | 23.01.96 |
| McArthur, James | 5.7 | Wigan | Glasgow | 07.10.87 |
| Milivojevic, Luka | 6.0 | Olympiacos | Kragujevac, Serb | 07.04.91 |
| Mutch, Jordon | 5.9 | QPR | Birmingham | 02.12.91 |
| Puncheon, Jason | 5.8 | Southampton | Croydon | 26.06.86 |
| Townsend, Andros | 6.0 | Newcastle | Leytonstone | 16.07.91 |
| Zaha, Wilfried | 5.10 | Manchester Utd | Abidjan, Iv C | 10.11.92 |
| **Forwards** | | | | |
| Benteke, Christian | 6.3 | Liverpool | Kinshasa, DR Cong | 03.12.90 |
| Sorloth, Alexander | 6.4 | Midtjylland | Trondheim, Nor | 05.12.95 |
| Wickham, Connor | 6.3 | Sunderland | Colchester | 31.03.93 |

## EVERTON

**Ground**: Goodison Park, Liverpool L4 4EL
**Telephone**: 0151 556 1878. **Club nickname**: Toffees
**Capacity**: 39,595. **Colours**: Blue and white. **Main sponsor**: SportPesa
**Record transfer fee**: £45m to Swansea for Gylfi Sigurdsson, Aug 2017
**Record fee received**: £75m from Manchester Utd for Romelu Lukaku, Jul 2017
**Record attendance**: 78,299 v Liverpool (Div 1) Sep 18, 1948
**League Championship**: Winners 1890–91, 1914–15, 1927–28, 1931–31, 1938–39, 1962–63, 1969–70, 1984–85, 1986–87
**FA Cup**: Winners 1906, 1933, 1966, 1984, 1995
**League Cup**: Runners-up 1977, 1984
**European competitions**: Winners Cup-Winners' Cup 1984–85
**Finishing positions in Premier League**: 1992–93 13th, 1993–94 17th, 1994–95 15th, 1995–96 6th 1996–97 15th 1997–98 17th 1998–99 14th, 1999–2000 13th, 2000–01 16th, 2001–02 15th, 2002–03 7th, 2003–04 17th, 2004–05 4th, 2005–06 11th, 2006–07 6th, 2007–08 5th, 2008–09 5th, 2009–10 8th, 20010–11 7th, 2011–12 7th, 2012–13 6th, 2013–14 5th, 2014–15 11th, 2015–16 11th, 2016–17 7th, 2017–18 8th
**Biggest win**: 9-1 v Manchester City (Div 1) Sep 3, 1906, v Plymouth (Div 2) Dec 27, 1930. Also: 11-2 v Derby (FA Cup 1) Jan 18, 1890
**Biggest defeat**: 0-7 v Portsmouth (Div 1) Sep 10, 1949, v Arsenal (Prem Lge) May 11, 2005
**Highest League scorer in a season**: Ralph 'Dixie' Dean 60 (1927–28)
**Most League goals in aggregate**: Ralph 'Dixie' Dean 349 (1925–37)
**Longest unbeaten League sequence**: 20 matches (1978)
**Longest sequence without a League win**: 14 matches (1937)
**Most capped player**: Neville Southall (Wales) 92

| | | | | |
|---|---|---|---|---|
| **Goalkeepers** | | | | |
| Pickford, Jordan | 6.1 | Sunderland | Washington, Co Dur | 07.03.94 |
| Stekelenburg, Maarten | 6.6 | Fulham | Haarlem, Hol | 22.09.82 |
| **Defenders** | | | | |
| Baines, Leighton | 5.7 | Wigan | Liverpool | 11.12.84 |
| Browning, Tyias | 5.11 | – | Liverpool | 27.05.94 |
| Coleman, Seamus | 5.10 | Sligo | Donegal, Ire | 11.10.88 |
| Holgate, Mason | 5.11 | Barnsley | Doncaster | 22.10.96 |
| Kenny, Jonjoe | 5.10 | – | Liverpool | 15.03.97 |
| Jagielka, Phil | 5.11 | Sheffield Utd | Manchester | 17.08.82 |
| Keane, Michael | 6.3 | Burnley | Stockport | 11.01.93 |

| | | | | |
|---|---|---|---|---|
| Martina, Cuco | 6.1 | Southampton | Rotterdam, Hol | 25.09.89 |
| Pennington, Matthew | 6.1 | – | Warrington | 06.10.94 |
| Williams, Ashley | 6.0 | Swansea | Wolverhampton | 23.08.84 |
| **Midfielders** | | | | |
| Baningime, Beni | 5.10 | – | Kinshasa, Dr Cong | 09.09.98 |
| Besic, Muhamed | 5.10 | Ferencvaros | Berlin, Ger | 10.09.92 |
| Bolasie, Yannick | 6.2 | Crystal Palace | Kinshasa, DR Cong | 24.05.89 |
| Davies, Tom | 5.11 | – | Liverpool | 30.06.98 |
| Gueye, Idrissa | 5.9 | Aston Villa | Dakar, Sen | 26.09.89 |
| Klaassen, Davy | 5.11 | Ajax | Hilversum, Hol | 21.02.93 |
| McCarthy, James | 5.11 | Wigan | Glasgow | 12.11.90 |
| Mirallas, Kevin | 6.0 | Olympiacos | Liege, Bel | 05.10.87 |
| Schneiderlin, Morgan | 5.11 | Manchester Utd | Zellwiller, Fr | 08.11.89 |
| Sigurdsson, Gylfi | 6.1 | Swansea | Hafnarfjordur, Ice | 08.09.89 |
| Vlasic, Nikola | 5.10 | Hajduk Split | Split, Cro | 04.10.97 |
| Williams, Joe | 6.1 | – | Liverpool | 08.12.96 |
| **Forwards** | | | | |
| Calvert-Lewin, Dominic | 6.2 | Sheffield Utd | Sheffield | 16.03.97 |
| Lookman, Ademola | 5.9 | Charlton | Wandsworth | 20.10.97 |
| Niasse, Oumar | 6.1 | Lokomotiv Moscow | Oukam, Sen | 18.04.90 |
| Rooney, Wayne | 5.10 | Manchester Utd | Liverpool | 24.10.85 |
| Sandro | 5.10 | Malaga | Las Palmas, Sp | 09.07.95 |
| Tusun, Cenk | 6.0 | Besiktas | Wetzlar, Ger | 07.06.91 |
| Walcott, Theo | 5.8 | Arsenal | Newbury | 16.03.89 |

## FULHAM

**Ground**: Craven Cottage, Stevenage Road, Lndon SW6 6HH
**Telephone**: 0870 442 1222. **Club nickname**: Cottagers
**Capacity: 25,700**: **Colours**: White and black. **Main sponsor**: Grosvenor Casinos
**Record transfer fee**: £25m to Nice for Jean Michael Seri, Jul 2018
**Record fee received**: £16.7m from Tottenham for Mousa Dembele, Aug 2012
**Record attendance**: 49,335 v Millwall (Div 2) Oct 8, 1938
**League Championship**: 7th 2008–09
**FA Cup**: Runners-up 1975
**League Cup**: 5th rd 1968, 1971, 2000
**European competitions:** Runners-up Europa League 2009–10
**Finishing positions in Premier League:** 2001–02 13th, 2002–03 14th, 2003–04 9th, 2004–05 13th, 2005–06 12th, 2006–07 16th, 2007–08 17th, 2008–09 7th, 2009–10 12th, 2010–11 8th, 2011–12 9th, 2012–13 12th, 2013–14 19th
**Biggest win**: 10-1 v Ipswich (Div 1) Dec 26, 1963
**Biggest defeat:** 0-10 v Liverpool (League Cup 2), Sep 23, 1986
**Highest League scorer in a season**: Frank Newton 43 (1931–32)
**Most League goals in aggregate**: Gordon Davies 159 (1978–84 and 1986–91)
**Longest unbeaten League sequence**: 23 matches (2017–18)
**Longest sequence without a League win**: 15 matches (1950)
**Most capped player**: Johnny Haynes (England) 56

| | | | | |
|---|---|---|---|---|
| **Goalkeepers** | | | | |
| Bettinelli, Marcus | 6.4 | Simpeleen | Camberwell | 24.05.92 |
| Button, David | 6.3 | Brentford | Stevenage | 27.02.89 |
| **Defenders** | | | | |
| Christie, Cyrus | 6.2 | Middlesbrough | Coventry | 30.09.92 |
| Le Marchand, Maxime | 5.11 | Nice | Saint-Malo, Fr | 11.10.89 |
| Marcelo | 6.4 | CD Lugo | Barcelona, Sp | 08.10.93 |

| | | | | |
|---|---|---|---|---|
| Odoi, Denis | 5.10 | Lokeren | Leuven, Bel | 27.05.88 |
| Ream, Tim | 6.1 | Bolton | St Louis, US | 05.10.87 |
| Sessegnon, Ryan | 5.10 | – | Roehampton | 18.05.00 |
| **Midfielders** | | | | |
| Ayite, Floyd | 5.9 | Bastia | Bordeaux, Fr | 15.12.88 |
| Cairney, Tom | 6.0 | Blackburn | Nottingham | 20.01.91 |
| Cisse, Ibrahima | 6.0 | Standard Liege | Liege, Bel | 28.02.94 |
| Edun, Tayo | 5.10 | – | Islington | 14.05.98 |
| Johansen, Stefan | 6.0 | Celtic | Vardo, Nor | 08.01.91 |
| Kebano, Neesken | 5.11 | Genk | Montereau, Fr | 10.03.92 |
| McDonald, Kevin | 6.2 | Wolves | Carnoustie | 04.11.88 |
| Seri, Jean Michael | 5.7 | Nice | Grand-Bereby, Iv C | 19.07.91 |
| **Forwards** | | | | |
| Fonte, Rui | 5.11 | Braga | Penafiel, Port | 23.04.90 |
| Kamara, Aboubakar | 5.10 | Amiens | Gonesse, Fr | 07.03.95 |
| Woodrow, Cauley | 6.1 | Luton | Hemel Hempstead | 02.12.94 |

## HUDDERSFIELD TOWN

**Ground**: John Smith's Stadium, Huddersfield HD1 6PX
**Telephone**: 0870 444 4677. **Club nickname**: Terriers.
**Capacity**: 24,169. **Colours**: Blue and White. **Main sponsor**: OPE Sports
**Record transfer fee**: £12m to Monaco for Terence Kongolo, Jun 2018
**Record fee received**: £8m from Blackburn for Jordan Rhodes, Aug 2012
**Record attendance**: Leeds Road: 67,037 v Arsenal (FA Cup 6) Feb 27, 1932; John Smith's Stadium: 24,426 v Manchester Utd (Prem Lge), Oct 21, 2017
**League Championship**: Winners 1923–24, 1924–25, 1925–26
**FA Cup**: Winners 1922
**League Cup**: Semi-finalists 1968
**Finishing position in Premier League:** 2017–18 16th
**Biggest win**: 10-1 v Blackpool (Div 1) Dec 13, 1930
**Biggest defeat:** 1-10 v Manchester City (Div 2) Nov 7, 1987
**Highest League scorer in a season**: Jordan Rhodes 36 (2011–12)
**Most League goals in aggregate:** George Brown (1921–29) 142, Jimmy Glazzard (1946–56) 142
**Longest unbeaten League sequence**: 43 matches (2011)
**Longest sequence without a League win**: 22 matches (1971–72)
**Most capped player**: Jimmy Nicholson (Northern Ireland) 31

| | | | | |
|---|---|---|---|---|
| **Goalkeepers** | | | | |
| Coleman, Joel | 6.4 | Oldham | Bolton | 06.09.95 |
| Hamer, Ben | 6.4 | Leicester | Taunton | 20.11.87 |
| Lossl, Jonas | 6.5 | Mainz | Kolding, Den | 01.02.89 |
| Schofield, Ryan | 6.3 | – | Huddersfield | 11.12.99 |
| **Defenders** | | | | |
| Durm, Erik | 6.0 | Borussia Dortmund | Pirmasens, Ger | 12.05.92 |
| Hadergjonaj, Florent | 6.0 | Ingolstadt | Langnau, Switz | 31.07.94 |
| Hefele, Michael | 6.3 | Dynamo Dresden | Pfaffenhofen, Ger | 01.09.90 |
| Kongolo, Terence | 6.2 | Monaco | Fribourg, Switz | 14.02.94 |
| Jorgensen, Mathias | 6.3 | FC Copenhagen | Copenhagen, Den | 23.04.90 |
| Lowe, Chris | 5.8 | Kaiserslautern | Plauen, Ger | 16.04.89 |
| Malone, Scott | 6.2 | Fulham | Rowley Regis | 25.03.91 |
| Schindler, Christopher | 6.2 | 1860 Munich | Munich, Ger | 29.04.90 |
| Smith, Tommy | 6.1 | Manchester City | Warrington | 14.04.92 |
| Stankovic, Jon Gorenc | 6.3 | Borussia Dortmund | Ljubljana, Sloven | 14.01.96 |

**Midfielders**

| | | | | |
|---|---|---|---|---|
| Bacuna, Juninho | 5.10 | Groningen | Groningen, Hol | 07.08.97 |
| Billing, Philip | 6.4 | – | Esbjerg, Den | 11.06.96 |
| Hogg, Jonathan | 5.7 | Watford | Middlesbrough | 06.12.88 |
| Ince, Tom | 5.10 | Derby | Stockport | 30.01.92 |
| Mooy, Aaron | 5.11 | Manchester City | Sydney, Aus | 15.09.90 |
| Pritchard, Alex | 5.8 | Norwich | Orsett | 03.05.93 |
| Sabiri, Abdelhamid | 6.0 | Nuremberg | Goulmima, Mor | 28.11.96 |
| Scannell, Sean | 5.9 | Crystal Palace | Croydon | 21.03.89 |
| Van La Parra, Rajiv | 5.11 | Wolves | Rotterdam, Hol | 04.06.91 |
| Williams, Danny | 6.0 | Reading | Karlsruhe, Ger | 08.03.89 |
| **Forwards** | | | | |
| Depoitre, Laurent | 6.3 | Porto | Tournai, Bel | 07.12.88 |
| Kachunga, Elias | 5.10 | Ingolstadt | Haan, Ger | 22.04.92 |
| Mounie, Steve | 6.3 | Montpellier | Parakin, Benin | 29.09.94 |
| Quaner, Collin | 6.3 | Union Berlin | Dusseldorf, Ger | 18.06.91 |
| Sobhi, Ramadan | 6.0 | Stoke | Cairo, Egy | 23.01.97 |

## LEICESTER CITY

**Ground**: King Power Stadium, Filbert Way, Leicester, LE2 7FL
**Telephone**: 0844 815 5000. **Club nickname**: Foxes
**Capacity**: 32,273. **Colours**: Blue and white. **Main sponsor**: King Power
**Record transfer fee**: £29.7m to Sporting Lisbon for Islam Slimani, Aug 2016
**Record fee received**: £60m from Manchester City for Riyad Mahrez, Jul 2018
**Record attendance**: Filbert Street: 47,298 v. Tottenham (FA Cup 5) Fb 18, 1928; King Power Stadium: 32,148 v Newcastle (Prem Lge) Dec 26, 2003. Also: 32,188 v Real Madrid (friendly) Jul 30, 2011
**League Championship**: Winners 2015–16
**FA Cup**: Runners-up 1949, 1961, 1963, 1969
**League Cup**: Winners 1964, 1997, 2000
**European competitions**: Champions League quarter-finals 2016–17
**Finishing positions in Premier League**: 1994–95 21st, 1996–97 9th, 1997–98 10th, 1998–99 10th, 1999–2000 8th, 2000–01 13th, 2001–02 20th, 2003–04 18th, 2014–15 14th, 2015–16 1st, 2016–17 12th, 2017–18 9th
**Biggest win**: 10-0 v Portsmouth (Div 1) Oct 20, 1928. Also: 13-0 v Notts Olympic (FA Cup) Oct 13, 1894
**Biggest defeat** (while Leicester Fosse): 0-12 v Nottm Forest (Div 1) Apr 21, 1909
**Highest League scorer in a season**: Arthur Rowley 44 (1956–57)
**Most League goals in aggregate**: Arthur Chandler 259 (1923–35)
**Longest unbeaten League sequence**: 23 matches (2008–09)
**Longest sequence without a League win**: 19 matches (1975)
**Most capped player**: Andy King (Wales) 47

**Goalkeepers**

| | | | | |
|---|---|---|---|---|
| Jakupovic, Eldin | 6.3 | Hull | Sarajevo, Bos | 02.10.84 |
| Schmeichel, Kasper | 6.0 | Leeds | Copenhagen, Den | 05.11.86 |
| **Defenders** | | | | |
| Benalouane, Yohan | 6.2 | Atalatna | Bagnols-sur-Ceze, Fr | 28.03.87 |
| Chilwell, Ben | 5.10 | – | Milton Keynes | 21.12.96 |
| Evans, Jonny | 6.2 | WBA | Belfast | 02.01.88 |
| Fuchs, Christian | 6.1 | Schalke | Neunkirchen, Aut | 07.04.86 |
| Maguire, Harry | 6.2 | Hull | Sheffield | 05.03.93 |
| Morgan, Wes | 6.1 | Nottm Forest | Nottingham | 21.01.84 |
| Simpson, Danny | 6.0 | QPR | Salford | 04.01.87 |

| **Midfielders** | | | | |
|---|---|---|---|---|
| Adrien Silva | 5.9 | Sporting Lisbon | Angouleme, Fr | 15.03.89 |
| Albrighton, Mark | 6.1 | Aston Villa | Tamworth | 18.11.89 |
| Amartey, Daniel | 6.0 | Copenhagen | Accra, Gh | 01.12.94 |
| Choudhury, Hamza | 5.10 | – | Loughborough | 01.10.97 |
| Diabate, Fousseni | 5.9 | Ajaccio | Aubervilliers, Fr | 18.10.95 |
| Gray, Demarai | 5.10 | Birmingham | Birmingham | 28.06.96 |
| Iborra, Vicente | 6.3 | Sevilla | Moncada, Sp | 16.01.88 |
| James, Matty | 5.10 | Manchester Utd | Bacup | 22.07.91 |
| Kapustka, Bartosz | 5.11 | Cracovia | Tarnow, Pol | 23.12.96 |
| King, Andy | 6.0 | – | Maidenhead | 29.10.88 |
| Maddison, James | 5.10 | Norwich | Coventry | 23.11.96 |
| Mendy, Nampalys | 5.6 | Nice | La Seyne, Fr | 23.06.92 |
| Ndidi, Wilfred | 6.0 | Genk | Lagos, Nig | 16.12.96 |
| **Forwards** | | | | |
| Barnes, Harvey | 5.9 | – | Burnley | 09.12.97 |
| Iheanacho, Kelechi | 6.2 | Manchester City | Owerri, Nig | 03.10.96 |
| Musa, Ahmed | 5.7 | CSKA Moscow | Jos, Nig | 14.10.92 |
| Okazaki, Shinji | 5.9 | Mainz | Takarazuka, Jap | 16.04.86 |
| Slimani, Islam | 6.2 | Sporting Lisbon | Algiers, Alg | 18.06.88 |
| Thomas, George | 5.8 | Coventry | Leicester | 24.03.97 |
| Ulloa, Leonardo | 6.2 | Brighton | General Roca, Arg | 26.07.86 |
| Vardy, Jamie | 5.10 | Fleetwood | Sheffield | 11.01.87 |

## LIVERPOOL

**Ground**: Anfield, Liverpool L4 OTH
**Telephone**: 0151 263 2361. **Club nickname**: Reds or Pool
**Capacity**: 53,394. **Colours**: Red. **Main sponsor**: Standard Chartered
**Record transfer fee**: £75 to Southampton for Virgil van Dijk Jan 2018
**Record fee received**: £142m from Barcelona for Philippe Coutinho, Jan 2018
**Record attendance**: 61,905 v Wolves, (FA Cup 4), Feb 2, 1952
**League Championship**: Winners 1900–01, 1905–06, 1921–22, 1922–23, 1946–47, 1963–64, 1965–66, 1972–73, 1975–76, 1976–77, 1978–79, 1979–80, 1981–82, 1982–83,1983–84, 1985–86, 1987–88, 1989–90
**FA Cup**: Winners 1965, 1974, 1986, 1989, 1992, 2001, 2006
**League Cup**: Winners 1981, 1982, 1983, 1984, 1995, 2001, 2003, 2012
**European competitions**: Winners European Cup/Champions League 1976–77, 1977–78,1980–81, 1983–84, 2004–05; UEFA Cup 1972–73, 1975–76, 2000–01; European Super Cup 1977, 2001, 2005
**Finishing positions in Premier League**: 1992–93 6th, 1993–94 8th, 1994–95 4th, 1995–96 3rd, 1996–97 4th, 1997–98 3rd, 1998–99 7th, 1999–2000 4th, 2000–01 3rd, 2001–02 2nd, 2002–03 5th, 2003–04 4th, 2004–05 5th, 2005–06 3rd, 2006–07 3rd, 2007–08 4th, 2008–09 2nd, 2009–10 7th, 2010–11 6th, 2011–12 8th, 2012–13 7th, 2013–14 2nd, 2014–15 6th, 2015–16 8th, 2016–17 4th, 2017–18 4th
**Biggest win**: 10-1 v Rotherham (Div 2) Feb 18, 1896. Also: 11-0 v Stromsgodset (Cup-Winners' Cup 1) Sep 17, 1974
**Biggest defeat**: 1-9 v Birmingham (Div 2) Dec 11, 1954
**Highest League scorer in a season**: Roger Hunt 41 (1961–62)
**Most League goals in aggregate**: Roger Hunt 245 (1959–69)
**Longest unbeaten League sequence**: 31 matches (1987–88))
**Longest sequence without a League win**: 14 matches (1953–54))
**Most capped player**: Steven Gerrard (England) 114

| | | | | |
|---|---|---|---|---|
| **Goalkeepers** | | | | |
| Karius, Loris | 6.3 | Mainz | Biberach, Ger | 22.06.93 |
| Mignolet, Simon | 6.4 | Sunderland | Sint-Truiden, Bel | 06.08.88 |
| Ward, Danny | 6.4 | Wrexham | Wrexham | 22.06.93 |
| **Defenders** | | | | |
| Clyne, Nathaniel | 5.9 | Southampton | Stockwell | 05.04.91 |
| Gomez, Joe | 6.1 | Charlton | Catford | 23.05.97 |
| Klavan, Ragnar | 6.2 | Augsburg | Viljandi, Est | 30.10.85 |
| Lovren, Dejan | 6.2 | Southampton | Zenica, Bos | 05.07.89 |
| Matip, Joel | 6.5 | Schalke | Bochum, Ger | 08.08.91 |
| Moreno, Alberto | 5.7 | Sevilla | Seville, Sp | 05.07.92 |
| Robertson, Andrew | 5.10 | Hull | Glasgow | 11.03.94 |
| Van Dijk, Virgil | 6.4 | Southampton | Breda, Hol | 08.07.91 |
| **Midfielders** | | | | |
| Fabinho | 6.2 | Monaco | Campinas, Bra | 23.10.93 |
| Grujic, Marko | 6.3 | Red Star Belgrade | Belgrade, Serb | 13.04.96 |
| Henderson, Jordan | 5.10 | Sunderland | Sunderland | 17.06.90 |
| Lallana, Adam | 5.10 | Southampton | Bournemouth | 10.05.88 |
| Markovic, Lazar | 5.9 | Benfica | Cacak, Serb | 02.03.94 |
| Milner, James | 5.11 | Manchester City | Leeds | 04.01.86 |
| Ojo, Sheyi | 5.10 | – | Hemel Hempstead | 19.06.97 |
| Oxlade-Chamberlain, Alex | 5.11 | Arsenal | Portsmouth | 15.08.93 |
| Salah, Mohamed | 5.9 | Roma | Basyoun, Egy | 15.06.92 |
| Shaqiri, Xherdan | 5.7 | Stoke | Gjilan, Kos | 10.10.91 |
| Wijnaldum, Georginio | 5.9 | Newcastle | Rotterdam, Hol | 11.11.90 |
| **Forwards** | | | | |
| Firmino, Roberto | 6.0 | Hoffenheim | Maceio, Br | 02.10.91 |
| Ings, Danny | 5.10 | Burnley | Winchester | 16.03.92 |
| Mane, Sadio | 5.9 | Southampton | Sedhiou, Sen | 10.04.92 |
| Origi, Divock | 6.1 | Lille | Ostend, Bel | 18.04.95 |
| Solanke, Dominic | 6.1 | Chelsea | Reading | 14.09.97 |
| Sturridge, Daniel | 6.2 | Chelsea | Birmingham | 01.09.89 |
| Woodburn, Ben | 5.11 | – | Nottingham | 15.10.99 |

## MANCHESTER CITY

**Ground**: Etihad Stadium, Etihad Campus, Manchester M11 3FF
**Telephone**: 0161 444 1894. **Club nickname**: City
**Capacity**: 55,017. **Colours**: Sky blue and white. **Main sponsor**: Etihad
**Record transfer fee**: £60m to Leicester for Riyad Mahrez, Jul 2018
**Record fee received**: £25m from Leicester for Kelechi Iheanacho, Jul 2017
**Record attendance**: Maine Road: 84,569 v Stoke (FA Cup 6) Mar 3, 1934 (British record for any game outside London or Glasgow). Etihad Stadium: 54,693 v Leicester (Prem Lge) February 6, 2016
**League Championship**: Winners 1936–37, 1967–68, 2011–12, 2013–14, 2017–18
**FA Cup**: Winners 1904, 1934, 1956, 1969, 2011
**League Cup**: Winners 1970, 1976, 2014, 2016, 2018
**European competitions**: Winners Cup-Winners' Cup 1969–70
**Finishing positions in Premier League**: 1992–93 9th, 1993–94 16th, 1994–95 17th, 1995–96 18th, 2000–01: 18th, 2002–03 9th, 2003–04 16th, 2004–05 8th, 2005–06 15th, 2006–07 14th, 2007–08 9th, 2008–09 10th, 2009–10 5th, 2010–11 3rd, 2011–12 1st, 2012–13 2nd, 2013–14 1st, 2014–15 2nd, 2015–16 4th, 2016–17 3rd, 2017–18 1st
**Biggest win**: 10-1 Huddersfield (Div 2) Nov 7, 1987. Also: 10-1 v Swindon (FA Cup 4) Jan 29, 1930
**Biggest defeat**: 1-9 v Everton (Div 1) Sep 3, 1906
**Highest League scorer in a season**: Tommy Johnson 38 (1928–29)

**Most League goals in aggregate**: Tommy Johnson, 158 (1919–30)
**Longest unbeaten League sequence**: 22 matches (1946–47) and (2017–18)
**Longest sequence without a League win**: 17 matches (1979–80)
**Most capped player**: Joe Hart (England) 63

| | | | | |
|---|---|---|---|---|
| **Goalkeepers** | | | | |
| Bravo, Claudio | 6.1 | Barcelona | Viluco, Chil | 13.04.83 |
| Ederson | 6.2 | Benfica | Osasco, Br | 17.08.93 |
| **Defenders** | | | | |
| Adarabioyo, Tosin | 6.5 | – | Manchester | 24.09.97 |
| Danilo | 6.0 | Real Madrid | Bicas, Br | 15.07.91 |
| Denayer, Jason | 6.1 | – | Jette, Bel | 28.06.95 |
| Kompany, Vincent | 6.4 | Hamburg | Uccle, Bel | 10.04.86 |
| Laporte, Aymeric | 6.3 | Athletic Bilbao | Agen, Fr | 27.05.94 |
| Maffeo, Pablo | 5.8 | Girona | Sant Joan, Sp | 12.07.97 |
| Mangala, Eliaquim | 6.2 | Porto | Colombes, Fr | 13.02.91 |
| Mendy, Benjamin | 6.0 | Monaco | Longjumeau, Fr | 17.07.94 |
| Otamendi, Nicolas | 6.0 | Valencia | Buenos Aires, Arg | 12.02.88 |
| Stones, John | 6.2 | Everton | Barnsley | 28.05.94 |
| Walker, Kyle | 6.0 | Tottenham | Sheffield | 28.05.90 |
| **Midfielders** | | | | |
| De Bruyne, Kevin | 5.11 | Wolfsburg | Drongen, Bel | 28.06.91 |
| Delph, Fabian | 5.9 | Aston Villa | Bradford | 21.11.89 |
| Diaz, Brahim | 5.7 | – | Malaga, Sp | 03.08.99 |
| Fernandinho | 5.10 | Shakhtar Donetsk | Londrina, Br | 04.05.85 |
| Garcia, Aleix | 5.8 | Villarreal | Ulldecona, Sp | 28.06.97 |
| Gundogan, Ilkay | 5.11 | Borussia Dortmund | Gelsenkirchen, Ger | 24.10.90 |
| Harrison, Jack | 5.9 | New York City | Stoke | 20.11.96 |
| Mahrez, Riyad | 5.10 | Leicester | Sarcelles, Fr | 21.02.91 |
| Moreno, Marlos | 5.7 | Nacional | Medellin, Col | 20.09.96 |
| Roberts, Patrick | 5.7 | Fulham | Kingston upon Thames | 05.02.97 |
| Sane, Leroy | 6.0 | Schalke | Essen, Ger | 11.01.96 |
| Silva, Bernardo | 5.8 | Monaco | Lisbon, Port | 10.08.94 |
| Silva, David | 5.7 | Valencia | Arguineguin, Sp | 08.01.86 |
| Zinchenko, Oleksandr | 5.9 | FC Ufa | Radomyshi, Ukr | 15.12.96 |
| **Forwards** | | | | |
| Aguero, Sergio | 5.8 | Atletico Madrid | Quilmes, Arg | 02.06.88 |
| Foden, Phil | 5.7 | – | Stockport | 28.05.00 |
| Gabriel Jesus | 5.9 | Palmeiras | Sao Paulo, Br | 03.04.97 |
| Sterling, Raheem | 5.7 | Liverpool | Kingston, Jam | 08.12.94 |

## MANCHESTER UNITED

**Ground**: Old Trafford Stadium, Sir Matt Busby Way, Manchester, M16 ORA
**Telephone**: 0161 868 8000. **Club nickname**: Red Devils
**Capacity**: 73,300. **Colours**: Red and white. **Main sponsor**: Chevrolet
**Record transfer fee**: £89.3m to Juventus for Paul Pogba, Aug 2016
**Record fee received**: £80m from Real Madrid for Cristiano Ronaldo, Jun 2009
**Record attendance**: 75,811 v Blackburn (Prem Lge), Mar 31, 2007. Also: 76,962 Wolves v Grimsby (FA Cup semi-final) Mar 25, 1939. Crowd of 83,260 saw Manchester Utd v Arsenal (Div 1) Jan 17, 1948 at Maine Road – Old Trafford out of action through bomb damage
**League Championship**: Winners 1907–08, 1910–11, 1951–52, 1955–56, 1956–7, 1964–65, 1966–67, 1992–93, 1993–94, 1995–96, 1996–97, 1998–99, 1999–2000, 2000–01, 2002–03, 2006–07, 2007–08, 2008–09, 2010–11, 2012–13
**FA Cup**: Winners 1909, 1948, 1963, 1977, 1983, 1985, 1990, 1994, 1996, 1999, 2004, 2016

**League Cup**: Winners 1992, 2006, 2009, 2010, 2017
**European competitions**: Winners European Cup/Champions League 1967–68, 1998–99, 2007–08; Cup-Winners' Cup 1990–91; European Super Cup 1991; Europa League 2016–17
**World Club Cup**: Winners 2008
**Finishing positions in Premier League**: 1992–93 1st, 1993–94 1st, 1994–95 2nd, 1995–96 1st, 1996–97 1st, 1997–98 2nd, 1998–99 1st, 1999–2000 1st, 2000–01 1st, 2001–02 3rd, 2002–03 1st, 2003–04 3rd, 2004–05 3rd, 2005–06 2nd, 2006–07 1st, 2007–08 1st, 2000–09 1st, 2009–10 2nd, 2010–11 1st, 2011–12 2nd, 2012–13 1st, 2013–14 7th, 2014–15 4th, 2015–16 5th, 2016–17 6th, 2017–18 2nd
**Biggest win**: As Newton Heath: 10-1 v Wolves (Div 1) Oct 15, 1892. As Manchester Utd: 9-0 v Ipswich (Prem Lge), Mar 4, 1995. Also: 10-0 v Anderlecht (European Cup prelim rd) Sep 26, 1956
**Biggest defeat**: 0-7 v Blackburn (Div 1) Apr 10, 1926, v Aston Villa (Div 1) Dec 27, 1930, v Wolves (Div 2) 26 Dec, 1931
**Highest League scorer in a season**: Dennis Viollet 32 (1959–60)
**Most League goals in aggregate**: Bobby Charlton 199 (1956–73)
**Longest unbeaten League sequence**: 29 matches (1998–99)
**Longest sequence without a League win**: 16 matches (1930)
**Most capped player**: Sir Bobby Charlton (England) 106

| | | | | |
|---|---|---|---|---|
| **Goalkeepers** | | | | |
| De Gea, David | 6.4 | Atletico Madrid | Madrid, Sp | 07.11.90 |
| Grant, Lee | 6.2 | Stoke | Hemel Hempstead | 27.01.83 |
| Romero, Sergio | 6.4 | Sampdoria | Bernardo, Arg | 22.02.87 |
| **Defenders** | | | | |
| Bailly, Eric | 6.1 | Villarreal | Bingerville, Iv C | 12.04.94 |
| Dalot, Diogo | 6.1 | Porto | Braga, Port | 18.03.99 |
| Darmian, Matteo | 6.0 | Torino | Legnano, It | 02.12.89 |
| Fosu-Mensah, Tim | 6.1 | – | Amsterdam, Hol | 02.01.98 |
| Jones, Phil | 5.11 | Blackburn | Blackburn | 21.02.92 |
| Lindelof, Victor | 6.2 | Benfica | Vasteras, Swe | 17.07.94 |
| Rojo, Marcos | 6.2 | Sporting Lisbon | La Plata, Arg | 20.03.90 |
| Shaw, Luke | 6.1 | Southamptonn | Kingston upon Thames | 12.07.95 |
| Smalling, Chris | 6.1 | Fulham | Greenwich | 22.11.89 |
| Tuanzebe, Axel | 6.1 | – | Bunia, Dr Cong | 14.11.97 |
| **Midfielders** | | | | |
| Blind, Daley | 5.11 | Ajax | Amsterdam, Hol | 09.03.90 |
| Fellaini, Marouane | 6.4 | Everton | Etterbeek, Bel | 22.11.87 |
| Herrera, Ander | 6.0 | Athletic Bilbao | Bilbao, Sp | 14.08.89 |
| Mata, Juan | 5.7 | Chelsea | Burgos, Sp | 28.04.88 |
| Matic, Nemanja | 6.4 | Chelsea | Sabac, Serb | 01.08.88 |
| McTominay, Scott | 6.4 | – | Lancaster | 08.12.96 |
| Pereira, Andreas | 5.10 | PSV Eindhoven | Duffel, Bel | 01.01.96 |
| Pogba, Paul | 6.3 | Juventus | Lagny-sur-Marne, Fr | 15.03.93 |
| Valencia, Antonio | 5.10 | Wigan | Lago Agrio, Ec | 04.08.85 |
| Young, Ashley | 5.10 | Aston Villa | Stevenage | 09.07.85 |
| **Forwards** | | | | |
| Fred | 5.7 | Shakhtar Donetsk | Belo Horizonte, Bra | 05.03.93 |
| Lingard, Jesse | 6.2 | – | Warrington | 15.12.92 |
| Lukaku, Romelu | 6.3 | Everton | Antwerp, Bel | 13.05.93 |
| Martial, Anthony | 5.11 | Monaco | Massy, Fr | 05.12.95 |
| Rashford, Marcus | 6.0 | – | Wythensawe | 31.10.97 |
| Sanchez, Alexis | 5.7 | Arsenal | Tocopilla, Chil | 19.12.88 |

## NEWCASTLE UNITED

**Ground**: St James' Park, Newcastle-upon-Tyne, NE1 4ST
**Telephone**: 0844 372 1892. **Club nickname**: Magpies
**Capacity**: 52,354. **Colours**: Black and white. **Main sponsor**: FUN88
**Record attendance**: 68,386 v Chelsea (Div 1) Sep 3, 1930
**Record transfer fee**: £16m to Real Madrid for Michael Owen, Aug 2005
**Record fee received**: £35m from Liverpool for Andy Carroll, Jan 2011
**League Championship**: Winners 1904–05, 1906–07, 1908–09, 1926–27
**FA Cup: Winners**: 1910, 1924, 1932, 1951, 1952,1955
**League Cup:** Runners-up 1976
**European competitions**: Winners Fairs Cup 1968–69; Anglo-Italian Cup 1972–73
**Finishing positions in Premier League**: 1993–94 3rd, 1994–95 6th, 1995–96 2nd, 1996–97 2nd, 1997–98 13th, 1998–99 13th, 1999–2000 11th, 2000–01 11th, 2001–02 4th, 2002–03 3rd, 2003–04 5th, 2004–05 14th, 2005–06 7th, 2006–07 13th, 2007–08 12th, 2008–09 18th, 2010–11 12th, 2011–12 5th, 2012–13 16th, 2013–14 10th, 2014–15 15th, 2015–16 18th, 2017–18 10th
**Biggest win**: 13-0 v Newport (Div 2) Oct 5, 1946
**Biggest defeat**: 0-9 v Burton (Div 2) Apr 15, 1895
**Highest League scorer in a season**: Hughie Gallacher 36 (1926–27)
**Most League goals in aggregate**: Jackie Milburn 177 (1946–57)
**Longest unbeaten League sequence**: 14 matches (1950)
**Longest sequence without a League win**: 21 matches (1978)
**Most capped player**: Shay Given (Republic of Irelnd) 83

| | | | | |
|---|---|---|---|---|
| **Goalkeepers** | | | | |
| Darlow, Karl | 6.1 | Nottm Forest | Northampton | 08.10.90 |
| Dubravka, Martin | 6.3 | Sparta Prague | Zilina, Slovak | 15.01.89 |
| Elliot, Rob | 6.3 | Charlton | Chatham | 30.04.86 |
| Woodman, Freddie | 6.2 | Crystal Palace | Croydon | 04.03.97 |
| **Defenders** | | | | |
| Clark, Ciaran | 6.2 | Aston Villa | Harrow | 26.09.89 |
| Dummett, Paul | 6.0 | – | Newcastle | 26.09.91 |
| Lascelles, Jamaal | 6.2 | Nottm Forest | Derby | 11.11.93 |
| Lazaar, Achraf | 6.1 | Palermo | Casablanca, Mor | 22.01.92 |
| Lejeune, Florian | 6.3 | Eibar | Paris, Fr | 20.05.91 |
| Manquillo, Javier | 6.0 | Atletico Madrid | Madrid, Sp | 05.05.94 |
| Mbemba, Chancel | 6.0 | Anderlecht | Kinshasa, DR Cong | 08.08.94 |
| Yedlin, DeAndre | 5.9 | Tottenham | Seattle, US | 09.07.93 |
| **Midfielders** | | | | |
| Aarons, Rolando | 5.9 | Bristol City | Kingston, Jam | 16.11.95 |
| Atsu, Christian | 5.8 | Chelsea | Ada Foah, Gh | 10.01.92 |
| Colback, Jack | 5.10 | Sunderland | Killingworth | 24.10.89 |
| Diame, Mohamed | 6.1 | Hull | Creteil, Fr | 14.06.87 |
| Hayden, Isaac | 6.1 | Arsenal | Chelmsford | 22.03.95 |
| Kenedy | 6.0 | Chelsea (loan) | Santa Rita, Bra | 08.02.96 |
| Ki Sung-Yeung | 6.2 | Swansea | Gwangju, S Kor | 24.01.89 |
| Merino, Mikel | 6.2 | Borussia Dortmund | Pamplona, Sp | 22.06.96 |
| Murphy, Jacob | 5.10 | Norwich | Wembley | 24.02.95 |
| Ritchie, Matt | 5.8 | Bournemouth | Gosport | 10.09.89 |
| Shelvey, Jonjo | 6.0 | Swansea | Romford | 27.02.92 |
| **Forwards** | | | | |
| Armstrong, Adam | 5.8 | – | Newcastle | 10.02.97 |
| Ayoze Perez | 5.11 | Tenerife | Santa Cruz, Ten | 23.07.93 |
| Gayle, Dwight | 5.10 | Crystal Palace | Walthamstow | 20.10.90 |

| | | | | |
|---|---|---|---|---|
| Joselu | 6.3 | Stoke | Stuttgart, Ger | 27.03.90 |
| Mitrovic, Aleksandar | 6.3 | Anderlecht | Smederevo, Serb | 16.09.94 |

## SOUTHAMPTON

**Ground**: St Mary's Stadium, Britannia Road, Southampton, SO14 5FP
**Telephone**: 0845 688 9448. **Club nickname**: Saints
**Capacity**: 32,384. **Colours**: Red and white. **Main sponsor**: Virgin Media
**Record transfer fee**: £19.1m to Monaco for Guido Carrillo, Jan 2018
**Record fee received**: £75m from Liverpool for Virgil van Dijk, Jan 2018
**Record attendance**: The Dell: 31,044 v Manchester Utd (Div 1) Oct 8, 1969. St Mary's: 32,363 v Coventry (Champ) Apr 28, 2012
**League Championship**: Runners-up 1983–84
**FA Cup**: Winners 1976
**League Cup**: Runners-up 1979, 2017
**European competitions**: Fairs Cup rd 3 1969–70; Cup-Winners' Cup rd 3 1976–77
**Finishing positions in Premier League**: 1992–93 18th, 1993–94 18th, 1994–5 10th, 1995–96 17th, 1996–97 16th, 1997–98 12th, 1998–99 17th, 1999–200 15th, 2000–01 10th, 2001–02 11th, 2002–03 8th, 2003–04 12th, 2004–05 20th, 2012–13 14th, 2013–14 8th, 2014–15 7th, 2015–16 6th, 2016–17 8 th, 2017–18 17th
**Biggest win**: 8-0 v Northampton (Div 3S) Dec 24, 1921, v Sunderland (Prem Lge) Oct 18, 2014
**Biggest defeat**: 0-8 v Tottenham (Div 2) Mar 28, 1936, v Everton (Div 1) Nov 20, 1971
**Highest League scorer in a season**: Derek Reeves 39 (1959–60)
**Most League goals in aggregate:** Mick Channon 185 (1966–82)
**Longest unbeaten League sequence**: 19 matches (1921)
**Longest unbeaten League sequence**: 20 matches (1969)
**Most capped player**: Peter Shilton (England) 49

| | | | | |
|---|---|---|---|---|
| **Goalkeepers** | | | | |
| Forster, Fraser | 6.7 | Celtic | Hexham | 17.03.88 |
| Gunn, Angus | 6.5 | Manchester City | Norwich | 22.01.96 |
| McCarthy, Alex | 6.4 | Crystal Palace | Guildford | 03.12.89 |
| **Defenders** | | | | |
| Bednarek, Jan | 6.2 | Lech Poznan | Slupca, Pol | 12.04.96 |
| Bertrand, Ryan | 5.10 | Chelsea | Southwark | 05.08.89 |
| Hoedt, Wesley | 6.2 | Lazio | Alkmaar, Hol | 06.03.94 |
| Soares, Cedric | 5.8 | Sporting Lisbon | Singen, Ger | 31.08.91 |
| Stephens, Jack | 6.1 | Plymouth | Torpoint | 27.01.94 |
| Targett, Matt | 6.0 | – | Eastleigh | 18.09.95 |
| Vestergaard, Jannik | 6.6 | Borussia M'gladbach | Copenhagen, Den | 03.08.92 |
| Yoshida, Maya | 6.2 | Venlo | Nagasaki, Jap | 24.08.88 |
| **Midfielders** | | | | |
| Armstrong, Stuart | 6.0 | Celtic | Inverness | 30.03.92 |
| Boufal, Sofiane | 5.9 | Lille | Paris, Fr | 17.09.93 |
| Clasie, Jordy | 5.7 | Feyenoord | Haarlem, Hol | 27.06.91 |
| Davis, Steven | 5.8 | Rangers | Ballymena | 01.01.85 |
| Elyounoussi, Mohamed | 5.10 | Basle | Al Hoceima, Mor | 04.08.94 |
| Hesketh, Jake | 5.6 | – | Stockport | 27.03.96 |
| Hojbjerg, Pierre-Emile | 6.1 | Bayern Munich | Copenhagen, Den | 05.08.95 |
| Lemina, Mario | 6.1 | Juventus | Libreville, Gab | 01.09.93 |
| McQueen, Sam | 5.11 | – | Southampton | 06.02.95 |
| Redmond, Nathan | 5.8 | Norwich | Birmingham | 06.03.94 |
| Romeu, Oriol | 6.0 | Chelsea | Ulldecona, Sp | 24.09.91 |
| Sims, Joshua | 5.9 | – | Yeovil | 28.03.97 |
| Ward-Prowse, James | 5.8 | – | Portsmouth | 01.11.94 |

**Forwards**

| | | | | |
|---|---|---|---|---|
| Austin, Charlie | 6.2 | QPR | Hungerford | 05.07.89 |
| Gabbiadini, Manolo | 6.1 | Napoli | Calcinate, It | 26.11.91 |
| Gallagher, Sam | 6.4 | – | Crediton | 15.09.95 |
| Long, Shane | 5.10 | Hull | Gortnahoe, Ire | 22.01.87 |

## TOTTENHAM HOTSPUR

**Ground**: Tottenham Stadium
**Telephone**: TBC. **Club nickname**: Spurs
**Capacity**: 62,062. **Colours**: White. **Main sponsor**: AIA
**Record transfer fee**: £42m to Ajax for Davinson Sanchez, Aug 2017
**Record fee received**: £85.3m from Real Madrid for Gareth Bale, Aug 2013
**Record attendance**: White Hart Lane: 75,038 v Sunderland (FA Cup 6) Mar 5, 1938. Wembley: 85,512 v Bayer Leverkusen (Champs Lge) Nov 2, 2016
**League Championship**: Winners 1950–51, 1960–61
**FA Cup**: Winners 1901, 1921, 1961, 1962, 1967, 1981, 1982, 1991
**League Cup**: Winners 1971, 1973, 1999, 2008
**European competitions**: Winners Cup-Winners' Cup 1962–63; UEFA Cup 1971–72, 1983–84
**Finishing positions in Premier League**: 1992–93 8th, 1993–94 15th, 1994–95 7th, 1995–96 8th, 1996–97 10th, 1997–98 14th, 1998–99 11th, 1999–2000 10th, 2000–01 12th, 2001–02 9th, 2002–03 10th, 2003–04 14th, 2004–05 9th, 2005–06 5th, 2006–07 5th, 2007–08 11th, 2008–09 8th, 2009–10 4th, 2010–11 5th, 2011–12 4th, 2012–13 5th, 2013–14 6th, 2014–15 5th, 2015–16 3rd, 2016–17 2nd, 2017–18 3rd
**Biggest win**: 9-0 v Bristol Rov (Div 2) Oct 22, 1977. Also: 13-2 v Crewe (FA Cup 4 replay) Feb 3, 1960
**Biggest defeat**: 0-7 v Liverpool (Div 1) Sep 2, 1979. Also: 0-8 v Cologne (Inter Toto Cup) Jul 22, 1995
**Highest League scorer in a season**: Jimmy Greaves 37 (1962–63)
**Most League goals in aggregate**: Jimmy Greaves 220 (1961–70)
**Longest unbeaten League sequence**: 22 matches (1949)
**Longest sequence without a League win**: 16 matches (1934–35)
**Most capped player**: Pat Jennings (Northern Ireland) 74

| | | | | |
|---|---|---|---|---|
| **Goalkeepers** | | | | |
| Gazzaniga, Paulo | 6.5 | Southampton | Murphy, Arg | 02.01.92 |
| Lloris, Hugo | 6.2 | Lyon | Nice, Fr | 26.12.86 |
| Vorm, Michel | 6.0 | Swansea | Nieuwegein, Hol | 20.10.83 |
| **Defenders** | | | | |
| Alderweireld, Toby | 6.2 | Atletico Madrid | Antwerp, Bel | 02.03.89 |
| Aurier, Serge | 5.9 | Paris SG | Ouragahio, Iv C | 24.12.92 |
| Davies, Ben | 5.6 | Swansea | Neath | 24.04.93 |
| Dier, Eric | 6.2 | Sporting Lisbon | Cheltenham | 15.01.94 |
| Foyth, Juan | 5.10 | Estudiantes | La Plata, Arg | 12.01.98 |
| Rose, Danny | 5.8 | Leeds | Doncaster | 02.07.90 |
| Sanchez, Davinson | 6.2 | Ajax | Caloto, Col | 12.06.96 |
| Trippier, Kieran | 5.10 | Burnley | Bury | 19.09.90 |
| Vertonghen, Jan | 6.2 | Ajax | Sint-Niklaas, Bel | 24.04.87 |
| Walker-Peters, Kyle | 5.8 | – | Edmonton | 13.04.97 |
| **Midfielders** | | | | |
| Alli, Dele | 6.1 | MK Dons | Milton Keynes | 11.04.96 |
| Dembele, Mousa | 6.1 | Fulham | Wilrijk, Bel | 16.07.87 |
| Eriksen, Christian | 5.10 | Ajax | Middelfart, Den | 14.02.92 |
| Lamela, Erik | 6.0 | Roma | Buenos Aires, Arg | 04.03.92 |
| Lucas Moura | 5.8 | Paris SG | Sao Paulo, Br | 13.08.92 |
| Nkoudou, Georges-Kevin | 5.8 | Marseille | Versailles, Fr | 13.02.95 |

| | | | | |
|---|---|---|---|---|
| Onomah, Josh | 5.11 | – | Enfield | 27.04.97 |
| Sissoko, Moussa | 6.2 | Newcastle | Le Blanc-Mesnil, Fr | 16.08.89 |
| Wanyama, Victor | 6.2 | Southampton | Nairobi, Ken | 25.06.91 |
| Winks, Harry | 5.10 | – | Hemel Hempstead | 02.02.96 |
| **Forwards** | | | | |
| Janssen, Vincent | 5.11 | Alkmaar | Heesch, Hol | 15.06.94 |
| Kane, Harry | 6.2 | – | Walthamstow | 28.07.93 |
| Llorente, Fernando | 6.5 | Swansea | Pamplona, Sp | 26.02.85 |
| Son Heung-Min | 6.1 | Bayer Leverkusen | Chuncheon, S Kor | 08.07.92 |

## WATFORD

**Ground**: Vicarage Road Stadium, Vicarage Road, Watford WD18 OER
**Telephone**: 01923 496000. **Club nickname**: Hornets
**Capacity**: 21,000. **Colours**: Yellow and black. **Main sponsor**: FxPro
**Record transfer fee**: £18.5m to Burnley for Andre Gray, Aug 2017
**Record fee received**: £20m from Changchun Yatai for Odion Ighalo, Jan 2017
**Record attendance**: 34,099 v Manchester Utd (FA Cup 4 rep) Feb 3, 1969
**League Championship**: Runners-up 1982–83
**FA Cup**: Runners-up 1984
**League Cup**: Semi-finals 1979, 2005
**European competitions**: UEFA Cup rd 3 1983–84
**Finishing positions in Premier League**: 1999–2000 20th, 2006–07 20th, 2015–16 13th, 2016–17 17th, 2017–18 14th
**Biggest win**: 8-0 v Sunderland (Div 1) Sep 25, 1982. Also: 10-1 v Lowestoft (FA Cup 1) Nov 27, 1926
**Biggest defeat**: 0-10 v Wolves (FA Cup 1 replay) Jan 24, 1912
**Highest League scorer in a season**: Cliff Holton 42 (1959–60)
**Most League goals in aggregate**: Luther Blissett 148 (1976–83, 1984–88, 1991–92)
**Longest unbeaten League sequence**: 22 matches (1996–97)
**Longest sequence without a League win**: 19 matches (1971–72)
**Most capped players**: John Barnes (England) 31, Kenny Jackett (Wales) 31

| | | | | |
|---|---|---|---|---|
| **Goalkeepers** | | | | |
| Arlauskis, Giedrius | 6.4 | Steaua Bucharest | Telsiai, Lith | 01.12.87 |
| Bachmann, Daniel | 6.3 | Stoke | Vienna, Aut | 09.07.94 |
| Foster, Ben | 6.2 | WBA | Leamington | 03.04.83 |
| Gomes, Heurelho | 6.2 | PSV Eindhoven | Joao Pinheiro, Br | 15.12.81 |
| **Defenders** | | | | |
| Britos, Miguel | 6.2 | Napoli | Maldonado, Uru | 17.07.85 |
| Cathcart, Craig | 6.2 | Blackpool | Belfast | 06.02.89 |
| Femenia, Kiko | 5.9 | Alaves | Sanet Negrals, Sp | 02.02.91 |
| Hoban, Tommie | 6.2 | – | Waltham Forest | 24.01.94 |
| Holebas, Jose | 6.1 | Roma | Aschaffenburg, Ger | 27.06.84 |
| Janmaat, Daryl | 6.1 | Newcastle | Leidschendam, Hol | 22.07.89 |
| Kabasele, Christian | 6.1 | Genk | Lubumbashi, DR Cong | 24.02.91 |
| Kaboul, Younes | 6.3 | Sunderland | St Julien, Fr | 04.01.86 |
| Mariappa, Adrian | 5.11 | Crystal Palace | Harrow | 03.10.86 |
| Masina, Adam | 6.2 | Bologna | Khouribga, Mor | 02.01.94 |
| Navarro, Marc | 6.2 | Espanyol | Barcelona, Sp | 02.07.95 |
| Prodl, Sebastian | 6.4 | Werder Bremen | Graz, Aut | 21.06.87 |
| Wilmot, Ben | 6.2 | Stevenage | Stevenage | 04.11.99 |
| Zeegelaar, Marvin | 6.1 | Sporting Lisbon | Amsterdam, Hol | 12.08.90 |
| **Midfielders** | | | | |
| Amrabat, Nordin | 5.11 | Malaga | Naarden, Hol | 31.03.87 |
| Capoue, Etienne | 6.2 | Tottenham | Niort, Fr | 11.07.88 |

| | | | | |
|---|---|---|---|---|
| Chalobah, Nathaniel | 6.1 | Chelsea | Freetown, SLeone | 12.12.94 |
| Cleverley, Tom | 5.10 | Everton | Basingstoke | 12.08.89 |
| Doucoure, Abdoulaye | 6.0 | Rennes | Meulan, Fr | 01.01.93 |
| Hughes, Will | 6.1 | Derby | Weybridge | 07.04.95 |
| Lukebakio, Dodi | 6.2 | Anderlecht | Asse, Bel | 24.09.97 |
| Pereyra, Roberto | 6.0 | Juventus | San Miguel, Arg | 07.01.91 |
| Sema, Ken | 5.10 | Ostersunds | Norrkoping, Swe | 30.09.93 |
| **Forwards** | | | | |
| Deeney, Troy | 6.0 | Walsall | Birmingham | 29.06.88 |
| Gray, Andre | 5.10 | Burnley | Wolverhampton | 26.06.91 |
| Okaka, Stefano | 6.1 | Anderlecht | Castiglione, It | 09.08.89 |
| Oulare, Obbi | 6.5 | Club Bruges | Waregem, Bel | 08.01.96 |
| Richarlison | 5.10 | Fluminense | Nova Venecia, Br | 10.05.97 |
| Sinclair, Jerome | 6.0 | Liverpool | Birmingham | 20.09.96 |
| Success, Isaac | 6.0 | Granada | Benin City, Nig | 07.01.96 |

## WEST HAM UNITED

**Ground**: Queen Elizabeth Olympic Park, London E20 2ST
**Telephone**: 0208 548 2748. **Club nickname**: Hammers
**Capacity**: 60,000. **Colours**: Claret and blue. **Main sponsor**: Betway
**Record transfer fee**: £36m to Lazio for Felipe Anderson, July 2018
**Record fee received**: £25m from Marseille for Dimitri Payet, Jan 2017
**Record attendance**: Upton Park: 43,322 v Tottenham (Div 1) Oct 17, 1970. Olympic Stadium: 56,996 v Manchester Utd (Prem Lge) Jan 2, 2017
**League Championship**: 3rd 1985–86
**FA Cup**: Winners 1964, 1975, 1980
**League Cup**: Runners-up 1966, 1981
**European competitions**: Winners Cup-Winners' Cup 1964–65
**Finishing positions in Premier League**: 1993–94 13th, 1994–95 14th, 1995–96 10th, 1996–97 14th, 1997–98 8th, 1998–99 5th, 1999–2000 9th, 2000–01 15th, 2001–02 7th, 2002–03 18th, 2005–06 9th, 2006–07 15th, 2007–08 10th, 2008–09: 9th, 2009 10 17th, 2010–11 20th, 2012–13 10th, 2013–14 13th, 2014–15 12th, 2015–16 7th, 2016–17 11th, 2017–18 13th
**Biggest win**: 8-0 v Rotherham (Div 2) Mar 8, 1958, v Sunderland (Div 1) Oct 19, 1968. Also: 10-0 v Bury (League Cup 2) Oct 25, 1983
**Biggest defeat**: 0-7 v Barnsley (Div 2) Sep 1, 1919, v Everton (Div 1) Oct 22, 1927, v Sheffield Wed (Div 1) Nov 28, 1959
**Highest League scorer in a season**: Vic Watson 42 (1929–30)
**Most League goals in aggregate**: Vic Watson 298 (1920–35)
**Longest unbeaten League sequence**: 27 matches (1980–81)
**Longest sequence without a League win**: 17 matches (1976)
**Most capped player**: Bobby Moore (England) 108

| | | | | |
|---|---|---|---|---|
| **Goalkeepers** | | | | |
| Adrian | 6.3 | Real Betis | Seville, Sp | 03.01.87 |
| Fabianski, Lukasz | 6.3 | Swansea | Kostrzyn, Pol | 18.04.85 |
| **Defenders** | | | | |
| Balbuena, Fabian | 6.2 | Corinthians | Ciudad del Este, Par | 23.08.91 |
| Byram, Sam | 5.11 | Leeds | Thurrock | 16.09.93 |
| Cresswell, Aaron | 5.7 | Ipswich | Liverpool | 15.12.89 |
| Diop, Issa | 6.4 | Toulouse | Toulouse | 09.01.97 |
| Felipe Anderson | 5.10 | Lazio | Santa Maria, Bra | 15.04.93 |
| Fonte, Jose | 6.2 | Southampton | Penafiel, Por | 22.12.83 |
| Fredericks, Ryan | 5.8 | Fulham | Potters Bar | 10.10.92 |

| | | | | |
|---|---|---|---|---|
| Masuaku, Arthur | 5.11 | Olympiacos | Lille, Fr | 07.11.93 |
| Ogbonna, Angelo | 6.3 | Juventus | Cassino, It | 23.05.88 |
| Oxford, Reece | 6.3 | Tottenham | Edmonton | 16.12.98 |
| Reid, Winston | 6.3 | Midtjylland | Auckland, NZ | 03.07.88 |
| Rice, Declan | 6.1 | – | London | 14.01.99 |
| Zabaleta, Pablo | 5.10 | Manchester City | Buenos Aires, Arg | 16.01.85 |
| **Midfielders** | | | | |
| Antonio, Michail | 5.11 | Nottm Forest | Wandsworth | 28.03.90 |
| Cullen, Josh | 5.9 | – | Westcliff-on-Sea | 07.04.96 |
| Fernandes, Edimilson | 6.3 | FC Sion | Sion, Switz | 15.04.96 |
| Haksabanovic, Sead | 5.9 | Halmstads | Sweden | 04.05.99 |
| Kouyate, Cheikhou | 6.4 | Anderlecht | Dakar, Sen | 21.12.89 |
| Lanzini, Manuel | 5.6 | Al Jazira | Ituzaingo, Arg | 15.02.93 |
| Noble, Mark | 5.11 | – | West Ham | 08.05.87 |
| Obiang, Pedro | 6.1 | Sampdoria | Alcala, Sp | 27.03.92 |
| Snodgrass, Robert | 6.0 | Hull | Glasgow | 07.09.87 |
| Wilshere, Jack | 5.8 | Arsenal | Stevenage | 01.01.92 |
| **Forwards** | | | | |
| Arnautovic, Marko | 6.4 | Stoke | Vienna, Aut | 19.04.89 |
| Carroll, Andy | 6.3 | Liverpool | Gateshead | 06.01.89 |
| Hernandez, Javier | 5.9 | Bayer Leverkusen | Guadalajara, Mex | 01.06.88 |
| Hugill, Jordan | 6.0 | Preston | Middlesbrough | 04.06.92 |
| Yarmolenko, Andriy | 6.2 | Borussia Dortmund | St Petersburg, Rus | 23.10.89 |

## WOLVERHAMPTON WANDERERS

**Ground**: Molineux Stadium, Waterloo Road, Wolverhampton WV1 4QR
**Telephone**: 0871 222 2220. **Club nickname**: Wolves
**Capacity: 31,700. Colours**: Gold and black. **Main sponsor:**
**Record attendance**: 61,315 v Liverpool (FA Cup 5) Feb 11, 1939
**Record transfer fee:** £15.8m to Porto for Ruben Neves, Jul 2017
**Record fee received:** £14m from Sunderland for Steven Fletcher, Aug 2012
**Record attendance:** 61,315 v Liverpool (FA Cup 5), Feb 11, 1935
**League Championship:** Winners 1953–54, 1957–58, 1958–59
**FA Cup:** Winners 1893, 1908, 1949, 1960
**League Cup:** Winners 1974, 1980
**European competitions:** UEFA Cup runners-up 1971–72
**Finishing positions in Premier League:** 2003–04 20th, 2009–10 15th, 2003–04 20th
**Biggest win:** 10-1 v Leicester (Div 2) Apr 15, 1938. Also: 14-0 v Crosswell's Brewery (FA Cup 2) Nov 13, 1886
**Biggest defeat:** 1-10 v Newton Heath (Div 1) Oct 15, 1892
**Highest League scorer in a season:** Dennis Westcott 38 (1946–47)
**Most League goals in aggregate:** Steve Bull 250 (1986–90)
**Longest unbeaten League sequence:** 20 matches (1923–24)
**Longest sequence without a League win:** 19 matches (1984–85)
**Most capped player:** Billy Wright (England) 105

| | | | | |
|---|---|---|---|---|
| **Goalkeepers** | | | | |
| Ikeme, Carl | 6.3 | – | Sutton Coldfield | 08.06.86 |
| Norris, Will | 6.5 | Cambridge | Watford | 12.08.93 |
| Rui Patricio | 6.2 | Sporting Lisbon | Marrazes, Port | 15.02.88 |
| Ruddy, Jack | 6.5 | Bury | Glasgow | 27.12.97 |
| Ruddy, John | 6.4 | Norwich | St Ives, Camb | 24.10.86 |
| **Defenders** | | | | |
| Batth, Danny | 6.3 | – | Brierley Hill | 21.09.90 |

| | | | | |
|---|---|---|---|---|
| Bennett, Ryan | 6.2 | Wolves | Orsett | 06.03.90 |
| Boly, Willy | 6.2 | Porto | Melun, Fr | 03.02.91 |
| Doherty, Matt | 5.11 | – | Dublin, Ire | 16.01.92 |
| Douglas, Barry | 5.9 | Konyaspor | Glasgow | 04.09.89 |
| Ebanks-Landell, Ethan | 6.2 | – | West Bromwich | 16.12.92 |
| Hause, Kortney | 6.3 | Wycombe | Goodmayes | 16.07.95 |
| Iorfa, Dominic | 6.4 | Southend | Southend | 24.06.95 |
| Ofosu-Ayeh, Phil | 6.0 | Eintracht Braunschweig | Moers, Ger | 15.09.91 |
| **Midfielders** | | | | |
| Cavaleiro, Ivan | 5.9 | Monaco | Vila Franca de Xira, Por | 18.10.93 |
| Coady, Conor | 6.1 | Huddersfield | St Helens | 25.02.93 |
| Diogo Jota | 5.10 | Atletico Madrid | Porto | 04.12.96 |
| Gibbs-White, Morgan | 5.11 | – | Stafford | 27.01.00 |
| Graham, Jordan | 6.0 | Aston Villa | Coventry | 05.03.95 |
| Helder Costa | 5.10 | Benfica | Luandra, Ang | 12.01.94 |
| Neves, Ruben | 5.11 | Porto | Santa Maria, Port | 13.03.97 |
| Ronan, Connor | 5.8 | – | Rochdale | 06.03.98 |
| Saiss, Romain | 6.3 | Angers | Bourg-de-Peage, Fr | 26.03.90 |
| Stevenson, Ben | 6.0 | Coventry | Leicester | 23.03.97 |
| Zyro, Michal | 6.2 | Legia Warsaw | Warsaw, Pol | 20.09.92 |
| **Forwards** | | | | |
| Enobakhare, Bright | 6.0 | – | Nigeria | 08.02.98 |
| Jimenez, Raul | 6.2 | Benfica (loan) | Tepeji del Rio, Mex | 05.05.91 |
| Mason, Joe | 5.10 | Cardiff | Plymouth | 13.05.91 |
| Mir, Rafael | 6.1 | Valencia | Murcia, Sp | 18.06.97 |

# ENGLISH FOOTBALL LEAGUE

(At time of going to press)

# CHAMPIONSHIP

## ASTON VILLA

**Ground**: Villa Park, Trinity Road, Birmingham, B6 6HE
**Telephone**: 0800 612 0970. **Club nickname**: Villans
**Colours**: Claret and blue. **Capacity**: 42,785
**Record attendance**: 76,588 v Derby (FA Cup 6) Mar 2, 1946

| | | | | |
|---|---|---|---|---|
| **Goalkeepers** | | | | |
| Bunn, Mark | 6.0 | Norwich | Southgate | 16.11.84 |
| Johnstone, Sam | 6.3 | Manchester Utd (loan) | Preston | 25.03.93 |
| Steer, Jed | 6.3 | Norwich | Norwich | 23.09.92 |
| **Defenders** | | | | |
| Bree, James | 5.10 | Barnsley | Wakefield | 11.10.97 |
| Chester, James | 5.11 | WBA | Warrington | 23.01.89 |
| Elphick, Tommy | 5.11 | Bournemouth | Brighton | 07.09.87 |
| Taylor, Neil | 5.9 | Swansea | St Asaph | 07.02.89 |
| **Midfielders** | | | | |
| Adomah, Albert | 6.1 | Middlesbrough | Lambeth | 13.12.87 |
| Bjarnason, Birkir | 6.0 | Basle | Akureyri, Ice | 27.05.88 |
| Elmohamady, Ahmed | 5.11 | Hull | Basyoun, Egy | 09.09.87 |

| | | | | |
|---|---|---|---|---|
| Gardner, Gary | 6.2 | – | Solihull | 29.06.92 |
| Grealish, Jack | 5.9 | – | Solihull | 10.09.95 |
| Green, Andre | 5.11 | – | Solihull | 26.07.98 |
| Hourihane, Conor | 6.0 | Barnsley | Cork, Ire | 02.02.91 |
| Jedinak, Mile | 6.3 | Crystal Palace | Sydney, Aus | 03.08.84 |
| Lansbury, Henri | 6.0 | Nottm Forest | Enfield | 12.10.90 |
| Lyden, Jordan | 6.0 | – | Perth, Aus | 30.01.96 |
| Tshibola, Aaron | 6.3 | Reading | Newham | 02.01.95 |
| Whelan, Glenn | 5.10 | Stoke | Dublin, Ire | 13.01.84 |
| **Forwards** | | | | |
| Davis, Keinan | 6.3 | – | Stevenage | 13.02.98 |
| Hepburn-Murphy, Russell | 5.8 | – | Birmingham | 28.08.98 |
| Hogan, Scott | 5.11 | Brentford | Salford | 13.04.92 |
| Kodjia, Jonathan | 6.2 | Bristol City | St Denis, Fr | 22.10.89 |

## BIRMINGHAM CITY

**Ground**: St Andrew's, Birmingham B9 4NH
**Telephone**: 0844 557 1875. **Club nickname**: Blues
**Colours**: Blue and white. **Capacity**: 30,016
**Record attendance**: 66,844 v Everton (FA Cup 5) Feb 11, 1939

| | | | | |
|---|---|---|---|---|
| **Goalkeepers** | | | | |
| Kuszczak, Tomasz | 6.3 | Wolves | Krosno, Pol | 20.03.82 |
| Stockdale, David | 6.3 | Brighton | Leeds | 28.09.85 |
| Trueman, Connal | 6.1 | – | Birmingham | 26.03.96 |
| **Defenders** | | | | |
| Colin, Maxime | 5.11 | Brentford | Arras, Fr | 15.11.91 |
| Dacres-Cogley, Joshua | 5.9 | – | – | 12.03.96 |
| Dean, Harlee | 5.10 | Brentford | Basingstoke | 26.07.91 |
| Grounds, Jonathan | 6.1 | Oldham | Thornaby | 02.02.88 |
| Harding, Wes | 5.11 | – | Leicester | 20.10.96 |
| Jota | 5.11 | Brentford | Pobra do Caraminal, Sp | 16.06.91 |
| Kieftenbeld, Maikel | 5.11 | Groningen | Lemelerveld, Hol | 26.06.90 |
| Morrison, Michael | 6.1 | Charlton | Bury St Edmunds | 03.03.88 |
| O'Keefe, Corey | 6.0 | – | Birmingham | 05.06.98 |
| Pedersen, Kristian | 6.2 | Union Berlin | Ringsted, Den | 04.08.94 |
| Roberts, Marc | 6.0 | Barnsley | Wakefield | 26.07.90 |
| **Midfielders** | | | | |
| Davis, David | 5.8 | Wolves | Smethwick | 20.02.91 |
| Gardner, Craig | 5.10 | WBA | Solihull | 25.11.86 |
| Maghoma, Jacques | 5.11 | Sheffield Wed | Lubumbashi, DR Cong | 23.10.87 |
| N'Doye, Cheikh | 6.3 | Angers | Rufisque, Sen | 29.03.86 |
| Solomon-Otabor, Viv | 5.9 | – | London | 02.01.96 |
| **Forwards** | | | | |
| Adams, Che | 5.10 | Sheffield Utd | Leicester | 13.07.96 |
| Jutkiewicz, Lukas | 6.1 | Burnley | Southampton | 20.03.89 |
| Vassell, Isaac | 5.8 | Luton | Newquay | 09.09.93 |

## BLACKBURN ROVERS

**Ground**: Ewood Park, Blackburn BB2 4JF
**Telephone**: 0871 702 1875. **Club nickname**: Rovers
**Colours**: Blue and white. **Capacity**: 31,367
**Record attendance**: 62,522 v Bolton (FA Cup 6) Mar 2, 1929

| | | | | |
|---|---|---|---|---|
| **Goalkeepers** | | | | |
| Leutwiler, Jayson | 6.4 | Shrewsbury | Neuchatel, Switz | 25.04.89 |
| Raya, David | 6.0 | Cornella | Barcelona, Sp | 15.09.95 |
| **Defenders** | | | | |
| Bell, Amari'i | 5.11 | Fleetwood | Burton | 05.05.94 |
| Caddis, Paul | 5.7 | Birmingham | Irvine | 19.04.88 |
| Downing, Paul | 6.1 | MK Dons | Taunton | 26.10.91 |
| Lenihan, Darragh | 5.10 | Belvedere | Dunboyne, Ire | 16.03.94 |
| Mulgrew, Charlie | 6.3 | Celtic | Glasgow | 06.03.86 |
| Nyambe, Ryan | 6.0 | – | Katima Mulilo, Nam | 04.12.97 |
| Wharton, Scott | – | – | Blackburn | 03.10.97 |
| Williams, Derrick | 6.2 | Bristol City | Waterford, Ire | 17.01.93 |
| **Midfielders** | | | | |
| Conway, Craig | 5.8 | Cardiff | Irvine | 02.05.85 |
| Dack, Bradley | 5.8 | Gillingham | Greenwich | 31.12.93 |
| Evans, Corry | 5.11 | Hull | Belfast | 30.07.90 |
| Gladwin, Ben | 6.3 | QPR | Reading | 08.06.92 |
| Rothwell, Joe | 6.1 | Oxford | Manchester | 11.01.95 |
| Smallwood, Richie | 5.11 | Rotherham | Redcar | 29.12.90 |
| Tomlinson, Willem | 5.11 | – | Burnley | 27.01.98 |
| Whittingham, Peter | 5.10 | Cardiff | Nuneaton | 08.09.84 |
| **Forwards** | | | | |
| Chapman, Harrison | 5.10 | Middlesbrough | Hartlepool | 15.11.97 |
| Graham, Danny | 6.1 | Sunderland | Gateshead | 12.08.85 |
| Samuel, Dominic | 6.0 | Reading | Southwark | 01.04.94 |

## BOLTON WANDERERS

**Ground**: Macron Stadium, Burnden Way, Lostock, Bolton BL6 6JW
**Telephone**: 0844 871 2932. **Club nickname**: Trotters
**Colours**: White and navy. **Capacity**: 28,723
**Record attendance**: Burnden Park: 69,912 v Manchester City (FA Cup 5) Feb 18, 1933.
Macron Stadium: 28,353 v Leicester (Prem Lge) Dec 28, 2003

| | | | | |
|---|---|---|---|---|
| **Goalkeepers** | | | | |
| Alnwick, Ben | 6.2 | Peterborough | Prudhoe | 01.01.87 |
| Turner, Jake | 6.4 | – | Wilmslow | 16.06.99 |
| **Defenders** | | | | |
| Beevers, Mark | 6.4 | Millwall | Barnsley | 21.11.89 |
| Darby, Stephen | 6.0 | Bradford | Liverpool | 06.10.88 |
| Little, Mark | 6.1 | Bristol City | Worcester | 20.08.88 |
| Olkowski, Pawel | 6.1 | Cologne | Ozimek, Pol | 13.02.90 |
| Wheater, David | 6.5 | Middlesbrough | Redcar | 14.02.87 |
| **Midfielders** | | | | |
| Ameobi, Sammy | 6.4 | Newcastle | Newcastle | 01.05.92 |
| Buckley, Will | 6.0 | Sunderland | Oldham | 12.08.88 |
| Lowe, Jason | 5.10 | Birmingham | Wigan | 02.09.91 |
| Morais, Filipe | 5.9 | Bradford | Benavente, Por | 21.11.85 |
| Noone, Craig | 6.3 | Cardiff | Kirkby | 17.11.87 |
| Oztumer, Erhun | 5.3 | Walsall | Greenwich | 29.05.91 |
| Vela, Josh | 5.11 | – | Salford | 14.12.93 |
| **Forwards** | | | | |
| Donaldson, Clayton | 6.1 | Sheffield Utd | Bradford | 07.02.84 |
| Le Fondre, Adam | 5.9 | Cardiff | Stockport | 02.12.86 |

## BRENTFORD

**Ground**: Griffin Park, Braemar Road, Brentford TW8 0NT
**Telephone**: 0845 345 6442. **Club nickname**: Bees
**Colours**: Red, white and black. **Capacity**: 12,763
**Record attendance**: 38,678 v Leicester (FA Cup 6) Feb 26, 1949

| | | | | |
|---|---|---|---|---|
| **Goalkeepers** | | | | |
| Bentley, Daniel | 6.2 | Southend | Basildon | 13.07.93 |
| Bonham, Jack | 6.4 | Watford | Stevenage | 14.09.93 |
| Daniels, Luke | 6.4 | Scunthorpe | Bolton | 05.01.88 |
| **Defenders** | | | | |
| Barbet, Yoann | 6.2 | Chamois | Libourne, Fr | 10.05.93 |
| Clarke, Josh | 5.8 | – | Walthamstow | 05.07.94 |
| Dalsgaard, Henrik | 6.3 | Zulte Waregem | Roum, Den | 27.07.89 |
| Egan, John | 6.2 | Gillingham | Cork, Ire | 20.10.92 |
| Field, Tom | 5.10 | – | Kingston upon Thames | 14.03.97 |
| Henry, Rico | 5.8 | Walsall | Birmingham | 08.07.97 |
| Konsa, Ezri | 6.0 | Charlton | Newham | 23.10.97 |
| Yennaris, Nico | 5.9 | Arsenal | Leytonstone | 24.05.93 |
| **Midfielders** | | | | |
| Canos, Sergi | 5.9 | Norwich | Nules, Sp | 02.02.97 |
| Judge, Alan | 6.0 | Blackburn | Dublin, Ire | 11.11.88 |
| MacLeod, Lewis | 5.9 | Rangers | Wishaw | 16.06.94 |
| Marcondes, Emiliano | 6.0 | Nordsjaelland | Hvidovre, Den | 09.03.95 |
| Maupay, Neal | 5.7 | St Etienne | Versailles, Fr | 14.08.96 |
| McEachran, Josh | 5.10 | Chelsea | Oxford | 01.03.93 |
| Mokotjo, Kamo | 5.7 | Twente | Odendaalsrus, SA | 11.03.91 |
| Sawyers, Romaine | 5.9 | Walsall | Birmingham | 02.11.91 |
| Woods, Ryan | 5.8 | Shrewsbury | Norton Canes | 13.12.93 |
| **Forwards** | | | | |
| Benrahma, Said | 5.8 | Nice | Temouchent, Alg | 10.08.95 |
| Jozefzoom, Florian | 5.8 | PSV Eindhoven | Saint-Laurent, Fr Guin | 09.02.91 |
| Shaibu, Justin | 6.0 | Koge | Denmark | 28.10.97 |
| Watkins, Ollie | 5.10 | Exeter | Torbay | 30.12.95 |

## BRISTOL CITY

**Ground**: Ashton Gate, Bristol BS3 2EJ
**Telephone**: 0871 222 6666. **Club nickname**: Robins
**Colours**: Red and white. **Capacity**: 27,000
**Record attendance**: 43,335 v Preston (FA Cup 5) Feb 16, 1935

| | | | | |
|---|---|---|---|---|
| **Goalkeepers** | | | | |
| Fielding, Frank | 6.0 | Derby | Blackburn | 04.04.88 |
| O'Leary, Max | 6.1 | – | Bath | 10.10.96 |
| **Defenders** | | | | |
| Baker, Nathan | 6.3 | Aston Villa | Worcester | 23.04.91 |
| Hunt, Jack | 5.9 | Sheffield Wed | Rothwell | 06.12.90 |
| Kelly, Lloyd | 5.10 | – | Bristol | 01.10.98 |
| Moore, Taylor | 6.1 | Lens | Walthamstow | 12.05.97 |
| Pisano, Eros | 6.1 | Hellas Verona | Busto Arsizio, It | 31.03.87 |
| Webster, Adam | 6.3 | Ipswich | Chichester | 04.01.95 |
| Wright, Bailey | 5.10 | Preston | Melbourne, Aus | 28.07.92 |

| | | | | |
|---|---|---|---|---|
| **Midfielders** | | | | |
| Adelakun, Hakeeb | 6.0 | Scunthorpe | Hackney | 11.06.96 |
| Bakinson, Tyreeq | 6.1 | Luton | Camden | 08.01.98 |
| Brownhill, Josh | 5.10 | Preston | Warrington | 19.12.95 |
| Bryan, Joe | 5.7 | – | Bristol | 17.09.93 |
| Eliasson, Niclas | 5.9 | Norrkoping | Sweden | 07.12.95 |
| Hegeler, Jens | 6.4 | Hertha Berlin | Cologne, Ger | 22.01.88 |
| O'Dowda, Callum | 5.11 | Oxford | Oxford | 23.04.95 |
| Pack, Marlon | 6.2 | Cheltenham | Portsmouth | 25.03.91 |
| Smith, Korey | 6.0 | Oldham | Hatfield | 31.01.91 |
| **Forwards** | | | | |
| Diedhiou, Famara | 6.2 | Angers | Saint-Louis, Sen | 15.12.92 |
| Djuric, Milan | 6.6 | Cesena | Tuzia, Bos | 22.05.90 |
| Holden, Rory | | Derry | Derry | 23.08.97 |
| Paterson, Jamie | 5.9 | Nottm Forest | Coventry | 20.12.91 |
| Taylor, Matty | 5.9 | Bristol Rov | Oxford | 30.03.90 |
| Weimann, Andreas | 6.2 | Derby | Vienna, Aut | 05.08.91 |
| Watkins, Marley | 6.1 | Norwich | Lewisham | 17.10.90 |

## DERBY COUNTY

**Ground**: Pride Park, Derby DE24 8XL
**Telephone**: 0871 472 1884. **Club nickname**: Rams
**Colours**: White and black. **Capacity**: 33,597
**Record attendance**: Baseball Ground: 41,826 v Tottenham (Div 1) Sep 20, 1969; Pride Park: 33,597 (England v Mexico) May 25, 2011; Club: 33,475 v Rangers (Ted McMinn testimonial) May 1, 2006

| | | | | |
|---|---|---|---|---|
| **Goalkeepers** | | | | |
| Carson, Scott | 6.3 | Wigan | Whitehaven | 03.09.85 |
| Mitchell, Jonathan | 6.2 | Newcastle | Hartlepool | 24.11.94 |
| Roos, Kelle | 6.5 | Nuneaton | Rijkevoort, Hol | 31.05.92 |
| **Defenders** | | | | |
| Davies, Curtis | 6.2 | Hull | Waltham Forest | 15.03.85 |
| Forsyth, Craig | 6.0 | Watford | Carnoustie | 24.02.89 |
| Keogh, Richard | 6.2 | Coventry | Harlow | 11.08.86 |
| Lowe, Max | 5.9 | – | Birmingham | 11.05.97 |
| Olsson, Marcus | 6.0 | Blackburn | Gavle, Swe | 17.05.88 |
| Pearce, Alex | 6.2 | Reading | Wallingford | 09.11.88 |
| Wisdom, Andre | 6.1 | Liverpool | Leeds | 09.05.93 |
| **Midfielders** | | | | |
| Anya, Ikechi | 5.7 | Watford | Glasgow | 03.01.88 |
| Butterfield, Jacob | 5.11 | Huddersfield | Bradford | 10.06.90 |
| Bryson, Craig | 5.8 | Kilmarnock | Rutherglen | 06.11.86 |
| Hanson, Jamie | 6.3 | – | Burton upon Trent | 10.11.95 |
| Huddlestone, Tom | 6.1 | Hull | Nottingham | 28.12.86 |
| Johnson, Bradley | 5.10 | Norwich | Hackney | 28.04.87 |
| Ledley, Joe | 6.0 | Crystal Palace | Cardiff | 23.01.87 |
| Thorne, George | 6.2 | WBA | Chatham | 04.01.93 |
| **Forwards** | | | | |
| Bennett, Mason | 5.10 | – | Shirebrook | 15.07.96 |
| Blackman, Nick | 6.1 | Reading | Whitefield | 11.11.89 |
| Jerome, Cameron | 6.1 | Norwich | Huddersfield | 14.08.86 |
| Lawrence, Tom | 5.10 | Leicester | Wrexham | 13.01.94 |
| Martin, Chris | 5.10 | Norwich | Beccles | 04.11.88 |

| | | | | |
|---|---|---|---|---|
| Nugent, David | 5.11 | Middlesbrough | Liverpool | 02.05.85 |
| Vydra, Matej | 5.11 | Watford | Chotebor, Cz | 01.05.92 |

## HULL CITY

**Ground**: KCOM Stadium, Anlaby Road, Hull, HU3 6HU
**Telephone**: 01482 504 600. **Club nickname:** Tigers
**Capacity:** 25,404. **Colours**: Amber and black
**Record attendance**: Boothferry Park: 55,019 v Manchester Utd (FA Cup 6) Feb 26, 1949. KC Stadium: 25,030 v Liverpool (Prem Lge) May 9, 2010. Also: 25,280 (England U21 v Holland) Feb 17, 2004

| | | | | |
|---|---|---|---|---|
| **Goalkeepers** | | | | |
| Mannion, Wilf | 6.1 | AFC Wimbledon | Hillingdon | 05.05.98 |
| Marshall, David | 6.3 | Cardiff | Glasgow | 05.03.85 |
| **Defenders** | | | | |
| Burke, Reece | 6.2 | West Ham | Newham | 02.09.96 |
| De Wijs, Jordy | 6.2 | PSV Eindhoven | Kortrijk, Bel | 08.01.95 |
| Kingsley, Stephen | 5.10 | Swansea | Stirling | 23.07.94 |
| Lichaj, Eric | 5.10 | Nottm Forest | Downers Grove, US | 17.11.88 |
| MacDonald, Angus | 6.2 | Barnsley | Winchester | 15.10.92 |
| Mazuch, Ondrej | 6.2 | Sparta Prague | Hodonin, Cz | 15.03.89 |
| Odubajo, Moses | 5.10 | Brentford | Greenwich | 28.07.93 |
| **Midfielders** | | | | |
| Batty, Daniel | 5.11 | – | Pontefract | 10.12.97 |
| Evandro | 5.10 | Porto | Blumenau, Br | 23.08.86 |
| Grosicki, Kamil | 5.11 | Rennes | Szczecin, Pol | 08.06.88 |
| Henriksen, Markus | 6.2 | Alkmaar | Trondheim, Nor | 25.07.92 |
| Irvine, Jackson | 6.2 | Burton | Melbourne, Aus | 07.03.93 |
| Stewart, Kevin | 5.7 | Liverpool | Enfield | 07.09.93 |
| Toral, Jon | 6.1 | Arsenal | Reus, Sp | 05.02.95 |
| Weir, James | 5.11 | Manchester Utd | Preston | 04.08.95 |
| **Forwards** | | | | |
| Bowen, Jarrod | 5.9 | Hereford | Leominster | 20.12.96 |
| Campbell, Fraizer | 5.11 | Crystal Palace | Huddersfield | 13.09.87 |
| Dicko, Nouha | 5.8 | Wolves | Paris, Fr | 14.05.92 |
| Keane, Will | 6.2 | Manchester Utd | Stockport | 11.01.93 |
| Milinkovic, David | 5.11 | Genoa | Antibes, Fr | 20.05.94 |

## IPSWICH TOWN

**Ground**: Portman Road, Ipswich IP1 2DA
**Telephone**: 01473 400500. **Club nickname**: Blues/Town
**Colours**: Blue and white. **Capacity:** 30,300
**Record attendance**: 38,010 v Leeds (FA Cup 6) Mar 8, 1975

| | | | | |
|---|---|---|---|---|
| **Goalkeepers** | | | | |
| Bialkowski, Bartosz | 6.0 | Notts Co | Braniewo, Pol | 06.07.87 |
| Gerken, Dean | 6.2 | Bristol City | Southend | 04.08.85 |
| **Defenders** | | | | |
| Chambers, Luke | 5.11 | Nottm Forest | Kettering | 29.08.85 |
| Cotter, Barry | 5.9 | Limerick | – | 04.12.98 |
| Chalobah, Trevor | 6.3 | Chelsea (loan) | Freetown, SLeone | 05.07.99 |
| Kenlock, Myles | 6.1 | – | Croydon | 29.11.96 |
| Knudsen, Jonas | 6.1 | Esbjerg | Esbjerg, Den | 16.09.92 |
| Spence, Jordan | 6.2 | MK Dons | Woodford | 24.05.90 |

**Midfielders**

| | | | | |
|---|---|---|---|---|
| Adeyemi, Tom | 6.1 | Cardiff | Norwich | 24.10.91 |
| Bishop, Ed | 5.11 | – | Cambridge | 15.07.96 |
| Downes, Flynn | 5.10 | – | Brentwood | 20.01.99 |
| Dozzell, Andre | 5.10 | – | Ipswich | 02.05.99 |
| Huws, Emyr | 5.10 | Cardiff | Llanelli | 30.09.93 |
| Roberts, Jordan | 6.1 | Crawley | Watford | 05.01.94 |
| Rowe, Danny | 6.0 | Macclesfield | Wythenshawe | 09.03.92 |
| Skuse, Cole | 5.9 | Bristol City | Bristol | 29.03.86 |
| Ward, Grant | 5.10 | Tottenham | Lewisham | 05.12.94 |
| **Forwards** | | | | |
| Garner, Joe | 5.10 | Rangers | Blackburn | 12.04.88 |
| McGoldrick, David | 6.1 | Nottm Forest | Nottingham | 29.11.87 |
| Sears, Freddie | 5.10 | Colchester | Hornchurch | 27.11.89 |
| Waghorn, Martyn | 5.10 | Rangers | South Shields | 23.01.93 |

## LEEDS UNITED

**Ground**: Elland Road, Leeds LS11 OES
**Telephone**: 0871 334 1919. **Club nickname**: Whites
**Colours**: White. **Capacity**: 37,900
**Record attendance**: 57,892 v Sunderland (FA Cup 5 rep) Mar 15, 1967

**Goalkeepers**

| | | | | |
|---|---|---|---|---|
| Blackman, Jamal | 6.6 | Chelsea (loan) | Croydon | 27.10.93 |
| Lonergan, Andy | 6.4 | Wolves | Preston | 19.10.83 |
| Peacock-Farrell, Bailey | 6.2 | – | Darlington | 29.10.96 |
| **Defenders** | | | | |
| Ayling, Luke | 6.1 | Bristol City | Lambeth | 25.08.91 |
| Berardi, Gaetano | 5.11 | Sampdoria | Sorengo, Swi | 21.08.88 |
| Buoy, Ouasim | 5.11 | Juventus | Amsterdam, Hol | 11.06.93 |
| Cooper, Liam | 6.0 | Chesterfield | Hull | 30.08.91 |
| De Bock, Laurens | 5.10 | Club Bruges | Dendermonde, Bel | 07.11.92 |
| Jansson, Pontus | 6.5 | Torino | Arlov, Swe | 13.02.91 |
| Pearce, Tom | 6.1 | Everton | Ormskirk | 12.04.98 |
| Shaughnessy, Conor | 6.3 | Reading | Galway, Ire | 30.06.96 |
| **Midfielders** | | | | |
| Alioski, Ezgjan | 5.8 | Lugano | Prilep, Maced | 12.02.92 |
| Anita, Vurnon | 5.6 | Newcastle | Willemstad, Cur | 04.04.89 |
| Baker, Lewis | 6.0 | Chelsea (loan) | Luton | 25.04.95 |
| Dallas, Stuart | 6.0 | Brentford | Cookstown | 19.04.91 |
| Forshaw, Adam | 6.1 | Middlesbrough | Liverpool | 08.10.91 |
| Hernandez, Pablo | 5.8 | Al-Arabi | Castellon, Sp | 11.04.85 |
| Ideguchi, Yosuke | 5.8 | Gamba Osaka | Fukuoka, Jap | 23.08.96 |
| Klich, Mateusz | 6.0 | FC Twente | Tarnow, Pol | 13.06.90 |
| O'Kane, Eunan | 5.8 | Bournemouth | Derry | 10.07.90 |
| Phillips, Kalvin | 5.10 | – | Leeds | 02.12.95 |
| Sacko, Hadi | 6.0 | Sporting Lisbon | Corbeil, Fr | 24.03.94 |
| Saiz, Samuel | 5.9 | Huesca | Madrid, Sp | 22.01.91 |
| **Forwards** | | | | |
| Antonsson, Marcus | 6.1 | Kalmar | Sweden | 08.05.91 |
| Doukara, Souleymane | 6.1 | Catania | Meudon, Fr | 29.09.91 |
| Ekuban, Caleb | 6.2 | Chievo | Villafranca, It | 23.03.94 |
| Roberts, Tyler | 5.11 | WBA | Gloucester | 12.01.99 |
| Roofe, Kemar | 5.10 | Oxford | Walsall | 06.01.93 |

## MIDDLESBROUGH

**Ground**: Riverside Stadium, Middlesbrough, TS3 6RS
**Telephone**: 0844 499 6789. **Club nickname**: Boro
**Capacity**: 35,100. **Colours**: Red
**Record attendance**: Ayresome Park: 53,596 v Newcastle (Div 1) Dec 27, 1949; Riverside Stadium: 35,000 (England v Slovakia) Jun 11, 2003. Club: 34,836 v Norwich (Prem Lge) Dec 28, 2004

| | | | | |
|---|---|---|---|---|
| **Goalkeepers** | | | | |
| Konstantopoulos, Dimi | 6.5 | AEK Athens | Thessaloniki, Gre | 29.11.79 |
| Randolph, Darren | 6.1 | West Ham | Bray, Ire | 12.05.87 |
| Ripley, Connor | 6.3 | – | Middlesbrough | 13.02.93 |
| **Defenders** | | | | |
| Ayala, Daniel | 6.3 | Norwich | El Saucejo, Sp | 07.11.90 |
| Barragan, Antonio | 6.1 | Valencia | Pontedueme, Sp | 12.06.87 |
| Fabio | 5.6 | Cardiff | Petropolis, Br | 09.07.90 |
| Flint, Aden | 6.2 | Bristol City | Pinxton | 11.07.89 |
| Friend, George | 6.0 | Doncaster | Barnstaple | 19.10.87 |
| Fry, Dael | 6.0 | – | Middlesbrough | 30.08.97 |
| Gibson, Ben | 6.1 | – | Nunthorpe | 05.01.93 |
| Shotton, Ryan | 6.3 | Birmingham | Stoke | 30.09.88 |
| **Midfielders** | | | | |
| Clayton, Adam | 5.9 | Huddersfield | Manchester | 14.01.89 |
| De Sart, Julien | 6.2 | Standard Liege | Waremme, Bel | 23.12.94 |
| Downing, Stewart | 6.0 | West Ham | Middlesbrough | 02.07.84 |
| Howson, Jonny | 5.11 | Norwich | Leeds | 21.05.88 |
| Johnson, Marvin | 5.10 | Oxford | Birmingham | 01.12.90 |
| Leadbitter, Grant | 5.9 | Ipswich | Chester-le-Street | 07.01.86 |
| McNair, Paddy | 6.0 | Sunderland | Ballyclare | 27.04.95 |
| Traore, Adama | 5.10 | Aston Villa | L'Hospitalet, Sp | 25.01.96 |
| **Forwards** | | | | |
| Assombalonga, Britt | 5.10 | Nottm Forest | Kinshasa, DR Cong | 06.12.92 |
| Bamford, Patrick | 6.1 | Chelsea | Grantham | 05.09.93 |
| Braithwaite, Martin | 5.11 | Toulouse | Esbjerg, Den | 05.06.91 |
| Fletcher, Ashley | 6.1 | West Ham | Keighley | 02.10.95 |
| Gestede, Rudy | 6.4 | Aston Villa | Nancy, Fr | 10.10.88 |

## MILLWALL

**Ground**: The Den, Zampa Road, London SE16 3LN
**Telephone**: 0207 232 1222. **Club nickname**: Lions
**Colours**: Blue. **Capacity**: 20,146
**Record attendance**: The Den: 48,672 v Derby (FA Cup 5) Feb 20, 1937. New Den: 20,093 v Arsenal (FA Cup 3) Jan 10, 1994

| | | | | |
|---|---|---|---|---|
| **Goalkeepers** | | | | |
| Archer, Jordan | 6.3 | Tottenham | Walthamstow | 12.04.93 |
| Amos, Ben | 6.3 | Bolton (loan) | Macclesfield | 10.04.90 |
| Martin, David | 6.2 | MK Dons | Romford | 22.01.86 |
| **Defenders** | | | | |
| Cooper, Jake | 6.4 | Reading | Bracknell | 03.02.95 |
| Hutchinson, Shaun | 6.2 | Fulham | Newcastle | 23.11.90 |
| McLaughlin, Conor | 6.0 | Fleetwood | Belfast | 26.07.91 |
| Meredith, James | 6.1 | Bradford | Albury, Aus | 04.04.88 |
| Romeo, Mahlon | 5.10 | Gillingham | Westminster | 19.09.95 |

| | | | | |
|---|---|---|---|---|
| Wallace, Murray | 6.2 | Scunthorpe | Glasgow | 10.01.93 |
| Webster, Byron | 6.4 | Yeovil | Leeds | 31.03.87 |
| **Midfielders** | | | | |
| Ferguson, Shane | 5.11 | Newcastle | Derry | 12.07.91 |
| Oyedinma, Fred | 6.1 | – | Plumstead | 24.11.96 |
| Saville, George | 5.9 | Wolves | Camberley | 01.06.93 |
| Thompson, Ben | 5.10 | – | Sidcup | 03.10.95 |
| Wallace, Jed | 5.10 | Wolves | Reading | 26.03.94 |
| Williams, Shaun | 6.0 | MK Dons | Dublin, Ire | 19.09.86 |
| **Forwards** | | | | |
| Elliott, Tom | 6.4 | AFC Wimbledon | Leeds | 09.11.90 |
| Gregory, Lee | 6.2 | Halifax | Sheffield | 26.08.88 |
| Morison, Steve | 6.2 | Leeds | Enfield | 29.08.83 |
| O'Brien, Aiden | 5.8 | – | Islington | 04.10.93 |

## NORWICH CITY

**Ground:** Carrow Road, Norwich NR1 1JE
**Telephone:** 01603 760760. **Club nickname:** Canaries
**Colours:** Yellow and green. **Capacity:** 27,220
**Record attendance:** 43,984 v Leicester City (FA Cup 6), Mar 30, 1963

| | | | | |
|---|---|---|---|---|
| **Goalkeepers** | | | | |
| Jones, Paul | 6.3 | Portsmouth | Maidstone | 28.06.86 |
| Matthews, Remi | 6.1 | – | Gorleston | 10.02.94 |
| McGovern, Michael | 6.3 | Hamilton | Enniskillen | 12.07.84 |
| **Defenders** | | | | |
| Hanley, Grant | 6.2 | Newcastle | Dumfries | 20.11.91 |
| Husband, James | 5.11 | Middlesbrough | Leeds | 03.01.94 |
| Klose, Timm | 6.4 | Wolfsburg | Frankfurt, Ger | 09.05.88 |
| Martin, Russell | 6.0 | Peterborough | Brighton | 04.01.86 |
| Passlack, Felix | 5.8 | Borussia Dormund (loan) | Bottrop, Ger | 29.05.98 |
| Pinto, Ivo | 6.1 | Dinamo Zagreb | Lourosa, Por | 07.01.90 |
| Raggett, Sean | 6.5 | Lincoln | Gillingham | 17.04.93 |
| Zimmermann, Christoph | 6.4 | Borussia Dortmund | Dusseldorf, Ger | 12.01.93 |
| **Midfielders** | | | | |
| Buendia, Emi | 5.8 | Getafe | Mar del Plata, Arg | 25.12.96 |
| Hernandez, Onel | 5.8 | Braunschweig | Moron, Cub | 01.12.93 |
| Leitner, Moritz | 5.9 | Augsburg | Munchen, Ger | 08.12.92 |
| Marshall, Ben | 6.0 | Wolves | Salford | 29.09.91 |
| McLean, Kenny | 6.0 | Aberdeen | Rutherglen | 08.01.92 |
| Stiepermann, Marco | 6.3 | Bochum | Dortmund, Ger | 09.02.91 |
| Tettey, Alexander | 5.11 | Rennes | Accra, Gh | 04.04.86 |
| Thompson, Louis | 5.11 | Swindon | Bristol | 19.12.94 |
| Trybull, Tom | 5.11 | Den Haag | Berlin, Ger | 09.03.93 |
| Vrancic, Mario | 6.1 | Darmstadt | Slavonski Brod, Croa | 23.05.89 |
| Wildschut, Yanic | 6.2 | Wigan | Amsterdam, Hol | 01.11.91 |
| **Forwards** | | | | |
| Morris, Carlton | 6.2 | – | Cambridge | 16.12.95 |
| Oliveira, Nelson | 6.1 | Benfica | Barcelos, Por | 08.08.91 |
| Pukki, Teemu | 5.11 | Brondby | Kotka, Fin | 29.03.90 |
| Rhodes, Jordan | 6.1 | Sheffield Wed (loan) | Oldham | 05.02.90 |
| Srbeny, Dennis | 6.3 | Paderborn | Berlin, Ger | 05.05.94 |

## NOTTINGHAM FOREST

**Ground**: City Ground, Pavilion Road, Nottingham NG2 5FJ
**Telephone**: 0115 982 4444. **Club nickname**: Forest
**Colours**: Red and white. **Capacity**: 30,576
**Record attendance**: 49,946 v Manchester Utd (Div 1) Oct 28, 1967

| | | | | |
|---|---|---|---|---|
| **Goalkeepers** | | | | |
| Evtimov, Dimitar | 6.3 | Etropole | Shumen, Bul | 07.09.93 |
| Henderson, Stephen | 6.3 | Charlton | Dublin, Ire | 02.05.88 |
| Kapinos, Stefanos | 6.4 | Olympiacos | Piraeus, Gre | 18.03.94 |
| Pantilimon, Costel | 6.8 | Watford | Bacau, Rom | 01.02.87 |
| **Defenders** | | | | |
| Darikwa, Tendayi | 6.2 | Burnley | Nottingham | 13.12.91 |
| Dawson, Michael | 6.2 | Hull | Northallerton | 18.11.83 |
| Figueiredo, Tobias | 6.2 | Sporting CP | Satao, Port | 02.02.94 |
| Fox, Danny | 6.0 | Southampton | Winsford | 29.05.86 |
| Fuentes, Juan | 5.10 | Osasuna | Cordoba, Sp | 05.01.90 |
| Lam, Thomas | 6.2 | Zwolle | Amsterdam, Hol | 18.12.93 |
| Lichaj, Eric | 5.10 | Aston Villa | Downers Grove, US | 17.11.88 |
| Mancienne, Michael | 6.0 | Hamburg | Feltham | 08.01.88 |
| Robinson, Jack | 5.7 | QPR | Warrington | 01.09.93 |
| Traore, Armand | 6.1 | QPR | Paris, Fr | 08.10.89 |
| Worrall, Joe | 6.4 | – | Hucknall | 10.01.97 |
| **Midfielders** | | | | |
| Ariyibi, Gboly | 6.0 | Chesterfield | Arlington, US | 18.01.95 |
| Bouchalakis, Andreas | 6.1 | Olympiacos | Heraklion, Gre | 05.04.93 |
| Bridcutt, Liam | 5.9 | Leeds | Reading | 08.05.89 |
| Cash, Matty | 6.1 | – | Slough | 07.08.97 |
| Diogo Goncalves | 6.3 | Benfica (loan) | Beja, Port | 06.02.97 |
| Guedioura, Adlene | 6.0 | Middlesbrough | La Roche, Fr | 12.11.85 |
| Joao Carvalho | 5.8 | Benfica | Castanheira, Port | 09.03.97 |
| Lolley, Joe | 5.10 | Huddersfield | Redditch | 25.08.92 |
| Osborn, Ben | 5.10 | – | Derby | 05.08.94 |
| McKay, Barrie | 5.9 | Rangers | Paisley | 30.12.94 |
| Ward, Jamie | 5.5 | Derby | Birmingham | 12.05.86 |
| Watson, Ben | 5.10 | Watford | Camberwell | 09.07.85 |
| **Forwards** | | | | |
| Brereton, Ben | 6.0 | – | Blythe Bridge | 18.04.99 |
| Clough, Zach | 5.8 | Bolton | Manchester | 08.03.95 |
| Gil Bastiao Dias | 6.0 | Monaco (loan) | Gafanha, Port | 28.09.96 |
| Grabban, Lewis | 6.0 | Bournemouth | Croydon | 12.01.88 |
| Murphy, Daryl | 6.2 | Newcastle | Waterford, Ire | 15.03.83 |
| Soudani, Hillal | 5.9 | Dinamo Zagreb | Chlef, Alg | 25.11.87 |
| Vellios, Apostolos | 6.4 | Iraklis | Thessaloniki, Gre | 08.01.92 |

## PRESTON NORTH END

**Ground**: Deepdale, Sir Tom Finney Way, Preston PR1 6RU
**Telephone**: 0844 856 1964. **Club nickname**: Lilywhites
**Colours**: White and navy. **Capacity**: 23,404
**Record attendance**: 42,684 v Arsenal (Div 1) Apr 23, 1938

| | | | | |
|---|---|---|---|---|
| **Goalkeepers** | | | | |
| Crowe, Michael | 6.2 | Ipswich | Bexley | 13.11.95 |
| Maxwell, Chris | 6.2 | Fleetwood | St Asaph | 30.07.90 |

| | | | | |
|---|---|---|---|---|
| Rudd, Declan | 6.3 | Norwich | Diss | 16.01.91 |
| **Defenders** | | | | |
| Boyle, Andy | 5.11 | Dundalk | Dublin, Ire | 07.03.91 |
| Clarke, Tom | 5.11 | Huddersfield | Halifax | 21.12.87 |
| Davies, Ben | 5.11 | – | Barrow | 11.08.95 |
| Hughes, Andrew | 5.11 | Peterborough | Cardiff | 05.06.92 |
| Huntington, Paul | 6.2 | Yeovil | Carlisle | 17.09.87 |
| O'Connor, Kevin | 6.2 | Cork | Enniscorthy, Ire | 07.05.95 |
| Storey, Jordan | 6.2 | Exeter | Yeovil | 02.09.97 |
| Vermijl, Marnick | 5.11 | Sheffield Wed | Peer, Bel | 13.01.92 |
| Woods, Calum | 5.11 | Huddersfield | Liverpool | 05.02.87 |
| **Midfielders** | | | | |
| Browne, Alan | 5.8 | Cork | Cork, Ire | 15.04.95 |
| Earl, Josh | 6.4 | – | Southport | 24.10.98 |
| Fisher, Darnell | 5.9 | Rotherham | Reading | 04.04.94 |
| Harrop, Josh | 5.9 | Manchester Utd | Stockport | 15.12.95 |
| Horgan, Daryl | 5.7 | Dundalk | Galway, Ire | 10.08.92 |
| Johnson, Daniel | 5.8 | Aston Villa | Kingston, Jam | 08.10.92 |
| Ledson, Ryan | 5.9 | Oxford | Liverpool | 19.08.97 |
| Pearson, Ben | 5.5 | Manchester Utd | Oldham | 04.01.95 |
| Pringle, Ben | 5.8 | Fulham | Newcastle | 25.07.89 |
| **Forwards** | | | | |
| Barkhuizen, Tom | 5.11 | Preston | Blackpool | 04.07.93 |
| Bodin, Billy | 5.11 | Bristol Rov | Swindon | 24.03.92 |
| Burke, Graham | 5.11 | Shamrock Rov | Dublin, Ire | 21.09.93 |
| Doyle, Eoin | 6.0 | Cardiff | Dublin, Ire | 12.03.88 |
| Gallagher, Paul | 6.0 | Leicester | Glasgow | 09.08.84 |
| Maguire, Sean | 5.9 | Cork | Luton | 01.05.94 |
| Moult, Louis | 6.0 | Motherwell | Stoke | 14.05.92 |
| Robinson, Callum | 5.10 | Aston Villa | Northampton | 02.02.95 |
| Simpson, Connor | 6.5 | Hartlepool | Guisborough | 24.01.00 |

## QUEENS PARK RANGERS

**Ground**: Loftus Road Stadium, South Africa Road, London W12 7PA
**Telephone**:0208 743 0262. **Club nickname**: Hoops
**Colours**: Blue and white. **Capcity**: 18,360
**Record attendance**: 35,353 v Leeds (Div 1) 27 Apr, 1974

| | | | | |
|---|---|---|---|---|
| **Goalkeepers** | | | | |
| Ingram, Matt | 6.3 | Wycombe | High Wycombe | 18.12.93 |
| **Defenders** | | | | |
| Baptiste, Alex | 5.11 | Middlesbrough | Sutton-in-Ashfield | 31.01.86 |
| Bidwell, Jake | 6.0 | Brentford | Southport | 21.03.93 |
| Furlong, Darnell | 5.11 | – | Luton | 31.10.95 |
| Hall, Grant | 6.4 | Tottenham | Brighton | 29.10.91 |
| Kakay, Osman | 5.11 | – | Westminster | 25.08.97 |
| Leistner, Toni | 6.3 | Union Berlin | Dresden, Ger | 19.08.90 |
| Lynch, Joel | 6.1 | Huddersfield | Eastbourne | 03.10.87 |
| **Midfielders** | | | | |
| Cousins, Jordan | 5.10 | Charlton | Greenwich | 06.03.94 |
| Freeman, Luke | 5.10 | Bristol City | Dartford | 22.03.92 |
| Goss, Sean | 5.10 | Manchester Utd | Wegberg, Ger | 01.10.95 |
| Luongo, Massimo | 5.10 | Swindon | Sydney, Aus | 25.09.92 |
| Manning, Ryan | 5.11 | Galway | Galway, Ire | 14.06.96 |

| | | | | |
|---|---|---|---|---|
| Osayi-Samuel, Bright | 5.9 | Blackpool | Nigeria | 01.02.97 |
| Scowen, Josh | 5.10 | Barnsley | Enfield | 28.03.93 |
| Smyth, Paul | | Linfield | Belfast | 10.09.97 |
| Wszolek, Pawel | 6.1 | Hellas Verona | Tczew, Pol | 30.04.92 |
| **Forwards** | | | | |
| Chair, Ilias | 5.4 | Lierse | Belgium | 30.10.97 |
| Eze, Eberechi | 5.8 | Millwall | Greenwich | 29.06.98 |
| Oteh, Aramide | 5.9 | Tottenham | Lewisham | 10.09.98 |
| Smith, Matt | 6.6 | Fulham | Birmingham | 07.06.89 |
| Sylla, Idrissa | 6.2 | Anderlecht | Conakry, Guin | 03.12.90 |
| Washington, Conor | 5.10 | Peterborough | Chatham | 18.05.92 |
| Wheeler, David | 5.11 | Exeter | Brighton | 04.10.90 |

## READING

**Ground**: Madejski Stadium, Junction 11 M4, Reading RG2 OFL
**Telephone**: 0118 968 1100. **Club nickname**: Royals
**Colours**: Blue and white. **Capacity**: 24,200
**Record attendance**: Elm Park: 33,042 v Brentford (FA Cup 5) Feb 19, 1927; Madejski Stadium: 24,184 v Everton (Prem Lge) Nov 17, 2012

| | | | | |
|---|---|---|---|---|
| **Goalkeepers** | | | | |
| Jaakkola, Anssi | 6.5 | Ajax Cape Town | Kemi, Fin | 13.03.87 |
| Mannone, Vito | 6.3 | Sunderland | Desio, It | 02.03.88 |
| **Defenders** | | | | |
| Blackett, Tyler | 6.1 | Manchester Utd | Manchester | 02.04.94 |
| Gunter, Chris | 5.11 | Nottm Forest | Newport | 21.07.89 |
| McShane, Paul | 6.0 | Hull | Kilpedder, Ire | 06.01.86 |
| Moore, Liam | 6.1 | Leicester | Leicester | 31.01.93 |
| Obita, Jordan | 5.11 | – | Oxford | 08.12.93 |
| O'Shea, John | 6.3 | Sunderland | Waterford, Ire | 30.04.81 |
| Richards, Omar | – | Fulham | Lewisham | 15.02.98 |
| Tiago, Ilori | 6.3 | Liverpool | Hampstead | 26.02.93 |
| **Midfielders** | | | | |
| Bacuna, Leandro | 6.2 | Aston Villa | Groningen, Hol | 21.08.91 |
| Clement, Pelle | 5.10 | Ajax | Amsterdam, Hol | 19.05.96 |
| Edwards, Dave | 5.11 | Wolves | Pontesbury | 03.02.85 |
| Evans, George | 6.1 | Manchester City | Cheadle | 13.12.94 |
| Harriott, Callum | 5.6 | Charlton | Norbury | 04.03.94 |
| Kelly, Liam | 5.6 | – | Basingstoke | 22.11.95 |
| McCleary, Garath | 5.11 | Nottm Forest | Bromley | 15.05.87 |
| Meyler, David | 6.2 | Hull | Cork, Ire | 29.05.89 |
| Popa, Adrian | 5.7 | Steaua Bucharest | Bucharest, Rom | 24.07.88 |
| Swift, John | 6.0 | Chelsea | Portsmouth | 23.06.95 |
| Van den Berg, Joey | 6.1 | Heerenveen | Nijeveen, Hol | 13.02.86 |
| **Forwards** | | | | |
| Aluko, Sone | 5.8 | Fulham | Hounslow | 19.12.89 |
| Barrow, Modou | 5.10 | Swansea | Banjul, Gam | 13.10.92 |
| Bodvarsson, Jon Dadi | 6.3 | Wolves | Selfoss, Ice | 25.05.92 |
| Kermorgant, Yann | 6.1 | Bournemouth | Vannes, Fr | 08.11.81 |
| McNulty, Marc | 5.10 | Coventry | Edinburgh | 14.09.92 |
| Smith, Sam | – | Manchester Utd | Manchester | 08.03.98 |

## ROTHERHAM UNITED

**Ground**: New York Stadium, New York Way, Rotherham S60 1AH
**Telephone**: 08444 140733. **Club nickname**: Millers
**Colours**: Red and white. **Capacity**: 12,021
**Record attendance**: Millmoor: 25,170 v Sheffield Wed (Div 2) Jan 26, 1952 and v Sheffield Wed (Div 2) Dec 13, 1952; Don Valley Stadium: 7,082 v Aldershot (Lge 2 play-off semi-final, 2nd leg) May 19, 2010; New York Stadium: 11,758 v Sheffield Utd (Lge 1) Sep 7, 2013

| | | | | |
|---|---|---|---|---|
| **Goalkeepers** | | | | |
| **Defenders** | | | | |
| Ajayi, Semi | 6.4 | Cardiff | Crayford | 09.11.93 |
| Ball, Dominic | 6.1 | Tottenham | Welwyn Garden City | 02.08.95 |
| Ihiekwe, Michael | 6.1 | Tranmere | Liverpool | 20.11.92 |
| Mattock, Joe | 6.0 | Sheffield Wed | Leicester | 15.05.90 |
| Purrington, Ben | 5.9 | Plymouth | Exeter | 05.05.96 |
| Robertson, Clark | 6.2 | Blackpool | Aberdeen | 05.09.93 |
| Vyner, Zak | 5.11 | Bristol City (loan) | Bath | 14.05.95 |
| Wood, Richard | 6.3 | Charlton | Ossett | 05.07.85 |
| **Midfielders** | | | | |
| Forde, Anthony | 5.9 | Walsall | Ballingarry, Ire | 16.11.93 |
| Newell, Joe | 5.11 | Peterborough | Tamworth | 15.03.93 |
| Palmer, Matt | 5.10 | Burton | Derby | 01.08.93 |
| Potter, Darren | 5.10 | MK Dons | Liverpool | 21.12.84 |
| Taylor, Jon | 5.11 | Peterborough | Liverpool | 20.07.92 |
| Vaulks, Will | 5.11 | Falkirk | Wirral | 13.09.93 |
| Williams, Ryan | 5.8 | Barnsley | Perth, Aus | 28.10.93 |
| **Forwards** | | | | |
| Ball, David | 6.0 | Fleetwood | Whitefield | 14.12.89 |
| Procter, Jamie | 6.2 | Bolton | Preston | 25.03.92 |
| Smith, Michael | 6.4 | Bury | Wallsend | 17.10.91 |
| Vassell, Kyle | 6.0 | Blackpool | Milton Keynes | 07.02.93 |
| Yates, Jerry | 5.9 | – | Doncaster | 10.11.96 |

## SHEFFIELD UNITED

**Ground**: Bramall Lane, Sheffield S2 4SU
**Telephone**: 0871 995 1899. **Club nickname**: Blades
**Colours**: Red and white. **Capacity**: 32,702
**Record attendance**: 68,287 v Leeds (FA Cup 5) Feb 15, 1936

| | | | | |
|---|---|---|---|---|
| **Goalkeepers** | | | | |
| Eastwood, Jake | 6.1 | – | Sheffield | 03.10.96 |
| Henderson, Dean | 6.3 | Manchester Utd (loan) | Whitehaven | 12.03.97 |
| Moore, Simon | 6.3 | Cardiff | Sandown, IOW | 19.05.90 |
| **Defenders** | | | | |
| Baldock, George | 5.9 | MK Dons | Buckingham | 09.03.93 |
| Basham, Chris | 5.11 | Blackpool | Hebburn | 18.02.88 |
| Freeman, Kieron | 6.1 | Derby | Bestwood | 21.03.92 |
| Lafferty, Daniel | 6.1 | Burnley | Derry | 01.04.89 |
| Leonard, Ryan | 6.1 | Southend | Plymouth | 24.05.92 |
| Lundstram, John | 5.11 | Oxford | Liverpool | 18.02.94 |
| O'Connell, Jack | 6.3 | Brentford | Liverpool | 29.03.94 |
| Stearman, Richard | 6.2 | Fulham | Wolverhampton | 19.08.87 |
| Stevens, Enda | 6.0 | Portsmouth | Dublin, Ire | 09.07.90 |

| | | | | |
|---|---|---|---|---|
| Wright, Jake | 6.1 | Oxford | Keighley | 11.03.86 |
| **Midfielders** | | | | |
| Coutts, Paul | 6.1 | Derby | Aberdeen | 22.07.88 |
| Duffy, Mark | 5.9 | Birmingham | Liverpool | 07.10.85 |
| Evans, Lee | 6.1 | Wolves | Newport | 24.07.94 |
| Fleck, John | 5.7 | Coventry | Glasgow | 24.08.91 |
| **Forwards** | | | | |
| Clarke, Leon | 6.2 | Bury | Birmingham | 10.02.85 |
| Evans, Ched | 6.0 | Chesterfield | St Asaph | 28.12.88 |
| Holmes, Ricky | 6.2 | Charlton | Uxbridge | 19.06.87 |
| Sharp, Billy | 5.9 | Leeds | Sheffield | 05.02.86 |

## SHEFFIELD WEDNESDAY

**Ground**: Hillsborough, Sheffield, S6 1SW
**Telephone**: 0871 995 1867. **Club nickname**: Owls
**Colours**: Blue and white. **Capacity**: 39,812
**Record attendance**: 72,841 v Manchester City (FA Cup 5) Feb 17, 1934

| | | | | |
|---|---|---|---|---|
| **Goalkeepers** | | | | |
| Dawson, Cameron | 6.0 | Sheffield Utd | Sheffield | 07.07.95 |
| Westwood, Keiren | 6.1 | Sunderland | Manchester | 23.10.84 |
| Wildsmith, Joe | 6.1 | – | Sheffield | 28.12.95 |
| **Defenders** | | | | |
| Baker, Ashley | – | Cardiff | Bridgend | 30.10.96 |
| Fox, Morgan | 6.1 | Charlton | Chelmsford | 21.09.93 |
| Hutchinson, Sam | 6.0 | Chelsea | Windsor | 03.08.89 |
| Lees, Tom | 6.1 | Leeds | Warwick | 18.11.90 |
| Nielsen, Frederik | 6.7 | Nottm Forest | Denmark | 07.02.98 |
| Palmer, Liam | 6.2 | – | Worksop | 19.09.91 |
| Pudil, Daniel | 6.1 | Watford | Prague, Cz | 27.09.85 |
| Thorniley, Jordan | 5.11 | Everton | Warrington | 24.11.96 |
| Van Aken, Joost | 6.4 | Heerenveen | Haarlem, Hol | 13.05.94 |
| **Midfielders** | | | | |
| Abdi, Almen | 5.11 | Watford | Prizren, Kos | 21.10.86 |
| Bannan, Barry | 5.11 | Crystal Palace | Airdrie | 01.12.89 |
| Boyd, George | 5.10 | Burnley | Chatham | 02.10.85 |
| Clare, Sean | 6.3 | – | Hackney | 18.09.96 |
| Jones, David | 6.0 | Burnley | Southport | 04.11.84 |
| Lee, Kieran | 6.1 | Oldham | Tameside | 22.06.88 |
| Pelupessy, Joel | 5.11 | Heracles | Nijverdal, Hol | 15.05.93 |
| Reach, Adam | 6.1 | Middlesbrough | Gateshead | 03.02.93 |
| Stobbs, Jack | 5.11 | – | Leeds | 27.02.97 |
| **Forwards** | | | | |
| Fletcher, Steven | 6.1 | Sunderland | Shrewsbury | 26.03.87 |
| Forestieri, Fernando | 5.8 | Watford | Rosario, Arg | 15.01.90 |
| Hooper, Gary | 5.10 | Norwich | Loughton | 26.01.88 |
| Lucas Joao | 6.4 | Nacional | Luanda, Ang | 04.09.93 |
| Matias, Marco | 5.10 | Nacional | Barreiro, Por | 10.05.89 |
| Nuhiu, Atdhe | 6.6 | Rapid Vienna | Prishtina, Kos | 29.07.89 |
| Winnall, Sam | 5.9 | Barnsley | Wolverhampton | 19.01.91 |

## STOKE CITY

**Ground**: bet365 Stadium, Stanley Matthews Way, Stoke-on-Trent ST4 7EG
**Telephone**: 01782 367598. **Club nickname**: Potters
**Colours**: Red and white. **Capacity**: 30,183.
**Record attendance**: Victoria Ground: 51,380 v Arsenal (Div 1) Mar 29, 1937. bet365 Stadium: 30,022 v Everton (Prem Lge) Mar 17, 2018

| | | | | |
|---|---|---|---|---|
| **Goalkeepers** | | | | |
| Butland, Jack | 6.4 | Birmingham | Bristol | 10.03.93 |
| Federici, Adam | 6.2 | Bournemouth | Nowra, Aus | 31.01.85 |
| Haugaard, Jakob | 6.6 | Midtjylland | Sundby, Den | 01.05.92 |
| **Defenders** | | | | |
| Bauer, Moritz | 5.11 | Rubin Kazan | Winterthur, Switz | 25.01.92 |
| Cameron, Geoff | 6.3 | Houston | Attleboro, US | 11.07.85 |
| Edwards, Tom | 5.9 | – | Stafford | 22.01.99 |
| Martins Indi, Bruno | 6.1 | Porto | Barreiro, Port | 08.02.92 |
| Pieters, Erik | 6.1 | PSV Eindhoven | Tiel, Hol | 07.08.88 |
| Shawcross, Ryan | 6.3 | Manchester Utd | Chester | 04.10.87 |
| Tymon, Josh | 5.10 | Hull | Hull | 22.05.99 |
| Wimmer, Kevin | 6.2 | Tottenham | Wels, Aut | 15.11.92 |
| **Midfielders** | | | | |
| Adam, Charlie | 6.1 | Liverpool | Dundee | 10.12.85 |
| Afellay, Ibrahim | 5.11 | Barcelona | Utrecht, Hol | 02.04.86 |
| Allen, Joe | 5.7 | Liverpool | Carmarthen | 14.03.90 |
| Fletcher, Darren | 6.0 | WBA | Edinburgh | 01.02.84 |
| Imbula, Giannelli | 6.1 | Porto | Vilvoorde, Bel | 12.09.92 |
| Ndiaye, Badou | 5.11 | Galatasaray | Dakar, Sen | 27.10.90 |
| Oghenekaro, Etebo | 5.9 | Feirense | Lagos, Nig | 09.11.95 |
| **Forwards** | | | | |
| Afobe, Benik | 6.0 | Wolves (loan) | Waltham Forest | 12.02.93 |
| Berahino, Saido | 5.10 | WBA | Bujumbura, Bur | 04.08.93 |
| Biram Diouf, Mame | 6.1 | Hannover | Dakar, Sen | 16.12.87 |
| Choupo-Moting. Eric | 6.3 | Schalke | Hamburg, Ger | 23.03.89 |
| Crouch, Peter | 6.7 | Tottenham | Macclesfield | 30.01.81 |
| Krkic, Bojan | 5.7 | Barcelona | Linyola, Sp | 28.08.90 |
| Ngoy, Julien | 6.2 | Bruges | Antwerp, Bel | 02.11.97 |

## SWANSEA CITY

**Ground**: Liberty Stadium, Morfa, Swansea SA1 2FA
**Telephone**: 01792 616600. **Club nickname**: Swans
**Colours**: White. **Capacity**: 20,972.
**Record attendance**: Vetch Field: 32,796 v Arsenal (FA Cup 4) Feb 17, 1968. Liberty Stadium: 20,972 v Liverpool (Prem Lge) May 1, 2016

| | | | | |
|---|---|---|---|---|
| **Goalkeepers** | | | | |
| Mulder, Erwin | 6.4 | Heerenveen | Pannerden, Hol | 03.03.89 |
| **Defenders** | | | | |
| Amat, Jordi | 6.0 | Espanyol | Canet de Mar, Sp | 21.03.92 |
| Bartley, Kyle | 6.1 | Arsenal | Stockport | 22.05.91 |
| Fernandez, Federico | 6.3 | Napoli | Tres Algarrobos, Arg | 21.02.89 |
| Mawson, Alfie | 6.2 | Barnsley | Hillingdon | 19.01.94 |
| Naughton, Kyle | 5.10 | Tottenham | Sheffield | 11.11.88 |
| Olsson, Martin | 5.10 | Norwich | Gavle, Swe | 17.05.88 |

| | | | | |
|---|---|---|---|---|
| Van der Hoorn, Mike | 6.3 | Ajax | Almere, Hol | 15.10.92 |
| **Midfielders** | | | | |
| Carroll, Tom | 5.10 | Tottenham | Watford | 28.05.92 |
| Clucas, Sam | 5.10 | Hull | Lincoln | 25.09.90 |
| Dyer, Nathan | 5.10 | Southampton | Trowbridge | 29.11.87 |
| Fer, Leroy | 6.2 | QPR | Zoetermeer, Hol | 05.01.90 |
| Fulton, Jay | 5.10 | Falkirk | Bolton | 04.04.94 |
| Mesa, Roque | 5.7 | Las Palmas | Las Palmas, Gran Can | 07.06.89 |
| Narsingh, Luciano | 5.10 | PSV Eindhoven | Amsterdam, Hol | 13.09.90 |
| Routledge, Wayne | 5.7 | Newcastle | Sidcup | 07.01.85 |
| **Forwards** | | | | |
| Asoro, Joel | 5.9 | Sunderland | Stockholm, Swe | 27.04.99 |
| Ayew, Andre | 5.10 | West Ham | Seclin, Fr | 17.12.89 |
| Ayew, Jordan | 6.0 | Aston Villa | Marseille, Fr | 11.09.91 |
| Bony, Wilfried | 6.0 | Manchester City | Bingerville, Iv C | 10.12.88 |
| Borja | 6.3 | Atletico Madrid | Madrid, Sp | 25.08.92 |
| McBurnie, Oliver | 6.2 | Bradford | Leeds | 04.06.96 |

## WEST BROMWICH ALBION

**Ground**: The Hawthorns, Halfords Lane, West Bromwich B71 4LF
**Telephone**: 0871 271 1100. **Club nickname**: Baggies
**Colours**: Blue and white. **Capacity**: 26,500.
**Record attendance**: 64,815 v Arsenal (FA Cup 6) Mar 6, 1937

| | | | | |
|---|---|---|---|---|
| **Goalkeepers** | | | | |
| Johnstone, Sam | 6.4 | Manchester Utd | Preston | 25.03.93 |
| **Defenders** | | | | |
| Bartley, Kyle | 6.1 | Swansea | Stockport | 22.05.91 |
| Dawson, Craig | 6.2 | Rochdale | Rochdale | 06.05.90 |
| Gibbs, Kieran | 5.10 | Arsenal | Lambeth | 26.09.89 |
| Hegazi, Ahmed | 6.4 | Al Ahly | Ismailia, Egy | 25.01.91 |
| Nyom, Allan | 6.2 | Watford | Neuilly-sur-Seine, Fr | 10.05.88 |
| **Midfielders** | | | | |
| Barry, Gareth | 6.0 | Everton | Hastings | 23.02.81 |
| Brunt, Chris | 6.1 | Sheffield Wed | Belfast | 14.12.84 |
| Burke, Oliver | 6.2 | Leipzig | Kircaldy | 07.04.97 |
| Chadli, Nacer | 6.2 | Tottenham | Liege, Bel | 02.08.89 |
| Field, Sam | 5.11 | – | Stourbridge | 08.05.98 |
| Harper, Rekeem | 6.0 | – | Birmingham | 08.03.00 |
| Leko, Jonathan | 6.0 | – | Kinshasa, DR Cong | 24.04.99 |
| Livermore, Jake | 6.0 | Hull | Enfield | 14.11.89 |
| McClean, James | 5.11 | Wigan | Derry | 22.04.89 |
| Phillips, Matt | 6.0 | QPR | Aylesbury | 13.03.91 |
| **Forwards** | | | | |
| Robson-Kanu, Hal | 6.0 | Reading | Acton | 21.05.89 |
| Rodriguez, Jay | 6.1 | Southampton | Burnley | 29.07.89 |
| Rondon, Salomon | 6.2 | Zenit St Petersburg | Caracas, Ven | 16.09.89 |

## WIGAN ATHLETIC

**Ground**: DW Stadium, Robin Park, Wigan WN5 0UZ
**Telephone**: 01942 774000. **Club nickname**: Latics
**Colours**: Blue and white. **Capacity**: 25,023
**Record attendance**: Springfield Park: 27,526 v Hereford (FA Cup 2) Dec 12, 1953; DW Stadium: 25,133 v Manchester Utd (Prem Lge) May 11, 2008

| | | | | |
|---|---|---|---|---|
| **Goalkeepers** | | | | |
| Jones, Jamie | 6.2 | Stevenage | Kirkby | 18.02.89 |
| Walton, Christian | 6.5 | Brighton (loan) | Truro | 09.11.95 |
| **Defenders** | | | | |
| Bruce, Alex | 5.11 | Bury | Norwich | 28.09.84 |
| Burn, Dan | 6.7 | Fulham | Blyth | 09.05.92 |
| Dunkley, Chey | 6.2 | Oxford | Wolverhampton | 13.02.92 |
| James, Reece | 5.11 | Chelsea (loan) | Redbridge | 08.12.99 |
| Thomas, Terell | 6.0 | Charlton | Redbridge | 13.10.97 |
| **Midfielders** | | | | |
| Byrne, Nathan | 5.11 | Wolves | St Albans | 05.06.92` |
| Colclough, Ryan | 6.0 | Crewe | Burslem | 27.12.94 |
| Da Silva-Lopes, Leon | 5.7 | Peterborough | Lisbon, Por | 30.11.98 |
| Flores, Jordan | 5.11 | – | Wigan | 04.10.95 |
| Jacobs, Michael | 5.9 | Wolves | Rothwell | 04.11.91 |
| Laurent, Josh | 6.2 | Hartlepool | Leystonstone | 06.05.95 |
| MacDonald, Shaun | 6.1 | Bournemouth | Swansea | 17.06.88 |
| Morsy, Sam | 5.9 | Chesterfield | Wolverhampton | 10.09.91 |
| Naismith, Kai | 6.1 | Portsmouth | Glasgow | 18.02.92 |
| Powell, Nick | 6.0 | Manchester Utd | Crewe | 23.03.94 |
| Power, Max | 5.11 | Tranmere | Birkenhead | 27.07.93 |
| Roberts, Gary | 5.10 | Portsmouth | Chester | 18.03.84 |
| Walker, Jamie | 5.10 | Hearts | Edinburgh | 25.06.93 |
| **Forwards** | | | | |
| Cole, Devante | 6.1 | Fleetwood | Alderley Edge | 10.05.95 |
| Grigg, Will | 5.11 | Brentford | Solihull | 03.07.91 |
| Massey, Gavin | 5.10 | Leyton Orient | Watford | 14.10.92 |
| Vaughan, James | 5.11 | Sunderland | Birmingham | 14.07.88 |

# LEAGUE ONE

## ACCRINGTON STANLEY

**Ground**: Wham Stadium, Livingstone Road, Accrington BB5 5BX
**Telephone**: 0871 434 1968. **Club nickname**: Stanley
**Colours**: Red and white. **Capacity**: 5,500
**Record attendance**: 4,368 v Colchester (FA Cup 3) Jan 3, 2004

| | | | | |
|---|---|---|---|---|
| **Goalkeepers** | | | | |
| Maxted, Jonathan | 6.0 | Guiseley | Tadcaster | 26.10.93 |
| **Defenders** | | | | |
| Conneely, Seamus | 6.1 | Sligo | Lambeth | 09.07.88 |
| Donacien, Janoi | 6.0 | Aston Villa | Castries, St Luc | 03.11.93 |
| Hughes, Mark | 6.3 | Stevenage | Kirkby | 09.12.86 |
| Callum Johnson | – | Middlesbrough | Yarm | 23.10.96 |
| Ogle, Reagan | 5.9 | – | Australia | 29.03.99 |
| Richards-Everton, Ben | 6.4 | Dunfermline | Birmingham | 17.10.91 |
| Rodgers, Harvey | 5.11 | Fleetwood | York | 20.10.96 |
| Sykes, Ross | 6.5 | – | Burnley | 26.03.99 |
| **Midfielders** | | | | |
| Brown, Scott | 5.9 | Grimsby | Runcorn | 08.05.85 |
| Clark, Jordan | 6.0 | Shrewsbury | Hoyland | 22.09.93 |
| Finley, Sam | 5.8 | Fylde | Liverpool | 04.08.92 |

| | | | | |
|---|---|---|---|---|
| McConville, Sean | 5.11 | Chester | Burscough | 06.03.89 |
| Mingoia, Piero | 5.6 | Cambridge | Enfield | 20.10.91 |
| Nolan, Liam | 5.10 | Southport | Liverpool | 20.09.94 |
| Sousa, Erico | 5.7 | Tranmere | Vale da Amoreira, Por | 12.03.95 |
| Williams, Danny | 5.9 | Dundee | Wigan | 25.01.88 |
| **Forwards** | | | | |
| Jackson, Kayden | 5.11 | Barnsley | Bradford | 22.02.94 |
| Kee, Billy | 5.9 | Scunthorpe | Leicester | 01.12.90 |

## AFC WIMBLEDON

**Ground**: Kingsmeadow, Kingston Road, Kingston upon Thames KT1 3PB
**Telephone**: 0208 547 3528. **Club nickname**: Dons
**Colours**: Blue. **Capacity**: 4,850
**Record attendance**: 4,749 v Exeter (Lge 2) Apr 23, 2013

| | | | | |
|---|---|---|---|---|
| **Goalkeepers** | | | | |
| King, Tom | 6.1 | Millwall (loan) | Plymouth | 09.03.95 |
| McDonnell, Joe | 5.11 | Basingstoke | Basingstoke | 19.05.94 |
| Tzanev, Nik | 6.4 | Brentford | Wellington, NZ | 23.12.96 |
| **Defenders** | | | | |
| Kalambay, Paul | 6.0 | – | Dulwich | 09.07.99 |
| Meades, Jon | 6.1 | Oxford | Cardiff | 02.03.92 |
| Nightingale, Will | 6.1 | – | Wandsworth | 02.08.95 |
| Oshilaja, Adedeji | 6.0 | Cardiff | Bermondsey | 26.02.93 |
| Sibbick, Toby | 6.0 | – | Isleworth | 23.05.99 |
| Watson, Tennai | 6.0 | Reading (loan) | Hillingdon | 04.03.97 |
| **Midfielders** | | | | |
| Barcham, Andy | 5.10 | Portsmouth | Basildon | 16.12.86 |
| Bellikli, Neset | 5.10 | – | Sutton | 09.07.98 |
| Egan, Alfie | 5.10 | – | Lambeth | 03.09.97 |
| Hartigan, Anthony | 5.10 | – | Kingston u Thames | 27.01.00 |
| Kaja, Egli | 5.10 | Kingstonian | Albania | 26.07.97 |
| Pinnock, Mitch | 6.3 | Dover | Gravesend | 12.12.94 |
| Soares, Tom | 6.0 | Bury | Reading | 10.07.86 |
| Trotter, Liam | 6.2 | Bolton | Ipswich | 24.08.88 |
| Wagstaff, Scott | 5.9 | Gillingham | Maidstone | 31.03.90 |
| Wordsworth, Anthony | 6.1 | Southend | Camden | 03.01.89 |
| **Forwards** | | | | |
| Appiah, Kwesi | 5.11 | Crystal Palace | Thamesmead | 12.08.90 |
| Hanson, James | 6.4 | Sheffield Utd | Bradford | 09.11.87 |
| McDonald, Cody | 6.0 | Gillingham | Witham | 30.05.86 |
| Pigott, Joe | 6.2 | Maidstone | Maidstone | 24.11.93 |

## BARNSLEY

**Ground**: Oakwell Stadium, Barnsley S71 1ET
**Telephone**: 01226 211211. **Club nickname**: Tykes
**Colours**: Red and white. **Capacity**: 23,009
**Record attendance**: 40,255 v Stoke (FA Cup 5) Feb 15, 1936

| | | | | |
|---|---|---|---|---|
| **Goalkeepers** | | | | |
| Davies, Adam | 6.1 | Sheffield Wed | Rinteln, Ger | 17.07.92 |
| Walton, Jack | 6.1 | – | Bury | 23.04.98 |

| **Defenders** | | | | |
|---|---|---|---|---|
| Cavare, Dimitri | 6.1 | Rennes | Pointe-a-Pitre, Guad | 05.02.95 |
| Fryers, Zeki | 6.0 | Crystal Palace | Manchester | 09.09.92 |
| Jackson, Adam | 6.3 | Middlesbrough | Darlington | 18.05.94 |
| Lindsay, Liam | 6.3 | Partick | Paisley | 12.10.95 |
| Pinnock, Ethan | 6.2 | Forest Green | Lambeth | 29.05.93 |
| McCarthy, Jason | 6.1 | Southampton | Southampton | 07.11.95 |
| Pinillos, Dani | 6.0 | Cordoba | Logrono, Sp | 22.10.92 |
| **Midfielders** | | | | |
| Hedges, Ryan | 6.1 | Swansea | Northampton | 08.07.95 |
| Isgrove, Lloyd | 5.10 | Southampton | Yeovil | 12.01.93 |
| McGeehan, Cameron | 5.11 | Luton | Kingston upon Thames | 06.04.95 |
| Moncur, George | 5.9 | Colchester | Swindon | 18.08.93 |
| Mowatt, Alex | 5.10 | Leeds | Doncaster | 13.02.95 |
| Potts, Brad | 6.2 | Blackpool | Hexham | 07.03.94 |
| **Forwards** | | | | |
| Bradshaw, Tom | 5.10 | Walsall | Shrewsbury | 27.07.92 |
| Moore, Kieffer | 6.5 | Ipswich | Torquay | 08.08.92 |
| Thiam, Mamadou | 5.11 | Dijon | Aubervilliers, Fr | 20.03.95 |

## BLACKPOOL

**Ground**: Bloomfield Road, Blackpool FY1 6JJ
**Telephone**: 0871 622 1953. **Club nickname**: Seasiders
**Colours**: Tangerine and white. **Capacity**: 17,338
**Record attendance**: 38,098 v Wolves (Div 1) Sep 17, 1955

| **Goalkeepers** | | | | |
|---|---|---|---|---|
| Boney, Myles | 5.11 | – | Blackpool | 01.02.98 |
| Howard, Mark | 6.0 | Bolton | Southwark | 21.09.86 |
| Mafoumbi, Christoffer | 6.5 | Free State | Roubaix, Fr | 03.03.94 |
| **Defenders** | | | | |
| Anderton, Nick | 6.2 | Barrow | Preston | 22.04.96 |
| Heneghan, Ben | 6.3 | Sheffield Utd (loan) | Manchester | 19.09.93 |
| Mellor, Kelvin | 6.2 | Plymouth | Crewe | 25.01.91 |
| Nottingham, Michael | 6.4 | Salford | Birmingham | 14.04.89 |
| O'Connor, Paudie | 6.3 | Leeds (loan) | Limerick, Ire | 14.07.97 |
| Tilt, Curtis | 6.4 | Wrexham | Walsall | 04.08.91 |
| Turton, Ollie | 5.11 | Crewe | Manchester | 06.12.92 |
| **Midfielders** | | | | |
| O'Sullivan, John | 5.11 | Carlisle | Dublin, Ire | 18.09.93 |
| Pritchard, Harry | | Maidenhead | High Wycombe | 14.09.92 |
| Ryan, Jimmy | 5.10 | Fleetwood | Maghull | 06.09.88 |
| Spearing, Jay | 5.6 | Bolton | Wallasey | 25.11.88 |
| Taylor, Chris | 6.0 | Bolton | Oldham | 20.12.86 |
| Thompson, Jordan | 5.9 | Rangers | Belfast | 03.01.97 |
| **Forwards** | | | | |
| Bunney, Joe | 5.10 | Northampton (loan) | Northwich | 26.09.93 |
| Clayton, Max | 5.9 | Bolton | Crewe | 09.08.94 |
| Cullen, Mark | 5.9 | Luton | Stakeford | 21.04.92 |
| Delfouneso, Nathan | 6.1 | Swindon | Birmingham | 02.02.91 |
| Dodoo, Joe | 6.0 | Rangers (loan) | Kumasi, Gha | 29.06.95 |
| Gnanduillet, Armand | 6.3 | Leyton Orient | Angers, Fr | 13.02.92 |
| Menga, Dolly | 5.11 | Braga | Verviers, Bel | 21.05.93 |

## BRADFORD CITY

**Ground**: Northern Commercials Stadium, Valley Parade, Bradford BD8 7DY
**Telephone**: 01274 773355. **Club nickname**: Bantams
**Colours**: Yellow and claret. **Capacity**: 25,136
**Record attendance:** 39,146 v Burnley (FA Cup 4) Mar 11, 1911

| | | | | |
|---|---|---|---|---|
| **Goalkeepers** | | | | |
| Doyle, Colin | 6.5 | Blackpool | Cork, Ire | 12.08.85 |
| O'Donnell, Richard | 6.2 | Northampton | Sheffield | 12.09.88 |
| **Defenders** | | | | |
| Chicksen, Adam | 5.8 | Charlton | Milton Keynes | 27.09.91 |
| Hanson, Jacob | 6.0 | Huddersfield | Kirkburton | 30.11.97 |
| Isherwood, Thomas | 6.4 | Bayern Munich | Sweden | 28.01.98 |
| Kilgallon, Matt | 6.1 | Blackburn | York | 08.01.84 |
| Knight-Percival, Nat | 6.0 | Shrewsbury | Cambridge | 31.03.87 |
| McGowan, Ryan | 6.3 | Al-Sharjah | Adelaide, Aus | 15.08.89 |
| Riley, Joe | 6.0 | Manchester Utd | Blackpool | 06.12.96 |
| Vincelot, Romain | 5.10 | Coventry | Poitiers, Fr | 29.10.85 |
| **Midfielders** | | | | |
| Akpan, Hope | 6.0 | Burton | Liverpool | 14.08.91 |
| Devine, Danny | 5.11 | – | Bradford | 04.09.97 |
| Gibson, Jordan | – | Rangers | Birmingham | 26.02.98 |
| O'Connor, Anthony | 6.2 | Aberdeen | Cork, Ire | 25.10.92 |
| Pybus, Dan | 5.11 | Sunderland | South Shields | 12.12.97 |
| Reeves, Jake | 5.7 | AFC Wimbledon | Greenwich | 30.05.93 |
| Robinson, Tyrell | 5.9 | Arsenal | Basildon | 16.09.97 |
| Wright, Josh | 6.0 | Southend | Bethnal Green | 06.11.89 |
| **Forwards** | | | | |
| Brunker, Kai | 6.2 | Freiburg | Germany | 10.06.94 |
| Grodowski, Joel | 6.1 | PSV Bork | Selm, Ger | 30.11.97 |
| Jones, Alex | 6.1 | Birmingham | Sutton Coldfield | 28.09.94 |
| McCartan, Shay | 5.10 | Accrington | Newry | 18.05.94 |
| Omari, Patrick | 6.1 | Barnsley | Slough | 24.05.96 |
| Wyke, Charlie | 5.11 | Carlisle | Middlesbrough | 06.12.92 |

## BRISTOL ROVERS

**Ground**: Memorial Stadium, Filton Avenue, Horfield, Bristol BS7 OBF
**Telephone**: 0117 909 6648. **Club nickname**: Pirates
**Colours**: Blue and white. **Capacity**: 12,011
**Record attendance**: Eastville: 38,472 v Preston (FA Cup 4) Jan 30, 1960. Memorial Stadium: 12,011 v WBA (FA Cup 6) Mar 9, 2008

| | | | | |
|---|---|---|---|---|
| **Goalkeepers** | | | | |
| Slocombe, Sam | 6.0 | Blackpool | Scunthorpe | 05.06.88 |
| Smith, Adam | 5.11 | Northampton | Sunderland | 23.01.92 |
| **Defenders** | | | | |
| Broadbent, Tom | 6.3 | Hayes | – | 15.02.92 |
| Clarke, James | 6.0 | Woking | Aylesbury | 17.11.89 |
| Craig, Tony | 6.0 | Millwall | Greenwich | 20.04.85 |
| Leadbitter, Daniel | 6.0 | Hereford | Newcastle | 24.06.91 |
| Lockyer, Tom | 6.1 | – | Cardiff | 03.12.94 |
| Menayesse, Rollin | 6.3 | Western SM | Kinshasa, DR Cong | 04.12.97 |
| Partington, Joe | 6.2 | Eastleigh | Portsmouth | 01.04.90 |

| **Midfielders** | | | | |
|---|---|---|---|---|
| Bennett, Kyle | 5.5 | Portsmouth | Telford | 09.09.90 |
| Clarke, Ollie | 5.11 | – | Bristol | 29.06.92 |
| Lines, Chris | 6.2 | Port Vale | Bristol | 30.11.85 |
| Matthews, Sam | 5.10 | Bournemouth | Poole | 01.03.97 |
| Rodman, Alex | 6.2 | Shrewsbury | Sutton Coldfield | 15.12.87 |
| Sercombe, Liam | 5.10 | Oxford | Exeter | 25.04.90 |
| Sinclair, Stuart | 5.8 | Salisbury | Houghton Conquest | 09.11.87 |
| Upson, Ed | 5.10 | MK Dons | Bury St Edmunds | 21.11.89 |
| Widdrington, Theo | 5.10 | Portsmouth | Southampton | 06.04.99 |
| **Forwards** | | | | |
| Gaffney, Rory | 6.0 | Cambridge Utd | Tuam, Ire | 23.10.89 |
| Harrison, Ellis | 5.11 | – | Newport | 29.01.94 |
| Mensah, Bernard | 5.8 | Aldershot | Hounslow | 29.12.94 |
| Nichols, Tom | 5.10 | Peterborough | Taunton | 28.08.93 |
| Reilly, Gavin | 5.11 | St Mirren | Dumfries | 10.05.93 |

## BURTON ALBION

**Ground**: Pirelli Stadium, Princess Way, Burton upon Trent DE13 AR
**Telephone**: 01283 565938. **Club nickname**: Brewers
**Colours**: Yellow and black. **Capacity**: 6,912
**Record attendance**: 6,192 v Oxford Utd (Blue Square Prem Lge) Apr 17, 2009

| **Goalkeepers** | | | | |
|---|---|---|---|---|
| Bywater, Stephen | 6.3 | Kerala | Oldham | 07.06.81 |
| Campbell, Harry | 6.1 | Bolton | Blackburn | 16.11.95 |
| **Defenders** | | | | |
| Brayford, John | 5.8 | Sheffield Utd | Stoke | 29.12.87 |
| Buxton, Jake | 5.11 | Wigan | Sutton-in-Ashfield | 04.03.85 |
| Egert, Tomas | 6.3 | Slovan Liberec | Prague, Cz | 01.08.94 |
| McFadzean, Kyle | 6.1 | MK Dons | Sheffield | 28.02.87 |
| McCrory, Damien | 6.2 | Dagenham | Croom, Ire | 23.02.90 |
| Turner, Ben | 6.4 | Cardiff | Birmingham | 21.08.88 |
| **Midfielders** | | | | |
| Allen, Jamie | 5.11 | Rochdale | Rochdale | 29.01.95 |
| Dyer, Lloyd | 5.8 | Burnley | Birmingham | 13.09.82 |
| Fox, Ben | 5.11 | – | Burton | 01.02.98 |
| Fraser, Scott | 6.0 | Dundee Utd | Dundee | 30.03.95 |
| Harness, Marcus | 6.0 | – | Coventry | 01.08.94 |
| Lund, Matt | 6.0 | Rochdale | Manchester | 21.11.90 |
| Miller, Will | 5.7 | Tottenham | Hackney | 08.06.96 |
| Templeton, David | 5.10 | Hamilton | Glasgow | 07.01.89 |
| **Forwards** | | | | |
| Akins, Lucas | 6.0 | Stevenage | Huddersfield | 25.02.89 |
| Boyce, Liam | 6.1 | Ross Co | Belfast | 08.04.91 |
| Sbarra, Joe | 5.10 | – | Lichfield | 21.12.98 |
| Sordell, Marvin | 5.10 | Coventry | Harrow | 17.02.91 |

## CHARLTON ATHLETIC

**Ground**: The Valley, Floyd Road, London SE7 8BL
**Telephone**: 0208 333 4000. **Club nickname**: Addicks
**Colours**: Red and white. **Capacity**: 27,111
**Record attendance**: 75,031 v Aston Villa (FA Cup 5) Feb 12, 1938

| | | | | |
|---|---|---|---|---|
| **Goalkeepers** | | | | |
| Phillips, Dillon | 6.2 | – | Hornchurch | 11.06.95 |
| **Defenders** | | | | |
| Bauer, Patrick | 6.4 | Maritimo | Backnang, Ger | 28.10.92 |
| Page, Lewis | 5.10 | West Ham | Enfield | 20.05.96 |
| Pearce, Jason | 5.11 | Wigan | Hillingdon | 06.12.87 |
| Sarr, Naby | 6.5 | Sporting Lisbon | Marseille, Fr | 13.08.93 |
| Solly, Chris | 5.8 | – | Rochester | 20.01.90 |
| **Midfielders** | | | | |
| Aribo, Joe | 6.0 | Staines | Camberwell | 21.07.96 |
| Dijksteel, Anfernee | 6.0 | – | Holland | 27.10.96 |
| Forster-Caskey, Jake | 5.10 | Brighton | Southend | 05.04.94 |
| Fosu-Henry, Tarique | 5.8 | Reading | Wandsworth | 05.11.95 |
| Kashi, Ahmed | 5.10 | Metz | Aubervilliers, Fr | 18.11.88 |
| Lapslie, George | 5.9 | – | Waltham Forest | 05.09.97 |
| Maloney, Taylor | 5.9 | – | Gravesend | 21.01.99 |
| Marshall, Mark | 5.7 | Bradford | Manchester, Jam | 05.05.87 |
| Reeves, Ben | 5.10 | MK Dons | Verwood | 19.11.91 |
| **Forwards** | | | | |
| Ahearne-Grant, Karlan | 6.0 | – | Greenwich | 19.12.97 |
| Clarke, Billy | 5.7 | Bradford | Cork, Ire | 13.12.87 |
| Magennis, Josh | 6.2 | Kilmarnock | Bangor, NI | 15.08.90 |
| Taylor, Lyle | 6.2 | AFC Wimbledon | Greenwich | 29.03.90 |
| Vetokele, Igor | 5.9 | Copenhagen | Ostend, Bel | 23.03.92 |

## COVENTRY CITY

**Ground**: Ricoh Arena, Phoenix Way, Coventry CV6 6GE.
**Telephone**: 02476 992326. **Club nickname**: Sky Blues
**Colours**: Sky blue. **Capacity**: 32,500
**Record attendance**: Highfield Road: 51,455 v Wolves (Div 2) Apr 29, 1967. Ricoh Arena: 31,407 v Chelsea (FA Cup 6), Mar 7, 2009

| | | | | |
|---|---|---|---|---|
| **Goalkeepers** | | | | |
| Burge, Lee | 5.11 | – | Hereford | 09.01.93 |
| Liam O'Brien | 6.4 | Portsmouth | Ruislip | 30.11.91 |
| **Defenders** | | | | |
| Brown, Junior | 5.9 | Shrewsbury | Crewe | 07.05.89 |
| Davies, Tom | 5.11 | Portsmouth | Warrington | 18.04.92 |
| Grimmer, Jack | 6.1 | Fulham | Aberdeen | 25.01.94 |
| Harries, Cian | 6.1 | – | Birmingham | 01.04.97 |
| Haynes, Ryan | 5.7 | – | Northampton | 27.09.95 |
| Hyam, Dominic | 6.2 | Reading | Dundee | 20.12.95 |
| McDonald, Rod | 6.3 | Northampton | Crewe | 11.04.92 |
| Sterling, Dujon | 5.11 | Chelsea (loan) | Islington | 24.10.99 |
| Willis, Jordan | 5.11 | – | Coventry | 24.08.94 |
| **Midfielders** | | | | |
| Andreu, Tony | 5.10 | Norwich | Cagnes-sur-Mer, Fr | 22.05.88 |
| Doyle, Michael | 5.10 | Portsmouth | Dublin, Ire | 08.07.81 |
| Jones, Jodi | 5.10 | Dagenham | Bow | 22.10.97 |
| Kelly, Liam | 5.10 | Leyton Orient | Milton Keynes | 10.02.90 |
| Ogogo, Abu | 5.10 | Shrewsbury | Epsom | 03.11.89 |
| Vincenti, Peter | 6.2 | Rochdale | St Peter, Jer | 07.07.86 |
| Westbrooke, Zain | 5.11 | Brentford | Chertsey | 28.10.96 |

**Forwards**

| | | | | |
|---|---|---|---|---|
| Beavon, Stuart | 5.7 | Burton | Reading | 05.05.84 |
| Biamou, Maxime | 6.1 | Sutton | Creteil, Fr | 13.11.90 |
| Clarke-Harris, Jonson | 6.0 | Rotherham | Leicester | 20.07.94 |
| Ponticelli, Jordan | 5.11 | – | Nuneaton | 10.09.98 |

## DONCASTER ROVERS

**Ground**: Keepmoat Stadium, Stadium Way, Doncaster DN4 5JW
**Telephone**: 01302 764664. **Club nickname**: Rovers
**Colours**: Red and white. **Capacity**: 15,231
**Record attendance**: Belle Vue: 37,149 v Hull (Div 3 N) Oct 2, 1948. Keepmoat Stadium: 15,001 v Leeds (Lge 1) Apr 1, 2008

| | | | | |
|---|---|---|---|---|
| **Goalkeepers** | | | | |
| Lawlor, Ian | 6.4 | Manchester City | Dublin, Ire | 27.10.94 |
| Marosi, Marko | 6.3 | Wigan | Slovakia | 23.10.93 |
| **Defenders** | | | | |
| Anderson, Tom | 6.3 | Burnley | Burnley | 02.09.93 |
| Andrew, Danny | 5.11 | Grimsby | Holbeach | 23.12.90 |
| Butler, Andy | 6.0 | Sheffield Utd | Doncaster | 04.11.83 |
| Mason, Niall | 5.11 | Aston Villa | Bromley | 10.01.97 |
| McCullough, Luke | 6.1 | Manchester Utd | Portadown | 15.02.94 |
| Wright, Joe | 6.4 | Huddersfield | Monk Fryston | 26.02.95 |
| **Midfielders** | | | | |
| Amos, Danny | 5.11 | – | Sheffield | 22.12.99 |
| Ben Khemis, Issam | 5.9 | Lorient | Paris, Fr | 10.01.96 |
| Blair, Matty | 5.10 | Mansfield | Warwick | 30.11.87 |
| Coppinger, James | 5.7 | Exeter | Middlesbrough | 10.01.81 |
| Crawford, Ali | 5.8 | Hamilton | Lanark | 30.07.91 |
| Rowe, Tommy | 5.11 | Wolves | Manchester | 01.05.89 |
| Whiteman, Ben | 6.0 | Sheffield Utd | Rochdale | 17.06.96 |
| **Forwards** | | | | |
| Beestin, Alfie | 5.10 | Tadcaster | Leeds | 01.10.97 |
| Kiwomya, Alex | 5.11 | Chelsea | Sheffield | 20.05.96 |
| Marquis, John | 6.1 | Millwall | Lewisham | 16.05.92 |
| May, Alfie | 5.10 | Hythe | Gravesend | 02.07.93 |
| Wilks, Mallik | 5.11 | Leeds (loan) | Leeds | 15.12.98 |

## FLEETWOOD TOWN

**Ground**: Highbury Stadium, Park Avenue, Fleetwod FY7 6TX
**Telephone**: 01253 775080. **Club nickname**: Fishermen
**Colours**: Red and white. **Capacity**: 5,311
**Record attendance**: 5,194 v York (Lge 2 play-off semi-final, 2nd leg) May 16, 2014

| | | | | |
|---|---|---|---|---|
| **Goalkeepers** | | | | |
| Cairns, Alex | 6.0 | Rotherham | Doncaster | 04.01.93 |
| Urwin, Matt | 6.1 | Fylde | Blackpool | 28.11.93 |
| **Defenders** | | | | |
| Bolger, Cian | 6.4 | Southend | Cellbridge, Ire | 12.03.92 |
| Coyle, Lewie | 5.9 | Leeds (loan) | Hull | 15.10.95 |
| Eastham, Ashley | 6.3 | Rochdale | Preston | 22.03.91 |
| Jones, Gethin | 5.10 | Everton | Perth, Aus | 13.10.95 |
| Maguire, Joe | 5.10 | Liverpool | Manchester | 18.01.96 |

| | | | | |
|---|---|---|---|---|
| Morgan, Craig | 6.0 | Wigan | Flint | 16.06.85 |
| Spurr, Tommy | 6.1 | Preston (loan) | Leeds | 30.09.87 |
| **Midfielders** | | | | |
| Dempsey, Kyle | 5.10 | Huddersfield | Whitehaven | 17.09.95 |
| Diagouraga, Toumani | 6.2 | Plymouth | Paris, Fr | 10.06.87 |
| Duckworth, Michael | 5.11 | Hartlepool | Rinteln, Ger | 28.04.92 |
| Grant, Bobby | 5.11 | Blackpool | Litherland | 01.07.90 |
| Holt, Jason | 5.6 | Rangers (loan) | Musselburgh | 19.02.93 |
| Schwabl, Markus | 6.0 | Aalen | Tegernsee, Ger | 26.08.90 |
| Sowerby, Jack | 5.9 | – | Preston | 23.03.95 |
| **Forwards** | | | | |
| Biggins, Harrison | – | Stocksbridge | Sheffield | 15.03.96 |
| Burns, Wes | 5.8 | Bristol City | Cardiff | 23.11.94 |
| Hunter, Ashley | 5.10 | Ilkeston | Derby | 29.09.95 |
| Madden, Paddy | 6.0 | Scunthorpe | Dublin, Ire | 04.03.90 |
| McAleny, Conor | 5.10 | Everton | Liverpool | 12.08.92 |
| Morelli, Joao | 5.11 | Middlesbrough | Sao Paulo, Br | 11.03.96 |

## GILLINGHAM

**Ground**: Mems Priestfield Stadium, Redfern Avenue, Gillingham ME7 4DD
**Telephone**: 01634 300000. **Club nickname**: Gills
**Colours**: Blue and white. **Capacity**: 11,582
**Record attendance**: 23,002 v QPR. (FA Cup 3) Jan 10, 1948

| | | | | |
|---|---|---|---|---|
| **Goalkeepers** | | | | |
| Hadler, Tom | 6.2 | – | Canterbury | 30.07.96 |
| Holy, Tomas | 6.9 | Sparta Prague | Rychnov, Cz | 10.12.91 |
| **Defenders** | | | | |
| Ehmer, Max | 6.2 | QPR | Frankfurt, Ger | 03.02.92 |
| Fuller, Barry | 5.10 | AFC Wimbledon | Ashford, Kent | 25.09.84 |
| Garmston, Bradley | 5.11 | WBA | Chorley | 18.01.94 |
| Lacey, Alex | 6.0 | Yeovil | Milton Keynes | 31.05.93 |
| O'Mara, Finn | 6.0 | – | Southwark | 03.02.99 |
| O'Neill, Luke | 6.0 | Southend | Slough | 20.08.91 |
| Zakuani, Gabriel | 6.1 | Northampton | Kinshasa, DR Cong | 31.05.86 |
| **Midfielders** | | | | |
| Bingham, Billy | 5.11 | Crewe | Greenwich | 15.07.90 |
| Byrne, Mark | 5.9 | Newport | Dublin, Ire | 09.11.88 |
| Charles-Cook, Regan | 5.9 | Charlton | Lewisham | 14.02.97 |
| List, Elliott | 5.10 | Crystal Palace | Camberwell | 12.05.97 |
| Nasseri, Navid | 5.9 | Syrianska | Manchester | 26.07.96 |
| Parrett, Dean | 5.9 | AFC Wimbledon | Hampstead | 16.11.91 |
| Oldaker, Darren | 5.9 | QPR | London | 01.04.99 |
| Rees, Josh | 5.9 | Bromley | Hemel Hempstead | 04.10.93 |
| Reilly, Callum | 6.1 | Bury | Warrington | 03.10.93 |
| **Forwards** | | | | |
| Eaves, Tom | 6.4 | Yeovil | Liverpool | 14.01.92 |
| Hanlan, Brandon | 6.0 | Charlton | Chelsea | 31.05.97 |
| Parker, Josh | 5.11 | Wealdstone | Slough | 01.12.90 |
| Wilkinson, Conor | 6.3 | Bolton | Croydon | 23.01.95 |

## LUTON TOWN

**Ground**: Kenilworth Road, Maple Road, Luton LU4 8AW
**Telephone**: 01582 411622. **Club nickname**: Hatters
**Colours**: Orange and black. **Capacity**: 10,226
**Record attendance**: 30,069 v Blackpool (FA Cup 6) Mar 4, 1959

| | | | | |
|---|---|---|---|---|
| **Goalkeepers** | | | | |
| Shea, James | 5.11 | AFC Wimbledon | Islington | 16.06.91 |
| Stech, Marek | 6.5 | Sparta Prague | Prague, Cz | 28.01.90 |
| **Defenders** | | | | |
| Bradley, Sonny | 6.4 | Plymouth | Hull | 13.09.91 |
| Jones, Lloyd | 6.3 | Liverpool | Plymouth | 07.10.95 |
| Justin, James | 6.3 | – | Luton | 11.07.97 |
| Musonda, Frankie | 6.0 | – | Bedford | 12.12.97 |
| Pearson, Matty | 6.3 | Barnsley | Keighley | 03.08.93 |
| Potts, Dan | 5.8 | West Ham | Romford | 13.04.94 |
| Rea, Glen | 6.1 | Brighton | Brighton | 03.09.94 |
| Senior, Jack | 5.8 | Huddersfield | Halifax | 13.01.97 |
| Sheehan, Alan | 5.11 | Bradford | Athlone, Ire | 14.09.86 |
| Stacey, Jack | 5.11 | Reading | Ascot | 06.04.96 |
| **Midfielders** | | | | |
| Berry, Luke | 5.9 | Cambridge | Cambridge | 12.07.92 |
| Gambin, Luke | 5.7 | Barnet | Sutton | 16.03.93 |
| Grant, Jorge | 5.9 | Nottm Forest (loan) | Banbury | 19.12.94 |
| McCormack, Alan | 5.8 | Brentford | Dublin, Ire | 10.01.84 |
| Ruddock, Pelly | 5.9 | West Ham | Hendon | 17.07.93 |
| Shinnie, Andrew | 5.11 | Birmingham | Aberdeen | 17.07.89 |
| **Forwards** | | | | |
| Collins, James | 6.2 | Crawley | Coventry | 01.12.90 |
| Cornick, Harry | 5.11 | Bournemouth | Poole | 06.03.95 |
| Hylton, Danny | 6.0 | Oxford | Camden | 25.02.89 |
| Jarvis, Aaron | 6.2 | Basingstoke | Basingstoke | 24.01.98 |
| Jervis, Jake | 6.3 | Plymouth | Birmingham | 17.09.91 |
| Lee, Elliot | 5.11 | Barnsley | Durham | 16.12.94 |

## OXFORD UNITED

**Ground**: Kassam Stadium, Grenoble Road, Oxford OX4 4XP
**Telephone**: 01865 337500. **Club nickname**: U's
**Colours**: Yellow. **Capacity**: 12,500
**Record attendance**: Manor Ground: 22,750 v Preston (FA Cup 6) Feb 29, 1964. Kassam Stadium: 12,243 v Leyton Orient (Lge 2) May 6, 2006

| | | | | |
|---|---|---|---|---|
| **Goalkeepers** | | | | |
| Eastwood, Simon | 6.2 | Blackburn | Luton | 26.06.89 |
| Shearer, Scott | 6.3 | Mansfield | Glasgow | 15.02.81 |
| **Defenders** | | | | |
| Carroll, Canice | 6.0 | – | Oxford | 26.01.99 |
| Dickie, Rob | 6.3 | Reading | Wokingham | 03.03.96 |
| Garbutt, Luke | 5.10 | Everton (loan) | Harrogate | 21.05.93 |
| Long, Sam | 5.10 | – | Oxford | 16.01.95 |
| McMahon, Tony | 5.10 | Bradford | Bishop Auckland | 24.03.86 |
| Mousinho, John | 6.1 | Burton | Isleworth | 30.04.86 |
| Nelson, Curtis | 6.0 | Plymouth | Newcastle-under-Lyme | 21.05.93 |

| | | | | |
|---|---|---|---|---|
| Raglan, Charlie | 6.0 | Chesterfield | Wythenshawe | 28.04.93 |
| **Midfielders** | | | | |
| Brannagan, Cameron | 5.11 | Liverpool | Manchester | 09.05.96 |
| Carruthers, Samir | 5.9 | Sheffield Utd (loan) | Islington | 04.04.93 |
| Henry, James | 6.1 | Wolves | Reading | 10.06.89 |
| Ruffels, Josh | 5.10 | Coventry | Oxford | 23.10.93 |
| Xemi | 6.1 | Barcelona | Sabadell, Sp | 02.02.95 |
| **Forwards** | | | | |
| Hall, Rob | 6.2 | Bolton | Aylesbury | 20.10.93 |
| Obika, Jonathan | 6.0 | Swindon | Enfield | 12.09.90 |
| Whyte, Gavin | 5.10 | Crusaders | Belfast | 31.01.96 |

## PETERBOROUGH UNITED

**Ground**: Abax Stadium, London Road, Peterborough PE2 8AL
**Telephone**: 01733 563947. **Club nickname**: Posh
**Colours**: Blue and white. **Capacity**: 14,319
**Record attendance**: 30,096 v Swansea (FA Cup 5) Feb 20, 1965

| | | | | |
|---|---|---|---|---|
| **Goalkeepers** | | | | |
| Chapman, Aaron | 6.8 | Accrington | Rotherham | 29.05.90 |
| O'Malley, Conor | 6.3 | St Patrick's | Westport, Ire | 01.08.94 |
| Tibbetts, Josh | 6.0 | Birmingham | Stourbridge | 02.11.94 |
| **Defenders** | | | | |
| Baldwin, Jack | 6.1 | Hartlepool | Barking | 30.06.93 |
| Bennett, Rhys | 6.3 | Mansfield | Manchester | 01.09.91 |
| Denton, Tyler | 5.8 | Leeds (loan) | Dewsbury | 06.09.95 |
| Freestone, Lewis | 6.1 | – | King's Lynn | 26.10.99 |
| Naismith, Jason | 6.2 | Ross Co | Paisley | 25.06.94 |
| Tafazolli, Ryan | 6.5 | Mansfield | Sutton | 28.09.91 |
| Yorwerth, Josh | 6.0 | Crawley | Bridgend | 28.02.95 |
| **Midfielders** | | | | |
| Anderson, Jermaine | 5.11 | – | Camden | 16.05.96 |
| Cooper, George | 5.9 | Crewe | Warrington | 02.11.96 |
| Daniel, Colin | 5.11 | Blackpool | Nottingham | 15.02.88 |
| Dembele, Siriki | 5.8 | Grimsby | Ivory Coast | 07.09.96 |
| Doughty, Michael | 6.1 | QPR | Westminster | 20.11.92 |
| Edwards, Gwion | 5.9 | Crawley | Lampeter | 01.03.93 |
| Grant, Anthony | 5.10 | Port Vale | Lambeth | 04.06.87 |
| King, Adam | 5.11 | Swansea (loan) | Edinburgh | 11.10.95 |
| O'Hara, Mark | 6.4 | Dundee | Barrhead | 12.12.95 |
| Reed, Louis | 5.8 | Sheffield Utd | Barnsley | 25.07.97 |
| Ward, Joe | | Woking | Chelmsford | 22.08.95 |
| Woodyard, Alex | 5.9 | Lincoln | Gravesend | 03.05.93 |
| **Forwards** | | | | |
| Cummings, Jason | 5.10 | Nottm Forest (loan) | Edinburgh | 01.08.95 |
| Lloyd, Danny | – | Stockport | Liverpool | 03.12.91 |
| Godden, Matt | 6.1 | Stevenage | Canterbury | 29.07.91 |
| Maddison, Marcus | 5.11 | Gateshead | Durham | 26.09.93 |
| Marriott, Jack | 5.9 | Luton | Beverley | 09.09.84 |
| Nabi, Adil | 5.9 | WBA | Birmingham | 28.02.94 |
| Stevens, Matty | 5.11 | Barnet | Surrey | 12.02.98 |

## PLYMOUTH ARGYLE

**Ground**: Home Park, Plymouth PL2 3DQ
**Telephone**: 01752 562561. **Club nickname**: Pilgrims
**Colours**: Green and white. **Capacity**: 16,388
**Record attendance**: 43,596 v Aston Villa (Div 2) Oct 10, 1936

| | | | | |
|---|---|---|---|---|
| **Goalkeepers** | | | | |
| Burgoyne, Harry | 6.4 | Wolves (loan) | Ludlow | 28.12.96 |
| Letheren, Kyle | 6.2 | York | Llanelli | 26.12.87 |
| **Defenders** | | | | |
| Canavan, Niall | 6.3 | Rochdale | Leeds | 11.04.91 |
| Edwards, Ryan | 5.11 | Morecambe | Liverpool | 07.10.93 |
| Grant, Peter | 6.2 | Falkirk | Bellshill | 11.03.94 |
| Riley, Joe | 6.0 | Shrewsbury | Salford | 13.10.91 |
| Sawyer, Gary | 6.0 | Leyton Orient | Bideford | 05.07.85 |
| Smith-Brown, Ashley | 5.10 | Manchester City | Manchester | 31.03.96 |
| Songo'o, Yann | 6.2 | Blackburn | Yaounde, Cam | 19.11.91 |
| Wootton, Scott | 6.2 | MK Dons | Birkenhead | 12.09.91 |
| **Midfielders** | | | | |
| Ainsworth, Lionel | 5.9 | Motherwell | Nottingham | 01.10.87 |
| Carey, Graham | 6.0 | Ross Co | Dublin, Ire | 02.05.89 |
| Fox, David | 5.10 | Crewe | Leek | 13.12.83 |
| Grant, Conor | 5.9 | Everton | Fazakerley | 18.04.95 |
| Lameiras, Ruben | 5.9 | Coventry | Lisbon, Por | 22.12.94 |
| Ness, Jamie | 6.1 | Scunthorpe | Irvine | 02.03.91 |
| Sarcevic, Antoni | 6.0 | Shrewsbury | Manchester | 13.03.92 |
| Wylde, Gregg | 5.10 | Millwall | Kirkintilloch | 23.03.91 |
| **Forwards** | | | | |
| Dyson, Callum | 6.2 | Everton | Fazakerley | 19.09.96 |
| Fletcher, Alex | 5.10 | – | Newton Abbot | 09.02.99 |
| Grant, Joel | 6.0 | Exeter | Acton | 26.08.87 |
| Ladapo, Freddie | 6.0 | Southend | Romford | 01.02.93 |
| Taylor, Ryan | 6.2 | Oxford | Rotherham | 04.05.88 |

## PORTSMOUTH

**Ground**: Fratton Park, Frogmore Road, Portsmouth, PO4 8RA
**Telephone**: 0239 273 1204. **Club nickname**: Pompey
**Colours**: Blue and white. **Capacity**: 20,700
**Record attendance**: 51,385 v Derby (FA Cup 6) Feb 26, 1949

| | | | | |
|---|---|---|---|---|
| **Goalkeepers** | | | | |
| Bass, Alex | 6.2 | – | Southampton | 01.04.98 |
| McGee, Luke | 6.2 | Tottenham | Edgware | 02.09.95 |
| MacGillivray, Craig | 6.2 | Shrewsbury | Harrogate | 12.01.93 |
| **Defenders** | | | | |
| Brown, Lee | 6.0 | Bristol Rov | Farnborough | 10.08.90 |
| Burgess, Christian | 6.5 | Peterborough | Barking | 07.10.91 |
| Casey, Matt | 6.5 | – | Southampton | 13.11.99 |
| Clarke, Matt | 5.11 | Ipswich | Ipswich | 22.09.96 |
| Haunstrup, Brandon | 5.8 | – | Waterlooville | 26.10.96 |
| Naylor, Tom | 6.0 | Burton | Sutton-in-Ashfield | 28.06.91 |
| Thompson, Nathan | 5.10 | Swindon | Chester | 22.04.91 |
| Whatmough, Jack | 6.0 | – | Gosport | 19.08.96 |

| **Midfielders** | | | | |
|---|---|---|---|---|
| Close, Ben | 5.9 | – | Portsmouth | 08.08.96 |
| Dennis, Louis | 6.1 | Bromley | Hendon | 09.10.92 |
| Donohue, Dion | 5.10 | Chesterfield | Anglesey | 26.08.93 |
| Evans, Gareth | 6.0 | Fleetwood | Macclesfield | 26.04.88 |
| Lowe, Jamal | 6.0 | Hampton | Harrow | 21.07.94 |
| May, Adam | 6.0 | – | Southampton | 06.12.97 |
| Rose, Danny | 5.8 | Northampton | Bristol | 21.02.88 |
| Smith, Dan | 6.0 | – | Lewisham | 05.09.99 |
| **Forwards** | | | | |
| Chaplin, Conor | 5.10 | – | Worthing | 16.02.97 |
| Curtis, Ronan | 6.0 | Derry | Donegal | 29.03.96 |
| Hawkins, Oliver | 6.3 | Dagenham | Ealing | 08.04.92 |
| Pitman, Brett | 6.0 | Ipswich | St Helier, Jer | 03.01.88 |

## ROCHDALE

**Ground**: Crown Oil Arena, Wilbutts Lane, Rochdale OL11 5DS
**Telephone**: 01706 644648. **Club nickname**: Dale
**Colours**: Blue and black. **Capacity**: 10,249
**Record attendance**: 24,231 v Notts Co (FA Cup 2) Dec 10, 1949

| **Goalkeepers** | | | | |
|---|---|---|---|---|
| Lillis, Josh | 6.0 | Scunthorpe | Derby | 24.06.87 |
| Moore, Brendan | 6.2 | Torquay | Elmira, USA | 16.04.92 |
| **Defenders** | | | | |
| Delaney, Ryan | 6.0 | Burton | Wexford, Ire | 06.09.96 |
| McGahey, Harrison | 6.1 | Sheffield Utd | Preston | 26.09.95 |
| McNulty, Jim | 6.0 | Bury | Liverpool | 13.02.85 |
| Ntlhe, Kgosi | 5.9 | Stevenage | Pretoria, SA | 21.02.94 |
| Rafferty, Joe | 6.0 | Liverpool | Liverpool | 06.10.93 |
| **Midfielders** | | | | |
| Adshead, Daniel | 5.7 | – | Manchester | 02.09.01 |
| Camps, Callum | 5.11 | – | Stockport | 14.03.96 |
| Cannon, Andy | 5.9 | – | Tameside | 14.03.96 |
| Done, Matt | 5.10 | Sheffield Utd | Oswestry | 22.07.88 |
| Dooley, Stephen | 5.11 | Coleraine | Ballymoney | 19.10.91 |
| Inman, Brad | 5.9 | Peterborough | Adelaide, Aus | 10.12.91 |
| Perkins, David | 5.6 | Wigan | Heysham | 21.06.82 |
| Rathbone, Oliver | 5.11 | Manchester Utd | Blackburn | 10.10.96 |
| Thompson, Joe | 6.0 | Carlisle | Rochdale | 05.03.89 |
| Williams, Jordan | 5.11 | Barrow | Warrington | 13.12.92 |
| **Forwards** | | | | |
| Andrew, Calvin | 6.2 | York | Luton | 19.12.86 |
| Henderson, Ian | 5.10 | Colchester | Thetford | 24.01.85 |
| Wilbraham, Aaron | 6.3 | Bolton | Knutsford | 21.10.79 |

## SCUNTHORPE UNITED

**Ground**: Glanford Park, Doncaster Road, Scunthorpe DN15 8TD
**Telephone**: 0871 221 1899. **Club nickname**: Iron
**Colours**: Claret and blue. **Capacity**: 9,183
**Record attendance**: Old Show Ground: 23,935 v Portsmouth (FA Cup 4) Jan 30, 1954. Glanford Park: 8,921 v Newcastle (Champ) Oct 20, 2009

| | | | | |
|---|---|---|---|---|
| **Goalkeepers** | | | | |
| Flatt, Jonathan | 6.1 | Wolves | Wolverhampton | 12.09.94 |
| Gilks, Matt | 6.1 | Wigan | Rochdale | 04.06.82 |
| Watson, Rory | 6.3 | Hull | York | 05.02.96 |
| **Defenders** | | | | |
| Burgess, Cameron | 6.4 | Fulham | Aberdeen | 21.10.95 |
| Butroid, Lewis | 5.9 | – | Gainsborough | 17.09.98 |
| Clarke, Jordan | 6.0 | Coventry | Coventry | 19.11.91 |
| Goode, Charlie | 6.5 | Hendon | Watford | 03.08.95 |
| McArdle, Rory | 6.1 | Bradford | Sheffield | 01.05.87 |
| Townsend, Conor | 5.6 | Hull | Hessle | 04.03.93 |
| **Midfielders** | | | | |
| Holmes, Duane | 5.6 | Huddersfield | Columbus, US | 06.11.94 |
| Lewis, Clayton | 5.7 | Auckland | Wellington NZ | 12.02.97 |
| Morris, Josh | 5.10 | Bradford | Preston | 30.09.91 |
| Ojo, Funso | 5.10 | Willem 11 | Antwerp, Bel | 28.08.91 |
| Sutton, Levi | 5.11 | – | Scunthorpe | 24.03.96 |
| **Forwards** | | | | |
| Humphrys, Stephen | 6.1 | Fulham (loan) | Oldham | 15.09.97 |
| Novak, Lee | 6.0 | Charlton | Newcastle | 28.09,88 |
| Olomola, Olufela | 5.7 | Southampton | London | 05.09.97 |
| Wootton, Kyle | 6.2 | – | Epworth | 11.10.96 |

## SHREWSBURY TOWN

**Ground**: Montgomery Waters Meadow, Oteley Road, Shrewsbury SY2 6ST
**Telephone**: 01743 289177. **Club nickname**: Shrews
**Colours**: Blue and yellow. **Capacity**: 9,875
**Record attendance**: Gay Meadow: 18,917 v Walsall (Div 3) Apr 26, 1961. Greenhous Meadow: 10,210 v Chelsea (Lge Cup 4) Oct 28, 2014

| | | | | |
|---|---|---|---|---|
| **Goalkeepers** | | | | |
| Gregory, Cameron | 6.3 | – | Sutton Coldfield | 20.01.00 |
| **efenders** | | | | |
| Beckles, Omar | 6.3 | Accrington | Kettering | 19.10.91 |
| Bolton, James | 6.0 | Gateshead | Stone | 13.08.94 |
| Hendrie, Luke | 6.2 | Burnley | Leeds | 27.08.94 |
| Kennedy, Kieran | 5.11 | Macclesfield | Urmston | 23.09.93 |
| Nsiala, Aristote | 6.4 | Hartlepool | Kinshasa, DR Cong | 25.03.92 |
| Sadler, Mat | 5.11 | Rotherham | Birmingham | 26.02.85 |
| **Midfielders** | | | | |
| Morris, Bryn | 6.0 | Middlesbrough | Hartlepool | 25.04.96 |
| Nolan, Jon | 5.10 | Chesterfield | Huyton | 22.04.92 |
| Whalley, Shaun | 5.9 | Luton | Whiston | 07.08.87 |
| **Forwards** | | | | |
| Amadi-Holloway, Aaron | 6.2 | Oldham | Cardiff | 01.02.93 |
| Jones, Sam | 6.2 | Grimsby | Barnsley | 18.09.91 |
| Gilliead, Alex | 6.0 | Newcastle | Shotley Bridge | 11.02.96 |
| Gnahoua, Arthur | 6.2 | Kidderminster | London | 18.09.92 |
| John-Lewis, Lenell | 5.10 | Newport | Hammersmith | 17.05.89 |
| Morris, Carlton | 6.2 | Norwich (loan) | Cambridge | 16.12.95 |
| Okenabirhie, Fejiri | 5.10 | Dagenham | Hendon | 25.02.96 |
| Payne, Stefan | 5.10 | Barnsley | Lambeth | 10.08.91 |

## SOUTHEND UNITED

**Ground**: Roots Hall, Victoria Avenue, Southend SS2 6NQ
**Telephone**: 01702 304050. **Club nickname**: Shrimpers
**Colours**: Blue and white. **Capacity**: 12,392
**Record attendance**: 31,090 v Liverpool (FA Cup 3) Jan 10, 1979

| | | | | |
|---|---|---|---|---|
| **Goalkeepers** | | | | |
| Oxley, Mark | 6.2 | Hibernian | Sheffield | 28.09.90 |
| Smith, Ted | 6.1 | – | Benfleet | 18.01.96 |
| **Defenders** | | | | |
| Coker, Ben | 5.11 | Colchester | Cambridge | 01.07.90 |
| Demetriou, Jason | 5.11 | Walsall | Newham | 18.11.87 |
| Ferdinand, Anton | 6.0 | Reading | Peckham | 18.02.85 |
| Hendrie, Stephen | 5.11 | West Ham | Glasgow | 08.01.95 |
| Kiernan, Rob | 6.1 | Rangers | Rickmansworth | 13.01.91 |
| Kyprianou, Harry | 6.0 | Watford | Enfield | 16.03.97 |
| Lennon, Harry | 6.3 | Charlton | Romford | 16.12.94 |
| White, John | 6.0 | Colchester | Colchester | 25.07.86 |
| **Midfielders** | | | | |
| Dieng, Timothee | 6.2 | Bradford | Grenoble, Fr | 09.04.92 |
| Hyam, Luke | 5.10 | Ipswich | Ipswich | 24.10.91 |
| Kightly, Michael | 5.11 | Burnley | Basildon | 24.01.86 |
| Leonard, Ryan | 6.1 | Plymouth | Plympton | 24.05.92 |
| Mantom, Sam | 5.9 | Scunthorpe | Stourbridge | 20.02.92 |
| McLaughlin, Stephen | 5.10 | Nottm Forest | Donegal, Ire | 14.06.90 |
| **Forwards** | | | | |
| Cox, Simon | 5.11 | Reading | Reading | 28.04.87 |
| Hopper, Tom | 6.1 | Scunthorpe | Boston | 14.12.93 |
| Robinson, Theo | 5.10 | Lincoln | Birmingham | 22.01.89 |

## SUNDERLAND

**Ground**: Stadium of Light, Sunderland SR5 1SU
**Telephone**: 0871 911 1200. **Club nickname**: Black Cats
**Capacity**: 48,707. **Colours**: Red and white
**Record attendance**: Roker Park: 75,118 v Derby (FA Cup 6 rep) Mar 8, 1933. Stadium of Light: 48,353 v Liverpool (Prem Lge) Apr 13, 2002

| | | | | |
|---|---|---|---|---|
| **Goalkeepers** | | | | |
| McLaughlin, Jon | 6.3 | Hearts | Edinburgh | 09.09.87 |
| Ruiter, Robbin | 6.5 | Utrecht | Amsterdam, Hol | 25.03.87 |
| Steele, Jason | 6.2 | Blackburn | Newton Aycliffe | 18.08.90 |
| **Defenders** | | | | |
| Flanagan, Tom | 6.2 | Burton | Hammersmith | 21.10.91 |
| James, Reece | 6.0 | Wigan | Bacup | 07.11.93 |
| Kone, Lamine | 6.3 | Lorient | Paris, Fr | 01.02.88 |
| Love, Donald | 5.10 | Manchester Utd | Rochdale | 02.12.94 |
| Matthews, Adam | 5.10 | Celtic | Swansea | 13.01.92 |
| Oviedo, Bryan | 5.8 | Everton | San Jose, C Rica | 18.02.90 |
| Ozturk, Alim | 6.3 | Boluspor | Alkmaar, Hol | 17.11.92 |
| **Midfielders** | | | | |
| Cattermole, Lee | 5.10 | Wigan | Stockton | 21.03.88 |
| Embleton, Elliot | 5.8 | – | Durham | 02.04.99 |
| Gooch, Lynden | 5.8 | – | Santa Cruz, US | 24.12.95 |
| Honeyman, George | 5.8 | – | Prudhoe | 02.09.94 |

| | | | | |
|---|---|---|---|---|
| Khazri, Wahbi | 6.0 | Bordeaux | Ajaccio, Fr | 08.02.91 |
| McGeady, Aiden | 5.11 | Everton | Paisley | 04.04.86 |
| McGeouch, Dylan | 5.10 | Hibernian | Glasgow | 15.01.93 |
| Robson, Ethan | 5.10 | – | Houghton-le-Spring | 25.10.96 |
| **Forwards** | | | | |
| Maguire, Chris | 5.8 | Bury | Bellshill | 16.01.89 |
| McManaman, Callum | 5.11 | WBA | Knowsley | 25.04.91 |
| Watmore, Duncan | 5.9 | Altrincham | Cheadle Hulme | 08.03.94 |

## WALSALL

**Ground**: Banks's Stadium, Bescot Crescent, Walsall WS1 4SA
**Telephone**: 01922 622791. **Club nickname**: Saddlers
**Colours**: Red and white. **Capacity**: 11,300
**Record attendance**: Fellows Park: 25,453 v Newcastle (Div 2) Aug 29, 1961. Banks's Stadium: 11,049 v Rotherham (Div 1) May 10, 2004

| | | | | |
|---|---|---|---|---|
| **Goalkeepers** | | | | |
| Dunn, Chris | 6.5 | Wrexham | Havering | 23.10.87 |
| Roberts, Liam | 6.0 | – | Walsall | 24.11.94 |
| **Defenders** | | | | |
| Cockerill-Mollett, Callum | 5.10 | – | Leicester | 15.01.99 |
| Devlin, Nicky | 6.0 | Ayr | Bishopbriggs | 17.10.93 |
| Edwards, Joe | 5.9 | Colchester | Gloucester | 31.10.90 |
| Guthrie, Jon | 5.10 | Crewe | Devizes | 29.07.92 |
| Leahy, Luke | 5.10 | Falkirk | Coventry | 19.11.92 |
| Roberts, Kory | 6.1 | – | Birmingham | 17.12.97 |
| **Midfielders** | | | | |
| Chambers, Adam | 5.10 | Leyton Orient | Sandwell | 20.11.80 |
| Dobson, George | 6.1 | Sparta Rotterdam | Harold Wood | 15.11.97 |
| Ginnelly, Josh | 5.8 | Burnley | Coventry | 24.03.97 |
| Ismail, Zeli | 5.9 | Bury | Kukes, Alb | 12.12.93 |
| Kinsella, Liam | 5.9 | – | Colchester | 23.02.96 |
| Morris, Kieron | 5.10 | – | Hereford | 03.06.94 |
| **Forwards** | | | | |
| Bakayoko, Amadou | 6.3 | – | Sierra Leone | 01.01.96 |
| Cook, Andy | 6.1 | Tranmere | Bishop Auckland | 18.10.90 |

## WYCOMBE WANDERERS

**Ground**: Adams Park, Hillbottom Road, High Wycombe HP12 4HJ
**Telephone**: 01494 472100. **Club nickname**: Chairboys
**Colours**: Light and dark blue. **Capacity**: 10,300
**Record attendance**: 10,000 v Chelsea (friendly) July 13, 2005

| | | | | |
|---|---|---|---|---|
| **Goalkeepers** | | | | |
| Allsop, Ryan | 6.3 | Bournemouth | Birmingham | 17.06.92 |
| Ma-Kalambay, Yves | 6.6 | Otelul Galati | Brussels, Bel | 31.01.86 |
| **Defenders** | | | | |
| Charles, Darius | 6.1 | AFC Wimbledon | Ealing | 10.12.87 |
| El–Abd, Adam | 6.0 | Shrewsbury | Brighton | 11.09.84 |
| Harriman, Michael | 5.6 | QPR | Chichester | 23.10.92 |
| Jacobson, Joe | 5.11 | Shrewsbury | Cardiff | 17.11.86 |
| Jombati, Sido | 6.1 | Cheltenham | Lisbon, Por | 20.08.87 |
| Stewart, Anthony | 6.0 | Crewe | Lambeth | 18.09.92 |

| | | | | |
|---|---|---|---|---|
| **Midfielders** | | | | |
| Bean, Marcus | 5.11 | Colchester | Hammersmith | 02.11.84 |
| Bloomfield, Matt | 5.8 | Ipswich | Felixstowe | 08.02.84 |
| Cowan-Hall, Paris | 5.8 | Millwall | Hillingdon | 05.10.90 |
| Freeman, Nick | 5.11 | Biggleswade | Stevenage | 07.11.95 |
| Gape, Dominic | 5.11 | Southampton | Burton Bradstock | 09.09.94 |
| O'Nien, Luke | 5.9 | Watford | Hemel Hempstead | 21.11.94 |
| Saunders, Sam | 5.8 | Brentford | Erith | 29.08.83 |
| **Forwards** | | | | |
| Akinfenwa, Adebayo | 6.0 | Wimbledon | Islington | 10.05.82 |
| Kashket, Scott | 5.9 | Leyton Orient | Chigwell | 25.02.96 |
| Mackail-Smith, Craig | 5.10 | Luton | Watford | 25.02.84 |
| Tyson, Nathan | 6.0 | Kilmarnock | Reading | 04.05.82 |

# LEAGUE TWO

## BURY

**Ground**: Gigg Lane, Bury BL9 9HR
**Telephone**: 08445 790009. **Club nickname**: Shakers
**Colours**: White and blue. **Capacity**: 11,640
**Record attendance**: 35,000 v Bolton (FA Cup 3) Jan 9, 1960

| | | | | |
|---|---|---|---|---|
| **Goalkeepers** | | | | |
| Hudson, Matthew | 6.4 | Preston (loan) | Southport | 29.07.98 |
| Murphy, Joe | 6.2 | Huddersfield | Dublin, Ire | 21.08.81 |
| **Defenders** | | | | |
| Aimson, Will | 5.10 | Blackpool | Christchurch | 01.01.94 |
| Aldred, Tom | 6.2 | Blackpool | Bolton | 11.09.90 |
| Edwards, Phil | 5.9 | Burton | Bootle | 08.11.85 |
| Leigh, Greg | 5.11 | Bradford | Manchester | 30.09.94 |
| Miller, Tom | 5.11 | Carlisle | Ely | 29.06.90 |
| O'Connell, Eoghan | 6.2 | Celtic | Cork, Ire | 13.08.95 |
| Skarz, Joe | 6.0 | Oxford | Huddersfield | 13.07.89 |
| Stokes, Chris | 6.1 | Coventry | Trowbridge | 08.03.91 |
| Thompson, Adam | 6.2 | Southend | Harlow | 28.09.92 |
| **Midfielders** | | | | |
| Adams, Nicky | 5.10 | Carlisle | Bolton | 16.10.83 |
| Cooney, Ryan | 5.10 | – | Manchester | 26.02.00 |
| Dawson, Stephen | 5.6 | Scunthorpe | Dublin, Ire | 04.12.85 |
| Mayor, Danny | 6.0 | Sheffield Wed | Leyland | 18.10.90 |
| O'Shea, Jay | 6.0 | Chesterfield | Dublin, Ire | 10.08.88 |
| Tsu Dai | 5.9 | – | Hong Kong | 24.07.99 |
| **Forwards** | | | | |
| Beckford, Jermaine | 6.2 | Preston | Ealing | 09.12.83 |
| Bunn, Harry | 5.9 | Huddersfield | Oldham | 21.11.92 |
| Dagnall, Chris | 5.8 | Crewe | Liverpool | 15.04.86 |
| Moore, Byron | 6.0 | Bristol Rov | Stoke | 24.08.88 |
| Omotayo, Gold | 5.10 | Whitehawk | Zurich, Switz | 27.01.94 |

## CAMBRIDGE UNITED

**Ground**: Abbey Stadium, Newmarket Road, Cambridge CB5 8LN
**Telephone**: 01223 566500. **Club nickname**: U's
**Colours**: Yellow and black. **Capacity**: 9,617

**Record attendance**: 14,000 v Chelsea (friendly) May 1, 1970

| | | | | |
|---|---|---|---|---|
| **Goalkeepers** | | | | |
| Forde, David | 6.2 | Millwall | Galway, Ire | 20.12.79 |
| Mitov, Dimitar | 6.2 | Charlton | – | 22.01.97 |
| **Defenders** | | | | |
| Carroll, Jake | 6.0 | Hartlepool | Dublin, Ire | 11.08.91 |
| Coulson, Josh | 6.3 | – | Cambridge | 28.01.89 |
| Darling, Harry | 5.11 | – | Cambridge | 08.08.99 |
| John, Louis | 6.3 | Sutton | Croydon | 19.04.94 |
| O'Neil, Liam | 5.11 | Chesterfield | Cambridge | 31.07.93 |
| Taft, George | 6.3 | Mansfield | Leicester | 29.07.93 |
| Taylor, Greg | 6.1 | Luton | Bedford | 15.01.90 |
| **Midfielders** | | | | |
| Deegan, Gary | 5.9 | Shrewsbury | Dublin, Ire | 28.09.87 |
| Halliday, Brad | 5.11 | Middlesbrough | Redcar | 10.07.95 |
| Lambe, Reggie | 5.9 | Carlisle | Hamilton, Berm | 04.02.91 |
| Lewis, Paul | 6.1 | Macclesfield | Liverpool | 17.12.94 |
| Osadebe, Emmanuel | 6.2 | Gillingham | Dundalk, Ire | 01.10.96 |
| **Forwards** | | | | |
| Amoo, David | 5.10 | Partick | Southwark | 13.04.91 |
| Azeez, Ade | 6.0 | Partick | Orpington | 08.01.94 |
| Brown, Jevani | 5.9 | St Neots | Letchworth | 16.10.94 |
| Corr, Barry | 6.3 | Southend | Wicklow, Ire | 02.04.85 |
| Dunk, Harrison | 6.0 | Bromley | London | 25.10.90 |
| Foy, Matthew | 5.7 | – | Huntingdon | 02.11.98 |
| Ibehre, Jabo | 6.2 | Carlisle | Islington | 28.01.83 |
| Maris, George | 5.11 | Barnsley | Sheffield | 06.03.96 |

## CARLISLE UNITED

**Ground**: Brunton Park, Warwick Road, Carlisle CA1 1LL
**Telephone**: 01228 526237. **Club nickname**: Cumbrians
**Colours**: Blue and white. **Capacity**: 17,949
**Record attendance**: 27,500 v Birmingham City (FA Cup 3) Jan 5, 1957, v Middlesbrough (FA Cup 5) Jan 7, 1970

| | | | | |
|---|---|---|---|---|
| **Goalkeepers** | | | | |
| Collin, Adam | 6.2 | Notts Co | Penrith | 09.12.84 |
| Fryer, Joe | 6.4 | Middlesbrough (loan) | Chester-le-Street | 14.11.95 |
| **Defenders** | | | | |
| Gillesphey, Macaulay | 6.0 | Newcastle | Ashington | 24.11.95 |
| Grainger, Danny | 5.10 | Dunfermline | Penrith | 28.07.86 |
| Liddle, Gary | 6.1 | Chesterield | Middlesbrough | 15.06.86 |
| Miller, Gary | 6.0 | Plymouth | Glasgow | 15.04.87 |
| Olsen, Kieron | 5.10 | – | Sunderland | 26.11.99 |
| Parkes, Tom | 6.3 | Leyton Orient | Sutton-in-Ashfield | 15.01.92 |
| **Midfielders** | | | | |
| Devitt, Jamie | 5.10 | Morecambe | Dublin, Ire | 06.07.90 |
| Egan, Jack | 5.9 | – | Salford | 16.10.98 |
| Etuhu, Kelvin | 6.1 | Bury | Kano, Nig | 30.05.88 |
| Glendon, George | 5.10 | Fleetwood | Manchester | 03.05.95 |
| Jones, Mike | 6.0 | Oldham | Birkenhead | 15.08.87 |
| Jordan Holt | 5.9 | – | Carlisle | 17.03.00 |
| Kennedy, Jason | 6.1 | Bradford | Roseworth | 11.09.86 |
| **Forwards** | | | | |

| | | | | |
|---|---|---|---|---|
| Bennett, Richard | 6.4 | Barrow | Oldham | 23.03.91 |
| Hope, Hallam | 5.11 | Bury | Manchester | 17.03.94 |
| Stockton, Cole | 6.1 | Hearts | Huyton | 13.03.94 |

## CHELTENHAM TOWN

**Ground**: LCI Stadium, Whaddon Road, Cheltenham GL52 5NA
**Telephone**: 01242 573558
**Colours**: Red and black. **Capacity**: 7,066
**Record attendance**: 8,326 v Reading (FA Cup 1) Nov 17, 1956

| | | | | |
|---|---|---|---|---|
| **Goalkeepers** | | | | |
| Flinders, Scott | 6.4 | Macclesfield | Rotherham | 12.06.86 |
| Lovett, Rhys | 6.2 | Rochdale | Birmingham | 15.06.97 |
| **Defenders** | | | | |
| Bower, Matt | 6.5 | – | Cheltenham | 11.12.98 |
| Boyle, Will | 6.2 | Huddersfield | Garforth | 01.09.95 |
| Broom, Ryan | 5.10 | Bristol Rov | Newport | 04.09.96 |
| Debayo, Josh | 6.0 | Leicester | Hendon | 17.10.96 |
| Forster, Jordon | 6.2 | Hibernian | Edinburgh | 23.09.93 |
| Hussey, Chris | 6.0 | Sheffield Utd | Hammersmith | 02.01.89 |
| Long, Sean | 5.10 | Lincoln | Dublin | 02.05.95 |
| Mullins, Johnny | 5.11 | Luton | Hampstead | 06.11.85 |
| **Midfielders** | | | | |
| Atangana, Nigel | 6.2 | Leyton Orient | Corbeil-Essonnes, Fr | 09.09.89 |
| Dawson, Kevin | 5.11 | Yeovil | Dublin, Ire | 30.06.90 |
| Thomas, Conor | 6.1 | ATK | Coventry | 29.10.93 |
| Tozer, Ben | 6.1 | Newport | Plymouth | 01.03.90 |
| **Forwards** | | | | |
| Eisa, Mohamed | 6.1 | Greenwich | Khartoum, Sud | 15.06.90 |
| Graham, Brian | 6.2 | Hibernian | Glasgow | 23.11.87 |
| Lloyd, George | 5.8 | – | Gloucester | 11.02.00 |
| Sellars, Jerell | 5.8 | Aston Villa | Lincoln | 11.12.95 |

## COLCHESTER UNITED

**Ground**: Weston Homes Community Stadium, United Way, Colchester CO4 5HE
**Telephone**: 01206 755100. **Club nickname**: U's
**Colours**: Blue and white. **Capacity**: 10,105
**Record attendance**: Layer Road:19,072 v Reading (FA Cup 1) Nov 27, 1948.
Community Stadium: 10,064 v Norwich (Lge 1) Jan 16, 2010

| | | | | |
|---|---|---|---|---|
| **Goalkeepers** | | | | |
| Barnes, Dillon | 6.4 | Bedford | Enfield | 08.04.96 |
| Walker, Sam | 6.6 | Chelsea | Gravesend | 02.10.91 |
| **Defenders** | | | | |
| Barnes, Aaron | 6.1 | Charlton | Croydon | 14.10.96 |
| Chesmain, Noah | 5.10 | Millwall | Waltham Forest | 16.12.97 |
| Eastman, Tom | 6.3 | Ipswich | Colchester | 21.10.91 |
| James, Cameron | 6.0 | – | Chelmsford | 11.02.98 |
| Kent, Frankie | 6.2 | – | Romford | 21.11.95 |
| Kinsella, Lewis | 5.9 | Aston Villa | Watford | 02.09.94 |
| Prosser, Luke | 6.3 | Southend | Enfield | 28.05.88 |
| Vincent-Young, Kane | 5.11 | Tottenham | Camden | 15.03.96 |
| **Midfielders** | | | | |
| Comley, Brandon | 5.11 | QPR | Islington | 18.11.95 |

| | | | | |
|---|---|---|---|---|
| Gondoh, Ryan | 6.0 | Maldon | Sutton | 06.06.97 |
| Lapslie, Tom | 5.6 | – | Waltham Forest | 05.10.95 |
| Murray, Sean | 5.9 | Swindon | Abbots Langley | 11.10.93 |
| Pell, Harry | 6.4 | Cheltenham | Tilbury | 21.10.91 |
| Senior, Courtney | 5.9 | Brentford | Croydon | 11.02.98 |
| Szmodics, Sammie | 5.7 | – | Colchester | 24.09.95 |
| **Forwards** | | | | |
| Dickenson, Brennan | 6.0 | Gillingham | Ferndown | 26.02.93 |
| Mandron, Mikael | 6.3 | Wigan | Boulogne, Fr | 11.10.94 |
| Norris, Luke | 6.1 | Swindon | Stevenage | 03.06.93 |
| Nouble, Frank | 6.3 | Newport | Lewisham | 24.09.91 |

## CRAWLEY TOWN

**Ground**: Checkatrade Stadium, Winfield Way, Crawley RH11 9RX
**Telephone**: 01293 410000. **Club nickname**: Reds
**Colours**: Red. **Capacity:** 6,134
**Record attendance**: 5,880 v Reading (FA Cup 3) Jan 5, 2013

| | | | | |
|---|---|---|---|---|
| **Goalkeepers** | | | | |
| Mersin, Yusuf | 6.4 | Kasimpasa | Greenwich | 23.09.94 |
| Morris, Glenn | 6.0 | Gillingham | Woolwich | 20.12.83 |
| **Defenders** | | | | |
| Connolly, Mark | 6.1 | Kilmarnock | Monaghan, Ire | 16.12.91 |
| McNerney, Joe | 6.4 | Woking | Chertsey | 24.01.90 |
| Randall, Mark | 6.0 | Newport | Milton Keynes | 28.09.89 |
| **Midfielders** | | | | |
| Bulman, Dannie | 5.8 | AFC Wimbledon | Ashford, Surrey | 24.01.79 |
| Cox, Dean | 5.4 | Leyton Orient | Haywards Heath | 12.08.87 |
| Francomb, George | 6.0 | AFC Wimbledon | Hackney | 08.09.91 |
| Payne, Josh | 6.0 | Eastleigh | Basingstoke | 25.11.90 |
| Sanoh, Moussa | 5.9 | Waalwijk | Nijmegen, Hol | 20.07.95 |
| Smith, Jimmy | 6.1 | Stevenage | Newham | 07.01.87 |
| Tajbakhsh, Aryan | 6.1 | Cray | Hendon | 20.10.90 |
| Young, Lewis | 5.9 | Bury | Stevenage | 27.09.89 |
| **Forwards** | | | | |
| Camara, Panutche | 6.1 | Dulwich Hamlet | Guin-Bassau | 28.02.97 |
| Palmer, Ollie | 6.5 | Lincoln | Epsom | 21.01.92 |
| Poleon, Dominic | 6.2 | Bradford | Newham | 07.09.93 |

## CREWE ALEXANDRA

**Ground**: Alexandra Stadium, Gresty Road, Crewe CW2 6EB
**Telephone**: 01270 213014. **Club nickname**: Railwaymen
**Colours**: Red and white. **Capacity**: 10,066
**Record attendance**: 20,000 v Tottenham (FA Cup 4) Jan 30, 1960

| | | | | |
|---|---|---|---|---|
| **Goalkeepers** | | | | |
| Garratt, Ben | 6.1 | – | Shrewsbury | 25.04.93 |
| Richards, David | 6.0 | Bristol City | Abergavenny | 31.12.93 |
| **Defenders** | | | | |
| Ng, Perry | 5.11 | – | Liverpool | 27.04.96 |
| Nolan, Eddie | 6.0 | Blackpool | Waterford, Ire | 05.08.88 |
| Ray, George | 6.0 | – | Warrington | 03.10.93 |
| Raynes, Michael | 6.3 | Carlisle | Wythenshawe | 15.10.87 |

| | | | | |
|---|---|---|---|---|
| **Midfielders** | | | | |
| Ainley, Callum | 5.8 | – | Middlewich | 02.11.97 |
| Finney, Oliver | 5.7 | – | Stoke | 15.12.97 |
| Green, Paul | 5.9 | Oldham | Pontefract | 10.04.83 |
| Jones, James | 5.9 | – | Winsford | 01.02.96 |
| Kirk, Charlie | 5.7 | – | Winsford | 24.12.97 |
| Lowery, Tom | – | – | Holmes Chapel | 31.12.97 |
| Pickering, Harry | – | – | Chester | 29.12.98 |
| Walker, Brad | 6.1 | Hartlepool | Billingham | 25.04.96 |
| Wintle, Ryan | 5.6 | Alsager | Newcastle-under-Lyme | 13.06.97 |
| **Forwards** | | | | |
| Bowery, Jordan | 6.1 | Leyton Orient | Nottingham | 02.07.91 |
| Dale, Owen | 5.9 | – | Warrington | 01.11.98 |
| Miller, Shaun | 5.10 | Carlisle | Alsager | 25.09.87 |
| Nicholls, Alex | 5.10 | Barnet | Stourbridge | 09.12.87 |
| Porter, Chris | 6.1 | Colchester | Wigan | 12.12.83 |
| Reilly, Lewis | 5.11 | – | Liverpool | 07.07.99 |

## EXETER CITY

**Ground**: St James Park, Stadium Way, Exeter EX4 6PX
**Telephone**: 01392 411243. **Club nickname**: Grecians
**Colours**: Red and white. **Capacity**: 8,830
**Record attendance**: 20,984 v Sunderland (FA Cup 6 replay) Mar 4, 1931

| | | | | |
|---|---|---|---|---|
| **Goalkeepers** | | | | |
| Hamon, James | 6.1 | Guernsey | Guernsey | 01.07.95 |
| Pym, Christy | 5.11 | – | Exeter | 24.04.95 |
| **Defenders** | | | | |
| Brown, Troy | 6.1 | Cheltenham | Croydon | 17.09.90 |
| Croll, Luke | 6.1 | Crystal Palace | Lambeth | 10.01.95 |
| Egan, Kyle | 5.11 | – | Bristol | 15.12.98 |
| Moxey, Dean | 5.11 | Bolton | Exeter | 14.01.86 |
| Sweeney, Pierce | 5.11 | Reading | Dublin, Ire | 11.09.94 |
| Woodman, Craig | 5.9 | Brentford | Tiverton | 22.12.82 |
| **Midfielders** | | | | |
| Boateng, Hiram | 5.7 | Crystal Palace | Wandsworth | 08.01.96 |
| Holmes, Lee | 5.9 | Preston | Mansfield | 02.04.87 |
| Law, Nicky | 5.10 | Bradford | Plymouth | 29.03.88 |
| Sparkes, Jack | 5.9 | – | Exeter | 29.09.00 |
| Taylor, Jake | 5.10 | Reading | Ascot | 01.12.91 |
| Tillson, Jordan | 6.0 | Bristol Rov | Bath | 05.03.93 |
| **Forwards** | | | | |
| Abrahams, Tristan | 5.19 | Norwich (loan) | Lewisham | 29.12.98 |
| Forte, Jonathan | 6.0 | Notts Co | Sheffield | 25.07.86 |
| Jay, Matt | 5.10 | – | Torbay | 27.02.96 |
| Stockley, Jayden | 6.3 | Aberdeen | Poole | 15.09.93 |

## FOREST GREEN ROVERS

**Ground**: New Lawn, Another Way, Nailsworth GL6 OFG
**Telephone**:01453 835291. **Club nickname**: Green Devils
**Capacity**: 5,140. **Record attendance**: 4,836 v Derby (FA Cup 3, Jan 3, 2009)

| | | | | |
|---|---|---|---|---|
| **Goalkeepers** | | | | |
| Montgomery, James | 6.2 | Gateshead | Sunderland | 20.04.94 |

| | | | | |
|---|---|---|---|---|
| Sanchez, Robert | 6.5 | Brighton (loan) | Cartagena, Sp | 18.11.97 |
| Thomas, Lewis | 6.0 | Swansea | Manselton | 20.09.97 |
| **Defenders** | | | | |
| Collins, Lee | 5.11 | Mansfield | Telford | 28.09.88 |
| Gunning, Gavin | 6.2 | Port Vale | Dublin, Ire | 26.01.91 |
| Hollis, Haydn | 6.4 | Notts Co | Selston | 14.10.92 |
| Laird, Scott | 5.9 | Scunthorpe | Taunton | 15.05.88 |
| Mills, Joseph | 5.9 | Perth Glory | Swindon | 30.10.89 |
| Rawson , Farrend | 6.2 | Derby | Nottingham | 11.07.96 |
| Shephard, Liam | 5.10 | Peterborough | Pentre | 22.11.94 |
| **Midfielders** | | | | |
| Archibald, Theo | 5.11 | Brentford (loan) | Glasgow | 05.03.98 |
| Brown, Reece | 5.9 | Birmingham | Dudley | 03.03.96 |
| Campbell, Tahvon | 5.8 | WBA | Birmingham | 10.01.97 |
| Cooper, Charlie | 5.9 | Birmingham | Stockton | 01.05.97 |
| Grubb, Dayle | 6.0 | Weston SM | Weston SM | 24.07.91 |
| James, Lloyd | 5.11 | Exeter | Bristol | 16.02.88 |
| Simpson, Jordan | 5.10 | Swindon | Swindon | 28.11.98 |
| Winchester, Carl | 6.0 | Cheltenham | Belfast | 12.04.93 |
| **Forwards** | | | | |
| Doidge, Christian | 6.1 | Dagenham | Newport | 25.08.92 |
| Pearce, Isaac | 5.6 | Fulham (loan) | Bristol | 27.10.98 |
| Reid, Reuben | 6.0 | Exeter | Bristol | 26.07.88 |
| Williams, George | 5.8 | Fulham | Milton Keynes | 07.09.95 |

## GRIMSBY TOWN

**Ground**: Blundell Park, Cleethorpes DN35 7PY
**Telephone**: 01472 605050
**Colours**: Black and white: **Capacity**: 9,052
**Record attendance**: 31,651 v Wolves (FA Cup 5) 20 February, 1937

| | | | | |
|---|---|---|---|---|
| **Goalkeepers** | | | | |
| McKeown, James | 6.1 | Peterborough | Birmingham | 24.07.89 |
| **Defenders** | | | | |
| Collins, Danny | 6.0 | Rotherham | Chester | 06.08.80 |
| Davis, Harry | 6.2 | St Mirren | Burnley | 24.09.91 |
| Dixon, Paul | 5.10 | Dundee Utd | Aberdeen | 22.11.86 |
| Fox, Andrew | 5.11 | Eskilstuna | Huntingdon | 15.01.93 |
| Famewo, Akin | 5.11 | Luton (loan) | Lewisham | 09.11.98 |
| Hall-Johnson, Reece | 5.8 | Braintree | Aylesbury | 09.05.95 |
| Whitmore, Alex | 6.1 | Chesterfield | Newcastle | 07.09.95 |
| **Midfielders** | | | | |
| Clifton, Harry | 5.11 | – | Grimsby | 12.06.98 |
| Cook, Jordan | 5.9 | Luton | Sunderland | 20.03.90 |
| Hessenthaler, Jake | 5.10 | Gillingham | Gravesend | 20.04.90 |
| Rose, Mitch | 5.9 | Newport | Doncaster | 04.07.94 |
| Welsh, John | 6.0 | Preston | Liverpool | 10.01.84 |
| Whitehouse, Elliott | 5.11 | Lincoln | Worksop | 27.10.93 |
| Woolford, Martyn | 6.0 | Fleetwood | Castleford | 13.10.85 |
| Wright, Max | 5.8 | – | Grimsby | 06.04.98 |
| **Forwards** | | | | |
| Cardwell, Harry | 6.2 | Reading | Beverley | 23.10.96 |
| Hooper, JJ | 6.1 | Port Vale | Greenwich | 09.10.93 |
| Robles, Louis | 6.0 | San Roque | Liverpool | 11.09.96 |

## LINCOLN CITY

**Ground:** Sincil Bank Stadium, Lincoln LN5 8LD
**Telephone:** 01522 880011. **Club nickname:** Imps
**Colours:** Red and white. **Capacity:** 10,130
**Record attendance:** 23,196 v Derby (League Cup 4) Nov 15, 1967

| | | | | |
|---|---|---|---|---|
| **Goalkeepers** | | | | |
| Smith, Grant | 6.1 | Boreham Wood | Reading | 20.11.93 |
| Vickers, Josh | 6.0 | Swansea | Basildon | 01.12.95 |
| **Defenders** | | | | |
| Eardley, Neal | 5.11 | Northampton | Llandudno | 06.11.88 |
| Habergham, Sam | 6.0 | Braintree | Doncaster | 20.02.92 |
| Toffolo, Harry | 6.0 | Millwall | Welwyn Garden City | 19.08.95 |
| Waterfall, Luke | 6.2 | Wrexham | Sheffield | 30.07.90 |
| **Midfielders** | | | | |
| Anderson, Harry | 5.7 | Peterborough | Slough | 09.01.97 |
| Bostwick, Michael | 6.1 | Peterborough | Greenwich | 17.05.88 |
| Frecklington, Lee | 5.8 | Rotherham | Lincoln | 08.09.85 |
| O'Connor, Michael | 6.1 | Notts Co | Belfast | 06.10.87 |
| **Forwards** | | | | |
| Akinde, John | 6.2 | Barnet | Gravesend | 08.07.89 |
| Bruno Andrade | 5.9 | Boreham Wood | Viseu, Port | 02.10.93 |
| Green, Matt | 6.0 | Mansfield | Bath | 02.01.87 |
| Pett, Tom | 5.8 | Stevenage | Potters Bar | 03.12.91 |
| Rhead, Matt | 6.4 | Mansfield | Stoke | 31.05.84 |

## MACCLESFIELD TOWN

**Ground:** Moss Rose Stadium, London Road, Macclesfield SK11 7SP
**Telephone:** 01625 264686. **Club nickname:** Silkmen
**Colours:** Blue and white. **Capacity:**
**Record attendance:** 9,003 v Winsford (Cheshire Senior Cup 2) Feb 14, 1948

| | | | | |
|---|---|---|---|---|
| **Goalkeepers** | | | | |
| **Defenders** | | | | |
| Evans, Callum | 5.10 | Forest Green | Bristol | 11.10.95 |
| Fitzpatrick, David | 5.10 | Southport | Manchester | 28.02.90 |
| Hodgkiss, Jared | 5.7 | Kidderminster | Stafford | 15.11.86 |
| Lowe, Keith | 6.2 | Kidderminster | Wolverhampton | 13.09.85 |
| Pilkington, George | 6.0 | Mansfield | Rugeley | 07.11.81 |
| **Midfielders** | | | | |
| Durrell, Elliot | 5.10 | Chester | Shrewsbury | 31.07.89 |
| Grimes, Jamie | 6.1 | Cheltenham | Nottingham | 22.12.90 |
| Lloyd, Ryan | 5.10 | Port Vale | Newcastle-u-Lyme | 01.02.94 |
| Whittaker, Danny | 5.10 | Chesterfield | Manchester | 14.11.80 |
| **Forwards** | | | | |
| Blissett, Nathan | 6.1 | Plymouth | West Bromwich | 29.06.90 |
| Marsh, Tyrone | 5.11 | Dover | Bedord | 24.12.93 |
| Smith, Harry | 6.5 | Millwall | Chatham | 18.05.95 |
| Wilson, Scott | 6.1 | Eastleigh | Bristol | 11.01.93 |

## MANSFIELD TOWN

**Ground**: One Call Stadium, Quarry Lane, Mansfield NG18 5DA
**Telephone**: 01623 482482. **Club nickname**: Stags
**Colours**: Amber and blue. **Capacity**: 10,000
**Record attendance**: 24,467 v Nottm Forest (FA Cup 3) Jan 10, 1953

| | | | | |
|---|---|---|---|---|
| **Goalkeepers** | | | | |
| Logan, Conrad | 6.2 | Rochdale | Ramelton, Ire | 18.04.86 |
| Olejnik, Bobby | 6.0 | Exeter | Vienna, Aut | 26.11.86 |
| **Defenders** | | | | |
| Benning, Malvind | 5.10 | Walsall | Sandwell | 02.11.93 |
| Diamond, Zander | 6.2 | Northampton | Alexandria, Sco | 03.12.85 |
| Kelleher, Fiacre | 6.4 | Oxford (loan) | Cork, Ire | 10.03.96 |
| Mirfin, David | 6.1 | Scunthorpe | Sheffield | 18.04.85 |
| Pearce, Krystian | 6.2 | Torquay | Birmingham | 05.01.90 |
| Preston, Matt | 6.0 | Swindon | Birmingham | 16.03.95 |
| White, Hayden | 6.1 | Peterborough | Greenwich | 15.04.95 |
| **Midfielders** | | | | |
| Anderson, Paul | 5.9 | Northampton | Leicester | 23.07.88 |
| Atkinson, Will | 5.10 | Southend | Beverley | 14.10.88 |
| Bishop, Neal | 6.0 | Scunthorpe | Stockton | 07.08.81 |
| Butcher, Calum | 6.0 | Millwall | Rochford | 26.02.91 |
| Chapman, Adam | 5.10 | Newport | Doncaster | 29.11.89 |
| Digby, Paul | 6.3 | Ipswich | Sheffield | 02.02.95 |
| Khan, Otis | 5.9 | Yeovil | Ashton-under-Lyne | 05.09.95 |
| MacDonald, Alex | 5.7 | Oxford | Warrington | 14.04.90 |
| Mellis, Jacob | 5.11 | Bury | Nottingham | 08.01.91 |
| **Forwards** | | | | |
| Angol, Lee | 6.2 | Peterborough | Sutton | 04.08.94 |
| Davies, Craig | 6.2 | Oldham | Burton | 09.01.86 |
| Hamilton CJ | 5.7 | Sheffield Utd | Harrow | 23.03.95 |
| Rose, Danny | 5.10 | Bury | Barnsley | 10.12.93 |
| Sterling-James, Omari | 5.10 | Solihull | Birmingham | 15.09.93 |
| Walker, Tyler | 5.10 | Nottm Forest (loan) | Nottingham | 07.10.96 |

## MILTON KEYNES DONS

**Ground**: stadiummk, Stadium Way West, Milton Keynes MK1 1ST
**Telephone**: 01908 622922. **Club nickname**: Dons
**Colours**: White. **Capacity**: 30,500
**Record attendance**: 28,127 v Chelsea (FA Cup 4) Jan 31, 2016

| | | | | |
|---|---|---|---|---|
| **Goalkeepers** | | | | |
| Nicholls, Lee | 6.3 | Wigan | Huyton | 05.10.92 |
| Sietsma, Wieger | 6.3 | Heerenveen | Groningen, Hol | 11.07.95 |
| **Defenders** | | | | |
| Brittain, Callum | 5.10 | – | Bedford | 12.03.98 |
| Lewington, Dean | 5.11 | Wimbledon | Kingston upon Thames | 18.05.84 |
| Moore-Taylor, Jordan | 5.10 | Exeter | Exeter | 21.01.94 |
| Tilney, Ben | 5.9 | – | Luton | 28.02.97 |
| Walsh, Joe | 5.11 | Crawley | Cardiff | 13.05.92 |
| Williams, George | 5.9 | Barnsley | Hillingdon | 14.04.93 |
| **Midfielders** | | | | |
| Aneke, Chuks | 6.3 | Zulte Waregem | Newham | 03.07.93 |
| Cisse, Ousseynou | 6.4 | Tours | Suresnes, Fr | 07.04.91 |

| | | | | |
|---|---|---|---|---|
| Furlong, Connor | 5.7 | – | Milton Keynes | 07.02.98 |
| Gilbey, Alex | 6.0 | Wigan | Dagenham | 09.12.94 |
| Hancox, Mitch | 5.10 | Macclesfield | Solihull | 09.11.93 |
| Harley, Ryan | 5.9 | Exeter | Bristol | 22.01.85 |
| Houghton, Jordan | 6.0 | Chelsea | Chertsey | 09.11.95 |
| Kasumu, David | 5.11 | – | Lambert | 05.10.99 |
| McGrandles, Conor | 6.0 | Norwich | Falkirk | 24.09.95 |
| Nesbitt, Aidan | 5.10 | Celtic | Paisley | 05.02.97 |
| Pawlett, Peter | 5.10 | Aberdeen | Hull | 03.02.91 |
| Rasulo, Giorgio | 5.10 | – | Banbury | 23.01.97 |
| Watson, Ryan | 6.1 | Barnet | Crewe | 07.07.93 |
| **Forwards** | | | | |
| Agard, Kieran | 5.10 | Bristol City | Newham | 10.10.89 |
| Logan, Hugo | 5.8 | – | Stevenage | 21.09.98 |
| Muirhead, Robbie | 6.3 | Hearts | Irvine | 08.03.96 |
| Nombe, Sam | 5.11 | – | Croydon | 22.10.98 |
| Simpson, Robbie | 6.1 | Exeter | Poole | 15.03.85 |
| Sow, Osman | 6.3 | Henan Jianye | Stockholm, Swe | 22.04.90 |
| Thomas-Asante, Brandon | 5.11 | – | Milton Keynes | 29.12.98 |

## MORECAMBE

**Ground**: Globe Arena, Christie Way, Westgate, Morecambe LA4 4TB
**Telephone**: 01524 411797. **Club nickname**: Shrimps
**Colours**: Red and white. **Capacity**: 6,476
**Record attendance**: Christie Park: 9,234 v Weymouth (FA Cup 3) Jan 6, 1962. Globe Arena: 5,003 v Burnley (League Cup 2) Aug 24, 2010

| | | | | |
|---|---|---|---|---|
| **Goalkeepers** | | | | |
| Halstead, Mark | 6.3 | Southport | Blackpool | 17.09.90 |
| Roche, Barry | 6.4 | Chesterfield | Dublin, Ire | 06.04.82 |
| **Defenders** | | | | |
| Conlan, Luke | 5.11 | Burnley | Portaferry | 31.10.94 |
| Cranston, Jordan | 5.11 | Cheltenham | Wednesfield | 11.11.93 |
| Mills, Zak | 5.10 | Grimsby | Peterborough | 28.05.92 |
| Old, Steve | 6.3 | GAIS | Palmerston, NZ | 17.02.86 |
| **Midfielders** | | | | |
| Ellison, Kevin | 6.0 | Rotherham | Liverpool | 23.02.79 |
| Fleming, Andy | 5.11 | Wrexham | Liverpool | 05.10.87 |
| Hedley, Ben | 5.10 | – | Gateshead | 18.10.98 |
| Kenyon, Alex | 6.0 | Stockport | Euxton | 17.07.92 |
| Tutte, Andrew | 5.9 | Bury | Liverpool | 21.09.90 |
| Wildig, Aaron | 5.9 | Shrewsbury | Hereford | 15.04.92 |
| **Forwards** | | | | |
| Campbell, Adam | 5.9 | Notts Co | North Shields | 01.01.95 |
| Hawley, Kyle | – | – | Oldham | 11.05.00 |
| Mandeville, Liam | 5.11 | Doncaster (loan) | Lincoln | 17.02.97 |
| Oates, Rhys | 6.2 | Hartlepool | Pontefract | 04.12.94 |
| Oliver, Vadaine | 6.1 | York | Sheffield | 21.10.91 |
| Oswell, Jason | 6.2 | Stockport | Northwich | 07.10.92 |
| Sinclair, James | 5.9 | GAIS | Newcastle | 22.10.87 |
| Thompson, Garry | 5.11 | Wycombe | Kendal | 24.11.80 |

## NEWPORT COUNTY

**Ground**: Rodney Parade, Newport NP19 OUU
**Telephone**: 01633 670690. **Club nickname**: Exiles
**Colours**: Amber and black. **Capacity**: 7,850
**Record attendance**: Somerton Park: 24,268 v Cardiff (Div 3S) Oct 16, 1937. Rodney Parade: 9,836 v Tottenham (FA Cup 4) Jan 27, 2018

| | | | | |
|---|---|---|---|---|
| **Goalkeepers** | | | | |
| Day, Joe | 6.0 | Peterborough | Brighton | 13.08.90 |
| **Defenders** | | | | |
| Bennett, Scott | 5.10 | Notts Co | Newquay | 30.11.90 |
| Butler, Dan | 5.9 | Torquay | Cowes | 26.08.94 |
| Demetriou, Mickey | 6.2 | Shrewsbury | Dorrington | 12.03.90 |
| Franks, Fraser | 6.2 | Stevenage | Hammersmith | 22.11.90 |
| O'Brien, Mark | 5.11 | Luton | Dublin, Ire | 20.11.92 |
| Pipe, David | 5.9 | Eastleigh | Caerphilly | 05.11.83 |
| **Midfielders** | | | | |
| Cooper, Charlie | 5.9 | Forest Green (loan) | Stockton | 01.05.97 |
| Dolan, Matt | 5.9 | Yeovil | Hartlepool | 11.02.93 |
| Labadie, Joss | 6.3 | Dagenham | Croydon | 30.08.90 |
| Willmott, Robbie | 5.9 | Chelmsford | Harlow | 16.05.90 |
| **Forwards** | | | | |
| Amond, Padraig | 5.11 | Hartlepool | Carlow, Ire | 15.04.88 |
| Reynolds, Lamar | 5.10 | Brentwood | Jamaica | 16.08.95 |

## NORTHAMPTON TOWN

**Ground**: Sixfields Stadium, Upton Way, Northampton NN5 5QA
**Telephone**: 01604 683700. **Club nickname**: Cobblers
**Colours**: Claret and white. **Capacity**: 7,750
**Record attendance:** County Ground: 24,523 v Fulham (Div 1) Apr 23, 1966. Sixfields Stadium: 7,798 v Manchester Utd (Lge Cup 3) Sep 21, 2016

| | | | | |
|---|---|---|---|---|
| **Goalkeepers** | | | | |
| Coddington, Luke | 6.1 | Huddersfield | Middlesbrough | 06.06.95 |
| Cornell, David | 6.0 | Oldham | Swansea | 28.03.91 |
| **Defenders** | | | | |
| Barnett, Leon | 6.1 | Bury | Luton | 30.11.85 |
| Buchanan, David | 5.9 | Preston | Rochdale | 06.05.86 |
| Facey, Shay | 5.10 | Manchester City | Stockport | 07.01.95 |
| Moloney, Brendan | 6.1 | Yeovil | Beaufort, Ire | 18.01.89 |
| Odoffin, Hakeem | 6.3 | Wolves | Barnet | 13.04.98 |
| Phillips, Aaron | 5.8 | Coventry | Warwick | 20.11.93 |
| Pierre, Aaron | 6.1 | Wycombe | Southall | 17.02.93 |
| Poole, Regan | 5.11 | Manchester Utd | Cardiff | 18.06.98 |
| Taylor, Ash | 6.0 | Aberdeen | Bromborough | 02.09.90 |
| Turnbull, Jordan | 6.1 | Coventry | Trowbridge | 30.10.94 |
| **Midfielders** | | | | |
| Bridge, Jack | 5.10 | Southend | Southend | 21.09.95 |
| Crooks, Matt | 6.1 | Rangers | Leeds | 20.01.94 |
| Foley, Sam | 6.0 | Port Vale | Upton-on-Severn | 17.10.86 |
| Kasim, Yaser | 5.11 | Swindon | Baghdad, Irq | 16.05.91 |
| McWilliams, Shaun | 5.11 | – | Northampton | 14.08.98 |
| O'Toole, John-Joe | 6.2 | Bristol Rov | Harrow | 30.09.88 |

| | | | | |
|---|---|---|---|---|
| Powell, Daniel | 6.2 | MK Dons | Luton | 12.03.91 |
| **Forwards** | | | | |
| Bowditch, Dean | 5.11 | MK Dons | Bishop's Stortford | 15.06.86 |
| Hoskins, Sam | 5.8 | Yeovil | Dorchester | 04.02.93 |
| Iaciofano, Joe | 5.10 | – | Northampton | 10.09.98 |
| Morias, Junior | 5.8 | Peterborough | Kingston, Jam | 04.07.95 |
| Van Veen, Kevin | 6.0 | Scunthorpe | Eindhovern, Hol | 01.06.91 |
| Waters, Billy | 5.9 | Cheltenham | Epsom | 15.10.94 |
| Williams, Andy | 5.10 | Doncaster | Hereford | 14.08.86 |

## NOTTS COUNTY

**Ground**: Meadow Lane, Nottingham NG2 3HJ
**Telephone**: 0115 952 9000. **Club nickname**: Magpies
**Colours**: White and black. **Capacity**: 20,300
**Record attendance**: 47,310 v York (FA Cup 6) Mar 12, 1955

| | | | | |
|---|---|---|---|---|
| **Goalkeepers** | | | | |
| Fitzsimons, Ross | 6.1 | Chelmsford | London | 28.05.94 |
| Pindroch, Branislav | 6.4 | Karvina | Banska, Slovak | 30.10.91 |
| **Defenders** | | | | |
| Bird, Pierce | 6.2 | Dunkirk | Nottingham | 16.04.99 |
| Brisley, Shaun | 6.2 | Carlisle | Macclesfield | 06.05.90 |
| Duffy, Richard | 5.11 | Port Vale | Swansea | 30.08.85 |
| Hall, Ben | 6.1 | Brighton (loan) | Enniskillen | 16.01.97 |
| Hewitt, Elliott | 5.11 | Ipswich | Bodelwyddan | 30.05.94 |
| Kellett, Andy | 5.8 | Wigan | Bolton | 10.11.93 |
| Jones, Dan | 6.2 | Chesterfield | Wordsley | 23.12.86 |
| Tootle, Matt | 5.9 | Shrewsbury | Knowsley | 11.10.90 |
| **Midfielders** | | | | |
| Crawford, Tom | 6.1 | Chester | Chester | 30.05.99 |
| Hawkridge, Terry | 5.6 | Lincoln | Nottingham | 23.02.90 |
| Husin, Noor | 5.10 | Crystal Palace | Mazar-i-Sharf, Afg | 03.03.97 |
| Patching, Will | 6.1 | Manchester City | Manchester | 18.10.98 |
| Thomas, Nathan | 5.10 | Sheffield Utd (loan) | Ingleby Barwick | 27.09.94 |
| Vaughan, David | 5.7 | Nottm Forest | Rhuddlan | 18.02.83 |
| **Forwards** | | | | |
| Alessandra, Lewis | 5.10 | Hartlepool | Heywood | 08.02.89 |
| Boldewijn, Enzio | 6.1 | Crawley | Almere, Hol | 17.11.92 |
| Dennis, Kristian | 5.11 | Chesterfield | Manchester | 12.03.90 |
| Hemmings Kane | 6.1 | Oxford | Burton | 08.04.92 |
| Stead, Jon | 6.3 | Huddersfield | Huddersfield | 07.04.83 |

## OLDHAM ATHLETIC

**Ground**: Boundary Park, Oldham OL1 2PA
**Telephone**: 0161 624 4972. **Club nickname**: Latics
**Colours**: Blue and white. **Capacity**: 13,500
**Record attendance**: 47,761 v Sheffield Wed (FA Cup 4) Jan 25, 1930

| | | | | |
|---|---|---|---|---|
| **Goalkeepers** | | | | |
| Placide, Johnny | 6.0 | Guingamp | Montfermeil, Fr | 29.01.88 |
| Zeus de la Paz | 6.2 | Cincinnati | Nijmegen, Hol | 11.03.95 |
| **Defenders** | | | | |
| Clarke, Peter | 6.0 | Bury | Southport | 03.01.82 |
| Dummigan, Cameron | 5.11 | Burnley | Lurgan | 02.06.96 |

| | | | | |
|---|---|---|---|---|
| Edmundson, George | 6.1 | – | Wythenshawe | 15.08.97 |
| Gerrard, Anthony | 6.2 | Shrewsbury | Liverpool | 06.02.86 |
| Hunt, Rob | 5.8 | Brighton | Dagenham | 07.07.95 |
| McLaughlin, Ryan | 5.9 | Liverpool | Belfast | 30.09.94 |
| Moimbe, Wilfried | 5.8 | Nantes | Vichy, Fr | 18.10.88 |
| Stott, Jamie | 6.1 | – | Failsworth | 22.12.97 |
| **Midfielders** | | | | |
| Baxter, Jose | 5.11 | Everton | Bootle | 07.02.92 |
| Byrne, Jack | 5.9 | Wigan | Dublin, Ire | 24.04.96 |
| Fane, Ousmane | 6.4 | Kidderminster | Paris, Fr | 13.12.93 |
| Flynn, Ryan | 5.7 | Sheffield Utd | Edinburgh | 04.09.88 |
| Gardner, Dan | 6.1 | Chesterfield | Gorton | 05.04.90 |
| Maouche, Mohamed | 5.11 | Tours | Ambilly, Fr | 10.01.93 |
| McEleny, Patrick | 6.0 | Dundalk | Derry | 26.09.92 |
| Missilou, Christopher | 5.11 | Le Puy | Auxerre, Fr | 18.07.92 |
| **Forwards** | | | | |
| Benteke, Jonathan | 6.1 | Omonia Nicosia | Liege, Bel | 28.04.95 |
| Duffus, Courtney | 6.2 | Everton | Cheltenham | 24.10.95 |
| Nepomuceno, Gevaro | 5.9 | Maritimo | Tilburg, Hol | 10.11.92 |

## PORT VALE

**Ground**: Vale Park, Hamil Road, Burslem, Stoke-on-Trent ST6 1AW
**Telephone**: 01782 655800. **Club nickname**: Valiants
**Colours**: Black and white. **Capacity**: 18,947
**Record attendance**: 49,768 v Aston Villa (FA Cup 5) Feb 20, 1960

| | | | | |
|---|---|---|---|---|
| **Goalkeepers** | | | | |
| Brown, Scott | 6.1 | Wycombe | Wolverhampton | 26.04.85 |
| Hornby, Sam | 6.2 | Burton | Sutton Coldfield | 14.02.95 |
| Lainton, Rob | 6.2 | Bury | Ashton-under-Lyme | 12.10.89 |
| **Defenders** | | | | |
| Davis, Joe | 6.3 | Fleetwood | Burnley | 10.11.93 |
| Gibbons, James | 5.9 | – | Stoke | 16.03.98 |
| Legge, Leon | 6.1 | Cambridge | Hastings | 28.04.85 |
| Kay, Antony | 5.11 | Bury | Barnsley | 21.10.82 |
| Smith, Nathan | 6.0 | – | Madeley | 03.04.96 |
| Vassell, Theo | 6.1 | Gateshead | Stoke | 02.01.97 |
| **Midfielders** | | | | |
| Daniels, Brendon | 5.11 | Alfreton | Stoke | 24.09.93 |
| Dodds, Louis | 5.11 | Chesterfield (loan) | Sheffield | 08.10.86 |
| Hannant, Luke | 5.11 | Gateshead | Great Yarmouth | 04.11.93 |
| Joyce, Luke | 5.11 | Carlisle | Bolton | 09.07.87 |
| Montano, Cristian | 5.11 | Bristol Rov | Cali, Col | 11.12.91 |
| Oyeleke, Manny | 5.9 | Aldershot | Wandsworth | 24.12.92 |
| Pugh, Danny | 6.0 | Blackpool | Cheadle Hulme | 19.10.82 |
| Tonge, Michael | 6.0 | Stevenage | Manchester | 07.04.83 |
| **Forwards** | | | | |
| Angus, Dior | 6.0 | Redditch | Coventry | 18.01.94 |
| Barnett, Tyrone | 6.3 | AFC Wimbledon | Stevenage | 28.10.85 |
| Kanu, Idris | 6.0 | Peterborough | – | 05.12.99 |
| Miller, Ricky | 6.2 | Peterborough | Hatfield | 13.03.89 |
| Pope, Tom | 6.3 | Bury | Stoke | 27.08.85 |
| Quigley, Scott | 6.4 | Blackpool (loan) | Shrewsbury | 02.09.92 |
| Worrall, David | 6.0 | Millwall | Manchester | 12.06.90 |

## STEVENAGE

**Ground**: Lamex Stadium, Broadhall Way, Stevenage SG2 8RH
**Telephone**: 01438 223223. **Club nickname**: Boro
**Colours**: White and red. **Capacity**: 6,920
**Record attendance**: 8,040 v Newcastle (FA Cup 4) January 25, 1998

| | | | | |
|---|---|---|---|---|
| **Goalkeepers** | | | | |
| Day, Chris | 6.2 | Millwall | Walthamstow | 28.07.75 |
| Farman, Paul | 6.5 | Lincoln | North Shields | 02.11.89 |
| **Defenders** | | | | |
| Cuthbert, Scott | 6.2 | Luton | Alexandria, Scot | 15.06.87 |
| Henry, Ronnie | 5.11 | Luton | Hemel Hempstead | 02.01.84 |
| Hunt, Johnny | 5.10 | Mansfield | Liverpool | 23.08.90 |
| Johnson, Ryan | 6.2 | – | Birmingham | 02.10.96 |
| O'Donnell, Dylan | 6.2 | Norwich | Stevenage | 14.02.01 |
| Slater, Luke | 5.11 | St Kevin's | Dublin, Ire | 02.03.98 |
| Vancooten, Terence | 6.1 | Reading | Kingston u Thames | 29.12.97 |
| Wildin, Luther | 5.10 | Nuneaton | Leicester | 03.12.97 |
| Wilkinson, Luke | 6.2 | Luton | Wells | 02.12.91 |
| **Midfielders** | | | | |
| Byrom, Joel | 6.0 | Mansfield | Oswaldtwistle | 14.09.86 |
| Campbell-Ryce, Jamal | 5.6 | Carlisle | Lambeth | 06.04.83 |
| Ferry, James | 5.11 | Brenford | – | 20.04.97 |
| McKee, Mark | 5.10 | Cliftonville | – | 01.02.98 |
| Sonupe, Emmanuel | 5.11 | Kidderminster | Denmark Hill | 21.03.96 |
| Timlin, Michael | 5.8 | Southend | Lambeth | 19.03.85 |
| **Forwards** | | | | |
| Georgiou, Andronicos | 5.11 | – | Enfield | 28.10.99 |
| Kennedy, Ben | 5.10 | – | Belfast | 12.01.97 |
| Newton, Dan | 5.10 | Tamworth | Liverpool | 01.02.98 |
| Revell, Alex | 6.3 | Northampton | Cambridge | 07.07.83 |
| White, Joe | 6.0 | Dagenham | Camden | 16.01.99 |

## SWINDON TOWN

**Ground**: County Ground, County Road, Swindon SN1 2ED
**Telephone**: 0871 423 6433. **Club nickname**: Robins
**Colours**: Red and white. **Capacity**: 15,728
**Record attendance**: 32,000 v Arsenal (FA Cup 3) Jan 15, 1972

| | | | | |
|---|---|---|---|---|
| **Goalkeepers** | | | | |
| McCormick, Luke | 6.0 | Plymouth | Coventry | 15.08.83 |
| Moore, Stuart | 6.2 | Barrow | Sandown, IOW | 08.09.94 |
| Vigouroux, Lawrence | 6.4 | Liverpool | Camden | 19.11.93 |
| **Defenders** | | | | |
| Conroy, Dion | 6.0 | Chelsea | Redhill | 11.12.95 |
| Dunne, James | 5.11 | Cambridge | Farnborough | 18.09.89 |
| Knoyle, Kyle | 5.10 | West Ham | Newham | 24.09.96 |
| Lancashire, Olly | 6.1 | Shrewsbury | Basingstoke | 13.12.88 |
| McGivern, Ryan | 5.10 | Northampton | Newry | 08.01.90 |
| Robertson, Chris | 6.3 | AFC Wimbledon | Dundee | 11.10.86 |
| Romanski, Joe | – | – | Reading | 03.02.00 |
| **Midfielders** | | | | |
| Alzate, Steven | 5.11 | Brighton (loan) | Camden | 08.09.98 |

| | | | | |
|---|---|---|---|---|
| Dunne, James | 5.11 | Cambridge | Farnborough | 18.09.89 |
| Edwards, Jordan | 6.0 | Bristol City | – | 26.10.99 |
| Iandolo, Ellis | 5.10 | – | Chatham | 22.08.97 |
| McGlashan, Jermaine | 5.7 | Southend | Croydon | 14.04.88 |
| Smith, Martin | 5.10 | Coleraine | Sunderland | 02.10.95 |
| Taylor, Matt | 5.10 | Northampton | Oxford | 27.11.81 |
| Twine, Scott | 5.9 | – | Swindon | 14.07.99 |
| **Forwards** | | | | |
| Abebayo, Elijah | 6.4 | Fulham (loan) | Brent | 07.01.98 |
| Anderson, Keshi | 5.10 | Crystal Palace | Luton | 06.04.95 |
| Richards, Marc | 5.11 | Northampton | Wolverhampton | 08.07.82 |
| Woolery, Kaiyne | 5.10 | Wigan | Hackney | 11.01.95 |

## TRANMERE ROVERS

**Ground**: Prenton Park, Prenton Road, West Birkenhead CH42 9PY
**Telephone**: 0871 221 2001. **Club nickname**: Rovers
**Colours**: White. **Capacity**: 16,567
**Record attendance**: 24,424 v Stoke (FA Cup 4) Feb 5, 1972

| | | | | |
|---|---|---|---|---|
| **Goalkeepers** | | | | |
| Davies, Scott | 6.0 | Fleetwood | Blackpool | 27.02.87 |
| Pilling, Luke | 5.11 | – | Birkenhead | 25.07.97 |
| **Defenders** | | | | |
| Ellis, Mark | 6.2 | Carlisle | Plymouth | 30.09.88 |
| Caprice, Jake | 5.11 | Leyton Orient | Lambeth | 11.11.92 |
| Cole, Larnell | 5.7 | Fulham | Manchester | 09.03.93 |
| McNulty, Steve | 6.1 | Luton | Liverpool | 26.09.83 |
| Monthe, Manny | 6.1 | Forest Green | Cameroon | 26.01.95 |
| Ridehalgh, Liam | 5.10 | Huddersfild | Halifax | 20.04.91 |
| Sutton, Ritchie | 6.0 | Mansfield | Stoke | 29.04.86 |
| **Midfielders** | | | | |
| Harris, Jay | 5.7 | Wrexham | Liverpool | 15.04.87 |
| Jennings, Connor | 6.0 | Wrexham | Manchester | 29.10.91 |
| Norburn, Ollie | 6.1 | Macclesfield | Bolton | 26.10.92 |
| **Forwards** | | | | |
| Mullin, Paul | 5.10 | Swindon | Liverpool | 06.11.94 |

## YEOVIL TOWN

**Ground**: Huish Park, Lufton Way, Yeovil BA22 8YF
**Telephone**: 01935 423662. **Club nickname**: Glovers
**Colours**: Green and white. **Capacity**: 9,665
**Record attendance**: 9,527 v Leeds (Lge 1) Apr 25, 2008

| | | | | |
|---|---|---|---|---|
| **Goalkeepers** | | | | |
| Maddison, Jonny | 6.1 | Leicester | Chester-le-Street | 04.09.94 |
| Nelson, Stuart | 6.1 | Gillingham | Stroud | 17.09.81 |
| **Defenders** | | | | |
| Dickinson, Carl | 6.1 | Notts Co | Swadlincote | 31.03.87 |
| Donnellan, Shaun | 6.0 | WBA | Barnet | 16.10.96 |
| James, Tom | 5.11 | Cardiff | Cardiff | 15.04.96 |
| Mugabi, Bevis | 6.2 | Southampton | Harrow | 01.05.95 |
| Warren, Gary | 5.11 | Inverness | Bristol | 16.08.84 |
| **Midfielders** | | | | |
| Bailey, James | 6.0 | Carlisle | Bollington | 18.09.88 |

| | | | | |
|---|---|---|---|---|
| Browne, Rhys | 5.9 | Grimsby | Romford | 16.11.95 |
| D'Almeida, Sessi | 5.10 | Blackpool | Bordeaux | 20.11.95 |
| Gobern, Oscar | 6.3 | Ross Co | Birmingham | 26.01.91 |
| Gray, Jake | 5.11 | Luton | Aylesbury | 25.12.95 |
| Santos, Alefe | 5.10 | Derby | Sao Paulo, Br | 01.03.95 |
| Smith, Connor | 5.11 | Plymouth | Mullingar, Ire | 18.02.93 |
| **Forwards** | | | | |
| Fisher, Alex | 6.3 | Motherwell | Westminster | 30.06.90 |
| Sowunmi, Omar | 6.6 | Ipswich | Colchester | 07.11.95 |
| Zoko, Francois | 6.0 | Blackpool | Daloa, Iv C | 13.09.83 |

# SCOTTISH PREMIERSHIP SQUADS 2018–19

(at time of going to press)

## ABERDEEN

**Ground**: Pittodrie Stadium, Pittodrie Street, Aberdeen AB24 5QH. **Capacity**: 22,199. **Telephone**: 01224 650400. **Manager**: Derek McInnes. **Colours**: Red and white. **Nickname**: Dons
**Goalkeepers**: Joe Lewis
**Defenders**: Andrew Considine, Michael Devlin, Shaleum Logan, Scott McKenna, Mark Reynolds, Graeme Shinnie
**Midfielders**: Lewis Ferguson, Chris Forrester, Stephen Gleeson, Gary Mackay-Steven, Niall McGinn, Frank Ross, Greg Tansey
**Forwards**: Sam Cosgrove, Adam Rooney, Stevie May, Connor McLennan, Scott Wright

## CELTIC

**Ground**: Celtic Park, Glasgow G40 3RE. **Capacity**: 60,832. **Telephone**: 0871 226 1888
**Manager**: Brendan Rodgers. **Colours**: Green and white. **Nickname**: Bhoys
**Goalkeepers**: Scott Bain, Dorus de Vries, Craig Gordon
**Defenders**: Kristoffer Ajer, Dedryck Boyata, Marvin Compper, Cristian Gamboa, Jack Hendry, Mikael Lustig, Calvin Miller, Anthony Ralston, Jozo Simunovic, Kieran Tierney
**Midfielders**: Scott Allan, Kundai Benyu, Nir Bitton, Scott Brown, Ryan Christie, James Forrest, Jonny Hayes, Eboue Kouassi, Callum McGregor, Lewis Morgan, Olivier Ntcham, Tom Rogic, Scott Sinclair
**Forwards**: Moussa Dembele, Odsonne Edouard. Leigh Griffiths, Calvin Miller

## DUNDEE

**Ground**: Kilmac Stadium, Sandeman Street, Dundee DD3 7JY. **Capacity**: 11,850. **Telephone**: 01382 889966. **Manager**: Neil McCann. **Colours**: Blue and white. **Nickname**: Dark Blues
**Goalkeepers**: Calum Ferie, Jack Hamilton, Elliot Parish
**Defenders**: Steven Caulker, Daniel Jefferies, Cammy Kerr, Genseric Kusunga, Josh Meekings, Darren O'Dea, Nathan Ralph
**Midfielders**: Roarie Deacon, Glen Kamara, Jack Lambert, Kharl Madianga, Paul McGowan, Elton Ngwatala, Lewis Spence, James Vincent
**Forwards**: Marcus Haber, Matthew Henvie, Jean Alassane Mendy, Sofien Moussa, Cedwyn Scott, Craig Wighton, Randy Wolters

## HAMILTON ACADEMICAL

**Ground**: New Douglas Park, Hamilton ML3 0FT. **Capacity**: 6,000. **Telephone**: 01698 368652.
**Manager**: Martin Canning. **Colours**: Red and white. **Nickname**: Accies
**Goalkeepers**: Ryan Fulton, Alex Marshall, Gary Woods
**Defenders**: Ziggy Gordon, Alex Gogic, Aaron McGowan, Scott McMann, Alex Penny, Lennard

Sowah, Kenny van der Weg, Shaun Want
**Midfielders**: Steven Boyd, Ronan Hughes, Doug Imrie, Ross Jenkins, Sam Kelly, Darren Lyon, Darian MacKinnon, Aaron Smith, Tom Taiwo
**Forwards**: Rakish Bingham, Mason Bloomfield (loan), Ross Cunningham, Mickel Miller, Marios Ogkmpoe, Antonio Rojano, Ryan Tierney

## HEART OF MIDLOTHIAN

**Ground**: Tynecastle Stadium, McLeod Street Edinburgh EH11 2NL. **Capacity**: 20,099
**Telephone**: 0871 663 1874. **Manager**: Craig Levein. **Colours**: Maroon and white. **Nickname:** Jam Tarts
**Goalkeepers:** Kelby Mason, Zdenek Zlamal
**Defenders**: Daniel Baur, Christophe Berra, Marcus Godinho, Ben Garuccio, Chris Hamilton, Peter Haring, Aaron Hughes, Liam Smith, Michael Smith, John Souttar
**Midfielders**: Danny Amankwaa, Oliver Bozanic, Jamie Brandon, Bobby Burns, Ross Callachan, Harry Cochrane, Don Cowie, Arnaud Djoum, Ryan Edwards, Olly Lee, Malaury Martin, Anthony McDonald, Lewis Moore, Jake Mulraney, Dario Zanatta
**Forwards**: Roy Currie, Uche Ikpeazu, Kyle Lafferty, Steven MacLean, Steven Naismith (loan), Conor Sammon

## HIBERNIAN

**Ground**: Easter Road Stadium, Albion Place, Edinburgh EH7 5QG. **Capacity**: 20,451.
**Telephone**: 0131 661 2159. **Manager**: Neil Lennon. **Colours**: Green and whote. **Nickname**: Hibees
**Goalkeepers**: Adam Bogdan (loan), Ross Laidlaw, Ofir Marciano
**Defenders**: Efe Ambrose, David Gray, Paul Hanlon, Darren McGregor, Ryan Porteous, Lewis Stevenson, Steven Whittaker
**Midfielders**: Marvin Bartley, Stevie Mallan, Scott Martin, John McGinn, Fraser Murray, Vykintas Slivka, Danny Swanson
**Forwards**: Martin Boyle, Florian Kamberi, Simon Murray, Oli Shaw, Deivydas Matulevicius, Anthony Stokes

## KILMARNOCK

**Ground**: Rugby Park, Kilmarnock KA 1 2DP. **Capacity**: 18,128. **Telephone**: 01563 545300
**Manager**: Steve Clarke. **Colours**: Blue and white. **Nickname**: Killie
**Goalkeepers**: Jamie MacDonald
**Defenders**: Scott Boyd, Kirk Broadfoot, Stuart Findlay, Gordon Greer, Daniel Higgins, Stephen O'Donnell, Greg Taylor, Calum Waters
**Midfielders**: Chris Burke, Gary Dicker, Adam Frizzell, Dean Hawkshaw, Jordan Jones, Youssouf Mulumbu, Alan Power, Dom Thomas, Iain Wilson
**Forwards**: Kris Boyd, Eamonn Brophy, Lee Erwin, Greg Kiltie, Rory McKenzie, Mikael Ndjoli (loan)

## LIVINGSTON

**Ground:** Tony Macaroni Arena, Alderstone Road, Livingston EH54 7DN. **Capacity:** 10,000
**Telephone:** 01506 417000. **Manager:** Kenny Miller. **Colours:** Gold and black. **Nickname:** Livvy's Lions
**Goalkeepers:** Neil Alexander, Liam Kelly, Jordan Pettigrew, Ross Stewart
**Defenders:** Callum Crane, Declan Gallagher, Craig Halkett, Jack McMillan, Ricki Lamie, Alan Lithgow, Steven Saunders
**Midfielders:** Cameron Blues, Shaun Byrne, Nicky Cadden, Rafaele De Vita, Craig Henderson, Jack Ogilvie, Keaghan Jacobs, Scott Pittman, Scott Robinson, Craig Sibbald
**Forwards: Jack Hamilton,** Ryan Hardie (loan), Matthew Knox, Lee Miller, Kyle Sampson

## MOTHERWELL

**Ground**: Fir Park, Firpark Street, Motherwell ML1 2QN. **Capacity**: 13,742. **Telephone**: 01698 333333. **Manager**: Stephen Robinson. **Colours**: Claret and amber. **Nickname**: Well
**Goalkeepers**: Trevor Carson, Rohan Ferguson, Mark Gillespie
**Defenders**: Liam Donnelly, Charles Dunne, Liam Grimshaw, Peter Hartley, Cedric Kipre, Adam Livingstone, Barry Maguire, Andy Rose, Richard Tait, Aaron Taylor-Sinclair
**Midfielders**: Gael Bigirimana, Lee Brown, Chris Cadden, Allan Campbell, Elliott Frear, Alex Rodriguez-Gorrin, Jake Hastie, Carl McHugh, David Turnbull
**Forwards**: Ryan Bowman, Danny Johnson, Curtis Main, George Newell, Craig Tanner

## RANGERS

**Ground**: Ibrox Park, Edmison Drive, Glasgow G51 2XD. **Capacity**: 50,411
**Telephone**: 0871 702 1972. **Manager**: Steven Gerrard. **Colours**: Blue. **Nickname**: Gers
**Goalkeepers**: Jak Alnwick, Wes Foderingham, Allan McGregor
**Defenders**: Fabio Cardoso, Jon Flanaghan, Connor Goldsen, Lee Hodson, Declan John, Nikola Katic, Ross McCrorie, James Tavernier, Lee Wallace, Aidan Wilson
**Midfielders**: Scott Arfield, Daniel Candeias, Lassana Coulibaly (loan), Greg Docherty, Graham Dorrans, Ovie Ejaria (loan), Harry Forrester, Andy Halliday, Jason Holt, Ryan Jack, Jordan Rossiter
**Forwards**: Eduardo Herrera, Alfredo Morelos, Jamie Murphy, Umar Sadiq (loan), Josh Windass

## ST JOHNSTONE

**Ground**: McDiarmid Park, Crieff Road, Perth PH1 2SJ. **Capacity**: 10,673. **Telephone**: 01738 459090. **Manager**: Tommy Wright. **Colours**: Blue and white. **Nickname**: Saints
**Goalkeepers**: Zander Clark, Mark Hurst
**Defenders**: Steven Anderson, Aaron Comrie, Brian Easton, Richard Foster, Liam Gordon, Jason Kerr, Joe Shaughnessy, Scott Tanser
**Midfielders**: Blair Alston, Liam Craig, Murray Davidson, Ali McCann, Kyle McCean, Stefan Scougall, David Wotherspoon, Drey Wright
**Forwards**: Callum Hendry, Greg Hurst, Chris Kane, David McMillan, Tony Watt

## ST MIRREN

**Ground**: Paisley Stadium, Greenhill Road, Paisley PA3 IRU. **Capacity**: 8,023
**Telephone**: 0141 889 2558. **Manager**: Alan Stubbs. **Colours**: Black and white. **Nickname**: Buddies
**Goalkeepers**: Jamie Langfield, Danny Rogers (loan), Craig Samson
**Defenders**: Jack Baird, Hayden Coulson (loan), Adam Eckersley, Josh Heaton, Gary MacKenzie, Andrew McDonald, Paul McGinn
**Midfielders**: Ethan Erhahon, Ryan Flynn, Jim Kellerman, Jeff King, Jordan Kirkpatrick, Cameron MacPherson, Kyle Magennis, Stephen McGinn, Ian McShane,
**Forwards**: Cody Cooke, Danny Mullen, Cammy Smith, Ross C Stewart

# ENGLISH FIXTURES 2018–2019

**Premier League and Football League**

## Friday 3 August

**Championship**

Reading v Derby

## Saturday 4 August

**Championship**

Birmingham v Norwich
Brentford v Rotherham
Bristol City v Nottm Forest
Ipswich v Blackburn
Millwall v Middlesbrough
Preston v QPR
Sheff Utd v Swansea
WBA v Bolton
Wigan v Sheff Wed

**League One**

Accrington v Gillingham
Barnsley v Oxford
Burton v Rochdale
Coventry v Scunthorpe
Fleetwood v AFC Wimbledon
Peterborough v Bristol Rov
Portsmouth v Luton
Shrewsbury v Bradford
Southend v Doncaster
Sunderland v Charlton
Walsall v Plymouth
Wycombe v Blackpool

**League Two**

Bury v Yeovil
Cheltenham v Crawley
Crewe v Morecambe
Exeter v Carlisle
Grimsby v Forest Green
Mansfield v Newport
Northampton v Lincoln
Notts Co v Colchester
Oldham v MK Dons
Port Vale v Cambridge
Stevenage v Tranmere
Swindon v Macclesfield

## Sunday 5 August

**Championship**

Leeds v Stoke

## Monday 6 August

**Championship**

Hull v Aston Villa

## Tuesday 7 August

**Championship**

Middlesbrough v Sheff Utd
Nottm Forest v WBA

## Friday 10 August

**Premier League**

Man Utd v Leicester

## Saturday 11 August

**Premier League**

Bournemouth v Cardiff
Fulham v Crystal Palace
Huddersfield v Chelsea
Newcastle v Tottenham
Watford v Brighton
Wolves v Everton

**Championship**

Aston Villa v Wigan
Blackburn v Millwall
Bolton v Bristol City
Derby v Leeds
Middlesbrough v Birmingham
Norwich v WBA
Nottm Forest v Reading
QPR v Sheff Utd
Rotherham v Ipswich
Sheff Wed v Hull
Stoke v Brentford
Swansea v Preston

**League One**

AFC Wimbledon v Coventry
Blackpool v Portsmouth
Bradford v Barnsley
Bristol Rov v Accrington
Charlton v Shrewsbury
Doncaster v Wycombe
Gillingham v Burton
Luton v Sunderland
Oxford v Fleetwood
Plymouth v Southend
Rochdale v Peterborough
Scunthorpe v Walsall

**League Two**

Cambridge v Notts Co
Carlisle v Northampton
Colchester v Port Vale
Crawley v Stevenage
Forest Green v Oldham
Lincoln v Swindon
Macclesfield v Grimsby
MK Dons v Bury
Morecambe v Exeter
Newport v Crewe
Tranmere v Cheltenham
Yeovil v Mansfield

## Sunday 12 August

**Premier League**

Arsenal v Man City
Liverpool v West Ham
Southampton v Burnley

## Friday 17 August

**Championship**

Birmingham v Swansea

**League Two**

Notts Co v Yeovil

## Saturday 18 August

**Premier League**

Burnley v Watford
Cardiff v Newcastle
Chelsea v Arsenal
Everton v Southampton
Leicester v Wolves
Tottenham v Fulham
West Ham v Bournemouth

**Championship**

Bristol City v Middlesbrough
Hull v Blackburn
Ipswich v Aston Villa
Leeds v Rotherham
Millwall v Derby
Preston v Stoke
Reading v Bolton
Sheff Utd v Norwich
WBA v QPR
Wigan v Nottm Forest

**League One**

Accrington v Charlton
Barnsley v AFC Wimbledon
Burton v Doncaster
Coventry v Plymouth
Fleetwood v Rochdale
Peterborough v Luton
Portsmouth v Oxford
Shrewsbury v Blackpool
Southend v Bradford
Walsall v Gillingham
Wycombe v Bristol Rov

**League Two**

Bury v Forest Green
Cheltenham v Carlisle
Crewe v MK Dons
Exeter v Newport
Grimsby v Lincoln
Mansfield v Colchester

Northampton v Cambridge
Oldham v Macclesfield
Port Vale v Crawley
Stevenage v Morecambe
Swindon v Tranmere

## Sunday 19 August

**Premier League**
Brighton v Man Utd
Man City v Huddersfield

**Championship**
Brenford v Sheff Wed

**League One**
Sunderland v Scunthorpe

## Monday 20 August

**Premier League**
Crystal Palace v Liverpool

## Tuesday 21 August

**Championship**
Derby v Ipswich
QPR v Bristol City
Rotherham v Hull
Swansea v Leeds

**League One**
AFC Wimbledon v Walsall
Blackpool v Coventry
Bradford v Burton
Bristol Rov v Portsmouth
Charlton v Peterborough
Doncaster v Shrewsbury
Luton v Southend
Oxford v Accrington
Plymouth v Wycombe
Rochdale v Barnsley

**League Two**
Cambridge v Exeter
Carlisle v Port Vale
Colchester v Crewe
Crawley v Swindon
Forest Green v Stevenage
Lincoln v Bury
Macclesfield v Cheltenham
MK Dons v Grimsby
Morecambe v Northampton
Newport v Notts Co
Tranmere v Mansfield
Yeovil v Oldham

## Wednesday 22 August

**Championship**
Aston Villa v Brentford
Blackburn v Reading
Bolton v Birmingham
Norwich v Preston
Sheff Wed v Millwall
Stoke v Wigan

**League One**
Gillingham v Sunderland
Scunthorpe v Fleetwood

## Friday 24 August

**Championship**
Middlesbrough v WBA

## Saturday 25 August

**Premier League**
Arsenal v West Ham
Bournemouth v Everton
Fulham v Burnley
Huddersfield v Cardiff
Liverpool v Brighton
Southampton v Leicester
Wolves v Man City

**Championship**
Aston Villa v Reading
Blackburn v Brentford
Bolton v Sheff Utd
Derby v Preston
Norwich v Leeds
Nottm Forest v Birmingham
QPR v Wigan
Rotherham v Millwall
Sheff Wed v Ipswich
Stoke v Hull
Swansea v Bristol City

**League One**
AFC Wimbledon v Sunderland
Blackpool v Accrington
Bradford v Wycombe
Bristol Rov v Southend
Charlton v Fleetwood
Doncaster v Portsmouth
Gillingham v Coventry
Luton v Shrewsbury
Oxford v Burton
Plymouth v Peterborough
Rochdale v Walsall
Scunthorpe v Barnsley

**League Two**
Cambridge v Cheltenham
Carlisle v Crewe
Colchester v Northampton
Crawley v Bury
Forest Green v Swindon
Lincoln v Notts Co
Macclesfield v Mansfield
MK Dons v Exeter
Morecambe v Oldham
Newport v Grimsby
Tranmere v Port Vale
Yeovil v Stevenage

## Sunday 26 August

**Premier League**
Newcastle v Chelsea
Watford v Crystal Palace

## Monday 27 August

**Premier League**
Man Utd v Tottenham

## Saturday 1 September

**Premier League**
Brighton v Fulham
Burnley v Man Utd
Chelsea v Bournemouth
Crystal Palace v Southampton
Everton v Huddersfield
Leicester v Liverpool
Man City v Newcastle
West Ham v Wolves

**Championship**
Birmingham v QPR
Brentford v Nottm Forest
Hull v Derby
Leeds v Middlesbrough
Millwall v Swansea
Preston v Bolton
Reading v Sheff Wed
Sheff Utd v Aston Villa
WBA v Stoke
Wigan v Rotherham

**League One**
Accrington v Scunthorpe
Barnsley v Gillingham
Burton v AFC Wimbledon
Coventry v Rochdale
Fleetwood v Bradford
Peterborough v Doncaster
Portsmouth v Plymouth
Shrewsbury v Bristol Rov
Southend v Charlton
Sunderland v Oxford
Walsall v Blackpool
Wycombe v Luton

**League Two**
Bury v Morecambe
Cheltenham v Colchester
Crewe v Macclesfield
Exeter v Lincoln
Grimsby v Yeovil

Mansfield v Carlisle
Northampton v Tranmere
Notts Co v Forest Green
Oldham v Crawley
Port Vale v Newport
Stevenage v Cambridge
Swindon v MK Dons

## Sunday 2 September

**Premier League**
Cardiff v Arsenal
Watford v Tottenham
**Championship**
Bristol City v Blackburn
Ipswich v Norwich

## Saturday 8 September

**League One**
Accrington v Burton
Barnsley v Walsall
Blackpool v Bradford
Bristol Rov v Plymouth
Charlton v Wycombe
Doncaster v Luton
Gillingham v AFC Wimbledon
Oxford v Coventry
Portsmouth v Shrewsbury
Scunthorpe v Rochdale
Southend v Peterborough
Sunderland v Fleetwood

**League Two**
Bury v Grimsby
Cambridge v Carlisle
Crewe v Mansfield
Exeter v Notts Co
Forest Green v Port Vale
Lincoln v Crawley
Morecambe v Swindon
Northampton v Cheltenham
Oldham v Newport
Stevenage v Macclesfield
Tranmere v Colchester
Yeovil v MK Dons

## Saturday 15 September

**Premier League**
Bournemouth v Leicester
Chelsea v Cardiff
Huddersfield v Crystal Palace
Man City v Fulham
Newcastle v Arsenal
Tottenham v Liverpool
Watford v Man Utd

**Championship**
Birmingham v WBA
Blackburn v Aston Villa
Bolton v QPR
Brentford v Wigan
Bristol City v Sheff Utd
Hull v Ipswich
Millwall v Leeds
Norwich v Middlesbrough
Preston v Reading
Rotherham v Derby
Sheff Wed v Stoke
Swansea v Nottm Forest

**League One**
AFC Wimbledon v Scunthorpe
Bradford v Charlton
Burton v Sunderland
Coventry v Barnsley
Fleetwood v Accrington
Luton v Bristol Rov
Peterborough v Portsmouth
Plymouth v Blackpool
Rochdale v Gillingham
Shrewsbury v Southend
Walsall v Doncaster
Wycombe v Oxford

**League Two**
Carlisle v Tranmere
Cheltenham v Crewe
Colchester v Cambridge
Crawley v Morecambe
Grimsby v Oldham
Macclesfield v Lincoln
Mansfield v Exeter
MK Dons v Forest Green
Newport v Yeovil
Notts Co v Stevenage
Port Vale v Northampton
Swindon v Bury

## Sunday 16 September

**Premier League**
Everton v West Ham
Wolves v Burnley

## Monday 17 September

**Premier League**
Southampton v Brighton

## Tuesday 18 September

**Championship**
Aston Villa v Rotherham
Derby v Blackburn
Ipswich v Brentford
Leeds v Preston
Stoke v Swansea
WBA v Bristol City
Wigan v Hull

## Wednesday 19 September

**Championship**
Middlesbrough v Bolton
Nottm Forest v Sheff Wed
QPR v Millwall
Reading v Norwich
Sheff Utd v Birmingham

## Saturday 22 September

**Premier League**
Brighton v Tottenham
Burnley v Bournemouth
Cardiff v Man City
Crystal Palace v Newcastle
Fulham v Watford
Leicester v Huddersfield
Liverpool v Southampton
Man Utd v Wolves

**Championship**
Aston Villa v Sheff Wed
Derby v Brentford
Ipswich v Bolton
Leeds v Birmingham
Middlesbrough v Swansea
Nottm Forest v Rotherham
QPR v Norwich
Reading v Hull
Sheff Utd v Preston
Stoke v Blackburn
WBA v Millwall
Wigan v Bristol City

**League One**
Accrington v AFC Wimbledon
Barnsley v Burton
Blackpool v Luton
Bristol Rov v Coventry
Charlton v Plymouth
Doncaster v Bradford
Gillingham v Peterborough
Oxford v Walsall
Portsmouth v Wycombe
Scunthorpe v Shrewsbury
Southend v Fleetwood
Sunderland v Rochdale

**League Two**
Bury v Carlisle
Cambridge v Mansfield
Crewe v Port Vale
Exeter v Cheltenham
Forest Green v Crawley
Lincoln v MK Dons
Morecambe v Macclesfield
Northampton v Notts Co

Oldham v Colchester
Stevenage v Grimsby
Tranmere v Newport
Yeovil v Swindon

## Sunday 23 September

**Premier League**
Arsenal v Everton
West Ham v Chelsea

## Saturday 29 September

**Premier League**
Arsenal v Watford
Chelsea v Liverpool
Everton v Fulham
Huddersfield v Tottenham
Man City v Brighton
Newcastle v Leicester
West Ham v Man Utd
Wolves v Southampton

**Championship**
Birmingham v Ipswich
Blackburn v Nottm Forest
Bolton v Derby
Brentford v Reading
Bristol City v Aston Villa
Hull v Middlesbrough
Millwall v Sheff Utd
Norwich v Wigan
Preston v WBA
Rotherham v Stoke
Sheff Wed v Leeds
Swansea v QPR

**League One**
AFC Wimbledon v Oxford
Bradford v Bristol Rov
Burton v Scunthorpe
Coventry v Sunderland
Fleetwood v Barnsley
Luton v Charlton
Peterborough v Blackpool
Plymouth v Doncaster
Rochdale v Portsmouth
Shrewsbury v Gillingham
Walsall v Accrington
Wycombe v Southend

**League Two**
Carlisle v Stevenage
Cheltenham v Lincoln
Colchester v Bury
Crawley v Yeovil
Grimsby v Morecambe
Macclesfield v Forest Green
Mansfield v Northampton
MK Dons v Tranmere
Newport v Cambridge
Notts Co v Crewe
Port Vale v Exeter
Swindon v Oldham

## Sunday 30 September

**Premier League**
Cardiff v Bunley

## Monday 1 October

**Premier League**
Bournemouth v Crystal Palace

## Tuesday 2 October

**Championship**
Aston Villa v Preston
Brentford v Birmingham
Hull v Leeds
Ipswich v Middlesbrough
Reading v QPR
Stoke v Bolton
Wigan v Swansea

**League One**
Accrington v Doncaster
AFC Wimbledon v Bradford
Barnsley v Plymouth
Burton v Southend
Coventry v Portsmouth
Fleetwood v Wycombe
Gillingham v Blackpool
Oxford v Luton
Rochdale v Bristol Rov
Scunthorpe v Charlton
Sunderland v Peterborough
Walsall v Shrewsbury

**League Two**
Cambridge v Forest Green
Carlisle v Grimsby
Cheltenham v Morecambe
Colchester v Yeovil
Crewe v Swindon
Exeter v Stevenage
Mansfield v Oldham
Newport v Macclesfield
Northampton v Bury
Notts Co v Crawley
Port Vale v MK Dons
Tranmere v Lincoln

## Wednesday 3 October

**Championship**
Blackburn v Sheff Utd
Derby v Norwich
Nottm Forest v Millwall
Rotherham v Bristol City
Sheff Wed v WBA

## Saturday 6 October

**Premier League**
Brighton v West Ham
Burnley v Huddersfield
Crystal Palace v Wolves
Fulham v Arsenal
Leicester v Everton
Liverpool v Man City
Man Utd v Newcastle
Southampton v Chelsea
Tottenham v Cardiff
Watford v Bournemouth

**Championship**
Birmingham v Rotherham
Bolton v Blackburn
Leeds v Brentford
Middlesbrough v Nottm Forest
Millwall v Aston Villa
Norwich v Stoke
Preston v Wigan
QPR v Derby
Sheff Utd v Hull
Swansea v Ipswich
WBA v Reading

**League One**
Blackpool v Rochdale
Bradford v Sunderland
Bristol Rov v Walsall
Charlton v Coventry
Doncaster v Fleetwood
Luton v Scunthorpe
Peterborough v Barnsley
Plymouth v AFC Wimbledon
Portsmouth v Gillingham
Shrewsbury v Accrington
Southend v Oxford
Wycombe v Burton

**League Two**
Bury v Mansfield
Crawley v Cambridge
Forest Green v Newport
Grimsby v Port Vale
Lincoln v Crewe
Macclesfield v Notts Co
MK Dons v Cheltenham
Morecambe v Tranmere
Oldham v Carlisle
Stevenage v Colchester
Swindon v Northampton
Yeovil v Exeter

## Sunday 7 October
**Championship**
Bristol City v Sheff Wed

## Friday 12 October
**League Two**
Tranmere v Macclesfield

## Saturday 13 October
**League One**
Accrington v Bradford
AFC Wimbledon v Portsmouth
Barnsley v Luton
Burton v Bristol Rov
Coventry v Wycombe
Fleetwood v Shrewsbury
Gillingham v Southend
Oxford v Plymouth
Rochdale v Doncaster
Scunthorpe v Peterborough
Sunderland v Blackpool
Walsall v Charlton

**League Two**
Cambridge v MK Dons
Carlisle v Morecambe
Cheltenham v Yeovil
Colchester v Crawley
Crewe v Bury
Exeter v Swindon
Mansfield v Grimsby
Newport v Stevenage
Northampton v Forest Green
Notts Co v Oldham
Port Vale v Lincoln

## Saturday 20 October
**Premier League**
Arsenal v Leicester
Bournemouth v Southampton
Cardiff v Fulham
Chelsea v Man Utd
Everton v Crystal Palace
Huddersfield v Liverpool
Man City v Burnley
Newcastle v Brighton
West Ham v Tottenham
Wolves v Watford

**Championship**
Aston Villa v Swansea
Blackburn v Leeds
Brentford v Bristol City
Derby v Sheff Utd
Hull v Preston
Ipswich v QPR
Nottm Forest v Norwich
Reading v Millwall
Rotherham v Bolton
Sheff Wed v Middlesbrough
Stoke v Birmingham
Wigan v WBA

**League One**
Blackpool v AFC Wimbledon
Bradford v Rochdale
Bristol Rov v Oxford
Charlton v Barnsley
Doncaster v Gillingham
Luton v Walsall
Peterborough v Accrington
Plymouth v Burton
Portsmouth v Fleetwood
Shrewsbury v Sunderland
Southend v Coventry
Wycombe v Scunthorpe

**League Two**
Bury v Notts Co
Crawley v Newport
Forest Green v Cheltenham
Grimsby v Exeter
Lincoln v Cambridge
Macclesfield v Carlisle
MK Dons v Northampton
Morecambe v Colchester
Oldham v Port Vale
Stevenage v Crewe
Swindon v Mansfield
Yeovil v Tranmere

## Tuesday 23 October
**Championship**
Birmingham v Reading
Middlesbrough v Rotherham
Millwall v Wigan
Norwich v Aston Villa
QPR v Sheff Wed
Sheff Utd v Stoke
Swansea v Blackburn

**League One**
Blackpool v Scunthorpe
Bradford v Coventry
Bristol Rov v AFC Wimbledon
Charlton v Oxford
Doncaster v Sunderland
Luton v Accrington
Peterborough v Fleetwood
Plymouth v Gillingham
Portsmouth v Burton
Shrewsbury v Barnsley
Southend v Walsall
Wycombe v Rochdale

**League Two**
Bury v Newport
Crawley v Exeter
Forest Green v Tranmere
Grimsby v Colchester
Lincoln v Carlisle
Macclesfield v Northampton
MK Dons v Notts Co
Morecambe v Mansfield
Oldham v Cheltenham
Stevenage v Port Vale
Swindon v Cambridge
Yeovil v Crewe

## Wednesday 24 October
**Championship**
Bolton v Nottm Forest
Bristol City v Hull
Leeds v Ipswich
Preston v Brentford
WBA v Derby

## Saturday 27 October
**Premier League**
Brighton v Wolves
Burnley v Chelsea
Crystal Palace v Arsenal
Fulham v Bournemouth
Leicester v West Ham
Liverpool v Cardiff
Man Utd v Everton
Southampton v Newcastle
Tottenham v Man City
Watford v Huddersfield

**Championship**
Birmingham v Sheff Wed
Bolton v Hull
Bristol City v Stoke
Leeds v Nottm Forest
Middlesbrough v Derby
Millwall v Ipswich
Norwich v Brentford
Preston v Rotherham
QPR v Aston Villa
Sheff Utd v Wigan
Swansea v Reading
WBA v Blackburn

**League One**
Accrington v Portsmouth
AFC Wimbledon v Luton
Barnsley v Bristol Rov
Burton v Peterborough
Coventry v Doncaster
Fleetwood v Blackpool
Gillingham v Bradford

Oxford v Shrewsbury
Rochdale v Charlton
Scunthorpe v Plymouth
Sunderland v Southend
Walsall v Wycombe

**League Two**
Cambridge v Macclesfield
Carlisle v Yeovil
Cheltenham v Stevenage
Colchester v Lincoln
Crewe v Grimsby
Exeter v Forest Green
Mansfield v MK Dons
Newport v Morecambe
Northampton v Oldham
Notts Co v Swindon
Port Vale v Bury
Tranmere v Crawley

## Saturday 3 November
**Premier League**
Arsenal v Liverpool
Bournemouth v Man Utd
Cardiff v Leicester
Chelsea v Crystal Palace
Everton v Brighton
Huddersfield v Fulham
Man City v Southampton
Newcastle v Watford
West Ham v Burnley
Wolves v Tottenham

**Championship**
Aston Villa v Bolton
Blackburn v QPR
Brentford v Millwall
Derby v Birmingham
Hull v WBA
Ipswich v Preston
Nottm Forest v Sheff Utd
Reading v Bristol City
Rotherham v Swansea
Sheff Wed v Norwich
Stoke v Middlesbrough
Wigan v Leeds

**League One**
AFC Wimbledon v Shrewsbury
Barnsley v Southend
Blackpool v Bristol Rov
Bradford v Portsmouth
Charlton v Doncaster
Coventry v Accrington
Gillingham v Fleetwood
Plymouth v Sunderland
Rochdale v Luton
Scunthorpe v Oxford
Walsall v Burton
Wycombe v Peterborough

**League Two**
Cambridge v Grimsby
Carlisle v Newport
Cheltenham v Mansfield
Colchester v Swindon
Crawley v MK Dons
Lincoln v Forest Green
Macclesfield v Bury
Morecambe v Yeovil
Northampton v Crewe
Port Vale v Notts Co
Stevenage v Oldham
Tranmere v Exeter

## Saturday 10 November
**Premier League**
Arsenal v Wolves
Cardiff v Brighton
Chelsea v Everton
Crystal Palace v Tottenham
Huddersfield v West Ham
Leicester v Burnley
Liverpool v Fulham
Man City v Man Utd
Newcastle v Bournemouth
Southampton v Watford

**Championship**
Birmingham v Hull
Blackburn v Rotherham
Bolton v Swansea
Bristol City v Preston
Derby v Aston Villa
Middlesbrough v Wigan
Norwich v Millwall
Nottm Forest v Stoke
QPR v Brentford
Reading v Ipswich
Sheff Utd v Sheff Wed
WBA v Leeds

## Saturday 17 November
**League One**
Accrington v Barnsley
Bristol Rov v Scunthorpe
Burton v Coventry
Doncaster v AFC Wimbledon
Fleetwood v Walsall
Luton v Plymouth
Oxford v Gillingham
Peterborough v Bradford
Portsmouth v Charlton
Shrewsbury v Rochdale
Southend v Blackpool
Sunderland v Wycombe

**League Two**
Bury v Stevenage
Crewe v Tranmere
Exeter v Northampton
Forest Green v Morecambe
Grimsby v Crawley
Mansfield v Port Vale
MK Dons v Macclesfield
Newport v Colchester
Notts Co v Cheltenham
Oldham v Cambridge
Swindon v Carlisle
Yeovil v Lincoln

## Saturday 24 November
**Premier League**
Bournemouth v Arsenal
Brighton v Leicester
Burnley v Newcastle
Everton v Cardiff
Fulham v Southampton
Man Utd v Crystal Palace
Tottenham v Chelsea
Watford v Liverpool
West Ham v Man City
Wolves v Huddersfield

**Championship**
Brentford v Middlesbrough
Hull v Nottm Forest
Ipswich v WBA
Leeds v Bristol City
Millwall v Bolton
Preston v Blackburn
Rotherham v Sheff Utd
Sheff Wed v Derby
Stoke v QPR
Swansea v Norwich
Wigan v Reading

**League One**
AFC Wimbledon v Southend
Barnsley v Doncaster
Blackpool v Burton
Bradford v Oxford
Charlton v Bristol Rov
Coventry v Peterborough
Gillingham v Luton
Plymouth v Fleetwood
Rochdale v Accrington
Scunthorpe v Portsmouth
Walsall v Sunderland
Wycombe v Shrewsbury

**League Two**
Cambridge v Bury
Carlisle v Forest Green
Cheltenham v Newport
Colchester v Exeter
Crawley v Crewe
Lincoln v Mansfield
Macclesfield v Yeovil
Morecambe v Notts Co
Northampton v Grimsby
Port Vale v Swindon
Stevenage v MK Dons
Tranmere v Oldham

## Sunday 25 November

**Championship**
Aston Villa v Birmingham

## Tuesday 27 November

**Championship**
Brentford v Sheff Utd
Hull v Norwich
Leeds v Reading
Preston v Middlesbrough
Rotherham v QPR
Sheff Wed v Bolton

**League One**
Accrington v Wycombe
Bristol Rov v Gillingham
Burton v Charlton
Doncaster v Blackpool
Fleetwood v Coventry
Luton v Bradford
Oxford v Rochdale
Peterborough v AFC Wimbledon
Portsmouth v Walsall
Shrewsbury v Plymouth
Southend v Scunthorpe
Sunderland v Barnsley

**League Two**
Bury v Cheltenham
Crewe v Cambridge
Exeter v Macclesfield
Forest Green v Colchester
Grimsby v Tranmere
Mansfield v Crawley
MK Dons v Morecambe
Newport v Northampton
Notts Co v Carlisle
Oldham v Lincoln
Swindon v Stevenage
Yeovil v Port Vale

## Wednesday 28 November

**Championship**
Aston Villa v Nottm Forest
Ipswich v Bristol City
Millwall v Birmingham
Stoke v Derby
Swansea v WBA
Wigan v Blackburn

## Saturday 1 December

**Premier League**
Arsenal v Tottenham
Cardiff v Wolves
Chelsea v Fulham
Crystal Palace v Burnley
Huddersfield v Brighton
Leicester v Watford
Liverpool v Everton
Man City v Bournemouth
Newcastle v West Ham
Southampton v Man Utd

**Championship**
Birmingham v Preston
Blackburn v Sheff Wed
Bolton v Wigan
Derby v Swansea
Middlesbrough v Aston Villa
Norwich v Rotherham
Nottm Forest v Ipswich
QPR v Hull
Reading v Stoke
Sheff Utd v Leeds
WBA v Brentford

## Sunday 2 December

**Championship**
Bristol City v Millwall

## Tuesday 4 December

**Premier League**
Bournemouth v Huddersfield
Brighton v Crystal Palace
Burnley v Liverpool
Fulham v Leicester
Man Utd v Arsenal
Watford v Man City
West Ham v Cardiff
Wolves v Chelsea

## Wednesday 5 December

**Premier League**
Everton v Newcastle
Tottenham v Southampton

## Saturday 8 December

**Premier League**
Arsenal v Huddersfield
Bournemouth v Liverpool
Burnley v Brighton
Cardiff v Southampton
Chelsea v Man City
Everton v Watford
Leicester v Tottenham
Man Utd v Fulham
Newcastle v Wolves
West Ham v Crystal Palace

**Championship**
Birmingham v Bristol City
Brentford v Swansea
Leeds v QPR
Middlesbrough v Blackburn
Millwall v Hull
Norwich v Bolton
Nottm Forest v Preston
Reading v Sheff Utd
Sheff Wed v Rotherham
Stoke v Ipswich
WBA v Aston Villa
Wigan v Derby

**League One**
Accrington v Sunderland
AFC Wimbledon v Rochdale
Blackpool v Charlton
Bristol Rov v Doncaster
Burton v Shrewsbury
Luton v Fleetwood
Peterborough v Oxford
Plymouth v Bradford
Portsmouth v Southend
Scunthorpe v Gillingham
Walsall v Coventry
Wycombe v Barnsley

**League Two**
Bury v Exeter
Cheltenham v Grimsby
Colchester v Macclesfield
Crawley v Northampton
Crewe v Oldham
Mansfield v Notts Co
MK Dons v Carlisle
Morecambe v Port Vale
Stevenage v Lincoln
Swindon v Newport
Tranmere v Cambridge
Yeovil v Forest Green

## Saturday 15 December

### Premier League
Brighton v Chelsea
Crystal Palace v Leicester
Fulham v West Ham
Huddersfield v Newcastle
Liverpool v Man Utd
Man City v Everton
Southampton v Arsenal
Tottenham v Burnley
Watford v Cardiff
Wolves v Bournemouth

### Championship
Aston Villa v Stoke
Blackburn v Birmingham
Bolton v Leeds
Bristol City v Norwich
Derby v Nottm Forest
Hull v Brentford
Ipswich v Wigan
Preston v Millwall
QPR v Middlesbrough
Rotherham v Reading
Sheff Utd v WBA
Swansea v Sheff Wed

### League One
Barnsley v Portsmouth
Bradford v Walsall
Charlton v AFC Wimbledon
Coventry v Luton
Doncaster v Scunthorpe
Fleetwood v Burton
Gillingham v Wycombe
Oxford v Blackpool
Rochdale v Plymouth
Shrewsbury v Peterborough
Southend v Accrington
Sunderland v Bristol Rov

### League Two
Cambridge v Yeovil
Carlisle v Colchester
Exeter v Crewe
Forest Green v Mansfield
Grimsby v Swindon
Lincoln v Morecambe
Macclesfield v Crawley
Newport v MK Dons
Northampton v Stevenage
Notts Co v Tranmere
Oldham v Bury
Port Vale v Cheltenham

## Saturday 22 December

### Premier League
Arsenal v Burnley
Bournemouth v Brighton
Cardiff v Man Utd
Chelsea v Leicester
Everton v Tottenham
Huddersfield v Southampton
Man City v Crystal Palace
Newcastle v Fulham
West Ham v Watford
Wolves v Liverpool

### Championship
Aston Villa v Leeds
Blackburn v Norwich
Brentford v Bolton
Derby v Bristol City
Hull v Swansea
Ipswich v Sheff Utd
Nottm Forest v QPR
Reading v Middlesbrough
Rotherham v WBA
Sheff Wed v Preston
Stoke v Millwall
Wigan v Birmingham

### League One
Blackpool v Barnsley
Bradford v Scunthorpe
Bristol Rov v Fleetwood
Charlton v Gillingham
Doncaster v Oxford
Luton v Burton
Peterborough v Walsall
Plymouth v Accrington
Portsmouth v Sunderland
Shrewsbury v Coventry
Southend v Rochdale
Wycombe v AFC Wimbledon

### League Two
Bury v Tranmere
Crawley v Carlisle
Forest Green v Crewe
Grimsby v Notts Co
Lincoln v Newport
Macclesfield v Port Vale
MK Dons v Colchester
Morecambe v Cambridge
Oldham v Exeter
Stevenage v Mansfield
Swindon v Cheltenham
Yeovil v Northampton

## Wednesday 26 December

### Premier League
Brighton v Arsenal
Burnley v Everton
Crystal Palace v Cardiff
Fulham v Wolves
Leicester v Man City
Liverpool v Newcastle
Man Utd v Huddersfield
Southampton v West Ham
Tottenham v Bournemouth
Watford v Chelsea

### Championship
Birmingham v Stoke
Bolton v Rotherham
Bristol City v Brentford
Leeds v Blackburn
Middlesbrough v Sheff Wed
Millwall v Reading
Norwich v Nottm Forest
Preston v Hull
QPR v Ipswich
Sheff Utd v Derby
Swansea v Aston Villa
WBA v Wigan

### League One
Accrington v Shrewsbury
AFC Wimbledon v Plymouth
Barnsley v Peterborough
Burton v Wycombe
Coventry v Charlton
Fleetwood v Doncaster
Gillingham v Portsmouth
Oxford v Southend
Rochdale v Blackpool
Scunthorpe v Luton
Sunderland v Bradford
Walsall v Bristol Rov

### League Two
Cambridge v Crawley
Carlisle v Oldham
Cheltenham v MK Dons
Colchester v Stevenage
Crewe v Lincoln
Exeter v Yeovil
Mansfield v Bury
Newport v Forest Green
Northampton v Swindon
Notts Co v Macclesfield
Port Vale v Grimsby
Tranmere v Morecambe

## Saturday 29 December

**Premier League**

Brighton v Everton
Burnley v West Ham
Crystal Palace v Chelsea
Fulham v Huddersfield
Leicester v Cardiff
Liverpool v Arsenal
Man Utd v Bournemouth
Southampton v Man City
Tottenham v Wolves
Watford v Newcastle

**Championship**

Birmingham v Brentford
Bolton v Stoke
Bristol City v Rotherham
Leeds v Hull
Middlesbrough v Ipswich
Millwall v Nottm Forest
Norwich v Derby
Preston v Aston Villa
QPR v Reading
Sheff Utd v Blackburn
Swansea v Wigan
WBA v Sheff Wed

**League One**

Accrington v Peterborough
AFC Wimbledon v Blackpool
Barnsley v Charlton
Burton v Plymouth
Coventry v Southend
Fleetwood v Portsmouth
Gillingham v Doncaster
Oxford v Bristol Rov
Rochdale v Bradford
Scunthorpe v Wycombe
Sunderland v Shrewsbury
Walsall v Luton

**League Two**

Cambridge v Lincoln
Carlisle v Macclesfield
Cheltenham v Forest Green
Colchester v Morecambe
Crewe v Stevenage
Exeter v Grimsby
Mansfield v Swindon
Newport v Crawley
Northampton v MK Dons
Notts Co v Bury
Port Vale v Oldham
Tranmere v Yeovil

## Tuesday 1 January

**Premier League**

Arsenal v Fulham
Bournemouth v Watford
Cardiff v Tottenham
Chelsea v Southampton
Everton v Leicester
Huddersfield v Burnley
Man City v Liverpool
Newcastle v Man Utd
West Ham v Brighton
Wolves v Crystal Palace

**Championship**

Aston Villa v QPR
Blackburn v WBA
Brentford v Norwich
Derby v Middlesbrough
Hull v Bolton
Ipswich v Millwall
Nottm Forest v Leeds
Reading v Swansea
Rotherham v Preston
Sheff Wed v Birmingham
Stoke v Bristol City
Wigan v Sheff Utd

**League One**

Blackpool v Sunderland
Bradford v Accrington
Bristol Rov v Burton
Charlton v Walsall
Doncaster v Rochdale
Luton v Barnsley
Peterborough v Scunthorpe
Plymouth v Oxford
Portsmouth v AFC Wimbledon
Shrewsbury v Fleetwood
Southend v Gillingham
Wycombe v Coventry

**League Two**

Bury v Crewe
Crawley v Colchester
Forest Green v Northampton
Grimsby v Mansfield
Lincoln V Port Vale
Macclesfield v Tranmere
MK Dons v Cambridge
Morecambe v Carlisle
Oldham v Notts Co
Stevenage v Newport
Swindon v Exeter
Yeovil v Cheltenham

## Saturday 5 January

**League One**

AFC Wimbledon v Fleetwood
Blackpool v Wycombe
Bradford v Shrewsbury
Bristol Rov v Peterborough
Charlton v Sunderland
Doncaster v Southend
Gillingham v Accrington
Luton v Portsmouth
Oxford v Barnsley
Plymouth v Walsall
Rochdale v Burton
Scunthorpe v Coventry

**League Two**

Cambridge v Stevenage
Carlisle v Mansfield
Colchester v Notts Co
Crawley v Cheltenham
Forest Green v Grimsby
Lincoln v Exeter
Macclesfield v Swindon
MK Dons v Oldham
Morecambe v Crewe
Newport v Port Vale
Tranmere v Northampton
Yeovil v Bury

## Saturday 12 January

**Premier League**

Brighton v Liverpool
Burnley v Fulham
Cardiff v Huddersfield
Chelsea v Newcastle
Crystal Palace v Watford
Everton v Bournemouth
Leicester v Southampton
Man City v Wolves
Tottenham v Man Utd
West Ham v Arsenal

**Championship**

Birmingham v Middlesbrough
Brentford v Stoke
Bristol City v Bolton
Hull v Sheff Wed
Ipswich v Rotherham
Leeds v Derby
Millwall v Blackburn
Preston v Swansea
Reading v Nottm Forest
Sheff Utd v QPR
WBA v Norwich
Wigan v Aston Villa

**League One**
Accrington v Bristol Rov
Barnsley v Bradford
Burton v Gillingham
Coventry v AFC Wimbledon
Fleetwood v Oxford
Peterborough v Rochdale
Portsmouth v Blackpool
Shrewsbury v Charlton
Southend v Plymouth
Sunderland v Luton
Walsall v Scunthorpe
Wycombe v Doncaster

**League Two**
Bury v MK Dons
Cheltenham v Tranmere
Crewe v Newport
Exeter v Morecambe
Grimsby v Macclesfield
Mansfield v Yeovil
Northampton v Carlisle
Notts Co v Cambridge
Oldham v Forest Green
Port Vale v Colchester
Stevenage v Crawley
Swindon v Lincoln

## Saturday 19 January

**Premier League**
Arsenal v Chelsea
Bournemouth v West Ham
Fulham v Tottenham
Huddersfield v Man City
Liverpool v Crystal Palace
Man Utd v Brighton
Newcastle v Cardiff
Southampton v Everton
Watford v Burnley
Wolves v Leicester

**Championship**
Aston Villa v Hull
Blackburn v Ipswich
Bolton v WBA
Derby v Reading
Middlesbrough v Millwall
Norwich v Birmingham
Nottm Forest v Bristol City
QPR v Preston
Rotherham v Brentford
Sheff Wed v Wigan
Stoke v Leeds
Swansea v Sheff Utd

**League One**
AFC Wimbledon v Barnsley
Blackpool v Shrewsbury
Bradford v Southend
Bristol Rov v Wycombe
Charlton v Accrington
Doncaster v Burton
Gillingham v Walsall
Luton v Peterborough
Oxford v Portsmouth
Plymouth v Coventry
Rochdale v Fleetwood
Scunthorpe v Sunderland

**League Two**
Cambridge v Northampton
Carlisle v Cheltenham
Colchester v Mansfield
Crawley v Port Vale
Forest Green v Bury
Lincoln v Grimsby
Macclesfield v Oldham
MK Dons v Crewe
Morecambe v Stevenage
Newport v Exeter
Tranmere v Swindon
Yeovil v Notts Co

## Saturday 26 January

**Championship**
Aston Villa v Ipswich
Blackburn v Hull
Bolton v Reading
Derby v Millwall
Middlesbrough v Bristol City
Norwich v Sheff Utd
Nottm Forest v Wigan
QPR v WBA
Rotherham v Leeds
Sheff Wed v Brentford
Stoke v Preston
Swansea v Birmingham

**League One**
Accrington v Oxford
Barnsley v Rochdale
Burton v Bradford
Coventry v Blackpool
Fleetwood v Scunthorpe
Peterborough v Charlton
Portsmouth v Bristol Rov
Shrewsbury v Doncaster
Southend v Luton
Sunderland v Gillingham
Walsall v AFC Wimbledon
Wycombe v Plymouth

**League Two**
Bury v Lincoln
Cheltenham v Macclesfield
Crewe v Colchester
Exeter v Cambridge
Grimsby v MK Dons
Mansfield v Tranmere
Northampton v Morecambe
Notts Co v Newport
Oldham v Yeovil
Port Vale v Carlisle
Stevenage v Forest Green
Swindon v Crawley

## Tuesday 29 January

**Premier League**
Arsenal v Cardiff
Bournemouth v Chelsea
Fulham v Brighton
Huddersfield v Everton
Man Utd v Burnley
Wolves v West Ham

## Wednesday 30 January

**Premier League**
Liverpool v Leicester
Newcastle v Man City
Southampton v Crystal Palace
Tottenham v Watford

## Saturday 2 February

**Premier League**
Brighton v Watford
Burnley v Southampton
Cardiff v Bournemouth
Chelsea v Huddersfield
Crystal Palace v Fulham
Everton v Wolves
Leicester v Man Utd
Man City v Arsenal
Tottenham v Newcastle
West Ham v Liverpool

**Championship**
Birmingham v Nottm Forest
Brentford v Blackburn
Bristol City v Swansea
Hull v Stoke
Ipswich v Sheff Wed
Leeds v Norwich
Millwall v Rotherham
Preston v Derby
Reading v Aston Villa
Sheff Utd v Bolton
WBA v Middlesbrough
Wigan v QPR

**League One**
Accrington v Blackpool
Barnsley v Scunthorpe
Burton v Oxford
Coventry v Gillingham
Fleetwood v Charlton

Peterborough v Plymouth
Portsmouth v Doncaster
Shrewsbury v Luton
Southend v Bristol Rov
Sunderland v AFC Wimbledon
Walsall v Rochdale
Wycombe v Bradford

**League Two**
Bury v Crawley
Cheltenham v Cambridge
Crewe v Carlisle
Exeter v MK Dons
Grimsby v Newport
Mansfield v Macclesfield
Northampton v Colchester
Notts Co v Lincoln
Oldham v Morecambe
Port Vale v Tranmere
Stevenage v Yeovil
Swindon v Forest Green

## Saturday 9 February
**Premier League**
Brighton v Burnley
Crystal Palace v West Ham
Fulham v Man Utd
Huddersfield v Arsenal
Liverpool v Bournemouth
Man City v Chelsea
Southampton v Cardiff
Tottenham v Leicester
Watford v Everton
Wolves v Newcastle

**Championship**
Aston Villa v Sheff Utd
Blackburn v Bristol City
Bolton v Preston
Derby v Hull
Middlesbrough v Leeds
Nottm Forest v Brentford
QPR v Birmingham
Rotherham v Wigan
Sheff Wed v Reading
Stoke v WBA
Swansea v Millwall

**League One**
AFC Wimbledon v Burton
Blackpool v Walsall
Bradford v Fleetwood
Bristol Rov v Shrewsbury
Charlton v Southend
Doncaster v Peterborough
Gillingham v Barnsley
Luton v Wycombe
Oxford v Sunderland
Plymouth v Portsmouth
Rochdale v Coventry
Scunthorpe v Accrington

**League Two**
Cambridge v Port Vale
Carlisle v Exeter
Colchester v Cheltenham
Crawley v Oldham
Forest Green v Notts Co
Lincoln v Northampton
Macclesfield v Crewe
MK Dons v Swindon
Morecambe v Bury
Newport v Mansfield
Tranmere v Stevenage
Yeovil v Grimsby

## Sunday 10 February
**Championship**
Norwich v Ipswich

## Tuesday 12 February
**Championship**
Birmingham v Bolton
Hull v Rotherham
Millwall v Sheff Wed
WBA v Nottm Forest

## Wednesday 13 February
**Championship**
Brentford v Aston Villa
Bristol City v QPR
Ipswich v Derby
Leeds v Swansea
Preston v Norwich
Reading v Blackburn
Sheff Utd v Middlesbrough
Wigan v Stoke

## Saturday 16 February
**Championship**
Aston Villa v WBA
Blackburn v Middlesbrough
Bolton v Norwich
Bristol City v Birmingham
Derby v Wigan
Hull v Millwall
Ipswich v Stoke
Preston v Nottm Forest
QPR v Leeds
Rotherham v Sheff Wed
Sheff Utd v Reading
Swansea v Brentford

**League One**
Barnsley v Wycombe
Bradford v Plymouth
Charlton v Blackpool
Coventry v Walsall
Doncaster v Bristol Rov
Fleetwood v Luton
Gillingham v Scunthorpe
Oxford v Peterborough
Rochdale v AFC Wimbledon
Shrewsbury v Burton
Southend v Portsmouth
Sunderland v Accrington

**League Two**
Cambridge v Tranmere
Carlisle v MK Dons
Exeter v Bury
Forest Green v Yeovil
Grimsby v Cheltenham
Lincoln v Stevenage
Macclesfield v Colchester
Newport v Swindon
Northampton v Crawley
Notts Co v Mansfield
Oldham v Crewe
Port Vale v Morecambe

## Saturday 23 February
**Premier League**
Arsenal v Southampton
Bournemouth v Wolves
Burnley v Tottenham
Cardiff v Watford
Chelsea v Brighton
Everton v Man City
Leicester v Crystal Palace
Man Utd v Liverpool
Newcastle v Huddersfield
West Ham v Fulham

**Championship**
Birmingham v Blackburn
Brentford v Hull
Leeds v Bolton
Middlesbrough v QPR
Millwall v Preston
Norwich v Bristol City
Nottm Forest v Derby
Reading v Rotherham
Sheff Wed v Swansea
Stoke v Aston Villa
WBA v Sheff Utd
Wigan v Ipswich

**League One**
Accrington v Southend
AFC Wimbledon v Charlton
Blackpool v Oxford
Bristol Rov v Sunderland

Burton v Fleetwood
Luton v Coventry
Peterborough v Shrewsbury
Plymouth v Rochdale
Portsmouth v Barnsley
Scunthorpe v Doncaster
Walsall v Bradford
Wycombe v Gillingham

**League Two**
Bury v Oldham
Cheltenham v Port Vale
Colchester v Carlisle
Crawley v Macclesfield
Crewe v Exeter
Mansfield v Forest Green
MK Dons v Newport
Morecambe v Lincoln
Stevenage v Northampton
Swindon v Grimsby
Tranmere v Notts Co
Yeovil v Cambridge

## Tuesday 26 February

**Premier League**
Arsenal v Bournemouth
Cardiff v Everton
Crystal Palace v Man Utd
Huddersfield v Wolves
Leicester v Brighton

## Wednesday 27 February

**Premier League**
Chelsea v Tottenham
Liverpool v Watford
Man City v West Ham
Newcastle v Burnley
Southampton v Fulham

## Saturday 2 March

**Premier League**
Bournemouth v Man City
Brighton v Huddersfield
Burnley v Crystal Palace
Everton v Liverpool
Fulham v Chelsea
Man Utd v Southampton
Tottenham v Arsenal
Watford v Leicester
West Ham v Newcastle
Wolves v Cardiff

**Championship**
Aston Villa v Derby
Brentford v QPR
Hull v Birmingham
Ipswich v Reading
Leeds v WBA
Millwall v Norwich
Preston v Bristol City
Rotherham v Blackburn
Sheff Wed v Sheff Utd
Stoke v Nottm Forest
Swansea v Bolton
Wigan v Middlesbrough

**League One**
Accrington v Coventry
Bristol Rov v Blackpool
Burton v Walsall
Doncaster v Charlton
Fleetwood v Gillingham
Luton v Rochdale
Oxford v Scunthorpe
Peterborough v Wycombe
Portsmouth v Bradford
Shrewsbury v AFC Wimbledon
Southend v Barnsley
Sunderland v Plymouth

**League Two**
Bury v Macclesfield
Crewe v Northampton
Exeter v Tranmere
Forest Green v Lincoln
Grimsby v Cambridge
Mansfield v Cheltenham
MK Dons v Crawley
Newport v Carlisle
Notts Co v Port Vale
Oldham v Stevenage
Swindon v Colchester
Yeovil v Morecambe

## Tuesday 5 March

**League Two**
Cheltenham v Bury

## Friday 8 March

**League Two**
Lincoln v Yeovil
Tranmere v Crewe

## Saturday 9 March

**Premier League**
Arsenal v Man Utd
Cardiff v West Ham
Chelsea v Wolves
Crystal Palace v Brighton
Huddersfield v Bournemouth
Leicester v Fulham
Liverpool v Burnley
Man City v Watford
Newcastle v Everton
Southampton v Tottenham

**Championship**
Blackburn v Preston
Bolton v Millwall
Bristol City v Leeds
Derby v Sheff Wed
Middlesbrough v Brentford
Norwich v Swansea
Nottm Forest v Hull
QPR v Stoke
Reading v Wigan
Sheff Utd v Rotherham
WBA v Ipswich

**League One**
AFC Wimbledon v Doncaster
Barnsley v Accrington
Blackpool v Southend
Bradford v Peterborough
Charlton v Portsmouth
Coventry v Burton
Gillingham v Oxford
Plymouth v Luton
Rochdale v Shrewsbury
Scunthorpe v Bristol Rov
Walsall v Fleetwood
Wycombe v Sunderland

**League Two**
Cambridge v Oldham
Carlisle v Swindon
Cheltenham v Notts Co
Colchester v Newport
Crawley v Grimsby
Macclesfield v MK Dons
Morecambe v Forest Green
Northampton v Exeter
Port Vale v Mansfield
Stevenage v Bury

## Sunday 10 March

**Championship**
Birmingham v Aston Villa

## Tuesday 12 March

**Championship**
Blackburn v Wigan
Bolton v Sheff Wed
Bristol City v Ipswich
Reading v Leeds
Sheff Utd v Brentford

**League One**
AFC Wimbledon v Peterborough
Barnsley v Sunderland
Blackpool v Doncaster
Bradford v Luton
Charlton v Burton
Coventry v Fleetwood

Gillingham v Bristol Rov
Plymouth v Shrewsbury
Rochdale v Oxford
Scunthorpe v Southend
Walsall v Portsmouth
Wycombe v Accrington

**League Two**
Cambridge v Crewe
Carlisle v Notts Co
Colchester v Forest Green
Crawley v Mansfield
Lincoln v Oldham
Macclesfield v Exeter
Morecambe v MK Dons
Northampton v Newport
Port Vale v Yeovil
Stevenage v Swindon
Tranmere v Grimsby

## Wednesday 13 March

**Championship**
Birmingham v Millwall
Derby v Stoke
Middlesbrough v Preston
Norwich v Hull
Nottm Forest v Aston Villa
QPR v Rotherham
WBA v Swansea

## Saturday 16 March

**Premier League**
Bournemouth v Newcastle
Brighton v Cardiff
Burnley v Leicester
Everton v Chelsea
Fulham v Liverpool
Man Utd v Man City
Tottenham v Crystal Palace
Watford v Southampton
West Ham v Huddersfield
Wolves v Arsenal

**Championship**
Aston Villa v Middlesbrough
Brentford v WBA
Hull v QPR
Ipswich v Nottm Forest
Leeds v Sheff Utd
Millwall v Bristol City
Preston v Birmingham
Rotherham v Norwich
Sheff Wed v Blackburn
Stoke v Reading
Swansea v Derby
Wigan v Bolton

**League One**
Accrington v Rochdale
Bristol Rov v Charlton
Burton v Blackpool
Doncaster v Barnsley
Fleetwood v Plymouth
Luton v Gillingham
Oxford v Bradford
Peterborough v Coventry
Portsmouth v Scunthorpe
Shrewsbury v Wycombe
Southend v AFC Wimbledon
Sunderland v Walsall

**League Two**
Bury v Cambridge
Crewe v Crawley
Exeter v Colchester
Forest Green v Carlisle
Grimsby v Northampton
Mansfield v Lincoln
MK Dons v Stevenage
Newport v Cheltenham
Notts Co v Morecambe
Oldham v Tranmere
Swindon v Port Vale
Yeovil v Macclesfield

## Saturday 23 March

**League One**
AFC Wimbledon v Gillingham
Bradford v Blackpool
Burton v Accrington
Coventry v Oxford
Fleetwood v Sunderland
Luton v Doncaster
Peterborough v Southend
Plymouth v Bristol Rov
Rochdale v Scunthorpe
Shrewsbury v Portsmouth
Walsall v Barnsley
Wycombe v Charlton

**League Two**
Carlisle v Cambridge
Cheltenham v Northampton
Colchester v Tranmere
Crawley v Lincoln
Grimsby v Bury
Macclesfield v Stevenage
Mansfield v Crewe
MK Dons v Yeovil
Newport v Oldham
Notts Co v Exeter
Port Vale v Forest Green
Swindon v Morecambe

## Saturday 30 March

**Premier League**
Arsenal v Newcastle
Brighton v Southampton
Burnley v Wolves
Cardiff v Chelsea
Crystal Palace v Huddersfield
Fulham v Man City
Leicester v Bournemouth
Liverpool v Tottenham
Man Utd v Watford
West Ham v Everton

**Championship**
Aston Villa v Blackburn
Derby v Rotherham
Ipswich v Hull
Leeds v Millwall
Middlesbrough v Norwich
Nottm Forest v Swansea
QPR v Bolton
Reading v Preston
Sheff Utd v Bristol City
Stoke v Sheff Wed
WBA v Birmingham
Wigan v Brentford

**League One**
Accrington v Fleetwood
Barnsley v Coventry
Blackpool v Plymouth
Bristol Rov v Luton
Charlton v Bradford
Doncaster v Walsall
Gillingham v Rochdale
Oxford v Wycombe
Portsmouth v Peterborough
Scunthorpe v AFC Wimbledon
Southend v Shrewsbury
Sunderland

**League Two**
Bury v Swindon
Cambridge v Colchester
Crewe v Cheltenham
Exeter v Mansfield
Forest Green v MK Dons
Lincoln v Macclesfield
Morecambe v Crawley
Northampton v Port Vale
Oldham v Grimsby
Stevenage v Notts Co
Tranmere v Carlisle
Yeovil v Newport

## Saturday 6 April

**Premier League**
Bournemouth v Burnley

Chelsea v West Ham
Everton v Arsenal
Huddersfield v Leicester
Man City v Cardiff
Newcastle v Crystal Palace
Southampton v Liverpool
Tottenham v Brighton
Watford v Fulham
Wolves v Man Utd

**Championship**
Birmingham v Leeds
Blackburn v Stoke
Bolton v Ipswich
Brentford v Derby
Bristol City v Wigan
Hull v Reading
Millwall v WBA
Norwich v QPR
Preston v Sheff Utd
Rotherham v Nottm Forest
Sheff Wed v Aston Villa
Swansea v Middlesbrough

**League One**
AFC Wimbledon v Accrington
Bradford v Doncaster
Burton v Barnsley
Coventry v Bristol Rov
Fleetwood v Southend
Luton v Blackpool
Peterborough v Gillingham
Plymouth v Charlton
Rochdale v Sunderland
Shrewsbury v Scunthorpe
Walsall v Oxford
Wycombe v Portsmouth

**League Two**
Carlisle v Bury
Cheltenham v Exeter
Colchester v Oldham
Crawley v Forest Green
Grimsby v Stevenage
Macclesfield v Morecambe
Mansfield v Cambridge
MK Dons v Lincoln
Newport v Tranmere
Notts Co v Northampton
Port Vale v Crewe
Swindon v Yeovil

## Tuesday 9 April
**Championship**
Blackburn v Derby
Bolton v Middlesbrough
Bristol City v WBA
Norwich v Reading
Preston v Leeds
Sheff Wed v Nottm Forest
Swansea v Stoke

## Wednesday 10 April
**Championship**
Birmingham v Sheff Utd
Brentford v Ipswich
Hull v Wigan
Millwall v QPR
Rotherham v Aston Villa

## Saturday 13 April
**Premier League**
Brighton v Bournemouth
Burnley v Cardiff
Crystal Palace v Man City
Fulham v Everton
Leicester v Newcastle
Liverpool v Chelsea
Man Utd v West Ham
Southampton v Wolves
Tottenham v Huddersfield
Watford v Arsenal

**Championship**
Aston Villa v Bristol City
Derby v Bolton
Ipswich v Birmingham
Leeds v Sheff Wed
Middlesbrough v Hull
Nottm Forest v Blackburn
QPR v Swansea
Reading v Brentford
Sheff Utd v Millwall
Stoke v Rotherham
WBA v Preston
Wigan v Norwich

**League One**
Accrington v Walsall
Barnsley v Fleetwood
Blackpool v Peterborough
Bristol Rov v Bradford
Charlton v Luton
Doncaster v Plymouth
Gillingham v Shrewsbury
Oxford v AFC Wimbledon
Portsmouth v Rochdale
Scunthorpe v Burton
Southend v Wycombe
Sunderland v Coventry

**League Two**
Bury v Colchester
Cambridge v Newport
Crewe v Notts Co
Exeter v Port Vale
Forest Green v Macclesfield
Lincoln v Cheltenham
Morecambe v Grimsby
Northampton v Mansfield
Oldham v Swindon
Stevenage v Carlisle
Tranmere v MK Dons
Yeovil v Crawley

## Friday 19 April
**Championship**
Birmingham v Derby
Bolton v Aston Villa
Bristol City v Reading
Leeds v Wigan
Middlesbrough v Stoke
Millwall v Brentford
Norwich v Sheff Wed
Preston v Ipswich
QPR v Blackburn
Sheff Utd v Nottm Forest
Swansea v Rotherham
WBA v Hull

**League One**
Accrington v Luton
AFC Wimbledon v Bristol Rov
Barnsley v Shrewsbury
Burton v Portsmouth
Coventry v Bradford
Fleetwood v Peterborough
Gillingham v Plymouth
Oxford v Charlton
Rochdale v Wycombe
Scunthorpe v Blackpool
Sunderland v Doncaster
Walsall v Southend

**League Two**
Cambridge v Swindon
Carlisle v Lincoln
Cheltenham v Oldham
Colchester v Grimsby
Crewe v Yeovil
Exeter v Crawley
Mansfield v Morecambe
Newport v Bury
Northampton v Macclesfield
Notts Co v MK Dons
Port Vale v Stevenage
Tranmere v Forest Green

## Saturday 20 April
**Premier League**
Arsenal v Crystal Palace
Bournemouth v Fulham
Cardiff v Liverpool

Chelsea v Burnley
Everton v Man Utd
Huddersfield v Watford
Man City v Tottenham
Newcastle v Southampton
West Ham v Leicester
Wolves v Brighton

## Monday 22 April

**Championship**
Aston Villa v Millwall
Blackburn v Bolton
Brentford v Leeds
Derby v QPR
Hull v Sheff Utd
Ipswich v Swansea
Nottm Forest v Middlesbrough
Reading v WBA
Rotherham v Birmingham
Sheff Wed v Bristol City
Stoke v Norwich
Wigan v Preston

**League One**
Blackpool v Fleetwood
Bradford v Gillingham
Bristol Rov v Rochdale
Charlton v Scunthorpe
Doncaster v Accrington
Luton v AFC Wimbledon
Peterborough v Sunderland
Plymouth v Barnsley
Portsmouth v Coventry
Shrewsbury v Oxford
Southend v Burton
Wycombe v Walsall

**League Two**
Bury v Northampton
Crawley v Notts Co
Forest Green v Cambridge
Grimsby v Carlisle
Lincoln v Tranmere
Macclesfield v Newport
MK Dons v Port Vale
Morecambe v Cheltenham
Oldham v Mansfield
Stevenage v Exeter
Swindon v Crewe
Yeovil v Colchester

## Saturday 27 April

**Premier League**
Brighton v Newcastle
Burnley v Man City
Crystal Palace v Everton
Fulham v Cardiff
Leicester v Arsenal
Liverpool v Huddersfield
Man Utd v Chelsea
Southampton v Bournemouth
Tottenham v West Ham
Watford v Wolves

**Championship**
Birmingham v Wigan
Bolton v Brentford
Bristol City v Derby
Leeds v Aston Villa
Middlesbrough v Reading
Millwall v Stoke
Norwich v Blackburn
Preston v Sheff Wed
QPR v Nottm Forest
Sheff Utd v Ipswich
Swansea v Hull
WBA v Rotherham

**League One**
Accrington v Plymouth
AFC Wimbledon v Wycombe
Barnsley v Blackpool
Burton v Luton
Coventry v Shrewsbury
Fleetwood v Bristol Rov
Gillingham v Charlton
Oxford v Doncaster
Rochdale v Southend
Scunthorpe v Bradford
Sunderland v Portsmouth
Walsall v Peterborough

**League Two**
Cambridge v Morecambe
Carlisle v Crawley
Cheltenham v Swindon
Colchester v MK Dons
Crewe v Forest Green
Exeter v Oldham
Mansfield v Stevenage
Newport v Lincoln
Northampton v Yeovil
Notts Co v Grimsby
Port Vale v Macclesfield
Tranmere v Bury

## Saturday 4 May

**Premier League**
Arsenal v Brighton
Bournemouth v Tottenham
Cardiff v Crystal Palace
Chelsea v Watford
Everton v Burnley
Huddersfield v Man Utd
Man City v Leicester
Newcastle v Liverpool
West Ham v Southampton
Wolves v Fulham

**League One**
Blackpool v Gillingham
Bradford v AFC Wimbledon
Bristol Rov v Barnsley
Charlton v Rochdale
Doncaster v Coventry
Luton v Oxford
Peterborough v Burton
Plymouth v Scunthorpe
Portsmouth v Accrington
Shrewsbury v Walsall
Southend v Sunderland
Wycombe v Fleetwood

**League Two**
Bury v Port Vale
Crawley v Tranmere
Forest Green v Exeter
Grimsby v Crewe
Lincoln v Colchester
Macclesfield v Cambridge
MK Dons v Mansfield
Morecambe v Newport
Oldham v Northampton
Stevenage v Cheltenham
Swindon v Notts Co
Yeovil v Carlisle

## Sunday 5 May

**Championship**
Aston Villa v Norwich
Blackburn v Swansea
Brentford v Preston
Derby v WBA
Hull v Bristol City
Ipswich v Leeds
Nottm Forest v Bolton
Reading v Birmingham
Rotherham v Middlesbrough
Sheff Wed v QPR
Stoke v Sheff Utd
Wigan v Millwall

## Sunday 12 May

**Premier League**
Brighton v Man City
Burnley v Arsenal
Crystal Palace v Bournemouth
Fulham v Newcastle
Leicester v Chelsea
Liverpool v Wolves
Man Utd v Cardiff
Southampton v Huddersfield
Tottenham v Everton
Watford v West Ham

# SCOTTISH FIXTURES 2018–2019

**Premiership Championship League One and League Two**

## Saturday 4 August

**Premiership**

Celtic v Livingston
Hamilton v Hearts
Hibernian v Motherwell
Kilmarnock v St Johnstone
St Mirren v Dundee

**Championship**

Ayr v Partick
Dundee Utd v Dunfermline
Falkirk v Inverness
Morton v Queen of South
Ross Co v Alloa

**League One**

East Fife v Dumbarton
Forfar v Airdrieonians
Montrose v Arbroath
Stenhousemuir v Brechin
Stranraer v Raith

**League Two**

Annan v Elgin
Berwick v Stirling
Clyde v Cowdenbeath
Edinburgh v Albion
Peterhead v Queen's Park

## Sunday 5 August

**Premiership**

Aberdeen v Rangers

## Saturday 11 August

**Premiership**

Dundee v Aberdeen
Hearts v Celtic
Livingston v Kilmarnock
Motherwell v Hamilton
Rangers v St Mirren
St Johnstone v Hibernian

**Championship**

Alloa v Morton
Dunfermline v Ross Co
Inverness v Ayr
Partick v Falkirk
Queen of South v Dundee Utd

**League One**

Airdrieonians v Montrose
Arbroath v Stranraer
Brechin v East Fife
Dumbarton v Forfar
Raith v Stenhousemuir

**League Two**

Albion v Peterhead
Cowdenbeath v Annan
Elgin v Edinburgh
Queen's Park v Berwick
Stirling v Clyde

## Saturday 18 August

**League One**

Dumbarton v Arbroath
Forfar v Stranraer
Montrose v Brechin
Raith v East Fife
Stenhousemuir v Airdrieonians

**League Two**

Albion v Elgin
Annan v Queen's Park
Cowdenbeath v Berwick
Edinburgh v Stirling
Peterhead v Clyde

## Saturday 25 August

**Premiership**

Celtic v Hamilton
Hibernian v Aberdeen
Kilmarnock v Hearts
St Johnstone v Dundee
St Mirren v Livingston

**Championship**

Ayr v Dunfermline
Dundee Utd v Partick
Falkirk v Queen of South
Inverness v Alloa
Morton v Ross Co

**League One**

Airdrieonians v Raith
Brechin v Dumbarton
East Fife v Arbroath
Forfar v Stenhousemuir
Stranraer v Montrose

**League Two**

Berwick v Annan
Clyde v Edinburgh
Elgin v Cowdenbeath
Queen's Park v Albion
Stirling v Peterhead

## Sunday 26 August

**Premiership**

Motherwell v Rangers

## Saturday 1 September

**Premiership**

Aberdeen v Kilmarnock
Dundee v Motherwell
Hamilton v St Johnstone
Hearts v St Mirren
Livingston v Hibernian

**Championship**

Alloa v Dundee Utd
Dunfermline v Inverness
Partick v Morton
Queen of South v Ayr
Ross Co v Falkirk

**League One**

Airdrieonians v Stranraer
Arbroath v Brechin
Montrose v East Fife
Raith v Forfar
Stenhousemuir v Dumbarton

**League Two**

Albion v Berwick
Annan v Clyde
Elgin v Stirling
Peterhead v Edinburgh
Queen's Park v Cowdenbeath

## Sunday 2 September

**Premiership**

Celtic v Rangers

## Saturday 15 September

**Premiership**

Hibernian v Kilmarnock
Livingston v Hamilton
Motherwell v Hearts
Rangers v Dundee
St Johnstone v Aberdeen
St Mirren v Celtic

**Championship**

Ayr v Falkirk
Dundee Utd v Morton
Dunfermline v Alloa
Inverness v Partick
Queen of South v Ross Co

**League One**

Arbroath v Forfar
Brechin v Raith
Dumbarton v Montrose
East Fife v Airdrieonians
Stranraer v Stenhousemuir

**League Two**
Berwick v Elgin
Clyde v Albion
Cowdenbeath v Peterhead
Edinburgh v Annan
Stirling v Queen's Park

## Saturday 22 September

**Premiership**
Aberdeen v Motherwell
Dundee v Hibernian
Hamilton v St Mirren
Hearts v Livingston
Kilmarnock v Celtic
Rangers v St Johnstone

**Championship**
Alloa v Ayr
Falkirk v Dundee Utd
Morton v Dunfermline
Partick v Queen of South
Ross Co v Inverness

**League One**
Airdrieonians v Dumbarton
Forfar v Brechin
Raith v Montrose
Stenhousemuir v Arbroath
Stranraer v East Fife

**League Two**
Clyde v Elgin
Cowdenbeath v Albion
Peterhead v Berwick
Queen's Park v Edinburgh
Stirling v Annan

## Saturday 29 September

**Premiership**
Celtic v Aberdeen
Hamilton v Dundee
Hearts v St Johnstone
Kilmarnock v Motherwell
Livingston v Rangers
St Mirren v Hibernian

**Championship**
Alloa v Falkirk
Dundee Utd v Ross Co
Dunfermline v Partick
Inverness v Queen of South
Morton v Ayr

**League One**
Arbroath v Airdrieonians
Brechin v Stranraer
Dumbarton v Raith
East Fife v Stenhousemuir
Montrose v Forfar

**League Two**
Albion v Stirling
Annan v Peterhead
Berwick v Clyde
Edinburgh v Cowdenbeath
Elgin v Queen's Park

## Saturday 6 October

**Premiership**
Aberdeen v St Mirren
Dundee v Kilmarnock
Hibernian v Hamilton
Motherwell v Livingston
Rangers v Hearts
St Johnstone v Celtic

**Championship**
Ayr v Dundee Utd
Falkirk v Dunfermline
Inverness v Morton
Partick v Ross Co
Queen of South v Alloa

**League One**
Airdrieonians v Brechin
Forfar v East Fife
Raith v Arbroath
Stenhousemuir v Montrose
Stranraer v Dumbarton

**League Two**
Annan v Albion
Cowdenbeath v Stirling
Edinburgh v Berwick
Peterhead v Elgin
Queen's Park v Clyde

## Saturday 20 October

**Premiership**
Celtic v Hibernian
Hamilton v Rangers
Hearts v Aberdeen
Livingston v Dundee
Motherwell v St Johnstone
St Mirren v Kilmarnock

**Championship**
Alloa v Partick
Dundee Utd v Inverness
Dunfermline v Queen of South
Morton v Falkirk
Ross Co v Ayr

**League One**
Arbroath v Dumbarton
East Fife v Brechin
Montrose v Airdrieonians
Raith v Stranraer
Stenhousemuir v Forfar

## Saturday 27 October

**Premiership**
Aberdeen v Livingston
Celtic v Motherwell
Dundee v Hearts
Hibernian v Rangers
Kilmarnock v Hamilton
St Johnstone v St Mirren

**Championship**
Alloa v Inverness
Dunfermline v Dundee Utd
Partick v Ayr
Queen of South v Falkirk
Ross Co v Morton

**League One**
Airdrieonians v Stenhousemuir
Brechin v Montrose
Dumbarton v East Fife
Forfar v Raith
Stranraer v Arbroath

**League Two**
Albion v Queen's Park
Berwick v Cowdenbeath
Clyde v Peterhead
Elgin v Annan
Stirling v Edinburgh

## Tuesday 30 October

**Championship**
Ayr v Alloa
Falkirk v Ross Co
Inverness v Dunfermline
Partick v Dundee Utd
Queen of South v Morton

## Wednesday 31 October

**Premiership**
Aberdeen v Hamilton
Dundee v Celtic
Hearts v Hibernian
Livingston v St Johnstone
Rangers v Kilmarnock
St Mirren v Motherwell

## Saturday 3 November

**Premiership**
Celtic v Hearts
Hamilton v Livingston
Hibernian v St Johnstone
Kilmarnock v Aberdeen
Motherwell v Dundee
St Mirren v Rangers

**Championship**
Alloa v Dunfermline
Dundee Utd v Queen of South

Falkirk v Ayr
Inverness v Ross Co
Morton v Partick

**League One**
Airdrieonians v Forfar
Arbroath v East Fife
Montrose v Dumbarton
Raith v Brechin
Stenhousemuir v Stranraer

**League Two**
Cowdenbeath v Elgin
Edinburgh v Clyde
Peterhead v Albion
Queen's Park v Annan
Stirling v Berwick

## Saturday 10 November

**Premiership**
Aberdeen v Hibernian
Dundee v St Mirren
Hearts v Kilmarnock
Livingston v Celtic
Rangers v Motherwell
St Johnstone v Hamilton

**Championship**
Ayr v Queen of South
Dunfermline v Falkirk
Morton v Alloa
Partick v Inverness
Ross Co v Dundee Utd

**League One**
Arbroath v Montrose
Brechin v Forfar
Dumbarton v Stenhousemuir
East Fife v Raith
Stranraer v Airdrieonians

**League Two**
Albion v Edinburgh
Annan v Cowdenbeath
Clyde v Stirling
Elgin v Berwick
Queen's Park v Peterhead

## Saturday 17 November

**Championship**
Ayr v Morton
Dundee Utd v Alloa
Falkirk v Partick
Queen of South v Inverness
Ross Co v Dunfermline

**League One**
Airdrieonians v East Fife
Brechin v Arbroath
Forfar v Dumbarton
Montrose v Stranraer
Stenhousemuir v Raith

**League Two**
Annan v Stirling
Berwick v Albion
Cowdenbeath v Queen's Park
Edinburgh v Peterhead
Elgin v Clyde

## Saturday 24 November

**Premiership**
Hamilton v Celtic
Hibernian v Dundee
Motherwell v Aberdeen
Rangers v Livingston
St Johnstone v Kilmarnock
St Mirren v Hearts

## Saturday 1 December

**Premiership**
Aberdeen v Dundee
Celtic v St Johnstone
Hearts v Rangers
Kilmarnock v Hibernian
Livingston v Motherwell
St Mirren v Hamilton

**Championship**
Alloa v Ross Co
Dundee Utd v Ayr
Dunfermline v Morton
Inverness v Falkirk
Queen of South v Partick

**League One**
Arbroath v Stenhousemuir
Dumbarton v Brechin
East Fife v Montrose
Raith v Airdrieonians
Stranraer v Forfar

**League Two**
Albion v Cowdenbeath
Clyde v Berwick
Edinburgh v Queen's Park
Peterhead v Annan
Stirling v Elgin

## Wednesday 5 December

**Premiership**
Dundee v Hamilton
Hibernian v St Mirren
Kilmarnock v Livingston
Motherwell v Celtic
Rangers v Aberdeen
St Johnstone v Hearts

## Saturday 8 December

**Premiership**
Aberdeen v St Johnstone
Celtic v Kilmarnock
Dundee v Rangers
Hamilton v Hibernian
Hearts v Motherwell
Livingston v St Mirren

**Championship**
Ayr v Inverness
Falkirk v Alloa
Morton v Dundee Utd
Partick v Dunfermline
Ross Co v Queen of South

**League One**
Brechin v Stenhousemuir
Dumbarton v Airdrieonians
East Fife v Stranraer
Forfar v Arbroath
Montrose v Raith

**League Two**
Annan v Edinburgh
Berwick v Peterhead
Cowdenbeath v Clyde
Elgin v Albion
Queen's Park v Stirling

## Saturday 15 December

**Premiership**
Hibernian v Celtic
Kilmarnock v Dundee
Livingston v Hearts
Rangers v Hamilton
St Johnstone v Motherwell
St Mirren v Aberdeen

**Championship**
Ayr v Ross Co
Falkirk v Morton
Inverness v Dundee Utd
Partick v Alloa
Queen of South v Dunfermline

**League One**
Airdrieonians v Arbroath
Forfar v Montrose
Raith v Dumbarton
Stenhousemuir v East Fife
Stranraer v Brechin

**League Two**
Berwick v Queen's Park
Clyde v Annan
Edinburgh v Elgin

Peterhead v Cowdenbeath
Stirling v Albion

## Saturday 22 December

**Premiership**
Aberdeen v Hearts
Celtic v Dundee
Hamilton v Kilmarnock
Hibernian v Livingston
Motherwell v St Mirren
St Johnstone v Rangers

**Championship**
Alloa v Queen of South
Dundee Utd v Falkirk
Dunfermline v Ayr
Morton v Inverness
Ross Co v Partick

**League One**
Arbroath v Raith
Brechin v Airdrieonians
Dumbarton v Stranraer
East Fife v Forfar
Montrose v Stenhousemuir

**League Two**
Albion v Clyde
Annan v Berwick
Cowdenbeath v Edinburgh
Peterhead v Stirling
Queen's Park v Elgin

## Wednesday 26 December

**Premiership**
Aberdeen v Celtic
Dundee v Livingston
Hearts v Hamilton
Motherwell v Kilmarnock
Rangers v Hibernian
St Mirren v St Johnstone

## Saturday 29 December

**Premiership**
Dundee v St Johnstone
Hamilton v Motherwell
Hibernian v Hearts
Kilmarnock v St Mirren
Livingston v Aberdeen
Rangers v Celtic

**Championship**
Alloa v Dundee Utd
Falkirk v Dunfermline
Partick v Morton
Queen of South v Ayr
Ross Co v Inverness

**League One**
Airdrieonians v Stranraer
Forfar v Brechin
Montrose v Arbroath
Raith v East Fife
Stenhousemuir v Dumbarton

**League Two**
Albion v Annan
Berwick v Edinburgh
Clyde v Queen's Park
Elgin v Peterhead
Stirling v Cowdenbeath

## Saturday 5 January

**Championship**
Ayr v Falkirk
Dundee Utd v Partick
Dunfermline v Alloa
Inverness v Queen of South
Morton v Ross Co

**League One**
Arbroath v Brechin
Dumbarton v Forfar
East Fife v Airdrieonians
Raith v Stenhousemuir
Stranraer v Montrose

**League Two**
Annan v Elgin
Cowdenbeath v Berwick
Edinburgh v Stirling
Peterhead v Clyde
Queen's Park v Albion

## Saturday 12 January

**Championship**
Alloa v Morton
Dundee Utd v Dunfermline
Inverness v Ayr
Partick v Falkirk
Queen of South v Ross Co

**League One**
Airdrieonians v Raith
Brechin v Dumbarton
Forfar v Stranraer
Montrose v East Fife
Stenhousemuir v Arbroath

**League Two**
Albion v Peterhead
Berwick v Clyde
Elgin v Cowdenbeath
Queen's Park v Edinburgh
Stirling v Annan

## Saturday 19 January

**League Two**
Clyde v Elgin
Cowdenbeath v Albion
Edinburgh v Annan
Peterhead v Berwick
Stirling v Queen's Park

## Wednesday 23 January

**Premiership**
Celtic v St Mirren
Hamilton v Aberdeen
Hearts v Dundee
Kilmarnock v Rangers
Motherwell v Hibernian
St Johnstone v Livingston

## Saturday 26 January

**Premiership**
Aberdeen v Kilmarnock
Celtic v Hamilton
Dundee v Motherwell
Hearts v St Johnstone
Livingston v Rangers
St Mirren v Hibernian

**Championship**
Ayr v Dundee Utd
Falkirk v Inverness
Morton v Dunfermline
Partick v Queen of South
Ross Co v Alloa

**League One**
Arbroath v Forfar
Brechin v Raith
Dumbarton v Montrose
Stenhousemuir v Airdrieonians
Stranraer v East Fife

**League Two**
Albion v Stirling
Annan v Peterhead
Clyde v Cowdenbeath
Elgin v Edinburgh
Queen's Park v Berwick

## Saturday 2 February

**Premiership**
Hamilton v Dundee
Hibernian v Aberdeen
Kilmarnock v Hearts
Motherwell v Livingston
Rangers v St Mirren
St Johnstone v Celtic

**Championship**
Alloa v Ayr
Dundee Utd v Morton

Dunfermline v Ross Co
Falkirk v Queen of South
Inverness v Partick

**League One**
Airdrieonians v Dumbarton
East Fife v Arbroath
Montrose v Brechin
Raith v Forfar
Stranraer v Stenhousemuir

**League Two**
Berwick v Annan
Cowdenbeath v Peterhead
Edinburgh v Albion
Elgin v Queen's Park
Stirling v Clyde

## Wednesday 6 February

**Premiership**
Aberdeen v Rangers
Celtic v Hibernian
Dundee v Kilmarnock
Hamilton v St Johnstone
Hearts v Livingston
St Mirren v Motherwell

## Saturday 9 February

**League One**
Arbroath v Stranraer
Brechin v East Fife
Dumbarton v Raith
Forfar v Airdrieonians
Stenhousemuir v Montrose

## Saturday 16 February

**Premiership**
Aberdeen v St Mirren
Hibernian v Hamilton
Kilmarnock v Celtic
Livingston v Dundee
Motherwell v Hearts
Rangers v St Johnstone

**Championship**
Alloa v Partick
Dunfermline v Inverness
Morton v Ayr
Queen of South v Dundee Utd
Ross Co v Falkirk

**League One**
Airdrieonians v Brechin
East Fife v Stenhousemuir
Montrose v Forfar
Raith v Arbroath
Stranraer v Dumbarton

**League Two**
Albion v Elgin
Annan v Clyde
Berwick v Stirling
Peterhead v Edinburgh
Queen's Park v Cowdenbeath

## Saturday 23 February

**Premiership**
Celtic v Motherwell
Dundee v Hibernian
Hamilton v Rangers
Hearts v St Mirren
Livingston v Kilmarnock
St Johnstone v Aberdeen

**Championship**
Ayr v Dunfermline
Falkirk v Dundee Utd
Inverness v Morton
Partick v Ross Co
Queen of South v Alloa

**League One**
Arbroath v Airdrieonians
Brechin v Stranraer
East Fife v Dumbarton
Forfar v Stenhousemuir
Raith v Montrose

**League Two**
Annan v Albion
Berwick v Elgin
Edinburgh v Cowdenbeath
Queen's Park v Clyde
Stirling v Peterhead

## Tuesday 26 February

**Championship**
Alloa v Falkirk
Dundee Utd v Inverness
Dunfermline v Partick
Morton v Queen of South
Ross Co v Ayr

## Wednesday 27 February

**Premiership**
Aberdeen v Hamilton
Hearts v Celtic
Kilmarnock v Motherwell
Rangers v Dundee
St Johnstone v Hibernian
St Mirren v Livingston

## Saturday 2 March

**Championship**
Ayr v Partick
Dundee Utd v Ross Co
Dunfermline v Queen of South
Inverness v Alloa
Morton v Falkirk

**League One**
Airdrieonians v Montrose
Dumbarton v Arbroath
Forfar v East Fife
Stenhousemuir v Brechin
Stranraer v Raith

**League Two**
Albion v Berwick
Annan v Queen's Park
Clyde v Edinburgh
Cowdenbeath v Stirling
Peterhead v Elgin

## Saturday 9 March

**Premiership**
Celtic v Aberdeen
Dundee v Hearts
Hibernian v Rangers
Livingston v St Johnstone
Motherwell v Hamilton
St Mirren v Kilmarnock

**Championship**
Alloa v Dunfermline
Falkirk v Ayr
Partick v Dundee Utd
Queen of South v Inverness
Ross Co v Morton

**League One**
Arbroath v Stenhousemuir
Brechin v Forfar
East Fife v Stranraer
Montrose v Dumbarton
Raith v Airdrieonians

**League Two**
Berwick v Cowdenbeath
Edinburgh v Queen's Park
Elgin v Clyde
Peterhead v Annan
Stirling v Albion

## Saturday 16 March

**Premiership**
Aberdeen v Livingston
Dundee v Celtic
Hamilton v Hearts
Hibernian v Motherwell
Rangers v Kilmarnock
St Johnstone v St Mirren

**Championship**
Ayr v Queen of South
Dunfermline v Dundee Utd

Falkirk v Partick
Inverness v Ross Co
Morton v Alloa

**League One**
Arbroath v East Fife
Brechin v Montrose
Dumbarton v Airdrieonians
Forfar v Raith
Stenhousemuir v Stranraer

**League Two**
Albion v Cowdenbeath
Annan v Edinburgh
Berwick v Peterhead
Clyde v Stirling
Queen's Park v Elgin

## Saturday 23 March

**Championship**
Ayr v Morton
Dundee Utd v Alloa
Partick v Inverness
Queen of South v Falkirk
Ross Co v Dunfermline

**League One**
Airdrieonians v Forfar
East Fife v Brechin
Montrose v Stenhousemuir
Raith v Dumbarton
Stranraer v Arbroath

**League Two**
Clyde v Annan
Cowdenbeath v Queen's Park
Edinburgh v Peterhead
Elgin v Albion
Stirling v Berwick

## Saturday 30 March

**Premiership**
Celtic v Rangers
Hearts v Aberdeen
Kilmarnock v Hamilton
Livingston v Hibernian
Motherwell v St Johnstone
St Mirren v Dundee

**Championship**
Alloa v Ross Co
Dundee Utd v Queen of South
Dunfermline v Ayr
Inverness v Falkirk
Morton v Partick

**League One**
Brechin v Airdrieonians
Dumbarton v Stenhousemuir
East Fife v Raith
Forfar v Arbroath
Montrose v Stranraer

**League Two**
Albion v Clyde
Berwick v Edinburgh
Elgin v Annan
Peterhead v Cowdenbeath
Queen's Park v Stirling

## Wednesday 3 April

**Premiership**
Aberdeen v Motherwell
Hibernian v Kilmarnock
Livingston v Hamilton
Rangers v Hearts
St Johnstone v Dundee
St Mirren v Celtic

## Saturday 6 April

**Premiership**
Celtic v Livingston
Dundee v Aberdeen
Hamilton v St Mirren
Hearts v Hibernian
Kilmarnock v St Johnstone
Motherwell v Rangers

**Championship**
Ayr v Inverness
Falkirk v Alloa
Partick v Dunfermline
Queen of South v Morton
Ross Co v Dundee Utd

**League One**
Airdrieonians v East Fife
Arbroath v Montrose
Dumbarton v Brechin
Stenhousemuir v Raith
Stranraer v Forfar

**League Two**
Albion v Queen's Park
Annan v Berwick
Clyde v Peterhead
Cowdenbeath v Edinburgh
Stirling v Elgin

## Saturday 13 April

**Championship**
Alloa v Queen of South
Dundee Utd v Ayr
Dunfermline v Falkirk
Morton v Inverness
Ross Co v Partick

**League One**
Airdrieonians v Stenhousemuir
Brechin v Arbroath
East Fife v Montrose
Forfar v Dumbarton
Raith v Stranraer

**League Two**
Annan v Stirling
Berwick v Queen's Park
Cowdenbeath v Elgin
Edinburgh v Clyde
Peterhead v Albion

## Saturday 20 April

**Championship**
Ayr v Ross Co
Falkirk v Morton
Inverness v Dundee Utd
Partick v Alloa
Queen of South v Dunfermline

**League One**
Arbroath v Raith
Dumbarton v East Fife
Montrose v Airdrieonians
Stenhousemuir v Forfar
Stranraer v Brechin

**League Two**
Albion v Edinburgh
Clyde v Berwick
Elgin v Peterhead
Queen's Park v Annan
Stirling v Cowdenbeath

## Saturday 27 April

**Championship**
Alloa v Inverness
Dundee Utd v Falkirk
Dunfermline v Morton
Partick v Ayr
Ross Co v Queen of South

**League One**
Airdrieonians v Arbroath
Dumbarton v Stranraer
Forfar v Montrose
Raith v Brechin
Stenhousemuir v East Fife

**League Two**
Annan v Cowdenbeath
Berwick v Albion
Clyde v Queen's Park
Edinburgh v Elgin
Peterhead v Stirling

**Saturday 4 May**

**Championship**

Ayr v Alloa
Falkirk v Ross Co
Inverness v Dunfermline
Morton v Dundee Utd
Queen of South v Partick

**League One**

Arbroath v Dumbarton
Brechin v Stenhousemuir
East Fife v Forfar
Montrose v Raith
Stranraer v Airdrieonians

**League Two**

Albion v Annan
Cowdenbeath v Clyde
Elgin v Berwick
Queen's Park v Peterhead
Stirling v Edinburgh

# NATIONAL LEAGUE

**Premier fixtures 2018–2019**

## Saturday 4 August

Aldershoft v Barnet
Barrow v Havant
Boreham Wood v Dag & Red
Braintree v Halifax
Dover v Wrexham
Eastleigh v Solihull
Ebbsfleet v Chesterfield
Fylde v Bromley
Harrogate v Sutton
Maidenhead v Gateshead
Maidstone v Hartlepool
Salford v Leyton Orient

## Tuesday 7 August

Barnet v Braintree
Bromley v Dover
Chesterfield v Aldershot
Dag & Red v Maidstone
Halifax v Barrow
Gateshead v Salford
Hartlepool v Harrogate
Havant v Boreham Wood
Leyton Orient v Ebbsfleet
Solihull v Maidenhead
Sutton v Eastleigh
Wrexham v Fylde

## Saturday 11 August

Barnet v Eastleigh
Bromley v Harrogate
Chesterfield v Braintree
Dag & Red v Maidenhead
Halifax v Maidstone
Gateshead v Dover
Hartlepool v Ebbsfleet
Havant v Fylde
Leyton Orient v Barrow
Solihull v Aldershot
Sutton v Salford
Wrexham v Boreham Wood

## Tuesday 14 August

Aldershot v Dag & Red
Barrow v Chesterfield
Boreham Wood v Gateshead
Braintree v Hartlepool
Dover v Havant
Eastleigh v Bromley
Ebbsfleet v Sutton
Fylde v Solihull
Harrogate v Barnet
Maidenhead v Wrexham
Maidstone v Leyton Orient
Salford v Halifax

## Saturday 18 August

Aldershot v Harrogate
Barnet v Ebbsfleet
Braintree v Havant
Bromley v Gateshead
Eastleigh v Wrexham
Fylde v Dover
Halifax v Dag & Red
Hartlepool v Maidenhead
Leyton Orient v Boreham Wood
Maidstone v Barrow
Salford v Chesterfield
Solihull v Sutton

## Saturday 25 August

Barrow v Braintree
Boreham Wood v Halifax
Chesterfield v Barnet
Dag & Red v Hartlepool
Dover v Eastleigh
Ebbsfleet v Aldershot
Gateshead v Leyton Orient
Harrogate v Solihull
Havant v Salford
Maidenhead v Maidstone
Sutton v Fylde
Wrexham v Bromley

## Monday 27 August

Aldershot v Sutton
Barnet v Dag & Red
Braintree v Maidenhead
Bromley v Havant
Eastleigh v Ebbsfleet
Fylde v Harrogate
Halifax v Gateshead
Hartlepool v Chesterfield
Leyton Orient v Dover
Maidstone v Boreham Wood
Salford v Barrow
Solihull v Wrexham

## Saturday 1 September

Barrow v Solihull
Boreham Wood v Braintree
Chesterfield v Leyton Orient
Dag & Red v Salford
Dover v Barnet
Ebbsfleet v Fylde
Gateshead v Maidstone
Harrogate v Eastleigh
Havant v Hartlepool
Maidenhead v Bromley
Sutton v Halifax
Wrexham v Aldershot

## Tuesday 4 September

Boreham Wood v Chesterfield
Bromley v Barnet
Dag & Red v Braintree
Dover v Ebbsfleet
Gateshead v Harrogate
Fylde v Salford
Hartlepool v Barrow
Havant v Aldershot
Leyton Orient v Solihull
Maidenhead v Eastleigh
Maidstone v Sutton
Wrexham v Halifax

## Saturday 8 September

Aldershot v Bromley
Barnet v Maidenhead
Barrow v Dag & Red
Braintree v Wrexham
Chesterfield v Dover
Eastleigh v Fylde
Ebbsfleet v Gateshead
Halifax v Leyton Orient

Harrogate v Havant
Salford v Maidstone
Solihull v Hartlepool
Sutton v Boreham Wood

**Saturday 15 September**
Boreham Wood v Barrow
Bromley v Salford
Dag & Red v Chesterfield
Dover v Solihull
Fylde v Aldershot
Gateshead v Braintree
Hartlepool v Eastleigh
Havant v Sutton
Leyton Orient v Barnet
Maidenhead v Halifax
Maidstone v Harrogate
Wrexham v Ebbsfleet

**Saturday 22 September**
Aldershot v Dover
Barnet v Fylde
Barrow v Maidenhead
Braintree v Maidstone
Chesterfield v Gateshead
Eastleigh v Dag & Red
Ebbsfleet v Havant
Halifax v Hartlepool
Harrogate v Leyton Orient
Salford v Boreham Wood
Solihull v Bromley
Sutton v Wrexham

**Tuesday 25 September**
Aldershot v Maidstone
Barnet v Havant
Barrow v Gateshead
Braintree v Leyton Orient
Chesterfield v Maidenhead
Eastleigh v Boreham Wood
Ebbsfleet v Bromley
Halifax v Fylde
Harrogate v Wrexham
Salford v Hartlepool
Solihull v Dag & Red
Sutton v Dover

**Saturday 29 September**
Boreham Wood v Harrogate
Bromley v Halifax
Dag & Red v Ebbsfleet
Dover v Barrow
Fylde v Braintree
Gateshead v Eastleigh
Hartlepool v Aldershot
Havant v Solihull

Leyton Orient v Sutton
Maidenhead v Salford
Maidstone v Chesterfield
Wrexham v Barnet

**Saturday 6 October**
Aldershot v Halifax
Barnet v Solihull
Barrow v Sutton
Braintree v Eastleigh
Chesterfield v Fylde
Dover v Salford
Ebbsfleet v Harrogate
Gateshead v Dag & Red
Hartlepool v Boreham Wood
Maidenhead v Leyton Orient
Maidstone v Bromley
Wrexham v Havant

**Saturday 13 October**
Boreham Wood v Maidenhead
Bromley v Barrow
Dag & Red v Wrexham
Eastleigh v Aldershot
Fylde v Maidstone
Halifax v Chesterfield
Harrogate v Dover
Havant v Gateshead
Leyton Orient v Hartlepool
Salford v Braintree
Solihull v Ebbsfleet
Sutton v Barnet

**Saturday 27 October**
Barrow v Barnet
Boreham Wood v Bromley
Braintree v Dover
Chesterfield v Wrexham
Dag & Red v Harrogate
Halifax v Eastleigh
Gateshead v Aldershot
Hartlepool v Sutton
Leyton Orient v Havant
Maidenhead v Fylde
Maidstone v Solihull
Salford v Ebbsfleet

**Tuesday 30 October**
Aldershot v Boreham Wood
Barnet v Salford
Bromley v Braintree
Dover v Dag & Red
Eastleigh v Leyton Orient
Ebbsfleet v Maidstone
Fylde v Gateshead
Harrogate v Barrow

Havant v Maidenhead
Solihull v Halifax
Sutton v Chesterfield
Wrexham v Hartlepool

**Saturday 3 November**
Aldershot v Braintree
Barnet v Maidstone
Bromley v Hartlepool
Dover v Maidenhead
Eastleigh v Salford
Ebbsfleet v Barrow
Fylde v Leyton Orient
Harrogate v Chesterfield
Havant v Halifax
Solihull v Boreham Wood
Sutton v Dag & Red
Wrexham v Gateshead

**Saturday 17 November**
Barrow v Eastleigh
Boreham Wood v Ebbsfleet
Braintree v Solihull
Chesterfield v Havant
Dag & Red v Fylde
Halifax v Dover
Gateshead v Sutton
Hartlepool v Barnet
Leyton Orient v Bromley
Maidenhead v Harrogate
Maidstone v Wrexham
Salford v Aldershot

**Saturday 24 November**
Aldershot v Barrow
Barnet v Gateshead
Bromley v Dag & Red
Dover v Hartlepool
Eastleigh v Chesterfield
Ebbsfleet v Halifax
Fylde v Boreham Wood
Harrogate v Braintree
Havant v Maidstone
Solihull v Salford
Sutton v Maidenhead
Wrexham v Leyton Orient

**Tuesday 27 November**
Barrow v Wrexham
Boreham Wood v Dover
Braintree v Sutton
Chesterfield v Bromley
Dag & Red v Havant
Halifax v Barnet
Gateshead v Solihull
Hartlepool v Fylde
Leyton Orient v Aldershot

Maidenhead v Ebbsfleet
Maidstone v Eastleigh
Salford v Harrogate

## Saturday 1 December
Aldershot v Ebbsfleet
Barnet v Chesterfield
Braintree v Barrow
Bromley v Wrexham
Eastleigh v Dover
Fylde v Sutton
Halifax v Boreham Wood
Hartlepool v Dag & Red
Leyton Orient v Gateshead
Maidstone v Maidenhead
Salford v Havant
Solihull v Harrogate

## Saturday 8 December
Barrow v Maidstone
Boreham Wood v Leyton Orient
Chesterfield v Salford
Dag & Red v Halifax
Dover v Fylde
Ebbsfleet v Barnet
Gateshead v Bromley
Harrogate v Aldershot
Havant v Braintree
Maidenhead v Hartlepool
Sutton v Solihull
Wrexham v Eastleigh

## Saturday 22 December
Aldershot v Wrexham
Barnet v Dover
Braintree v Boreham Wood
Bromley v Maidenhead
Eastleigh v Harrogate
Fylde v Ebbsfleet
Halifax v Sutton
Hartlepool v Havant
Leyton Orient v Chesterfield
Maidstone v Gateshead
Salford v Dag & Red
Solihull v Barrow

## Wednesday 26 December
Barrow v Fylde
Boreham Wood v Barnet
Chesterfield v Solihull
Dag & Red v Leyton Orient
Dover v Maidstone
Ebbsfleet v Braintree
Gateshead v Hartlepool
Harrogate v Halifax
Havant v Eastleigh
Maidenhead v Aldershot
Sutton v Bromley
Wrexham v Salford

## Saturday 29 December
Barrow v Salford
Boreham Wood v Maidstone
Chesterfield v Hartlepool
Dag & Red v Barnet
Dover v Leyton Orient
Ebbsfleet v Eastleigh
Gateshead v Halifax
Harrogate v Fylde
Havant v Bromley
Maidenhead v Braintree
Sutton v Aldershot
Wrexham v Solihull

## Tuesday 1 January
Aldershot v Maidenhead
Barnet v Boreham Wood
Braintree v Ebbsfleet
Bromley v Sutton
Eastleigh v Havant
Fylde v Barrow
Halifax v Harrogate
Hartlepool v Gateshead
Leyton Orient v Dag & Red
Maidstone v Dover
Salford v Wrexham
Solihull v Chesterfield

## Saturday 5 January
Barnet v Aldershot
Bromley v Fylde
Chesterfield v Ebbsfleet
Dag & Red v Boreham Wood
Halifax v Braintree
Gateshead v Maidenhead
Hartlepool v Maidstone
Havant v Barrow
Leyton Orient v Salford
Solihull v Eastleigh
Sutton v Harrogate
Wrexham v Dover

## Saturday 19 January
Aldershot v Chesterfield
Barrow v Halifax
Boreham Wood v Havant
Braintree v Barnet
Dover v Bromley
Eastleigh v Sutton
Ebbsfleet v Leyton Orient
Fylde v Wrexham
Harrogate v Hartlepool
Maidenhead v Solihull
Maidstone v Dag & Red
Salford v Gateshead

## Saturday 26 January
Barnet v Harrogate
Bromley v Eastleigh
Chesterfield v Barrow
Dag & Red v Aldershot
Halifax v Salford
Gateshead v Boreham Wood
Hartlepool v Braintree
Havant v Dover
Leyton Orient v Maidstone
Solihull v Fylde
Sutton v Ebbsfleet
Wrexham v Maidenhead

## Saturday 2 February
Aldershot v Solihull
Barrow v Leyton Orient
Boreham Wood v Wrexham
Braintree v Chesterfield
Dover v Gateshead
Eastleigh v Barnet
Ebbsfleet v Hartlepool
Fylde v Havant
Harrogate v Bromley
Maidenhead v Dag & Red
Maidstone v Halifax
Salford v Sutton

## Saturday 9 February
Aldershot v Eastleigh
Barnet v Sutton
Barrow v Bromley
Braintree v Salford
Chesterfield v Halifax
Dover v Harrogate
Ebbsfleet v Solihull
Gateshead v Havant
Hartlepool v Leyton Orient
Maidenhead v Boreham Wood
Maidstone v Fylde
Wrexham v Dag & Red

## Saturday 16 February
Boreham Wood v Hartlepool
Bromley v Maidstone
Dag & Red v Gateshead
Eastleigh v Braintree
Fylde v Chesterfield
Halifax v Aldershot
Harrogate v Ebbsfleet
Havant v Wrexham
Leyton Orient v Maidenhead
Salford v Dover
Solihull v Barnet
Sutton v Barrow

### Saturday 23 February
Barrow v Ebbsfleet
Boreham Wood v Solihull
Braintree v Aldershot
Chesterfield v Harrogate
Dag & Red v Sutton
Halifax v Havant
Gateshead v Wrexham
Hartlepool v Bromley
Leyton Orient v Fylde
Maidenhead v Dover
Maidstone v Barnet
Salford v Eastleigh

### Saturday 2 March
Aldershot v Gateshead
Barnet v Barrow
Bromley v Boreham Wood
Dover v Braintree
Eastleigh v Halifax
Ebbsfleet v Salford
Fylde v Maidenhead
Harrogate v Dag & Red
Havant v Leyton Orient
Solihull v Maidstone
Sutton v Hartlepool
Wrexham v Chesterfield

### Saturday 9 March
Barrow v Aldershot
Boreham Wood v Fylde
Braintree v Harrogate
Chesterfield v Eastleigh
Dag & Red v Bromley
Halifax v Ebbsfleet
Gateshead v Barnet
Hartlepool v Dover
Leyton Orient v Wrexham
Maidenhead v Sutton
Maidstone v Havant
Salford v Solihull

### Tuesday 12 March
Aldershot v Leyton Orient
Barnet v Halifax
Bromley v Chesterfield
Dover v Boreham Wood
Eastleigh v Maidstone
Ebbsfleet v Maidenhead
Fylde v Hartlepool
Harrogate v Salford
Havant v Dag & Red
Solihull v Gateshead
Sutton v Braintree
Wrexham v Barrow

### Saturday 16 March
Aldershot v Salford
Barnet v Hartlepool
Bromley v Leyton Orient
Dover v Halifax
Eastleigh v Barrow
Ebbsfleet v Boreham Wood
Fylde v Dag & Red
Harrogate v Maidenhead
Havant v Chesterfield
Solihull v Braintree
Sutton v Gateshead
Wrexham v Maidstone

### Saturday 23 March
Barrow v Harrogate
Boreham Wood v Aldershot
Braintree v Bromley
Chesterfield v Sutton
Dag & Red v Dover
Halifax v Solihull
Gateshead v Fylde
Hartlepool v Wrexham
Leyton Orient v Eastleigh
Maidenhead v Havant
Maidstone v Ebbsfleet
Salford v Barnet

### Saturday 30 March
Aldershot v Fylde
Barnet v Leyton Orient
Barrow v Boreham Wood
Braintree v Gateshead
Chesterfield v Dag & Red
Eastleigh v Hartlepool
Ebbsfleet v Wrexham
Halifax v Maidenhead
Harrogate v Maidstone
Salford v Bromley
Solihull v Dover
Sutton v Havant

### Saturday 6 April
Boreham Wood v Sutton
Bromley v Aldershot
Dag & Red v Barrow
Dover v Chesterfield
Fylde v Eastleigh
Gateshead v Ebbsfleet
Hartlepool v Solihull
Havant v Harrogate
Leyton Orient v Halifax
Maidenhead v Barnet
Maidstone v Salford
Wrexham v Braintree

### Saturday 13 April
Aldershot v Hartlepool
Barnet v Wrexham
Barrow v Dover
Braintree v Fylde
Chesterfield v Maidstone
Eastleigh v Gateshead
Ebbsfleet v Dag & Red
Halifax v Bromley
Harrogate v Boreham Wood
Salford v Maidenhead
Solihull v Havant
Sutton v Leyton Orient

### Friday 19 April
Boreham Wood v Salford
Bromley v Solihull
Dag & Red v Eastleigh
Dover v Aldershot
Fylde v Barnet
Gateshead v Chesterfield
Hartlepool v Halifax
Havant v Ebbsfleet
Leyton Orient v Harrogate
Maidenhead v Barrow
Maidstone v Braintree
Wrexham v Sutton

### Monday 22 April
Aldershot v Havant
Barnet v Bromley
Barrow v Hartlepool
Braintree v Dag & Red
Chesterfield v Boreham Wood
Eastleigh v Maidenhead
Ebbsfleet v Dover
Halifax v Wrexham
Harrogate v Gateshead
Salford v Fylde
Solihull v Leyton Orient
Sutton v Maidstone

### Saturday 27 April
Boreham Wood v Eastleigh
Bromley v Ebbsfleet
Dag & Red v Solihull
Dover v Sutton
Fylde v Halifax
Gateshead v Barrow
Hartlepool v Salford
Havant v Barnet
Leyton Orient v Braintree
Maidenhead v Chesterfield
Maidstone v Aldershot
Wrexham v Harrogate